GW01372465

# The CRB Encyclopedia of Commodity and Financial Prices, Second Edition
# 2009

## Commodity Research Bureau

**WILEY**

John Wiley & Sons, Inc.

Copyright © 2009 by Commodity Research Bureau, a Barchart.com, Inc. company. All rights reserved.

Published by John Wiley & Sons, Inc., Hoboken, New Jersey
Published simultaneously in Canada.

No part of this publication may be reproduced, stored in a retrieval system, or transmitted in any form or by any means, electronic, mechanical, photocopying, recording, scanning, or otherwise, except as permitted under Section 107 or 108 of the 1976 United States Copyright Act, without either the prior written permission of the Publisher, or authorization through payment of the appropriate per-copy fee to the Copyright Clearance Center, Inc., 222 Rosewood Drive, Danvers, MA 01923, (978) 750-8400, fax (978) 646-8600, or on the web at www.copyright.com. Requests to the Publisher for permission should be addressed to the Permissions Department, John Wiley & Sons, Inc., 111 River Street, Hoboken, NJ 07030, (201) 748-6011, fax (201) 748-6008, or online at http://www.wiley.com/go/permissions.

Limit of Liability/Disclaimer of Warranty: While the publisher and author have used their best efforts in preparing this book, they make no representations or warranties with respect to the accuracy or completeness of the contents of this book and specifically disclaim any implied warranties of merchantability or fitness for a particular purpose. No warranty may be created or extended by sales representatives or written sales materials. The advice and strategies contained herein may not be suitable for your situation. You should consult with a professional where appropriate. Neither the publisher nor author shall be liable for any loss of profit or any other commercial damages, including but not limited to special, incidental, consequential, or other damages.

For general information on our other products and services or for technical support, please contact our Customer Care Department within the United States at (800) 762-2974, outside the United States at (317) 572-3993 or fax (317) 572-4002.

Wiley also publishes its books in a variety of electronic formats. Some content that appears in print may not be available in electronic books. For more information about Wiley products, visit our web site at www.wiley.com.

ISBN 978-0-470-34406-4

Printed in the United States of America

10  9  8  7  6  5  4  3  2  1



CRB believes that the information and opinions contained herein are reliable, but CRB does not make any warranties whatsoever, expressed or implied, and CRB assumes no liability for reliance on or use of information and opinion contained herein.

Commodity Research Bureau Editorial Board


Editor in Chief             Contributing Author
Christopher J. Lown         Richard W. Asplund



Commodity Research Bureau
330 South Wells Street, Suite 612
Chicago, Illinois 60606-7110 USA
800.621.5271 or +1.312.554.8456
Fax: +1.312.939.4135
Website: www.crbtrader.com
Email: info@crbtrader.com

# Table of Contents

PAGE
- 5 Introduction
- 6 Key World and Market Events

### 10 Currencies
- 12 US Dollar Index
- 16 Australian Dollar
- 21 British Pound
- 26 Canadian Dollar
- 32 Euro FX
- 36 Japanese Yen
- 42 Mexican Peso
- 46 Swiss Franc
- 52 Cross-Rates

### 60 Energy
- 62 Crude Oil, WTI
- 68 Gasoline, RBOB
- 73 Heating Oil
- 78 Natural Gas
- 84 Propane

### 88 Financial Instruments
- 90 EuroDollars, 3-Month
- 92 Federal Funds, 30-Day
- 94 Libor, 1-Month
- 96 Treasury Note, 2-Year
- 100 Treasury Note, 5-Year
- 104 Treasury Note, 10-Year
- 108 Treasury Note, 30-Year
- 112 International Interest Rates
- 120 Economic Indicators

### 138 Foods & Fibers
- 140 Cocoa
- 146 Coffee
- 152 Orange Juice
- 154 Sugar
- 160 Cotton
- 166 Lumber

### 172 Grains & Oilseeds
- 176 Corn
- 182 Oats
- 188 Rice
- 194 Wheat, Chicago
- 200 Wheat, Kansas City
- 204 Wheat, Minneapolis
- 208 Canola
- 210 Soybeans
- 216 Soybean Meal
- 222 Soybean Oil

### 228 Indices - Commodities
- 230 Reuters CCI
- 232 Reuters/Jefferies-CRB Index
- 234 Reuters CCI Industrials Sub-Index
- 236 Reuters CCI Grains & Oilseeds Sub-Index
- 238 Reuters CCI Livestock & Meats Sub-Index
- 240 Reuters CCI Energy Sub-Index
- 242 Reuters CCI Precious Metals Sub-Index
- 244 Reuters CCI Softs Sub-Index
- 246 CRB Spot Index
- 248 CRB Spot Metals Sub-Index
- 250 CRB Spot Textiles Sub-Index
- 252 CRB Spot Raw Industrials Sub-Index
- 254 CRB Spot Foodstuffs Sub-Index
- 256 CRB Spot Fats & Oils Sub-Index
- 258 CRB Spot Livestock Sub-Index
- 260 S&P Goldman Sachs Commodity Index

### 262 Indices - Stocks
- 266 Dow Jones Industrials Index
- 270 Dow Jones Transports Index
- 272 Dow Jones Utilities Index
- 274 CBOE Volatility Index
- 276 NASDAQ 100 Index
- 278 NASDAQ Composite Index
- 280 S&P 500 Index
- 284 S&P MidCap 400 Index
- 286 S&P 100 Index
- 288 Russell 2000 Index
- 290 Value Line Index
- 292 International Stock Indexes

### 304 Livestock & Meats
- 306 Cattle, Feeder
- 312 Cattle, Live
- 318 Hogs, Lean
- 324 Pork Bellies
- 330 Hides
- 332 Tallow

### 334 Metals
- 336 Aluminum
- 342 Copper
- 350 Gold
- 356 Lead
- 358 Nickel
- 360 Palladium
- 364 Platinum
- 368 Silver
- 374 Tin
- 376 Zinc

### 378 CD Instructions

# AgriCharts
## a Barchart Company

Call a Sales Rep at 877-247-4394
info@agricharts.com

## Everything you need for your website

Your Website Solution:

- ☑ **Markets**
  ...including advanced quotes and charts

- ☑ **News**
  ...real-time updates and commentary

- ☑ **Weather**
  ...local, regional, national

- ☑ **Your Content & Bids**
  ...easy-to-use

AgriCharts is a division of Barchart.com, Inc. and Commodity Research Bureau (CRB)—two firms well regarded for their market information, data and website services. With a heritage dating back to 1934, Barchart and CRB have been providing services to the agricultural and financial industries for nearly 75 years!

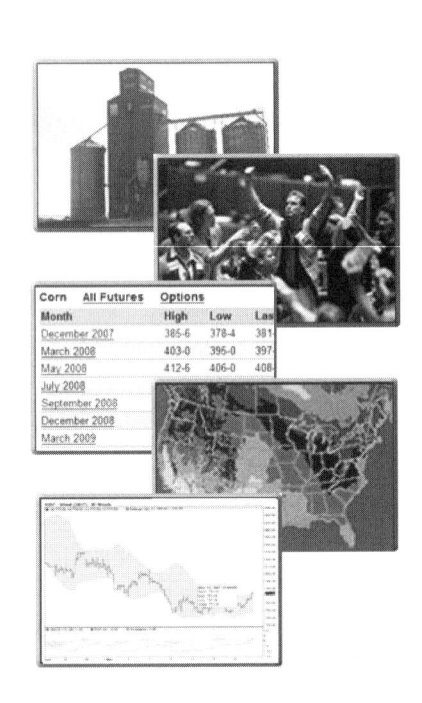

### A better website. A better price. A better choice.
### Choose AgriCharts.

To learn more, call AgriCharts at 877-247-4394!
Visit us at www.agricharts.com

AgriCharts is a division of
Barchart.com, Inc. & Commodity Research Bureau

**AgriCharts**
7350 Hickman Road
Des Moines, IA 50322
877-247-4394 or 515-276-7400

# Introduction

The purpose of this book is to present the "big picture" for the commodity and financial markets by providing a (1) a complete array of long-term price charts, (2) a brief written history and outlook for each commodity and financial sector, and (3) a CD-ROM with comprehensive supporting data.

The long-term charts in this book are difficult to find anywhere else. Commodity Research Bureau (CRB) has been in business since 1934 and CRB has developed the most complete database of commodity and financial price history available in the industry. Many of the chart services that are available on the web, and even the more expensive terminal-based chart services, have limited price histories and a limited graphical ability to display long-term charts. This book fills that gap by providing a handy reference guide with easy-to-access long-term price charts. This book also includes inflation-adjusted charts for a variety of commodity markets, which provide an interesting perspective on long-term prices.

The brief written histories of the key commodity and financial sectors give market participants an easy way to get up to speed on the main events that have moved the markets in the post-war period. Understanding what has happened in the past is critical for forecasting the markets looking ahead. In just a few pages, readers can quickly gain an overview of what has been happening in each major commodity and financial sector and also gain an important understanding of the key factors that are likely to drive each market in the future.

In the historical commentary, we often use data from the *CRB Commodity Yearbook 2009* to explain the supply/demand factors that have moved the markets. The *CRB Commodity Yearbook 2009* is the companion book for this publication since it contains a host of fundamental data on the commodity and financial markets. This data provides an important means to gain a deeper understanding of the fundamental supply/demand factors that move the markets.

---

The outlook for the world economy changed dramatically in September 2008 when the global banking crisis emerged in force with the bankruptcy of Lehman Brothers. Prior to the Lehman bankruptcy, the U.S. banking system and economy were muddling through the housing slump that began in 2006. However, the Lehman bankruptcy kicked off a dramatic chain of events including a plunge in global stock markets, soaring credit spreads, a near collapse of the U.S. and European banking systems, and a plunge in commodity prices.

The U.S. Federal Reserve and Treasury rode to the rescue with a wide variety of programs including liquidity injections and guarantees for the banking system. Yet the U.S. economy fell off a cliff in late 2008, with Q4 GDP showing a decline of –3.8% overall and a –5.1% decline excluding the unwanted inventory buildup.

The banking crisis that emerged in late 2008 was clearly the worst crisis since the Great Depression. However, unlike the Great Depression, Federal Reserve and Treasury officials in late 2008 took aggressive and innovative action to try to contain the crisis. While some mistakes were made along the way, U.S. officials clearly helped to reduce the severity of the situation.

Yet as of early 2009, there was no sign that the crisis and global economic recession would soon be over. The initial cause of the crisis, declining U.S. home prices, continued unabated in early 2009. Moreover, real estate prices were also falling sharply in other countries such as the U.K. and Ireland. Declining home prices and the sharp sell-off in the global stock markets decimated household wealth and caused consumers to cut back sharply on spending. Businesses responded with huge numbers of layoffs, thus boosting unemployment and causing even more spending cutbacks by consumers.

The U.S. housing melt-down was the event that kicked off the global credit crisis. However, the crisis erupted into a severe global event because of the high degree of leverage in the global financial system and because of increased counterparty risks in the huge derivatives market. The Lehman bankruptcy quickly caused the crisis to escalate to a global scale as European and Asian financial institutions and investors saw that the U.S. government was unable or unwilling to bail out a key player in the global financial system. The Lehman bankruptcy quickly led to The Reserve fund, one of the largest institutional money market firms, to fall below par value or "break the buck," which then resulted in a run on money market funds, until the Fed and the Treasury halted that run by temporarily guaranteeing investor deposits held in money market funds.

The Treasury and the Fed were also forced to go to Congress to obtain $700 billion in funds that could be used to bail out the U.S. banking system on a more systematic basis. The Treasury used the first $350 million installment of the "Troubled Asset Relief Program" (TARP) to inject capital directly into banks, thus boosting their solvency in an attempt to get them to keep lending to businesses and consumers. The Federal Reserve also provided liquidity directly into the financial markets, thus bypassing banks, by buying commercial paper, mortgage securities, and securitized consumer and small-business loans.

As of early 2009, the situation remained grim and most market participants were expecting the global recession to last at least through mid-2009. In addition, most market participants were expecting weak U.S. economic growth to extend into 2010. The long-term lesson of the global economy is that financial crises eventually pass and the economy eventually gets back on its feet. But the size of the current financial crisis suggests that the economic recovery will be slow and painful.

Richard Asplund, CRB Chief Economist

# Key World and Market Events

**Federal Reserve Established**—1913—Congress creates the modern Federal Reserve after a series of runs on national banks makes clear the need for a centralized monetary authority to manage the money supply and act as the lender of last resort to commercial banks.

**World War I begins**—1914-1918—First World War lasts from August 1914 to November 1918.

**1929 Stock Market Crash**—October 28-29, 1929—Dow Jones Industrial Average plunges 23.6% in just two days and then plunges by an overall 90% to the low in 1932.

**Smoot-Hawley Act**—1930—Congress passes the protectionist Smoot-Hawley Act which helps cause the 1929 Stock Market Crash and deepens the Great Depression by causing a sharp drop in US trade.

**Great Depression**—1929-33—The Great Depression lasts nearly 4 years (Aug 1929 to March 1933) and devastates the US economy and social structure. The Great Depression is later shown to result in part from an inadvertent deflationary monetary policy by the Federal Reserve.

**Bretton Woods Conference**—July 22, 1944—US and UK, looking ahead to the end of World War II, meet in Bretton Woods, New Hampshire and create a post-war monetary system based on fixed exchange rates and the fixed convertibility of the dollar into gold. The Bretton Woods conference also sets the stage for the creation of the World Bank, the International Monetary Fund (IMF), and the General Agreement on Tariffs and Trade (GATT). The Bretton Woods currency system is highly successful for over two decades but finally breaks down in 1971 under stress from US inflation and trade deficit and the need for more global flexibility.

**World War II ends**—1945—World War II ends in Europe on May 8, 1945, with the surrender of Germany and Italy. World War II ends in the Pacific with Japan's surrender on August 15, 1945.

**Korean War**—1950-53—Korean War lasts from 1950-1953 as US fights communism.

**William McChesney Martin becomes Fed Chairman**—April 2, 1951—William McChesney Martin Jr. begins his long 19-year term as Fed Chairman (through Jan 31, 1970).

**OPEC is formed**—September 1960—OPEC is formed among several Middle East Arab countries to gain negotiating leverage with the major oil companies.

**Berlin Wall is built**—1961—Soviet Union builds Berlin Wall as Cold War emerges between the Soviet Union and the US and its allies.

**Cuban Missile Crisis**—October 16, 1962—Cold War reaches its peak with the Cuban Missile Crisis which ends with the Soviet Union removing its missiles from Cuba.

**Kennedy assassination**—November 22, 1963—President Kennedy is assassinated in Dallas by Lee Harvey Oswald. Vice President Lyndon Johnson becomes President.

**Gulf of Tonkin incident**—August 1964—US military involvement in Vietnam starts to escalate into an all-out war after a North Vietnamese gunboat fires on an American destroyer. Major US involvement in the Vietnam War finally ends 9 years later in 1973 with the Paris Peace Accords.

**1967 Arab-Israeli War**—June 5-10, 1967—Israel launches a pre-emptive attack in a war with Egypt, Syria and Jordan, and takes control of Sinai Peninsula, the West Bank, and about half of the Golan Heights. Sinai is returned to Egypt when Israel and Egypt declare peace in the Camp David Accords, signed on September 17, 1978.

**Arthur Burns becomes Fed Chairman**—February 1, 1970—Arthur Burns begins his 8-year term as Fed Chairman (through Jan 31, 1978).

**Nixon closes the gold window, ending Bretton Woods**—August 15, 1971—President Nixon announces that the US government will no longer exchange gold for dollars. That effectively ends the Bretton Woods monetary system that had been in place since 1945. Major currencies are freely floating by 1973. Along with the gold announcement, Nixon also announces 90-day wage and price controls and a 10% import surcharge in an attempt to curb inflation and the US trade deficit.

**Nixon travels to China**—February 21-28, 1972—Nixon travels to China to seek rapprochement with the Communist nation. US and China announce they will work toward full diplomatic relations. China's long isolation starts to thaw.

**Soviet Grain Purchases**—Summer 1972—The Soviet Union during the summer of 1972 purchases a huge amount of corn, wheat, soybeans and soybean meal from the US in response to poor domestic crops, thus causing grain and soybean prices to soar in late 1972 and early 1973.

**Yom Kippur War**—October 6, 1973—Israel barely wins the war that started with a surprise attack on Yom Kippur by Egypt and Syria in an attempt to win back Sinai and Golan Heights, respectively.

# KEY WORLD AND MARKET EVENTS

**Arab Oil Embargo**—October 17, 1973—Arab members of OPEC halt exports of oil to the US in retaliation for supporting Israel during the Yom Kippur War. Oil prices triple from $3.50 to the $10-11 per barrel range by 1974-75. The embargo lasts only 5 months (until March 1974) but the long-term impact is severe.

**1973-75 US recession and stock bear market**—Serious US stock bear market emerges in response to the Arab Oil Embargo and the major US economic recession from Nov-1973 to March-1975.

**President Nixon resigns**—August 4, 1974—President Nixon resigns due to the Watergate scandal. Vice President Gerald Ford becomes President.

**US citizens can legally own gold**—1975—US allows its citizens to own gold bullion. Owning gold was illegal from 1933-1974 except for jewelry and coin collecting.

**China begins economic liberalization**—1978—The People's Republic of China starts reforming its economy from a centrally-planned economy to a market-oriented economy, but retains communist political structure. Rapid Chinese economic growth begins (average annual Chinese GDP growth is +9.7% from 1978-2005).

**C. William Miller becomes Fed Chairman**—March 8, 1978—C. William Miller is appointed Fed Chairman by President Jimmy Carter and begins his short 1-year term.

**Paul Volcker becomes Fed Chairman**—August 6, 1979—Paul Volcker is appointed Federal Reserve Chairman by President Jimmy Carter and begins his 8-year term. Volcker cracks down on money supply to force inflation lower, causing double dip recessions in 1980 and 1981-82. The federal funds rate target peaks at 20% in March 1980 and again in May 1981.

**Shah is deposed by Iranian Revolution**—January 16, 1979—Shah of Iran is deposed by popular protest and is replaced by an Islamic theocracy headed by Ayatollah Khomeini, who arrives in Iran on February 1, 1979, two weeks after the Shah fled on January 16, 1979. Oil prices surge as Iran's oil production is devastated by the revolution.

**1979 Oil Crisis**—Crude oil prices more than double from about $15 to $40 per barrel on oil supply disruptions caused initially by the Iranian revolution, which severely cut Iranian oil production. Americans experience long lines at the gas pumps as shortages are worsened by President Carter's gasoline price controls.

**Soviet Grain Embargo**—January 4, 1980—President Carter announces an embargo on grain exports to the Soviet Union in retaliation for the Soviet Union's invasion of Afghanistan.

**Gold and silver hit record highs**—January 1980—Gold reaches a record high of $850.00 (London PM gold fix on Jan 21, 1980) and silver in New York reaches a record high of $48.00 (NY daily close) due to inflationary 1970s, but precious metals prices then plunge as Volcker cracks down on inflation.

**1980 US Recession**—US recession (January 1980 to July 1980) is caused by Fed's crack-down on money supply and inflation and the surge in oil prices tied to the Iranian revolution. First dip of the "double-dip" recession.

**Iran-Iraq War begins**—September 22, 1980—The Iran-Iraq War lasts from 1980-1988 and causes sharp cutbacks in Iranian and Iraqi oil production and puts new upward pressure on oil prices. A ceasefire is finally declared on August 20, 1988.

**1981-82 US Recession**—US economy enters another recession (the second dip of the "double-dip recession") from July 1981 to November 1982 as the US economy continues to suffer from high oil prices and the Fed's crack-down on inflation.

**Latin American Debt Crisis**—Early-1980s—Latin America countries (Brazil, Argentina and Mexico in particular) are unable to pay large debts owed to global banks due to world recession and oil price spike.

**President Reagan's first term begins**—January 20, 1981—Ronald Reagan's 8-year term as President begins with his mission of "supply side economics." Reagan terminates oil price controls and forces a 25% tax cut through Congress, which eventually produces a huge federal budget deficit but also stimulates the economy.

**US stocks begin bull market**—1982—After plunging on an inflation-adjusted basis from 1973-1982, the US stock market finally enters a long-term bull market that lasts until 2000, with corrections in 1987 and 1990.

**Plaza Accord**—September 1985—G5 nations agree on plan to drive the dollar lower via currency market intervention.

**Louvre Accord**—February 21-22, 1987—G5 nations agreed to stabilize currencies and halt the dollar's decline

**Greenspan becomes Fed Chairman**—August 11, 1987—Alan Greenspan is appointed as Federal Reserve Chairman by President Reagan and begins his long 18-1/2 year term (through January 31, 2006).

**1987 "Black Monday" Stock Market Crash**—October 19, 1987—US stock market crashes 20.5% but recovers its losses within just 9 months as Fed successfully manages the crisis by flooding the banking system with liquidity.

# KEY WORLD AND MARKET EVENTS

**Berlin Wall Falls**—November 9, 1989—Berlin Wall, which was originally built in 1961 by the Soviets to separate East and West Germany, falls. Unification of East and West Germany follows in 1990, creating economic dislocations for Germany.

**Nikkei index peaks and Japan's bubble later bursts**—December 1989—Japan's stock market peaks and the stock and property bubble starts to burst. Japan suffers more than a decade of deflation and sub-par economic growth. The Nikkei index plunges by three-quarters and Tokyo land prices fall by one-half.

**Iraq invades Kuwait**—August 2, 1990—Iraqi dictator Saddam Hussein invades Kuwait to take control of oil fields, with likely intention to move on to Saudi Arabia.

**"Desert Storm" Gulf War**—January 17, 1991—US and coalition forces go to war against Iraq to force Iraq out of Kuwait. US stops short of Baghdad and leaves Saddam Hussein in power.

**1990-91 US Recession**—US economy is in recession from July 1990 to March 1991 due mainly to the oil price spike caused by Iraq's invasion of Kuwait and the subsequent US-Coalition war against Iraq.

**Soviet Union dissolves**—December 26, 1991—The Supreme Soviet, the highest governmental body of the Soviet Union, dissolves itself and Russia and other republics later become independent nations.

**S&L Bailout**—1991—Congress bails out the US savings and loan banking sector which is insolvent due to high short-term rates and rampant speculation. Bailout costs some $350 billion but is disposed of fairly quickly by the Resolution Trust Corporation.

**NAFTA**—1993—US Congress approves North American Free Trade Zone among the US, Mexico and Canada.

**Mexican Peso Crisis**—1994—Mexican peso collapses by 40% in two weeks. President Clinton bails out Mexico with a $50 billion loan and the fall-out is contained.

**Uruguay Round is completed**—April 1994—After 7-1/2 years, the Uruguay Round of world trade talks finally concludes successfully with agreement among 125 countries, creating the World Trade Organization (replacing the General Agreement on Tariffs and Trade, or GATT) and promoting a major expansion in world trade. Previous world trade agreements include the Tokyo Round (1979), the Kennedy Round (1967), and five others.

**Asian financial crisis**—July 1997—Run starts on East Asian Tiger currencies causing a collapse in the East Asian stock markets and an economic recession. Countries most affected were Thailand, South Korea and the Philippines.

**Russian debt default**—August 17, 1998—Russia defaults on its foreign sovereign debt and devalues the ruble due to high debt from Soviet era, limited success with market reforms, high inflation, and low currency reserves due in part to spending $6 billion to defend the ruble during the Asian currency crisis in 1997. The ruble is floated in the wake of the crisis.

**LTCM hedge fund bailout**—September 1998—Federal Reserve orchestrates bailout of Long-Term Capital Management hedge fund in order to prevent systemic financial system crisis.

**European Monetary Union**—January 1, 1999—European Monetary Union is completed and the Euro comes into existence to replace individual currencies such as the mark, franc and lira. The European Central Bank takes over responsibility for Euro-Zone monetary policy.

**US stock market hits record high but bubble subsequently bursts**—March 2000—The S&P 500, the Nasdaq Composite and other key stock market indices hit record highs in March 2000 but subsequently enter a bear market.

**2001 US Recession**—US economy enters recession from March 2001 to November 2001 due to bursting of equity bubble and post-Y2K technology spending bust.

**9/11 terrorist attacks on US**—September 11, 2001—Al-Qaeda attacks US with airplanes crashing into World Trade Center and the Pentagon. As a result, US enters two wars (Afghanistan and Iraq) and military spending, along with the US budget deficit, soar.

**US invades Afghanistan**—October 7, 2001—US invades Afghanistan to oust Taliban government and deny safe haven to al-Qaeda.

**Doha Round begins**—November 2001—In an attempt to extend Uruguay Round success, the Doha Round of world trade talks begins but little progress is made through early 2006 due to objections by Brazil and others about G7 government agricultural subsidies to local farmers.

**Congress passes Sarbanes-Oxley**—July 30, 2002—Congress passes Sarbanes-Oxley Act which creates corporate governance reforms and enhanced financial disclosure in response to the string of corporate frauds that developed during the stock bubble, including Enron (bankruptcy Dec 2001), Worldcom (bankruptcy July 2002), Tyco, and others.

# KEY WORLD AND MARKET EVENTS

**SARS outbreak begins**—February 2003—SARS, a new and deadly type of pneumonia, is first reported in Asia in February 2003 and quickly spreads to various locations around the world, hurting economic growth in Asia, Canada and elsewhere. The disease is contained, however, and no cases are reported after late- 2004.

**US launches war against Iraq's Saddam Hussein**—March 20, 2003—US and UK begin "Operation Iraqi Freedom" against Iraq and topple Saddam Hussein, who is captured by US forces on December 13, 2003, and hung after a trial in an Iraqi court.

**First case of Mad Cow is found in US**—December 2003—The US first case of Mad Cow disease (BSE) is found in a Canadian-born dairy cow in Washington state. More than 50 countries suspend imports of US cattle and beef products.

**Avian flu emerges**—August 2004—Sporadic outbreaks of avian flu are seen in August-October 2004 in Vietnam and Thailand. Avian flu progressively spreads into other parts of Asia and then to Africa and Europe by early 2006.

**China revalues Yuan and moves to crawling peg**—July 21, 2005—China announces a one-time revaluation in the yuan by 2.1%, and then allows the yuan to crawl higher in a nod to international demands that China allow its currency to rise to help curb its soaring trade surplus.

**Hurricane Katrina**—August 29, 2005—Hurricane Katrina makes landfall near New Orleans and causes widespread devastation including the flooding and shutdown of New Orleans.

**Bernanke becomes Fed Chairman**—February 1, 2006—Economist, former Fed Governor and Bush-advisor, Ben Bernanke, is appointed Fed Chairman by President George W. Bush, taking over from Alan Greenspan, who retired after an 18-1/2 year term.

**Two Bear Stearns hedge funds are insolvent**—June 2007—The U.S. mortgage crisis accelerates after two Bear Stearns mortgage-backed hedge funds become insolvent, requiring a $3.2 billion loan from the Bear Stearns parent company. The funds nevertheless end up filing bankruptcy in August 2007.

**BNP Paribas freezes hedge fund redemptions**—August 10, 2007—BNP Paribas freezes redemptions from three mortgage security hedge funds, sparking a run on other hedge funds by institutional investors.

**US officially enters recession in December 2007**—In a decision announced a year later in December 2008, the National Bureau of Economic Research declares that a U.S. recession began in December 2007.

**First fiscal stimulus plan**—February 8, 2008—Congress approves and President Bush signs a $168 billion fiscal stimulus program.

**Bear Stearns bailout**—March 14, 2008—Bear Stearns, under distress, is acquired by JPMorgan Chase for $1.4 billion with support from US government.

Fannie Mae and Freddie Mac are seized--September 8, 2008—The US government effectively nationalizes Fannie Mae and Freddie Mac due to insolvency and funding problems.

**Lehman Brothers declares bankruptcy**—September 15, 2008—Lehman Brothers declares bankruptcy, causing the US mortgage crisis to balloon into a financial crisis of global proportions. Barclays later buys the bulk of Lehman for $1.75 billion. On the same day, Merrill Lynch, under distress, is acquired by Bank of America for $50 billion.

**AIG receives support**—September 17, 2008—Insurance-giant AIG, facing bankruptcy, receives a federal bailout.

**Goldman Sachs and Morgan Stanley convert to commercial bank status**—September 22, 2008—Goldman Sachs and Morgan Stanley convert to commercial bank status to gain direct access to Federal Reserve funding, sounding the death knell for the Wall Street investment bank model.

**$700 billion TARP bank bailout**—October 4, 2008—President Bush signs into law the $700 billion Troubled Asset Relief Program (TARP), which is subsequently used to inject capital into banks.

**Fed money market rescue**—October 22, 2008—Federal Reserve announces a $540 billion program to backstop the US money market industry to prevent a larger run by investors.

**Fed announces $800 billion rescue package**—November 26, 2008—The Federal Reserve announces a program to buy $500 billion of mortgage securities and $100 billion of debt of Fannie Mae and Freddie Mac, which brings mortgage rates down sharply. Fed says it will also aid the purchase of up to $200 billion of securitized consumer and small-business loans to thaw markets.

**Barack Obama becomes President**—January 20, 2009—Barack Obama takes office as the 44th President of the United States, winning the election with his promise of change.

**Obama stimulus plan**—February 2009—Congress approves and President Obama signs a $787 billion fiscal stimulus bill to revive the U.S. economy.

# Currencies

**Current Dollar Outlook**

The dollar in the latter half of 2008 staged a sharp rally sparked by the US banking crisis. During the global financial crisis, which began in earnest after the bankruptcy of Lehman Brothers in mid-September 2008, investors and financial institutions the world over scrambled for liquidity in dollars. With a complete lack of trust among investors and financial institutions, there was a run towards the world's reserve currency. The US Federal Reserve was forced to provide huge quantities of dollars, both within the US and also in Europe and Asia through swap lines set up with overseas central banks. The dollar was also pushed higher in late 2008 by US investors who scrambled to sell their overseas stock investments during the crisis and then had to convert foreign currencies back into dollars into order to repatriate their cash.

The question for the dollar going forward is what will happen when the financial crisis starts to ease. At that point, there will potentially be a huge quantity of unwanted emergency dollar liquidity in the global financial system. The Federal Reserve's target rate as of early 2009 of zero to 0.25% was lower than any other G7 nation except for Japan. If the Fed does not drain that liquidity as the crisis eases, then there may be a big oversupply of dollars.

**Dollar History**

**Modern floating rate currency era begins in 1973**

Exchange rates from 1945 to 1971 were fixed by the Bretton Woods agreement. Major world currencies were fixed in terms of the dollar, which was the system's "reserve currency" and the dollar in turn was fixed and convertible into gold by the US government at $35 per ounce. The Bretton Woods era of fixed exchange rates effectively ended on August 15, 1971, when President Nixon announced that the US government would close the gold window and no longer exchange gold for dollars. With the gold convertibility of the system removed, the system of fixed exchange rates slowly broke down and by 1973 the major world currencies were trading in a floating-rate currency system where the market, rather than a government, determines the value of a currency.

The Bretton Woods system broke down mainly because the US by the early 1970s was seeing increased inflation and a balance of payments deficit. When currencies started floating freely in 1973, the US dollar depreciated through most of the rest of the 1970s due to the relatively high US inflation rate seen during the 1970s, which averaged +7.1% annually, up sharply from +2.3% in the 1960s and +2.1% in the 1950s.

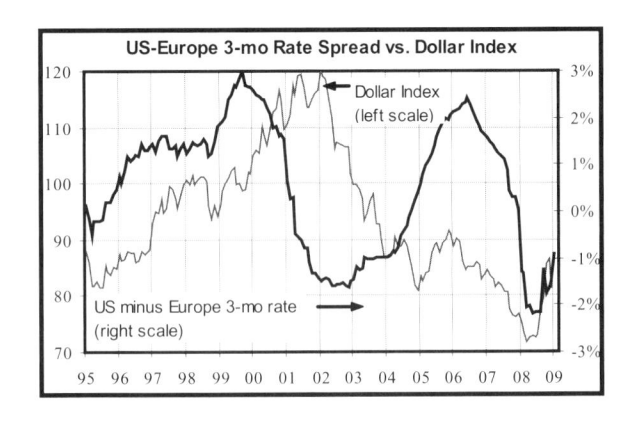

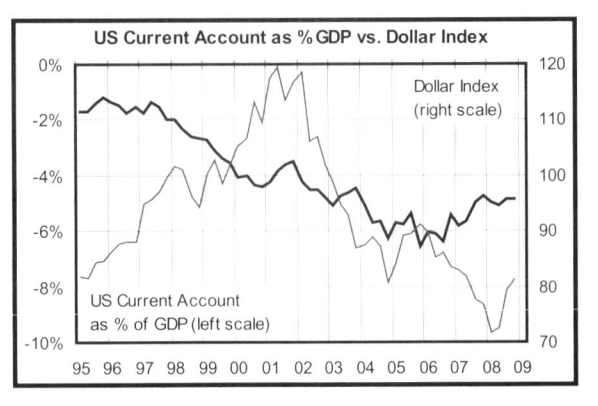

**Dollar strength during the Volcker Era**

Paul Volcker was appointed Federal Reserve Chairman in August 1979 and he raised interest rates sharply to crack down on money supply growth and to halt runaway inflation. Sharply higher US interest rates quickly allowed the dollar to stabilize in the 1979-1980 period. The dollar then rallied sharply starting in mid-1980 as US inflation started to fall and as investors bought dollars to take advantage of high US yields.

**Plaza Accord of 1985**

The dollar index nearly doubled in value from mid-1981 to the record high in 1985, driven higher by (1) declining US inflation, (2) a stimulative fiscal policy caused by the Reagan tax cuts and budget deficits, and (3) the sharp rally in the US stock market which attracted foreign capital into the US. The Reagan administration took a lassie-faire attitude to the surge in the dollar and made little effort to curb the dollar's gains.

By 1985, however, US manufacturers and the US auto industry in particular were screaming because their export goods were no longer competitive in the world market. US exports plunged and imports rose, thus causing the US current account deficit to soar to a then-record of 3.2% of

GDP by the end of 1985. The Reagan administration finally arranged the Plaza Accord in September 1985 where the G5 countries (US, UK, West Germany, France and Canada) agreed to force a depreciation in the dollar, mainly through currency market intervention. The central banks spent $10 billion intervening in the currency markets. The outcome was very successful and the dollar fell sharply, giving back all of its 1981-85 rally. The sharp decline became alarming, however, as some market commentators started spinning doomsday scenarios involving a dollar melt-down. In order to halt the plunge in the dollar seen in 1985-87, the G5 nations signed the Louvre Accord in February 1987, in which they agreed to halt the decline in the dollar.

The Louvre Accord was successful in halting the plunge in the dollar. However, the dollar from 1987 through 1995 continued to trade on a weak note, undercut by the declining trend in US interest rates during that time-frame and the generally high US current account deficit.

**1995-2002 rally and the introduction of the euro**

The dollar then rallied sharply during the 1995-2002 period after the Fed raised its funds rate target to the 6% area in 1994, thus giving the dollar a strong interest rate differential advantage. In addition, foreign demand for dollars was strong as foreign investors scrambled to buy internet and technology stocks during the US stock market boom.

The euro was introduced January 1, 1999 as part of the European Economic and Monetary Union (EMU). Eleven European countries initially participated in the common currency, which replaced each nation's individual currencies. The idea was to create a common economic area with a free flow of trade and to eliminate the inefficiencies caused by having individual currencies. The European Central Bank took over the duties of setting monetary policy for the Euro-Zone countries. The euro has been a success and has become a critical component of the global financial system.

**2002-08 plunge in the dollar**

The dollar index from early 2002 through early 2008 plunged by a total of 41%. The early part of that sell-off was due to several key factors: (1) the bursting of the US equity bubble and the weak US economy from 200103, (2) the Fed's sharp cut in the federal funds rate target to an extraordinary low 1.00% by June 2003, and (3) the sharp increase in the US current account deficit from about 4% of GDP in 2002 to 6.3% by the end 2004.

The US current account deficit was driven higher by a variety of long-term structural factors including (1) the huge US appetite for foreign imported oil, (2) the improved comparative advantage of nations such as China and India, which have cheap labor and the resources to employ that labor into export powerhouses, and (3) the poor US household savings rate and the massive US federal budget deficit, which meant the US had to import a huge amount of capital to cover its capital needs (boosting the capital account surplus and the US current account deficit as well). The US current account deficit finally started stabilizing in 2006 due to strong overseas economic growth and strong demand for US exports.

The dollar staged a bull market rally in 2005, despite the high US current account deficit, mainly because of the sharp rise in US interest rate differentials, as seen in the nearby interest rate spread chart (i.e., the 3-month US Eurodollar Libor rate minus the European Libor rate). Higher US short-term interest rates encouraged foreign investors to put their cash into the US money markets to earn a higher yield than they could earn in Europe or Japan. The Fed's tighter monetary policy also meant that the Fed was pumping fewer dollar reserves into the nation's banking system, making dollars a bit less plentiful.

The US Federal Reserve started raising its federal funds rate target in June 2004 from the 1.00% level that prevailed during the previous 12 months. The Fed from June 2004 through July 2006 raised its funds rate target by a total of 425 basis points, from 1.00% to 5.25%.

The 2005 rally in the dollar was short-lived and the dollar resumed its decline in 2006 and 2007. The decline in the dollar in 2006-07 was driven by new concerns about the US economy after the housing bubble burst. The US housing market topped out in 2006 and the Fed started cutting interest rates in September 2007 when Bear Stearns and BNP Paribas ran into trouble with their hedge funds that held mortgage-backed securities. The Fed's rate cuts undercut US interest rate differentials and reduced demand for dollars. The dollar was also undercut by the sell-off in the stock market, which started in late 2007. Foreign investors started withdrawing capital from the US stock market due to concern about the direction of the US economy with the weight of the mortgage crisis. The dollar hit a record low in March 2008. The dollar then rallied sharply through the remainder of 2008 after the global financial crisis emerged and sparked strong global demand for emergency liquidity in dollars. The dollar was also supported by the decline in the US trade deficit in late 2008 due to the decline in oil prices.

# U.S. DOLLAR INDEX

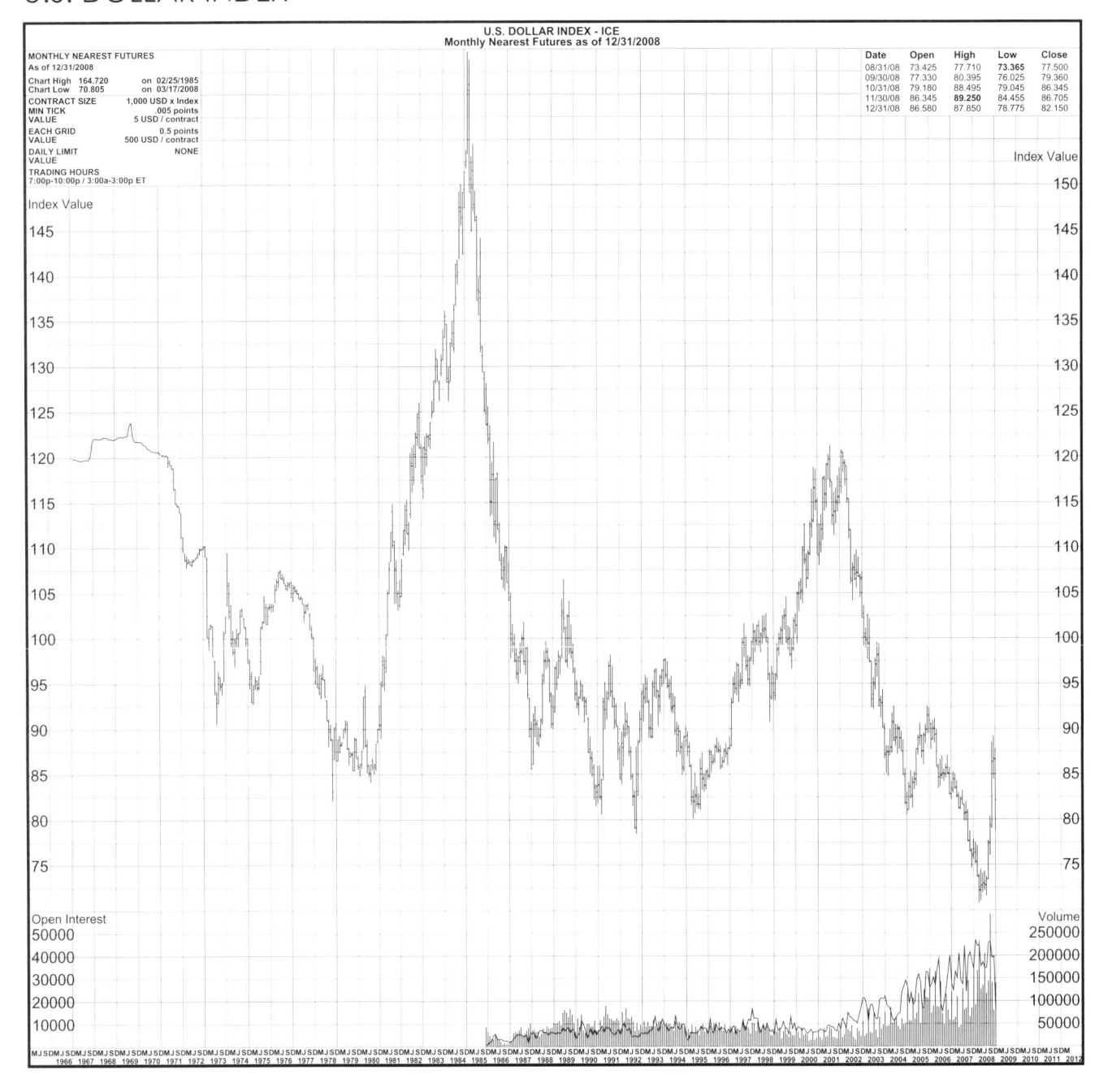

**U.S. DOLLAR INDEX - ICE**
Monthly Nearest Futures as of 12/31/2008

MONTHLY NEAREST FUTURES
As of 12/31/2008
Chart High 164.720 on 02/25/1985
Chart Low 70.805 on 03/17/2008
CONTRACT SIZE 1,000 USD x Index
MIN TICK .005 points
VALUE 5 USD / contract
EACH GRID 0.5 points
VALUE 500 USD / contract
DAILY LIMIT NONE
VALUE
TRADING HOURS
7:00p-10:00p / 3:00a-3:00p ET

| Date | Open | High | Low | Close |
|---|---|---|---|---|
| 08/31/08 | 73.425 | 77.710 | 73.365 | 77.500 |
| 09/30/08 | 77.330 | 80.395 | 76.025 | 79.360 |
| 10/31/08 | 79.180 | 88.495 | 79.045 | 86.345 |
| 11/30/08 | 86.345 | 89.250 | 84.455 | 86.705 |
| 12/31/08 | 86.580 | 87.850 | 78.775 | 82.150 |

## Annual High, Low and Settle of U.S. Dollar Index Futures    Index Value

| Year | High | Low | Settle | Year | High | Low | Settle | Year | High | Low | Settle |
|---|---|---|---|---|---|---|---|---|---|---|---|
| 1967 | 121.79 | 119.63 | 121.79 | 1981 | 114.88 | 88.95 | 104.69 | 1995 | 89.79 | 80.14 | 84.83 |
| 1968 | 122.22 | 121.95 | 121.96 | 1982 | 126.02 | 104.62 | 117.91 | 1996 | 89.20 | 84.51 | 87.86 |
| 1969 | 123.82 | 121.74 | 121.74 | 1983 | 134.05 | 115.43 | 131.79 | 1997 | 101.68 | 88.01 | 99.57 |
| 1970 | 121.75 | 120.55 | 120.64 | 1984 | 151.47 | 126.18 | 151.47 | 1998 | 102.82 | 90.74 | 93.96 |
| 1971 | 120.55 | 111.16 | 111.21 | 1985 | 164.72 | 123.24 | 123.55 | 1999 | 104.60 | 93.12 | 101.42 |
| 1972 | 111.27 | 107.76 | 110.14 | 1986 | 125.62 | 104.20 | 104.24 | 2000 | 118.90 | 99.40 | 109.28 |
| 1973 | 110.31 | 90.54 | 102.39 | 1987 | 105.02 | 85.55 | 85.66 | 2001 | 121.29 | 108.04 | 117.21 |
| 1974 | 109.50 | 96.86 | 97.29 | 1988 | 99.70 | 86.07 | 92.29 | 2002 | 120.80 | 102.26 | 102.26 |
| 1975 | 104.81 | 92.82 | 103.51 | 1989 | 106.52 | 91.75 | 93.93 | 2003 | 103.67 | 86.70 | 87.26 |
| 1976 | 107.60 | 102.91 | 104.56 | 1990 | 95.44 | 81.46 | 83.89 | 2004 | 92.50 | 80.48 | 81.00 |
| 1977 | 106.01 | 96.44 | 96.44 | 1991 | 98.23 | 80.60 | 84.69 | 2005 | 92.53 | 81.11 | 90.96 |
| 1978 | 97.87 | 82.07 | 86.50 | 1992 | 94.20 | 78.43 | 93.87 | 2006 | 91.18 | 82.18 | 83.43 |
| 1979 | 91.02 | 85.43 | 85.82 | 1993 | 97.69 | 88.92 | 97.63 | 2007 | 85.25 | 74.65 | 76.70 |
| 1980 | 94.88 | 84.12 | 90.39 | 1994 | 97.85 | 84.95 | 88.69 | 2008 | 89.25 | 70.81 | 82.15 |

Futures begin trading 11/20/1985.    *Source: IntercontinentalExchange (ICE); formerly New York Board of Trade (NYBOT)*

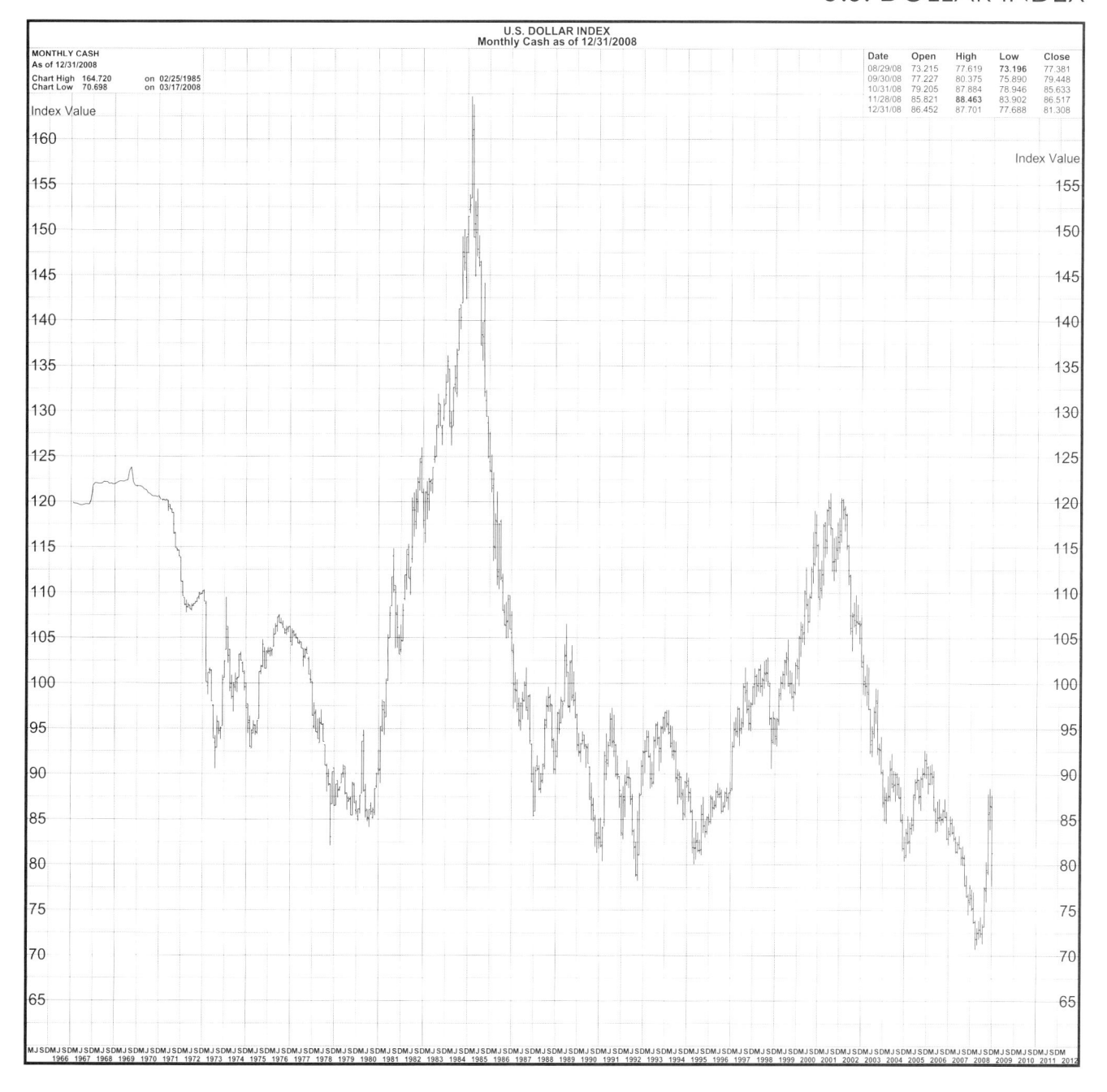

# U.S. DOLLAR INDEX

**U.S. DOLLAR INDEX**
Monthly Cash as of 12/31/2008

MONTHLY CASH
As of 12/31/2008
Chart High 164.720 on 02/25/1985
Chart Low 70.698 on 03/17/2008

| Date | Open | High | Low | Close |
|---|---|---|---|---|
| 08/29/08 | 73.215 | 77.619 | **73.196** | 77.381 |
| 09/30/08 | 77.227 | 80.375 | 75.890 | 79.448 |
| 10/31/08 | 79.205 | 87.884 | 78.946 | 85.633 |
| 11/28/08 | 85.821 | **88.463** | 83.902 | 86.517 |
| 12/31/08 | 86.452 | 87.701 | 77.688 | 81.308 |

## Annual High, Low and Settle of U.S. Dollar Index    Index Value

| Year | High | Low | Settle | Year | High | Low | Settle | Year | High | Low | Settle |
|---|---|---|---|---|---|---|---|---|---|---|---|
| 1967 | 121.79 | 119.63 | 121.79 | 1981 | 114.88 | 88.95 | 104.69 | 1995 | 89.63 | 80.05 | 84.76 |
| 1968 | 122.22 | 121.95 | 121.96 | 1982 | 126.02 | 104.62 | 117.91 | 1996 | 89.14 | 84.48 | 88.18 |
| 1969 | 123.82 | 121.74 | 121.74 | 1983 | 134.05 | 115.43 | 131.79 | 1997 | 101.79 | 88.15 | 99.65 |
| 1970 | 121.75 | 120.55 | 120.64 | 1984 | 151.47 | 126.18 | 151.47 | 1998 | 102.88 | 90.57 | 94.17 |
| 1971 | 120.55 | 111.16 | 111.21 | 1985 | 164.72 | 123.24 | 123.46 | 1999 | 104.88 | 93.05 | 101.87 |
| 1972 | 111.27 | 107.76 | 110.14 | 1986 | 125.21 | 103.55 | 103.58 | 2000 | 119.07 | 99.71 | 109.56 |
| 1973 | 110.31 | 90.54 | 102.39 | 1987 | 104.35 | 85.33 | 85.42 | 2001 | 121.02 | 108.09 | 116.82 |
| 1974 | 109.50 | 96.86 | 97.29 | 1988 | 99.61 | 85.87 | 92.50 | 2002 | 120.51 | 101.80 | 101.85 |
| 1975 | 104.81 | 92.82 | 103.51 | 1989 | 106.56 | 91.77 | 93.21 | 2003 | 103.20 | 86.36 | 86.92 |
| 1976 | 107.60 | 102.91 | 104.56 | 1990 | 94.72 | 81.27 | 83.07 | 2004 | 92.29 | 80.39 | 80.85 |
| 1977 | 106.01 | 96.44 | 96.44 | 1991 | 97.32 | 80.34 | 83.52 | 2005 | 92.63 | 80.77 | 91.17 |
| 1978 | 97.87 | 82.07 | 86.50 | 1992 | 92.52 | 78.19 | 92.36 | 2006 | 91.16 | 82.24 | 83.72 |
| 1979 | 91.02 | 85.43 | 85.82 | 1993 | 96.85 | 88.37 | 96.84 | 2007 | 85.43 | 74.48 | 76.70 |
| 1980 | 94.88 | 84.12 | 90.39 | 1994 | 97.10 | 84.91 | 88.73 | 2008 | 88.46 | 70.70 | 81.31 |

*Source: IntercontinentalExchange (ICE); formerly New York Board of Trade (NYBOT)*

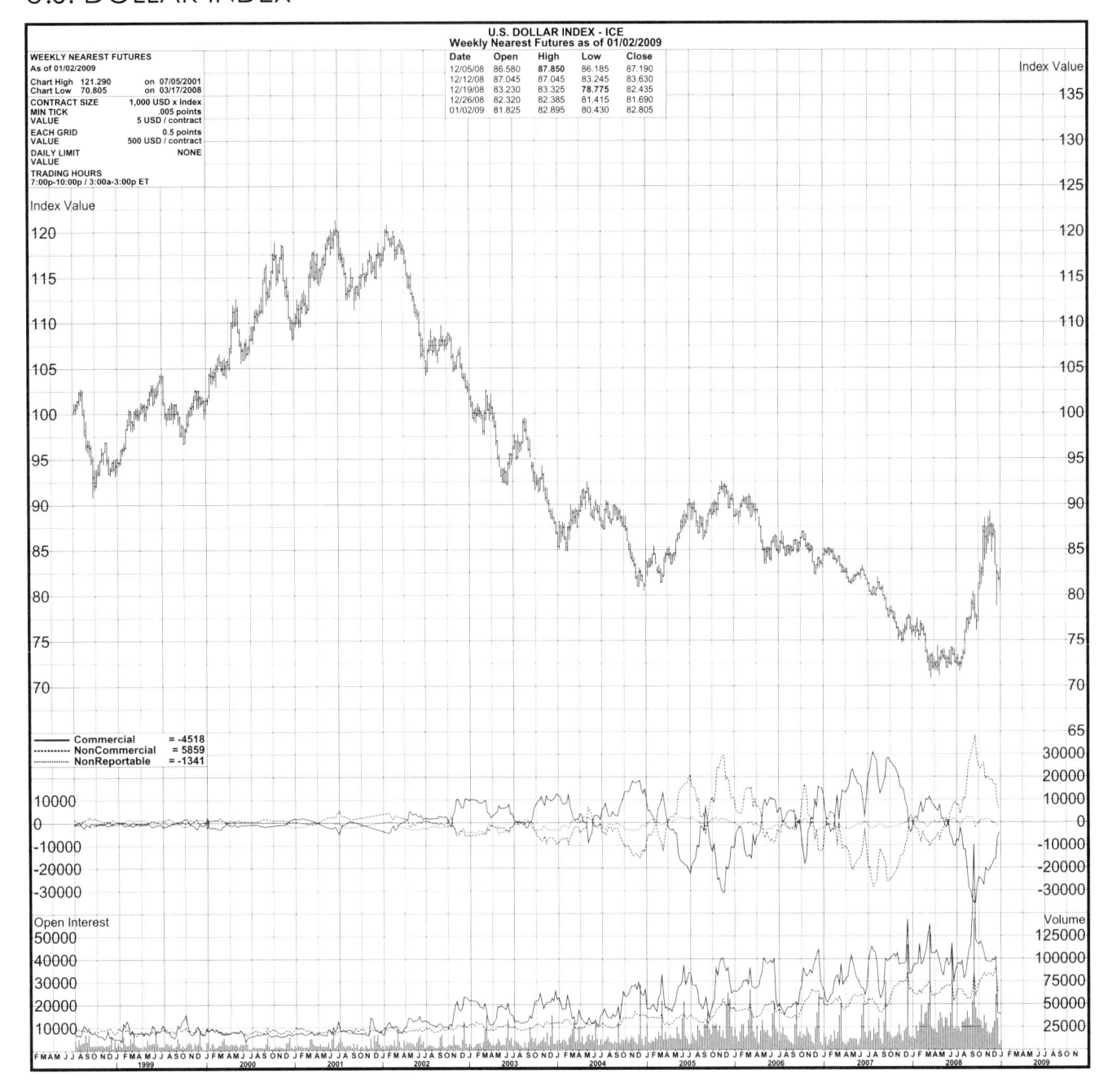

# U.S. DOLLAR INDEX

**U.S. DOLLAR INDEX - ICE**
Weekly Nearest Futures as of 01/02/2009

| Date | Open | High | Low | Close |
|---|---|---|---|---|
| 12/05/08 | 86.580 | 87.850 | 86.185 | 87.190 |
| 12/12/08 | 87.045 | 87.045 | 83.245 | 83.630 |
| 12/19/08 | 83.230 | 83.325 | 78.775 | 82.435 |
| 12/26/08 | 82.320 | 82.385 | 81.415 | 81.690 |
| 01/02/09 | 81.825 | 82.895 | 80.430 | 82.805 |

**WEEKLY NEAREST FUTURES** As of 01/02/2009
- Chart High 121.290 on 07/05/2001
- Chart Low 70.805 on 03/17/2008
- CONTRACT SIZE 1,000 USD x Index
- MIN TICK .005 points
- VALUE 5 USD / contract
- EACH GRID 0.5 points
- VALUE 500 USD / contract
- DAILY LIMIT NONE
- TRADING HOURS 7:00p-10:00p / 3:00a-3:00p ET

Commercial = -4518
NonCommercial = 5859
NonReportable = -1341

## Quarterly High, Low and Settle of U.S. Dollar Index Futures — Index Value

| Quarter | High | Low | Settle | Quarter | High | Low | Settle | Quarter | High | Low | Settle |
|---|---|---|---|---|---|---|---|---|---|---|---|
| 03/2000 | 106.63 | 99.40 | 105.16 | 03/2003 | 103.67 | 97.62 | 99.49 | 03/2006 | 91.18 | 87.69 | 89.39 |
| 06/2000 | 112.66 | 103.85 | 106.58 | 06/2003 | 102.19 | 92.16 | 95.11 | 06/2006 | 90.03 | 83.41 | 84.90 |
| 09/2000 | 116.52 | 106.44 | 113.00 | 09/2003 | 99.57 | 92.43 | 93.23 | 09/2006 | 87.05 | 84.17 | 85.68 |
| 12/2000 | 118.90 | 109.27 | 109.28 | 12/2003 | 94.32 | 86.70 | 87.26 | 12/2006 | 87.08 | 82.18 | 83.43 |
| 03/2001 | 117.78 | 108.04 | 117.63 | 03/2004 | 89.95 | 84.77 | 87.95 | 03/2007 | 85.25 | 82.38 | 82.66 |
| 06/2001 | 120.37 | 114.01 | 119.75 | 06/2004 | 92.50 | 87.30 | 89.00 | 06/2007 | 83.26 | 81.10 | 81.69 |
| 09/2001 | 121.29 | 111.35 | 113.96 | 09/2004 | 90.49 | 87.20 | 87.51 | 09/2007 | 82.00 | 77.58 | 77.63 |
| 12/2001 | 118.85 | 112.62 | 117.21 | 12/2004 | 88.79 | 80.48 | 81.00 | 12/2007 | 78.80 | 74.65 | 76.70 |
| 03/2002 | 120.80 | 116.00 | 119.06 | 03/2005 | 85.46 | 81.11 | 84.05 | 03/2008 | 77.49 | 70.81 | 72.17 |
| 06/2002 | 118.95 | 105.97 | 106.55 | 06/2005 | 89.35 | 83.31 | 88.98 | 06/2008 | 74.50 | 71.05 | 72.80 |
| 09/2002 | 109.75 | 104.12 | 107.26 | 09/2005 | 90.66 | 86.02 | 89.35 | 09/2008 | 80.40 | 71.56 | 79.36 |
| 12/2002 | 108.95 | 102.26 | 102.26 | 12/2005 | 92.53 | 88.35 | 90.96 | 12/2008 | 89.25 | 78.78 | 82.15 |

*Source: IntercontinentalExchange (ICE); formerly New York Board of Trade (NYBOT)*

# U.S. DOLLAR INDEX

**WEEKLY CASH**
As of 01/02/2009
Chart High 121.020 on 07/06/2001
Chart Low 70.698 on 03/17/2008

**U.S. DOLLAR INDEX**
Weekly Cash as of 01/02/2009

| Date | Open | High | Low | Close |
|---|---|---|---|---|
| 12/05/08 | 86.452 | **87.701** | 86.095 | 87.121 |
| 12/12/08 | 86.886 | 86.914 | 83.210 | 83.644 |
| 12/19/08 | 83.697 | 83.826 | **77.688** | 81.298 |
| 12/26/08 | 81.038 | 81.494 | 80.349 | 80.892 |
| 01/02/09 | 80.881 | 81.921 | 79.631 | 81.839 |

## Quarterly High, Low and Settle of U.S. Dollar Index    Index Value

| Quarter | High | Low | Settle | Quarter | High | Low | Settle | Quarter | High | Low | Settle |
|---|---|---|---|---|---|---|---|---|---|---|---|
| 03/2000 | 106.86 | 99.71 | 105.44 | 03/2003 | 103.20 | 97.57 | 99.06 | 03/2006 | 91.16 | 87.83 | 89.73 |
| 06/2000 | 112.86 | 104.23 | 106.84 | 06/2003 | 101.81 | 91.88 | 94.73 | 06/2006 | 90.40 | 83.60 | 85.22 |
| 09/2000 | 116.75 | 106.70 | 113.25 | 09/2003 | 99.49 | 92.10 | 92.85 | 09/2006 | 87.33 | 84.39 | 85.97 |
| 12/2000 | 119.07 | 109.46 | 109.56 | 12/2003 | 94.13 | 86.36 | 86.92 | 12/2006 | 87.30 | 82.24 | 83.72 |
| 03/2001 | 117.63 | 108.09 | 117.37 | 03/2004 | 89.84 | 84.56 | 87.61 | 03/2007 | 85.43 | 82.64 | 82.93 |
| 06/2001 | 120.33 | 113.86 | 119.43 | 06/2004 | 92.29 | 87.02 | 88.80 | 06/2007 | 83.27 | 81.25 | 81.92 |
| 09/2001 | 121.02 | 111.31 | 113.48 | 09/2004 | 90.29 | 87.00 | 87.36 | 09/2007 | 82.13 | 77.67 | 77.72 |
| 12/2001 | 118.26 | 112.27 | 116.82 | 12/2004 | 88.64 | 80.39 | 80.85 | 12/2007 | 78.89 | 74.48 | 76.70 |
| 03/2002 | 120.51 | 115.54 | 118.62 | 03/2005 | 85.44 | 80.77 | 84.06 | 03/2008 | 77.35 | 70.70 | 71.80 |
| 06/2002 | 118.75 | 105.37 | 106.11 | 06/2005 | 89.48 | 83.36 | 89.11 | 06/2008 | 74.31 | 71.19 | 72.46 |
| 09/2002 | 109.77 | 103.54 | 106.87 | 09/2005 | 90.77 | 85.99 | 89.52 | 09/2008 | 80.38 | 71.31 | 79.45 |
| 12/2002 | 108.74 | 101.80 | 101.85 | 12/2005 | 92.63 | 88.53 | 91.17 | 12/2008 | 88.46 | 77.69 | 81.31 |

*Source: IntercontinentalExchange (ICE); formerly New York Board of Trade (NYBOT)*

# AUSTRALIAN DOLLAR

**Annual High, Low and Settle of Australian Dollar Futures**     In USD per AUD

| Year | High | Low | Settle | Year | High | Low | Settle | Year | High | Low | Settle |
|---|---|---|---|---|---|---|---|---|---|---|---|
| 1967 | 1.1185 | 1.1088 | 1.1185 | 1981 | 1.1890 | 1.1225 | 1.1280 | 1995 | .7725 | .7055 | .7401 |
| 1968 | 1.1198 | 1.1084 | 1.1089 | 1982 | 1.1308 | .9339 | .9801 | 1996 | .8210 | .7276 | .7936 |
| 1969 | 1.1143 | 1.1081 | 1.1143 | 1983 | .9910 | .8542 | .8985 | 1997 | .8005 | .6475 | .6518 |
| 1970 | 1.1184 | 1.1087 | 1.1112 | 1984 | .9668 | .8187 | .8258 | 1998 | .7005 | .5465 | .6085 |
| 1971 | 1.1888 | 1.1124 | 1.1887 | 1985 | .8230 | .6350 | .6822 | 1999 | .6743 | .6123 | .6583 |
| 1972 | 1.2732 | 1.1880 | 1.2732 | 1986 | .7490 | .5715 | .6650 | 2000 | .6693 | .5075 | .5590 |
| 1973 | 1.4885 | 1.2710 | 1.4825 | 1987 | .7395 | .6288 | .7170 | 2001 | .5725 | .4774 | .5074 |
| 1974 | 1.4875 | 1.3025 | 1.3245 | 1988 | .8810 | .6940 | .8450 | 2002 | .5773 | .5033 | .5548 |
| 1975 | 1.3655 | 1.2518 | 1.2545 | 1989 | .8880 | .7315 | .7760 | 2003 | .7475 | .5578 | .7455 |
| 1976 | 1.2610 | 1.0054 | 1.0890 | 1990 | .8335 | .7330 | .7656 | 2004 | .7980 | .6730 | .7790 |
| 1977 | 1.1410 | 1.0822 | 1.1380 | 1991 | .7985 | .7493 | .7565 | 2005 | .7992 | .7214 | .7325 |
| 1978 | 1.1860 | 1.1230 | 1.1500 | 1992 | .7670 | .6775 | .6869 | 2006 | .7931 | .7006 | .7866 |
| 1979 | 1.1518 | 1.0902 | 1.1057 | 1993 | .7242 | .6392 | .6770 | 2007 | .9382 | .7665 | .8726 |
| 1980 | 1.1814 | 1.0670 | 1.1814 | 1994 | .7795 | .6762 | .7730 | 2008 | .9770 | .5975 | .6997 |

Futures begin trading 01/13/1987.     Source: CME Group; Chicago Mercantile Exchange

# AUSTRALIAN DOLLAR

**AUSTRALIAN DOLLAR / U.S. DOLLAR**
Monthly Cash as of 12/31/2008

| Date | Open | High | Low | Close |
|---|---|---|---|---|
| 08/29/08 | .9423 | .9424 | .8494 | .8579 |
| 09/30/08 | .8580 | .8581 | .7804 | .7916 |
| 10/31/08 | .7923 | .8020 | .6010 | .6673 |
| 11/28/08 | .6710 | .7017 | .6077 | .6548 |
| 12/31/08 | .6503 | .7132 | .6295 | .7029 |

MONTHLY CASH
As of 12/31/2008
Chart High 1.4885 on 12/07/1973
Chart Low .4778 on 04/02/2001

## Annual High, Low and Settle of Australian Dollar    In USD per AUD

| Year | High | Low | Settle | Year | High | Low | Settle | Year | High | Low | Settle |
|---|---|---|---|---|---|---|---|---|---|---|---|
| 1967 | 1.1185 | 1.1088 | 1.1185 | 1981 | 1.1890 | 1.1225 | 1.1280 | 1995 | .7764 | .7077 | .7437 |
| 1968 | 1.1198 | 1.1084 | 1.1089 | 1982 | 1.1308 | .9339 | .9801 | 1996 | .8211 | .7313 | .7943 |
| 1969 | 1.1143 | 1.1081 | 1.1143 | 1983 | .9910 | .8542 | .8985 | 1997 | .8012 | .6463 | .6515 |
| 1970 | 1.1184 | 1.1087 | 1.1112 | 1984 | .9668 | .8187 | .8258 | 1998 | .6880 | .5503 | .6101 |
| 1971 | 1.1888 | 1.1124 | 1.1887 | 1985 | .8230 | .6350 | .6822 | 1999 | .6745 | .6106 | .6568 |
| 1972 | 1.2732 | 1.1880 | 1.2732 | 1986 | .7490 | .5715 | .6650 | 2000 | .6685 | .5075 | .5585 |
| 1973 | 1.4885 | 1.2710 | 1.4825 | 1987 | .7395 | .6380 | .7215 | 2001 | .5725 | .4778 | .5106 |
| 1974 | 1.4875 | 1.3025 | 1.3245 | 1988 | .8833 | .6955 | .8540 | 2002 | .5796 | .5052 | .5615 |
| 1975 | 1.3655 | 1.2518 | 1.2545 | 1989 | .8967 | .7270 | .7880 | 2003 | .7537 | .5614 | .7521 |
| 1976 | 1.2610 | 1.0054 | 1.0890 | 1990 | .8480 | .7392 | .7718 | 2004 | .8003 | .6777 | .7825 |
| 1977 | 1.1410 | 1.0822 | 1.1380 | 1991 | .8038 | .7500 | .7595 | 2005 | .7990 | .7234 | .7335 |
| 1978 | 1.1860 | 1.1230 | 1.1500 | 1992 | .7705 | .6783 | .6885 | 2006 | .7930 | .7016 | .7894 |
| 1979 | 1.1518 | 1.0902 | 1.1057 | 1993 | .7253 | .6413 | .6793 | 2007 | .9398 | .7681 | .8748 |
| 1980 | 1.1814 | 1.0670 | 1.1814 | 1994 | .7789 | .6773 | .7764 | 2008 | .9849 | .6010 | .7029 |

Data continued from page 20.    *Source: Forex*

17

# AUSTRALIAN DOLLAR

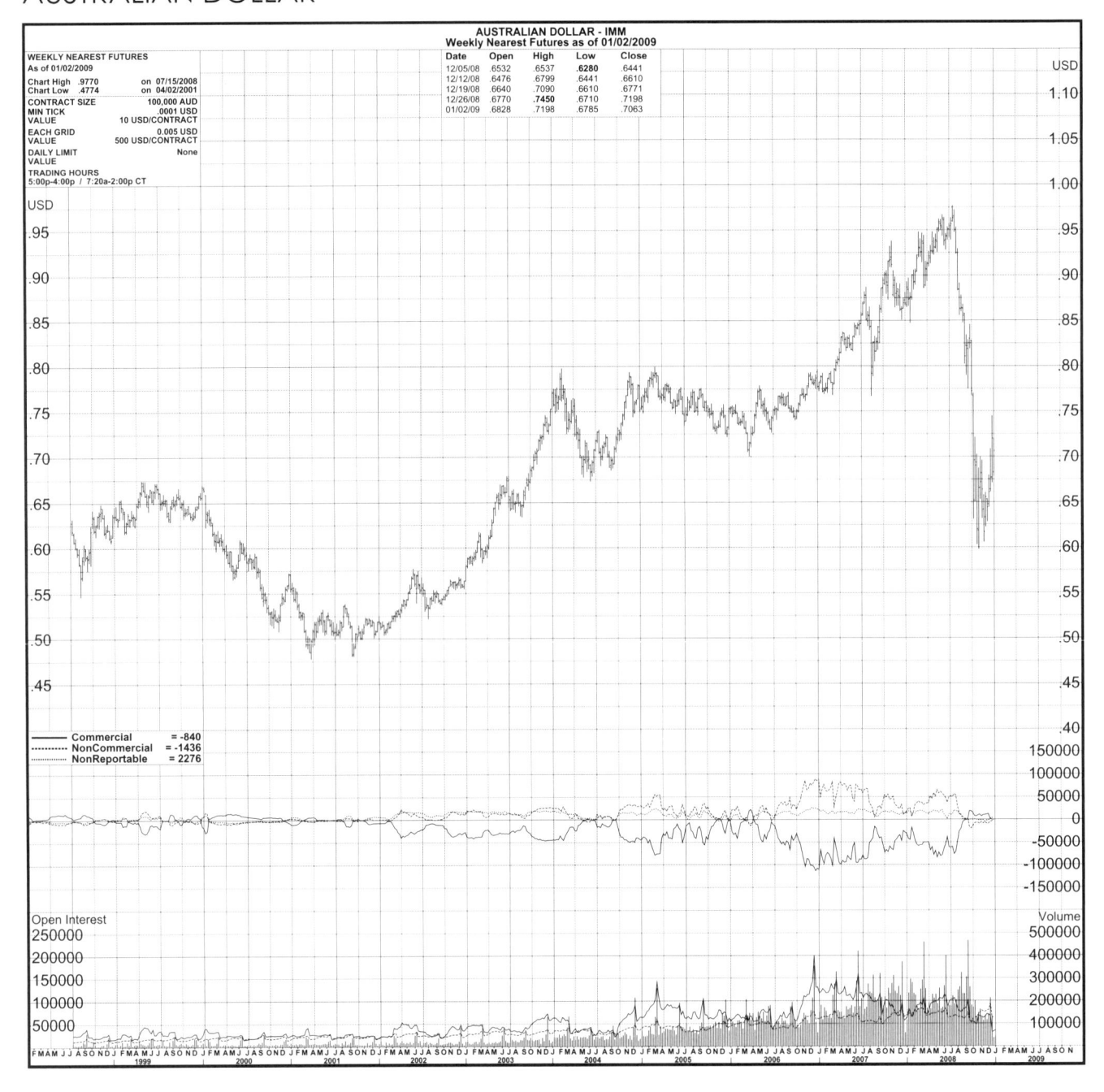

**WEEKLY NEAREST FUTURES**
As of 01/02/2009
Chart High .9770 on 07/15/2008
Chart Low .4774 on 04/02/2001
CONTRACT SIZE 100,000 AUD
MIN TICK .0001 USD
VALUE 10 USD/CONTRACT
EACH GRID 0.005 USD
VALUE 500 USD/CONTRACT
DAILY LIMIT None
VALUE
TRADING HOURS
5:00p-4:00p / 7:20a-2:00p CT

**AUSTRALIAN DOLLAR - IMM**
Weekly Nearest Futures as of 01/02/2009

| Date | Open | High | Low | Close |
|---|---|---|---|---|
| 12/05/08 | .6532 | .6537 | .6280 | .6441 |
| 12/12/08 | .6476 | .6799 | .6441 | .6610 |
| 12/19/08 | .6640 | .7090 | .6610 | .6771 |
| 12/26/08 | .6770 | .7450 | .6710 | .7198 |
| 01/02/09 | .6828 | .7198 | .6785 | .7063 |

Commercial = -840
NonCommercial = -1436
NonReportable = 2276

## Quarterly High, Low and Settle of Australian Dollar Futures   In USD per AUD

| Quarter | High | Low | Settle | Quarter | High | Low | Settle | Quarter | High | Low | Settle |
|---|---|---|---|---|---|---|---|---|---|---|---|
| 03/2000 | .6693 | .5962 | .6082 | 03/2003 | .6178 | .5578 | .5987 | 03/2006 | .7579 | .7006 | .7157 |
| 06/2000 | .6107 | .5651 | .5980 | 06/2003 | .6703 | .5887 | .6674 | 06/2006 | .7789 | .7107 | .7428 |
| 09/2000 | .6025 | .5360 | .5431 | 09/2003 | .6817 | .6335 | .6746 | 09/2006 | .7718 | .7393 | .7444 |
| 12/2000 | .5598 | .5075 | .5590 | 12/2003 | .7475 | .6700 | .7455 | 12/2006 | .7931 | .7404 | .7866 |
| 03/2001 | .5725 | .4848 | .4852 | 03/2004 | .7980 | .7255 | .7589 | 03/2007 | .8108 | .7678 | .8072 |
| 06/2001 | .5329 | .4774 | .5084 | 06/2004 | .7649 | .6730 | .6910 | 06/2007 | .8504 | .8048 | .8460 |
| 09/2001 | .5389 | .4802 | .4895 | 09/2004 | .7304 | .6850 | .7233 | 09/2007 | .8871 | .7665 | .8857 |
| 12/2001 | .5237 | .4888 | .5074 | 12/2004 | .7938 | .7140 | .7790 | 12/2007 | .9382 | .8508 | .8726 |
| 03/2002 | .5320 | .5033 | .5309 | 03/2005 | .7992 | .7475 | .7685 | 03/2008 | .9481 | .8469 | .9041 |
| 06/2002 | .5773 | .5231 | .5600 | 06/2005 | .7819 | .7469 | .7564 | 06/2008 | .9670 | .8938 | .9493 |
| 09/2002 | .5680 | .5214 | .5392 | 09/2005 | .7761 | .7336 | .7601 | 09/2008 | .9770 | .7748 | .7886 |
| 12/2002 | .5682 | .5369 | .5548 | 12/2005 | .7622 | .7214 | .7325 | 12/2008 | .7990 | .5975 | .6997 |

*Source: CME Group; Chicago Mercantile Exchange*

# AUSTRALIAN DOLLAR

**AUSTRALIAN DOLLAR / U.S. DOLLAR**
Weekly Cash as of 01/02/2009

| Date | Open | High | Low | Close |
|---|---|---|---|---|
| 12/05/08 | .6503 | .6549 | .6295 | .6471 |
| 12/12/08 | .6462 | .6803 | .6452 | .6641 |
| 12/19/08 | .6645 | .7132 | .6612 | .6803 |
| 12/26/08 | .6847 | .6895 | .6759 | .6842 |
| 01/02/09 | .6852 | .7118 | .6835 | .7114 |

WEEKLY CASH
As of 01/02/2009
Chart High  .9849  on 07/15/2008
Chart Low   .4778  on 04/02/2001

## Quarterly High, Low and Settle of Australian Dollar    In USD per AUD

| Quarter | High | Low | Settle | Quarter | High | Low | Settle | Quarter | High | Low | Settle |
|---|---|---|---|---|---|---|---|---|---|---|---|
| 03/2000 | .6685 | .6010 | .6075 | 03/2003 | .6179 | .5614 | .6041 | 03/2006 | .7586 | .7016 | .7157 |
| 06/2000 | .6103 | .5650 | .5964 | 06/2003 | .6738 | .5924 | .6726 | 06/2006 | .7792 | .7117 | .7428 |
| 09/2000 | .6018 | .5367 | .5425 | 09/2003 | .6871 | .6343 | .6808 | 09/2006 | .7720 | .7402 | .7455 |
| 12/2000 | .5594 | .5075 | .5585 | 12/2003 | .7537 | .6760 | .7521 | 12/2006 | .7930 | .7414 | .7894 |
| 03/2001 | .5725 | .4853 | .4854 | 03/2004 | .8003 | .7258 | .7655 | 03/2007 | .8127 | .7681 | .8086 |
| 06/2001 | .5316 | .4778 | .5111 | 06/2004 | .7692 | .6777 | .6972 | 06/2007 | .8521 | .8067 | .8480 |
| 09/2001 | .5390 | .4823 | .4912 | 09/2004 | .7348 | .6857 | .7278 | 09/2007 | .8886 | .7683 | .8876 |
| 12/2001 | .5251 | .4900 | .5106 | 12/2004 | .7947 | .7187 | .7825 | 12/2007 | .9398 | .8556 | .8748 |
| 03/2002 | .5357 | .5052 | .5334 | 03/2005 | .7990 | .7507 | .7731 | 03/2008 | .9497 | .8527 | .9134 |
| 06/2002 | .5796 | .5258 | .5635 | 06/2005 | .7841 | .7477 | .7605 | 06/2008 | .9668 | .9032 | .9585 |
| 09/2002 | .5713 | .5230 | .5434 | 09/2005 | .7765 | .7370 | .7629 | 09/2008 | .9849 | .7804 | .7916 |
| 12/2002 | .5692 | .5402 | .5615 | 12/2005 | .7646 | .7234 | .7335 | 12/2008 | .8020 | .6010 | .7029 |

*Source: Forex*

# AUSTRALIAN DOLLAR

**AUSTRALIAN DOLLAR / U.S. DOLLAR**
Quarterly Cash as of 12/31/2008

| Date | Open | High | Low | Close |
|---|---|---|---|---|
| 12/31/07 | .8883 | .9398 | .8556 | .8748 |
| 03/31/08 | .8762 | .9497 | .8527 | .9134 |
| 06/30/08 | .9132 | .9668 | .9032 | .9585 |
| 09/30/08 | .9585 | .9849 | .7804 | .7916 |
| 12/31/08 | .7923 | .8020 | **.6010** | .7029 |

QUARTERLY CASH
As of 12/31/2008
Chart High 2.4161 on 12/31/1928
Chart Low .4778 on 04/02/2001

## Annual High, Low and Settle of Australian Dollar    In USD per AUD

| Year | High | Low | Settle | Year | High | Low | Settle | Year | High | Low | Settle |
|---|---|---|---|---|---|---|---|---|---|---|---|
| 1925 | | | | 1939 | 1.8667 | 1.5633 | 1.5657 | 1953 | 1.1231 | 1.1167 | 1.1197 |
| 1926 | | | | 1940 | 1.6079 | 1.3040 | 1.6075 | 1954 | 1.1229 | 1.1105 | 1.1105 |
| 1927 | | | | 1941 | 1.6085 | 1.6056 | 1.6075 | 1955 | 1.1166 | 1.1090 | 1.1166 |
| 1928 | 2.4161 | 2.4161 | 2.4161 | 1942 | 1.6075 | 1.6075 | 1.6075 | 1956 | 1.1186 | 1.1086 | 1.1096 |
| 1929 | 2.4042 | 2.4042 | 2.4042 | 1943 | 1.6075 | 1.6075 | 1.6075 | 1957 | 1.1179 | 1.1087 | 1.1179 |
| 1930 | 2.2930 | 2.2930 | 2.2930 | 1944 | ---- | ---- | ---- | 1958 | 1.1224 | 1.1169 | 1.1171 |
| 1931 | 1.8648 | 1.3425 | 1.3425 | 1945 | 1.6071 | 1.6035 | 1.6071 | 1959 | 1.1221 | 1.1149 | 1.1149 |
| 1932 | 1.4970 | 1.3075 | 1.3089 | 1946 | 1.6071 | 1.6054 | 1.6054 | 1960 | 1.1209 | 1.1155 | 1.1185 |
| 1933 | 2.0488 | 1.3360 | 2.0375 | 1947 | 1.6061 | 1.6045 | 1.6061 | 1961 | 1.1217 | 1.1105 | 1.1194 |
| 1934 | 2.0527 | 1.9576 | 1.9614 | 1948 | 1.6062 | 1.6058 | 1.6062 | 1962 | 1.1216 | 1.1159 | 1.1169 |
| 1935 | 1.9726 | 1.8928 | 1.9564 | 1949 | 1.6062 | 1.1158 | 1.1158 | 1963 | 1.1175 | 1.1142 | 1.1142 |
| 1936 | 2.0053 | 1.9477 | 1.9550 | 1950 | 1.1158 | 1.1155 | 1.1155 | 1964 | 1.1153 | 1.1090 | 1.1118 |
| 1937 | 1.9908 | 1.9463 | 1.9905 | 1951 | 1.1158 | 1.1131 | 1.1131 | 1965 | 1.1170 | 1.1119 | 1.1164 |
| 1938 | 1.9991 | 1.8603 | 1.8603 | 1952 | 1.1205 | 1.1087 | 1.1179 | 1966 | 1.1171 | 1.1111 | 1.1116 |

Data through 02/14/1966 is theoretical based on AUP / 2.    Data continued on page 17.    *Source: Forex*

# BRITISH POUND

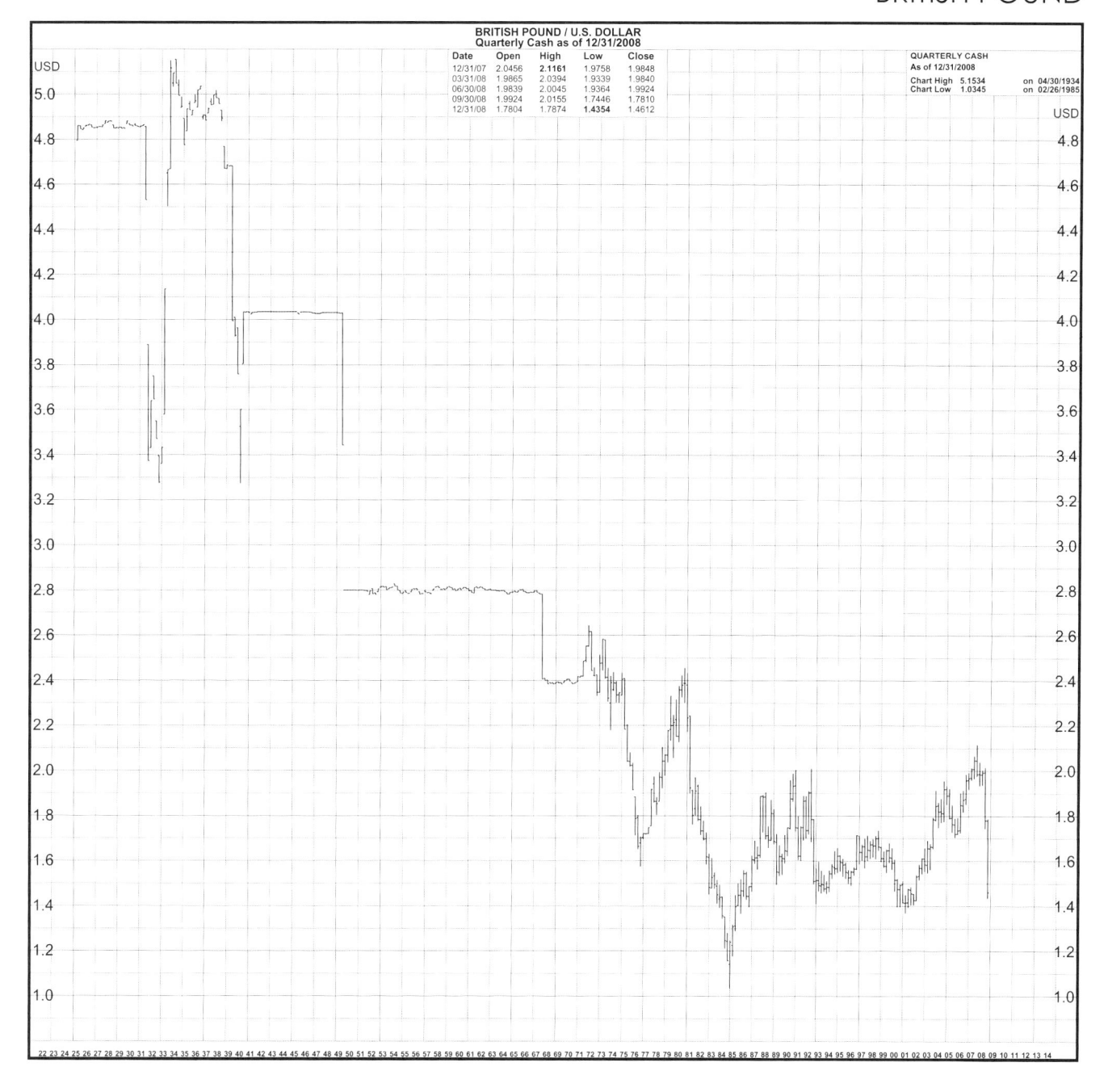

**BRITISH POUND / U.S. DOLLAR**
Quarterly Cash as of 12/31/2008

| Date | Open | High | Low | Close |
|---|---|---|---|---|
| 12/31/07 | 2.0456 | 2.1161 | 1.9758 | 1.9848 |
| 03/31/08 | 1.9865 | 2.0394 | 1.9339 | 1.9840 |
| 06/30/08 | 1.9839 | 2.0045 | 1.9364 | 1.9924 |
| 09/30/08 | 1.9924 | 2.0155 | 1.7446 | 1.7810 |
| 12/31/08 | 1.7804 | 1.7874 | 1.4354 | 1.4612 |

QUARTERLY CASH
As of 12/31/2008
Chart High 5.1534 on 04/30/1934
Chart Low 1.0345 on 02/26/1985

## Annual High, Low and Settle of British Pound    In USD per GBP

| Year | High | Low | Settle | Year | High | Low | Settle | Year | High | Low | Settle |
|---|---|---|---|---|---|---|---|---|---|---|---|
| 1925 | 4.8604 | 4.7724 | 4.8498 | 1939 | 4.6857 | 3.9247 | 3.9301 | 1953 | 2.8190 | 2.8028 | 2.8103 |
| 1926 | 4.8661 | 4.8488 | 4.8513 | 1940 | 4.0356 | 3.2736 | 4.0350 | 1954 | 2.8281 | 2.7874 | 2.7874 |
| 1927 | 4.8825 | 4.8503 | 4.8825 | 1941 | 4.0350 | 4.0248 | 4.0350 | 1955 | 2.8026 | 2.7836 | 2.8026 |
| 1928 | 4.8820 | 4.8492 | 4.8524 | 1942 | 4.0350 | 4.0348 | 4.0350 | 1956 | 2.8077 | 2.7825 | 2.7850 |
| 1929 | 4.8816 | 4.8482 | 4.8816 | 1943 | 4.0350 | 4.0350 | 4.0350 | 1957 | 2.8058 | 2.7827 | 2.8058 |
| 1930 | 4.8707 | 4.8564 | 4.8566 | 1944 | 4.0350 | 4.0350 | 4.0350 | 1958 | 2.8171 | 2.8033 | 2.8034 |
| 1931 | 4.8649 | 3.3737 | 3.3737 | 1945 | 4.0350 | 4.0249 | 4.0337 | 1959 | 2.8165 | 2.7984 | 2.7984 |
| 1932 | 3.7500 | 3.2753 | 3.2787 | 1946 | 4.0338 | 4.0294 | 4.0294 | 1960 | 2.8135 | 2.7997 | 2.8073 |
| 1933 | 5.1497 | 3.3614 | 5.1159 | 1947 | 4.0313 | 4.0271 | 4.0313 | 1961 | 2.8154 | 2.7874 | 2.8096 |
| 1934 | 5.1534 | 4.9408 | 4.9458 | 1948 | 4.0315 | 4.0307 | 4.0315 | 1962 | 2.8153 | 2.8009 | 2.8033 |
| 1935 | 4.9699 | 4.7762 | 4.9288 | 1949 | 4.0314 | 2.8007 | 2.8007 | 1963 | 2.8048 | 2.7965 | 2.7965 |
| 1936 | 5.0363 | 4.8880 | 4.9078 | 1950 | 2.8007 | 2.8000 | 2.8000 | 1964 | 2.7994 | 2.7834 | 2.7906 |
| 1937 | 4.9964 | 4.8851 | 4.9964 | 1951 | 2.8007 | 2.7949 | 2.7949 | 1965 | 2.8037 | 2.7908 | 2.8021 |
| 1938 | 5.0180 | 4.6703 | 4.6703 | 1952 | 2.8079 | 2.7812 | 2.8059 | 1966 | 2.8039 | 2.7888 | 2.7901 |

Data continued on page 23.    *Source: Forex*

# BRITISH POUND

**BRITISH POUND - IMM**
Monthly Nearest Futures as of 12/31/2008

| Date | Open | High | Low | Close |
|---|---|---|---|---|
| 08/31/08 | 1.9774 | 1.9779 | 1.8150 | 1.8156 |
| 09/30/08 | 1.8169 | 1.8624 | 1.7442 | 1.7840 |
| 10/31/08 | 1.7879 | 1.7921 | 1.5224 | 1.6106 |
| 11/30/08 | 1.6032 | 1.6363 | 1.4551 | 1.5371 |
| 12/31/08 | 1.5371 | 1.5700 | **1.4329** | 1.4557 |

**MONTHLY NEAREST FUTURES** As of 12/31/2008

| | | |
|---|---|---|
| Chart High | 2.7992 | on 04/28/1967 |
| Chart Low | 1.0345 | on 02/26/1985 |
| CONTRACT SIZE | | 62,500 GBP |
| MIN TICK | | .0001 USD |
| VALUE | | 6.25 USD / contract |
| EACH GRID | | 0.01 USD |
| VALUE | | 625 USD / contract |
| DAILY LIMIT VALUE | | None |
| TRADING HOURS | | 5:00p-4:00p / 7:20a-2:00p CT |

## Annual High, Low and Settle of British Pound Futures — In USD per GBP

| Year | High | Low | Settle | Year | High | Low | Settle | Year | High | Low | Settle |
|---|---|---|---|---|---|---|---|---|---|---|---|
| 1967 | 2.7992 | 2.4063 | 2.4063 | 1981 | 2.4475 | 1.7645 | 1.9040 | 1995 | 1.6570 | 1.5200 | 1.5514 |
| 1968 | 2.4092 | 2.3842 | 2.3842 | 1982 | 1.9340 | 1.5820 | 1.6295 | 1996 | 1.7128 | 1.4880 | 1.7124 |
| 1969 | 2.3973 | 2.3840 | 2.3973 | 1983 | 1.6310 | 1.4105 | 1.4625 | 1997 | 1.7114 | 1.5650 | 1.6466 |
| 1970 | 2.4061 | 2.3853 | 2.3906 | 1984 | 1.4975 | 1.1525 | 1.1540 | 1998 | 1.7300 | 1.6042 | 1.6568 |
| 1971 | 2.5538 | 2.3938 | 2.5520 | 1985 | 1.4975 | 1.0345 | 1.4390 | 1999 | 1.6798 | 1.5476 | 1.6190 |
| 1972 | 2.6440 | 2.3270 | 2.3342 | 1986 | 1.5525 | 1.3600 | 1.4720 | 2000 | 1.6578 | 1.3952 | 1.4948 |
| 1973 | 2.5880 | 2.2550 | 2.2940 | 1987 | 1.8845 | 1.4530 | 1.8825 | 2001 | 1.5700 | 1.3652 | 1.4486 |
| 1974 | 2.4270 | 2.1340 | 2.2910 | 1988 | 1.9045 | 1.6456 | 1.7992 | 2002 | 1.6052 | 1.4004 | 1.6022 |
| 1975 | 2.4300 | 1.9920 | 2.0040 | 1989 | 1.8180 | 1.4940 | 1.5888 | 2003 | 1.7843 | 1.5390 | 1.7739 |
| 1976 | 2.0255 | 1.5290 | 1.6640 | 1990 | 1.9740 | 1.5640 | 1.9094 | 2004 | 1.9500 | 1.7436 | 1.9071 |
| 1977 | 1.9250 | 1.6670 | 1.9195 | 1991 | 1.9898 | 1.5824 | 1.8448 | 2005 | 1.9318 | 1.7046 | 1.7187 |
| 1978 | 2.0985 | 1.7960 | 2.0410 | 1992 | 2.0088 | 1.4780 | 1.4986 | 2006 | 1.9853 | 1.7186 | 1.9572 |
| 1979 | 2.3245 | 1.9685 | 2.2015 | 1993 | 1.5904 | 1.4050 | 1.4684 | 2007 | 2.1138 | 1.9183 | 1.9785 |
| 1980 | 2.4485 | 2.1280 | 2.4185 | 1994 | 1.6436 | 1.4522 | 1.5670 | 2008 | 2.0397 | 1.4329 | 1.4557 |

Futures begin trading 05/16/1972.   Source: CME Group; Chicago Mercantile Exchange

# BRITISH POUND

**BRITISH POUND / U.S. DOLLAR**
Monthly Cash as of 12/31/2008

| Date | Open | High | Low | Close |
|---|---|---|---|---|
| 08/29/08 | 1.9841 | 1.9841 | 1.8175 | 1.8217 |
| 09/30/08 | 1.8201 | 1.8668 | 1.7446 | 1.7810 |
| 10/31/08 | 1.7804 | 1.7874 | 1.5268 | 1.6083 |
| 11/28/08 | 1.6116 | 1.6403 | 1.4557 | 1.5377 |
| 12/31/08 | 1.5377 | 1.5722 | 1.4354 | 1.4612 |

MONTHLY CASH
As of 12/31/2008
Chart High 2.7992 on 04/28/1967
Chart Low 1.0345 on 02/26/1985

## Annual High, Low and Settle of British Pound    In USD per GBP

| Year | High | Low | Settle | Year | High | Low | Settle | Year | High | Low | Settle |
|---|---|---|---|---|---|---|---|---|---|---|---|
| 1967 | 2.7992 | 2.4063 | 2.4063 | 1981 | 2.4320 | 1.7610 | 1.9100 | 1995 | 1.6570 | 1.5213 | 1.5507 |
| 1968 | 2.4092 | 2.3842 | 2.3842 | 1982 | 1.9390 | 1.5840 | 1.6180 | 1996 | 1.7163 | 1.4898 | 1.7140 |
| 1969 | 2.3973 | 2.3840 | 2.3973 | 1983 | 1.6310 | 1.4105 | 1.4500 | 1997 | 1.7145 | 1.5678 | 1.6480 |
| 1970 | 2.4061 | 2.3853 | 2.3906 | 1984 | 1.4950 | 1.1560 | 1.1575 | 1998 | 1.7365 | 1.6085 | 1.6628 |
| 1971 | 2.5538 | 2.3938 | 2.5520 | 1985 | 1.5015 | 1.0345 | 1.4475 | 1999 | 1.6791 | 1.5475 | 1.6150 |
| 1972 | 2.6440 | 2.3312 | 2.3478 | 1986 | 1.5590 | 1.3660 | 1.4865 | 2000 | 1.6581 | 1.3955 | 1.4926 |
| 1973 | 2.5843 | 2.3055 | 2.3222 | 1987 | 1.8875 | 1.4640 | 1.8870 | 2001 | 1.5100 | 1.3688 | 1.4555 |
| 1974 | 2.4370 | 2.1780 | 2.3460 | 1988 | 1.9055 | 1.6565 | 1.8115 | 2002 | 1.6133 | 1.4044 | 1.6100 |
| 1975 | 2.4343 | 2.0173 | 2.0237 | 1989 | 1.8305 | 1.4935 | 1.6110 | 2003 | 1.7944 | 1.5463 | 1.7860 |
| 1976 | 2.0358 | 1.5745 | 1.7006 | 1990 | 1.9875 | 1.5885 | 1.9320 | 2004 | 1.9553 | 1.7482 | 1.9188 |
| 1977 | 1.9195 | 1.6950 | 1.9170 | 1991 | 2.0040 | 1.5995 | 1.8655 | 2005 | 1.9326 | 1.7047 | 1.7208 |
| 1978 | 2.1050 | 1.8040 | 2.0420 | 1992 | 2.0100 | 1.4965 | 1.5095 | 2006 | 1.9847 | 1.7191 | 1.9578 |
| 1979 | 2.3325 | 1.9780 | 2.2130 | 1993 | 1.5971 | 1.4082 | 1.4760 | 2007 | 2.1161 | 1.9186 | 1.9848 |
| 1980 | 2.4555 | 2.1255 | 2.3875 | 1994 | 1.6440 | 1.4545 | 1.5660 | 2008 | 2.0394 | 1.4354 | 1.4612 |

Data continued from page 21.    *Source: Forex*

# BRITISH POUND

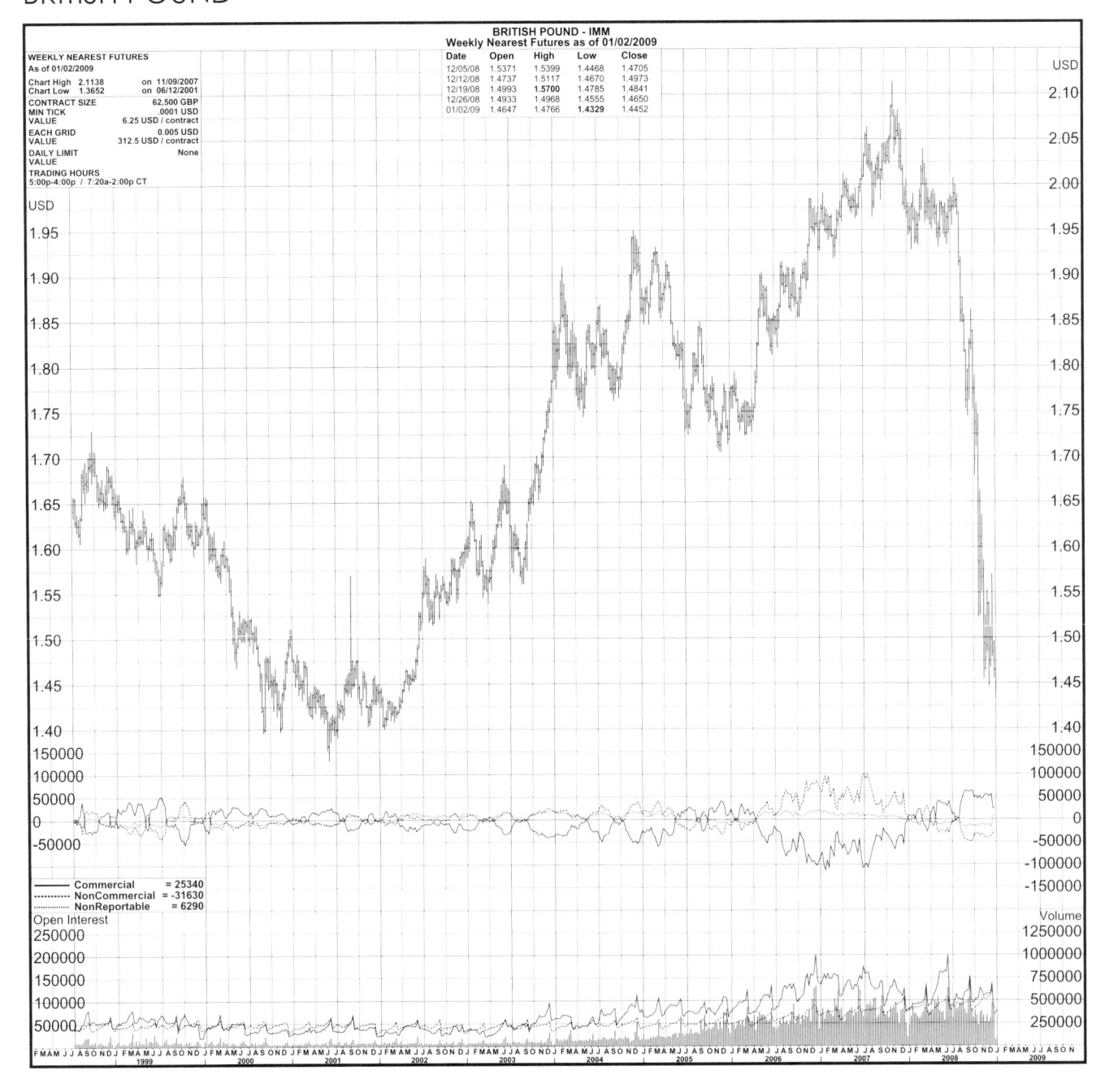

**BRITISH POUND - IMM**
Weekly Nearest Futures as of 01/02/2009

| Date | Open | High | Low | Close |
|---|---|---|---|---|
| 12/05/08 | 1.5371 | 1.5399 | 1.4468 | 1.4705 |
| 12/12/08 | 1.4737 | 1.5117 | 1.4670 | 1.4973 |
| 12/19/08 | 1.4993 | 1.5700 | 1.4785 | 1.4841 |
| 12/26/08 | 1.4933 | 1.4968 | 1.4555 | 1.4650 |
| 01/02/09 | 1.4647 | 1.4766 | 1.4329 | 1.4452 |

**WEEKLY NEAREST FUTURES**
As of 01/02/2009
Chart High 2.1138 on 11/09/2007
Chart Low 1.3652 on 06/12/2001
CONTRACT SIZE 62,500 GBP
MIN TICK .0001 USD
VALUE 6.25 USD / contract
EACH GRID 0.005 USD
VALUE 312.5 USD / contract
DAILY LIMIT None
VALUE
TRADING HOURS
5:00p-4:00p / 7:20a-2:00p CT

Commercial = 25340
NonCommercial = -31630
NonReportable = 6290

## Quarterly High, Low and Settle of British Pound Futures    In USD per GBP

| Quarter | High | Low | Settle | Quarter | High | Low | Settle | Quarter | High | Low | Settle |
|---|---|---|---|---|---|---|---|---|---|---|---|
| 03/2000 | 1.6578 | 1.5620 | 1.5940 | 03/2003 | 1.6524 | 1.5448 | 1.5724 | 03/2006 | 1.7938 | 1.7186 | 1.7380 |
| 06/2000 | 1.6090 | 1.4670 | 1.5186 | 06/2003 | 1.6920 | 1.5390 | 1.6468 | 06/2006 | 1.9035 | 1.7265 | 1.8508 |
| 09/2000 | 1.5236 | 1.3952 | 1.4770 | 09/2003 | 1.6672 | 1.5596 | 1.6536 | 09/2006 | 1.9161 | 1.8200 | 1.8730 |
| 12/2000 | 1.5000 | 1.3966 | 1.4948 | 12/2003 | 1.7843 | 1.6444 | 1.7739 | 12/2006 | 1.9853 | 1.8529 | 1.9572 |
| 03/2001 | 1.5110 | 1.4150 | 1.4158 | 03/2004 | 1.9102 | 1.7720 | 1.8316 | 03/2007 | 1.9914 | 1.9183 | 1.9669 |
| 06/2001 | 1.4486 | 1.3652 | 1.4094 | 06/2004 | 1.8490 | 1.7436 | 1.8057 | 06/2007 | 2.0128 | 1.9584 | 2.0055 |
| 09/2001 | 1.5700 | 1.3900 | 1.4668 | 09/2004 | 1.8683 | 1.7612 | 1.8023 | 09/2007 | 2.0636 | 1.9638 | 2.0419 |
| 12/2001 | 1.4772 | 1.4028 | 1.4486 | 12/2004 | 1.9500 | 1.7650 | 1.9071 | 12/2007 | 2.1138 | 1.9712 | 1.9785 |
| 03/2002 | 1.4486 | 1.4004 | 1.4190 | 03/2005 | 1.9318 | 1.8456 | 1.8826 | 03/2008 | 2.0397 | 1.9280 | 1.9712 |
| 06/2002 | 1.5308 | 1.4184 | 1.5244 | 06/2005 | 1.9168 | 1.7829 | 1.7863 | 06/2008 | 1.9966 | 1.9313 | 1.9819 |
| 09/2002 | 1.5900 | 1.5086 | 1.5626 | 09/2005 | 1.8492 | 1.7242 | 1.7603 | 09/2008 | 2.0074 | 1.7442 | 1.7840 |
| 12/2002 | 1.6052 | 1.5362 | 1.6022 | 12/2005 | 1.7894 | 1.7046 | 1.7187 | 12/2008 | 1.7921 | 1.4329 | 1.4557 |

*Source: CME Group; Chicago Mercantile Exchange*

# BRITISH POUND

**BRITISH POUND / U.S. DOLLAR**
Weekly Cash as of 01/02/2009

| Date | Open | High | Low | Close |
|---|---|---|---|---|
| 12/05/08 | 1.5377 | 1.5397 | 1.4472 | 1.4715 |
| 12/12/08 | 1.4740 | 1.5117 | 1.4681 | 1.4962 |
| 12/19/08 | 1.4946 | 1.5722 | 1.4812 | 1.4934 |
| 12/26/08 | 1.4943 | 1.4989 | 1.4577 | 1.4628 |
| 01/02/09 | 1.4630 | 1.4830 | 1.4354 | 1.4544 |

WEEKLY CASH
As of 01/02/2009
Chart High 2.1161 on 11/09/2007
Chart Low 1.3688 on 06/12/2001

## Quarterly High, Low and Settle of British Pound   In USD per GBP

| Quarter | High | Low | Settle | Quarter | High | Low | Settle | Quarter | High | Low | Settle |
|---|---|---|---|---|---|---|---|---|---|---|---|
| 03/2000 | 1.6581 | 1.5620 | 1.5919 | 03/2003 | 1.6570 | 1.5539 | 1.5838 | 03/2006 | 1.7935 | 1.7191 | 1.7365 |
| 06/2000 | 1.6070 | 1.4655 | 1.5163 | 06/2003 | 1.6904 | 1.5463 | 1.6555 | 06/2006 | 1.9024 | 1.7251 | 1.8483 |
| 09/2000 | 1.5216 | 1.3955 | 1.4749 | 09/2003 | 1.6760 | 1.5610 | 1.6631 | 09/2006 | 1.9144 | 1.8178 | 1.8716 |
| 12/2000 | 1.4979 | 1.3966 | 1.4926 | 12/2003 | 1.7944 | 1.6534 | 1.7860 | 12/2006 | 1.9847 | 1.8518 | 1.9578 |
| 03/2001 | 1.5100 | 1.4158 | 1.4161 | 03/2004 | 1.9142 | 1.7788 | 1.8443 | 03/2007 | 1.9917 | 1.9186 | 1.9676 |
| 06/2001 | 1.4498 | 1.3688 | 1.4155 | 06/2004 | 1.8605 | 1.7482 | 1.8192 | 06/2007 | 2.0133 | 1.9592 | 2.0077 |
| 09/2001 | 1.4785 | 1.3936 | 1.4740 | 09/2004 | 1.8772 | 1.7709 | 1.8124 | 09/2007 | 2.0654 | 1.9656 | 2.0461 |
| 12/2001 | 1.4844 | 1.4044 | 1.4555 | 12/2004 | 1.9553 | 1.7747 | 1.9188 | 12/2007 | 2.1161 | 1.9758 | 1.9848 |
| 03/2002 | 1.4559 | 1.4044 | 1.4259 | 03/2005 | 1.9326 | 1.8509 | 1.8901 | 03/2008 | 2.0394 | 1.9339 | 1.9840 |
| 06/2002 | 1.5380 | 1.4248 | 1.5304 | 06/2005 | 1.9218 | 1.7872 | 1.7914 | 06/2008 | 2.0045 | 1.9364 | 1.9924 |
| 09/2002 | 1.5847 | 1.5153 | 1.5688 | 09/2005 | 1.8500 | 1.7272 | 1.7639 | 09/2008 | 2.0155 | 1.7446 | 1.7810 |
| 12/2002 | 1.6133 | 1.5415 | 1.6100 | 12/2005 | 1.7903 | 1.7047 | 1.7208 | 12/2008 | 1.7874 | 1.4354 | 1.4612 |

*Source: Forex*

# CANADIAN DOLLAR

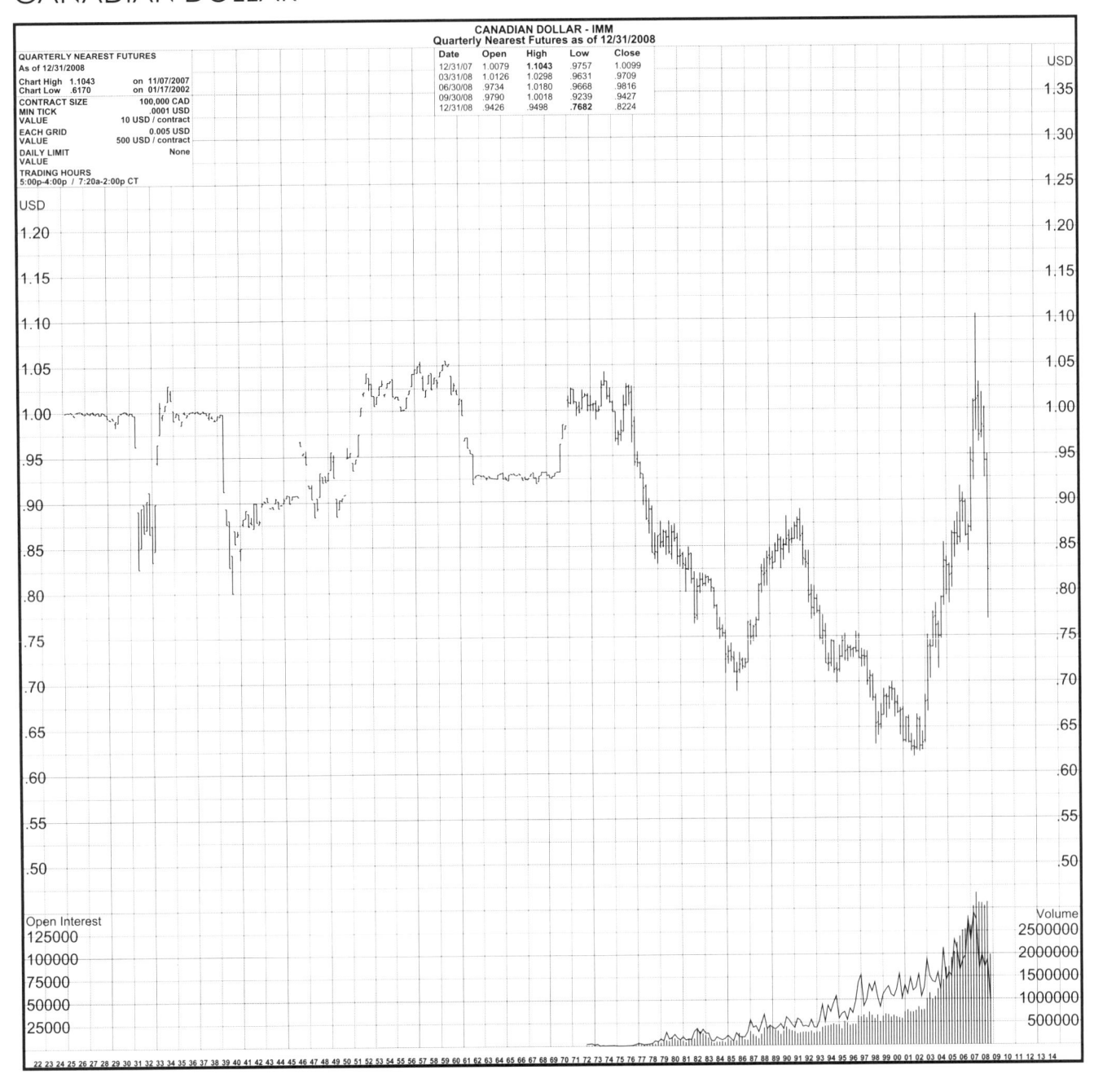

**QUARTERLY NEAREST FUTURES**
As of 12/31/2008
Chart High 1.1043 on 11/07/2007
Chart Low .6170 on 01/17/2002
CONTRACT SIZE 100,000 CAD
MIN TICK .0001 USD
VALUE 10 USD / contract
EACH GRID 0.005 USD
VALUE 500 USD / contract
DAILY LIMIT None
VALUE
TRADING HOURS
5:00p-4:00p / 7:20a-2:00p CT

**CANADIAN DOLLAR - IMM**
Quarterly Nearest Futures as of 12/31/2008

| Date | Open | High | Low | Close |
|---|---|---|---|---|
| 12/31/07 | 1.0079 | 1.1043 | .9757 | 1.0099 |
| 03/31/08 | 1.0126 | 1.0298 | .9631 | .9709 |
| 06/30/08 | .9734 | 1.0180 | .9668 | .9816 |
| 09/30/08 | .9790 | 1.0018 | .9239 | .9427 |
| 12/31/08 | .9426 | .9498 | .7682 | .8224 |

## Annual High, Low and Settle of Canadian Dollar — In USD per CAD

| Year | High | Low | Settle | Year | High | Low | Settle | Year | High | Low | Settle |
|---|---|---|---|---|---|---|---|---|---|---|---|
| 1925 | 1.0009 | .9969 | .9996 | 1939 | .9977 | .8762 | .8762 | 1953 | 1.0301 | 1.0055 | 1.0275 |
| 1926 | 1.0014 | .9963 | .9993 | 1940 | .8802 | .8007 | .8656 | 1954 | 1.0344 | 1.0157 | 1.0329 |
| 1927 | 1.0014 | .9984 | .9990 | 1941 | .8913 | .8369 | .8739 | 1955 | 1.0350 | 1.0005 | 1.0005 |
| 1928 | 1.0004 | .9976 | .9979 | 1942 | .8996 | .8717 | .8788 | 1956 | 1.0409 | 1.0008 | 1.0409 |
| 1929 | .9975 | .9834 | .9907 | 1943 | .9064 | .8940 | .8940 | 1957 | 1.0547 | 1.0230 | 1.0230 |
| 1930 | 1.0012 | .9889 | .9990 | 1944 | .9051 | .8933 | .8975 | 1958 | 1.0416 | 1.0154 | 1.0366 |
| 1931 | .9998 | .8271 | .8271 | 1945 | .9083 | .8991 | .9073 | 1959 | 1.0551 | 1.0258 | 1.0512 |
| 1932 | .9123 | .8513 | .8660 | 1946 | .9678 | .9060 | .9544 | 1960 | 1.0515 | 1.0178 | 1.0178 |
| 1933 | 1.0118 | .8351 | 1.0055 | 1947 | .9569 | .8836 | .8836 | 1961 | 1.0127 | .9589 | .9589 |
| 1934 | 1.0294 | .9917 | 1.0131 | 1948 | .9323 | .8906 | .9225 | 1962 | .9568 | .9191 | .9292 |
| 1935 | 1.0018 | .9858 | .9905 | 1949 | .9552 | .8841 | .8841 | 1963 | .9285 | .9233 | .9262 |
| 1936 | 1.0012 | .9950 | 1.0006 | 1950 | .9604 | .8921 | .9491 | 1964 | .9310 | .9247 | .9304 |
| 1937 | 1.0015 | .9986 | .9995 | 1951 | .9741 | .9348 | .9741 | 1965 | .9311 | .9228 | .9294 |
| 1938 | 1.0002 | .9906 | .9906 | 1952 | 1.0417 | .9949 | 1.0300 | 1966 | .9304 | .9232 | .9232 |

Data continued on page 28.   *Source: Forex*

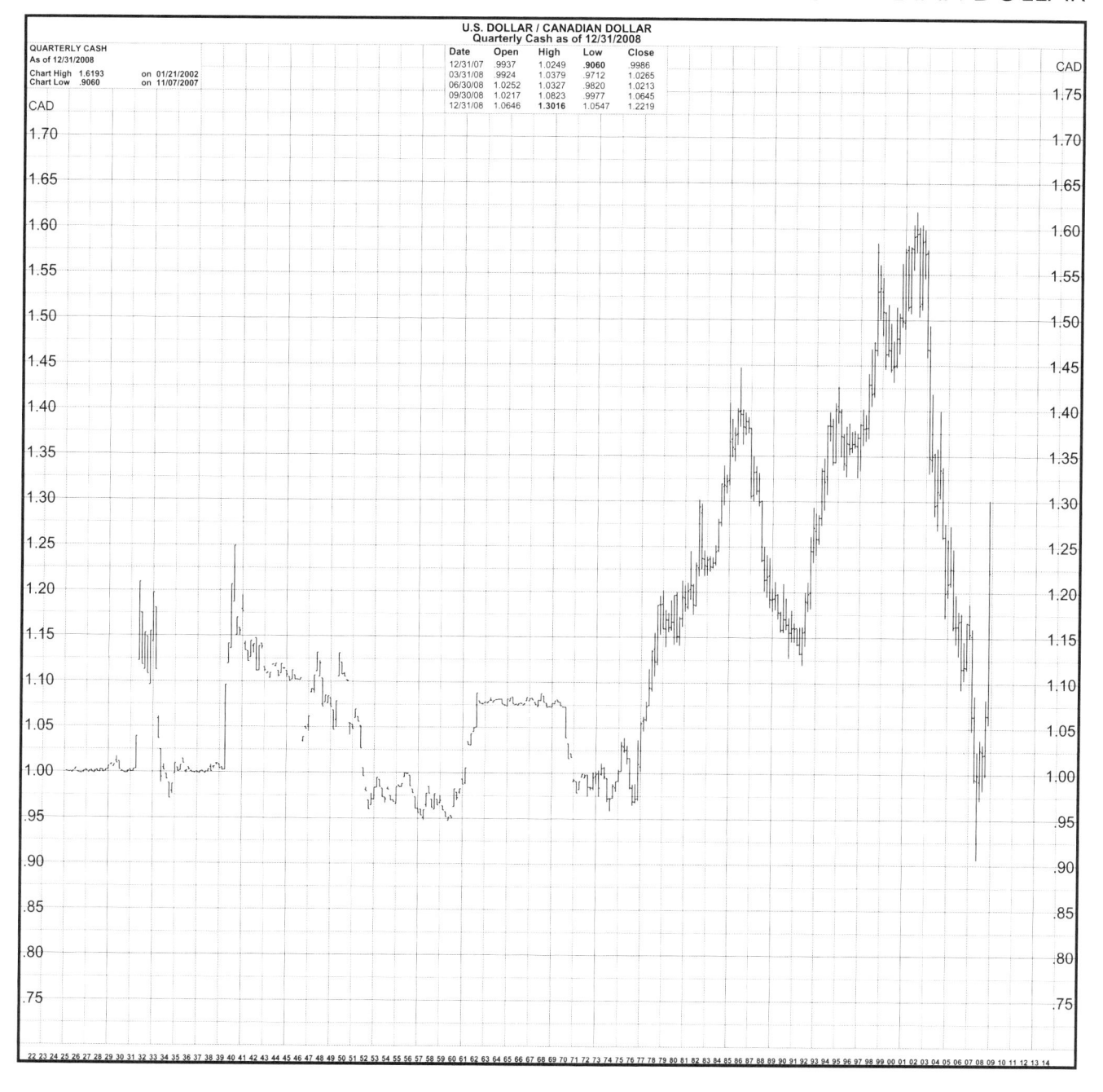

# CANADIAN DOLLAR

**U.S. DOLLAR / CANADIAN DOLLAR**
Quarterly Cash as of 12/31/2008

| Date | Open | High | Low | Close |
|---|---|---|---|---|
| 12/31/07 | .9937 | 1.0249 | .9060 | .9986 |
| 03/31/08 | .9924 | 1.0379 | .9712 | 1.0265 |
| 06/30/08 | 1.0252 | 1.0327 | .9820 | 1.0213 |
| 09/30/08 | 1.0217 | 1.0823 | .9977 | 1.0645 |
| 12/31/08 | 1.0646 | 1.3016 | 1.0547 | 1.2219 |

QUARTERLY CASH As of 12/31/2008
Chart High 1.6193 on 01/21/2002
Chart Low .9060 on 11/07/2007

## Annual High, Low and Settle of Canadian Dollar   In CAD per USD

| Year | High | Low | Settle | Year | High | Low | Settle | Year | High | Low | Settle |
|---|---|---|---|---|---|---|---|---|---|---|---|
| 1925 | 1.0031 | .9991 | 1.0004 | 1939 | 1.1413 | 1.0023 | 1.1413 | 1953 | .9945 | .9708 | .9732 |
| 1926 | 1.0037 | .9986 | 1.0007 | 1940 | 1.2489 | 1.1361 | 1.1553 | 1954 | .9845 | .9667 | .9681 |
| 1927 | 1.0016 | .9986 | 1.0010 | 1941 | 1.1949 | 1.1220 | 1.1443 | 1955 | .9995 | .9662 | .9995 |
| 1928 | 1.0024 | .9996 | 1.0021 | 1942 | 1.1472 | 1.1116 | 1.1379 | 1956 | .9992 | .9607 | .9607 |
| 1929 | 1.0169 | 1.0025 | 1.0094 | 1943 | 1.1186 | 1.1033 | 1.1186 | 1957 | .9775 | .9481 | .9775 |
| 1930 | 1.0112 | .9988 | 1.0010 | 1944 | 1.1194 | 1.1049 | 1.1142 | 1958 | .9848 | .9601 | .9647 |
| 1931 | 1.2090 | 1.0002 | 1.2090 | 1945 | 1.1122 | 1.1010 | 1.1022 | 1959 | .9748 | .9478 | .9513 |
| 1932 | 1.1747 | 1.0961 | 1.1547 | 1946 | 1.1038 | 1.0333 | 1.0478 | 1960 | .9825 | .9510 | .9825 |
| 1933 | 1.1975 | .9883 | .9945 | 1947 | 1.1317 | 1.0450 | 1.1317 | 1961 | 1.0429 | .9875 | 1.0429 |
| 1934 | 1.0084 | .9714 | .9871 | 1948 | 1.1228 | 1.0726 | 1.0840 | 1962 | 1.0880 | 1.0452 | 1.0762 |
| 1935 | 1.0144 | .9982 | 1.0096 | 1949 | 1.1311 | 1.0469 | 1.1311 | 1963 | 1.0831 | 1.0770 | 1.0797 |
| 1936 | 1.0050 | .9988 | .9994 | 1950 | 1.1210 | 1.0412 | 1.0536 | 1964 | 1.0814 | 1.0741 | 1.0748 |
| 1937 | 1.0014 | .9985 | 1.0005 | 1951 | 1.0697 | 1.0266 | 1.0266 | 1965 | 1.0837 | 1.0740 | 1.0760 |
| 1938 | 1.0095 | .9998 | 1.0095 | 1952 | 1.0051 | .9600 | .9709 | 1966 | 1.0832 | 1.0748 | 1.0832 |

Data continued on page 29.   *Source: Forex*

# CANADIAN DOLLAR

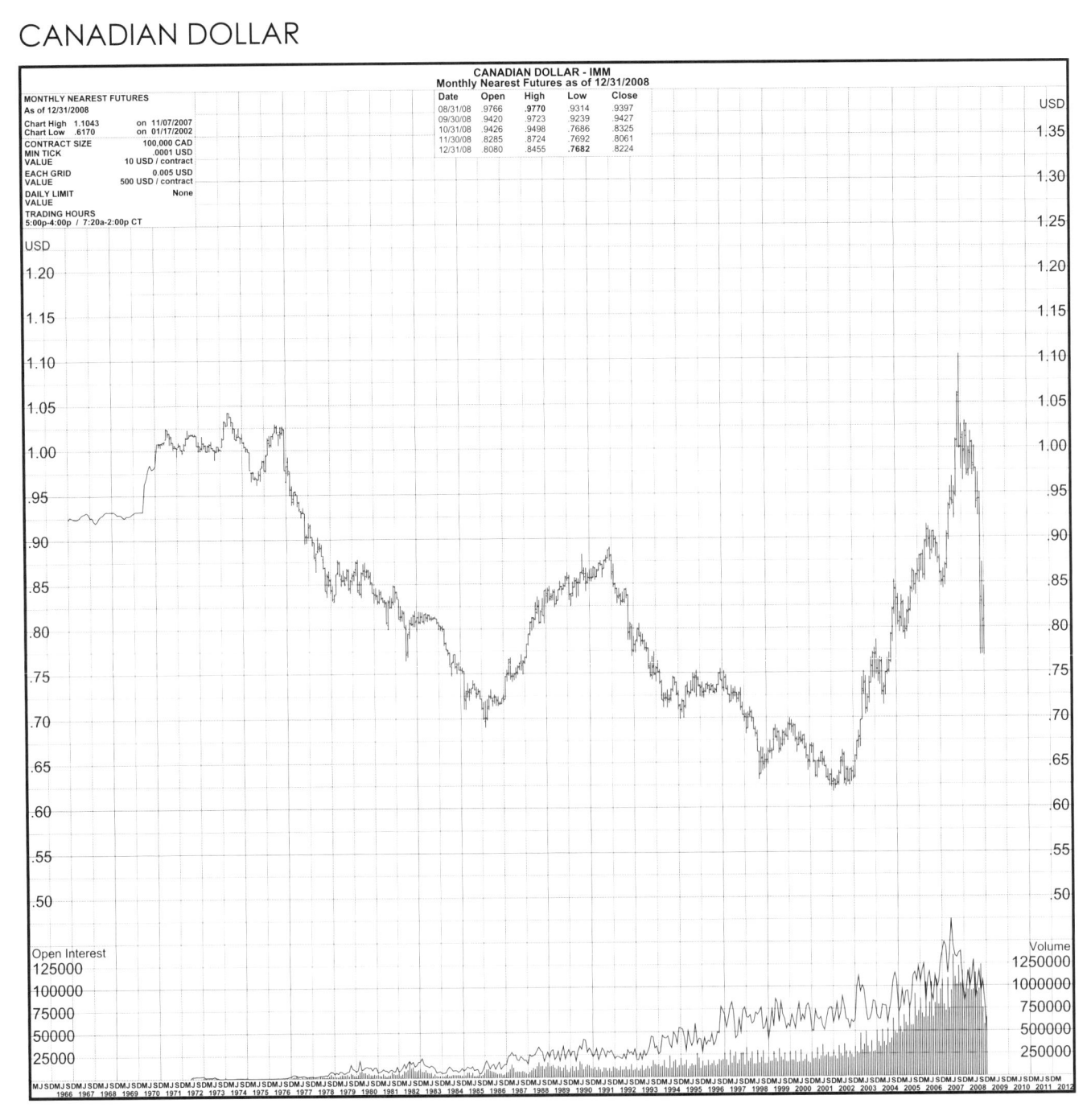

**MONTHLY NEAREST FUTURES**
As of 12/31/2008

Chart High  1.1043   on 11/07/2007
Chart Low   .6170   on 01/17/2002
CONTRACT SIZE       100,000 CAD
MIN TICK VALUE       .0001 USD
                    10 USD / contract
EACH GRID VALUE     0.005 USD
                    500 USD / contract
DAILY LIMIT VALUE   None
TRADING HOURS       5:00p-4:00p / 7:20a-2:00p CT

**CANADIAN DOLLAR - IMM**
Monthly Nearest Futures as of 12/31/2008

| Date | Open | High | Low | Close |
|---|---|---|---|---|
| 08/31/08 | .9766 | .9770 | .9314 | .9397 |
| 09/30/08 | .9420 | .9723 | .9239 | .9427 |
| 10/31/08 | .9426 | .9498 | .7686 | .8325 |
| 11/30/08 | .8285 | .8724 | .7692 | .8061 |
| 12/31/08 | .8080 | .8455 | .7682 | .8224 |

## Annual High, Low and Settle of Canadian Dollar Futures    In USD per CAD

| Year | High | Low | Settle | Year | High | Low | Settle | Year | High | Low | Settle |
|---|---|---|---|---|---|---|---|---|---|---|---|
| 1967 | .9315 | .9238 | .9256 | 1981 | .8490 | .7992 | .8406 | 1995 | .7530 | .6983 | .7331 |
| 1968 | .9321 | .9196 | .9318 | 1982 | .8420 | .7641 | .8128 | 1996 | .7551 | .7216 | .7332 |
| 1969 | .9321 | .9253 | .9308 | 1983 | .8196 | .7990 | .8043 | 1997 | .7524 | .6954 | .7007 |
| 1970 | .9842 | .9318 | .9828 | 1984 | .8042 | .7469 | .7538 | 1998 | .7120 | .6305 | .6520 |
| 1971 | 1.0248 | .9933 | 1.0024 | 1985 | .7569 | .7097 | .7114 | 1999 | .6947 | .6473 | .6922 |
| 1972 | 1.0260 | .9961 | 1.0051 | 1986 | .7328 | .6898 | .7210 | 2000 | .6992 | .6403 | .6679 |
| 1973 | 1.0160 | .9892 | 1.0001 | 1987 | .7715 | .7213 | .7679 | 2001 | .6719 | .6225 | .6276 |
| 1974 | 1.0427 | 1.0040 | 1.0090 | 1988 | .8440 | .7667 | .8362 | 2002 | .6640 | .6170 | .6322 |
| 1975 | 1.0100 | .9610 | .9775 | 1989 | .8625 | .8233 | .8561 | 2003 | .7772 | .6318 | .7694 |
| 1976 | 1.0296 | .9640 | .9822 | 1990 | .8828 | .8246 | .8555 | 2004 | .8530 | .7135 | .8322 |
| 1977 | .9924 | .8951 | .9141 | 1991 | .8906 | .8520 | .8602 | 2005 | .8753 | .7855 | .8620 |
| 1978 | .9181 | .8355 | .8437 | 1992 | .8718 | .7685 | .7815 | 2006 | .9152 | .8489 | .8602 |
| 1979 | .8777 | .8305 | .8597 | 1993 | .8060 | .7401 | .7557 | 2007 | 1.1043 | .8427 | 1.0099 |
| 1980 | .8780 | .8294 | .8385 | 1994 | .7638 | .7088 | .7128 | 2008 | 1.0298 | .7682 | .8224 |

Futures begin trading 05/16/1972.    Data continued from page 26.    *Source: CME Group; Chicago Mercantile Exchange*

# CANADIAN DOLLAR

**U.S. DOLLAR / CANADIAN DOLLAR**
Monthly Cash as of 12/31/2008

| Date | Open | High | Low | Close |
|---|---|---|---|---|
| 08/29/08 | 1.0247 | 1.0729 | 1.0227 | 1.0641 |
| 09/30/08 | 1.0628 | 1.0823 | 1.0298 | 1.0645 |
| 10/31/08 | 1.0646 | 1.3016 | 1.0547 | 1.2121 |
| 11/28/08 | 1.2105 | 1.2981 | 1.1465 | 1.2393 |
| 12/31/08 | 1.2361 | 1.3005 | 1.1822 | 1.2219 |

MONTHLY CASH
As of 12/31/2008
Chart High 1.6193 on 01/21/2002
Chart Low .9060 on 11/07/2007

## Annual High, Low and Settle of Canadian Dollar — In CAD per USD

| Year | High | Low | Settle | Year | High | Low | Settle | Year | High | Low | Settle |
|---|---|---|---|---|---|---|---|---|---|---|---|
| 1967 | 1.0825 | 1.0735 | 1.0804 | 1981 | 1.2453 | 1.1753 | 1.1860 | 1995 | 1.4268 | 1.3276 | 1.3641 |
| 1968 | 1.0874 | 1.0728 | 1.0732 | 1982 | 1.3017 | 1.1844 | 1.2291 | 1996 | 1.3865 | 1.3265 | 1.3703 |
| 1969 | 1.0807 | 1.0728 | 1.0743 | 1983 | 1.2517 | 1.2180 | 1.2444 | 1997 | 1.4415 | 1.3346 | 1.4289 |
| 1970 | 1.0732 | 1.0161 | 1.0175 | 1984 | 1.3397 | 1.2442 | 1.3218 | 1998 | 1.5848 | 1.4048 | 1.5349 |
| 1971 | .9990 | .9785 | .9990 | 1985 | 1.4086 | 1.3180 | 1.3986 | 1999 | 1.5468 | 1.4428 | 1.4458 |
| 1972 | 1.0014 | .9747 | .9953 | 1986 | 1.4475 | 1.3625 | 1.3808 | 2000 | 1.5627 | 1.4318 | 1.4987 |
| 1973 | 1.0112 | .9747 | .9963 | 1987 | 1.3805 | 1.2945 | 1.2990 | 2001 | 1.6052 | 1.4901 | 1.5918 |
| 1974 | .9947 | .9587 | .9911 | 1988 | 1.3010 | 1.1830 | 1.1922 | 2002 | 1.6193 | 1.5035 | 1.5730 |
| 1975 | 1.0393 | .9910 | 1.0167 | 1989 | 1.2118 | 1.1560 | 1.1585 | 2003 | 1.5776 | 1.2840 | 1.2956 |
| 1976 | 1.0368 | .9648 | 1.0101 | 1990 | 1.2097 | 1.1273 | 1.1600 | 2004 | 1.4002 | 1.1719 | 1.1997 |
| 1977 | 1.1151 | 1.0022 | 1.0942 | 1991 | 1.1661 | 1.1195 | 1.1556 | 2005 | 1.2734 | 1.1429 | 1.1626 |
| 1978 | 1.1959 | 1.0905 | 1.1862 | 1992 | 1.2936 | 1.1405 | 1.2708 | 2006 | 1.1797 | 1.0931 | 1.1663 |
| 1979 | 1.2021 | 1.1392 | 1.1667 | 1993 | 1.3481 | 1.2408 | 1.3218 | 2007 | 1.1876 | .9060 | .9986 |
| 1980 | 1.2127 | 1.1409 | 1.1946 | 1994 | 1.4088 | 1.3078 | 1.4017 | 2008 | 1.3016 | .9712 | 1.2219 |

Data continued from page 27. *Source: Forex*

# CANADIAN DOLLAR

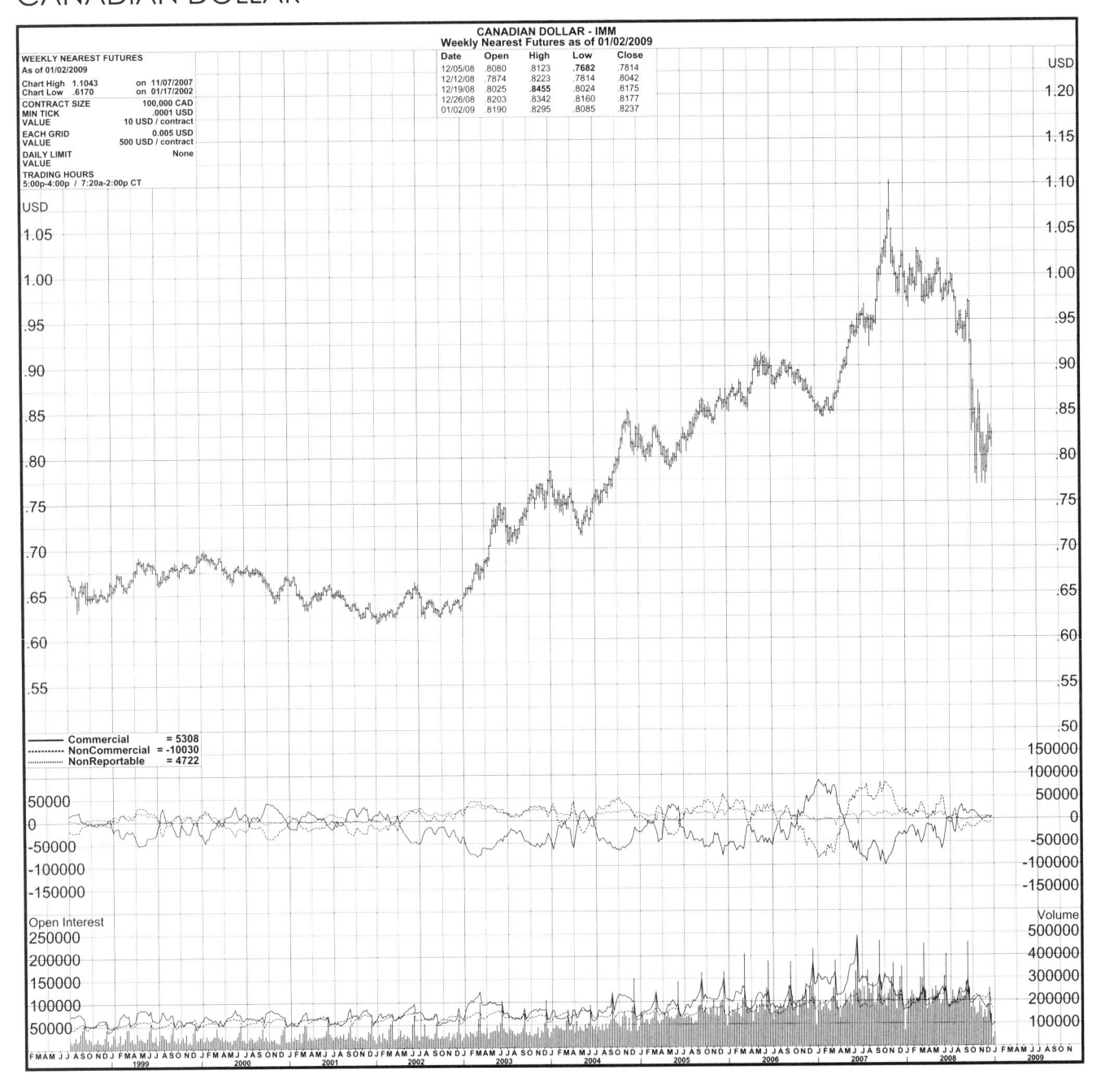

**WEEKLY NEAREST FUTURES**
As of 01/02/2009

| | | |
|---|---|---|
| Chart High | 1.1043 | on 11/07/2007 |
| Chart Low | .6170 | on 01/17/2002 |
| CONTRACT SIZE | | 100,000 CAD |
| MIN TICK VALUE | | .0001 USD / 10 USD / contract |
| EACH GRID VALUE | | 0.005 USD / 500 USD / contract |
| DAILY LIMIT VALUE | | None |
| TRADING HOURS | | 5:00p-4:00p / 7:20a-2:00p CT |

**CANADIAN DOLLAR - IMM**
Weekly Nearest Futures as of 01/02/2009

| Date | Open | High | Low | Close |
|---|---|---|---|---|
| 12/05/08 | .8080 | .8123 | .7682 | .7814 |
| 12/12/08 | .7874 | .8223 | .7814 | .8042 |
| 12/19/08 | .8025 | .8455 | .8024 | .8175 |
| 12/26/08 | .8203 | .8342 | .8160 | .8177 |
| 01/02/09 | .8190 | .8295 | .8085 | .8237 |

Commercial = 5308
NonCommercial = -10030
NonReportable = 4722

## Quarterly High, Low and Settle of Canadian Dollar Futures    In USD per CAD

| Quarter | High | Low | Settle | Quarter | High | Low | Settle | Quarter | High | Low | Settle |
|---|---|---|---|---|---|---|---|---|---|---|---|
| 03/2000 | .6992 | .6782 | .6911 | 03/2003 | .6853 | .6318 | .6774 | 03/2006 | .8854 | .8489 | .8579 |
| 06/2000 | .6922 | .6604 | .6767 | 06/2003 | .7513 | .6666 | .7374 | 06/2006 | .9152 | .8513 | .8971 |
| 09/2000 | .6844 | .6641 | .6660 | 09/2003 | .7458 | .7027 | .7377 | 09/2006 | .9076 | .8742 | .8967 |
| 12/2000 | .6712 | .6403 | .6679 | 12/2003 | .7772 | .7372 | .7694 | 12/2006 | .8993 | .8587 | .8602 |
| 03/2001 | .6719 | .6325 | .6346 | 03/2004 | .7863 | .7356 | .7611 | 03/2007 | .8717 | .8427 | .8691 |
| 06/2001 | .6610 | .6320 | .6600 | 06/2004 | .7656 | .7135 | .7494 | 06/2007 | .9570 | .8638 | .9426 |
| 09/2001 | .6627 | .6315 | .6328 | 09/2004 | .7935 | .7465 | .7920 | 09/2007 | 1.0098 | .9205 | 1.0072 |
| 12/2001 | .6422 | .6225 | .6276 | 12/2004 | .8530 | .7830 | .8322 | 12/2007 | 1.1043 | .9757 | 1.0099 |
| 03/2002 | .6349 | .6170 | .6269 | 03/2005 | .8370 | .7945 | .8269 | 03/2008 | 1.0298 | .9631 | .9709 |
| 06/2002 | .6640 | .6235 | .6586 | 06/2005 | .8295 | .7855 | .8163 | 06/2008 | 1.0180 | .9668 | .9816 |
| 09/2002 | .6608 | .6223 | .6287 | 09/2005 | .8650 | .8027 | .8624 | 09/2008 | 1.0018 | .9239 | .9427 |
| 12/2002 | .6450 | .6240 | .6322 | 12/2005 | .8753 | .8357 | .8620 | 12/2008 | .9498 | .7682 | .8224 |

*Source: CME Group; Chicago Mercantile Exchange*

# CANADIAN DOLLAR

**WEEKLY CASH**
As of 01/02/2009
Chart High 1.6193 on 01/21/2002
Chart Low .9060 on 11/07/2007

**U.S. DOLLAR / CANADIAN DOLLAR**
Weekly Cash as of 01/02/2009

| Date | Open | High | Low | Close |
|---|---|---|---|---|
| 12/05/08 | 1.2361 | 1.3005 | 1.2307 | 1.2690 |
| 12/12/08 | 1.2685 | 1.2754 | 1.2156 | 1.2481 |
| 12/19/08 | 1.2461 | 1.2470 | 1.1822 | 1.2187 |
| 12/26/08 | 1.2154 | 1.2270 | 1.1988 | 1.2221 |
| 01/02/09 | 1.2206 | 1.2351 | 1.2067 | 1.2077 |

## Quarterly High, Low and Settle of Canadian Dollar   In CAD per USD

| Quarter | High | Low | Settle | Quarter | High | Low | Settle | Quarter | High | Low | Settle |
|---|---|---|---|---|---|---|---|---|---|---|---|
| 03/2000 | .6981 | .6772 | .6896 | 03/2003 | .6854 | .6339 | .6813 | 03/2006 | .8850 | .8477 | .8562 |
| 06/2000 | .6905 | .6605 | .6754 | 06/2003 | .7513 | .6692 | .7418 | 06/2006 | .9148 | .8495 | .8962 |
| 09/2000 | .6834 | .6633 | .6650 | 09/2003 | .7499 | .7048 | .7407 | 09/2006 | .9065 | .8726 | .8945 |
| 12/2000 | .6700 | .6401 | .6669 | 12/2003 | .7788 | .7385 | .7718 | 12/2006 | .8972 | .8570 | .8574 |
| 03/2001 | .6710 | .6333 | .6345 | 03/2004 | .7885 | .7359 | .7625 | 03/2007 | .8694 | .8420 | .8663 |
| 06/2001 | .6620 | .6321 | .6601 | 06/2004 | .7670 | .7142 | .7490 | 06/2007 | .9551 | .8621 | .9401 |
| 09/2001 | .6634 | .6327 | .6329 | 09/2004 | .7941 | .7472 | .7930 | 09/2007 | 1.0085 | .9204 | 1.0055 |
| 12/2001 | .6430 | .6230 | .6282 | 12/2004 | .8533 | .7840 | .8335 | 12/2007 | 1.1038 | .9758 | 1.0014 |
| 03/2002 | .6353 | .6176 | .6270 | 03/2005 | .8370 | .7946 | .8268 | 03/2008 | 1.0296 | .9635 | .9742 |
| 06/2002 | .6651 | .6241 | .6598 | 06/2005 | .8286 | .7853 | .8158 | 06/2008 | 1.0183 | .9683 | .9791 |
| 09/2002 | .6618 | .6230 | .6304 | 09/2005 | .8629 | .8013 | .8608 | 09/2008 | 1.0023 | .9240 | .9394 |
| 12/2002 | .6471 | .6252 | .6357 | 12/2005 | .8750 | .8349 | .8601 | 12/2008 | .9481 | .7683 | .8184 |

*Source: Forex*

# EURO FX

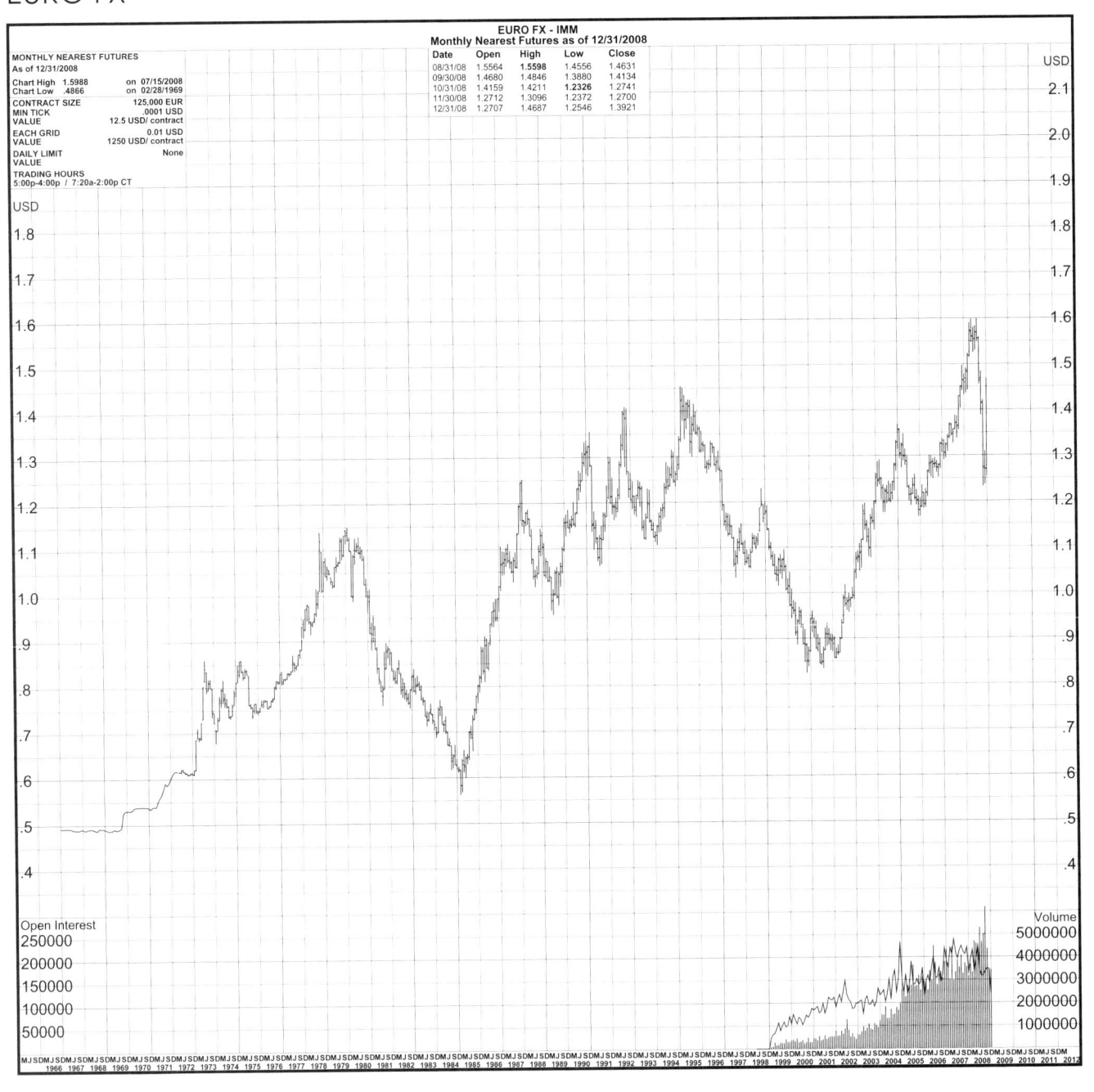

**MONTHLY NEAREST FUTURES**
As of 12/31/2008
Chart High 1.5988 on 07/15/2008
Chart Low .4866 on 02/28/1969
CONTRACT SIZE 125,000 EUR
MIN TICK .0001 USD
VALUE 12.5 USD/ contract
EACH GRID 0.01 USD
VALUE 1250 USD/ contract
DAILY LIMIT None
VALUE
TRADING HOURS
5:00p-4:00p / 7:20a-2:00p CT

**EURO FX - IMM**
**Monthly Nearest Futures as of 12/31/2008**

| Date | Open | High | Low | Close |
|---|---|---|---|---|
| 08/31/08 | 1.5564 | 1.5598 | 1.4556 | 1.4631 |
| 09/30/08 | 1.4680 | 1.4846 | 1.3880 | 1.4134 |
| 10/31/08 | 1.4159 | 1.4211 | 1.2326 | 1.2741 |
| 11/30/08 | 1.2712 | 1.3096 | 1.2372 | 1.2700 |
| 12/31/08 | 1.2707 | 1.4687 | 1.2546 | 1.3921 |

## Annual High, Low and Settle of Euro FX Futures   In USD per EUR

| Year | High | Low | Settle | Year | High | Low | Settle | Year | High | Low | Settle |
|---|---|---|---|---|---|---|---|---|---|---|---|
| 1967 | .4923 | .4884 | .4907 | 1981 | 1.0149 | .7583 | .8735 | 1995 | 1.4549 | 1.2496 | 1.3620 |
| 1968 | .4923 | .4874 | .4895 | 1982 | .8770 | .7528 | .8221 | 1996 | 1.3670 | 1.2431 | 1.2690 |
| 1969 | .5306 | .4866 | .5306 | 1983 | .8397 | .7037 | .7170 | 1997 | 1.2712 | 1.0345 | 1.0874 |
| 1970 | .5386 | .5302 | .5367 | 1984 | .7712 | .6171 | .6196 | 1998 | 1.2320 | 1.0537 | 1.1768 |
| 1971 | .5998 | .5343 | .5998 | 1985 | .8031 | .5621 | .8015 | 1999 | 1.1925 | 1.0000 | 1.0160 |
| 1972 | .6219 | .6085 | .6110 | 1986 | 1.0195 | .7863 | 1.0187 | 2000 | 1.0464 | .8245 | .9428 |
| 1973 | .8606 | .6087 | .7233 | 1987 | 1.2469 | 1.0084 | 1.2454 | 2001 | .9615 | .8342 | .8878 |
| 1974 | .8166 | .6773 | .8107 | 1988 | 1.2521 | 1.0160 | 1.1044 | 2002 | 1.0473 | .8549 | 1.0471 |
| 1975 | .8592 | .7329 | .7467 | 1989 | 1.1677 | .9550 | 1.1566 | 2003 | 1.2623 | 1.0302 | 1.2534 |
| 1976 | .8304 | .7467 | .8297 | 1990 | 1.3369 | 1.1270 | 1.3109 | 2004 | 1.3687 | 1.1745 | 1.3558 |
| 1977 | .9330 | .8050 | .9320 | 1991 | 1.3559 | 1.0617 | 1.2885 | 2005 | 1.3593 | 1.1661 | 1.1880 |
| 1978 | 1.1395 | .9062 | 1.0749 | 1992 | 1.4101 | 1.1614 | 1.2073 | 2006 | 1.3373 | 1.1835 | 1.3236 |
| 1979 | 1.1448 | 1.0167 | 1.1328 | 1993 | 1.2493 | 1.1189 | 1.1245 | 2007 | 1.4977 | 1.2901 | 1.4590 |
| 1980 | 1.1495 | .9625 | .9965 | 1994 | 1.3160 | 1.1067 | 1.2624 | 2008 | 1.5988 | 1.2326 | 1.3921 |

Cash data through 05/19/1998 is theoretical based on DEM * 1.95583.   Futures begin trading 05/20/1998.   *Source: CME Group; Chicago Mercantile Exchange*

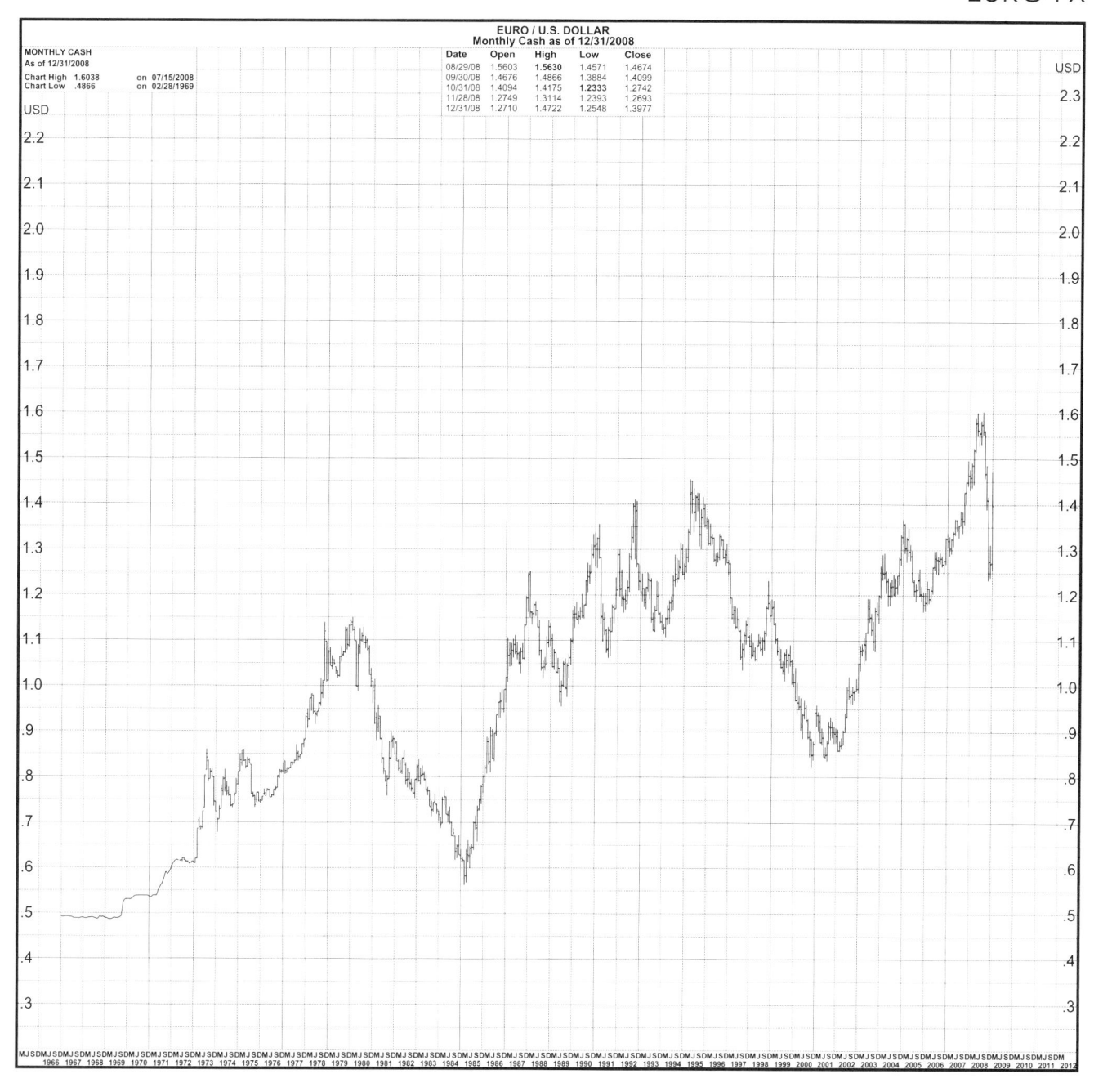

# EURO FX

**MONTHLY CASH**
As of 12/31/2008
Chart High 1.6038 on 07/15/2008
Chart Low .4866 on 02/28/1969

**EURO / U.S. DOLLAR**
Monthly Cash as of 12/31/2008

| Date | Open | High | Low | Close |
|---|---|---|---|---|
| 08/29/08 | 1.5603 | 1.5630 | 1.4571 | 1.4674 |
| 09/30/08 | 1.4676 | 1.4866 | 1.3884 | 1.4099 |
| 10/31/08 | 1.4094 | 1.4175 | 1.2333 | 1.2742 |
| 11/28/08 | 1.2749 | 1.3114 | 1.2393 | 1.2693 |
| 12/31/08 | 1.2710 | 1.4722 | 1.2548 | 1.3977 |

## Annual High, Low and Settle of Euro FX    In USD per EUR

| Year | High | Low | Settle | Year | High | Low | Settle | Year | High | Low | Settle |
|---|---|---|---|---|---|---|---|---|---|---|---|
| 1967 | .4923 | .4884 | .4907 | 1981 | 1.0149 | .7583 | .8735 | 1995 | 1.4549 | 1.2496 | 1.3620 |
| 1968 | .4923 | .4874 | .4895 | 1982 | .8770 | .7528 | .8221 | 1996 | 1.3670 | 1.2431 | 1.2690 |
| 1969 | .5306 | .4866 | .5306 | 1983 | .8397 | .7037 | .7170 | 1997 | 1.2712 | 1.0345 | 1.0874 |
| 1970 | .5386 | .5302 | .5367 | 1984 | .7712 | .6171 | .6196 | 1998 | 1.2320 | 1.0537 | 1.1717 |
| 1971 | .5998 | .5343 | .5998 | 1985 | .8031 | .5621 | .8015 | 1999 | 1.1890 | .9992 | 1.0088 |
| 1972 | .6219 | .6085 | .6110 | 1986 | 1.0195 | .7863 | 1.0187 | 2000 | 1.0413 | .8230 | .9422 |
| 1973 | .8606 | .6087 | .7233 | 1987 | 1.2469 | 1.0084 | 1.2454 | 2001 | .9592 | .8352 | .8912 |
| 1974 | .8166 | .6773 | .8107 | 1988 | 1.2521 | 1.0160 | 1.1044 | 2002 | 1.0505 | .8565 | 1.0493 |
| 1975 | .8592 | .7329 | .7467 | 1989 | 1.1677 | .9550 | 1.1566 | 2003 | 1.2649 | 1.0336 | 1.2588 |
| 1976 | .8304 | .7467 | .8297 | 1990 | 1.3369 | 1.1270 | 1.3109 | 2004 | 1.3666 | 1.1760 | 1.3567 |
| 1977 | .9330 | .8050 | .9320 | 1991 | 1.3559 | 1.0617 | 1.2885 | 2005 | 1.3581 | 1.1641 | 1.1837 |
| 1978 | 1.1395 | .9062 | 1.0749 | 1992 | 1.4101 | 1.1614 | 1.2073 | 2006 | 1.3367 | 1.1802 | 1.3197 |
| 1979 | 1.1448 | 1.0167 | 1.1328 | 1993 | 1.2493 | 1.1189 | 1.1245 | 2007 | 1.4967 | 1.2868 | 1.4587 |
| 1980 | 1.1495 | .9625 | .9965 | 1994 | 1.3160 | 1.1067 | 1.2624 | 2008 | 1.6038 | 1.2333 | 1.3977 |

Data through 12/31/1998 is theoretical based on DEM * 1.95583.    *Source: Forex*

# EURO FX

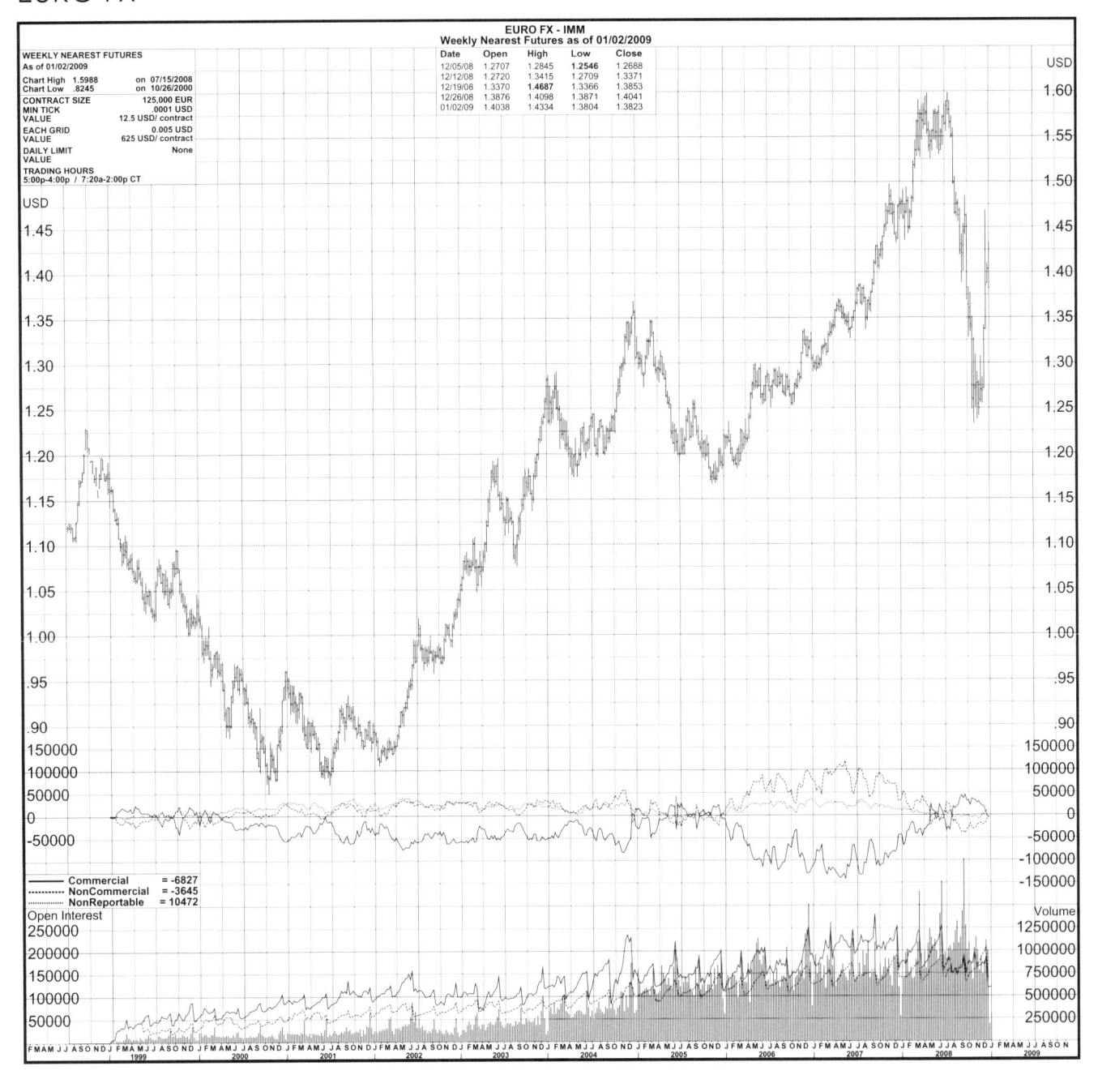

**WEEKLY NEAREST FUTURES**
As of 01/02/2009
Chart High 1.5988 on 07/15/2008
Chart Low .8245 on 10/26/2000
CONTRACT SIZE 125,000 EUR
MIN TICK .0001 USD
VALUE 12.5 USD/ contract
EACH GRID 0.005 USD
VALUE 625 USD/ contract
DAILY LIMIT None
VALUE
TRADING HOURS
5:00p-4:00p / 7:20a-2:00p CT

**EURO FX - IMM**
Weekly Nearest Futures as of 01/02/2009

| Date | Open | High | Low | Close |
|---|---|---|---|---|
| 12/05/08 | 1.2707 | 1.2845 | 1.2546 | 1.2688 |
| 12/12/08 | 1.2720 | 1.3415 | 1.2709 | 1.3371 |
| 12/19/08 | 1.3370 | 1.4687 | 1.3366 | 1.3853 |
| 12/26/08 | 1.3876 | 1.4098 | 1.3871 | 1.4041 |
| 01/02/09 | 1.4038 | 1.4334 | 1.3804 | 1.3823 |

Commercial = -6827
NonCommercial = -3645
NonReportable = 10472

## Quarterly High, Low and Settle of Euro FX Futures   In USD per EUR

| Quarter | High | Low | Settle | Quarter | High | Low | Settle | Quarter | High | Low | Settle |
|---|---|---|---|---|---|---|---|---|---|---|---|
| 03/2000 | 1.0464 | .9440 | .9607 | 03/2003 | 1.1082 | 1.0302 | 1.0868 | 03/2006 | 1.2359 | 1.1835 | 1.2179 |
| 06/2000 | .9805 | .8861 | .9581 | 06/2003 | 1.1960 | 1.0534 | 1.1469 | 06/2006 | 1.3003 | 1.2089 | 1.2850 |
| 09/2000 | .9639 | .8478 | .8854 | 09/2003 | 1.1715 | 1.0759 | 1.1620 | 09/2006 | 1.2961 | 1.2503 | 1.2739 |
| 12/2000 | .9430 | .8245 | .9428 | 12/2003 | 1.2623 | 1.1365 | 1.2534 | 12/2006 | 1.3373 | 1.2525 | 1.3236 |
| 03/2001 | .9615 | .8761 | .8796 | 03/2004 | 1.2919 | 1.2025 | 1.2280 | 03/2007 | 1.3458 | 1.2901 | 1.3394 |
| 06/2001 | .9094 | .8411 | .8482 | 06/2004 | 1.2366 | 1.1745 | 1.2178 | 06/2007 | 1.3715 | 1.3266 | 1.3568 |
| 09/2001 | .9339 | .8342 | .9084 | 09/2004 | 1.2449 | 1.1959 | 1.2432 | 09/2007 | 1.4300 | 1.3370 | 1.4293 |
| 12/2001 | .9221 | .8712 | .8878 | 12/2004 | 1.3687 | 1.2219 | 1.3558 | 12/2007 | 1.4977 | 1.4033 | 1.4590 |
| 03/2002 | .9040 | .8549 | .8682 | 03/2005 | 1.3593 | 1.2735 | 1.2982 | 03/2008 | 1.5907 | 1.4355 | 1.5729 |
| 06/2002 | .9956 | .8686 | .9885 | 06/2005 | 1.3143 | 1.2012 | 1.2137 | 06/2008 | 1.5985 | 1.5255 | 1.5690 |
| 09/2002 | 1.0185 | .9571 | .9834 | 09/2005 | 1.2598 | 1.1900 | 1.2059 | 09/2008 | 1.5988 | 1.3880 | 1.4134 |
| 12/2002 | 1.0473 | .9666 | 1.0471 | 12/2005 | 1.2249 | 1.1661 | 1.1880 | 12/2008 | 1.4687 | 1.2326 | 1.3921 |

*Source: CME Group; Chicago Mercantile Exchange*

# EURO FX

**EURO / U.S. DOLLAR**
Weekly Cash as of 01/02/2009

| Date | Open | High | Low | Close |
|------|------|------|-----|-------|
| 12/05/08 | 1.2710 | 1.2849 | **1.2548** | 1.2735 |
| 12/12/08 | 1.2723 | 1.3416 | 1.2716 | 1.3381 |
| 12/19/08 | 1.3363 | **1.4722** | 1.3352 | 1.3908 |
| 12/26/08 | 1.3924 | 1.4124 | 1.3904 | 1.4040 |
| 01/02/09 | 1.4068 | 1.4362 | 1.3842 | 1.3910 |

WEEKLY CASH
As of 01/02/2009
Chart High 1.6038 on 07/15/2008
Chart Low .8230 on 10/26/2000

## Quarterly High, Low and Settle of Euro FX — In USD per EUR

| Quarter | High | Low | Settle | Quarter | High | Low | Settle | Quarter | High | Low | Settle |
|---------|------|-----|--------|---------|------|-----|--------|---------|------|-----|--------|
| 03/2000 | 1.0413 | .9406 | .9554 | 03/2003 | 1.1083 | 1.0336 | 1.0931 | 03/2006 | 1.2324 | 1.1802 | 1.2116 |
| 06/2000 | .9751 | .8847 | .9525 | 06/2003 | 1.1933 | 1.0562 | 1.1514 | 06/2006 | 1.2980 | 1.2035 | 1.2788 |
| 09/2000 | .9595 | .8443 | .8831 | 09/2003 | 1.1739 | 1.0764 | 1.1661 | 09/2006 | 1.2939 | 1.2457 | 1.2681 |
| 12/2000 | .9425 | .8230 | .9422 | 12/2003 | 1.2649 | 1.1377 | 1.2588 | 12/2006 | 1.3367 | 1.2484 | 1.3197 |
| 03/2001 | .9592 | .8759 | .8759 | 03/2004 | 1.2929 | 1.2046 | 1.2307 | 03/2007 | 1.3411 | 1.2868 | 1.3356 |
| 06/2001 | .9087 | .8414 | .8493 | 06/2004 | 1.2389 | 1.1760 | 1.2196 | 06/2007 | 1.3680 | 1.3264 | 1.3535 |
| 09/2001 | .9330 | .8352 | .9112 | 09/2004 | 1.2462 | 1.1970 | 1.2439 | 09/2007 | 1.4278 | 1.3360 | 1.4259 |
| 12/2001 | .9244 | .8737 | .8912 | 12/2004 | 1.3666 | 1.2225 | 1.3567 | 12/2007 | 1.4967 | 1.4016 | 1.4587 |
| 03/2002 | .9063 | .8565 | .8718 | 03/2005 | 1.3581 | 1.2732 | 1.2958 | 03/2008 | 1.5897 | 1.4368 | 1.5781 |
| 06/2002 | .9988 | .8713 | .9913 | 06/2005 | 1.3125 | 1.1981 | 1.2102 | 06/2008 | 1.6017 | 1.5286 | 1.5748 |
| 09/2002 | 1.0212 | .9610 | .9875 | 09/2005 | 1.2589 | 1.1868 | 1.2029 | 09/2008 | 1.6038 | 1.3884 | 1.4099 |
| 12/2002 | 1.0505 | .9688 | 1.0493 | 12/2005 | 1.2205 | 1.1641 | 1.1837 | 12/2008 | 1.4722 | 1.2333 | 1.3977 |

*Source: Forex*

# JAPANESE YEN

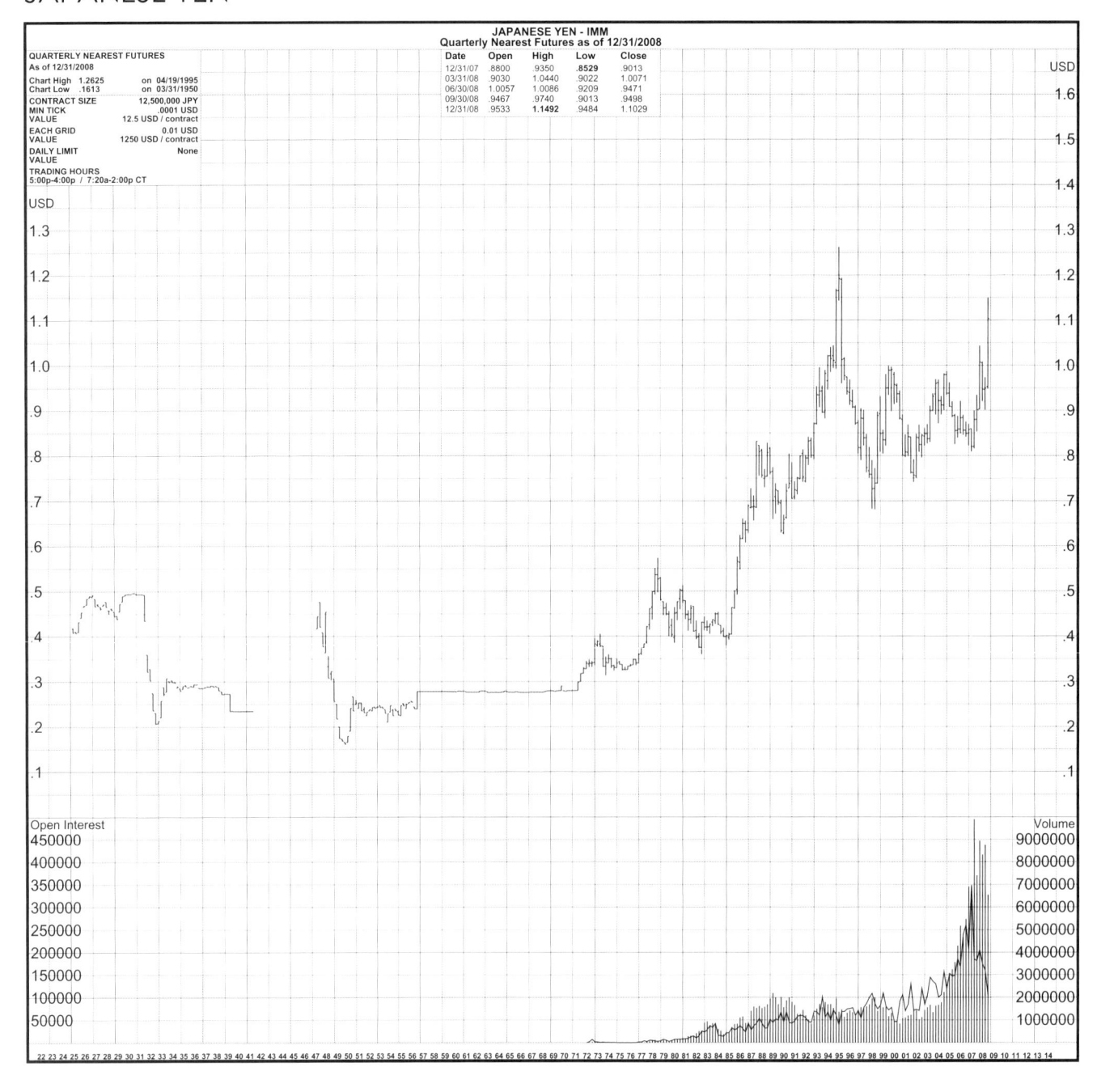

**QUARTERLY NEAREST FUTURES**
As of 12/31/2008
Chart High 1.2625 on 04/19/1995
Chart Low .1613 on 03/31/1950
CONTRACT SIZE 12,500,000 JPY
MIN TICK .0001 USD
VALUE 12.5 USD / contract
EACH GRID 0.01 USD
VALUE 1250 USD / contract
DAILY LIMIT None
VALUE
TRADING HOURS
5:00p-4:00p / 7:20a-2:00p CT

**JAPANESE YEN - IMM**
Quarterly Nearest Futures as of 12/31/2008

| Date | Open | High | Low | Close |
|---|---|---|---|---|
| 12/31/07 | .8800 | .9350 | .8529 | .9013 |
| 03/31/08 | .9030 | 1.0440 | .9022 | 1.0071 |
| 06/30/08 | 1.0057 | 1.0086 | .9209 | .9471 |
| 09/30/08 | .9467 | .9740 | .9013 | .9498 |
| 12/31/08 | .9533 | 1.1492 | .9484 | 1.1029 |

## Annual High, Low and Settle of Japanese Yen — In USD per JPY

| Year | High | Low | Settle | Year | High | Low | Settle | Year | High | Low | Settle |
|---|---|---|---|---|---|---|---|---|---|---|---|
| 1925 | .4657 | .4655 | .4657 | 1939 | .7849 | .7796 | .7843 | 1953 | .4663 | .4663 | .4663 |
| 1926 | .4657 | .4645 | .4655 | 1940 | .7847 | .7810 | .7819 | 1954 | .4663 | .4663 | .4663 |
| 1927 | .4672 | .4633 | .4672 | 1941 | .7819 | .7815 | .7817 | 1955 | .4663 | .4639 | .4639 |
| 1928 | .4680 | .4657 | .4659 | 1942 | ---- | ---- | ---- | 1956 | .4665 | .4639 | .4659 |
| 1929 | .4682 | .4635 | .4682 | 1943 | ---- | ---- | ---- | 1957 | .4657 | .4653 | .4655 |
| 1930 | .4672 | .4657 | .4663 | 1944 | ---- | ---- | ---- | 1958 | .4676 | .4653 | .4676 |
| 1931 | .4657 | .4545 | .4620 | 1945 | ---- | ---- | ---- | 1959 | .4688 | .4674 | .4688 |
| 1932 | .4653 | .4626 | .4653 | 1946 | .1117 | .0931 | .1117 | 1960 | .4690 | .4688 | .4688 |
| 1933 | .7479 | .4649 | .7299 | 1947 | .1087 | .0833 | .0833 | 1961 | .4927 | .4688 | .4890 |
| 1934 | .7911 | .7352 | .7860 | 1948 | .1305 | .0833 | .0954 | 1962 | .4905 | .4880 | .4895 |
| 1935 | .7904 | .7835 | .7866 | 1949 | .3912 | .1150 | .3233 | 1963 | .4923 | .4884 | .4923 |
| 1936 | .7958 | .7839 | .7868 | 1950 | .4663 | .3683 | .4663 | 1964 | .4923 | .4919 | .4919 |
| 1937 | .7894 | .7837 | .7882 | 1951 | .4663 | .4663 | .4663 | 1965 | .4919 | .4874 | .4888 |
| 1938 | .7905 | .7817 | .7839 | 1952 | .4663 | .4663 | .4663 | 1966 | .4923 | .4868 | .4923 |

Data continued on page 38.   *Source: Forex*

# JAPANESE YEN

**QUARTERLY CASH**
As of 12/31/2008
Chart High 620.00 on 03/31/1950
Chart Low 79.78 on 04/19/1995

**U.S. DOLLAR / JAPANESE YEN**
Quarterly Cash as of 12/31/2008

| Date | Open | High | Low | Close |
|---|---|---|---|---|
| 12/31/07 | 114.77 | 117.95 | 107.22 | 111.69 |
| 03/31/08 | 111.63 | 112.04 | 96.67 | 99.70 |
| 06/30/08 | 99.71 | 108.59 | 99.60 | 106.19 |
| 09/30/08 | 106.20 | 110.66 | 103.56 | 106.21 |
| 12/31/08 | 106.12 | 106.54 | 87.14 | 90.66 |

## Annual High, Low and Settle of Japanese Yen    In JPY per USD

| Year | High | Low | Settle | Year | High | Low | Settle | Year | High | Low | Settle |
|---|---|---|---|---|---|---|---|---|---|---|---|
| 1925 | 260.08 | 231.54 | 231.54 | 1939 | 426.62 | 366.30 | 426.62 | 1953 | 435.00 | 405.00 | 435.00 |
| 1926 | 226.40 | 203.79 | 204.33 | 1940 | 426.80 | 426.62 | 426.62 | 1954 | 475.00 | 405.00 | 424.00 |
| 1927 | 217.49 | 203.50 | 216.50 | 1941 | 426.62 | 426.62 | 426.62 | 1955 | 445.00 | 398.00 | 401.00 |
| 1928 | 221.98 | 209.60 | 217.91 | 1942 | ---- | ---- | ---- | 1956 | 418.00 | 359.84 | 359.84 |
| 1929 | 227.89 | 204.25 | 204.25 | 1943 | ---- | ---- | ---- | 1957 | 359.84 | 359.84 | 359.84 |
| 1930 | 203.71 | 201.53 | 201.53 | 1944 | ---- | ---- | ---- | 1958 | 359.84 | 359.84 | 359.84 |
| 1931 | 230.10 | 202.27 | 230.10 | 1945 | ---- | ---- | ---- | 1959 | 360.23 | 359.84 | 360.23 |
| 1932 | 484.97 | 277.85 | 482.39 | 1946 | ---- | ---- | ---- | 1960 | 361.27 | 358.81 | 359.58 |
| 1933 | 482.16 | 325.31 | 325.31 | 1947 | 240.00 | 210.00 | 238.00 | 1961 | 362.06 | 358.94 | 362.06 |
| 1934 | 348.68 | 329.92 | 346.98 | 1948 | 330.00 | 220.00 | 310.00 | 1962 | 362.06 | 358.42 | 358.42 |
| 1935 | 357.40 | 341.06 | 347.95 | 1949 | 595.00 | 327.00 | 595.00 | 1963 | 362.98 | 358.55 | 362.84 |
| 1936 | 350.75 | 340.02 | 350.75 | 1950 | 620.00 | 375.00 | 425.00 | 1964 | 362.71 | 359.20 | 359.20 |
| 1937 | 351.00 | 343.76 | 343.88 | 1951 | 432.50 | 385.00 | 432.50 | 1965 | 362.45 | 358.94 | 361.14 |
| 1938 | 367.51 | 344.23 | 367.51 | 1952 | 445.00 | 410.00 | 415.00 | 1966 | 362.71 | 361.01 | 362.58 |

Data continued on page 39.    *Source: Forex*

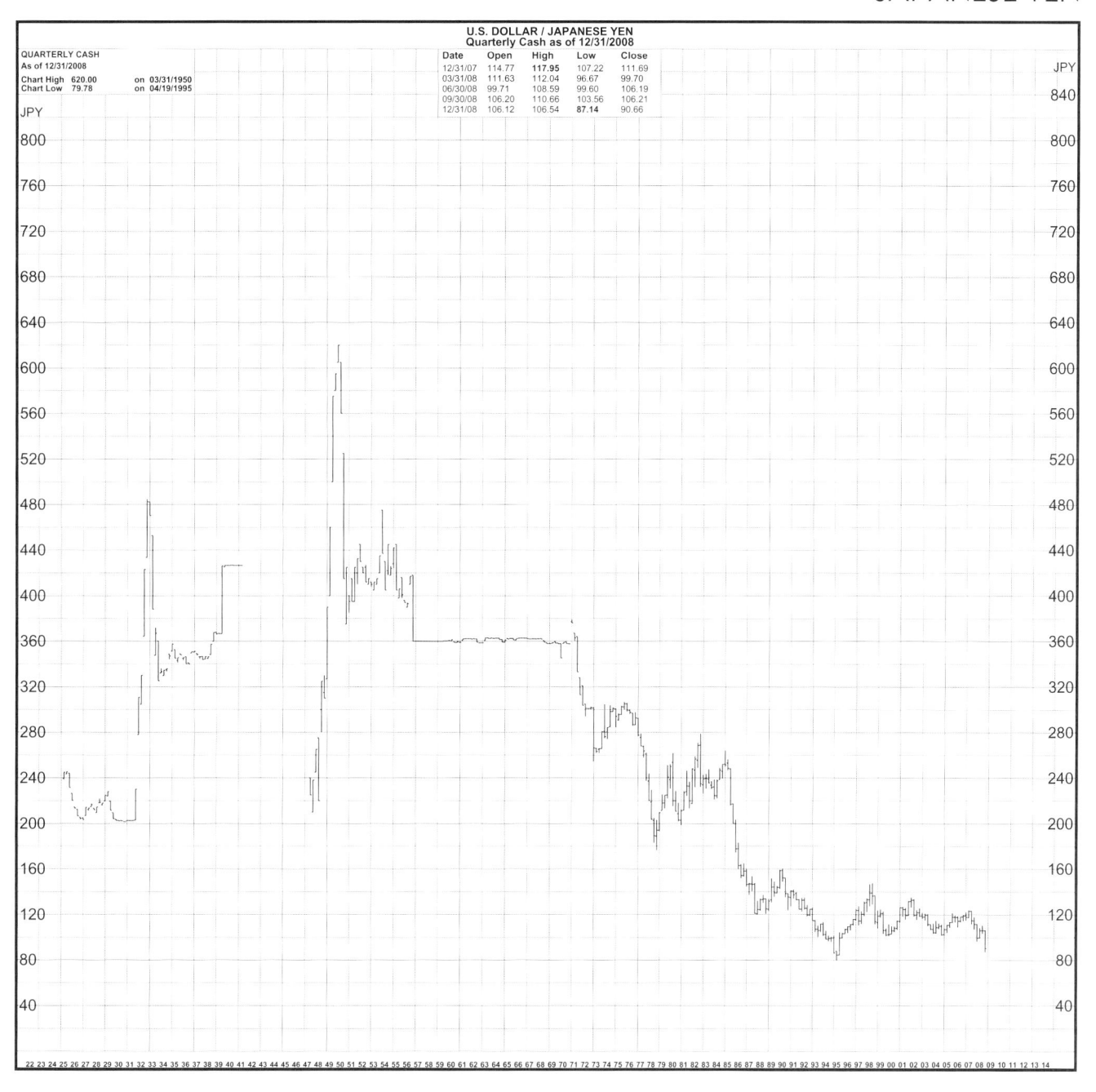

# JAPANESE YEN

## JAPANESE YEN - IMM
### Monthly Nearest Futures as of 12/31/2008

| Date | Open | High | Low | Close |
|---|---|---|---|---|
| 08/31/08 | .9291 | .9344 | .9013 | .9202 |
| 09/30/08 | .9200 | .9740 | .9164 | .9498 |
| 10/31/08 | .9533 | 1.1033 | .9484 | 1.0140 |
| 11/30/08 | 1.0144 | 1.0696 | .9953 | 1.0465 |
| 12/31/08 | 1.0466 | 1.1492 | 1.0461 | 1.1029 |

**MONTHLY NEAREST FUTURES** As of 12/31/2008
- Chart High 1.2625 on 04/19/1995
- Chart Low .2758 on 12/30/1966
- CONTRACT SIZE 12,500,000 JPY
- MIN TICK .0001 USD
- VALUE 12.5 USD / contract
- EACH GRID 0.005 USD
- VALUE 625 USD / contract
- DAILY LIMIT VALUE None
- TRADING HOURS 5:00p-4:00p / 7:20a-2:00p CT

## Annual High, Low and Settle of Japanese Yen Futures    In USD per JPY

| Year | High | Low | Settle | Year | High | Low | Settle | Year | High | Low | Settle |
|---|---|---|---|---|---|---|---|---|---|---|---|
| 1967 | .4923 | .4884 | .4907 | 1981 | .5128 | .4115 | .4624 | 1995 | 1.2625 | .9601 | .9773 |
| 1968 | .4923 | .4874 | .4895 | 1982 | .4669 | .3596 | .4315 | 1996 | .9755 | .8676 | .8713 |
| 1969 | .5306 | .4866 | .5306 | 1983 | .4438 | .4048 | .4371 | 1997 | .9050 | .7623 | .7736 |
| 1970 | .5386 | .5302 | .5367 | 1984 | .4543 | .3984 | .3987 | 1998 | .8974 | .6807 | .8884 |
| 1971 | .5998 | .5343 | .5998 | 1985 | .5018 | .3794 | .5004 | 1999 | .9990 | .8040 | .9892 |
| 1972 | .3480 | .3175 | .3410 | 1986 | .6608 | .4922 | .6354 | 2000 | .9974 | .8794 | .8827 |
| 1973 | .4055 | .3320 | .3329 | 1987 | .8320 | .6283 | .8316 | 2001 | .8907 | .7600 | .7629 |
| 1974 | .3600 | .3130 | .3310 | 1988 | .8288 | .7296 | .8069 | 2002 | .8685 | .7415 | .8447 |
| 1975 | .3503 | .3240 | .3260 | 1989 | .8187 | .6588 | .6968 | 2003 | .9384 | .8220 | .9318 |
| 1976 | .3500 | .3260 | .3407 | 1990 | .8046 | .6254 | .7384 | 2004 | .9825 | .8710 | .9797 |
| 1977 | .4228 | .3406 | .4216 | 1991 | .7993 | .7031 | .7991 | 2005 | .9873 | .8252 | .8551 |
| 1978 | .5735 | .4140 | .5270 | 1992 | .8419 | .7402 | .8004 | 2006 | .9217 | .8390 | .8484 |
| 1979 | .5306 | .3995 | .4197 | 1993 | .9959 | .7915 | .8959 | 2007 | .9350 | .8087 | .9013 |
| 1980 | .5056 | .3847 | .5025 | 1994 | 1.0442 | .8818 | 1.0108 | 2008 | 1.1492 | .9013 | 1.1029 |

Futures begin trading 05/16/1972.    Data continued from page 36.    *Source: CME Group; Chicago Mercantile Exchange*

# JAPANESE YEN

**U.S. DOLLAR / JAPANESE YEN**
Monthly Cash as of 12/31/2008

| Date | Open | High | Low | Close |
|---|---|---|---|---|
| 08/29/08 | 107.93 | 110.66 | 107.29 | 108.77 |
| 09/30/08 | 108.68 | 109.19 | 103.56 | 106.21 |
| 10/31/08 | 106.12 | 106.54 | 90.98 | 98.58 |
| 11/28/08 | 98.83 | 100.55 | 93.58 | 95.60 |
| 12/31/08 | 95.52 | 95.61 | 87.14 | 90.66 |

MONTHLY CASH
As of 12/31/2008
Chart High 379.00 on 02/26/1971
Chart Low 79.78 on 04/19/1995

## Annual High, Low and Settle of Japanese Yen — In JPY per USD

| Year | High | Low | Settle | Year | High | Low | Settle | Year | High | Low | Settle |
|---|---|---|---|---|---|---|---|---|---|---|---|
| 1967 | 362.58 | 361.93 | 361.93 | 1981 | 246.36 | 198.60 | 219.92 | 1995 | 104.65 | 79.78 | 103.46 |
| 1968 | 362.32 | 357.91 | 357.91 | 1982 | 278.70 | 217.20 | 234.85 | 1996 | 116.43 | 103.18 | 115.93 |
| 1969 | 359.58 | 357.78 | 357.78 | 1983 | 247.64 | 226.50 | 231.74 | 1997 | 131.58 | 110.63 | 130.20 |
| 1970 | 359.32 | 345.30 | 357.65 | 1984 | 251.95 | 221.04 | 251.95 | 1998 | 147.62 | 111.73 | 113.88 |
| 1971 | 379.00 | 313.00 | 313.00 | 1985 | 263.85 | 199.92 | 200.08 | 1999 | 124.78 | 101.30 | 102.18 |
| 1972 | 321.00 | 294.12 | 301.75 | 1986 | 203.58 | 151.85 | 158.10 | 2000 | 115.05 | 101.36 | 114.34 |
| 1973 | 302.39 | 254.45 | 280.27 | 1987 | 159.75 | 120.90 | 121.10 | 2001 | 132.08 | 113.57 | 131.56 |
| 1974 | 304.88 | 273.97 | 301.11 | 1988 | 137.30 | 120.30 | 125.00 | 2002 | 135.14 | 115.54 | 118.79 |
| 1975 | 306.84 | 284.58 | 305.16 | 1989 | 151.90 | 123.20 | 143.95 | 2003 | 121.88 | 106.74 | 107.38 |
| 1976 | 306.00 | 285.96 | 292.83 | 1990 | 160.40 | 123.75 | 135.45 | 2004 | 114.89 | 101.83 | 102.43 |
| 1977 | 292.83 | 237.47 | 240.10 | 1991 | 142.10 | 124.79 | 124.84 | 2005 | 121.40 | 101.69 | 117.96 |
| 1978 | 243.90 | 176.30 | 194.14 | 1992 | 134.95 | 118.65 | 124.80 | 2006 | 119.87 | 108.98 | 119.03 |
| 1979 | 251.19 | 193.12 | 240.73 | 1993 | 126.21 | 100.40 | 111.83 | 2007 | 124.14 | 107.22 | 111.69 |
| 1980 | 261.85 | 201.98 | 203.00 | 1994 | 113.58 | 96.15 | 99.71 | 2008 | 112.04 | 87.14 | 90.66 |

Data continued from page 37.   *Source: Forex*

39

# JAPANESE YEN

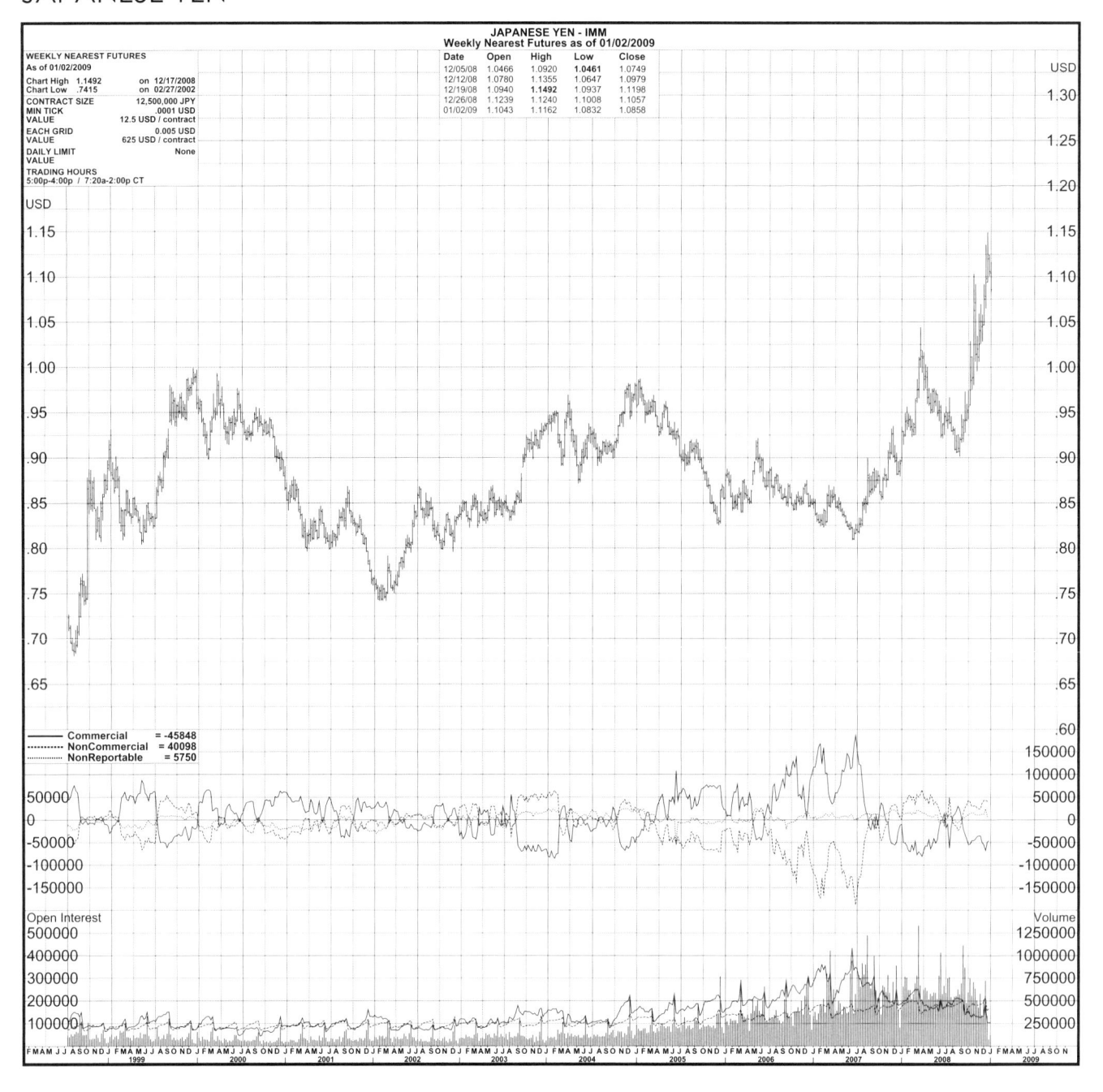

**JAPANESE YEN - IMM**
Weekly Nearest Futures as of 01/02/2009

| Date | Open | High | Low | Close |
|---|---|---|---|---|
| 12/05/08 | 1.0466 | 1.0920 | **1.0461** | 1.0749 |
| 12/12/08 | 1.0780 | 1.1355 | 1.0647 | 1.0979 |
| 12/19/08 | 1.0940 | **1.1492** | 1.0937 | 1.1198 |
| 12/26/08 | 1.1239 | 1.1240 | 1.1008 | 1.1057 |
| 01/02/09 | 1.1043 | 1.1162 | 1.0832 | 1.0858 |

**WEEKLY NEAREST FUTURES**
As of 01/02/2009
- Chart High: 1.1492 on 12/17/2008
- Chart Low: .7415 on 02/27/2002
- CONTRACT SIZE: 12,500,000 JPY
- MIN TICK: .0001 USD
- VALUE: 12.5 USD / contract
- EACH GRID: 0.005 USD
- VALUE: 625 USD / contract
- DAILY LIMIT VALUE: None
- TRADING HOURS: 5:00p-4:00p / 7:20a-2:00p CT

Commercial = -45848
NonCommercial = 40098
NonReportable = 5750

## Quarterly High, Low and Settle of Japanese Yen Futures    In USD per JPY

| Quarter | High | Low | Settle | Quarter | High | Low | Settle | Quarter | High | Low | Settle |
|---|---|---|---|---|---|---|---|---|---|---|---|
| 03/2000 | .9974 | .8978 | .9908 | 03/2003 | .8607 | .8220 | .8482 | 03/2006 | .8880 | .8390 | .8585 |
| 06/2000 | .9855 | .9142 | .9577 | 06/2003 | .8698 | .8265 | .8369 | 06/2006 | .9217 | .8487 | .8832 |
| 09/2000 | .9600 | .9175 | .9373 | 09/2003 | .9111 | .8296 | .8996 | 09/2006 | .8901 | .8454 | .8559 |
| 12/2000 | .9445 | .8794 | .8827 | 12/2003 | .9384 | .8979 | .9318 | 12/2006 | .8754 | .8412 | .8484 |
| 03/2001 | .8907 | .8005 | .8008 | 03/2004 | .9695 | .8904 | .9604 | 03/2007 | .8701 | .8229 | .8575 |
| 06/2001 | .8470 | .7962 | .8079 | 06/2004 | .9688 | .8710 | .9220 | 06/2007 | .8599 | .8087 | .8201 |
| 09/2001 | .8688 | .7983 | .8415 | 09/2004 | .9322 | .8905 | .9127 | 09/2007 | .8995 | .8158 | .8797 |
| 12/2001 | .8416 | .7600 | .7629 | 12/2004 | .9825 | .9002 | .9797 | 12/2007 | .9350 | .8529 | .9013 |
| 03/2002 | .7920 | .7415 | .7567 | 03/2005 | .9873 | .9343 | .9383 | 03/2008 | 1.0440 | .9022 | 1.0071 |
| 06/2002 | .8481 | .7501 | .8403 | 06/2005 | .9629 | .9074 | .9092 | 06/2008 | 1.0086 | .9209 | .9471 |
| 09/2002 | .8685 | .8082 | .8243 | 09/2005 | .9208 | .8844 | .8877 | 09/2008 | .9740 | .9013 | .9498 |
| 12/2002 | .8478 | .7956 | .8447 | 12/2005 | .8920 | .8252 | .8551 | 12/2008 | 1.1492 | .9484 | 1.1029 |

*Source: CME Group; Chicago Mercantile Exchange*

# JAPANESE YEN

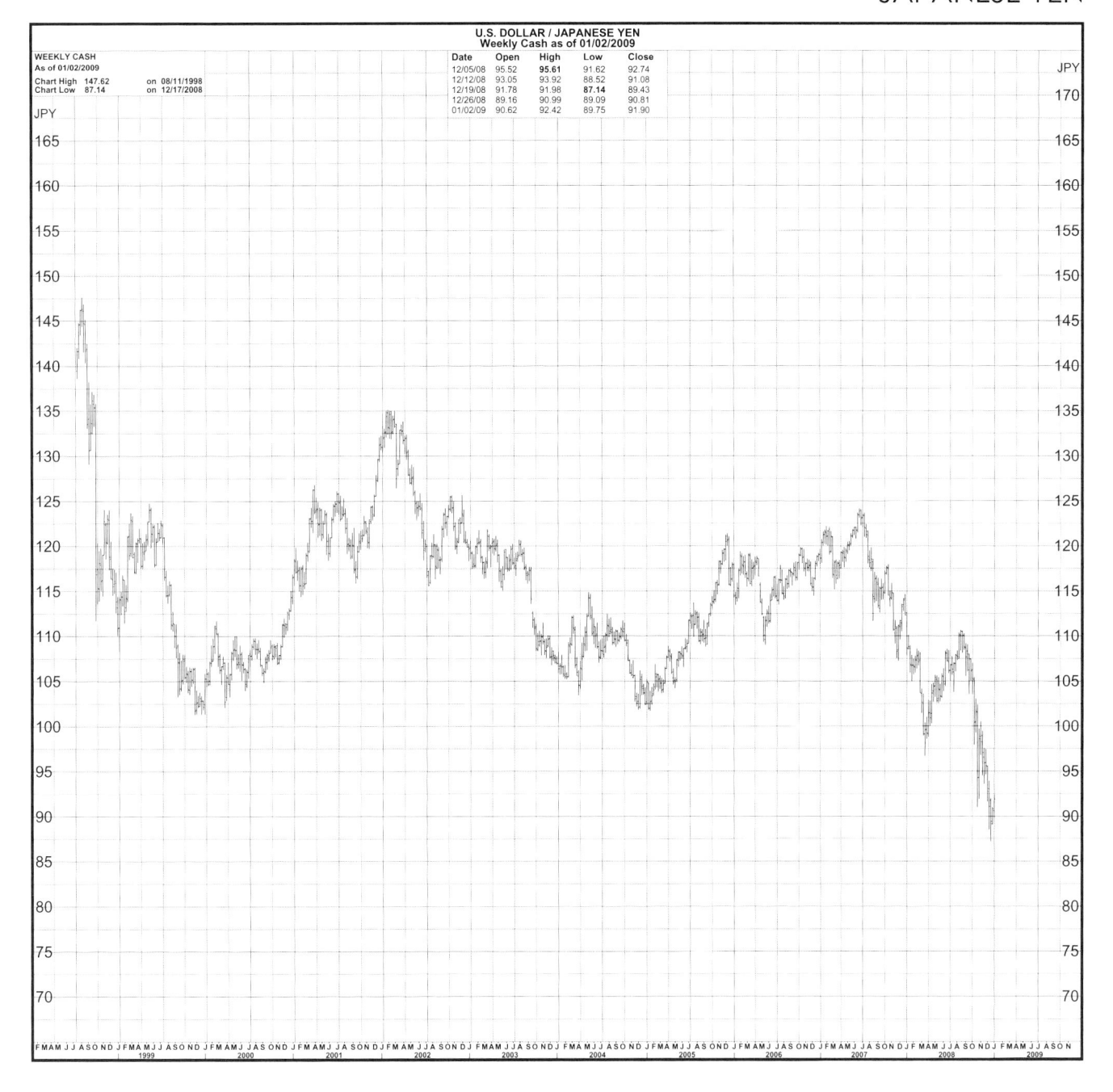

**U.S. DOLLAR / JAPANESE YEN**
Weekly Cash as of 01/02/2009

| Date | Open | High | Low | Close |
|---|---|---|---|---|
| 12/05/08 | 95.52 | 95.61 | 91.62 | 92.74 |
| 12/12/08 | 93.05 | 93.92 | 88.52 | 91.08 |
| 12/19/08 | 91.78 | 91.98 | 87.14 | 89.43 |
| 12/26/08 | 89.16 | 90.99 | 89.09 | 90.81 |
| 01/02/09 | 90.62 | 92.42 | 89.75 | 91.90 |

WEEKLY CASH
As of 01/02/2009
Chart High 147.62 on 08/11/1998
Chart Low 87.14 on 12/17/2008

## Quarterly High, Low and Settle of Japanese Yen   In JPY per USD

| Quarter | High | Low | Settle | Quarter | High | Low | Settle | Quarter | High | Low | Settle |
|---|---|---|---|---|---|---|---|---|---|---|---|
| 03/2000 | 111.73 | 101.36 | 102.75 | 03/2003 | 121.88 | 116.35 | 117.91 | 03/2006 | 119.40 | 113.44 | 117.69 |
| 06/2000 | 110.03 | 102.85 | 106.05 | 06/2003 | 121.12 | 115.07 | 119.75 | 06/2006 | 118.90 | 108.98 | 114.42 |
| 09/2000 | 109.80 | 104.83 | 108.09 | 09/2003 | 120.69 | 110.12 | 111.49 | 09/2006 | 118.28 | 113.47 | 118.15 |
| 12/2000 | 115.05 | 106.84 | 114.34 | 12/2003 | 111.60 | 106.74 | 107.38 | 12/2006 | 119.87 | 114.45 | 119.03 |
| 03/2001 | 126.34 | 113.57 | 126.25 | 03/2004 | 112.33 | 103.41 | 104.39 | 03/2007 | 122.19 | 115.16 | 117.85 |
| 06/2001 | 126.81 | 118.37 | 124.72 | 06/2004 | 114.89 | 103.49 | 108.80 | 06/2007 | 124.14 | 117.46 | 123.07 |
| 09/2001 | 126.12 | 115.84 | 119.41 | 09/2004 | 112.50 | 107.59 | 110.07 | 09/2007 | 123.68 | 111.64 | 114.87 |
| 12/2001 | 132.08 | 119.30 | 131.56 | 12/2004 | 111.47 | 101.83 | 102.43 | 12/2007 | 117.95 | 107.22 | 111.69 |
| 03/2002 | 135.14 | 126.40 | 132.73 | 03/2005 | 107.70 | 101.69 | 107.22 | 03/2008 | 112.04 | 96.67 | 99.70 |
| 06/2002 | 133.84 | 118.40 | 119.54 | 06/2005 | 110.99 | 104.20 | 110.90 | 06/2008 | 108.59 | 99.60 | 106.19 |
| 09/2002 | 124.21 | 115.54 | 121.79 | 09/2005 | 113.72 | 108.78 | 113.47 | 09/2008 | 110.66 | 103.56 | 106.21 |
| 12/2002 | 125.69 | 118.31 | 118.79 | 12/2005 | 121.40 | 113.02 | 117.96 | 12/2008 | 106.54 | 87.14 | 90.66 |

*Source: Forex*

# MEXICAN PESO

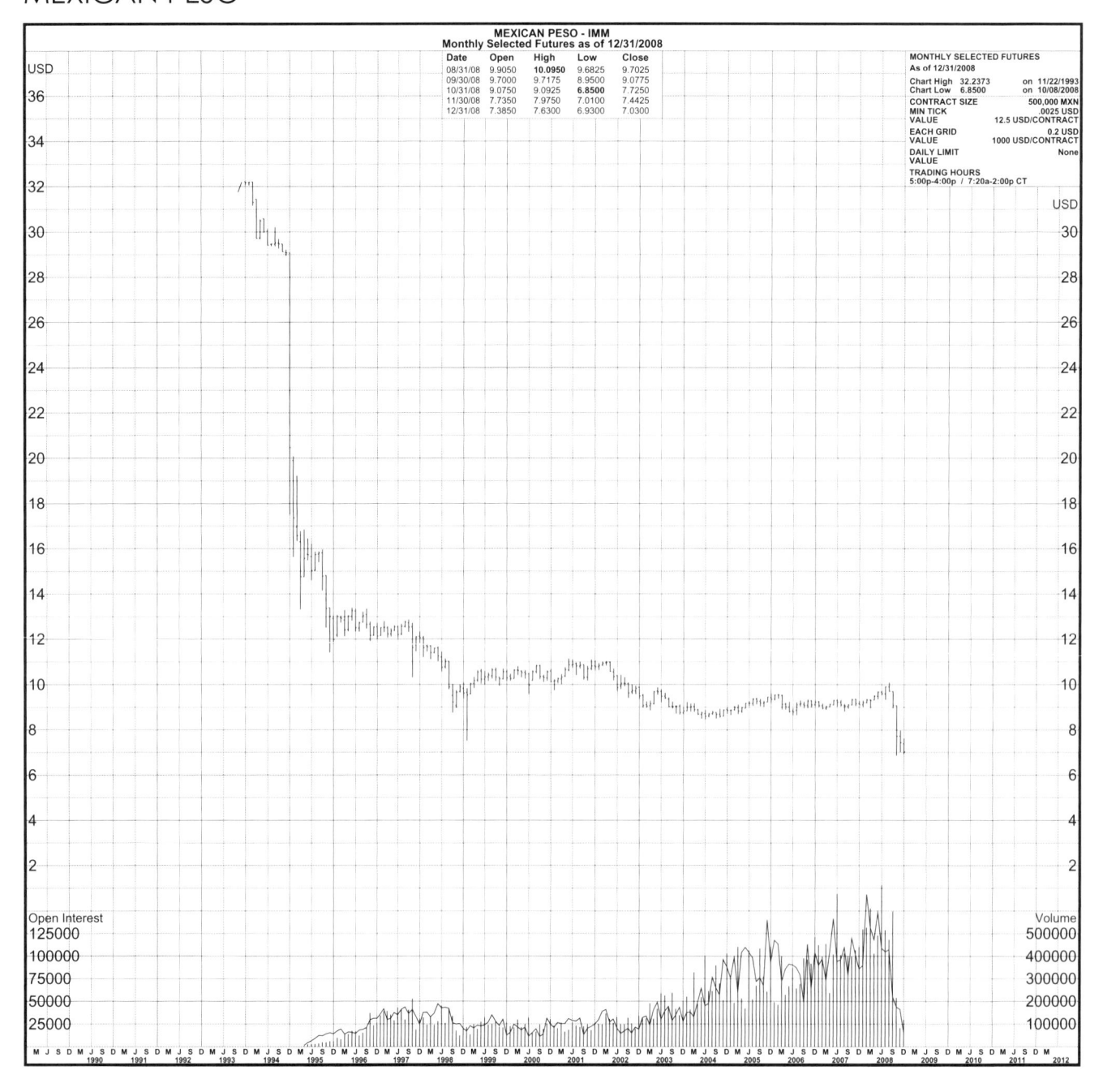

**MEXICAN PESO - IMM**
Monthly Selected Futures as of 12/31/2008

| Date | Open | High | Low | Close |
|---|---|---|---|---|
| 08/31/08 | 9.9050 | 10.0950 | 9.6825 | 9.7025 |
| 09/30/08 | 9.7000 | 9.7175 | 8.9500 | 9.0775 |
| 10/31/08 | 9.0750 | 9.0925 | 6.8500 | 7.7250 |
| 11/30/08 | 7.7350 | 7.9750 | 7.0100 | 7.4425 |
| 12/31/08 | 7.3850 | 7.6300 | 6.9300 | 7.0300 |

**MONTHLY SELECTED FUTURES**
As of 12/31/2008

Chart High 32.2373 on 11/22/1993
Chart Low 6.8500 on 10/08/2008
CONTRACT SIZE 500,000 MXN
MIN TICK .0025 USD
VALUE 12.5 USD/CONTRACT
EACH GRID 0.2 USD
VALUE 1000 USD/CONTRACT
DAILY LIMIT None
VALUE
TRADING HOURS
5:00p-4:00p / 7:20a-2:00p CT

## Annual High, Low and Settle of Mexican Peso Futures   In USD per MXN

| Year | High | Low | Settle | Year | High | Low | Settle | Year | High | Low | Settle |
|---|---|---|---|---|---|---|---|---|---|---|---|
| 1967 | | | | 1981 | | | | 1995 | 20.0803 | 11.4000 | 11.9800 |
| 1968 | | | | 1982 | | | | 1996 | 13.4000 | 11.9100 | 12.1350 |
| 1969 | | | | 1983 | | | | 1997 | 12.8800 | 10.3000 | 12.0600 |
| 1970 | | | | 1984 | | | | 1998 | 12.1400 | 8.7500 | 9.6100 |
| 1971 | | | | 1985 | | | | 1999 | 10.7400 | 7.5000 | 10.2900 |
| 1972 | | | | 1986 | | | | 2000 | 10.8600 | 9.5700 | 10.1275 |
| 1973 | | | | 1987 | | | | 2001 | 11.1400 | 9.7400 | 10.7825 |
| 1974 | | | | 1988 | | | | 2002 | 11.0300 | 9.3600 | 9.4925 |
| 1975 | | | | 1989 | | | | 2003 | 9.8800 | 8.6650 | 8.8300 |
| 1976 | | | | 1990 | | | | 2004 | 9.2350 | 8.4600 | 8.8575 |
| 1977 | | | | 1991 | | | | 2005 | 9.6025 | 8.6425 | 9.3475 |
| 1978 | | | | 1992 | | | | 2006 | 9.5775 | 8.6300 | 9.2200 |
| 1979 | | | | 1993 | 32.2373 | 30.8642 | 32.1750 | 2007 | 9.3750 | 8.8075 | 9.1075 |
| 1980 | | | | 1994 | 32.2061 | 17.4978 | 20.4708 | 2008 | 10.0950 | 6.8500 | 7.0300 |

Futures begin trading 04/25/1995.   *Source: CME Group; Chicago Mercantile Exchange*

# MEXICAN PESO

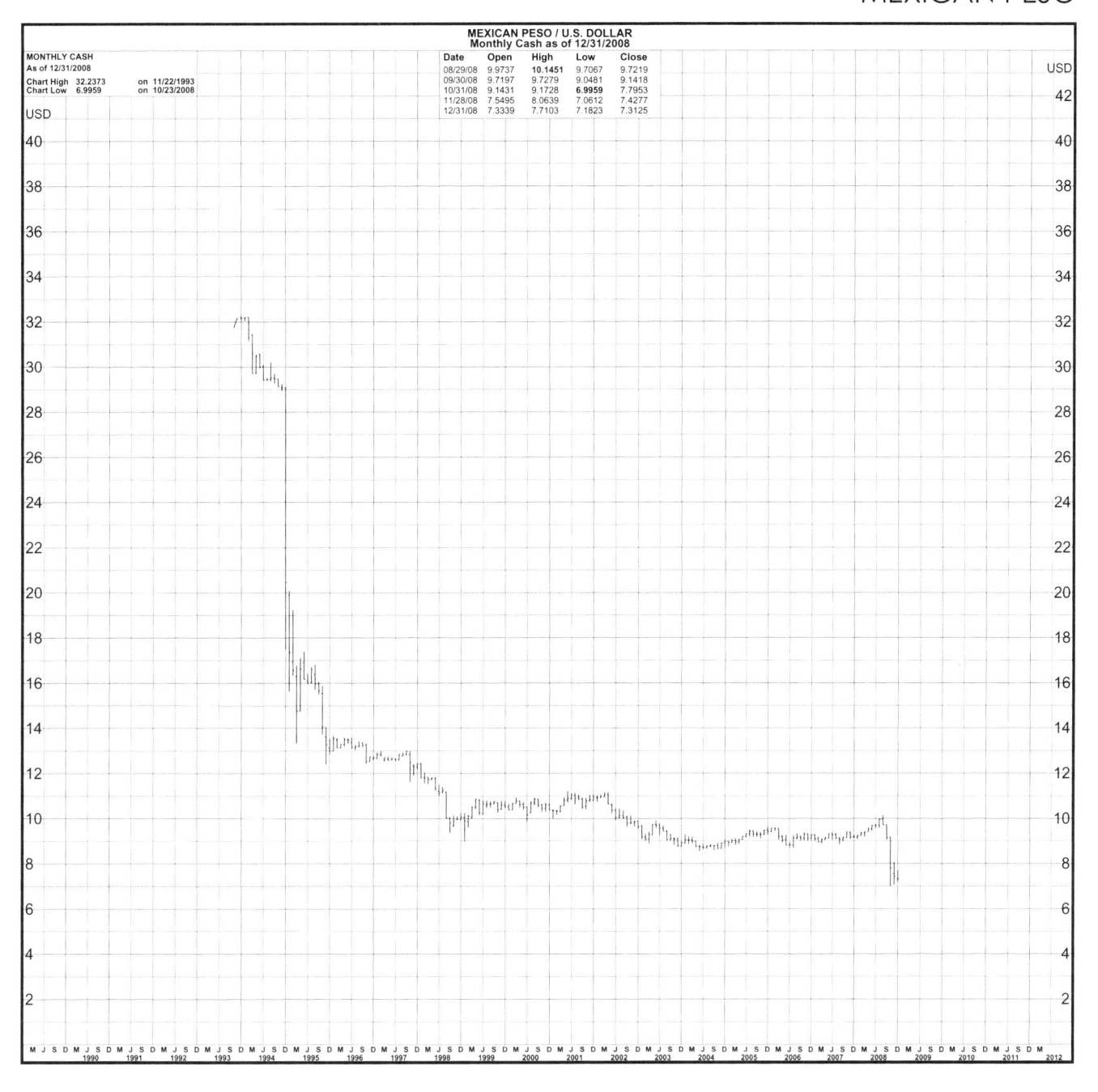

**MEXICAN PESO / U.S. DOLLAR**
Monthly Cash as of 12/31/2008

| Date | Open | High | Low | Close |
|---|---|---|---|---|
| 08/29/08 | 9.9737 | 10.1451 | 9.7067 | 9.7219 |
| 09/30/08 | 9.7197 | 9.7279 | 9.0481 | 9.1418 |
| 10/31/08 | 9.1431 | 9.1728 | 6.9959 | 7.7953 |
| 11/28/08 | 7.5495 | 8.0639 | 7.0612 | 7.4277 |
| 12/31/08 | 7.3339 | 7.7103 | 7.1823 | 7.3125 |

MONTHLY CASH
As of 12/31/2008
Chart High 32.2373 on 11/22/1993
Chart Low 6.9959 on 10/23/2008

## Annual High, Low and Settle of Mexican Peso   In USD per MXN

| Year | High | Low | Settle | Year | High | Low | Settle | Year | High | Low | Settle |
|---|---|---|---|---|---|---|---|---|---|---|---|
| 1967 | | | | 1981 | | | | 1995 | 20.0803 | 12.4069 | 13.0039 |
| 1968 | | | | 1982 | | | | 1996 | 13.6426 | 12.4224 | 12.6968 |
| 1969 | | | | 1983 | | | | 1997 | 12.9870 | 11.6279 | 12.4069 |
| 1970 | | | | 1984 | | | | 1998 | 12.4688 | 9.3589 | 10.0650 |
| 1971 | | | | 1985 | | | | 1999 | 10.8640 | 8.9710 | 10.5290 |
| 1972 | | | | 1986 | | | | 2000 | 10.9390 | 9.8570 | 10.3950 |
| 1973 | | | | 1987 | | | | 2001 | 11.2110 | 10.0050 | 10.9200 |
| 1974 | | | | 1988 | | | | 2002 | 11.1669 | 9.5279 | 9.6339 |
| 1975 | | | | 1989 | | | | 2003 | 9.9162 | 8.7276 | 8.9049 |
| 1976 | | | | 1990 | | | | 2004 | 9.2878 | 8.5417 | 8.9804 |
| 1977 | | | | 1991 | | | | 2005 | 9.6167 | 8.7443 | 9.4091 |
| 1978 | | | | 1992 | | | | 2006 | 9.5938 | 8.6818 | 9.2535 |
| 1979 | | | | 1993 | 32.2373 | 30.8642 | 32.1750 | 2007 | 9.3995 | 8.8276 | 9.1651 |
| 1980 | | | | 1994 | 32.2061 | 17.4978 | 20.4708 | 2008 | 10.1451 | 6.9959 | 7.3125 |

*Source: Forex*

# MEXICAN PESO

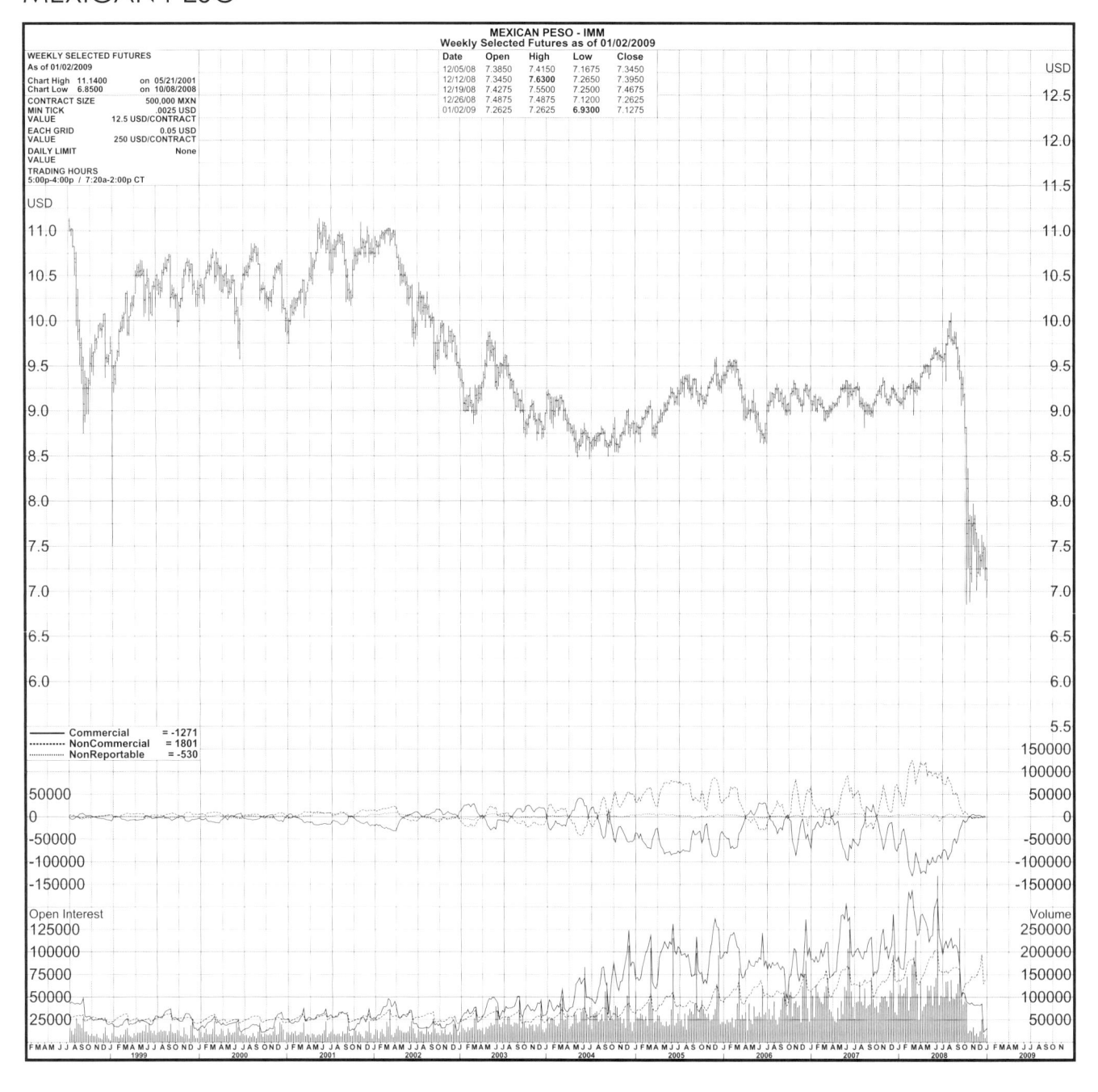

**MEXICAN PESO - IMM**
Weekly Selected Futures as of 01/02/2009

| Date | Open | High | Low | Close |
|---|---|---|---|---|
| 12/05/08 | 7.3850 | 7.4150 | 7.1675 | 7.3450 |
| 12/12/08 | 7.3450 | 7.6300 | 7.2650 | 7.3950 |
| 12/19/08 | 7.4275 | 7.5500 | 7.2500 | 7.4675 |
| 12/26/08 | 7.4875 | 7.4875 | 7.1200 | 7.2625 |
| 01/02/09 | 7.2625 | 7.2625 | 6.9300 | 7.1275 |

**WEEKLY SELECTED FUTURES**
As of 01/02/2009
Chart High 11.1400 on 05/21/2001
Chart Low 6.8500 on 10/08/2008
CONTRACT SIZE 500,000 MXN
MIN TICK .0025 USD
VALUE 12.5 USD/CONTRACT
EACH GRID 0.05 USD
VALUE 250 USD/CONTRACT
DAILY LIMIT None
VALUE
TRADING HOURS
5:00p-4:00p / 7:20a-2:00p CT

Commercial = -1271
NonCommercial = 1801
NonReportable = -530

## Quarterly High, Low and Settle of Mexican Peso Futures   In USD per MXN

| Quarter | High | Low | Settle | Quarter | High | Low | Settle | Quarter | High | Low | Settle |
|---|---|---|---|---|---|---|---|---|---|---|---|
| 03/2000 | 10.8050 | 10.1500 | 10.6125 | 03/2003 | 9.5800 | 8.8500 | 9.1500 | 03/2006 | 9.5775 | 8.8900 | 9.1225 |
| 06/2000 | 10.6300 | 9.5700 | 9.9625 | 06/2003 | 9.8800 | 9.1100 | 9.4775 | 06/2006 | 9.2400 | 8.6300 | 8.7900 |
| 09/2000 | 10.8600 | 10.1700 | 10.3450 | 09/2003 | 9.6300 | 8.9350 | 9.0250 | 09/2006 | 9.3050 | 8.6375 | 9.0700 |
| 12/2000 | 10.6800 | 10.0800 | 10.1275 | 12/2003 | 9.1250 | 8.6650 | 8.8300 | 12/2006 | 9.3425 | 8.9525 | 9.2200 |
| 03/2001 | 10.4600 | 9.7400 | 10.3175 | 03/2004 | 9.2350 | 8.7900 | 8.8950 | 03/2007 | 9.2750 | 8.8775 | 9.0225 |
| 06/2001 | 11.1400 | 10.3150 | 10.8850 | 06/2004 | 8.9225 | 8.4600 | 8.5975 | 06/2007 | 9.3450 | 9.0125 | 9.2175 |
| 09/2001 | 10.9900 | 10.2000 | 10.3050 | 09/2004 | 8.8375 | 8.4900 | 8.6825 | 09/2007 | 9.3200 | 8.8075 | 9.1000 |
| 12/2001 | 11.1000 | 10.1600 | 10.7825 | 12/2004 | 9.0250 | 8.5300 | 8.8575 | 12/2007 | 9.3750 | 9.0525 | 9.1075 |
| 03/2002 | 11.0300 | 10.6250 | 10.9675 | 03/2005 | 9.1200 | 8.6425 | 8.8300 | 03/2008 | 9.3725 | 8.9500 | 9.3050 |
| 06/2002 | 11.0100 | 9.7100 | 9.8650 | 06/2005 | 9.2650 | 8.7400 | 9.1700 | 06/2008 | 9.7150 | 9.3050 | 9.5950 |
| 09/2002 | 10.4275 | 9.4000 | 9.6250 | 09/2005 | 9.4125 | 9.0450 | 9.1850 | 09/2008 | 10.0950 | 8.9500 | 9.0775 |
| 12/2002 | 10.0000 | 9.3600 | 9.4925 | 12/2005 | 9.6025 | 9.0150 | 9.3475 | 12/2008 | 9.0925 | 6.8500 | 7.0300 |

*Source: CME Group; Chicago Mercantile Exchange*

# MEXICAN PESO

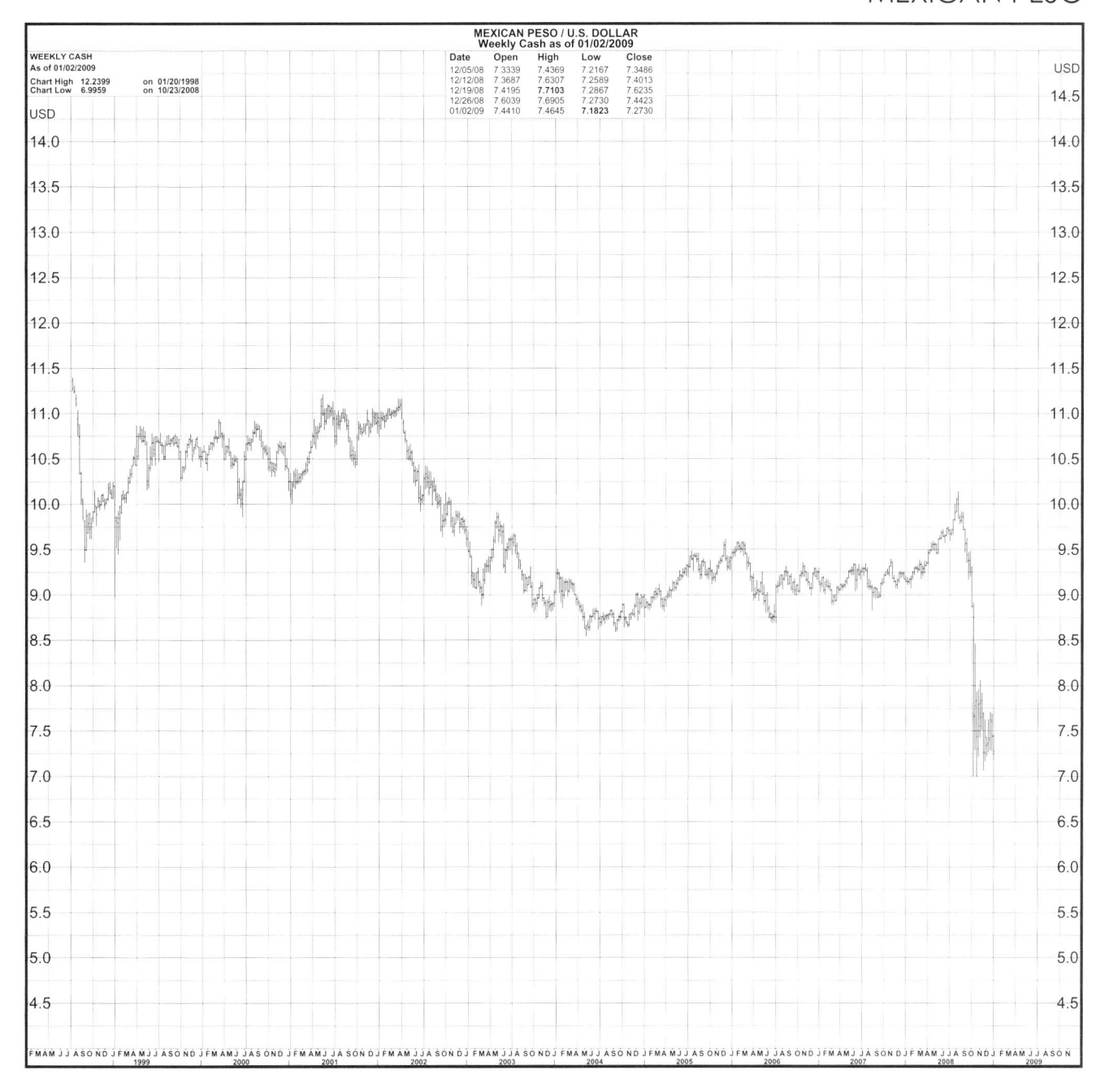

**MEXICAN PESO / U.S. DOLLAR**
Weekly Cash as of 01/02/2009

| Date | Open | High | Low | Close |
|---|---|---|---|---|
| 12/05/08 | 7.3339 | 7.4369 | 7.2167 | 7.3486 |
| 12/12/08 | 7.3687 | 7.6307 | 7.2589 | 7.4013 |
| 12/19/08 | 7.4195 | 7.7103 | 7.2867 | 7.6235 |
| 12/26/08 | 7.6039 | 7.6905 | 7.2730 | 7.4423 |
| 01/02/09 | 7.4410 | 7.4645 | 7.1823 | 7.2730 |

WEEKLY CASH
As of 01/02/2009
Chart High 12.2399 on 01/20/1998
Chart Low 6.9959 on 10/23/2008

## Quarterly High, Low and Settle of Mexican Peso    In USD per MXN

| Quarter | High | Low | Settle | Quarter | High | Low | Settle | Quarter | High | Low | Settle |
|---|---|---|---|---|---|---|---|---|---|---|---|
| 03/2000 | 10.9390 | 10.3690 | 10.7810 | 03/2003 | 9.7087 | 8.8775 | 9.2687 | 03/2006 | 9.5938 | 9.0342 | 9.1896 |
| 06/2000 | 10.7980 | 9.8570 | 10.1620 | 06/2003 | 9.9162 | 9.2366 | 9.5630 | 06/2006 | 9.2561 | 8.6818 | 8.8183 |
| 09/2000 | 10.9220 | 10.2410 | 10.5910 | 09/2003 | 9.6840 | 9.0119 | 9.0988 | 09/2006 | 9.3165 | 8.6843 | 9.1027 |
| 12/2000 | 10.7010 | 10.3020 | 10.3950 | 12/2003 | 9.1501 | 8.7276 | 8.9049 | 12/2006 | 9.3615 | 8.9931 | 9.2535 |
| 03/2001 | 10.5880 | 10.0050 | 10.5690 | 03/2004 | 9.2878 | 8.8498 | 8.9807 | 03/2007 | 9.2985 | 8.8840 | 9.0564 |
| 06/2001 | 11.2110 | 10.5600 | 11.0610 | 06/2004 | 8.9914 | 8.5417 | 8.7048 | 06/2007 | 9.3489 | 9.0381 | 9.2527 |
| 09/2001 | 11.1360 | 10.4220 | 10.5110 | 09/2004 | 8.8460 | 8.5953 | 8.7866 | 09/2007 | 9.3475 | 8.8276 | 9.1443 |
| 12/2001 | 11.0619 | 10.4004 | 10.9200 | 12/2004 | 9.0319 | 8.6357 | 8.9804 | 12/2007 | 9.3995 | 9.0659 | 9.1651 |
| 03/2002 | 11.1669 | 10.7486 | 11.0681 | 03/2005 | 9.1226 | 8.7443 | 8.9526 | 03/2008 | 9.4082 | 9.0742 | 9.3960 |
| 06/2002 | 11.1632 | 9.9182 | 10.0492 | 06/2005 | 9.3190 | 8.8684 | 9.3046 | 06/2008 | 9.7477 | 9.3942 | 9.6989 |
| 09/2002 | 10.4306 | 9.6316 | 9.7953 | 09/2005 | 9.4882 | 9.1611 | 9.2920 | 09/2008 | 10.1451 | 9.0481 | 9.1418 |
| 12/2002 | 10.1317 | 9.5279 | 9.6339 | 12/2005 | 9.6167 | 9.1124 | 9.4091 | 12/2008 | 9.1728 | 6.9959 | 7.3125 |

*Source: Forex*

# SWISS FRANC

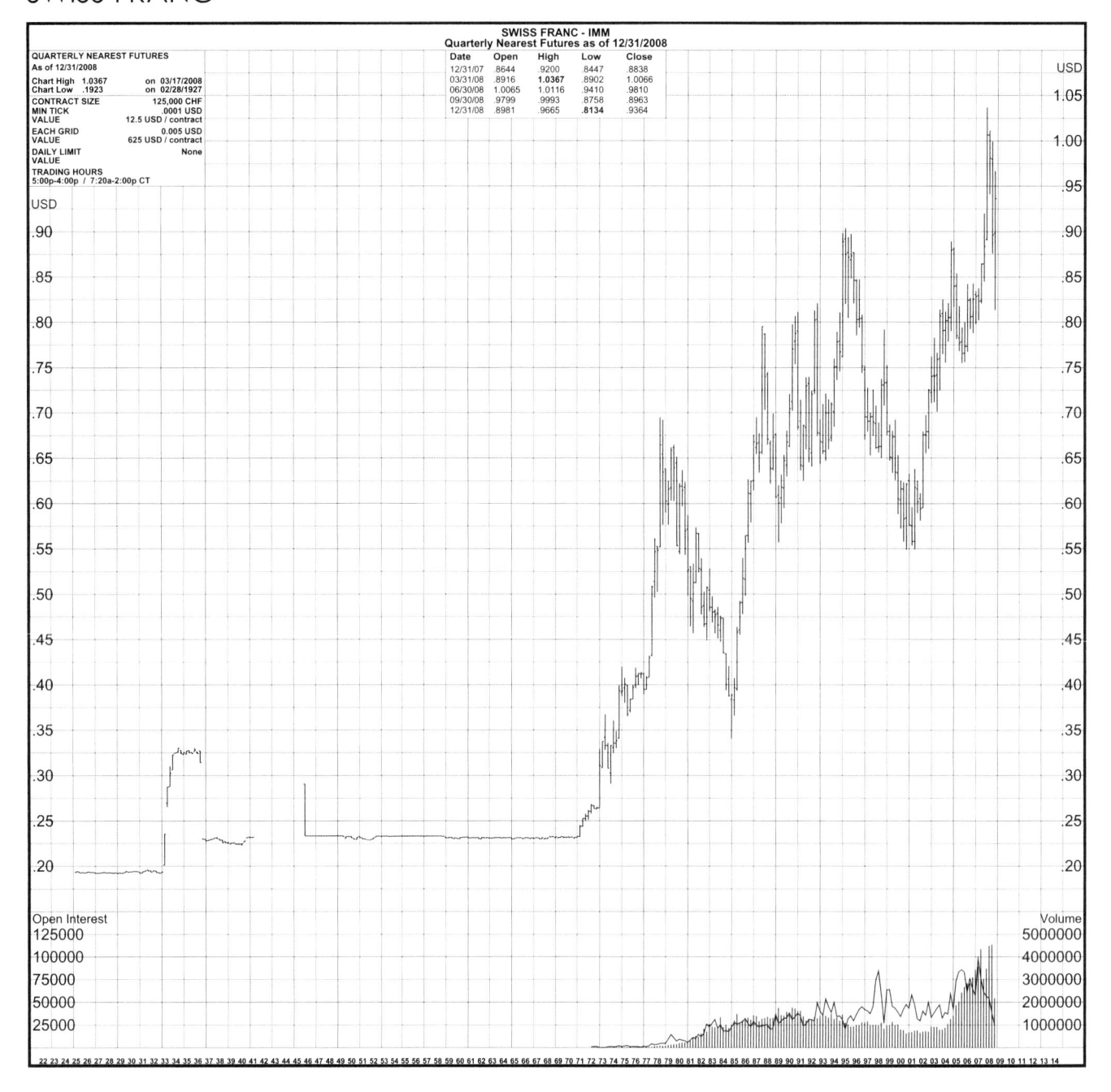

**QUARTERLY NEAREST FUTURES**
As of 12/31/2008
Chart High 1.0367 on 03/17/2008
Chart Low .1923 on 02/28/1927
CONTRACT SIZE 125,000 CHF
MIN TICK .0001 USD
VALUE 12.5 USD / contract
EACH GRID 0.005 USD
VALUE 625 USD / contract
DAILY LIMIT None
VALUE
TRADING HOURS
5:00p-4:00p / 7:20a-2:00p CT

**SWISS FRANC - IMM**
Quarterly Nearest Futures as of 12/31/2008

| Date | Open | High | Low | Close |
|---|---|---|---|---|
| 12/31/07 | .8644 | .9200 | .8447 | .8838 |
| 03/31/08 | .8916 | 1.0367 | .8902 | 1.0066 |
| 06/30/08 | 1.0065 | 1.0116 | .9410 | .9810 |
| 09/30/08 | .9799 | .9993 | .8758 | .8963 |
| 12/31/08 | .8981 | .9665 | .8134 | .9364 |

## Annual High, Low and Settle of Swiss Franc    In USD per CHF

| Year | High | Low | Settle | Year | High | Low | Settle | Year | High | Low | Settle |
|---|---|---|---|---|---|---|---|---|---|---|---|
| 1925 | .1941 | .1926 | .1930 | 1939 | .2267 | .2242 | .2242 | 1953 | .2333 | .2325 | .2329 |
| 1926 | .1936 | .1925 | .1932 | 1940 | .2320 | .2225 | .2320 | 1954 | .2333 | .2331 | .2333 |
| 1927 | .1932 | .1923 | .1932 | 1941 | .2322 | .2320 | .2321 | 1955 | .2334 | .2332 | .2334 |
| 1928 | .1928 | .1924 | .1927 | 1942 | ---- | ---- | ---- | 1956 | .2334 | .2333 | .2334 |
| 1929 | .1944 | .1923 | .1944 | 1943 | ---- | ---- | ---- | 1957 | .2334 | .2331 | .2334 |
| 1930 | .1944 | .1929 | .1940 | 1944 | ---- | ---- | ---- | 1958 | .2334 | .2330 | .2332 |
| 1931 | .1960 | .1924 | .1948 | 1945 | ---- | ---- | ---- | 1959 | .2320 | .2304 | .2313 |
| 1932 | .1951 | .1924 | .1924 | 1946 | .2907 | .2336 | .2336 | 1960 | .2323 | .2305 | .2323 |
| 1933 | .3102 | .1928 | .3025 | 1947 | .2336 | .2336 | .2336 | 1961 | .2322 | .2310 | .2317 |
| 1934 | .3302 | .3064 | .3241 | 1948 | .2336 | .2336 | .2336 | 1962 | .2317 | .2301 | .2317 |
| 1935 | .3275 | .3231 | .3243 | 1949 | .2336 | .2308 | .2329 | 1963 | .2317 | .2310 | .2317 |
| 1936 | .3303 | .2298 | .2298 | 1950 | .2329 | .2294 | .2320 | 1964 | .2317 | .2311 | .2317 |
| 1937 | .2315 | .2279 | .2312 | 1951 | .2330 | .2288 | .2290 | 1965 | .2316 | .2300 | .2316 |
| 1938 | .2323 | .2260 | .2261 | 1952 | .2333 | .2288 | .2333 | 1966 | .2317 | .2304 | .2313 |

Data continued on page 48.    *Source: Forex*

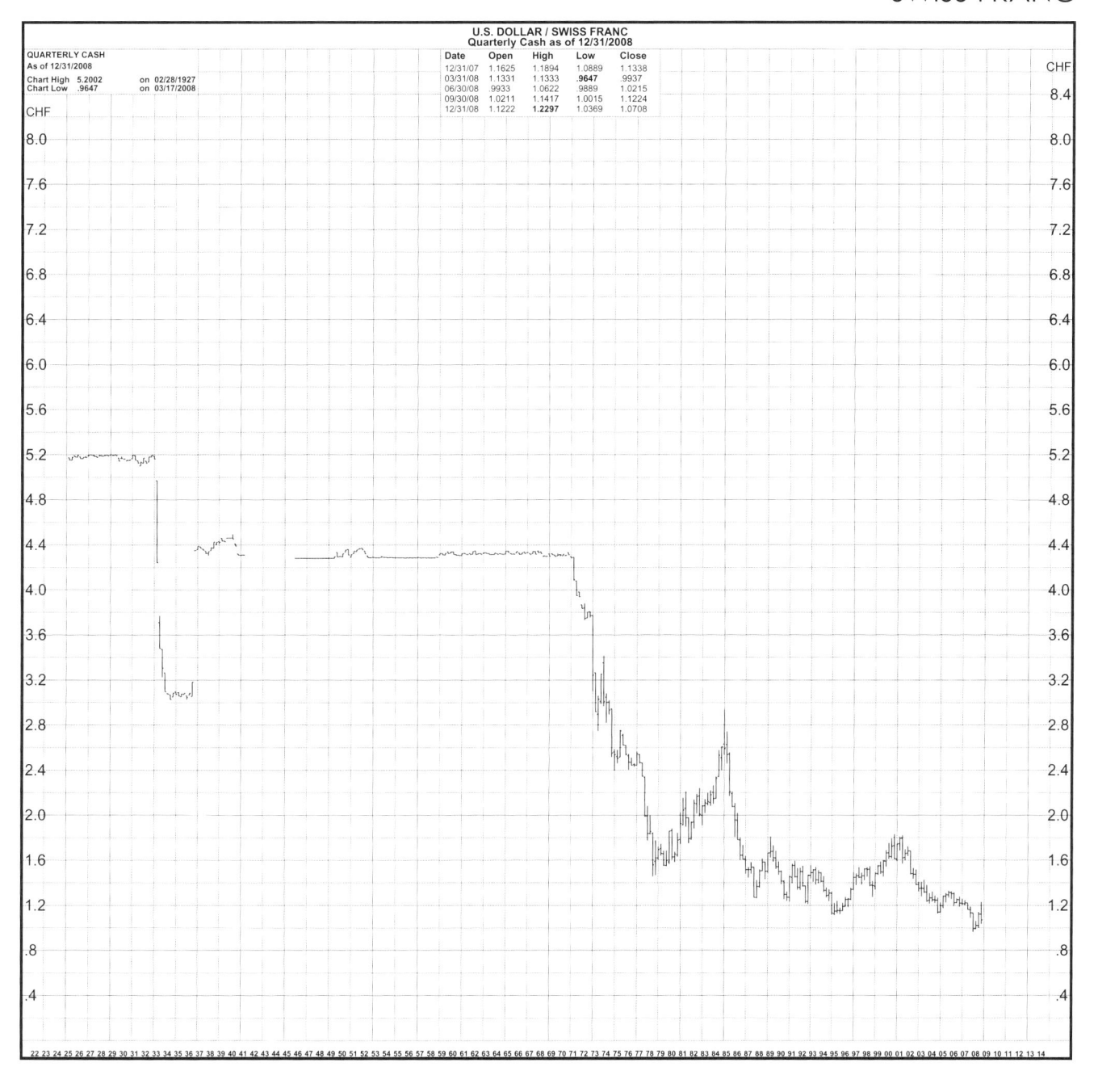

# SWISS FRANC

```
                    U.S. DOLLAR / SWISS FRANC
                     Quarterly Cash as of 12/31/2008
QUARTERLY CASH     Date      Open    High    Low     Close
As of 12/31/2008   12/31/07  1.1625  1.1894  1.0889  1.1338
Chart High 5.2002  on 02/28/1927    03/31/08  1.1331  1.1333  .9647   .9937
Chart Low   .9647  on 03/17/2008    06/30/08  .9933   1.0622  .9889   1.0215
                                    09/30/08  1.0211  1.1417  1.0015  1.1224
CHF                                 12/31/08  1.2222  1.2297  1.0369  1.0708
```

## Annual High, Low and Settle of Swiss Franc     In CHF per USD

| Year | High | Low | Settle | Year | High | Low | Settle | Year | High | Low | Settle |
|------|------|------|--------|------|------|------|--------|------|------|------|--------|
| 1925 | 5.1921 | 5.1520 | 5.1813 | 1939 | 4.4603 | 4.4111 | 4.4603 | 1953 | 4.3011 | 4.2863 | 4.2937 |
| 1926 | 5.1948 | 5.1653 | 5.1760 | 1940 | 4.4944 | 4.3103 | 4.3103 | 1954 | 4.2900 | 4.2863 | 4.2863 |
| 1927 | 5.2002 | 5.1760 | 5.1760 | 1941 | 4.3103 | 4.3066 | 4.3085 | 1955 | 4.2882 | 4.2845 | 4.2845 |
| 1928 | 5.1975 | 5.1867 | 5.1894 | 1942 | ---- | ---- | ---- | 1956 | 4.2863 | 4.2845 | 4.2845 |
| 1929 | 5.2002 | 5.1440 | 5.1440 | 1943 | ---- | ---- | ---- | 1957 | 4.2900 | 4.2845 | 4.2845 |
| 1930 | 5.1840 | 5.1440 | 5.1546 | 1944 | ---- | ---- | ---- | 1958 | 4.2918 | 4.2845 | 4.2882 |
| 1931 | 5.1975 | 5.1020 | 5.1335 | 1945 | ---- | ---- | ---- | 1959 | 4.3403 | 4.3103 | 4.3234 |
| 1932 | 5.1975 | 5.1256 | 5.1975 | 1946 | 4.2808 | 3.4400 | 4.2808 | 1960 | 4.3384 | 4.3048 | 4.3048 |
| 1933 | 5.1867 | 3.2237 | 3.3058 | 1947 | 4.2808 | 4.2808 | 4.2808 | 1961 | 4.3290 | 4.3066 | 4.3159 |
| 1934 | 3.2637 | 3.0285 | 3.0855 | 1948 | 4.2808 | 4.2808 | 4.2808 | 1962 | 4.3459 | 4.3159 | 4.3159 |
| 1935 | 3.0950 | 3.0534 | 3.0836 | 1949 | 4.3328 | 4.2808 | 4.2937 | 1963 | 4.3290 | 4.3159 | 4.3159 |
| 1936 | 4.3516 | 3.0276 | 4.3516 | 1950 | 4.3592 | 4.2937 | 4.3103 | 1964 | 4.3271 | 4.3159 | 4.3159 |
| 1937 | 4.3879 | 4.3197 | 4.3253 | 1951 | 4.3706 | 4.2918 | 4.3668 | 1965 | 4.3478 | 4.3178 | 4.3178 |
| 1938 | 4.4248 | 4.3048 | 4.4228 | 1952 | 4.3706 | 4.2863 | 4.2863 | 1966 | 4.3403 | 4.3159 | 4.3234 |

Data continued on page 49.     Source: *Forex*

# SWISS FRANC

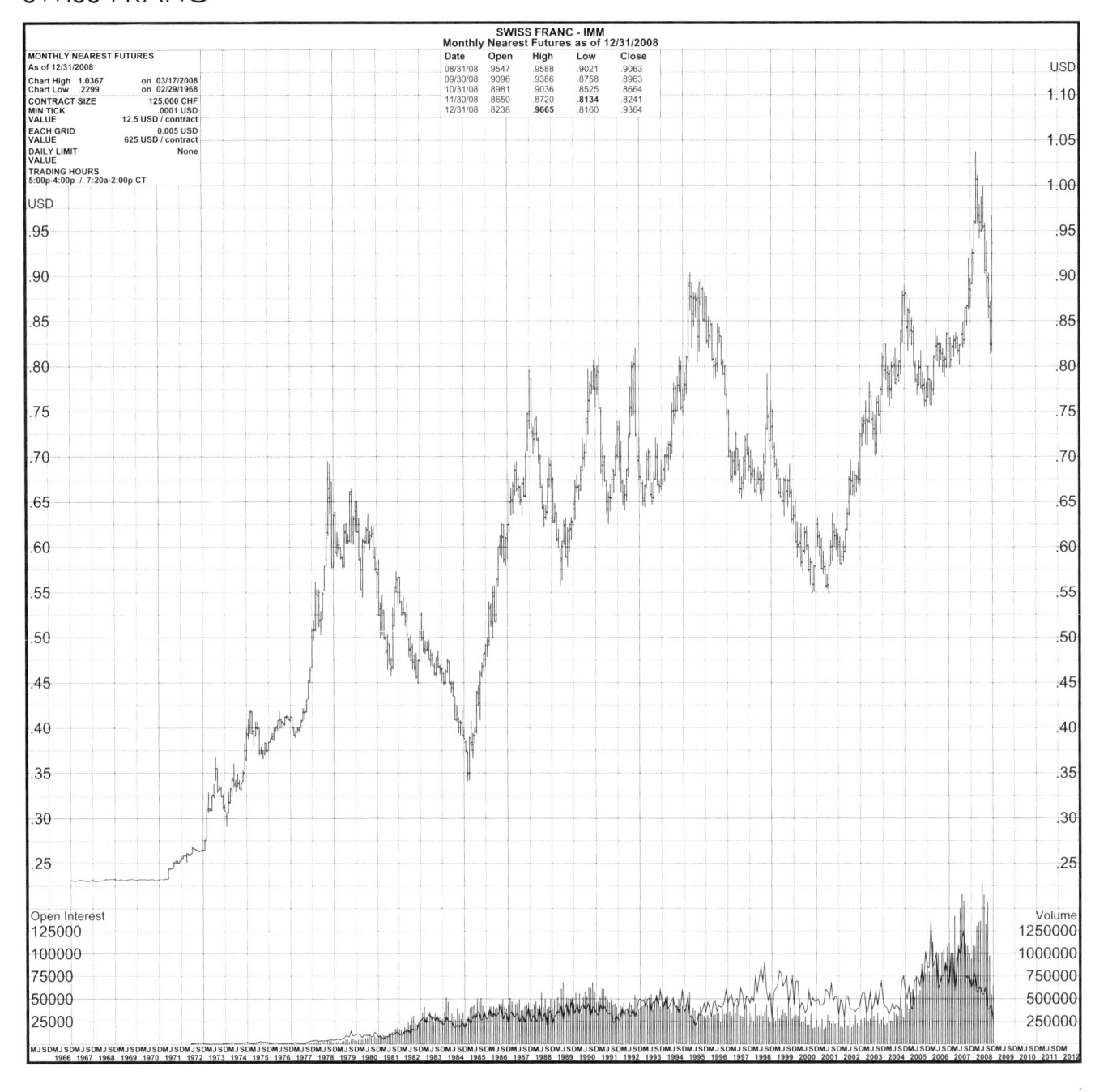

**MONTHLY NEAREST FUTURES**
As of 12/31/2008
Chart High 1.0367 on 03/17/2008
Chart Low .2299 on 02/29/1968
CONTRACT SIZE 125,000 CHF
MIN TICK .0001 USD
VALUE 12.5 USD / contract
EACH GRID 0.005 USD
VALUE 625 USD / contract
DAILY LIMIT None
VALUE
TRADING HOURS
5:00p-4:00p / 7:20a-2:00p CT

**SWISS FRANC - IMM**
Monthly Nearest Futures as of 12/31/2008

| Date | Open | High | Low | Close |
|---|---|---|---|---|
| 08/31/08 | .9547 | .9588 | .9021 | .9063 |
| 09/30/08 | .9096 | .9386 | .8758 | .8963 |
| 10/31/08 | .8981 | .9036 | .8525 | .8664 |
| 11/30/08 | .8650 | .8720 | .8134 | .8241 |
| 12/31/08 | .8238 | .9665 | .8160 | .9364 |

## Annual High, Low and Settle of Swiss Franc Futures   In USD per CHF

| Year | High | Low | Settle | Year | High | Low | Settle | Year | High | Low | Settle |
|---|---|---|---|---|---|---|---|---|---|---|---|
| 1967 | .2317 | .2303 | .2316 | 1981 | .5865 | .4566 | .5668 | 1995 | .9038 | .7616 | .8731 |
| 1968 | .2327 | .2299 | .2326 | 1982 | .5675 | .4486 | .5070 | 1996 | .8772 | .7439 | .7520 |
| 1969 | .2327 | .2312 | .2320 | 1983 | .5280 | .4507 | .4658 | 1997 | .7520 | .6529 | .6897 |
| 1970 | .2326 | .2309 | .2319 | 1984 | .4763 | .3870 | .3879 | 1998 | .7920 | .6503 | .7331 |
| 1971 | .2580 | .2316 | .2554 | 1985 | .4928 | .3408 | .4908 | 1999 | .7525 | .6258 | .6347 |
| 1972 | .2685 | .2511 | .2644 | 1986 | .6268 | .4779 | .6247 | 2000 | .6536 | .5488 | .6217 |
| 1973 | .3676 | .2642 | .3078 | 1987 | .7955 | .6144 | .7950 | 2001 | .6382 | .5492 | .6020 |
| 1974 | .3993 | .2908 | .3935 | 1988 | .7877 | .6215 | .6728 | 2002 | .7265 | .5808 | .7249 |
| 1975 | .4202 | .3652 | .3838 | 1989 | .6773 | .5569 | .6474 | 2003 | .8138 | .7010 | .8066 |
| 1976 | .4189 | .3843 | .4122 | 1990 | .8068 | .6296 | .7875 | 2004 | .8892 | .7554 | .8796 |
| 1977 | .5094 | .3895 | .5079 | 1991 | .8108 | .6254 | .7300 | 2005 | .8826 | .7548 | .7656 |
| 1978 | .6951 | .4961 | .6347 | 1992 | .8209 | .6405 | .6781 | 2006 | .8428 | .7560 | .8254 |
| 1979 | .6648 | .5764 | .6394 | 1993 | .7212 | .6436 | .6702 | 2007 | .9200 | .7979 | .8838 |
| 1980 | .6516 | .5430 | .5697 | 1994 | .8108 | .6680 | .7673 | 2008 | 1.0367 | .8134 | .9364 |

Futures begin trading 05/16/1972.   Data continued from page 46.   *Source: CME Group; Chicago Mercantile Exchange*

# SWISS FRANC

**U.S. DOLLAR / SWISS FRANC**
Monthly Cash as of 12/31/2008

| Date | Open | High | Low | Close |
|---|---|---|---|---|
| 08/29/08 | 1.0471 | 1.1088 | 1.0435 | 1.1009 |
| 09/30/08 | 1.1003 | 1.1417 | 1.0698 | 1.1224 |
| 10/31/08 | 1.1222 | 1.1749 | 1.1128 | 1.1593 |
| 11/28/08 | 1.1570 | 1.2297 | 1.1473 | 1.2143 |
| 12/31/08 | 1.2152 | 1.2251 | 1.0369 | 1.0708 |

MONTHLY CASH
As of 12/31/2008
Chart High 4.3497 on 02/29/1968
Chart Low .9647 on 03/17/2008

## Annual High, Low and Settle of Swiss Franc — In CHF per USD

| Year | High | Low | Settle | Year | High | Low | Settle | Year | High | Low | Settle |
|---|---|---|---|---|---|---|---|---|---|---|---|
| 1967 | 4.3422 | 4.3159 | 4.3178 | 1981 | 2.2123 | 1.7421 | 1.7901 | 1995 | 1.3188 | 1.1123 | 1.1534 |
| 1968 | 4.3497 | 4.2974 | 4.2992 | 1982 | 2.2416 | 1.7790 | 2.0092 | 1996 | 1.3538 | 1.1490 | 1.3413 |
| 1969 | 4.3253 | 4.2974 | 4.3103 | 1983 | 2.2212 | 1.9113 | 2.1815 | 1997 | 1.5387 | 1.3398 | 1.4616 |
| 1970 | 4.3309 | 4.2992 | 4.3122 | 1984 | 2.6102 | 2.1003 | 2.6068 | 1998 | 1.5470 | 1.2747 | 1.3751 |
| 1971 | 4.2950 | 3.9400 | 3.9400 | 1985 | 2.9385 | 2.0712 | 2.0777 | 1999 | 1.6021 | 1.3404 | 1.5913 |
| 1972 | 3.8775 | 3.7286 | 3.7693 | 1986 | 2.1097 | 1.6025 | 1.6090 | 2000 | 1.8300 | 1.5427 | 1.6140 |
| 1973 | 3.7707 | 2.7473 | 3.2531 | 1987 | 1.6360 | 1.2695 | 1.2700 | 2001 | 1.8219 | 1.5680 | 1.6585 |
| 1974 | 3.4153 | 2.5157 | 2.5523 | 1988 | 1.6155 | 1.2630 | 1.5010 | 2002 | 1.7225 | 1.3810 | 1.3835 |
| 1975 | 2.7563 | 2.3981 | 2.6212 | 1989 | 1.8090 | 1.4870 | 1.5410 | 2003 | 1.4274 | 1.2310 | 1.2398 |
| 1976 | 2.6192 | 2.4050 | 2.4456 | 1990 | 1.5895 | 1.2395 | 1.2720 | 2004 | 1.3227 | 1.1285 | 1.1398 |
| 1977 | 2.5654 | 1.9861 | 1.9940 | 1991 | 1.5936 | 1.2319 | 1.3585 | 2005 | 1.3286 | 1.1369 | 1.3139 |
| 1978 | 2.0833 | 1.4550 | 1.6200 | 1992 | 1.5496 | 1.2105 | 1.4665 | 2006 | 1.3239 | 1.1881 | 1.2192 |
| 1979 | 1.7437 | 1.5451 | 1.5987 | 1993 | 1.5520 | 1.3823 | 1.4883 | 2007 | 1.2572 | 1.0889 | 1.1338 |
| 1980 | 1.8801 | 1.5637 | 1.7771 | 1994 | 1.4950 | 1.2363 | 1.3088 | 2008 | 1.2297 | .9647 | 1.0708 |

Data continued from page 47.   Source: Forex

# SWISS FRANC

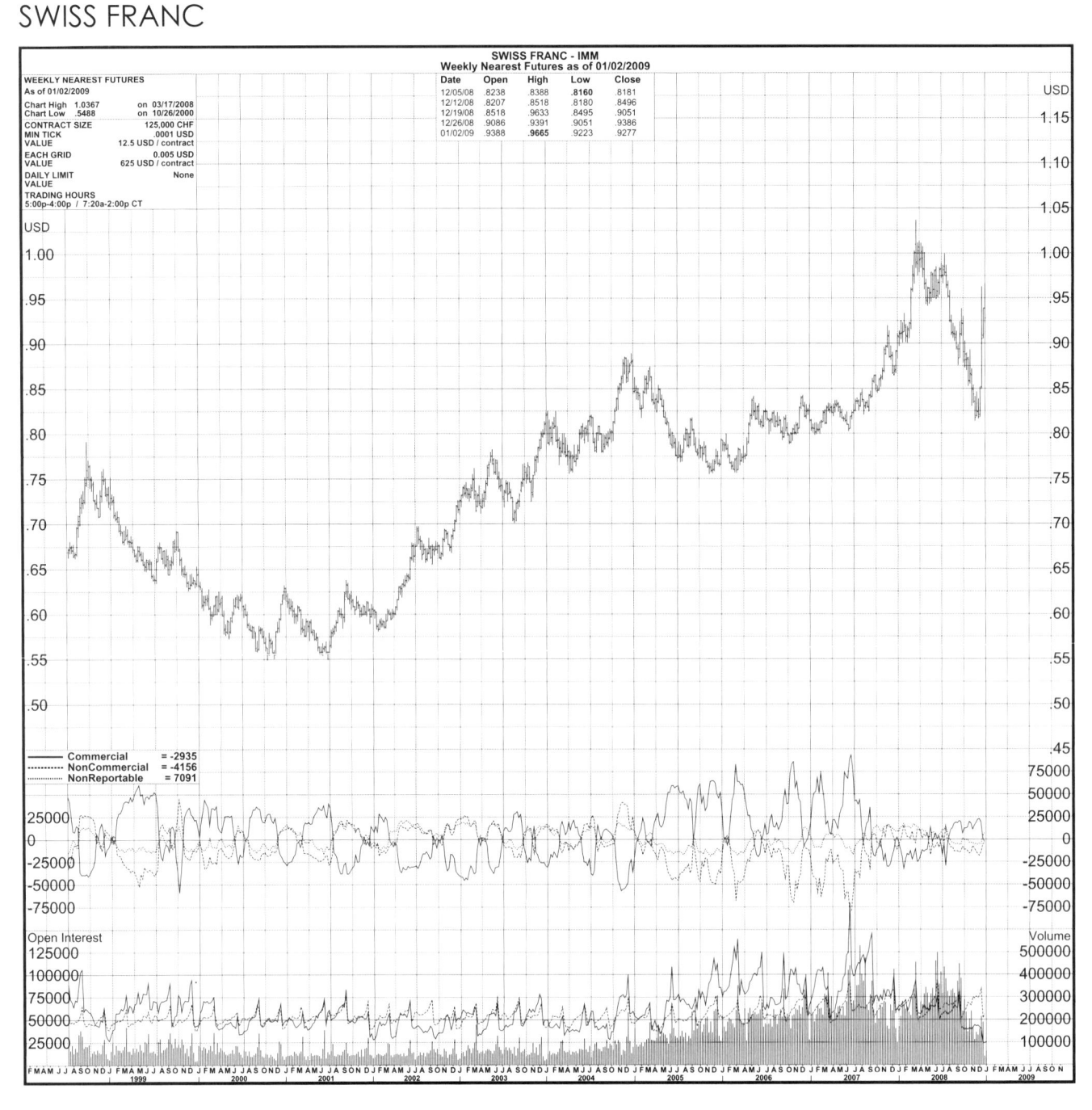

**SWISS FRANC - IMM**
Weekly Nearest Futures as of 01/02/2009

| Date | Open | High | Low | Close |
|---|---|---|---|---|
| 12/05/08 | .8238 | .8388 | .8160 | .8181 |
| 12/12/08 | .8207 | .8518 | .8180 | .8496 |
| 12/19/08 | .8518 | .9633 | .8495 | .9051 |
| 12/26/08 | .9086 | .9391 | .9051 | .9386 |
| 01/02/09 | .9388 | .9665 | .9223 | .9277 |

**WEEKLY NEAREST FUTURES**
As of 01/02/2009
Chart High 1.0367 on 03/17/2008
Chart Low .5488 on 10/26/2000
CONTRACT SIZE 125,000 CHF
MIN TICK .0001 USD
VALUE 12.5 USD / contract
EACH GRID 0.005 USD
VALUE 625 USD / contract
DAILY LIMIT None
VALUE
TRADING HOURS
5:00p-4:00p / 7:20a-2:00p CT

Commercial = -2935
NonCommercial = -4156
NonReportable = 7091

## Quarterly High, Low and Settle of Swiss Franc Futures — In USD per CHF

| Quarter | High | Low | Settle | Quarter | High | Low | Settle | Quarter | High | Low | Settle |
|---|---|---|---|---|---|---|---|---|---|---|---|
| 03/2000 | .6536 | .5880 | .6055 | 03/2003 | .7621 | .7107 | .7404 | 03/2006 | .8001 | .7560 | .7735 |
| 06/2000 | .6255 | .5721 | .6162 | 06/2003 | .7829 | .7115 | .7406 | 06/2006 | .8421 | .7672 | .8241 |
| 09/2000 | .6235 | .5576 | .5828 | 09/2003 | .7664 | .7010 | .7589 | 09/2006 | .8270 | .7923 | .8060 |
| 12/2000 | .6225 | .5488 | .6217 | 12/2003 | .8138 | .7247 | .8066 | 12/2006 | .8428 | .7879 | .8254 |
| 03/2001 | .6326 | .5750 | .5762 | 03/2004 | .8249 | .7648 | .7908 | 03/2007 | .8340 | .7979 | .8283 |
| 06/2001 | .5959 | .5535 | .5580 | 06/2004 | .8116 | .7554 | .8017 | 06/2007 | .8375 | .8020 | .8232 |
| 09/2001 | .6382 | .5492 | .6178 | 09/2004 | .8209 | .7785 | .8054 | 09/2007 | .8650 | .8205 | .8645 |
| 12/2001 | .6255 | .5890 | .6020 | 12/2004 | .8892 | .7900 | .8796 | 12/2007 | .9200 | .8447 | .8838 |
| 03/2002 | .6115 | .5808 | .5943 | 03/2005 | .8826 | .8169 | .8395 | 03/2008 | 1.0367 | .8902 | 1.0066 |
| 06/2002 | .6795 | .5951 | .6756 | 06/2005 | .8543 | .7813 | .7850 | 06/2008 | 1.0116 | .9410 | .9810 |
| 09/2002 | .6975 | .6552 | .6791 | 09/2005 | .8178 | .7680 | .7772 | 09/2008 | .9993 | .8758 | .8963 |
| 12/2002 | .7265 | .6601 | .7249 | 12/2005 | .7943 | .7548 | .7656 | 12/2008 | .9665 | .8134 | .9364 |

*Source: CME Group; Chicago Mercantile Exchange*

# SWISS FRANC

**U.S. DOLLAR / SWISS FRANC**
Weekly Cash as of 01/02/2009

| Date | Open | High | Low | Close |
|---|---|---|---|---|
| 12/05/08 | 1.2152 | 1.2251 | 1.1928 | 1.2200 |
| 12/12/08 | 1.2189 | 1.2220 | 1.1742 | 1.1777 |
| 12/19/08 | 1.1726 | 1.1775 | 1.0413 | 1.1037 |
| 12/26/08 | 1.1040 | 1.1062 | 1.0669 | 1.0695 |
| 01/02/09 | 1.0701 | 1.0847 | 1.0369 | 1.0820 |

WEEKLY CASH
As of 01/02/2009
Chart High 1.8300 on 10/26/2000
Chart Low .9647 on 03/17/2008

## Quarterly High, Low and Settle of Swiss Franc — In CHF per USD

| Quarter | High | Low | Settle | Quarter | High | Low | Settle | Quarter | High | Low | Settle |
|---|---|---|---|---|---|---|---|---|---|---|---|
| 03/2000 | 1.6888 | 1.5427 | 1.6633 | 03/2003 | 1.4083 | 1.3231 | 1.3496 | 03/2006 | 1.3239 | 1.2558 | 1.3043 |
| 06/2000 | 1.7529 | 1.6109 | 1.6340 | 06/2003 | 1.4079 | 1.2785 | 1.3511 | 06/2006 | 1.3137 | 1.1921 | 1.2233 |
| 09/2000 | 1.7925 | 1.6151 | 1.7242 | 09/2003 | 1.4274 | 1.3096 | 1.3184 | 09/2006 | 1.2622 | 1.2184 | 1.2506 |
| 12/2000 | 1.8300 | 1.6110 | 1.6140 | 12/2003 | 1.3805 | 1.2310 | 1.2398 | 12/2006 | 1.2770 | 1.1881 | 1.2192 |
| 03/2001 | 1.7435 | 1.5904 | 1.7428 | 03/2004 | 1.3078 | 1.2140 | 1.2664 | 03/2007 | 1.2572 | 1.2031 | 1.2152 |
| 06/2001 | 1.8079 | 1.6846 | 1.7938 | 06/2004 | 1.3227 | 1.2323 | 1.2503 | 06/2007 | 1.2469 | 1.1996 | 1.2214 |
| 09/2001 | 1.8219 | 1.5680 | 1.6207 | 09/2004 | 1.2859 | 1.2207 | 1.2450 | 09/2007 | 1.2233 | 1.1627 | 1.1638 |
| 12/2001 | 1.6959 | 1.5986 | 1.6585 | 12/2004 | 1.2685 | 1.1285 | 1.1398 | 12/2007 | 1.1894 | 1.0889 | 1.1338 |
| 03/2002 | 1.7225 | 1.6357 | 1.6813 | 03/2005 | 1.2262 | 1.1369 | 1.1966 | 03/2008 | 1.1333 | .9647 | .9937 |
| 06/2002 | 1.6822 | 1.4738 | 1.4809 | 06/2005 | 1.2877 | 1.1739 | 1.2815 | 06/2008 | 1.0622 | .9889 | 1.0215 |
| 09/2002 | 1.5304 | 1.4360 | 1.4750 | 09/2005 | 1.3081 | 1.2241 | 1.2936 | 09/2008 | 1.1417 | 1.0015 | 1.1224 |
| 12/2002 | 1.5170 | 1.3810 | 1.3835 | 12/2005 | 1.3286 | 1.2674 | 1.3139 | 12/2008 | 1.2297 | 1.0369 | 1.0708 |

*Source: Forex*

# EURO / SWISS FRANC

**EURO / SWISS FRANC**
Monthly Cash as of 12/31/2008

| Date | Open | High | Low | Close |
|---|---|---|---|---|
| 08/29/08 | 1.6338 | 1.6351 | 1.6092 | 1.6161 |
| 09/30/08 | 1.6159 | 1.6182 | 1.5666 | 1.5819 |
| 10/31/08 | 1.5813 | 1.5830 | 1.4314 | 1.4767 |
| 11/28/08 | 1.4782 | 1.5530 | 1.4715 | 1.5407 |
| 12/31/08 | 1.5414 | 1.5881 | 1.4759 | 1.4947 |

MONTHLY CASH
As of 12/31/2008
Chart High 2.4801 on 10/31/1973
Chart Low 1.4314 on 10/27/2008

## Annual High, Low and Settle of Euro / Swiss Franc    In CHF per EUR

| Year | High | Low | Settle | Year | High | Low | Settle | Year | High | Low | Settle |
|---|---|---|---|---|---|---|---|---|---|---|---|
| 1967 | 2.1317 | 2.1123 | 2.1159 | 1981 | 1.8404 | 1.5261 | 1.5636 | 1995 | 1.7085 | 1.5086 | 1.5709 |
| 1968 | 2.1247 | 2.0939 | 2.1012 | 1982 | 1.7023 | 1.5244 | 1.6517 | 1996 | 1.7098 | 1.5518 | 1.7080 |
| 1969 | 2.2903 | 2.0951 | 2.2877 | 1983 | 1.7130 | 1.5440 | 1.5642 | 1997 | 1.7258 | 1.5795 | 1.5966 |
| 1970 | 2.3276 | 2.2798 | 2.3131 | 1984 | 1.6891 | 1.5323 | 1.6152 | 1998 | 1.6675 | 1.5489 | 1.6218 |
| 1971 | 2.3632 | 2.2495 | 2.3632 | 1985 | 1.7072 | 1.5590 | 1.6425 | 1999 | 1.6302 | 1.5783 | 1.5998 |
| 1972 | 2.3775 | 2.2919 | 2.3030 | 1986 | 1.7041 | 1.5353 | 1.6390 | 2000 | 1.6174 | 1.4942 | 1.5210 |
| 1973 | 2.4801 | 2.1494 | 2.3530 | 1987 | 1.7174 | 1.5582 | 1.5816 | 2001 | 1.5480 | 1.4399 | 1.4780 |
| 1974 | 2.3744 | 2.0359 | 2.0691 | 1988 | 1.6870 | 1.5381 | 1.6576 | 2002 | 1.4882 | 1.4442 | 1.4503 |
| 1975 | 2.1221 | 1.9545 | 1.9573 | 1989 | 1.8126 | 1.6274 | 1.7823 | 2003 | 1.5748 | 1.4484 | 1.5605 |
| 1976 | 2.0326 | 1.8155 | 2.0291 | 1990 | 1.8535 | 1.5685 | 1.6674 | 2004 | 1.5867 | 1.5037 | 1.5463 |
| 1977 | 2.0994 | 1.8386 | 1.8584 | 1991 | 1.7820 | 1.5959 | 1.7504 | 2005 | 1.5661 | 1.5295 | 1.5555 |
| 1978 | 1.9746 | 1.4547 | 1.7413 | 1992 | 1.8398 | 1.6420 | 1.7705 | 2006 | 1.6105 | 1.5407 | 1.6090 |
| 1979 | 1.8566 | 1.7212 | 1.8110 | 1993 | 1.8547 | 1.6264 | 1.6736 | 2007 | 1.6828 | 1.5933 | 1.6538 |
| 1980 | 1.8928 | 1.6928 | 1.7709 | 1994 | 1.6997 | 1.5963 | 1.6522 | 2008 | 1.6557 | 1.4314 | 1.4947 |

*Source: Forex*

# EURO / SWISS FRANC

**EURO / SWISS FRANC**
Weekly Cash as of 01/02/2009

| Date | Open | High | Low | Close |
|---|---|---|---|---|
| 12/05/08 | 1.5414 | 1.5545 | 1.5165 | 1.5537 |
| 12/12/08 | 1.5527 | 1.5818 | 1.5500 | 1.5759 |
| 12/19/08 | 1.5710 | 1.5881 | 1.5295 | 1.5361 |
| 12/26/08 | 1.5377 | 1.5423 | 1.5007 | 1.5019 |
| 01/02/09 | 1.5042 | 1.5059 | 1.4759 | 1.5053 |

WEEKLY CASH
As of 01/02/2009
Chart High 1.6828 on 10/11/2007
Chart Low 1.4314 on 10/27/2008

## Quarterly High, Low and Settle of Euro / Swiss Franc   In CHF per EUR

| Quarter | High | Low | Settle | Quarter | High | Low | Settle | Quarter | High | Low | Settle |
|---|---|---|---|---|---|---|---|---|---|---|---|
| 03/2000 | 1.6174 | 1.5843 | 1.5894 | 03/2003 | 1.4811 | 1.4484 | 1.4751 | 03/2006 | 1.5821 | 1.5407 | 1.5803 |
| 06/2000 | 1.5932 | 1.5393 | 1.5567 | 06/2003 | 1.5563 | 1.4744 | 1.5558 | 06/2006 | 1.5858 | 1.5452 | 1.5645 |
| 09/2000 | 1.5667 | 1.5056 | 1.5229 | 09/2003 | 1.5624 | 1.5280 | 1.5372 | 09/2006 | 1.5967 | 1.5591 | 1.5859 |
| 12/2000 | 1.5364 | 1.4942 | 1.5210 | 12/2003 | 1.5748 | 1.5368 | 1.5605 | 12/2006 | 1.6105 | 1.5811 | 1.6090 |
| 03/2001 | 1.5471 | 1.5058 | 1.5269 | 03/2004 | 1.5867 | 1.5466 | 1.5587 | 03/2007 | 1.6290 | 1.5933 | 1.6230 |
| 06/2001 | 1.5480 | 1.5126 | 1.5238 | 06/2004 | 1.5693 | 1.5037 | 1.5243 | 06/2007 | 1.6673 | 1.6210 | 1.6533 |
| 09/2001 | 1.5284 | 1.4399 | 1.4770 | 09/2004 | 1.5544 | 1.5132 | 1.5487 | 09/2007 | 1.6689 | 1.6179 | 1.6598 |
| 12/2001 | 1.4915 | 1.4514 | 1.4780 | 12/2004 | 1.5557 | 1.5078 | 1.5463 | 12/2007 | 1.6828 | 1.6300 | 1.6538 |
| 03/2002 | 1.4882 | 1.4571 | 1.4661 | 03/2005 | 1.5634 | 1.5344 | 1.5504 | 03/2008 | 1.6557 | 1.5333 | 1.5684 |
| 06/2002 | 1.4785 | 1.4490 | 1.4686 | 06/2005 | 1.5574 | 1.5295 | 1.5509 | 06/2008 | 1.6377 | 1.5665 | 1.6087 |
| 09/2002 | 1.4747 | 1.4442 | 1.4565 | 09/2005 | 1.5661 | 1.5400 | 1.5559 | 09/2008 | 1.6369 | 1.5666 | 1.5819 |
| 12/2002 | 1.4789 | 1.4497 | 1.4503 | 12/2005 | 1.5653 | 1.5354 | 1.5555 | 12/2008 | 1.5881 | 1.4314 | 1.4947 |

*Source: Forex*

# EURO / BRITISH POUND

MONTHLY CASH
As of 12/31/2008
Chart High .98020 on 12/29/2008
Chart Low .17568 on 07/31/1967

| Date | Open | High | Low | Close |
|---|---|---|---|---|
| 08/29/08 | .78640 | .80760 | .77949 | .80540 |
| 09/30/08 | .80560 | .81880 | .78430 | .79150 |
| 10/31/08 | .79130 | .81950 | .76950 | .79230 |
| 11/28/08 | .79270 | .86620 | .78430 | .82520 |
| 12/31/08 | .82580 | .98020 | .82430 | .95630 |

## Annual High, Low and Settle of Euro / British Pound    In GBP per EUR

| Year | High | Low | Settle | Year | High | Low | Settle | Year | High | Low | Settle |
|---|---|---|---|---|---|---|---|---|---|---|---|
| 1967 | .2052 | .1757 | .2052 | 1981 | .4794 | .3856 | .4573 | 1995 | .9012 | .8034 | .8783 |
| 1968 | .2073 | .2044 | .2065 | 1982 | .5127 | .4447 | .5081 | 1996 | .8820 | .7420 | .7420 |
| 1969 | .2223 | .2040 | .2219 | 1983 | .5546 | .4804 | .4945 | 1997 | .7557 | .6371 | .6630 |
| 1970 | .2273 | .2212 | .2258 | 1984 | .5399 | .4916 | .5353 | 1998 | .7164 | .6303 | .7104 |
| 1971 | .2378 | .2231 | .2348 | 1985 | .5576 | .4801 | .5537 | 1999 | .7183 | .6199 | .6253 |
| 1972 | .2619 | .2347 | .2602 | 1986 | .6934 | .5478 | .6853 | 2000 | .6415 | .5685 | .6309 |
| 1973 | .3446 | .2587 | .3115 | 1987 | .7130 | .6487 | .6600 | 2001 | .6444 | .5953 | .6123 |
| 1974 | .3462 | .3041 | .3456 | 1988 | .6602 | .6034 | .6097 | 2002 | .6543 | .6072 | .6517 |
| 1975 | .3797 | .3448 | .3690 | 1989 | .7233 | .5946 | .7179 | 2003 | .7254 | .6470 | .7049 |
| 1976 | .5180 | .3690 | .4879 | 1990 | .7193 | .6426 | .6785 | 2004 | .7108 | .6545 | .7071 |
| 1977 | .5062 | .4683 | .4862 | 1991 | .6907 | .6526 | .6907 | 2005 | .7095 | .6611 | .6879 |
| 1978 | .5418 | .4742 | .5264 | 1992 | .8163 | .6645 | .7998 | 2006 | .7022 | .6671 | .6741 |
| 1979 | .5309 | .4609 | .5119 | 1993 | .8416 | .7552 | .7619 | 2007 | .7389 | .6536 | .7348 |
| 1980 | .5114 | .4117 | .4174 | 1994 | .8230 | .7463 | .8061 | 2008 | .9802 | .7344 | .9563 |

*Source: Forex*

# EURO / BRITISH POUND

**WEEKLY CASH**
As of 01/02/2009
Chart High .98020 on 12/29/2008
Chart Low .56850 on 05/04/2000
GBP

EURO / BRITISH POUND
Weekly Cash as of 01/02/2009

| Date | Open | High | Low | Close |
|---|---|---|---|---|
| 12/05/08 | .82580 | .87250 | .82430 | .86530 |
| 12/12/08 | .86650 | .89970 | .85780 | .89440 |
| 12/19/08 | .89400 | .95580 | .88850 | .93090 |
| 12/26/08 | .93340 | .96170 | .92980 | .96030 |
| 01/02/09 | .96420 | .98020 | .94320 | .95650 |

## Quarterly High, Low and Settle of Euro / British Pound    In GBP per EUR

| Quarter | High | Low | Settle | Quarter | High | Low | Settle | Quarter | High | Low | Settle |
|---|---|---|---|---|---|---|---|---|---|---|---|
| 03/2000 | .6329 | .5956 | .5999 | 03/2003 | .6927 | .6470 | .6900 | 03/2006 | .6985 | .6784 | .6978 |
| 06/2000 | .6415 | .5685 | .6279 | 06/2003 | .7254 | .6813 | .6957 | 06/2006 | .7022 | .6753 | .6918 |
| 09/2000 | .6359 | .5934 | .5985 | 09/2003 | .7153 | .6859 | .7012 | 09/2006 | .6962 | .6685 | .6776 |
| 12/2000 | .6312 | .5738 | .6309 | 12/2003 | .7120 | .6806 | .7049 | 12/2006 | .6795 | .6671 | .6741 |
| 03/2001 | .6444 | .6133 | .6183 | 03/2004 | .7059 | .6612 | .6673 | 03/2007 | .6868 | .6536 | .6788 |
| 06/2001 | .6315 | .5953 | .5997 | 06/2004 | .6816 | .6545 | .6704 | 06/2007 | .6858 | .6709 | .6743 |
| 09/2001 | .6365 | .5955 | .6179 | 09/2004 | .6879 | .6580 | .6864 | 09/2007 | .7028 | .6679 | .6971 |
| 12/2001 | .6300 | .6040 | .6123 | 12/2004 | .7108 | .6843 | .7071 | 12/2007 | .7389 | .6895 | .7348 |
| 03/2002 | .6279 | .6072 | .6114 | 03/2005 | .7095 | .6849 | .6856 | 03/2008 | .7981 | .7344 | .7954 |
| 06/2002 | .6521 | .6090 | .6479 | 06/2005 | .6904 | .6611 | .6756 | 06/2008 | .8098 | .7767 | .7904 |
| 09/2002 | .6502 | .6241 | .6294 | 09/2005 | .6989 | .6713 | .6819 | 09/2008 | .8188 | .7795 | .7915 |
| 12/2002 | .6543 | .6249 | .6517 | 12/2005 | .6908 | .6707 | .6879 | 12/2008 | .9802 | .7695 | .9563 |

*Source: Forex*

# BRITISH POUND / JAPANESE YEN

**BRITISH POUND / JAPANESE YEN**
Monthly Cash as of 12/31/2008

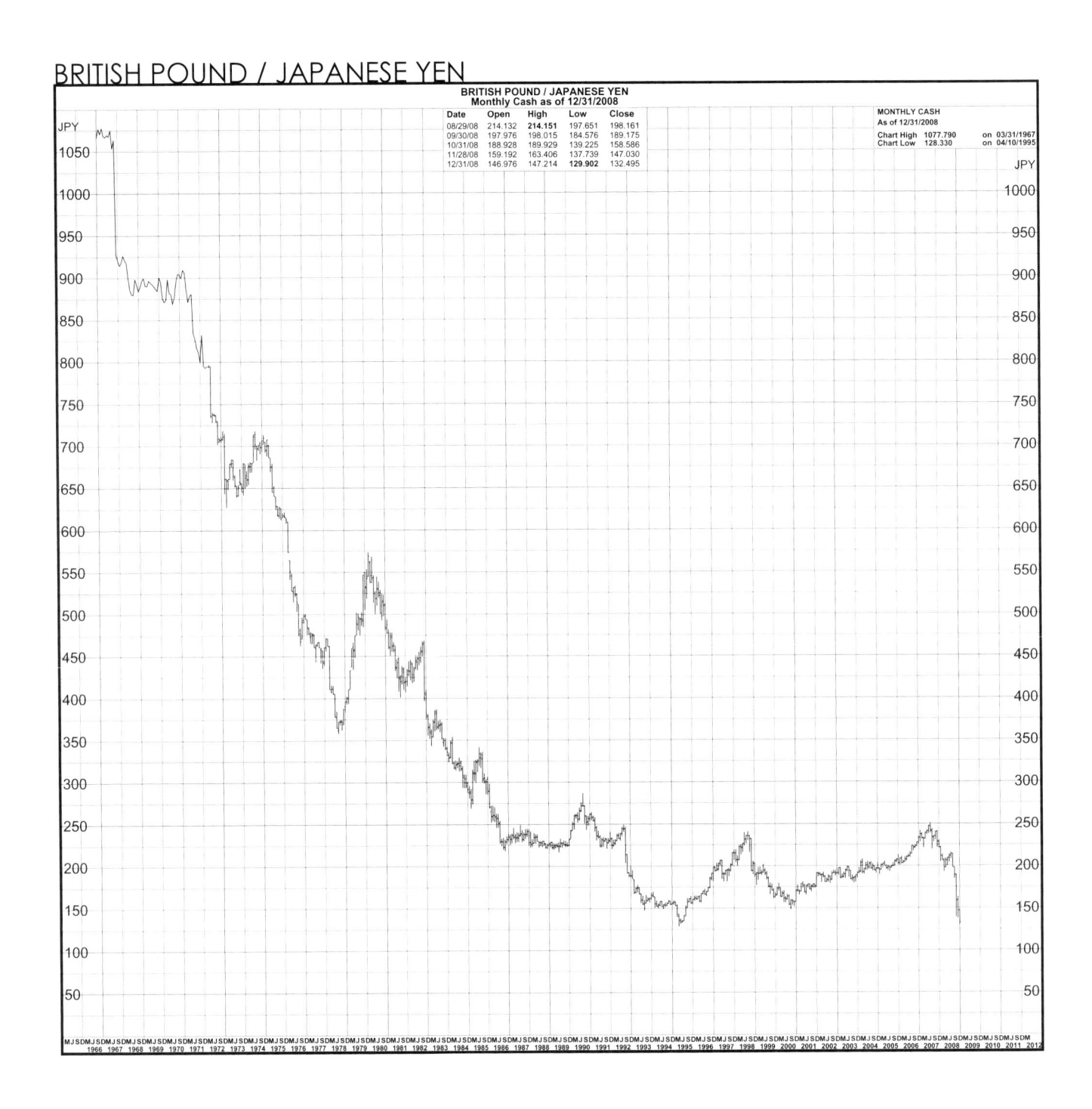

| Date | Open | High | Low | Close |
|---|---|---|---|---|
| 08/29/08 | 214.132 | 214.151 | 197.651 | 198.161 |
| 09/30/08 | 197.976 | 198.015 | 184.576 | 189.175 |
| 10/31/08 | 188.928 | 189.929 | 139.225 | 158.586 |
| 11/28/08 | 159.192 | 163.406 | 137.739 | 147.030 |
| 12/31/08 | 146.976 | 147.214 | 129.902 | 132.495 |

MONTHLY CASH As of 12/31/2008
Chart High 1077.790 on 03/31/1967
Chart Low 128.330 on 04/10/1995

## Annual High, Low and Settle of British Pound / Japanese Yen    In JPY per GBP

| Year | High | Low | Settle | Year | High | Low | Settle | Year | High | Low | Settle |
|---|---|---|---|---|---|---|---|---|---|---|---|
| 1967 | 1,077.79 | 920.49 | 920.49 | 1981 | 494.40 | 401.18 | 420.05 | 1995 | 164.52 | 128.33 | 160.48 |
| 1968 | 926.28 | 879.65 | 884.00 | 1982 | 468.62 | 375.34 | 379.99 | 1996 | 198.89 | 156.47 | 198.75 |
| 1969 | 900.38 | 884.20 | 900.38 | 1983 | 387.18 | 331.17 | 336.02 | 1997 | 218.95 | 181.36 | 215.20 |
| 1970 | 904.26 | 869.33 | 904.26 | 1984 | 354.56 | 288.01 | 291.63 | 1998 | 240.91 | 186.54 | 189.40 |
| 1971 | 909.44 | 799.69 | 799.69 | 1985 | 341.77 | 268.91 | 289.62 | 1999 | 201.89 | 161.05 | 165.05 |
| 1972 | 832.26 | 701.75 | 708.45 | 1986 | 298.53 | 218.36 | 235.02 | 2000 | 179.76 | 148.28 | 170.71 |
| 1973 | 717.92 | 627.23 | 650.84 | 1987 | 249.24 | 225.18 | 228.52 | 2001 | 191.61 | 165.45 | 191.43 |
| 1974 | 718.14 | 641.89 | 706.41 | 1988 | 241.90 | 220.83 | 226.56 | 2002 | 197.23 | 179.23 | 191.35 |
| 1975 | 713.43 | 612.80 | 617.55 | 1989 | 233.14 | 216.37 | 231.82 | 2003 | 199.50 | 179.48 | 191.77 |
| 1976 | 621.45 | 462.27 | 497.98 | 1990 | 286.94 | 232.81 | 262.16 | 2004 | 208.05 | 190.15 | 196.51 |
| 1977 | 500.67 | 435.58 | 460.26 | 1991 | 264.46 | 220.62 | 232.66 | 2005 | 213.02 | 189.60 | 202.95 |
| 1978 | 472.50 | 358.29 | 396.43 | 1992 | 249.19 | 186.70 | 188.46 | 2006 | 234.78 | 200.59 | 233.05 |
| 1979 | 550.35 | 393.06 | 532.74 | 1993 | 195.37 | 147.29 | 165.10 | 2007 | 251.09 | 219.45 | 221.68 |
| 1980 | 573.72 | 481.32 | 484.66 | 1994 | 169.63 | 149.13 | 156.18 | 2008 | 222.75 | 129.90 | 132.50 |

*Source: Forex*

# BRITISH POUND / JAPANESE YEN

**WEEKLY CASH**
As of 01/02/2009
Chart High 251.092 on 07/20/2007
Chart Low 129.902 on 12/30/2008

**BRITISH POUND / JAPANESE YEN**
Weekly Cash as of 01/02/2009

| Date | Open | High | Low | Close |
|---|---|---|---|---|
| 12/05/08 | 146.976 | **147.214** | 133.328 | 136.513 |
| 12/12/08 | 137.170 | 140.821 | 133.070 | 136.280 |
| 12/19/08 | 136.643 | 139.250 | 132.353 | 133.573 |
| 12/26/08 | 133.335 | 134.736 | 132.102 | 132.865 |
| 01/02/09 | 132.269 | 134.685 | **129.902** | 133.695 |

## Quarterly High, Low and Settle of British Pound / Japanese Yen    In JPY per GBP

| Quarter | High | Low | Settle | Quarter | High | Low | Settle | Quarter | High | Low | Settle |
|---|---|---|---|---|---|---|---|---|---|---|---|
| 03/2000 | 179.76 | 162.78 | 163.88 | 03/2003 | 198.01 | 184.29 | 186.75 | 03/2006 | 211.16 | 200.59 | 204.34 |
| 06/2000 | 170.88 | 156.33 | 160.83 | 06/2003 | 199.50 | 185.16 | 198.23 | 06/2006 | 213.72 | 203.94 | 211.49 |
| 09/2000 | 166.40 | 148.28 | 159.46 | 09/2003 | 199.16 | 181.37 | 185.40 | 09/2006 | 223.85 | 209.56 | 221.12 |
| 12/2000 | 171.83 | 151.56 | 170.71 | 12/2003 | 191.93 | 179.48 | 191.77 | 12/2006 | 234.78 | 220.48 | 233.05 |
| 03/2001 | 179.07 | 165.50 | 178.82 | 03/2004 | 208.05 | 190.25 | 192.47 | 03/2007 | 241.47 | 221.11 | 231.85 |
| 06/2001 | 181.41 | 165.45 | 176.58 | 06/2004 | 205.08 | 190.15 | 197.90 | 06/2007 | 247.94 | 231.28 | 247.13 |
| 09/2001 | 178.91 | 169.21 | 176.05 | 09/2004 | 204.75 | 193.70 | 199.47 | 09/2007 | 251.09 | 219.45 | 235.03 |
| 12/2001 | 191.61 | 173.47 | 191.43 | 12/2004 | 203.68 | 191.05 | 196.51 | 12/2007 | 241.38 | 220.98 | 221.68 |
| 03/2002 | 192.43 | 180.25 | 189.25 | 03/2005 | 202.72 | 189.60 | 202.61 | 03/2008 | 222.75 | 192.85 | 197.73 |
| 06/2002 | 192.58 | 180.07 | 182.98 | 06/2005 | 205.35 | 194.20 | 198.68 | 06/2008 | 213.92 | 197.24 | 211.62 |
| 09/2002 | 193.25 | 179.23 | 191.05 | 09/2005 | 203.47 | 192.80 | 200.12 | 09/2008 | 215.87 | 184.58 | 189.18 |
| 12/2002 | 197.23 | 187.72 | 191.35 | 12/2005 | 213.02 | 199.21 | 202.95 | 12/2008 | 189.93 | 129.90 | 132.50 |

*Source: Forex*

# EURO / JAPANESE YEN

**EURO / JAPANESE YEN**
Monthly Cash as of 12/31/2008

| Date | Open | High | Low | Close |
|---|---|---|---|---|
| 08/29/08 | 168.37 | 169.46 | 159.22 | 159.66 |
| 09/30/08 | 159.51 | 159.73 | 147.05 | 149.71 |
| 10/31/08 | 149.55 | 150.59 | 113.65 | 125.62 |
| 11/28/08 | 126.21 | 130.96 | 116.48 | 121.30 |
| 12/31/08 | 121.45 | 130.95 | 115.88 | 126.75 |

MONTHLY CASH
As of 12/31/2008
Chart High 285.34 on 12/03/1979
Chart Low 88.97 on 10/26/2000

## Annual High, Low and Settle of Euro / Japanese Yen — In JPY per EUR

| Year | High | Low | Settle | Year | High | Low | Settle | Year | High | Low | Settle |
|---|---|---|---|---|---|---|---|---|---|---|---|
| 1967 | 190.52 | 185.82 | 188.95 | 1981 | 205.21 | 175.92 | 192.10 | 1995 | 144.37 | 110.60 | 140.91 |
| 1968 | 190.13 | 181.17 | 182.58 | 1982 | 213.63 | 188.51 | 193.06 | 1996 | 149.11 | 132.46 | 147.63 |
| 1969 | 199.81 | 182.64 | 199.81 | 1983 | 197.66 | 164.93 | 166.16 | 1997 | 148.01 | 121.75 | 142.62 |
| 1970 | 204.74 | 193.74 | 204.17 | 1984 | 181.35 | 149.67 | 156.11 | 1998 | 162.57 | 132.36 | 135.10 |
| 1971 | 205.73 | 187.74 | 187.74 | 1985 | 169.36 | 146.12 | 160.36 | 1999 | 135.16 | 102.10 | 103.25 |
| 1972 | 195.55 | 182.91 | 184.37 | 1986 | 163.59 | 140.66 | 161.05 | 2000 | 111.96 | 88.97 | 107.75 |
| 1973 | 228.58 | 174.63 | 202.72 | 1987 | 169.45 | 148.39 | 150.81 | 2001 | 117.30 | 99.98 | 117.23 |
| 1974 | 244.11 | 198.71 | 244.11 | 1988 | 158.75 | 134.13 | 138.05 | 2002 | 125.60 | 111.30 | 124.64 |
| 1975 | 251.20 | 221.37 | 227.86 | 1989 | 168.32 | 132.30 | 166.49 | 2003 | 140.96 | 124.13 | 135.17 |
| 1976 | 242.96 | 221.89 | 242.96 | 1990 | 188.93 | 159.76 | 177.56 | 2004 | 141.63 | 125.83 | 138.98 |
| 1977 | 243.99 | 209.72 | 223.77 | 1991 | 179.11 | 144.59 | 160.86 | 2005 | 143.61 | 130.61 | 139.62 |
| 1978 | 233.94 | 177.43 | 208.68 | 1992 | 175.41 | 148.60 | 150.67 | 2006 | 157.18 | 137.11 | 157.09 |
| 1979 | 285.34 | 205.94 | 272.70 | 1993 | 155.73 | 115.15 | 125.75 | 2007 | 168.95 | 149.26 | 162.88 |
| 1980 | 278.06 | 201.11 | 202.29 | 1994 | 128.94 | 112.99 | 125.87 | 2008 | 169.96 | 113.65 | 126.75 |

*Source: Forex*

# EURO / JAPANESE YEN

**EURO / JAPANESE YEN**
Weekly Cash as of 01/02/2009

WEEKLY CASH
As of 01/02/2009
Chart High 169.96 on 07/23/2008
Chart Low 88.97 on 10/26/2000

| Date | Open | High | Low | Close |
|---|---|---|---|---|
| 12/05/08 | 121.45 | 121.45 | **115.88** | 118.14 |
| 12/12/08 | 118.12 | 122.72 | 117.89 | 121.83 |
| 12/19/08 | 122.15 | **130.95** | 121.69 | 124.42 |
| 12/26/08 | 124.37 | 127.75 | 123.98 | 127.47 |
| 01/02/09 | 127.51 | 129.70 | 125.39 | 127.87 |

## Quarterly High, Low and Settle of Euro / Japanese Yen   In JPY per EUR

| Quarter | High | Low | Settle | Quarter | High | Low | Settle | Quarter | High | Low | Settle |
|---|---|---|---|---|---|---|---|---|---|---|---|
| 03/2000 | 111.96 | 97.56 | 98.19 | 03/2003 | 130.78 | 124.13 | 128.88 | 03/2006 | 143.42 | 137.11 | 142.59 |
| 06/2000 | 103.15 | 94.93 | 101.03 | 06/2003 | 140.96 | 127.50 | 137.88 | 06/2006 | 146.65 | 140.21 | 146.33 |
| 09/2000 | 103.28 | 90.09 | 95.47 | 09/2003 | 138.59 | 125.07 | 129.99 | 09/2006 | 150.74 | 145.03 | 149.82 |
| 12/2000 | 107.86 | 88.97 | 107.75 | 12/2003 | 135.24 | 124.19 | 135.17 | 12/2006 | 157.18 | 148.50 | 157.09 |
| 03/2001 | 113.20 | 104.18 | 110.61 | 03/2004 | 139.04 | 126.58 | 128.46 | 03/2007 | 159.65 | 150.76 | 157.39 |
| 06/2001 | 113.72 | 99.98 | 105.95 | 06/2004 | 137.88 | 125.83 | 132.71 | 06/2007 | 166.95 | 156.94 | 166.58 |
| 09/2001 | 110.75 | 104.71 | 108.82 | 09/2004 | 137.56 | 131.25 | 136.89 | 09/2007 | 168.95 | 149.26 | 163.82 |
| 12/2001 | 117.30 | 106.72 | 117.23 | 12/2004 | 141.63 | 134.06 | 138.98 | 12/2007 | 167.74 | 158.74 | 162.88 |
| 03/2002 | 119.68 | 111.30 | 115.67 | 03/2005 | 140.72 | 133.00 | 138.91 | 03/2008 | 164.05 | 151.72 | 157.33 |
| 06/2002 | 119.50 | 113.46 | 118.53 | 06/2005 | 140.49 | 130.61 | 134.23 | 06/2008 | 169.46 | 156.34 | 167.22 |
| 09/2002 | 121.96 | 114.25 | 120.24 | 09/2005 | 138.85 | 132.54 | 136.48 | 09/2008 | 169.96 | 147.05 | 149.71 |
| 12/2002 | 125.60 | 120.01 | 124.64 | 12/2005 | 143.61 | 135.86 | 139.62 | 12/2008 | 150.59 | 113.65 | 126.75 |

*Source: Forex*

# Energy

## Crude Oil Market Outlook

Crude oil prices as of early 2009 were trading near the depressed level of $40 per barrel. Once the current global recession ends, however, there is a good chance for a sustained upward rebound in oil prices. When strong demand reemerges, oil producers may be caught flat-footed in responding to that demand, particularly since they were under-investing in new capacity even before the global recession emerged in 2008. Moreover, oil producers will not invest in new capacity until prices reach relatively high levels above $70 per barrel because the cost of developing new reserves is now much higher than in the past. The world is not running out of oil, but it is running out of easy-to-find and cheap oil. The high cost of developing new oil wells almost assures higher oil prices in the future when the global economy stabilizes.

## Crude Oil Price History

### 1973 oil crisis

The world oil market from the 1930s through the early 1970s was tightly controlled by the major oil companies, which were referred to as the "Seven Sisters." However, in the early 1970s, Middle East countries started to nationalize oil facilities and take control of their own oil production destiny. This gave the Arab countries the leverage to announce an oil embargo against the US in 1973 in retaliation for US support for Israel during the Yom Kippur War, when Israel suffered a surprise attack by Egypt and Syria.

In the space of a few months, prices for West Texas Intermediate oil spiked higher and roughly tripled from $3.56 per barrel in mid-1973 to $10.11 in early 1974. The shock to US consumers came not only from the hike in prices but also from shortages and long lines at the gas pumps. Shortages quickly arose because of ill-conceived US oil price controls and rationing that were imposed by President Nixon and Congress in the early 1970s. Those price controls discouraged exploration and production and reduced the supply of gasoline available to US consumers at the gas pump (President Reagan finally dismantled oil price controls and regulation in 1981). The oil embargo on US oil exports by Arab countries did not work particularly well from a technical standpoint since the US could simply buy oil from other sellers from the pool of oil that sloshes around world. However, the embargo did succeed in raising prices sharply and alerting the world to OPEC's impressive pricing power.

OPEC was initially formed in 1960 in order to present a united front in negotiations with the major oil companies. OPEC currently has 12 members (Saudi Arabia, Iran, Venezuela, Iraq, UAE, Kuwait, Nigeria, Libya, Indonesia, Algeria, Qatar, Angola). OPEC members together account for some two-thirds of world oil reserves. Although OPEC is not a true cartel since it does not account for 100% of oil production, OPEC seeks to stabilize world oil prices by acting as the "swing producer," increasing or decreasing production in order to keep the market relatively stable. OPEC wants to maximize its long-term oil revenues, but OPEC does not want to push oil prices too high because a price spike would (1) cause oil demand to plunge from a world recession, (2) cause non-OPEC oil production to become economical in higher-cost areas, and (3) encourage the development of alternative sources of energy.

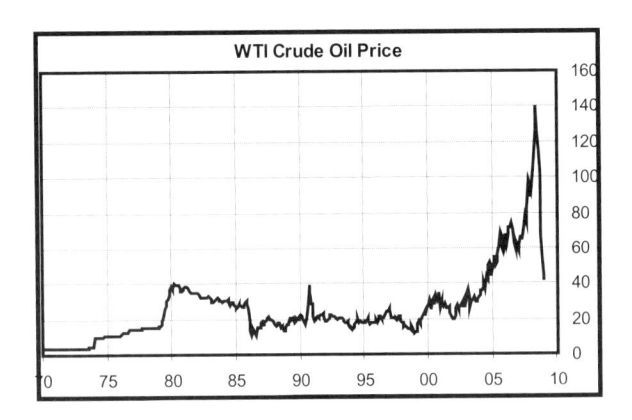

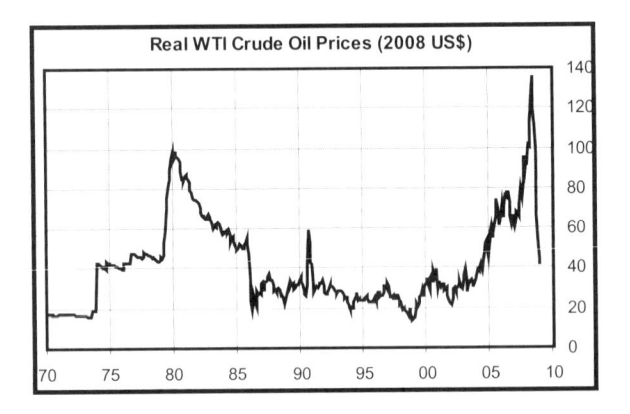

### 1979 oil crisis

After the 1973 Arab Oil Embargo was over, oil prices did not fall back but instead rose steadily through the latter half of the 1970s as OPEC enforced its newly-found pricing power and as oil demand grew. Oil prices then spiked higher in 1979 on the Iranian revolution against the Shah of Iran in January 1979, which devastated Iranian oil production. The Iran-Iraq war, which began in September 1980, then caused a sharp reduction in both Iranian and Iraqi oil output. OPEC production plunged by half, from 30 million barrels per day (bpd) in 1978 to only 15 million bpd by 1984. In response to those events, oil prices spiked higher in 1979 from about $15 per barrel in late-1978 to $38 per barrel at the end of 1979 and to a then-record of $39.50 in June 1980 (which is equivalent to $101 per barrel in current 2008 dollars). After peaking in 1980, oil prices then moved steadily lower through 1985 as the world adjusted to the Iranian-Iraqi oil production disruptions and as other sources of supply came on line. In addition, oil prices were undercut by the double-dip US recessions seen in 1980 and 1981-82.

# ENERGY

**1986 oil price collapse**

Oil prices then plunged in 1986 to $10 per barrel as Iranian and Iraqi oil production started to come back on line, even though the Iraq-Iraq war did not officially end until 1988. Iranian oil production started rising sharply in 1986 from about 2.0 mln bpd in 1985 to 3.2 mln bpd by early 1989. Iraqi production nearly doubled from 1.5 mln bpd in 1984 to 2.7 mln bpd by early 1987. Other OPEC members failed to cut production fast enough to accommodate rising Iran-Iraq production, thus causing a collapse in oil prices. Oil prices finally recovered in 1987 back to the $20 area after OPEC reinstated some production discipline.

**1990 spike on first Gulf war**

Oil prices were relatively steady and averaged $19 per barrel from the late-1980s through 1996. There was a brief upward spike to nearly $40 per barrel seen in 1990 when the US and coalition forces went to war against Iraq to push Saddam Hussein out of Kuwait and to protect Saudi Arabia and its oil fields.

**1998 oil price collapse and 1999-2000 recovery**

After moving sideways near $20 per barrel during much of the 1990s, oil prices in 1997-99 plunged due to (1) reduced Asian oil demand tied to the 1997 Asian currency crisis, (2) a four-fold increase in Iraqi production (from 500,000 bpd at the end of 1996 to 2 million bpd in mid 1998) as the UN oil-for-food program allowed for a restoration of Iraq's oil production, and (3) the failure of OPEC to cut production fast enough to accommodate increased Iraqi production. Saudi Arabia in particular was reluctant to allow its production to fall below 8.0 mln bpd. However, after oil prices plunged to $10 per barrel and some OPEC nations were forced to borrow heavily to meet their financial obligations, OPEC finally agreed to new production discipline and oil prices then more than tripled from $10 to over $30 by 2000. However, oil prices then fell sharply in 2000-01 from the $30 area to a low of $16.70 in November 2001 due to reduced oil demand caused by the US recession in 2001 and soft global economy that followed the bursting of the equity bubble.

**2002-06 supply/demand squeeze**

From the low of $16.17 per barrel seen in November 2001, oil prices then more than quadrupled to a record high of $70 per barrel in August 2005. That rally was driven by (1) stronger worldwide demand with the global economic recovery and particularly strong oil import demand from China (China's oil imports doubled from 60 million tons in mid-2002 to over 120 million tons in early 2005), (2) various temporary supply disruptions, and (3) the lack of any significant world excess capacity that could be quickly ramped up to meet new demand.

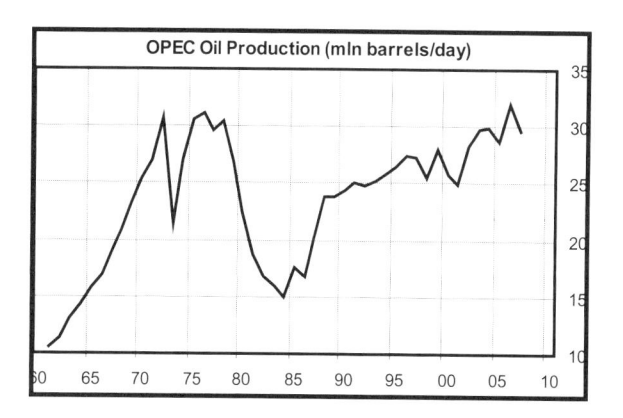

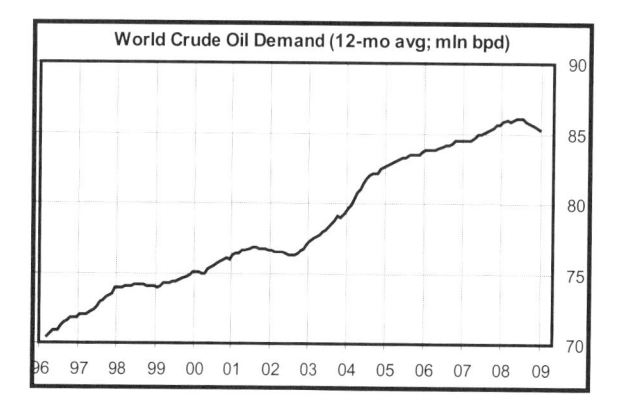

In addition, US oil production in the Gulf of Mexico was severely disrupted by Hurricane Ivan in September 2004, which caused long-term and severe damage to oilrigs and undersea oil pipelines. Hurricanes Katrina and Rita, a year later in August and September 2005, then caused even more damage to oil rigs and undersea pipelines. US production in the Gulf of Mexico was completely shut down right after Katrina and 25% of production remained offline even 6 months after Katrina.

**2007-08 blow-off top to $147**

The crude oil price rally accelerated into high gear in 2007 and 2008 with the record high of $147.27 reached in July 2008. In retrospect, it is clear that this rally was driven mostly by speculative fever rather than by any rational analysis of supply and demand. In response to the surge in oil prices, OPEC sharply boosted production by 15% from 26.4 million bpd in May 2007 to a record high of 30.305 million bpd in August 2008.

When the global recession and financial crisis emerged in mid-2008, oil prices plunged as demand collapsed and speculators bailed out of their long positions. OPEC in late-2008 and early-2009 responded to the plunge in oil prices with a production cut-back to the 26 million bpd area, but the production cut was not fast enough to prevent a collapse in oil prices. As of early 2009, the crude oil market was suffering from weak demand and a big inventory overhang.

# CRUDE OIL

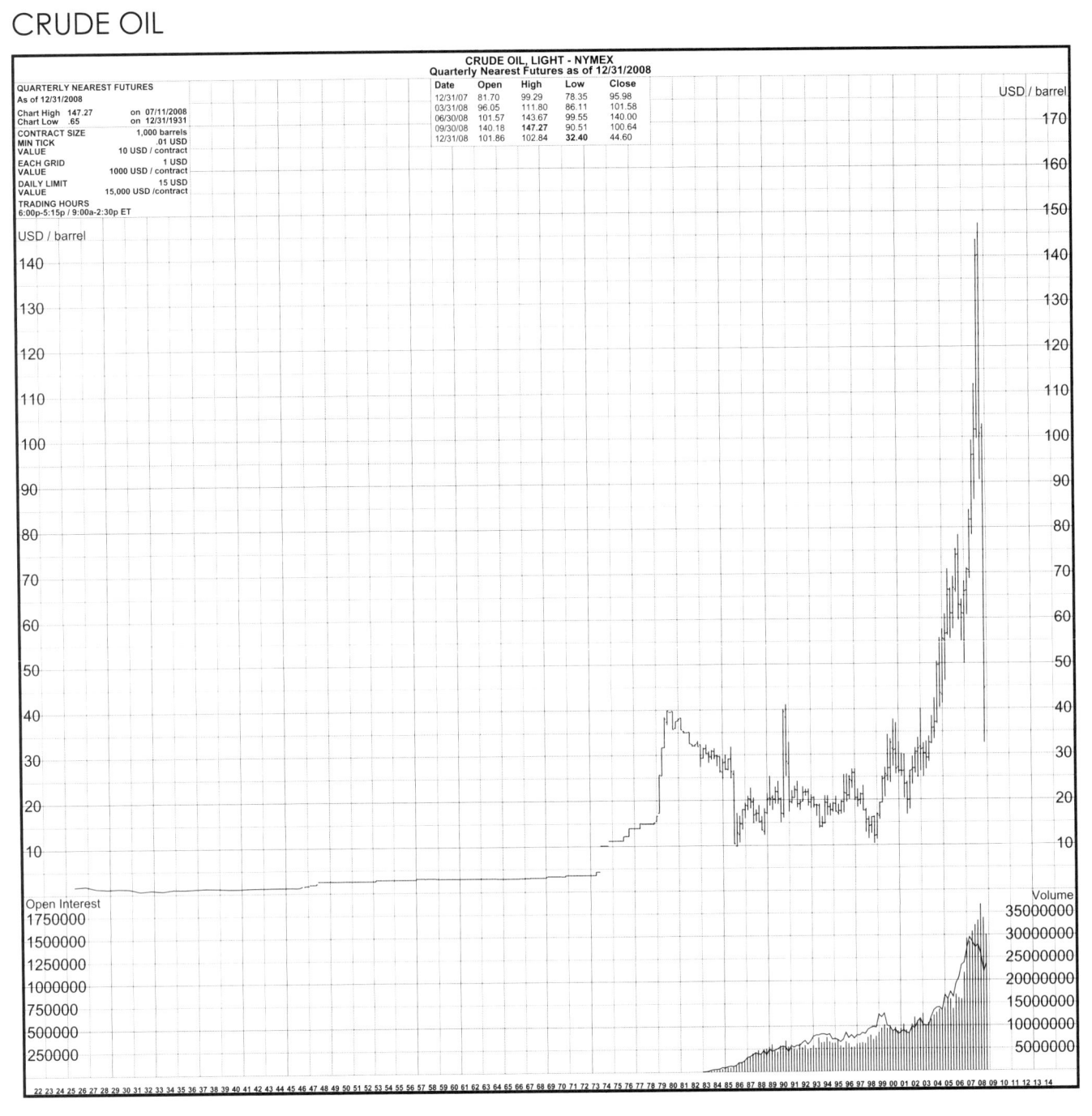

**CRUDE OIL, LIGHT - NYMEX**
Quarterly Nearest Futures as of 12/31/2008

| Date | Open | High | Low | Close |
|---|---|---|---|---|
| 12/31/07 | 81.70 | 99.29 | 78.35 | 95.98 |
| 03/31/08 | 96.05 | 111.80 | 86.11 | 101.58 |
| 06/30/08 | 101.57 | 143.67 | 99.55 | 140.00 |
| 09/30/08 | 140.18 | 147.27 | 90.51 | 100.64 |
| 12/31/08 | 101.86 | 102.84 | 32.40 | 44.60 |

**QUARTERLY NEAREST FUTURES**
As of 12/31/2008
Chart High 147.27 on 07/11/2008
Chart Low .65 on 12/31/1931
CONTRACT SIZE 1,000 barrels
MIN TICK .01 USD
VALUE 10 USD / contract
EACH GRID 1 USD
VALUE 1000 USD / contract
DAILY LIMIT 15 USD
VALUE 15,000 USD /contract
TRADING HOURS
6:00p-5:15p / 9:00a-2:30p ET

## Annual High, Low and Settle of Crude Oil   In USD per Barrel

| Year | High | Low | Settle | Year | High | Low | Settle | Year | High | Low | Settle |
|---|---|---|---|---|---|---|---|---|---|---|---|
| 1925 | 1.68 | 1.68 | 1.68 | 1939 | 1.02 | 1.02 | 1.02 | 1953 | 2.82 | 2.57 | 2.82 |
| 1926 | 1.88 | 1.88 | 1.88 | 1940 | 1.02 | 1.02 | 1.02 | 1954 | 2.82 | 2.82 | 2.82 |
| 1927 | 1.30 | 1.30 | 1.30 | 1941 | 1.14 | 1.14 | 1.14 | 1955 | 2.82 | 2.82 | 2.82 |
| 1928 | 1.17 | 1.17 | 1.17 | 1942 | 1.19 | 1.19 | 1.19 | 1956 | 2.82 | 2.82 | 2.82 |
| 1929 | 1.27 | 1.27 | 1.27 | 1943 | 1.20 | 1.20 | 1.20 | 1957 | 3.07 | 2.82 | 3.00 |
| 1930 | 1.19 | 1.19 | 1.19 | 1944 | 1.21 | 1.21 | 1.21 | 1958 | 3.07 | 3.00 | 3.00 |
| 1931 | 0.65 | 0.65 | 0.65 | 1945 | 1.22 | 1.22 | 1.22 | 1959 | 3.00 | 2.97 | 2.97 |
| 1932 | 0.87 | 0.87 | 0.87 | 1946 | 1.62 | 1.17 | 1.62 | 1960 | 2.97 | 2.97 | 2.97 |
| 1933 | 0.67 | 0.67 | 0.67 | 1947 | 2.07 | 1.62 | 2.07 | 1961 | 2.97 | 2.97 | 2.97 |
| 1934 | 1.00 | 1.00 | 1.00 | 1948 | 2.57 | 2.57 | 2.57 | 1962 | 2.97 | 2.97 | 2.97 |
| 1935 | 0.97 | 0.97 | 0.97 | 1949 | 2.57 | 2.57 | 2.57 | 1963 | 2.97 | 2.97 | 2.97 |
| 1936 | 1.09 | 1.09 | 1.09 | 1950 | 2.57 | 2.57 | 2.57 | 1964 | 2.97 | 2.92 | 2.92 |
| 1937 | 1.18 | 1.18 | 1.18 | 1951 | 2.57 | 2.57 | 2.57 | 1965 | 2.92 | 2.92 | 2.92 |
| 1938 | 1.13 | 1.13 | 1.13 | 1952 | 2.57 | 2.57 | 2.57 | 1966 | 2.97 | 2.92 | 2.97 |

Data continued on page 64.   *Source: CME Group; New York Mercantile Exchange*

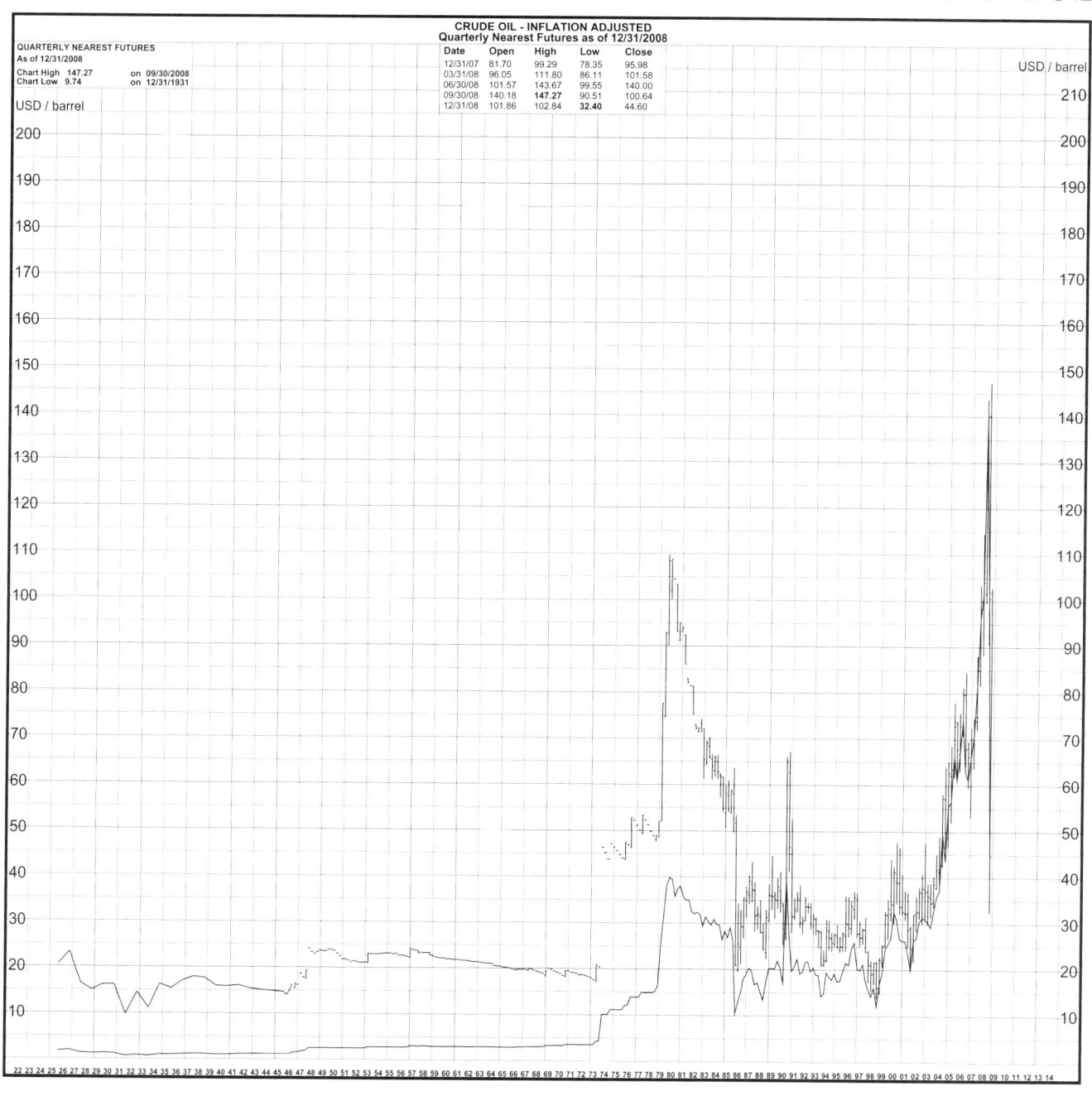

# CRUDE OIL

**QUARTERLY NEAREST FUTURES**
As of 12/31/2008
Chart High 147.27 on 09/30/2008
Chart Low 9.74 on 12/31/1931
USD / barrel

**CRUDE OIL - INFLATION ADJUSTED**
Quarterly Nearest Futures as of 12/31/2008

| Date | Open | High | Low | Close |
|---|---|---|---|---|
| 12/31/07 | 81.70 | 99.29 | 78.35 | 95.98 |
| 03/31/08 | 96.05 | 111.80 | 86.11 | 101.58 |
| 06/30/08 | 101.57 | 143.67 | 99.55 | 140.00 |
| 09/30/08 | 140.18 | 147.27 | 90.51 | 100.64 |
| 12/31/08 | 101.86 | 102.84 | 32.40 | 44.60 |

## Annual High, Low and Settle of Crude Oil    In USD per Barrel

| Year | High | Low | Settle | Year | High | Low | Settle | Year | High | Low | Settle |
|---|---|---|---|---|---|---|---|---|---|---|---|
| 1925 | 1.68 | 1.68 | 1.68 | 1939 | 1.02 | 1.02 | 1.02 | 1953 | 2.82 | 2.57 | 2.82 |
| 1926 | 1.88 | 1.88 | 1.88 | 1940 | 1.02 | 1.02 | 1.02 | 1954 | 2.82 | 2.82 | 2.82 |
| 1927 | 1.30 | 1.30 | 1.30 | 1941 | 1.14 | 1.14 | 1.14 | 1955 | 2.82 | 2.82 | 2.82 |
| 1928 | 1.17 | 1.17 | 1.17 | 1942 | 1.19 | 1.19 | 1.19 | 1956 | 2.82 | 2.82 | 2.82 |
| 1929 | 1.27 | 1.27 | 1.27 | 1943 | 1.20 | 1.20 | 1.20 | 1957 | 3.07 | 2.82 | 3.00 |
| 1930 | 1.19 | 1.19 | 1.19 | 1944 | 1.21 | 1.21 | 1.21 | 1958 | 3.07 | 3.00 | 3.00 |
| 1931 | 0.65 | 0.65 | 0.65 | 1945 | 1.22 | 1.22 | 1.22 | 1959 | 3.00 | 2.97 | 2.97 |
| 1932 | 0.87 | 0.87 | 0.87 | 1946 | 1.62 | 1.17 | 1.62 | 1960 | 2.97 | 2.97 | 2.97 |
| 1933 | 0.67 | 0.67 | 0.67 | 1947 | 2.07 | 1.62 | 2.07 | 1961 | 2.97 | 2.97 | 2.97 |
| 1934 | 1.00 | 1.00 | 1.00 | 1948 | 2.57 | 2.57 | 2.57 | 1962 | 2.97 | 2.97 | 2.97 |
| 1935 | 0.97 | 0.97 | 0.97 | 1949 | 2.57 | 2.57 | 2.57 | 1963 | 2.97 | 2.97 | 2.97 |
| 1936 | 1.09 | 1.09 | 1.09 | 1950 | 2.57 | 2.57 | 2.57 | 1964 | 2.97 | 2.92 | 2.92 |
| 1937 | 1.18 | 1.18 | 1.18 | 1951 | 2.57 | 2.57 | 2.57 | 1965 | 2.92 | 2.92 | 2.92 |
| 1938 | 1.13 | 1.13 | 1.13 | 1952 | 2.57 | 2.57 | 2.57 | 1966 | 2.97 | 2.92 | 2.97 |

Data continued on page 65.    *Source: CME Group; New York Mercantile Exchange*

# CRUDE OIL

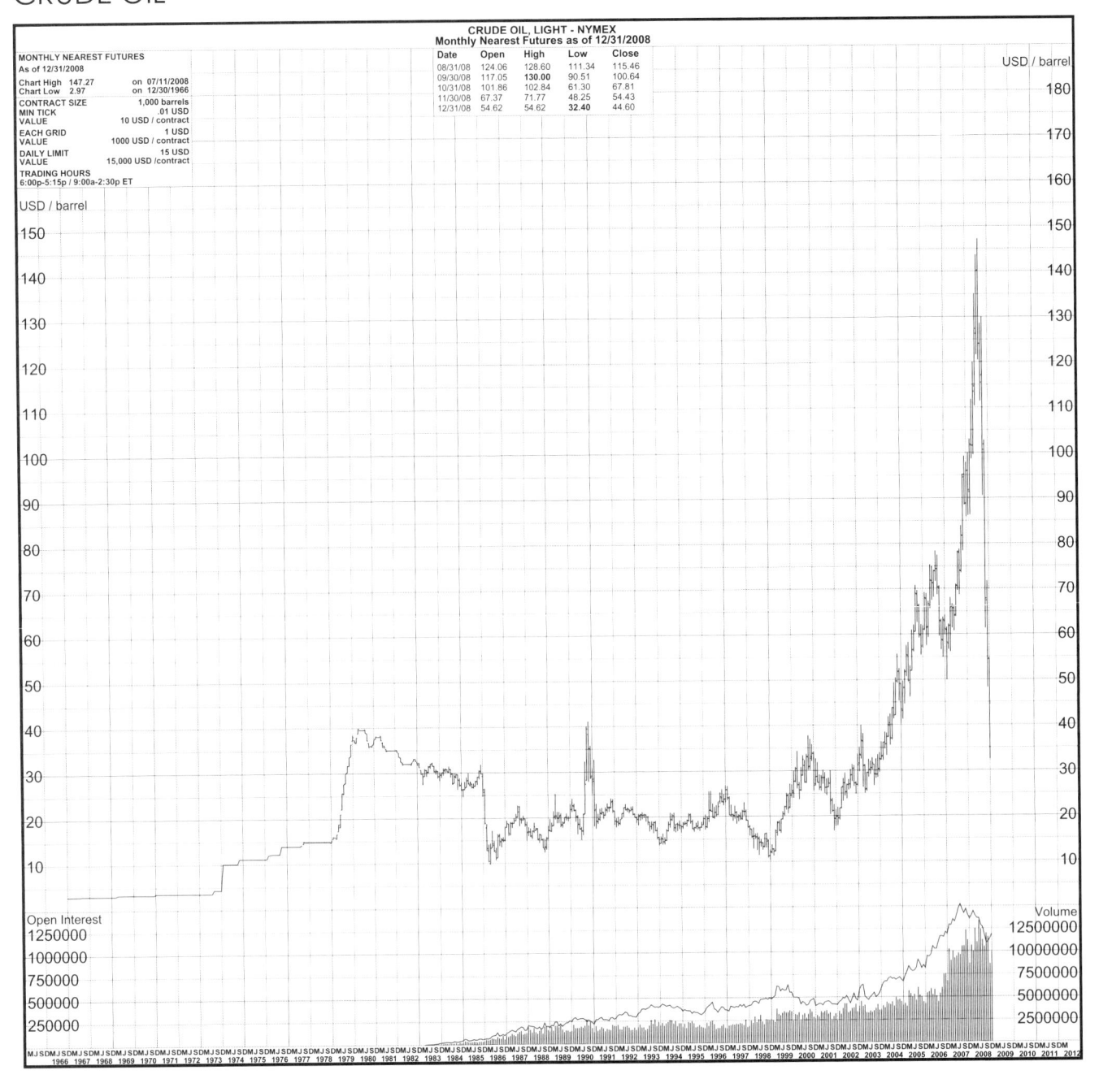

**CRUDE OIL, LIGHT - NYMEX**
Monthly Nearest Futures as of 12/31/2008

| Date | Open | High | Low | Close |
|---|---|---|---|---|
| 08/31/08 | 124.06 | 128.60 | 111.34 | 115.46 |
| 09/30/08 | 117.05 | 130.00 | 90.51 | 100.64 |
| 10/31/08 | 101.86 | 102.84 | 61.30 | 67.81 |
| 11/30/08 | 67.37 | 71.77 | 48.25 | 54.43 |
| 12/31/08 | 54.62 | 54.62 | 32.40 | 44.60 |

**MONTHLY NEAREST FUTURES**
As of 12/31/2008
- Chart High 147.27 on 07/11/2008
- Chart Low 2.97 on 12/30/1966
- CONTRACT SIZE: 1,000 barrels
- MIN TICK: .01 USD
- VALUE: 10 USD / contract
- EACH GRID: 1 USD
- VALUE: 1000 USD /contract
- DAILY LIMIT: 15 USD
- VALUE: 15,000 USD /contract
- TRADING HOURS: 6:00p-5:15p / 9:00a-2:30p ET

## Annual High, Low and Settle of Crude Oil Futures    In USD per Barrel

| Year | High | Low | Settle | Year | High | Low | Settle | Year | High | Low | Settle |
|---|---|---|---|---|---|---|---|---|---|---|---|
| 1967 | 3.07 | 2.97 | 3.07 | 1981 | 38.25 | 34.87 | 35.00 | 1995 | 20.82 | 16.60 | 19.55 |
| 1968 | 3.07 | 3.07 | 3.07 | 1982 | 35.12 | 31.87 | 31.87 | 1996 | 26.80 | 17.08 | 25.92 |
| 1969 | 3.35 | 3.07 | 3.35 | 1983 | 32.35 | 27.40 | 29.60 | 1997 | 26.74 | 17.50 | 17.64 |
| 1970 | 3.56 | 3.31 | 3.56 | 1984 | 31.50 | 26.04 | 26.41 | 1998 | 18.06 | 10.35 | 12.05 |
| 1971 | 3.56 | 3.56 | 3.56 | 1985 | 31.82 | 24.66 | 26.30 | 1999 | 27.15 | 11.26 | 25.60 |
| 1972 | 3.56 | 3.56 | 3.56 | 1986 | 26.60 | 9.75 | 17.94 | 2000 | 37.80 | 23.70 | 26.80 |
| 1973 | 4.31 | 3.56 | 4.31 | 1987 | 22.76 | 14.90 | 16.70 | 2001 | 32.70 | 16.70 | 19.84 |
| 1974 | 11.16 | 10.11 | 11.16 | 1988 | 18.92 | 12.28 | 17.24 | 2002 | 33.65 | 17.85 | 31.20 |
| 1975 | 11.16 | 11.16 | 11.16 | 1989 | 25.30 | 16.91 | 21.82 | 2003 | 39.99 | 25.04 | 32.52 |
| 1976 | 13.90 | 11.16 | 13.90 | 1990 | 41.15 | 15.06 | 28.44 | 2004 | 55.67 | 32.20 | 43.45 |
| 1977 | 14.97 | 13.78 | 14.85 | 1991 | 32.75 | 17.45 | 19.12 | 2005 | 70.85 | 41.25 | 61.04 |
| 1978 | 15.14 | 14.72 | 15.14 | 1992 | 22.95 | 17.72 | 19.50 | 2006 | 78.40 | 54.86 | 61.05 |
| 1979 | 38.47 | 15.48 | 38.01 | 1993 | 21.14 | 13.75 | 14.17 | 2007 | 99.29 | 49.90 | 95.98 |
| 1980 | 39.81 | 35.75 | 37.48 | 1994 | 20.98 | 13.88 | 17.76 | 2008 | 147.27 | 32.40 | 44.60 |

Data continued from page 62.    Futures begin trading 03/30/1983.    *Source: CME Group; New York Mercantile Exchange*

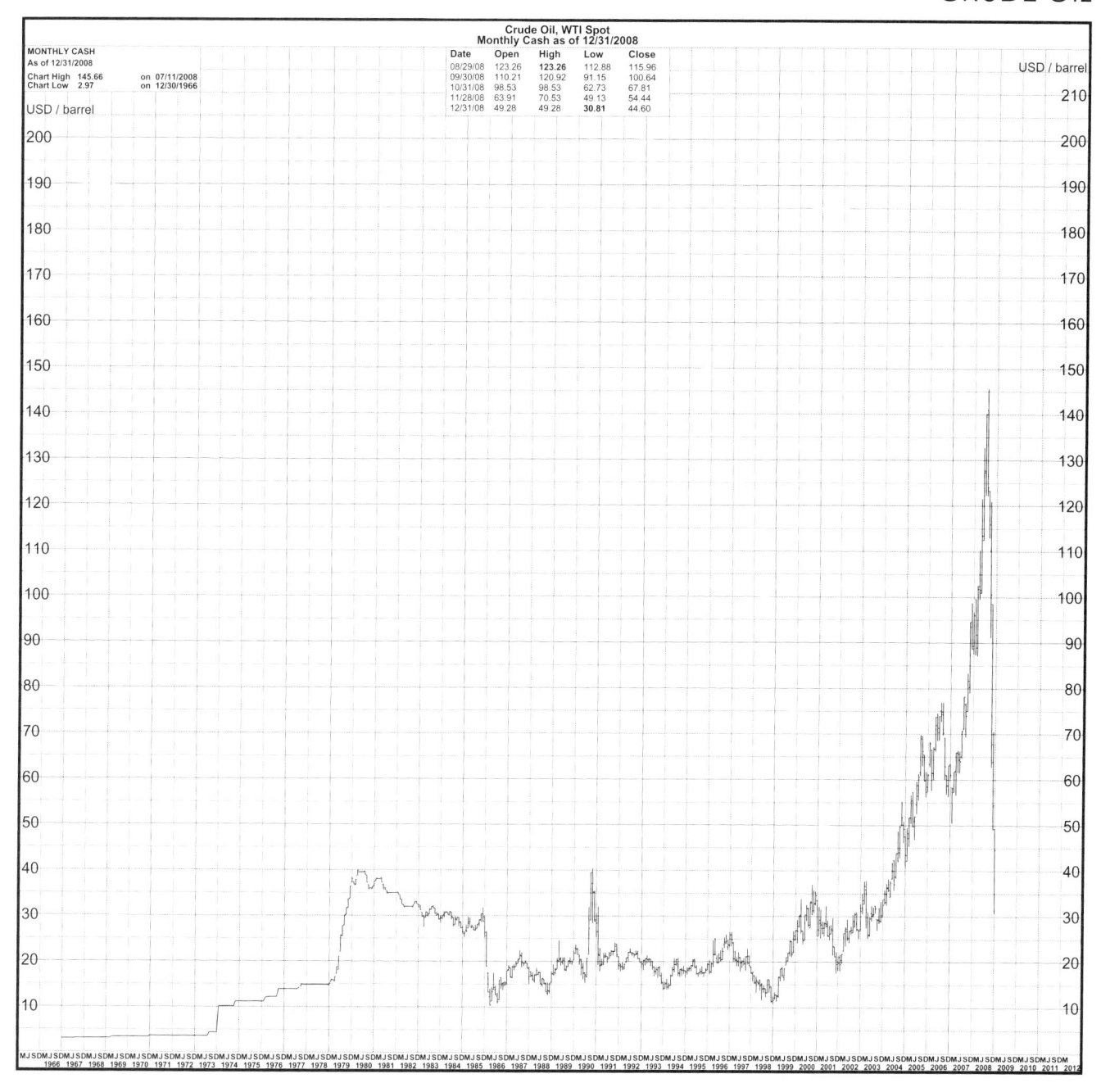

# CRUDE OIL

**Crude Oil, WTI Spot**
Monthly Cash as of 12/31/2008

| Date | Open | High | Low | Close |
|---|---|---|---|---|
| 08/29/08 | 123.26 | 123.26 | 112.88 | 115.96 |
| 09/30/08 | 110.21 | 120.92 | 91.15 | 100.64 |
| 10/31/08 | 98.53 | 98.53 | 62.73 | 67.81 |
| 11/28/08 | 63.91 | 70.53 | 49.13 | 54.44 |
| 12/31/08 | 49.28 | 49.28 | 30.81 | 44.60 |

MONTHLY CASH
As of 12/31/2008
Chart High 145.66 on 07/11/2008
Chart Low 2.97 on 12/30/1966
USD / barrel

## Annual High, Low and Settle of Crude Oil   In USD per Barrel

| Year | High | Low | Settle | Year | High | Low | Settle | Year | High | Low | Settle |
|---|---|---|---|---|---|---|---|---|---|---|---|
| 1967 | 3.07 | 2.97 | 3.07 | 1981 | 38.25 | 34.87 | 35.00 | 1995 | 20.71 | 16.67 | 19.47 |
| 1968 | 3.07 | 3.07 | 3.07 | 1982 | 35.12 | 31.87 | 31.87 | 1996 | 26.56 | 17.26 | 25.91 |
| 1969 | 3.35 | 3.07 | 3.35 | 1983 | 32.25 | 27.40 | 29.60 | 1997 | 26.61 | 17.53 | 17.63 |
| 1970 | 3.56 | 3.31 | 3.56 | 1984 | 31.00 | 26.05 | 26.40 | 1998 | 17.81 | 10.80 | 11.66 |
| 1971 | 3.56 | 3.56 | 3.56 | 1985 | 31.80 | 25.20 | 26.30 | 1999 | 26.94 | 11.36 | 26.92 |
| 1972 | 3.56 | 3.56 | 3.56 | 1986 | 26.55 | 10.40 | 17.95 | 2000 | 37.00 | 23.84 | 25.76 |
| 1973 | 4.31 | 3.56 | 4.31 | 1987 | 22.40 | 15.15 | 16.70 | 2001 | 32.30 | 17.48 | 19.78 |
| 1974 | 11.16 | 10.11 | 11.16 | 1988 | 18.60 | 12.60 | 17.25 | 2002 | 32.73 | 17.98 | 31.23 |
| 1975 | 11.16 | 11.16 | 11.16 | 1989 | 24.65 | 17.05 | 21.80 | 2003 | 37.83 | 25.23 | 32.55 |
| 1976 | 13.90 | 11.16 | 13.90 | 1990 | 40.40 | 15.30 | 28.45 | 2004 | 55.23 | 32.48 | 43.46 |
| 1977 | 14.97 | 13.78 | 14.85 | 1991 | 32.00 | 17.85 | 19.10 | 2005 | 69.82 | 42.13 | 61.04 |
| 1978 | 15.14 | 14.72 | 15.14 | 1992 | 22.89 | 17.85 | 19.48 | 2006 | 77.03 | 56.27 | 61.06 |
| 1979 | 38.47 | 15.48 | 38.01 | 1993 | 21.43 | 13.79 | 14.13 | 2007 | 98.83 | 50.49 | 96.01 |
| 1980 | 39.81 | 35.75 | 37.48 | 1994 | 20.87 | 13.86 | 17.78 | 2008 | 145.66 | 30.81 | 44.60 |

Data continued from page 63.   *Source: CME Group; New York Mercantile Exchange*

# CRUDE OIL

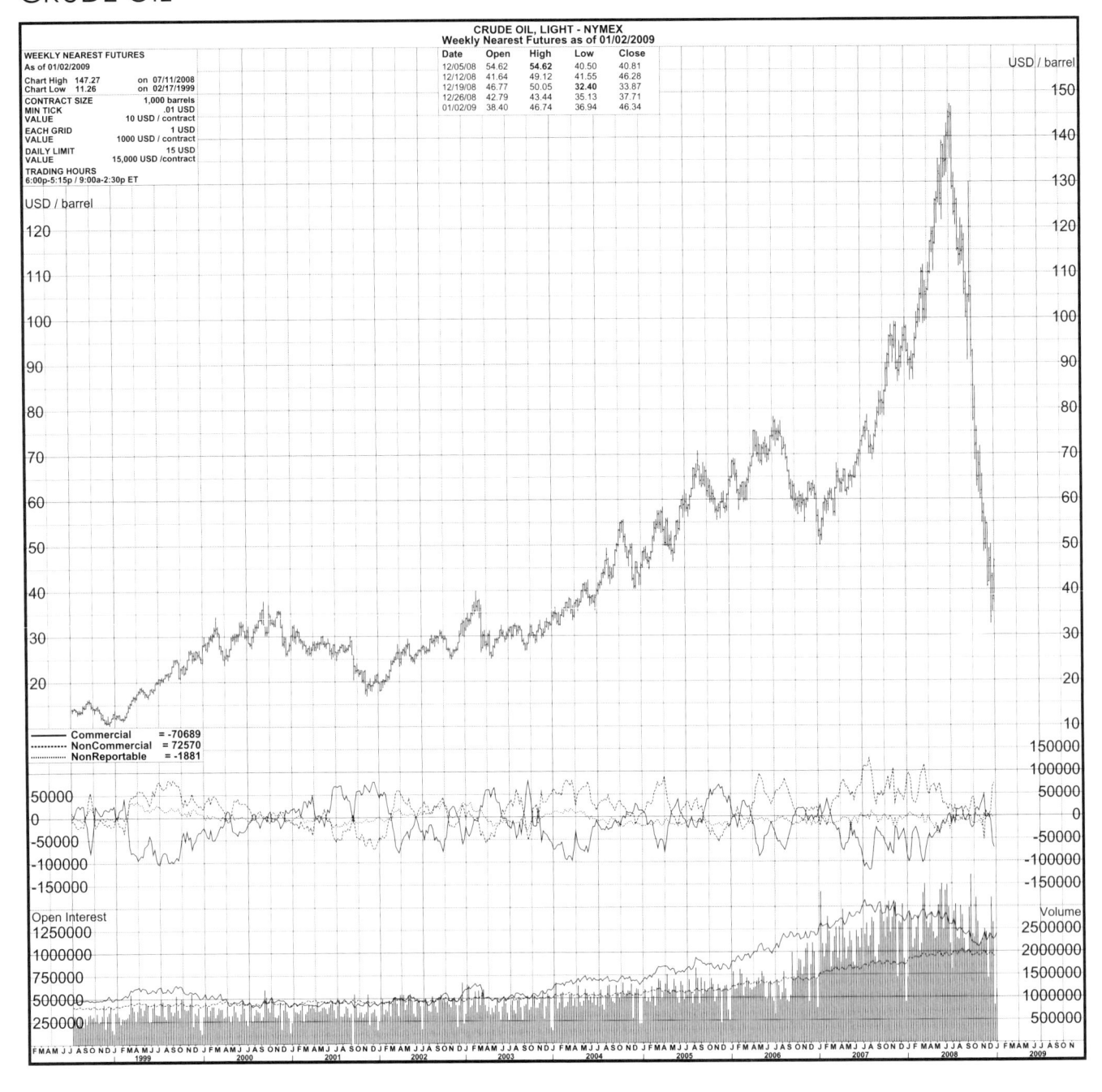

**CRUDE OIL, LIGHT - NYMEX**
Weekly Nearest Futures as of 01/02/2009

| Date | Open | High | Low | Close |
|---|---|---|---|---|
| 12/05/08 | 54.62 | 54.62 | 40.50 | 40.81 |
| 12/12/08 | 41.64 | 49.12 | 41.55 | 46.28 |
| 12/19/08 | 46.77 | 50.05 | 32.40 | 33.87 |
| 12/26/08 | 42.79 | 43.44 | 35.13 | 37.71 |
| 01/02/09 | 38.40 | 46.74 | 36.94 | 46.34 |

**WEEKLY NEAREST FUTURES**
As of 01/02/2009
Chart High 147.27 on 07/11/2008
Chart Low 11.26 on 02/17/1999
CONTRACT SIZE 1,000 barrels
MIN TICK .01 USD
VALUE 10 USD / contract
EACH GRID 1 USD
VALUE 1000 USD / contract
DAILY LIMIT 15 USD
VALUE 15,000 USD / contract
TRADING HOURS
6:00p-5:15p / 9:00a-2:30p ET

Commercial = -70689
NonCommercial = 72570
NonReportable = -1881

## Quarterly High, Low and Settle of Crude Oil Futures    In USD per Barrel

| Quarter | High | Low | Settle | Quarter | High | Low | Settle | Quarter | High | Low | Settle |
|---|---|---|---|---|---|---|---|---|---|---|---|
| 03/2000 | 34.37 | 24.02 | 26.90 | 03/2003 | 39.99 | 26.30 | 31.04 | 03/2006 | 69.20 | 57.55 | 66.63 |
| 06/2000 | 33.40 | 23.70 | 32.50 | 06/2003 | 32.50 | 25.04 | 30.19 | 06/2006 | 75.35 | 65.60 | 73.93 |
| 09/2000 | 37.80 | 27.26 | 30.84 | 09/2003 | 32.85 | 26.65 | 29.20 | 09/2006 | 78.40 | 59.52 | 62.91 |
| 12/2000 | 37.00 | 25.58 | 26.80 | 12/2003 | 33.93 | 28.26 | 32.52 | 12/2006 | 64.15 | 54.86 | 61.05 |
| 03/2001 | 32.70 | 25.70 | 26.29 | 03/2004 | 38.50 | 32.20 | 35.76 | 03/2007 | 68.09 | 49.90 | 65.87 |
| 06/2001 | 30.20 | 25.10 | 26.25 | 06/2004 | 42.45 | 33.30 | 37.05 | 06/2007 | 71.06 | 60.68 | 70.68 |
| 09/2001 | 29.98 | 20.30 | 23.43 | 09/2004 | 50.47 | 36.69 | 49.64 | 09/2007 | 83.90 | 68.63 | 81.66 |
| 12/2001 | 23.98 | 16.70 | 19.84 | 12/2004 | 55.67 | 40.25 | 43.45 | 12/2007 | 99.29 | 78.35 | 95.98 |
| 03/2002 | 26.38 | 17.85 | 26.31 | 03/2005 | 57.60 | 41.25 | 55.40 | 03/2008 | 111.80 | 86.11 | 101.58 |
| 06/2002 | 29.54 | 23.31 | 26.86 | 06/2005 | 60.95 | 46.20 | 56.50 | 06/2008 | 143.67 | 99.55 | 140.00 |
| 09/2002 | 31.39 | 25.73 | 30.45 | 09/2005 | 70.85 | 56.10 | 66.24 | 09/2008 | 147.27 | 90.51 | 100.64 |
| 12/2002 | 33.65 | 24.82 | 31.20 | 12/2005 | 66.62 | 55.40 | 61.04 | 12/2008 | 102.84 | 32.40 | 44.60 |

*Source: CME Group; New York Mercantile Exchange*

# CRUDE OIL

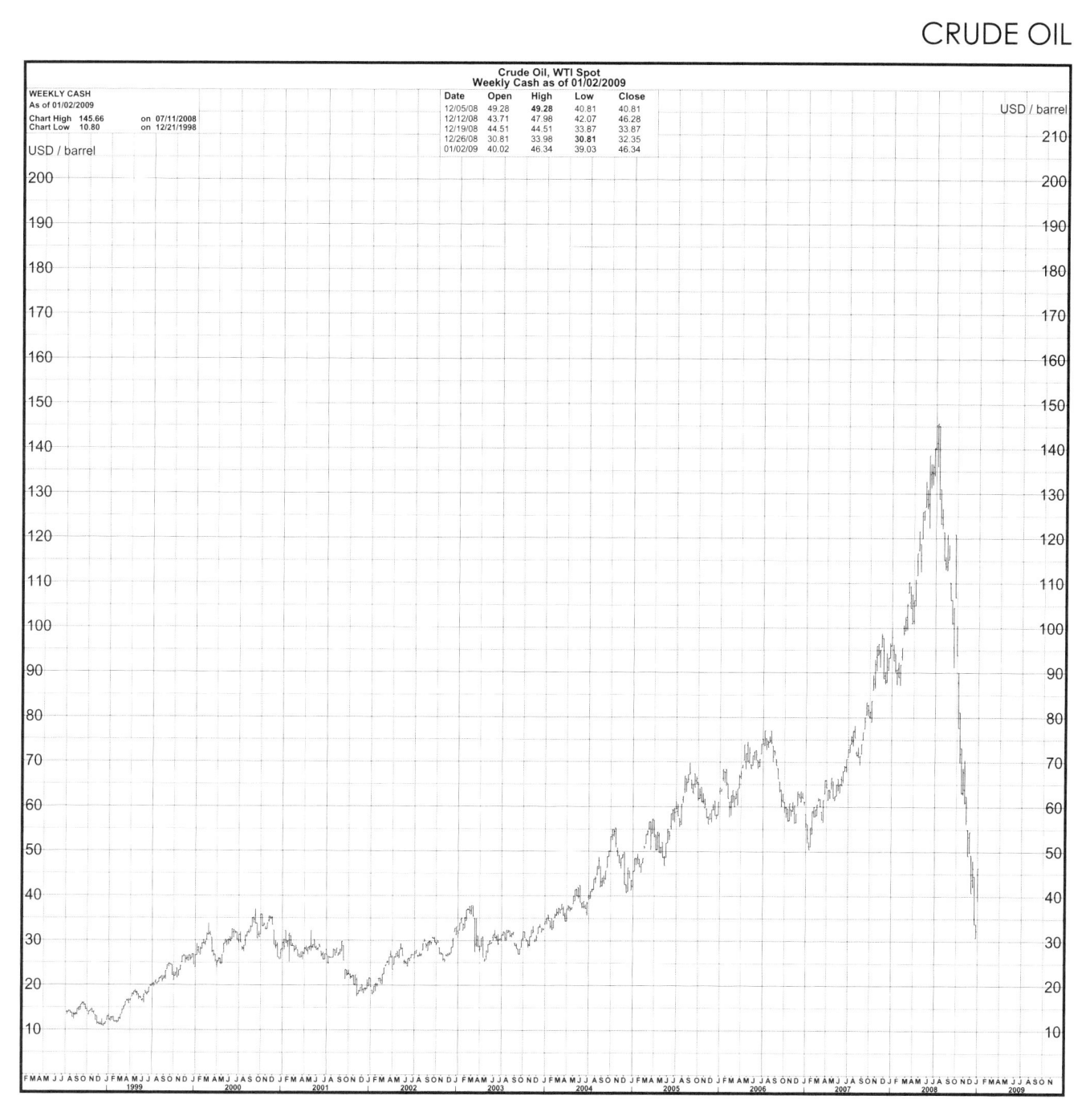

**Crude Oil, WTI Spot**
Weekly Cash as of 01/02/2009

| Date | Open | High | Low | Close |
|---|---|---|---|---|
| 12/05/08 | 49.28 | 49.28 | 40.81 | 40.81 |
| 12/12/08 | 43.71 | 47.98 | 42.07 | 46.28 |
| 12/19/08 | 44.51 | 44.51 | 33.87 | 33.87 |
| 12/26/08 | 30.81 | 33.98 | 30.81 | 32.35 |
| 01/02/09 | 40.02 | 46.34 | 39.03 | 46.34 |

WEEKLY CASH
As of 01/02/2009
Chart High 145.66 on 07/11/2008
Chart Low 10.80 on 12/21/1998

USD / barrel

## Quarterly High, Low and Settle of Crude Oil — In USD per Barrel

| Quarter | High | Low | Settle | Quarter | High | Low | Settle | Quarter | High | Low | Settle |
|---|---|---|---|---|---|---|---|---|---|---|---|
| 03/2000 | 33.85 | 24.04 | 26.80 | 03/2003 | 37.83 | 27.50 | 31.03 | 03/2006 | 68.36 | 57.66 | 66.66 |
| 06/2000 | 32.60 | 23.84 | 31.80 | 06/2003 | 32.38 | 25.23 | 30.18 | 06/2006 | 74.62 | 66.24 | 73.98 |
| 09/2000 | 37.00 | 27.48 | 30.45 | 09/2003 | 32.38 | 26.93 | 29.23 | 09/2006 | 77.03 | 60.11 | 62.92 |
| 12/2000 | 35.76 | 25.76 | 25.76 | 12/2003 | 33.73 | 28.48 | 32.55 | 12/2006 | 63.44 | 56.27 | 61.06 |
| 03/2001 | 32.15 | 25.17 | 26.46 | 03/2004 | 38.18 | 32.48 | 35.78 | 03/2007 | 66.04 | 50.49 | 65.88 |
| 06/2001 | 32.30 | 25.62 | 25.74 | 06/2004 | 42.35 | 34.28 | 37.05 | 06/2007 | 70.69 | 61.48 | 70.69 |
| 09/2001 | 29.78 | 21.45 | 23.43 | 09/2004 | 49.91 | 38.38 | 49.65 | 09/2007 | 83.36 | 69.32 | 81.67 |
| 12/2001 | 23.33 | 17.48 | 19.78 | 12/2004 | 55.23 | 40.72 | 43.46 | 12/2007 | 98.83 | 79.03 | 96.01 |
| 03/2002 | 26.33 | 17.98 | 26.33 | 03/2005 | 56.62 | 42.13 | 55.41 | 03/2008 | 110.33 | 87.15 | 101.59 |
| 06/2002 | 29.38 | 23.48 | 26.88 | 06/2005 | 59.65 | 46.81 | 56.50 | 06/2008 | 140.21 | 100.98 | 140.00 |
| 09/2002 | 30.83 | 26.08 | 30.45 | 09/2005 | 69.82 | 55.49 | 66.25 | 09/2008 | 145.66 | 91.15 | 100.64 |
| 12/2002 | 32.73 | 25.15 | 31.23 | 12/2005 | 65.48 | 56.15 | 61.04 | 12/2008 | 98.53 | 30.81 | 44.60 |

*Source: CME Group; New York Mercantile Exchange*

# GASOLINE, RBOB

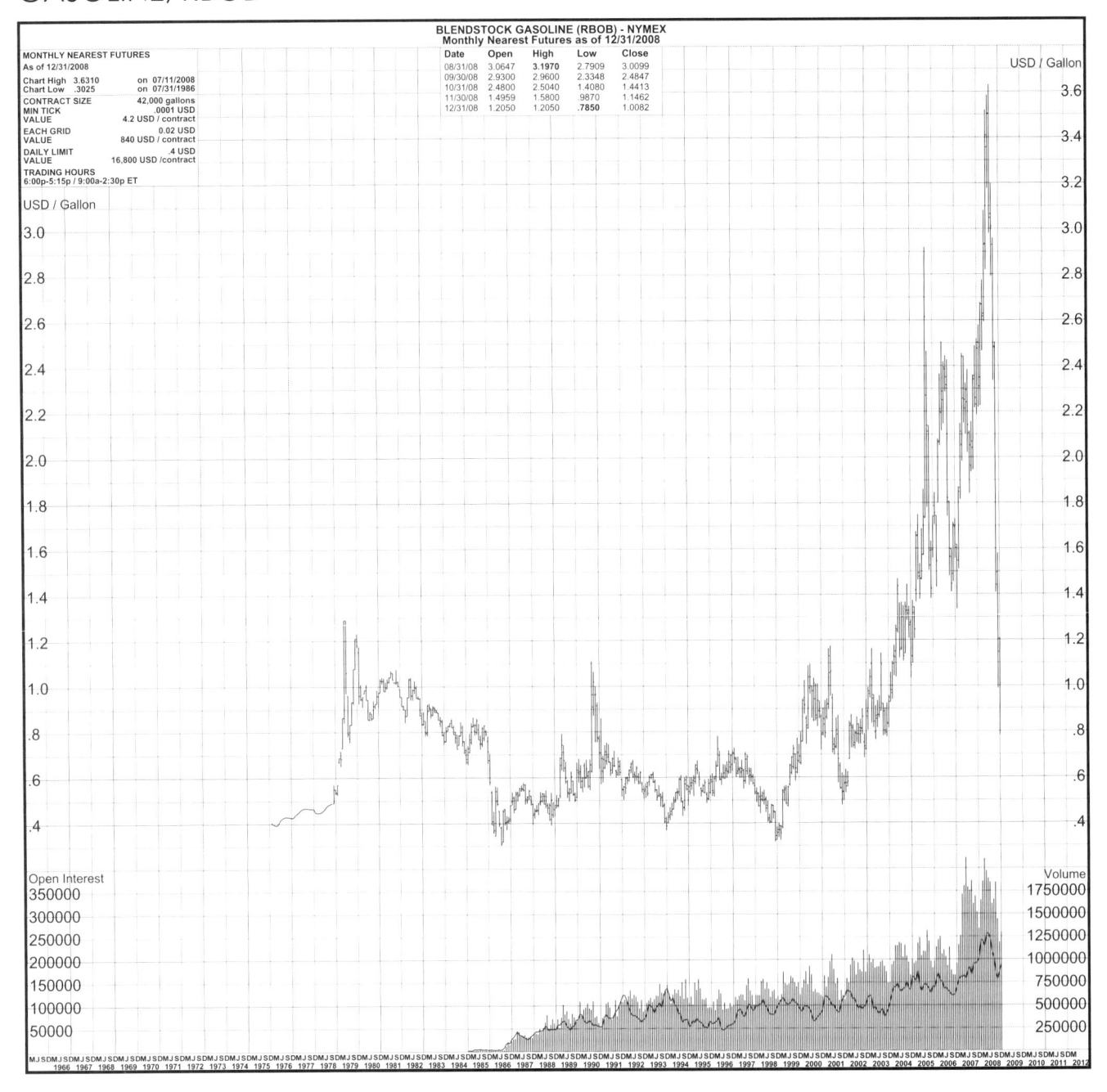

**MONTHLY NEAREST FUTURES**
As of 12/31/2008
Chart High 3.6310 on 07/11/2008
Chart Low .3025 on 07/31/1986
CONTRACT SIZE 42,000 gallons
MIN TICK .0001 USD
VALUE 4.2 USD / contract
EACH GRID 0.02 USD
VALUE 840 USD / contract
DAILY LIMIT .4 USD
VALUE 16,800 USD /contract
TRADING HOURS
6:00p-5:15p / 9:00a-2:30p ET

**BLENDSTOCK GASOLINE (RBOB) - NYMEX**
Monthly Nearest Futures as of 12/31/2008

| Date | Open | High | Low | Close |
|---|---|---|---|---|
| 08/31/08 | 3.0647 | 3.1970 | 2.7909 | 3.0099 |
| 09/30/08 | 2.9300 | 2.9600 | 2.3348 | 2.4847 |
| 10/31/08 | 2.4800 | 2.5040 | 1.4080 | 1.4413 |
| 11/30/08 | 1.4959 | 1.5800 | .9870 | 1.1462 |
| 12/31/08 | 1.2050 | 1.2050 | .7850 | 1.0082 |

### Annual High, Low and Settle of Gasoline, RBOB Futures     In USD per Gallon

| Year | High | Low | Settle | Year | High | Low | Settle | Year | High | Low | Settle |
|---|---|---|---|---|---|---|---|---|---|---|---|
| 1967 | | | | 1981 | 1.0750 | .9550 | .9550 | 1995 | .6740 | .4870 | .5886 |
| 1968 | | | | 1982 | 1.0400 | .8325 | .8325 | 1996 | .7810 | .5150 | .7067 |
| 1969 | | | | 1983 | .9275 | .7475 | .7600 | 1997 | .7290 | .5250 | .5281 |
| 1970 | | | | 1984 | .7290 | .6605 | .6810 | 1998 | .5600 | .3160 | .3570 |
| 1971 | | | | 1985 | .8650 | .6560 | .7140 | 1999 | .7720 | .3240 | .6910 |
| 1972 | | | | 1986 | .7085 | .3025 | .4790 | 2000 | 1.0960 | .6540 | .7858 |
| 1973 | | | | 1987 | .5785 | .3950 | .4367 | 2001 | 1.1750 | .4780 | .5725 |
| 1974 | | | | 1988 | .5450 | .3895 | .4788 | 2002 | .9400 | .5310 | .8648 |
| 1975 | | | | 1989 | .7920 | .4660 | .6322 | 2003 | 1.1630 | .7630 | .9492 |
| 1976 | .4300 | .3920 | .4260 | 1990 | 1.1100 | .5350 | .7092 | 2004 | 1.4700 | .9290 | 1.0887 |
| 1977 | .4670 | .4270 | .4650 | 1991 | .8600 | .5175 | .5487 | 2005 | 2.9200 | 1.0980 | 1.7400 |
| 1978 | .5700 | .4470 | .5375 | 1992 | .6775 | .5025 | .5404 | 2006 | 2.5050 | 1.4100 | 1.6021 |
| 1979 | 1.2900 | .5250 | 1.1800 | 1993 | .6250 | .3670 | .3877 | 2007 | 2.5175 | 1.3351 | 2.4758 |
| 1980 | 1.1750 | .8500 | .9725 | 1994 | .6105 | .4010 | .5590 | 2008 | 3.6310 | .7850 | 1.0082 |

Futures begin trading 12/03/1984; through December 2005 contract "Unleaded"; January 2006 contract to date "RBOB".
*Source: CME Group; New York Mercantile Exchange*

# GASOLINE, RBOB

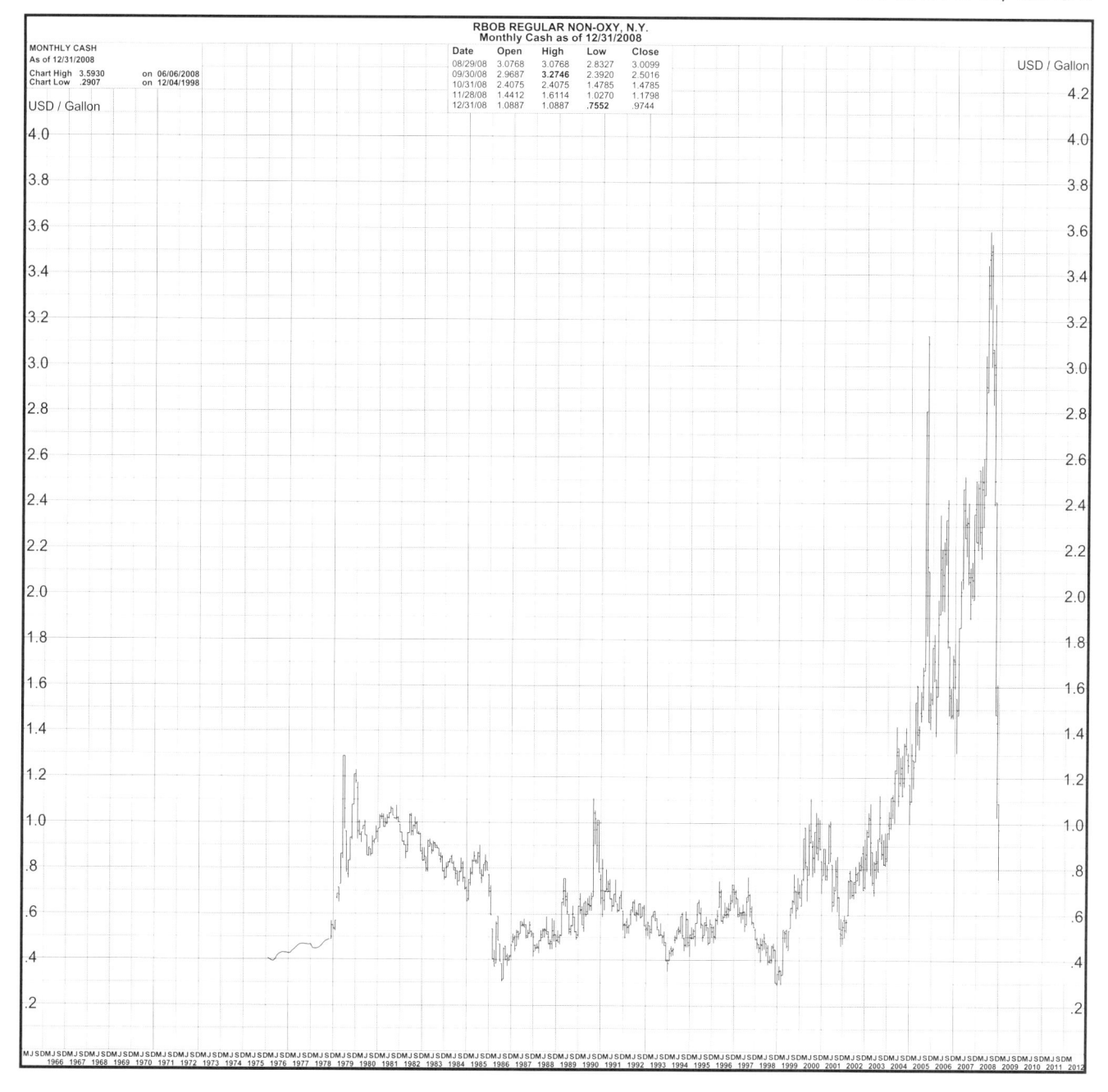

**RBOB REGULAR NON-OXY, N.Y.**
Monthly Cash as of 12/31/2008

| Date | Open | High | Low | Close |
|---|---|---|---|---|
| 08/29/08 | 3.0768 | 3.0768 | 2.8327 | 3.0099 |
| 09/30/08 | 2.9687 | 3.2746 | 2.3920 | 2.5016 |
| 10/31/08 | 2.4075 | 2.4075 | 1.4785 | 1.4785 |
| 11/28/08 | 1.4412 | 1.6114 | 1.0270 | 1.1798 |
| 12/31/08 | 1.0887 | 1.0887 | .7552 | .9744 |

MONTHLY CASH
As of 12/31/2008
Chart High 3.5930 on 06/06/2008
Chart Low .2907 on 12/04/1998

### Annual High, Low and Settle of Gasoline, RBOB    In USD per Gallon

| Year | High | Low | Settle | Year | High | Low | Settle | Year | High | Low | Settle |
|---|---|---|---|---|---|---|---|---|---|---|---|
| 1967 | | | | 1981 | 1.0750 | .9550 | .9550 | 1995 | .6663 | .4605 | .5251 |
| 1968 | | | | 1982 | 1.0400 | .8325 | .8325 | 1996 | .7464 | .4755 | .6915 |
| 1969 | | | | 1983 | .9275 | .7475 | .7600 | 1997 | .7639 | .4924 | .4924 |
| 1970 | | | | 1984 | .8575 | .6525 | .6575 | 1998 | .5167 | .2907 | .3408 |
| 1971 | | | | 1985 | .9000 | .6575 | .7125 | 1999 | .7788 | .2930 | .6755 |
| 1972 | | | | 1986 | .7260 | .3050 | .4625 | 2000 | 1.1093 | .6380 | .7553 |
| 1973 | | | | 1987 | .5800 | .4130 | .4360 | 2001 | 1.0120 | .4622 | .5478 |
| 1974 | | | | 1988 | .5900 | .4270 | .4850 | 2002 | .9328 | .5010 | .8468 |
| 1975 | | | | 1989 | .7575 | .4675 | .6350 | 2003 | 1.1231 | .6831 | .9580 |
| 1976 | .4300 | .3920 | .4260 | 1990 | 1.1075 | .5225 | .7035 | 2004 | 1.4240 | .9297 | 1.0885 |
| 1977 | .4670 | .4270 | .4650 | 1991 | .8420 | .5300 | .5525 | 2005 | 3.1340 | 1.0965 | 1.7700 |
| 1978 | .5700 | .4470 | .5375 | 1992 | .6655 | .4950 | .5400 | 2006 | 2.4199 | 1.3812 | 1.6446 |
| 1979 | 1.2900 | .5250 | 1.1800 | 1993 | .6160 | .3499 | .3855 | 2007 | 2.5216 | 1.3078 | 2.4708 |
| 1980 | 1.1750 | .8500 | .9725 | 1994 | .6155 | .3970 | .5115 | 2008 | 3.5930 | .7552 | .9744 |

*Source: CME Group; New York Mercantile Exchange*

# GASOLINE, RBOB

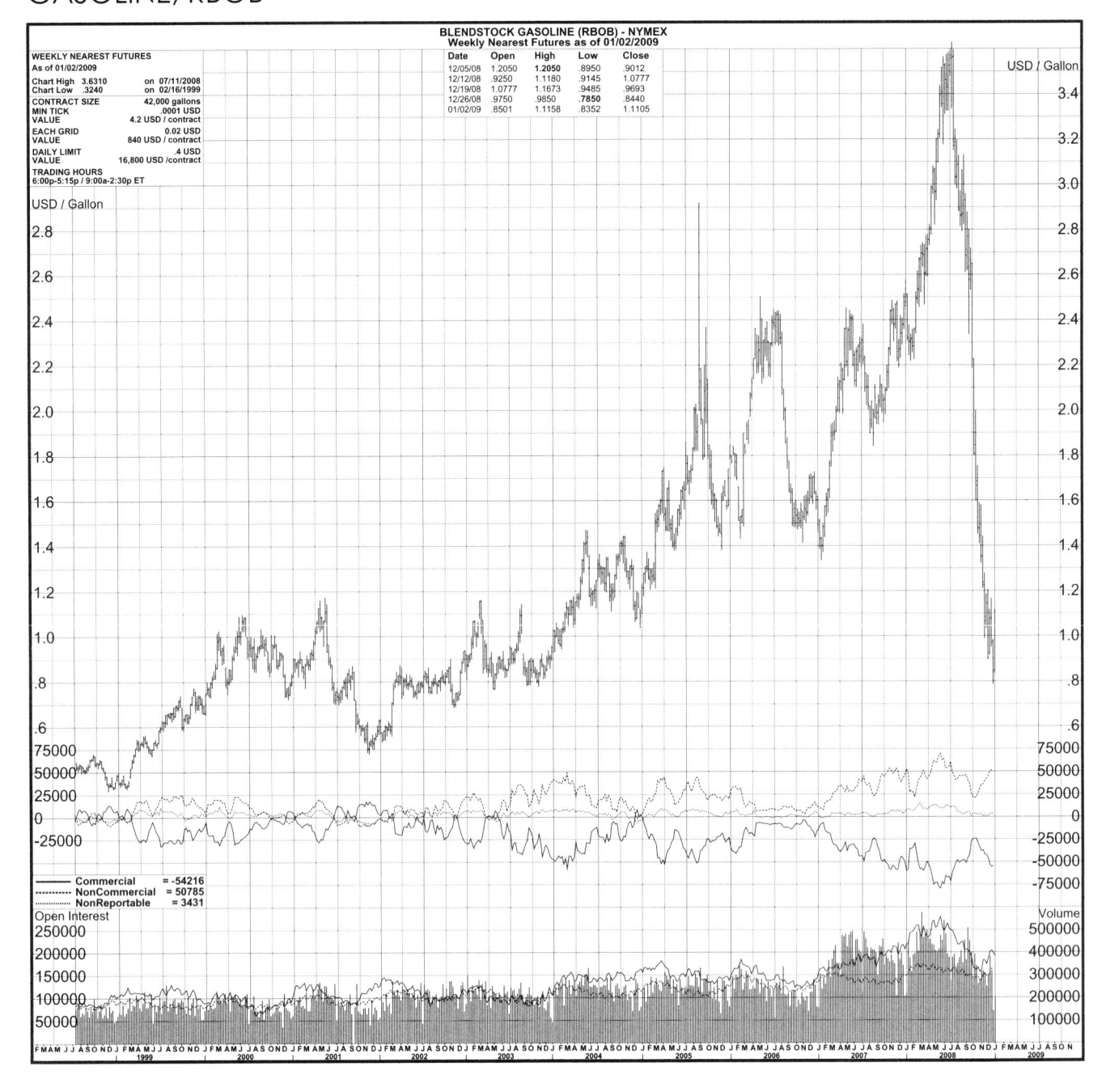

## Quarterly High, Low and Settle of Gasoline, RBOB Futures   In USD per Gallon

| Quarter | High | Low | Settle | Quarter | High | Low | Settle | Quarter | High | Low | Settle |
| --- | --- | --- | --- | --- | --- | --- | --- | --- | --- | --- | --- |
| 03/2000 | 1.0250 | .6540 | .9169 | 03/2003 | 1.1630 | .8050 | .9444 | 03/2006 | 2.0805 | 1.4310 | 2.0645 |
| 06/2000 | 1.0960 | .7430 | 1.0378 | 06/2003 | .9600 | .7630 | .8699 | 06/2006 | 2.5050 | 2.0500 | 2.3931 |
| 09/2000 | 1.0350 | .8415 | .8694 | 09/2003 | 1.1436 | .7790 | .8865 | 09/2006 | 2.4450 | 1.4800 | 1.5632 |
| 12/2000 | 1.0100 | .7200 | .7858 | 12/2003 | .9590 | .7760 | .9492 | 12/2006 | 1.7300 | 1.4100 | 1.6021 |
| 03/2001 | .9450 | .7700 | .9190 | 03/2004 | 1.1775 | .9290 | 1.1244 | 03/2007 | 2.1488 | 1.3351 | 2.1115 |
| 06/2001 | 1.1750 | .7050 | .7211 | 06/2004 | 1.4700 | 1.0380 | 1.1562 | 06/2007 | 2.4550 | 1.9820 | 2.2942 |
| 09/2001 | .8700 | .5750 | .6799 | 09/2004 | 1.3660 | 1.1075 | 1.3444 | 09/2007 | 2.3836 | 1.8400 | 2.0683 |
| 12/2001 | .6630 | .4780 | .5725 | 12/2004 | 1.4450 | 1.0350 | 1.0887 | 12/2007 | 2.5175 | 1.9450 | 2.4758 |
| 03/2002 | .8450 | .5310 | .8249 | 03/2005 | 1.6750 | 1.0980 | 1.6549 | 03/2008 | 2.7752 | 2.2183 | 2.6163 |
| 06/2002 | .8740 | .7220 | .7938 | 06/2005 | 1.7491 | 1.3770 | 1.5721 | 06/2008 | 3.5850 | 2.5920 | 3.5015 |
| 09/2002 | .8640 | .7440 | .8135 | 09/2005 | 2.9200 | 1.5700 | 2.1381 | 09/2008 | 3.6310 | 2.3348 | 2.4847 |
| 12/2002 | .9400 | .6840 | .8648 | 12/2005 | 2.1390 | 1.3805 | 1.7100 | 12/2008 | 2.5040 | .7850 | 1.0082 |

Through December 2005 contract "Unleaded"; January 2006 contract to date "RBOB".   *Source: CME Group; New York Mercantile Exchange*

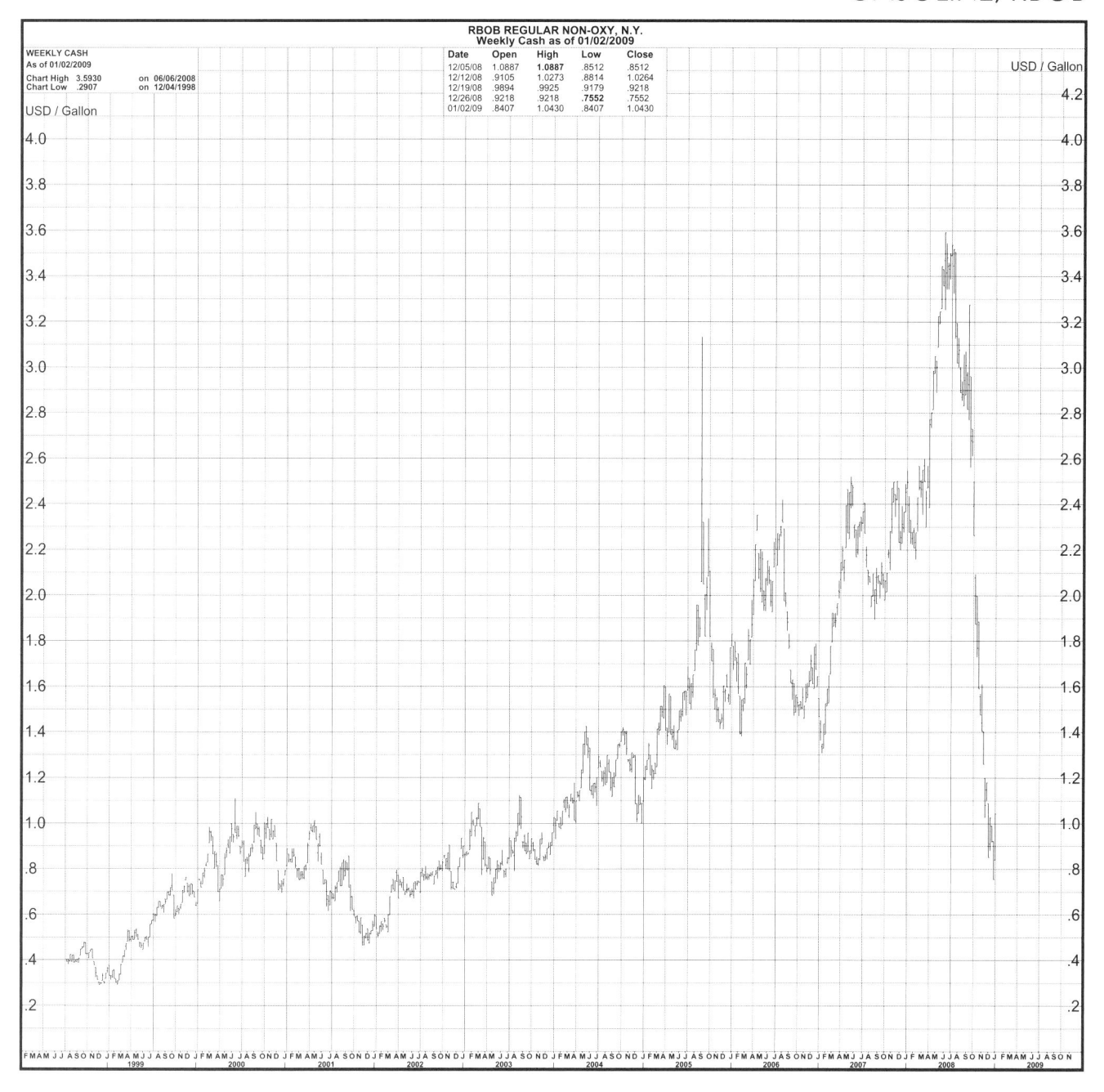

# GASOLINE, RBOB

**RBOB REGULAR NON-OXY, N.Y.**
Weekly Cash as of 01/02/2009

| Date | Open | High | Low | Close |
|---|---|---|---|---|
| 12/05/08 | 1.0887 | 1.0887 | .8512 | .8512 |
| 12/12/08 | .9105 | 1.0273 | .8814 | 1.0264 |
| 12/19/08 | .9894 | .9925 | .9179 | .9218 |
| 12/26/08 | .9218 | .9218 | .7552 | .7552 |
| 01/02/09 | .8407 | 1.0430 | .8407 | 1.0430 |

WEEKLY CASH
As of 01/02/2009
Chart High  3.5930  on 06/06/2008
Chart Low   .2907   on 12/04/1998

### Quarterly High, Low and Settle of Gasoline, RBOB    In USD per Gallon

| Quarter | High | Low | Settle | Quarter | High | Low | Settle | Quarter | High | Low | Settle |
|---|---|---|---|---|---|---|---|---|---|---|---|
| 03/2000 | .9843 | .6380 | .8294 | 03/2003 | 1.0880 | .7717 | .9169 | 03/2006 | 1.9807 | 1.3812 | 1.8718 |
| 06/2000 | 1.1093 | .6591 | .9441 | 06/2003 | .8829 | .6831 | .8277 | 06/2006 | 2.3519 | 1.9157 | 2.1826 |
| 09/2000 | 1.0493 | .7658 | .8682 | 09/2003 | 1.1231 | .7896 | .8678 | 09/2006 | 2.4199 | 1.4729 | 1.5632 |
| 12/2000 | 1.0274 | .6939 | .7553 | 12/2003 | .9595 | .8128 | .9580 | 12/2006 | 1.7894 | 1.4590 | 1.6446 |
| 03/2001 | .8897 | .7514 | .7992 | 03/2004 | 1.1283 | .9297 | 1.1017 | 03/2007 | 2.0655 | 1.3078 | 2.0155 |
| 06/2001 | 1.0120 | .6144 | .6581 | 06/2004 | 1.4240 | 1.0030 | 1.1234 | 06/2007 | 2.5216 | 2.0277 | 2.3179 |
| 09/2001 | .8555 | .6142 | .6762 | 09/2004 | 1.3529 | 1.1176 | 1.3407 | 09/2007 | 2.4046 | 1.8937 | 2.0670 |
| 12/2001 | .6789 | .4622 | .5478 | 12/2004 | 1.4204 | 1.0010 | 1.0885 | 12/2007 | 2.5020 | 1.9813 | 2.4708 |
| 03/2002 | .7534 | .5010 | .7474 | 03/2005 | 1.5313 | 1.0965 | 1.5313 | 03/2008 | 2.5986 | 2.1586 | 2.3863 |
| 06/2002 | .7961 | .6702 | .7364 | 06/2005 | 1.6048 | 1.3223 | 1.4731 | 06/2008 | 3.5930 | 2.4392 | 3.4916 |
| 09/2002 | .8340 | .6952 | .7973 | 09/2005 | 3.1340 | 1.5001 | 2.1231 | 09/2008 | 3.5372 | 2.3920 | 2.5016 |
| 12/2002 | .9328 | .7079 | .8468 | 12/2005 | 2.1047 | 1.4119 | 1.7700 | 12/2008 | 2.4075 | .7552 | .9744 |

*Source: CME Group; New York Mercantile Exchange*

# GASOLINE, RBOB

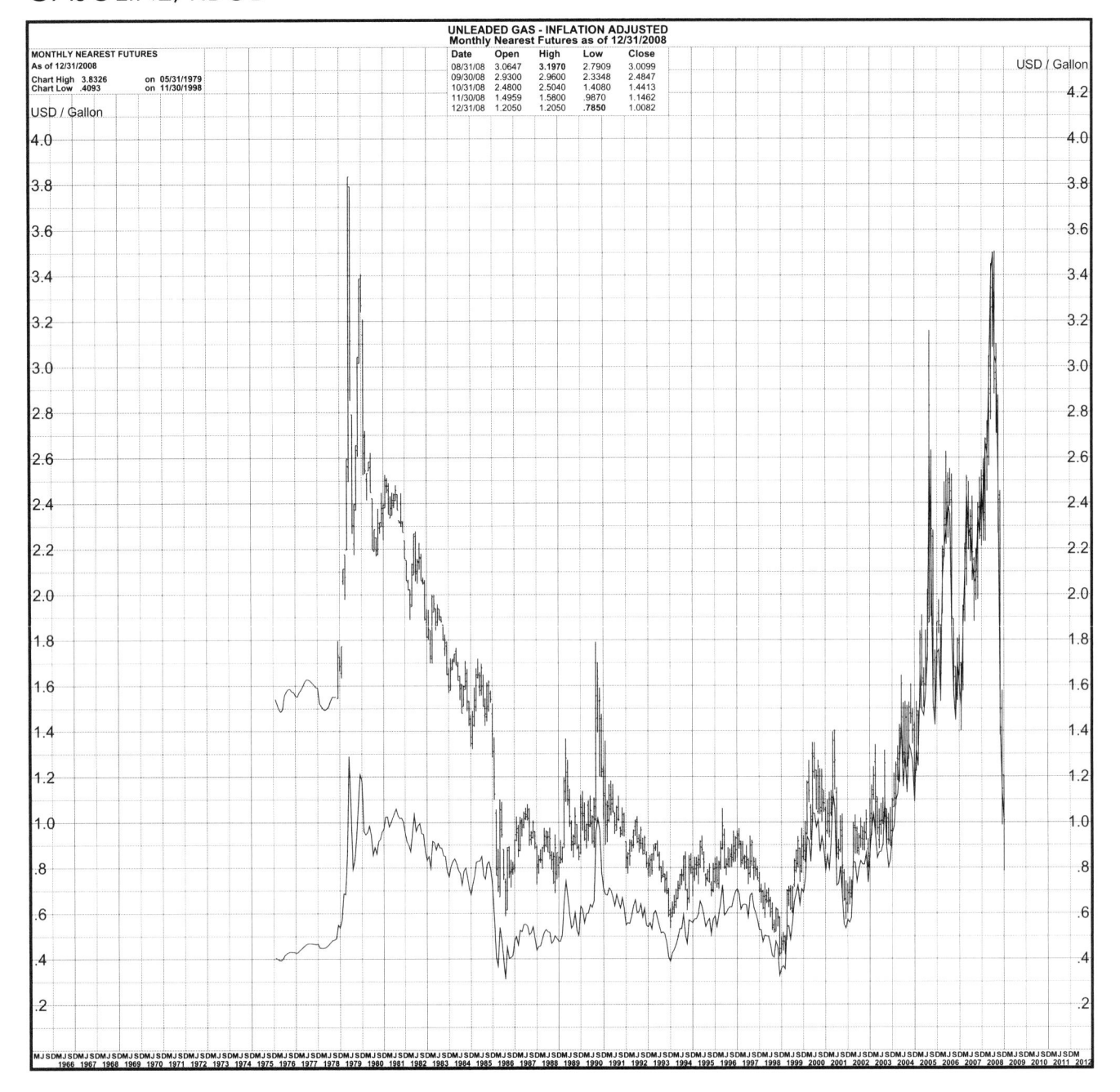

**MONTHLY NEAREST FUTURES**
As of 12/31/2008
Chart High 3.8326 on 05/31/1979
Chart Low .4093 on 11/30/1998

USD / Gallon

**UNLEADED GAS - INFLATION ADJUSTED**
Monthly Nearest Futures as of 12/31/2008

| Date | Open | High | Low | Close |
|---|---|---|---|---|
| 08/31/08 | 3.0647 | **3.1970** | 2.7909 | 3.0099 |
| 09/30/08 | 2.9300 | 2.9600 | 2.3348 | 2.4847 |
| 10/31/08 | 2.4800 | 2.5040 | 1.4080 | 1.4413 |
| 11/30/08 | 1.4959 | 1.5800 | .9870 | 1.1462 |
| 12/31/08 | 1.2050 | 1.2050 | **.7850** | 1.0082 |

# HEATING OIL

**HEATING OIL #2 - INFLATION ADJUSTED**
Monthly Nearest Futures as of 12/31/2008

| Date | Open | High | Low | Close |
|---|---|---|---|---|
| 08/31/08 | 3.4552 | 3.5381 | 3.0240 | 3.1819 |
| 09/30/08 | 3.2600 | 3.2965 | 2.6712 | 2.8636 |
| 10/31/08 | 2.9250 | 2.9500 | 1.8880 | 2.0063 |
| 11/30/08 | 2.0842 | 2.2113 | 1.6400 | 1.6737 |
| 12/31/08 | 1.7271 | 1.7271 | 1.1914 | 1.4057 |

MONTHLY NEAREST FUTURES
As of 12/31/2008
Chart High 4.0161 on 07/31/2008
Chart Low .3771 on 02/28/1999

# HEATING OIL

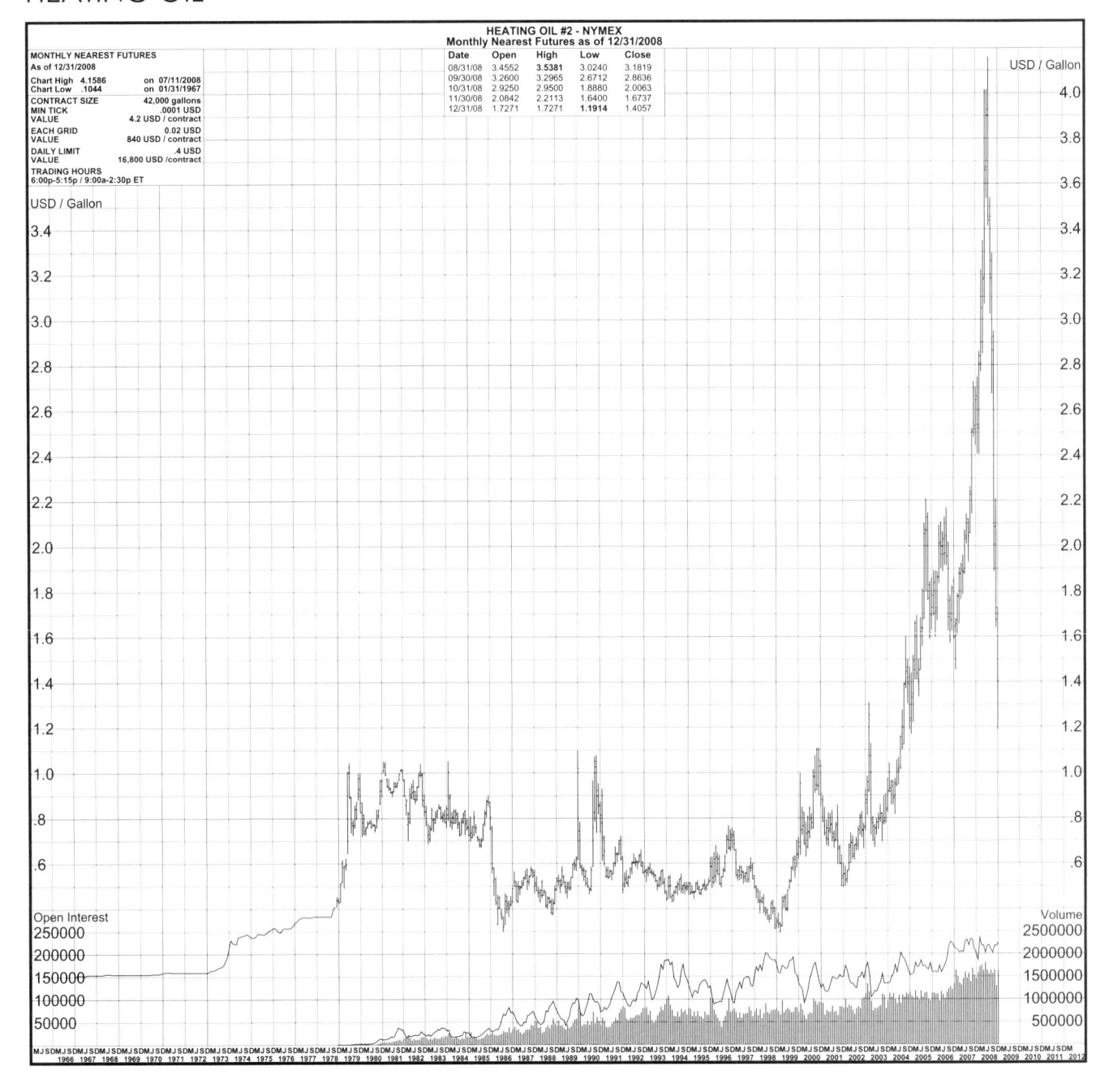

**HEATING OIL #2 - NYMEX**
Monthly Nearest Futures as of 12/31/2008

| Date | Open | High | Low | Close |
|---|---|---|---|---|
| 08/31/08 | 3.4552 | 3.5381 | 3.0240 | 3.1819 |
| 09/30/08 | 3.2600 | 3.2965 | 2.6712 | 2.8636 |
| 10/31/08 | 2.9250 | 2.9500 | 1.8880 | 2.0063 |
| 11/30/08 | 2.0842 | 2.2113 | 1.6400 | 1.6737 |
| 12/31/08 | 1.7271 | 1.7271 | 1.1914 | 1.4057 |

**MONTHLY NEAREST FUTURES** As of 12/31/2008
- Chart High 4.1586 on 07/11/2008
- Chart Low .1044 on 01/31/1967
- CONTRACT SIZE 42,000 gallons
- MIN TICK .0001 USD
- VALUE 4.2 USD / contract
- EACH GRID 0.02 USD
- VALUE 840 USD / contract
- DAILY LIMIT .4 USD
- VALUE 16,800 USD /contract
- TRADING HOURS 6:00p-5:15p / 9:00a-2:30p ET

## Annual High, Low and Settle of Heating Oil #2 Futures    In USD per Gallon

| Year | High | Low | Settle | Year | High | Low | Settle | Year | High | Low | Settle |
|---|---|---|---|---|---|---|---|---|---|---|---|
| 1967 | .1080 | .1044 | .1080 | 1981 | 1.0530 | .8945 | .9710 | 1995 | .6265 | .4405 | .5863 |
| 1968 | .1120 | .1080 | .1100 | 1982 | 1.0420 | .7001 | .8281 | 1996 | .7675 | .4890 | .7284 |
| 1969 | .1100 | .1100 | .1100 | 1983 | .8630 | .6850 | .8424 | 1997 | .7450 | .4890 | .4908 |
| 1970 | .1160 | .1100 | .1160 | 1984 | 1.0530 | .7185 | .7240 | 1998 | .4985 | .3080 | .3400 |
| 1971 | .1200 | .1185 | .1185 | 1985 | .9015 | .6685 | .8055 | 1999 | .7150 | .2920 | .6903 |
| 1972 | .1185 | .1185 | .1185 | 1986 | .7680 | .2995 | .4890 | 2000 | 1.1100 | .6275 | .9066 |
| 1973 | .2270 | .1209 | .2270 | 1987 | .5870 | .4260 | .5144 | 2001 | .8979 | .4930 | .5507 |
| 1974 | .2895 | .2450 | .2754 | 1988 | .5440 | .3700 | .5348 | 2002 | .9255 | .4990 | .8655 |
| 1975 | .3137 | .2739 | .3137 | 1989 | 1.1000 | .4440 | 1.0187 | 2003 | 1.3100 | .6690 | .9127 |
| 1976 | .3383 | .2954 | .3383 | 1990 | 1.0780 | .4630 | .8131 | 2004 | 1.6030 | .8150 | 1.2297 |
| 1977 | .3670 | .3430 | .3660 | 1991 | .9300 | .4660 | .4829 | 2005 | 2.2100 | 1.1680 | 1.7280 |
| 1978 | .4540 | .3550 | .4300 | 1992 | .6615 | .4915 | .5640 | 2006 | 2.1700 | 1.5700 | 1.5979 |
| 1979 | 1.0450 | .4300 | .8275 | 1993 | .6005 | .4325 | .4416 | 2007 | 2.7272 | 1.4530 | 2.6444 |
| 1980 | .9736 | .7170 | .9690 | 1994 | .5540 | .4260 | .5131 | 2008 | 4.1586 | 1.1914 | 1.4057 |

Futures begin trading 11/14/1978.    Source: CME Group; New York Mercantile Exchange

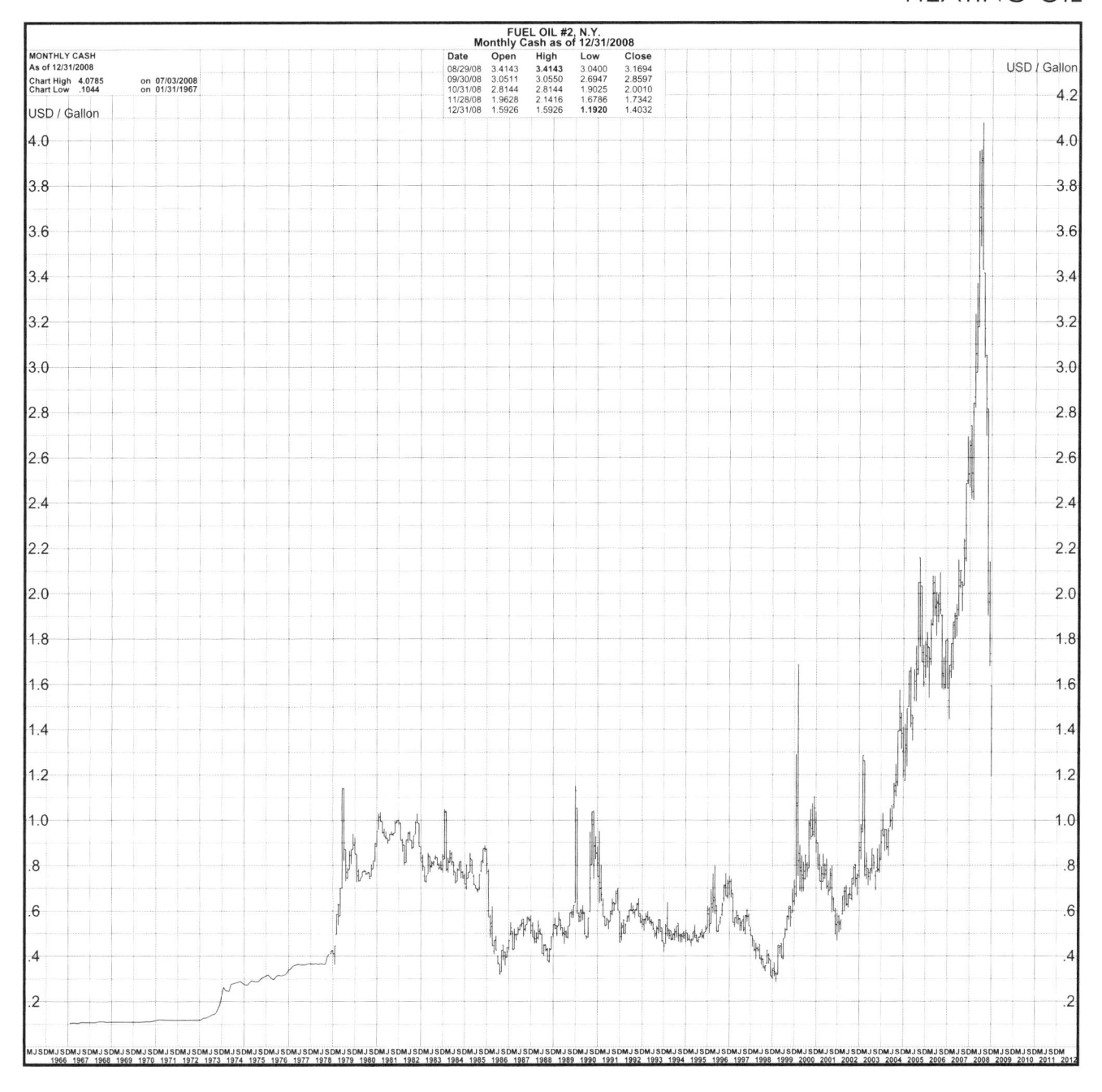

# HEATING OIL

**FUEL OIL #2, N.Y.**
Monthly Cash as of 12/31/2008

| Date | Open | High | Low | Close |
|---|---|---|---|---|
| 08/29/08 | 3.4143 | 3.4143 | 3.0400 | 3.1694 |
| 09/30/08 | 3.0511 | 3.0550 | 2.6947 | 2.8597 |
| 10/31/08 | 2.8144 | 2.8144 | 1.9025 | 2.0010 |
| 11/28/08 | 1.9628 | 2.1416 | 1.6786 | 1.7342 |
| 12/31/08 | 1.5926 | 1.5926 | 1.1920 | 1.4032 |

MONTHLY CASH
As of 12/31/2008
Chart High 4.0785 on 07/03/2008
Chart Low .1044 on 01/31/1967
USD / Gallon

## Annual High, Low and Settle of Heating Oil   In USD per Gallon

| Year | High | Low | Settle | Year | High | Low | Settle | Year | High | Low | Settle |
|---|---|---|---|---|---|---|---|---|---|---|---|
| 1967 | .1080 | .1044 | .1080 | 1981 | 1.0375 | .8950 | .9875 | 1995 | .6221 | .4410 | .5853 |
| 1968 | .1120 | .1080 | .1100 | 1982 | 1.0300 | .8000 | .8325 | 1996 | .7990 | .5024 | .7282 |
| 1969 | .1100 | .1100 | .1100 | 1983 | .8550 | .7225 | .8400 | 1997 | .7409 | .4906 | .4906 |
| 1970 | .1160 | .1100 | .1160 | 1984 | 1.0500 | .7175 | .7175 | 1998 | .4921 | .3008 | .3355 |
| 1971 | .1200 | .1185 | .1185 | 1985 | .8875 | .6800 | .8075 | 1999 | .7350 | .2842 | .7055 |
| 1972 | .1185 | .1185 | .1185 | 1986 | .7835 | .3175 | .4675 | 2000 | 1.6878 | .6595 | .9074 |
| 1973 | .2270 | .1209 | .2270 | 1987 | .5800 | .4275 | .5125 | 2001 | .8983 | .4691 | .5495 |
| 1974 | .2895 | .2450 | .2754 | 1988 | .5585 | .3700 | .5385 | 2002 | .9017 | .5049 | .8648 |
| 1975 | .3137 | .2739 | .3137 | 1989 | 1.1500 | .4520 | 1.1300 | 2003 | 1.2847 | .6898 | .9027 |
| 1976 | .3383 | .2954 | .3383 | 1990 | 1.0535 | .4725 | .8095 | 2004 | 1.5758 | .8405 | 1.2165 |
| 1977 | .3670 | .3430 | .3660 | 1991 | .9510 | .4595 | .4615 | 2005 | 2.1585 | 1.1740 | 1.7243 |
| 1978 | .4275 | .3550 | .4100 | 1992 | .6555 | .4670 | .5610 | 2006 | 2.0944 | 1.5400 | 1.5829 |
| 1979 | 1.1400 | .3620 | .8500 | 1993 | .5975 | .4172 | .4440 | 2007 | 2.6941 | 1.4432 | 2.6531 |
| 1980 | .9500 | .7250 | .9500 | 1994 | .6375 | .4530 | .5140 | 2008 | 4.0785 | 1.1920 | 1.4032 |

*Source: CME Group; New York Mercantile Exchange*

# HEATING OIL

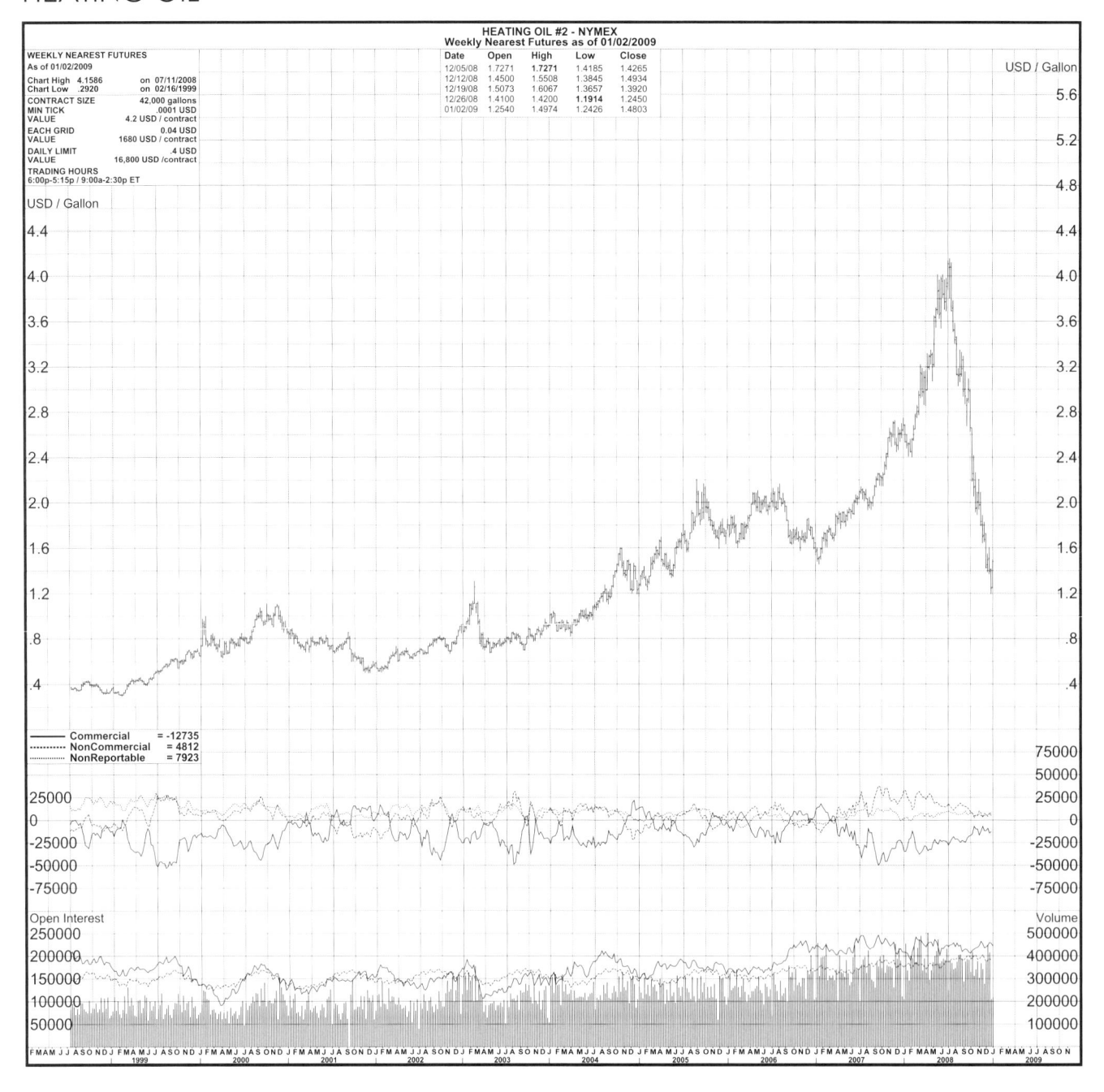

## Quarterly High, Low and Settle of Heating Oil #2 Futures    In USD per Gallon

| Quarter | High | Low | Settle | Quarter | High | Low | Settle | Quarter | High | Low | Settle |
|---|---|---|---|---|---|---|---|---|---|---|---|
| 03/2000 | .9975 | .6355 | .7833 | 03/2003 | 1.3100 | .7250 | .7924 | 03/2006 | 1.8920 | 1.5970 | 1.8618 |
| 06/2000 | .8500 | .6275 | .8414 | 06/2003 | .8070 | .6690 | .7808 | 06/2006 | 2.1080 | 1.8338 | 1.9642 |
| 09/2000 | 1.0760 | .7490 | .9240 | 09/2003 | .8605 | .6938 | .7778 | 09/2006 | 2.1700 | 1.6249 | 1.6846 |
| 12/2000 | 1.1100 | .8500 | .9066 | 12/2003 | .9760 | .7690 | .9127 | 12/2006 | 1.8611 | 1.5700 | 1.5979 |
| 03/2001 | .8979 | .6770 | .7550 | 03/2004 | 1.0430 | .8560 | .8864 | 03/2007 | 1.9055 | 1.4530 | 1.8794 |
| 06/2001 | .8350 | .6735 | .7125 | 06/2004 | 1.0674 | .8150 | 1.0055 | 06/2007 | 2.0710 | 1.7638 | 2.0319 |
| 09/2001 | .8575 | .5950 | .6635 | 09/2004 | 1.3960 | 1.0120 | 1.3917 | 09/2007 | 2.2640 | 1.9290 | 2.2379 |
| 12/2001 | .6793 | .4930 | .5507 | 12/2004 | 1.6030 | 1.1900 | 1.2297 | 12/2007 | 2.7272 | 2.1415 | 2.6444 |
| 03/2002 | .6865 | .4990 | .6689 | 03/2005 | 1.6700 | 1.1680 | 1.6576 | 03/2008 | 3.2220 | 2.4042 | 3.0492 |
| 06/2002 | .7350 | .5995 | .6796 | 06/2005 | 1.6950 | 1.3340 | 1.6191 | 06/2008 | 4.0153 | 2.8489 | 3.9029 |
| 09/2002 | .8183 | .6540 | .8018 | 09/2005 | 2.2100 | 1.5560 | 2.0673 | 09/2008 | 4.1586 | 2.6712 | 2.8636 |
| 12/2002 | .9255 | .6630 | .8655 | 12/2005 | 2.1470 | 1.5875 | 1.7280 | 12/2008 | 2.9500 | 1.1914 | 1.4057 |

*Source: CME Group; New York Mercantile Exchange*

# HEATING OIL

**FUEL OIL #2, N.Y.**
Weekly Cash as of 01/02/2009

| Date | Open | High | Low | Close |
|---|---|---|---|---|
| 12/05/08 | 1.5926 | **1.5926** | 1.3890 | 1.3890 |
| 12/12/08 | 1.4529 | 1.4716 | 1.3677 | 1.4534 |
| 12/19/08 | 1.4351 | 1.4353 | 1.3504 | 1.3682 |
| 12/26/08 | 1.2625 | 1.3225 | **1.1920** | 1.1920 |
| 01/02/09 | 1.2778 | 1.4653 | 1.2778 | 1.4653 |

WEEKLY CASH
As of 01/02/2009
Chart High 4.0785 on 07/03/2008
Chart Low .2842 on 02/16/1999
USD / Gallon

## Quarterly High, Low and Settle of Heating Oil      In USD per Gallon

| Quarter | High | Low | Settle | Quarter | High | Low | Settle | Quarter | High | Low | Settle |
|---|---|---|---|---|---|---|---|---|---|---|---|
| 03/2000 | 1.6878 | .6595 | .7896 | 03/2003 | 1.2847 | .7512 | .7952 | 03/2006 | 1.8856 | 1.5400 | 1.8641 |
| 06/2000 | .8465 | .6816 | .8447 | 06/2003 | .8571 | .7110 | .7791 | 06/2006 | 2.0792 | 1.8124 | 1.9575 |
| 09/2000 | 1.0498 | .7468 | .9253 | 09/2003 | .8732 | .6898 | .7748 | 09/2006 | 2.0944 | 1.5797 | 1.6471 |
| 12/2000 | 1.1052 | .8551 | .9074 | 12/2003 | .9562 | .7666 | .9027 | 12/2006 | 1.7952 | 1.5739 | 1.5829 |
| 03/2001 | .8983 | .6895 | .7630 | 03/2004 | 1.0330 | .8628 | .8822 | 03/2007 | 1.8745 | 1.4432 | 1.8742 |
| 06/2001 | .8512 | .6952 | .7068 | 06/2004 | 1.0629 | .8405 | 1.0096 | 06/2007 | 2.1496 | 1.8015 | 2.0331 |
| 09/2001 | .7983 | .5926 | .6605 | 09/2004 | 1.3930 | 1.0506 | 1.3930 | 09/2007 | 2.2421 | 1.9193 | 2.2316 |
| 12/2001 | .6591 | .4691 | .5495 | 12/2004 | 1.5758 | 1.1882 | 1.2165 | 12/2007 | 2.6941 | 2.1408 | 2.6531 |
| 03/2002 | .6652 | .5049 | .6652 | 03/2005 | 1.6579 | 1.1740 | 1.6579 | 03/2008 | 3.2345 | 2.4103 | 3.0592 |
| 06/2002 | .7133 | .5975 | .6733 | 06/2005 | 1.6760 | 1.3491 | 1.6124 | 06/2008 | 3.9602 | 2.9772 | 3.9100 |
| 09/2002 | .7960 | .6450 | .7893 | 09/2005 | 2.1585 | 1.5227 | 2.0486 | 09/2008 | 4.0785 | 2.6947 | 2.8597 |
| 12/2002 | .9017 | .6680 | .8648 | 12/2005 | 2.0334 | 1.5872 | 1.7243 | 12/2008 | 2.8144 | 1.1920 | 1.4032 |

*Source: CME Group; New York Mercantile Exchange*

# NATURAL GAS

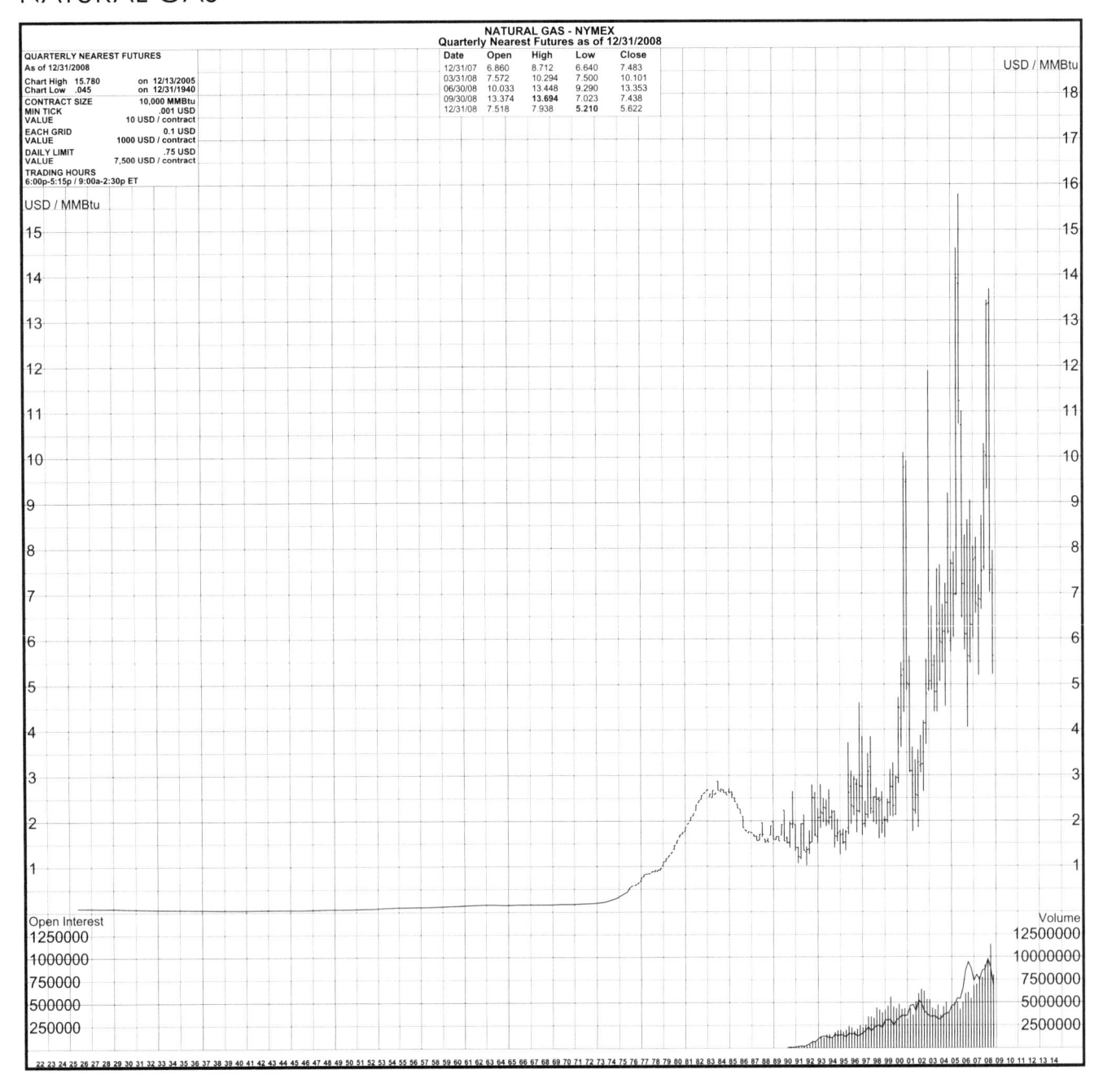

**NATURAL GAS - NYMEX**
Quarterly Nearest Futures as of 12/31/2008

| Date | Open | High | Low | Close |
|---|---|---|---|---|
| 12/31/07 | 6.860 | 8.712 | 6.640 | 7.483 |
| 03/31/08 | 7.572 | 10.294 | 7.500 | 10.101 |
| 06/30/08 | 10.033 | 13.448 | 9.290 | 13.353 |
| 09/30/08 | 13.374 | 13.694 | 7.023 | 7.438 |
| 12/31/08 | 7.518 | 7.938 | 5.210 | 5.622 |

**QUARTERLY NEAREST FUTURES**
As of 12/31/2008
Chart High 15.780 on 12/13/2005
Chart Low .045 on 12/31/1940
CONTRACT SIZE 10,000 MMBtu
MIN TICK .001 USD
VALUE 10 USD / contract
EACH GRID 0.1 USD
VALUE 1000 USD / contract
DAILY LIMIT .75 USD
VALUE 7,500 USD / contract
TRADING HOURS
6:00p-5:15p / 9:00a-2:30p ET

## Annual High, Low and Settle of Natural Gas — In USD per MMBtu

| Year | High | Low | Settle | Year | High | Low | Settle | Year | High | Low | Settle |
|---|---|---|---|---|---|---|---|---|---|---|---|
| 1925 | .094 | .094 | .094 | 1939 | .049 | .049 | .049 | 1953 | .092 | .092 | .092 |
| 1926 | .095 | .095 | .095 | 1940 | .045 | .045 | .045 | 1954 | .101 | .101 | .101 |
| 1927 | .088 | .088 | .088 | 1941 | .049 | .049 | .049 | 1955 | .104 | .104 | .104 |
| 1928 | .089 | .089 | .089 | 1942 | .051 | .051 | .051 | 1956 | .108 | .108 | .108 |
| 1929 | .082 | .082 | .082 | 1943 | .052 | .052 | .052 | 1957 | .110 | .110 | .110 |
| 1930 | .076 | .076 | .076 | 1944 | .051 | .051 | .051 | 1958 | .120 | .120 | .120 |
| 1931 | .070 | .070 | .070 | 1945 | .049 | .049 | .049 | 1959 | .130 | .130 | .130 |
| 1932 | .064 | .064 | .064 | 1946 | .053 | .053 | .053 | 1960 | .140 | .140 | .140 |
| 1933 | .062 | .062 | .062 | 1947 | .060 | .060 | .060 | 1961 | .150 | .150 | .150 |
| 1934 | .060 | .060 | .060 | 1948 | .065 | .065 | .065 | 1962 | .160 | .160 | .160 |
| 1935 | .058 | .058 | .058 | 1949 | .063 | .063 | .063 | 1963 | .160 | .160 | .160 |
| 1936 | .055 | .055 | .055 | 1950 | .065 | .065 | .065 | 1964 | .150 | .150 | .150 |
| 1937 | .051 | .051 | .051 | 1951 | .073 | .073 | .073 | 1965 | .160 | .160 | .160 |
| 1938 | .049 | .049 | .049 | 1952 | .078 | .078 | .078 | 1966 | .160 | .160 | .160 |

Henry Hub.  Data continued on page 80.  *Source: CME Group; New York Mercantile Exchange*

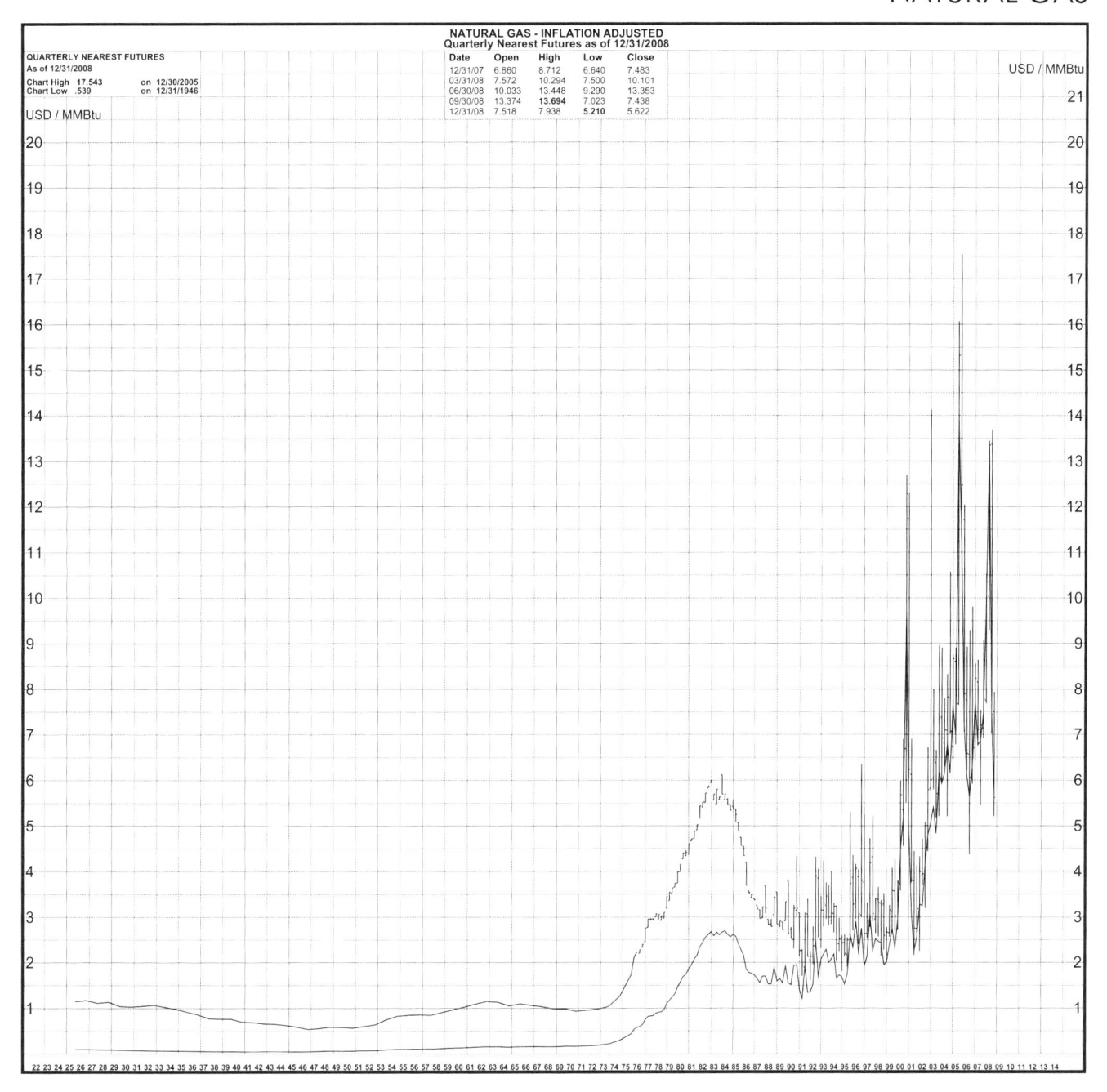

# NATURAL GAS

**QUARTERLY NEAREST FUTURES**
As of 12/31/2008
Chart High 17.543 on 12/30/2005
Chart Low .539 on 12/31/1946
USD / MMBtu

**NATURAL GAS - INFLATION ADJUSTED**
Quarterly Nearest Futures as of 12/31/2008

| Date | Open | High | Low | Close |
|---|---|---|---|---|
| 12/31/07 | 6.860 | 8.712 | 6.640 | 7.483 |
| 03/31/08 | 7.572 | 10.294 | 7.500 | 10.101 |
| 06/30/08 | 10.033 | 13.448 | 9.290 | 13.353 |
| 09/30/08 | 13.374 | 13.694 | 7.023 | 7.438 |
| 12/31/08 | 7.518 | 7.938 | 5.210 | 5.622 |

## Annual High, Low and Settle of Natural Gas   In USD per MMBtu

| Year | High | Low | Settle | Year | High | Low | Settle | Year | High | Low | Settle |
|---|---|---|---|---|---|---|---|---|---|---|---|
| 1925 | .094 | .094 | .094 | 1939 | .049 | .049 | .049 | 1953 | .092 | .092 | .092 |
| 1926 | .095 | .095 | .095 | 1940 | .045 | .045 | .045 | 1954 | .101 | .101 | .101 |
| 1927 | .088 | .088 | .088 | 1941 | .049 | .049 | .049 | 1955 | .104 | .104 | .104 |
| 1928 | .089 | .089 | .089 | 1942 | .051 | .051 | .051 | 1956 | .108 | .108 | .108 |
| 1929 | .082 | .082 | .082 | 1943 | .052 | .052 | .052 | 1957 | .110 | .110 | .110 |
| 1930 | .076 | .076 | .076 | 1944 | .051 | .051 | .051 | 1958 | .120 | .120 | .120 |
| 1931 | .070 | .070 | .070 | 1945 | .049 | .049 | .049 | 1959 | .130 | .130 | .130 |
| 1932 | .064 | .064 | .064 | 1946 | .053 | .053 | .053 | 1960 | .140 | .140 | .140 |
| 1933 | .062 | .062 | .062 | 1947 | .060 | .060 | .060 | 1961 | .150 | .150 | .150 |
| 1934 | .060 | .060 | .060 | 1948 | .065 | .065 | .065 | 1962 | .160 | .160 | .160 |
| 1935 | .058 | .058 | .058 | 1949 | .063 | .063 | .063 | 1963 | .160 | .160 | .160 |
| 1936 | .055 | .055 | .055 | 1950 | .065 | .065 | .065 | 1964 | .150 | .150 | .150 |
| 1937 | .051 | .051 | .051 | 1951 | .073 | .073 | .073 | 1965 | .160 | .160 | .160 |
| 1938 | .049 | .049 | .049 | 1952 | .078 | .078 | .078 | 1966 | .160 | .160 | .160 |

Henry Hub.   Data continued on page 81.   *Source: CME Group; New York Mercantile Exchange*

# NATURAL GAS

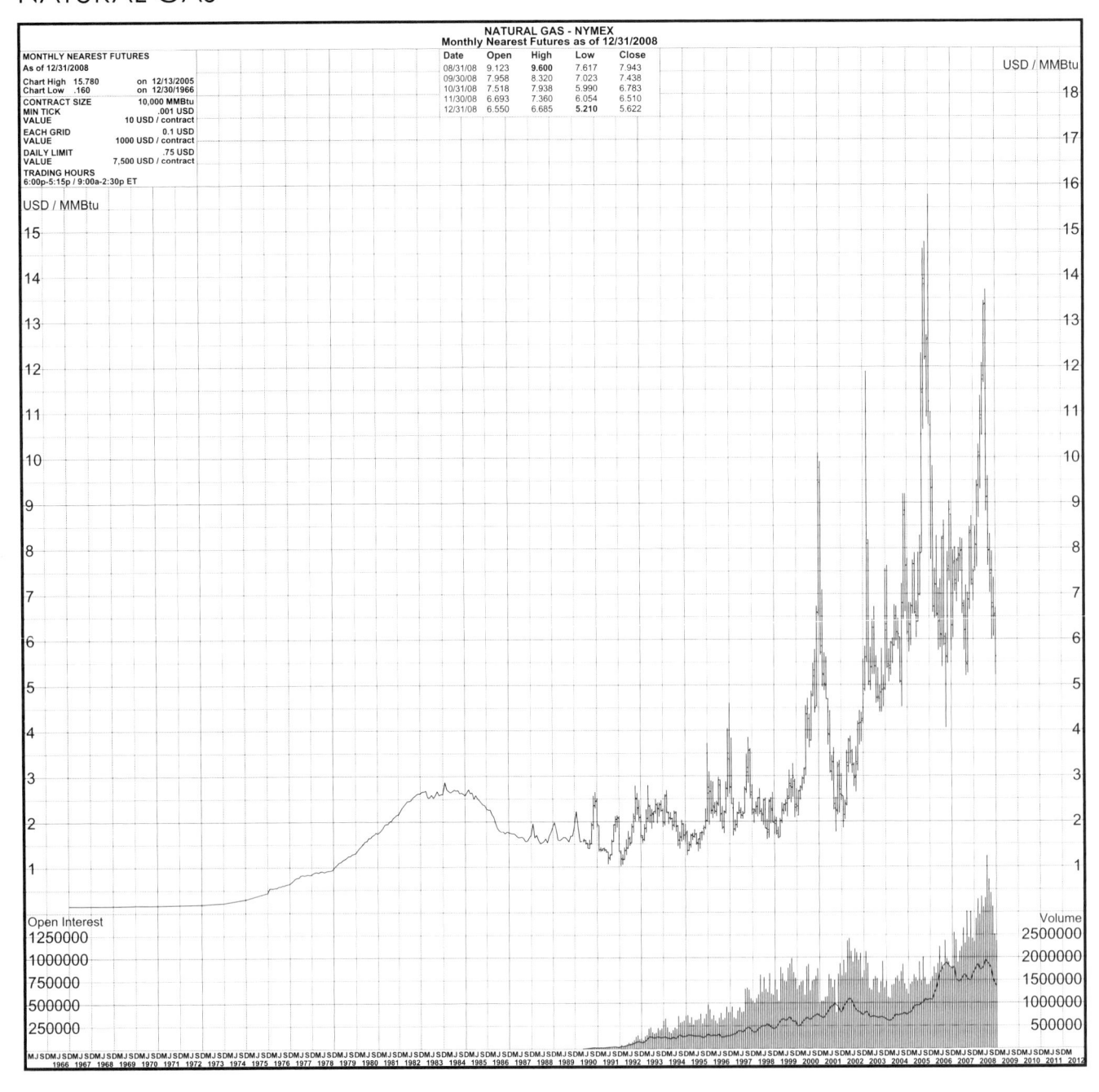

**NATURAL GAS - NYMEX**
Monthly Nearest Futures as of 12/31/2008

| Date | Open | High | Low | Close |
|---|---|---|---|---|
| 08/31/08 | 9.123 | 9.600 | 7.617 | 7.943 |
| 09/30/08 | 7.958 | 8.320 | 7.023 | 7.438 |
| 10/31/08 | 7.518 | 7.938 | 5.990 | 6.783 |
| 11/30/08 | 6.693 | 7.360 | 6.054 | 6.510 |
| 12/31/08 | 6.550 | 6.685 | 5.210 | 5.622 |

**MONTHLY NEAREST FUTURES**
As of 12/31/2008
Chart High  15.780  on 12/13/2005
Chart Low  .160  on 12/30/1966
CONTRACT SIZE  10,000 MMBtu
MIN TICK  .001 USD
VALUE  10 USD / contract
EACH GRID  0.1 USD
VALUE  1000 USD / contract
DAILY LIMIT  .75 USD
VALUE  7,500 USD / contract
TRADING HOURS
6:00p-5:15p / 9:00a-2:30p ET

## Annual High, Low and Settle of Natural Gas Futures     In USD per MMBtu

| Year | High | Low | Settle | Year | High | Low | Settle | Year | High | Low | Settle |
|---|---|---|---|---|---|---|---|---|---|---|---|
| 1967 | .160 | .160 | .160 | 1981 | 2.160 | 1.770 | 2.160 | 1995 | 3.720 | 1.250 | 2.619 |
| 1968 | .160 | .160 | .160 | 1982 | 2.620 | 2.230 | 2.620 | 1996 | 4.600 | 1.735 | 2.757 |
| 1969 | .170 | .170 | .170 | 1983 | 2.680 | 2.520 | 2.610 | 1997 | 3.850 | 1.680 | 2.264 |
| 1970 | .170 | .170 | .170 | 1984 | 2.870 | 2.570 | 2.570 | 1998 | 2.725 | 1.600 | 1.945 |
| 1971 | .180 | .180 | .180 | 1985 | 2.710 | 2.280 | 2.280 | 1999 | 3.275 | 1.625 | 2.329 |
| 1972 | .190 | .190 | .190 | 1986 | 2.260 | 1.730 | 1.760 | 2000 | 10.100 | 2.125 | 9.775 |
| 1973 | .220 | .220 | .220 | 1987 | 1.740 | 1.560 | 1.700 | 2001 | 9.916 | 1.760 | 2.570 |
| 1974 | .300 | .300 | .300 | 1988 | 1.960 | 1.520 | 1.890 | 2002 | 5.560 | 1.850 | 4.789 |
| 1975 | .440 | .440 | .440 | 1989 | 1.980 | 1.550 | 1.920 | 2003 | 11.899 | 4.390 | 6.189 |
| 1976 | .640 | .540 | .640 | 1990 | 2.650 | 1.396 | 1.950 | 2004 | 9.200 | 4.520 | 6.149 |
| 1977 | .840 | .670 | .840 | 1991 | 2.140 | 1.060 | 1.343 | 2005 | 15.780 | 5.710 | 11.225 |
| 1978 | .960 | .870 | .960 | 1992 | 2.790 | 1.020 | 1.687 | 2006 | 11.000 | 4.050 | 6.299 |
| 1979 | 1.310 | 1.020 | 1.310 | 1993 | 2.800 | 1.521 | 1.997 | 2007 | 8.712 | 5.192 | 7.483 |
| 1980 | 1.760 | 1.370 | 1.740 | 1994 | 2.690 | 1.395 | 1.725 | 2008 | 13.694 | 5.210 | 5.622 |

Futures begin trading 04/04/1990.     Source: *CME Group; New York Mercantile Exchange*

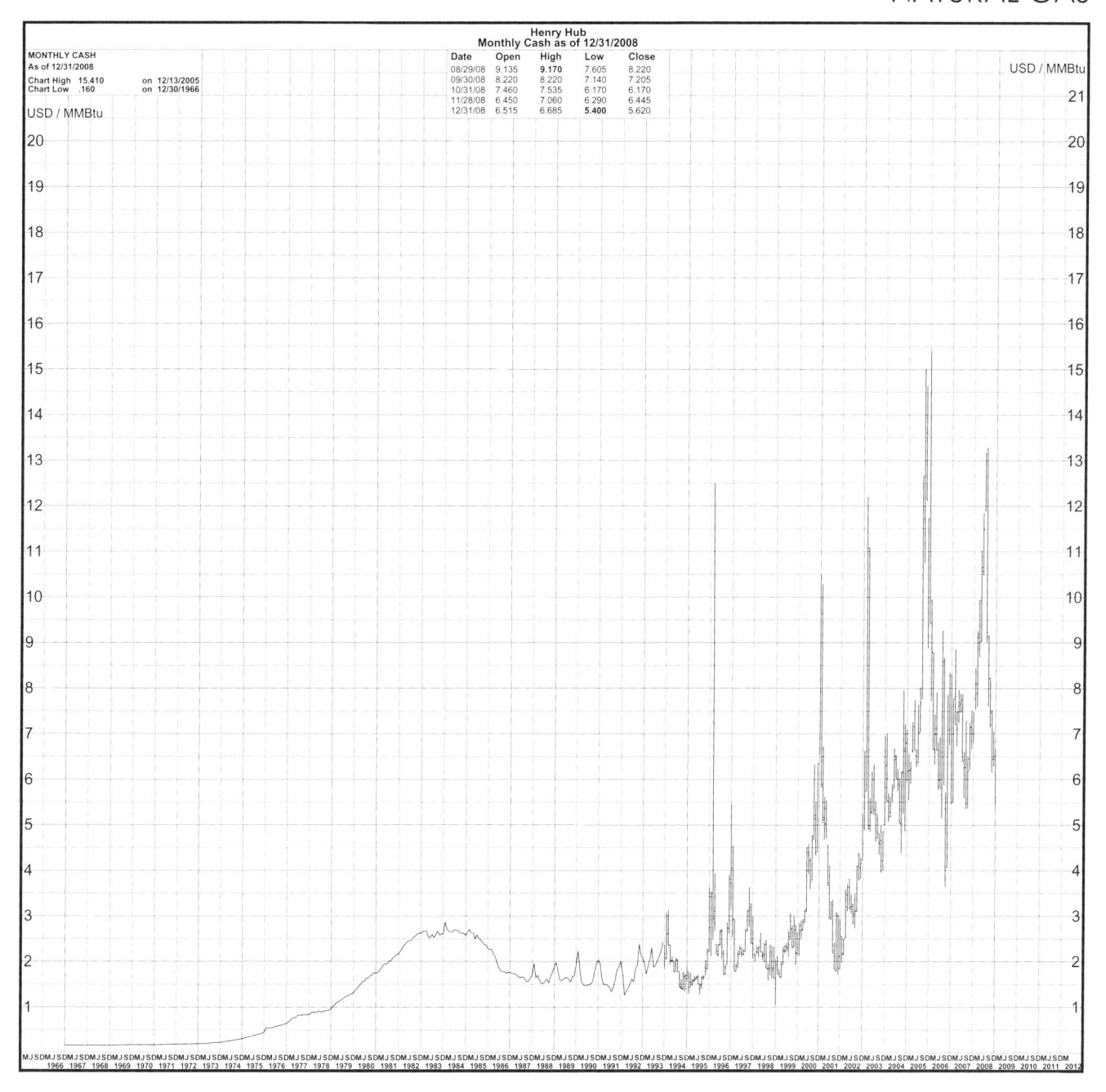

# NATURAL GAS

**Henry Hub Monthly Cash as of 12/31/2008**

| Date | Open | High | Low | Close |
|---|---|---|---|---|
| 08/29/08 | 9.135 | 9.170 | 7.605 | 8.220 |
| 09/30/08 | 8.220 | 8.220 | 7.140 | 7.205 |
| 10/31/08 | 7.460 | 7.535 | 6.170 | 6.170 |
| 11/28/08 | 6.450 | 7.060 | 6.290 | 6.445 |
| 12/31/08 | 6.515 | 6.685 | 5.400 | 5.620 |

MONTHLY CASH As of 12/31/2008
Chart High 15.410 on 12/13/2005
Chart Low .160 on 12/30/1966
USD / MMBtu

## Annual High, Low and Settle of Natural Gas — In USD per MMBtu

| Year | High | Low | Settle | Year | High | Low | Settle | Year | High | Low | Settle |
|---|---|---|---|---|---|---|---|---|---|---|---|
| 1967 | .160 | .160 | .160 | 1981 | 2.160 | 1.770 | 2.160 | 1995 | 3.625 | 1.280 | 2.750 |
| 1968 | .160 | .160 | .160 | 1982 | 2.620 | 2.230 | 2.620 | 1996 | 12.500 | 1.695 | 4.050 |
| 1969 | .170 | .170 | .170 | 1983 | 2.680 | 2.520 | 2.610 | 1997 | 4.550 | 1.785 | 2.265 |
| 1970 | .170 | .170 | .170 | 1984 | 2.870 | 2.570 | 2.570 | 1998 | 2.635 | 1.035 | 1.935 |
| 1971 | .180 | .180 | .180 | 1985 | 2.710 | 2.280 | 2.280 | 1999 | 3.075 | 1.645 | 2.305 |
| 1972 | .190 | .190 | .190 | 1986 | 2.260 | 1.730 | 1.760 | 2000 | 10.500 | 2.140 | 10.415 |
| 1973 | .220 | .220 | .220 | 1987 | 1.740 | 1.560 | 1.700 | 2001 | 10.295 | 1.695 | 2.720 |
| 1974 | .300 | .300 | .300 | 1988 | 1.960 | 1.520 | 1.890 | 2002 | 5.250 | 1.980 | 4.585 |
| 1975 | .440 | .440 | .440 | 1989 | 1.980 | 1.550 | 1.920 | 2003 | 12.200 | 3.965 | 5.825 |
| 1976 | .640 | .540 | .640 | 1990 | 2.230 | 1.470 | 2.040 | 2004 | 7.960 | 4.385 | 6.185 |
| 1977 | .840 | .670 | .840 | 1991 | 2.000 | 1.340 | 2.000 | 2005 | 15.410 | 5.560 | 9.435 |
| 1978 | .960 | .870 | .960 | 1992 | 2.380 | 1.260 | 2.070 | 2006 | 9.945 | 3.655 | 5.475 |
| 1979 | 1.310 | 1.020 | 1.310 | 1993 | 2.430 | 1.720 | 2.080 | 2007 | 8.860 | 5.350 | 7.465 |
| 1980 | 1.760 | 1.370 | 1.740 | 1994 | 3.130 | 1.345 | 1.705 | 2008 | 13.275 | 5.400 | 5.620 |

Henry Hub.   Data continued from page 78.   *Source: CME Group; New York Mercantile Exchange*

# NATURAL GAS

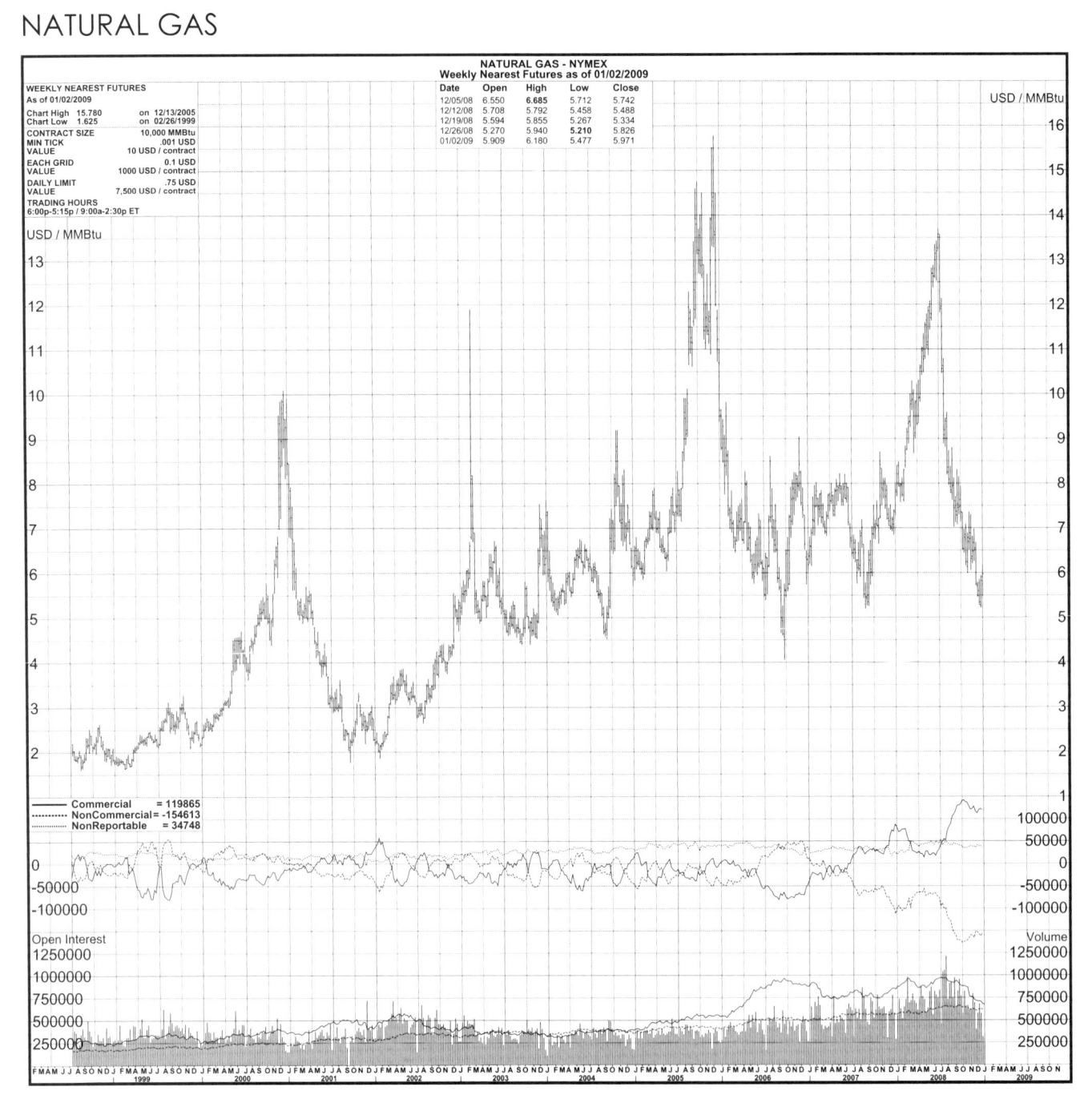

## Quarterly High, Low and Settle of Natural Gas Futures    In USD per Gallon

| Quarter | High | Low | Settle | Quarter | High | Low | Settle | Quarter | High | Low | Settle |
|---------|------|-----|--------|---------|------|-----|--------|---------|------|-----|--------|
| 03/2000 | 2.980 | 2.125 | 2.945 | 03/2003 | 11.899 | 4.850 | 5.060 | 03/2006 | 11.000 | 6.450 | 7.210 |
| 06/2000 | 4.715 | 2.815 | 4.476 | 06/2003 | 6.719 | 4.865 | 5.411 | 06/2006 | 8.280 | 5.750 | 6.104 |
| 09/2000 | 5.479 | 3.610 | 5.186 | 09/2003 | 5.640 | 4.390 | 4.830 | 09/2006 | 8.619 | 4.050 | 5.620 |
| 12/2000 | 10.100 | 4.380 | 9.775 | 12/2003 | 7.550 | 4.390 | 6.189 | 12/2006 | 9.050 | 5.460 | 6.299 |
| 03/2001 | 9.916 | 4.870 | 5.025 | 03/2004 | 7.630 | 5.060 | 5.933 | 03/2007 | 8.035 | 6.030 | 7.730 |
| 06/2001 | 5.620 | 3.055 | 3.096 | 06/2004 | 6.760 | 5.460 | 6.155 | 06/2007 | 8.230 | 6.551 | 6.773 |
| 09/2001 | 3.620 | 1.760 | 2.244 | 09/2004 | 7.230 | 4.520 | 6.795 | 09/2007 | 7.192 | 5.192 | 6.870 |
| 12/2001 | 3.340 | 2.140 | 2.570 | 12/2004 | 9.200 | 6.100 | 6.149 | 12/2007 | 8.712 | 6.640 | 7.483 |
| 03/2002 | 3.560 | 1.850 | 3.283 | 03/2005 | 7.740 | 5.710 | 7.653 | 03/2008 | 10.294 | 7.500 | 10.101 |
| 06/2002 | 3.875 | 3.050 | 3.245 | 06/2005 | 7.915 | 6.030 | 6.981 | 06/2008 | 13.448 | 9.290 | 13.353 |
| 09/2002 | 4.200 | 2.640 | 4.138 | 09/2005 | 14.600 | 6.949 | 13.921 | 09/2008 | 13.694 | 7.023 | 7.438 |
| 12/2002 | 5.560 | 3.670 | 4.789 | 12/2005 | 15.780 | 10.720 | 11.225 | 12/2008 | 7.938 | 5.210 | 5.622 |

*Source: CME Group; New York Mercantile Exchange*

# NATURAL GAS

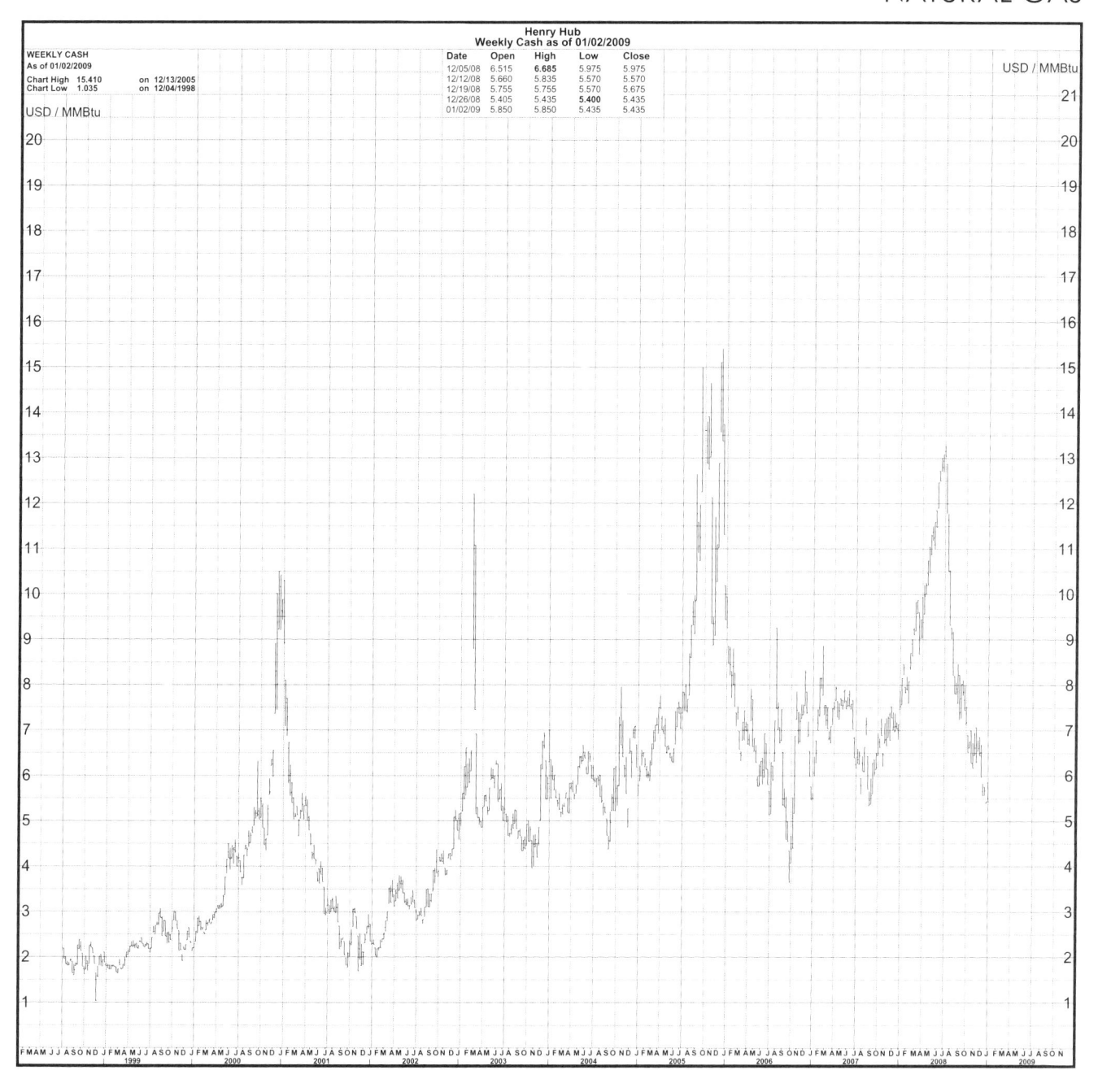

**WEEKLY CASH**
As of 01/02/2009
Chart High 15.410 on 12/13/2005
Chart Low 1.035 on 12/04/1998

USD / MMBtu

**Henry Hub**
Weekly Cash as of 01/02/2009

| Date | Open | High | Low | Close |
|---|---|---|---|---|
| 12/05/08 | 6.515 | 6.685 | 5.975 | 5.975 |
| 12/12/08 | 5.660 | 5.835 | 5.570 | 5.570 |
| 12/19/08 | 5.755 | 5.755 | 5.570 | 5.675 |
| 12/26/08 | 5.405 | 5.435 | 5.400 | 5.435 |
| 01/02/09 | 5.850 | 5.850 | 5.435 | 5.435 |

USD / MMBtu

## Quarterly High, Low and Settle of Natural Gas     In USD per Gallon

| Quarter | High | Low | Settle | Quarter | High | Low | Settle | Quarter | High | Low | Settle |
|---|---|---|---|---|---|---|---|---|---|---|---|
| 03/2000 | 2.935 | 2.140 | 2.870 | 03/2003 | 12.200 | 4.880 | 4.985 | 03/2006 | 9.945 | 6.325 | 6.985 |
| 06/2000 | 4.585 | 2.845 | 4.330 | 06/2003 | 6.335 | 4.860 | 5.330 | 06/2006 | 7.920 | 5.765 | 5.805 |
| 09/2000 | 6.325 | 3.585 | 5.130 | 09/2003 | 5.530 | 4.345 | 4.580 | 09/2006 | 9.250 | 3.655 | 3.655 |
| 12/2000 | 10.500 | 4.340 | 10.415 | 12/2003 | 6.950 | 3.965 | 5.825 | 12/2006 | 8.325 | 4.075 | 5.475 |
| 03/2001 | 10.295 | 4.670 | 5.355 | 03/2004 | 7.015 | 5.080 | 5.445 | 03/2007 | 8.860 | 5.500 | 7.480 |
| 06/2001 | 5.545 | 2.955 | 2.955 | 06/2004 | 6.680 | 5.485 | 6.030 | 06/2007 | 7.970 | 6.395 | 6.395 |
| 09/2001 | 3.355 | 1.820 | 1.820 | 09/2004 | 6.235 | 4.385 | 6.165 | 09/2007 | 7.295 | 5.350 | 6.180 |
| 12/2001 | 3.085 | 1.695 | 2.720 | 12/2004 | 7.960 | 4.865 | 6.185 | 12/2007 | 7.525 | 6.205 | 7.465 |
| 03/2002 | 3.585 | 1.980 | 3.205 | 03/2005 | 7.275 | 5.560 | 7.170 | 03/2008 | 9.935 | 7.530 | 9.935 |
| 06/2002 | 3.805 | 3.050 | 3.215 | 06/2005 | 7.760 | 6.290 | 7.025 | 06/2008 | 13.155 | 9.030 | 13.155 |
| 09/2002 | 4.100 | 2.730 | 4.100 | 09/2005 | 15.000 | 7.035 | 15.000 | 09/2008 | 13.275 | 7.140 | 7.205 |
| 12/2002 | 5.250 | 3.780 | 4.585 | 12/2005 | 15.410 | 8.880 | 9.435 | 12/2008 | 7.535 | 5.400 | 5.620 |

*Henry Hub.    Source: CME Group; New York Mercantile Exchange*

# PROPANE

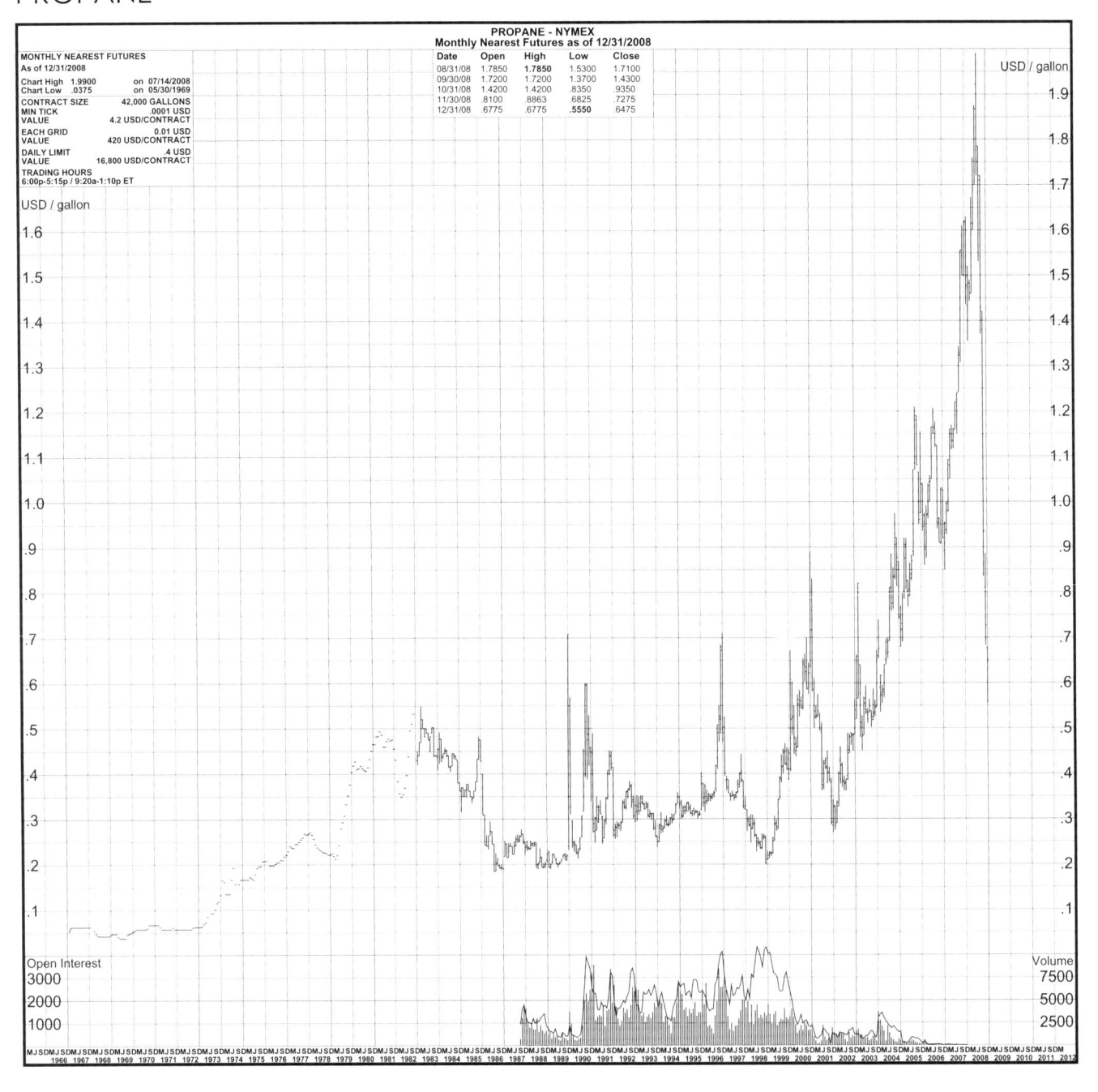

**PROPANE - NYMEX**
Monthly Nearest Futures as of 12/31/2008

| Date | Open | High | Low | Close |
|---|---|---|---|---|
| 08/31/08 | 1.7850 | 1.7850 | 1.5300 | 1.7100 |
| 09/30/08 | 1.7200 | 1.7200 | 1.3700 | 1.4300 |
| 10/31/08 | 1.4200 | 1.4200 | .8350 | .9350 |
| 11/30/08 | .8100 | .8863 | .6825 | .7275 |
| 12/31/08 | .6775 | .6775 | .5550 | .6475 |

**MONTHLY NEAREST FUTURES**
As of 12/31/2008
Chart High 1.9900 on 07/14/2008
Chart Low .0375 on 05/30/1969
CONTRACT SIZE 42,000 GALLONS
MIN TICK .0001 USD
VALUE 4.2 USD/CONTRACT
EACH GRID 0.01 USD
VALUE 420 USD/CONTRACT
DAILY LIMIT .4 USD
VALUE 16,800 USD/CONTRACT
TRADING HOURS
6:00p-5:15p / 9:20a-1:10p ET

## Annual High, Low and Settle of Propane Futures    In USD per Gallon

| Year | High | Low | Settle | Year | High | Low | Settle | Year | High | Low | Settle |
|---|---|---|---|---|---|---|---|---|---|---|---|
| 1967 | .0625 | .0519 | .0625 | 1981 | .4930 | .4550 | .4550 | 1995 | .4025 | .3000 | .3935 |
| 1968 | .0625 | .0425 | .0455 | 1982 | .5320 | .3490 | .5320 | 1996 | .7100 | .3150 | .4900 |
| 1969 | .0525 | .0375 | .0525 | 1983 | .5500 | .4075 | .4550 | 1997 | .5260 | .3200 | .3292 |
| 1970 | .0673 | .0545 | .0673 | 1984 | .4925 | .3625 | .3625 | 1998 | .3200 | .2000 | .2125 |
| 1971 | .0673 | .0573 | .0573 | 1985 | .4825 | .3150 | .4275 | 1999 | .4675 | .2125 | .4450 |
| 1972 | .0621 | .0573 | .0621 | 1986 | .4000 | .1850 | .1900 | 2000 | .8900 | .4050 | .8650 |
| 1973 | .1328 | .0621 | .1328 | 1987 | .2775 | .2150 | .2375 | 2001 | .8300 | .2700 | .3260 |
| 1974 | .1928 | .1348 | .1664 | 1988 | .2525 | .1890 | .2235 | 2002 | .5650 | .2750 | .5400 |
| 1975 | .2075 | .1662 | .2075 | 1989 | .7085 | .1900 | .7080 | 2003 | .8200 | .4510 | .6600 |
| 1976 | .2213 | .1975 | .2213 | 1990 | .6000 | .2125 | .4478 | 2004 | .9740 | .5350 | .7450 |
| 1977 | .2680 | .2290 | .2670 | 1991 | .4900 | .2450 | .2750 | 2005 | 1.2100 | .6800 | 1.0375 |
| 1978 | .2700 | .2210 | .2210 | 1992 | .3850 | .2560 | .3300 | 2006 | 1.2075 | .8600 | .9200 |
| 1979 | .4040 | .2120 | .4040 | 1993 | .3535 | .2385 | .2495 | 2007 | 1.6200 | .8500 | 1.6200 |
| 1980 | .4650 | .4060 | .4650 | 1994 | .3600 | .2485 | .3329 | 2008 | 1.9900 | .5550 | .6475 |

Futures begin trading 08/21/1987.    Source: CME Group; New York Mercantile Exchange

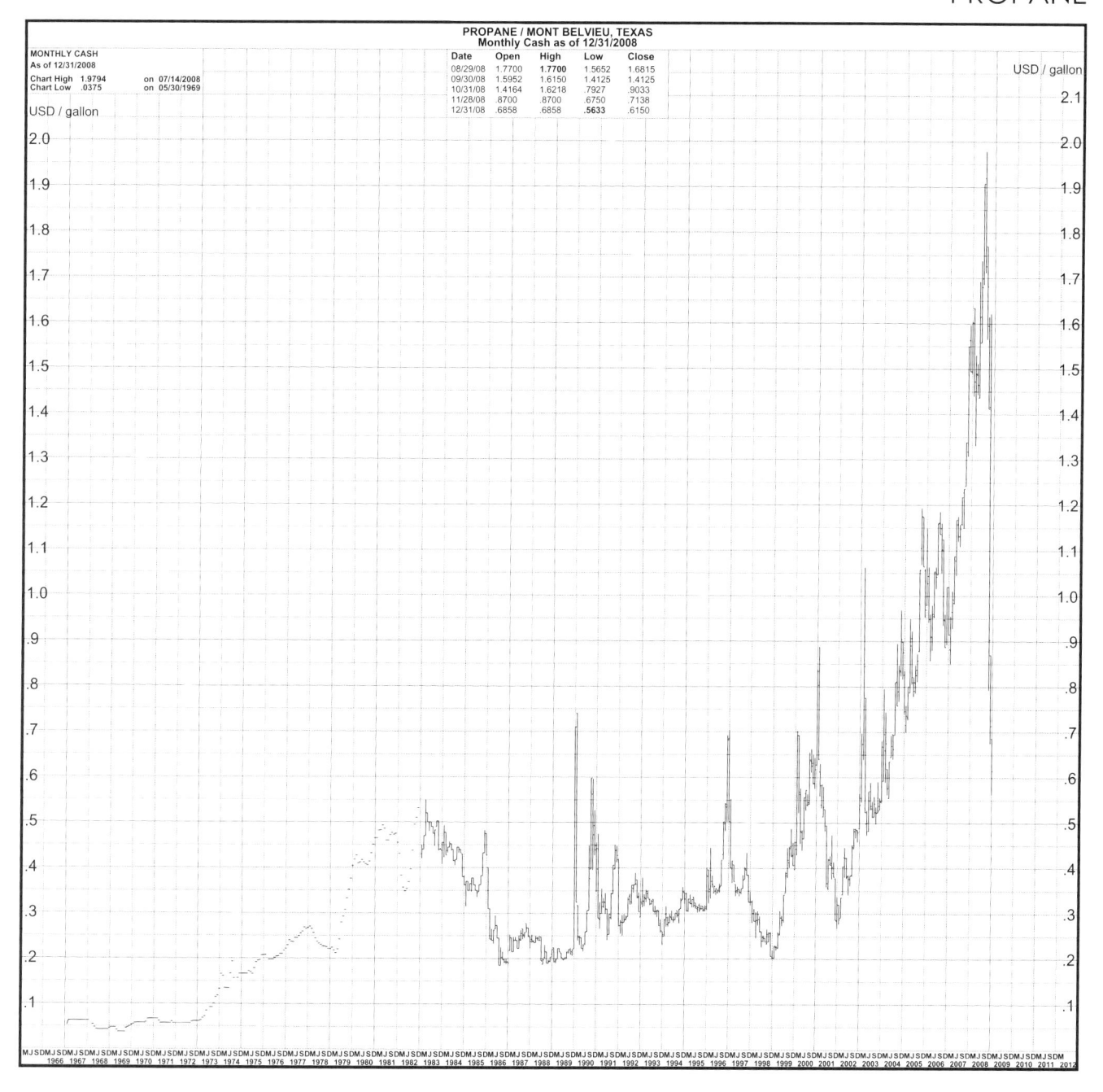

# PROPANE

**PROPANE / MONT BELVIEU, TEXAS**
Monthly Cash as of 12/31/2008

| Date | Open | High | Low | Close |
|---|---|---|---|---|
| 08/29/08 | 1.7700 | 1.7700 | 1.5652 | 1.6815 |
| 09/30/08 | 1.5952 | 1.6150 | 1.4125 | 1.4125 |
| 10/31/08 | 1.4164 | 1.6218 | .7927 | .9033 |
| 11/28/08 | .8700 | .8700 | .6750 | .7138 |
| 12/31/08 | .6858 | .6858 | .5633 | .6150 |

MONTHLY CASH
As of 12/31/2008
Chart High 1.9794 on 07/14/2008
Chart Low .0375 on 05/30/1969
USD / gallon

## Annual High, Low and Settle of Propane    In USD per Gallon

| Year | High | Low | Settle | Year | High | Low | Settle | Year | High | Low | Settle |
|---|---|---|---|---|---|---|---|---|---|---|---|
| 1967 | .0625 | .0519 | .0625 | 1981 | .4930 | .4550 | .4550 | 1995 | .4013 | .3025 | .3825 |
| 1968 | .0625 | .0425 | .0455 | 1982 | .5320 | .3490 | .5320 | 1996 | .7050 | .3225 | .5025 |
| 1969 | .0525 | .0375 | .0525 | 1983 | .5500 | .4075 | .4550 | 1997 | .5525 | .3188 | .3263 |
| 1970 | .0673 | .0545 | .0673 | 1984 | .4925 | .3625 | .3625 | 1998 | .3298 | .2025 | .2025 |
| 1971 | .0673 | .0573 | .0573 | 1985 | .4825 | .3150 | .4275 | 1999 | .4869 | .2025 | .4575 |
| 1972 | .0621 | .0573 | .0621 | 1986 | .4000 | .1850 | .1900 | 2000 | .8375 | .4288 | .8338 |
| 1973 | .1328 | .0621 | .1328 | 1987 | .2775 | .2150 | .2375 | 2001 | .8875 | .2675 | .3200 |
| 1974 | .1928 | .1348 | .1664 | 1988 | .2525 | .1875 | .2200 | 2002 | .5650 | .2775 | .5400 |
| 1975 | .2075 | .1662 | .2075 | 1989 | .7100 | .1900 | .7100 | 2003 | 1.0625 | .4725 | .6675 |
| 1976 | .2213 | .1975 | .2213 | 1990 | .7400 | .2163 | .4425 | 2004 | .9688 | .5550 | .7463 |
| 1977 | .2680 | .2290 | .2670 | 1991 | .4750 | .2410 | .2735 | 2005 | 1.1932 | .7000 | 1.0275 |
| 1978 | .2700 | .2210 | .2210 | 1992 | .3890 | .2510 | .3250 | 2006 | 1.1850 | .8575 | .9150 |
| 1979 | .4040 | .2120 | .4040 | 1993 | .3790 | .2312 | .2535 | 2007 | 1.6054 | .8500 | 1.6019 |
| 1980 | .4650 | .4060 | .4650 | 1994 | .3585 | .2500 | .3325 | 2008 | 1.9794 | .5633 | .6150 |

*Source: CME Group; New York Mercantile Exchange*

# PROPANE

## Quarterly High, Low and Settle of Propane Futures    In USD per Gallon

| Quarter | High | Low | Settle | Quarter | High | Low | Settle | Quarter | High | Low | Settle |
|---|---|---|---|---|---|---|---|---|---|---|---|
| 03/2000 | .6725 | .4050 | .4800 | 03/2003 | .8200 | .4800 | .5125 | 03/2006 | 1.0400 | .8600 | .9700 |
| 06/2000 | .5850 | .4375 | .5775 | 06/2003 | .5950 | .4510 | .5400 | 06/2006 | 1.1650 | .9620 | 1.1650 |
| 09/2000 | .6650 | .5405 | .6250 | 09/2003 | .5650 | .5025 | .5250 | 09/2006 | 1.2075 | .9400 | .9525 |
| 12/2000 | .8900 | .5750 | .8650 | 12/2003 | .6725 | .5180 | .6600 | 12/2006 | 1.0300 | .9075 | .9200 |
| 03/2001 | .8300 | .5000 | .5280 | 03/2004 | .7400 | .5350 | .5800 | 03/2007 | 1.0925 | .8500 | 1.0925 |
| 06/2001 | .5750 | .3625 | .3750 | 06/2004 | .7000 | .5675 | .6675 | 06/2007 | 1.1700 | 1.0500 | 1.1575 |
| 09/2001 | .4500 | .3640 | .4025 | 09/2004 | .8850 | .6925 | .8335 | 09/2007 | 1.3425 | 1.1500 | 1.3225 |
| 12/2001 | .4150 | .2700 | .3260 | 12/2004 | .9740 | .7400 | .7450 | 12/2007 | 1.6200 | 1.3075 | 1.6200 |
| 03/2002 | .4050 | .2750 | .4000 | 03/2005 | .9200 | .6800 | .8750 | 03/2008 | 1.6300 | 1.3550 | 1.4600 |
| 06/2002 | .4600 | .3625 | .3775 | 06/2005 | .9200 | .7675 | .8300 | 06/2008 | 1.8750 | 1.4600 | 1.8675 |
| 09/2002 | .4900 | .3625 | .4810 | 09/2005 | 1.2100 | .8250 | 1.1800 | 09/2008 | 1.9900 | 1.3700 | 1.4300 |
| 12/2002 | .5650 | .4500 | .5400 | 12/2005 | 1.1900 | .9500 | 1.0375 | 12/2008 | 1.4200 | .5550 | .6475 |

*Source: CME Group; New York Mercantile Exchange*

# PROPANE

**PROPANE / MONT BELVIEU, TEXAS**
Weekly Cash as of 01/02/2009

| Date | Open | High | Low | Close |
|---|---|---|---|---|
| 12/05/08 | .6858 | .6858 | .5834 | .5869 |
| 12/12/08 | .5700 | .6394 | .5633 | .5950 |
| 12/19/08 | .6168 | .6620 | .6168 | .6256 |
| 12/26/08 | .6325 | .6325 | .5900 | .5900 |
| 01/02/09 | .5900 | .6688 | .5900 | .6688 |

WEEKLY CASH As of 01/02/2009
Chart High 1.9794 on 07/14/2008
Chart Low .2025 on 12/31/1998

## Quarterly High, Low and Settle of Propane    In USD per Gallon

| Quarter | High | Low | Settle | Quarter | High | Low | Settle | Quarter | High | Low | Settle |
|---|---|---|---|---|---|---|---|---|---|---|---|
| 03/2000 | .7025 | .4288 | .4813 | 03/2003 | 1.0625 | .5238 | .5238 | 03/2006 | 1.0639 | .8575 | .9600 |
| 06/2000 | .5725 | .4388 | .5725 | 06/2003 | .5894 | .4725 | .5375 | 06/2006 | 1.1600 | .9519 | 1.1600 |
| 09/2000 | .6625 | .5375 | .6250 | 09/2003 | .5582 | .4981 | .5225 | 09/2006 | 1.1850 | .9350 | .9481 |
| 12/2000 | .8375 | .5750 | .8338 | 12/2003 | .6800 | .5232 | .6675 | 12/2006 | 1.0200 | .8875 | .9150 |
| 03/2001 | .8875 | .5325 | .5838 | 03/2004 | .7957 | .5619 | .5763 | 03/2007 | 1.0875 | .8500 | 1.0875 |
| 06/2001 | .5800 | .3588 | .3669 | 06/2004 | .6950 | .5550 | .6625 | 06/2007 | 1.1750 | 1.0450 | 1.1475 |
| 09/2001 | .4725 | .3525 | .4025 | 09/2004 | .8950 | .6938 | .8363 | 09/2007 | 1.3383 | 1.1491 | 1.3383 |
| 12/2001 | .4138 | .2675 | .3200 | 12/2004 | .9688 | .7400 | .7463 | 12/2007 | 1.6054 | 1.3075 | 1.6019 |
| 03/2002 | .4038 | .2775 | .4038 | 03/2005 | .9500 | .7000 | .8907 | 03/2008 | 1.6338 | 1.3313 | 1.4650 |
| 06/2002 | .4450 | .3413 | .3763 | 06/2005 | .9225 | .7788 | .8257 | 06/2008 | 1.9075 | 1.4367 | 1.9075 |
| 09/2002 | .4882 | .3613 | .4813 | 09/2005 | 1.1932 | .8113 | 1.1750 | 09/2008 | 1.9794 | 1.4125 | 1.4125 |
| 12/2002 | .5650 | .4575 | .5400 | 12/2005 | 1.1738 | .9525 | 1.0275 | 12/2008 | 1.6218 | .5633 | .6150 |

*Source: CME Group; New York Mercantile Exchange*

# FINANCIAL INSTRUMENTS

### Current US Interest Rate Outlook

As of February 2009, the US economy was in a deep recession and the economic outlook for 2009 looked grim. The US Federal Reserve pegged the federal funds target at the unprecedented target range of zero to 0.25%. The Fed stood ready to expand its liquidity measures and Congress had just pass a $787 billion stimulus program. The Obama Administration was working on new plans to rescue banks and curb foreclosures. Yet, US consumers and businesses remained paralyzed by the worst financial crisis seen since the Great Depression.

Market participants as of early 2009 were generally expecting US interest rates to remain extremely low through 2009 and even into 2010. The market consensus was that the US recession (which officially began in December 2007) would last at least through mid-2009 and that the US economy would recover at a snail's pace through 2010 due to the massive problems including debt-saturated consumers, falling home prices, a glut of homes on the market, devastated household wealth, extremely tight credit conditions, and a crippled banking system. With the weak economy, most observers expected the Fed to keep short-term interest rates very low through 2009 and 2010.

Most observers expected longer-term T-note yields to also remain low at least through 2009. The Fed, by keeping short-term rates pegged at a very low levels, will ensure to some extent that long-term rates should remain low as well. In addition, the Fed as of early 2009 was considering "quantitative easing," which would involve the purchase of long-term T-notes. The purchase of those T-notes would keep long-term T-note yields low, thus anchoring private rates at low levels as well.

However, long-term Treasury yields cannot remain low forever. When the crisis subsides and the economy improves, the T-note market will then start worrying about inflation and will be expecting the Fed to decisively roll back its extraordinarily easy monetary policy. The market knows that the Fed helped cause the housing bubble in the first place with its 1% interest rate policy in 20032004. The T-note market will be hoping that the Fed can manage its exit from low interest rates without causing another bubble or an outburst of inflation.

### US Interest Rate History

#### The 1970s to 1990s

US interest rates rose sharply during the period of 1965 to the early 1980s mainly because the Fed let inflation get out of control. The CPI rose sharply in 1973-75 to +11.8%, fell back in 1976-77, but then soared to a peak of +13.6% in 1980. Upward pressure on inflation in the 1970s stemmed from (1) deficit spending for the Vietnam War and President Johnson's Great Society, (2) the end of the Bretton Woods fixed-currency system in 1971, which resulted in the dollar's depreciation, and (3) the Arab oil embargo in 1973.

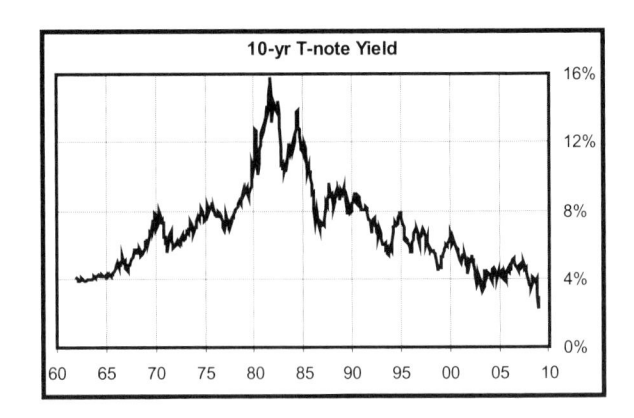

The Fed should have tightened monetary policy during that time, but instead kept interest rates targeted too low and allowed inflation to reach runaway levels. Finally, President Jimmy Carter appointed Paul Volcker as Fed Chairman in 1979. Mr. Volcker used strict monetarist policies to clamp down on reserve and money supply growth, which is the root cause of inflation. The Fed raised its federal funds rate target as high as 20% in 1980 and again in 1981. The Fed's tight monetary policy caused US interest rates to spike higher and caused a double-dip recession in 1980 (Jan-July) and 1981-82 (July 1981 to Nov 1982).

Throughout the remainder of the 1980s, the 10-year T-note yield moved steadily lower as inflation stabilized in the 4-6% range and as the US economy experience a long period of expansion. That expansion was interrupted by a recession in 1990-91, which was caused by the first Iraq war and its related oil spike. Yet over the 19822003 time frame, the 10-year T-note yield moved steadily lower on the Fed's impressive inflation-fighting regime. US interest rates were able to fall even further in the 1990s as the CPI was able to stabilize at the low average of 2.5-3.0%. The 10-year T-note yield in the 1990s eased from 8% at the end of 1989 to as low as 4.16% by the end of 1998.

### Interest Rates During the 2000 Equity Bubble

The latter half of the 1990s was the time of the extraordinary Internet and technology boom. US GDP in the latter half of the 1990s averaged +4.0%, which was significantly stronger than the long-run average of +3.4%. The Fed allowed GDP to run at the high level of +4.0% in the late 1990s because Fed Chairman Greenspan recognized that productivity showed a permanent upward shift in the late-1990s due to technology improvements.

However, the technology boom, along with low interest rates and speculative Internet fever, produced a massive bubble in the stock market. The Fed by mid-1999 realized that it needed to start taking away the punch bowl and raised the funds rate target from 4.75% in mid-1999 to a 10-year high of 6.5% by mid-2000. The Fed's tighter monetary policy finally popped the stock market bubble in early 2000. The plunge in the stock market that started in 2000, along with the post Y2K technology spending bust, led to a US recession in 2001 (March-November).

In response, the Fed in 2001 slashed its funds rate target from 6.5% to 1.75%, and then cut the funds rate further to 1.00% by July 2003 due to the additional shock to the economy from the al-Qaeda terrorist attack on September 11, 2001. The war between the US and Iraq in 2003 provided another negative factor for the US economy during that period. The Fed eased monetary policy sharply in order to prevent the possibility of deflation, which the Fed knew had devastated the Japanese economy in the 1990s. The Fed's easy monetary policy, combined with a benign inflation environment, allowed the 10-year T-note yield to fall to a low of 3.07% in June 2003, a level in long-term yields not seen since the 1960s.

By mid-2004, the Fed recognized that the US economy had finally entered a period of sustained expansion and the Fed started to raise the federal funds rate target in 25 basis point increments at each consecutive Federal Open Market Committee meeting. The US economy continued to perform well in the 2004-05 period despite the Fed's tighter monetary policy and the sharp rise in oil prices that occurred over that timeframe. The Fed from June 2004 through July 2006 raised the funds rate target by a total of 425 basis points to 5.25%.

**2006-09 housing bubble bursts and global crisis ensues**

The Fed's 2-year-long 425-basis-point rate hike finally had an impact in curbing the housing market, which had been in a speculative fever during 2003-06. Home sales started sliding in late 2005 and home prices hit a peak and started falling after mid-2006. In addition, borrowers started to default on sub-prime mortgages where monthly payments adjusted sharply higher once the teaser periods were over. The increasing defaults on sub-prime mortgages caused heavy losses in mortgage-backed securities, producing major losses for banks and hedge funds that held those securities. Bear Stearns in June 2007 had to guarantee two of its hedge funds holding mortgage securities that became insolvent and BNP Paribas halted investor redemptions from three of its mortgage-related hedge funds in August 2007.

As the scope of the mortgage crisis became clear, the Fed started cutting interest rates to soften the blow. The Fed implemented its first rate cut in September 2007 and cut the funds rate to 2.00% by April 2008. The Bush administration's fiscal stimulus program provided some support for the US economy in the first half of 2008 and the Fed left the funds rate unchanged at 2.00% through September 2008.

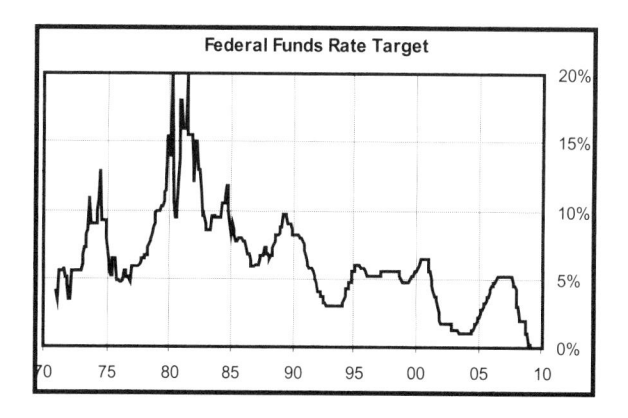

However, the crisis then reached epic proportions in September 2008 when Lehman Brothers was forced into bankruptcy by the weight of its bad mortgage portfolio, funding difficulties, and a lack of market confidence. The US and global stock markets plunged and panic emerged among US individual and institutional investors, who started pulling cash out of hedge funds, the stock market, overseas investments, and anything else that had any element of risk. Trust among investors completely evaporated and many investors moved their cash into government-guaranteed securities or deposits. Investors were focused on survival.

In response to the crisis, the interbank lending market almost completely shut down as banks hoarded what cash they had and refused to lend it out to other banks. The 3-month Libor rate, which is the rate at which banks loan each other money, soared by about 200 basis points to a peak of 4.82%.

The US Treasury and Federal Reserve were forced into a host of radical measures including (1) pumping huge quantities of cash into the US and global banking system to keep banks liquid, (2) guaranteeing money market funds, (3) buying commercial paper to keep the market functioning for providing credit to large corporations, and (4) buying mortgage securities to provide capital to the mortgage markets. The Fed in October 2008 cut its funds rate target to 1.00% and in December 2008 cut its funds rate target to the range of zero to 0.25%. The Fed also promised to keep short-term rates near zero for an extended period of time.

By late 2008, the Treasury and the Fed had contained the worst of the crisis in the financial markets. The stock market stabilized and credit spreads started to decline. However, the pain was spreading from the financial markets into the real economy. US GDP fell -0.5% in Q3-2008 and -3.8% in Q4. The market was looking for steep GDP declines in the first half of 2009.

# EURODOLLARS, 3-MONTH

**EURODOLLARS - IMM**
Monthly Selected Futures as of 12/31/2008

| Date | Open | High | Low | Close |
|---|---|---|---|---|
| 08/31/08 | 97.1950 | 97.2000 | 97.1300 | 97.1775 |
| 09/30/08 | 97.1725 | 97.4100 | 96.2350 | 96.5450 |
| 10/31/08 | 96.5900 | 97.8700 | 96.5550 | 97.7550 |
| 11/30/08 | 97.7750 | 98.1700 | 97.5800 | 97.8750 |
| 12/31/08 | 97.8750 | 98.9900 | 97.8100 | 98.9400 |

**MONTHLY SELECTED FUTURES** As of 12/31/2008
- Chart High 99.1000 on 06/19/2003
- Chart Low 78.0600 on 12/11/1980
- CONTRACT SIZE 1,000,000 USD
- MIN TICK .005 points
- VALUE 12.5 USD / contracts
- EACH GRID 0.1 points
- VALUE 250 USD / contracts
- DAILY LIMIT None
- TRADING HOURS 5:00p-4:00p / 7:20a-2:00p CT

## Annual High, Low and Settle of Eurodollars, 3-Month Futures — In Point of 100%

| Year | High | Low | Settle | Year | High | Low | Settle | Year | High | Low | Settle |
|---|---|---|---|---|---|---|---|---|---|---|---|
| 1967 | | | | 1981 | 86.7600 | 84.6900 | 85.5800 | 1995 | 94.6900 | 92.7300 | 94.6800 |
| 1968 | | | | 1982 | 90.7000 | 82.8400 | 90.7000 | 1996 | 94.8600 | 94.0200 | 94.4400 |
| 1969 | | | | 1983 | 91.2700 | 89.0200 | 89.6500 | 1997 | 94.5300 | 93.9550 | 94.2250 |
| 1970 | | | | 1984 | 91.0800 | 86.6300 | 90.4800 | 1998 | 95.3050 | 94.2000 | 95.0450 |
| 1971 | | | | 1985 | 92.5900 | 89.2500 | 92.2500 | 1999 | 95.1500 | 93.8000 | 93.8350 |
| 1972 | | | | 1986 | 94.3600 | 91.7400 | 93.8900 | 2000 | 94.1550 | 93.0100 | 94.1100 |
| 1973 | | | | 1987 | 94.1200 | 90.1500 | 92.4400 | 2001 | 98.1600 | 94.1350 | 98.0250 |
| 1974 | | | | 1988 | 93.2700 | 90.4200 | 90.6200 | 2002 | 98.7000 | 97.3700 | 98.6800 |
| 1975 | | | | 1989 | 92.2200 | 88.7600 | 91.9800 | 2003 | 99.1000 | 98.6150 | 98.7750 |
| 1976 | | | | 1990 | 92.8800 | 91.0800 | 92.8000 | 2004 | 98.8950 | 97.0650 | 97.0950 |
| 1977 | | | | 1991 | 96.0100 | 92.5200 | 95.9600 | 2005 | 97.1300 | 95.1900 | 95.2250 |
| 1978 | | | | 1992 | 97.0100 | 95.0900 | 96.3600 | 2006 | 95.3200 | 94.3150 | 94.6800 |
| 1979 | | | | 1993 | 96.8600 | 96.3400 | 96.4900 | 2007 | 95.7800 | 93.9600 | 95.7650 |
| 1980 | | | | 1994 | 96.6900 | 92.7500 | 92.7700 | 2008 | 98.9900 | 95.7500 | 98.9400 |

Futures begin trading 12/09/1981.  *Source: CME Group; Chicago Mercantile Exchange*

# EURODOLLARS, 3-MONTH

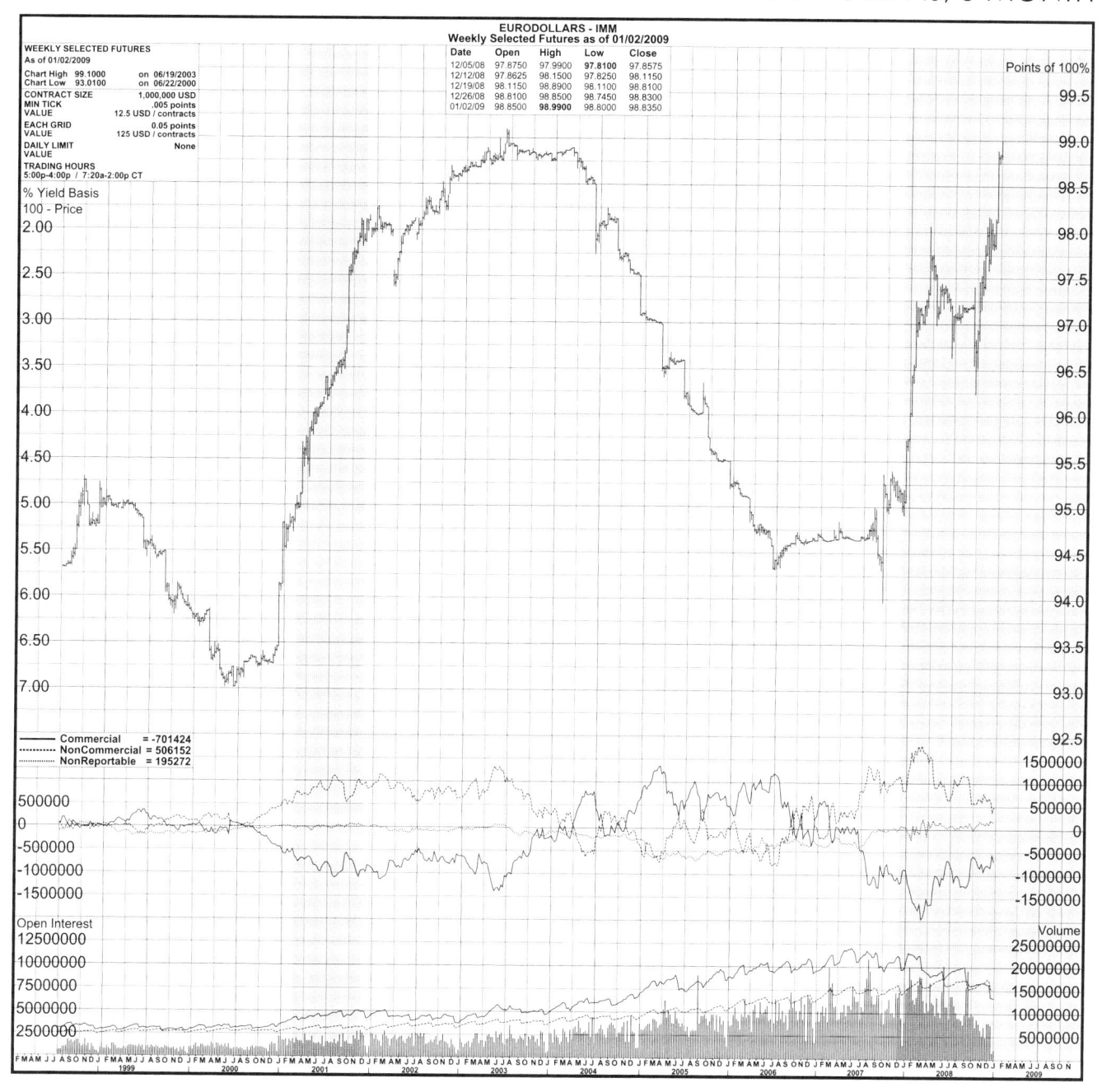

## Quarterly High, Low and Settle of Eurodollars, 3-Month Futures   In Point of 100%

| Quarter | High | Low | Settle | Quarter | High | Low | Settle | Quarter | High | Low | Settle |
|---|---|---|---|---|---|---|---|---|---|---|---|
| 03/2000 | 93.8700 | 93.2900 | 93.3450 | 03/2003 | 98.8850 | 98.6150 | 98.8500 | 03/2006 | 95.3200 | 94.7800 | 94.7950 |
| 06/2000 | 93.5000 | 93.0100 | 93.0650 | 06/2003 | 99.1000 | 98.6950 | 98.9250 | 06/2006 | 94.8200 | 94.3150 | 94.4200 |
| 09/2000 | 93.3600 | 93.0450 | 93.2600 | 09/2003 | 98.9500 | 98.7550 | 98.8650 | 09/2006 | 94.7300 | 94.3250 | 94.6650 |
| 12/2000 | 94.1550 | 93.2350 | 94.1100 | 12/2003 | 98.8850 | 98.7450 | 98.7750 | 12/2006 | 94.7200 | 94.5800 | 94.6800 |
| 03/2001 | 95.6850 | 94.1350 | 95.5900 | 03/2004 | 98.8950 | 98.7500 | 98.8300 | 03/2007 | 94.8450 | 94.6200 | 94.7350 |
| 06/2001 | 96.3950 | 95.3000 | 96.1850 | 06/2004 | 98.8350 | 97.7400 | 97.9800 | 06/2007 | 94.7400 | 94.6350 | 94.6700 |
| 09/2001 | 97.6150 | 96.1750 | 97.5400 | 09/2004 | 98.2450 | 97.6700 | 97.6950 | 09/2007 | 95.3650 | 93.9600 | 95.1550 |
| 12/2001 | 98.1600 | 97.5200 | 98.0250 | 12/2004 | 97.7650 | 97.0650 | 97.0950 | 12/2007 | 95.7800 | 94.9100 | 95.7650 |
| 03/2002 | 98.2600 | 97.3700 | 97.4700 | 03/2005 | 97.1300 | 96.4000 | 96.4850 | 03/2008 | 98.0650 | 95.7500 | 97.7300 |
| 06/2002 | 98.1275 | 97.4450 | 98.0450 | 06/2005 | 96.6850 | 96.1400 | 96.1500 | 06/2008 | 97.7400 | 96.6300 | 97.0700 |
| 09/2002 | 98.5250 | 98.0350 | 98.5100 | 09/2005 | 96.3450 | 95.6100 | 95.6150 | 09/2008 | 97.4100 | 96.2350 | 96.5450 |
| 12/2002 | 98.7000 | 98.2050 | 98.6800 | 12/2005 | 95.6350 | 95.1900 | 95.2250 | 12/2008 | 98.9900 | 96.5550 | 98.9400 |

*Source: CME Group*

# FEDERAL FUNDS, 30-DAY

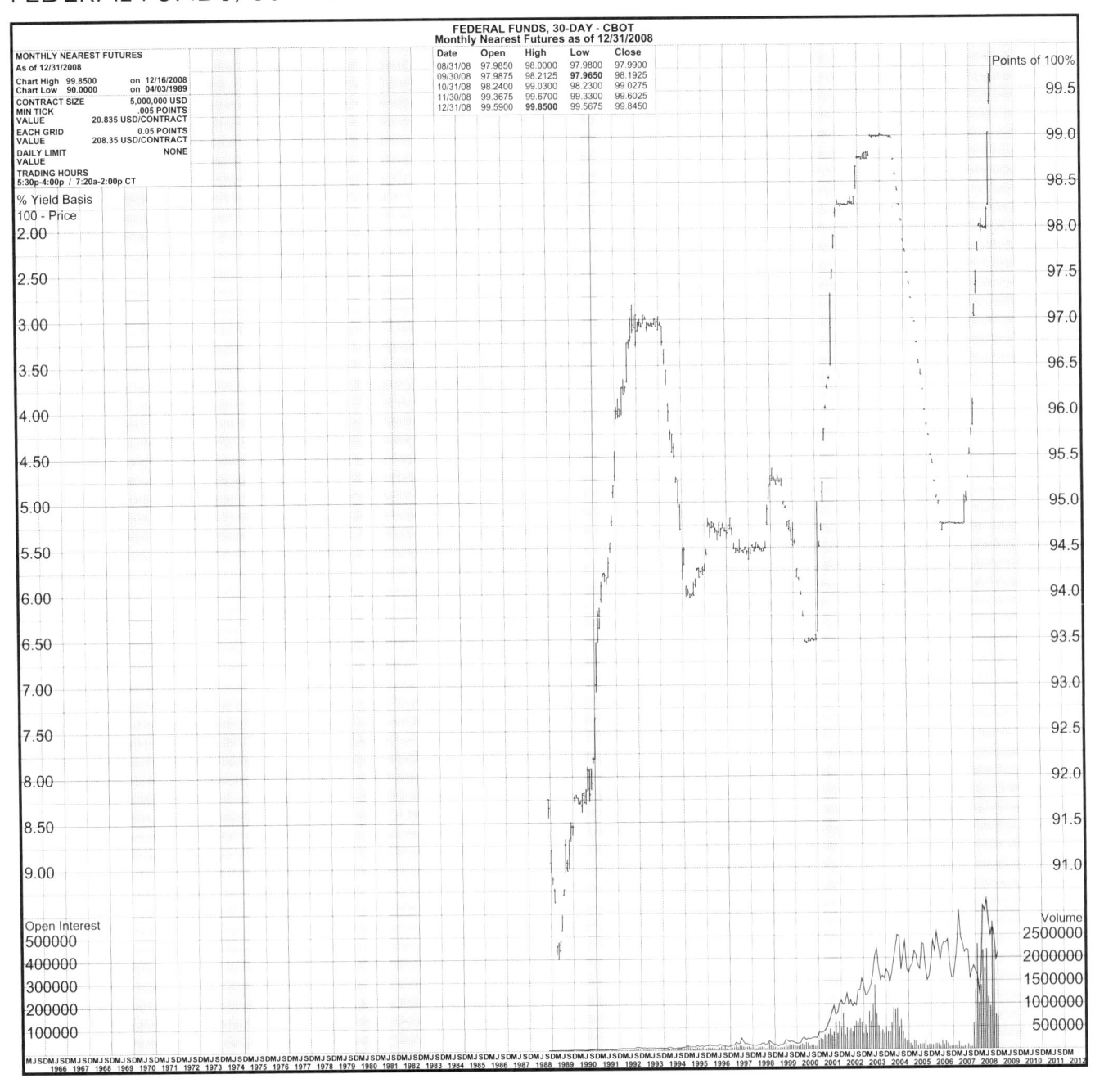

**FEDERAL FUNDS, 30-DAY - CBOT**
Monthly Nearest Futures as of 12/31/2008

| Date | Open | High | Low | Close |
|---|---|---|---|---|
| 08/31/08 | 97.9850 | 98.0000 | 97.9800 | 97.9900 |
| 09/30/08 | 97.9875 | 98.2125 | 97.9650 | 98.1925 |
| 10/31/08 | 98.2400 | 99.0300 | 98.2300 | 99.0275 |
| 11/30/08 | 99.3675 | 99.6700 | 99.3300 | 99.6025 |
| 12/31/08 | 99.5900 | 99.8500 | 99.5675 | 99.8450 |

MONTHLY NEAREST FUTURES
As of 12/31/2008
Chart High 99.8500 on 12/16/2008
Chart Low 90.0000 on 04/03/1989
CONTRACT SIZE 5,000,000 USD
MIN TICK .005 POINTS
VALUE 20.835 USD/CONTRACT
EACH GRID 0.05 POINTS
VALUE 208.35 USD/CONTRACT
DAILY LIMIT NONE
VALUE
TRADING HOURS
5:30p-4:00p / 7:20a-2:00p CT

% Yield Basis
100 - Price

## Annual High, Low and Settle of Federal Funds, 30-Day Futures   In Point of 100%

| Year | High | Low | Settle | Year | High | Low | Settle | Year | High | Low | Settle |
|---|---|---|---|---|---|---|---|---|---|---|---|
| 1967 | | | | 1981 | | | | 1995 | 94.5100 | 93.9500 | 94.3200 |
| 1968 | | | | 1982 | | | | 1996 | 94.8250 | 94.4150 | 94.6600 |
| 1969 | | | | 1983 | | | | 1997 | 94.8200 | 94.3650 | 94.4900 |
| 1970 | | | | 1984 | | | | 1998 | 95.2850 | 94.4300 | 95.2850 |
| 1971 | | | | 1985 | | | | 1999 | 95.3700 | 94.5100 | 94.6900 |
| 1972 | | | | 1986 | | | | 2000 | 94.5950 | 93.4450 | 93.4900 |
| 1973 | | | | 1987 | | | | 2001 | 98.2100 | 93.5750 | 98.1800 |
| 1974 | | | | 1988 | 91.7900 | 90.9500 | 91.2000 | 2002 | 98.7750 | 98.2150 | 98.7600 |
| 1975 | | | | 1989 | 91.5100 | 90.0000 | 91.4500 | 2003 | 99.0200 | 98.7350 | 99.0150 |
| 1976 | | | | 1990 | 92.6400 | 91.6100 | 92.6400 | 2004 | 99.0100 | 97.8350 | 97.8400 |
| 1977 | | | | 1991 | 95.5600 | 92.9300 | 95.5500 | 2005 | 97.7600 | 95.8300 | 95.8500 |
| 1978 | | | | 1992 | 97.1700 | 95.9100 | 97.0500 | 2006 | 95.7350 | 94.6650 | 94.7650 |
| 1979 | | | | 1993 | 97.0500 | 96.8700 | 97.0300 | 2007 | 95.7900 | 94.7400 | 95.7550 |
| 1980 | | | | 1994 | 96.9800 | 94.1600 | 94.4800 | 2008 | 99.8500 | 95.8250 | 99.8450 |

Futures begin trading 10/06/1988.   *Source: CME Group; Chicago Board of Trade*

# FEDERAL FUNDS, 30-DAY

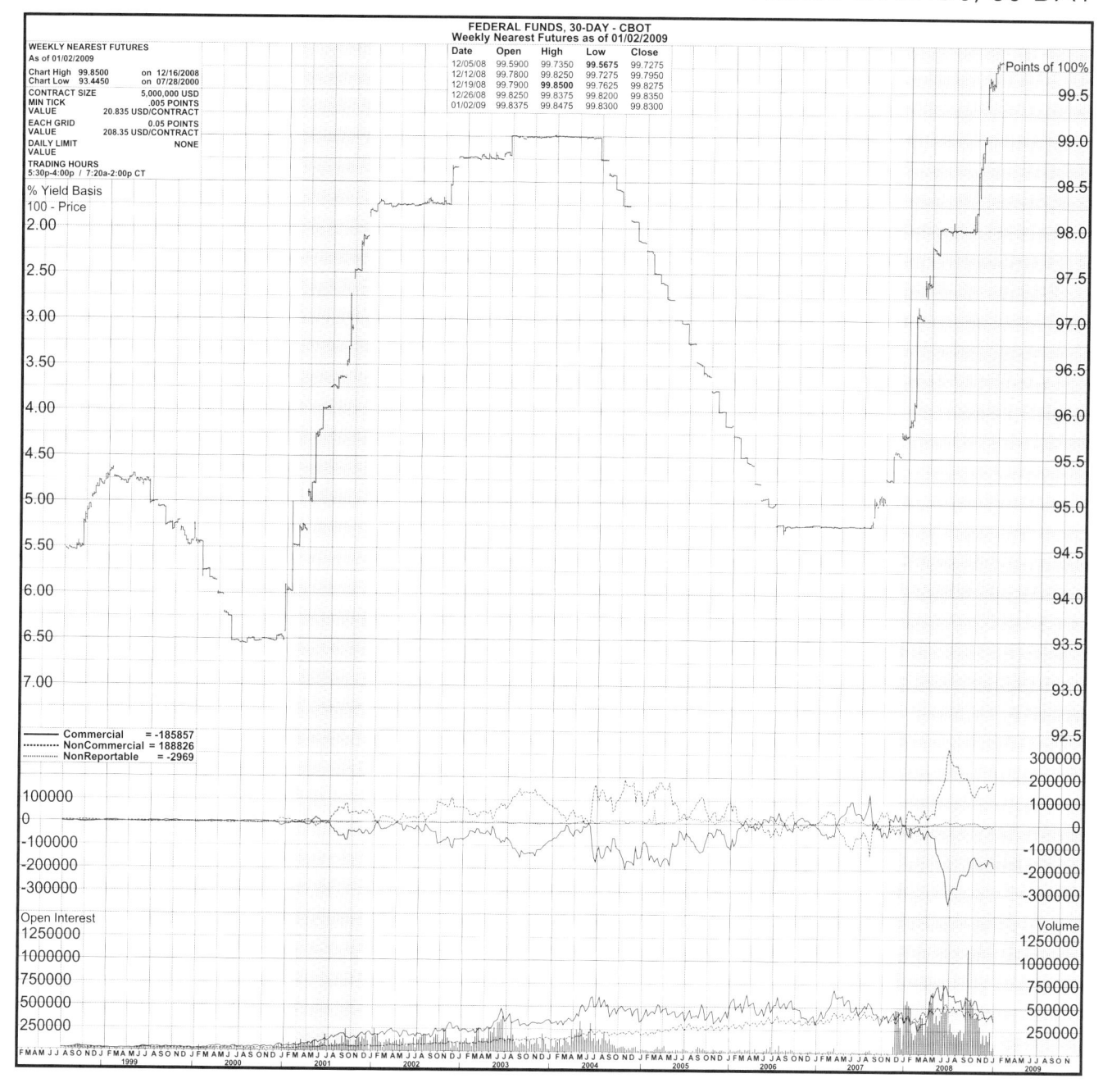

**FEDERAL FUNDS, 30-DAY - CBOT**
Weekly Nearest Futures as of 01/02/2009

| Date | Open | High | Low | Close |
|---|---|---|---|---|
| 12/05/08 | 99.5900 | 99.7350 | 99.5675 | 99.7275 |
| 12/12/08 | 99.7800 | 99.8250 | 99.7275 | 99.7950 |
| 12/19/08 | 99.7900 | 99.8500 | 99.7625 | 99.8275 |
| 12/26/08 | 99.8250 | 99.8375 | 99.8200 | 99.8350 |
| 01/02/09 | 99.8375 | 99.8475 | 99.8300 | 99.8300 |

**WEEKLY NEAREST FUTURES**
As of 01/02/2009
Chart High 99.8500 on 12/16/2008
Chart Low 93.4450 on 07/28/2000
CONTRACT SIZE 5,000,000 USD
MIN TICK .005 POINTS
VALUE 20.835 USD/CONTRACT
EACH GRID 0.05 POINTS
VALUE 208.35 USD/CONTRACT
DAILY LIMIT NONE
VALUE
TRADING HOURS
5:30p-4:00p / 7:20a-2:00p CT

Commercial = -185857
NonCommercial = 188826
NonReportable = -2969

## Quarterly High, Low and Settle of Federal Funds, 30-Day Futures    In Point of 100%

| Quarter | High | Low | Settle | Quarter | High | Low | Settle | Quarter | High | Low | Settle |
|---|---|---|---|---|---|---|---|---|---|---|---|
| 03/2000 | 94.5950 | 94.1350 | 94.1400 | 03/2003 | 98.8050 | 98.7350 | 98.7500 | 03/2006 | 95.7350 | 95.4100 | 95.4150 |
| 06/2000 | 94.0200 | 93.4650 | 93.4700 | 06/2003 | 98.8300 | 98.7400 | 98.7850 | 06/2006 | 95.2250 | 94.9550 | 94.9950 |
| 09/2000 | 93.5150 | 93.4450 | 93.4800 | 09/2003 | 99.0100 | 98.9650 | 98.9900 | 09/2006 | 94.7700 | 94.6650 | 94.7500 |
| 12/2000 | 93.5500 | 93.4700 | 93.4900 | 12/2003 | 99.0200 | 98.9800 | 99.0150 | 12/2006 | 94.7700 | 94.7450 | 94.7650 |
| 03/2001 | 95.0000 | 93.5750 | 94.6850 | 03/2004 | 99.0100 | 98.9900 | 98.9950 | 03/2007 | 94.7600 | 94.7400 | 94.7450 |
| 06/2001 | 96.0500 | 94.9900 | 96.0200 | 06/2004 | 99.0000 | 98.9700 | 98.9750 | 06/2007 | 94.7600 | 94.7450 | 94.7500 |
| 09/2001 | 97.2800 | 96.2300 | 96.8950 | 09/2004 | 98.7450 | 98.3950 | 98.4000 | 09/2007 | 95.1000 | 94.7450 | 95.0250 |
| 12/2001 | 98.2100 | 97.4350 | 98.1800 | 12/2004 | 98.2550 | 97.8350 | 97.8400 | 12/2007 | 95.7900 | 95.2450 | 95.7550 |
| 03/2002 | 98.3050 | 98.2150 | 98.2550 | 03/2005 | 97.7600 | 97.3700 | 97.3750 | 03/2008 | 97.5150 | 95.8250 | 97.3950 |
| 06/2002 | 98.2600 | 98.2350 | 98.2400 | 06/2005 | 97.2300 | 96.9600 | 96.9650 | 06/2008 | 98.0900 | 97.7250 | 98.0050 |
| 09/2002 | 98.3300 | 98.2450 | 98.2500 | 09/2005 | 96.7450 | 96.3750 | 96.3800 | 09/2008 | 98.2125 | 97.9650 | 98.1925 |
| 12/2002 | 98.7750 | 98.2450 | 98.7600 | 12/2005 | 96.2300 | 95.8300 | 95.8500 | 12/2008 | 99.8500 | 98.2300 | 99.8450 |

*Source: CME Group*

# LIBOR, 1-MONTH

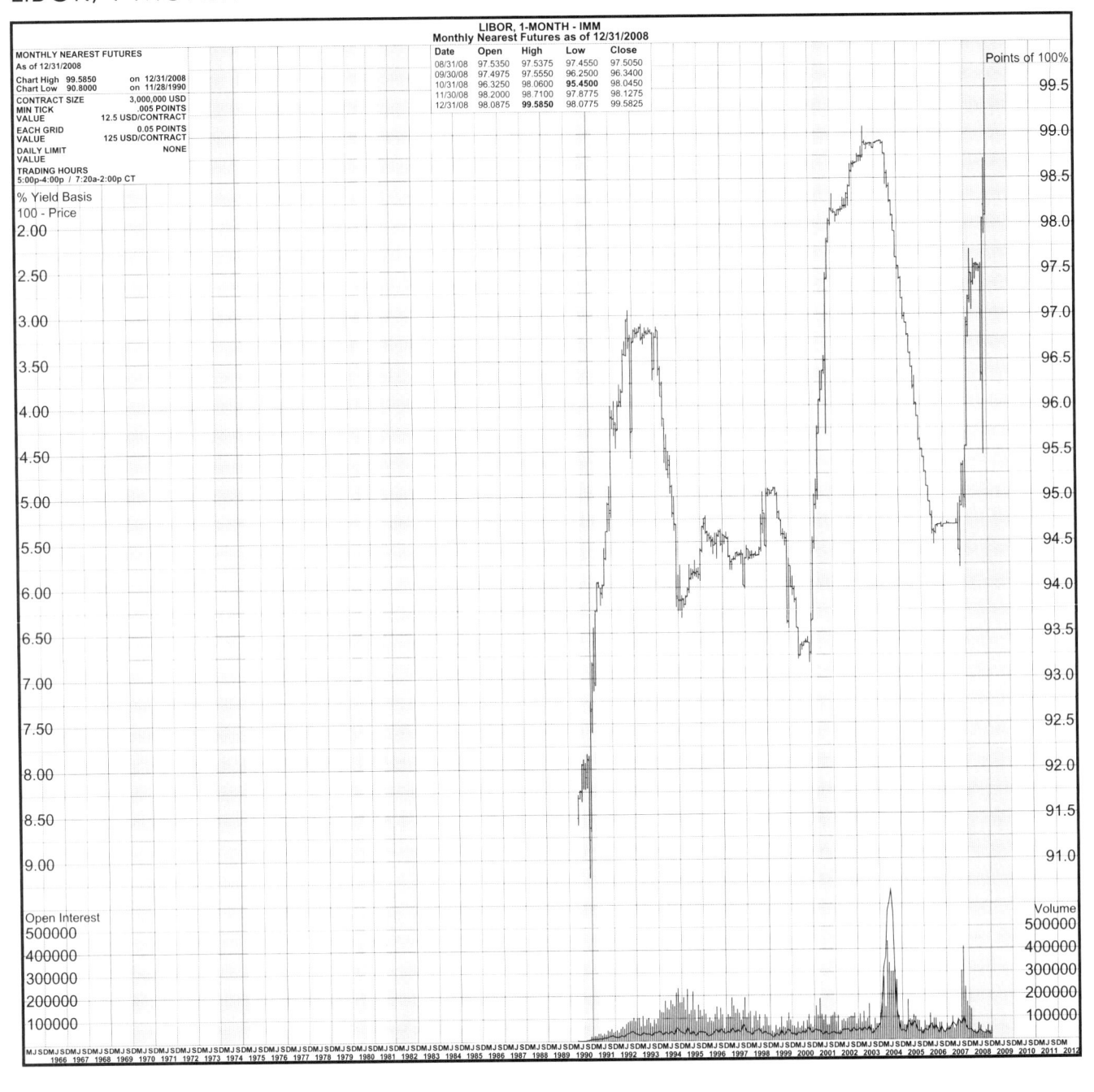

**MONTHLY NEAREST FUTURES**
As of 12/31/2008
Chart High 99.5850 on 12/31/2008
Chart Low 90.8000 on 11/28/1990
CONTRACT SIZE 3,000,000 USD
MIN TICK .005 POINTS
VALUE 12.5 USD/CONTRACT
EACH GRID 0.05 POINTS
VALUE 125 USD/CONTRACT
DAILY LIMIT NONE
VALUE
TRADING HOURS
5:00p-4:00p / 7:20a-2:00p CT

**LIBOR, 1-MONTH - IMM**
Monthly Nearest Futures as of 12/31/2008

| Date | Open | High | Low | Close |
|---|---|---|---|---|
| 08/31/08 | 97.5350 | 97.5375 | 97.4550 | 97.5050 |
| 09/30/08 | 97.4975 | 97.5550 | 96.2500 | 96.3400 |
| 10/31/08 | 96.3250 | 98.0600 | 95.4500 | 98.0450 |
| 11/30/08 | 98.2000 | 98.7100 | 97.8775 | 98.1275 |
| 12/31/08 | 98.0875 | 99.5850 | 98.0775 | 99.5825 |

## Annual High, Low and Settle of Libor, 1-Month Futures   In Point of 100%

| Year | High | Low | Settle | Year | High | Low | Settle | Year | High | Low | Settle |
|---|---|---|---|---|---|---|---|---|---|---|---|
| 1967 | | | | 1981 | | | | 1995 | 94.4300 | 93.6600 | 94.4100 |
| 1968 | | | | 1982 | | | | 1996 | 94.7900 | 94.3100 | 94.5700 |
| 1969 | | | | 1983 | | | | 1997 | 94.6100 | 93.9800 | 94.3200 |
| 1970 | | | | 1984 | | | | 1998 | 95.0850 | 94.2900 | 95.0200 |
| 1971 | | | | 1985 | | | | 1999 | 95.0975 | 93.5375 | 94.2300 |
| 1972 | | | | 1986 | | | | 2000 | 94.2300 | 93.1600 | 93.6225 |
| 1973 | | | | 1987 | | | | 2001 | 98.1700 | 93.6300 | 98.1650 |
| 1974 | | | | 1988 | | | | 2002 | 98.6800 | 98.0150 | 98.6575 |
| 1975 | | | | 1989 | | | | 2003 | 99.0750 | 98.6125 | 98.8850 |
| 1976 | | | | 1990 | 92.7400 | 90.8000 | 92.6400 | 2004 | 98.9150 | 97.4850 | 97.5275 |
| 1977 | | | | 1991 | 96.0000 | 92.4000 | 95.8700 | 2005 | 97.5325 | 95.4975 | 95.5100 |
| 1978 | | | | 1992 | 97.0600 | 95.4200 | 96.7000 | 2006 | 95.5175 | 94.4600 | 94.6775 |
| 1979 | | | | 1993 | 96.9100 | 96.2800 | 96.7600 | 2007 | 95.5400 | 94.2075 | 95.5350 |
| 1980 | | | | 1994 | 96.8800 | 93.7300 | 93.8600 | 2008 | 99.5850 | 95.4500 | 99.5825 |

Futures begin trading 04/05/1990.   *Source: CME Group; Chicago Mercantile Exchange*

# LIBOR, 1-MONTH

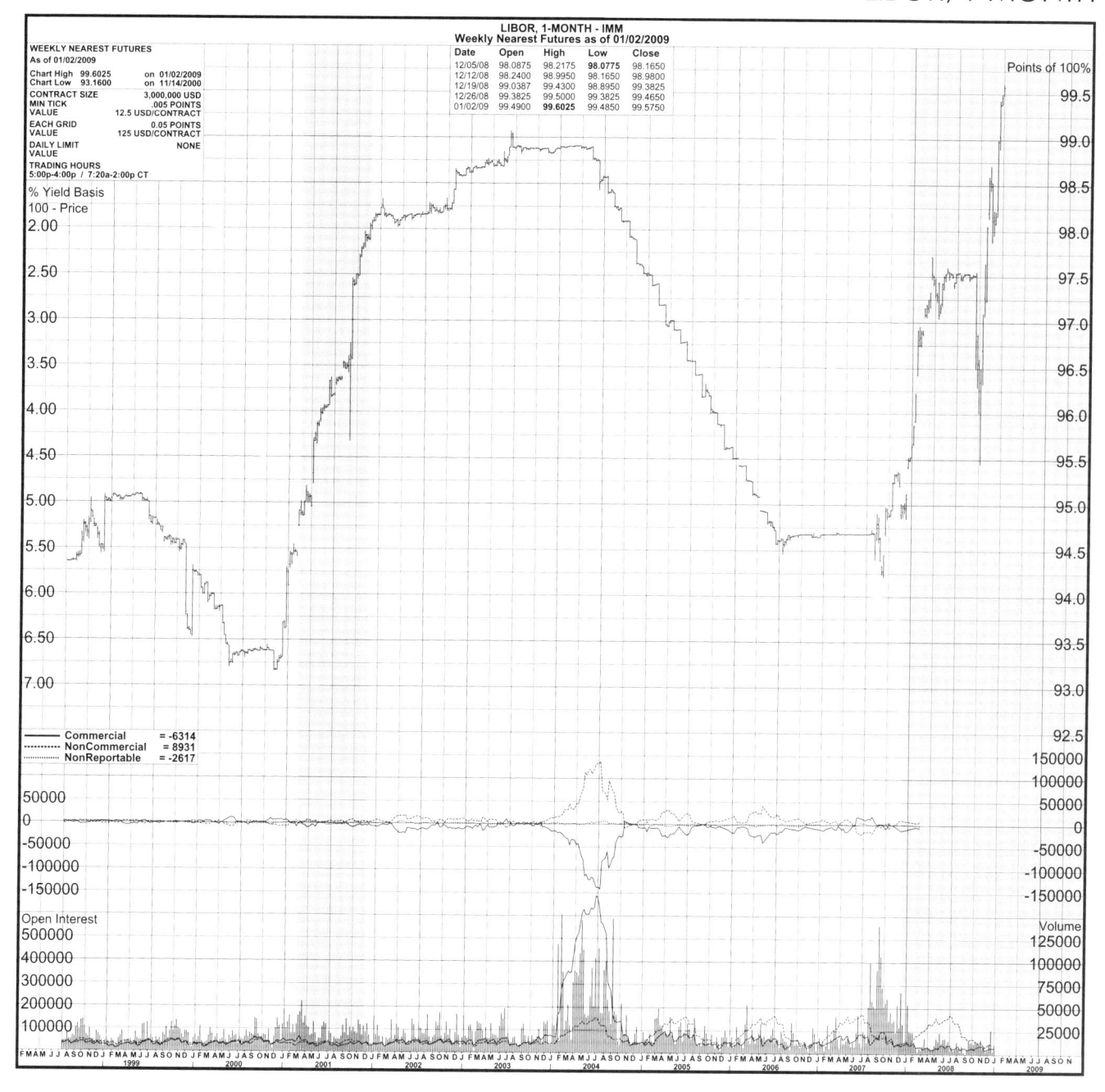

## Quarterly High, Low and Settle of Libor, 1-Month Futures    In Point of 100%

| Quarter | High | Low | Settle | Quarter | High | Low | Settle | Quarter | High | Low | Settle |
|---|---|---|---|---|---|---|---|---|---|---|---|
| 03/2000 | 94.2300 | 93.8200 | 93.8575 | 03/2003 | 98.7725 | 98.6125 | 98.7350 | 03/2006 | 95.5175 | 95.0950 | 95.0975 |
| 06/2000 | 93.8800 | 93.2000 | 93.3625 | 06/2003 | 99.0750 | 98.6750 | 98.8875 | 06/2006 | 95.1000 | 94.5650 | 94.6150 |
| 09/2000 | 93.4250 | 93.3000 | 93.3950 | 09/2003 | 98.9150 | 98.8150 | 98.8800 | 09/2006 | 94.6825 | 94.4600 | 94.6750 |
| 12/2000 | 93.7050 | 93.1600 | 93.6225 | 12/2003 | 98.8900 | 98.8250 | 98.8850 | 12/2006 | 94.7000 | 94.6425 | 94.6775 |
| 03/2001 | 95.1850 | 93.6300 | 95.0525 | 03/2004 | 98.9150 | 98.8750 | 98.9100 | 03/2007 | 94.7100 | 94.6775 | 94.6825 |
| 06/2001 | 96.3750 | 94.9500 | 96.1650 | 06/2004 | 98.9100 | 98.4250 | 98.5500 | 06/2007 | 94.6850 | 94.6775 | 94.6825 |
| 09/2001 | 97.4600 | 95.6800 | 97.3850 | 09/2004 | 98.5850 | 98.0750 | 98.0950 | 09/2007 | 94.9825 | 94.2075 | 94.9225 |
| 12/2001 | 98.1700 | 97.3800 | 98.1650 | 12/2004 | 98.0950 | 97.4850 | 97.5275 | 12/2007 | 95.5400 | 94.8500 | 95.5350 |
| 03/2002 | 98.3300 | 98.0150 | 98.0875 | 03/2005 | 97.5325 | 96.9350 | 96.9775 | 03/2008 | 97.7150 | 95.5325 | 97.4475 |
| 06/2002 | 98.1900 | 98.0800 | 98.1550 | 06/2005 | 97.0150 | 96.5675 | 96.5700 | 06/2008 | 97.6025 | 97.0400 | 97.5325 |
| 09/2002 | 98.3400 | 98.1500 | 98.3275 | 09/2005 | 96.5850 | 95.9900 | 96.0125 | 09/2008 | 97.5550 | 96.2500 | 96.3400 |
| 12/2002 | 98.6800 | 98.1900 | 98.6575 | 12/2005 | 96.0200 | 95.4975 | 95.5100 | 12/2008 | 99.5850 | 95.4500 | 99.5825 |

*Source: CME Group*

# TREASURY NOTES, 2-YEAR

**MONTHLY NEAREST FUTURES**
As of 12/31/2008
Chart High 110-11 on 12/17/2008
Chart Low 95-105 on 06/26/1990
CONTRACT SIZE 200,000 USD @ 6%
MIN TICK 1/128
VALUE 15.625 USD/CONTRACT
EACH GRID 16/128 1/128
VALUE 250 USD/CONTRACT
DAILY LIMIT None
VALUE
TRADING HOURS
5:30p-4:00p / 7:20a-2:00p CT

**T-NOTE, 2-YEAR - CBOT**
Monthly Nearest Futures as of 12/31/2008

| Date | Open | High | Low | Close |
|---|---|---|---|---|
| 08/31/08 | 106-5 | 106-84 | **105-100** | 106-60 |
| 09/30/08 | 106-64 | 107-126 | 106-16 | 107-45 |
| 10/31/08 | 106-102 | 108-14 | 106-68 | 107-53 |
| 11/30/08 | 107-56 | 109-66 | 107-47 | 109-24 |
| 12/31/08 | 109-17 | **110-11** | 109- | 109-98 |

## Annual High, Low and Settle of Treasury Notes, 2-Year Futures    In Nominal Value

| Year | High | Low | Settle | Year | High | Low | Settle | Year | High | Low | Settle |
|---|---|---|---|---|---|---|---|---|---|---|---|
| 1967 | | | | 1981 | | | | 1995 | 101 160/256 | 96 118/256 | 101 084/256 |
| 1968 | | | | 1982 | | | | 1996 | 102 012/256 | 97 204/256 | 100 084/256 |
| 1969 | | | | 1983 | | | | 1997 | 101 014/256 | 98 186/256 | 100 106/256 |
| 1970 | | | | 1984 | | | | 1998 | 103 180/256 | 99 248/256 | 102 124/256 |
| 1971 | | | | 1985 | | | | 1999 | 102 150/256 | 99 066/256 | 99 078/256 |
| 1972 | | | | 1986 | | | | 2000 | 101 162/256 | 98 048/256 | 101 148/256 |
| 1973 | | | | 1987 | | | | 2001 | 106 094/256 | 101 176/256 | 104 126/256 |
| 1974 | | | | 1988 | | | | 2002 | 107 240/256 | 103 050/256 | 107 152/256 |
| 1975 | | | | 1989 | | | | 2003 | 108 222/256 | 106 172/256 | 107 006/256 |
| 1976 | | | | 1990 | 98 096/256 | 95 210/256 | 98 000/256 | 2004 | 108 036/256 | 104 180/256 | 104 204/256 |
| 1977 | | | | 1991 | 102 050/256 | 97 130/256 | 102 050/256 | 2005 | 104 216/256 | 102 108/256 | 102 172/256 |
| 1978 | | | | 1992 | 104 022/256 | 99 102/256 | 102 028/256 | 2006 | 102 218/256 | 101 042/256 | 101 238/256 |
| 1979 | | | | 1993 | 103 220/256 | 101 232/256 | 102 168/256 | 2007 | 105 108/256 | 101 108/256 | 105 000/256 |
| 1980 | | | | 1994 | 103 048/256 | 96 080/256 | 96 140/256 | 2008 | 110 022/256 | 105 006/256 | 109 196/256 |

Futures begin trading 06/22/1990.    *Source: CME Group; Chicago Board of Trade*

# TREASURY NOTES, 2-YEAR

**T-Note Yield, 2-Year**
Monthly Cash as of 12/31/2008

| Date | Open | High | Low | Close |
|---|---|---|---|---|
| 08/29/08 | 2.507 | 2.628 | 2.204 | 2.367 |
| 09/30/08 | 2.367 | 2.522 | 1.355 | 1.968 |
| 10/31/08 | 1.960 | 1.968 | 1.317 | 1.572 |
| 11/28/08 | 1.564 | 1.588 | .955 | .981 |
| 12/31/08 | .980 | 1.074 | .604 | .764 |

MONTHLY CASH
As of 12/31/2008
Chart High 16.950 on 09/08/1981
Chart Low .604 on 12/17/2008

## Annual High, Low and Settle of Treasury Notes, 2-Year Yield   In Percent

| Year | High | Low | Settle | Year | High | Low | Settle | Year | High | Low | Settle |
|---|---|---|---|---|---|---|---|---|---|---|---|
| 1967 | | | | 1981 | 16.950 | 12.110 | 13.630 | 1995 | 7.732 | 5.141 | 5.150 |
| 1968 | | | | 1982 | 15.180 | 9.480 | 9.480 | 1996 | 6.517 | 4.771 | 5.859 |
| 1969 | | | | 1983 | 11.410 | 9.090 | 10.850 | 1997 | 6.536 | 5.427 | 5.617 |
| 1970 | | | | 1984 | 13.170 | 9.830 | 10.020 | 1998 | 5.726 | 3.566 | 4.511 |
| 1971 | | | | 1985 | 10.890 | 7.940 | 7.980 | 1999 | 6.386 | 4.379 | 6.218 |
| 1972 | | | | 1986 | 8.380 | 5.880 | 6.310 | 2000 | 6.947 | 5.056 | 5.108 |
| 1973 | | | | 1987 | 9.430 | 6.110 | 7.760 | 2001 | 5.108 | 2.287 | 3.047 |
| 1974 | | | | 1988 | 9.229 | 6.984 | 9.133 | 2002 | 3.753 | 1.558 | 1.598 |
| 1975 | | | | 1989 | 9.929 | 7.373 | 7.840 | 2003 | 2.140 | 1.056 | 1.819 |
| 1976 | 7.260 | 5.310 | 5.340 | 1990 | 9.075 | 7.075 | 7.130 | 2004 | 3.138 | 1.446 | 3.065 |
| 1977 | 7.260 | 5.420 | 7.220 | 1991 | 7.231 | 4.661 | 4.751 | 2005 | 4.502 | 3.049 | 4.400 |
| 1978 | 9.980 | 7.240 | 9.980 | 1992 | 5.915 | 3.572 | 4.542 | 2006 | 5.275 | 4.292 | 4.808 |
| 1979 | 12.630 | 8.920 | 11.230 | 1993 | 4.658 | 3.644 | 4.225 | 2007 | 5.128 | 2.791 | 3.047 |
| 1980 | 15.360 | 8.360 | 13.060 | 1994 | 7.768 | 3.999 | 7.680 | 2008 | 3.114 | .604 | .764 |

*Source: Federal Reserve Board*

# TREASURY NOTES, 2-YEAR

## Quarterly High, Low and Settle of Treasury Notes, 2-Year Futures — In Nominal Value

| Quarter | High | Low | Settle | Quarter | High | Low | Settle | Quarter | High | Low | Settle |
|---------|------|-----|--------|---------|------|-----|--------|---------|------|-----|--------|
| 03/2000 | 99 076/256 | 98 104/256 | 98 252/256 | 03/2003 | 108 104/256 | 106 214/256 | 107 196/256 | 03/2006 | 102 218/256 | 101 224/256 | 101 238/256 |
| 06/2000 | 99 180/256 | 98 048/256 | 99 048/256 | 06/2003 | 108 222/256 | 107 084/256 | 108 038/256 | 06/2006 | 102 014/256 | 101 042/256 | 101 092/256 |
| 09/2000 | 100 020/256 | 99 008/256 | 100 016/256 | 09/2003 | 108 088/256 | 106 242/256 | 107 204/256 | 09/2006 | 102 058/256 | 101 052/256 | 102 028/256 |
| 12/2000 | 101 162/256 | 99 210/256 | 101 148/256 | 12/2003 | 107 230/256 | 106 172/256 | 107 006/256 | 12/2006 | 102 140/256 | 101 200/256 | 101 238/256 |
| 03/2001 | 103 032/256 | 101 176/256 | 102 254/256 | 03/2004 | 108 036/256 | 106 194/256 | 107 150/256 | 03/2007 | 102 138/256 | 101 168/256 | 102 094/256 |
| 06/2001 | 103 152/256 | 102 084/256 | 102 146/256 | 06/2004 | 107 154/256 | 105 112/256 | 105 228/256 | 06/2007 | 102 126/256 | 101 108/256 | 101 204/256 |
| 09/2001 | 105 176/256 | 102 136/256 | 105 034/256 | 09/2004 | 106 116/256 | 105 056/256 | 105 250/256 | 09/2007 | 103 178/256 | 101 160/256 | 103 126/256 |
| 12/2001 | 106 094/256 | 104 032/256 | 104 126/256 | 12/2004 | 106 002/256 | 104 180/256 | 104 204/256 | 12/2007 | 105 108/256 | 102 230/256 | 105 000/256 |
| 03/2002 | 105 110/256 | 103 050/256 | 103 076/256 | 03/2005 | 104 216/256 | 103 168/256 | 103 204/256 | 03/2008 | 108 070/256 | 105 006/256 | 107 140/256 |
| 06/2002 | 106 000/256 | 103 062/256 | 105 132/256 | 06/2005 | 104 108/256 | 103 104/256 | 104 008/256 | 06/2008 | 107 122/256 | 105 006/256 | 106 006/256 |
| 09/2002 | 107 132/256 | 104 236/256 | 107 116/256 | 09/2005 | 104 008/256 | 102 250/256 | 103 020/256 | 09/2008 | 107 252/256 | 105 078/256 | 107 090/256 |
| 12/2002 | 107 240/256 | 106 112/256 | 107 152/256 | 12/2005 | 103 000/256 | 102 108/256 | 102 172/256 | 12/2008 | 110 022/256 | 106 136/256 | 109 196/256 |

*Source: CME Group; Chicago Board of Trade*

# TREASURY NOTES, 2-YEAR

**T-Note Yield, 2-Year**
Weekly Cash as of 01/02/2009

| Date | Open | High | Low | Close |
|---|---|---|---|---|
| 12/05/08 | .980 | 1.020 | .772 | .930 |
| 12/12/08 | .922 | 1.074 | .663 | .759 |
| 12/19/08 | .758 | .822 | .604 | .722 |
| 12/26/08 | .737 | 1.057 | .737 | .883 |
| 01/02/09 | .883 | .891 | .710 | .867 |

WEEKLY CASH
As of 01/02/2009
Chart High 6.947 on 05/18/2000
Chart Low .604 on 12/17/2008

## Quarterly High, Low and Settle of Treasury Notes, 2-Year Yield    In Percent

| Quarter | High | Low | Settle | Quarter | High | Low | Settle | Quarter | High | Low | Settle |
|---|---|---|---|---|---|---|---|---|---|---|---|
| 03/2000 | 6.734 | 6.252 | 6.474 | 03/2003 | 1.872 | 1.314 | 1.490 | 03/2006 | 4.841 | 4.292 | 4.816 |
| 06/2000 | 6.947 | 6.093 | 6.349 | 06/2003 | 1.732 | 1.056 | 1.300 | 06/2006 | 5.275 | 4.792 | 5.150 |
| 09/2000 | 6.476 | 5.932 | 5.983 | 09/2003 | 2.072 | 1.221 | 1.466 | 09/2006 | 5.250 | 4.616 | 4.683 |
| 12/2000 | 6.067 | 5.056 | 5.108 | 12/2003 | 2.140 | 1.426 | 1.819 | 12/2006 | 4.923 | 4.458 | 4.808 |
| 03/2001 | 5.108 | 4.086 | 4.159 | 03/2004 | 1.972 | 1.446 | 1.572 | 03/2007 | 4.991 | 4.450 | 4.574 |
| 06/2001 | 4.554 | 3.862 | 4.213 | 06/2004 | 2.938 | 1.564 | 2.677 | 06/2007 | 5.128 | 4.558 | 4.858 |
| 09/2001 | 4.240 | 2.713 | 2.815 | 09/2004 | 2.815 | 2.323 | 2.605 | 09/2007 | 5.009 | 3.808 | 3.984 |
| 12/2001 | 3.356 | 2.287 | 3.047 | 12/2004 | 3.138 | 2.450 | 3.065 | 12/2007 | 4.285 | 2.791 | 3.047 |
| 03/2002 | 3.753 | 2.689 | 3.715 | 03/2005 | 3.899 | 3.049 | 3.783 | 03/2008 | 3.103 | 1.236 | 1.614 |
| 06/2002 | 3.740 | 2.572 | 2.827 | 06/2005 | 3.816 | 3.418 | 3.633 | 06/2008 | 3.114 | 1.550 | 2.616 |
| 09/2002 | 2.932 | 1.675 | 1.691 | 09/2005 | 4.181 | 3.567 | 4.165 | 09/2008 | 2.831 | 1.355 | 1.968 |
| 12/2002 | 2.214 | 1.558 | 1.598 | 12/2005 | 4.502 | 4.149 | 4.400 | 12/2008 | 1.968 | .604 | .764 |

*Source: Federal Reserve Board*

# TREASURY NOTES, 5-YEAR

**MONTHLY NEAREST FUTURES**
As of 12/31/2008
Chart High 122 63/64 on 12/17/2008
Chart Low 86 22/64 on 03/21/1989
CONTRACT SIZE 100,000 USD @ 6%
MIN TICK VALUE 1/128
15.625 USD/CONTRACT
EACH GRID VALUE 32/128 1/128
500 USD/CONTRACT
DAILY LIMIT VALUE None
TRADING HOURS 5:30p-4:00p / 7:20a-2:00p CT

**T-NOTE, 5-YEAR - CBOT**
Monthly Nearest Futures as of 12/31/2008

| Date | Open | High | Low | Close |
|---|---|---|---|---|
| 08/31/08 | 111 30/64 | 112 49/64 | 110 53/64 | 112 29/64 |
| 09/30/08 | 112 27/64 | 115 32/64 | 111 55/64 | 113 44/64 |
| 10/31/08 | 112 23/64 | 114 52/64 | 111 15/64 | 113 17/64 |
| 11/30/08 | 113 18/64 | 119 28/64 | 113 4/64 | 119 22/64 |
| 12/31/08 | 119 20/64 | 122 63/64 | 119 14/64 | 120 63/64 |

## Annual High, Low and Settle of Treasury Notes, 5-Year Futures   In Nominal Value

| Year | High | Low | Settle | Year | High | Low | Settle | Year | High | Low | Settle |
|---|---|---|---|---|---|---|---|---|---|---|---|
| 1967 | | | | 1981 | | | | 1995 | 102 058/128 | 92 016/128 | 102 056/128 |
| 1968 | | | | 1982 | | | | 1996 | 103 076/128 | 95 120/128 | 99 040/128 |
| 1969 | | | | 1983 | | | | 1997 | 101 046/128 | 96 048/128 | 100 110/128 |
| 1970 | | | | 1984 | | | | 1998 | 107 052/128 | 100 076/128 | 105 044/128 |
| 1971 | | | | 1985 | | | | 1999 | 105 052/128 | 98 002/128 | 98 002/128 |
| 1972 | | | | 1986 | | | | 2000 | 103 112/128 | 96 064/128 | 103 072/128 |
| 1973 | | | | 1987 | | | | 2001 | 110 058/128 | 102 112/128 | 105 106/128 |
| 1974 | | | | 1988 | 91 024/128 | 87 124/128 | 88 052/128 | 2002 | 114 074/128 | 103 046/128 | 113 032/128 |
| 1975 | | | | 1989 | 94 098/128 | 86 044/128 | 93 008/128 | 2003 | 117 102/128 | 110 060/128 | 111 080/128 |
| 1976 | | | | 1990 | 93 098/128 | 88 022/128 | 93 026/128 | 2004 | 115 036/128 | 107 108/128 | 109 068/128 |
| 1977 | | | | 1991 | 100 032/128 | 91 076/128 | 100 018/128 | 2005 | 110 000/128 | 105 046/128 | 106 044/128 |
| 1978 | | | | 1992 | 102 090/128 | 94 078/128 | 99 040/128 | 2006 | 106 116/128 | 102 126/128 | 105 016/128 |
| 1979 | | | | 1993 | 106 014/128 | 99 006/128 | 103 002/128 | 2007 | 111 030/128 | 103 008/128 | 110 058/128 |
| 1980 | | | | 1994 | 104 078/128 | 92 004/128 | 92 076/128 | 2008 | 122 126/128 | 109 017/128 | 120 126/128 |

Futures begin trading 05/271988.   *Source: CME Group; Chicago Board of Trade*

# TREASURY NOTES, 5-YEAR

**MONTHLY CASH**
As of 12/31/2008
Chart High 16.270 on 09/30/1981
Chart Low 1.185 on 12/17/2008

T-Note Yield, 5-Year
Monthly Cash as of 12/31/2008

| Date | Open | High | Low | Close |
|---|---|---|---|---|
| 08/29/08 | 3.216 | 3.375 | 2.984 | 3.089 |
| 09/30/08 | 3.122 | 3.154 | 2.348 | 2.986 |
| 10/31/08 | 2.888 | 3.077 | 2.332 | 2.821 |
| 11/28/08 | 2.775 | 2.784 | 1.908 | 1.944 |
| 12/31/08 | 1.870 | 1.881 | 1.185 | 1.551 |

## Annual High, Low and Settle of Treasury Notes, 5-Year Yield — In Percent

| Year | High | Low | Settle | Year | High | Low | Settle | Year | High | Low | Settle |
|---|---|---|---|---|---|---|---|---|---|---|---|
| 1967 | 5.910 | 4.380 | 5.780 | 1981 | 16.270 | 12.210 | 13.970 | 1995 | 7.935 | 5.374 | 5.388 |
| 1968 | 6.360 | 5.420 | 6.330 | 1982 | 15.020 | 10.090 | 10.090 | 1996 | 6.917 | 5.120 | 6.199 |
| 1969 | 8.330 | 6.110 | 8.220 | 1983 | 11.950 | 9.720 | 11.570 | 1997 | 6.899 | 5.602 | 5.701 |
| 1970 | 8.300 | 5.850 | 5.980 | 1984 | 13.840 | 10.830 | 11.080 | 1998 | 5.807 | 3.889 | 4.542 |
| 1971 | 7.030 | 4.740 | 5.500 | 1985 | 11.700 | 8.480 | 8.490 | 1999 | 6.353 | 4.387 | 6.346 |
| 1972 | 6.320 | 5.470 | 6.260 | 1986 | 9.000 | 6.390 | 6.820 | 2000 | 6.834 | 4.880 | 4.967 |
| 1973 | 8.130 | 6.230 | 6.830 | 1987 | 10.110 | 6.540 | 8.414 | 2001 | 5.108 | 3.246 | 4.334 |
| 1974 | 8.790 | 6.720 | 7.360 | 1988 | 9.244 | 7.542 | 9.146 | 2002 | 4.877 | 2.533 | 2.730 |
| 1975 | 8.560 | 6.930 | 7.500 | 1989 | 9.761 | 7.394 | 7.856 | 2003 | 3.617 | 1.997 | 3.218 |
| 1976 | 7.820 | 5.990 | 6.130 | 1990 | 9.137 | 7.526 | 7.636 | 2004 | 4.101 | 2.608 | 3.607 |
| 1977 | 7.580 | 6.160 | 7.540 | 1991 | 8.082 | 5.895 | 5.924 | 2005 | 4.578 | 3.551 | 4.355 |
| 1978 | 9.350 | 7.580 | 9.320 | 1992 | 7.186 | 5.087 | 6.029 | 2006 | 5.263 | 4.229 | 4.701 |
| 1979 | 11.500 | 8.700 | 10.380 | 1993 | 6.073 | 4.536 | 5.193 | 2007 | 5.241 | 3.219 | 3.455 |
| 1980 | 14.120 | 8.860 | 12.590 | 1994 | 7.904 | 4.927 | 7.823 | 2008 | 3.744 | 1.185 | 1.551 |

*Source: Federal Researve Board*

# TREASURY NOTES, 5-YEAR

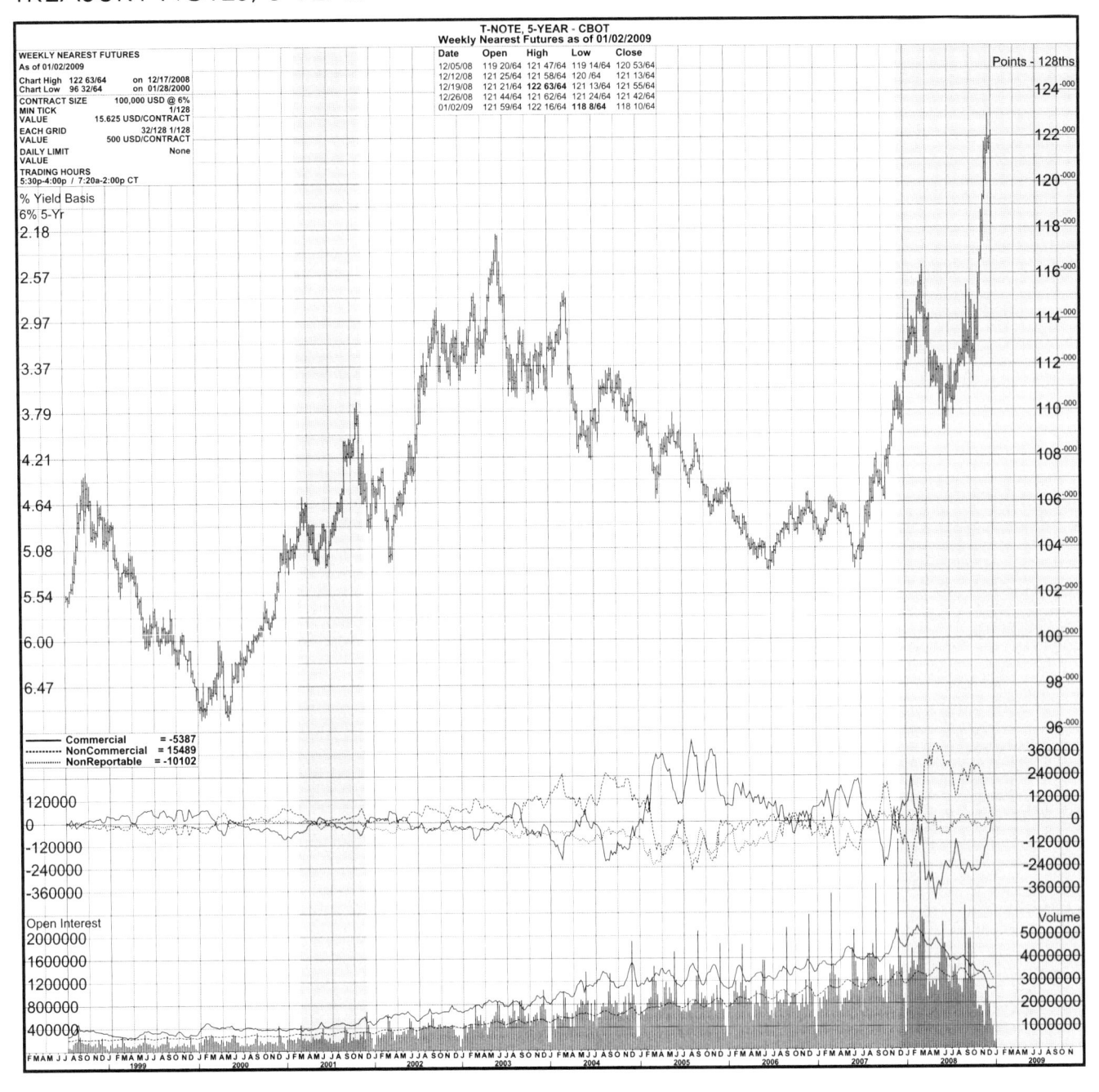

**T-NOTE, 5-YEAR - CBOT**
Weekly Nearest Futures as of 01/02/2009

| Date | Open | High | Low | Close |
|---|---|---|---|---|
| 12/05/08 | 119 20/64 | 121 47/64 | 119 14/64 | 120 53/64 |
| 12/12/08 | 121 25/64 | 121 58/64 | 120 /64 | 121 13/64 |
| 12/19/08 | 121 21/64 | 122 63/64 | 121 13/64 | 121 55/64 |
| 12/26/08 | 121 44/64 | 121 62/64 | 121 24/64 | 121 42/64 |
| 01/02/09 | 121 59/64 | 122 16/64 | 118 8/64 | 118 10/64 |

**WEEKLY NEAREST FUTURES**
As of 01/02/2009
Chart High 122 63/64 on 12/17/2008
Chart Low 96 32/64 on 01/28/2000
CONTRACT SIZE 100,000 USD @ 6%
MIN TICK VALUE 1/128 — 15.625 USD/CONTRACT
EACH GRID VALUE 32/128 1/128 — 500 USD/CONTRACT
DAILY LIMIT VALUE None
TRADING HOURS 5:30p-4:00p / 7:20a-2:00p CT

Commercial = -5387
NonCommercial = 15489
NonReportable = -10102

## Quarterly High, Low and Settle of Treasury Notes, 5-Year Futures — In Nominal Value

| Quarter | High | Low | Settle | Quarter | High | Low | Settle | Quarter | High | Low | Settle |
|---|---|---|---|---|---|---|---|---|---|---|---|
| 03/2000 | 98 080/128 | 96 064/128 | 98 064/128 | 03/2003 | 115 028/128 | 111 044/128 | 113 064/128 | 03/2006 | 106 116/128 | 104 038/128 | 104 056/128 |
| 06/2000 | 100 002/128 | 96 064/128 | 99 002/128 | 06/2003 | 117 102/128 | 112 046/128 | 115 016/128 | 06/2006 | 104 076/128 | 103 000/128 | 103 056/128 |
| 09/2000 | 100 090/128 | 98 054/128 | 100 070/128 | 09/2003 | 115 062/128 | 110 072/128 | 113 060/128 | 09/2006 | 105 106/128 | 102 126/128 | 105 054/128 |
| 12/2000 | 103 112/128 | 100 020/128 | 103 072/128 | 12/2003 | 113 076/128 | 110 060/128 | 111 080/128 | 12/2006 | 106 058/128 | 104 068/128 | 105 016/128 |
| 03/2001 | 106 038/128 | 102 112/128 | 105 066/128 | 03/2004 | 115 036/128 | 110 106/128 | 113 072/128 | 03/2007 | 106 038/128 | 104 024/128 | 105 092/128 |
| 06/2001 | 106 008/128 | 103 022/128 | 103 044/128 | 06/2004 | 113 084/128 | 107 108/128 | 108 088/128 | 06/2007 | 105 120/128 | 103 008/128 | 104 004/128 |
| 09/2001 | 108 096/128 | 103 032/128 | 108 024/128 | 09/2004 | 111 118/128 | 108 070/128 | 110 096/128 | 09/2007 | 108 018/128 | 103 052/128 | 107 042/128 |
| 12/2001 | 110 058/128 | 104 088/128 | 105 106/128 | 12/2004 | 111 100/128 | 109 014/128 | 109 068/128 | 12/2007 | 111 030/128 | 106 006/128 | 110 058/128 |
| 03/2002 | 107 074/128 | 103 046/128 | 103 094/128 | 03/2005 | 110 000/128 | 106 016/128 | 107 012/128 | 03/2008 | 116 048/128 | 110 008/128 | 114 030/128 |
| 06/2002 | 108 096/128 | 103 064/128 | 107 054/128 | 06/2005 | 109 122/128 | 106 106/128 | 108 114/128 | 06/2008 | 114 051/128 | 109 017/128 | 111 000/128 |
| 09/2002 | 114 056/128 | 107 024/128 | 114 036/128 | 09/2005 | 109 064/128 | 106 076/128 | 106 110/128 | 09/2008 | 115 063/128 | 109 101/128 | 113 088/128 |
| 12/2002 | 114 074/128 | 111 016/128 | 113 032/128 | 12/2005 | 106 124/128 | 105 046/128 | 106 044/128 | 12/2008 | 122 126/128 | 111 030/128 | 120 126/128 |

*Source: CME Group; Chicago Board of Trade*

# TREASURY NOTES, 5-YEAR

**WEEKLY CASH**
As of 01/02/2009
Chart High 6.834 on 05/09/2000
Chart Low 1.185 on 12/17/2008

T-Note Yield, 5-Year
Weekly Cash as of 01/02/2009

| Date | Open | High | Low | Close |
|---|---|---|---|---|
| 12/05/08 | 1.870 | 1.881 | 1.485 | 1.667 |
| 12/12/08 | 1.768 | 1.776 | 1.496 | 1.553 |
| 12/19/08 | 1.566 | 1.580 | 1.185 | 1.352 |
| 12/26/08 | 1.382 | 1.583 | 1.352 | 1.497 |
| 01/02/09 | 1.467 | 1.730 | 1.369 | 1.727 |

## Quarterly High, Low and Settle of Treasury Notes, 5-Year Yield    In Percent

| Quarter | High | Low | Settle | Quarter | High | Low | Settle | Quarter | High | Low | Settle |
|---|---|---|---|---|---|---|---|---|---|---|---|
| 03/2000 | 6.807 | 6.278 | 6.320 | 03/2003 | 3.204 | 2.474 | 2.738 | 03/2006 | 4.846 | 4.229 | 4.814 |
| 06/2000 | 6.834 | 5.936 | 6.171 | 06/2003 | 3.010 | 1.997 | 2.423 | 06/2006 | 5.263 | 4.785 | 5.098 |
| 09/2000 | 6.316 | 5.803 | 5.833 | 09/2003 | 3.617 | 2.346 | 2.823 | 09/2006 | 5.199 | 4.489 | 4.587 |
| 12/2000 | 5.938 | 4.880 | 4.967 | 12/2003 | 3.519 | 2.792 | 3.218 | 12/2006 | 4.821 | 4.347 | 4.701 |
| 03/2001 | 5.092 | 4.351 | 4.557 | 03/2004 | 3.401 | 2.608 | 2.781 | 03/2007 | 4.900 | 4.377 | 4.537 |
| 06/2001 | 5.108 | 4.411 | 4.934 | 06/2004 | 4.101 | 2.776 | 3.808 | 06/2007 | 5.241 | 4.495 | 4.936 |
| 09/2001 | 4.962 | 3.246 | 3.780 | 09/2004 | 3.875 | 3.212 | 3.370 | 09/2007 | 5.110 | 3.955 | 4.229 |
| 12/2001 | 4.696 | 3.448 | 4.334 | 12/2004 | 3.774 | 3.205 | 3.607 | 12/2007 | 4.463 | 3.219 | 3.455 |
| 03/2002 | 4.877 | 4.038 | 4.824 | 03/2005 | 4.385 | 3.559 | 4.174 | 03/2008 | 3.467 | 2.164 | 2.467 |
| 06/2002 | 4.875 | 3.789 | 4.062 | 06/2005 | 4.224 | 3.551 | 3.725 | 06/2008 | 3.744 | 2.512 | 3.341 |
| 09/2002 | 4.104 | 2.548 | 2.578 | 09/2005 | 4.288 | 3.735 | 4.195 | 09/2008 | 3.568 | 2.348 | 2.986 |
| 12/2002 | 3.404 | 2.533 | 2.730 | 12/2005 | 4.578 | 4.182 | 4.355 | 12/2008 | 3.077 | 1.185 | 1.551 |

*Source: Federal Reserve Board*

# TREASURY NOTES, 10-YEAR

**T-NOTE, 10-YEAR - CBOT**
Monthly Nearest Futures as of 12/31/2008

| Date | Open | High | Low | Close |
|---|---|---|---|---|
| 08/31/08 | 115 2/64 | 117 13/64 | 114 4/64 | 116 44/64 |
| 09/30/08 | 116 42/64 | 120 33/64 | 114 1/64 | 114 40/64 |
| 10/31/08 | 114 47/64 | 118 4/64 | 111 25/64 | 113 5/64 |
| 11/30/08 | 113 7/64 | 123 11/64 | 112 55/64 | 122 57/64 |
| 12/31/08 | 122 58/64 | 130 51/64 | 122 37/64 | 125 48/64 |

**MONTHLY NEAREST FUTURES** As of 12/31/2008
Chart High 130 51/64 on 12/17/2008
Chart Low 60 30/64 on 06/23/1982
CONTRACT SIZE 100,000 USD @ 6%
MIN TICK 1/64
VALUE 15.625 USD/CONTRACT
EACH GRID 32/64 1/64
VALUE 500 USD/CONTRACT
DAILY LIMIT None
VALUE
TRADING HOURS
5:30p-4:00p / 7:20a-2:00p CT

## Annual High, Low and Settle of Treasury Notes, 10-Year Futures    In Nominal Value

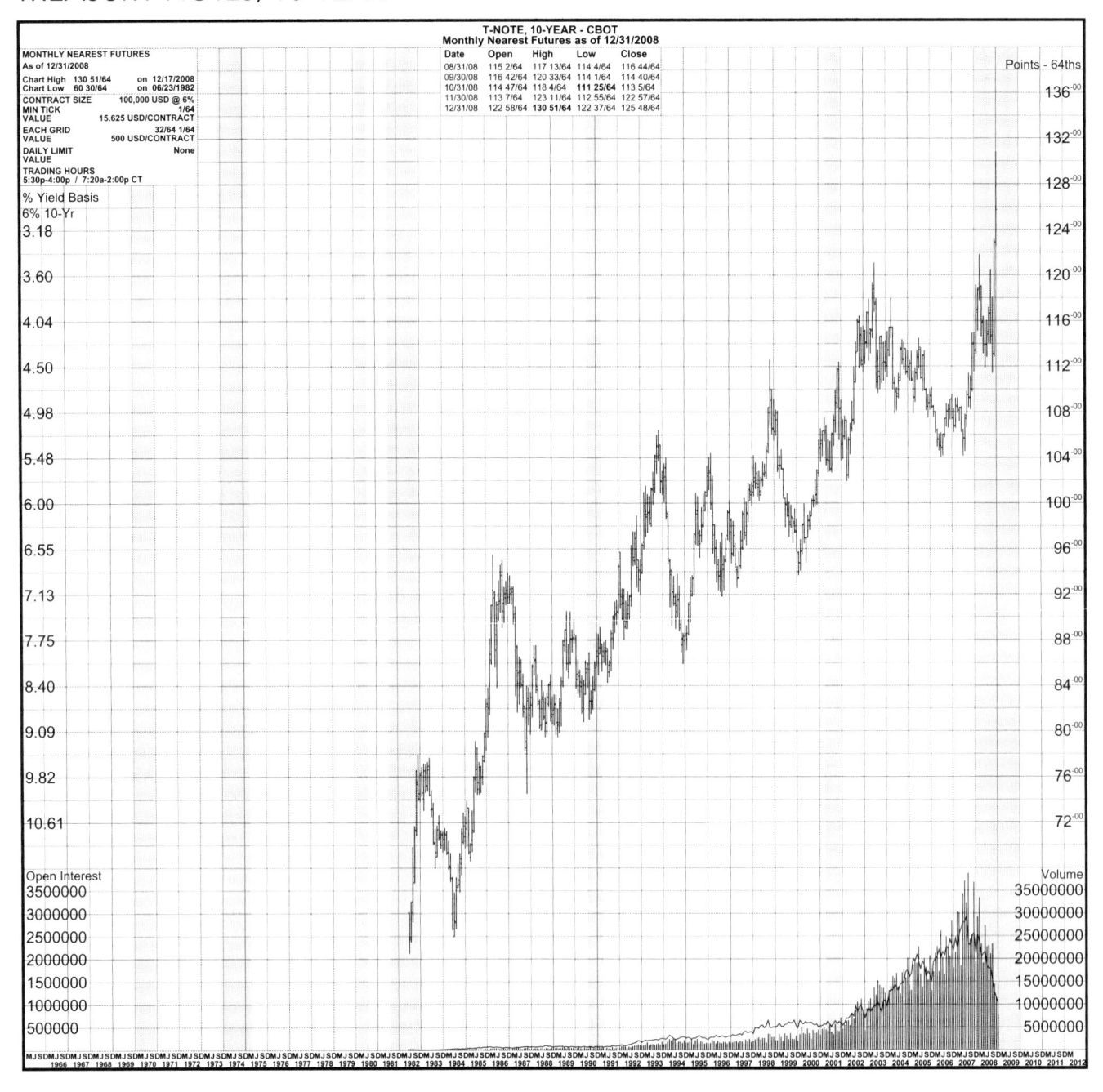

| Year | High | Low | Settle | Year | High | Low | Settle | Year | High | Low | Settle |
|---|---|---|---|---|---|---|---|---|---|---|---|
| 1967 | | | | 1981 | | | | 1995 | 103 18/64 | 87 04/64 | 102 24/64 |
| 1968 | | | | 1982 | 77 56/64 | 60 30/64 | 76 10/64 | 1996 | 104 28/64 | 91 50/64 | 97 32/64 |
| 1969 | | | | 1983 | 77 44/64 | 67 60/64 | 70 30/64 | 1997 | 101 56/64 | 92 36/64 | 101 32/64 |
| 1970 | | | | 1984 | 72 56/64 | 61 62/64 | 71 26/64 | 1998 | 112 40/64 | 100 10/64 | 106 18/64 |
| 1971 | | | | 1985 | 82 54/64 | 68 34/64 | 82 12/64 | 1999 | 108 14/64 | 95 46/64 | 95 55/64 |
| 1972 | | | | 1986 | 95 34/64 | 79 28/64 | 91 50/64 | 2000 | 105 36/64 | 93 43/64 | 104 55/64 |
| 1973 | | | | 1987 | 93 44/64 | 74 32/64 | 82 62/64 | 2001 | 112 26/64 | 102 44/64 | 105 09/64 |
| 1974 | | | | 1988 | 87 36/64 | 79 28/64 | 81 28/64 | 2002 | 116 28/64 | 101 58/64 | 115 03/64 |
| 1975 | | | | 1989 | 90 36/64 | 79 28/64 | 88 32/64 | 2003 | 121 06/64 | 109 39/64 | 112 17/64 |
| 1976 | | | | 1990 | 88 40/64 | 80 50/64 | 87 00/64 | 2004 | 117 62/64 | 107 51/64 | 111 60/64 |
| 1977 | | | | 1991 | 94 44/64 | 84 16/64 | 94 30/64 | 2005 | 114 32/64 | 107 31/64 | 109 26/64 |
| 1978 | | | | 1992 | 98 60/64 | 87 62/64 | 94 38/64 | 2006 | 110 13/64 | 104 02/64 | 107 30/64 |
| 1979 | | | | 1993 | 106 28/64 | 93 50/64 | 102 14/64 | 2007 | 115 01/64 | 104 08/64 | 113 25/64 |
| 1980 | | | | 1994 | 104 02/64 | 85 56/64 | 88 22/64 | 2008 | 130 51/64 | 111 25/64 | 125 48/64 |

Futures begin trading 05/03/1982.    *Source: CME Group; Chicago Board of Trade*

# TREASURY NOTES, 10-YEAR

**T-Note Yield, 10-Year**
Monthly Cash as of 12/31/2008

| Date | Open | High | Low | Close |
|---|---|---|---|---|
| 08/29/08 | 3.942 | 4.090 | 3.763 | 3.813 |
| 09/30/08 | 3.847 | 3.905 | 3.250 | 3.827 |
| 10/31/08 | 3.748 | 4.109 | 3.400 | 3.970 |
| 11/28/08 | 3.937 | 3.964 | 2.930 | 2.957 |
| 12/31/08 | 2.883 | 2.887 | 2.038 | 2.244 |

MONTHLY CASH As of 12/31/2008
Chart High 15.840 on 09/30/1981
Chart Low 2.038 on 12/18/2008

## Annual High, Low and Settle of Treasury Notes, 10-Year Yield    In Percent

| Year | High | Low | Settle | Year | High | Low | Settle | Year | High | Low | Settle |
|---|---|---|---|---|---|---|---|---|---|---|---|
| 1967 | 5.870 | 4.450 | 5.700 | 1981 | 15.840 | 12.110 | 13.980 | 1995 | 7.928 | 5.574 | 5.581 |
| 1968 | 6.270 | 5.340 | 6.160 | 1982 | 14.950 | 10.360 | 10.360 | 1996 | 7.123 | 5.501 | 6.418 |
| 1969 | 8.050 | 5.950 | 7.880 | 1983 | 12.200 | 10.120 | 11.820 | 1997 | 7.016 | 5.659 | 5.725 |
| 1970 | 8.220 | 6.210 | 6.500 | 1984 | 13.990 | 11.240 | 11.550 | 1998 | 5.849 | 4.084 | 4.654 |
| 1971 | 6.950 | 5.380 | 5.890 | 1985 | 12.020 | 8.990 | 9.000 | 1999 | 6.453 | 4.558 | 6.440 |
| 1972 | 6.620 | 5.850 | 6.410 | 1986 | 9.490 | 6.950 | 7.230 | 2000 | 6.834 | 4.998 | 5.102 |
| 1973 | 7.580 | 6.400 | 6.900 | 1987 | 10.230 | 7.010 | 8.830 | 2001 | 5.563 | 4.101 | 5.033 |
| 1974 | 8.160 | 6.930 | 7.400 | 1988 | 9.410 | 8.110 | 9.133 | 2002 | 5.475 | 3.559 | 3.818 |
| 1975 | 8.590 | 7.220 | 7.760 | 1989 | 9.550 | 7.634 | 7.917 | 2003 | 4.668 | 3.074 | 4.257 |
| 1976 | 8.000 | 6.800 | 6.810 | 1990 | 9.113 | 7.880 | 8.063 | 2004 | 4.904 | 3.650 | 4.216 |
| 1977 | 7.820 | 6.840 | 7.780 | 1991 | 8.434 | 6.659 | 6.701 | 2005 | 4.693 | 3.803 | 4.395 |
| 1978 | 9.160 | 7.820 | 9.150 | 1992 | 7.723 | 6.164 | 6.701 | 2006 | 5.245 | 4.289 | 4.710 |
| 1979 | 11.020 | 8.760 | 10.330 | 1993 | 6.789 | 5.143 | 5.790 | 2007 | 5.316 | 3.840 | 4.035 |
| 1980 | 13.650 | 9.470 | 12.430 | 1994 | 8.062 | 5.548 | 7.820 | 2008 | 4.324 | 2.038 | 2.244 |

*Source: Federal Reserve Board*

# TREASURY NOTES, 10-YEAR

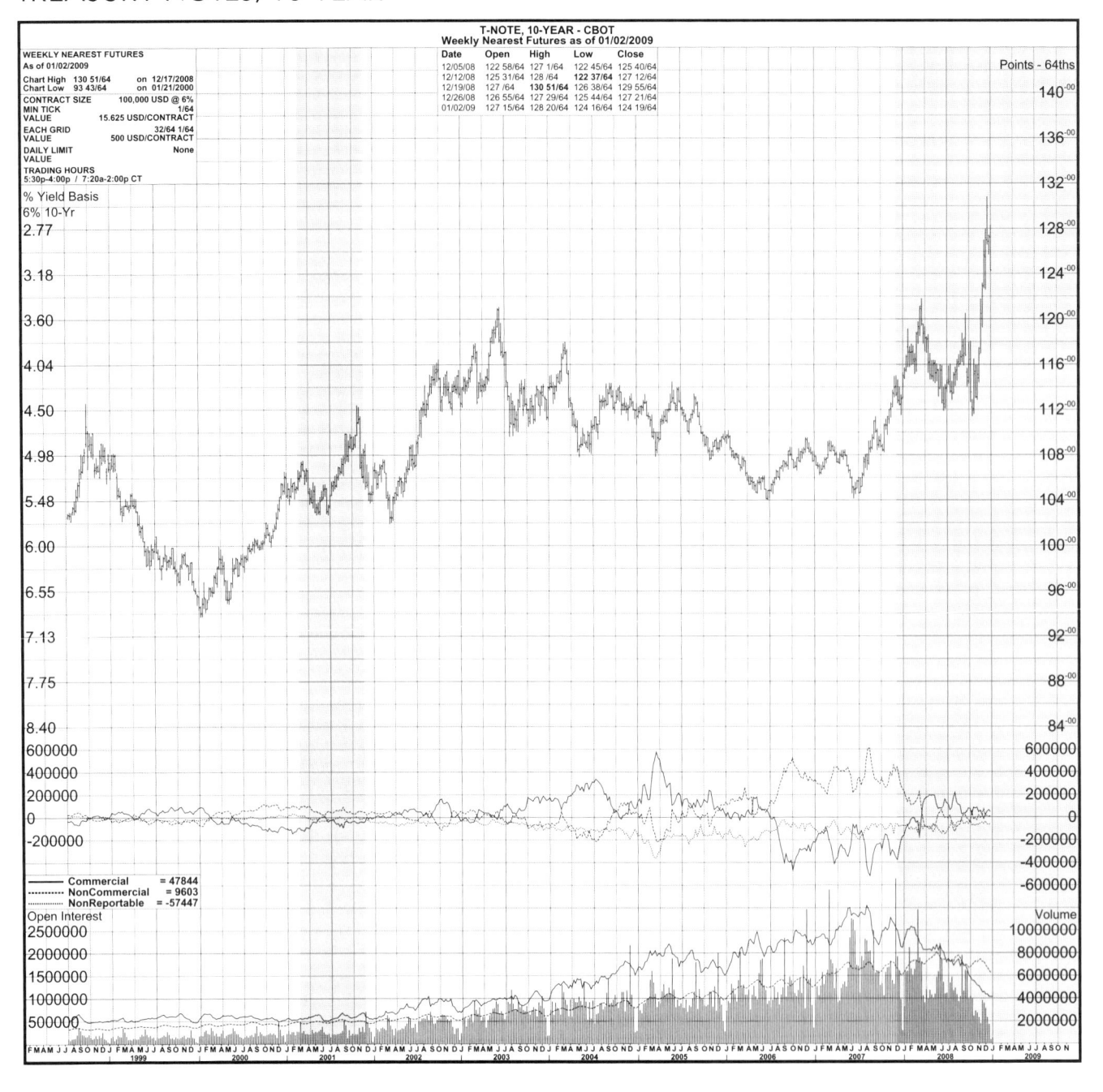

**Quarterly High, Low and Settle of Treasury Notes, 10-Year Futures**  In Nominal Value

| Quarter | High | Low | Settle | Quarter | High | Low | Settle | Quarter | High | Low | Settle |
|---|---|---|---|---|---|---|---|---|---|---|---|
| 03/2000 | 98 14/64 | 93 43/64 | 98 05/64 | 03/2003 | 117 58/64 | 112 11/64 | 114 56/64 | 03/2006 | 110 13/64 | 106 08/64 | 106 25/64 |
| 06/2000 | 99 60/64 | 94 52/64 | 98 31/64 | 06/2003 | 121 06/64 | 113 08/64 | 117 28/64 | 06/2006 | 106 34/64 | 104 02/64 | 104 55/64 |
| 09/2000 | 100 46/64 | 97 40/64 | 100 14/64 | 09/2003 | 117 61/64 | 109 39/64 | 114 40/64 | 09/2006 | 108 48/64 | 104 10/64 | 108 04/64 |
| 12/2000 | 105 36/64 | 99 43/64 | 104 55/64 | 12/2003 | 114 48/64 | 110 31/64 | 112 17/64 | 12/2006 | 109 36/64 | 106 38/64 | 107 30/64 |
| 03/2001 | 107 33/64 | 103 38/64 | 106 13/64 | 03/2004 | 117 62/64 | 111 02/64 | 115 26/64 | 03/2007 | 109 19/64 | 106 13/64 | 108 08/64 |
| 06/2001 | 106 55/64 | 102 44/64 | 103 01/64 | 06/2004 | 115 32/64 | 107 51/64 | 109 21/64 | 06/2007 | 108 32/64 | 104 08/64 | 105 45/64 |
| 09/2001 | 109 59/64 | 102 44/64 | 108 50/64 | 09/2004 | 114 24/64 | 109 11/64 | 112 40/64 | 09/2007 | 111 27/64 | 104 35/64 | 109 18/64 |
| 12/2001 | 112 26/64 | 103 46/64 | 105 09/64 | 12/2004 | 114 10/64 | 110 63/64 | 111 60/64 | 12/2007 | 115 01/64 | 108 13/64 | 113 25/64 |
| 03/2002 | 107 43/64 | 101 58/64 | 102 29/64 | 03/2005 | 113 25/64 | 107 53/64 | 109 17/64 | 03/2008 | 121 52/64 | 113 04/64 | 118 61/64 |
| 06/2002 | 108 61/64 | 102 12/64 | 107 15/64 | 06/2005 | 114 32/64 | 108 54/64 | 113 30/64 | 06/2008 | 119 06/64 | 111 56/64 | 113 59/64 |
| 09/2002 | 116 13/64 | 106 56/64 | 115 58/64 | 09/2005 | 113 43/64 | 109 50/64 | 109 59/64 | 09/2008 | 120 33/64 | 112 54/64 | 114 40/64 |
| 12/2002 | 116 28/64 | 111 32/64 | 115 03/64 | 12/2005 | 110 05/64 | 107 31/64 | 109 26/64 | 12/2008 | 130 51/64 | 111 25/64 | 125 48/64 |

*Source: CME Group; Chicago Board of Trade*

# TREASURY NOTES, 10-YEAR

**WEEKLY CASH**
As of 01/02/2009
Chart High 6.834 on 01/28/2000
Chart Low 2.038 on 12/18/2008

T-Note Yield, 10-Year
Weekly Cash as of 01/02/2009

| Date | Open | High | Low | Close |
|---|---|---|---|---|
| 12/05/08 | 2.883 | 2.887 | 2.508 | 2.657 |
| 12/12/08 | 2.753 | 2.760 | 2.538 | 2.589 |
| 12/19/08 | 2.582 | 2.582 | 2.038 | 2.131 |
| 12/26/08 | 2.141 | 2.240 | 2.108 | 2.137 |
| 01/02/09 | 2.135 | 2.417 | 2.050 | 2.416 |

## Quarterly High, Low and Settle of Treasury Notes, 10-Year Yield   In Percent

| Quarter | High | Low | Settle | Quarter | High | Low | Settle | Quarter | High | Low | Settle |
|---|---|---|---|---|---|---|---|---|---|---|---|
| 03/2000 | 6.834 | 5.994 | 6.000 | 03/2003 | 4.203 | 3.549 | 3.823 | 03/2006 | 4.884 | 4.289 | 4.853 |
| 06/2000 | 6.593 | 5.700 | 6.018 | 06/2003 | 4.080 | 3.074 | 3.528 | 06/2006 | 5.245 | 4.835 | 5.138 |
| 09/2000 | 6.184 | 5.656 | 5.799 | 09/2003 | 4.668 | 3.459 | 3.937 | 09/2006 | 5.241 | 4.530 | 4.633 |
| 12/2000 | 5.897 | 4.998 | 5.102 | 12/2003 | 4.491 | 3.912 | 4.257 | 12/2006 | 4.848 | 4.404 | 4.710 |
| 03/2001 | 5.365 | 4.687 | 4.923 | 03/2004 | 4.418 | 3.650 | 3.837 | 03/2007 | 4.906 | 4.473 | 4.648 |
| 06/2001 | 5.563 | 4.846 | 5.392 | 06/2004 | 4.904 | 3.831 | 4.617 | 06/2007 | 5.316 | 4.602 | 5.033 |
| 09/2001 | 5.438 | 4.501 | 4.572 | 09/2004 | 4.641 | 3.963 | 4.119 | 09/2007 | 5.201 | 4.301 | 4.579 |
| 12/2001 | 5.395 | 4.101 | 5.033 | 12/2004 | 4.420 | 3.943 | 4.216 | 12/2007 | 4.719 | 3.840 | 4.035 |
| 03/2002 | 5.473 | 4.791 | 5.415 | 03/2005 | 4.693 | 3.977 | 4.496 | 03/2008 | 4.052 | 3.281 | 3.432 |
| 06/2002 | 5.475 | 4.600 | 4.822 | 06/2005 | 4.541 | 3.803 | 3.945 | 06/2008 | 4.324 | 3.430 | 3.979 |
| 09/2002 | 4.867 | 3.567 | 3.607 | 09/2005 | 4.435 | 3.942 | 4.328 | 09/2008 | 4.174 | 3.250 | 3.827 |
| 12/2002 | 4.351 | 3.559 | 3.818 | 12/2005 | 4.682 | 4.317 | 4.395 | 12/2008 | 4.109 | 2.038 | 2.244 |

*Source: Federal Reserve Board*

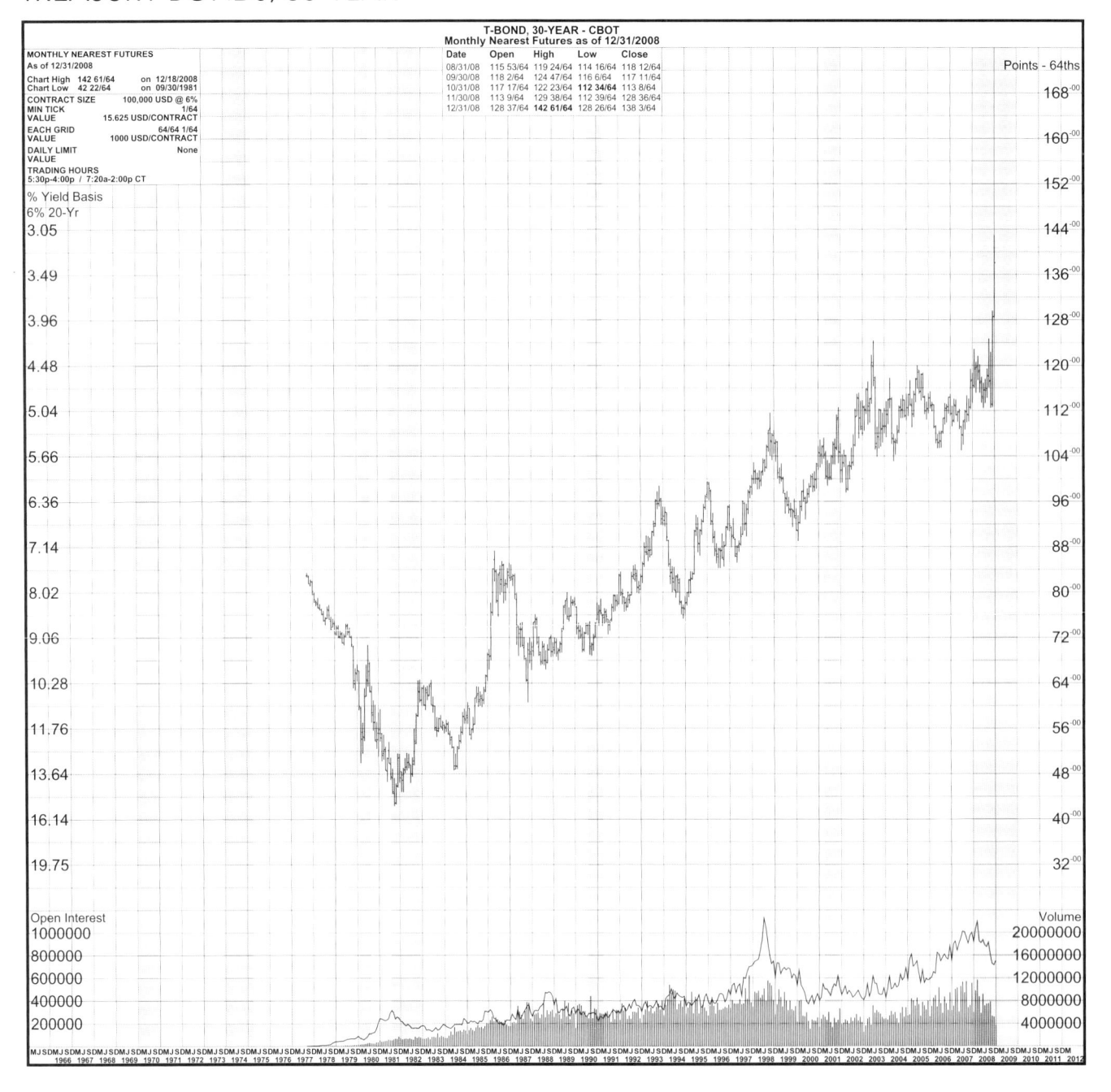

# TREASURY BONDS, 30-YEAR

**MONTHLY NEAREST FUTURES**
As of 12/31/2008
Chart High 142 61/64 on 12/18/2008
Chart Low 42 22/64 on 09/30/1981
CONTRACT SIZE 100,000 USD @ 6%
MIN TICK 1/64
VALUE 15.625 USD/CONTRACT
EACH GRID 64/64 1/64
VALUE 1000 USD/CONTRACT
DAILY LIMIT None
VALUE
TRADING HOURS
5:30p-4:00p / 7:20a-2:00p CT

% Yield Basis
6% 20-Yr

**T-BOND, 30-YEAR - CBOT**
Monthly Nearest Futures as of 12/31/2008

| Date | Open | High | Low | Close |
|---|---|---|---|---|
| 08/31/08 | 115 53/64 | 119 24/64 | 114 16/64 | 118 12/64 |
| 09/30/08 | 118 2/64 | 124 47/64 | 116 6/64 | 117 11/64 |
| 10/31/08 | 117 17/64 | 122 23/64 | 112 34/64 | 113 8/64 |
| 11/30/08 | 113 9/64 | 129 38/64 | 112 39/64 | 128 36/64 |
| 12/31/08 | 128 37/64 | 142 61/64 | 128 26/64 | 138 3/64 |

## Annual High, Low and Settle of Treasury Bonds, 30-Year Futures    In Nominal Value

| Year | High | Low | Settle | Year | High | Low | Settle | Year | High | Low | Settle |
|---|---|---|---|---|---|---|---|---|---|---|---|
| 1967 | | | | 1981 | 59 15/32 | 42 11/32 | 47 09/32 | 1995 | 99 17/32 | 77 19/32 | 99 13/32 |
| 1968 | | | | 1982 | 64 20/32 | 44 25/32 | 63 03/32 | 1996 | 99 15/32 | 84 07/32 | 91 22/32 |
| 1969 | | | | 1983 | 64 20/32 | 54 15/32 | 56 08/32 | 1997 | 100 21/32 | 85 06/32 | 100 01/32 |
| 1970 | | | | 1984 | 59 17/32 | 48 19/32 | 58 09/32 | 1998 | 111 21/32 | 98 02/32 | 106 09/32 |
| 1971 | | | | 1985 | 69 11/32 | 53 30/32 | 69 00/32 | 1999 | 106 31/32 | 90 25/32 | 90 30/32 |
| 1972 | | | | 1986 | 87 12/32 | 66 11/32 | 82 17/32 | 2000 | 105 23/32 | 89 00/32 | 104 20/32 |
| 1973 | | | | 1987 | 84 29/32 | 60 18/32 | 70 11/32 | 2001 | 112 19/32 | 98 24/32 | 101 17/32 |
| 1974 | | | | 1988 | 76 04/32 | 66 11/32 | 70 09/32 | 2002 | 115 04/32 | 97 16/32 | 112 22/32 |
| 1975 | | | | 1989 | 80 01/32 | 67 31/32 | 77 28/32 | 2003 | 124 12/32 | 103 27/32 | 109 10/32 |
| 1976 | | | | 1990 | 78 06/32 | 68 26/32 | 76 03/32 | 2004 | 117 26/32 | 103 02/32 | 112 16/32 |
| 1977 | 83 19/32 | 79 17/32 | 80 07/32 | 1991 | 83 06/32 | 72 16/32 | 83 04/32 | 2005 | 119 30/32 | 109 00/32 | 114 06/32 |
| 1978 | 80 02/32 | 72 17/32 | 72 26/32 | 1992 | 84 30/32 | 76 16/32 | 82 24/32 | 2006 | 115 13/32 | 105 11/32 | 111 14/32 |
| 1979 | 74 16/32 | 62 21/32 | 66 08/32 | 1993 | 98 26/32 | 81 19/32 | 93 12/32 | 2007 | 119 12/32 | 104 31/32 | 116 12/32 |
| 1980 | 70 23/32 | 49 28/32 | 55 25/32 | 1994 | 95 02/32 | 75 09/32 | 78 02/32 | 2008 | 142 30/32 | 112 14/32 | 138 02/32 |

Futures begin trading 08/22/1977.    *Source: CME Group; Chicago Board of Trade*

# TREASURY BONDS, 30-YEAR

**MONTHLY CASH**
As of 12/31/2008
Chart High 15.210 on 10/26/1981
Chart Low 2.519 on 12/18/2008

T-Bond Yield, 30-Year
Monthly Cash as of 12/31/2008

| Date | Open | High | Low | Close |
|---|---|---|---|---|
| 08/29/08 | 4.572 | 4.722 | 4.364 | 4.412 |
| 09/30/08 | 4.442 | 4.476 | 3.895 | 4.305 |
| 10/31/08 | 4.237 | 4.375 | 3.884 | 4.369 |
| 11/28/08 | 4.374 | 4.374 | 3.468 | 3.487 |
| 12/31/08 | 3.385 | 3.388 | 2.519 | 2.691 |

## Annual High, Low and Settle of Treasury Bonds, 30-Year Yield   In Percent

| Year | High | Low | Settle | Year | High | Low | Settle | Year | High | Low | Settle |
|---|---|---|---|---|---|---|---|---|---|---|---|
| 1967 | 5.440 | 4.400 | 5.360 | 1981 | 15.210 | 11.670 | 13.650 | 1995 | 7.962 | 5.938 | 5.956 |
| 1968 | 5.650 | 5.040 | 5.650 | 1982 | 14.800 | 10.330 | 10.430 | 1996 | 7.250 | 5.922 | 6.639 |
| 1969 | 6.810 | 5.740 | 6.810 | 1983 | 12.150 | 10.270 | 11.870 | 1997 | 7.189 | 5.850 | 5.915 |
| 1970 | 6.990 | 5.970 | 5.970 | 1984 | 13.940 | 11.320 | 11.540 | 1998 | 6.092 | 4.685 | 5.092 |
| 1971 | 5.960 | 5.440 | 5.620 | 1985 | 11.970 | 9.270 | 9.270 | 1999 | 6.491 | 5.030 | 6.479 |
| 1972 | 6.560 | 5.570 | 6.340 | 1986 | 9.650 | 7.120 | 7.490 | 2000 | 6.762 | 5.380 | 5.457 |
| 1973 | 7.450 | 6.530 | 7.010 | 1987 | 10.250 | 7.290 | 8.950 | 2001 | 5.919 | 4.661 | 5.472 |
| 1974 | 8.290 | 7.180 | 7.620 | 1988 | 9.542 | 8.320 | 8.995 | 2002 | 5.872 | 4.606 | 4.783 |
| 1975 | 8.330 | 7.520 | 8.050 | 1989 | 9.337 | 7.753 | 7.973 | 2003 | 5.495 | 4.135 | 5.068 |
| 1976 | 7.910 | 7.200 | 7.200 | 1990 | 9.203 | 7.962 | 8.240 | 2004 | 5.597 | 4.620 | 4.822 |
| 1977 | 8.060 | 7.350 | 8.030 | 1991 | 8.622 | 7.394 | 7.396 | 2005 | 4.931 | 4.151 | 4.547 |
| 1978 | 8.990 | 8.070 | 8.960 | 1992 | 8.146 | 7.201 | 7.403 | 2006 | 5.307 | 4.460 | 4.818 |
| 1979 | 10.530 | 8.800 | 10.110 | 1993 | 7.493 | 5.771 | 6.341 | 2007 | 5.408 | 4.279 | 4.459 |
| 1980 | 13.170 | 9.490 | 11.980 | 1994 | 8.187 | 6.154 | 7.883 | 2008 | 4.813 | 2.519 | 2.691 |

*Source: Federal Reserve Board*

# TREASURY BONDS, 30-YEAR

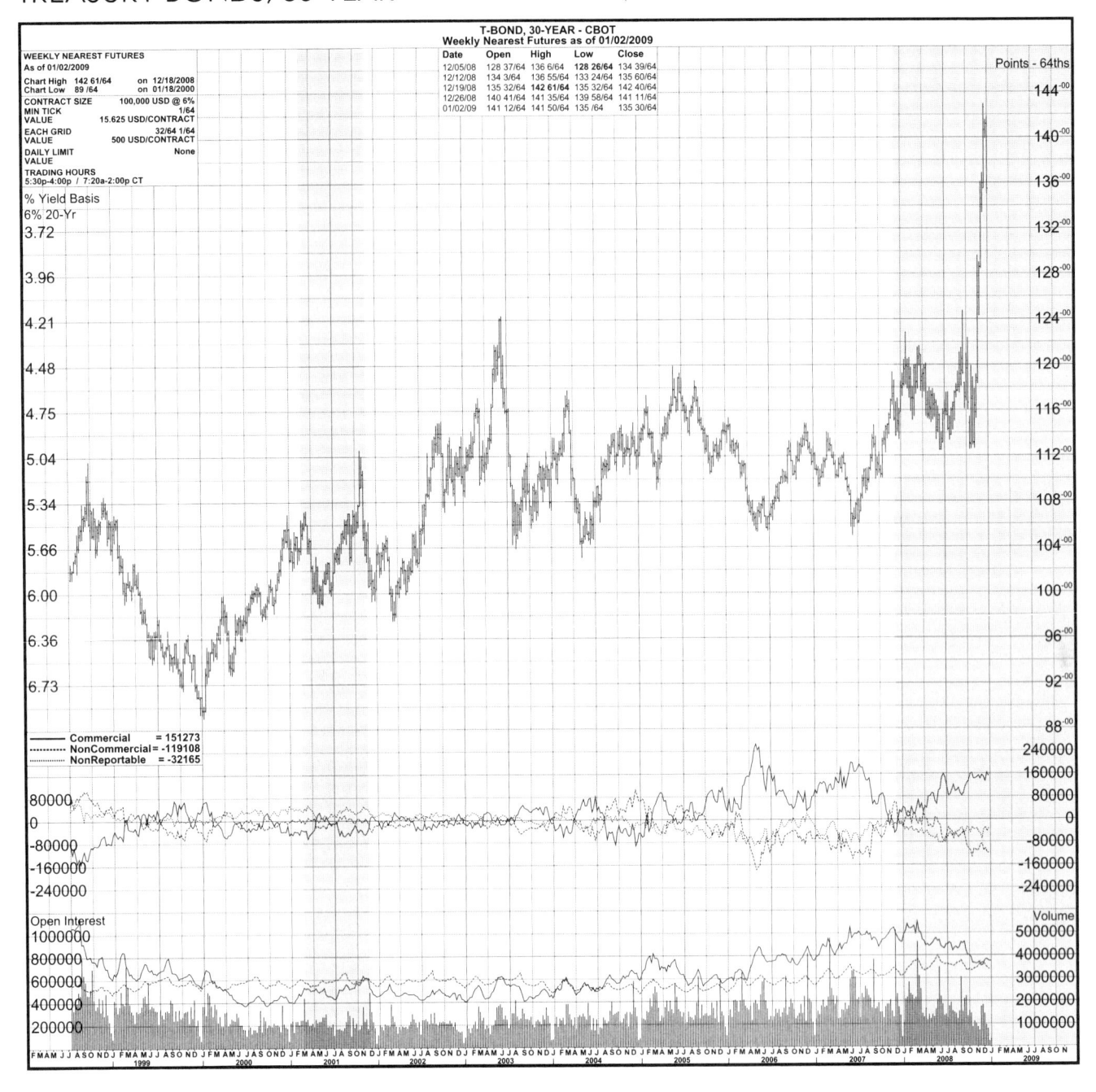

**T-BOND, 30-YEAR - CBOT**
Weekly Nearest Futures as of 01/02/2009

| Date | Open | High | Low | Close |
|---|---|---|---|---|
| 12/05/08 | 128 37/64 | 136 6/64 | 128 26/64 | 134 39/64 |
| 12/12/08 | 134 3/64 | 136 55/64 | 133 24/64 | 135 60/64 |
| 12/19/08 | 135 32/64 | 142 61/64 | 135 32/64 | 142 40/64 |
| 12/26/08 | 140 41/64 | 141 35/64 | 139 58/64 | 141 11/64 |
| 01/02/09 | 141 12/64 | 141 50/64 | 135 /64 | 135 30/64 |

**WEEKLY NEAREST FUTURES**
As of 01/02/2009
Chart High 142 61/64 on 12/18/2008
Chart Low 89 /64 on 01/18/2000
CONTRACT SIZE 100,000 USD @ 6%
MIN TICK VALUE 1/64 — 15.625 USD/CONTRACT
EACH GRID VALUE 32/64 1/64 — 500 USD/CONTRACT
DAILY LIMIT VALUE None
TRADING HOURS 5:30p-4:00p / 7:20a-2:00p CT

% Yield Basis 6% 20-Yr

Commercial = 151273
NonCommercial = -119108
NonReportable = -32165

## Quarterly High, Low and Settle of Treasury Bonds, 30-Year Futures — In Nominal Value

| Quarter | High | Low | Settle | Quarter | High | Low | Settle | Quarter | High | Low | Settle |
|---|---|---|---|---|---|---|---|---|---|---|---|
| 03/2000 | 97 28/32 | 89 00/32 | 97 22/32 | 03/2003 | 117 05/32 | 108 13/32 | 112 24/32 | 03/2006 | 115 13/32 | 108 26/32 | 109 05/32 |
| 06/2000 | 99 28/32 | 92 24/32 | 97 11/32 | 06/2003 | 124 12/32 | 109 26/32 | 117 11/32 | 06/2006 | 109 14/32 | 105 11/32 | 106 21/32 |
| 09/2000 | 101 00/32 | 96 19/32 | 98 21/32 | 09/2003 | 118 01/32 | 103 27/32 | 112 05/32 | 09/2006 | 113 11/32 | 105 14/32 | 112 13/32 |
| 12/2000 | 105 23/32 | 97 23/32 | 104 20/32 | 12/2003 | 112 15/32 | 105 20/32 | 109 10/32 | 12/2006 | 114 29/32 | 109 27/32 | 111 14/32 |
| 03/2001 | 107 08/32 | 101 31/32 | 104 06/32 | 03/2004 | 117 26/32 | 107 08/32 | 114 02/32 | 03/2007 | 114 04/32 | 109 06/32 | 111 08/32 |
| 06/2001 | 104 28/32 | 98 24/32 | 100 10/32 | 06/2004 | 114 12/32 | 103 02/32 | 106 12/32 | 06/2007 | 112 10/32 | 104 31/32 | 107 24/32 |
| 09/2001 | 107 02/32 | 99 25/32 | 105 16/32 | 09/2004 | 114 03/32 | 106 04/32 | 112 07/32 | 09/2007 | 114 23/32 | 105 31/32 | 111 11/32 |
| 12/2001 | 112 19/32 | 99 08/32 | 101 17/32 | 12/2004 | 115 00/32 | 110 11/32 | 112 16/32 | 12/2007 | 119 12/32 | 110 02/32 | 116 12/32 |
| 03/2002 | 105 04/32 | 97 16/32 | 98 05/32 | 03/2005 | 117 12/32 | 109 00/32 | 111 12/32 | 03/2008 | 122 28/32 | 115 03/32 | 118 26/32 |
| 06/2002 | 105 16/32 | 97 27/32 | 102 25/32 | 06/2005 | 119 30/32 | 110 25/32 | 118 24/32 | 06/2008 | 120 04/32 | 112 14/32 | 115 19/32 |
| 09/2002 | 114 31/32 | 102 08/32 | 114 08/32 | 09/2005 | 119 04/32 | 113 24/32 | 114 13/32 | 09/2008 | 124 24/32 | 113 11/32 | 117 06/32 |
| 12/2002 | 115 04/32 | 107 02/32 | 112 22/32 | 12/2005 | 115 00/32 | 110 12/32 | 114 06/32 | 12/2008 | 142 30/32 | 112 17/32 | 138 02/32 |

*Source: CME Group; Chicago Board of Trade*

# TREASURY BONDS, 30-YEAR

**T-Bond Yield, 30-Year**
Weekly Cash as of 01/02/2009

| Date | Open | High | Low | Close |
|---|---|---|---|---|
| 12/05/08 | 3.385 | **3.388** | 3.007 | 3.110 |
| 12/12/08 | 3.143 | 3.182 | 3.003 | 3.064 |
| 12/19/08 | 3.081 | 3.081 | **2.519** | 2.562 |
| 12/26/08 | 2.603 | 2.702 | 2.561 | 2.613 |
| 01/02/09 | 2.612 | 2.823 | 2.558 | 2.815 |

WEEKLY CASH
As of 01/02/2009
Chart High 6.762 on 01/20/2000
Chart Low 2.519 on 12/18/2008

## Quarterly High, Low and Settle of Treasury Bonds, 30-Year Yield   In Percent

| Quarter | High | Low | Settle | Quarter | High | Low | Settle | Quarter | High | Low | Settle |
|---|---|---|---|---|---|---|---|---|---|---|---|
| 03/2000 | 6.762 | 5.826 | 5.831 | 03/2003 | 5.094 | 4.603 | 4.837 | 03/2006 | 4.921 | 4.460 | 4.893 |
| 06/2000 | 6.252 | 5.623 | 5.894 | 06/2003 | 5.056 | 4.135 | 4.566 | 06/2006 | 5.307 | 4.872 | 5.186 |
| 09/2000 | 5.976 | 5.628 | 5.884 | 09/2003 | 5.495 | 4.526 | 4.884 | 09/2006 | 5.292 | 4.676 | 4.767 |
| 12/2000 | 5.950 | 5.380 | 5.457 | 12/2003 | 5.331 | 4.873 | 5.068 | 12/2006 | 4.976 | 4.525 | 4.818 |
| 03/2001 | 5.691 | 5.217 | 5.458 | 03/2004 | 5.219 | 4.620 | 4.777 | 03/2007 | 5.021 | 4.623 | 4.848 |
| 06/2001 | 5.919 | 5.429 | 5.736 | 06/2004 | 5.597 | 4.777 | 5.313 | 06/2007 | 5.408 | 4.758 | 5.126 |
| 09/2001 | 5.776 | 5.297 | 5.411 | 09/2004 | 5.352 | 4.757 | 4.891 | 09/2007 | 5.291 | 4.617 | 4.833 |
| 12/2001 | 5.721 | 4.661 | 5.472 | 12/2004 | 5.066 | 4.703 | 4.822 | 12/2007 | 4.928 | 4.279 | 4.459 |
| 03/2002 | 5.872 | 5.311 | 5.815 | 03/2005 | 4.931 | 4.351 | 4.766 | 03/2008 | 4.720 | 4.102 | 4.306 |
| 06/2002 | 5.863 | 5.321 | 5.519 | 06/2005 | 4.825 | 4.151 | 4.219 | 06/2008 | 4.813 | 4.275 | 4.531 |
| 09/2002 | 5.559 | 4.606 | 4.662 | 09/2005 | 4.618 | 4.205 | 4.568 | 09/2008 | 4.722 | 3.895 | 4.305 |
| 12/2002 | 5.214 | 4.631 | 4.783 | 12/2005 | 4.879 | 4.479 | 4.547 | 12/2008 | 4.375 | 2.519 | 2.691 |

*Source: Federal Reserve Board*

# STERLING, 3-MONTH

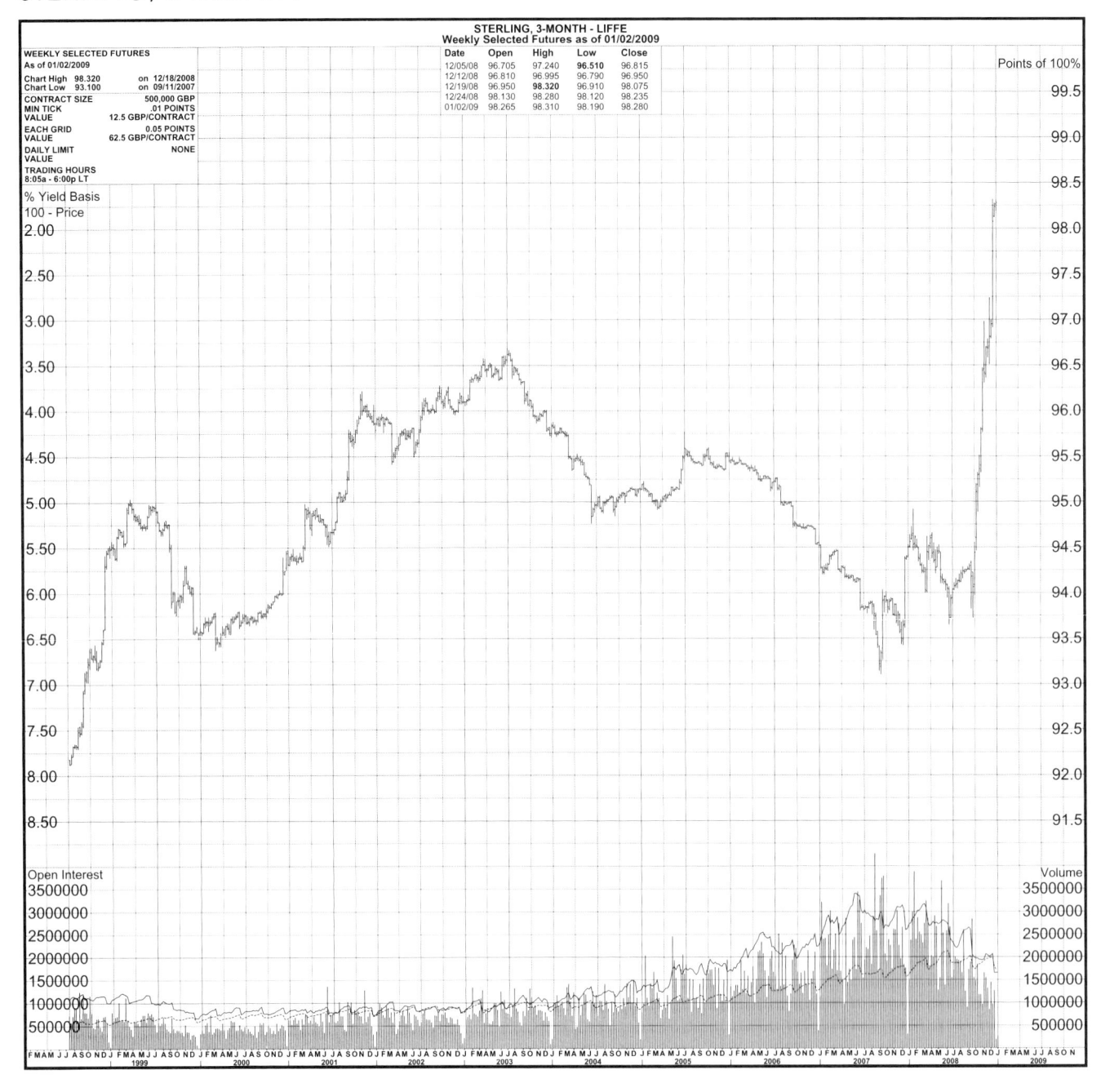

## Quarterly High, Low and Settle of Sterling, 3-Month Futures    In Point of 100%

| Quarter | High | Low | Settle | Quarter | High | Low | Settle | Quarter | High | Low | Settle |
|---|---|---|---|---|---|---|---|---|---|---|---|
| 03/2000 | 93.800 | 93.370 | 93.460 | 03/2003 | 96.560 | 96.050 | 96.550 | 03/2006 | 95.540 | 95.330 | 95.370 |
| 06/2000 | 93.810 | 93.410 | 93.680 | 06/2003 | 96.610 | 96.330 | 96.570 | 06/2006 | 95.410 | 95.110 | 95.210 |
| 09/2000 | 93.820 | 93.640 | 93.780 | 09/2003 | 96.690 | 96.070 | 96.210 | 09/2006 | 95.270 | 94.710 | 94.770 |
| 12/2000 | 94.400 | 93.720 | 94.240 | 12/2003 | 96.220 | 95.760 | 95.800 | 12/2006 | 94.760 | 94.520 | 94.550 |
| 03/2001 | 94.980 | 94.250 | 94.870 | 03/2004 | 95.880 | 95.420 | 95.460 | 03/2007 | 94.560 | 94.200 | 94.230 |
| 06/2001 | 94.950 | 94.510 | 94.540 | 06/2004 | 95.530 | 94.760 | 94.950 | 06/2007 | 94.300 | 93.800 | 93.840 |
| 09/2001 | 95.800 | 94.540 | 95.670 | 09/2004 | 95.070 | 94.840 | 95.030 | 09/2007 | 94.040 | 93.100 | 93.960 |
| 12/2001 | 96.220 | 95.590 | 95.880 | 12/2004 | 95.170 | 94.980 | 95.140 | 12/2007 | 94.430 | 93.420 | 94.420 |
| 03/2002 | 96.070 | 95.410 | 95.520 | 03/2005 | 95.230 | 94.910 | 94.990 | 03/2008 | 94.920 | 94.000 | 94.555 |
| 06/2002 | 95.820 | 95.480 | 95.630 | 06/2005 | 95.510 | 94.980 | 95.500 | 06/2008 | 94.660 | 93.645 | 93.900 |
| 09/2002 | 96.280 | 95.600 | 96.230 | 09/2005 | 95.770 | 95.390 | 95.500 | 09/2008 | 94.350 | 93.715 | 94.130 |
| 12/2002 | 96.270 | 95.950 | 96.160 | 12/2005 | 95.600 | 95.340 | 95.500 | 12/2008 | 98.320 | 94.105 | 98.235 |

*Source: Euronext LIFFE*

# CANADIAN BANKERS' ACCEPTANCE, 3-MONTH

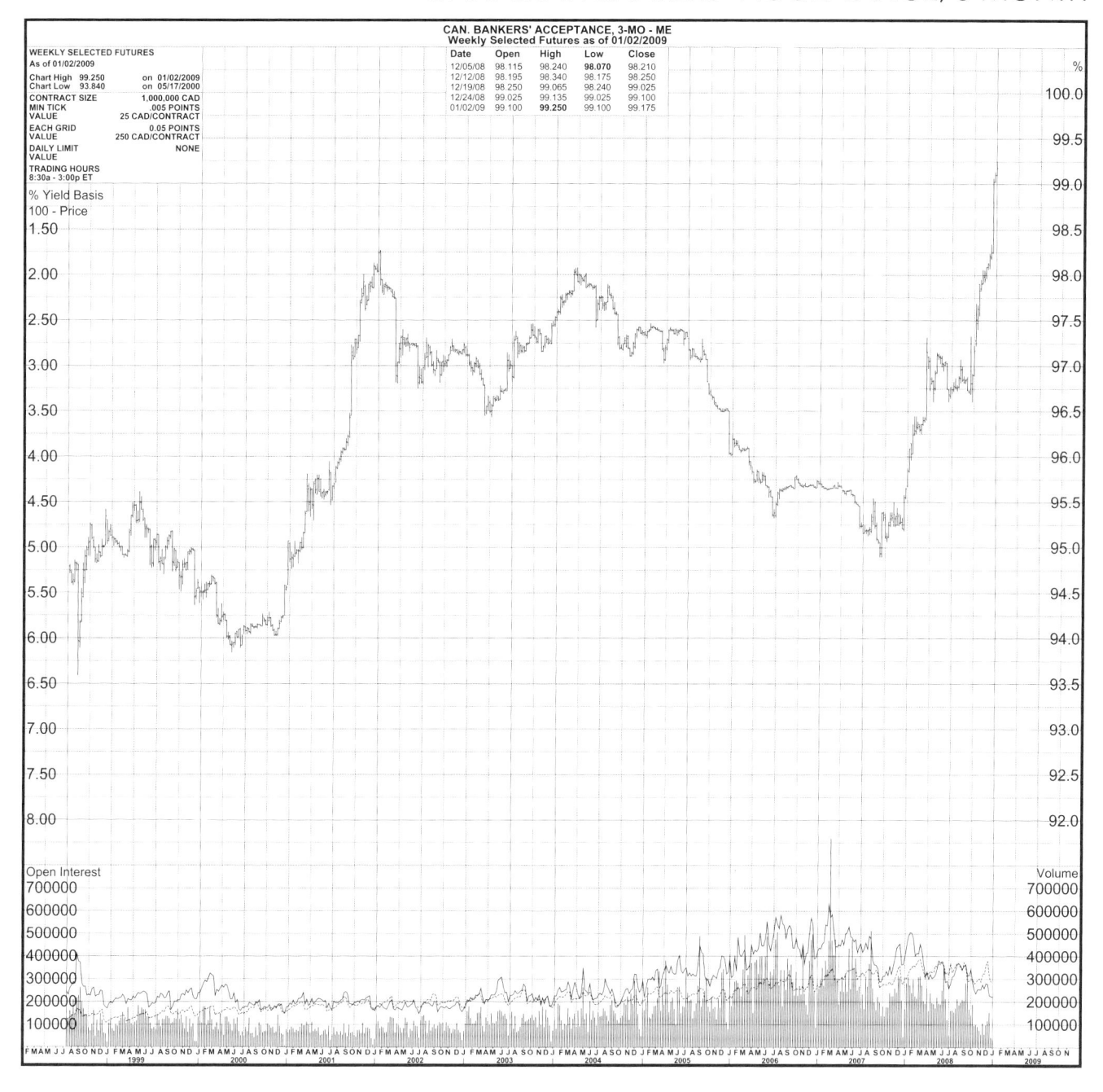

**CAN. BANKERS' ACCEPTANCE, 3-MO - ME**
Weekly Selected Futures as of 01/02/2009

| Date | Open | High | Low | Close |
|---|---|---|---|---|
| 12/05/08 | 98.115 | 98.240 | 98.070 | 98.210 |
| 12/12/08 | 98.195 | 98.340 | 98.175 | 98.250 |
| 12/19/08 | 98.250 | 99.065 | 98.240 | 99.025 |
| 12/24/08 | 99.025 | 99.135 | 99.025 | 99.100 |
| 01/02/09 | 99.100 | 99.250 | 99.100 | 99.175 |

**WEEKLY SELECTED FUTURES**
As of 01/02/2009
Chart High 99.250 on 01/02/2009
Chart Low 93.840 on 05/17/2000
CONTRACT SIZE 1,000,000 CAD
MIN TICK .005 POINTS
VALUE 25 CAD/CONTRACT
EACH GRID 0.05 POINTS
VALUE 250 CAD/CONTRACT
DAILY LIMIT NONE
VALUE
TRADING HOURS 8:30a - 3:00p ET

% Yield Basis
100 - Price

## Quarterly High, Low and Settle of Canadian Bankers' Acceptance   In Point of 100%

| Quarter | High | Low | Settle | Quarter | High | Low | Settle | Quarter | High | Low | Settle |
|---|---|---|---|---|---|---|---|---|---|---|---|
| 03/2000 | 94.700 | 94.140 | 94.190 | 03/2003 | 97.180 | 96.450 | 96.560 | 03/2006 | 96.240 | 95.805 | 95.840 |
| 06/2000 | 94.380 | 93.840 | 94.020 | 06/2003 | 97.150 | 96.430 | 97.005 | 06/2006 | 95.860 | 95.320 | 95.380 |
| 09/2000 | 94.270 | 94.040 | 94.200 | 09/2003 | 97.460 | 96.820 | 97.435 | 09/2006 | 95.800 | 95.335 | 95.750 |
| 12/2000 | 94.590 | 94.020 | 94.560 | 12/2003 | 97.495 | 97.150 | 97.475 | 12/2006 | 95.765 | 95.655 | 95.705 |
| 03/2001 | 95.810 | 94.590 | 95.470 | 03/2004 | 98.075 | 97.470 | 98.060 | 03/2007 | 95.740 | 95.630 | 95.670 |
| 06/2001 | 95.950 | 95.290 | 95.520 | 06/2004 | 98.080 | 97.420 | 97.670 | 06/2007 | 95.685 | 95.205 | 95.235 |
| 09/2001 | 97.230 | 95.510 | 97.080 | 09/2004 | 97.900 | 97.175 | 97.215 | 09/2007 | 95.550 | 94.895 | 95.360 |
| 12/2001 | 98.130 | 97.090 | 98.110 | 12/2004 | 97.430 | 97.100 | 97.370 | 12/2007 | 95.730 | 95.060 | 95.700 |
| 03/2002 | 98.270 | 96.800 | 97.040 | 03/2005 | 97.470 | 97.025 | 97.160 | 03/2008 | 97.315 | 95.730 | 97.060 |
| 06/2002 | 97.400 | 96.750 | 96.860 | 06/2005 | 97.430 | 97.155 | 97.320 | 06/2008 | 97.150 | 96.600 | 96.730 |
| 09/2002 | 97.310 | 96.790 | 97.070 | 09/2005 | 97.310 | 96.675 | 96.695 | 09/2008 | 97.330 | 96.600 | 96.920 |
| 12/2002 | 97.300 | 96.930 | 97.200 | 12/2005 | 96.740 | 96.015 | 96.015 | 12/2008 | 99.245 | 96.900 | 99.210 |

*Source: Montreal Exchange*

113

# EIROBOR, 3-MONTH

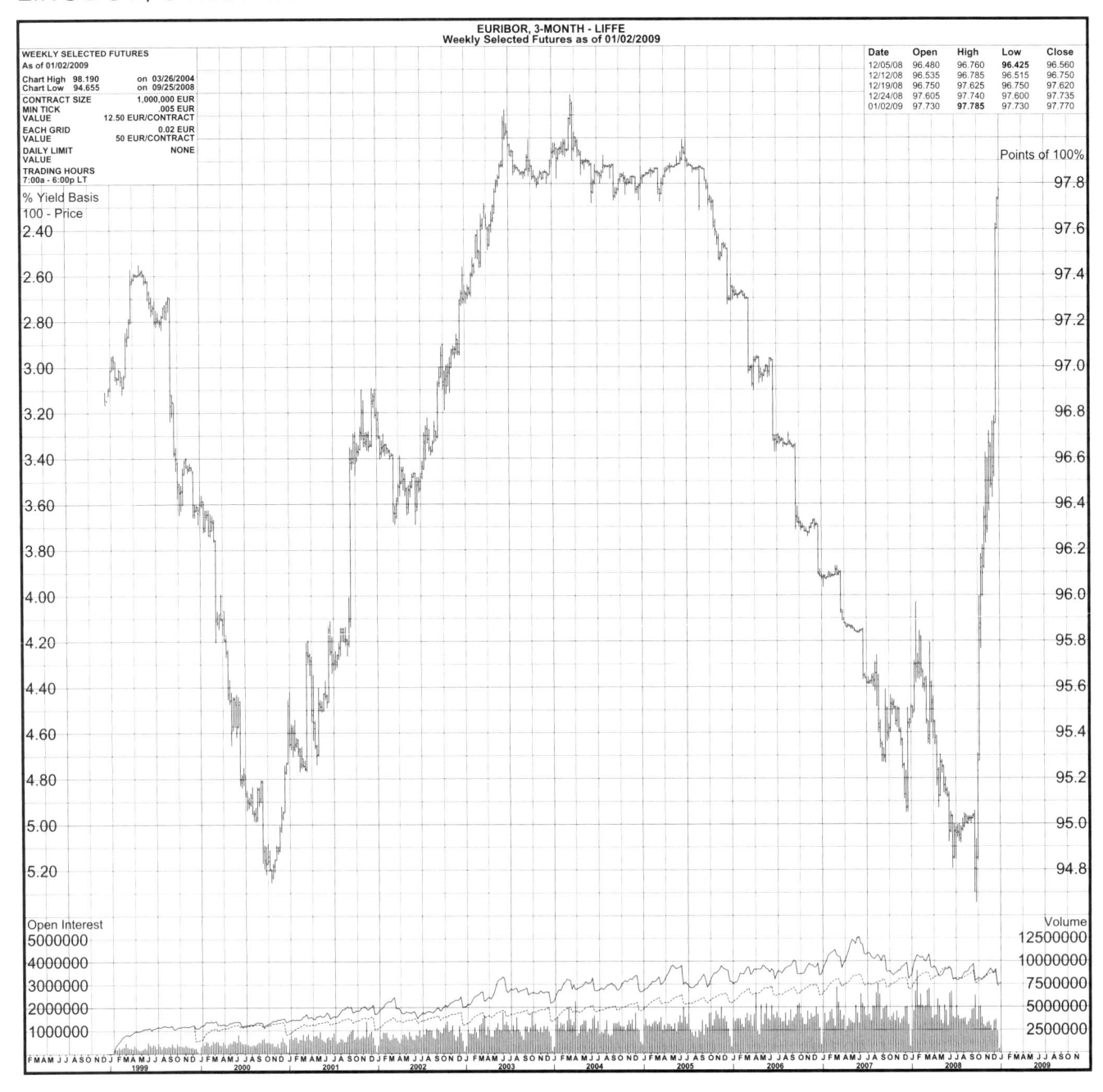

## Quarterly High, Low and Settle of Euribor, 3-Month Futures    In Points of 100%

| Quarter | High | Low | Settle | Quarter | High | Low | Settle | Quarter | High | Low | Settle |
|---|---|---|---|---|---|---|---|---|---|---|---|
| 03/2000 | 96.445 | 95.795 | 95.920 | 03/2003 | 97.700 | 97.275 | 97.690 | 03/2006 | 97.390 | 96.910 | 96.925 |
| 06/2000 | 96.010 | 95.160 | 95.210 | 06/2003 | 98.125 | 97.510 | 98.030 | 06/2006 | 97.050 | 96.625 | 96.680 |
| 09/2000 | 95.250 | 94.805 | 94.845 | 09/2003 | 98.065 | 97.820 | 97.975 | 09/2006 | 96.715 | 96.285 | 96.320 |
| 12/2000 | 95.270 | 94.745 | 95.270 | 12/2003 | 97.990 | 97.780 | 97.890 | 12/2006 | 96.340 | 96.080 | 96.085 |
| 03/2001 | 95.805 | 95.230 | 95.735 | 03/2004 | 98.190 | 97.820 | 98.125 | 03/2007 | 96.130 | 95.885 | 95.890 |
| 06/2001 | 95.890 | 95.260 | 95.755 | 06/2004 | 98.145 | 97.715 | 97.820 | 06/2007 | 95.900 | 95.630 | 95.640 |
| 09/2001 | 96.650 | 95.660 | 96.585 | 09/2004 | 97.925 | 97.725 | 97.775 | 09/2007 | 95.740 | 95.265 | 95.395 |
| 12/2001 | 96.910 | 96.525 | 96.855 | 12/2004 | 97.850 | 97.725 | 97.795 | 12/2007 | 95.565 | 95.050 | 95.470 |
| 03/2002 | 96.905 | 96.310 | 96.360 | 03/2005 | 97.875 | 97.720 | 97.790 | 03/2008 | 95.970 | 95.345 | 95.505 |
| 06/2002 | 96.615 | 96.310 | 96.485 | 06/2005 | 97.995 | 97.790 | 97.945 | 06/2008 | 95.510 | 94.805 | 94.925 |
| 09/2002 | 97.050 | 96.450 | 97.000 | 09/2005 | 97.995 | 97.680 | 97.785 | 09/2008 | 95.090 | 94.655 | 94.990 |
| 12/2002 | 97.440 | 96.810 | 97.350 | 12/2005 | 97.795 | 97.270 | 97.295 | 12/2008 | 97.785 | 94.900 | 97.770 |

*Source: Euronext LIFFE*

# EURO-BUND (FGBL)

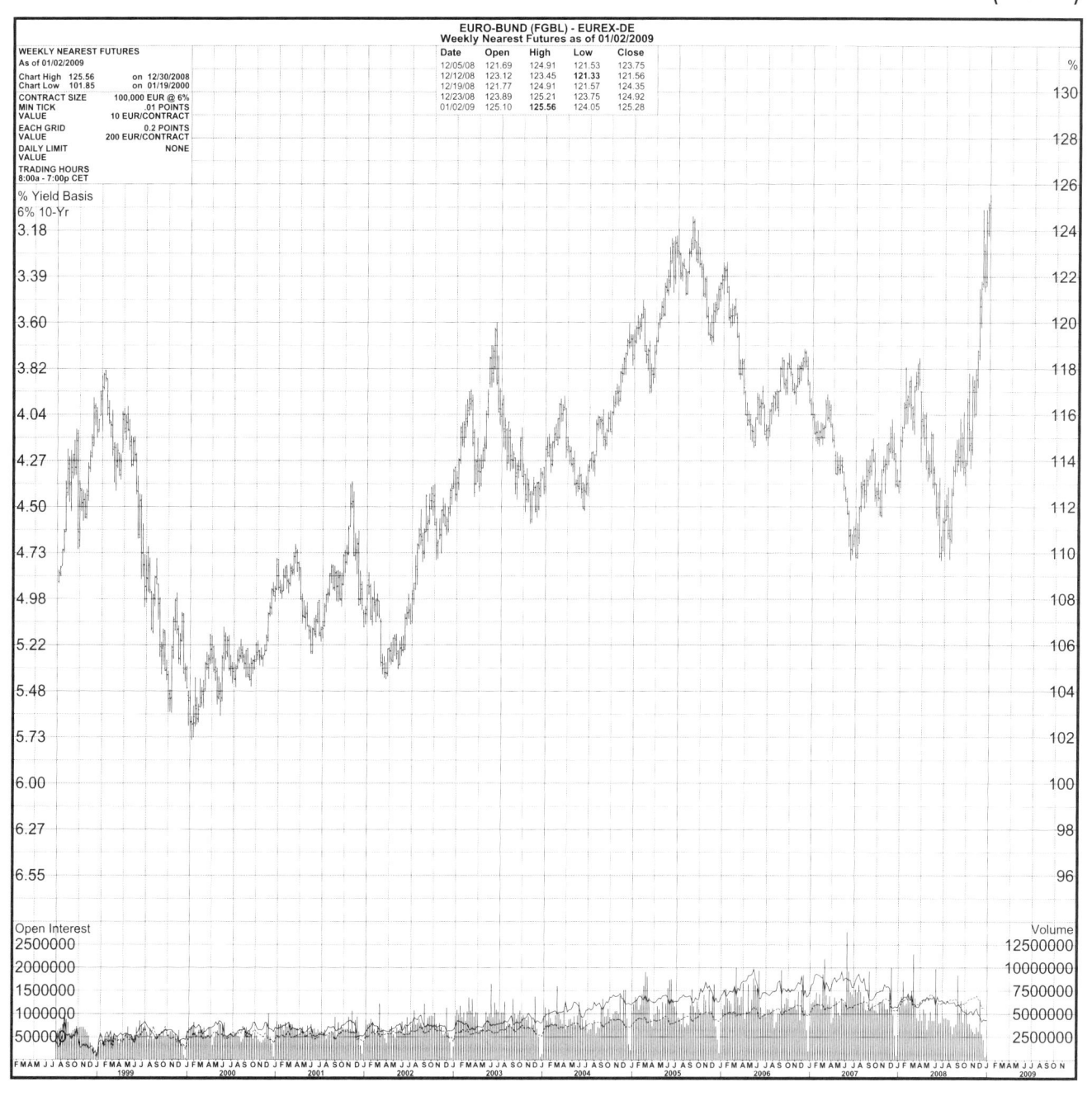

## Quarterly High, Low and Settle of Euro-Bund (FGBL) Futures    In Nominal Value

| Quarter | High | Low | Settle | Quarter | High | Low | Settle | Quarter | High | Low | Settle |
|---|---|---|---|---|---|---|---|---|---|---|---|
| 03/2000 | 105.70 | 101.85 | 105.41 | 03/2003 | 117.10 | 112.18 | 114.72 | 03/2006 | 122.65 | 116.85 | 117.17 |
| 06/2000 | 106.78 | 102.90 | 105.07 | 06/2003 | 120.00 | 112.65 | 116.83 | 06/2006 | 117.26 | 114.55 | 115.32 |
| 09/2000 | 106.26 | 104.15 | 105.30 | 09/2003 | 117.14 | 112.29 | 115.16 | 09/2006 | 118.70 | 114.65 | 118.10 |
| 12/2000 | 108.74 | 104.91 | 108.45 | 12/2003 | 115.45 | 111.24 | 113.12 | 12/2006 | 118.88 | 115.96 | 116.03 |
| 03/2001 | 110.39 | 108.00 | 109.56 | 03/2004 | 116.81 | 112.53 | 116.07 | 03/2007 | 116.89 | 114.62 | 114.92 |
| 06/2001 | 109.63 | 105.61 | 106.51 | 06/2004 | 116.21 | 111.81 | 113.15 | 06/2007 | 115.14 | 109.66 | 110.75 |
| 09/2001 | 109.51 | 106.12 | 108.65 | 09/2004 | 116.23 | 112.93 | 115.65 | 09/2007 | 114.98 | 109.75 | 112.68 |
| 12/2001 | 113.11 | 106.75 | 106.79 | 12/2004 | 119.97 | 115.12 | 118.59 | 12/2007 | 115.83 | 111.54 | 113.11 |
| 03/2002 | 109.16 | 104.50 | 104.78 | 03/2005 | 120.98 | 116.89 | 118.61 | 03/2008 | 118.48 | 112.85 | 115.98 |
| 06/2002 | 108.23 | 104.63 | 107.42 | 06/2005 | 123.78 | 118.51 | 123.50 | 06/2008 | 116.13 | 109.65 | 110.57 |
| 09/2002 | 112.94 | 106.89 | 112.75 | 09/2005 | 124.60 | 121.16 | 122.53 | 09/2008 | 116.13 | 109.70 | 115.07 |
| 12/2002 | 113.70 | 109.67 | 113.54 | 12/2005 | 122.71 | 119.03 | 121.84 | 12/2008 | 125.56 | 113.67 | 124.84 |

*Source: Eurex*

# JAPANESE GOVERNMENT BOND, 10-YEAR

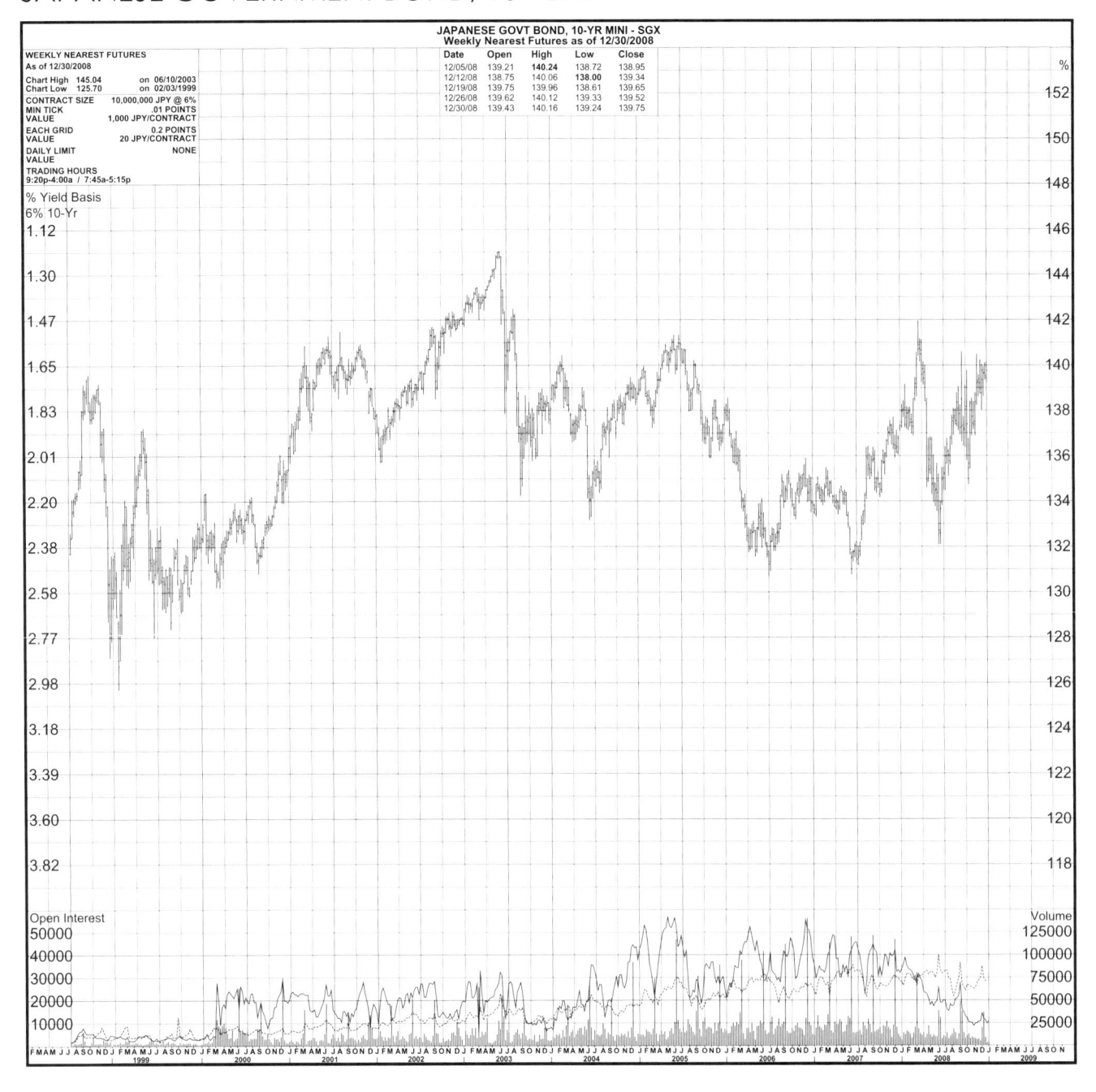

**JAPANESE GOVT BOND, 10-YR MINI - SGX**
Weekly Nearest Futures as of 12/30/2008

| Date | Open | High | Low | Close |
|---|---|---|---|---|
| 12/05/08 | 139.21 | 140.24 | 138.72 | 138.95 |
| 12/12/08 | 138.75 | 140.06 | 138.00 | 139.34 |
| 12/19/08 | 139.75 | 139.96 | 138.61 | 139.65 |
| 12/26/08 | 139.62 | 140.12 | 139.33 | 139.52 |
| 12/30/08 | 139.43 | 140.16 | 139.24 | 139.75 |

**WEEKLY NEAREST FUTURES**
As of 12/30/2008
Chart High 145.04 on 06/10/2003
Chart Low 125.70 on 02/03/1999
CONTRACT SIZE 10,000,000 JPY @ 6%
MIN TICK .01 POINTS
VALUE 1,000 JPY/CONTRACT
EACH GRID 0.2 POINTS
VALUE 20 JPY/CONTRACT
DAILY LIMIT NONE
VALUE
TRADING HOURS 9:20p-4:00a / 7:45a-5:15p

## Quarterly High, Low and Settle of Japanese Government Bonds, 10-Year Futures — In Nominal Value

| Quarter | High | Low | Settle | Quarter | High | Low | Settle | Quarter | High | Low | Settle |
|---|---|---|---|---|---|---|---|---|---|---|---|
| 03/2000 | 134.40 | 130.17 | 131.54 | 03/2003 | 143.45 | 141.70 | 143.06 | 03/2006 | 138.56 | 132.81 | 133.26 |
| 06/2000 | 133.95 | 130.62 | 132.75 | 06/2003 | 145.04 | 141.20 | 141.74 | 06/2006 | 134.14 | 131.50 | 131.65 |
| 09/2000 | 134.21 | 130.80 | 132.38 | 09/2003 | 142.50 | 134.24 | 137.14 | 09/2006 | 135.38 | 130.71 | 134.90 |
| 12/2000 | 136.08 | 132.48 | 134.90 | 12/2003 | 138.96 | 135.77 | 137.84 | 12/2006 | 135.89 | 133.18 | 133.93 |
| 03/2001 | 140.88 | 134.65 | 139.31 | 03/2004 | 140.45 | 136.89 | 137.36 | 03/2007 | 135.50 | 133.30 | 134.19 |
| 06/2001 | 141.30 | 137.10 | 140.46 | 06/2004 | 139.03 | 133.16 | 135.01 | 06/2007 | 134.68 | 130.76 | 132.04 |
| 09/2001 | 141.50 | 138.50 | 139.47 | 09/2004 | 138.49 | 134.09 | 138.04 | 09/2007 | 136.44 | 131.16 | 134.99 |
| 12/2001 | 140.94 | 137.85 | 138.20 | 12/2004 | 139.50 | 136.77 | 138.38 | 12/2007 | 137.72 | 134.15 | 136.76 |
| 03/2002 | 138.16 | 135.72 | 137.96 | 03/2005 | 139.96 | 137.22 | 139.40 | 03/2008 | 141.96 | 136.87 | 140.46 |
| 06/2002 | 139.45 | 137.48 | 139.15 | 06/2005 | 141.35 | 138.95 | 141.27 | 06/2008 | 140.71 | 132.08 | 135.24 |
| 09/2002 | 141.69 | 138.44 | 140.38 | 09/2005 | 141.35 | 137.36 | 137.67 | 09/2008 | 140.60 | 134.46 | 137.32 |
| 12/2002 | 142.39 | 140.26 | 142.09 | 12/2005 | 138.49 | 135.90 | 137.35 | 12/2008 | 140.50 | 134.72 | 139.75 |

*Source: Singapore Exchange*

# EUROSWISS, 3-MONTH

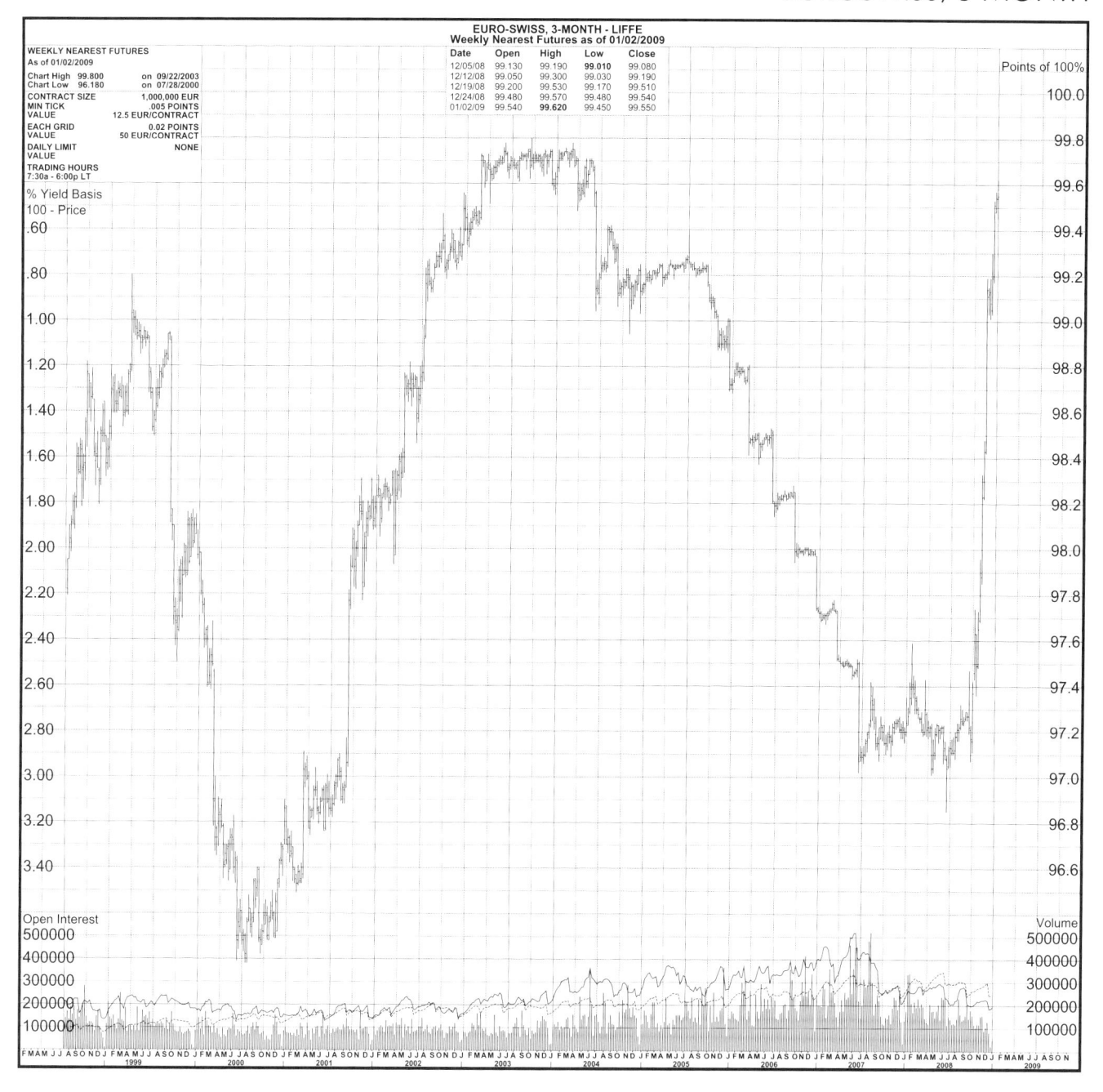

**EURO-SWISS, 3-MONTH - LIFFE**
Weekly Nearest Futures as of 01/02/2009

| Date | Open | High | Low | Close |
|---|---|---|---|---|
| 12/05/08 | 99.130 | 99.190 | 99.010 | 99.080 |
| 12/12/08 | 99.050 | 99.300 | 99.030 | 99.190 |
| 12/19/08 | 99.200 | 99.530 | 99.170 | 99.510 |
| 12/24/08 | 99.480 | 99.570 | 99.480 | 99.540 |
| 01/02/09 | 99.540 | 99.620 | 99.450 | 99.550 |

WEEKLY NEAREST FUTURES
As of 01/02/2009
Chart High 99.800 on 09/22/2003
Chart Low 96.180 on 07/28/2000
CONTRACT SIZE 1,000,000 EUR
MIN TICK .005 POINTS
VALUE 12.5 EUR/CONTRACT
EACH GRID 0.02 POINTS
VALUE 50 EUR/CONTRACT
DAILY LIMIT NONE
VALUE
TRADING HOURS
7:30a - 6:00p LT

% Yield Basis
100 - Price

## Quarterly High, Low and Settle of Euro-Swiss, 3-Month Futures    In Points of 100%

| Quarter | High | Low | Settle | Quarter | High | Low | Settle | Quarter | High | Low | Settle |
|---|---|---|---|---|---|---|---|---|---|---|---|
| 03/2000 | 98.080 | 96.650 | 96.730 | 03/2003 | 99.730 | 99.320 | 99.690 | 03/2006 | 98.820 | 98.410 | 98.480 |
| 06/2000 | 96.910 | 96.190 | 96.360 | 06/2003 | 99.780 | 99.510 | 99.680 | 06/2006 | 98.530 | 98.140 | 98.190 |
| 09/2000 | 96.600 | 96.180 | 96.280 | 09/2003 | 99.800 | 99.610 | 99.720 | 09/2006 | 98.280 | 97.940 | 97.970 |
| 12/2000 | 96.710 | 96.260 | 96.680 | 12/2003 | 99.750 | 99.570 | 99.620 | 12/2006 | 98.020 | 97.720 | 97.730 |
| 03/2001 | 97.110 | 96.490 | 97.040 | 03/2004 | 99.780 | 99.550 | 99.690 | 03/2007 | 97.780 | 97.510 | 97.510 |
| 06/2001 | 97.090 | 96.740 | 96.890 | 06/2004 | 99.710 | 99.040 | 99.100 | 06/2007 | 97.530 | 97.020 | 97.090 |
| 09/2001 | 97.970 | 96.820 | 97.900 | 09/2004 | 99.420 | 99.060 | 99.160 | 09/2007 | 97.420 | 97.060 | 97.200 |
| 12/2001 | 98.310 | 97.770 | 98.120 | 12/2004 | 99.250 | 98.940 | 99.160 | 12/2007 | 97.270 | 97.090 | 97.210 |
| 03/2002 | 98.350 | 97.930 | 98.230 | 03/2005 | 99.253 | 99.150 | 99.210 | 03/2008 | 97.590 | 97.180 | 97.230 |
| 06/2002 | 98.820 | 98.210 | 98.650 | 06/2005 | 99.290 | 99.180 | 99.270 | 06/2008 | 97.240 | 96.850 | 97.100 |
| 09/2002 | 99.470 | 98.630 | 99.390 | 09/2005 | 99.380 | 99.080 | 99.090 | 09/2008 | 97.470 | 97.050 | 97.220 |
| 12/2002 | 99.560 | 99.180 | 99.510 | 12/2005 | 99.120 | 98.690 | 98.720 | 12/2008 | 99.620 | 97.150 | 99.530 |

*Source: Euronext LIFFE*

# PRIME RATE AND DISCOUNT RATE

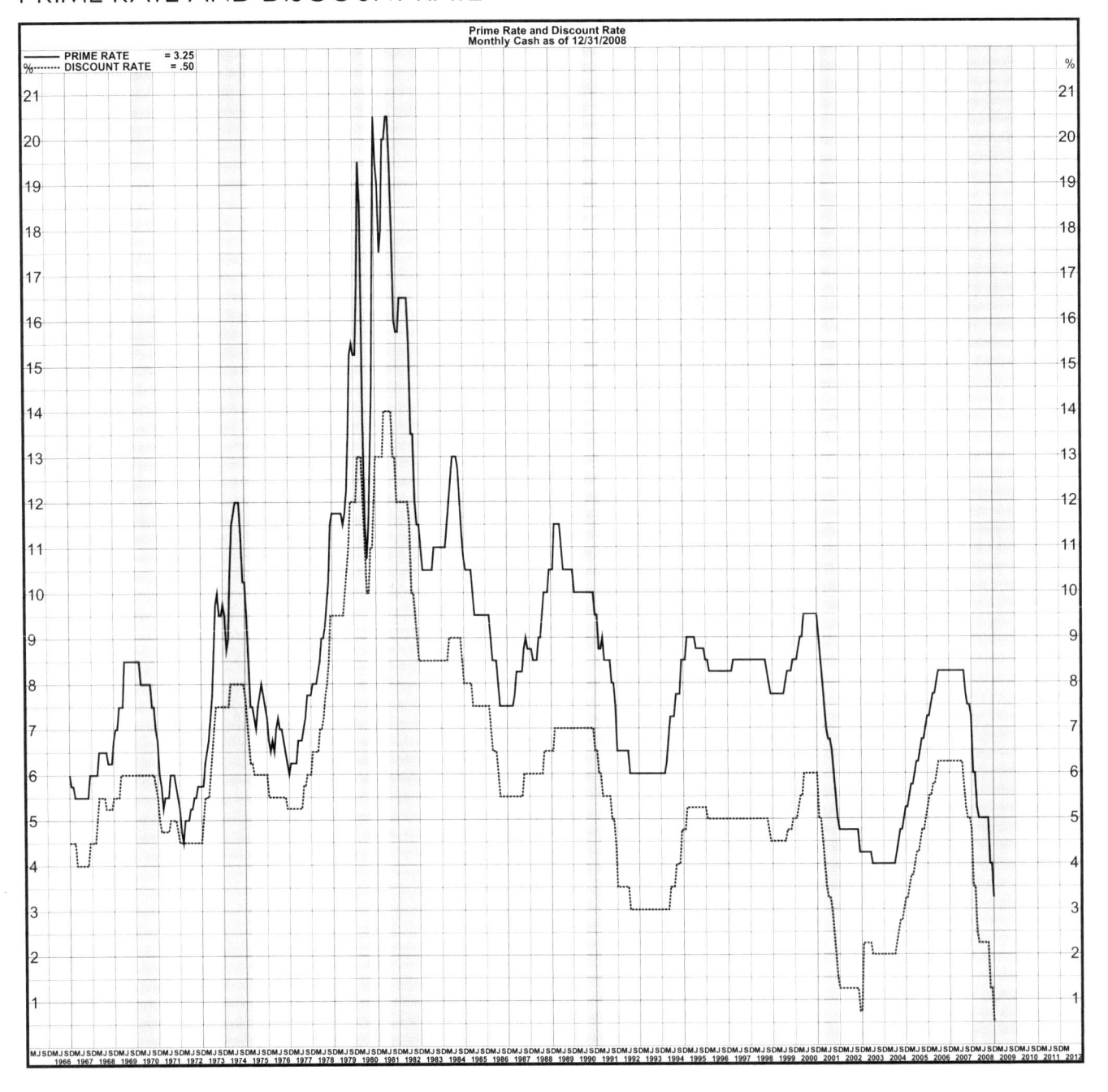

## Annual High, Low and Close of Prime Rate — In Percent

| Year | High | Low | Settle | Year | High | Low | Settle | Year | High | Low | Settle |
|---|---|---|---|---|---|---|---|---|---|---|---|
| 1967 | 6.00 | 5.50 | 6.00 | 1981 | 20.50 | 15.75 | 15.75 | 1995 | 9.00 | 8.50 | 8.50 |
| 1968 | 6.75 | 6.00 | 6.75 | 1982 | 17.00 | 11.50 | 11.50 | 1996 | 8.50 | 8.25 | 8.25 |
| 1969 | 8.50 | 7.00 | 8.50 | 1983 | 11.50 | 10.50 | 11.00 | 1997 | 8.50 | 8.25 | 8.50 |
| 1970 | 8.50 | 6.75 | 6.75 | 1984 | 13.00 | 10.75 | 10.75 | 1998 | 8.50 | 7.75 | 7.75 |
| 1971 | 6.50 | 5.25 | 5.25 | 1985 | 10.75 | 9.50 | 9.50 | 1999 | 8.50 | 7.75 | 8.50 |
| 1972 | 5.75 | 4.50 | 5.75 | 1986 | 9.50 | 7.50 | 7.50 | 2000 | 9.50 | 8.50 | 9.50 |
| 1973 | 10.00 | 5.75 | 9.75 | 1987 | 9.25 | 7.50 | 8.75 | 2001 | 9.50 | 4.75 | 4.75 |
| 1974 | 12.00 | 8.75 | 10.25 | 1988 | 10.50 | 8.50 | 10.50 | 2002 | 4.75 | 4.25 | 4.25 |
| 1975 | 10.00 | 7.00 | 7.25 | 1989 | 11.50 | 10.50 | 10.50 | 2003 | 4.25 | 4.00 | 4.00 |
| 1976 | 7.25 | 6.00 | 6.00 | 1990 | 10.50 | 9.50 | 9.50 | 2004 | 5.25 | 4.00 | 5.25 |
| 1977 | 7.75 | 6.00 | 7.75 | 1991 | 9.50 | 6.50 | 6.50 | 2005 | 7.25 | 5.25 | 7.25 |
| 1978 | 11.75 | 7.75 | 11.75 | 1992 | 6.50 | 6.00 | 6.00 | 2006 | 8.25 | 7.25 | 8.25 |
| 1979 | 15.75 | 11.50 | 15.25 | 1993 | 6.00 | 6.00 | 6.00 | 2007 | 8.25 | 7.25 | 7.25 |
| 1980 | 21.50 | 10.75 | 20.50 | 1994 | 8.50 | 6.00 | 8.50 | 2008 | 7.25 | 3.25 | 3.25 |

*Source: Federal Reserve Board*

# PRIME RATE AND DISCOUNT RATE

**Prime Rate and Discount Rate**
Weekly Cash as of 01/02/2009

- PRIME RATE = 3.25
- DISCOUNT RATE = .50

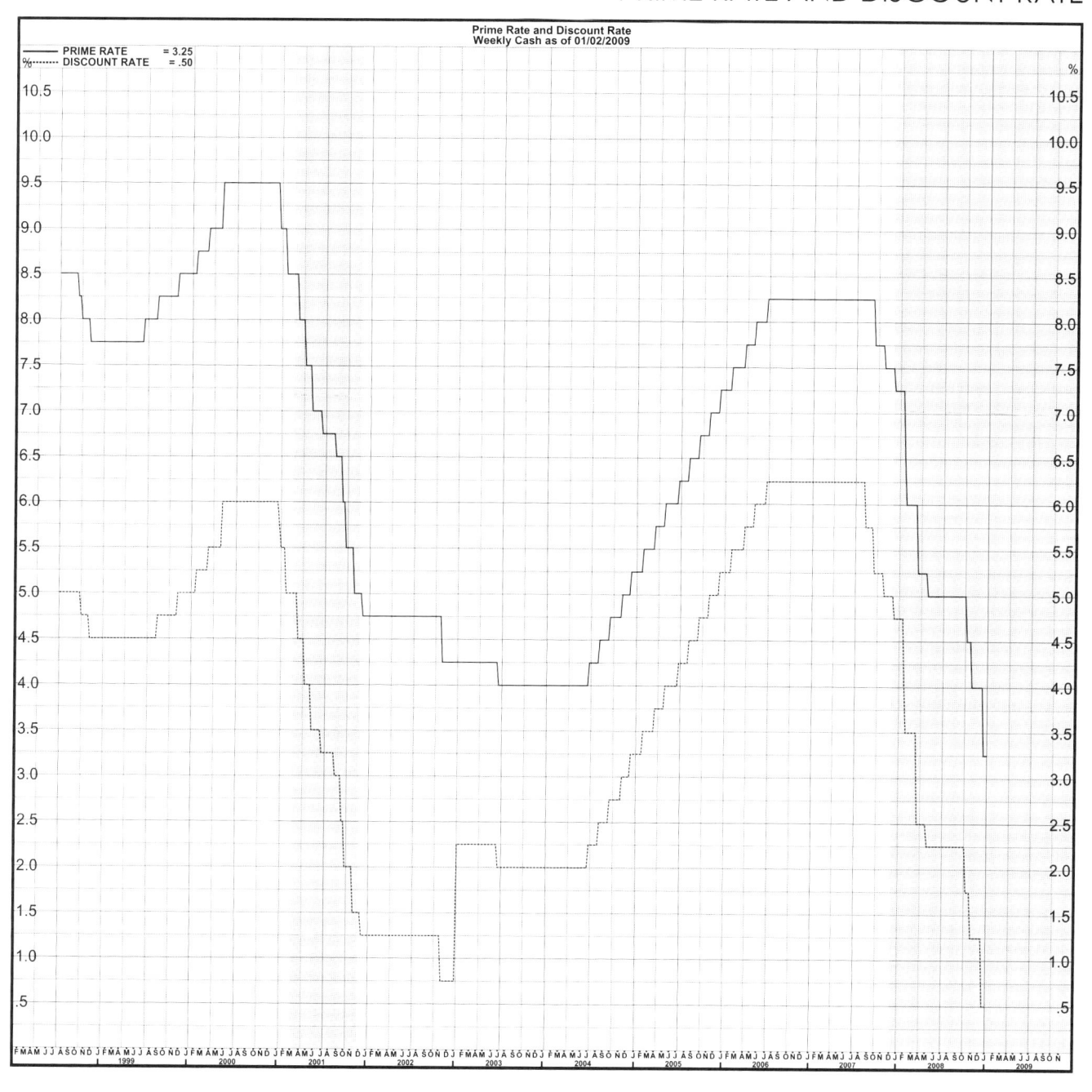

## Annual High, Low and Close of Discount Rate — In Percent

| Year | High | Low | Settle | Year | High | Low | Settle | Year | High | Low | Settle |
|---|---|---|---|---|---|---|---|---|---|---|---|
| 1967 | 4.50 | 4.00 | 4.50 | 1981 | 14.00 | 12.00 | 12.00 | 1995 | 5.25 | 4.75 | 5.25 |
| 1968 | 5.50 | 5.00 | 5.50 | 1982 | 12.00 | 8.50 | 8.50 | 1996 | 5.25 | 5.00 | 5.00 |
| 1969 | 6.00 | 6.00 | 6.00 | 1983 | 8.50 | 8.50 | 8.50 | 1997 | 5.00 | 5.00 | 5.00 |
| 1970 | 5.75 | 5.50 | 5.50 | 1984 | 9.00 | 8.00 | 8.00 | 1998 | 5.00 | 4.50 | 4.50 |
| 1971 | 5.25 | 4.50 | 4.50 | 1985 | 8.00 | 7.50 | 7.50 | 1999 | 5.00 | 4.50 | 5.00 |
| 1972 | 4.50 | 4.50 | 4.50 | 1986 | 7.50 | 5.50 | 5.50 | 2000 | 6.00 | 5.00 | 6.00 |
| 1973 | 7.50 | 5.00 | 7.50 | 1987 | 6.00 | 5.50 | 6.00 | 2001 | 6.00 | 1.25 | 1.25 |
| 1974 | 8.00 | 7.75 | 7.75 | 1988 | 6.50 | 6.00 | 6.50 | 2002 | 1.25 | 0.75 | 0.75 |
| 1975 | 7.25 | 6.00 | 6.00 | 1989 | 7.00 | 6.50 | 7.00 | 2003 | 2.25 | 0.75 | 2.00 |
| 1976 | 6.00 | 5.25 | 5.25 | 1990 | 7.00 | 6.50 | 6.50 | 2004 | 3.25 | 2.00 | 3.25 |
| 1977 | 6.00 | 5.25 | 6.00 | 1991 | 6.50 | 3.50 | 3.50 | 2005 | 5.25 | 3.25 | 5.25 |
| 1978 | 9.50 | 6.00 | 9.50 | 1992 | 3.50 | 3.00 | 3.00 | 2006 | 6.25 | 5.25 | 6.25 |
| 1979 | 12.00 | 9.50 | 12.00 | 1993 | 3.00 | 3.00 | 3.00 | 2007 | 6.25 | 4.75 | 4.75 |
| 1980 | 13.00 | 10.00 | 13.00 | 1994 | 4.75 | 3.00 | 4.75 | 2008 | 4.75 | 0.50 | 0.50 |

*Source: Federal Reserve Board*

# CONSUMER PRICE INDEX

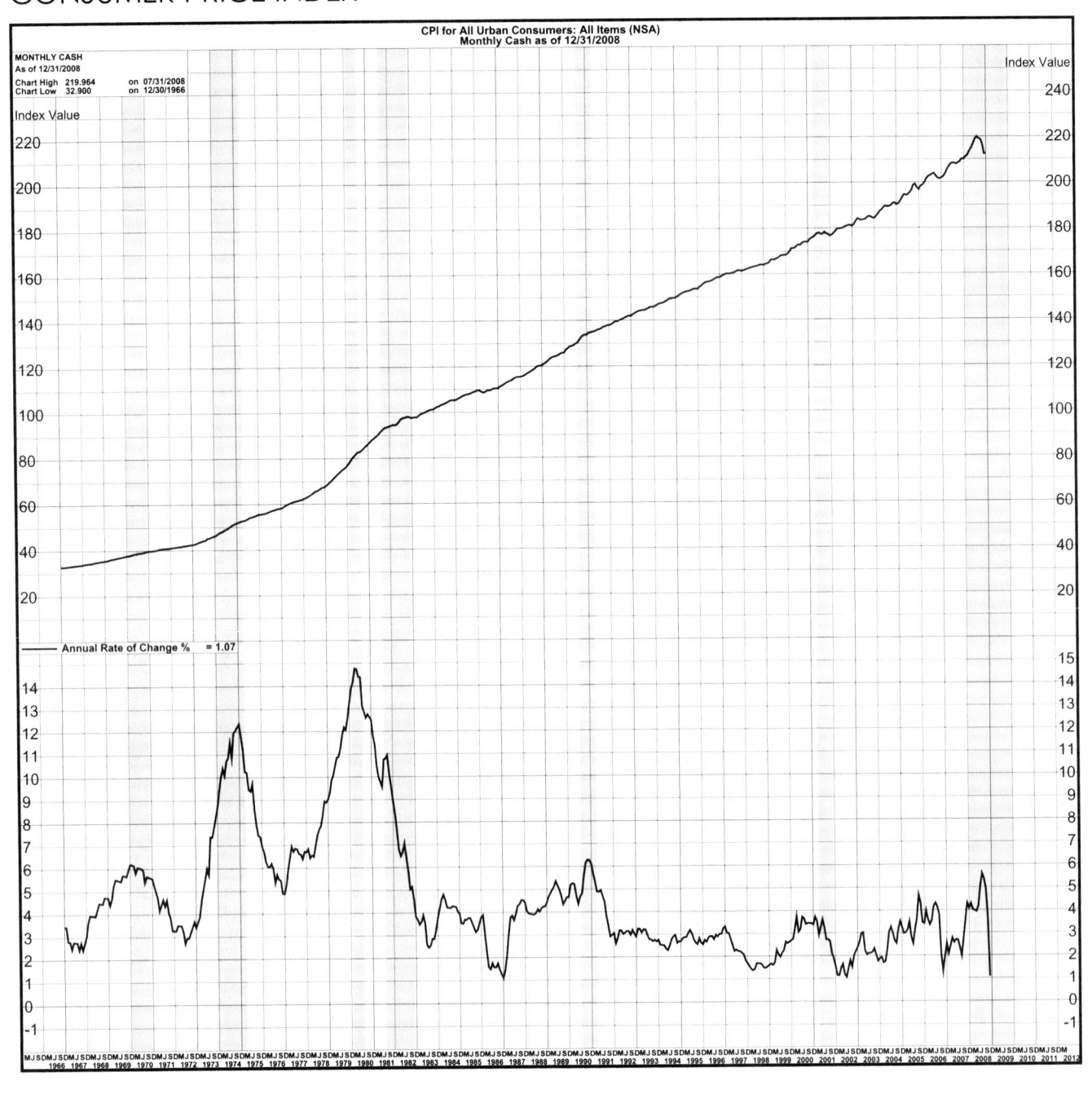

CPI for All Urban Consumers: All Items (NSA)
Monthly Cash as of 12/31/2008

MONTHLY CASH
As of 12/31/2008
Chart High 219.964 on 07/31/2008
Chart Low 32.900 on 12/30/1966

Annual Rate of Change % = 1.07

## Annual High, Low and Close of CPI: All Items — In Index Value

| Year | High | Low | Settle | Year | High | Low | Settle | Year | High | Low | Settle |
|---|---|---|---|---|---|---|---|---|---|---|---|
| 1967 | 33.9 | 32.9 | 33.9 | 1981 | 94.0 | 87.0 | 94.0 | 1995 | 153.7 | 150.3 | 153.5 |
| 1968 | 35.5 | 34.1 | 35.5 | 1982 | 98.2 | 94.3 | 97.6 | 1996 | 158.6 | 154.4 | 158.6 |
| 1969 | 37.7 | 35.6 | 37.7 | 1983 | 101.3 | 97.8 | 101.3 | 1997 | 161.6 | 159.1 | 161.3 |
| 1970 | 39.8 | 37.8 | 39.8 | 1984 | 105.3 | 101.9 | 105.3 | 1998 | 164.0 | 161.6 | 163.9 |
| 1971 | 41.1 | 39.8 | 41.1 | 1985 | 109.3 | 105.5 | 109.3 | 1999 | 168.3 | 164.3 | 168.3 |
| 1972 | 42.5 | 41.1 | 42.5 | 1986 | 110.5 | 108.6 | 110.5 | 2000 | 174.1 | 168.8 | 174.0 |
| 1973 | 46.2 | 42.6 | 46.2 | 1987 | 115.4 | 111.2 | 115.4 | 2001 | 178.3 | 175.1 | 176.7 |
| 1974 | 51.9 | 46.6 | 51.9 | 1988 | 120.5 | 115.7 | 120.5 | 2002 | 181.3 | 177.1 | 180.9 |
| 1975 | 55.5 | 52.1 | 55.5 | 1989 | 126.1 | 121.1 | 126.1 | 2003 | 185.2 | 181.7 | 184.3 |
| 1976 | 58.2 | 55.6 | 58.2 | 1990 | 133.8 | 127.4 | 133.8 | 2004 | 191.0 | 185.2 | 190.3 |
| 1977 | 62.1 | 58.5 | 62.1 | 1991 | 137.9 | 134.6 | 137.9 | 2005 | 199.2 | 190.7 | 196.8 |
| 1978 | 67.7 | 62.5 | 67.7 | 1992 | 142.0 | 138.1 | 141.9 | 2006 | 203.9 | 198.3 | 201.8 |
| 1979 | 76.7 | 68.3 | 76.7 | 1993 | 145.8 | 142.6 | 145.8 | 2007 | 210.2 | 202.4 | 210.0 |
| 1980 | 86.3 | 77.8 | 86.3 | 1994 | 149.7 | 146.2 | 149.7 | 2008 | 220.0 | 211.1 | 212.4 |

Not seasonally adjusted. Source: U.S. Department of Labor: Bureau of Labor Statistics

# CONSUMER PRICE INDEX

**PPI: All Commodities (NSA)**
Monthly Cash as of 12/31/2008

MONTHLY CASH
As of 12/31/2008
Chart High 205.5 on 07/31/2008
Chart Low 33.1 on 04/28/1967

Annual Rate of Change % = -.84

## Annual High, Low and Close of CPI: All Items   In Index Value

| Year | High | Low | Settle | Year | High | Low | Settle | Year | High | Low | Settle |
|---|---|---|---|---|---|---|---|---|---|---|---|
| 1967 | 34.0 | 32.9 | 34.0 | 1981 | 94.1 | 87.2 | 94.1 | 1995 | 153.9 | 150.5 | 153.9 |
| 1968 | 35.6 | 34.1 | 35.6 | 1982 | 98.1 | 94.4 | 97.7 | 1996 | 159.1 | 154.7 | 159.1 |
| 1969 | 37.7 | 35.7 | 37.7 | 1983 | 101.4 | 97.9 | 101.4 | 1997 | 161.8 | 159.4 | 161.8 |
| 1970 | 39.8 | 37.9 | 39.8 | 1984 | 105.5 | 102.1 | 105.5 | 1998 | 164.4 | 162.0 | 164.4 |
| 1971 | 41.1 | 39.9 | 41.1 | 1985 | 109.5 | 105.7 | 109.5 | 1999 | 168.8 | 164.7 | 168.8 |
| 1972 | 42.5 | 41.2 | 42.5 | 1986 | 110.8 | 108.7 | 110.8 | 2000 | 174.6 | 169.3 | 174.6 |
| 1973 | 46.3 | 42.7 | 46.3 | 1987 | 115.6 | 111.4 | 115.6 | 2001 | 178.1 | 175.6 | 177.3 |
| 1974 | 51.9 | 46.8 | 51.9 | 1988 | 120.7 | 116.0 | 120.7 | 2002 | 181.6 | 177.7 | 181.6 |
| 1975 | 55.6 | 52.3 | 55.6 | 1989 | 126.3 | 121.2 | 126.3 | 2003 | 185.0 | 182.3 | 185.0 |
| 1976 | 58.4 | 55.8 | 58.4 | 1990 | 134.2 | 127.5 | 134.2 | 2004 | 191.2 | 185.9 | 191.2 |
| 1977 | 62.3 | 58.7 | 62.3 | 1991 | 138.2 | 134.7 | 138.2 | 2005 | 199.1 | 191.3 | 197.7 |
| 1978 | 67.9 | 62.7 | 67.9 | 1992 | 142.3 | 138.3 | 142.3 | 2006 | 203.8 | 199.0 | 202.8 |
| 1979 | 76.9 | 68.5 | 76.9 | 1993 | 146.3 | 142.8 | 146.3 | 2007 | 211.7 | 203.2 | 211.7 |
| 1980 | 86.4 | 78.0 | 86.4 | 1994 | 150.1 | 146.3 | 150.1 | 2008 | 219.2 | 212.5 | 213.1 |

Seasonally adjusted.   Source: U.S. Department of Labor: Bureau of Labor Statistics

# PRODUCER PRICE INDEX

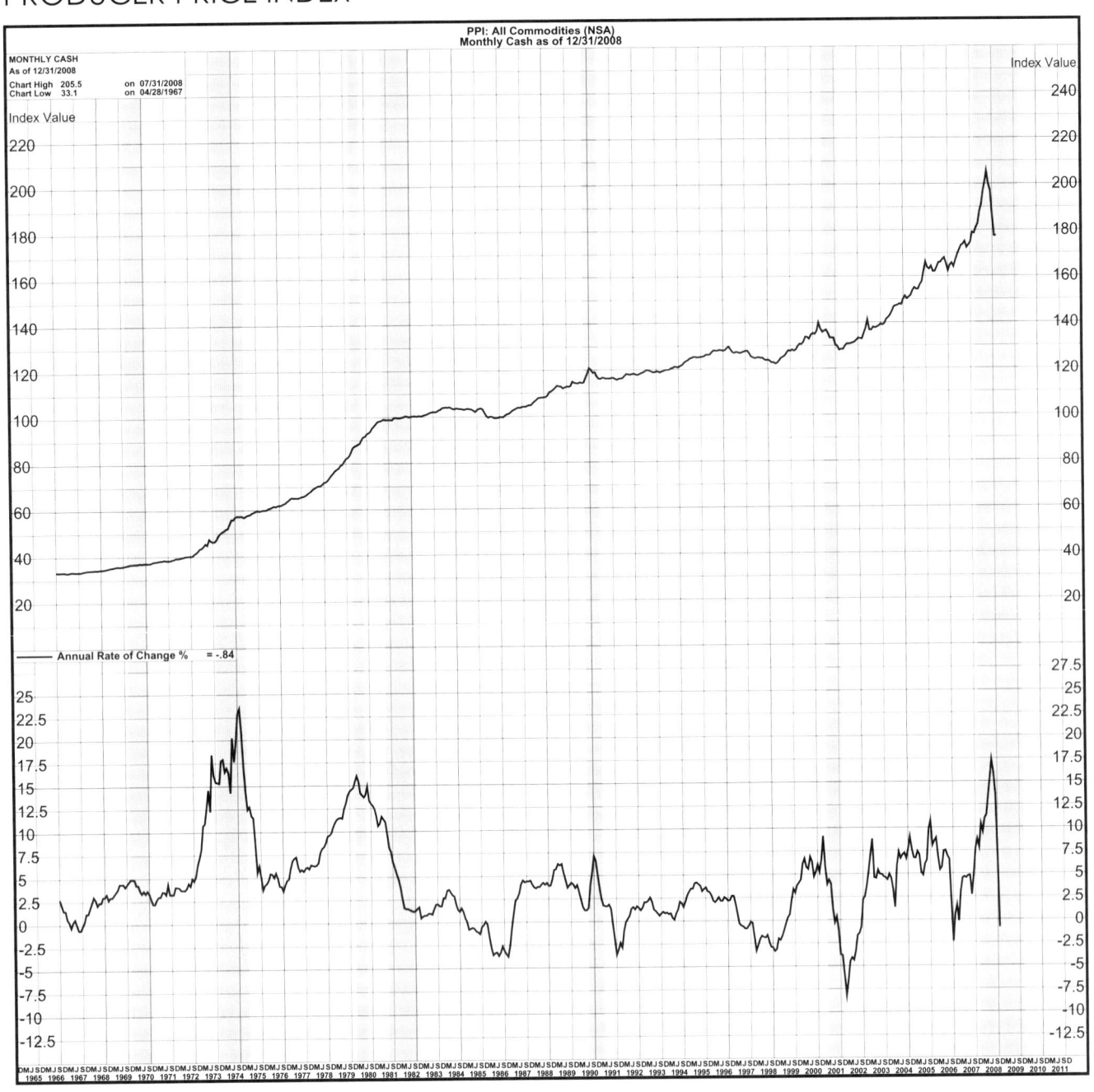

*PPI: All Commodities (NSA)*
*Monthly Cash as of 12/31/2008*

MONTHLY CASH
As of 12/31/2008
Chart High 205.5 on 07/31/2008
Chart Low 33.1 on 04/28/1967

Annual Rate of Change % = -.84

### Annual High, Low and Close of PPI: All commodities    In Index Value

| Year | High | Low | Settle | Year | High | Low | Settle | Year | High | Low | Settle |
|------|------|-----|--------|------|------|-----|--------|------|------|-----|--------|
| 1967 | 33.7 | 33.1 | 33.7 | 1981 | 99.0 | 95.2 | 98.8 | 1995 | 125.7 | 122.9 | 125.7 |
| 1968 | 34.6 | 33.8 | 34.6 | 1982 | 100.5 | 99.6 | 100.5 | 1996 | 129.1 | 126.2 | 129.1 |
| 1969 | 36.3 | 34.8 | 36.3 | 1983 | 102.3 | 100.2 | 102.3 | 1997 | 129.7 | 126.8 | 126.8 |
| 1970 | 37.1 | 36.5 | 37.1 | 1984 | 104.2 | 102.9 | 103.5 | 1998 | 125.4 | 122.8 | 122.8 |
| 1971 | 38.6 | 37.3 | 38.6 | 1985 | 103.6 | 102.1 | 103.6 | 1999 | 128.3 | 122.3 | 127.8 |
| 1972 | 41.1 | 38.8 | 41.1 | 1986 | 103.2 | 99.3 | 99.7 | 2000 | 136.2 | 128.3 | 136.2 |
| 1973 | 47.5 | 41.6 | 47.4 | 1987 | 104.2 | 100.5 | 104.2 | 2001 | 140.0 | 128.1 | 128.1 |
| 1974 | 57.4 | 49.0 | 57.3 | 1988 | 109.0 | 104.6 | 109.0 | 2002 | 133.2 | 128.4 | 132.9 |
| 1975 | 59.8 | 56.9 | 59.7 | 1989 | 113.2 | 110.5 | 113.0 | 2003 | 141.2 | 135.3 | 139.5 |
| 1976 | 62.5 | 59.9 | 62.5 | 1990 | 120.8 | 114.1 | 118.7 | 2004 | 151.4 | 141.4 | 150.2 |
| 1977 | 66.2 | 62.8 | 66.2 | 1991 | 119.0 | 115.9 | 115.9 | 2005 | 166.2 | 150.9 | 163.0 |
| 1978 | 72.7 | 66.8 | 72.7 | 1992 | 118.1 | 115.6 | 117.6 | 2006 | 167.9 | 161.9 | 165.6 |
| 1979 | 83.4 | 73.8 | 83.4 | 1993 | 119.7 | 118.0 | 118.6 | 2007 | 179.0 | 164.0 | 178.6 |
| 1980 | 93.8 | 85.2 | 93.8 | 1994 | 121.9 | 119.1 | 121.9 | 2008 | 205.5 | 177.5 | 177.5 |

Not seasonally adjusted.    *Source: U.S. Department of Labor: Bureau of Labor Statistics*

# PRODUCER PRICE INDEX

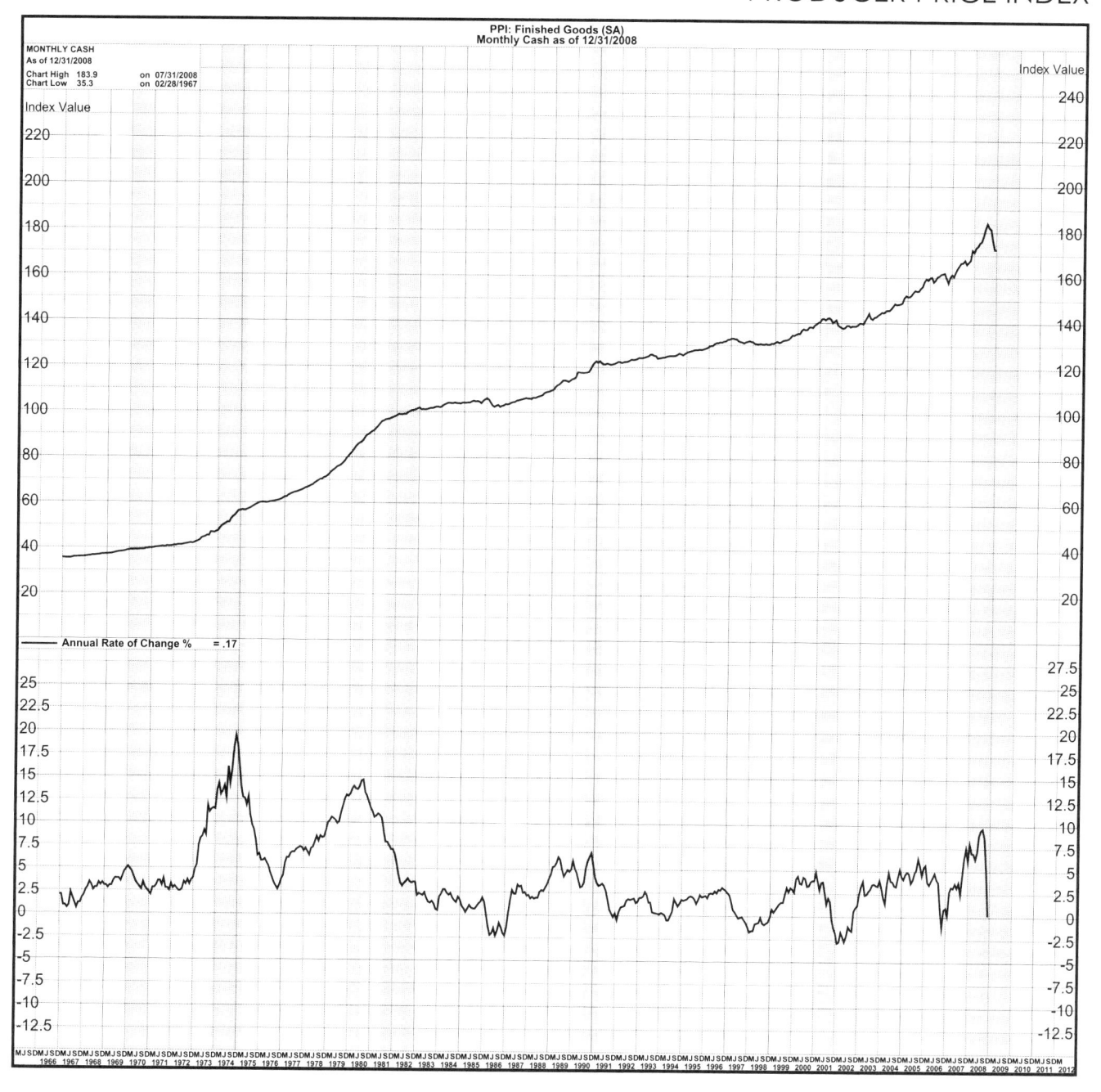

**PPI: Finished Goods (SA)**
Monthly Cash as of 12/31/2008

MONTHLY CASH
As of 12/31/2008
Chart High 183.9 on 07/31/2008
Chart Low 35.3 on 02/28/1967

Annual Rate of Change % = .17

## Annual High, Low and Close of PPI: Finished Goods — In Index Value

| Year | High | Low | Settle | Year | High | Low | Settle | Year | High | Low | Settle |
|---|---|---|---|---|---|---|---|---|---|---|---|
| 1967 | 36.0 | 35.3 | 36.0 | 1981 | 98.3 | 92.8 | 98.3 | 1995 | 129.3 | 126.9 | 129.3 |
| 1968 | 37.1 | 36.1 | 37.1 | 1982 | 101.8 | 98.8 | 101.8 | 1996 | 132.9 | 129.7 | 132.9 |
| 1969 | 38.9 | 37.2 | 38.9 | 1983 | 102.3 | 101.0 | 102.3 | 1997 | 133.0 | 130.9 | 131.4 |
| 1970 | 39.8 | 39.0 | 39.8 | 1984 | 104.0 | 103.0 | 104.0 | 1998 | 131.3 | 130.4 | 131.3 |
| 1971 | 41.1 | 39.9 | 41.1 | 1985 | 106.0 | 103.8 | 106.0 | 1999 | 135.2 | 131.2 | 135.2 |
| 1972 | 42.7 | 41.0 | 42.7 | 1986 | 105.5 | 102.3 | 103.6 | 2000 | 140.5 | 135.2 | 140.5 |
| 1973 | 47.6 | 43.0 | 47.6 | 1987 | 106.2 | 104.1 | 105.8 | 2001 | 142.2 | 138.0 | 138.0 |
| 1974 | 56.4 | 48.8 | 56.4 | 1988 | 110.0 | 106.3 | 110.0 | 2002 | 140.0 | 137.7 | 139.7 |
| 1975 | 60.1 | 56.6 | 60.1 | 1989 | 115.5 | 111.1 | 115.5 | 2003 | 145.3 | 141.2 | 145.3 |
| 1976 | 62.4 | 59.9 | 62.4 | 1990 | 122.6 | 117.4 | 122.0 | 2004 | 152.1 | 145.6 | 151.7 |
| 1977 | 66.7 | 62.5 | 66.7 | 1991 | 122.6 | 121.1 | 122.3 | 2005 | 159.9 | 151.7 | 159.9 |
| 1978 | 72.8 | 67.0 | 72.8 | 1992 | 124.2 | 122.0 | 124.2 | 2006 | 162.1 | 157.8 | 161.5 |
| 1979 | 82.2 | 73.7 | 82.2 | 1993 | 125.7 | 123.9 | 124.4 | 2007 | 172.3 | 160.6 | 171.4 |
| 1980 | 91.8 | 83.4 | 91.8 | 1994 | 126.6 | 124.8 | 126.6 | 2008 | 183.9 | 172.6 | 172.6 |

Seasonally adjusted.   Source: U.S. Department of Labor: Bureau of Labor Statistics

# U.S. UNEMPLOYMENT RATE

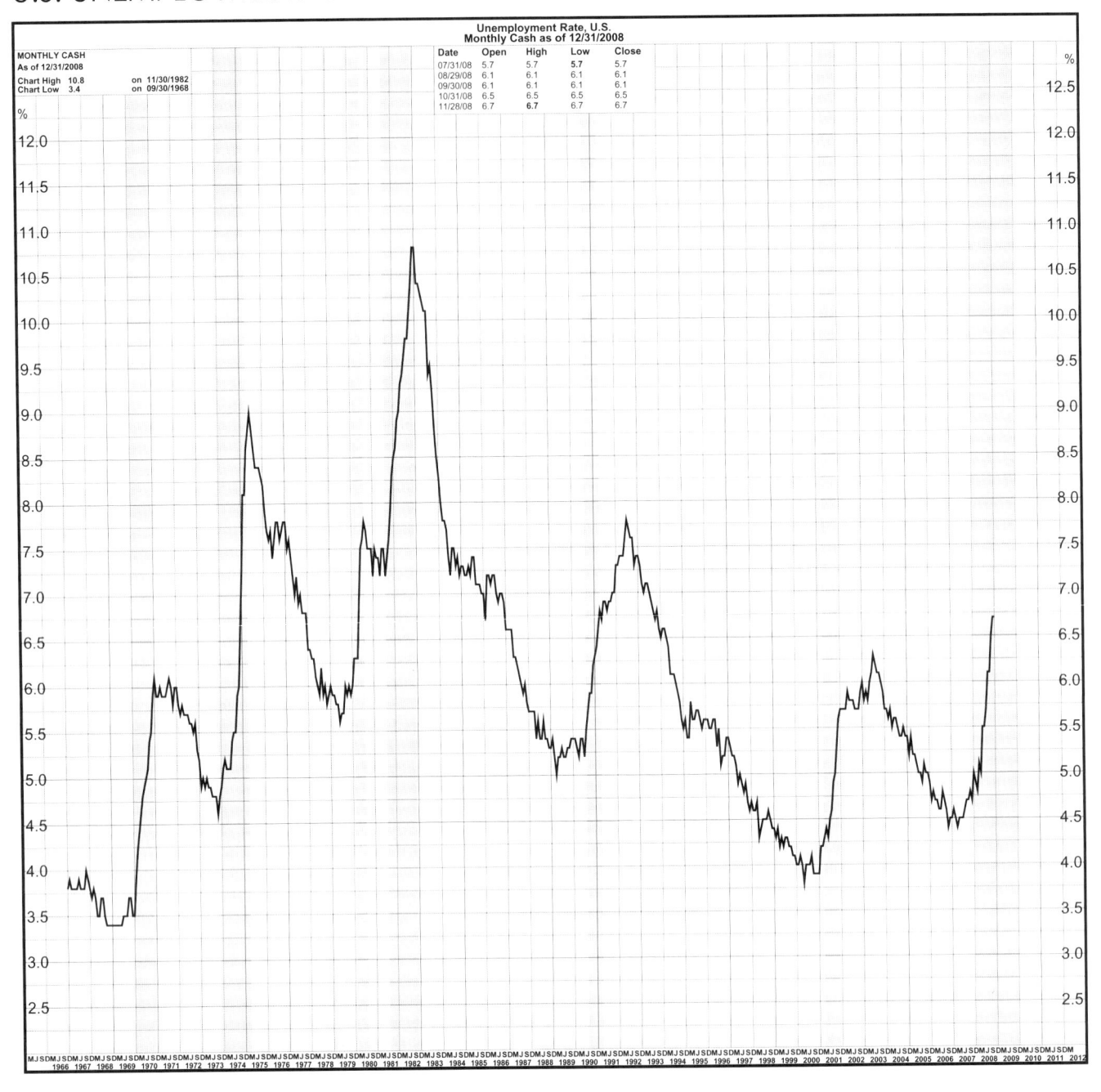

**Annual High, Low and Close of U.S. Unemployment Rate**  In Percent

| Year | High | Low | Settle | Year | High | Low | Settle | Year | High | Low | Settle |
|---|---|---|---|---|---|---|---|---|---|---|---|
| 1967 | 4.0 | 3.8 | 3.8 | 1981 | 8.5 | 7.2 | 8.5 | 1995 | 5.8 | 5.4 | 5.6 |
| 1968 | 3.8 | 3.4 | 3.4 | 1982 | 10.8 | 8.6 | 10.8 | 1996 | 5.6 | 5.1 | 5.4 |
| 1969 | 3.7 | 3.4 | 3.5 | 1983 | 10.4 | 8.3 | 8.3 | 1997 | 5.3 | 4.6 | 4.7 |
| 1970 | 6.1 | 3.9 | 6.1 | 1984 | 8.0 | 7.2 | 7.3 | 1998 | 4.7 | 4.3 | 4.4 |
| 1971 | 6.1 | 5.8 | 6.0 | 1985 | 7.4 | 7.0 | 7.0 | 1999 | 4.4 | 4.0 | 4.0 |
| 1972 | 5.8 | 5.2 | 5.2 | 1986 | 7.2 | 6.6 | 6.6 | 2000 | 4.1 | 3.8 | 3.9 |
| 1973 | 5.0 | 4.6 | 4.9 | 1987 | 6.6 | 5.7 | 5.7 | 2001 | 5.7 | 4.2 | 5.7 |
| 1974 | 7.2 | 5.1 | 7.2 | 1988 | 5.7 | 5.3 | 5.3 | 2002 | 6.0 | 5.7 | 6.0 |
| 1975 | 9.0 | 8.1 | 8.2 | 1989 | 5.4 | 5.0 | 5.4 | 2003 | 6.3 | 5.7 | 5.7 |
| 1976 | 7.9 | 7.4 | 7.8 | 1990 | 6.3 | 5.2 | 6.3 | 2004 | 5.7 | 5.4 | 5.4 |
| 1977 | 7.6 | 6.4 | 6.4 | 1991 | 7.3 | 6.4 | 7.3 | 2005 | 5.4 | 4.9 | 4.9 |
| 1978 | 6.4 | 5.8 | 6.0 | 1992 | 7.8 | 7.3 | 7.4 | 2006 | 4.8 | 4.4 | 4.5 |
| 1979 | 6.0 | 5.6 | 6.0 | 1993 | 7.3 | 6.5 | 6.5 | 2007 | 5.0 | 4.4 | 5.0 |
| 1980 | 7.8 | 6.3 | 7.2 | 1994 | 6.6 | 5.5 | 5.5 | 2008 | 7.2 | 4.8 | 7.2 |

*Source: U.S. Department of Labor: Bureau of Labor Statistics*

# U.S. UNEMPLOYED

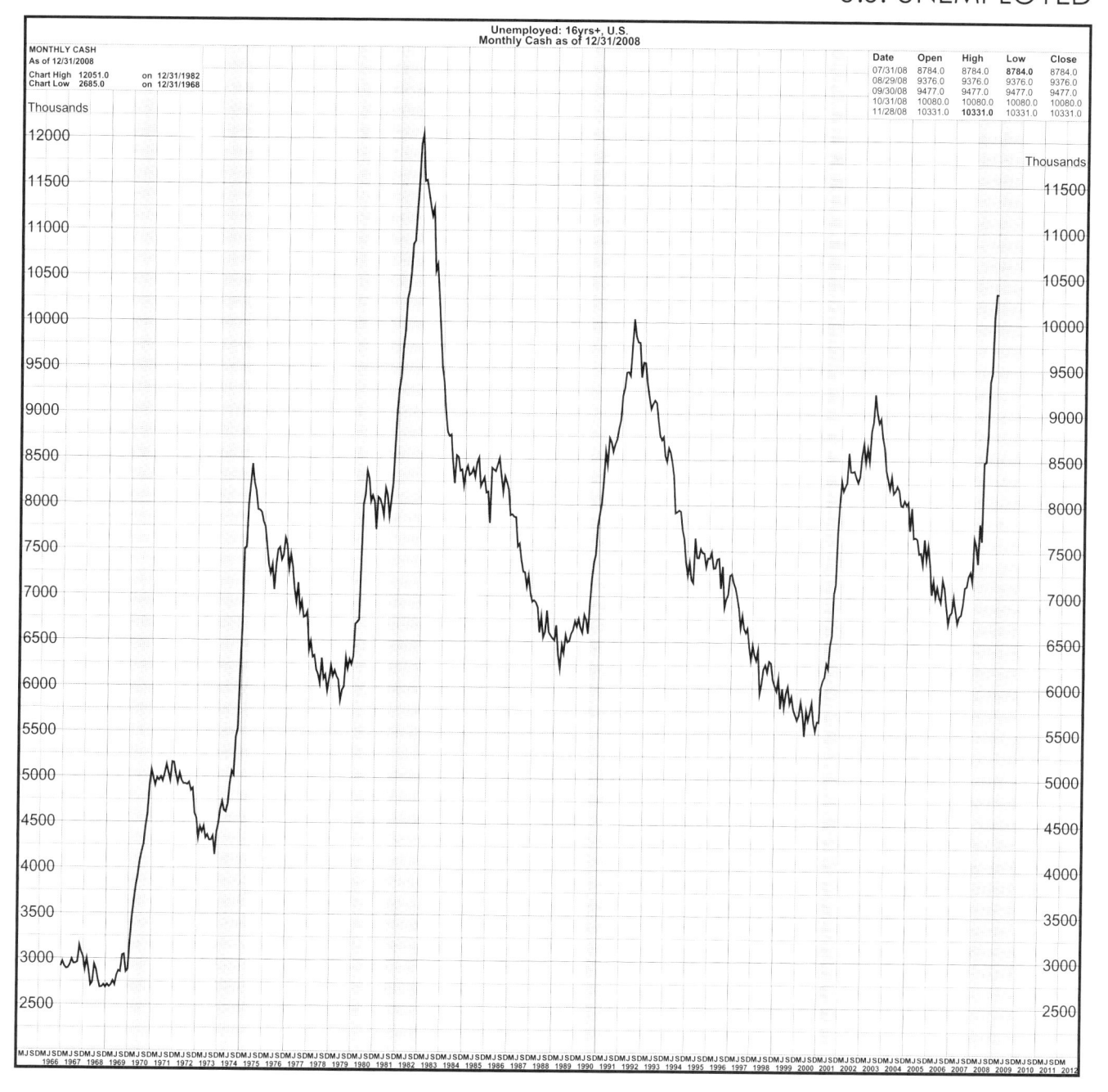

Unemployed: 16yrs+, U.S.
Monthly Cash as of 12/31/2008

MONTHLY CASH
As of 12/31/2008
Chart High 12051.0 on 12/31/1982
Chart Low 2685.0 on 12/31/1968

| Date | Open | High | Low | Close |
|---|---|---|---|---|
| 07/31/08 | 8784.0 | 8784.0 | 8784.0 | 8784.0 |
| 08/29/08 | 9376.0 | 9376.0 | 9376.0 | 9376.0 |
| 09/30/08 | 9477.0 | 9477.0 | 9477.0 | 9477.0 |
| 10/31/08 | 10080.0 | 10080.0 | 10080.0 | 10080.0 |
| 11/28/08 | 10331.0 | 10331.0 | 10331.0 | 10331.0 |

## Annual High, Low and Close of U.S. Unemployed, 16yrs+   In Thousands

| Year | High | Low | Settle | Year | High | Low | Settle | Year | High | Low | Settle |
|---|---|---|---|---|---|---|---|---|---|---|---|
| 1967 | 3,143 | 2,889 | 3,018 | 1981 | 9,267 | 7,863 | 9,267 | 1995 | 7,645 | 7,153 | 7,423 |
| 1968 | 3,001 | 2,685 | 2,685 | 1982 | 12,051 | 9,397 | 12,051 | 1996 | 7,491 | 6,882 | 7,253 |
| 1969 | 3,049 | 2,692 | 2,884 | 1983 | 11,545 | 9,331 | 9,331 | 1997 | 7,158 | 6,308 | 6,476 |
| 1970 | 5,076 | 3,201 | 5,076 | 1984 | 9,008 | 8,198 | 8,358 | 1998 | 6,422 | 5,941 | 6,032 |
| 1971 | 5,161 | 4,903 | 5,154 | 1985 | 8,513 | 8,128 | 8,138 | 1999 | 6,111 | 5,653 | 5,653 |
| 1972 | 5,038 | 4,543 | 4,543 | 1986 | 8,508 | 7,795 | 7,883 | 2000 | 5,858 | 5,481 | 5,634 |
| 1973 | 4,489 | 4,144 | 4,489 | 1987 | 7,892 | 6,936 | 6,936 | 2001 | 8,281 | 6,017 | 8,281 |
| 1974 | 6,636 | 4,618 | 6,636 | 1988 | 6,953 | 6,518 | 6,518 | 2002 | 8,691 | 8,165 | 8,691 |
| 1975 | 8,433 | 7,501 | 7,744 | 1989 | 6,725 | 6,205 | 6,667 | 2003 | 9,228 | 8,399 | 8,399 |
| 1976 | 7,620 | 7,053 | 7,545 | 1990 | 7,901 | 6,590 | 7,901 | 2004 | 8,330 | 8,005 | 8,047 |
| 1977 | 7,443 | 6,386 | 6,386 | 1991 | 9,198 | 8,015 | 9,198 | 2005 | 7,988 | 7,367 | 7,375 |
| 1978 | 6,489 | 5,947 | 6,228 | 1992 | 10,040 | 9,283 | 9,557 | 2006 | 7,205 | 6,715 | 6,849 |
| 1979 | 6,325 | 5,840 | 6,325 | 1993 | 9,325 | 8,477 | 8,477 | 2007 | 7,655 | 6,724 | 7,655 |
| 1980 | 8,363 | 6,683 | 7,718 | 1994 | 8,630 | 7,230 | 7,230 | 2008 | 11,108 | 7,381 | 11,108 |

*Source: U.S. Department of Labor: Bureau of Labor Statistics*

# U.S. CIVILIAN LABOR FORCE

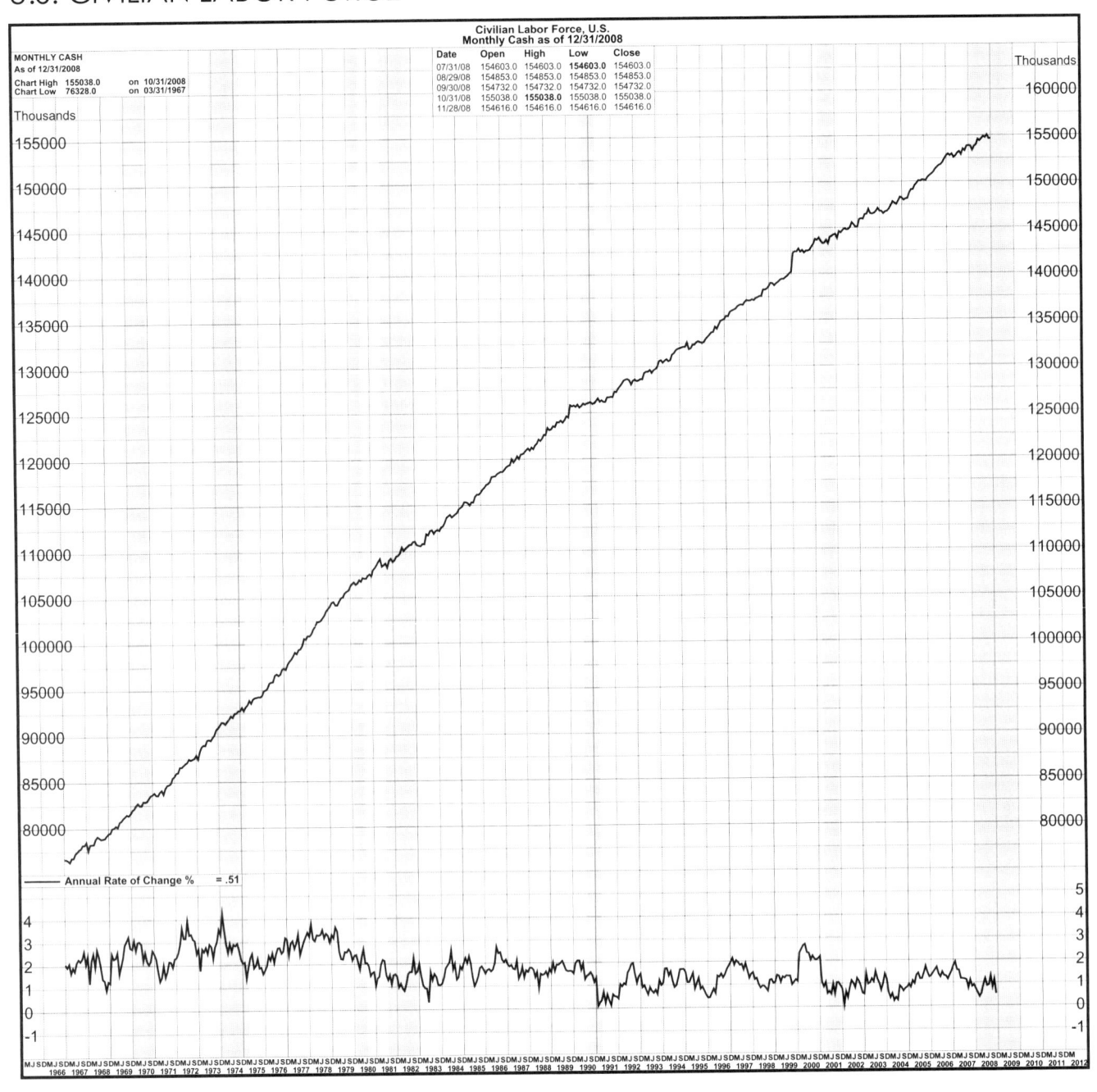

| Date | Open | High | Low | Close |
|---|---|---|---|---|
| 07/31/08 | 154603.0 | 154603.0 | 154603.0 | 154603.0 |
| 08/29/08 | 154853.0 | 154853.0 | 154853.0 | 154853.0 |
| 09/30/08 | 154732.0 | 154732.0 | 154732.0 | 154732.0 |
| 10/31/08 | 155038.0 | 155038.0 | 155038.0 | 155038.0 |
| 11/28/08 | 154616.0 | 154616.0 | 154616.0 | 154616.0 |

MONTHLY CASH As of 12/31/2008
Chart High 155038.0 on 10/31/2008
Chart Low 76328.0 on 03/31/1967

## Annual High, Low and Close of U.S. Civilian Labor Force — In Thousands

| Year | High | Low | Settle | Year | High | Low | Settle | Year | High | Low | Settle |
|---|---|---|---|---|---|---|---|---|---|---|---|
| 1967 | 78,491 | 76,328 | 78,491 | 1981 | 109,236 | 108,026 | 108,912 | 1995 | 132,716 | 131,851 | 132,511 |
| 1968 | 79,463 | 77,578 | 79,463 | 1982 | 111,083 | 109,089 | 111,083 | 1996 | 135,113 | 132,616 | 135,113 |
| 1969 | 81,624 | 79,523 | 81,624 | 1983 | 112,327 | 110,587 | 112,327 | 1997 | 137,155 | 135,400 | 137,155 |
| 1970 | 83,670 | 81,981 | 83,670 | 1984 | 114,581 | 112,209 | 114,581 | 1998 | 138,634 | 137,095 | 138,634 |
| 1971 | 85,625 | 83,575 | 85,625 | 1985 | 116,354 | 114,725 | 116,354 | 1999 | 140,177 | 138,730 | 140,177 |
| 1972 | 87,943 | 85,978 | 87,943 | 1986 | 118,634 | 116,682 | 118,611 | 2000 | 143,248 | 142,267 | 143,248 |
| 1973 | 90,890 | 87,487 | 90,890 | 1987 | 120,729 | 118,845 | 120,729 | 2001 | 144,324 | 143,301 | 144,324 |
| 1974 | 92,780 | 91,199 | 92,780 | 1988 | 122,637 | 120,913 | 122,622 | 2002 | 145,573 | 143,858 | 145,091 |
| 1975 | 94,409 | 92,776 | 94,409 | 1989 | 124,637 | 123,135 | 124,497 | 2003 | 147,109 | 145,914 | 146,808 |
| 1976 | 97,348 | 94,934 | 97,348 | 1990 | 126,142 | 125,573 | 126,142 | 2004 | 148,313 | 146,529 | 148,203 |
| 1977 | 100,576 | 97,208 | 100,491 | 1991 | 126,701 | 125,955 | 126,664 | 2005 | 150,183 | 147,979 | 150,153 |
| 1978 | 103,809 | 100,837 | 103,809 | 1992 | 128,613 | 127,207 | 128,554 | 2006 | 152,775 | 150,114 | 152,775 |
| 1979 | 106,258 | 104,057 | 106,258 | 1993 | 129,941 | 128,400 | 129,941 | 2007 | 153,866 | 152,587 | 153,866 |
| 1980 | 107,568 | 106,442 | 107,352 | 1994 | 131,951 | 130,400 | 131,951 | 2008 | 154,878 | 153,374 | 154,447 |

*Source: U.S. Department of Labor: Bureau of Labor Statistics*

# U.S. NON-FARM PAYROLLS

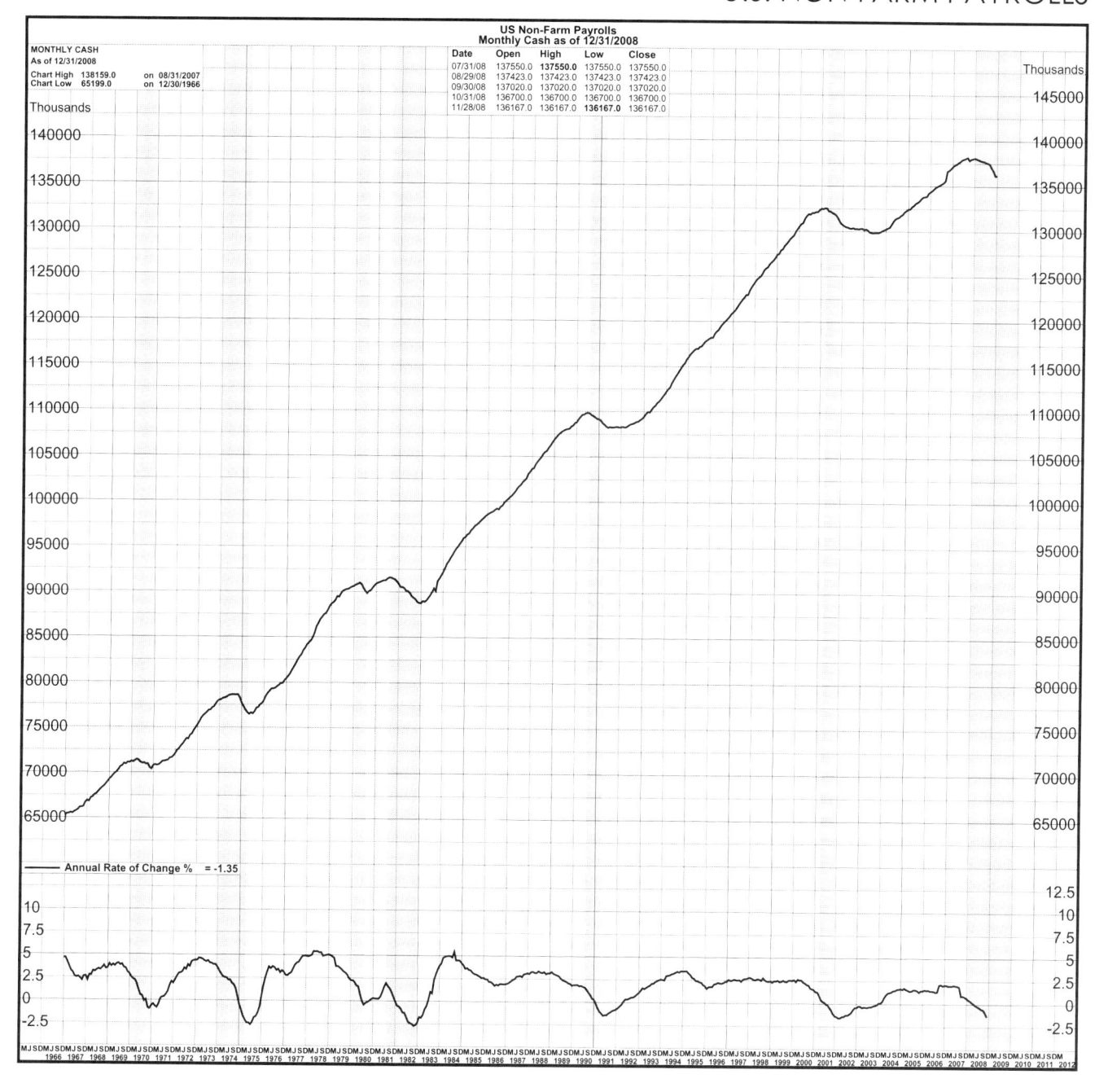

| | | MONTHLY CASH | | | |
|---|---|---|---|---|---|
| As of 12/31/2008 | | | | | |
| Chart High 138159.0 | on 08/31/2007 | | | | |
| Chart Low 65199.0 | on 12/30/1966 | | | | |

US Non-Farm Payrolls
Monthly Cash as of 12/31/2008

| Date | Open | High | Low | Close |
|---|---|---|---|---|
| 07/31/08 | 137550.0 | **137550.0** | 137550.0 | 137550.0 |
| 08/29/08 | 137423.0 | 137423.0 | 137423.0 | 137423.0 |
| 09/30/08 | 137020.0 | 137020.0 | 137020.0 | 137020.0 |
| 10/31/08 | 136700.0 | 136700.0 | 136700.0 | 136700.0 |
| 11/28/08 | 136167.0 | 136167.0 | **136167.0** | 136167.0 |

Annual Rate of Change %  = -1.35

## Annual High, Low and Close of U.S. Non-Farm Payrolls   In Thousands

| Year | High | Low | Settle | Year | High | Low | Settle | Year | High | Low | Settle |
|---|---|---|---|---|---|---|---|---|---|---|---|
| 1967 | 66,900 | 65,407 | 66,900 | 1981 | 91,594 | 90,884 | 90,884 | 1995 | 118,210 | 116,377 | 118,210 |
| 1968 | 69,245 | 66,805 | 69,245 | 1982 | 90,557 | 88,756 | 88,756 | 1996 | 121,003 | 118,192 | 121,003 |
| 1969 | 71,240 | 69,438 | 71,240 | 1983 | 92,210 | 88,903 | 92,210 | 1997 | 124,361 | 121,232 | 124,361 |
| 1970 | 71,453 | 70,409 | 70,790 | 1984 | 96,087 | 92,657 | 96,087 | 1998 | 127,364 | 124,629 | 127,364 |
| 1971 | 72,108 | 70,805 | 72,108 | 1985 | 98,587 | 96,353 | 98,587 | 1999 | 130,536 | 127,477 | 130,536 |
| 1972 | 75,270 | 72,445 | 75,270 | 1986 | 100,484 | 98,710 | 100,484 | 2000 | 132,484 | 130,781 | 132,484 |
| 1973 | 78,035 | 75,620 | 78,035 | 1987 | 103,634 | 100,655 | 103,634 | 2001 | 132,546 | 130,705 | 130,705 |
| 1974 | 78,634 | 77,657 | 77,657 | 1988 | 106,871 | 103,728 | 106,871 | 2002 | 130,581 | 130,161 | 130,161 |
| 1975 | 78,017 | 76,463 | 78,017 | 1989 | 108,809 | 107,133 | 108,809 | 2003 | 130,255 | 129,827 | 130,255 |
| 1976 | 80,448 | 78,506 | 80,448 | 1990 | 109,820 | 109,118 | 109,118 | 2004 | 132,449 | 130,372 | 132,449 |
| 1977 | 84,408 | 80,692 | 84,408 | 1991 | 108,998 | 108,203 | 108,261 | 2005 | 134,376 | 132,471 | 134,376 |
| 1978 | 88,674 | 84,595 | 88,674 | 1992 | 109,418 | 108,242 | 109,418 | 2006 | 137,167 | 134,530 | 137,167 |
| 1979 | 90,669 | 88,811 | 90,669 | 1993 | 112,203 | 109,725 | 112,203 | 2007 | 138,159 | 137,329 | 138,078 |
| 1980 | 90,991 | 89,832 | 90,936 | 1994 | 116,056 | 112,473 | 116,056 | 2008 | 138,002 | 135,489 | 135,489 |

*Source: U.S. Department of Labor: Bureau of Labor Statistics*

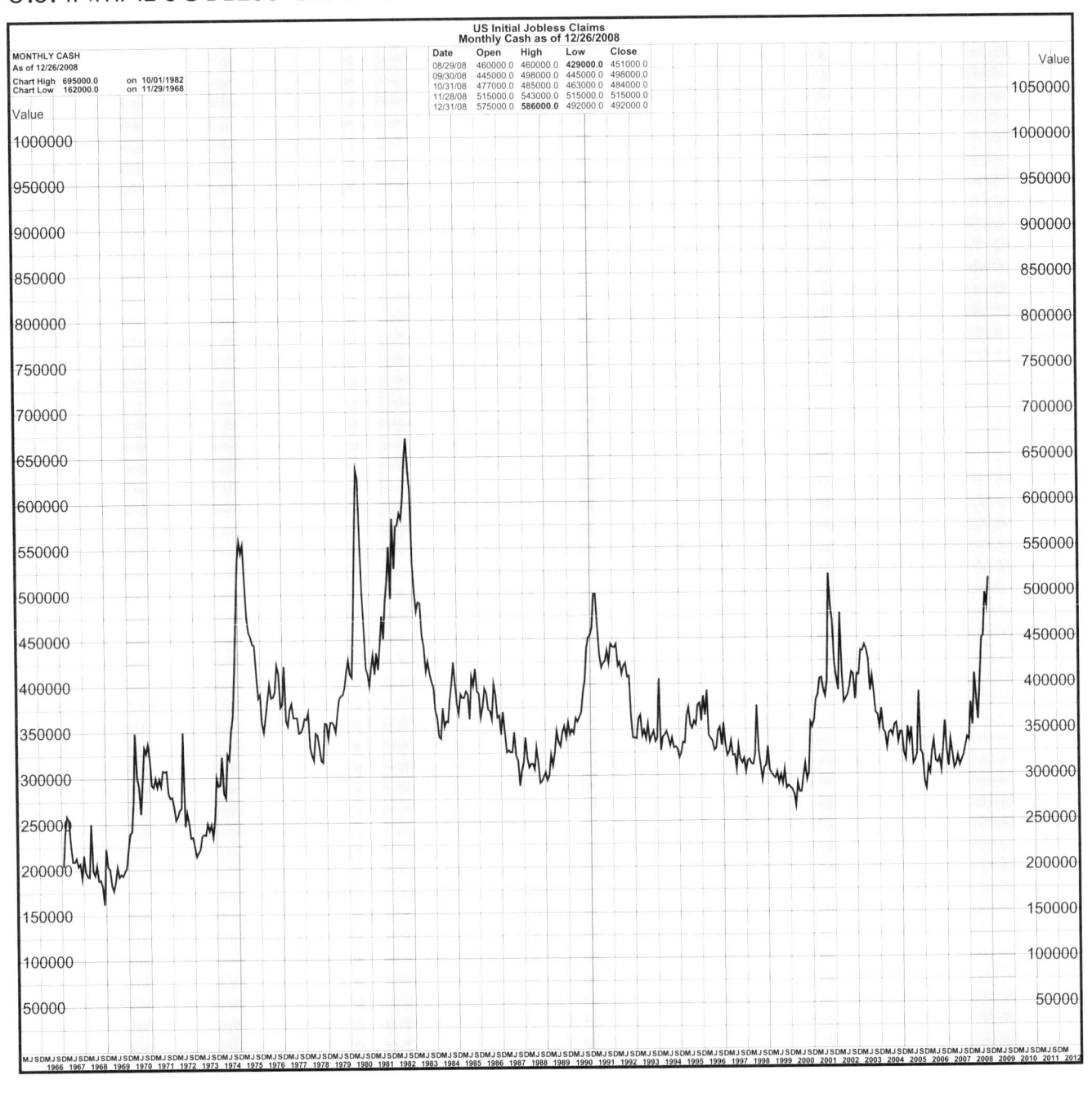

# U.S. INITIAL JOBLESS CLAIMS

**MONTHLY CASH**
As of 12/26/2008
Chart High 695000.0 on 10/01/1982
Chart Low 162000.0 on 11/29/1968

US Initial Jobless Claims
Monthly Cash as of 12/26/2008

| Date | Open | High | Low | Close |
|---|---|---|---|---|
| 08/29/08 | 460000.0 | 460000.0 | 429000.0 | 451000.0 |
| 09/30/08 | 445000.0 | 498000.0 | 445000.0 | 498000.0 |
| 10/31/08 | 477000.0 | 485000.0 | 463000.0 | 484000.0 |
| 11/28/08 | 515000.0 | 543000.0 | 515000.0 | 515000.0 |
| 12/31/08 | 575000.0 | 586000.0 | 492000.0 | 492000.0 |

## Annual High, Low and Close of U.S. Initial Jobless Claims    In Number

| Year | High | Low | Settle | Year | High | Low | Settle | Year | High | Low | Settle |
|---|---|---|---|---|---|---|---|---|---|---|---|
| 1967 | 310,000 | 191,000 | 216,000 | 1981 | 558,000 | 392,000 | 495,000 | 1995 | 390,000 | 324,000 | 359,000 |
| 1968 | 251,000 | 162,000 | 223,000 | 1982 | 695,000 | 489,000 | 534,000 | 1996 | 426,000 | 326,000 | 357,000 |
| 1969 | 232,000 | 177,000 | 223,000 | 1983 | 515,000 | 362,000 | 372,000 | 1997 | 347,000 | 301,000 | 303,000 |
| 1970 | 374,000 | 230,000 | 321,000 | 1984 | 439,000 | 333,000 | 379,000 | 1998 | 376,000 | 294,000 | 331,000 |
| 1971 | 359,000 | 244,000 | 279,000 | 1985 | 426,000 | 359,000 | 390,000 | 1999 | 345,000 | 268,000 | 286,000 |
| 1972 | 350,000 | 225,000 | 225,000 | 1986 | 416,000 | 344,000 | 345,000 | 2000 | 365,000 | 257,000 | 352,000 |
| 1973 | 326,000 | 214,000 | 300,000 | 1987 | 370,000 | 289,000 | 315,000 | 2001 | 520,000 | 317,000 | 421,000 |
| 1974 | 537,000 | 269,000 | 537,000 | 1988 | 361,000 | 284,000 | 304,000 | 2002 | 477,000 | 377,000 | 410,000 |
| 1975 | 575,000 | 365,000 | 391,000 | 1989 | 407,000 | 282,000 | 358,000 | 2003 | 447,000 | 351,000 | 351,000 |
| 1976 | 423,000 | 333,000 | 380,000 | 1990 | 474,000 | 331,000 | 454,000 | 2004 | 372,000 | 321,000 | 346,000 |
| 1977 | 565,000 | 334,000 | 364,000 | 1991 | 509,000 | 408,000 | 441,000 | 2005 | 435,000 | 292,000 | 292,000 |
| 1978 | 429,000 | 304,000 | 358,000 | 1992 | 564,000 | 313,000 | 341,000 | 2006 | 358,000 | 281,000 | 325,000 |
| 1979 | 471,000 | 336,000 | 428,000 | 1993 | 415,000 | 290,000 | 341,000 | 2007 | 359,000 | 287,000 | 337,000 |
| 1980 | 642,000 | 394,000 | 399,000 | 1994 | 406,000 | 314,000 | 319,000 | 2008 | 586,000 | 302,000 | 491,000 |

*Source: U.S. Department of Labor: Bureau of Labor Statistics*

# U.S. INITIAL JOBLESS CLAIMS

**WEEKLY CASH**
As of 01/02/2009
Chart High 586000.0 on 12/19/2008
Chart Low 257000.0 on 04/14/2000

US Initial Jobless Claims
Weekly Cash as of 01/02/2009

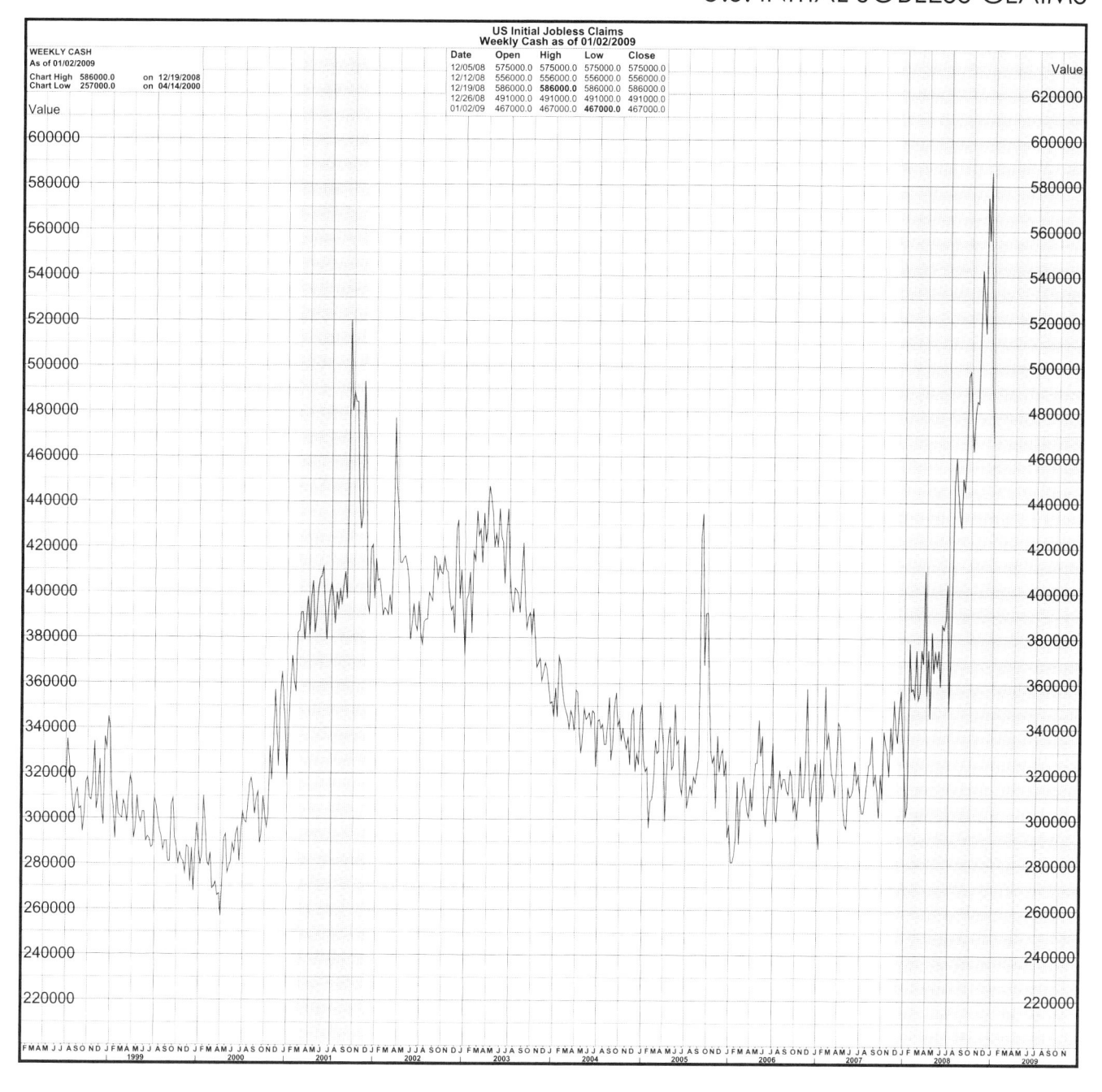

| Date | Open | High | Low | Close |
|---|---|---|---|---|
| 12/05/08 | 575000.0 | 575000.0 | 575000.0 | 575000.0 |
| 12/12/08 | 556000.0 | 556000.0 | 556000.0 | 556000.0 |
| 12/19/08 | 586000.0 | 586000.0 | 586000.0 | 586000.0 |
| 12/26/08 | 491000.0 | 491000.0 | 491000.0 | 491000.0 |
| 01/02/09 | 467000.0 | 467000.0 | 467000.0 | 467000.0 |

### Quarterly High, Low and Close of U.S. Initial Jobless Claims   In Number

| Quarter | High | Low | Settle | Quarter | High | Low | Settle | Quarter | High | Low | Settle |
|---|---|---|---|---|---|---|---|---|---|---|---|
| 03/2000 | 310,000 | 266,000 | 266,000 | 03/2003 | 436,000 | 372,000 | 435,000 | 03/2006 | 319,000 | 281,000 | 301,000 |
| 06/2000 | 296,000 | 257,000 | 281,000 | 06/2003 | 447,000 | 404,000 | 426,000 | 06/2006 | 344,000 | 297,000 | 314,000 |
| 09/2000 | 318,000 | 289,000 | 294,000 | 09/2003 | 437,000 | 384,000 | 389,000 | 09/2006 | 334,000 | 299,000 | 304,000 |
| 12/2000 | 365,000 | 296,000 | 352,000 | 12/2003 | 393,000 | 351,000 | 351,000 | 12/2006 | 358,000 | 300,000 | 325,000 |
| 03/2001 | 391,000 | 317,000 | 388,000 | 03/2004 | 372,000 | 340,000 | 345,000 | 03/2007 | 359,000 | 287,000 | 323,000 |
| 06/2001 | 411,000 | 379,000 | 393,000 | 06/2004 | 357,000 | 329,000 | 347,000 | 06/2007 | 343,000 | 296,000 | 320,000 |
| 09/2001 | 520,000 | 386,000 | 520,000 | 09/2004 | 356,000 | 323,000 | 356,000 | 09/2007 | 337,000 | 301,000 | 320,000 |
| 12/2001 | 493,000 | 391,000 | 421,000 | 12/2004 | 349,000 | 321,000 | 346,000 | 12/2007 | 357,000 | 309,000 | 337,000 |
| 03/2002 | 477,000 | 390,000 | 477,000 | 03/2005 | 352,000 | 296,000 | 352,000 | 03/2008 | 410,000 | 302,000 | 410,000 |
| 06/2002 | 446,000 | 379,000 | 383,000 | 06/2005 | 351,000 | 299,000 | 311,000 | 06/2008 | 404,000 | 345,000 | 404,000 |
| 09/2002 | 416,000 | 377,000 | 412,000 | 09/2005 | 435,000 | 305,000 | 391,000 | 09/2008 | 498,000 | 348,000 | 498,000 |
| 12/2002 | 432,000 | 382,000 | 410,000 | 12/2005 | 391,000 | 292,000 | 292,000 | 12/2008 | 586,000 | 463,000 | 491,000 |

*Source: U.S. Department of Labor: Bureau of Labor Statistics*

# U.S. AVERAGE HOURLY EARNINGS

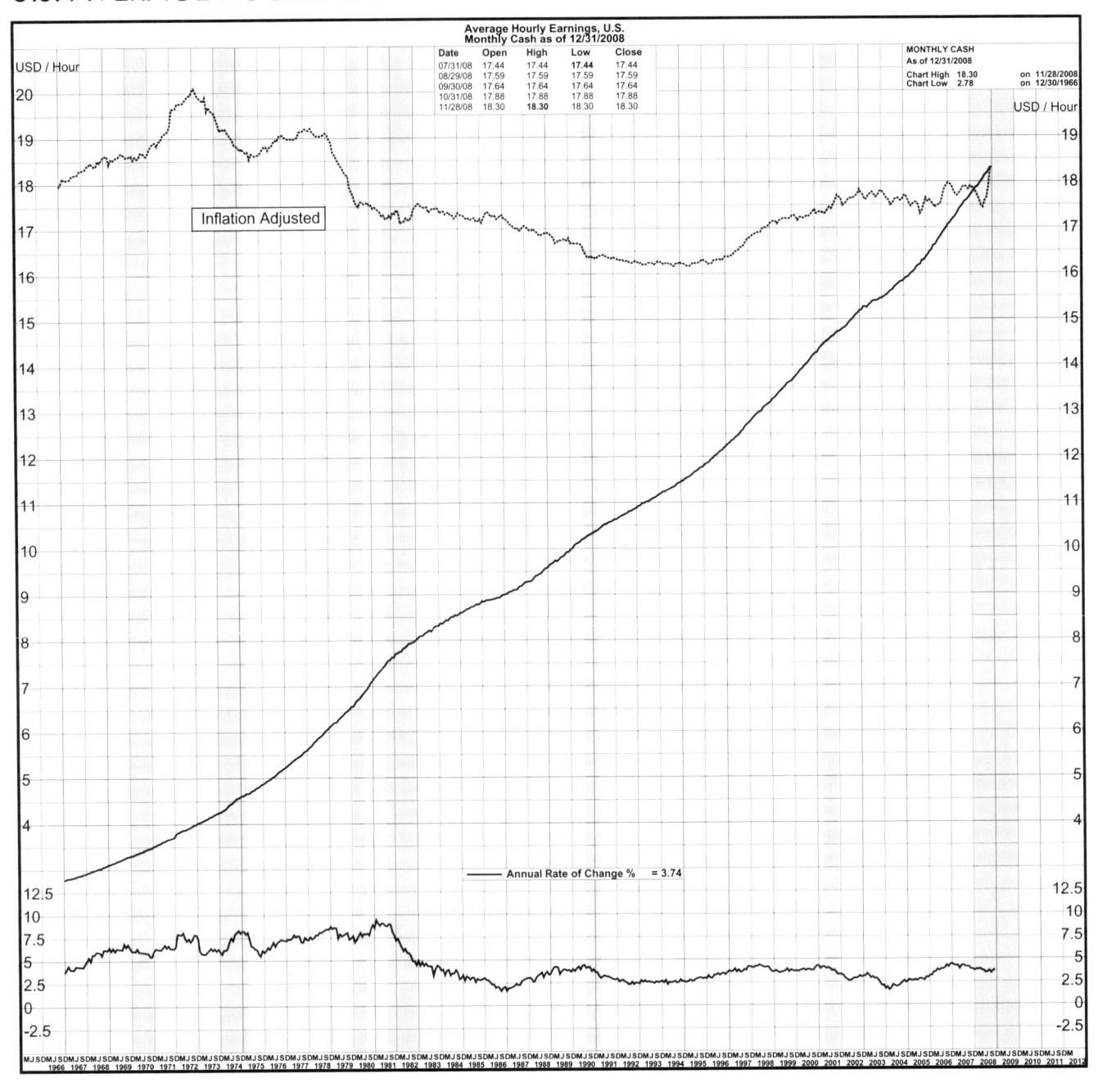

## Annual High, Low and Close of U.S. Average Hourly Earnings    In Dollars per Hour

| Year | High | Low | Settle | Year | High | Low | Settle | Year | High | Low | Settle |
|------|------|------|--------|------|------|------|--------|------|------|------|--------|
| 1967 | 2.92 | 2.79 | 2.92 | 1981 | 7.63 | 7.18 | 7.63 | 1995 | 11.79 | 11.47 | 11.79 |
| 1968 | 3.11 | 2.94 | 3.11 | 1982 | 8.01 | 7.71 | 8.01 | 1996 | 12.23 | 11.84 | 12.23 |
| 1969 | 3.30 | 3.12 | 3.30 | 1983 | 8.32 | 8.05 | 8.32 | 1997 | 12.73 | 12.27 | 12.73 |
| 1970 | 3.50 | 3.31 | 3.50 | 1984 | 8.60 | 8.36 | 8.60 | 1998 | 13.19 | 12.77 | 13.19 |
| 1971 | 3.73 | 3.52 | 3.73 | 1985 | 8.86 | 8.60 | 8.86 | 1999 | 13.68 | 13.25 | 13.68 |
| 1972 | 4.01 | 3.80 | 4.01 | 1986 | 9.00 | 8.84 | 9.00 | 2000 | 14.26 | 13.73 | 14.26 |
| 1973 | 4.25 | 4.03 | 4.25 | 1987 | 9.27 | 9.01 | 9.27 | 2001 | 14.73 | 14.27 | 14.73 |
| 1974 | 4.60 | 4.26 | 4.60 | 1988 | 9.59 | 9.28 | 9.59 | 2002 | 15.19 | 14.73 | 15.19 |
| 1975 | 4.87 | 4.61 | 4.87 | 1989 | 9.97 | 9.64 | 9.97 | 2003 | 15.45 | 15.19 | 15.45 |
| 1976 | 5.22 | 4.89 | 5.22 | 1990 | 10.33 | 10.00 | 10.33 | 2004 | 15.85 | 15.48 | 15.85 |
| 1977 | 5.60 | 5.25 | 5.60 | 1991 | 10.63 | 10.36 | 10.63 | 2005 | 16.35 | 15.90 | 16.35 |
| 1978 | 6.09 | 5.65 | 6.09 | 1992 | 10.88 | 10.63 | 10.88 | 2006 | 17.07 | 16.40 | 17.07 |
| 1979 | 6.56 | 6.13 | 6.56 | 1993 | 11.17 | 10.92 | 11.17 | 2007 | 17.70 | 17.10 | 17.70 |
| 1980 | 7.12 | 6.56 | 7.12 | 1994 | 11.46 | 11.19 | 11.46 | 2008 | 18.36 | 17.75 | 18.36 |

*Source: U.S. Department of Labor: Bureau of Labor Statistics*

# ISM MANUFACTURING: PMI COMPOSITE INDEX

**ISM Manufacturing: PMI Composite Index**
Monthly Cash as of 12/31/2008

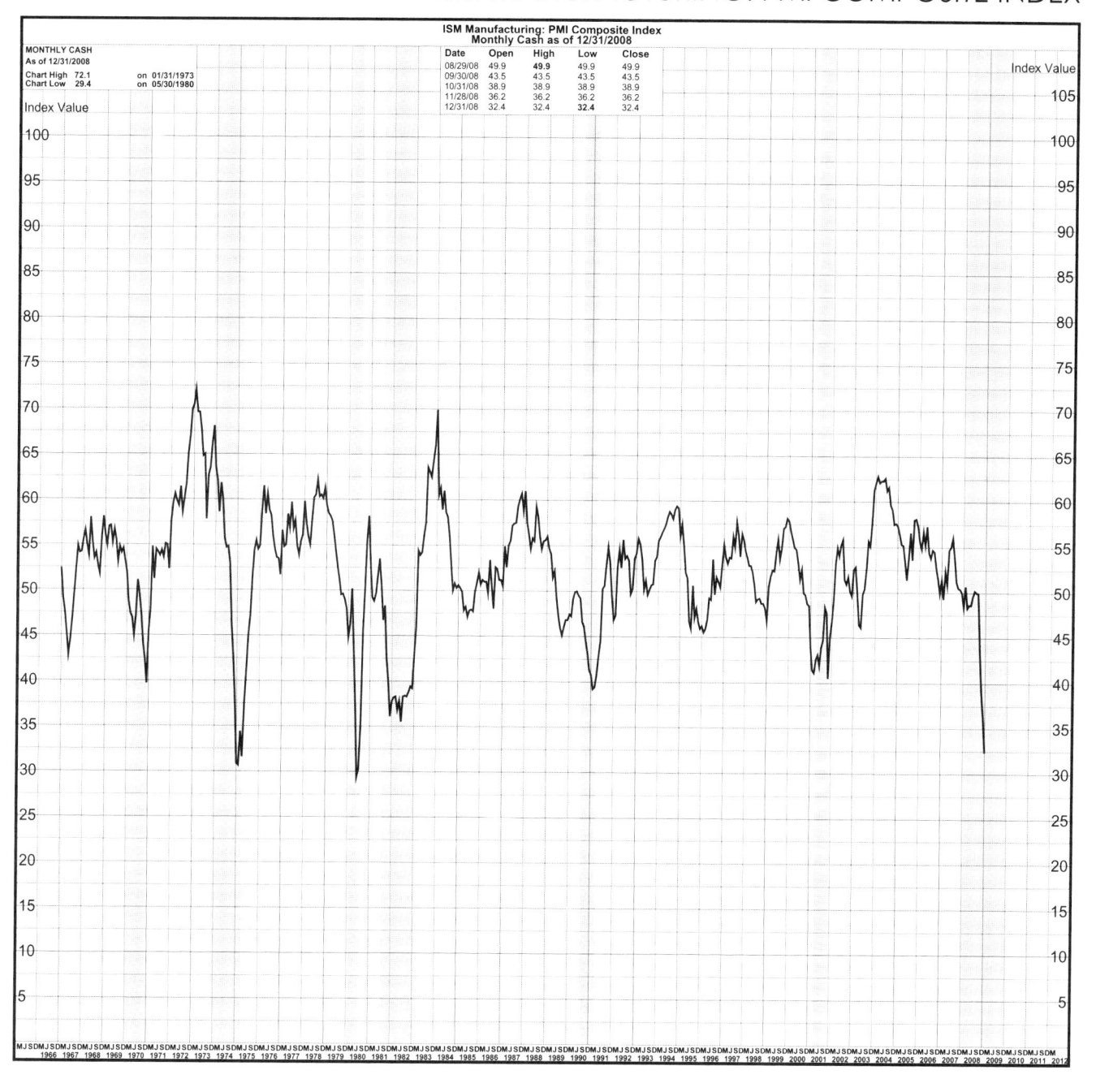

| Date | Open | High | Low | Close |
|---|---|---|---|---|
| 08/29/08 | 49.9 | 49.9 | 49.9 | 49.9 |
| 09/30/08 | 43.5 | 43.5 | 43.5 | 43.5 |
| 10/31/08 | 38.9 | 38.9 | 38.9 | 38.9 |
| 11/28/08 | 36.2 | 36.2 | 36.2 | 36.2 |
| 12/31/08 | 32.4 | 32.4 | 32.4 | 32.4 |

MONTHLY CASH
As of 12/31/2008
Chart High 72.1 on 01/31/1973
Chart Low 29.4 on 05/30/1980

## Annual High, Low and Close of ISM Manufacturing: PMI Index    In Index Value

| Year | High | Low | Settle | Year | High | Low | Settle | Year | High | Low | Settle |
|---|---|---|---|---|---|---|---|---|---|---|---|
| 1967 | 55.6 | 42.8 | 55.6 | 1981 | 53.5 | 36.1 | 37.8 | 1995 | 57.4 | 45.9 | 46.2 |
| 1968 | 58.1 | 51.8 | 56.1 | 1982 | 42.8 | 35.5 | 42.8 | 1996 | 55.2 | 45.5 | 55.2 |
| 1969 | 57.1 | 52.0 | 52.0 | 1983 | 69.9 | 46.0 | 69.9 | 1997 | 57.7 | 53.1 | 54.5 |
| 1970 | 51.1 | 39.7 | 45.4 | 1984 | 61.3 | 50.0 | 50.6 | 1998 | 53.8 | 46.8 | 46.8 |
| 1971 | 57.6 | 47.9 | 57.6 | 1985 | 52.0 | 47.1 | 50.7 | 1999 | 58.1 | 50.6 | 57.8 |
| 1972 | 70.5 | 58.6 | 70.5 | 1986 | 53.4 | 48.0 | 50.5 | 2000 | 56.7 | 43.9 | 43.9 |
| 1973 | 72.1 | 57.8 | 63.6 | 1987 | 61.0 | 52.6 | 61.0 | 2001 | 48.3 | 40.5 | 46.7 |
| 1974 | 62.1 | 30.9 | 30.9 | 1988 | 59.3 | 54.6 | 56.0 | 2002 | 55.8 | 49.1 | 52.5 |
| 1975 | 55.5 | 30.7 | 54.9 | 1989 | 54.7 | 45.1 | 47.4 | 2003 | 62.1 | 46.1 | 62.1 |
| 1976 | 61.5 | 51.7 | 56.6 | 1990 | 50.0 | 40.8 | 40.8 | 2004 | 62.8 | 57.3 | 57.3 |
| 1977 | 59.8 | 53.9 | 59.8 | 1991 | 54.9 | 39.2 | 46.8 | 2005 | 58.1 | 51.4 | 55.6 |
| 1978 | 62.2 | 55.0 | 59.4 | 1992 | 55.7 | 47.3 | 54.2 | 2006 | 57.3 | 49.9 | 51.4 |
| 1979 | 58.5 | 44.8 | 44.8 | 1993 | 55.8 | 49.6 | 55.6 | 2007 | 56.0 | 48.4 | 48.4 |
| 1980 | 58.2 | 29.4 | 53.0 | 1994 | 59.4 | 56.0 | 56.1 | 2008 | 50.7 | 32.4 | 32.4 |

*Source: Institute for Supply Management*

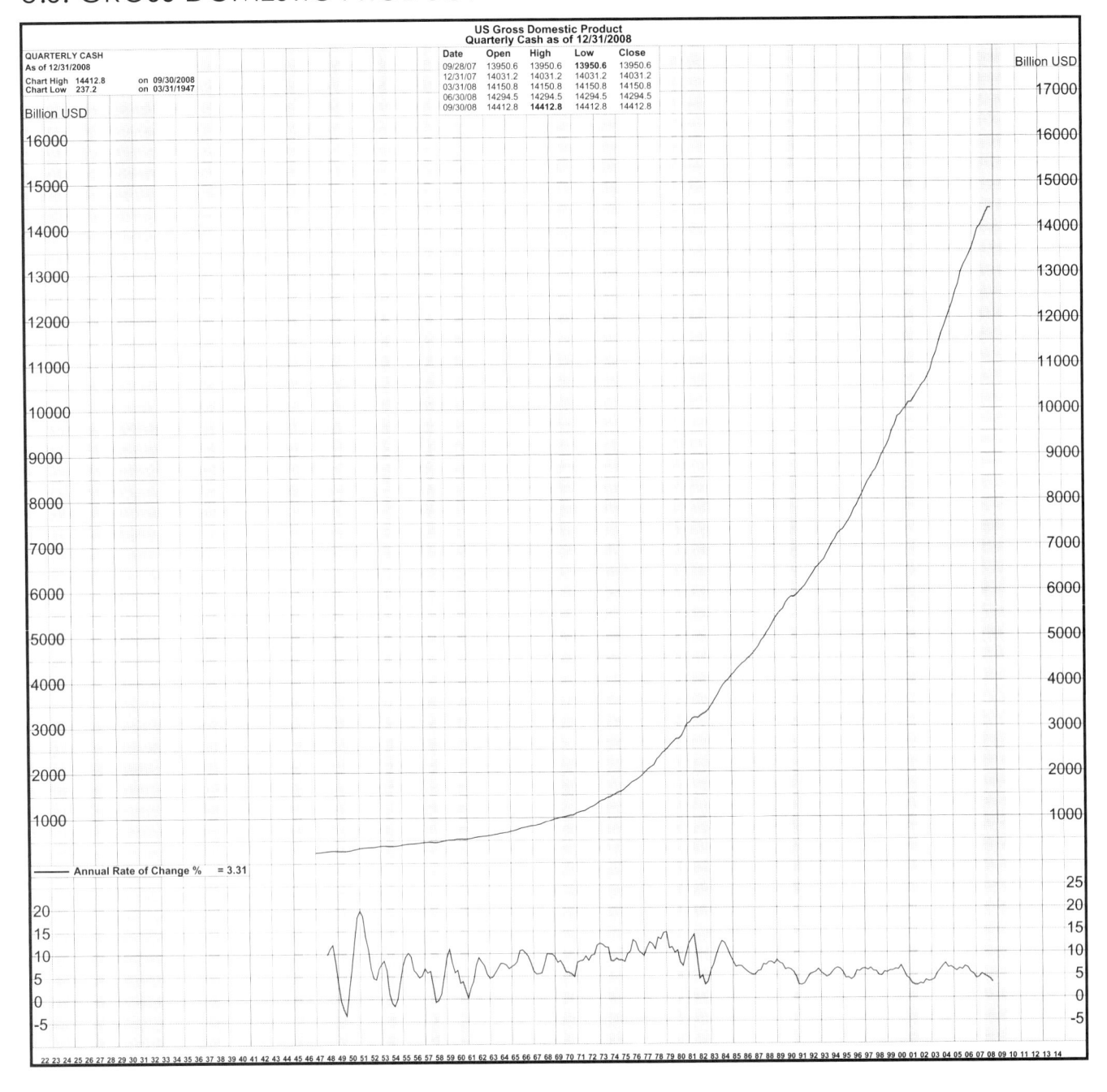

# U.S. GROSS DOMESTIC PRODUCT

**QUARTERLY CASH**
As of 12/31/2008
Chart High 14412.8 on 09/30/2008
Chart Low 237.2 on 03/31/1947

US Gross Domestic Product
Quarterly Cash as of 12/31/2008

| Date | Open | High | Low | Close |
|---|---|---|---|---|
| 09/28/07 | 13950.6 | 13950.6 | 13950.6 | 13950.6 |
| 12/31/07 | 14031.2 | 14031.2 | 14031.2 | 14031.2 |
| 03/31/08 | 14150.8 | 14150.8 | 14150.8 | 14150.8 |
| 06/30/08 | 14294.5 | 14294.5 | 14294.5 | 14294.5 |
| 09/30/08 | 14412.8 | 14412.8 | 14412.8 | 14412.8 |

Annual Rate of Change % = 3.31

## Annual High, Low and Close of U.S. Gross Domestic Product — In Billions of Dollars

| Year | High | Low | Settle | Year | High | Low | Settle | Year | High | Low | Settle |
|---|---|---|---|---|---|---|---|---|---|---|---|
| 1967 | 852.8 | 817.9 | 852.8 | 1981 | 3,196.4 | 3,052.7 | 3,196.4 | 1995 | 7,522.5 | 7,298.3 | 7,522.5 |
| 1968 | 936.3 | 879.9 | 936.3 | 1982 | 3,314.4 | 3,186.8 | 3,314.4 | 1996 | 8,000.4 | 7,624.1 | 8,000.4 |
| 1969 | 1,004.6 | 961.0 | 1,004.6 | 1983 | 3,690.4 | 3,382.9 | 3,690.4 | 1997 | 8,471.2 | 8,113.8 | 8,471.2 |
| 1970 | 1,052.9 | 1,017.3 | 1,052.9 | 1984 | 4,036.3 | 3,809.6 | 4,036.3 | 1998 | 8,953.8 | 8,586.7 | 8,953.8 |
| 1971 | 1,151.7 | 1,098.3 | 1,151.7 | 1985 | 4,321.8 | 4,119.5 | 4,321.8 | 1999 | 9,519.5 | 9,066.6 | 9,519.5 |
| 1972 | 1,287.0 | 1,190.6 | 1,287.0 | 1986 | 4,546.1 | 4,385.6 | 4,546.1 | 2000 | 9,953.6 | 9,629.4 | 9,953.6 |
| 1973 | 1,432.3 | 1,335.5 | 1,432.3 | 1987 | 4,886.3 | 4,613.8 | 4,886.3 | 2001 | 10,226.3 | 10,021.5 | 10,226.3 |
| 1974 | 1,553.4 | 1,447.0 | 1,553.4 | 1988 | 5,253.7 | 4,951.9 | 5,253.7 | 2002 | 10,591.1 | 10,333.3 | 10,591.1 |
| 1975 | 1,714.6 | 1,570.0 | 1,714.6 | 1989 | 5,584.3 | 5,367.1 | 5,584.3 | 2003 | 11,236.0 | 10,717.0 | 11,236.0 |
| 1976 | 1,885.3 | 1,772.6 | 1,885.3 | 1990 | 5,849.4 | 5,716.4 | 5,848.8 | 2004 | 11,995.2 | 11,457.1 | 11,995.2 |
| 1977 | 2,111.6 | 1,939.3 | 2,111.6 | 1991 | 6,095.8 | 5,888.0 | 6,095.8 | 2005 | 12,766.1 | 12,198.8 | 12,766.1 |
| 1978 | 2,417.0 | 2,150.0 | 2,417.0 | 1992 | 6,484.3 | 6,196.1 | 6,484.3 | 2006 | 13,392.3 | 13,008.4 | 13,392.3 |
| 1979 | 2,660.5 | 2,464.4 | 2,660.5 | 1993 | 6,800.2 | 6,542.7 | 6,800.2 | 2007 | 14,031.2 | 13,551.9 | 14,031.2 |
| 1980 | 2,916.9 | 2,725.3 | 2,916.9 | 1994 | 7,232.2 | 6,911.0 | 7,232.2 | 2008 | 14,412.8 | 14,150.8 | 14,412.8 |

*Source: U.S. Department of Commerce: Bureau of Economic Analysis*

# U.S. GROSS FEDERAL DEBT

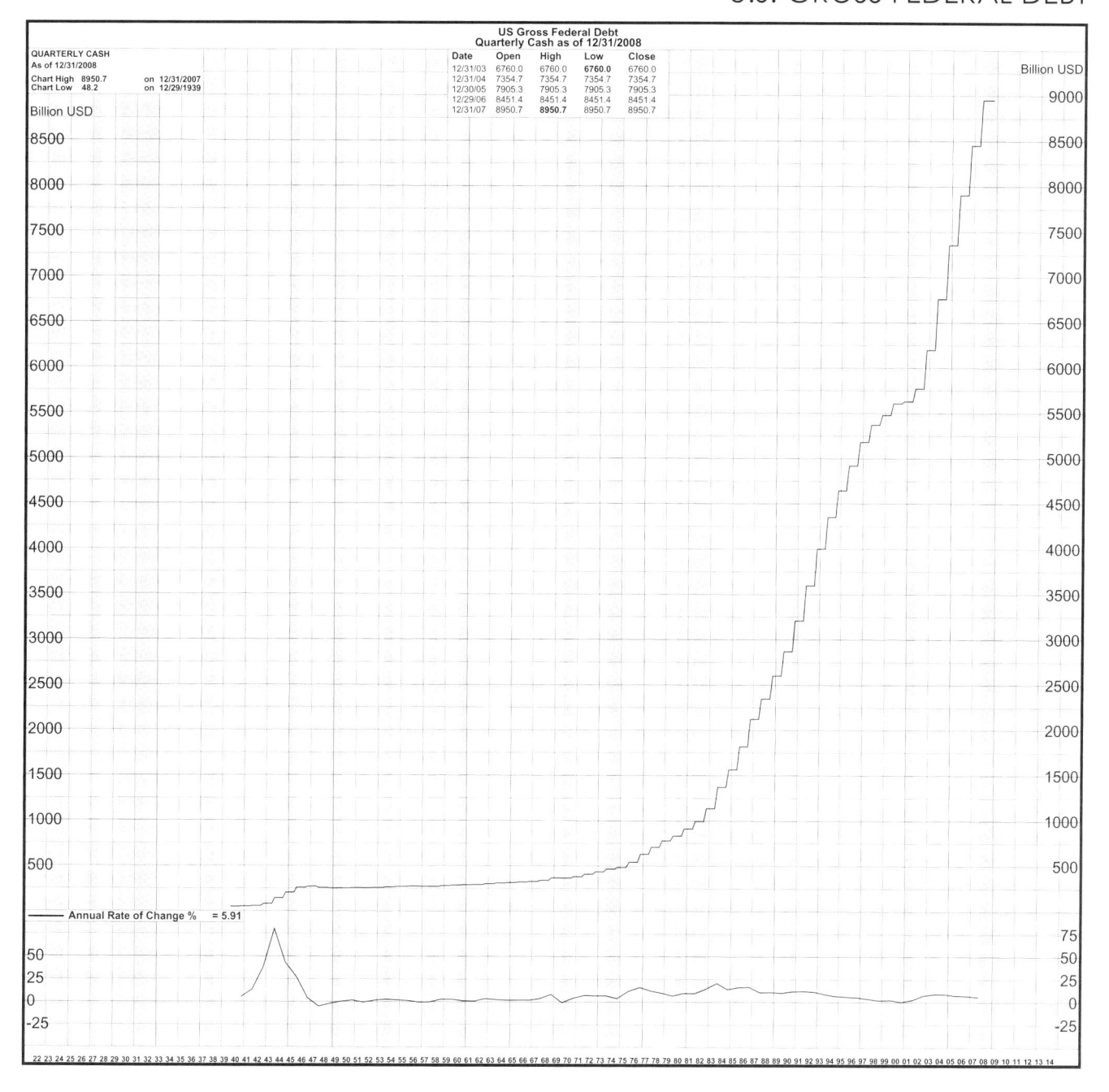

**QUARTERLY CASH**
As of 12/31/2008
Chart High 8950.7 on 12/31/2007
Chart Low 48.2 on 12/29/1939
Billion USD

| US Gross Federal Debt Quarterly Cash as of 12/31/2008 |
| Date | Open | High | Low | Close |
|---|---|---|---|---|
| 12/31/03 | 6760.0 | 6760.0 | 6760.0 | 6760.0 |
| 12/31/04 | 7354.7 | 7354.7 | 7354.7 | 7354.7 |
| 12/30/05 | 7905.3 | 7905.3 | 7905.3 | 7905.3 |
| 12/29/06 | 8451.4 | 8451.4 | 8451.4 | 8451.4 |
| 12/31/07 | 8950.7 | 8950.7 | 8950.7 | 8950.7 |

Annual Rate of Change % = 5.91

## Annual U.S. Gross Federal Debt — In Billions of Dollars

| Year | Close | Year | Close | Year | Close | Year | Close | Year | Close | Year | Close |
|---|---|---|---|---|---|---|---|---|---|---|---|
| 1925 |  | 1939 | 48.2  | 1953 | 266.0 | 1967 | 340.4 | 1981 | 994.8   | 1995 | 4,920.6 |
| 1926 |  | 1940 | 50.7  | 1954 | 270.8 | 1968 | 368.7 | 1982 | 1,137.3 | 1996 | 5,181.5 |
| 1927 |  | 1941 | 57.5  | 1955 | 274.4 | 1969 | 365.8 | 1983 | 1,371.7 | 1997 | 5,369.2 |
| 1928 |  | 1942 | 79.2  | 1956 | 272.7 | 1970 | 380.9 | 1984 | 1,564.6 | 1998 | 5,478.2 |
| 1929 |  | 1943 | 142.6 | 1957 | 272.3 | 1971 | 408.2 | 1985 | 1,817.4 | 1999 | 5,605.5 |
| 1930 |  | 1944 | 204.1 | 1958 | 279.7 | 1972 | 435.9 | 1986 | 2,120.5 | 2000 | 5,628.7 |
| 1931 |  | 1945 | 260.1 | 1959 | 287.5 | 1973 | 466.3 | 1987 | 2,346.0 | 2001 | 5,769.9 |
| 1932 |  | 1946 | 271.0 | 1960 | 290.5 | 1974 | 483.9 | 1988 | 2,601.1 | 2002 | 6,198.4 |
| 1933 |  | 1947 | 257.1 | 1961 | 292.6 | 1975 | 541.9 | 1989 | 2,867.8 | 2003 | 6,760.0 |
| 1934 |  | 1948 | 252.0 | 1962 | 302.9 | 1976 | 629.0 | 1990 | 3,206.3 | 2004 | 7,354.7 |
| 1935 |  | 1949 | 252.6 | 1963 | 310.3 | 1977 | 706.4 | 1991 | 3,598.2 | 2005 | 7,905.3 |
| 1936 |  | 1950 | 256.9 | 1964 | 316.1 | 1978 | 776.6 | 1992 | 4,001.8 | 2006 | 8,451.4 |
| 1937 |  | 1951 | 255.3 | 1965 | 322.3 | 1979 | 829.5 | 1993 | 4,351.0 | 2007 | 8,950.7 |
| 1938 |  | 1952 | 259.1 | 1966 | 328.5 | 1980 | 909.0 | 1994 | 4,643.3 | 2008 |  |

*Source: The White House: Council of Economic Advisors*

# U.S. FEDERAL SURPLUS OR DEFICIT

**US Federal Surplus or Deficit**
Quarterly Cash as of 12/31/2008

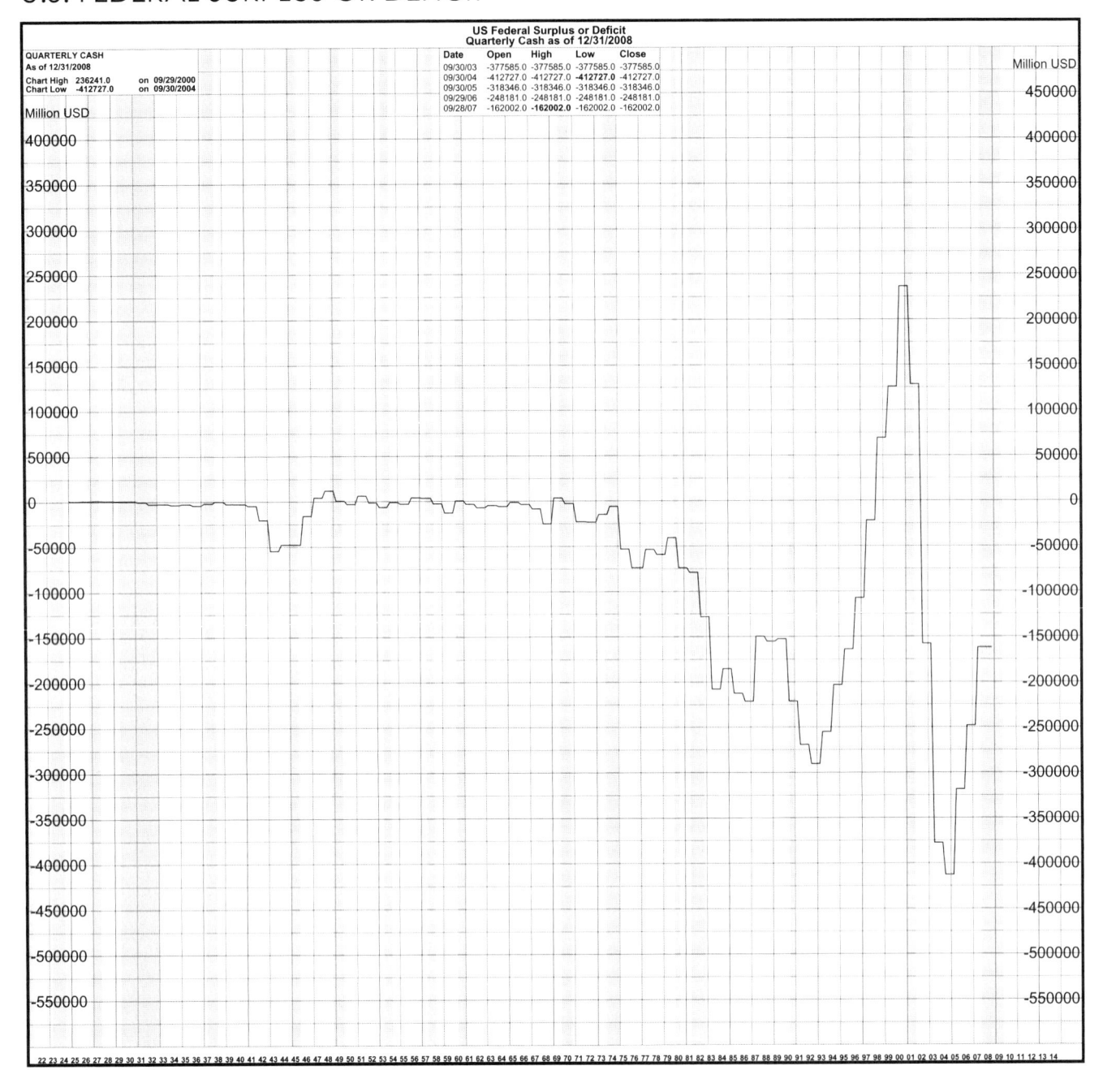

| Date | Open | High | Low | Close |
|---|---|---|---|---|
| 09/30/03 | -377585.0 | -377585.0 | -377585.0 | -377585.0 |
| 09/30/04 | -412727.0 | -412727.0 | -412727.0 | -412727.0 |
| 09/30/05 | -318346.0 | -318346.0 | -318346.0 | -318346.0 |
| 09/29/06 | -248181.0 | -248181.0 | -248181.0 | -248181.0 |
| 09/28/07 | -162002.0 | -162002.0 | -162002.0 | -162002.0 |

QUARTERLY CASH
As of 12/31/2008
Chart High 236241.0 on 09/29/2000
Chart Low -412727.0 on 09/30/2004

## Annual U.S. Federal Surplus or Deficit   In Millions of Dollars

| Year | Close | Year | Close | Year | Close | Year | Close | Year | Close | Year | Close |
|---|---|---|---|---|---|---|---|---|---|---|---|
| 1925 | 717 | 1939 | -2,846 | 1953 | -6,493 | 1967 | -8,643 | 1981 | -78,968 | 1995 | -163,952 |
| 1926 | 865 | 1940 | -2,920 | 1954 | -1,154 | 1968 | -25,161 | 1982 | -127,977 | 1996 | -107,431 |
| 1927 | 1,155 | 1941 | -4,941 | 1955 | -2,993 | 1969 | 3,242 | 1983 | -207,802 | 1997 | -21,884 |
| 1928 | 939 | 1942 | -20,503 | 1956 | 3,947 | 1970 | -2,842 | 1984 | -185,367 | 1998 | 69,270 |
| 1929 | 734 | 1943 | -54,554 | 1957 | 3,412 | 1971 | -23,033 | 1985 | -212,308 | 1999 | 125,610 |
| 1930 | 738 | 1944 | -47,557 | 1958 | -2,769 | 1972 | -23,373 | 1986 | -221,227 | 2000 | 236,241 |
| 1931 | -462 | 1945 | -47,553 | 1959 | -12,849 | 1973 | -14,908 | 1987 | -149,730 | 2001 | 128,236 |
| 1932 | -2,735 | 1946 | -15,936 | 1960 | 301 | 1974 | -6,135 | 1988 | -155,178 | 2002 | -157,758 |
| 1933 | -2,602 | 1947 | 4,018 | 1961 | -3,335 | 1975 | -53,242 | 1989 | -152,639 | 2003 | -377,585 |
| 1934 | -3,586 | 1948 | 11,796 | 1962 | -7,146 | 1976 | -73,732 | 1990 | -221,036 | 2004 | -412,727 |
| 1935 | -2,803 | 1949 | 580 | 1963 | -4,756 | 1977 | -53,659 | 1991 | -269,238 | 2005 | -318,346 |
| 1936 | -4,304 | 1950 | -3,119 | 1964 | -5,915 | 1978 | -59,185 | 1992 | -290,321 | 2006 | -248,181 |
| 1937 | -2,193 | 1951 | 6,102 | 1965 | -1,411 | 1979 | -40,726 | 1993 | -255,051 | 2007 | -162,002 |
| 1938 | -89 | 1952 | -1,519 | 1966 | -3,698 | 1980 | -73,830 | 1994 | -203,186 | 2008 | |

*Source: The White House:*

# U.S. RETAIL SALES (EXCEPT AUTOS)

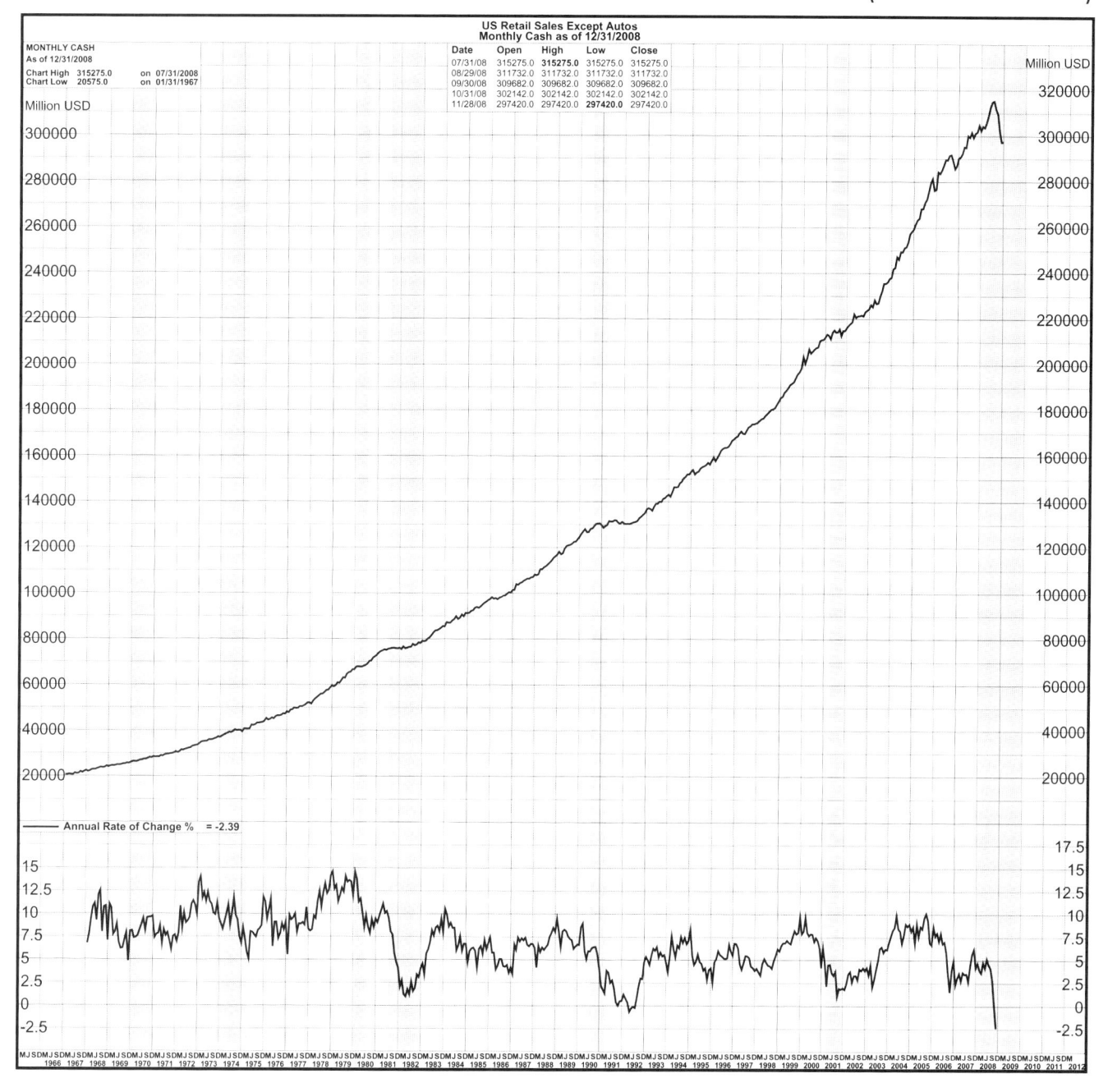

**Annual High, Low and Close of U.S. Retail Sales, Except Autos**    In Millions of Dollars

| Year | High | Low | Settle | Year | High | Low | Settle | Year | High | Low | Settle |
|------|------|-----|--------|------|------|-----|--------|------|------|-----|--------|
| 1967 | 22,431 | 20,575 | 22,431 | 1981 | 76,020 | 73,970 | 76,020 | 1995 | 159,533 | 152,039 | 159,533 |
| 1968 | 24,415 | 21,961 | 24,014 | 1982 | 79,095 | 75,481 | 79,095 | 1996 | 168,243 | 157,931 | 168,243 |
| 1969 | 25,960 | 24,394 | 25,960 | 1983 | 85,534 | 78,920 | 85,408 | 1997 | 174,675 | 168,637 | 174,675 |
| 1970 | 28,494 | 26,325 | 28,494 | 1984 | 91,288 | 87,027 | 91,146 | 1998 | 185,466 | 175,486 | 185,466 |
| 1971 | 30,678 | 28,330 | 30,678 | 1985 | 97,340 | 91,352 | 97,340 | 1999 | 203,493 | 185,933 | 203,493 |
| 1972 | 33,717 | 30,298 | 33,717 | 1986 | 101,366 | 97,248 | 101,366 | 2000 | 211,968 | 200,548 | 211,968 |
| 1973 | 37,211 | 34,384 | 36,928 | 1987 | 108,160 | 101,539 | 108,160 | 2001 | 216,123 | 211,323 | 216,123 |
| 1974 | 40,224 | 37,455 | 39,428 | 1988 | 116,869 | 107,927 | 116,869 | 2002 | 224,381 | 217,134 | 224,381 |
| 1975 | 44,107 | 40,601 | 44,107 | 1989 | 124,644 | 117,030 | 124,644 | 2003 | 238,132 | 225,259 | 238,132 |
| 1976 | 48,143 | 44,502 | 48,143 | 1990 | 130,530 | 125,981 | 129,765 | 2004 | 259,384 | 241,876 | 259,384 |
| 1977 | 52,170 | 47,752 | 52,170 | 1991 | 131,920 | 128,683 | 130,476 | 2005 | 281,332 | 261,623 | 276,667 |
| 1978 | 59,577 | 51,638 | 59,577 | 1992 | 136,677 | 130,261 | 136,677 | 2006 | 291,703 | 283,567 | 290,265 |
| 1979 | 66,693 | 59,189 | 66,693 | 1993 | 143,105 | 136,063 | 143,105 | 2007 | 304,705 | 290,762 | 302,353 |
| 1980 | 73,021 | 67,810 | 73,021 | 1994 | 153,249 | 142,199 | 153,249 | 2008 | 315,275 | 297,420 | 297,420 |

*Source: U.S. Department of Commerece: Census Bureau*

# U.S. INTERNATIONAL TRADE BALANCE

**Quarterly U.S. Trade Balance, Goods and Services**   In Millions of Dollars

| Quarter | Close | Quarter | Close | Quarter | Close | Quarter | Close | Quarter | Close | Quarter | Close |
|---|---|---|---|---|---|---|---|---|---|---|---|
| 03/1991 |  | 03/1994 | -6,466 | 03/1997 | -8,477 | 03/2000 | -31,732 | 03/2003 | -43,543 | 03/2006 | -62,096 |
| 06/1991 |  | 06/1994 | -8,380 | 06/1997 | -7,174 | 06/2000 | -31,279 | 06/2003 | -39,882 | 06/2006 | -64,519 |
| 09/1991 |  | 09/1994 | -8,310 | 09/1997 | -9,254 | 09/2000 | -34,474 | 09/2003 | -41,645 | 09/2006 | -64,603 |
| 12/1991 |  | 12/1994 | -8,456 | 12/1997 | -11,250 | 12/2000 | -34,154 | 12/2003 | -43,742 | 12/2006 | -60,306 |
| 03/1992 | -6,777 | 03/1995 | -9,708 | 03/1998 | -12,796 | 03/2001 | -32,700 | 03/2004 | -46,966 | 03/2007 | -62,688 |
| 06/1992 | -6,929 | 06/1995 | -10,623 | 06/1998 | -13,189 | 06/2001 | -29,498 | 06/2004 | -54,894 | 06/2007 | -59,634 |
| 09/1992 | -7,031 | 09/1995 | -5,924 | 09/1998 | -14,714 | 09/2001 | -30,782 | 09/2004 | -51,939 | 09/2007 | -56,945 |
| 12/1992 | -5,719 | 12/1995 | -6,271 | 12/1998 | -14,608 | 12/2001 | -26,679 | 12/2004 | -54,672 | 12/2007 | -57,579 |
| 03/1993 | -6,466 | 03/1996 | -7,756 | 03/1999 | -18,424 | 03/2002 | -30,920 | 03/2005 | -54,055 | 03/2008 | -56,964 |
| 06/1993 | -8,380 | 06/1996 | -7,460 | 06/1999 | -23,502 | 06/2002 | -35,329 | 06/2005 | -59,493 | 06/2008 | -58,689 |
| 09/1993 | -8,310 | 09/1996 | -10,195 | 09/1999 | -23,527 | 09/2002 | -36,842 | 09/2005 | -65,585 | 09/2008 | -56,559 |
| 12/1993 | -8,456 | 12/1996 | -10,475 | 12/1999 | -26,367 | 12/2002 | -42,917 | 12/2005 | -65,074 | 10/2008 | -57,190 |

*Source: U.S. Department of Commerce: Bureau of Economic Analysis*

# U.S. HOUSING STARTS

**Annual High, Low and Close of U.S Housing Starts**   In Thousands of Units

| Year | High | Low | Settle | Year | High | Low | Settle | Year | High | Low | Settle |
|------|------|------|------|------|------|------|------|------|------|------|------|
| 1967 | 1,538 | 1,056 | 1,308 | 1981 | 1,547 | 837 | 910 | 1995 | 1,461 | 1,249 | 1,431 |
| 1968 | 1,630 | 1,380 | 1,548 | 1982 | 1,372 | 843 | 1,303 | 1996 | 1,557 | 1,370 | 1,370 |
| 1969 | 1,769 | 1,229 | 1,327 | 1983 | 1,910 | 1,472 | 1,688 | 1997 | 1,566 | 1,355 | 1,566 |
| 1970 | 1,893 | 1,085 | 1,893 | 1984 | 2,260 | 1,586 | 1,612 | 1998 | 1,792 | 1,525 | 1,792 |
| 1971 | 2,295 | 1,741 | 2,295 | 1985 | 1,942 | 1,632 | 1,942 | 1999 | 1,748 | 1,553 | 1,708 |
| 1972 | 2,494 | 2,221 | 2,366 | 1986 | 1,972 | 1,623 | 1,833 | 2000 | 1,737 | 1,463 | 1,532 |
| 1973 | 2,481 | 1,526 | 1,526 | 1987 | 1,784 | 1,400 | 1,400 | 2001 | 1,670 | 1,540 | 1,568 |
| 1974 | 1,752 | 975 | 975 | 1988 | 1,573 | 1,271 | 1,563 | 2002 | 1,829 | 1,592 | 1,788 |
| 1975 | 1,360 | 904 | 1,321 | 1989 | 1,621 | 1,251 | 1,251 | 2003 | 2,083 | 1,629 | 2,057 |
| 1976 | 1,804 | 1,367 | 1,804 | 1990 | 1,551 | 969 | 969 | 2004 | 2,062 | 1,807 | 2,050 |
| 1977 | 2,142 | 1,527 | 2,142 | 1991 | 1,103 | 798 | 1,079 | 2005 | 2,228 | 1,833 | 2,002 |
| 1978 | 2,197 | 1,718 | 2,044 | 1992 | 1,297 | 1,099 | 1,227 | 2006 | 2,265 | 1,478 | 1,629 |
| 1979 | 1,913 | 1,498 | 1,498 | 1993 | 1,533 | 1,083 | 1,533 | 2007 | 1,491 | 1,000 | 1,000 |
| 1980 | 1,523 | 927 | 1,482 | 1994 | 1,564 | 1,272 | 1,455 | 2008 | 1,107 | 625 | 625 |

Seasonally adjusted.   *Source: U.S. Department of Commerce: Census Bureau*

# FOODS & FIBERS

### Sugar

Sugar prices from early 2004 through early 2006 more than tripled from 5.27 cents per pound to a 28-year high of 19.73 cents. That rally was driven by (1) strong worldwide demand for sugar for human consumption and for ethanol production in Brazil, (2) three straight years of inventory declines during 2003 through 2005 due to the combination of strong demand and flat production, and (3) speculative buying. However, world sugar production then responded to the higher prices and rose sharply by 13% in 2005, causing world sugar inventories to rise even more sharply by 43%. Sugar production rose by another 1% in 2007 and inventories rose another 8%. The rise in production and inventories in 2006-07 led to the sharp sell-off in sugar prices. Sugar prices then rallied in late 2007 and early 2008 as part of the general commodity bull market, but fell back again in spring 2008. The financial crisis in late 2008 sparked a sell-off in sugar prices, but sugar prices afterwards remained generally firm due to expectations for steady sugar demand for both human consumption and ethanol production. Historically, key sugar market events include:

**1974 rally**—Sugar rallies to a record 66 cents per pound on strong demand, extremely low inventories in 1974, and general commodity market strength tied to inflation and speculation.

**1980 rally**—Sugar rallies to 45 cents per pound on a drop in sugar production in 1980 and general commodity strength tied to speculation and the spike in US inflation to a record high of 14% in 1980.

**1988-90 rally**—Sugar rallies to 16 cents per pound as strong demand outpaces production for five consecutive years and as production deficits cause inventories to fall to the lowest levels since 1980-81.

**1994 rally**—Sugar rallies to the 15 cent per pound area as sugar production dips in 1993-94, causing inventories to drop to low levels in 1994.

**1997-99 bear market**—Sugar prices fall to 10-year lows after Asian currency crisis causes a sharp drop in demand and sugar inventories reach near-record highs.

**2004-06 bull market**—Sugar prices soar on strong demand, tight supplies, and the commodity bull market.

### Coffee

Coffee prices rallied fairly steadily over the 2002-07 period due to a steady increase in demand combined with flat production. World coffee inventories during that period remained at relatively tight levels below 25 million bags (1 bag = 60 kg or 132.3 lbs), thus supporting prices. Coffee prices were also swept up in the general commodity bull market. Coffee prices posted an 11-year high of 166.75 cents per pound in February 2008 but then fell through the remainder of 2008 on the financial crisis and global recession. Historically, key coffee market events include:

**1976-1977 rally**—Coffee prices rally to record high of 337.5 cents per pound on a devastating frost in Brazil in 1975 and general commodity market strength.

**1979 rally**—Coffee prices rally to 230 cents per pound on light frost in Brazil and general commodity price strength.

**1981-1985 trading range**—Coffee prices trade in a narrow range due to International Coffee Agreement (ICA) quotas.

**1985-1986 rally**—Coffee prices spike higher to 275 cents per pound on extreme drought in Brazil and a sharp draw-down in inventories.

**1989-1993 bear market**—Coffee prices fall as ICA quotas end and as ending stocks are near record highs.

**1994 rally**—Coffee prices spike higher on a severe frost in Brazil.

**1997 rally**—Coffee prices spike higher on strong demand and steady inventory draw-downs in 1995-97.

**1998-2001 bear market**—Coffee prices fall on growing world supply.

**2002-2006 bull market**—Coffee prices more than triple due to strong demand, lagging production due to poor tree tending during bear market, inventory draw-downs, and general commodity strength.

### Cocoa

Cocoa prices rallied sharply in 2000-02 on strong demand and a sharp drop in ending stocks in the 2000-01 and 2001-02 marketing years. However, cocoa prices then fell back and traded in a relatively narrow range of $1300-1800 per metric ton from 2003 through 2006. Cocoa prices settled back in 2003-06 after relatively big crops during those market years, which allowed world inventories to move higher. Cocoa prices in 2007-08 rallied sharply to a 22-year high of $3,385 per metric ton in July 2008 due to a drop in 2006/07 production and the general commodity bull market Cocoa prices fell back in late 2008 on the commodity bust, long liquidation pressure, and an increase in the 2007/08 cocoa crop. Historically, key cocoa market events include:

**1976-78 rally**—Cocoa prices rally sharply on a series of poor crops in the early 1970s which caused the stocks-to-grindings ratio to drop from 35% at the beginning of the 1970s to a record low of 18% in the 1976-77 marketing year. The cocoa market came into the 1970s with poor production capacity because low cocoa prices seen in the 1950s and 1960s caused poor investment in and maintenance of cocoa farms.

**1984-92 bear market**—Starting in the 1984-85 marketing year, cocoa production grows sharply, causing a big increase in inventories. The stocks-to-grindings ratio reaches a record high of 66% in 1991-92.

**1993-98 Brazil production plunges**—Brazilian cocoa production is devastated by the fungus "witch's broom," causing annual production to drop by 50% from 305,000 metric tons in 1992-93 to 124,000 MT in 1999-2000.

**2001-02 rally**—Cocoa prices rally on strong demand and a sharp drop in the ending stocks in the 2000-01 and 2001-02 marketing years.

**2004 Ivory Coast ceasefire violation**—Cocoa prices rally sharply in November 2004 when Ivory Coast government troops bomb a French peacekeeping force and the French military responds by destroying all the Ivory Coast's military aircraft. The incident causes a temporary disruption of cocoa shipments from the Ivory Coast.

### Orange Juice

Orange juice futures prices nearly quadrupled from 55 cents per pound in mid-2004 to a 31-year high of 209.50 cents by March 2007, which was just below the record high of 220 cents/lb posted in November 1977. That rally was driven by the one-third drop in Florida orange production seen in the 2004-05 and 2005-06 marketing years due to severe hurricane damage. After posting the March 2007 high, orange juice prices then plunged by 68% to a 4-year low of 67.10 cents in late 2008 due to revived Florida orange production, a sharp reduction in consumer demand for orange juice, and the overall commodity bear market. Historically, key orange market events include:

**1980s Florida freezes**—Major freezes in Florida in the 1980s (particularly in December 1983 and 1985) destroy one-third of Florida's orange trees and lead to a sharp reduction in Florida and US orange production in 1981 through 1992. Orange juice futures prices spiked higher numerous times during the 1980s.

**1988 Brazilian production record**—Brazilian orange production surges to a then-record high in 1998-90 and grows further in the 1990s, adding to world supply and curbing orange juice price spikes in 1990s. Brazil's share of world orange production grows to 37% in 2004 from 10% in 1970, while the US share falls to 18% in 2004 from 45% in 1970.

**1990s California freezes**—Freezes in 1991 and 1998 cause California orange production to plunge by 60% in 1990-91 and 40% in 1998-99 from the 5-year trend.

**1992 Florida production surge**—Starting in 1992, Florida orange production surges and remains high through most of the rest of the 1990s, leading to generally weak prices.

**2003-04 bear market**—Orange juice futures prices plunge to a 29-year low on a near-record crop in 2003-04 and the Atkins diet fad which reduced demand for high-carb orange juice.

**2004-05 hurricanes**—Four hurricanes in 2004 and Hurricane Wilma in 2005 devastate Florida orange groves and result in production dropping by one-third in 2004-05 and 2005-06.

### Cotton

Cotton prices in 2002-03 rallied sharply as demand for cotton rose, mainly because of increased clothing demand in China and India. Due to those higher prices, global cotton production rose sharply by 26% in 2004 and remained near that higher level through 2007. Cotton prices were stable during 2004-06 as supply and demand were roughly in balance and world inventories were stable near 60 million bales. Cotton prices then rallied sharply in late 2007 and early 2008, posting a 13-year high of 91.38 cents per pound in March 2008. Cotton was swept up in the sharp rally in grain and oilseed prices that was caused by (1) the big switch in acres to corn for ethanol production in 2007, and (2) the overall commodity bull market. Cotton prices then plunged by an overall 60% to 36.7 cents in Nov 2008 due to the overall commodity bear market and sharply reduced demand for cotton. The USDA in early 2009 cut its global cotton consumption forecast to a 71-year low of 112.6 million bales. Historically, key cotton market events include:

**1970s price spikes**—Cotton prices spike higher along with other US field crops in the 1970s due to inflation and general strength in commodity prices.

**1983 and 1988 droughts**—Cotton prices in 1983 and again in 1988 spike higher in response to US droughts.

**1994-95 rally**—Cotton prices rally to their modern day record of $1.172 per pound in April 1996 as a result of strong demand and sharply reduced crops in various Asian producing countries (China, Pakistan, India, Uzbekistan and Turkmenistan) due to dry weather, insect infestation and disease. The rally came despite a record US cotton crop in the 1994-95 marketing year.

**2001 bear market**—Cotton prices fall sharply in 2001 to 30 cents per pound as the US produces a then-record crop of 20.3 million bales. World ending stocks rise to a near-record high in the 2001-02 marketing year.

# COCOA

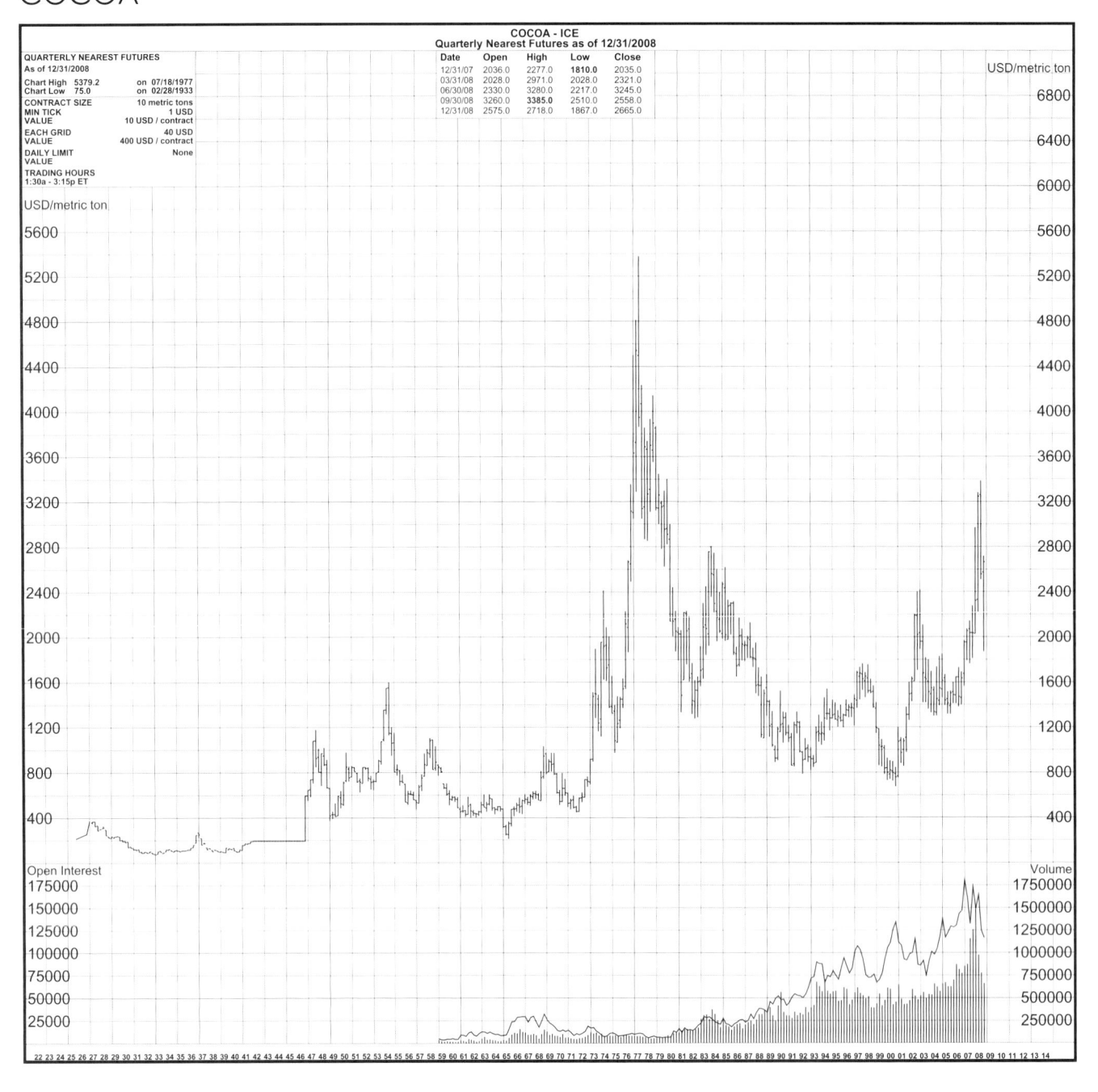

**COCOA - ICE**
Quarterly Nearest Futures as of 12/31/2008

| Date | Open | High | Low | Close |
|---|---|---|---|---|
| 12/31/07 | 2036.0 | 2277.0 | 1810.0 | 2035.0 |
| 03/31/08 | 2028.0 | 2971.0 | 2028.0 | 2321.0 |
| 06/30/08 | 2330.0 | 3280.0 | 2217.0 | 3245.0 |
| 09/30/08 | 3260.0 | 3385.0 | 2510.0 | 2558.0 |
| 12/31/08 | 2575.0 | 2718.0 | 1867.0 | 2665.0 |

**QUARTERLY NEAREST FUTURES**
As of 12/31/2008
- Chart High 5379.2 on 07/18/1977
- Chart Low 75.0 on 02/28/1933
- CONTRACT SIZE: 10 metric tons
- MIN TICK VALUE: 1 USD / 10 USD / contract
- EACH GRID VALUE: 40 USD / 400 USD / contract
- DAILY LIMIT VALUE: None
- TRADING HOURS: 1:30a - 3:15p ET

## Annual High, Low and Settle of Cocoa Futures    In Dollars per Metric Ton

| Year | High | Low | Settle | Year | High | Low | Settle | Year | High | Low | Settle |
|---|---|---|---|---|---|---|---|---|---|---|---|
| 1925 | 213 | 213 | 213 | 1939 | 133 | 92 | 128 | 1953 | 1,075 | 645 | 1,075 |
| 1926 | 255 | 255 | 255 | 1940 | 130 | 93 | 116 | 1954 | 1,601 | 948 | 1,061 |
| 1927 | 626 | 287 | 287 | 1941 | 188 | 112 | 188 | 1955 | 1,149 | 683 | 711 |
| 1928 | 330 | 222 | 224 | 1942 | 192 | 187 | 192 | 1956 | 703 | 513 | 560 |
| 1929 | 238 | 201 | 201 | 1943 | 192 | 192 | 192 | 1957 | 970 | 472 | 871 |
| 1930 | 205 | 134 | 134 | 1944 | 192 | 192 | 192 | 1958 | 1,105 | 816 | 891 |
| 1931 | 131 | 88 | 88 | 1945 | 192 | 192 | 192 | 1959 | 865 | 597 | 609 |
| 1932 | 102 | 82 | 82 | 1946 | 595 | 192 | 595 | 1960 | 644 | 484 | 489 |
| 1933 | 107 | 75 | 91 | 1947 | 1,179 | 551 | 926 | 1961 | 586 | 403 | 503 |
| 1934 | 122 | 99 | 108 | 1948 | 1,020 | 661 | 667 | 1962 | 525 | 401 | 454 |
| 1935 | 113 | 101 | 109 | 1949 | 667 | 375 | 592 | 1963 | 608 | 440 | 572 |
| 1936 | 246 | 113 | 246 | 1950 | 979 | 485 | 755 | 1964 | 569 | 430 | 477 |
| 1937 | 268 | 119 | 119 | 1951 | 857 | 626 | 716 | 1965 | 478 | 210 | 473 |
| 1938 | 129 | 98 | 100 | 1952 | 847 | 650 | 714 | 1966 | 578 | 412 | 553 |

Fut
*Source: IntercontinentalExchange (ICE); formerly New York Board of Trade*

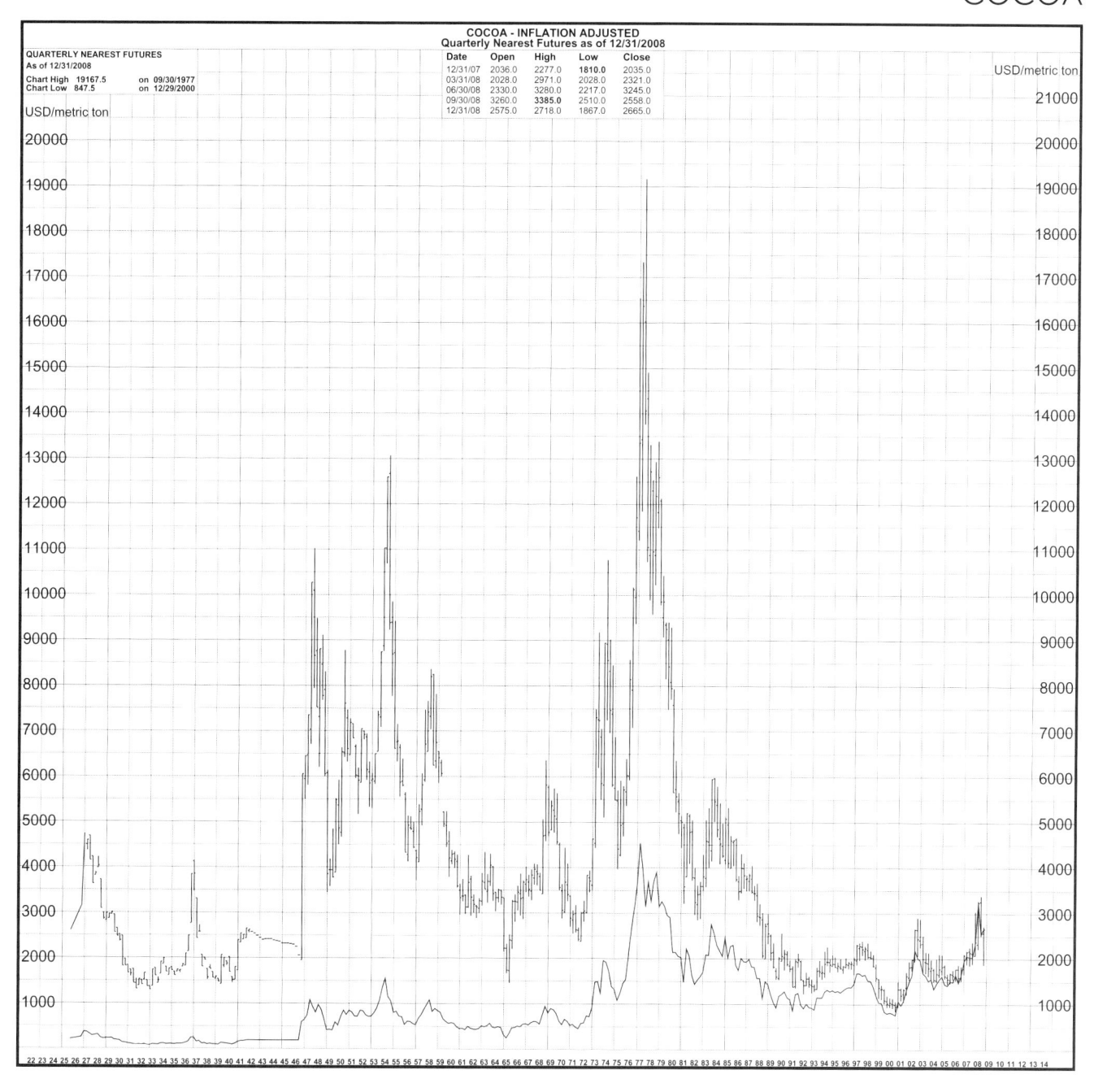

# COCOA

**QUARTERLY NEAREST FUTURES**
As of 12/31/2008
Chart High 19167.5 on 09/30/1977
Chart Low 847.5 on 12/29/2000
USD/metric ton

**COCOA - INFLATION ADJUSTED**
Quarterly Nearest Futures as of 12/31/2008

| Date | Open | High | Low | Close |
|---|---|---|---|---|
| 12/31/07 | 2036.0 | 2277.0 | 1810.0 | 2035.0 |
| 03/31/08 | 2028.0 | 2971.0 | 2028.0 | 2321.0 |
| 06/30/08 | 2330.0 | 3280.0 | 2217.0 | 3245.0 |
| 09/30/08 | 3260.0 | 3385.0 | 2510.0 | 2558.0 |
| 12/31/08 | 2575.0 | 2718.0 | 1867.0 | 2665.0 |

## Annual High, Low and Settle of Cocoa    In Dollars per Metric Ton

| Year | High | Low | Settle | Year | High | Low | Settle | Year | High | Low | Settle |
|---|---|---|---|---|---|---|---|---|---|---|---|
| 1925 | 213 | 213 | 213 | 1939 | 133 | 92 | 128 | 1953 | 1,075 | 645 | 1,075 |
| 1926 | 255 | 255 | 255 | 1940 | 130 | 93 | 116 | 1954 | 1,601 | 948 | 1,061 |
| 1927 | 626 | 287 | 287 | 1941 | 188 | 112 | 188 | 1955 | 1,149 | 683 | 711 |
| 1928 | 330 | 222 | 224 | 1942 | 192 | 187 | 192 | 1956 | 703 | 513 | 560 |
| 1929 | 238 | 201 | 201 | 1943 | 192 | 192 | 192 | 1957 | 970 | 472 | 871 |
| 1930 | 205 | 134 | 134 | 1944 | 192 | 192 | 192 | 1958 | 1,105 | 816 | 891 |
| 1931 | 131 | 88 | 88 | 1945 | 192 | 192 | 192 | 1959 | 865 | 648 | 648 |
| 1932 | 102 | 82 | 82 | 1946 | 595 | 192 | 595 | 1960 | 672 | 518 | 521 |
| 1933 | 107 | 75 | 91 | 1947 | 1,179 | 551 | 926 | 1961 | 623 | 430 | 538 |
| 1934 | 122 | 99 | 108 | 1948 | 1,020 | 661 | 667 | 1962 | 554 | 430 | 477 |
| 1935 | 113 | 101 | 109 | 1949 | 667 | 375 | 592 | 1963 | 639 | 466 | 598 |
| 1936 | 246 | 113 | 246 | 1950 | 979 | 485 | 755 | 1964 | 592 | 472 | 516 |
| 1937 | 268 | 119 | 119 | 1951 | 857 | 626 | 716 | 1965 | 529 | 251 | 513 |
| 1938 | 129 | 98 | 100 | 1952 | 847 | 650 | 714 | 1966 | 623 | 463 | 601 |

Ivory Coast.    Data prior to 10/17/1980 converted from cents per pound.    Data continued on page 143.
*Source: IntercontinentalExchange (ICE); formerly New York Board of Trade*

# COCOA

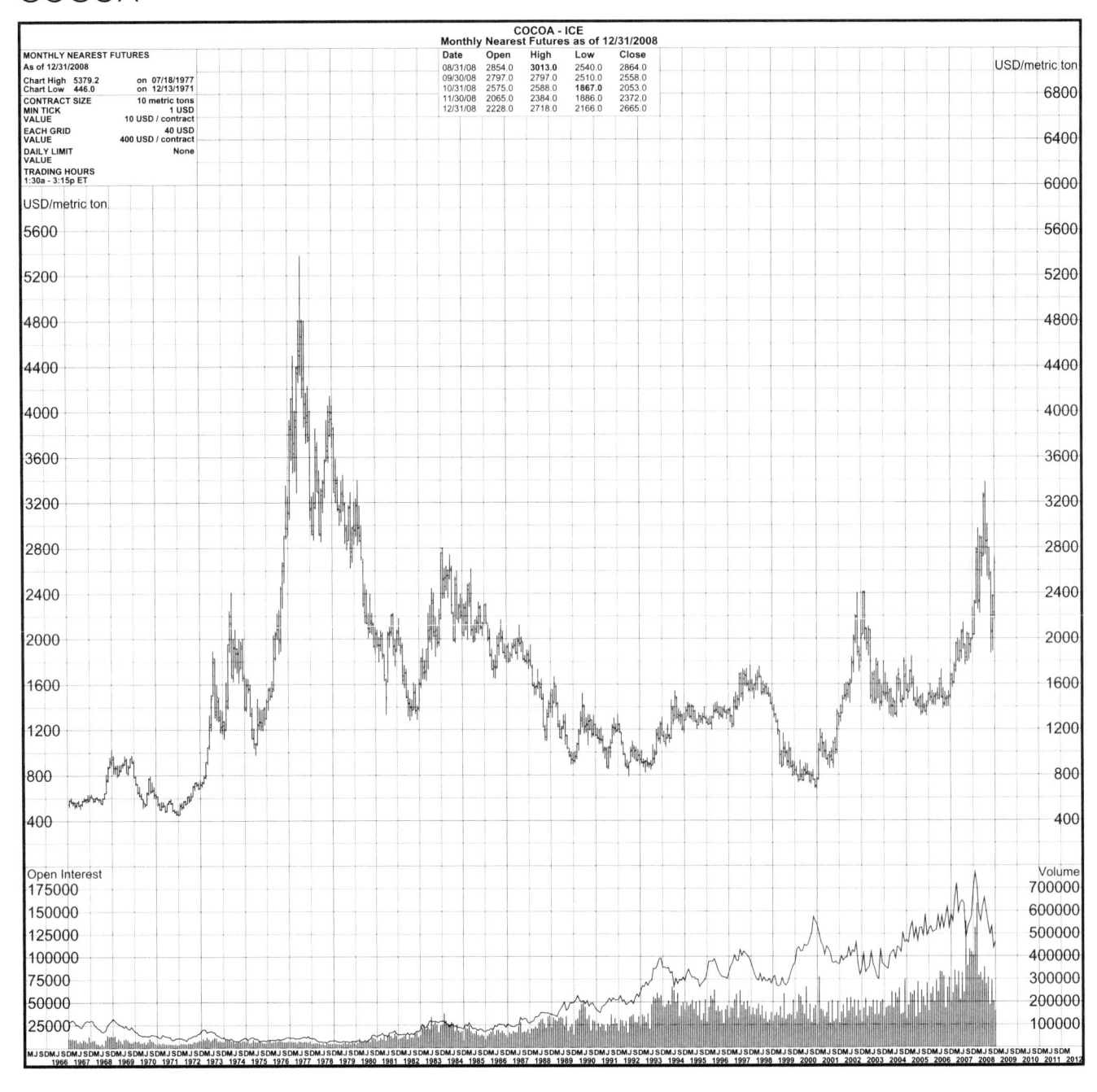

## COCOA - ICE
### Monthly Nearest Futures as of 12/31/2008

| Date | Open | High | Low | Close |
|---|---|---|---|---|
| 08/31/08 | 2854.0 | 3013.0 | 2540.0 | 2864.0 |
| 09/30/08 | 2797.0 | 2797.0 | 2510.0 | 2558.0 |
| 10/31/08 | 2575.0 | 2588.0 | 1867.0 | 2053.0 |
| 11/30/08 | 2065.0 | 2384.0 | 1886.0 | 2372.0 |
| 12/31/08 | 2228.0 | 2718.0 | 2166.0 | 2665.0 |

**MONTHLY NEAREST FUTURES** As of 12/31/2008
- Chart High 5379.2 on 07/18/1977
- Chart Low 446.0 on 12/13/1971
- CONTRACT SIZE: 10 metric tons
- MIN TICK: 1 USD
- VALUE: 10 USD / contract
- EACH GRID: 40 USD
- VALUE: 400 USD / contract
- DAILY LIMIT VALUE: None
- TRADING HOURS: 1:30a - 3:15p ET

## Annual High, Low and Settle of Cocoa Futures — In Dollars per Metric Ton

| Year | High | Low | Settle | Year | High | Low | Settle | Year | High | Low | Settle |
|---|---|---|---|---|---|---|---|---|---|---|---|
| 1967 | 633 | 504 | 614 | 1981 | 2,230 | 1,330 | 2,054 | 1995 | 1,442 | 1,200 | 1,258 |
| 1968 | 1,032 | 549 | 944 | 1982 | 2,184 | 1,275 | 1,603 | 1996 | 1,447 | 1,196 | 1,374 |
| 1969 | 974 | 777 | 786 | 1983 | 2,759 | 1,565 | 2,755 | 1997 | 1,766 | 1,210 | 1,630 |
| 1970 | 795 | 511 | 620 | 1984 | 2,805 | 1,960 | 2,052 | 1998 | 1,758 | 1,368 | 1,379 |
| 1971 | 619 | 446 | 455 | 1985 | 2,620 | 1,963 | 2,298 | 1999 | 1,422 | 782 | 837 |
| 1972 | 765 | 453 | 720 | 1986 | 2,315 | 1,648 | 1,935 | 2000 | 929 | 674 | 758 |
| 1973 | 1,896 | 694 | 1,237 | 1987 | 2,128 | 1,732 | 1,814 | 2001 | 1,380 | 752 | 1,310 |
| 1974 | 2,414 | 1,116 | 1,381 | 1988 | 1,950 | 1,103 | 1,500 | 2002 | 2,405 | 1,260 | 2,021 |
| 1975 | 1,657 | 972 | 1,450 | 1989 | 1,670 | 890 | 925 | 2003 | 2,420 | 1,360 | 1,515 |
| 1976 | 3,357 | 1,371 | 3,114 | 1990 | 1,525 | 905 | 1,150 | 2004 | 1,830 | 1,299 | 1,547 |
| 1977 | 5,379 | 3,047 | 3,138 | 1991 | 1,337 | 850 | 1,245 | 2005 | 1,850 | 1,315 | 1,504 |
| 1978 | 4,142 | 2,852 | 3,897 | 1992 | 1,254 | 785 | 936 | 2006 | 1,732 | 1,380 | 1,635 |
| 1979 | 3,869 | 2,623 | 2,954 | 1993 | 1,310 | 820 | 1,144 | 2007 | 2,277 | 1,566 | 2,035 |
| 1980 | 3,401 | 1,870 | 2,050 | 1994 | 1,543 | 1,041 | 1,280 | 2008 | 3,385 | 1,867 | 2,665 |

Data prior to Dec 1980 contract converted from cents per pound. Data continued from page 140.

*Source: IntercontinentalExchange (ICE); formerly New York Board of Trade*

# COCOA

**Cocoa, Ivory Coast — Monthly Cash as of 12/31/2008**

| Date | Open | High | Low | Close |
|---|---|---|---|---|
| 08/29/08 | 3301.0 | 3301.0 | 2894.0 | 3165.0 |
| 09/30/08 | 3001.0 | 3072.0 | 2853.0 | 3059.0 |
| 10/31/08 | 3012.0 | 3012.0 | 2299.0 | 2396.0 |
| 11/28/08 | 2277.0 | 2652.0 | 2254.0 | 2652.0 |
| 12/31/08 | 2542.0 | 3060.0 | 2542.0 | 3060.0 |

MONTHLY CASH As of 12/31/2008
Chart High 5732.0 on 09/14/1977
Chart Low 480.0 on 11/02/1966
USD/metric ton

## Annual High, Low and Settle of Cocoa — In Dollars per Metric Ton

| Year | High | Low | Settle | Year | High | Low | Settle | Year | High | Low | Settle |
|---|---|---|---|---|---|---|---|---|---|---|---|
| 1967 | 711 | 573 | 692 | 1981 | 2,425 | 1,571 | 2,246 | 1995 | 1,751 | 1,419 | 1,419 |
| 1968 | 1,121 | 634 | 1,047 | 1982 | 2,542 | 1,562 | 1,832 | 1996 | 1,623 | 1,393 | 1,534 |
| 1969 | 1,105 | 904 | 909 | 1983 | 2,962 | 1,755 | 2,962 | 1997 | 1,930 | 1,412 | 1,802 |
| 1970 | 918 | 617 | 708 | 1984 | 2,926 | 2,156 | 2,215 | 1998 | 1,949 | 1,583 | 1,583 |
| 1971 | 700 | 510 | 510 | 1985 | 2,680 | 2,163 | 2,580 | 1999 | 1,616 | 988 | 1,017 |
| 1972 | 862 | 518 | 821 | 1986 | 2,597 | 1,967 | 2,155 | 2000 | 1,106 | 876 | 930 |
| 1973 | 2,089 | 796 | 1,488 | 1987 | 2,377 | 1,975 | 2,052 | 2001 | 1,596 | 925 | 1,565 |
| 1974 | 2,877 | 1,378 | 1,786 | 1988 | 2,435 | 1,744 | 2,317 | 2002 | 2,711 | 1,524 | 2,336 |
| 1975 | 2,006 | 1,290 | 1,709 | 1989 | 2,247 | 1,097 | 1,128 | 2003 | 2,686 | 1,614 | 1,763 |
| 1976 | 3,594 | 1,565 | 3,456 | 1990 | 1,661 | 1,099 | 1,348 | 2004 | 2,044 | 1,526 | 1,770 |
| 1977 | 5,732 | 3,390 | 5,512 | 1991 | 1,496 | 1,027 | 1,413 | 2005 | 2,074 | 1,535 | 1,714 |
| 1978 | 4,387 | 3,086 | 4,101 | 1992 | 1,415 | 1,007 | 1,154 | 2006 | 2,017 | 1,677 | 1,898 |
| 1979 | 4,255 | 3,406 | 3,417 | 1993 | 1,695 | 1,098 | 1,499 | 2007 | 2,447 | 1,826 | 2,414 |
| 1980 | 3,825 | 2,100 | 2,285 | 1994 | 1,795 | 1,403 | 1,582 | 2008 | 3,593 | 2,254 | 3,060 |

Ivory Coast. Data prior to 10/17/1980 converted from cents per pound. Data continued from page 141.
*Source: IntercontinentalExchange (ICE); formerly New York Board of Trade*

# COCOA

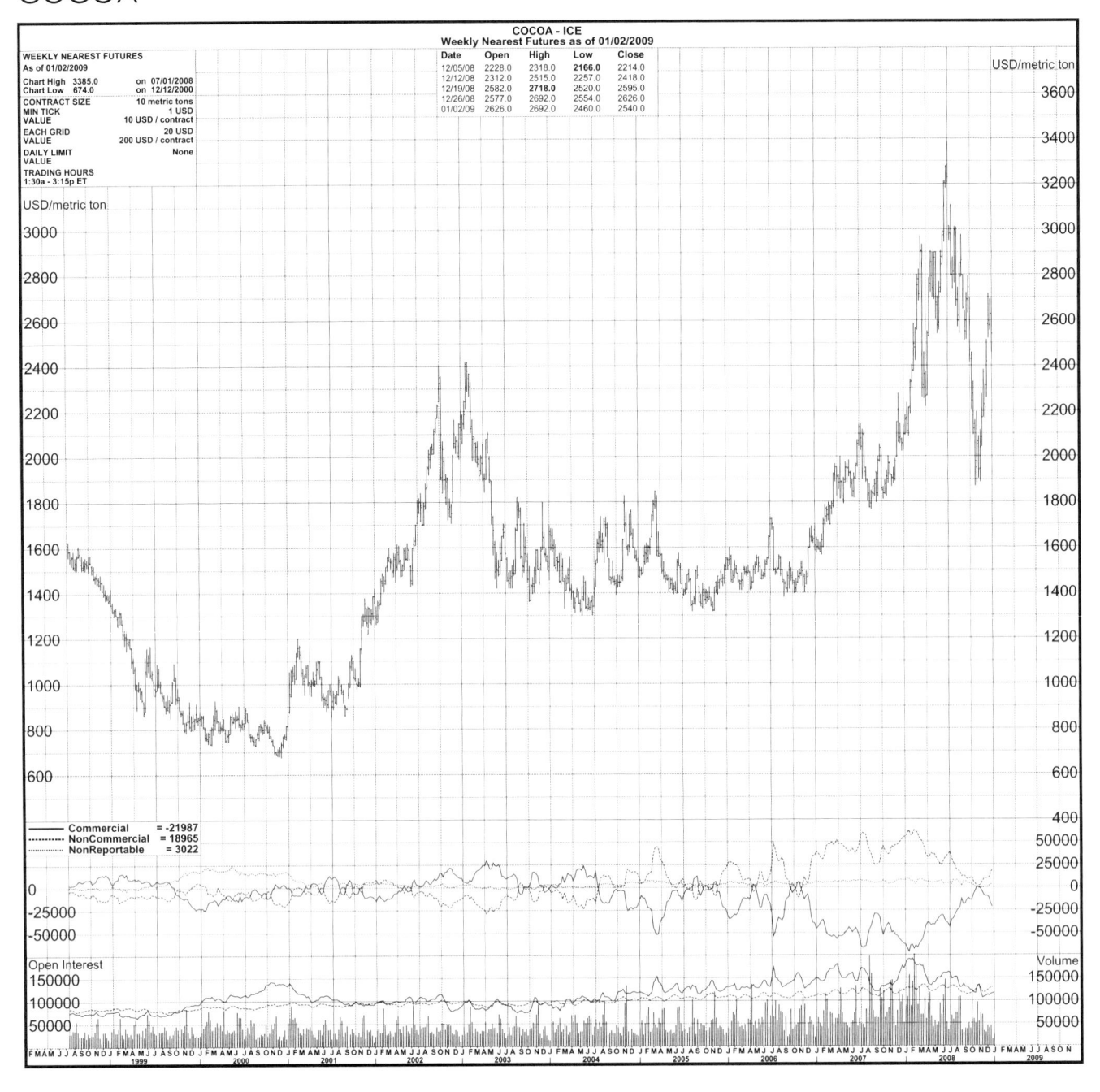

## COCOA - ICE
### Weekly Nearest Futures as of 01/02/2009

| Date | Open | High | Low | Close |
|---|---|---|---|---|
| 12/05/08 | 2228.0 | 2318.0 | 2166.0 | 2214.0 |
| 12/12/08 | 2312.0 | 2515.0 | 2257.0 | 2418.0 |
| 12/19/08 | 2582.0 | 2718.0 | 2520.0 | 2595.0 |
| 12/26/08 | 2577.0 | 2692.0 | 2554.0 | 2626.0 |
| 01/02/09 | 2626.0 | 2692.0 | 2460.0 | 2540.0 |

**WEEKLY NEAREST FUTURES**
As of 01/02/2009
Chart High 3385.0 on 07/01/2008
Chart Low 674.0 on 12/12/2000
CONTRACT SIZE 10 metric tons
MIN TICK 1 USD
VALUE 10 USD / contract
EACH GRID 20 USD
VALUE 200 USD / contract
DAILY LIMIT None
VALUE
TRADING HOURS
1:30a - 3:15p ET

Commercial = -21987
NonCommercial = 18965
NonReportable = 3022

## Quarterly High, Low and Settle of Cocoa Futures   In Dollars per Metric Ton

| Quarter | High | Low | Settle | Quarter | High | Low | Settle | Quarter | High | Low | Settle |
|---|---|---|---|---|---|---|---|---|---|---|---|
| 03/2000 | 929 | 730 | 800 | 03/2003 | 2,420 | 1,892 | 1,960 | 03/2006 | 1,600 | 1,410 | 1,489 |
| 06/2000 | 905 | 740 | 820 | 06/2003 | 2,110 | 1,420 | 1,681 | 06/2006 | 1,650 | 1,410 | 1,646 |
| 09/2000 | 898 | 725 | 797 | 09/2003 | 1,820 | 1,420 | 1,626 | 09/2006 | 1,732 | 1,380 | 1,472 |
| 12/2000 | 846 | 674 | 758 | 12/2003 | 1,800 | 1,360 | 1,515 | 12/2006 | 1,694 | 1,396 | 1,635 |
| 03/2001 | 1,202 | 752 | 1,073 | 03/2004 | 1,698 | 1,328 | 1,549 | 03/2007 | 1,969 | 1,566 | 1,953 |
| 06/2001 | 1,109 | 880 | 974 | 06/2004 | 1,562 | 1,299 | 1,336 | 06/2007 | 2,074 | 1,790 | 2,054 |
| 09/2001 | 1,100 | 854 | 1,077 | 09/2004 | 1,738 | 1,300 | 1,453 | 09/2007 | 2,143 | 1,763 | 2,036 |
| 12/2001 | 1,380 | 977 | 1,310 | 12/2004 | 1,830 | 1,390 | 1,547 | 12/2007 | 2,277 | 1,810 | 2,035 |
| 03/2002 | 1,598 | 1,260 | 1,494 | 03/2005 | 1,850 | 1,464 | 1,613 | 03/2008 | 2,971 | 2,028 | 2,321 |
| 06/2002 | 1,648 | 1,428 | 1,630 | 06/2005 | 1,669 | 1,392 | 1,440 | 06/2008 | 3,280 | 2,217 | 3,245 |
| 09/2002 | 2,206 | 1,610 | 2,191 | 09/2005 | 1,519 | 1,316 | 1,413 | 09/2008 | 3,385 | 2,510 | 2,558 |
| 12/2002 | 2,405 | 1,705 | 2,021 | 12/2005 | 1,525 | 1,315 | 1,504 | 12/2008 | 2,718 | 1,867 | 2,665 |

*Source: IntercontinentalExchange (ICE); formerly New York Board of Trade*

# COCOA

**Cocoa, Ivory Coast**
Weekly Cash as of 01/02/2009

| Date | Open | High | Low | Close |
|---|---|---|---|---|
| 12/05/08 | 2542.0 | 2626.0 | 2542.0 | 2584.0 |
| 12/12/08 | 2669.0 | 2780.0 | 2665.0 | 2780.0 |
| 12/19/08 | 2940.0 | 3052.0 | 2940.0 | 2975.0 |
| 12/26/08 | 2947.0 | 3028.0 | 2947.0 | 3028.0 |
| 01/02/09 | 2946.0 | 3060.0 | 2924.0 | 2935.0 |

WEEKLY CASH
As of 01/02/2009
Chart High 3593.0 on 07/01/2008
Chart Low 876.0 on 12/11/2000
USD/metric ton

## Quarterly High, Low and Settle of Cocoa    In Dollars per Metric Ton

| Quarter | High | Low | Settle | Quarter | High | Low | Settle | Quarter | High | Low | Settle |
|---|---|---|---|---|---|---|---|---|---|---|---|
| 03/2000 | 1,081 | 933 | 980 | 03/2003 | 2,686 | 2,200 | 2,247 | 03/2006 | 1,828 | 1,677 | 1,757 |
| 06/2000 | 1,106 | 932 | 1,012 | 06/2003 | 2,319 | 1,734 | 1,924 | 06/2006 | 1,914 | 1,686 | 1,914 |
| 09/2000 | 1,087 | 940 | 975 | 09/2003 | 2,049 | 1,710 | 1,899 | 09/2006 | 2,017 | 1,713 | 1,760 |
| 12/2000 | 1,048 | 876 | 930 | 12/2003 | 1,948 | 1,614 | 1,763 | 12/2006 | 1,949 | 1,683 | 1,898 |
| 03/2001 | 1,405 | 925 | 1,311 | 03/2004 | 1,920 | 1,611 | 1,713 | 03/2007 | 2,241 | 1,826 | 2,241 |
| 06/2001 | 1,363 | 1,108 | 1,166 | 06/2004 | 1,735 | 1,526 | 1,566 | 06/2007 | 2,375 | 2,086 | 2,375 |
| 09/2001 | 1,312 | 1,116 | 1,312 | 09/2004 | 1,960 | 1,547 | 1,655 | 09/2007 | 2,422 | 2,112 | 2,356 |
| 12/2001 | 1,596 | 1,234 | 1,565 | 12/2004 | 2,044 | 1,596 | 1,770 | 12/2007 | 2,447 | 2,138 | 2,414 |
| 03/2002 | 1,843 | 1,524 | 1,777 | 03/2005 | 2,074 | 1,679 | 1,832 | 03/2008 | 3,232 | 2,354 | 2,614 |
| 06/2002 | 1,955 | 1,719 | 1,949 | 06/2005 | 1,801 | 1,605 | 1,652 | 06/2008 | 3,499 | 2,523 | 3,499 |
| 09/2002 | 2,521 | 1,977 | 2,521 | 09/2005 | 1,774 | 1,535 | 1,614 | 09/2008 | 3,593 | 2,853 | 3,059 |
| 12/2002 | 2,711 | 2,029 | 2,336 | 12/2005 | 1,714 | 1,536 | 1,714 | 12/2008 | 3,060 | 2,254 | 3,060 |

Ivory Coast.    *Source: IntercontinentalExchange (ICE); formerly New York Board of Trade*

# COFFEE

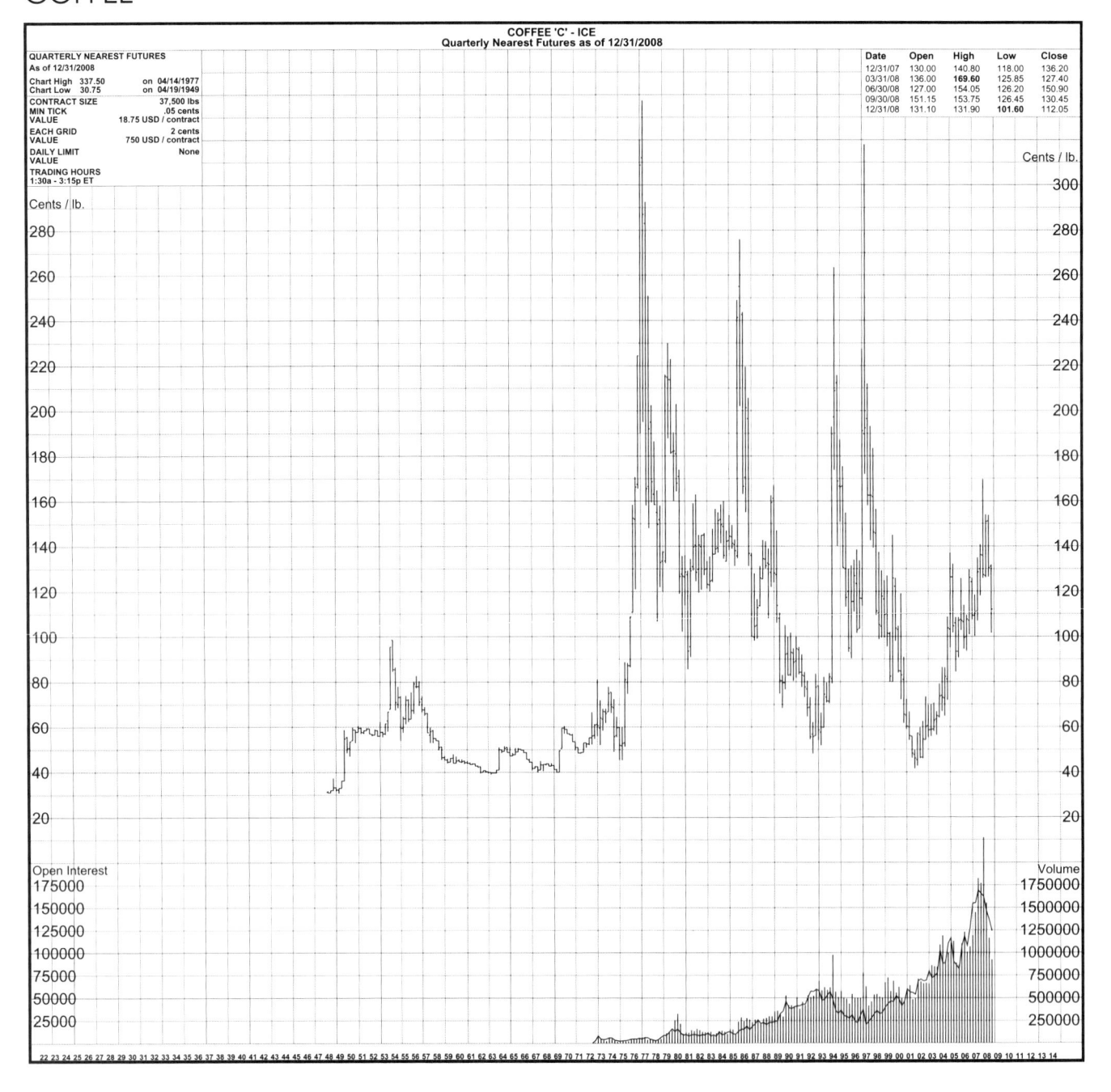

```
COFFEE 'C' - ICE
Quarterly Nearest Futures as of 12/31/2008
```

QUARTERLY NEAREST FUTURES
As of 12/31/2008
Chart High 337.50 on 04/14/1977
Chart Low  30.75 on 04/19/1949
CONTRACT SIZE       37,500 lbs
MIN TICK            .05 cents
VALUE           18.75 USD / contract
EACH GRID           2 cents
VALUE           750 USD / contract
DAILY LIMIT         None
VALUE
TRADING HOURS
1:30a - 3:15p ET

| Date | Open | High | Low | Close |
|---|---|---|---|---|
| 12/31/07 | 130.00 | 140.80 | 118.00 | 136.20 |
| 03/31/08 | 136.00 | 169.60 | 125.85 | 127.40 |
| 06/30/08 | 127.00 | 154.05 | 126.20 | 150.90 |
| 09/30/08 | 151.15 | 153.75 | 126.45 | 130.45 |
| 12/31/08 | 131.10 | 131.90 | 101.60 | 112.05 |

## Annual High, Low and Settle of Coffee   In Cents per Pound

| Year | High | Low | Settle | Year | High | Low | Settle | Year | High | Low | Settle |
|---|---|---|---|---|---|---|---|---|---|---|---|
| 1925 | | | | 1939 | | | | 1953 | 66.87 | 55.50 | 66.87 |
| 1926 | | | | 1940 | | | | 1954 | 98.50 | 67.50 | 73.25 |
| 1927 | | | | 1941 | | | | 1955 | 74.00 | 54.00 | 63.50 |
| 1928 | | | | 1942 | | | | 1956 | 82.75 | 63.50 | 71.25 |
| 1929 | | | | 1943 | | | | 1957 | 73.75 | 53.00 | 58.00 |
| 1930 | | | | 1944 | | | | 1958 | 58.75 | 45.50 | 46.50 |
| 1931 | | | | 1945 | | | | 1959 | 48.00 | 44.00 | 44.00 |
| 1932 | | | | 1946 | | | | 1960 | 47.00 | 43.62 | 44.25 |
| 1933 | | | | 1947 | | | | 1961 | 45.00 | 42.75 | 42.75 |
| 1934 | | | | 1948 | 37.35 | 31.00 | 33.25 | 1962 | 43.00 | 39.50 | 40.25 |
| 1935 | | | | 1949 | 58.75 | 30.75 | 54.75 | 1963 | 41.00 | 39.00 | 41.00 |
| 1936 | | | | 1950 | 59.75 | 47.00 | 57.75 | 1964 | 51.50 | 41.00 | 48.75 |
| 1937 | | | | 1951 | 60.50 | 57.00 | 59.25 | 1965 | 51.00 | 47.25 | 50.25 |
| 1938 | | | | 1952 | 59.25 | 55.75 | 56.00 | 1966 | 50.25 | 44.25 | 44.50 |

Colombian, NY.   Data continued on page 148.   *Source: IntercontinentalExchange (ICE); formerly New York Board of Trade*

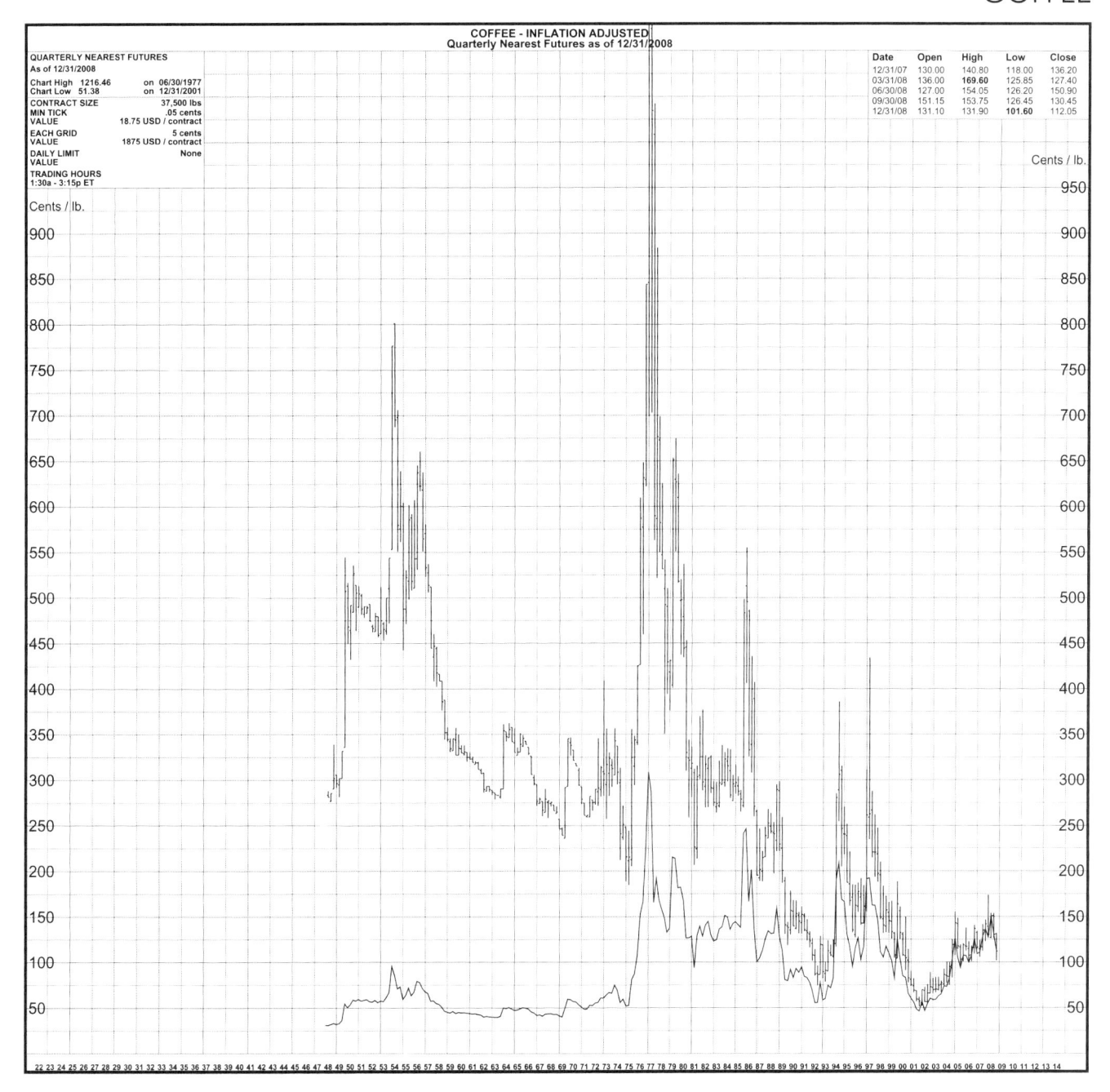

# COFFEE

| | | | | | |
|---|---|---|---|---|---|
| QUARTERLY NEAREST FUTURES | | Date | Open | High | Low | Close |
| As of 12/31/2008 | | 12/31/07 | 130.00 | 140.80 | 118.00 | 136.20 |
| Chart High 1216.46 on 06/30/1977 | | 03/31/08 | 136.00 | 169.60 | 125.85 | 127.40 |
| Chart Low 51.38 on 12/31/2001 | | 06/30/08 | 127.00 | 154.05 | 126.20 | 150.90 |
| CONTRACT SIZE 37,500 lbs | | 09/30/08 | 151.15 | 153.75 | 126.45 | 130.45 |
| MIN TICK .05 cents | | 12/31/08 | 131.10 | 131.90 | 101.60 | 112.05 |
| VALUE 18.75 USD / contract | | | | | | |
| EACH GRID 5 cents | | | | | | |
| VALUE 1875 USD / contract | | | | | | |
| DAILY LIMIT None | | | | | | |
| VALUE | | | | | | |
| TRADING HOURS | | | | | | |
| 1:30a - 3:15p ET | | | | | | |

## Annual High, Low and Settle of Coffee    In Cents per Pound

| Year | High | Low | Settle | Year | High | Low | Settle | Year | High | Low | Settle |
|---|---|---|---|---|---|---|---|---|---|---|---|
| 1925 | | | | 1939 | | | | 1953 | 66.87 | 55.50 | 66.87 |
| 1926 | | | | 1940 | | | | 1954 | 98.50 | 67.50 | 73.25 |
| 1927 | | | | 1941 | | | | 1955 | 74.00 | 54.00 | 63.50 |
| 1928 | | | | 1942 | | | | 1956 | 82.75 | 63.50 | 71.25 |
| 1929 | | | | 1943 | | | | 1957 | 73.75 | 53.00 | 58.00 |
| 1930 | | | | 1944 | | | | 1958 | 58.75 | 45.50 | 46.50 |
| 1931 | | | | 1945 | | | | 1959 | 48.00 | 44.00 | 44.00 |
| 1932 | | | | 1946 | | | | 1960 | 47.00 | 43.62 | 44.25 |
| 1933 | | | | 1947 | | | | 1961 | 45.00 | 42.75 | 42.75 |
| 1934 | | | | 1948 | 37.35 | 31.00 | 33.25 | 1962 | 43.00 | 39.50 | 40.25 |
| 1935 | | | | 1949 | 58.75 | 30.75 | 54.75 | 1963 | 41.00 | 39.00 | 41.00 |
| 1936 | | | | 1950 | 59.75 | 47.00 | 57.75 | 1964 | 51.50 | 41.00 | 48.75 |
| 1937 | | | | 1951 | 60.50 | 57.00 | 59.25 | 1965 | 51.00 | 47.25 | 50.25 |
| 1938 | | | | 1952 | 59.25 | 55.75 | 56.00 | 1966 | 50.25 | 44.25 | 44.50 |

Colombian, NY.    Data continued on page 149.    *Source: IntercontinentalExchange (ICE); formerly New York Board of Trade*

# COFFEE

**COFFEE 'C' - ICE**
Monthly Nearest Futures as of 12/31/2008

| Date | Open | High | Low | Close |
|---|---|---|---|---|
| 08/31/08 | 139.50 | 147.85 | 131.20 | 141.90 |
| 09/30/08 | 139.50 | 143.60 | 126.45 | 130.45 |
| 10/31/08 | 131.10 | 131.90 | 105.05 | 113.00 |
| 11/30/08 | 114.00 | 118.50 | 106.25 | 114.10 |
| 12/31/08 | 113.15 | 113.20 | 101.60 | 112.05 |

**MONTHLY NEAREST FUTURES** As of 12/31/2008
Chart High 337.50 on 04/14/1977
Chart Low 40.00 on 08/01/1967
CONTRACT SIZE 37,500 lbs
MIN TICK .05 cents
VALUE 18.75 USD / contract
EACH GRID 2 cents
VALUE 750 USD / contract
DAILY LIMIT VALUE None
TRADING HOURS 1:30a - 3:15p ET

## Annual High, Low and Settle of Coffee 'C' Futures   In Cents per Pound

| Year | High | Low | Settle | Year | High | Low | Settle | Year | High | Low | Settle |
|---|---|---|---|---|---|---|---|---|---|---|---|
| 1967 | 45.00 | 40.00 | 43.25 | 1981 | 159.00 | 85.50 | 139.71 | 1995 | 187.25 | 93.15 | 94.90 |
| 1968 | 44.00 | 40.50 | 43.00 | 1982 | 162.90 | 119.50 | 129.83 | 1996 | 138.50 | 90.40 | 116.90 |
| 1969 | 59.50 | 40.00 | 59.50 | 1983 | 156.50 | 120.10 | 138.79 | 1997 | 318.00 | 113.60 | 162.45 |
| 1970 | 60.50 | 53.50 | 53.50 | 1984 | 160.00 | 133.20 | 142.25 | 1998 | 183.50 | 98.75 | 117.75 |
| 1971 | 53.50 | 48.25 | 53.00 | 1985 | 249.00 | 131.25 | 241.29 | 1999 | 145.00 | 80.00 | 125.90 |
| 1972 | 61.25 | 52.25 | 60.90 | 1986 | 276.00 | 131.20 | 136.83 | 2000 | 126.00 | 61.55 | 65.55 |
| 1973 | 81.00 | 52.00 | 66.00 | 1987 | 136.90 | 98.10 | 125.96 | 2001 | 72.50 | 41.50 | 46.20 |
| 1974 | 77.90 | 49.00 | 59.62 | 1988 | 162.50 | 108.00 | 159.34 | 2002 | 73.50 | 42.70 | 60.20 |
| 1975 | 88.75 | 45.25 | 87.22 | 1989 | 166.90 | 68.30 | 79.57 | 2003 | 70.75 | 55.30 | 64.95 |
| 1976 | 224.50 | 86.40 | 224.45 | 1990 | 105.00 | 76.60 | 88.65 | 2004 | 108.70 | 64.00 | 103.75 |
| 1977 | 337.50 | 148.00 | 192.03 | 1991 | 100.00 | 73.25 | 77.70 | 2005 | 137.00 | 84.45 | 107.10 |
| 1978 | 202.50 | 106.60 | 132.88 | 1992 | 83.55 | 48.10 | 77.55 | 2006 | 129.75 | 93.50 | 126.20 |
| 1979 | 230.05 | 120.00 | 181.56 | 1993 | 82.20 | 51.70 | 71.55 | 2007 | 140.80 | 100.35 | 136.20 |
| 1980 | 203.00 | 102.10 | 126.80 | 1994 | 263.50 | 70.55 | 168.85 | 2008 | 169.60 | 101.60 | 112.05 |

Futures begin trading 08/16/1972.   Data continued from page 146.   *Source: IntercontinentalExchange (ICE); formerly New York Board of Trade*

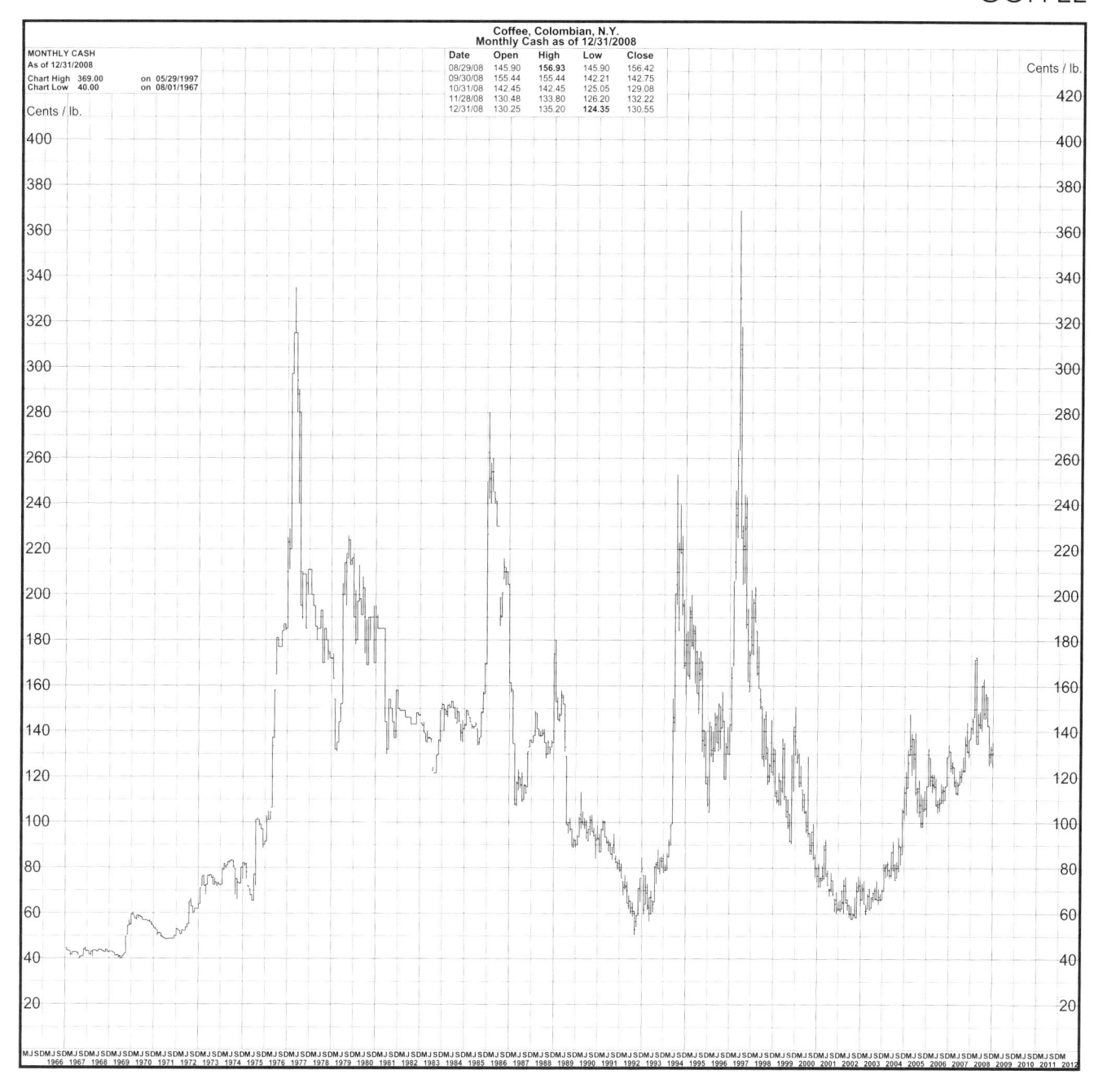

# COFFEE

**Coffee, Colombian, N.Y.**
Monthly Cash as of 12/31/2008

| Date | Open | High | Low | Close |
|---|---|---|---|---|
| 08/29/08 | 145.90 | **156.93** | 145.90 | 156.42 |
| 09/30/08 | 155.44 | 155.44 | 142.21 | 142.75 |
| 10/31/08 | 142.45 | 142.45 | 125.05 | 129.08 |
| 11/28/08 | 130.48 | 133.80 | 126.20 | 132.22 |
| 12/31/08 | 130.25 | 135.20 | **124.35** | 130.55 |

MONTHLY CASH
As of 12/31/2008
Chart High 369.00 on 05/29/1997
Chart Low 40.00 on 08/01/1967

## Annual High, Low and Settle of Coffee   In Cents per Pound

| Year | High | Low | Settle | Year | High | Low | Settle | Year | High | Low | Settle |
|---|---|---|---|---|---|---|---|---|---|---|---|
| 1967 | 45.00 | 40.00 | 43.25 | 1981 | 191.00 | 130.00 | 150.00 | 1995 | 200.00 | 107.00 | 108.00 |
| 1968 | 44.00 | 40.50 | 43.00 | 1982 | 150.00 | 143.00 | 147.00 | 1996 | 157.50 | 104.50 | 143.00 |
| 1969 | 59.50 | 40.00 | 59.50 | 1983 | 152.50 | 121.50 | 151.75 | 1997 | 369.00 | 140.00 | 178.00 |
| 1970 | 60.50 | 53.50 | 53.50 | 1984 | 153.50 | 135.05 | 143.00 | 1998 | 203.50 | 116.50 | 127.00 |
| 1971 | 53.50 | 48.25 | 53.00 | 1985 | 249.50 | 134.00 | 226.50 | 1999 | 151.00 | 90.75 | 135.50 |
| 1972 | 66.50 | 50.75 | 64.00 | 1986 | 280.00 | 161.25 | 161.25 | 2000 | 132.50 | 73.50 | 76.50 |
| 1973 | 77.00 | 64.00 | 72.50 | 1987 | 161.25 | 107.00 | 135.00 | 2001 | 92.50 | 60.00 | 62.00 |
| 1974 | 83.50 | 66.00 | 82.00 | 1988 | 174.00 | 128.00 | 174.00 | 2002 | 76.50 | 57.50 | 66.25 |
| 1975 | 102.00 | 65.50 | 91.50 | 1989 | 180.00 | 89.00 | 90.00 | 2003 | 74.50 | 59.50 | 70.00 |
| 1976 | 225.00 | 91.50 | 223.00 | 1990 | 113.50 | 84.00 | 93.00 | 2004 | 116.00 | 70.00 | 113.25 |
| 1977 | 335.00 | 185.00 | 211.00 | 1991 | 101.00 | 78.00 | 79.00 | 2005 | 147.75 | 98.00 | 115.98 |
| 1978 | 211.00 | 170.00 | 172.00 | 1992 | 84.50 | 50.50 | 79.50 | 2006 | 134.12 | 104.15 | 131.32 |
| 1979 | 226.00 | 131.00 | 190.00 | 1993 | 88.00 | 56.50 | 78.00 | 2007 | 144.14 | 112.07 | 141.48 |
| 1980 | 213.00 | 169.00 | 190.00 | 1994 | 253.00 | 78.50 | 178.00 | 2008 | 172.75 | 124.35 | 130.55 |

Colombian, NY.   Data continued from page 147.   *Source: IntercontinentalExchange (ICE); formerly New York Board of Trade*

# COFFEE

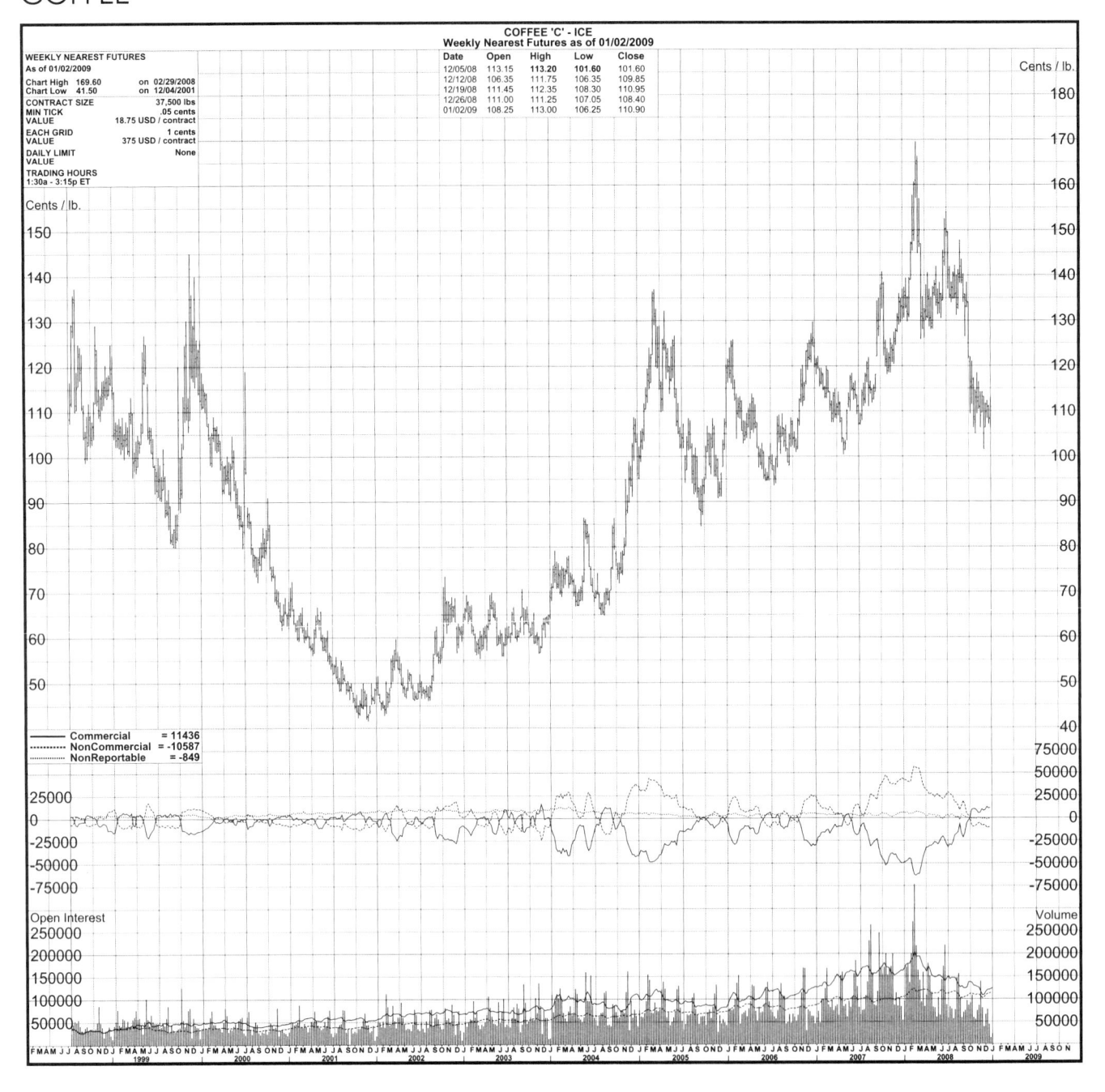

**Quarterly High, Low and Settle of Coffee 'C' Futures**  In Cents per Pound

| Quarter | High | Low | Settle | Quarter | High | Low | Settle | Quarter | High | Low | Settle |
|---------|------|-----|--------|---------|------|-----|--------|---------|------|-----|--------|
| 03/2000 | 126.00 | 98.00 | 103.70 | 03/2003 | 69.50 | 55.30 | 58.65 | 03/2006 | 125.90 | 102.80 | 107.00 |
| 06/2000 | 104.70 | 84.00 | 84.85 | 06/2003 | 70.00 | 55.80 | 58.90 | 06/2006 | 113.90 | 94.50 | 99.50 |
| 09/2000 | 119.00 | 72.20 | 83.00 | 09/2003 | 70.75 | 58.00 | 62.90 | 09/2006 | 109.50 | 93.50 | 107.65 |
| 12/2000 | 91.00 | 61.55 | 65.55 | 12/2003 | 66.90 | 56.40 | 64.95 | 12/2006 | 129.75 | 100.90 | 126.20 |
| 03/2001 | 72.50 | 59.00 | 60.30 | 03/2004 | 79.20 | 64.00 | 73.75 | 03/2007 | 125.90 | 107.45 | 109.25 |
| 06/2001 | 66.80 | 54.10 | 56.10 | 06/2004 | 86.50 | 66.80 | 73.10 | 06/2007 | 118.40 | 100.35 | 111.00 |
| 09/2001 | 56.00 | 46.25 | 48.30 | 09/2004 | 86.40 | 64.80 | 82.35 | 09/2007 | 135.00 | 106.90 | 128.65 |
| 12/2001 | 50.00 | 41.50 | 46.20 | 12/2004 | 108.70 | 71.90 | 103.75 | 12/2007 | 140.80 | 118.00 | 136.20 |
| 03/2002 | 57.40 | 42.70 | 57.20 | 03/2005 | 137.00 | 95.10 | 126.40 | 03/2008 | 169.60 | 125.85 | 127.40 |
| 06/2002 | 59.70 | 46.10 | 46.50 | 06/2005 | 132.25 | 101.70 | 104.65 | 06/2008 | 154.05 | 126.20 | 150.90 |
| 09/2002 | 62.50 | 46.00 | 54.50 | 09/2005 | 108.50 | 84.45 | 93.45 | 09/2008 | 153.75 | 126.45 | 130.45 |
| 12/2002 | 73.50 | 54.25 | 60.20 | 12/2005 | 108.50 | 90.75 | 107.10 | 12/2008 | 131.90 | 101.60 | 112.05 |

*Source: IntercontinentalExchange (ICE); formerly New York Board of Trade*

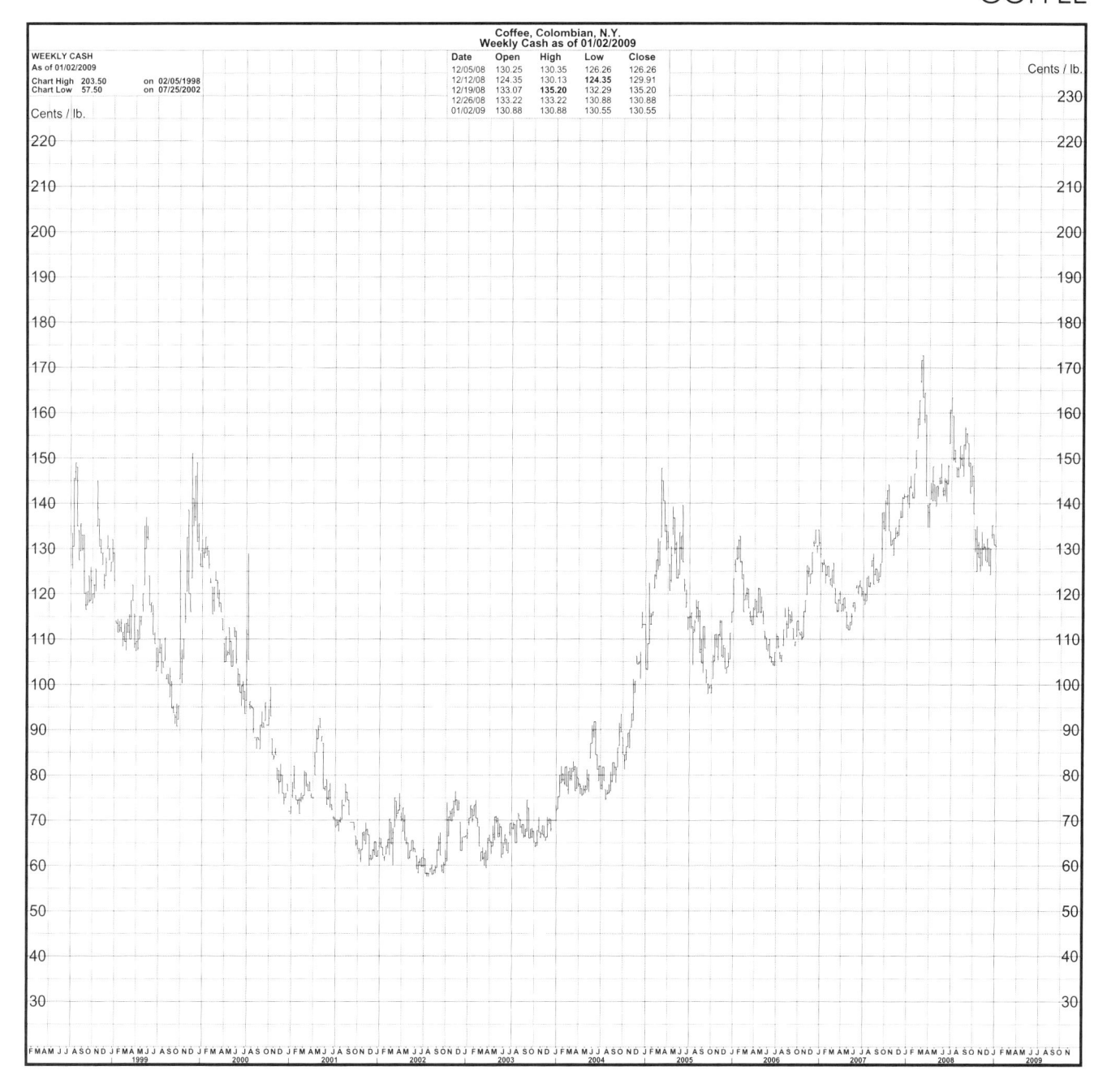

# COFFEE

**Coffee, Colombian, N.Y. Weekly Cash as of 01/02/2009**

| Date | Open | High | Low | Close |
|---|---|---|---|---|
| 12/05/08 | 130.25 | 130.35 | 126.26 | 126.26 |
| 12/12/08 | 124.35 | 130.13 | 124.35 | 129.91 |
| 12/19/08 | 133.07 | 135.20 | 132.29 | 135.20 |
| 12/26/08 | 133.22 | 133.22 | 130.88 | 130.88 |
| 01/02/09 | 130.88 | 130.88 | 130.55 | 130.55 |

WEEKLY CASH As of 01/02/2009
Chart High 203.50 on 02/05/1998
Chart Low 57.50 on 07/25/2002
Cents / lb.

## Quarterly High, Low and Settle of Coffee    In Cents per Pound

| Quarter | High | Low | Settle | Quarter | High | Low | Settle | Quarter | High | Low | Settle |
|---|---|---|---|---|---|---|---|---|---|---|---|
| 03/2000 | 132.50 | 115.50 | 116.00 | 03/2003 | 74.50 | 59.50 | 61.25 | 03/2006 | 132.73 | 113.17 | 116.90 |
| 06/2000 | 114.50 | 95.25 | 96.75 | 06/2003 | 71.00 | 61.75 | 67.25 | 06/2006 | 121.30 | 104.15 | 107.03 |
| 09/2000 | 129.00 | 85.75 | 96.00 | 09/2003 | 74.50 | 65.00 | 66.00 | 09/2006 | 117.19 | 104.93 | 113.95 |
| 12/2000 | 99.50 | 73.50 | 76.50 | 12/2003 | 70.75 | 64.00 | 70.00 | 12/2006 | 134.12 | 109.78 | 131.32 |
| 03/2001 | 82.00 | 71.50 | 76.50 | 03/2004 | 83.00 | 70.00 | 81.75 | 03/2007 | 131.32 | 115.95 | 117.84 |
| 06/2001 | 92.50 | 72.25 | 72.50 | 06/2004 | 91.75 | 75.50 | 79.00 | 06/2007 | 123.03 | 112.07 | 120.06 |
| 09/2001 | 78.00 | 67.50 | 68.50 | 09/2004 | 93.50 | 74.50 | 89.50 | 09/2007 | 138.13 | 117.69 | 134.45 |
| 12/2001 | 69.50 | 60.00 | 62.00 | 12/2004 | 116.00 | 81.25 | 113.25 | 12/2007 | 144.14 | 128.58 | 141.48 |
| 03/2002 | 75.00 | 60.00 | 72.25 | 03/2005 | 147.75 | 103.25 | 132.25 | 03/2008 | 172.75 | 134.60 | 138.02 |
| 06/2002 | 76.00 | 58.25 | 60.00 | 06/2005 | 139.50 | 112.00 | 113.25 | 06/2008 | 160.67 | 134.60 | 160.40 |
| 09/2002 | 67.25 | 57.50 | 58.50 | 09/2005 | 118.75 | 98.00 | 99.76 | 09/2008 | 163.29 | 142.21 | 142.75 |
| 12/2002 | 76.50 | 58.25 | 66.25 | 12/2005 | 115.98 | 98.11 | 115.98 | 12/2008 | 142.45 | 124.35 | 130.55 |

Colombian, NY.    *Source: IntercontinentalExchange (ICE); formerly New York Board of Trade*

# ORANGE JUICE

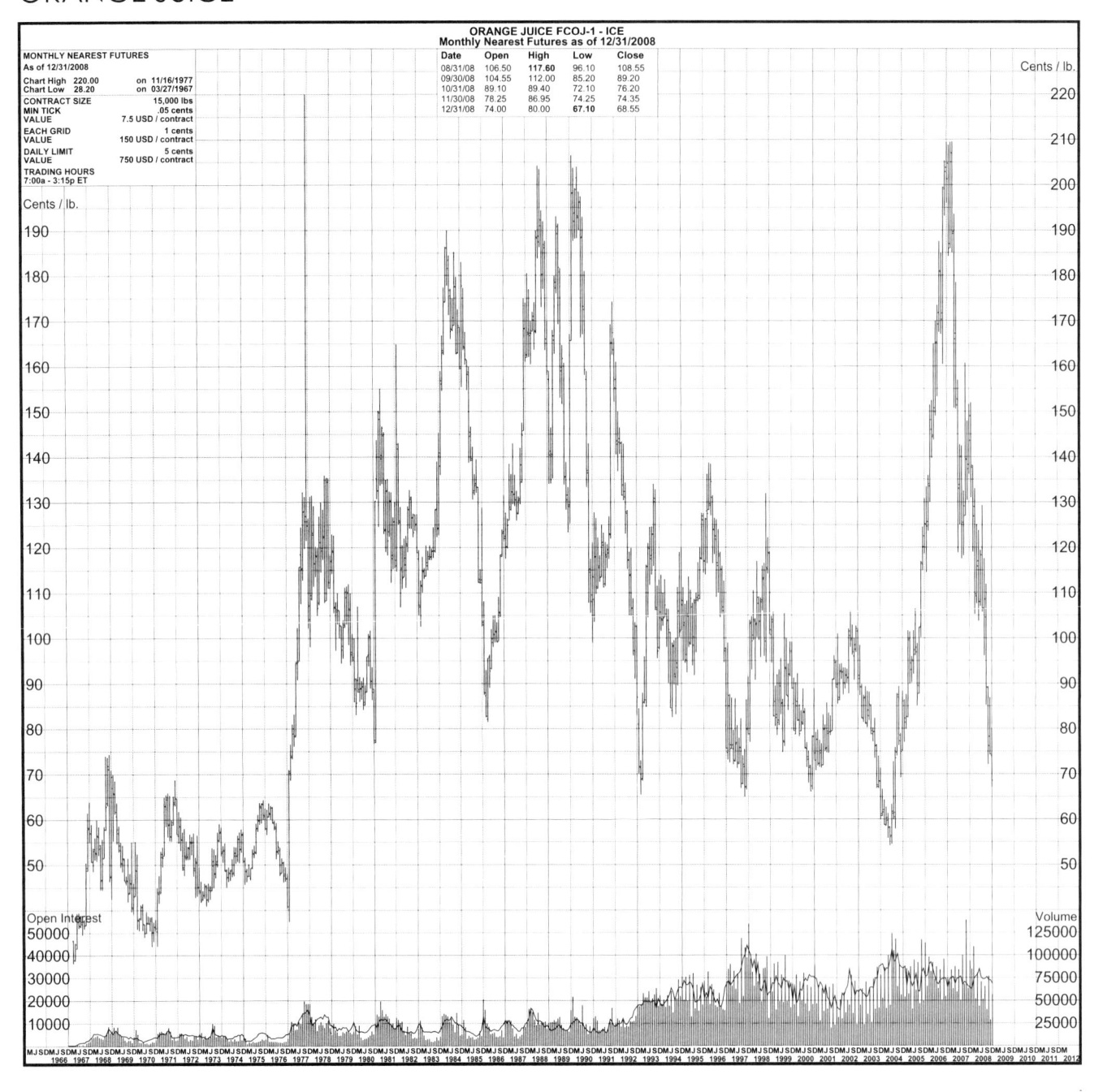

**Annual High, Low and Settle of Orange Juice Futures**  In Cents per Pound

| Year | High | Low | Settle | Year | High | Low | Settle | Year | High | Low | Settle |
|---|---|---|---|---|---|---|---|---|---|---|---|
| 1967 | 63.95 | 28.20 | 57.00 | 1981 | 155.10 | 76.90 | 117.20 | 1995 | 127.60 | 91.75 | 117.00 |
| 1968 | 74.40 | 42.50 | 69.50 | 1982 | 164.85 | 106.75 | 118.90 | 1996 | 138.75 | 75.60 | 75.65 |
| 1969 | 69.90 | 39.10 | 43.00 | 1983 | 145.25 | 102.50 | 140.90 | 1997 | 99.00 | 65.00 | 80.00 |
| 1970 | 55.15 | 31.90 | 36.00 | 1984 | 190.00 | 136.00 | 159.95 | 1998 | 131.95 | 77.00 | 101.80 |
| 1971 | 68.75 | 32.00 | 56.70 | 1985 | 183.00 | 102.60 | 103.50 | 1999 | 105.75 | 74.80 | 88.95 |
| 1972 | 61.80 | 42.75 | 44.35 | 1986 | 131.50 | 81.45 | 122.00 | 2000 | 92.25 | 66.15 | 74.60 |
| 1973 | 59.10 | 40.85 | 52.60 | 1987 | 175.00 | 117.50 | 161.95 | 2001 | 96.20 | 70.80 | 89.10 |
| 1974 | 57.85 | 45.10 | 50.75 | 1988 | 204.25 | 158.00 | 158.95 | 2002 | 106.00 | 85.40 | 91.75 |
| 1975 | 64.35 | 45.60 | 58.00 | 1989 | 193.10 | 123.30 | 165.65 | 2003 | 98.50 | 60.05 | 60.75 |
| 1976 | 63.65 | 40.50 | 40.80 | 1990 | 206.50 | 99.00 | 113.50 | 2004 | 89.40 | 54.20 | 86.10 |
| 1977 | 220.00 | 37.40 | 107.10 | 1991 | 174.25 | 103.50 | 155.15 | 2005 | 130.80 | 77.00 | 125.20 |
| 1978 | 136.00 | 98.00 | 115.05 | 1992 | 161.00 | 83.00 | 87.00 | 2006 | 209.40 | 114.50 | 201.25 |
| 1979 | 122.95 | 93.95 | 95.75 | 1993 | 134.00 | 65.45 | 104.40 | 2007 | 209.50 | 117.50 | 143.60 |
| 1980 | 107.00 | 76.75 | 77.40 | 1994 | 119.90 | 82.50 | 107.30 | 2008 | 152.00 | 67.10 | 68.55 |

Futures begin trading 02/01/1967.    Source: IntercontinentalExchange (ICE); formerly New York Board of Trade

# ORANGE JUICE

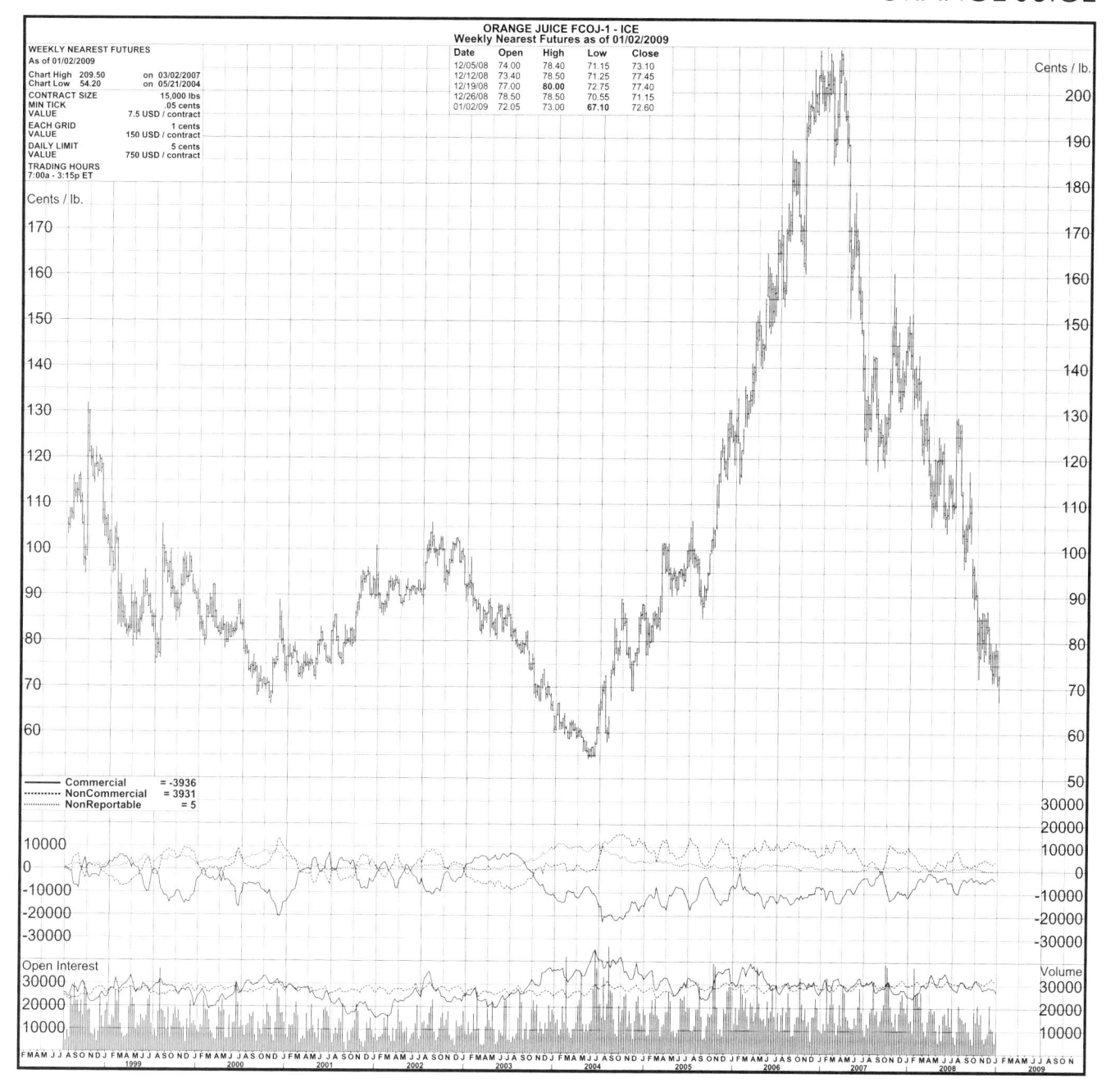

## Quarterly High, Low and Settle of Orange Juice Futures    In Cents per Pound

| Quarter | High | Low | Settle | Quarter | High | Low | Settle | Quarter | High | Low | Settle |
|---|---|---|---|---|---|---|---|---|---|---|---|
| 03/2000 | 92.25 | 78.75 | 81.80 | 03/2003 | 98.50 | 81.40 | 86.75 | 03/2006 | 151.50 | 114.50 | 148.15 |
| 06/2000 | 88.90 | 78.25 | 83.75 | 06/2003 | 89.40 | 80.25 | 85.30 | 06/2006 | 170.00 | 139.70 | 165.05 |
| 09/2000 | 84.50 | 68.00 | 71.45 | 09/2003 | 85.30 | 73.50 | 76.15 | 09/2006 | 187.60 | 153.25 | 170.30 |
| 12/2000 | 89.00 | 66.15 | 74.60 | 12/2003 | 76.50 | 60.05 | 60.75 | 12/2006 | 209.40 | 160.35 | 201.25 |
| 03/2001 | 79.75 | 70.80 | 75.15 | 03/2004 | 66.70 | 58.55 | 60.30 | 03/2007 | 209.50 | 184.20 | 189.25 |
| 06/2001 | 83.10 | 71.35 | 75.50 | 06/2004 | 63.40 | 54.20 | 61.75 | 06/2007 | 193.60 | 118.85 | 133.00 |
| 09/2001 | 85.80 | 74.60 | 79.35 | 09/2004 | 87.90 | 57.85 | 87.50 | 09/2007 | 142.80 | 117.50 | 129.10 |
| 12/2001 | 96.20 | 79.50 | 89.10 | 12/2004 | 89.40 | 69.20 | 86.10 | 12/2007 | 160.80 | 127.00 | 143.60 |
| 03/2002 | 101.00 | 85.40 | 92.50 | 03/2005 | 101.70 | 77.00 | 99.55 | 03/2008 | 152.00 | 105.25 | 109.65 |
| 06/2002 | 93.50 | 87.50 | 91.20 | 06/2005 | 101.70 | 89.85 | 96.35 | 06/2008 | 125.10 | 103.75 | 118.35 |
| 09/2002 | 106.00 | 87.75 | 96.95 | 09/2005 | 106.50 | 85.10 | 102.30 | 09/2008 | 129.30 | 85.20 | 89.20 |
| 12/2002 | 102.70 | 88.50 | 91.75 | 12/2005 | 130.80 | 100.20 | 125.20 | 12/2008 | 89.40 | 67.10 | 68.55 |

*Source: IntercontinentalExchange (ICE); formerly New York Board of Trade*

# SUGAR

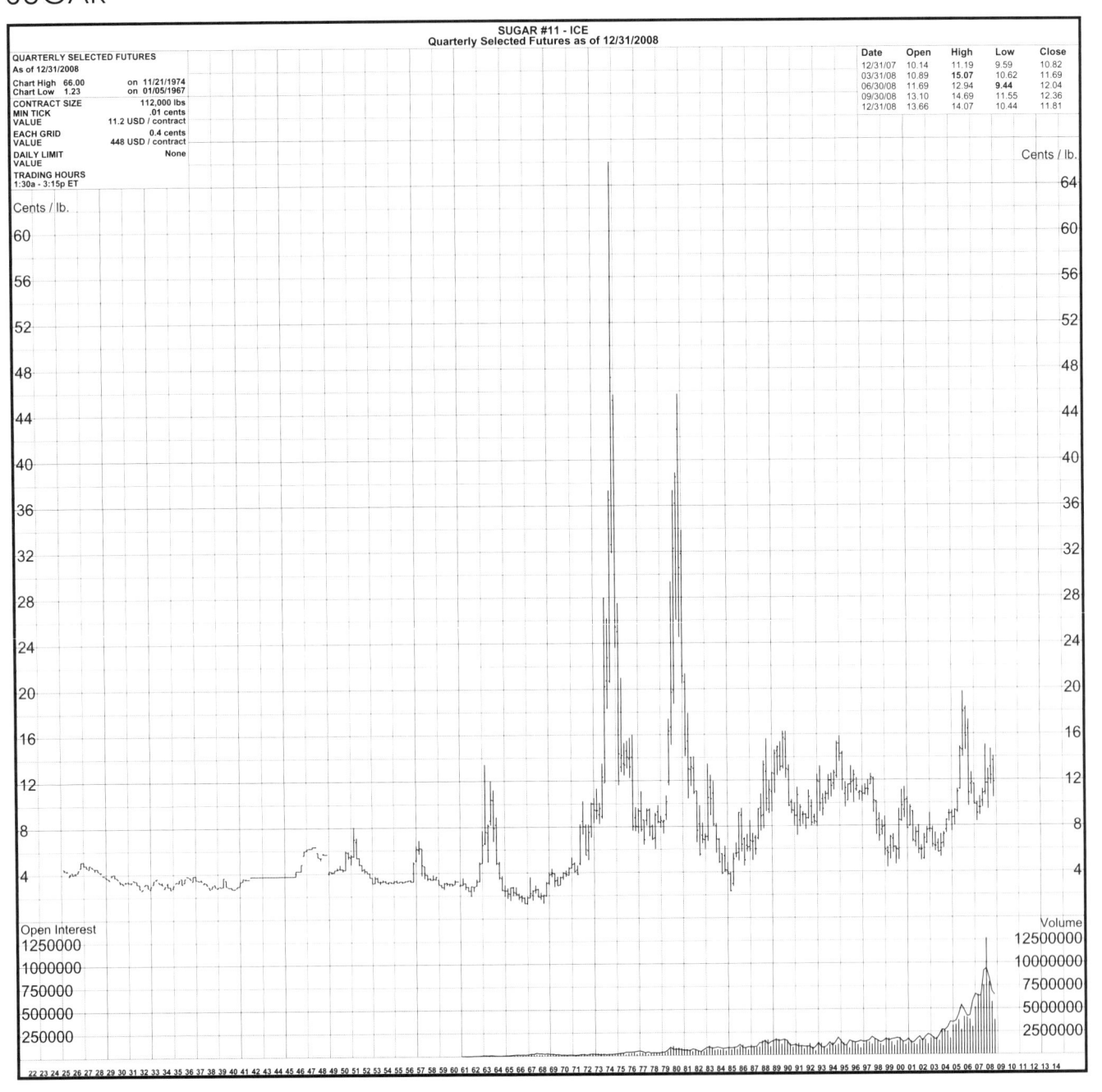

## SUGAR #11 - ICE
### Quarterly Selected Futures as of 12/31/2008

| QUARTERLY SELECTED FUTURES | | |
|---|---|---|
| As of 12/31/2008 | | |
| Chart High 66.00 | on 11/21/1974 | |
| Chart Low 1.23 | on 01/05/1967 | |
| CONTRACT SIZE | 112,000 lbs | |
| MIN TICK | .01 cents | |
| VALUE | 11.2 USD / contract | |
| EACH GRID | 0.4 cents | |
| VALUE | 448 USD / contract | |
| DAILY LIMIT VALUE | None | |
| TRADING HOURS | 1:30a - 3:15p ET | |

| Date | Open | High | Low | Close |
|---|---|---|---|---|
| 12/31/07 | 10.14 | 11.19 | 9.59 | 10.82 |
| 03/31/08 | 10.89 | 15.07 | 10.62 | 11.69 |
| 06/30/08 | 11.69 | 12.94 | 9.44 | 12.04 |
| 09/30/08 | 13.10 | 14.69 | 11.55 | 12.36 |
| 12/31/08 | 13.66 | 14.07 | 10.44 | 11.81 |

## Annual High, Low and Settle of Sugar #11 Futures — In Cents per Pound

| Year | High | Low | Settle | Year | High | Low | Settle | Year | High | Low | Settle |
|---|---|---|---|---|---|---|---|---|---|---|---|
| 1925 | 4.70 | 3.90 | 4.10 | 1939 | 3.65 | 2.77 | 2.93 | 1953 | 3.77 | 3.05 | 3.25 |
| 1926 | 5.10 | 4.00 | 5.10 | 1940 | 2.91 | 2.64 | 2.91 | 1954 | 3.43 | 3.05 | 3.17 |
| 1927 | 5.10 | 4.50 | 4.60 | 1941 | 3.60 | 2.93 | 3.50 | 1955 | 3.41 | 3.13 | 3.23 |
| 1928 | 4.50 | 3.90 | 3.90 | 1942 | 3.74 | 3.72 | 3.74 | 1956 | 5.00 | 3.22 | 4.85 |
| 1929 | 4.01 | 3.52 | 3.76 | 1943 | 3.74 | 3.74 | 3.74 | 1957 | 6.85 | 3.50 | 3.85 |
| 1930 | 3.70 | 3.14 | 3.29 | 1944 | 3.75 | 3.74 | 3.75 | 1958 | 3.85 | 3.35 | 3.67 |
| 1931 | 3.49 | 3.14 | 3.14 | 1945 | 3.75 | 3.75 | 3.75 | 1959 | 3.40 | 2.55 | 3.05 |
| 1932 | 3.16 | 2.59 | 2.83 | 1946 | 5.94 | 3.76 | 5.94 | 1960 | 3.40 | 2.85 | 3.25 |
| 1933 | 3.62 | 2.72 | 3.23 | 1947 | 6.32 | 6.02 | 6.32 | 1961 | 3.58 | 2.41 | 2.41 |
| 1934 | 3.32 | 2.67 | 2.67 | 1948 | 5.82 | 5.14 | 5.67 | 1962 | 4.95 | 1.95 | 4.80 |
| 1935 | 3.62 | 2.79 | 3.13 | 1949 | 4.50 | 3.90 | 4.33 | 1963 | 13.45 | 4.83 | 10.37 |
| 1936 | 3.82 | 3.27 | 3.82 | 1950 | 5.95 | 4.15 | 5.45 | 1964 | 11.24 | 2.42 | 2.50 |
| 1937 | 3.83 | 3.18 | 3.24 | 1951 | 8.05 | 4.70 | 4.77 | 1965 | 2.91 | 1.56 | 2.30 |
| 1938 | 3.21 | 2.69 | 2.88 | 1952 | 4.75 | 3.62 | 3.62 | 1966 | 2.76 | 1.32 | 1.32 |

Futures data begins 01/04/1961.   Contract months: March, May, July, October.   Data continued on page 156.
*Source: IntercontinentalExchange (ICE); formerly New York Board of Trade*

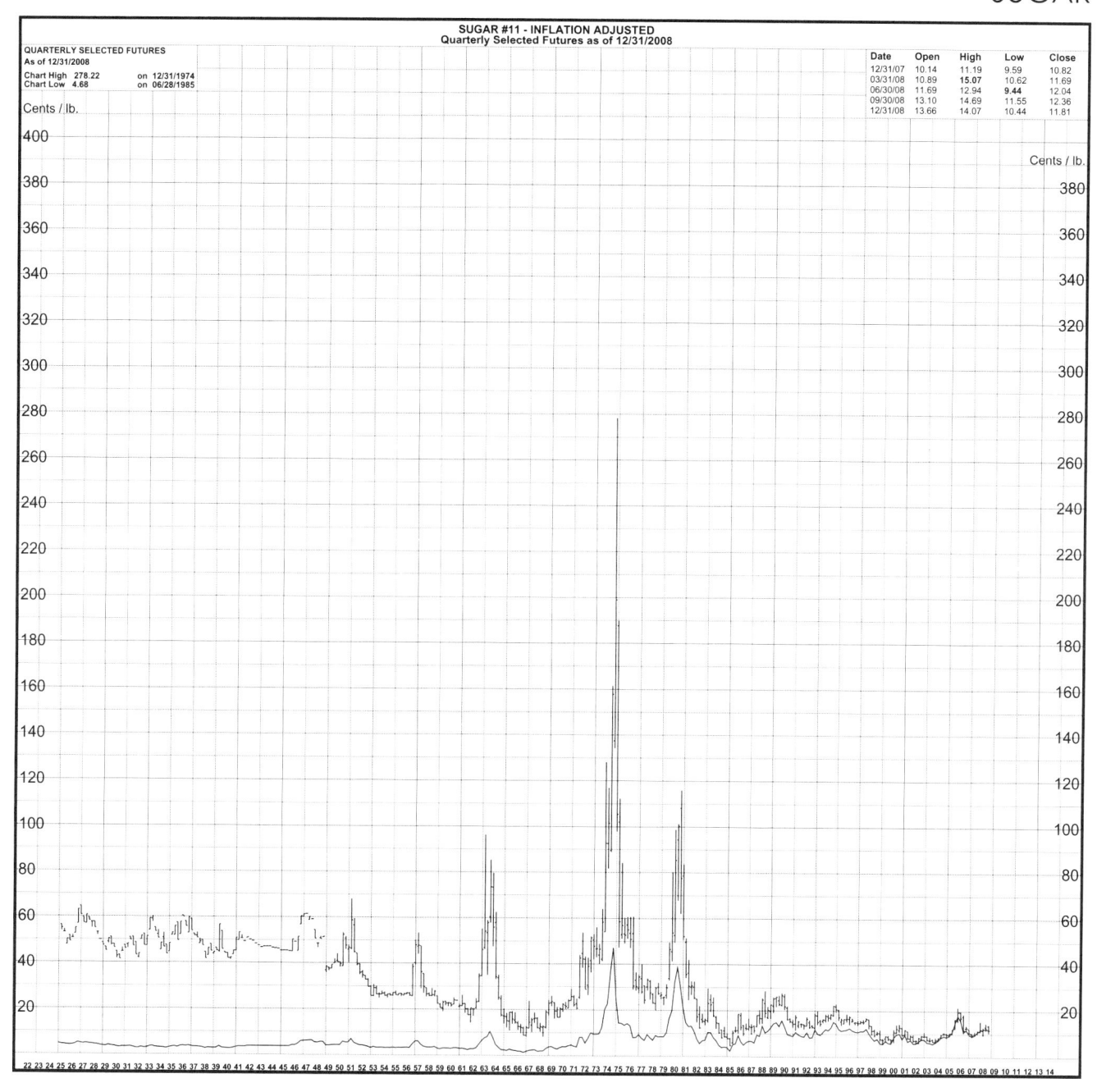

# SUGAR

## SUGAR #11 - INFLATION ADJUSTED
### Quarterly Selected Futures as of 12/31/2008

QUARTERLY SELECTED FUTURES
As of 12/31/2008
Chart High 278.22 on 12/31/1974
Chart Low 4.68 on 06/28/1985
Cents / lb.

| Date | Open | High | Low | Close |
|---|---|---|---|---|
| 12/31/07 | 10.14 | 11.19 | 9.59 | 10.82 |
| 03/31/08 | 10.89 | 15.07 | 10.62 | 11.69 |
| 06/30/08 | 11.69 | 12.94 | 9.44 | 12.04 |
| 09/30/08 | 13.10 | 14.69 | 11.55 | 12.36 |
| 12/31/08 | 13.66 | 14.07 | 10.44 | 11.81 |

## Annual High, Low and Settle of Sugar    In Cents per Pound

| Year | High | Low | Settle | Year | High | Low | Settle | Year | High | Low | Settle |
|---|---|---|---|---|---|---|---|---|---|---|---|
| 1925 | 4.70 | 3.90 | 4.10 | 1939 | 3.65 | 2.77 | 2.93 | 1953 | 3.77 | 3.05 | 3.25 |
| 1926 | 5.10 | 4.00 | 5.10 | 1940 | 2.91 | 2.64 | 2.91 | 1954 | 3.43 | 3.05 | 3.17 |
| 1927 | 5.10 | 4.50 | 4.60 | 1941 | 3.60 | 2.93 | 3.50 | 1955 | 3.41 | 3.13 | 3.23 |
| 1928 | 4.50 | 3.90 | 3.90 | 1942 | 3.74 | 3.72 | 3.74 | 1956 | 5.00 | 3.22 | 4.85 |
| 1929 | 4.01 | 3.52 | 3.76 | 1943 | 3.74 | 3.74 | 3.74 | 1957 | 6.85 | 3.50 | 3.85 |
| 1930 | 3.70 | 3.14 | 3.29 | 1944 | 3.75 | 3.74 | 3.75 | 1958 | 3.85 | 3.35 | 3.67 |
| 1931 | 3.49 | 3.14 | 3.14 | 1945 | 3.75 | 3.75 | 3.75 | 1959 | 3.40 | 2.55 | 3.05 |
| 1932 | 3.16 | 2.59 | 2.83 | 1946 | 5.94 | 3.76 | 5.94 | 1960 | 3.40 | 2.85 | 3.25 |
| 1933 | 3.62 | 2.72 | 3.23 | 1947 | 6.32 | 6.02 | 6.32 | 1961 | 3.42 | 2.43 | 2.43 |
| 1934 | 3.32 | 2.67 | 2.67 | 1948 | 5.82 | 5.14 | 5.67 | 1962 | 4.75 | 2.05 | 4.75 |
| 1935 | 3.62 | 2.79 | 3.13 | 1949 | 4.50 | 3.90 | 4.33 | 1963 | 12.60 | 4.80 | 10.25 |
| 1936 | 3.82 | 3.27 | 3.82 | 1950 | 5.95 | 4.15 | 5.45 | 1964 | 11.18 | 2.53 | 2.53 |
| 1937 | 3.83 | 3.18 | 3.24 | 1951 | 8.05 | 4.70 | 4.77 | 1965 | 2.91 | 1.60 | 2.10 |
| 1938 | 3.21 | 2.69 | 2.88 | 1952 | 4.75 | 3.62 | 3.62 | 1966 | 2.60 | 1.34 | 1.34 |

World Raw #11, NY.    Data continued on page 157.    *Source: IntercontinentalExchange (ICE); formerly New York Board of Trade*

155

# SUGAR

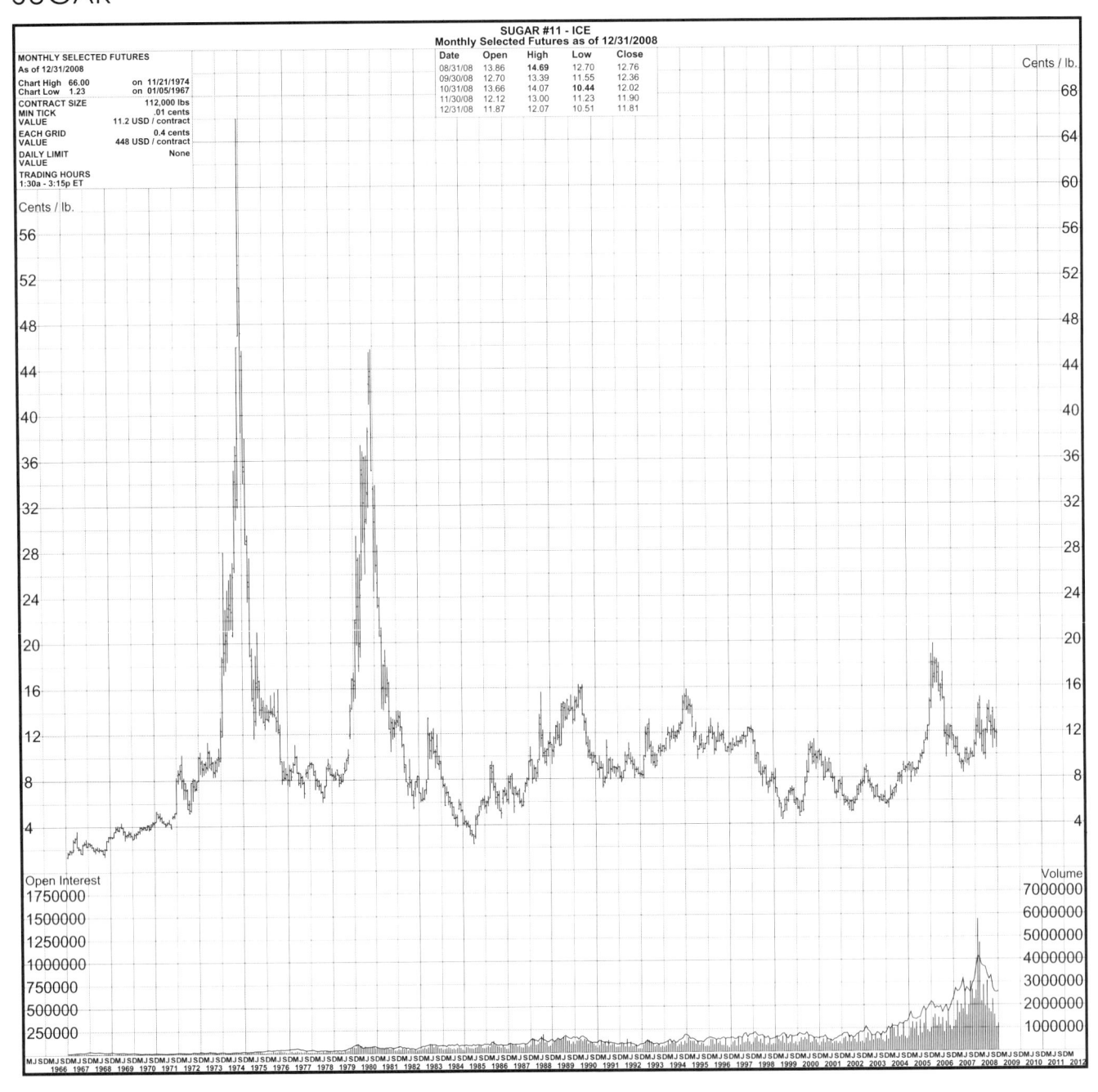

**SUGAR #11 - ICE**
Monthly Selected Futures as of 12/31/2008

| Date | Open | High | Low | Close |
|---|---|---|---|---|
| 08/31/08 | 13.86 | 14.69 | 12.70 | 12.76 |
| 09/30/08 | 12.70 | 13.39 | 11.55 | 12.36 |
| 10/31/08 | 13.66 | 14.07 | 10.44 | 12.02 |
| 11/30/08 | 12.12 | 13.00 | 11.23 | 11.90 |
| 12/31/08 | 11.87 | 12.07 | 10.51 | 11.81 |

**MONTHLY SELECTED FUTURES** As of 12/31/2008
- Chart High 66.00 on 11/21/1974
- Chart Low 1.23 on 01/05/1967
- CONTRACT SIZE 112,000 lbs
- MIN TICK .01 cents
- VALUE 11.2 USD / contract
- EACH GRID 0.4 cents
- VALUE 448 USD / contract
- DAILY LIMIT VALUE None
- TRADING HOURS 1:30a - 3:15p ET

## Annual High, Low and Settle of Sugar #11 Futures    In Cents per Pound

| Year | High | Low | Settle | Year | High | Low | Settle | Year | High | Low | Settle |
|---|---|---|---|---|---|---|---|---|---|---|---|
| 1967 | 3.63 | 1.23 | 2.52 | 1981 | 33.85 | 10.41 | 13.18 | 1995 | 15.83 | 9.62 | 11.60 |
| 1968 | 3.20 | 1.31 | 3.08 | 1982 | 14.10 | 5.40 | 6.85 | 1996 | 13.25 | 10.05 | 11.00 |
| 1969 | 4.36 | 2.74 | 2.88 | 1983 | 13.47 | 6.05 | 8.18 | 1997 | 12.55 | 10.10 | 12.22 |
| 1970 | 4.48 | 2.92 | 4.36 | 1984 | 8.29 | 3.79 | 4.16 | 1998 | 12.22 | 6.60 | 7.86 |
| 1971 | 8.25 | 3.79 | 7.99 | 1985 | 6.56 | 2.30 | 5.62 | 1999 | 8.82 | 4.36 | 6.12 |
| 1972 | 10.25 | 5.08 | 10.00 | 1986 | 9.58 | 4.52 | 6.16 | 2000 | 11.40 | 4.62 | 10.20 |
| 1973 | 13.53 | 8.25 | 12.33 | 1987 | 9.55 | 5.00 | 9.49 | 2001 | 10.49 | 6.11 | 7.39 |
| 1974 | 66.00 | 11.83 | 47.20 | 1988 | 15.64 | 7.56 | 11.15 | 2002 | 8.05 | 4.97 | 7.61 |
| 1975 | 45.70 | 11.60 | 13.37 | 1989 | 15.38 | 9.26 | 13.16 | 2003 | 9.13 | 5.66 | 5.67 |
| 1976 | 16.00 | 7.58 | 8.03 | 1990 | 16.28 | 9.08 | 9.37 | 2004 | 9.37 | 5.27 | 9.04 |
| 1977 | 11.10 | 6.40 | 9.40 | 1991 | 11.40 | 7.18 | 9.00 | 2005 | 14.89 | 7.50 | 14.68 |
| 1978 | 9.88 | 6.05 | 8.43 | 1992 | 11.14 | 7.66 | 8.41 | 2006 | 19.73 | 9.70 | 11.75 |
| 1979 | 17.40 | 7.37 | 16.31 | 1993 | 13.26 | 7.96 | 10.77 | 2007 | 11.66 | 8.36 | 10.82 |
| 1980 | 45.75 | 15.10 | 30.58 | 1994 | 15.38 | 10.23 | 15.17 | 2008 | 15.07 | 9.44 | 11.81 |

Contract months: March, May, July, October.   Data continued fom page 154.
*Source: IntercontinentalExchange (ICE); formerly New York Board of Trade*

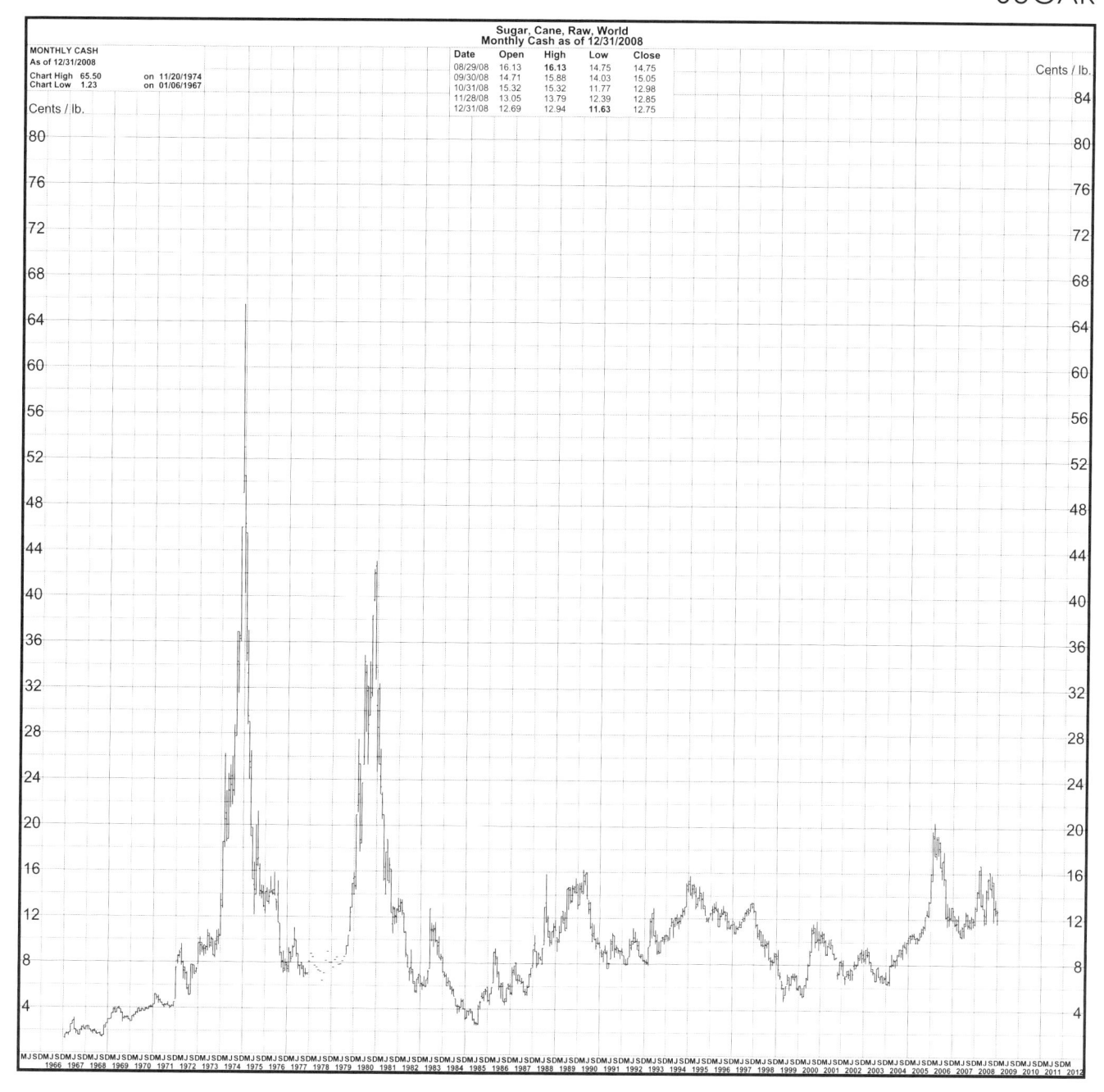

# SUGAR

**MONTHLY CASH**
As of 12/31/2008
Chart High  65.50  on 11/20/1974
Chart Low    1.23  on 01/06/1967
Cents / lb.

Sugar, Cane, Raw, World
Monthly Cash as of 12/31/2008

| Date | Open | High | Low | Close |
|---|---|---|---|---|
| 08/29/08 | 16.13 | **16.13** | 14.75 | 14.75 |
| 09/30/08 | 14.71 | 15.88 | 14.03 | 15.05 |
| 10/31/08 | 15.32 | 15.32 | 11.77 | 12.98 |
| 11/28/08 | 13.05 | 13.79 | 12.39 | 12.85 |
| 12/31/08 | 12.69 | 12.94 | **11.63** | 12.75 |

## Annual High, Low and Settle of Sugar     In Cents per Pound

| Year | High | Low | Settle | Year | High | Low | Settle | Year | High | Low | Settle |
|---|---|---|---|---|---|---|---|---|---|---|---|
| 1967 | 3.10 | 1.23 | 2.30 | 1981 | 32.43 | 10.56 | 12.96 | 1995 | 15.74 | 11.66 | 12.48 |
| 1968 | 2.95 | 1.37 | 2.95 | 1982 | 13.60 | 5.37 | 6.20 | 1996 | 13.53 | 11.04 | 11.82 |
| 1969 | 4.08 | 2.70 | 2.80 | 1983 | 12.75 | 5.64 | 7.23 | 1997 | 13.46 | 10.66 | 12.70 |
| 1970 | 4.25 | 2.80 | 4.25 | 1984 | 7.25 | 3.08 | 3.16 | 1998 | 12.70 | 7.56 | 8.54 |
| 1971 | 7.50 | 3.90 | 7.50 | 1985 | 5.90 | 2.56 | 4.75 | 1999 | 9.33 | 4.79 | 6.13 |
| 1972 | 9.65 | 5.10 | 9.65 | 1986 | 9.31 | 4.34 | 5.43 | 2000 | 11.84 | 5.17 | 10.64 |
| 1973 | 14.00 | 8.35 | 13.40 | 1987 | 9.21 | 5.19 | 9.21 | 2001 | 10.99 | 6.76 | 7.96 |
| 1974 | 65.50 | 12.70 | 46.30 | 1988 | 15.83 | 7.61 | 10.93 | 2002 | 9.43 | 6.30 | 8.42 |
| 1975 | 45.50 | 12.15 | 14.15 | 1989 | 15.49 | 9.03 | 13.14 | 2003 | 9.60 | 6.33 | 6.35 |
| 1976 | 15.90 | 7.05 | 7.45 | 1990 | 16.25 | 9.24 | 9.42 | 2004 | 10.49 | 6.22 | 10.45 |
| 1977 | 11.75 | 6.69 | 11.75 | 1991 | 10.72 | 7.58 | 9.04 | 2005 | 16.03 | 9.89 | 15.98 |
| 1978 | 15.17 | 12.63 | 14.25 | 1992 | 11.16 | 7.85 | 8.23 | 2006 | 20.46 | 11.36 | 12.80 |
| 1979 | 15.91 | 8.69 | 15.47 | 1993 | 12.93 | 7.85 | 10.52 | 2007 | 13.22 | 10.41 | 13.02 |
| 1980 | 43.13 | 14.38 | 28.55 | 1994 | 15.29 | 10.04 | 15.02 | 2008 | 16.70 | 11.54 | 12.75 |

World Raw #11, NY.    Data continued fom page 155.    *Source: IntercontinentalExchange (ICE); formerly New York Board of Trade*

# SUGAR

## Quarterly High, Low and Settle of Sugar #11 Futures    In Cents per Pound

| Quarter | High | Low | Settle | Quarter | High | Low | Settle | Quarter | High | Low | Settle |
|---|---|---|---|---|---|---|---|---|---|---|---|
| 03/2000 | 6.18 | 4.62 | 5.90 | 03/2003 | 9.13 | 7.38 | 7.68 | 03/2006 | 19.73 | 14.00 | 17.90 |
| 06/2000 | 9.50 | 5.00 | 8.50 | 06/2003 | 7.90 | 6.07 | 6.33 | 06/2006 | 18.39 | 14.57 | 15.79 |
| 09/2000 | 11.15 | 8.35 | 9.77 | 09/2003 | 7.39 | 5.75 | 6.20 | 09/2006 | 17.25 | 9.70 | 10.85 |
| 12/2000 | 11.40 | 8.67 | 10.20 | 12/2003 | 6.79 | 5.66 | 5.67 | 12/2006 | 12.65 | 10.66 | 11.75 |
| 03/2001 | 10.49 | 7.70 | 7.75 | 03/2004 | 7.26 | 5.27 | 6.40 | 03/2007 | 11.66 | 9.79 | 9.88 |
| 06/2001 | 9.82 | 7.93 | 9.59 | 06/2004 | 7.43 | 6.05 | 7.24 | 06/2007 | 10.06 | 8.36 | 9.07 |
| 09/2001 | 9.29 | 6.54 | 6.70 | 09/2004 | 8.55 | 7.33 | 8.50 | 09/2007 | 10.56 | 8.90 | 9.56 |
| 12/2001 | 7.85 | 6.11 | 7.39 | 12/2004 | 9.37 | 8.35 | 9.04 | 12/2007 | 11.19 | 9.59 | 10.82 |
| 03/2002 | 8.05 | 5.50 | 5.93 | 03/2005 | 9.33 | 7.50 | 8.70 | 03/2008 | 15.07 | 10.62 | 11.69 |
| 06/2002 | 6.30 | 4.97 | 5.91 | 06/2005 | 9.42 | 8.02 | 9.34 | 06/2008 | 12.94 | 9.44 | 12.04 |
| 09/2002 | 7.27 | 5.01 | 6.89 | 09/2005 | 11.20 | 9.10 | 10.95 | 09/2008 | 14.69 | 11.55 | 12.36 |
| 12/2002 | 7.89 | 6.38 | 7.61 | 12/2005 | 14.89 | 11.12 | 14.68 | 12/2008 | 14.07 | 10.44 | 11.81 |

Contract months: March, May, July, October.    *Source: IntercontinentalExchange (ICE); formerly New York Board of Trade*

# SUGAR

**WEEKLY CASH**
As of 01/02/2009
Chart High 20.46 on 02/03/2006
Chart Low 4.79 on 04/28/1999
Cents / lb.

Sugar, Cane, Raw, World
Weekly Cash as of 01/02/2009

| Date | Open | High | Low | Close |
|---|---|---|---|---|
| 12/05/08 | 12.69 | 12.69 | 11.63 | 11.63 |
| 12/12/08 | 11.92 | 12.94 | 11.92 | 12.68 |
| 12/19/08 | 12.62 | 12.82 | 12.01 | 12.01 |
| 12/26/08 | 11.87 | 11.98 | 11.78 | 11.98 |
| 01/02/09 | 12.08 | 12.81 | 12.08 | 12.81 |

## Quarterly High, Low and Settle of Sugar    In Cents per Pound

| Quarter | High | Low | Settle | Quarter | High | Low | Settle | Quarter | High | Low | Settle |
|---|---|---|---|---|---|---|---|---|---|---|---|
| 03/2000 | 6.23 | 5.17 | 6.23 | 03/2003 | 9.60 | 8.10 | 8.31 | 03/2006 | 20.46 | 15.39 | 19.02 |
| 06/2000 | 9.27 | 6.02 | 8.85 | 06/2003 | 8.29 | 6.58 | 6.58 | 06/2006 | 19.28 | 15.52 | 17.05 |
| 09/2000 | 11.60 | 9.08 | 10.01 | 09/2003 | 7.89 | 6.47 | 7.08 | 09/2006 | 17.91 | 11.36 | 12.31 |
| 12/2000 | 11.84 | 9.26 | 10.64 | 12/2003 | 7.43 | 6.33 | 6.35 | 12/2006 | 13.14 | 11.46 | 12.80 |
| 03/2001 | 10.99 | 8.85 | 8.85 | 03/2004 | 8.96 | 6.22 | 8.07 | 03/2007 | 12.44 | 10.89 | 11.03 |
| 06/2001 | 10.28 | 8.83 | 10.25 | 06/2004 | 8.92 | 7.77 | 8.92 | 06/2007 | 11.77 | 10.41 | 11.73 |
| 09/2001 | 9.78 | 8.46 | 8.64 | 09/2004 | 9.83 | 8.51 | 9.83 | 09/2007 | 12.72 | 11.23 | 11.83 |
| 12/2001 | 8.43 | 6.76 | 7.96 | 12/2004 | 10.49 | 9.02 | 10.45 | 12/2007 | 13.22 | 11.19 | 13.02 |
| 03/2002 | 8.46 | 6.30 | 7.47 | 03/2005 | 10.86 | 9.98 | 10.55 | 03/2008 | 16.70 | 12.83 | 13.23 |
| 06/2002 | 7.74 | 6.67 | 7.19 | 06/2005 | 10.88 | 9.89 | 10.88 | 06/2008 | 14.68 | 11.54 | 14.51 |
| 09/2002 | 8.95 | 7.60 | 8.61 | 09/2005 | 12.26 | 10.55 | 12.26 | 09/2008 | 16.13 | 13.76 | 15.05 |
| 12/2002 | 9.43 | 8.17 | 8.42 | 12/2005 | 16.03 | 12.23 | 15.98 | 12/2008 | 15.32 | 11.63 | 12.75 |

World Raw #11, NY.    *Source: IntercontinentalExchange (ICE); formerly New York Board of Trade*

# COTTON

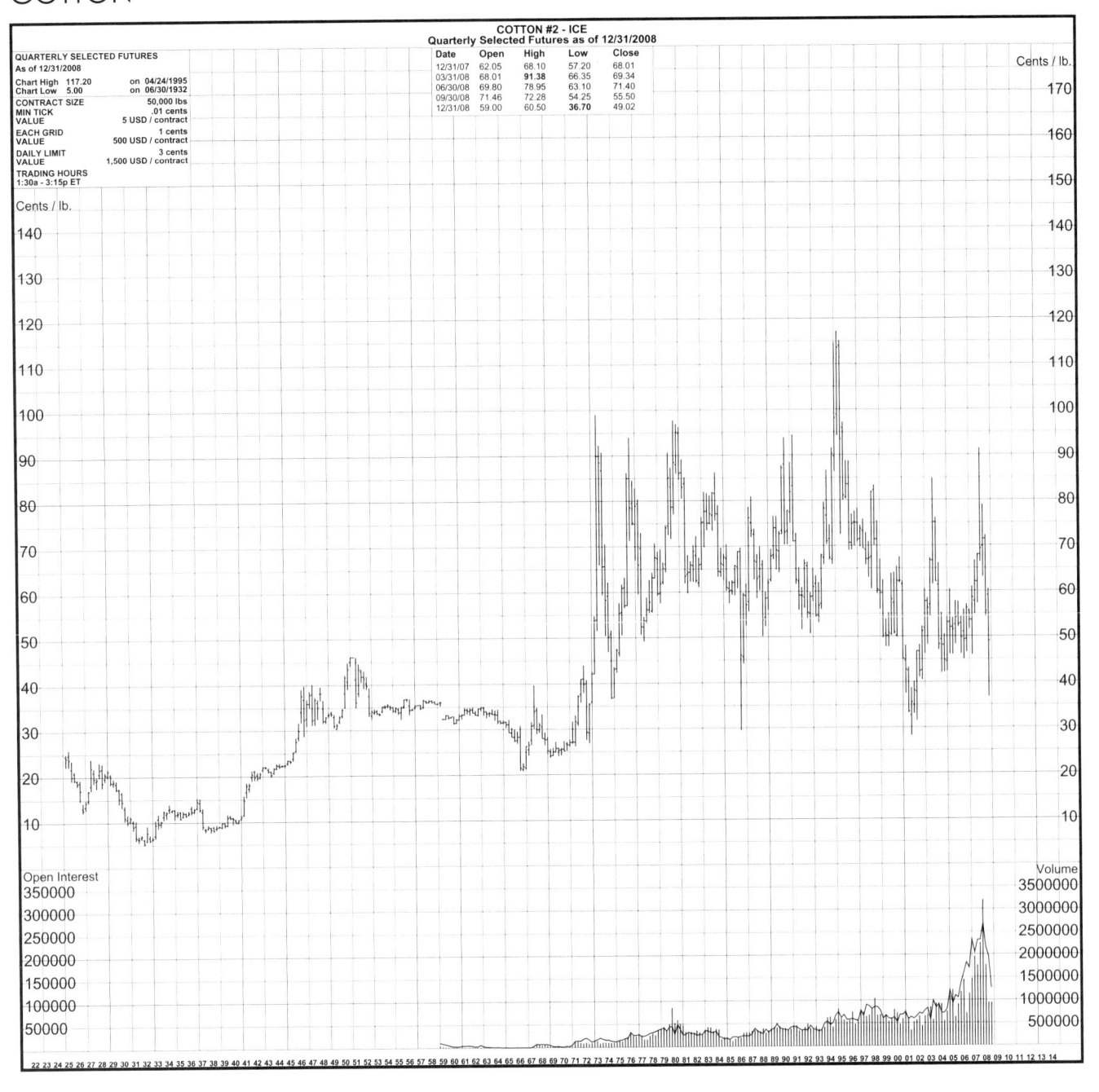

**COTTON #2 - ICE**
Quarterly Selected Futures as of 12/31/2008

| Date | Open | High | Low | Close |
|---|---|---|---|---|
| 12/31/07 | 62.05 | 68.10 | 57.20 | 68.01 |
| 03/31/08 | 68.01 | 91.38 | 66.35 | 69.34 |
| 06/30/08 | 69.80 | 78.95 | 63.10 | 71.40 |
| 09/30/08 | 71.46 | 72.28 | 54.25 | 55.50 |
| 12/31/08 | 59.00 | 60.50 | 36.70 | 49.02 |

**QUARTERLY SELECTED FUTURES**
As of 12/31/2008
Chart High 117.20 on 04/24/1995
Chart Low 5.00 on 06/30/1932
CONTRACT SIZE 50,000 lbs
MIN TICK .01 cents
EACH GRID VALUE 5 USD / contract
EACH GRID VALUE 1 cents
DAILY LIMIT 3 cents
VALUE 500 USD / contract
VALUE 1,500 USD / contract
TRADING HOURS 1:30a - 3:15p ET

## Annual High, Low and Settle of Cotton #2 Futures — In Cents per Pound

| Year | High | Low | Settle | Year | High | Low | Settle | Year | High | Low | Settle |
|---|---|---|---|---|---|---|---|---|---|---|---|
| 1925 | 25.51 | 19.31 | 19.31 | 1939 | 10.56 | 8.79 | 10.56 | 1953 | 33.41 | 32.49 | 32.63 |
| 1926 | 20.04 | 11.81 | 11.81 | 1940 | 10.80 | 9.38 | 9.86 | 1954 | 34.94 | 33.21 | 34.94 |
| 1927 | 21.19 | 12.72 | 18.99 | 1941 | 17.26 | 10.10 | 17.26 | 1955 | 34.05 | 32.93 | 33.70 |
| 1928 | 21.25 | 17.60 | 19.07 | 1942 | 20.23 | 18.57 | 19.67 | 1956 | 35.52 | 31.94 | 32.02 |
| 1929 | 19.78 | 16.64 | 16.64 | 1943 | 21.20 | 19.68 | 19.68 | 1957 | 33.40 | 31.96 | 33.40 |
| 1930 | 16.56 | 9.55 | 9.55 | 1944 | 21.64 | 20.17 | 21.55 | 1958 | 33.35 | 32.95 | 32.95 |
| 1931 | 10.54 | 5.97 | 5.99 | 1945 | 24.51 | 21.59 | 24.51 | 1959 | 33.31 | 29.92 | 33.21 |
| 1932 | 7.55 | 5.13 | 5.85 | 1946 | 36.88 | 24.71 | 32.38 | 1960 | 33.20 | 31.12 | 32.12 |
| 1933 | 10.67 | 5.99 | 10.05 | 1947 | 37.52 | 31.56 | 35.79 | 1961 | 34.84 | 31.98 | 34.12 |
| 1934 | 13.36 | 11.09 | 12.94 | 1948 | 37.55 | 31.18 | 32.17 | 1962 | 34.93 | 32.95 | 34.64 |
| 1935 | 12.89 | 10.76 | 12.02 | 1949 | 32.97 | 29.61 | 30.30 | 1963 | 35.10 | 32.50 | 33.60 |
| 1936 | 13.30 | 11.66 | 13.17 | 1950 | 42.59 | 31.03 | 42.59 | 1964 | 34.50 | 31.15 | 31.43 |
| 1937 | 14.77 | 8.26 | 8.58 | 1951 | 45.23 | 34.97 | 42.23 | 1965 | 32.10 | 28.25 | 28.25 |
| 1938 | 9.34 | 8.41 | 8.74 | 1952 | 41.88 | 33.09 | 33.09 | 1966 | 30.75 | 20.80 | 21.80 |

Futures data begins 07/01/1959. Data continued on page 162. *Source: IntercontinentalExchange (ICE); formerly New York Board of Trade*

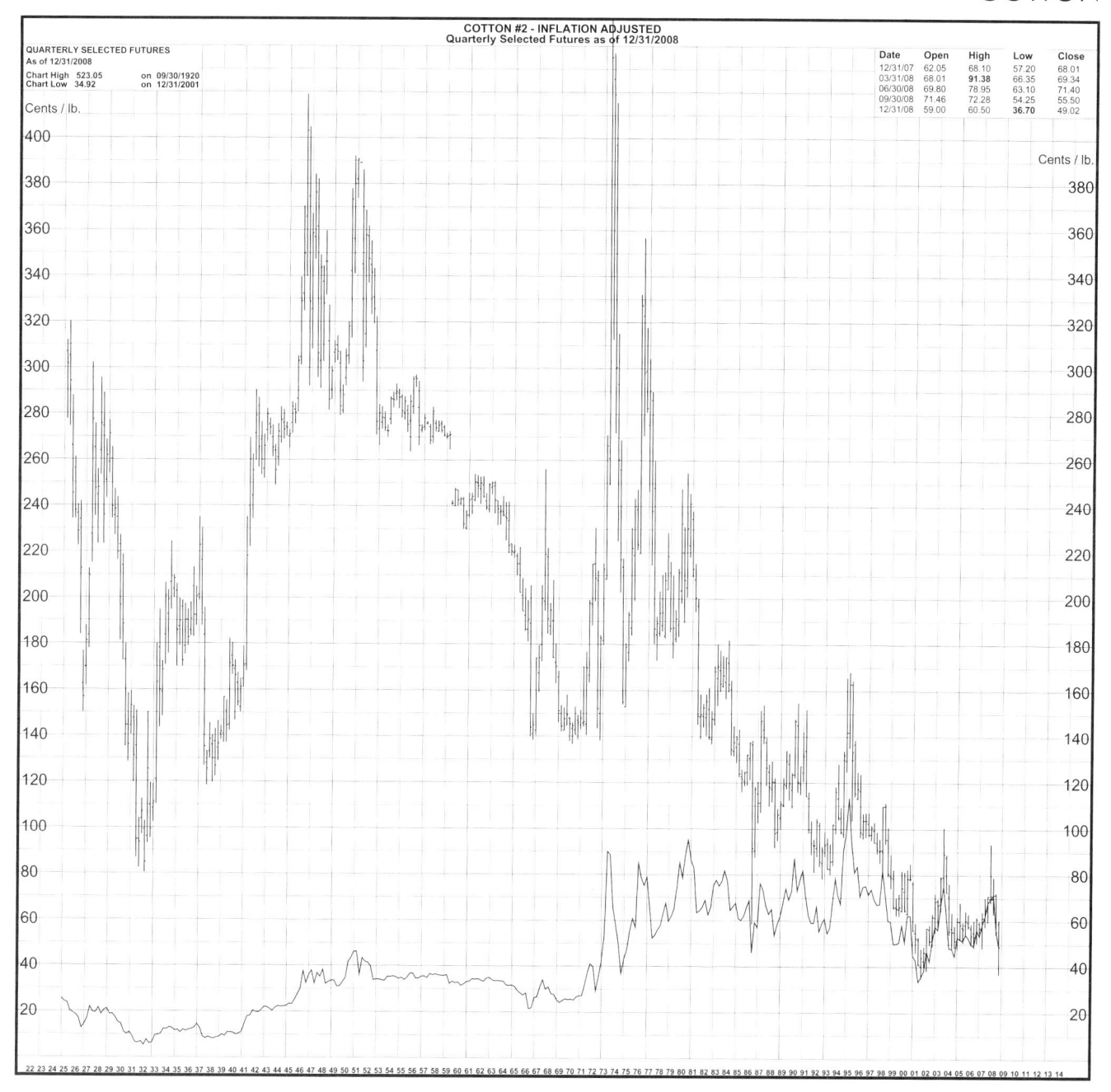

# COTTON

**COTTON #2 - INFLATION ADJUSTED**
Quarterly Selected Futures as of 12/31/2008

QUARTERLY SELECTED FUTURES
As of 12/31/2008
Chart High 523.05 on 09/30/1920
Chart Low 34.92 on 12/31/2001
Cents / lb.

| Date | Open | High | Low | Close |
|---|---|---|---|---|
| 12/31/07 | 62.05 | 68.10 | 57.20 | 68.01 |
| 03/31/08 | 68.01 | 91.38 | 66.35 | 69.34 |
| 06/30/08 | 69.80 | 78.95 | 63.10 | 71.40 |
| 09/30/08 | 71.46 | 72.28 | 54.25 | 55.50 |
| 12/31/08 | 59.00 | 60.50 | 36.70 | 49.02 |

## Annual High, Low and Settle of Cotton    In Cents per Pound

| Year | High | Low | Settle | Year | High | Low | Settle | Year | High | Low | Settle |
|---|---|---|---|---|---|---|---|---|---|---|---|
| 1925 | 25.51 | 19.31 | 19.31 | 1939 | 10.56 | 8.79 | 10.56 | 1953 | 33.41 | 32.49 | 32.63 |
| 1926 | 20.04 | 11.81 | 11.81 | 1940 | 10.80 | 9.38 | 9.86 | 1954 | 34.94 | 33.21 | 34.94 |
| 1927 | 21.19 | 12.72 | 18.99 | 1941 | 17.26 | 10.10 | 17.26 | 1955 | 34.05 | 32.93 | 33.70 |
| 1928 | 21.25 | 17.60 | 19.07 | 1942 | 20.23 | 18.57 | 19.67 | 1956 | 35.52 | 31.94 | 32.02 |
| 1929 | 19.78 | 16.64 | 16.64 | 1943 | 21.20 | 19.68 | 19.68 | 1957 | 33.40 | 31.96 | 33.40 |
| 1930 | 16.56 | 9.55 | 9.55 | 1944 | 21.64 | 20.17 | 21.55 | 1958 | 33.35 | 32.95 | 32.95 |
| 1931 | 10.54 | 5.97 | 5.99 | 1945 | 24.51 | 21.59 | 24.51 | 1959 | 33.06 | 29.92 | 30.09 |
| 1932 | 7.55 | 5.13 | 5.85 | 1946 | 36.88 | 24.71 | 32.38 | 1960 | 30.59 | 28.57 | 28.57 |
| 1933 | 10.67 | 5.99 | 10.05 | 1947 | 37.52 | 31.56 | 35.79 | 1961 | 32.35 | 28.60 | 32.34 |
| 1934 | 13.36 | 11.09 | 12.94 | 1948 | 37.55 | 31.18 | 32.17 | 1962 | 32.93 | 31.77 | 31.89 |
| 1935 | 12.89 | 10.76 | 12.02 | 1949 | 32.97 | 29.61 | 30.30 | 1963 | 32.83 | 31.80 | 31.84 |
| 1936 | 13.30 | 11.66 | 13.17 | 1950 | 42.59 | 31.03 | 42.59 | 1964 | 32.05 | 29.23 | 29.23 |
| 1937 | 14.77 | 8.26 | 8.58 | 1951 | 45.23 | 34.97 | 42.23 | 1965 | 29.57 | 28.12 | 28.12 |
| 1938 | 9.34 | 8.41 | 8.74 | 1952 | 41.88 | 33.09 | 33.09 | 1966 | 28.13 | 20.17 | 20.17 |

1-1/16" 7-Market average.    Data continued on page 163.    *Source: IntercontinentalExchange (ICE); formerly New York Board of Trade*

# COTTON

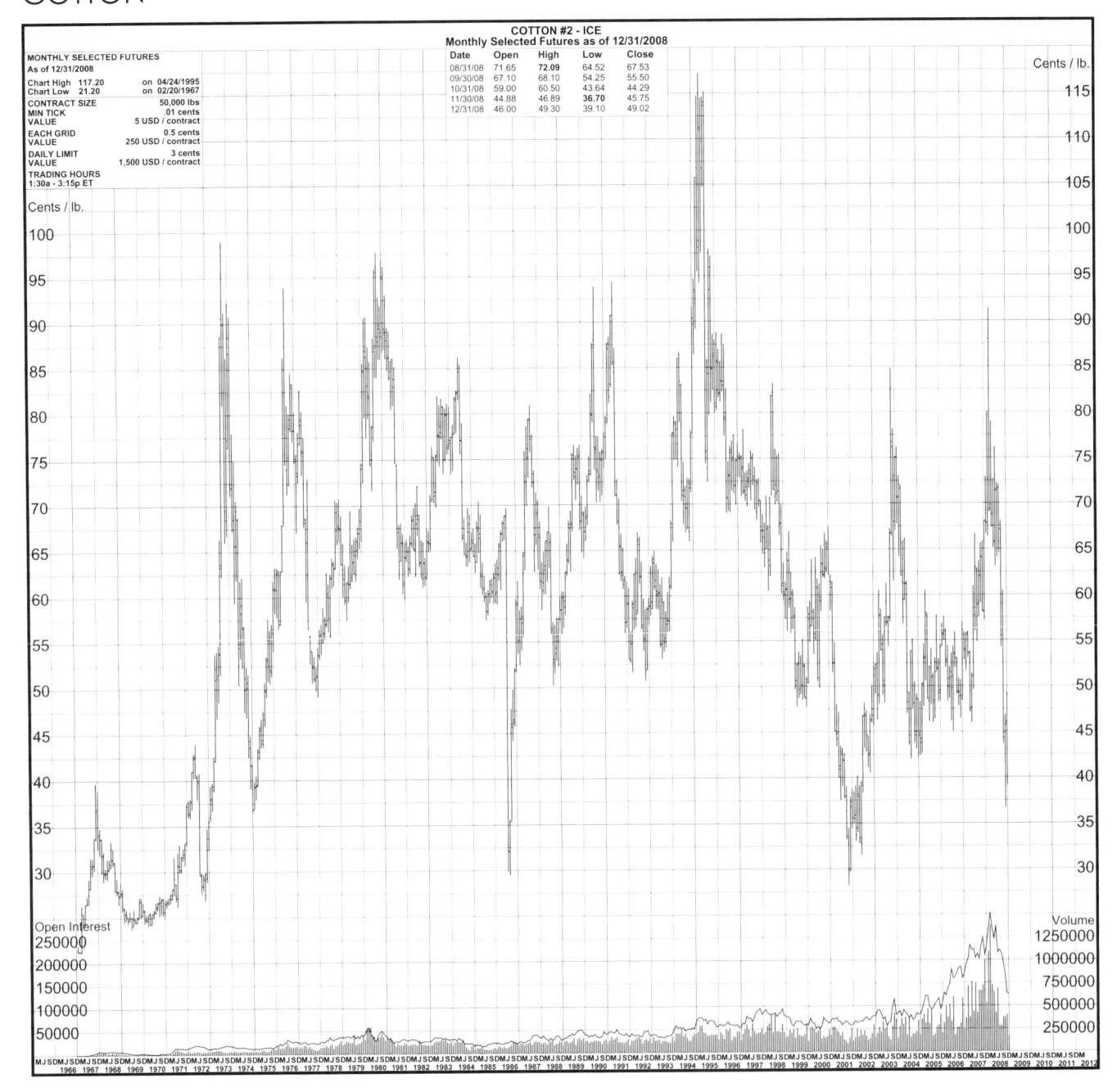

**MONTHLY SELECTED FUTURES**
As of 12/31/2008
Chart High 117.20 on 04/24/1995
Chart Low 21.20 on 02/20/1967
CONTRACT SIZE 50,000 lbs
MIN TICK .01 cents
VALUE 5 USD / contract
EACH GRID 0.5 cents
VALUE 250 USD / contract
DAILY LIMIT 3 cents
VALUE 1,500 USD / contract
TRADING HOURS 1:30a - 3:15p ET

**COTTON #2 - ICE**
Monthly Selected Futures as of 12/31/2008

| Date | Open | High | Low | Close |
|---|---|---|---|---|
| 08/31/08 | 71.65 | 72.09 | 64.52 | 67.53 |
| 09/30/08 | 67.10 | 68.10 | 54.25 | 55.50 |
| 10/31/08 | 59.00 | 60.50 | 43.64 | 44.29 |
| 11/30/08 | 44.88 | 46.89 | 36.70 | 45.75 |
| 12/31/08 | 46.00 | 49.30 | 39.10 | 49.02 |

## Annual High, Low and Settle of Cotton #2 Futures    In Cents per Pound

| Year | High | Low | Settle | Year | High | Low | Settle | Year | High | Low | Settle |
|---|---|---|---|---|---|---|---|---|---|---|---|
| 1967 | 39.70 | 21.20 | 33.95 | 1981 | 96.20 | 59.67 | 64.27 | 1995 | 117.20 | 72.50 | 81.05 |
| 1968 | 34.79 | 26.45 | 27.67 | 1982 | 72.24 | 61.00 | 65.92 | 1996 | 88.80 | 69.00 | 75.15 |
| 1969 | 28.19 | 23.75 | 25.75 | 1983 | 81.95 | 64.90 | 77.11 | 1997 | 78.25 | 65.75 | 67.07 |
| 1970 | 27.41 | 24.08 | 26.58 | 1984 | 86.25 | 63.30 | 66.17 | 1998 | 83.30 | 59.45 | 60.36 |
| 1971 | 37.46 | 26.15 | 37.20 | 1985 | 70.45 | 57.40 | 62.06 | 1999 | 67.00 | 47.75 | 50.74 |
| 1972 | 43.98 | 26.84 | 35.50 | 1986 | 69.70 | 29.50 | 59.28 | 2000 | 67.50 | 49.80 | 62.28 |
| 1973 | 99.00 | 35.60 | 88.50 | 1987 | 80.90 | 52.50 | 66.76 | 2001 | 62.20 | 28.20 | 35.59 |
| 1974 | 90.79 | 36.53 | 36.80 | 1988 | 69.85 | 50.20 | 58.49 | 2002 | 52.25 | 31.47 | 51.16 |
| 1975 | 61.75 | 36.85 | 60.87 | 1989 | 76.60 | 55.85 | 69.07 | 2003 | 84.80 | 46.30 | 75.07 |
| 1976 | 93.95 | 56.50 | 75.20 | 1990 | 93.90 | 64.15 | 77.80 | 2004 | 76.18 | 42.00 | 44.77 |
| 1977 | 82.75 | 49.10 | 53.69 | 1991 | 94.45 | 55.85 | 59.17 | 2005 | 60.50 | 42.40 | 54.19 |
| 1978 | 70.73 | 53.19 | 67.57 | 1992 | 67.00 | 50.68 | 58.86 | 2006 | 57.65 | 45.00 | 56.19 |
| 1979 | 74.70 | 57.50 | 74.06 | 1993 | 68.18 | 53.10 | 67.88 | 2007 | 68.10 | 45.94 | 68.01 |
| 1980 | 97.77 | 71.60 | 95.12 | 1994 | 91.60 | 65.90 | 90.35 | 2008 | 91.38 | 36.70 | 49.02 |

Data continued from page 160.    Source: *IntercontinentalExchange (ICE); formerly New York Board of Trade*

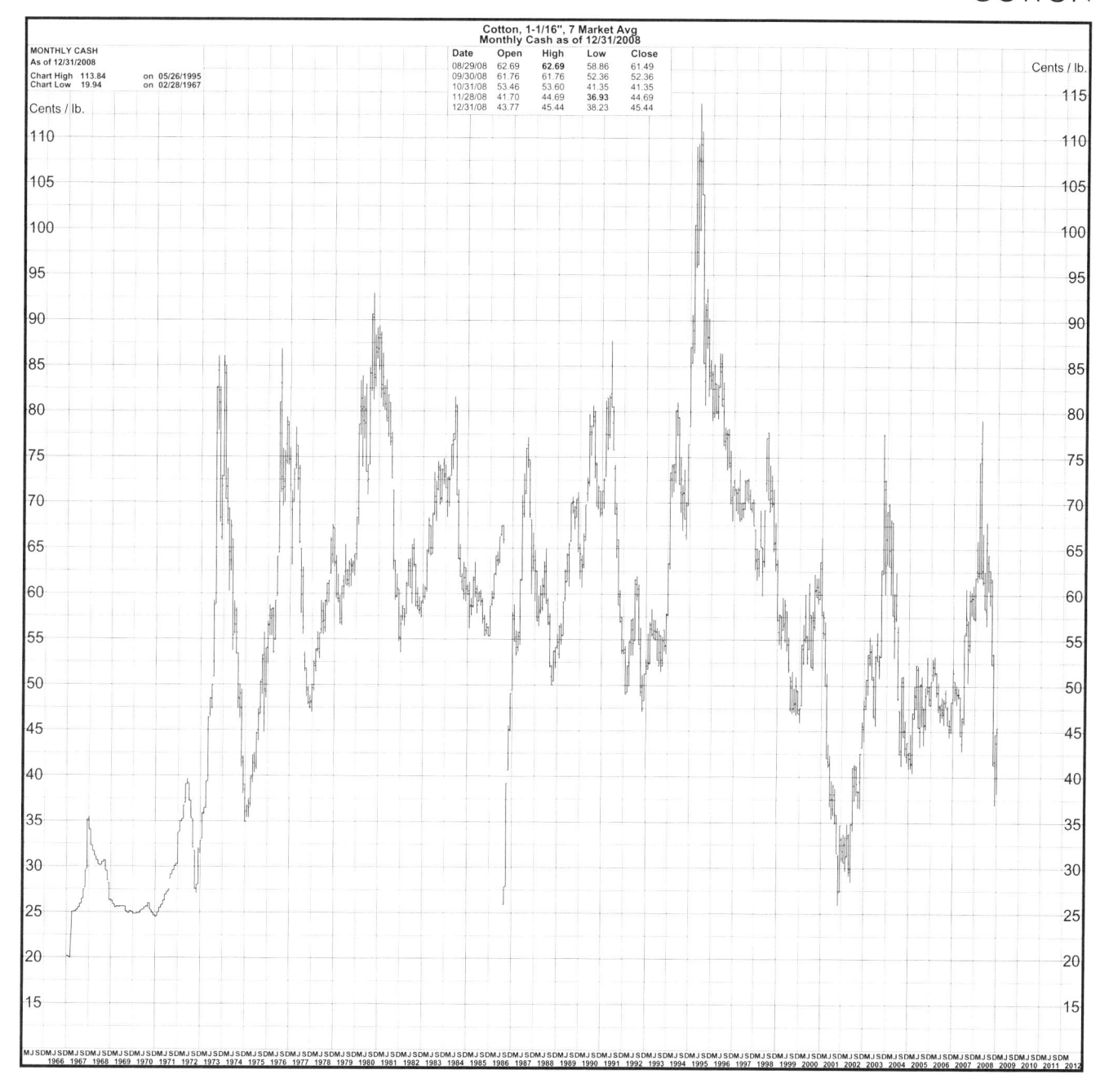

# COTTON

**Cotton, 1-1/16", 7 Market Avg — Monthly Cash as of 12/31/2008**

| Date | Open | High | Low | Close |
|---|---|---|---|---|
| 08/29/08 | 62.69 | 62.69 | 58.86 | 61.49 |
| 09/30/08 | 61.76 | 61.76 | 52.36 | 52.36 |
| 10/31/08 | 53.46 | 53.60 | 41.35 | 41.35 |
| 11/28/08 | 41.70 | 44.69 | 36.93 | 44.69 |
| 12/31/08 | 43.77 | 45.44 | 38.23 | 45.44 |

MONTHLY CASH — As of 12/31/2008
Chart High 113.84 on 05/26/1995
Chart Low 19.94 on 02/28/1967

## Annual High, Low and Settle of Cotton — In Cents per Pound

| Year | High | Low | Settle | Year | High | Low | Settle | Year | High | Low | Settle |
|---|---|---|---|---|---|---|---|---|---|---|---|
| 1967 | 35.44 | 19.94 | 34.09 | 1981 | 88.72 | 53.51 | 56.65 | 1995 | 113.84 | 78.99 | 79.86 |
| 1968 | 34.01 | 26.22 | 26.25 | 1982 | 66.04 | 56.40 | 59.68 | 1996 | 86.48 | 68.00 | 71.43 |
| 1969 | 26.25 | 24.83 | 24.83 | 1983 | 74.84 | 59.33 | 71.61 | 1997 | 73.71 | 62.73 | 63.84 |
| 1970 | 25.99 | 24.46 | 24.53 | 1984 | 81.61 | 59.17 | 60.31 | 1998 | 77.79 | 57.06 | 57.19 |
| 1971 | 33.67 | 24.58 | 33.67 | 1985 | 63.50 | 55.34 | 58.60 | 1999 | 59.70 | 45.94 | 47.53 |
| 1972 | 39.69 | 27.08 | 32.81 | 1986 | 67.48 | 25.94 | 57.60 | 2000 | 66.27 | 47.84 | 57.70 |
| 1973 | 86.08 | 33.05 | 85.27 | 1987 | 77.17 | 53.18 | 62.48 | 2001 | 58.22 | 25.94 | 31.10 |
| 1974 | 84.98 | 34.93 | 34.93 | 1988 | 64.96 | 50.05 | 54.71 | 2002 | 48.48 | 28.44 | 47.83 |
| 1975 | 56.93 | 35.39 | 56.48 | 1989 | 71.19 | 52.91 | 64.41 | 2003 | 77.66 | 45.56 | 69.09 |
| 1976 | 86.84 | 53.43 | 71.87 | 1990 | 80.67 | 60.69 | 71.29 | 2004 | 69.99 | 40.87 | 42.67 |
| 1977 | 78.26 | 47.02 | 49.62 | 1991 | 87.82 | 53.39 | 53.55 | 2005 | 53.20 | 40.39 | 50.49 |
| 1978 | 67.57 | 49.27 | 63.47 | 1992 | 62.02 | 47.11 | 52.11 | 2006 | 53.25 | 44.34 | 51.46 |
| 1979 | 68.33 | 56.46 | 68.33 | 1993 | 63.34 | 51.48 | 63.34 | 2007 | 61.86 | 42.84 | 61.86 |
| 1980 | 92.96 | 67.54 | 88.37 | 1994 | 87.07 | 62.74 | 87.07 | 2008 | 79.16 | 36.93 | 45.44 |

1-1/16" 7-Market average. Data continued from page 161. *Source: IntercontinentalExchange (ICE); formerly New York Board of Trade*

# COTTON

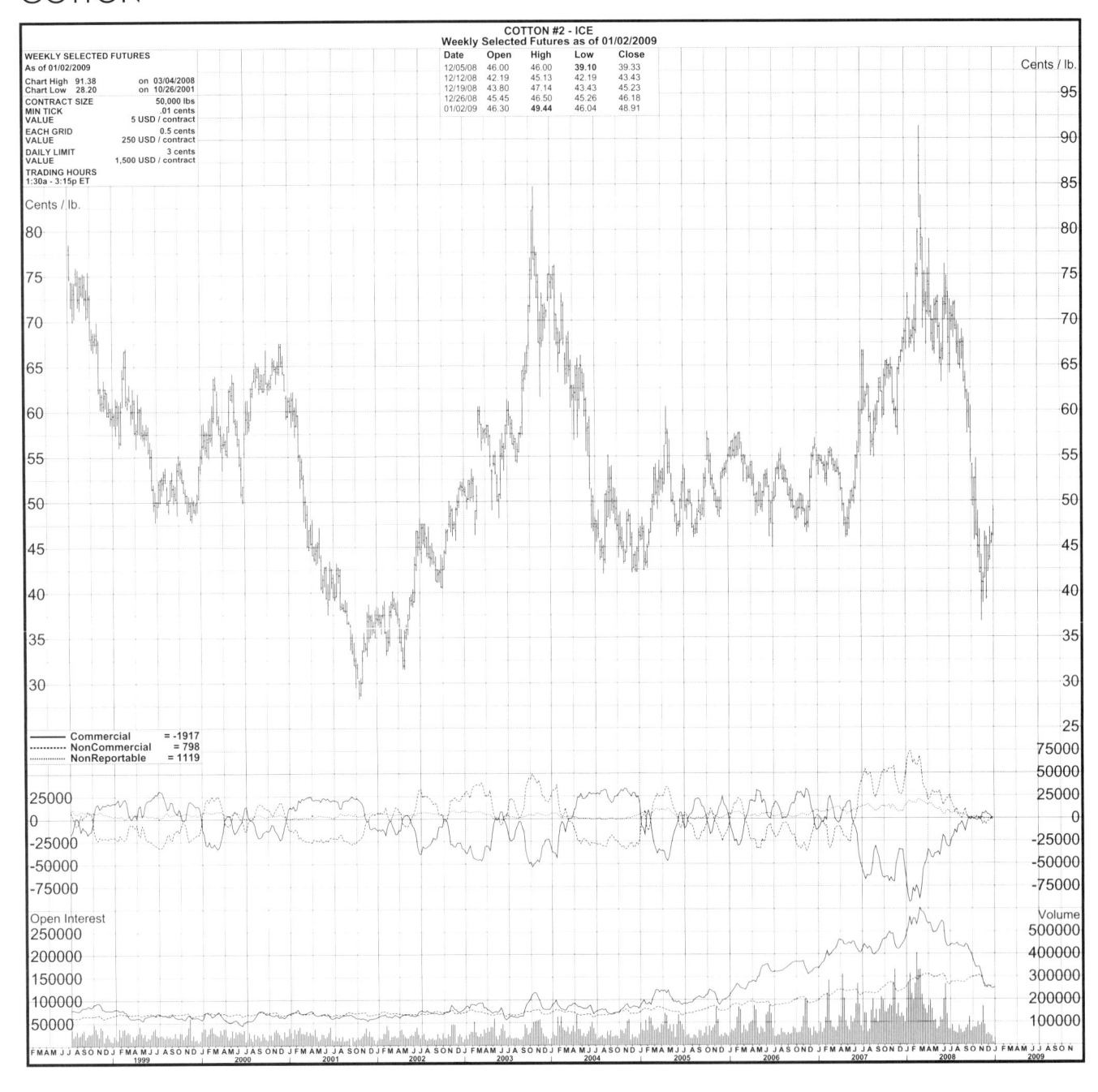

## Quarterly High, Low and Settle of Cotton #2 Futures   In Cents per Pound

| Quarter | High | Low | Settle | Quarter | High | Low | Settle | Quarter | High | Low | Settle |
|---|---|---|---|---|---|---|---|---|---|---|---|
| 03/2000 | 63.95 | 50.25 | 58.14 | 03/2003 | 60.55 | 46.30 | 57.71 | 03/2006 | 57.65 | 52.02 | 52.65 |
| 06/2000 | 64.15 | 50.50 | 50.88 | 06/2003 | 58.50 | 48.15 | 56.20 | 06/2006 | 54.45 | 46.12 | 49.75 |
| 09/2000 | 65.45 | 49.80 | 62.25 | 09/2003 | 67.25 | 54.30 | 66.75 | 09/2006 | 55.90 | 45.00 | 49.30 |
| 12/2000 | 67.50 | 61.80 | 62.28 | 12/2003 | 84.80 | 61.50 | 75.07 | 12/2006 | 57.05 | 46.50 | 56.19 |
| 03/2001 | 62.20 | 45.05 | 45.09 | 03/2004 | 76.18 | 62.10 | 62.10 | 03/2007 | 55.95 | 51.65 | 53.57 |
| 06/2001 | 48.10 | 37.50 | 42.75 | 06/2004 | 66.19 | 47.00 | 48.25 | 06/2007 | 61.00 | 45.94 | 58.50 |
| 09/2001 | 43.25 | 33.15 | 33.50 | 09/2004 | 55.20 | 42.00 | 48.10 | 09/2007 | 66.70 | 54.81 | 62.05 |
| 12/2001 | 38.75 | 28.20 | 35.59 | 12/2004 | 50.50 | 42.10 | 44.77 | 12/2007 | 68.10 | 57.20 | 68.01 |
| 03/2002 | 40.19 | 33.01 | 38.16 | 03/2005 | 54.60 | 42.40 | 53.03 | 03/2008 | 91.38 | 66.35 | 69.34 |
| 06/2002 | 46.80 | 31.47 | 46.80 | 06/2005 | 60.50 | 46.10 | 52.00 | 06/2008 | 78.95 | 63.10 | 71.40 |
| 09/2002 | 48.20 | 41.05 | 42.40 | 09/2005 | 54.10 | 46.00 | 51.50 | 09/2008 | 72.28 | 54.25 | 55.50 |
| 12/2002 | 52.25 | 40.50 | 51.16 | 12/2005 | 57.80 | 48.25 | 54.19 | 12/2008 | 60.50 | 36.70 | 49.02 |

*Source: IntercontinentalExchange (ICE); formerly New York Board of Trade*

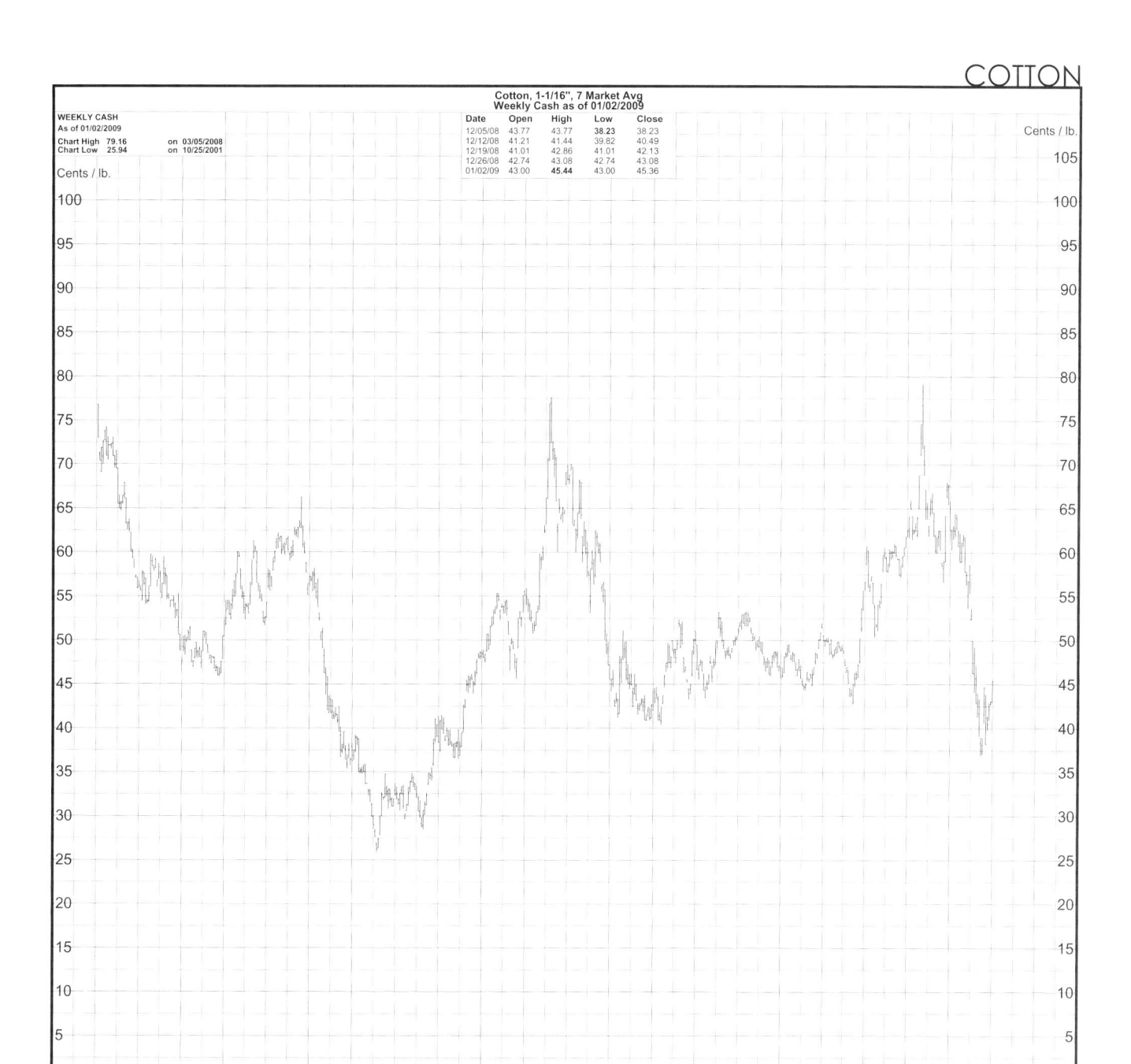

# COTTON

**WEEKLY CASH**
As of 01/02/2009
Chart High 79.16 on 03/05/2008
Chart Low 25.94 on 10/25/2001
Cents / lb.

Cotton, 1-1/16", 7 Market Avg
Weekly Cash as of 01/02/2009

| Date | Open | High | Low | Close |
|---|---|---|---|---|
| 12/05/08 | 43.77 | 43.77 | 38.23 | 38.23 |
| 12/12/08 | 41.21 | 41.44 | 39.82 | 40.49 |
| 12/19/08 | 41.01 | 42.86 | 41.01 | 42.13 |
| 12/26/08 | 42.74 | 43.08 | 42.74 | 43.08 |
| 01/02/09 | 43.00 | 45.44 | 43.00 | 45.36 |

## Quarterly High, Low and Settle of Cotton    In Cents per Pound

| Quarter | High | Low | Settle | Quarter | High | Low | Settle | Quarter | High | Low | Settle |
|---|---|---|---|---|---|---|---|---|---|---|---|
| 03/2000 | 60.04 | 47.84 | 55.28 | 03/2003 | 55.34 | 47.47 | 53.76 | 03/2006 | 53.25 | 48.84 | 49.32 |
| 06/2000 | 61.30 | 52.04 | 52.04 | 06/2003 | 54.56 | 45.56 | 53.18 | 06/2006 | 50.41 | 46.01 | 47.14 |
| 09/2000 | 62.25 | 51.68 | 59.74 | 09/2003 | 62.69 | 50.80 | 62.69 | 09/2006 | 49.63 | 45.68 | 45.68 |
| 12/2000 | 66.27 | 57.70 | 57.70 | 12/2003 | 77.66 | 60.06 | 69.09 | 12/2006 | 51.97 | 44.34 | 51.46 |
| 03/2001 | 58.22 | 42.03 | 42.03 | 03/2004 | 69.99 | 57.71 | 57.71 | 03/2007 | 50.53 | 47.93 | 49.09 |
| 06/2001 | 43.63 | 35.39 | 37.57 | 06/2004 | 62.43 | 48.43 | 48.64 | 06/2007 | 55.64 | 42.84 | 55.64 |
| 09/2001 | 39.24 | 31.63 | 31.63 | 09/2004 | 51.11 | 41.19 | 44.43 | 09/2007 | 60.67 | 50.34 | 59.39 |
| 12/2001 | 34.73 | 25.94 | 31.10 | 12/2004 | 46.19 | 40.87 | 42.67 | 12/2007 | 61.86 | 57.25 | 61.86 |
| 03/2002 | 34.86 | 29.66 | 33.33 | 03/2005 | 49.97 | 40.39 | 49.02 | 03/2008 | 79.16 | 61.41 | 61.92 |
| 06/2002 | 41.04 | 28.44 | 41.04 | 06/2005 | 52.30 | 43.28 | 50.23 | 06/2008 | 67.98 | 56.58 | 65.77 |
| 09/2002 | 41.39 | 36.61 | 38.37 | 09/2005 | 51.06 | 43.46 | 48.94 | 09/2008 | 64.38 | 52.36 | 52.36 |
| 12/2002 | 48.48 | 36.56 | 47.83 | 12/2005 | 53.20 | 47.89 | 50.49 | 12/2008 | 53.60 | 36.93 | 45.44 |

1-1/16" 7-Market average.    *Source: IntercontinentalExchange (ICE); formerly New York Board of Trade*

# LUMBER

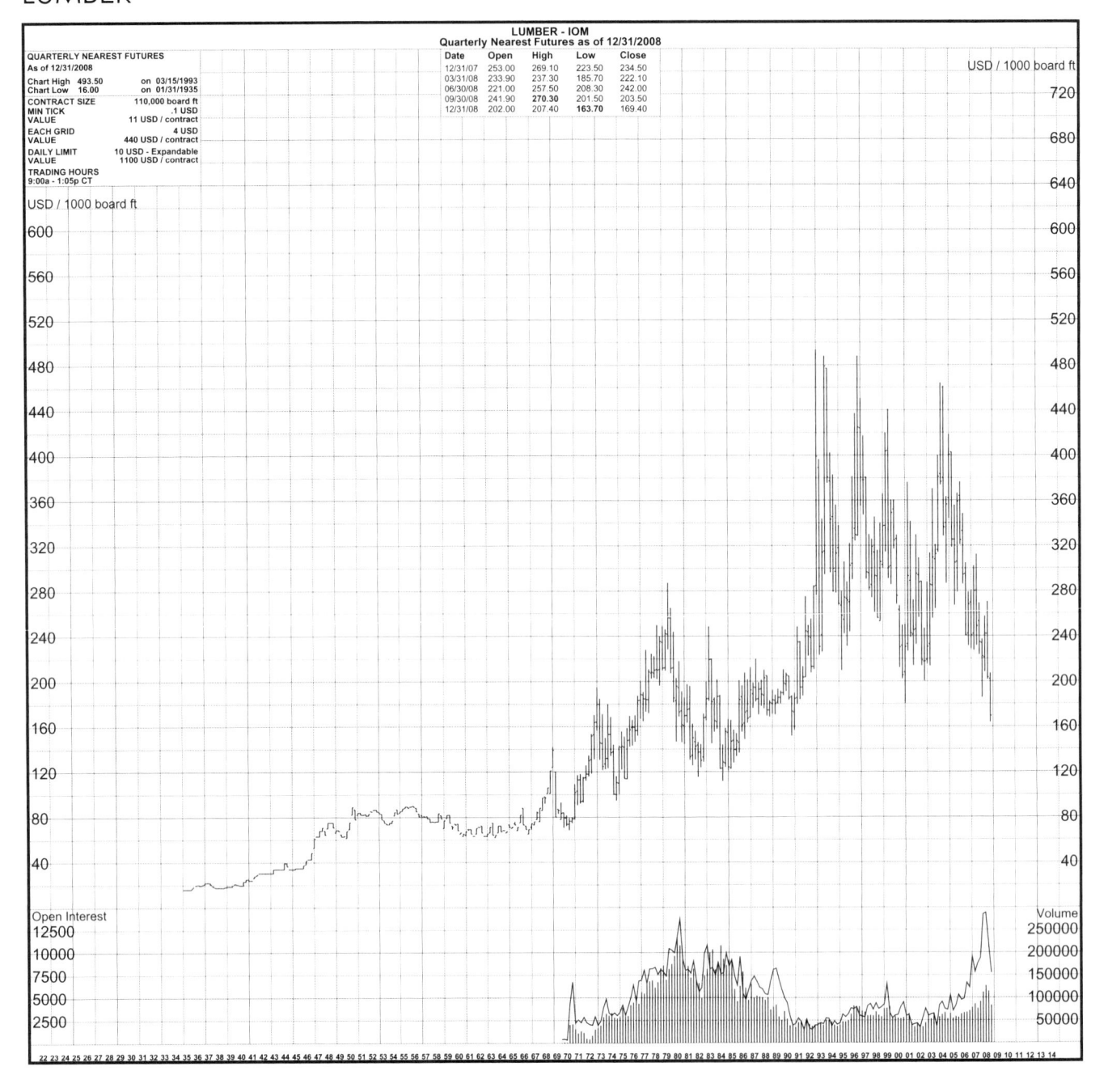

**LUMBER - IOM**
Quarterly Nearest Futures as of 12/31/2008

| Date | Open | High | Low | Close |
|---|---|---|---|---|
| 12/31/07 | 253.00 | 269.10 | 223.50 | 234.50 |
| 03/31/08 | 233.90 | 237.30 | 185.70 | 222.10 |
| 06/30/08 | 221.00 | 257.50 | 208.30 | 242.00 |
| 09/30/08 | 241.90 | 270.30 | 201.50 | 203.50 |
| 12/31/08 | 202.00 | 207.40 | 163.70 | 169.40 |

**QUARTERLY NEAREST FUTURES**
As of 12/31/2008
Chart High 493.50 on 03/15/1993
Chart Low 16.00 on 01/31/1935
CONTRACT SIZE 110,000 board ft
MIN TICK .1 USD
VALUE 11 USD / contract
EACH GRID 4 USD
VALUE 440 USD / contract
DAILY LIMIT 10 USD - Expandable
VALUE 1100 USD / contract
TRADING HOURS 9:00a - 1:05p CT

**Annual High, Low and Settle of Lumber**  In Dollars per 1,000 Board Feet

| Year | High | Low | Settle | Year | High | Low | Settle | Year | High | Low | Settle |
|---|---|---|---|---|---|---|---|---|---|---|---|
| 1925 | | | | 1939 | 21.07 | 18.42 | 21.07 | 1953 | 84.67 | 73.12 | 73.41 |
| 1926 | | | | 1940 | 24.99 | 19.60 | 24.99 | 1954 | 86.85 | 73.40 | 83.05 |
| 1927 | | | | 1941 | 29.20 | 24.01 | 29.20 | 1955 | 89.32 | 83.97 | 88.10 |
| 1928 | | | | 1942 | 30.38 | 30.38 | 30.38 | 1956 | 89.92 | 80.65 | 80.65 |
| 1929 | | | | 1943 | 33.81 | 30.38 | 33.81 | 1957 | 81.99 | 75.61 | 75.61 |
| 1930 | | | | 1944 | 39.20 | 33.81 | 33.81 | 1958 | 83.20 | 75.59 | 78.66 |
| 1931 | | | | 1945 | 34.79 | 33.81 | 34.79 | 1959 | 82.00 | 69.00 | 71.00 |
| 1932 | | | | 1946 | 48.31 | 34.79 | 48.31 | 1960 | 74.00 | 63.00 | 65.00 |
| 1933 | | | | 1947 | 70.59 | 52.74 | 70.59 | 1961 | 69.00 | 63.00 | 63.00 |
| 1934 | | | | 1948 | 75.24 | 64.35 | 70.79 | 1962 | 72.00 | 63.00 | 63.00 |
| 1935 | 16.00 | 16.00 | 16.00 | 1949 | 68.31 | 62.72 | 63.21 | 1963 | 75.00 | 62.00 | 64.00 |
| 1936 | 20.29 | 18.13 | 20.29 | 1950 | 88.95 | 61.48 | 78.09 | 1964 | 72.00 | 66.00 | 67.00 |
| 1937 | 22.05 | 18.50 | 18.50 | 1951 | 83.94 | 81.37 | 81.37 | 1965 | 76.00 | 68.00 | 71.00 |
| 1938 | 18.01 | 17.64 | 18.01 | 1952 | 86.58 | 81.51 | 84.95 | 1966 | 88.00 | 65.00 | 69.00 |

Spruce-Pine-Fir 2x4.   Data continued on page 168.   *Source: CME Group; Chicago Mercantile Exchange*

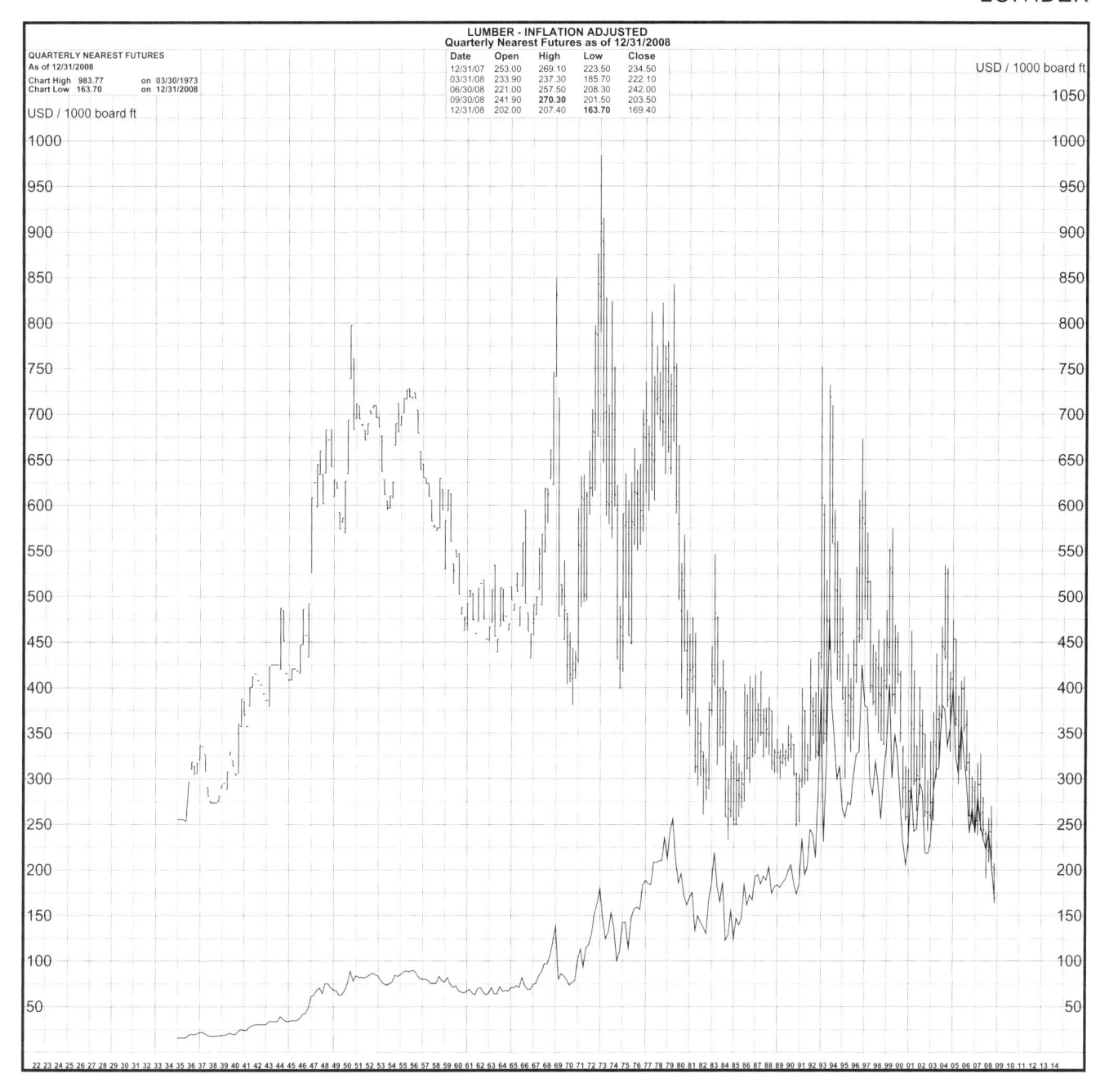

# LUMBER

QUARTERLY NEAREST FUTURES
As of 12/31/2008
Chart High 983.77 on 03/30/1973
Chart Low 163.70 on 12/31/2008
USD / 1000 board ft

LUMBER - INFLATION ADJUSTED
Quarterly Nearest Futures as of 12/31/2008

| Date | Open | High | Low | Close |
|---|---|---|---|---|
| 12/31/07 | 253.00 | 269.10 | 223.50 | 234.50 |
| 03/31/08 | 233.90 | 237.30 | 185.70 | 222.10 |
| 06/30/08 | 221.00 | 257.50 | 208.30 | 242.00 |
| 09/30/08 | 241.90 | 270.30 | 201.50 | 203.50 |
| 12/31/08 | 202.00 | 207.40 | 163.70 | 169.40 |

USD / 1000 board ft

## Annual High, Low and Settle of Lumber    In Dollars per 1,000 Board Feet

| Year | High | Low | Settle | Year | High | Low | Settle | Year | High | Low | Settle |
|---|---|---|---|---|---|---|---|---|---|---|---|
| 1925 | | | | 1939 | 21.07 | 18.42 | 21.07 | 1953 | 84.67 | 73.12 | 73.41 |
| 1926 | | | | 1940 | 24.99 | 19.60 | 24.99 | 1954 | 86.85 | 73.40 | 83.05 |
| 1927 | | | | 1941 | 29.20 | 24.01 | 29.20 | 1955 | 89.32 | 83.97 | 88.10 |
| 1928 | | | | 1942 | 30.38 | 30.38 | 30.38 | 1956 | 89.92 | 80.65 | 80.65 |
| 1929 | | | | 1943 | 33.81 | 30.38 | 33.81 | 1957 | 81.99 | 75.61 | 75.61 |
| 1930 | | | | 1944 | 39.20 | 33.81 | 33.81 | 1958 | 83.20 | 75.59 | 78.66 |
| 1931 | | | | 1945 | 34.79 | 33.81 | 34.79 | 1959 | 82.00 | 69.00 | 71.00 |
| 1932 | | | | 1946 | 48.31 | 34.79 | 48.31 | 1960 | 74.00 | 63.00 | 65.00 |
| 1933 | | | | 1947 | 70.59 | 52.74 | 70.59 | 1961 | 69.00 | 63.00 | 63.00 |
| 1934 | | | | 1948 | 75.24 | 64.35 | 70.79 | 1962 | 72.00 | 63.00 | 63.00 |
| 1935 | 16.00 | 16.00 | 16.00 | 1949 | 68.31 | 62.72 | 63.21 | 1963 | 75.00 | 62.00 | 64.00 |
| 1936 | 20.29 | 18.13 | 20.29 | 1950 | 88.95 | 61.48 | 78.09 | 1964 | 72.00 | 66.00 | 67.00 |
| 1937 | 22.05 | 18.50 | 18.50 | 1951 | 83.94 | 81.37 | 81.37 | 1965 | 76.00 | 68.00 | 71.00 |
| 1938 | 18.01 | 17.64 | 18.01 | 1952 | 86.58 | 81.51 | 84.95 | 1966 | 88.00 | 65.00 | 69.00 |

Spruce-Pine-Fir 2x4.    Data continued on page 169.    *Source: CME Group; Chicago Mercantile Exchange*

167

# LUMBER

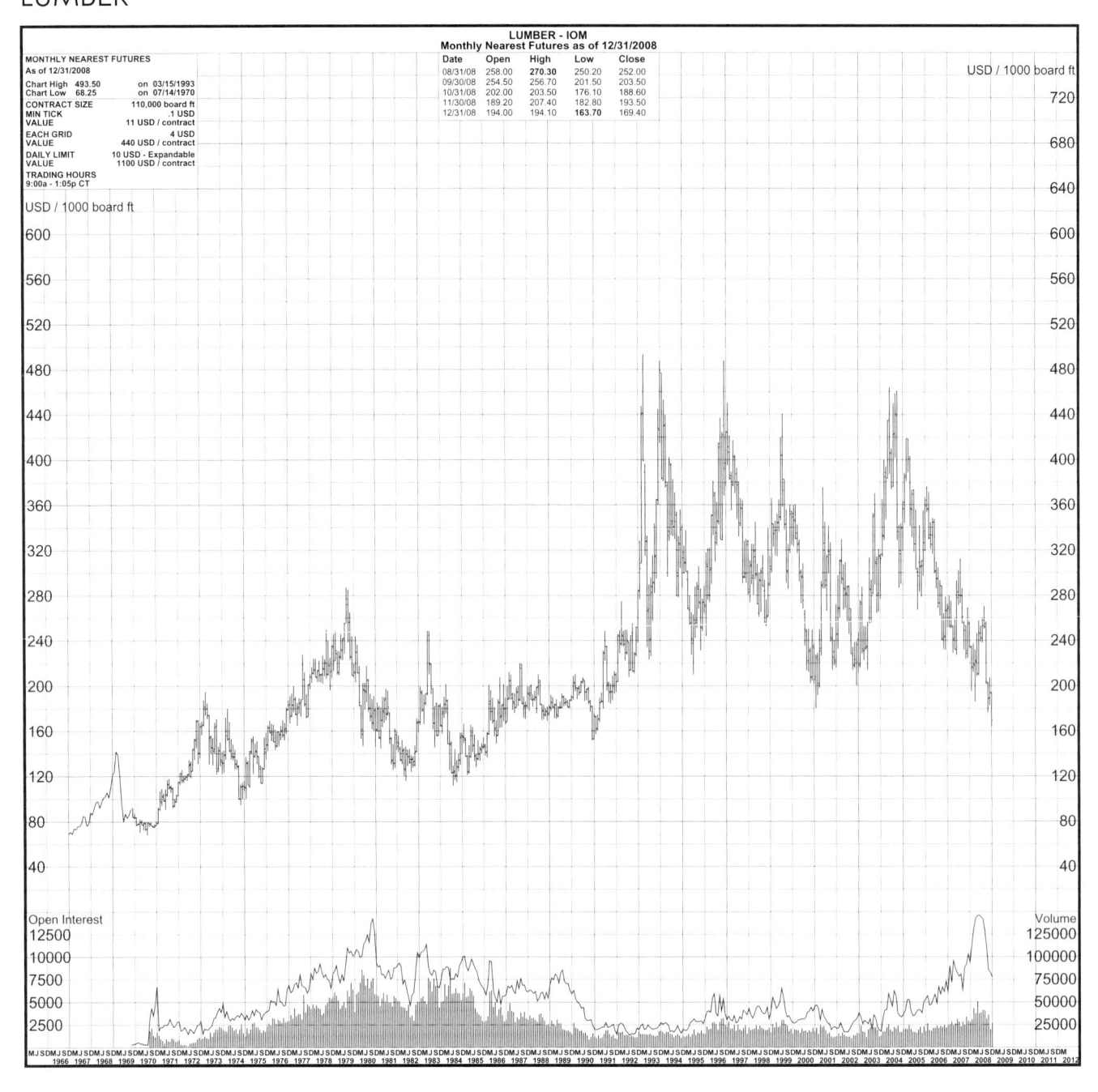

**LUMBER - IOM**
Monthly Nearest Futures as of 12/31/2008

| Date | Open | High | Low | Close |
|---|---|---|---|---|
| 08/31/08 | 258.00 | 270.30 | 250.20 | 252.00 |
| 09/30/08 | 254.50 | 256.70 | 201.50 | 203.50 |
| 10/31/08 | 202.00 | 203.50 | 176.10 | 188.60 |
| 11/30/08 | 189.20 | 207.40 | 182.80 | 193.50 |
| 12/31/08 | 194.00 | 194.10 | 163.70 | 169.40 |

**MONTHLY NEAREST FUTURES**
As of 12/31/2008
Chart High 493.50 on 03/15/1993
Chart Low 68.25 on 07/14/1970
CONTRACT SIZE 110,000 board ft
MIN TICK .1 USD
VALUE 11 USD / contract
EACH GRID 4 USD
VALUE 440 USD / contract
DAILY LIMIT 10 USD - Expandable
VALUE 1100 USD / contract
TRADING HOURS 9:00a - 1:05p CT

### Annual High, Low and Settle of Lumber Futures   In Dollars per 1,000 Board Feet

| Year | High | Low | Settle | Year | High | Low | Settle | Year | High | Low | Settle |
|---|---|---|---|---|---|---|---|---|---|---|---|
| 1967 | 88.00 | 69.00 | 88.00 | 1981 | 197.60 | 125.50 | 149.90 | 1995 | 337.90 | 209.60 | 271.50 |
| 1968 | 121.00 | 86.00 | 121.00 | 1982 | 171.40 | 115.50 | 167.50 | 1996 | 488.00 | 243.70 | 424.70 |
| 1969 | 142.00 | 78.00 | 83.50 | 1983 | 248.50 | 145.00 | 165.00 | 1997 | 450.50 | 280.60 | 282.90 |
| 1970 | 84.00 | 68.25 | 78.70 | 1984 | 201.90 | 111.70 | 155.40 | 1998 | 345.40 | 253.00 | 305.60 |
| 1971 | 118.20 | 78.00 | 114.60 | 1985 | 166.50 | 121.10 | 147.20 | 1999 | 440.80 | 285.60 | 349.00 |
| 1972 | 170.30 | 112.30 | 163.60 | 1986 | 207.90 | 136.60 | 167.10 | 2000 | 360.50 | 202.10 | 205.50 |
| 1973 | 194.70 | 121.50 | 131.80 | 1987 | 219.70 | 168.00 | 192.90 | 2001 | 376.00 | 180.40 | 245.10 |
| 1974 | 180.00 | 94.60 | 110.60 | 1988 | 210.30 | 168.50 | 181.20 | 2002 | 329.80 | 200.50 | 217.70 |
| 1975 | 158.70 | 100.50 | 147.52 | 1989 | 193.50 | 170.30 | 189.90 | 2003 | 370.40 | 213.50 | 312.60 |
| 1976 | 187.50 | 142.20 | 183.20 | 1990 | 210.70 | 151.60 | 173.30 | 2004 | 464.00 | 286.70 | 356.40 |
| 1977 | 228.00 | 164.60 | 208.40 | 1991 | 248.30 | 157.00 | 203.50 | 2005 | 418.50 | 267.00 | 359.00 |
| 1978 | 249.90 | 196.20 | 235.30 | 1992 | 284.70 | 203.50 | 284.10 | 2006 | 376.40 | 231.30 | 268.00 |
| 1979 | 287.30 | 207.10 | 211.50 | 1993 | 493.50 | 223.00 | 479.00 | 2007 | 312.30 | 223.50 | 234.50 |
| 1980 | 243.80 | 146.00 | 161.40 | 1994 | 477.00 | 278.00 | 313.20 | 2008 | 270.30 | 163.70 | 169.40 |

Futures begin trading 10/01/1969.   *Source: CME Group; Chicago Mercantile Exchange*

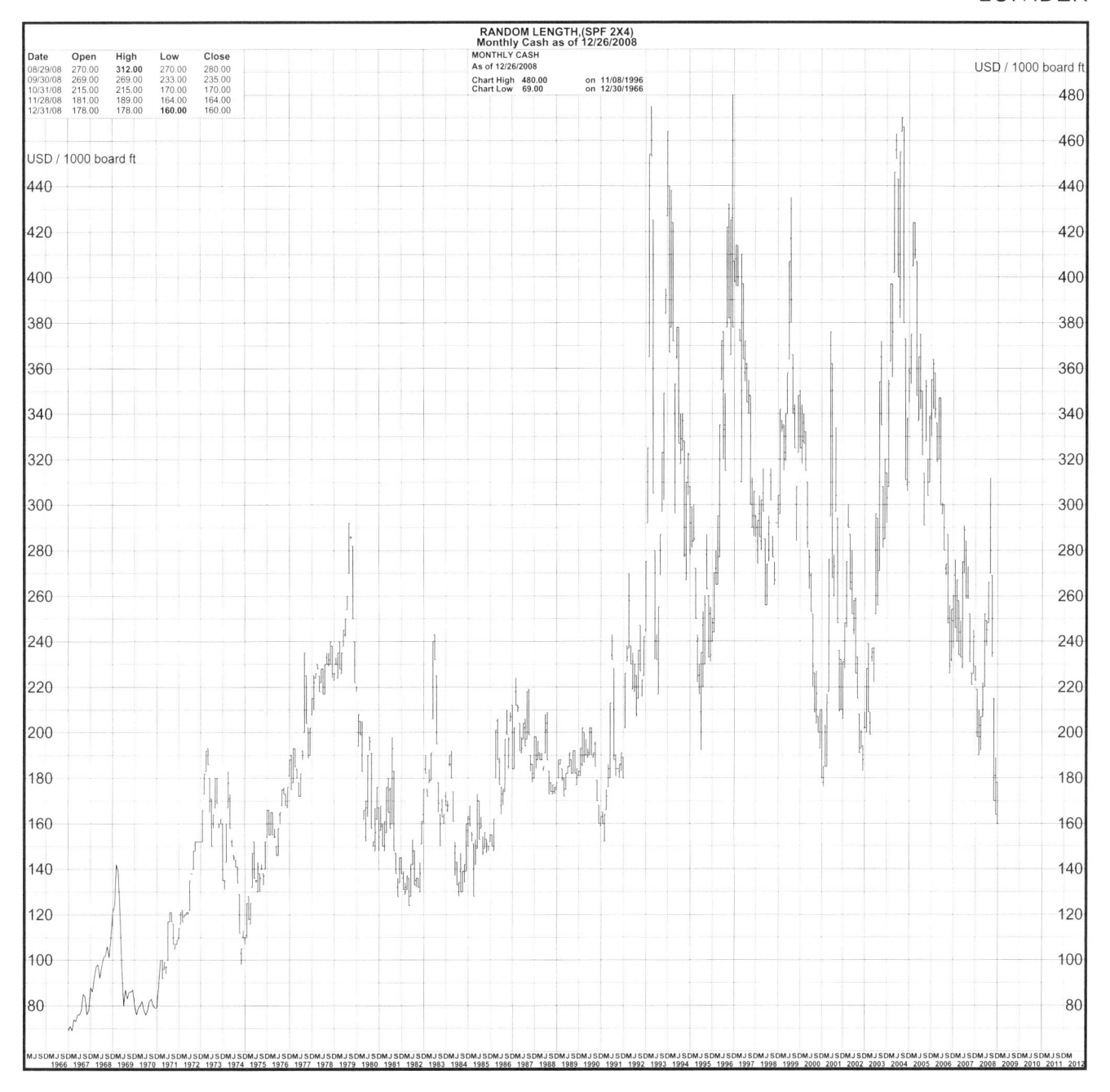

# LUMBER

## Annual High, Low and Settle of Lumber   In Dollars per 1,000 Board Feet

| Year | High | Low | Settle | Year | High | Low | Settle | Year | High | Low | Settle |
|---|---|---|---|---|---|---|---|---|---|---|---|
| 1967 | 88.00 | 69.00 | 88.00 | 1981 | 198.00 | 128.00 | 138.00 | 1995 | 300.00 | 192.00 | 248.00 |
| 1968 | 121.00 | 86.00 | 121.00 | 1982 | 175.00 | 124.00 | 175.00 | 1996 | 480.00 | 244.00 | 398.00 |
| 1969 | 142.00 | 80.00 | 80.00 | 1983 | 243.00 | 150.00 | 168.00 | 1997 | 414.00 | 286.00 | 290.00 |
| 1970 | 83.00 | 76.00 | 79.00 | 1984 | 192.00 | 128.00 | 163.00 | 1998 | 316.00 | 256.00 | 304.00 |
| 1971 | 121.00 | 89.00 | 114.00 | 1985 | 173.00 | 128.00 | 155.00 | 1999 | 435.00 | 284.00 | 325.00 |
| 1972 | 152.00 | 116.00 | 152.00 | 1986 | 212.00 | 148.00 | 184.00 | 2000 | 344.00 | 180.00 | 180.00 |
| 1973 | 193.00 | 135.00 | 135.00 | 1987 | 224.00 | 178.00 | 198.00 | 2001 | 376.00 | 176.00 | 231.00 |
| 1974 | 183.00 | 98.00 | 110.00 | 1988 | 209.00 | 173.00 | 178.00 | 2002 | 300.00 | 183.00 | 202.00 |
| 1975 | 166.00 | 110.00 | 166.00 | 1989 | 192.00 | 172.00 | 183.00 | 2003 | 372.00 | 199.00 | 303.00 |
| 1976 | 188.00 | 146.00 | 188.00 | 1990 | 202.00 | 159.00 | 163.00 | 2004 | 470.00 | 306.00 | 358.00 |
| 1977 | 235.00 | 172.00 | 215.00 | 1991 | 243.00 | 152.00 | 180.00 | 2005 | 424.00 | 291.00 | 355.00 |
| 1978 | 240.00 | 210.00 | 226.00 | 1992 | 275.00 | 202.00 | 275.00 | 2006 | 364.00 | 226.00 | 260.00 |
| 1979 | 292.00 | 218.00 | 220.00 | 1993 | 475.00 | 217.00 | 464.00 | 2007 | 291.00 | 221.00 | 223.00 |
| 1980 | 208.00 | 148.00 | 154.00 | 1994 | 440.00 | 267.00 | 292.00 | 2008 | 312.00 | 160.00 | 160.00 |

Spruce-Pine-Fir 2x4.   Data continued from page 166.   *Source: CME Group; Chicago Mercantile Exchange*

# LUMBER

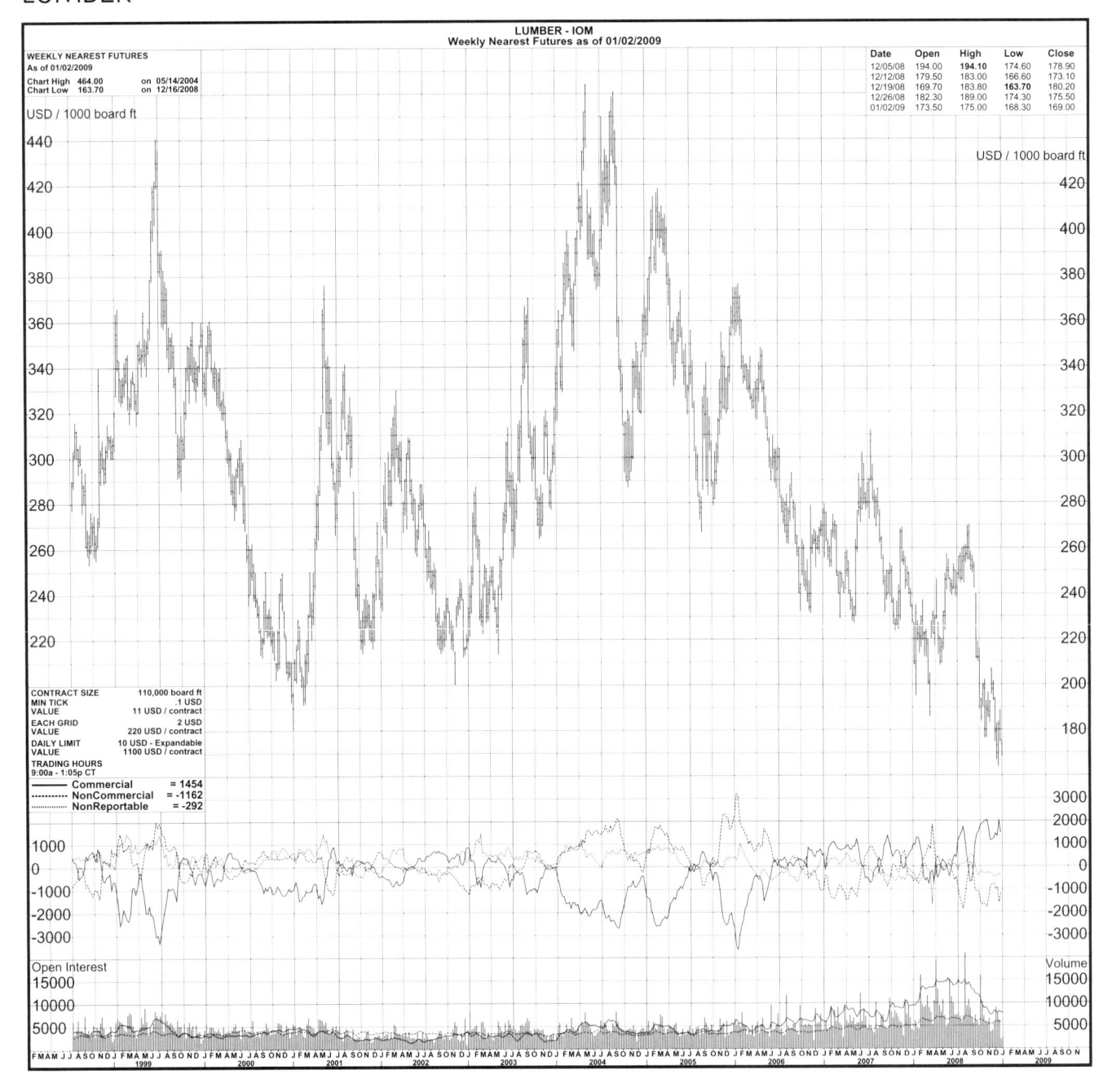

**Quarterly High, Low and Settle of Lumber Futures**  In Dollars per 1,000 Board Feet

| Quarter | High | Low | Settle | Quarter | High | Low | Settle | Quarter | High | Low | Settle |
|---|---|---|---|---|---|---|---|---|---|---|---|
| 03/2000 | 360.50 | 317.00 | 324.70 | 03/2003 | 287.60 | 215.60 | 230.60 | 03/2006 | 376.40 | 320.90 | 324.90 |
| 06/2000 | 329.50 | 268.00 | 275.50 | 06/2003 | 313.50 | 213.50 | 285.50 | 06/2006 | 348.40 | 286.10 | 294.50 |
| 09/2000 | 267.00 | 212.10 | 230.10 | 09/2003 | 370.40 | 255.50 | 309.50 | 09/2006 | 304.80 | 240.10 | 240.60 |
| 12/2000 | 249.70 | 202.10 | 205.50 | 12/2003 | 321.00 | 264.10 | 312.60 | 12/2006 | 279.00 | 231.30 | 268.00 |
| 03/2001 | 250.10 | 180.40 | 230.50 | 03/2004 | 400.00 | 314.00 | 381.10 | 03/2007 | 279.50 | 229.00 | 240.50 |
| 06/2001 | 376.00 | 226.50 | 293.30 | 06/2004 | 464.00 | 373.50 | 376.50 | 06/2007 | 302.30 | 227.00 | 279.80 |
| 09/2001 | 341.50 | 238.70 | 242.50 | 09/2004 | 461.00 | 328.40 | 336.20 | 09/2007 | 312.30 | 231.50 | 248.70 |
| 12/2001 | 272.00 | 213.80 | 245.10 | 12/2004 | 363.30 | 286.70 | 356.40 | 12/2007 | 269.10 | 223.50 | 234.50 |
| 03/2002 | 329.80 | 232.50 | 295.20 | 03/2005 | 418.50 | 344.00 | 400.70 | 03/2008 | 237.30 | 185.70 | 222.10 |
| 06/2002 | 309.30 | 256.30 | 287.50 | 06/2005 | 402.90 | 318.50 | 325.30 | 06/2008 | 257.50 | 208.30 | 242.00 |
| 09/2002 | 288.50 | 213.70 | 218.60 | 09/2005 | 355.80 | 267.00 | 304.90 | 09/2008 | 270.30 | 201.50 | 203.50 |
| 12/2002 | 247.00 | 200.50 | 217.70 | 12/2005 | 366.50 | 278.70 | 359.00 | 12/2008 | 207.40 | 163.70 | 169.40 |

*Source: CME Group; Chicago Mercantile Exchange*

# LUMBER

**Random Length, (SPF 2X4) Weekly Cash as of 01/02/2009**

| Date | Open | High | Low | Close |
|---|---|---|---|---|
| 12/05/08 | 178.00 | 178.00 | 178.00 | 178.00 |
| 12/12/08 | 160.00 | 160.00 | 160.00 | 160.00 |
| 12/19/08 | 160.00 | 160.00 | 160.00 | 160.00 |
| 12/26/08 | 160.00 | 160.00 | 160.00 | 160.00 |
| 01/02/09 | 160.00 | 160.00 | 160.00 | 160.00 |

**Weekly Cash** As of 01/02/2009
Chart High 470.00 on 08/27/2004
Chart Low 160.00 on 12/12/2008
USD / 1000 board ft

## Quarterly High, Low and Settle of Lumber    In Dollars per 1,000 Board Feet

| Quarter | High | Low | Settle | Quarter | High | Low | Settle | Quarter | High | Low | Settle |
|---|---|---|---|---|---|---|---|---|---|---|---|
| 03/2000 | 344.00 | 315.00 | 315.00 | 03/2003 | 239.00 | 199.00 | 199.00 | 03/2006 | 364.00 | 319.00 | 319.00 |
| 06/2000 | 310.00 | 253.00 | 253.00 | 06/2003 | 296.00 | 222.00 | 296.00 | 06/2006 | 347.00 | 296.00 | 300.00 |
| 09/2000 | 252.00 | 204.00 | 217.00 | 09/2003 | 372.00 | 256.00 | 335.00 | 09/2006 | 300.00 | 248.00 | 248.00 |
| 12/2000 | 210.00 | 180.00 | 180.00 | 12/2003 | 320.00 | 281.00 | 303.00 | 12/2006 | 260.00 | 226.00 | 260.00 |
| 03/2001 | 217.00 | 176.00 | 213.00 | 03/2004 | 397.00 | 308.00 | 376.00 | 03/2007 | 276.00 | 234.00 | 234.00 |
| 06/2001 | 376.00 | 218.00 | 268.00 | 06/2004 | 463.00 | 400.00 | 400.00 | 06/2007 | 291.00 | 228.00 | 289.00 |
| 09/2001 | 334.00 | 248.00 | 248.00 | 09/2004 | 470.00 | 380.00 | 380.00 | 09/2007 | 284.00 | 231.00 | 231.00 |
| 12/2001 | 236.00 | 206.00 | 231.00 | 12/2004 | 373.00 | 306.00 | 358.00 | 12/2007 | 245.00 | 221.00 | 223.00 |
| 03/2002 | 300.00 | 228.00 | 290.00 | 03/2005 | 424.00 | 353.00 | 412.00 | 03/2008 | 219.00 | 190.00 | 207.00 |
| 06/2002 | 287.00 | 243.00 | 258.00 | 06/2005 | 407.00 | 337.00 | 350.00 | 06/2008 | 252.00 | 207.00 | 245.00 |
| 09/2002 | 259.00 | 191.00 | 191.00 | 09/2005 | 355.00 | 291.00 | 352.00 | 09/2008 | 312.00 | 233.00 | 235.00 |
| 12/2002 | 209.00 | 183.00 | 202.00 | 12/2005 | 355.00 | 304.00 | 355.00 | 12/2008 | 215.00 | 160.00 | 160.00 |

Spruce-Pine-Fir 2x4.    *Source: CME Group; Chicago Mercantile Exchange*

# GRAINS & OILSEEDS

**Biofuels boost the long-term outlook for ag prices**

The emergence of biofuels as a significant source of transportation fuel has substantially improved the long-term outlook for grain and oilseed prices and for farm income. As the nearby chart illustrates, the long-term decline in the inflation-adjusted real prices of grain and soybean prices was finally broken, thanks largely to demand from ethanol and biodiesel producers.

In the United States, corn is the main feedstock for ethanol production. In 2008, ethanol producers used 3.6 billion bushels of corn to produce ethanol, which accounted for 30% of the US corn crop. The sharp increase in demand for corn from ethanol producers was a major factory in pushing corn prices sharply higher from late 2006 through mid-2008.

That sharp rally in corn prices sparked carry-over price increases for soybeans and to a lesser extent wheat. As corn prices rose, farmers planted more corn since they could earn a much higher return from planting corn than from other crops, thus taking acres away from soybeans and pushing soybean prices higher. In fact, corn planting in 2007 rose sharply by +19% to 93.5 million acres, while soybean planting fell by -14% to 64.7 million acres. The situation in 2008 partially reversed after soybean prices rallied sharply as well. In 2008, US farmers cut back corn planting by –8% to 86.0 million acres and boosted soybean acres by +17.0% to 75.7 million acres. This ethanol effect on crop planting can be seen in the nearby chart entitled "US Acres Planted."

Biofuels are here to stay for as long as the world depends primarily on internal combustion engines for transportation. There is a strong push for electric and fuel cell vehicles, but the widespread adoption of vehicles that do not use internal combustion engines will take decades. In the meantime, governments around the world are pushing biofuels as an alternative to gasoline and diesel fuel since biofuels are renewable, cleaner, and come from domestic sources.

The US government currently has a Renewable Fuel Standard (RFS) in place that requires renewable fuel usage to reach 36 billion gallons by 2022, which would be about 25% of the US fuel supply. The RFS requires the use of 15 billion gallons of corn-based ethanol by 2022 and the remainder from "advanced biofuels" such as ethanol produced from "cellulosic" sources including switch grass, corn stover waste, wood chips and others. The RFS requires 10.5 billion gallons of corn-based ethanol to be used in 2009, composing about 7% of US vehicle fuel supply, up from 9 billion gallons in 2008.

The bottom line is that biofuel producer demand for corn and other feedstocks is likely to provide a floor under grain and soybean prices over at least the next decade. The other key long-term drivers supporting grain and soybean prices include world population growth and the improving diets of people in the developing world.

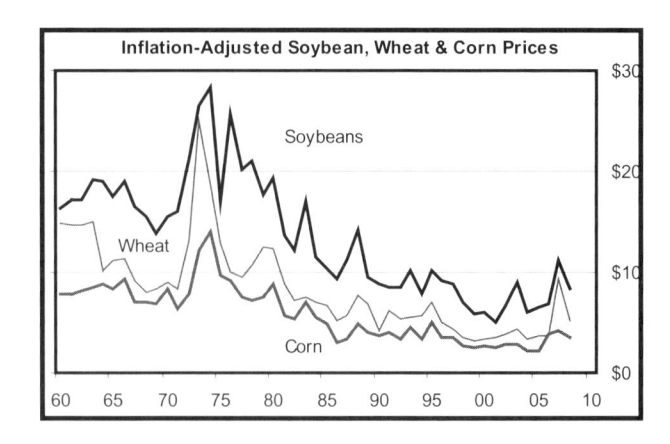

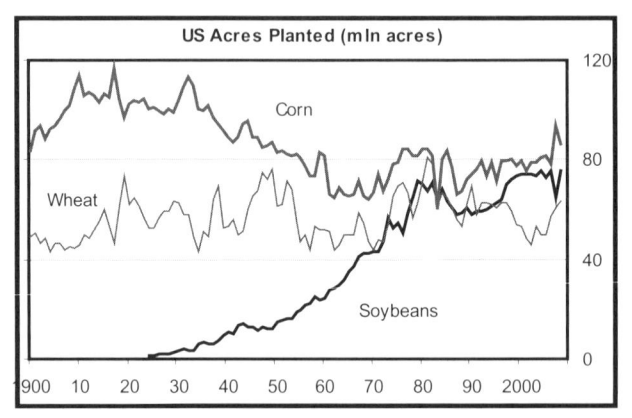

**Long-term US acreage planting trends**

The nearby chart of US planting trends, which incorporates data from the *CRB Commodity Yearbook 2009*, shows how corn a century ago in 1900 was the dominant crop in the US, with corn acreage almost twice that of wheat acreage. Acres planted with wheat have fluctuated in a wide range but have moved basically sideways in the past 100 years and current wheat planting acreage in the US isn't much different than it was back in 1900.

The most striking aspect of the chart is the rise in the popularity of soybeans in the 1930s and 1940s, and particularly after World War II. In fact, US farmland planted with soybeans is now only mildly below that of corn. Corn acres fell from 1930 through the 1970s to accommodate the higher acres planted with soybeans.

Soybeans after World War II became known as the "Miracle Bean." Soybean prices were higher than corn prices and soybeans were generally easier to grow. Demand for soybeans surged due in part to the high protein content in soybeans. Soybean meal, with its high protein content, could be used as a super-charger for animal feed. Soybean oil found very strong demand since it is nearly tasteless and colorless and is ideal for use in processed foods. Soybean oil is now used to produce biodiesel fuel as well.

# GRAINS & OILSEEDS

### Grain & Soybean Price History

Grain and soybean prices during the 1950s and 1960s were undoubtedly considered by farmers at the time to be volatile as prices were buffeted by the usual fluctuations in supply due mainly to the weather. The US government tried to support and stabilize prices in order to support US farmers. However, by modern standards of volatility, grain and soybean prices during the 1950s and 1960s were remarkably stable. That stability ended in the early-1970s, however, when grain and soybean prices soared to levels that were unimaginable at the time.

In theory, the volatility of grain and soybean prices should be trending lower. The rise of South America as a major producer now provides a counter-cyclical harvest supply during the winter season in the Northern Hemisphere and also diversifies world production from a weather standpoint. Yet a quick look at the charts shows that grain and soybean prices are now even more volatile than they were back in the 1980s and 1990s.

### 1972 Soviet grain purchases and inflation

Starting in the summer of 1972, grain and soybean prices started to rally sharply. Soybean prices nearly quadrupled from $3.50 per bushel to a record high of $12.90 per bushel (nearest-futures) in early 1973. Corn prices more than tripled from $1.20 per bushel in mid 1972 to nearly $4 in 1973. Wheat prices more than tripled to as high as $6 per bushel from about $1.60 in mid-1972.

The main factor driving that rally was the fact that the Soviet Union secretly purchased 24 million metric tons of wheat, corn, soybeans and soybean meal during the summer of 1972. The Soviets were forced to make the purchases because of domestic shortages caused by poor crops in the Soviet Union starting in 1970. When the Soviet purchases came to light in late 1972 and early 1973, grain and soybean prices soared. Soybean inventories were so depleted that President Nixon had to impose an embargo on soy meal exports so that the US would have enough soy meal for its own needs.

Prices were also boosted in the first half of the 1970s by the general surge in inflation seen in response to the Federal Reserve's expansionary monetary policy and the surge in crude oil prices caused by the Arab oil embargo in October 1973. US inflation soared to 11% in 1975.

The surge in grain and soybean prices in 1972-73 caused the US government to drop its former policy of trying to restrict production in order to support prices. Instead, the US government adopted policies encouraging US farmers to plant as much acreage as they could to meet demand. In addition, Brazil during the early 1970s quickly ramped up its soybean production to take advantage of high prices. Brazilian soybean production soared by roughly six-fold from about 2 million metric tons in 1970-71 to 12.5 million metric tons just 6 years later in 1976-77. This burst of world production created a production surplus of grain and soybeans, which led to extremely volatile prices through the 1970s.

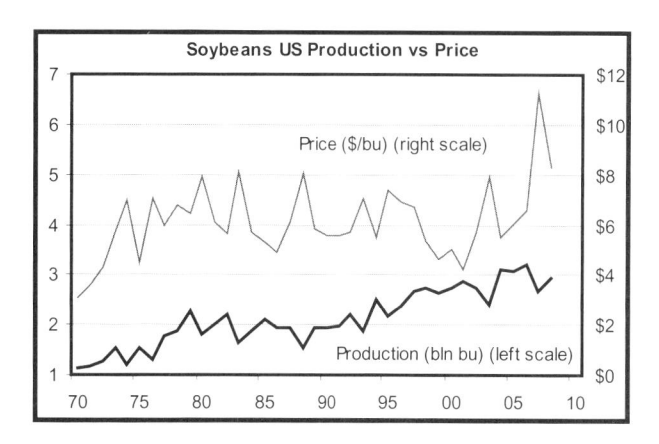

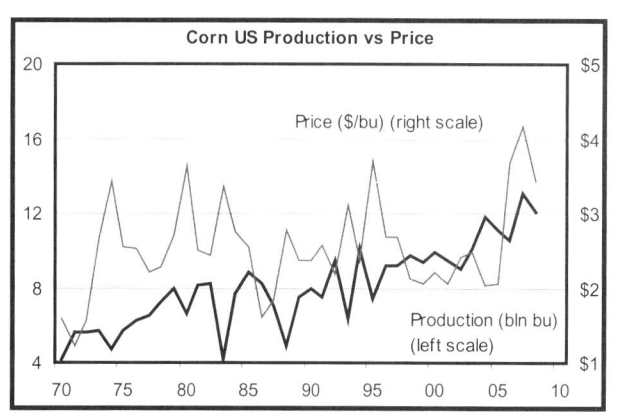

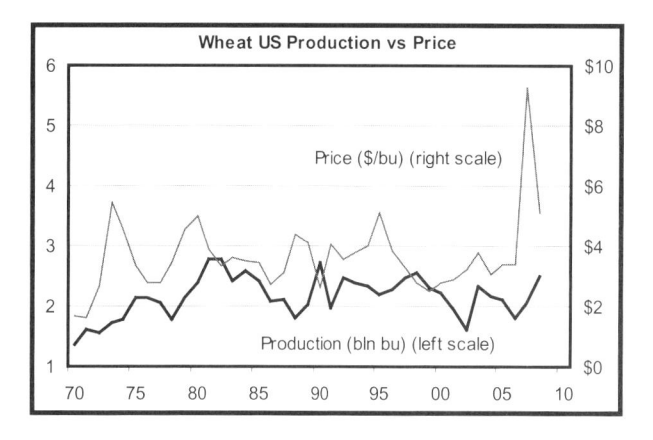

### 1979 Soviet Grain Embargo

The Soviet Union in the latter half of 1979 entered the market again to make huge purchases of US grain and soybeans, thus pushing prices higher. However, in January 1980, President Carter announced a grain embargo against the Soviet Union in retaliation for its invasion of Afghanistan. The US government was able to prevent a

# GRAINS & OILSEEDS

melt-down in prices in response to the embargo by placing the canceled Soviet grain purchases into government loan and reserve programs. The restrictions that kept those inventories locked in loan and reserve programs were so tight that the inventories were not available on the open market when a drought occurred during the summer of 1980. The drought, combined with restricted inventories, resulted in a sharp rally in grain and soybean prices in the first three quarters of 1980. Prices then fell sharply in late 1980 and into 1981-82 after the drought eased and large crops were harvested in 1981 and 1982. There was also the continued overhang from large government inventories. The plunge in grain and soybean prices in 1981-82 caused a farm recession tied to low prices and the buildup of debt that occurred in the 1970s as farmers expanded output.

**1983 PIK program and drought**

In order to allow huge US government inventories of grain and soybeans caused by the Soviet grain embargo to be worked down, the US government created the "PIK" program (payment-in-kind) where the government paid farmers in grain for not planting crops. However, this program took acreage out of production just as a severe drought hit during the summer of 1983, caused by El Nino conditions in the Pacific. The combination of the PIK program and the severe drought caused grain and soybean prices to soar in 1983.

Grain and soybean prices then fell sharply in 1984-86 as US production returned to normal and as the PIK grain that was paid to farmers came onto the market. This caused the return of the recessionary conditions for farmers that started in the early 1980s. There were widespread bankruptcies in the agriculture industry during the mid-1980s. The first Farm Aid concert was organized in 1985 by Willie Nelson, Neil Young and John Mellencamp in an effort to help American farmers during those recessionary times (see www.FarmAid.org).

**1988 Drought**

Grain and soybean prices soared during spring-1988 as a severe winter drought extended into spring. However, rain in July eased conditions and improved yields, and prices quickly dropped back to more normal levels.

**1993 Midwestern Flood**

Grain and soybean prices were subdued in 1991-92 with generally favorable weather and large crops in 1992. However, the Midwest was swamped with rain in 1993 in a "500-year flood" that destroyed a significant part of Midwestern crops, thus leading to a moderate rally in grain and soybean prices in 1993.

**1996-97 demand-driven rally**

Grain and soybean prices rallied in 1995-97 mainly because of strong demand by China, which in 1995 became a net importer, rather than an exporter, of corn. China also became a big buyer of vegetable oils and wheat.

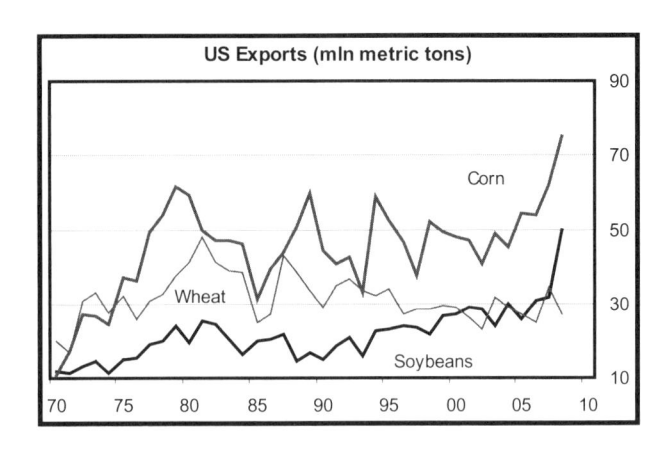

**1998-2000 bear market**

US crops were relatively large during 1997-2002, which led to relatively high inventories and depressed prices in that time frame.

**2003-04 spike on poor weather and low inventories**

Inventory levels were already headed downward in 2000-02 when a spell of hot and dry weather hit in 2003. The US soybean crop in 2003 was the smallest in seven years. Demand remained relatively strong, however, driving inventories to extremely low levels that produced the sharp rally in late 2003 and early-2004. Corn showed a smaller rally in 2003-04 since corn escaped from the hot and dry weather and the 2003-04 crop was large at 10.1 billion bushels.

**2004-05 large crops produce subdued prices**

The summer of 2004 saw ideal growing conditions with plenty of rain and cool temperatures. The result was record crops for soybeans and corn, and a large wheat crop as well. Crop sizes were large again in 2005 despite drought conditions in the Central Midwest. The result was a buildup in inventories into 2005 with a record carry-over in soybeans and a 12-year high carry-over in corn. The high production and carry-overs resulted in depressed soybean and corn prices in 2004 and 2005. At the time, there were great concerns about soybean rust disease which first reached the US in late 2004 (see www.usda.gov/soybeanrust). Fortunately, soybean rust turned out to be a minor problem during the summer of 2005 and did not cause significant yield losses.

**2006-08 rally**

Corn, wheat and soybean prices soared starting in 2006 mainly because ethanol demand suddenly became a major factor in driving corn prices higher. The strong demand for corn in fact led to a sharp 34% decline in the 2006-

07 US carry-over to a 3-year low of 1.304 billion bushels. Ethanol producers scrambled to buy cash corn during fall 2006 and winter 2007 in order to ensure they could keep their ethanol plants running at full capacity. As a result of the rally in corn prices to the $4 per bushel area by winter 2007, US farmers sharply boosted their corn planting in spring 2007 by 19.4% to a record 93.5 million acres in the spring of 2007. The huge number of acres planted with corn during spring 2007, combined with favorable weather during summer 2007, led to a big 24% increase in the 2007-08 corn crop to a record 13.038 billion bushels. The 2007 corn crop was large enough to meet the increased demand of ethanol producers and corn prices therefore eased to the low-$3 per bushel area by summer 2007. In fact, the US carry-over in 2007-08 rose 24.5% to 1.624 billion bushels, which was just above the 5-year average of 1.59 billion bushels.

Soybean prices during most of 2006 traded sideways near $6 per bushel. The US soybean crop during the summer of 2006 rose 4.4% to a record 3.197 billion bushels. However, the situation changed dramatically during the winter of 2007 when strong corn prices led US farmers to cut soybean planting by -14.3% to an 11-year low of 64.74 million acres. This led to a sharp -16.3% decline in the size of the summer 2007 soybean crop to 2.68 billion bushels. The small 2007 soybean crop, combined with firm global demand for soybeans, caused a sharp 64.3% drop in the US soybean carry-over in 2007/08 to 205 billion bushels, which was about one-third below the 5-year average of 320 billion bushels. The sharp drawdown in soybean supplies caused soybean prices to nearly double during 2007 from $6.83 per bushel at the end of 2006 to $12 per bushel by the end of 2007.

After moving basically sideways during 2002-05 in the $3-4 per bushel range, wheat prices started to rally in the later part of 2006 along with corn and soybean prices. Wheat prices closed 2006 at $5.01 per bushel, up 48% from the 2005 close of $3.39. The US wheat crop in 2006-07 was hurt by hot and dry weather in the southern Plains and fell -14.2% yr/yr to 1.806 billion bushels. That was the second smallest crop in the US in the past 25 years and caused the US wheat carry-over in 2006-07 to fall sharply by -17.3% to 472 million bushels, which was the tightest inventory level in 10 years. However, growing conditions were also poor in Europe where heat caused significant damage to the wheat crop. The situation was even worse in Australia where a severe drought slashed wheat production by about one-third. The end result was a sharp -18% decline in the global carry-over of wheat in 2006-07 to 120.8 metric tons.

Wheat prices on the CBOT nearest futures chart trended lower in the first third of 2007 to post a 1-1/2 year low of $4.12 per bushel in April 2007. Wheat prices then staged a remarkable rally that took prices up to record highs, finally closing 2007 at $8.85 per bushel, up +77% y/y. Wheat prices continued higher into 2008 and in February 2008 posted an all-time high of $13.00 per bushel. Strong demand and sharply lower supplies were the main driving factors for wheat prices in 2007. Drought hurt the wheat crops in Australia, Canada, and Russia and US production was hurt by a spring freeze followed by excessive precipitation. The US wheat crop in 2007-08 climbed by +14.1% yr/yr to 2.067 billion bushels, but that wasn't enough to make up for increased global demand, which caused the global carry-over in 2007-08 to fall by -11.7% to a 30-year low of 110.4 metric tons. With increased global demand for U.S. wheat, U.S carry-over in 2007-08 fell sharply by -47% to a 60-year low of 242 million bushels. As global supplies tightened, China and Russia raised their export taxes sharply to keep their own wheat at home to quell surging domestic prices.

Corn, soybean and wheat prices in early 2008 extended the rallies to record highs. Wheat on a nearest-futures basis posted a record high of $13.00 per bushel in February 2008. Corn then hit its record high of $7.625 per bushel four months later in June 2008. Soybeans finally posted their record high of $16.60 per bushel in July 2008. After posting those record highs, corn, soybean and wheat prices all went into an all-out plunge. From the 2008 record highs through the lows established in December, corn plunged by an overall 62%, soybeans by 53%, and wheat by 65%.

There is no doubt that grain and soybean prices were caught up in the speculative frenzy that engulfed the entire commodity market, reaching prices that were far in excess of what was reasonable based on fundamentals alone. Many commodity index funds and commodity-based exchange traded funds were launched during the 2006-08 commodity bull market and that gave investors an easy way to speculate in the commodity markets.

Grain and wheat prices had already sold off sharply even before the banking crisis emerged in mid-September 2008 with the bankruptcy of Lehman Brothers. The weather during the summer of 2008 was favorable and crop sizes were relatively large, near or above their respective 5-year averages. However, when the banking crisis emerged, grain and soybean prices sold off even further as investors sold everything in sight to preserve capital. Moreover, demand for corn, soybeans and wheat weakened with the global recession. Corn was also hurt by a sharp drop in ethanol production, which became unprofitable in late 2008 and early-2009 when gasoline prices fell sharply and took ethanol prices lower as well.

The outlook for grain and soybean prices looking forward from early-2009 is still relatively weak given that the global economy is in a severe recession at present. However, speculators have been washed out of the markets and prices have generally stabilized. The longer-term outlook for corn, soybean and wheat prices looks firm given that biofuel demand continues to underpin the markets and that food and livestock feed demand is likely to rebound as soon as the global recession ends.

# CORN

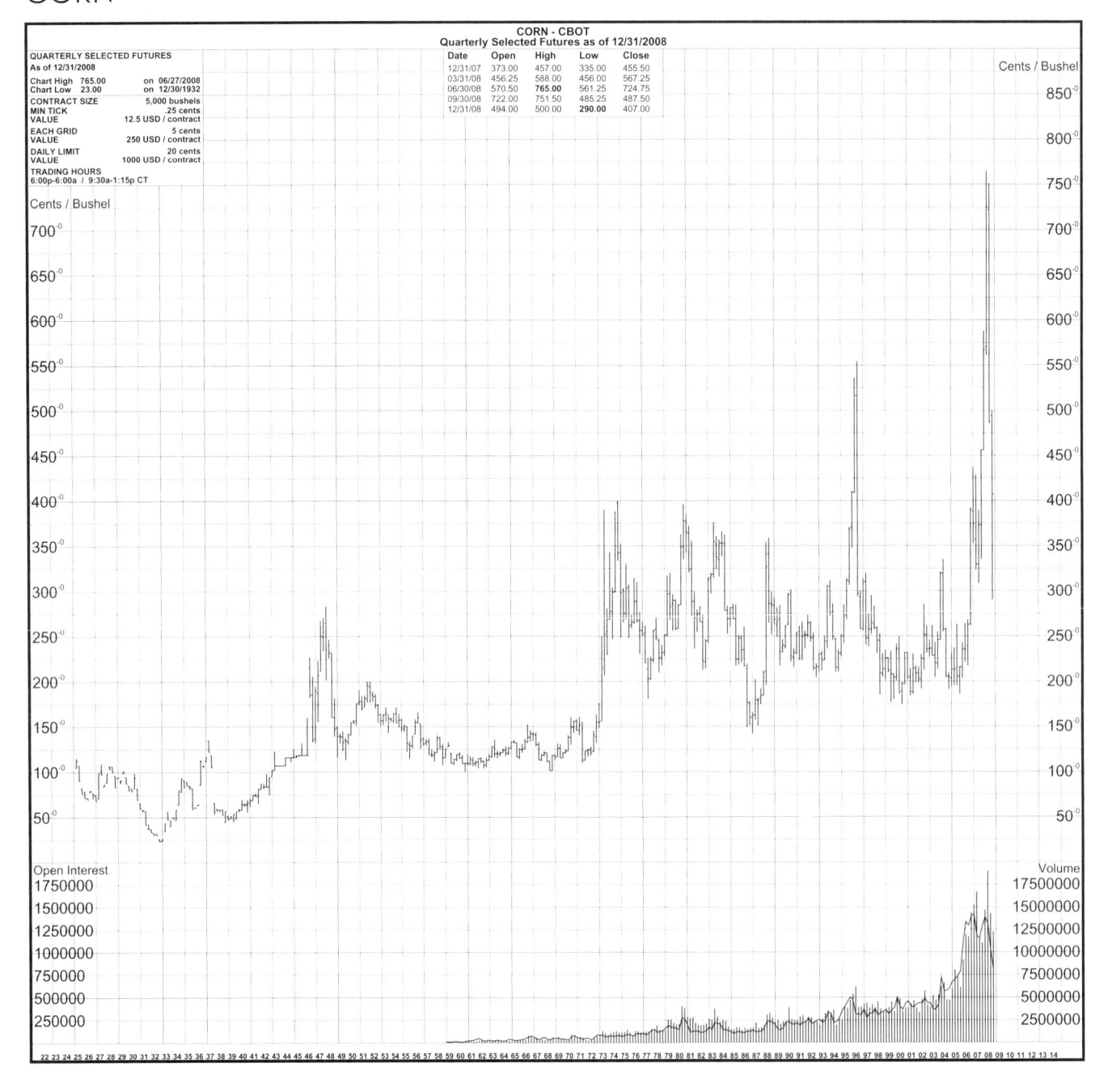

**CORN - CBOT**
Quarterly Selected Futures as of 12/31/2008

| Date | Open | High | Low | Close |
|---|---|---|---|---|
| 12/31/07 | 373.00 | 457.00 | 335.00 | 455.50 |
| 03/31/08 | 456.25 | 588.00 | 456.00 | 567.25 |
| 06/30/08 | 570.50 | 765.00 | 561.25 | 724.75 |
| 09/30/08 | 722.00 | 751.50 | 485.25 | 487.50 |
| 12/31/08 | 494.00 | 500.00 | 290.00 | 407.00 |

**QUARTERLY SELECTED FUTURES**
As of 12/31/2008
Chart High 765.00 on 06/27/2008
Chart Low 23.00 on 12/30/1932
CONTRACT SIZE 5,000 bushels
MIN TICK .25 cents
VALUE 12.5 USD / contract
EACH GRID 5 cents
VALUE 250 USD / contract
DAILY LIMIT 20 cents
VALUE 1000 USD / contract
TRADING HOURS
6:00p-6:00a / 9:30a-1:15p CT

### Annual High, Low and Settle of Corn Futures — In Cents per Bushel

| Year | High | Low | Settle | Year | High | Low | Settle | Year | High | Low | Settle |
|---|---|---|---|---|---|---|---|---|---|---|---|
| 1925 | 123.88 | 76.50 | 76.50 | 1939 | 56.25 | 45.00 | 56.25 | 1953 | 171.88 | 143.00 | 159.00 |
| 1926 | 80.25 | 70.00 | 75.13 | 1940 | 69.50 | 55.50 | 65.50 | 1954 | 171.75 | 149.38 | 157.38 |
| 1927 | 109.25 | 68.50 | 86.38 | 1941 | 82.00 | 62.00 | 81.00 | 1955 | 159.13 | 114.50 | 128.75 |
| 1928 | 107.50 | 83.38 | 83.38 | 1942 | 98.25 | 74.50 | 94.00 | 1956 | 166.50 | 125.63 | 135.00 |
| 1929 | 101.25 | 87.38 | 87.50 | 1943 | 123.00 | 95.25 | 107.00 | 1957 | 138.38 | 116.13 | 118.13 |
| 1930 | 98.88 | 69.50 | 69.50 | 1944 | 116.00 | 107.00 | 116.00 | 1958 | 140.25 | 107.25 | 115.50 |
| 1931 | 65.38 | 37.13 | 37.13 | 1945 | 132.25 | 115.50 | 118.50 | 1959 | 133.25 | 107.38 | 113.88 |
| 1932 | 37.00 | 23.00 | 23.00 | 1946 | 227.00 | 118.50 | 135.25 | 1960 | 122.00 | 100.25 | 109.38 |
| 1933 | 55.88 | 23.13 | 46.50 | 1947 | 271.00 | 131.75 | 264.00 | 1961 | 119.13 | 105.75 | 110.75 |
| 1934 | 93.25 | 47.25 | 93.25 | 1948 | 283.38 | 139.00 | 147.88 | 1962 | 116.25 | 103.50 | 112.75 |
| 1935 | 90.75 | 59.00 | 59.00 | 1949 | 150.50 | 113.00 | 134.25 | 1963 | 136.00 | 112.25 | 120.13 |
| 1936 | 113.50 | 60.75 | 107.25 | 1950 | 176.25 | 130.25 | 176.00 | 1964 | 128.50 | 117.00 | 126.38 |
| 1937 | 135.00 | 53.38 | 56.13 | 1951 | 200.13 | 168.63 | 195.75 | 1965 | 135.25 | 113.75 | 124.88 |
| 1938 | 59.25 | 44.75 | 57.00 | 1952 | 199.63 | 154.25 | 163.13 | 1966 | 152.38 | 121.00 | 142.00 |

Futures data begins 07/01/1959. Data continued on page 178. *Source: CME Group; Chicago Board of Trade*

# CORN

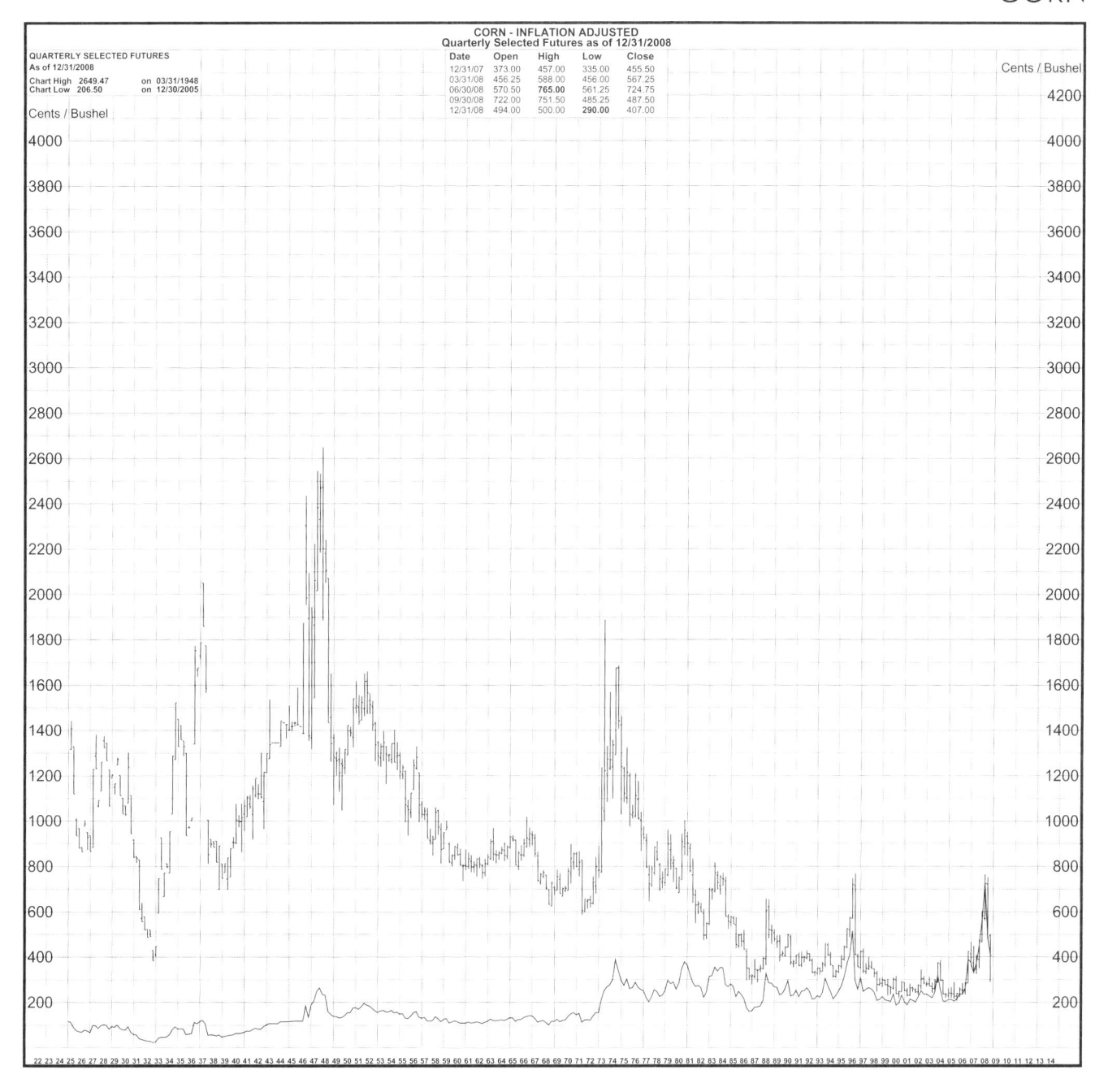

**CORN - INFLATION ADJUSTED**
Quarterly Selected Futures as of 12/31/2008

| Date | Open | High | Low | Close |
|---|---|---|---|---|
| 12/31/07 | 373.00 | 457.00 | 335.00 | 455.50 |
| 03/31/08 | 456.25 | 588.00 | 456.00 | 567.25 |
| 06/30/08 | 570.50 | 765.00 | 561.25 | 724.75 |
| 09/30/08 | 722.00 | 751.50 | 485.25 | 487.50 |
| 12/31/08 | 494.00 | 500.00 | 290.00 | 407.00 |

QUARTERLY SELECTED FUTURES
As of 12/31/2008
Chart High 2649.47 on 03/31/1948
Chart Low 206.50 on 12/30/2005
Cents / Bushel

## Annual High, Low and Settle of Corn — In Cents per Bushel

| Year | High | Low | Settle | Year | High | Low | Settle | Year | High | Low | Settle |
|---|---|---|---|---|---|---|---|---|---|---|---|
| 1925 | 123.88 | 76.50 | 76.50 | 1939 | 56.25 | 45.00 | 56.25 | 1953 | 171.88 | 143.00 | 159.00 |
| 1926 | 80.25 | 70.00 | 75.13 | 1940 | 69.50 | 55.50 | 65.50 | 1954 | 171.75 | 149.38 | 157.38 |
| 1927 | 109.25 | 68.50 | 86.38 | 1941 | 82.00 | 62.00 | 81.00 | 1955 | 159.13 | 114.50 | 128.75 |
| 1928 | 107.50 | 83.38 | 83.38 | 1942 | 98.25 | 74.50 | 94.00 | 1956 | 166.50 | 125.63 | 135.00 |
| 1929 | 101.25 | 87.38 | 87.50 | 1943 | 123.00 | 95.25 | 107.00 | 1957 | 138.38 | 116.13 | 118.13 |
| 1930 | 98.88 | 69.50 | 69.50 | 1944 | 116.00 | 107.00 | 116.00 | 1958 | 140.25 | 107.25 | 115.50 |
| 1931 | 65.38 | 37.13 | 37.13 | 1945 | 132.25 | 115.50 | 118.50 | 1959 | 133.25 | 108.75 | 116.00 |
| 1932 | 37.00 | 23.00 | 23.00 | 1946 | 227.00 | 118.50 | 135.25 | 1960 | 125.00 | 94.50 | 110.50 |
| 1933 | 55.88 | 23.13 | 46.50 | 1947 | 271.00 | 131.75 | 264.00 | 1961 | 119.00 | 104.75 | 111.50 |
| 1934 | 93.25 | 47.25 | 93.25 | 1948 | 283.38 | 139.00 | 147.88 | 1962 | 119.25 | 108.00 | 117.00 |
| 1935 | 90.75 | 59.00 | 59.00 | 1949 | 150.50 | 113.00 | 134.25 | 1963 | 138.50 | 116.00 | 124.50 |
| 1936 | 113.50 | 60.75 | 107.25 | 1950 | 176.25 | 130.25 | 176.00 | 1964 | 130.50 | 115.00 | 129.50 |
| 1937 | 135.00 | 53.38 | 56.13 | 1951 | 200.13 | 168.63 | 195.75 | 1965 | 139.00 | 114.50 | 126.50 |
| 1938 | 59.25 | 44.75 | 57.00 | 1952 | 199.63 | 154.25 | 163.13 | 1966 | 153.50 | 125.50 | 144.00 |

Chicago #3 Yellow through 12/1939; Chicago #2 Yellow 01/02/1940 to date.    Data continued on page 179.    *Source: U.S. Department of Agriculture*

# CORN

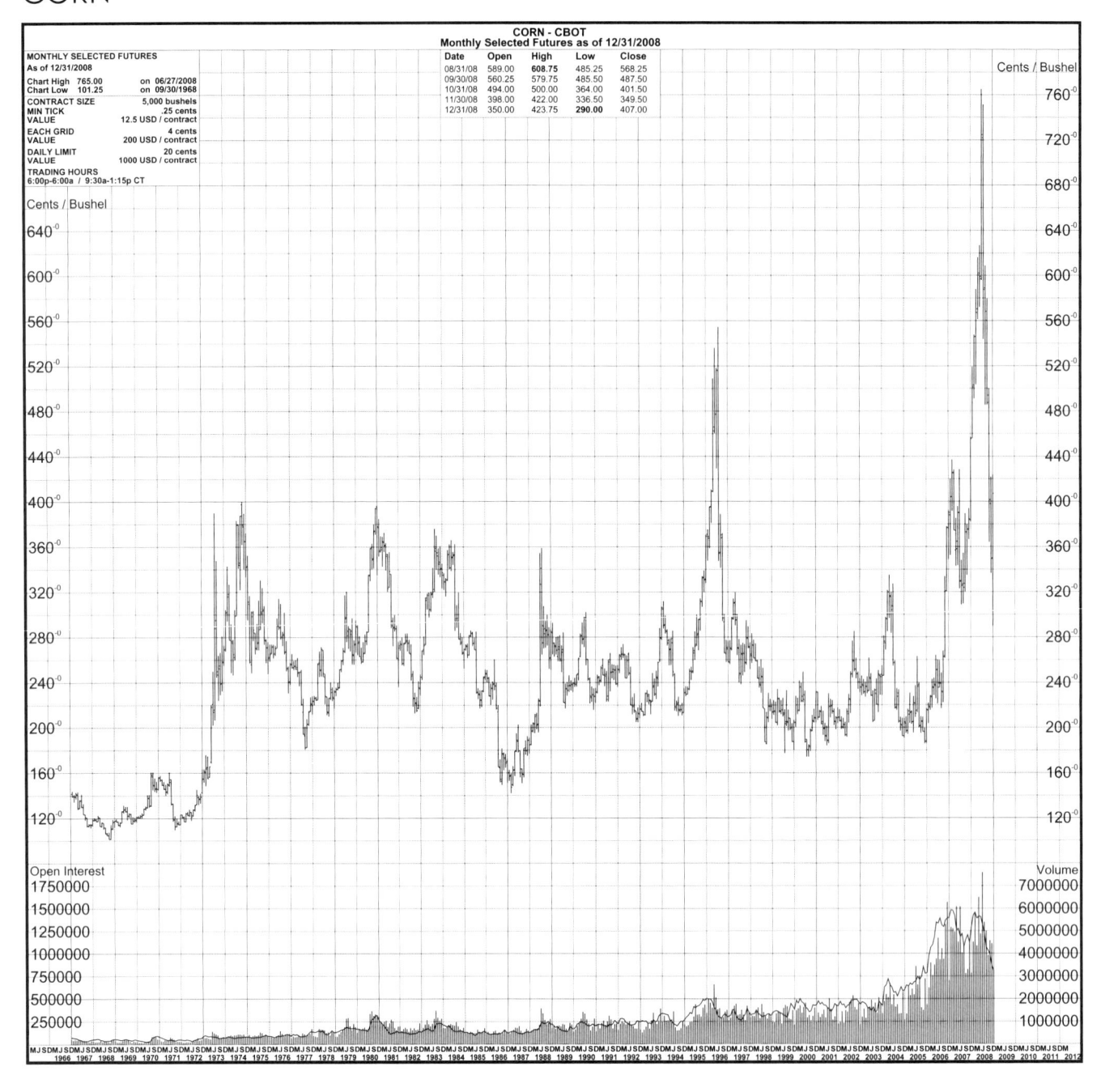

## CORN - CBOT
### Monthly Selected Futures as of 12/31/2008

| Date | Open | High | Low | Close |
|---|---|---|---|---|
| 08/31/08 | 589.00 | 608.75 | 485.25 | 568.25 |
| 09/30/08 | 560.25 | 579.75 | 485.50 | 487.50 |
| 10/31/08 | 494.00 | 500.00 | 364.00 | 401.50 |
| 11/30/08 | 398.00 | 422.00 | 336.50 | 349.50 |
| 12/31/08 | 350.00 | 423.75 | 290.00 | 407.00 |

**MONTHLY SELECTED FUTURES**
As of 12/31/2008
Chart High 765.00 on 06/27/2008
Chart Low 101.25 on 09/30/1968
CONTRACT SIZE 5,000 bushels
MIN TICK .25 cents
VALUE 12.5 USD / contract
EACH GRID 4 cents
VALUE 200 USD / contract
DAILY LIMIT 20 cents
VALUE 1000 USD / contract
TRADING HOURS
6:00p-6:00a / 9:30a-1:15p CT

### Annual High, Low and Settle of Corn Futures    In Cents per Bushel

| Year | High | Low | Settle | Year | High | Low | Settle | Year | High | Low | Settle |
|---|---|---|---|---|---|---|---|---|---|---|---|
| 1967 | 144.00 | 111.63 | 118.38 | 1981 | 384.75 | 236.00 | 270.50 | 1995 | 370.50 | 227.75 | 369.25 |
| 1968 | 122.75 | 101.25 | 117.88 | 1982 | 283.50 | 212.50 | 244.75 | 1996 | 554.50 | 257.75 | 258.25 |
| 1969 | 131.50 | 112.50 | 121.13 | 1983 | 376.00 | 242.25 | 337.25 | 1997 | 320.00 | 238.25 | 265.00 |
| 1970 | 160.75 | 120.13 | 155.50 | 1984 | 366.00 | 252.25 | 269.25 | 1998 | 283.50 | 185.00 | 213.50 |
| 1971 | 160.75 | 109.50 | 123.38 | 1985 | 286.00 | 217.00 | 248.25 | 1999 | 234.25 | 177.00 | 204.50 |
| 1972 | 163.50 | 116.87 | 155.00 | 1986 | 260.50 | 149.25 | 160.00 | 2000 | 249.50 | 174.00 | 231.75 |
| 1973 | 390.00 | 148.50 | 268.75 | 1987 | 202.75 | 142.00 | 184.75 | 2001 | 232.00 | 184.00 | 209.00 |
| 1974 | 400.00 | 246.50 | 342.00 | 1988 | 359.00 | 184.25 | 284.50 | 2002 | 285.50 | 191.50 | 235.75 |
| 1975 | 352.50 | 247.75 | 261.50 | 1989 | 292.75 | 217.00 | 239.75 | 2003 | 262.00 | 204.50 | 246.00 |
| 1976 | 314.50 | 230.50 | 256.50 | 1990 | 302.25 | 215.50 | 231.75 | 2004 | 335.25 | 191.00 | 204.75 |
| 1977 | 265.50 | 180.75 | 223.75 | 1991 | 266.00 | 223.00 | 251.50 | 2005 | 263.25 | 185.75 | 215.75 |
| 1978 | 271.50 | 209.75 | 231.75 | 1992 | 274.00 | 204.50 | 216.50 | 2006 | 392.00 | 203.50 | 390.25 |
| 1979 | 320.75 | 228.00 | 289.50 | 1993 | 306.75 | 210.00 | 306.00 | 2007 | 457.00 | 308.50 | 455.50 |
| 1980 | 396.00 | 256.50 | 378.00 | 1994 | 311.75 | 210.00 | 231.00 | 2008 | 765.00 | 290.00 | 407.00 |

Data continued from page 176.    *Source: CME Group; Chicago Board of Trade*

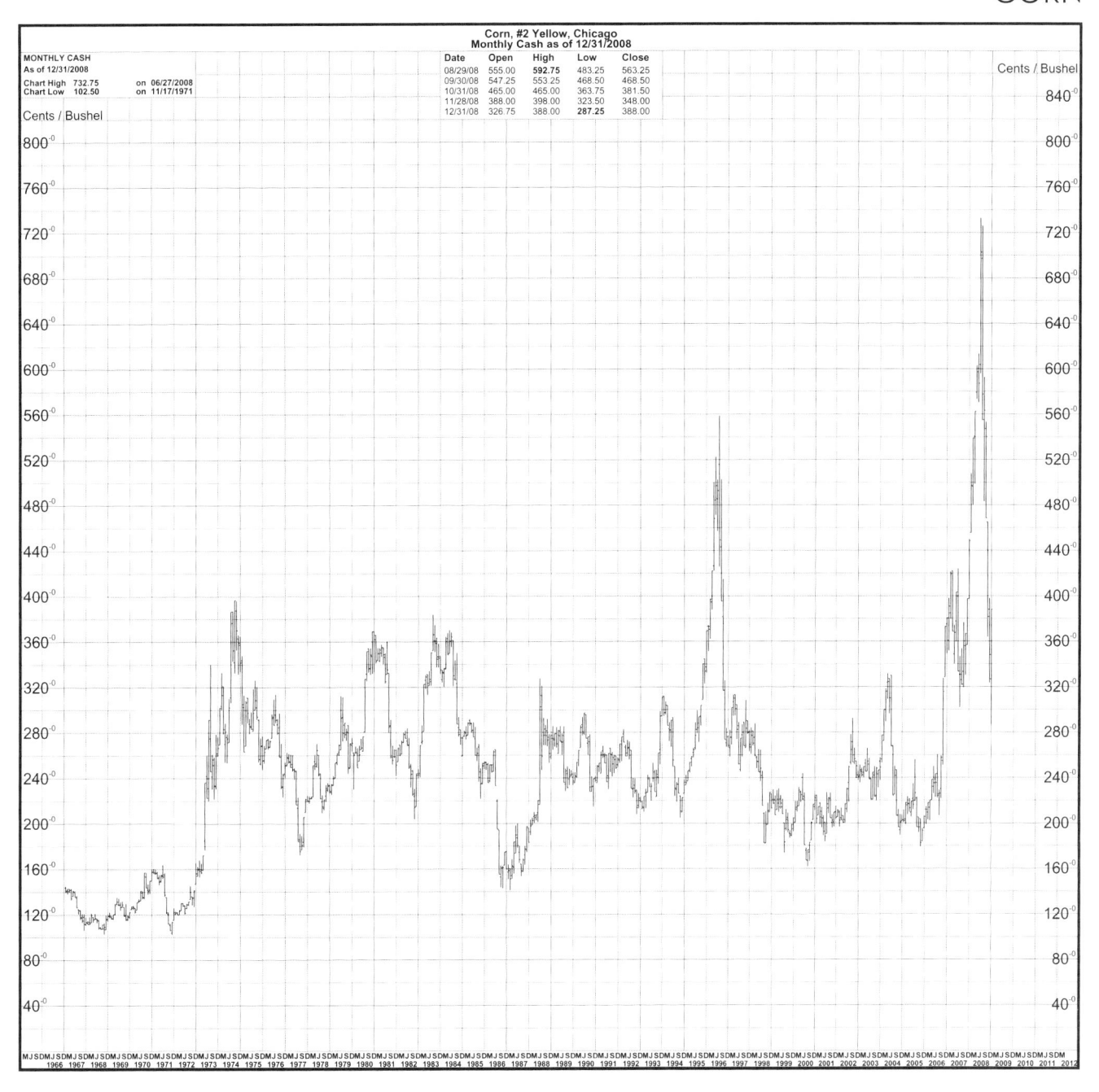

# CORN

**Corn, #2 Yellow, Chicago**
Monthly Cash as of 12/31/2008

| Date | Open | High | Low | Close |
|---|---|---|---|---|
| 08/29/08 | 555.00 | 592.75 | 483.25 | 563.25 |
| 09/30/08 | 547.25 | 553.25 | 468.50 | 468.50 |
| 10/31/08 | 465.00 | 465.00 | 363.75 | 381.50 |
| 11/28/08 | 388.00 | 398.00 | 323.50 | 348.00 |
| 12/31/08 | 326.75 | 388.00 | 287.25 | 388.00 |

MONTHLY CASH
As of 12/31/2008
Chart High 732.75 on 06/27/2008
Chart Low 102.50 on 11/17/1971
Cents / Bushel

## Annual High, Low and Settle of Corn — In Cents per Bushel

| Year | High | Low | Settle | Year | High | Low | Settle | Year | High | Low | Settle |
|---|---|---|---|---|---|---|---|---|---|---|---|
| 1967 | 145.00 | 106.50 | 113.50 | 1981 | 365.75 | 242.00 | 251.50 | 1995 | 369.25 | 233.50 | 369.25 |
| 1968 | 121.50 | 103.00 | 119.00 | 1982 | 284.00 | 204.00 | 242.75 | 1996 | 558.50 | 266.50 | 268.25 |
| 1969 | 135.25 | 115.00 | 122.25 | 1983 | 383.75 | 240.75 | 335.25 | 1997 | 313.25 | 245.25 | 269.00 |
| 1970 | 159.88 | 121.50 | 157.50 | 1984 | 370.25 | 259.25 | 275.25 | 1998 | 287.75 | 182.25 | 213.25 |
| 1971 | 163.75 | 102.50 | 122.25 | 1985 | 291.75 | 221.75 | 254.25 | 1999 | 230.50 | 173.75 | 204.50 |
| 1972 | 165.50 | 120.00 | 156.25 | 1986 | 265.00 | 143.00 | 160.00 | 2000 | 243.75 | 161.75 | 222.25 |
| 1973 | 340.00 | 153.00 | 266.50 | 1987 | 199.75 | 141.25 | 183.25 | 2001 | 227.25 | 183.50 | 205.00 |
| 1974 | 396.50 | 253.50 | 341.75 | 1988 | 327.50 | 189.50 | 277.50 | 2002 | 292.50 | 196.75 | 240.75 |
| 1975 | 347.75 | 247.75 | 255.50 | 1989 | 285.50 | 228.25 | 237.25 | 2003 | 265.75 | 219.75 | 249.00 |
| 1976 | 313.75 | 223.25 | 251.75 | 1990 | 297.25 | 214.50 | 237.75 | 2004 | 331.50 | 189.50 | 202.75 |
| 1977 | 262.75 | 172.25 | 220.25 | 1991 | 268.25 | 230.00 | 256.50 | 2005 | 256.00 | 179.00 | 205.75 |
| 1978 | 270.25 | 209.50 | 228.75 | 1992 | 282.75 | 208.00 | 219.00 | 2006 | 380.25 | 199.00 | 380.25 |
| 1979 | 312.50 | 225.50 | 271.00 | 1993 | 311.00 | 210.00 | 311.00 | 2007 | 449.75 | 302.00 | 448.50 |
| 1980 | 369.00 | 230.25 | 362.00 | 1994 | 311.75 | 204.75 | 236.00 | 2008 | 732.75 | 287.25 | 388.00 |

Chicago #2 Yellow. Data continued from page 177. *Source: U.S. Department of Agriculture*

179

# CORN

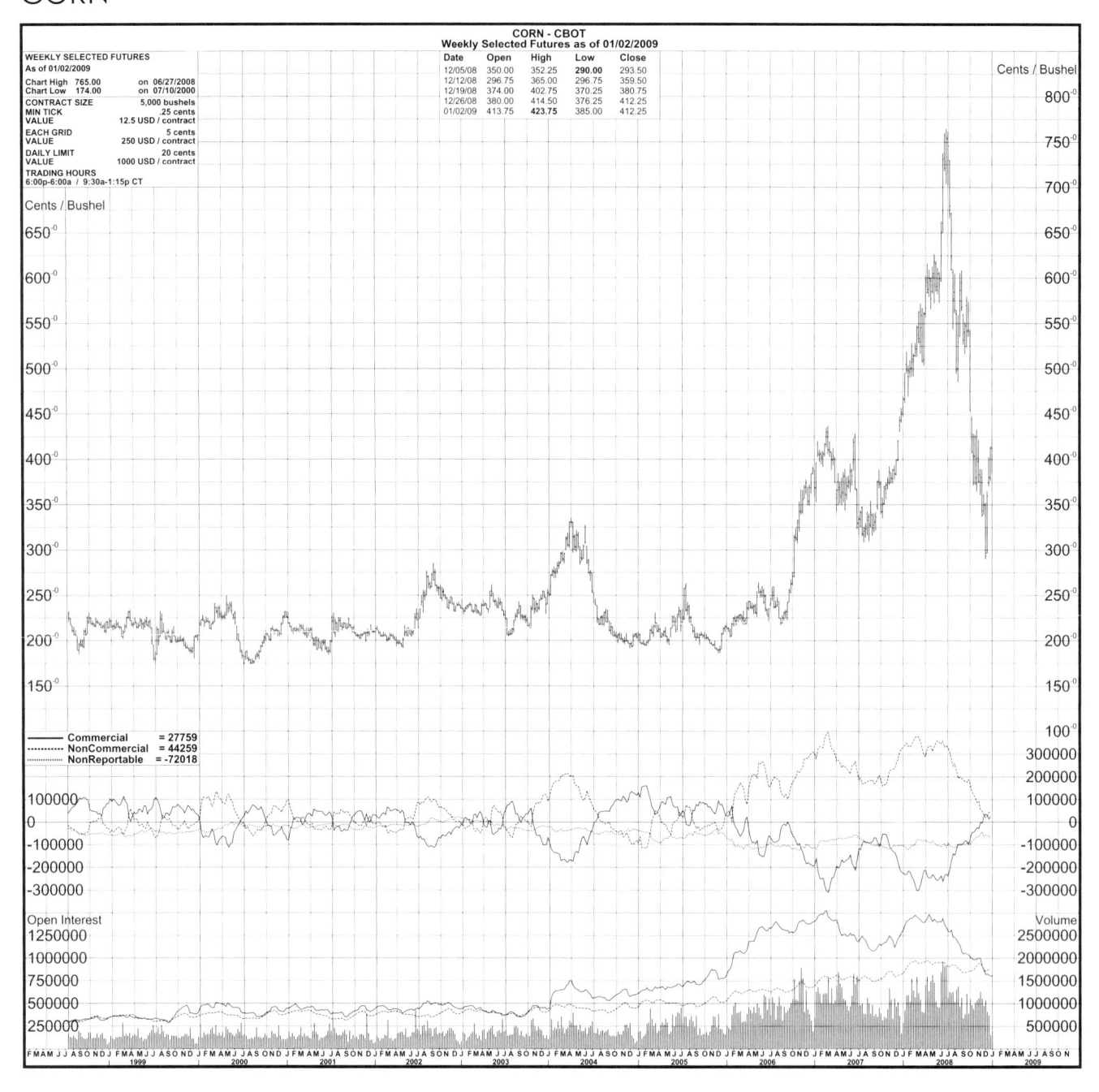

## Quarterly High, Low and Settle of Corn Futures   In Cents per Bushel

| Quarter | High | Low | Settle | Quarter | High | Low | Settle | Quarter | High | Low | Settle |
|---------|------|-----|--------|---------|------|-----|--------|---------|------|-----|--------|
| 03/2000 | 241.75 | 200.50 | 236.00 | 03/2003 | 246.00 | 227.25 | 236.50 | 03/2006 | 243.00 | 203.50 | 236.00 |
| 06/2000 | 249.50 | 186.50 | 187.50 | 06/2003 | 262.00 | 228.00 | 228.50 | 06/2006 | 264.25 | 221.00 | 235.50 |
| 09/2000 | 199.00 | 174.00 | 197.75 | 09/2003 | 243.50 | 204.50 | 220.25 | 09/2006 | 268.00 | 216.75 | 262.50 |
| 12/2000 | 232.00 | 196.75 | 231.75 | 12/2003 | 255.00 | 213.25 | 246.00 | 12/2006 | 392.00 | 261.50 | 390.25 |
| 03/2001 | 232.00 | 202.50 | 203.25 | 03/2004 | 321.75 | 245.75 | 320.00 | 03/2007 | 437.25 | 352.50 | 374.50 |
| 06/2001 | 214.75 | 184.00 | 188.75 | 06/2004 | 335.25 | 254.50 | 257.50 | 06/2007 | 428.75 | 323.00 | 329.50 |
| 09/2001 | 230.50 | 185.75 | 214.50 | 09/2004 | 259.25 | 204.00 | 205.50 | 09/2007 | 389.50 | 308.50 | 373.00 |
| 12/2001 | 217.50 | 198.25 | 209.00 | 12/2004 | 209.50 | 191.00 | 204.75 | 12/2007 | 457.00 | 335.00 | 455.50 |
| 03/2002 | 216.25 | 198.50 | 202.50 | 03/2005 | 231.00 | 194.00 | 213.00 | 03/2008 | 588.00 | 456.00 | 567.25 |
| 06/2002 | 230.00 | 191.50 | 225.50 | 06/2005 | 237.50 | 195.25 | 212.25 | 06/2008 | 765.00 | 561.25 | 724.75 |
| 09/2002 | 285.50 | 212.50 | 251.50 | 09/2005 | 263.25 | 195.00 | 205.50 | 09/2008 | 751.50 | 485.25 | 487.50 |
| 12/2002 | 261.75 | 231.25 | 235.75 | 12/2005 | 217.00 | 185.75 | 215.75 | 12/2008 | 500.00 | 290.00 | 407.00 |

*Source: CME Group; Chicago Board of Trade*

# CORN

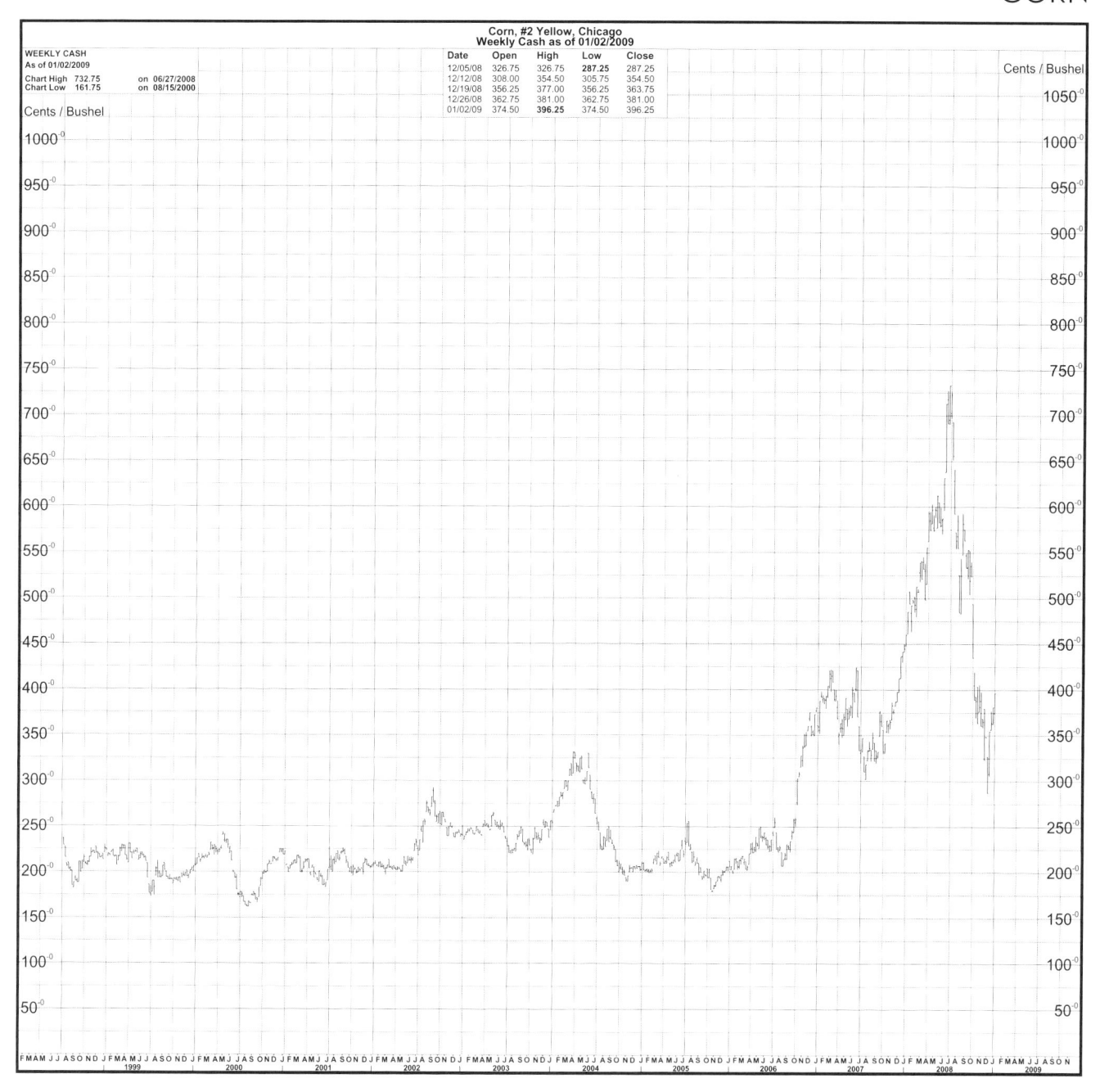

**WEEKLY CASH**
As of 01/02/2009
Chart High 732.75 on 06/27/2008
Chart Low 161.75 on 08/15/2000
Cents / Bushel

**Corn, #2 Yellow, Chicago**
Weekly Cash as of 01/02/2009

| Date | Open | High | Low | Close |
|---|---|---|---|---|
| 12/05/08 | 326.75 | 326.75 | 287.25 | 287.25 |
| 12/12/08 | 308.00 | 354.50 | 305.75 | 354.50 |
| 12/19/08 | 356.25 | 377.00 | 356.25 | 363.75 |
| 12/26/08 | 362.75 | 381.00 | 362.75 | 381.00 |
| 01/02/09 | 374.50 | 396.25 | 374.50 | 396.25 |

## Quarterly High, Low and Settle of Corn   In Cents per Bushel

| Quarter | High | Low | Settle | Quarter | High | Low | Settle | Quarter | High | Low | Settle |
|---|---|---|---|---|---|---|---|---|---|---|---|
| 03/2000 | 231.75 | 200.75 | 229.00 | 03/2003 | 251.25 | 235.50 | 249.50 | 03/2006 | 220.00 | 199.00 | 220.00 |
| 06/2000 | 243.75 | 180.75 | 180.75 | 06/2003 | 265.75 | 238.50 | 238.50 | 06/2006 | 250.00 | 220.50 | 235.50 |
| 09/2000 | 182.75 | 161.75 | 182.75 | 09/2003 | 250.00 | 220.50 | 223.25 | 09/2006 | 260.25 | 206.75 | 257.50 |
| 12/2000 | 224.75 | 184.75 | 222.25 | 12/2003 | 257.75 | 219.75 | 249.00 | 12/2006 | 380.25 | 251.00 | 380.25 |
| 03/2001 | 225.00 | 198.75 | 205.25 | 03/2004 | 318.50 | 253.00 | 316.00 | 03/2007 | 422.00 | 351.50 | 368.50 |
| 06/2001 | 214.25 | 183.50 | 188.25 | 06/2004 | 331.50 | 267.50 | 267.50 | 06/2007 | 424.00 | 333.50 | 333.50 |
| 09/2001 | 227.25 | 190.75 | 204.50 | 09/2004 | 268.00 | 206.50 | 206.50 | 09/2007 | 376.50 | 302.00 | 360.00 |
| 12/2001 | 215.25 | 196.00 | 205.00 | 12/2004 | 212.25 | 189.50 | 202.75 | 12/2007 | 449.75 | 330.25 | 448.50 |
| 03/2002 | 213.50 | 196.75 | 202.50 | 03/2005 | 223.50 | 199.00 | 217.00 | 03/2008 | 562.25 | 455.50 | 562.25 |
| 06/2002 | 231.00 | 200.25 | 230.00 | 06/2005 | 234.75 | 205.50 | 216.25 | 06/2008 | 732.75 | 570.25 | 702.75 |
| 09/2002 | 292.50 | 218.50 | 253.50 | 09/2005 | 256.00 | 191.75 | 196.50 | 09/2008 | 726.00 | 468.50 | 468.50 |
| 12/2002 | 266.00 | 237.75 | 240.75 | 12/2005 | 206.25 | 179.00 | 205.75 | 12/2008 | 465.00 | 287.25 | 388.00 |

Chicago #2 Yellow.   *Source: U.S. Department of Agriculture*

# OATS

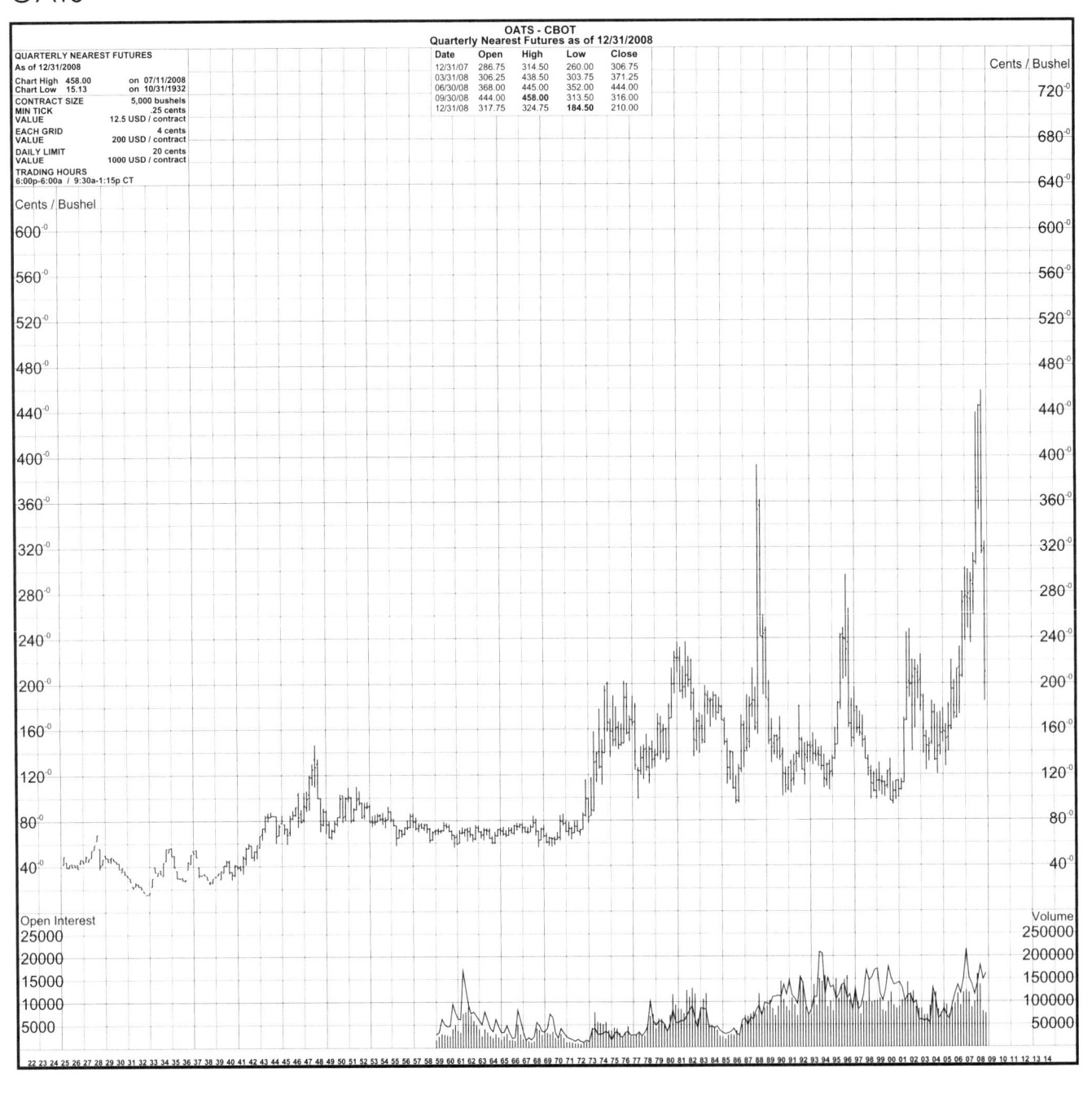

**OATS - CBOT**
Quarterly Nearest Futures as of 12/31/2008

| Date | Open | High | Low | Close |
|---|---|---|---|---|
| 12/31/07 | 286.75 | 314.50 | 260.00 | 306.75 |
| 03/31/08 | 306.25 | 438.50 | 303.75 | 371.25 |
| 06/30/08 | 368.00 | 445.00 | 352.00 | 444.00 |
| 09/30/08 | 444.00 | 458.00 | 313.50 | 316.00 |
| 12/31/08 | 317.75 | 324.75 | 184.50 | 210.00 |

**QUARTERLY NEAREST FUTURES**
As of 12/31/2008
Chart High 458.00 on 07/11/2008
Chart Low 15.13 on 10/31/1932
CONTRACT SIZE 5,000 bushels
MIN TICK .25 cents
VALUE 12.5 USD / contract
EACH GRID 4 cents
VALUE 200 USD / contract
DAILY LIMIT 20 cents
VALUE 1000 USD / contract
TRADING HOURS
6:00p-6:00a / 9:30a-1:15p CT

## Annual High, Low and Settle of Oats Futures — In Cents per Bushel

| Year | High | Low | Settle | Year | High | Low | Settle | Year | High | Low | Settle |
|---|---|---|---|---|---|---|---|---|---|---|---|
| 1925 | 57.75 | 39.25 | 41.88 | 1939 | 40.75 | 28.75 | 40.75 | 1953 | 94.25 | 74.50 | 84.25 |
| 1926 | 46.50 | 38.38 | 46.50 | 1940 | 45.75 | 28.00 | 41.25 | 1954 | 92.50 | 73.25 | 88.00 |
| 1927 | 54.25 | 43.50 | 54.25 | 1941 | 57.00 | 33.00 | 55.50 | 1955 | 88.50 | 57.50 | 71.50 |
| 1928 | 68.00 | 37.38 | 46.50 | 1942 | 59.75 | 44.75 | 58.50 | 1956 | 86.50 | 65.00 | 84.00 |
| 1929 | 50.38 | 43.25 | 45.00 | 1943 | 87.00 | 56.50 | 83.25 | 1957 | 86.50 | 69.63 | 73.25 |
| 1930 | 44.75 | 32.50 | 33.63 | 1944 | 87.75 | 60.00 | 75.00 | 1958 | 77.50 | 60.50 | 69.38 |
| 1931 | 32.38 | 20.75 | 24.75 | 1945 | 85.00 | 59.00 | 82.00 | 1959 | 81.75 | 67.25 | 75.63 |
| 1932 | 24.63 | 15.13 | 15.38 | 1946 | 105.00 | 74.00 | 79.00 | 1960 | 77.75 | 56.00 | 64.88 |
| 1933 | 39.25 | 15.13 | 34.63 | 1947 | 130.00 | 79.00 | 125.00 | 1961 | 74.00 | 58.50 | 71.75 |
| 1934 | 55.75 | 31.75 | 55.75 | 1948 | 146.75 | 70.00 | 88.13 | 1962 | 76.00 | 61.13 | 73.63 |
| 1935 | 56.25 | 29.00 | 29.25 | 1949 | 89.13 | 63.25 | 77.63 | 1963 | 75.38 | 62.38 | 70.75 |
| 1936 | 50.38 | 26.63 | 50.38 | 1950 | 103.25 | 75.13 | 99.50 | 1964 | 73.00 | 59.00 | 71.63 |
| 1937 | 54.38 | 30.25 | 32.38 | 1951 | 110.00 | 78.00 | 98.38 | 1965 | 74.25 | 65.13 | 70.88 |
| 1938 | 33.50 | 24.00 | 29.25 | 1952 | 106.25 | 81.25 | 92.50 | 1966 | 78.00 | 67.13 | 76.13 |

Futures data begins 07/01/1959.    Data continued on page 184.    *Source: CME Group; Chicago Board of Trade*

# OATS

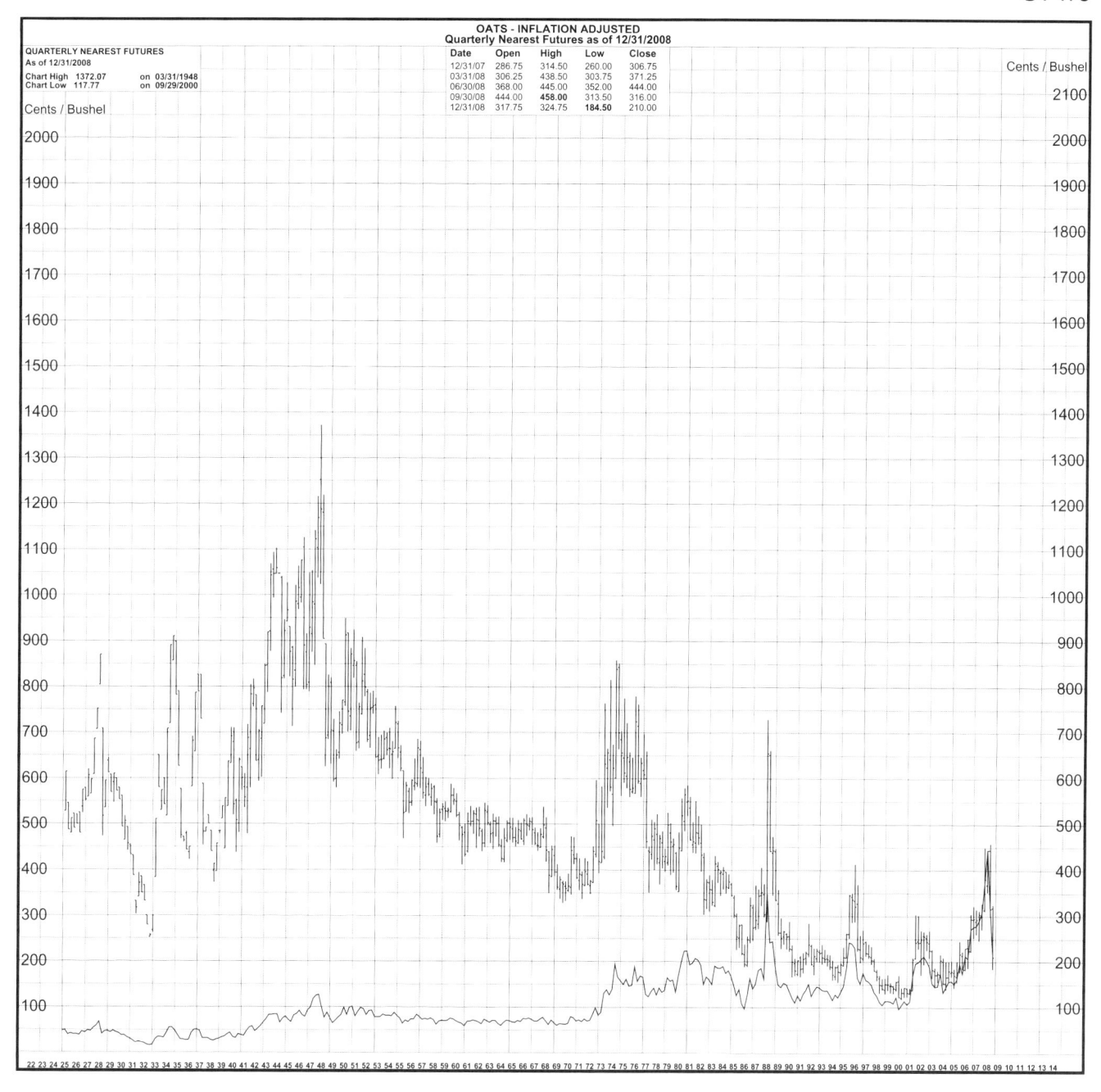

## OATS - INFLATION ADJUSTED
Quarterly Nearest Futures as of 12/31/2008

| Date | Open | High | Low | Close |
|---|---|---|---|---|
| 12/31/07 | 286.75 | 314.50 | 260.00 | 306.75 |
| 03/31/08 | 306.25 | 438.50 | 303.75 | 371.25 |
| 06/30/08 | 368.00 | 445.00 | 352.00 | 444.00 |
| 09/30/08 | 444.00 | 458.00 | 313.50 | 316.00 |
| 12/31/08 | 317.75 | 324.75 | 184.50 | 210.00 |

QUARTERLY NEAREST FUTURES
As of 12/31/2008
Chart High 1372.07 on 03/31/1948
Chart Low 117.77 on 09/29/2000

## Annual High, Low and Settle of Oats   In Cents per Bushel

| Year | High | Low | Settle | Year | High | Low | Settle | Year | High | Low | Settle |
|---|---|---|---|---|---|---|---|---|---|---|---|
| 1925 | | | | 1939 | 37.00 | 27.25 | 37.00 | 1953 | 84.88 | 73.00 | 79.13 |
| 1926 | | | | 1940 | 40.50 | 25.63 | 34.75 | 1954 | 82.50 | 69.88 | 78.00 |
| 1927 | | | | 1941 | 51.38 | 33.25 | 51.38 | 1955 | 77.13 | 57.88 | 65.75 |
| 1928 | | | | 1942 | 55.63 | 44.25 | 52.75 | 1956 | 78.00 | 63.25 | 77.38 |
| 1929 | | | | 1943 | 80.25 | 57.38 | 80.25 | 1957 | 77.88 | 64.00 | 65.50 |
| 1930 | | | | 1944 | 82.00 | 60.50 | 70.63 | 1958 | 66.50 | 59.13 | 63.38 |
| 1931 | | | | 1945 | 78.25 | 59.00 | 76.13 | 1959 | 72.13 | 63.13 | 71.50 |
| 1932 | | | | 1946 | 84.50 | 75.38 | 81.25 | 1960 | 71.75 | 60.25 | 61.63 |
| 1933 | | | | 1947 | 126.13 | 79.75 | 126.13 | 1961 | 72.00 | 59.63 | 72.00 |
| 1934 | | | | 1948 | 136.63 | 70.25 | 80.88 | 1962 | 72.00 | 61.38 | 72.00 |
| 1935 | | | | 1949 | 78.25 | 62.50 | 74.75 | 1963 | 70.38 | 63.25 | 68.25 |
| 1936 | 52.63 | 39.50 | 52.63 | 1950 | 91.75 | 74.13 | 91.75 | 1964 | 69.75 | 62.00 | 69.75 |
| 1937 | 54.38 | 29.00 | 29.38 | 1951 | 99.75 | 77.75 | 99.75 | 1965 | 70.25 | 64.25 | 67.25 |
| 1938 | 31.25 | 24.25 | 28.75 | 1952 | 96.38 | 83.13 | 87.25 | 1966 | 75.25 | 67.88 | 74.63 |

Minneapolis #2 Milling.   Data continued on page 185.   *Source: U.S. Department of Agriculture*

# OATS

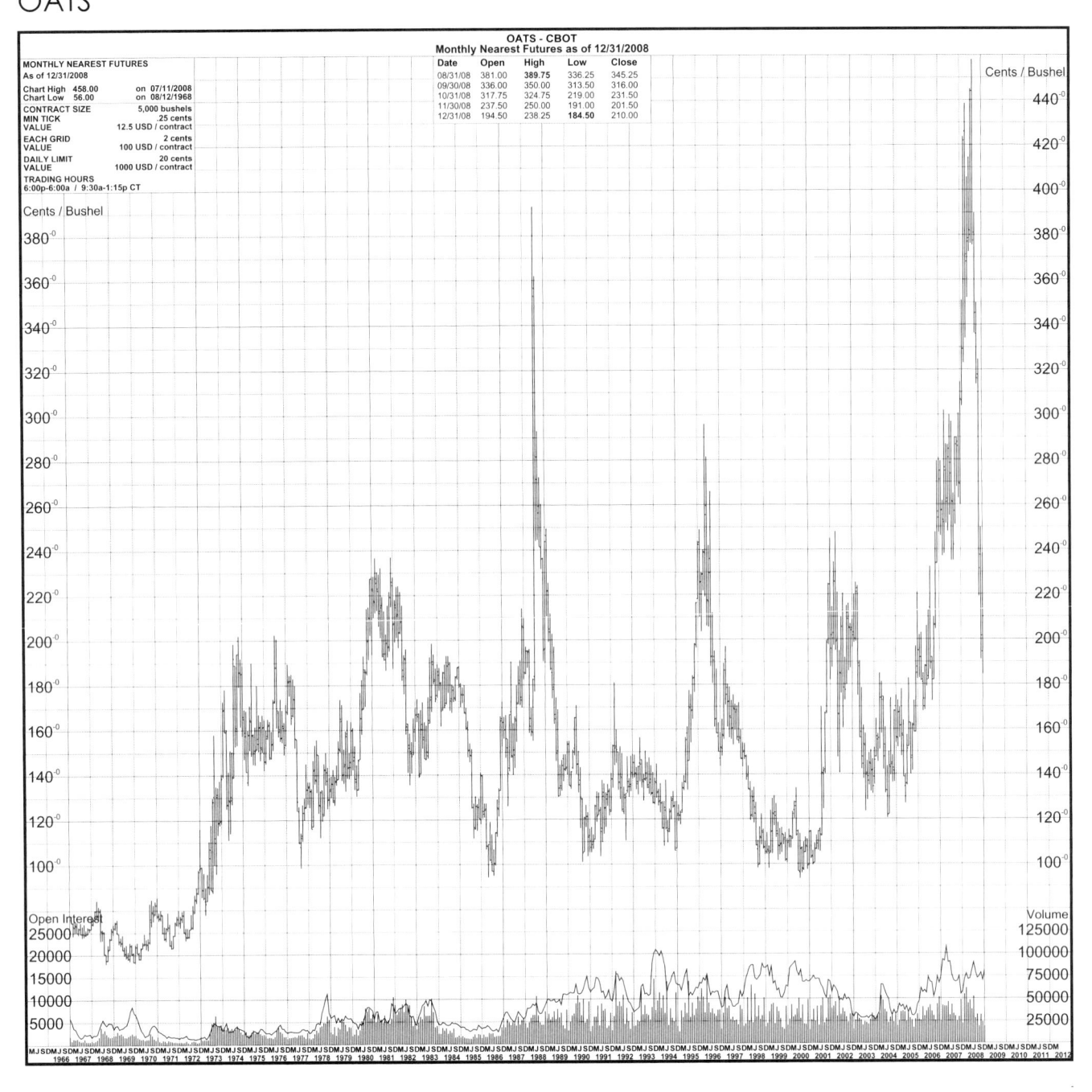

## OATS - CBOT
### Monthly Nearest Futures as of 12/31/2008

| Date | Open | High | Low | Close |
|---|---|---|---|---|
| 08/31/08 | 381.00 | 389.75 | 336.25 | 345.25 |
| 09/30/08 | 336.00 | 350.00 | 313.50 | 316.00 |
| 10/31/08 | 317.75 | 324.75 | 219.00 | 231.50 |
| 11/30/08 | 237.50 | 250.00 | 191.00 | 201.50 |
| 12/31/08 | 194.50 | 238.25 | 184.50 | 210.00 |

**MONTHLY NEAREST FUTURES**
As of 12/31/2008
Chart High 458.00 on 07/11/2008
Chart Low 56.00 on 08/12/1968
CONTRACT SIZE 5,000 bushels
MIN TICK .25 cents
VALUE 12.5 USD / contract
EACH GRID 2 cents
VALUE 100 USD / contract
DAILY LIMIT 20 cents
VALUE 1000 USD / contract
TRADING HOURS
6:00p-6:00a / 9:30a-1:15p CT

## Annual High, Low and Settle of Oats Futures — In Cents per Bushel

| Year | High | Low | Settle | Year | High | Low | Settle | Year | High | Low | Settle |
|---|---|---|---|---|---|---|---|---|---|---|---|
| 1967 | 77.75 | 67.75 | 73.88 | 1981 | 237.00 | 186.50 | 207.00 | 1995 | 243.75 | 117.50 | 242.25 |
| 1968 | 84.38 | 56.00 | 72.13 | 1982 | 224.25 | 135.50 | 166.75 | 1996 | 296.00 | 143.50 | 152.00 |
| 1969 | 75.88 | 56.50 | 63.63 | 1983 | 198.50 | 138.75 | 186.00 | 1997 | 197.00 | 143.25 | 149.75 |
| 1970 | 85.75 | 58.00 | 77.25 | 1984 | 193.00 | 161.50 | 180.25 | 1998 | 153.75 | 98.25 | 105.50 |
| 1971 | 80.00 | 62.75 | 74.50 | 1985 | 181.00 | 111.50 | 139.50 | 1999 | 130.50 | 98.00 | 109.25 |
| 1972 | 116.00 | 66.25 | 98.75 | 1986 | 172.50 | 94.25 | 163.25 | 2000 | 134.00 | 93.50 | 114.25 |
| 1973 | 158.00 | 77.75 | 138.50 | 1987 | 214.00 | 126.00 | 185.50 | 2001 | 245.00 | 99.50 | 195.75 |
| 1974 | 202.00 | 111.00 | 166.00 | 1988 | 393.00 | 155.00 | 243.75 | 2002 | 248.00 | 140.50 | 201.75 |
| 1975 | 190.00 | 135.50 | 146.25 | 1989 | 249.50 | 130.25 | 153.50 | 2003 | 225.50 | 123.50 | 146.25 |
| 1976 | 202.50 | 145.00 | 168.50 | 1990 | 171.00 | 101.00 | 110.25 | 2004 | 185.00 | 120.50 | 156.25 |
| 1977 | 189.50 | 98.50 | 134.50 | 1991 | 140.50 | 103.50 | 138.00 | 2005 | 220.75 | 127.00 | 195.00 |
| 1978 | 155.75 | 112.00 | 133.00 | 1992 | 181.00 | 110.50 | 145.25 | 2006 | 280.75 | 168.00 | 271.00 |
| 1979 | 173.75 | 126.50 | 159.75 | 1993 | 156.50 | 126.75 | 136.75 | 2007 | 314.50 | 235.00 | 306.75 |
| 1980 | 228.50 | 130.50 | 223.00 | 1994 | 144.75 | 106.00 | 121.75 | 2008 | 458.00 | 184.50 | 210.00 |

Data continued from page 182.   Source: *CME Group; Chicago Board of Trade*

# OATS

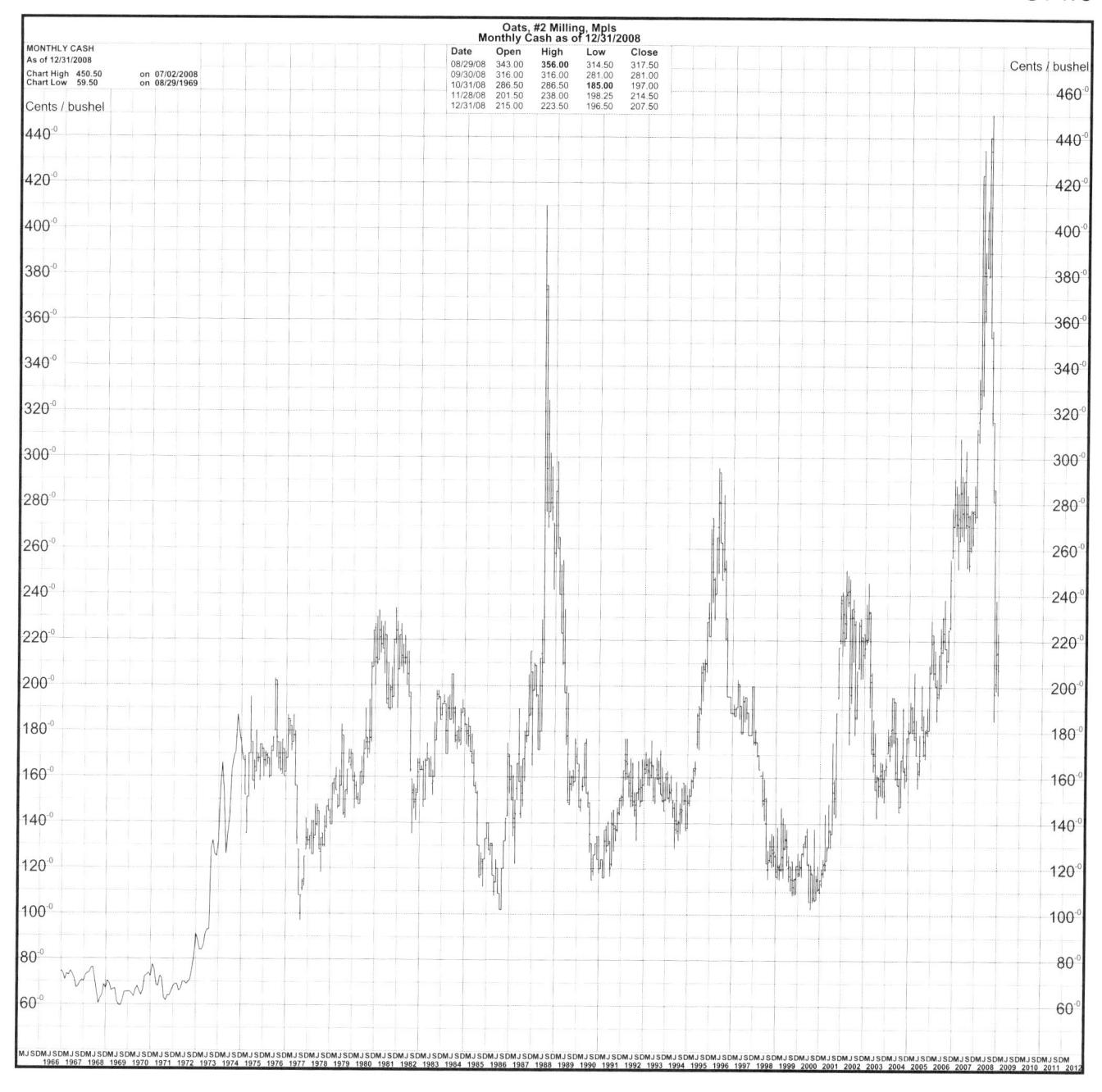

**Oats, #2 Milling, Mpls**
**Monthly Cash as of 12/31/2008**

| Date | Open | High | Low | Close |
|---|---|---|---|---|
| 08/29/08 | 343.00 | 356.00 | 314.50 | 317.50 |
| 09/30/08 | 316.00 | 316.00 | 281.00 | 281.00 |
| 10/31/08 | 286.50 | 286.50 | 185.00 | 197.00 |
| 11/28/08 | 201.50 | 238.00 | 198.25 | 214.50 |
| 12/31/08 | 215.00 | 223.50 | 196.50 | 207.50 |

MONTHLY CASH
As of 12/31/2008
Chart High 450.50 on 07/02/2008
Chart Low 59.50 on 08/29/1969
Cents / bushel

## Annual High, Low and Settle of Oats — In Cents per Bushel

| Year | High | Low | Settle | Year | High | Low | Settle | Year | High | Low | Settle |
|---|---|---|---|---|---|---|---|---|---|---|---|
| 1967 | 74.63 | 67.25 | 70.13 | 1981 | 234.00 | 189.00 | 207.00 | 1995 | 268.75 | 147.50 | 262.25 |
| 1968 | 76.25 | 60.38 | 67.00 | 1982 | 227.00 | 135.00 | 163.00 | 1996 | 295.50 | 188.25 | 188.25 |
| 1969 | 70.38 | 59.50 | 65.63 | 1983 | 198.00 | 147.00 | 192.00 | 1997 | 203.00 | 174.50 | 175.50 |
| 1970 | 73.88 | 63.50 | 72.25 | 1984 | 205.00 | 170.00 | 183.00 | 1998 | 181.25 | 115.50 | 116.75 |
| 1971 | 77.50 | 61.75 | 68.00 | 1985 | 186.00 | 112.00 | 140.00 | 1999 | 147.00 | 108.50 | 118.25 |
| 1972 | 91.00 | 66.00 | 91.00 | 1986 | 175.00 | 102.00 | 159.00 | 2000 | 138.25 | 102.75 | 115.25 |
| 1973 | 132.00 | 84.00 | 132.00 | 1987 | 215.00 | 122.00 | 198.00 | 2001 | 241.50 | 112.25 | 223.75 |
| 1974 | 187.00 | 126.00 | 174.00 | 1988 | 410.00 | 172.00 | 285.00 | 2002 | 251.00 | 174.50 | 216.75 |
| 1975 | 195.00 | 135.00 | 167.00 | 1989 | 298.00 | 148.00 | 166.00 | 2003 | 245.50 | 142.50 | 165.25 |
| 1976 | 203.00 | 159.00 | 168.00 | 1990 | 177.00 | 115.00 | 120.00 | 2004 | 195.50 | 145.25 | 179.75 |
| 1977 | 187.00 | 97.00 | 132.00 | 1991 | 152.50 | 116.00 | 151.50 | 2005 | 229.00 | 155.50 | 219.00 |
| 1978 | 150.00 | 118.00 | 139.00 | 1992 | 177.00 | 132.25 | 163.75 | 2006 | 291.25 | 184.75 | 284.50 |
| 1979 | 183.00 | 139.00 | 158.00 | 1993 | 176.25 | 145.50 | 161.75 | 2007 | 313.00 | 250.75 | 310.75 |
| 1980 | 227.00 | 146.00 | 212.00 | 1994 | 163.00 | 128.75 | 149.00 | 2008 | 450.50 | 185.00 | 207.50 |

Data continued from page 183. Minneapolis #2 Milling. *Source: U.S. Department of Agriculture*

# OATS

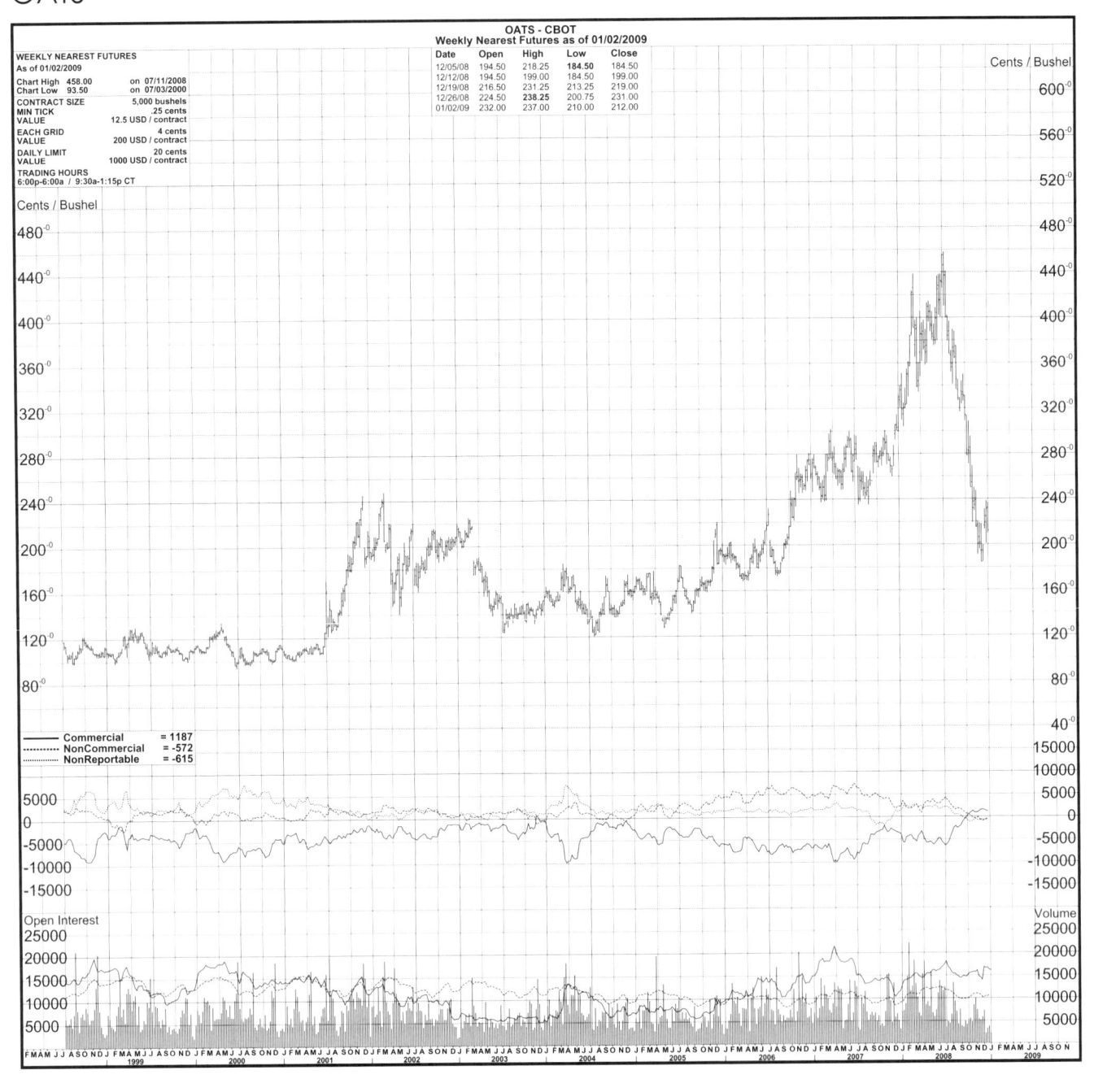

## OATS - CBOT
### Weekly Nearest Futures as of 01/02/2009

| Date | Open | High | Low | Close |
|---|---|---|---|---|
| 12/05/08 | 194.50 | 218.25 | 184.50 | 184.50 |
| 12/12/08 | 194.50 | 199.00 | 184.50 | 199.00 |
| 12/19/08 | 216.50 | 231.25 | 213.25 | 219.00 |
| 12/26/08 | 224.50 | 238.25 | 200.75 | 231.00 |
| 01/02/09 | 232.00 | 237.00 | 210.00 | 212.00 |

**WEEKLY NEAREST FUTURES**
As of 01/02/2009
Chart High 458.00 on 07/11/2008
Chart Low 93.50 on 07/03/2000
CONTRACT SIZE 5,000 bushels
MIN TICK .25 cents
VALUE 12.5 USD / contract
EACH GRID 4 cents
VALUE 200 USD / contract
DAILY LIMIT 20 cents
VALUE 1000 USD / contract
TRADING HOURS 6:00p-6:00a / 9:30a-1:15p CT

Commercial = 1187
NonCommercial = -572
NonReportable = -615

## Quarterly High, Low and Settle of Oats Futures   In Cents per Bushel

| Quarter | High | Low | Settle | Quarter | High | Low | Settle | Quarter | High | Low | Settle |
|---|---|---|---|---|---|---|---|---|---|---|---|
| 03/2000 | 123.50 | 107.00 | 122.25 | 03/2003 | 225.50 | 175.00 | 189.25 | 03/2006 | 203.00 | 168.00 | 173.50 |
| 06/2000 | 134.00 | 96.75 | 96.75 | 06/2003 | 190.50 | 138.00 | 153.25 | 06/2006 | 213.00 | 168.50 | 212.75 |
| 09/2000 | 113.50 | 93.50 | 105.25 | 09/2003 | 158.25 | 123.50 | 145.00 | 09/2006 | 232.50 | 172.50 | 206.25 |
| 12/2000 | 114.50 | 97.50 | 114.25 | 12/2003 | 151.75 | 131.25 | 146.25 | 12/2006 | 280.75 | 204.50 | 271.00 |
| 03/2001 | 114.75 | 99.50 | 106.50 | 03/2004 | 185.00 | 145.50 | 174.00 | 03/2007 | 302.00 | 237.00 | 276.50 |
| 06/2001 | 116.00 | 105.50 | 113.00 | 06/2004 | 181.25 | 131.50 | 132.75 | 06/2007 | 300.00 | 248.00 | 278.50 |
| 09/2001 | 170.00 | 112.50 | 167.00 | 09/2004 | 174.00 | 120.50 | 144.25 | 09/2007 | 297.00 | 235.00 | 289.75 |
| 12/2001 | 245.00 | 166.75 | 195.75 | 12/2004 | 175.00 | 136.25 | 156.25 | 12/2007 | 314.50 | 260.00 | 306.75 |
| 03/2002 | 248.00 | 187.50 | 199.00 | 03/2005 | 178.00 | 148.00 | 157.75 | 03/2008 | 438.50 | 303.75 | 371.25 |
| 06/2002 | 221.00 | 140.50 | 205.50 | 06/2005 | 164.00 | 127.00 | 151.25 | 06/2008 | 445.00 | 352.00 | 444.00 |
| 09/2002 | 220.50 | 160.50 | 211.75 | 09/2005 | 182.75 | 140.00 | 161.50 | 09/2008 | 458.00 | 313.50 | 316.00 |
| 12/2002 | 216.00 | 186.00 | 201.75 | 12/2005 | 220.75 | 158.50 | 195.00 | 12/2008 | 324.75 | 184.50 | 210.00 |

*Source: CME Group; Chicago Board of Trade*

# OATS

Oats, #2 Milling, Mpls
Weekly Cash as of 01/02/2009

| Date | Open | High | Low | Close |
|---|---|---|---|---|
| 12/05/08 | 215.00 | 219.50 | **196.50** | 196.50 |
| 12/12/08 | 205.50 | 213.50 | 205.50 | 213.50 |
| 12/19/08 | 216.00 | **223.50** | 216.00 | 216.50 |
| 12/26/08 | 216.50 | 216.50 | 212.50 | 216.25 |
| 01/02/09 | 214.50 | 214.50 | 207.50 | 209.50 |

WEEKLY CASH
As of 01/02/2009
Chart High 450.50 on 07/02/2008
Chart Low 102.75 on 07/03/2000
Cents / bushel

## Quarterly High, Low and Settle of Oats    In Cents per Bushel

| Quarter | High | Low | Settle | Quarter | High | Low | Settle | Quarter | High | Low | Settle |
|---|---|---|---|---|---|---|---|---|---|---|---|
| 03/2000 | 131.25 | 116.50 | 131.25 | 03/2003 | 245.50 | 191.00 | 205.25 | 03/2006 | 222.75 | 184.75 | 195.75 |
| 06/2000 | 138.25 | 105.75 | 105.75 | 06/2003 | 206.25 | 155.00 | 155.00 | 06/2006 | 230.50 | 194.75 | 220.25 |
| 09/2000 | 137.75 | 102.75 | 106.25 | 09/2003 | 167.25 | 142.50 | 161.50 | 09/2006 | 238.25 | 202.00 | 224.75 |
| 12/2000 | 121.50 | 106.75 | 115.25 | 12/2003 | 169.00 | 149.25 | 165.25 | 12/2006 | 291.25 | 225.25 | 284.50 |
| 03/2001 | 144.25 | 112.25 | 122.00 | 03/2004 | 195.50 | 167.50 | 181.50 | 03/2007 | 308.75 | 251.50 | 285.00 |
| 06/2001 | 148.75 | 123.75 | 135.50 | 06/2004 | 195.25 | 157.00 | 157.00 | 06/2007 | 303.50 | 264.00 | 271.00 |
| 09/2001 | 188.50 | 135.50 | 188.50 | 09/2004 | 191.00 | 145.25 | 163.25 | 09/2007 | 284.00 | 250.75 | 277.25 |
| 12/2001 | 241.50 | 194.75 | 223.75 | 12/2004 | 184.50 | 155.75 | 179.75 | 12/2007 | 313.00 | 262.00 | 310.75 |
| 03/2002 | 251.00 | 217.75 | 237.00 | 03/2005 | 206.25 | 177.00 | 177.00 | 03/2008 | 434.75 | 307.00 | 364.75 |
| 06/2002 | 247.25 | 174.50 | 233.00 | 06/2005 | 185.50 | 155.50 | 168.00 | 06/2008 | 440.50 | 360.00 | 440.50 |
| 09/2002 | 229.00 | 178.75 | 226.75 | 09/2005 | 201.00 | 168.25 | 180.50 | 09/2008 | 450.50 | 281.00 | 281.00 |
| 12/2002 | 229.50 | 203.25 | 216.75 | 12/2005 | 229.00 | 178.75 | 219.00 | 12/2008 | 286.50 | 185.00 | 207.50 |

Minneapolis #2 Milling.    *Source: U.S. Department of Agriculture*

# RICE

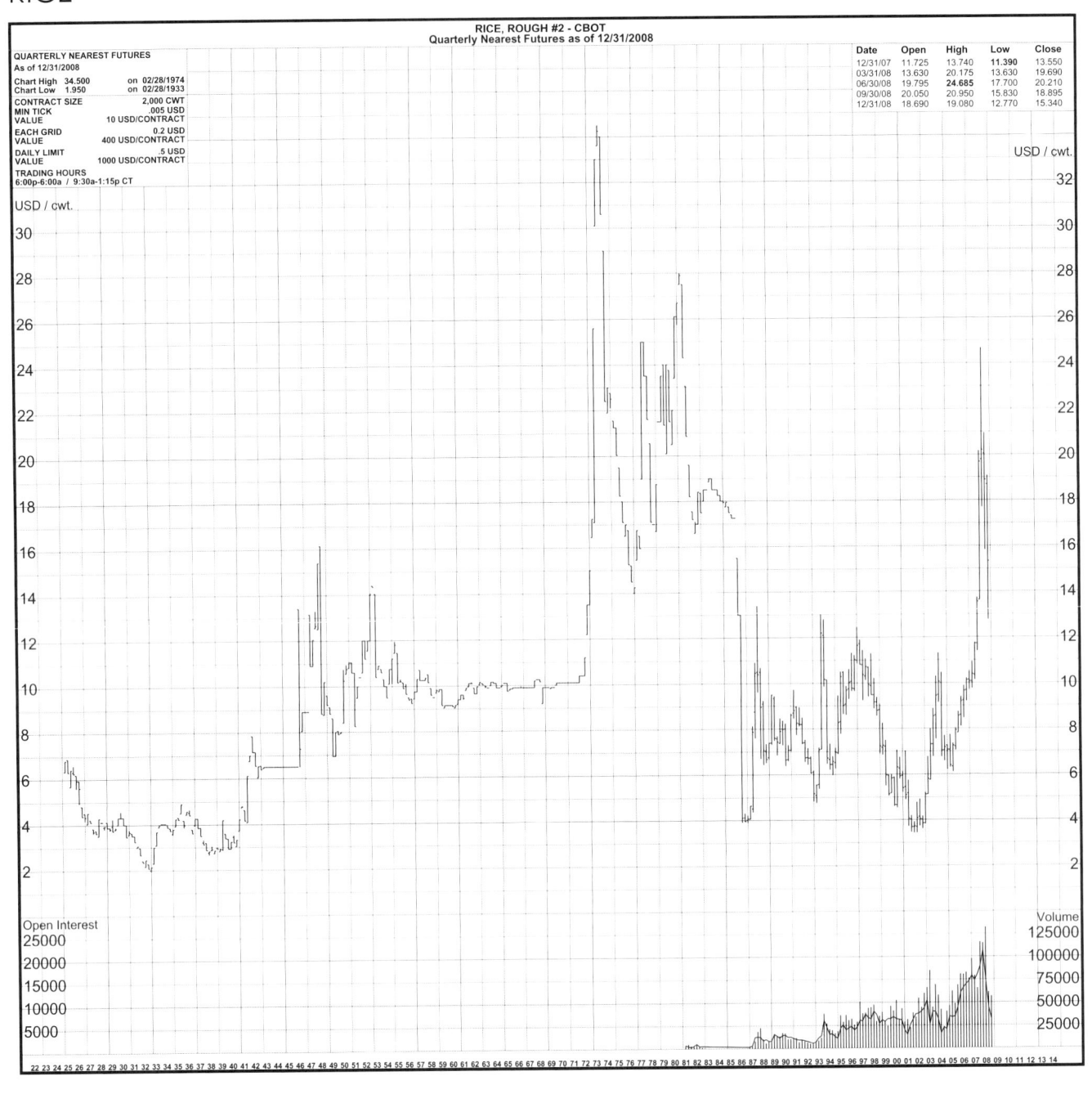

RICE, ROUGH #2 - CBOT
Quarterly Nearest Futures as of 12/31/2008

| Date | Open | High | Low | Close |
|------|------|------|-----|-------|
| 12/31/07 | 11.725 | 13.740 | 11.390 | 13.550 |
| 03/31/08 | 13.630 | 20.175 | 13.630 | 19.690 |
| 06/30/08 | 19.795 | 24.685 | 17.700 | 20.210 |
| 09/30/08 | 20.050 | 20.950 | 15.830 | 18.895 |
| 12/31/08 | 18.690 | 19.080 | 12.770 | 15.340 |

**QUARTERLY NEAREST FUTURES**
As of 12/31/2008
Chart High 34.500 on 02/28/1974
Chart Low 1.950 on 02/28/1933
CONTRACT SIZE 2,000 CWT
MIN TICK VALUE .005 USD / 10 USD/CONTRACT
EACH GRID VALUE 0.2 USD / 400 USD/CONTRACT
DAILY LIMIT VALUE .5 USD / 1000 USD/CONTRACT
TRADING HOURS 6:00p-6:00a / 9:30a-1:15p CT

## Annual High, Low and Settle of Rice    In Dollars per Cwt.

| Year | High | Low | Settle | Year | High | Low | Settle | Year | High | Low | Settle |
|------|------|-----|--------|------|------|-----|--------|------|------|-----|--------|
| 1925 | 6.88 | 5.69 | 6.41 | 1939 | 4.19 | 2.82 | 3.38 | 1953 | 14.40 | 10.40 | 10.90 |
| 1926 | 6.59 | 4.38 | 4.38 | 1940 | 3.52 | 2.93 | 3.32 | 1954 | 10.75 | 9.50 | 10.75 |
| 1927 | 4.52 | 3.62 | 3.69 | 1941 | 6.12 | 3.71 | 6.12 | 1955 | 11.95 | 10.10 | 10.20 |
| 1928 | 4.28 | 3.50 | 3.94 | 1942 | 7.84 | 6.05 | 6.53 | 1956 | 10.15 | 9.25 | 9.25 |
| 1929 | 4.25 | 3.72 | 3.84 | 1943 | 6.55 | 6.40 | 6.50 | 1957 | 10.70 | 9.45 | 10.25 |
| 1930 | 4.56 | 3.46 | 3.46 | 1944 | 6.50 | 6.50 | 6.50 | 1958 | 10.50 | 9.50 | 9.50 |
| 1931 | 3.75 | 3.00 | 3.06 | 1945 | 6.50 | 6.50 | 6.50 | 1959 | 9.85 | 9.05 | 9.15 |
| 1932 | 2.97 | 2.08 | 2.08 | 1946 | 13.40 | 6.50 | 8.90 | 1960 | 9.15 | 9.05 | 9.15 |
| 1933 | 3.99 | 1.95 | 3.99 | 1947 | 13.15 | 8.90 | 12.05 | 1961 | 9.90 | 9.20 | 9.90 |
| 1934 | 4.03 | 3.72 | 3.72 | 1948 | 16.15 | 8.75 | 10.20 | 1962 | 10.15 | 9.65 | 9.95 |
| 1935 | 4.90 | 3.56 | 4.90 | 1949 | 9.60 | 6.95 | 8.00 | 1963 | 10.15 | 9.90 | 9.90 |
| 1936 | 4.65 | 3.61 | 3.61 | 1950 | 10.95 | 7.90 | 10.75 | 1964 | 10.15 | 9.90 | 9.90 |
| 1937 | 4.26 | 3.12 | 3.12 | 1951 | 11.05 | 8.25 | 10.00 | 1965 | 10.10 | 9.75 | 9.85 |
| 1938 | 3.19 | 2.66 | 2.85 | 1952 | 12.00 | 10.40 | 12.00 | 1966 | 9.95 | 9.85 | 9.90 |

Louisiana #2 Long grain.    Data continued on page 191.    *Source: U.S. Department of Agriculture*

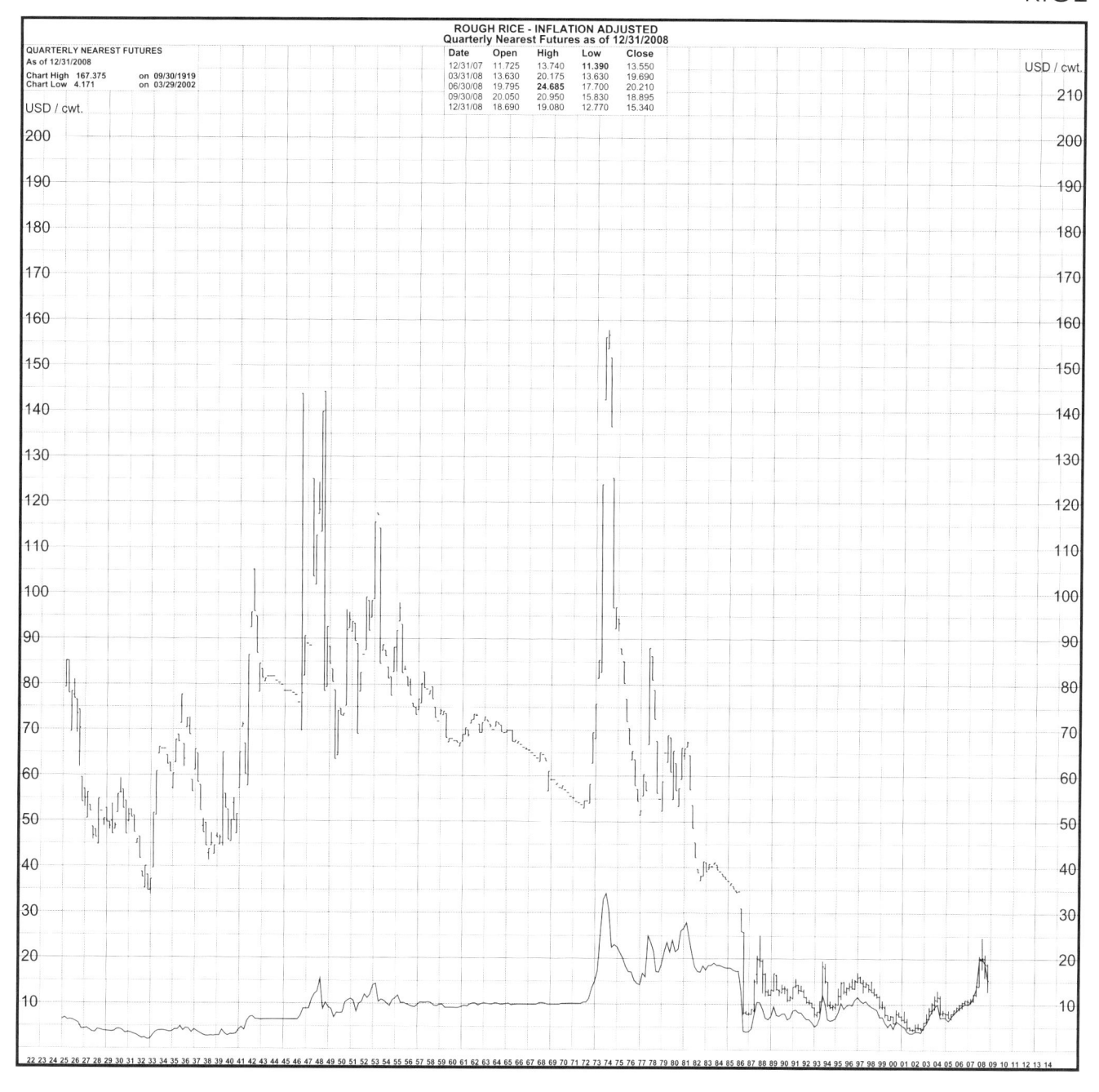

# RICE

## ROUGH RICE - INFLATION ADJUSTED
Quarterly Nearest Futures as of 12/31/2008

| Date | Open | High | Low | Close |
|---|---|---|---|---|
| 12/31/07 | 11.725 | 13.740 | 11.390 | 13.550 |
| 03/31/08 | 13.630 | 20.175 | 13.630 | 19.690 |
| 06/30/08 | 19.795 | 24.685 | 17.700 | 20.210 |
| 09/30/08 | 20.050 | 20.950 | 15.830 | 18.895 |
| 12/31/08 | 18.690 | 19.080 | 12.770 | 15.340 |

**Quarterly Nearest Futures**
As of 12/31/2008
Chart High 167.375 on 09/30/1919
Chart Low 4.171 on 03/29/2002
USD / cwt.

## Annual High, Low and Settle of Rice  In Dollars per Cwt.

| Year | High | Low | Settle | Year | High | Low | Settle | Year | High | Low | Settle |
|---|---|---|---|---|---|---|---|---|---|---|---|
| 1925 | 6.88 | 5.69 | 6.41 | 1939 | 4.19 | 2.82 | 3.38 | 1953 | 14.40 | 10.40 | 10.90 |
| 1926 | 6.59 | 4.38 | 4.38 | 1940 | 3.52 | 2.93 | 3.32 | 1954 | 10.75 | 9.50 | 10.75 |
| 1927 | 4.52 | 3.62 | 3.69 | 1941 | 6.12 | 3.71 | 6.12 | 1955 | 11.95 | 10.10 | 10.20 |
| 1928 | 4.28 | 3.50 | 3.94 | 1942 | 7.84 | 6.05 | 6.53 | 1956 | 10.15 | 9.25 | 9.25 |
| 1929 | 4.25 | 3.72 | 3.84 | 1943 | 6.55 | 6.40 | 6.50 | 1957 | 10.70 | 9.45 | 10.25 |
| 1930 | 4.56 | 3.46 | 3.46 | 1944 | 6.50 | 6.50 | 6.50 | 1958 | 10.50 | 9.50 | 9.50 |
| 1931 | 3.75 | 3.00 | 3.06 | 1945 | 6.50 | 6.50 | 6.50 | 1959 | 9.85 | 9.05 | 9.15 |
| 1932 | 2.97 | 2.08 | 2.08 | 1946 | 13.40 | 6.50 | 8.90 | 1960 | 9.15 | 9.05 | 9.15 |
| 1933 | 3.99 | 1.95 | 3.99 | 1947 | 13.15 | 8.90 | 12.05 | 1961 | 9.90 | 9.20 | 9.90 |
| 1934 | 4.03 | 3.72 | 3.72 | 1948 | 16.15 | 8.75 | 10.20 | 1962 | 10.15 | 9.65 | 9.95 |
| 1935 | 4.90 | 3.56 | 4.90 | 1949 | 9.60 | 6.95 | 8.00 | 1963 | 10.15 | 9.90 | 9.90 |
| 1936 | 4.65 | 3.61 | 3.61 | 1950 | 10.95 | 7.90 | 10.75 | 1964 | 10.15 | 9.90 | 9.90 |
| 1937 | 4.26 | 3.12 | 3.12 | 1951 | 11.05 | 8.25 | 10.00 | 1965 | 10.10 | 9.75 | 9.85 |
| 1938 | 3.19 | 2.66 | 2.85 | 1952 | 12.00 | 10.40 | 12.00 | 1966 | 9.95 | 9.85 | 9.90 |

Louisiana #2 Long grain.   Data continued on page 191.   *Source: U.S. Department of Agriculture*

# RICE

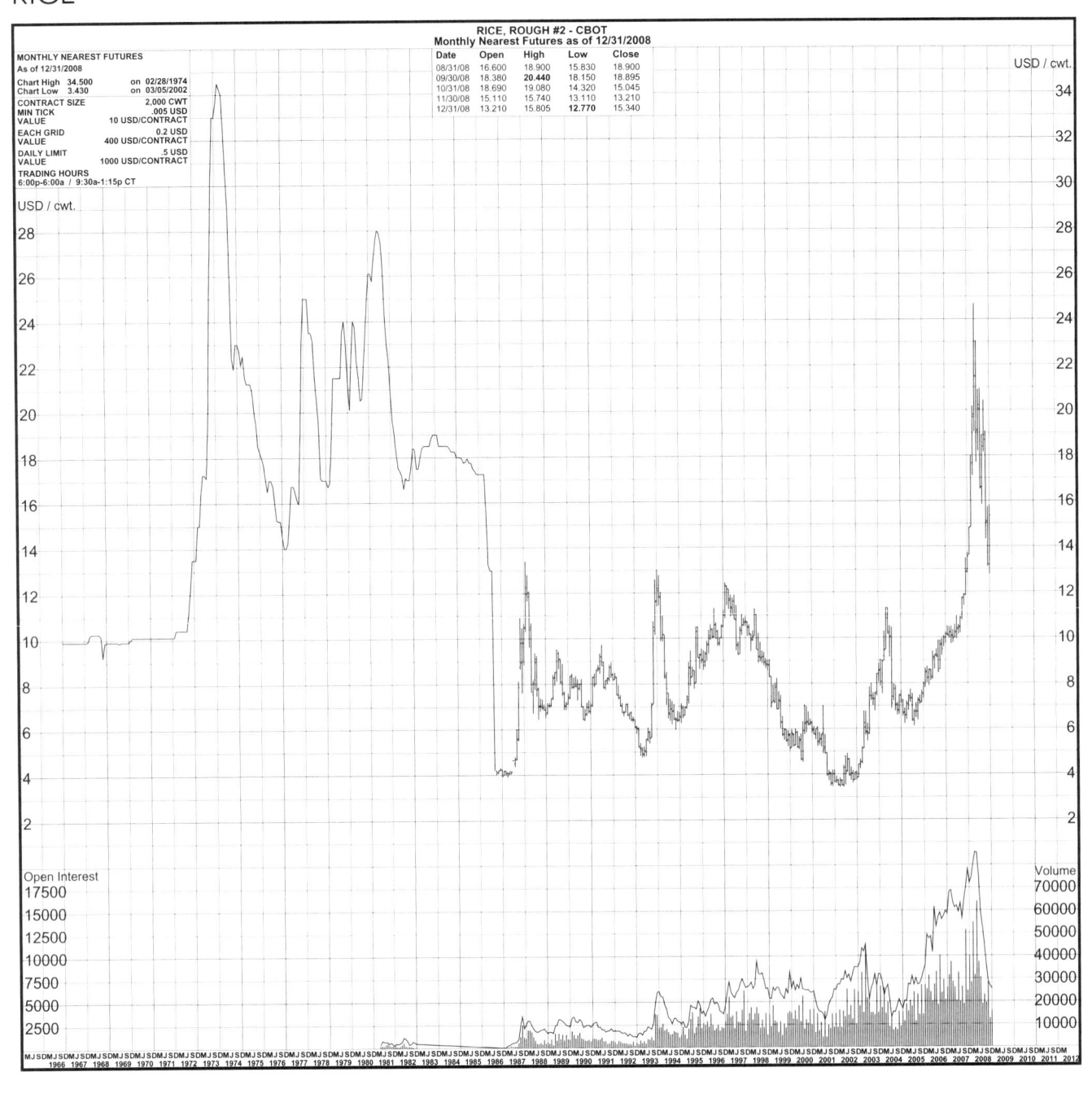

**RICE, ROUGH #2 - CBOT**
Monthly Nearest Futures as of 12/31/2008

| Date | Open | High | Low | Close |
|---|---|---|---|---|
| 08/31/08 | 16.600 | 18.900 | 15.830 | 18.900 |
| 09/30/08 | 18.380 | 20.440 | 18.150 | 18.895 |
| 10/31/08 | 18.690 | 19.080 | 14.320 | 15.045 |
| 11/30/08 | 15.110 | 15.740 | 13.110 | 13.210 |
| 12/31/08 | 13.210 | 15.805 | **12.770** | 15.340 |

**MONTHLY NEAREST FUTURES**
As of 12/31/2008
Chart High 34.500 on 02/28/1974
Chart Low 3.430 on 03/05/2002
CONTRACT SIZE 2,000 CWT
MIN TICK .005 USD
VALUE 10 USD/CONTRACT
EACH GRID 0.2 USD
VALUE 400 USD/CONTRACT
DAILY LIMIT .5 USD
VALUE 1000 USD/CONTRACT
TRADING HOURS
6:00p-6:00a / 9:30a-1:15p CT

## Annual High, Low and Settle of Rice, Rough Futures   In Dollars per Cwt.

| Year | High | Low | Settle | Year | High | Low | Settle | Year | High | Low | Settle |
|---|---|---|---|---|---|---|---|---|---|---|---|
| 1967 | 9.90 | 9.90 | 9.90 | 1981 | 28.00 | 20.85 | 20.85 | 1995 | 10.520 | 6.260 | 9.030 |
| 1968 | 10.25 | 9.20 | 9.90 | 1982 | 19.60 | 16.60 | 18.40 | 1996 | 11.330 | 8.600 | 11.030 |
| 1969 | 9.90 | 9.85 | 9.90 | 1983 | 19.00 | 17.50 | 19.00 | 1997 | 12.450 | 9.250 | 10.720 |
| 1970 | 10.10 | 10.00 | 10.10 | 1984 | 19.00 | 18.00 | 18.00 | 1998 | 11.300 | 8.560 | 8.790 |
| 1971 | 10.10 | 10.10 | 10.10 | 1985 | 18.00 | 17.25 | 17.25 | 1999 | 9.070 | 5.060 | 5.140 |
| 1972 | 13.50 | 10.10 | 13.50 | 1986 | 4.320 | 3.905 | 3.950 | 2000 | 7.060 | 4.540 | 5.920 |
| 1973 | 33.00 | 13.50 | 33.00 | 1987 | 10.920 | 3.900 | 10.460 | 2001 | 7.030 | 3.460 | 3.690 |
| 1974 | 34.50 | 21.90 | 23.00 | 1988 | 13.400 | 6.430 | 6.670 | 2002 | 4.920 | 3.430 | 3.850 |
| 1975 | 22.75 | 18.25 | 18.25 | 1989 | 9.520 | 6.670 | 7.430 | 2003 | 8.880 | 3.840 | 8.540 |
| 1976 | 18.00 | 14.50 | 14.50 | 1990 | 8.470 | 6.380 | 7.070 | 2004 | 11.320 | 6.580 | 7.180 |
| 1977 | 25.00 | 14.00 | 25.00 | 1991 | 9.730 | 7.020 | 8.190 | 2005 | 8.030 | 6.110 | 7.935 |
| 1978 | 25.00 | 17.00 | 17.00 | 1992 | 8.500 | 6.050 | 6.070 | 2006 | 10.220 | 7.820 | 10.130 |
| 1979 | 24.00 | 16.70 | 21.35 | 1993 | 13.000 | 4.760 | 12.200 | 2007 | 13.740 | 9.715 | 13.550 |
| 1980 | 26.10 | 20.10 | 26.10 | 1994 | 12.795 | 5.970 | 6.570 | 2008 | 24.685 | 12.770 | 15.340 |

Futures begin trading 08/20/1986.   Source: CME Group; Chicago Board of Trade

# RICE

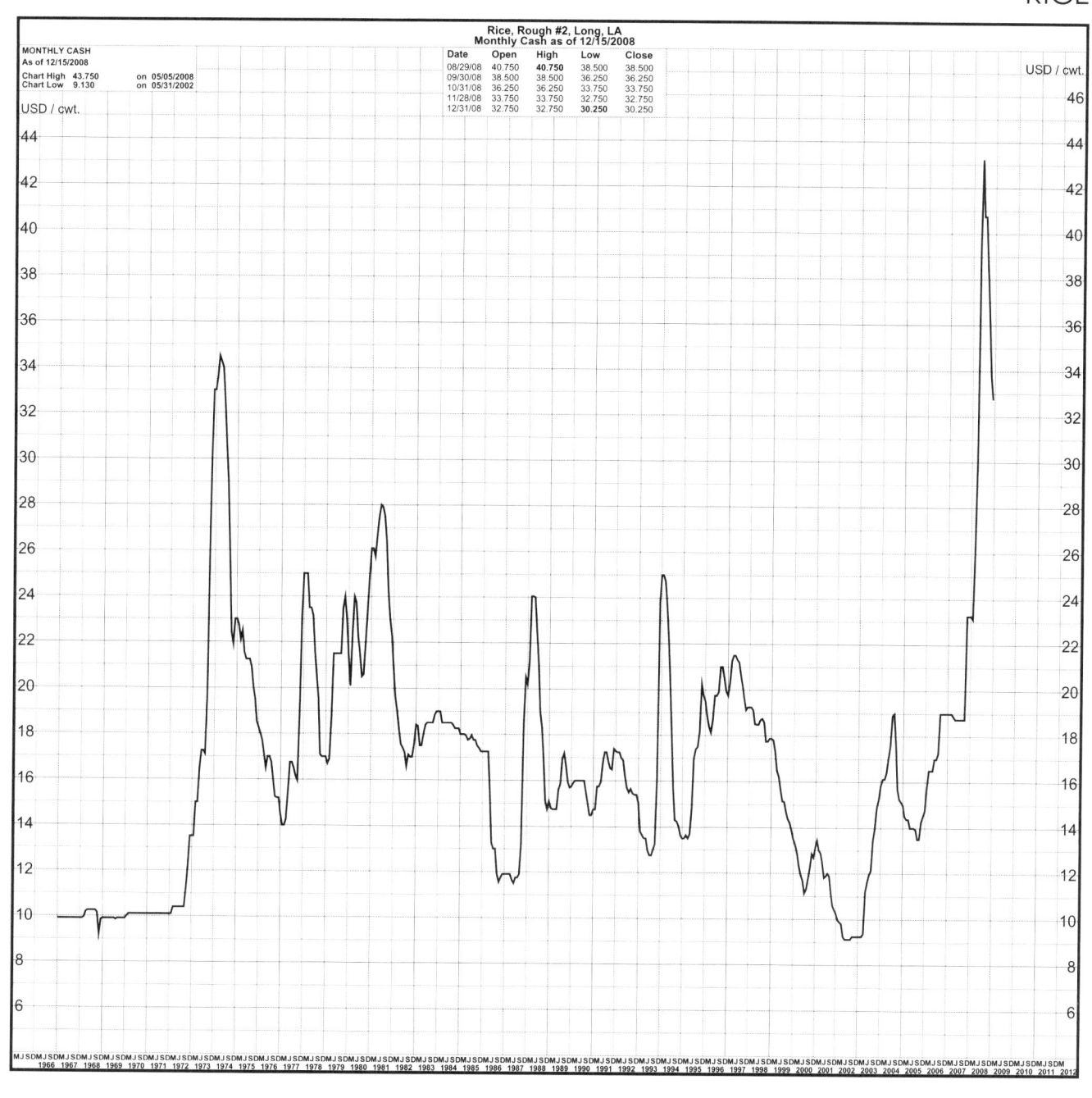

**MONTHLY CASH**
As of 12/15/2008
Chart High 43.750 on 05/05/2008
Chart Low 9.130 on 05/31/2002
USD/cwt.

Rice, Rough #2, Long, LA
Monthly Cash as of 12/15/2008

| Date | Open | High | Low | Close |
|---|---|---|---|---|
| 08/29/08 | 40.750 | 40.750 | 38.500 | 38.500 |
| 09/30/08 | 38.500 | 38.500 | 36.250 | 36.250 |
| 10/31/08 | 36.250 | 36.250 | 33.750 | 33.750 |
| 11/28/08 | 33.750 | 33.750 | 32.750 | 32.750 |
| 12/31/08 | 32.750 | 32.750 | 30.250 | 30.250 |

## Annual High, Low and Settle of Rice    In Dollars per Cwt.

| Year | High | Low | Settle | Year | High | Low | Settle | Year | High | Low | Settle |
|---|---|---|---|---|---|---|---|---|---|---|---|
| 1967 | 9.90 | 9.90 | 9.90 | 1981 | 28.00 | 20.85 | 20.85 | 1995 | 20.25 | 13.50 | 19.50 |
| 1968 | 10.25 | 9.20 | 9.90 | 1982 | 19.60 | 16.60 | 18.40 | 1996 | 21.00 | 18.13 | 19.75 |
| 1969 | 9.90 | 9.85 | 9.90 | 1983 | 19.00 | 17.50 | 19.00 | 1997 | 21.50 | 19.13 | 19.25 |
| 1970 | 10.10 | 10.00 | 10.10 | 1984 | 19.00 | 18.00 | 18.00 | 1998 | 19.25 | 17.75 | 17.88 |
| 1971 | 10.10 | 10.10 | 10.10 | 1985 | 18.00 | 17.25 | 17.25 | 1999 | 17.81 | 13.50 | 13.50 |
| 1972 | 13.50 | 10.10 | 13.50 | 1986 | 17.25 | 11.55 | 11.90 | 2000 | 13.25 | 11.13 | 13.13 |
| 1973 | 33.00 | 13.50 | 33.00 | 1987 | 20.50 | 11.50 | 20.20 | 2001 | 13.45 | 10.25 | 10.25 |
| 1974 | 34.50 | 21.90 | 23.00 | 1988 | 24.05 | 14.75 | 15.10 | 2002 | 9.97 | 9.13 | 9.25 |
| 1975 | 22.75 | 18.25 | 18.25 | 1989 | 17.20 | 14.75 | 15.75 | 2003 | 15.85 | 9.25 | 15.85 |
| 1976 | 18.00 | 14.50 | 14.50 | 1990 | 16.00 | 14.50 | 14.75 | 2004 | 19.00 | 15.00 | 15.00 |
| 1977 | 25.00 | 14.00 | 25.00 | 1991 | 17.40 | 14.75 | 17.30 | 2005 | 14.85 | 13.50 | 14.47 |
| 1978 | 25.00 | 17.00 | 17.00 | 1992 | 17.25 | 15.05 | 15.05 | 2006 | 19.00 | 15.25 | 19.00 |
| 1979 | 24.00 | 16.70 | 21.35 | 1993 | 25.00 | 12.75 | 25.00 | 2007 | 23.25 | 18.75 | 23.25 |
| 1980 | 26.10 | 20.10 | 26.10 | 1994 | 25.00 | 13.50 | 13.50 | 2008 | 43.75 | 22.75 | 30.25 |

Louisiana #2 Long grain.    Data continued from page 188.    *Source: U.S. Department of Agriculture*

# RICE

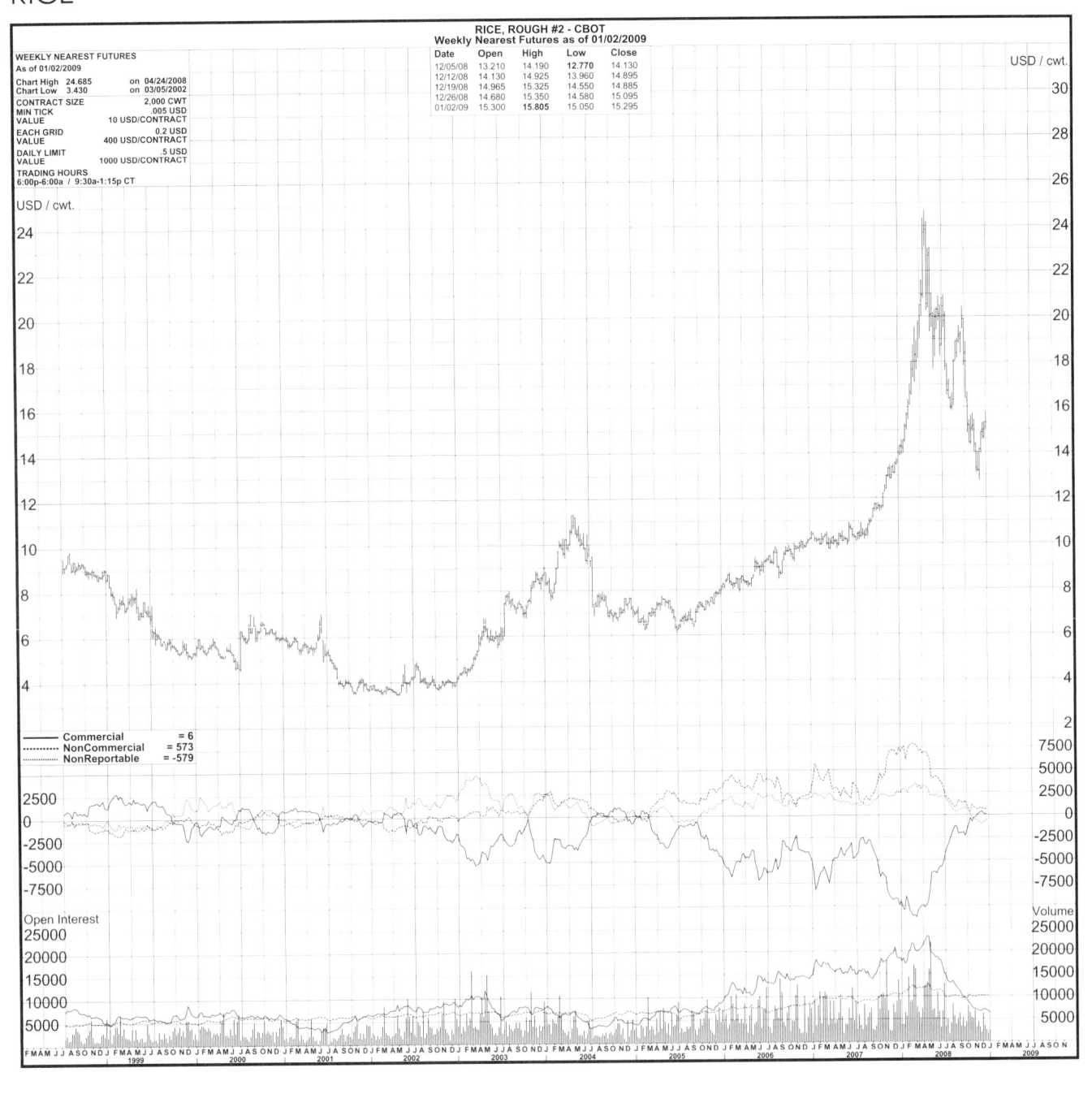

## RICE, ROUGH #2 - CBOT
### Weekly Nearest Futures as of 01/02/2009

| Date | Open | High | Low | Close |
|---|---|---|---|---|
| 12/05/08 | 13.210 | 14.190 | 12.770 | 14.130 |
| 12/12/08 | 14.130 | 14.925 | 13.960 | 14.895 |
| 12/19/08 | 14.965 | 15.325 | 14.550 | 14.885 |
| 12/26/08 | 14.680 | 15.350 | 14.580 | 15.095 |
| 01/02/09 | 15.300 | 15.805 | 15.050 | 15.295 |

**WEEKLY NEAREST FUTURES** As of 01/02/2009
- Chart High 24.685 on 04/24/2008
- Chart Low 3.430 on 03/05/2002
- CONTRACT SIZE 2,000 CWT
- MIN TICK .005 USD
- VALUE 10 USD/CONTRACT
- EACH GRID 0.2 USD
- VALUE 400 USD/CONTRACT
- DAILY LIMIT .5 USD
- VALUE 1000 USD/CONTRACT
- TRADING HOURS 6:00p-6:00a / 9:30a-1:15p CT

Commercial = 6
NonCommercial = 573
NonReportable = -579

## Quarterly High, Low and Settle of Rice, Rough    In Dollars per Cwt.

| Quarter | High | Low | Settle | Quarter | High | Low | Settle | Quarter | High | Low | Settle |
|---|---|---|---|---|---|---|---|---|---|---|---|
| 03/2000 | 5.990 | 5.180 | 5.835 | 03/2003 | 5.220 | 3.840 | 5.120 | 03/2006 | 8.750 | 7.820 | 8.560 |
| 06/2000 | 5.890 | 4.600 | 4.670 | 06/2003 | 6.780 | 5.130 | 5.800 | 06/2006 | 9.410 | 8.090 | 9.200 |
| 09/2000 | 7.060 | 4.540 | 6.310 | 09/2003 | 8.000 | 5.750 | 7.310 | 09/2006 | 9.890 | 8.460 | 9.665 |
| 12/2000 | 6.750 | 5.800 | 5.920 | 12/2003 | 8.880 | 6.770 | 8.540 | 12/2006 | 10.220 | 9.200 | 10.130 |
| 03/2001 | 6.120 | 5.220 | 5.400 | 03/2004 | 10.300 | 7.540 | 9.450 | 03/2007 | 10.520 | 9.715 | 10.080 |
| 06/2001 | 7.030 | 4.900 | 5.100 | 06/2004 | 11.320 | 9.140 | 10.060 | 06/2007 | 10.950 | 9.760 | 10.390 |
| 09/2001 | 5.750 | 3.720 | 4.050 | 09/2004 | 10.470 | 6.760 | 7.040 | 09/2007 | 11.770 | 10.130 | 11.730 |
| 12/2001 | 4.190 | 3.460 | 3.690 | 12/2004 | 7.690 | 6.580 | 7.180 | 12/2007 | 13.740 | 11.390 | 13.550 |
| 03/2002 | 3.920 | 3.430 | 3.720 | 03/2005 | 7.280 | 6.210 | 7.070 | 03/2008 | 20.175 | 13.630 | 19.690 |
| 06/2002 | 4.785 | 3.430 | 4.080 | 06/2005 | 7.740 | 6.300 | 6.400 | 06/2008 | 24.685 | 17.700 | 20.210 |
| 09/2002 | 4.920 | 3.730 | 4.035 | 09/2005 | 7.360 | 6.110 | 7.260 | 09/2008 | 20.950 | 15.830 | 18.895 |
| 12/2002 | 4.170 | 3.610 | 3.850 | 12/2005 | 8.030 | 7.050 | 7.935 | 12/2008 | 19.080 | 12.770 | 15.340 |

*Source: CME Group; Chicago Board of Trade*

# RICE

**WEEKLY CASH**
As of 12/15/2008
Chart High 43.750 on 05/05/2008
Chart Low 9.130 on 05/31/2002

USD / cwt.

Rice, Rough #2, Long, LA
Weekly Cash as of 12/15/2008

| Date | Open | High | Low | Close |
|---|---|---|---|---|
| 11/17/08 | 33.750 | 33.750 | 33.750 | 33.750 |
| 11/24/08 | 32.750 | 32.750 | 32.750 | 32.750 |
| 12/01/08 | 32.750 | 32.750 | 32.750 | 32.750 |
| 12/08/08 | 31.250 | 31.250 | 31.250 | 31.250 |
| 12/15/08 | 30.250 | 30.250 | 30.250 | 30.250 |

## Quarterly High, Low and Settle of Rice   In Dollars per Cwt.

| Quarter | High | Low | Settle | Quarter | High | Low | Settle | Quarter | High | Low | Settle |
|---|---|---|---|---|---|---|---|---|---|---|---|
| 03/2000 | 13.25 | 12.33 | 12.33 | 03/2003 | 9.38 | 9.25 | 9.38 | 03/2006 | 16.50 | 15.25 | 16.50 |
| 06/2000 | 11.94 | 11.13 | 11.13 | 06/2003 | 11.95 | 11.19 | 11.95 | 06/2006 | 17.00 | 16.50 | 17.00 |
| 09/2000 | 12.22 | 11.30 | 12.22 | 09/2003 | 14.00 | 12.13 | 14.00 | 09/2006 | 19.00 | 17.00 | 19.00 |
| 12/2000 | 13.13 | 12.69 | 13.13 | 12/2003 | 15.85 | 14.88 | 15.85 | 12/2006 | 19.00 | 19.00 | 19.00 |
| 03/2001 | 13.45 | 12.88 | 12.88 | 03/2004 | 16.40 | 16.13 | 16.40 | 03/2007 | 19.00 | 18.88 | 18.88 |
| 06/2001 | 12.45 | 11.81 | 11.88 | 06/2004 | 18.90 | 17.03 | 18.90 | 06/2007 | 18.88 | 18.75 | 18.75 |
| 09/2001 | 12.00 | 11.16 | 11.16 | 09/2004 | 19.00 | 15.69 | 15.69 | 09/2007 | 18.75 | 18.75 | 18.75 |
| 12/2001 | 10.59 | 10.25 | 10.25 | 12/2004 | 15.25 | 15.00 | 15.00 | 12/2007 | 23.25 | 18.75 | 23.25 |
| 03/2002 | 9.97 | 9.81 | 9.81 | 03/2005 | 14.85 | 14.38 | 14.38 | 03/2008 | 30.00 | 22.75 | 30.00 |
| 06/2002 | 9.25 | 9.13 | 9.13 | 06/2005 | 14.00 | 14.00 | 14.00 | 06/2008 | 43.75 | 31.00 | 40.75 |
| 09/2002 | 9.25 | 9.13 | 9.25 | 09/2005 | 13.94 | 13.50 | 13.50 | 09/2008 | 40.75 | 36.25 | 36.25 |
| 12/2002 | 9.25 | 9.25 | 9.25 | 12/2005 | 14.75 | 13.95 | 14.75 | 12/2008 | 36.25 | 30.25 | 30.25 |

Louisiana #2 Long grain.   *Source: U.S. Department of Agriculture*

# WHEAT, CHICAGO

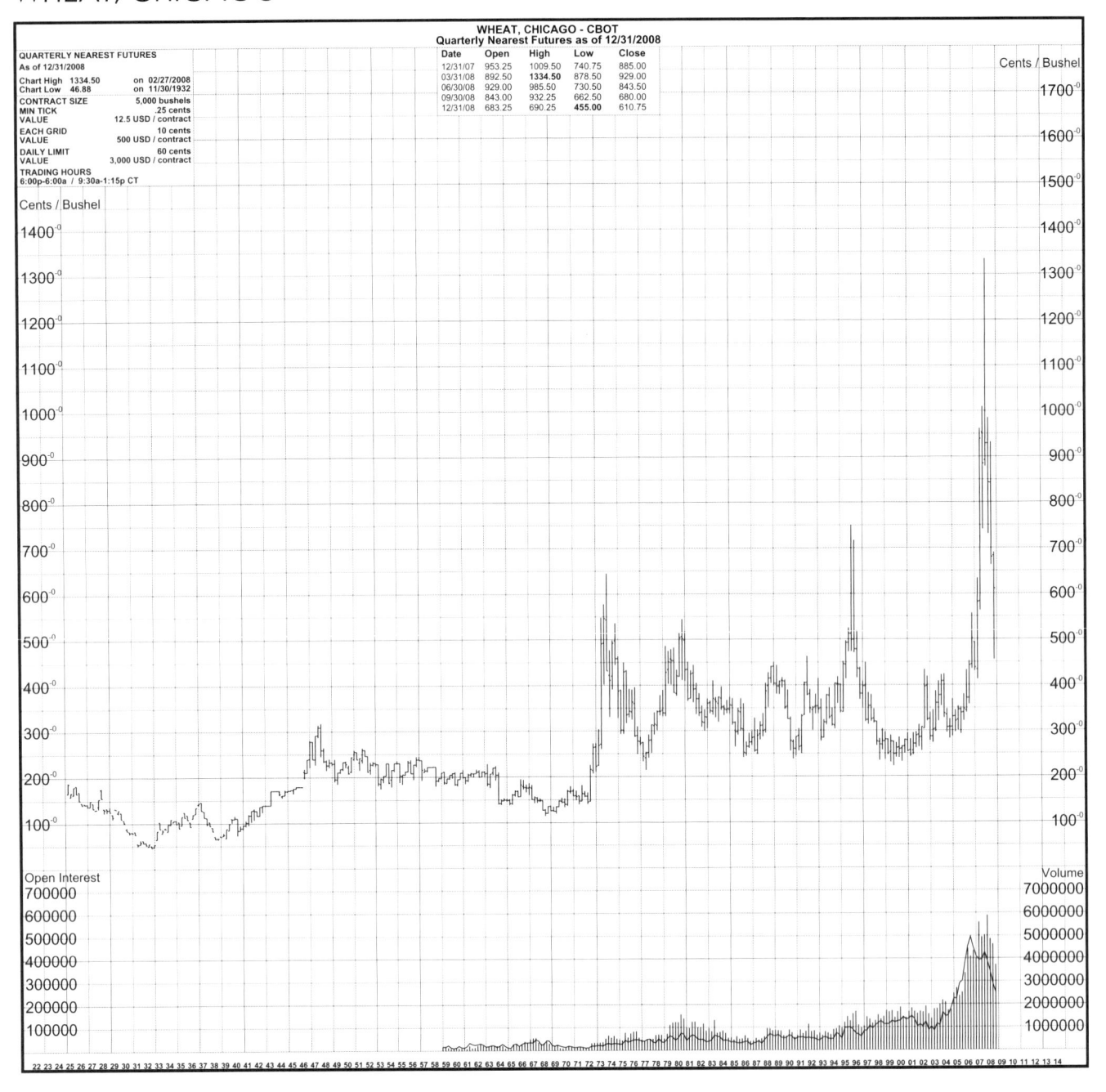

**WHEAT, CHICAGO - CBOT**
Quarterly Nearest Futures as of 12/31/2008

| Date | Open | High | Low | Close |
|---|---|---|---|---|
| 12/31/07 | 953.25 | 1009.50 | 740.75 | 885.00 |
| 03/31/08 | 892.50 | 1334.50 | 878.50 | 929.00 |
| 06/30/08 | 929.00 | 985.50 | 730.50 | 843.50 |
| 09/30/08 | 843.00 | 932.25 | 662.50 | 680.00 |
| 12/31/08 | 683.25 | 690.25 | 455.00 | 610.75 |

**QUARTERLY NEAREST FUTURES**
As of 12/31/2008
Chart High 1334.50 on 02/27/2008
Chart Low 46.88 on 11/30/1932
CONTRACT SIZE 5,000 bushels
MIN TICK .25 cents
VALUE 12.5 USD / contract
EACH GRID 10 cents
VALUE 500 USD / contract
DAILY LIMIT 60 cents
VALUE 3,000 USD / contract
TRADING HOURS
6:00p-6:00a / 9:30a-1:15p CT

## Annual High, Low and Settle of Wheat Futures   In Cents per Bushel

| Year | High | Low | Settle | Year | High | Low | Settle | Year | High | Low | Settle |
|---|---|---|---|---|---|---|---|---|---|---|---|
| 1925 | 200.00 | 159.00 | 180.00 | 1939 | 99.00 | 68.00 | 99.00 | 1953 | 230.75 | 174.00 | 202.75 |
| 1926 | 182.38 | 140.63 | 141.38 | 1940 | 116.00 | 73.00 | 89.00 | 1954 | 230.00 | 178.25 | 230.00 |
| 1927 | 149.50 | 129.75 | 130.38 | 1941 | 127.50 | 86.25 | 127.50 | 1955 | 235.00 | 184.00 | 211.75 |
| 1928 | 176.50 | 122.75 | 129.63 | 1942 | 138.75 | 107.00 | 138.75 | 1956 | 244.50 | 194.00 | 238.00 |
| 1929 | 136.13 | 109.50 | 128.75 | 1943 | 170.50 | 138.75 | 170.50 | 1957 | 245.00 | 192.50 | 221.50 |
| 1930 | 123.75 | 76.63 | 79.75 | 1944 | 172.38 | 155.25 | 169.50 | 1958 | 222.00 | 179.75 | 197.50 |
| 1931 | 82.75 | 49.38 | 58.00 | 1945 | 180.00 | 164.25 | 179.00 | 1959 | 212.00 | 184.00 | 204.25 |
| 1932 | 62.63 | 46.88 | 46.88 | 1946 | 239.00 | 179.00 | 239.00 | 1960 | 211.00 | 180.00 | 208.63 |
| 1933 | 102.88 | 48.25 | 83.88 | 1947 | 315.00 | 221.00 | 309.00 | 1961 | 215.75 | 184.63 | 207.25 |
| 1934 | 109.13 | 83.00 | 105.88 | 1948 | 318.50 | 215.00 | 232.25 | 1962 | 217.00 | 198.50 | 211.13 |
| 1935 | 124.00 | 90.00 | 113.00 | 1949 | 239.50 | 184.75 | 217.75 | 1963 | 228.63 | 176.00 | 219.50 |
| 1936 | 134.00 | 93.00 | 134.00 | 1950 | 244.50 | 207.00 | 243.75 | 1964 | 224.00 | 138.75 | 149.88 |
| 1937 | 146.00 | 96.00 | 99.00 | 1951 | 263.50 | 214.75 | 259.00 | 1965 | 170.75 | 138.00 | 168.63 |
| 1938 | 103.00 | 64.00 | 67.00 | 1952 | 259.00 | 206.50 | 230.75 | 1966 | 195.00 | 156.25 | 175.75 |

Futures data begins 07/01/1959.   Data continued on page 196.   *Source: CME Group; Chicago Board of Trade*

# WHEAT, CHICAGO

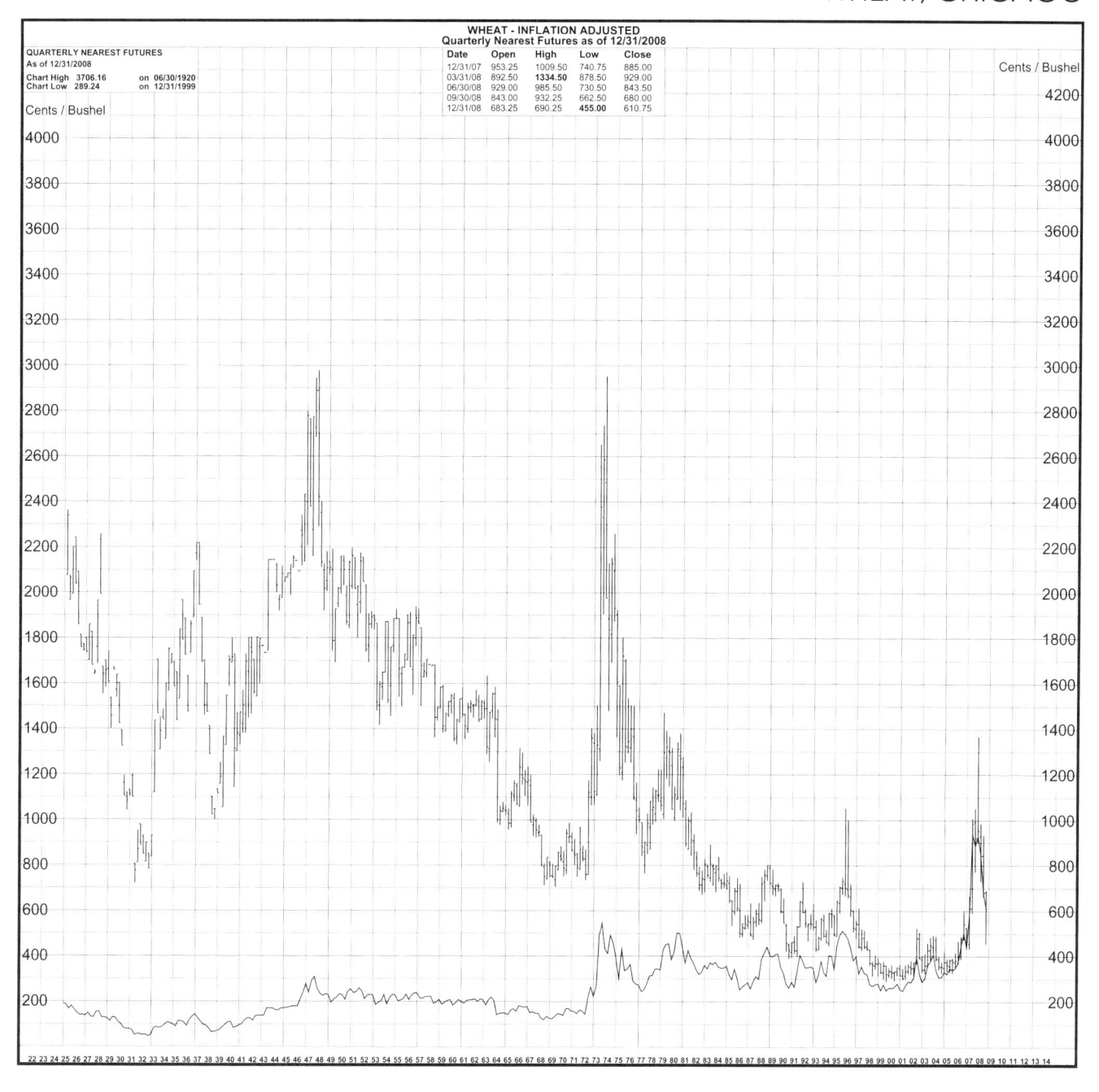

QUARTERLY NEAREST FUTURES
As of 12/31/2008
Chart High  3706.16  on 06/30/1920
Chart Low   289.24   on 12/31/1999
Cents / Bushel

WHEAT - INFLATION ADJUSTED
Quarterly Nearest Futures as of 12/31/2008

| Date | Open | High | Low | Close |
|---|---|---|---|---|
| 12/31/07 | 953.25 | 1009.50 | 740.75 | 885.00 |
| 03/31/08 | 892.50 | 1334.50 | 878.50 | 929.00 |
| 06/30/08 | 929.00 | 985.00 | 730.50 | 843.50 |
| 09/30/08 | 843.00 | 932.25 | 662.50 | 680.00 |
| 12/31/08 | 683.25 | 690.25 | 455.00 | 610.75 |

## Annual High, Low and Settle of Wheat   In Cents per Bushel

| Year | High | Low | Settle | Year | High | Low | Settle | Year | High | Low | Settle |
|---|---|---|---|---|---|---|---|---|---|---|---|
| 1925 | 200.00 | 159.00 | 180.00 | 1939 | 99.00 | 68.00 | 99.00 | 1953 | 230.75 | 174.00 | 202.75 |
| 1926 | 182.38 | 140.63 | 141.38 | 1940 | 116.00 | 73.00 | 89.00 | 1954 | 230.00 | 178.25 | 230.00 |
| 1927 | 149.50 | 129.75 | 130.38 | 1941 | 127.50 | 86.25 | 127.50 | 1955 | 235.00 | 184.00 | 211.75 |
| 1928 | 176.50 | 122.75 | 129.63 | 1942 | 138.75 | 107.00 | 138.75 | 1956 | 244.50 | 194.00 | 238.00 |
| 1929 | 136.13 | 109.50 | 128.75 | 1943 | 170.50 | 138.75 | 170.50 | 1957 | 245.00 | 192.50 | 221.50 |
| 1930 | 123.75 | 76.63 | 79.75 | 1944 | 172.38 | 155.25 | 169.50 | 1958 | 222.00 | 179.75 | 197.50 |
| 1931 | 82.75 | 49.38 | 58.00 | 1945 | 180.00 | 164.25 | 179.00 | 1959 | 212.00 | 184.00 | 203.25 |
| 1932 | 62.63 | 46.88 | 46.88 | 1946 | 239.00 | 179.00 | 239.00 | 1960 | 211.75 | 183.00 | 211.75 |
| 1933 | 102.88 | 48.25 | 83.88 | 1947 | 315.00 | 221.00 | 309.00 | 1961 | 215.00 | 186.00 | 208.25 |
| 1934 | 109.13 | 83.00 | 105.88 | 1948 | 318.50 | 215.00 | 232.25 | 1962 | 219.38 | 198.63 | 213.75 |
| 1935 | 124.00 | 90.00 | 113.00 | 1949 | 239.50 | 184.75 | 217.75 | 1963 | 228.63 | 179.00 | 222.13 |
| 1936 | 134.00 | 93.00 | 134.00 | 1950 | 244.50 | 207.00 | 243.75 | 1964 | 225.75 | 140.75 | 153.00 |
| 1937 | 146.00 | 96.00 | 99.00 | 1951 | 263.50 | 214.75 | 259.00 | 1965 | 173.50 | 141.88 | 169.50 |
| 1938 | 103.00 | 64.00 | 67.00 | 1952 | 259.00 | 206.50 | 230.75 | 1966 | 194.00 | 159.00 | 176.00 |

Chicago #2 Soft Red.   Data continued on page 197.   *Source: U.S. Department of Agriculture*

# WHEAT, CHICAGO

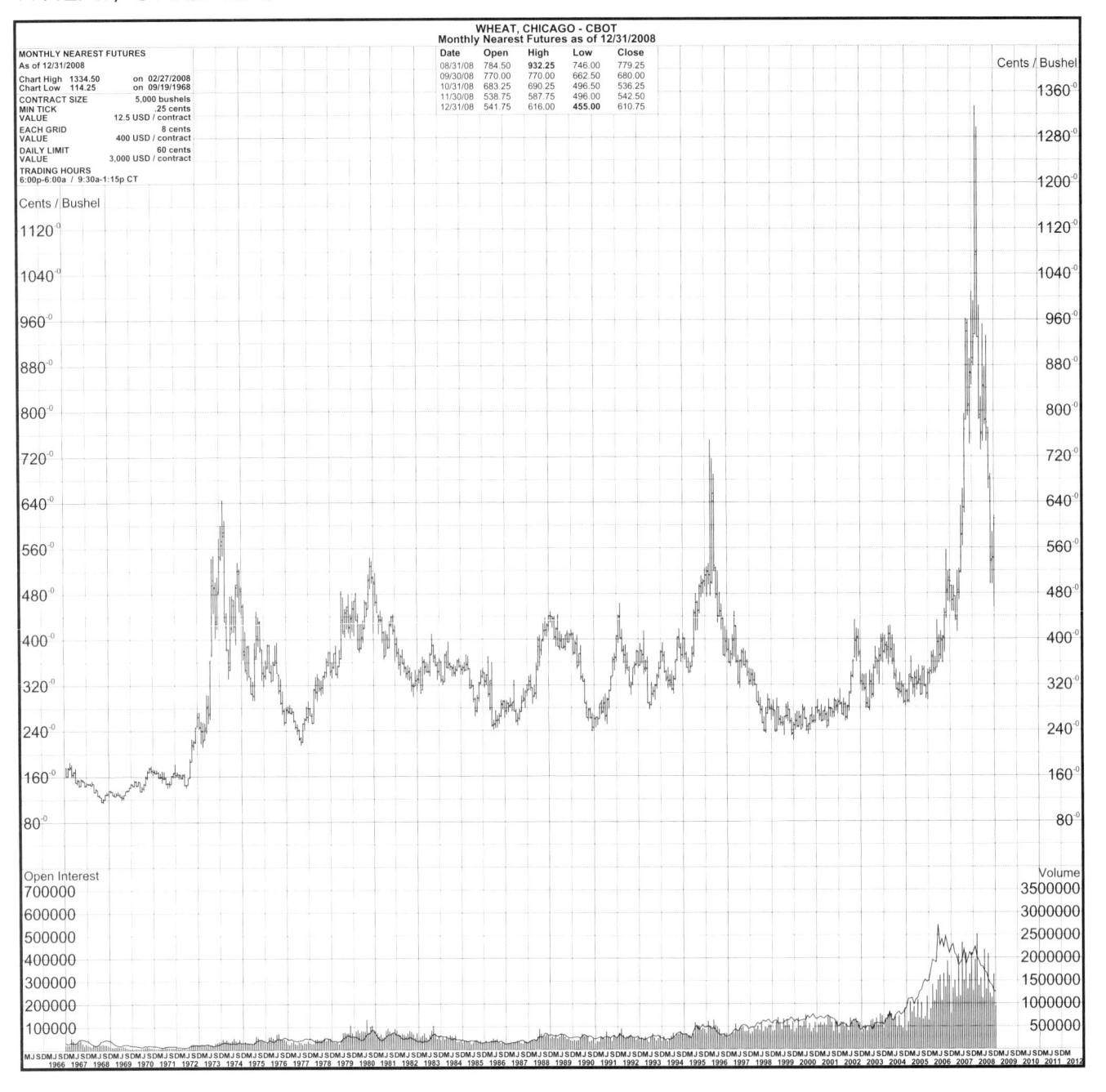

**WHEAT, CHICAGO - CBOT**
Monthly Nearest Futures as of 12/31/2008

| Date | Open | High | Low | Close |
|---|---|---|---|---|
| 08/31/08 | 784.50 | 932.25 | 746.00 | 779.25 |
| 09/30/08 | 770.00 | 770.00 | 662.50 | 680.00 |
| 10/31/08 | 683.25 | 690.25 | 496.50 | 536.25 |
| 11/30/08 | 538.75 | 587.75 | 496.00 | 542.50 |
| 12/31/08 | 541.75 | 616.00 | 455.00 | 610.75 |

**MONTHLY NEAREST FUTURES**
As of 12/31/2008
Chart High 1334.50 on 02/27/2008
Chart Low 114.25 on 09/19/1968
CONTRACT SIZE 5,000 bushels
MIN TICK .25 cents
VALUE 12.5 USD / contract
EACH GRID 8 cents
VALUE 400 USD / contract
DAILY LIMIT 60 cents
VALUE 3,000 USD / contract
TRADING HOURS
6:00p-6:00a / 9:30a-1:15p CT

## Annual High, Low and Settle of Wheat Futures    In Cents per Bushel

| Year | High | Low | Settle | Year | High | Low | Settle | Year | High | Low | Settle |
|---|---|---|---|---|---|---|---|---|---|---|---|
| 1967 | 186.25 | 142.38 | 147.88 | 1981 | 517.50 | 362.00 | 391.50 | 1995 | 525.00 | 339.50 | 512.25 |
| 1968 | 153.25 | 114.25 | 135.50 | 1982 | 405.00 | 299.25 | 330.75 | 1996 | 750.00 | 368.00 | 381.25 |
| 1969 | 148.25 | 119.50 | 147.38 | 1983 | 410.50 | 305.00 | 363.50 | 1997 | 449.00 | 313.00 | 325.75 |
| 1970 | 179.38 | 133.25 | 168.50 | 1984 | 397.00 | 319.50 | 347.75 | 1998 | 348.00 | 234.50 | 276.25 |
| 1971 | 182.00 | 139.75 | 163.13 | 1985 | 374.00 | 264.50 | 343.25 | 1999 | 297.00 | 222.50 | 248.50 |
| 1972 | 272.75 | 140.00 | 264.00 | 1986 | 371.00 | 241.50 | 274.50 | 2000 | 285.50 | 232.00 | 279.50 |
| 1973 | 578.00 | 211.00 | 546.00 | 1987 | 329.00 | 248.00 | 310.75 | 2001 | 297.00 | 242.50 | 289.00 |
| 1974 | 645.00 | 331.00 | 458.00 | 1988 | 441.50 | 286.50 | 440.00 | 2002 | 434.00 | 255.50 | 325.00 |
| 1975 | 463.50 | 293.00 | 335.75 | 1989 | 449.00 | 379.50 | 409.25 | 2003 | 409.00 | 273.00 | 377.00 |
| 1976 | 396.00 | 249.00 | 277.50 | 1990 | 412.00 | 238.00 | 260.50 | 2004 | 424.00 | 282.50 | 307.50 |
| 1977 | 292.00 | 214.25 | 279.25 | 1991 | 407.00 | 244.50 | 404.75 | 2005 | 370.00 | 287.00 | 339.25 |
| 1978 | 378.75 | 251.75 | 343.25 | 1992 | 463.25 | 301.50 | 353.75 | 2006 | 557.00 | 321.50 | 501.00 |
| 1979 | 486.00 | 332.00 | 454.25 | 1993 | 415.00 | 277.00 | 378.25 | 2007 | 1,009.50 | 412.00 | 885.00 |
| 1980 | 544.50 | 376.50 | 501.00 | 1994 | 418.75 | 303.50 | 401.50 | 2008 | 1,334.50 | 455.00 | 610.75 |

Data continued from page 194.    Source: CME Group; Chicago Board of Trade

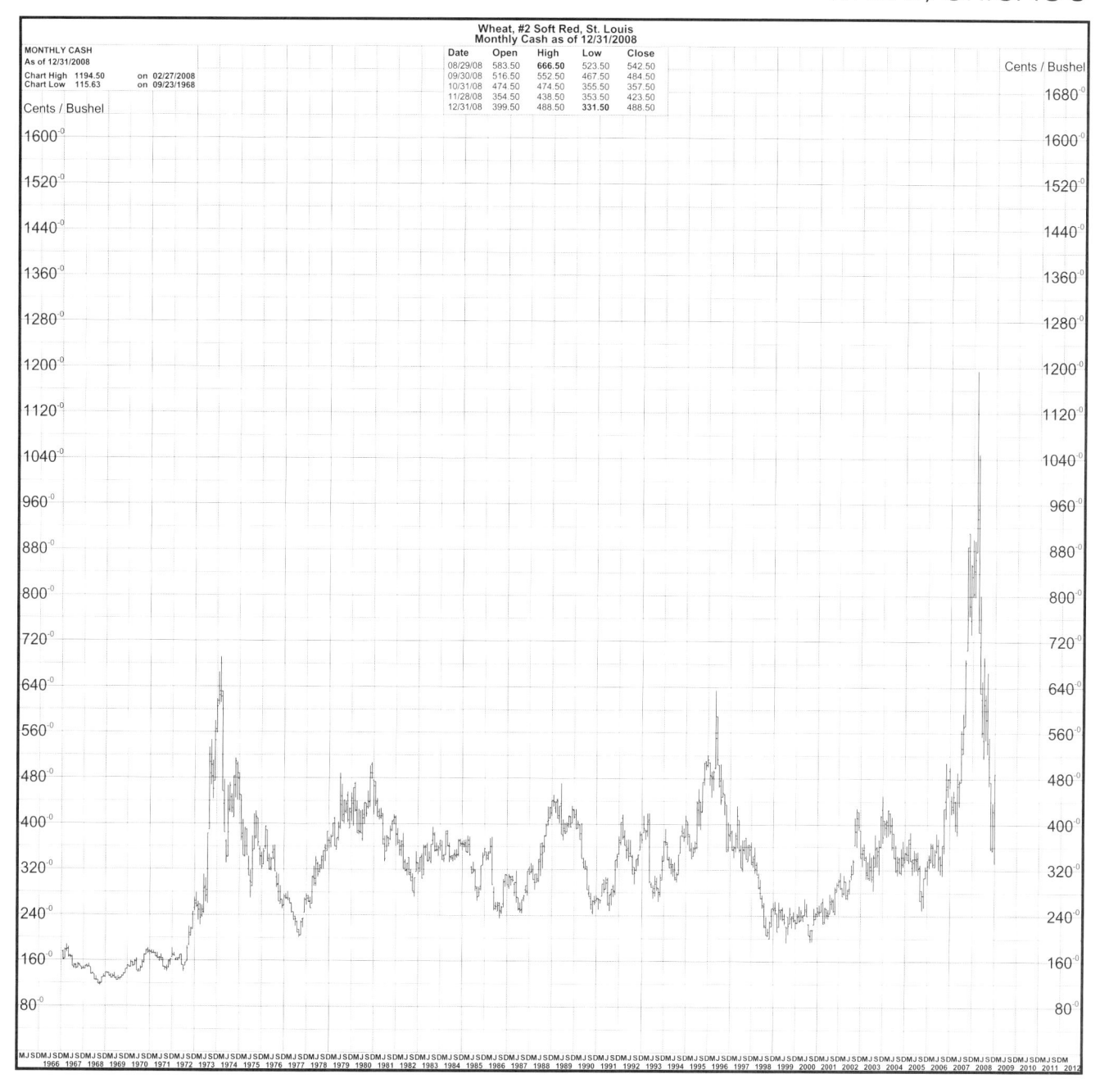

# WHEAT, CHICAGO

**MONTHLY CASH**
As of 12/31/2008
Chart High 1194.50 on 02/27/2008
Chart Low 115.63 on 09/23/1968
Cents / Bushel

Wheat, #2 Soft Red, St. Louis
Monthly Cash as of 12/31/2008

| Date | Open | High | Low | Close |
|---|---|---|---|---|
| 08/29/08 | 583.50 | 666.50 | 523.50 | 542.50 |
| 09/30/08 | 516.50 | 552.50 | 467.50 | 484.50 |
| 10/31/08 | 474.50 | 474.50 | 355.50 | 357.50 |
| 11/28/08 | 354.50 | 438.50 | 353.50 | 423.50 |
| 12/31/08 | 399.50 | 488.50 | 331.50 | 488.50 |

## Annual High, Low and Settle of Wheat — In Cents per Bushel

| Year | High | Low | Settle | Year | High | Low | Settle | Year | High | Low | Settle |
|---|---|---|---|---|---|---|---|---|---|---|---|
| 1967 | 187.75 | 142.50 | 145.00 | 1981 | 473.50 | 333.50 | 381.50 | 1995 | 520.00 | 340.00 | 513.00 |
| 1968 | 153.88 | 115.63 | 138.38 | 1982 | 392.00 | 272.00 | 322.00 | 1996 | 634.50 | 352.00 | 384.00 |
| 1969 | 151.00 | 124.63 | 150.50 | 1983 | 394.50 | 304.00 | 370.50 | 1997 | 432.50 | 317.00 | 330.00 |
| 1970 | 181.88 | 139.25 | 174.50 | 1984 | 388.50 | 332.50 | 365.00 | 1998 | 359.50 | 200.50 | 251.00 |
| 1971 | 181.75 | 140.00 | 170.00 | 1985 | 379.50 | 265.00 | 356.50 | 1999 | 265.50 | 192.00 | 228.50 |
| 1972 | 270.00 | 140.00 | 264.25 | 1986 | 377.00 | 234.50 | 293.50 | 2000 | 270.50 | 193.50 | 248.00 |
| 1973 | 618.50 | 222.00 | 605.00 | 1987 | 325.00 | 243.50 | 312.00 | 2001 | 304.50 | 226.50 | 300.50 |
| 1974 | 691.50 | 330.50 | 450.50 | 1988 | 441.50 | 284.50 | 441.50 | 2002 | 428.50 | 268.50 | 341.50 |
| 1975 | 449.75 | 269.50 | 324.75 | 1989 | 471.50 | 371.00 | 412.50 | 2003 | 450.00 | 283.50 | 377.50 |
| 1976 | 395.25 | 250.75 | 272.50 | 1990 | 426.50 | 242.50 | 269.00 | 2004 | 426.50 | 310.50 | 350.50 |
| 1977 | 281.25 | 201.00 | 273.00 | 1991 | 378.50 | 248.00 | 371.50 | 2005 | 386.50 | 249.50 | 327.50 |
| 1978 | 386.00 | 252.00 | 369.25 | 1992 | 417.00 | 294.50 | 372.50 | 2006 | 508.50 | 309.50 | 475.50 |
| 1979 | 488.75 | 353.50 | 444.25 | 1993 | 419.50 | 264.00 | 369.00 | 2007 | 910.50 | 380.50 | 804.50 |
| 1980 | 507.00 | 369.00 | 466.00 | 1994 | 416.00 | 298.00 | 407.00 | 2008 | 1,194.50 | 331.50 | 488.50 |

Chicago #2 Red through 04/29/1982, St. Louis #2 Red 04/30/1982 to date. Data continued from page 195. *Source: U.S. Department of Agriculture*

# WHEAT, CHICAGO

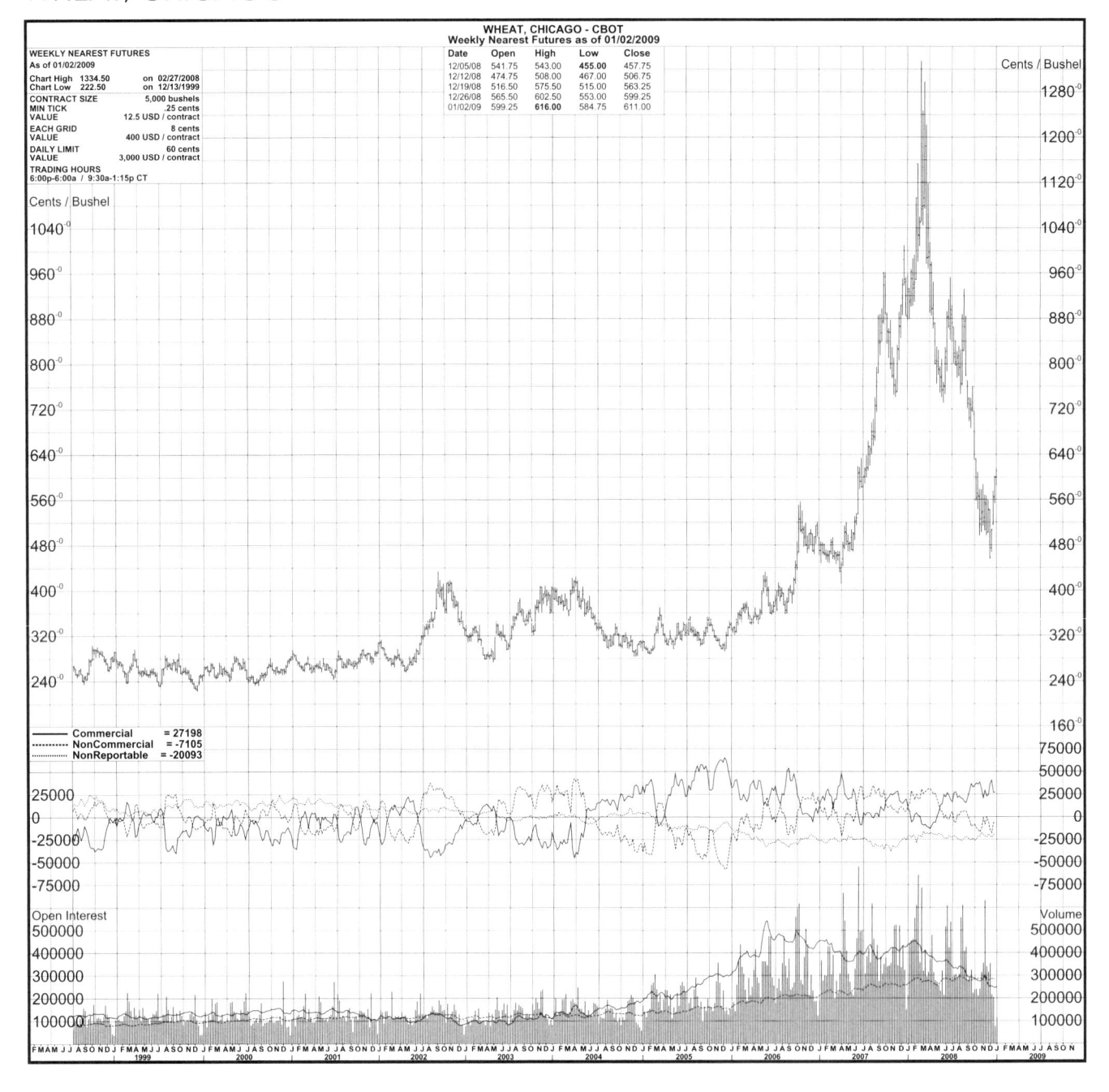

**Quarterly High, Low and Settle of Wheat Futures**   In Cents per Bushel

| Quarter | High | Low | Settle | Quarter | High | Low | Settle | Quarter | High | Low | Settle |
|---|---|---|---|---|---|---|---|---|---|---|---|
| 03/2000 | 273.50 | 241.00 | 262.25 | 03/2003 | 339.50 | 277.50 | 286.75 | 03/2006 | 380.00 | 321.50 | 347.75 |
| 06/2000 | 285.50 | 240.50 | 259.50 | 06/2003 | 345.75 | 273.00 | 301.75 | 06/2006 | 433.00 | 339.50 | 371.50 |
| 09/2000 | 266.00 | 232.00 | 265.00 | 09/2003 | 387.00 | 297.00 | 360.25 | 09/2006 | 453.00 | 357.25 | 443.00 |
| 12/2000 | 280.50 | 250.50 | 279.50 | 12/2003 | 409.00 | 321.00 | 377.00 | 12/2006 | 557.00 | 435.25 | 501.00 |
| 03/2001 | 294.50 | 254.00 | 255.00 | 03/2004 | 422.75 | 354.00 | 408.00 | 03/2007 | 494.00 | 431.00 | 438.00 |
| 06/2001 | 281.75 | 242.50 | 246.75 | 06/2004 | 424.00 | 328.00 | 338.00 | 06/2007 | 633.75 | 412.00 | 582.00 |
| 09/2001 | 295.00 | 246.25 | 270.75 | 09/2004 | 348.00 | 295.50 | 306.75 | 09/2007 | 961.75 | 562.50 | 939.00 |
| 12/2001 | 297.00 | 261.50 | 289.00 | 12/2004 | 326.00 | 282.50 | 307.50 | 12/2007 | 1,009.50 | 740.75 | 885.00 |
| 03/2002 | 313.25 | 263.75 | 285.00 | 03/2005 | 370.00 | 287.00 | 331.00 | 03/2008 | 1,334.50 | 878.50 | 929.00 |
| 06/2002 | 308.00 | 255.50 | 307.00 | 06/2005 | 345.50 | 296.50 | 321.50 | 06/2008 | 985.50 | 730.50 | 843.50 |
| 09/2002 | 434.00 | 304.00 | 396.50 | 09/2005 | 354.00 | 300.75 | 346.25 | 09/2008 | 932.25 | 662.50 | 680.00 |
| 12/2002 | 419.00 | 321.00 | 325.00 | 12/2005 | 352.00 | 292.50 | 339.25 | 12/2008 | 690.25 | 455.00 | 610.75 |

*Source: CME Group; Chicago Board of Trade*

# WHEAT, CHICAGO

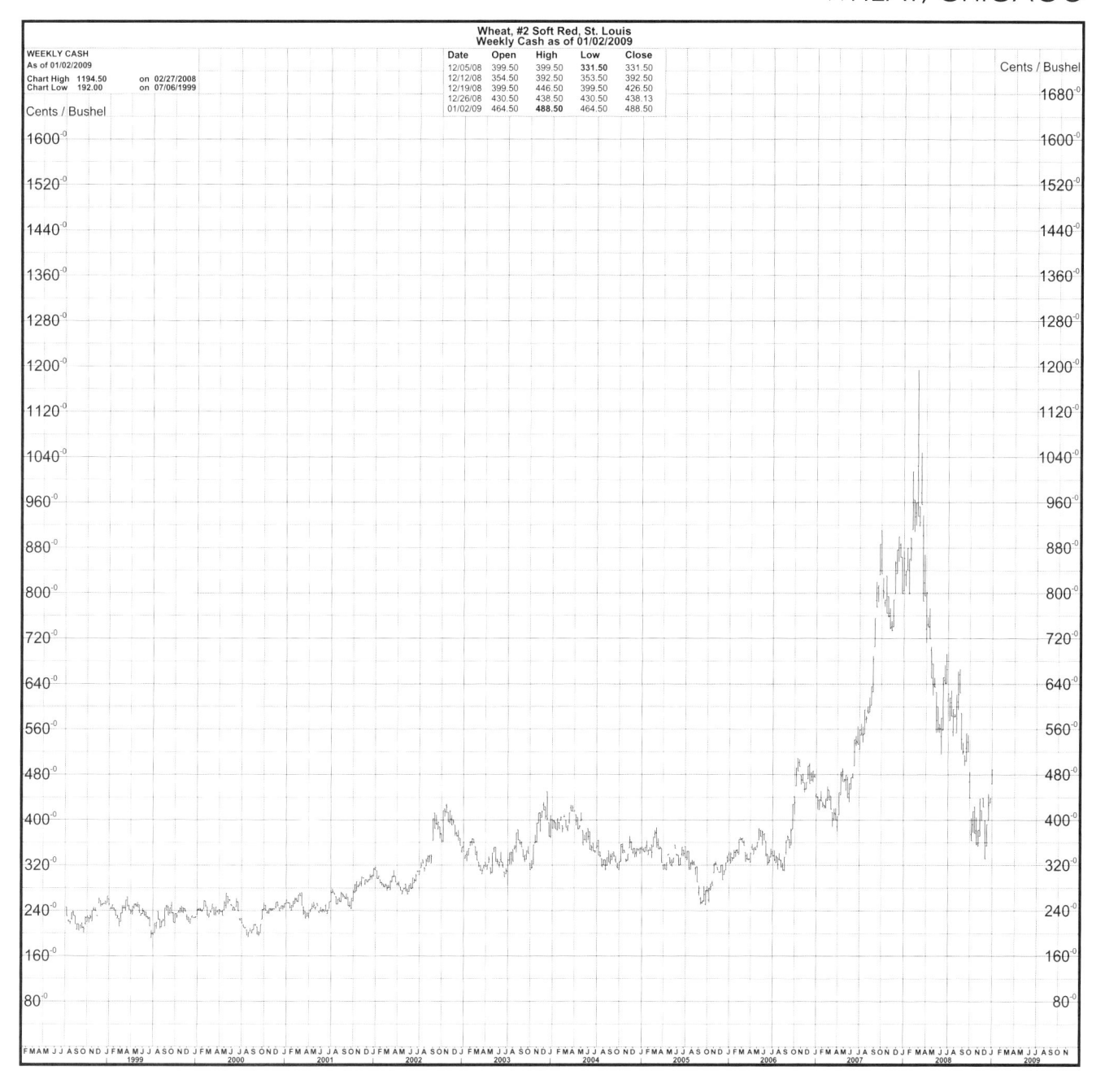

**WEEKLY CASH**
As of 01/02/2009
Chart High 1194.50 on 02/27/2008
Chart Low 192.00 on 07/06/1999

Cents / Bushel

**Wheat, #2 Soft Red, St. Louis**
**Weekly Cash as of 01/02/2009**

| Date | Open | High | Low | Close |
|---|---|---|---|---|
| 12/05/08 | 399.50 | 399.50 | 331.50 | 331.50 |
| 12/12/08 | 354.50 | 392.50 | 353.50 | 392.50 |
| 12/19/08 | 399.50 | 446.50 | 399.50 | 426.50 |
| 12/26/08 | 430.50 | 438.50 | 430.50 | 438.13 |
| 01/02/09 | 464.50 | 488.50 | 464.50 | 488.50 |

Cents / Bushel

## Quarterly High, Low and Settle of Wheat — In Cents per Bushel

| Quarter | High | Low | Settle | Quarter | High | Low | Settle | Quarter | High | Low | Settle |
|---|---|---|---|---|---|---|---|---|---|---|---|
| 03/2000 | 257.50 | 227.50 | 246.00 | 03/2003 | 366.50 | 304.50 | 316.50 | 03/2006 | 368.50 | 323.50 | 330.50 |
| 06/2000 | 270.50 | 231.50 | 239.50 | 06/2003 | 351.50 | 299.50 | 304.50 | 06/2006 | 384.50 | 320.50 | 340.50 |
| 09/2000 | 226.50 | 193.50 | 215.50 | 09/2003 | 382.50 | 283.50 | 346.50 | 09/2006 | 428.00 | 309.50 | 428.00 |
| 12/2000 | 255.50 | 225.00 | 248.00 | 12/2003 | 450.00 | 312.00 | 377.50 | 12/2006 | 508.50 | 410.50 | 475.50 |
| 03/2001 | 271.50 | 226.50 | 226.50 | 03/2004 | 426.50 | 377.50 | 425.50 | 03/2007 | 459.50 | 388.50 | 400.50 |
| 06/2001 | 254.45 | 226.50 | 241.00 | 06/2004 | 421.50 | 341.50 | 341.50 | 06/2007 | 565.50 | 380.50 | 533.50 |
| 09/2001 | 278.50 | 244.00 | 248.50 | 09/2004 | 364.50 | 310.50 | 317.50 | 09/2007 | 886.50 | 524.50 | 886.50 |
| 12/2001 | 304.50 | 242.50 | 300.50 | 12/2004 | 371.50 | 312.50 | 350.50 | 12/2007 | 910.50 | 732.50 | 804.50 |
| 03/2002 | 316.50 | 274.50 | 300.50 | 03/2005 | 386.50 | 332.50 | 336.50 | 03/2008 | 1,194.50 | 736.50 | 736.50 |
| 06/2002 | 304.50 | 268.50 | 301.50 | 06/2005 | 355.50 | 311.50 | 337.50 | 06/2008 | 801.50 | 515.50 | 610.50 |
| 09/2002 | 412.50 | 303.50 | 387.50 | 09/2005 | 352.50 | 249.50 | 275.50 | 09/2008 | 666.50 | 467.50 | 484.50 |
| 12/2002 | 428.50 | 341.50 | 341.50 | 12/2005 | 337.50 | 254.50 | 327.50 | 12/2008 | 488.50 | 331.50 | 488.50 |

St. Louis #2 Soft Red.    *Source: U.S. Department of Agriculture*

# WHEAT, KANSAS CITY

**WHEAT, KANSAS CITY - KCBT**
Monthly Nearest Futures as of 12/31/2008

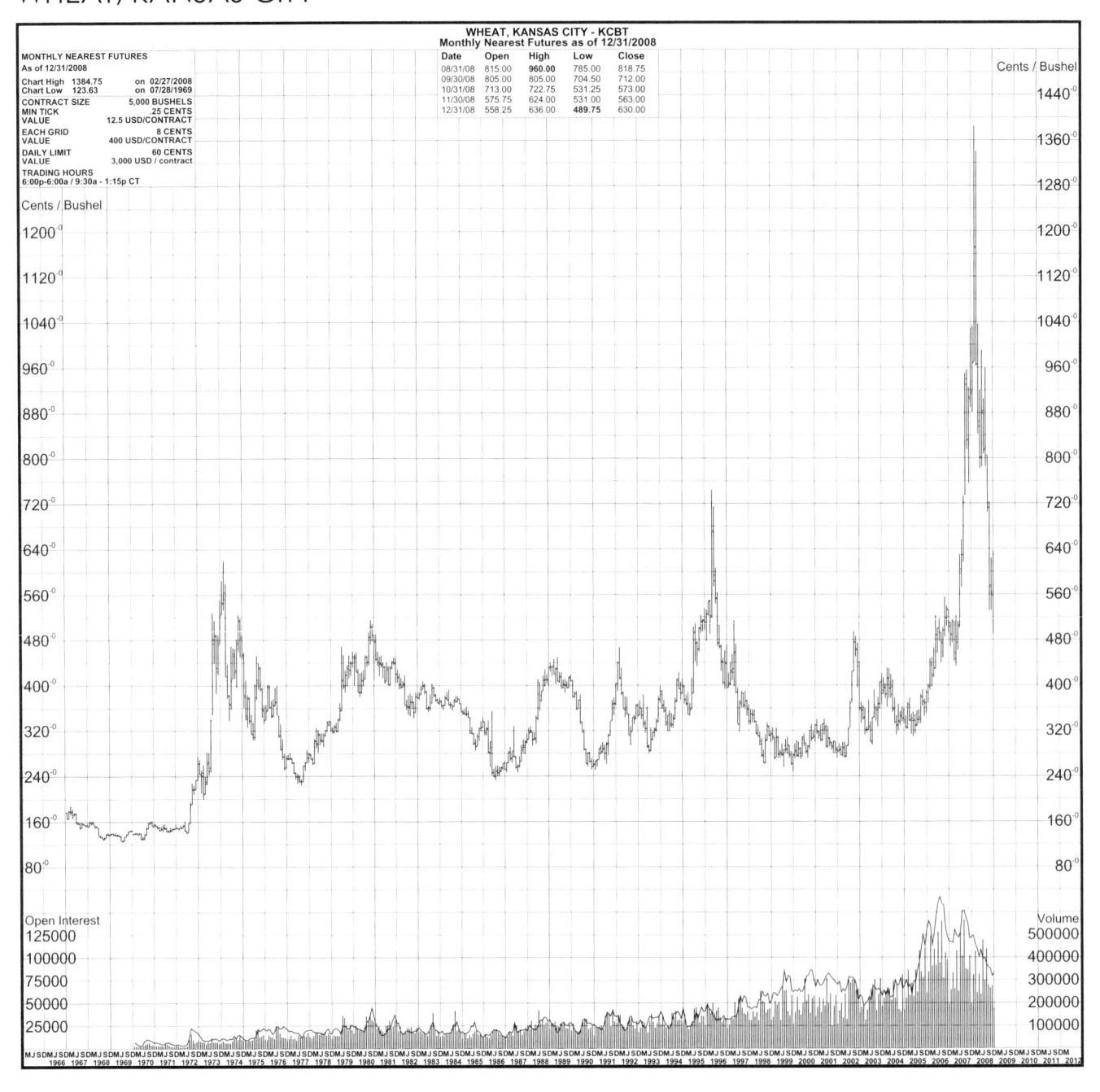

| Date | Open | High | Low | Close |
|---|---|---|---|---|
| 08/31/08 | 815.00 | 960.00 | 785.00 | 818.75 |
| 09/30/08 | 805.00 | 805.00 | 704.50 | 712.00 |
| 10/31/08 | 713.00 | 722.75 | 531.25 | 573.00 |
| 11/30/08 | 575.75 | 624.00 | 531.00 | 563.00 |
| 12/31/08 | 558.25 | 636.00 | 489.75 | 630.00 |

**MONTHLY NEAREST FUTURES**
As of 12/31/2008
Chart High 1384.75 on 02/27/2008
Chart Low 123.63 on 07/28/1969
CONTRACT SIZE 5,000 BUSHELS
MIN TICK .25 CENTS
VALUE 12.5 USD/CONTRACT
EACH GRID 8 CENTS
VALUE 400 USD/CONTRACT
DAILY LIMIT 60 CENTS
VALUE 3,000 USD / contract
TRADING HOURS 6:00p-6:00a / 9:30a - 1:15p CT

## Annual High, Low and Settle of Wheat   In Cents per Bushel

| Year | High | Low | Settle | Year | High | Low | Settle | Year | High | Low | Settle |
|---|---|---|---|---|---|---|---|---|---|---|---|
| 1967 | 188.75 | 147.88 | 152.50 | 1981 | 490.50 | 400.50 | 419.50 | 1995 | 535.00 | 346.50 | 509.50 |
| 1968 | 162.25 | 128.63 | 138.50 | 1982 | 428.75 | 342.50 | 378.25 | 1996 | 744.00 | 393.00 | 395.25 |
| 1969 | 145.88 | 123.63 | 144.38 | 1983 | 407.75 | 353.00 | 372.75 | 1997 | 514.00 | 317.00 | 335.50 |
| 1970 | 162.00 | 127.63 | 154.63 | 1984 | 393.00 | 354.00 | 354.00 | 1998 | 358.00 | 262.00 | 314.00 |
| 1971 | 156.88 | 141.63 | 149.50 | 1985 | 363.00 | 284.50 | 336.00 | 1999 | 326.00 | 248.00 | 276.25 |
| 1972 | 275.00 | 139.63 | 262.25 | 1986 | 354.75 | 232.50 | 252.00 | 2000 | 331.50 | 270.00 | 330.00 |
| 1973 | 550.00 | 200.00 | 523.00 | 1987 | 328.00 | 246.50 | 303.75 | 2001 | 340.00 | 271.50 | 284.00 |
| 1974 | 619.00 | 338.50 | 452.50 | 1988 | 433.50 | 293.50 | 431.00 | 2002 | 495.00 | 271.25 | 359.75 |
| 1975 | 459.00 | 303.25 | 338.50 | 1989 | 449.50 | 386.25 | 408.50 | 2003 | 420.50 | 294.50 | 384.75 |
| 1976 | 402.00 | 250.00 | 272.00 | 1990 | 409.50 | 252.25 | 261.00 | 2004 | 431.00 | 312.00 | 338.00 |
| 1977 | 286.75 | 225.00 | 278.25 | 1991 | 404.00 | 250.25 | 402.75 | 2005 | 392.50 | 309.50 | 387.00 |
| 1978 | 338.00 | 260.50 | 321.00 | 1992 | 467.00 | 294.00 | 347.25 | 2006 | 556.00 | 368.00 | 509.75 |
| 1979 | 469.00 | 315.00 | 450.00 | 1993 | 399.00 | 281.00 | 389.25 | 2007 | 1,029.25 | 433.00 | 913.50 |
| 1980 | 515.50 | 380.00 | 477.25 | 1994 | 423.25 | 318.00 | 399.00 | 2008 | 1,384.75 | 489.75 | 630.00 |

Futures data begins 01/04/1970.   Source: *Kansas City Board of Trade*

# WHEAT, KANSAS CITY

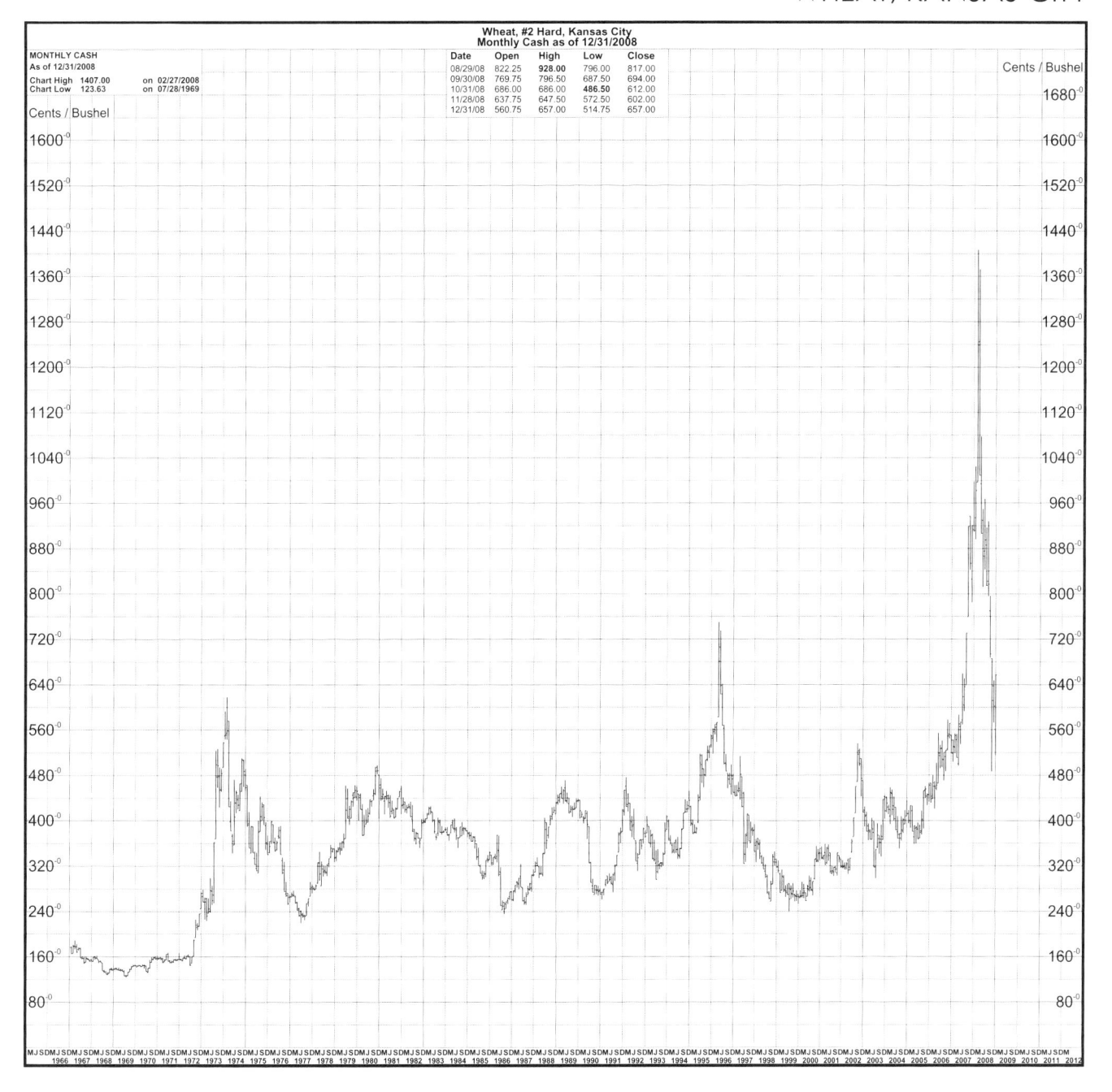

**Wheat, #2 Hard, Kansas City**
Monthly Cash as of 12/31/2008

| Date | Open | High | Low | Close |
|---|---|---|---|---|
| 08/29/08 | 822.25 | 928.00 | 796.00 | 817.00 |
| 09/30/08 | 769.75 | 796.50 | 687.50 | 694.00 |
| 10/31/08 | 686.00 | 686.00 | 486.50 | 612.00 |
| 11/28/08 | 637.75 | 647.50 | 572.50 | 602.00 |
| 12/31/08 | 560.75 | 657.00 | 514.75 | 657.00 |

MONTHLY CASH
As of 12/31/2008
Chart High 1407.00 on 02/27/2008
Chart Low 123.63 on 07/28/1969

Cents / Bushel

## Annual High, Low and Settle of Wheat — In Cents per Bushel

| Year | High | Low | Settle | Year | High | Low | Settle | Year | High | Low | Settle |
|---|---|---|---|---|---|---|---|---|---|---|---|
| 1967 | 188.75 | 147.88 | 152.50 | 1981 | 475.00 | 404.25 | 427.00 | 1995 | 551.00 | 376.50 | 549.00 |
| 1968 | 162.25 | 128.63 | 138.50 | 1982 | 441.50 | 351.50 | 398.75 | 1996 | 750.00 | 445.50 | 449.75 |
| 1969 | 145.88 | 123.63 | 144.38 | 1983 | 426.00 | 365.25 | 384.25 | 1997 | 514.00 | 324.00 | 345.00 |
| 1970 | 161.13 | 131.75 | 156.25 | 1984 | 404.00 | 351.50 | 378.50 | 1998 | 369.00 | 257.75 | 317.50 |
| 1971 | 167.50 | 148.63 | 155.38 | 1985 | 380.50 | 296.00 | 343.75 | 1999 | 329.25 | 238.75 | 265.75 |
| 1972 | 274.00 | 144.25 | 272.25 | 1986 | 374.50 | 235.50 | 260.00 | 2000 | 355.00 | 258.25 | 350.50 |
| 1973 | 537.50 | 223.63 | 537.50 | 1987 | 324.00 | 251.50 | 304.25 | 2001 | 358.50 | 302.00 | 318.50 |
| 1974 | 618.50 | 342.50 | 458.75 | 1988 | 432.75 | 299.00 | 431.50 | 2002 | 536.25 | 305.50 | 415.25 |
| 1975 | 463.25 | 308.25 | 340.50 | 1989 | 471.50 | 406.50 | 435.50 | 2003 | 444.00 | 298.00 | 417.25 |
| 1976 | 398.50 | 252.00 | 266.50 | 1990 | 436.75 | 267.75 | 270.50 | 2004 | 458.75 | 350.25 | 412.00 |
| 1977 | 292.50 | 219.75 | 283.75 | 1991 | 420.00 | 261.00 | 419.00 | 2005 | 465.75 | 358.00 | 462.50 |
| 1978 | 357.50 | 277.50 | 334.50 | 1992 | 476.50 | 310.88 | 372.00 | 2006 | 578.00 | 421.00 | 541.75 |
| 1979 | 463.00 | 328.50 | 452.50 | 1993 | 409.00 | 296.00 | 407.00 | 2007 | 998.00 | 496.75 | 911.50 |
| 1980 | 498.00 | 373.50 | 458.00 | 1994 | 453.00 | 332.00 | 436.00 | 2008 | 1,407.00 | 486.50 | 657.00 |

Kansas City #2 Hard Winter    Source: Kansas City Board of Trade

# WHEAT, KANSAS CITY

**WHEAT, KANSAS CITY - KCBT**
Weekly Nearest Futures as of 01/02/2009

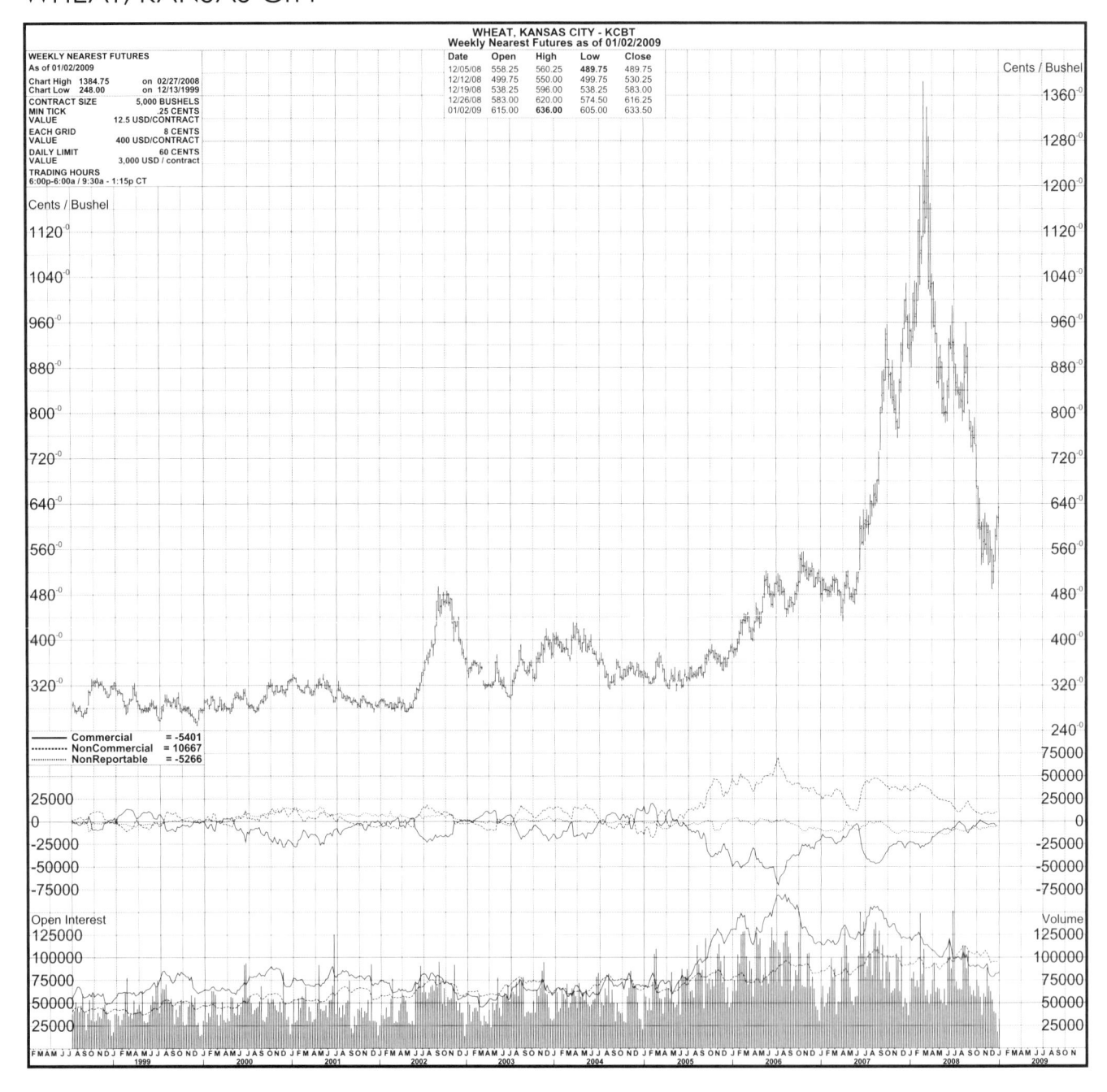

| Date | Open | High | Low | Close |
|---|---|---|---|---|
| 12/05/08 | 558.25 | 560.25 | 489.75 | 489.75 |
| 12/12/08 | 499.75 | 550.00 | 499.75 | 530.25 |
| 12/19/08 | 538.25 | 596.00 | 538.25 | 583.00 |
| 12/26/08 | 583.00 | 620.00 | 574.50 | 616.25 |
| 01/02/09 | 615.00 | 636.00 | 605.00 | 633.50 |

**WEEKLY NEAREST FUTURES**
As of 01/02/2009
Chart High 1384.75 on 02/27/2008
Chart Low 248.00 on 12/13/1999
CONTRACT SIZE 5,000 BUSHELS
MIN TICK .25 CENTS
VALUE 12.5 USD/CONTRACT
EACH GRID 8 CENTS
VALUE 400 USD/CONTRACT
DAILY LIMIT 60 CENTS
VALUE 3,000 USD / contract
TRADING HOURS 6:00p-6:00a / 9:30a - 1:15p CT

Commercial = -5401
NonCommercial = 10667
NonReportable = -5266

## Quarterly High, Low and Settle of Wheat Futures    In Cents per Bushel

| Quarter | High | Low | Settle | Quarter | High | Low | Settle | Quarter | High | Low | Settle |
|---|---|---|---|---|---|---|---|---|---|---|---|
| 03/2000 | 302.50 | 270.25 | 286.50 | 03/2003 | 370.75 | 312.25 | 320.75 | 03/2006 | 449.00 | 368.00 | 418.50 |
| 06/2000 | 315.00 | 270.00 | 302.00 | 06/2003 | 375.00 | 299.50 | 300.25 | 06/2006 | 522.50 | 413.00 | 499.75 |
| 09/2000 | 320.00 | 271.00 | 320.00 | 09/2003 | 392.50 | 294.50 | 356.75 | 09/2006 | 518.00 | 440.25 | 496.00 |
| 12/2000 | 331.50 | 298.50 | 330.00 | 12/2003 | 420.50 | 326.00 | 384.75 | 12/2006 | 556.00 | 485.00 | 509.75 |
| 03/2001 | 340.00 | 298.00 | 301.50 | 03/2004 | 431.00 | 362.00 | 412.50 | 03/2007 | 516.00 | 442.25 | 456.50 |
| 06/2001 | 333.50 | 289.25 | 293.00 | 06/2004 | 430.00 | 352.00 | 358.50 | 06/2007 | 630.25 | 433.00 | 596.50 |
| 09/2001 | 317.50 | 281.00 | 292.50 | 09/2004 | 378.00 | 312.00 | 336.75 | 09/2007 | 949.50 | 573.00 | 929.25 |
| 12/2001 | 302.00 | 271.50 | 284.00 | 12/2004 | 362.50 | 328.25 | 338.00 | 12/2007 | 1,029.25 | 755.50 | 913.50 |
| 03/2002 | 300.00 | 273.50 | 290.00 | 03/2005 | 378.00 | 322.00 | 338.00 | 03/2008 | 1,384.75 | 880.75 | 965.00 |
| 06/2002 | 325.00 | 271.25 | 322.50 | 06/2005 | 352.50 | 309.50 | 328.00 | 06/2008 | 1,036.25 | 782.00 | 883.00 |
| 09/2002 | 495.00 | 325.00 | 475.25 | 09/2005 | 384.00 | 326.50 | 380.25 | 09/2008 | 960.00 | 704.50 | 712.00 |
| 12/2002 | 487.00 | 355.00 | 359.75 | 12/2005 | 392.50 | 345.00 | 387.00 | 12/2008 | 722.75 | 489.75 | 630.00 |

*Source: Kansas City Board of Trade*

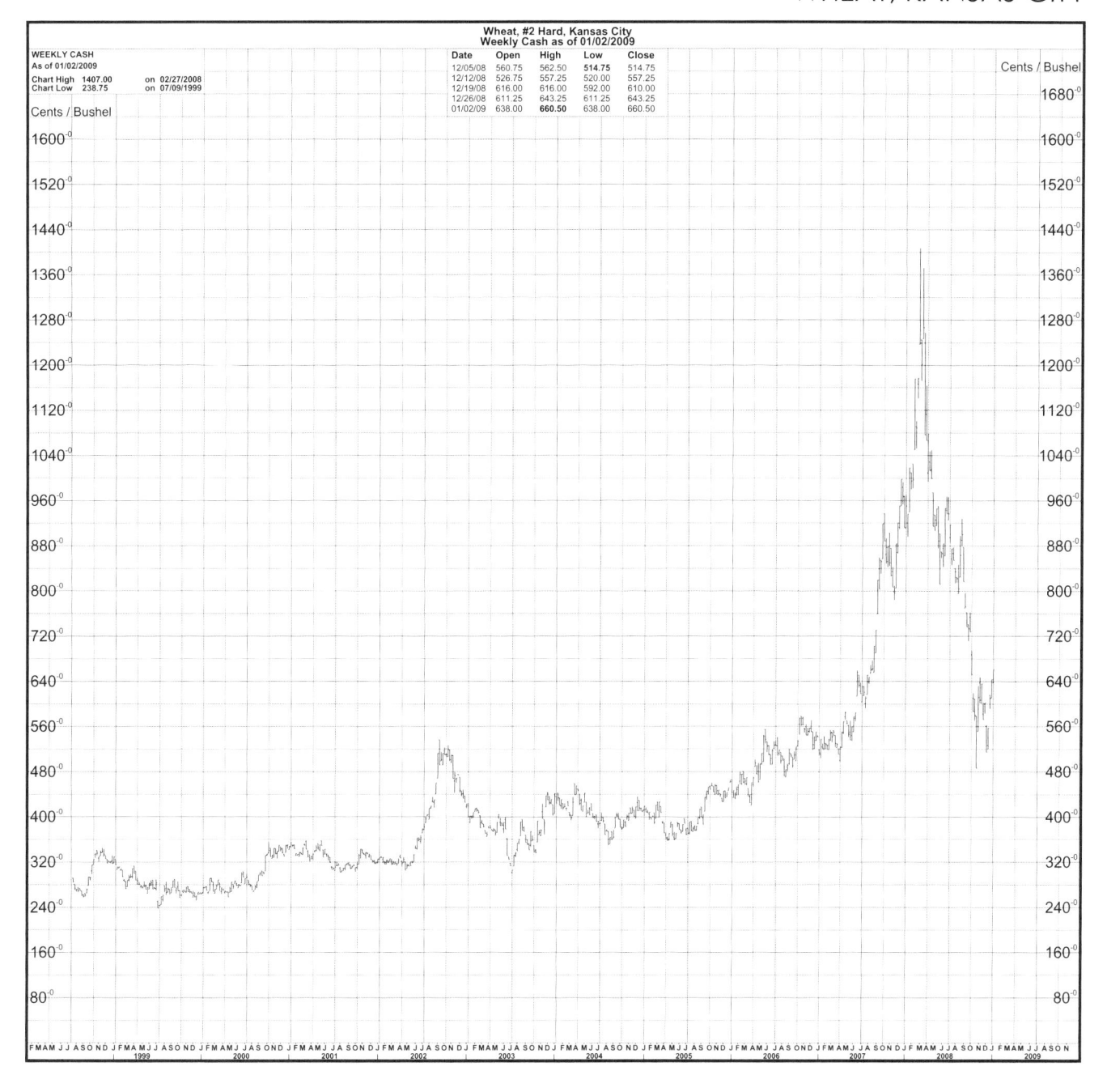

# WHEAT, KANSAS CITY

**Wheat, #2 Hard, Kansas City**
Weekly Cash as of 01/02/2009

| Date | Open | High | Low | Close |
|---|---|---|---|---|
| 12/05/08 | 560.75 | 562.50 | 514.75 | 514.75 |
| 12/12/08 | 526.75 | 557.25 | 520.00 | 557.25 |
| 12/19/08 | 616.00 | 616.00 | 592.00 | 610.00 |
| 12/26/08 | 611.25 | 643.25 | 611.25 | 643.25 |
| 01/02/09 | 638.00 | 660.50 | 638.00 | 660.50 |

WEEKLY CASH
As of 01/02/2009
Chart High 1407.00 on 02/27/2008
Chart Low 238.75 on 07/09/1999
Cents / Bushel

## Quarterly High, Low and Settle of Wheat   In Cents per Bushel

| Quarter | High | Low | Settle | Quarter | High | Low | Settle | Quarter | High | Low | Settle |
|---|---|---|---|---|---|---|---|---|---|---|---|
| 03/2000 | 291.75 | 263.00 | 275.00 | 03/2003 | 425.00 | 364.75 | 382.25 | 03/2006 | 480.50 | 421.00 | 460.50 |
| 06/2000 | 303.00 | 258.25 | 293.50 | 06/2003 | 405.00 | 317.75 | 317.75 | 06/2006 | 554.50 | 453.25 | 526.75 |
| 09/2000 | 331.50 | 267.50 | 331.50 | 09/2003 | 395.00 | 298.00 | 361.25 | 09/2006 | 541.00 | 470.50 | 524.00 |
| 12/2000 | 355.00 | 326.00 | 350.50 | 12/2003 | 444.00 | 336.00 | 417.25 | 12/2006 | 578.00 | 518.50 | 541.75 |
| 03/2001 | 358.50 | 322.00 | 322.00 | 03/2004 | 458.75 | 393.50 | 449.50 | 03/2007 | 553.50 | 503.50 | 511.00 |
| 06/2001 | 357.75 | 307.00 | 310.50 | 06/2004 | 454.75 | 383.00 | 383.00 | 06/2007 | 659.50 | 496.75 | 618.50 |
| 09/2001 | 320.25 | 302.00 | 314.00 | 09/2004 | 408.00 | 350.25 | 383.25 | 09/2007 | 918.75 | 593.00 | 918.75 |
| 12/2001 | 343.00 | 302.50 | 318.50 | 12/2004 | 436.00 | 377.50 | 412.00 | 12/2007 | 998.00 | 784.50 | 911.50 |
| 03/2002 | 330.00 | 313.50 | 323.50 | 03/2005 | 426.50 | 380.50 | 380.50 | 03/2008 | 1,407.00 | 896.00 | 1,009.50 |
| 06/2002 | 367.25 | 305.50 | 363.25 | 06/2005 | 396.75 | 358.00 | 367.00 | 06/2008 | 1,078.00 | 812.25 | 895.00 |
| 09/2002 | 536.25 | 371.25 | 516.75 | 09/2005 | 452.75 | 368.50 | 452.75 | 09/2008 | 928.00 | 687.50 | 694.00 |
| 12/2002 | 526.75 | 415.25 | 415.25 | 12/2005 | 465.75 | 427.00 | 462.50 | 12/2008 | 686.00 | 486.50 | 657.00 |

Kansas City #2 Hard Winter    *Source: Kansas City Board of Trade*

# WHEAT, MINNEAPOLIS

**WHEAT, MINNEAPOLIS - MGEX**
Monthly Nearest Futures as of 12/31/2008

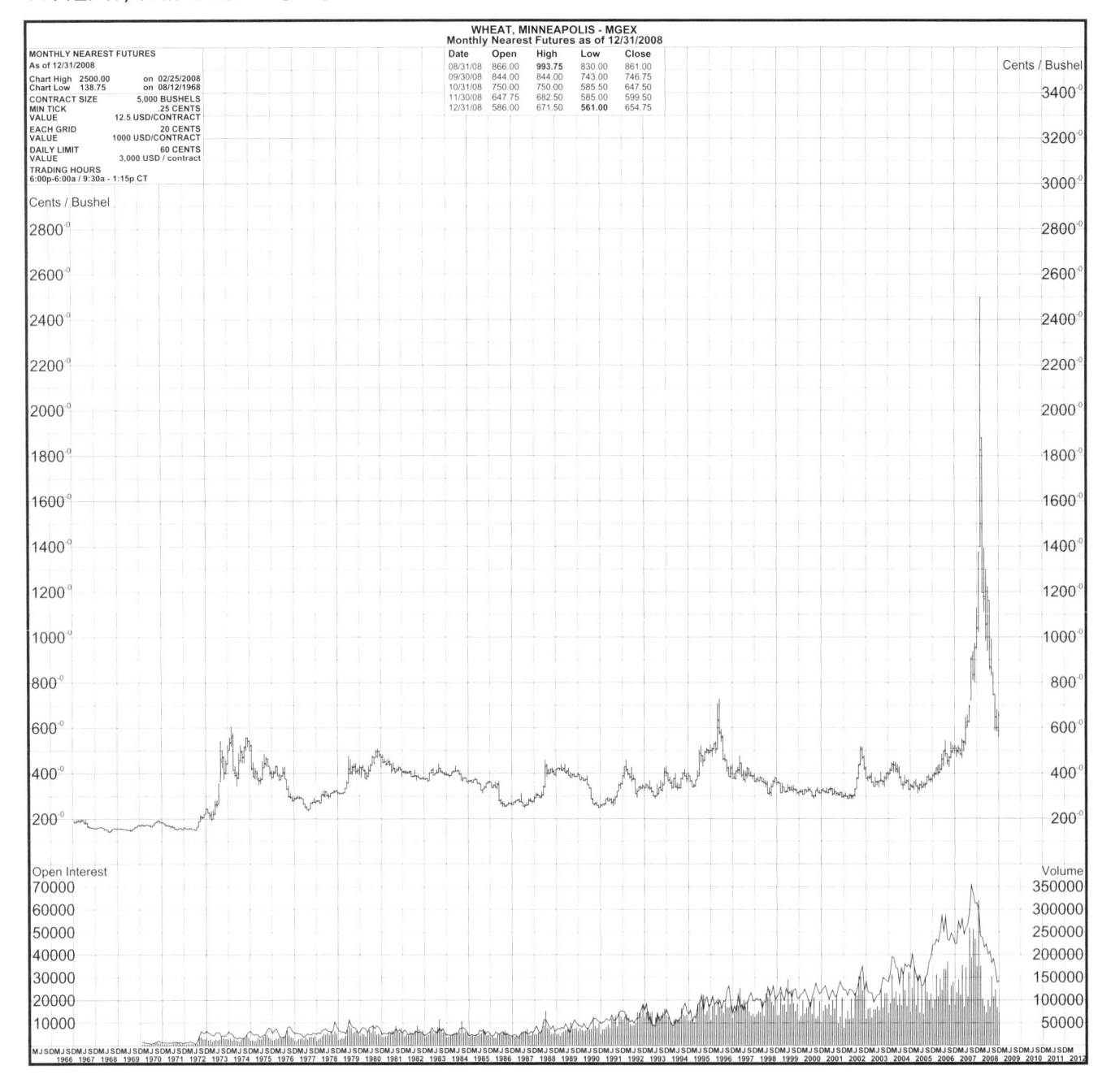

| Date | Open | High | Low | Close |
|---|---|---|---|---|
| 08/31/08 | 866.00 | 993.75 | 830.00 | 861.00 |
| 09/30/08 | 844.00 | 844.00 | 743.50 | 746.75 |
| 10/31/08 | 750.00 | 750.00 | 585.50 | 647.50 |
| 11/30/08 | 647.75 | 682.50 | 585.00 | 599.50 |
| 12/31/08 | 586.00 | 671.50 | 561.00 | 654.75 |

MONTHLY NEAREST FUTURES
As of 12/31/2008
Chart High 2500.00 on 02/25/2008
Chart Low 138.75 on 08/12/1968
CONTRACT SIZE 5,000 BUSHELS
MIN TICK .25 CENTS
VALUE 12.5 USD/CONTRACT
EACH GRID 20 CENTS
VALUE 1000 USD/CONTRACT
DAILY LIMIT 60 CENTS
VALUE 3,000 USD / contract
TRADING HOURS
6:00p-6:00a / 9:30a - 1:15p CT

## Annual High, Low and Settle of Wheat Futures   In Cents per Bushel

| Year | High | Low | Settle | Year | High | Low | Settle | Year | High | Low | Settle |
|---|---|---|---|---|---|---|---|---|---|---|---|
| 1967 | | | | 1981 | 484.00 | 383.00 | 406.50 | 1995 | 527.00 | 336.50 | 499.50 |
| 1968 | | | | 1982 | 415.75 | 366.00 | 375.00 | 1996 | 732.00 | 377.50 | 377.75 |
| 1969 | | | | 1983 | 444.00 | 363.00 | 394.25 | 1997 | 478.50 | 357.00 | 364.00 |
| 1970 | 196.00 | 164.75 | 184.63 | 1984 | 434.00 | 353.50 | 367.00 | 1998 | 389.00 | 299.00 | 359.25 |
| 1971 | 185.25 | 152.00 | 161.50 | 1985 | 380.25 | 309.75 | 360.50 | 1999 | 366.00 | 303.00 | 318.00 |
| 1972 | 249.00 | 149.75 | 243.50 | 1986 | 367.00 | 251.00 | 262.75 | 2000 | 341.00 | 286.50 | 327.25 |
| 1973 | 543.50 | 191.50 | 493.00 | 1987 | 315.00 | 245.00 | 290.75 | 2001 | 336.25 | 290.00 | 300.00 |
| 1974 | 609.00 | 342.00 | 522.00 | 1988 | 460.00 | 288.50 | 417.00 | 2002 | 518.00 | 285.00 | 377.25 |
| 1975 | 528.00 | 348.00 | 383.00 | 1989 | 442.25 | 379.50 | 393.50 | 2003 | 408.00 | 338.00 | 393.75 |
| 1976 | 435.00 | 276.00 | 289.25 | 1990 | 395.00 | 245.00 | 259.50 | 2004 | 449.50 | 325.00 | 346.00 |
| 1977 | 301.00 | 232.50 | 278.00 | 1991 | 390.00 | 252.25 | 389.00 | 2005 | 395.00 | 310.50 | 392.00 |
| 1978 | 327.00 | 267.75 | 314.50 | 1992 | 460.00 | 292.75 | 335.75 | 2006 | 545.00 | 377.50 | 518.50 |
| 1979 | 477.25 | 306.75 | 425.00 | 1993 | 430.00 | 287.75 | 403.50 | 2007 | 1,130.00 | 464.00 | 1,036.25 |
| 1980 | 510.00 | 370.50 | 472.00 | 1994 | 419.50 | 324.00 | 390.00 | 2008 | 2,500.00 | 561.00 | 654.75 |

Futures data begins 01/02/1979.   Source: *Minneapolis Grain Exchange*

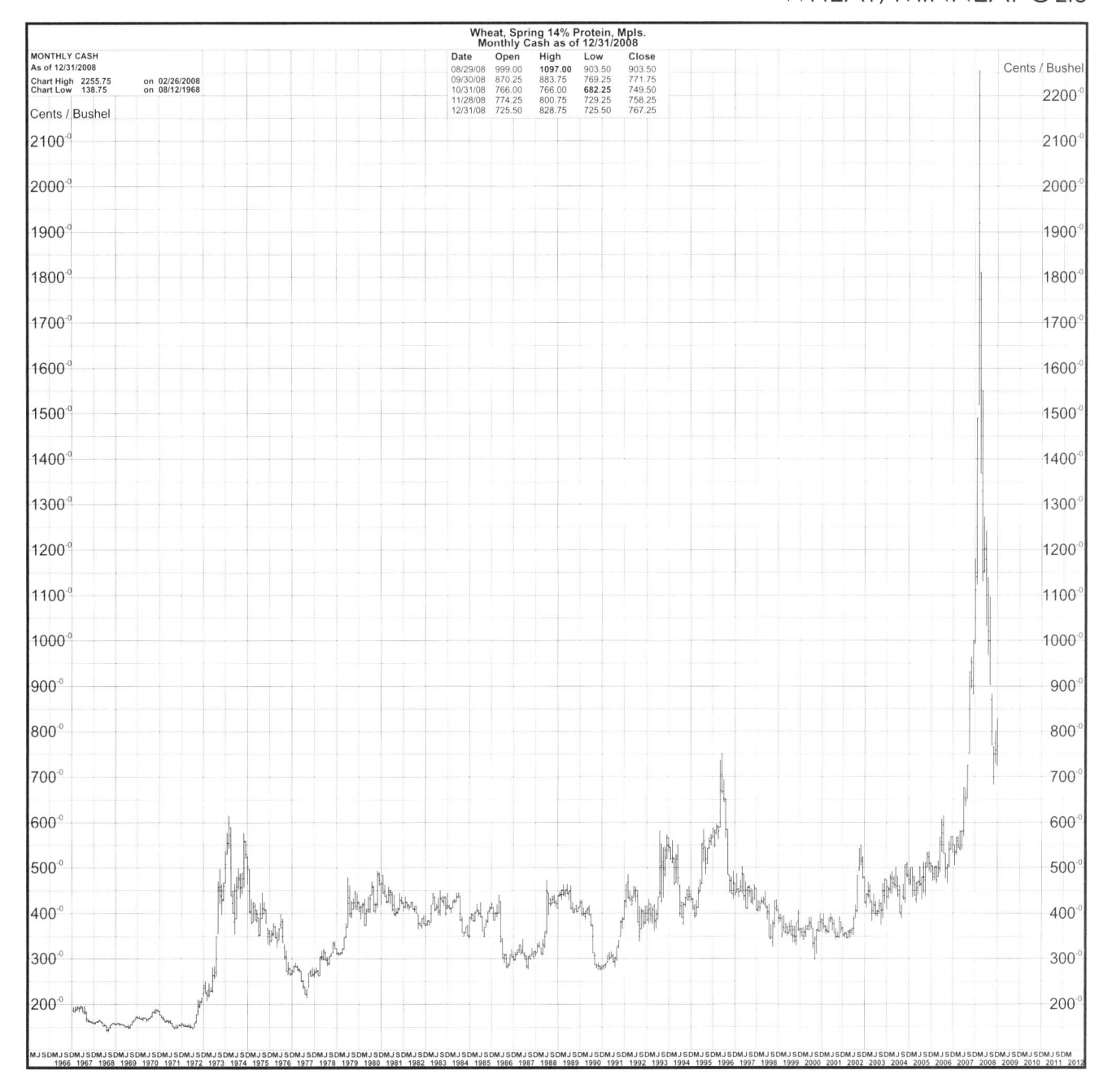

# WHEAT, MINNEAPOLIS

**Wheat, Spring 14% Protein, Mpls.**
**Monthly Cash as of 12/31/2008**

| Date | Open | High | Low | Close |
|---|---|---|---|---|
| 08/29/08 | 999.00 | 1097.00 | 903.50 | 903.50 |
| 09/30/08 | 870.25 | 883.75 | 769.25 | 771.75 |
| 10/31/08 | 766.00 | 766.00 | 682.25 | 749.50 |
| 11/28/08 | 774.25 | 800.75 | 729.25 | 758.25 |
| 12/31/08 | 725.50 | 828.75 | 725.50 | 767.25 |

MONTHLY CASH As of 12/31/2008
Chart High 2255.75 on 02/26/2008
Chart Low 138.75 on 08/12/1968

## Annual High, Low and Settle of Wheat   In Cents per Bushel

| Year | High | Low | Settle | Year | High | Low | Settle | Year | High | Low | Settle |
|---|---|---|---|---|---|---|---|---|---|---|---|
| 1967 | 197.00 | 157.13 | 158.50 | 1981 | 484.50 | 395.75 | 414.38 | 1995 | 587.00 | 389.25 | 587.00 |
| 1968 | 166.63 | 138.75 | 156.63 | 1982 | 437.63 | 365.00 | 377.00 | 1996 | 751.75 | 430.50 | 441.75 |
| 1969 | 174.63 | 146.00 | 170.00 | 1983 | 450.75 | 373.50 | 417.13 | 1997 | 503.75 | 406.50 | 406.50 |
| 1970 | 190.75 | 161.13 | 176.63 | 1984 | 445.75 | 345.75 | 391.00 | 1998 | 448.50 | 325.50 | 390.38 |
| 1971 | 177.00 | 146.00 | 158.25 | 1985 | 425.00 | 346.75 | 420.50 | 1999 | 408.00 | 329.00 | 365.50 |
| 1972 | 241.50 | 146.00 | 241.50 | 1986 | 440.00 | 279.00 | 297.75 | 2000 | 400.00 | 297.50 | 384.75 |
| 1973 | 537.00 | 207.25 | 508.00 | 1987 | 344.00 | 276.25 | 310.75 | 2001 | 400.00 | 342.00 | 352.50 |
| 1974 | 616.00 | 354.00 | 503.00 | 1988 | 474.00 | 308.50 | 438.00 | 2002 | 549.00 | 345.00 | 422.25 |
| 1975 | 497.50 | 328.50 | 339.00 | 1989 | 464.75 | 400.00 | 423.50 | 2003 | 475.50 | 374.50 | 436.25 |
| 1976 | 399.00 | 262.50 | 274.25 | 1990 | 430.00 | 273.50 | 283.50 | 2004 | 513.00 | 388.75 | 473.50 |
| 1977 | 291.88 | 214.00 | 271.00 | 1991 | 428.00 | 276.50 | 428.00 | 2005 | 536.50 | 421.75 | 504.50 |
| 1978 | 339.25 | 262.50 | 312.50 | 1992 | 486.25 | 337.50 | 385.75 | 2006 | 616.00 | 465.25 | 550.88 |
| 1979 | 479.50 | 305.13 | 412.88 | 1993 | 582.25 | 360.25 | 546.00 | 2007 | 1,180.50 | 504.75 | 1,111.25 |
| 1980 | 494.50 | 373.00 | 465.75 | 1994 | 561.25 | 374.25 | 432.50 | 2008 | 2,255.75 | 682.25 | 767.25 |

Minneapolis #1 Dark 15% through 12/1978, Minneapolis #1 Dark 14% 01/1979 to date.   *Source: Minneapolis Grain Exchange*

# WHEAT, MINNEAPOLIS

**WHEAT, MINNEAPOLIS - MGEX**
Weekly Nearest Futures as of 01/02/2009

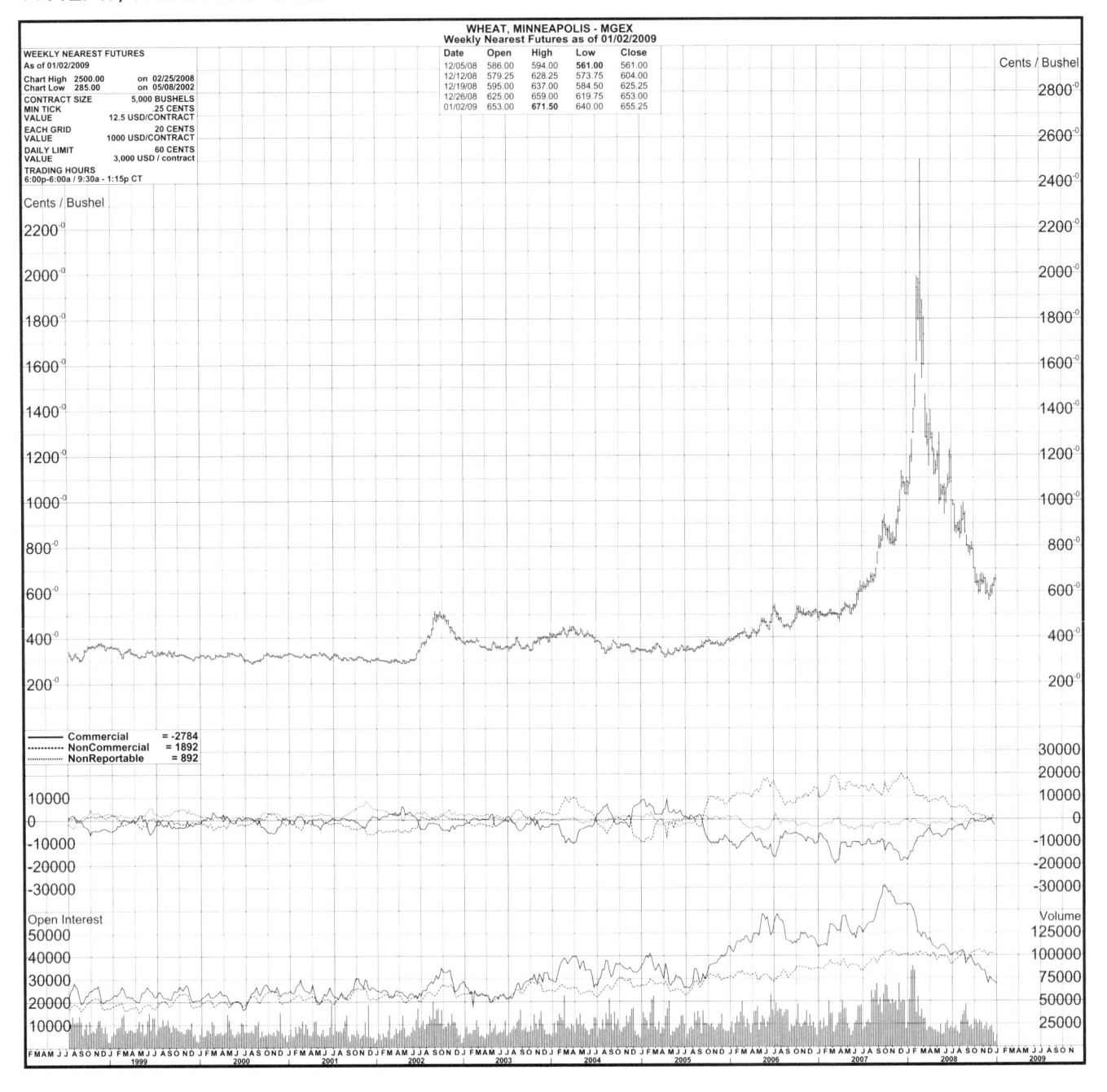

| Date | Open | High | Low | Close |
|---|---|---|---|---|
| 12/05/08 | 586.00 | 594.00 | 561.00 | 561.00 |
| 12/12/08 | 579.25 | 628.25 | 573.75 | 604.00 |
| 12/19/08 | 595.00 | 637.00 | 584.50 | 625.25 |
| 12/26/08 | 625.00 | 659.00 | 619.75 | 653.00 |
| 01/02/09 | 653.00 | 671.50 | 640.00 | 655.25 |

**WEEKLY NEAREST FUTURES**
As of 01/02/2009
Chart High 2500.00 on 02/25/2008
Chart Low 285.00 on 05/08/2002
CONTRACT SIZE 5,000 BUSHELS
MIN TICK .25 CENTS
VALUE 12.5 USD/CONTRACT
EACH GRID 20 CENTS
VALUE 1000 USD/CONTRACT
DAILY LIMIT 60 CENTS
VALUE 3,000 USD / contract
TRADING HOURS
6:00p-6:00a / 9:30a - 1:15p CT

Commercial = -2784
NonCommercial = 1892
NonReportable = 892

## Quarterly High, Low and Settle of Wheat Futures   In Cents per Bushel

| Quarter | High | Low | Settle | Quarter | High | Low | Settle | Quarter | High | Low | Settle |
|---|---|---|---|---|---|---|---|---|---|---|---|
| 03/2000 | 331.00 | 304.50 | 327.00 | 03/2003 | 402.00 | 352.00 | 361.25 | 03/2006 | 438.00 | 377.50 | 404.25 |
| 06/2000 | 341.00 | 314.50 | 322.75 | 06/2003 | 385.00 | 341.00 | 363.00 | 06/2006 | 498.00 | 400.00 | 496.00 |
| 09/2000 | 325.00 | 286.50 | 324.50 | 09/2003 | 406.50 | 349.00 | 364.00 | 09/2006 | 545.00 | 426.50 | 468.75 |
| 12/2000 | 340.00 | 309.00 | 327.25 | 12/2003 | 408.00 | 338.00 | 393.75 | 12/2006 | 538.00 | 465.00 | 518.50 |
| 03/2001 | 336.25 | 310.00 | 313.50 | 03/2004 | 448.00 | 396.00 | 436.75 | 03/2007 | 524.00 | 469.00 | 485.00 |
| 06/2001 | 334.25 | 302.00 | 310.00 | 06/2004 | 449.50 | 375.00 | 381.00 | 06/2007 | 649.00 | 464.00 | 623.00 |
| 09/2001 | 333.00 | 297.00 | 306.75 | 09/2004 | 390.00 | 327.00 | 358.25 | 09/2007 | 914.25 | 600.00 | 905.75 |
| 12/2001 | 320.00 | 290.00 | 300.00 | 12/2004 | 374.50 | 325.00 | 346.00 | 12/2007 | 1,130.00 | 799.50 | 1,036.25 |
| 03/2002 | 315.50 | 287.00 | 303.00 | 03/2005 | 376.00 | 326.00 | 343.75 | 03/2008 | 2,500.00 | 1,019.50 | 1,194.00 |
| 06/2002 | 333.00 | 285.00 | 329.00 | 06/2005 | 367.50 | 310.50 | 339.00 | 06/2008 | 1,395.00 | 938.00 | 1,175.00 |
| 09/2002 | 518.00 | 332.00 | 506.25 | 09/2005 | 389.00 | 333.25 | 383.00 | 09/2008 | 1,162.25 | 743.00 | 746.75 |
| 12/2002 | 517.50 | 375.50 | 377.25 | 12/2005 | 395.00 | 359.00 | 392.00 | 12/2008 | 750.00 | 561.00 | 654.75 |

*Source: Minneapolis Grain Exchange*

# WHEAT, MINNEAPOLIS

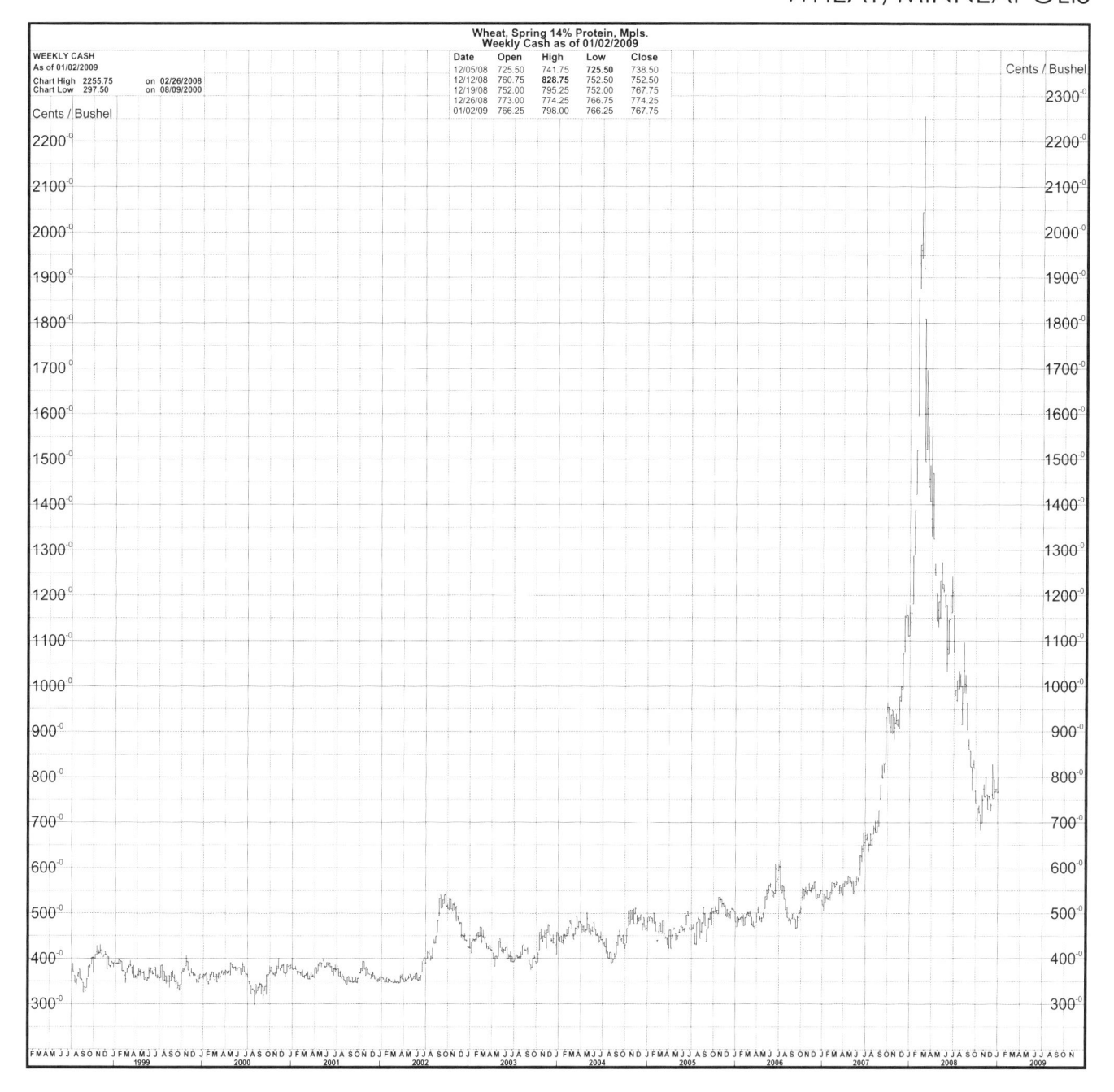

**Wheat, Spring 14% Protein, Mpls.**
Weekly Cash as of 01/02/2009

| Date | Open | High | Low | Close |
|---|---|---|---|---|
| 12/05/08 | 725.50 | 741.75 | 725.50 | 738.50 |
| 12/12/08 | 760.75 | 828.75 | 752.50 | 752.50 |
| 12/19/08 | 752.00 | 795.25 | 752.00 | 767.75 |
| 12/26/08 | 773.00 | 774.25 | 766.75 | 774.25 |
| 01/02/09 | 766.25 | 798.00 | 766.25 | 767.75 |

WEEKLY CASH As of 01/02/2009
Chart High 2255.75 on 02/26/2008
Chart Low 297.50 on 08/09/2000

## Quarterly High, Low and Settle of Wheat — In Cents per Bushel

| Quarter | High | Low | Settle | Quarter | High | Low | Settle | Quarter | High | Low | Settle |
|---|---|---|---|---|---|---|---|---|---|---|---|
| 03/2000 | 373.00 | 341.25 | 373.00 | 03/2003 | 469.75 | 412.75 | 428.75 | 03/2006 | 504.75 | 465.50 | 473.25 |
| 06/2000 | 392.50 | 363.50 | 371.50 | 06/2003 | 443.50 | 382.25 | 404.25 | 06/2006 | 609.00 | 479.50 | 575.50 |
| 09/2000 | 367.25 | 297.50 | 364.50 | 09/2003 | 431.00 | 374.50 | 406.50 | 09/2006 | 616.00 | 465.25 | 506.25 |
| 12/2000 | 400.00 | 359.00 | 384.75 | 12/2003 | 475.50 | 388.50 | 436.25 | 12/2006 | 568.50 | 501.00 | 550.88 |
| 03/2001 | 400.00 | 354.75 | 359.50 | 03/2004 | 492.25 | 431.25 | 466.75 | 03/2007 | 570.75 | 504.75 | 545.00 |
| 06/2001 | 399.25 | 356.50 | 377.50 | 06/2004 | 502.25 | 435.38 | 441.00 | 06/2007 | 677.00 | 537.50 | 677.00 |
| 09/2001 | 387.25 | 342.00 | 347.75 | 09/2004 | 464.75 | 388.75 | 433.25 | 09/2007 | 930.75 | 634.50 | 930.75 |
| 12/2001 | 393.75 | 345.50 | 352.50 | 12/2004 | 513.00 | 422.50 | 473.50 | 12/2007 | 1,180.50 | 882.50 | 1,111.25 |
| 03/2002 | 363.75 | 345.00 | 358.00 | 03/2005 | 500.75 | 434.75 | 438.75 | 03/2008 | 2,255.75 | 1,122.50 | 1,369.00 |
| 06/2002 | 394.00 | 346.25 | 388.25 | 06/2005 | 503.50 | 421.75 | 464.50 | 06/2008 | 1,550.75 | 1,032.00 | 1,155.50 |
| 09/2002 | 541.25 | 389.00 | 541.25 | 09/2005 | 513.25 | 430.25 | 510.50 | 09/2008 | 1,138.50 | 769.25 | 771.75 |
| 12/2002 | 549.00 | 422.25 | 422.25 | 12/2005 | 536.50 | 488.00 | 504.50 | 12/2008 | 828.75 | 682.25 | 767.25 |

Minneapolis #1 Dark 14%.   *Source: Minneapolis Grain Exchange*

# CANOLA

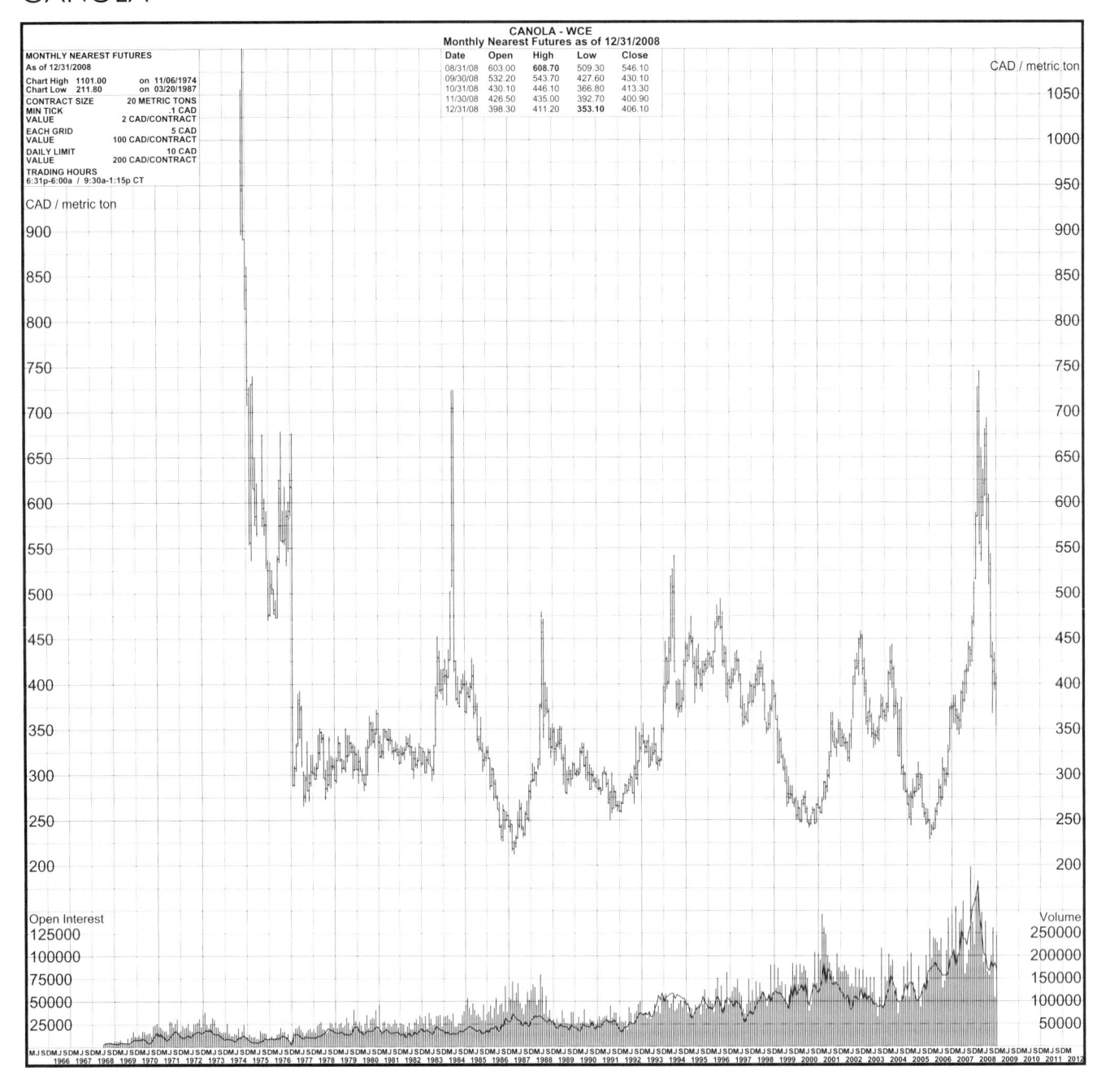

**CANOLA - WCE**
Monthly Nearest Futures as of 12/31/2008

| Date | Open | High | Low | Close |
|---|---|---|---|---|
| 08/31/08 | 603.00 | 608.70 | 509.30 | 546.10 |
| 09/30/08 | 532.20 | 543.70 | 427.60 | 430.10 |
| 10/31/08 | 430.10 | 446.10 | 366.80 | 413.30 |
| 11/30/08 | 426.50 | 435.00 | 392.70 | 400.90 |
| 12/31/08 | 398.30 | 411.20 | 353.10 | 406.10 |

**MONTHLY NEAREST FUTURES**
As of 12/31/2008
Chart High 1101.00 on 11/06/1974
Chart Low 211.80 on 03/20/1987
CONTRACT SIZE 20 METRIC TONS
MIN TICK .1 CAD
VALUE 2 CAD/CONTRACT
EACH GRID 5 CAD
VALUE 100 CAD/CONTRACT
DAILY LIMIT 10 CAD
VALUE 200 CAD/CONTRACT
TRADING HOURS
6:31p-6:00a / 9:30a-1:15p CT

## Annual High, Low and Settle of Canola Futures — In CAD per Metric Ton

| Year | High | Low | Settle | Year | High | Low | Settle | Year | High | Low | Settle |
|---|---|---|---|---|---|---|---|---|---|---|---|
| 1967 | | | | 1981 | 351.20 | 311.00 | 313.00 | 1995 | 475.50 | 378.50 | 432.50 |
| 1968 | | | | 1982 | 345.00 | 295.00 | 312.30 | 1996 | 494.50 | 379.10 | 396.00 |
| 1969 | | | | 1983 | 453.00 | 292.80 | 416.10 | 1997 | 437.50 | 352.00 | 380.90 |
| 1970 | | | | 1984 | 724.00 | 368.90 | 369.30 | 1998 | 436.50 | 344.50 | 386.20 |
| 1971 | | | | 1985 | 429.20 | 303.10 | 326.30 | 1999 | 390.70 | 250.00 | 254.00 |
| 1972 | | | | 1986 | 331.50 | 226.90 | 242.70 | 2000 | 282.20 | 241.00 | 263.30 |
| 1973 | | | | 1987 | 293.20 | 211.80 | 292.60 | 2001 | 369.00 | 256.60 | 331.00 |
| 1974 | 1,101.00 | 777.60 | 814.00 | 1988 | 480.00 | 287.00 | 346.70 | 2002 | 459.00 | 313.00 | 416.60 |
| 1975 | 861.00 | 470.00 | 476.40 | 1989 | 354.00 | 278.50 | 301.60 | 2003 | 428.90 | 328.50 | 364.50 |
| 1976 | 679.00 | 472.40 | 618.00 | 1990 | 335.40 | 283.50 | 285.00 | 2004 | 444.00 | 267.00 | 267.50 |
| 1977 | 677.00 | 265.00 | 302.00 | 1991 | 309.00 | 250.00 | 260.00 | 2005 | 314.00 | 228.00 | 230.10 |
| 1978 | 351.50 | 272.50 | 294.00 | 1992 | 353.60 | 257.80 | 342.70 | 2006 | 378.00 | 231.90 | 372.00 |
| 1979 | 351.00 | 290.50 | 306.00 | 1993 | 398.00 | 304.00 | 395.90 | 2007 | 512.20 | 343.10 | 505.00 |
| 1980 | 372.00 | 282.00 | 335.70 | 1994 | 542.20 | 362.20 | 441.00 | 2008 | 744.50 | 353.10 | 406.10 |

Futures data begins 04/30/1974.   Source: IntercontinentalExchange (ICE); formerly Winnipeg Commodity Exchange

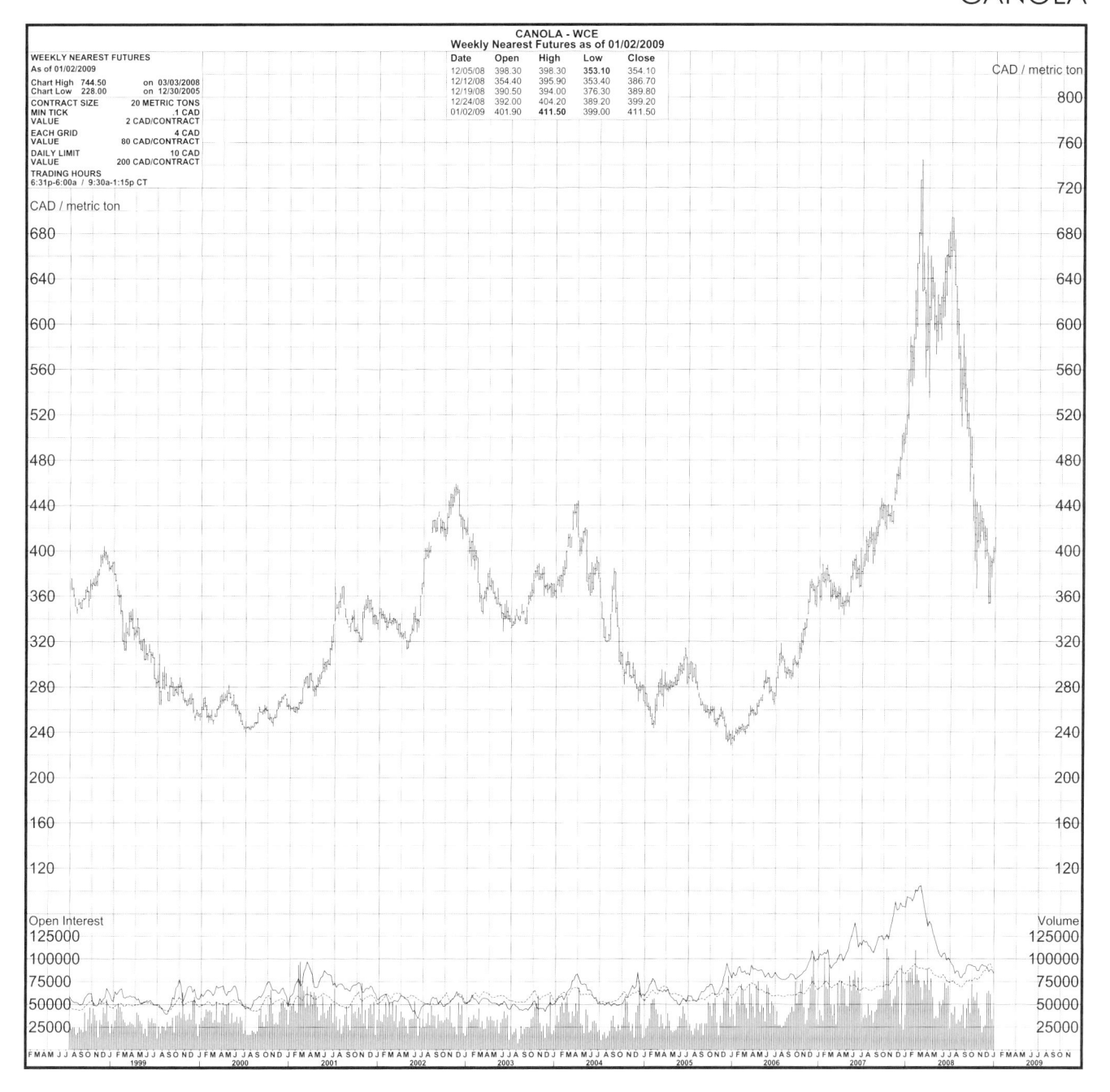

# CANOLA

**CANOLA - WCE**
Weekly Nearest Futures as of 01/02/2009

| Date | Open | High | Low | Close |
|---|---|---|---|---|
| 12/05/08 | 398.30 | 398.30 | 353.10 | 354.10 |
| 12/12/08 | 354.40 | 395.90 | 353.40 | 386.70 |
| 12/19/08 | 390.50 | 394.00 | 376.30 | 389.80 |
| 12/24/08 | 392.00 | 404.20 | 389.20 | 399.20 |
| 01/02/09 | 401.90 | 411.50 | 399.00 | 411.50 |

**WEEKLY NEAREST FUTURES**
As of 01/02/2009
Chart High 744.50 on 03/03/2008
Chart Low 228.00 on 12/30/2005
CONTRACT SIZE 20 METRIC TONS
MIN TICK .1 CAD
VALUE 2 CAD/CONTRACT
EACH GRID 4 CAD
VALUE 80 CAD/CONTRACT
DAILY LIMIT 10 CAD
VALUE 200 CAD/CONTRACT
TRADING HOURS
6:31p-6:00a / 9:30a-1:15p CT

## Quarterly High, Low and Settle of Canola Futures    In CAD per Metric Ton

| Quarter | High | Low | Settle | Quarter | High | Low | Settle | Quarter | High | Low | Settle |
|---|---|---|---|---|---|---|---|---|---|---|---|
| 03/2000 | 272.20 | 246.80 | 267.70 | 03/2003 | 428.90 | 344.00 | 368.40 | 03/2006 | 263.80 | 231.90 | 259.60 |
| 06/2000 | 282.20 | 246.50 | 246.90 | 06/2003 | 385.00 | 328.50 | 340.00 | 06/2006 | 295.00 | 254.20 | 274.30 |
| 09/2000 | 264.50 | 241.00 | 260.80 | 09/2003 | 365.00 | 332.00 | 361.80 | 09/2006 | 318.80 | 272.20 | 300.10 |
| 12/2000 | 274.50 | 245.00 | 263.30 | 12/2003 | 388.90 | 358.30 | 364.50 | 12/2006 | 378.00 | 296.50 | 372.00 |
| 03/2001 | 292.80 | 256.60 | 291.00 | 03/2004 | 441.30 | 357.30 | 423.50 | 03/2007 | 388.00 | 347.80 | 362.40 |
| 06/2001 | 325.00 | 271.50 | 316.80 | 06/2004 | 444.00 | 360.80 | 380.20 | 06/2007 | 403.00 | 343.10 | 381.70 |
| 09/2001 | 369.00 | 319.50 | 329.70 | 09/2004 | 385.10 | 299.50 | 307.20 | 09/2007 | 446.70 | 378.90 | 438.10 |
| 12/2001 | 361.00 | 319.00 | 331.00 | 12/2004 | 311.00 | 267.00 | 267.50 | 12/2007 | 512.20 | 418.40 | 505.00 |
| 03/2002 | 349.80 | 326.40 | 335.00 | 03/2005 | 295.50 | 243.20 | 280.90 | 03/2008 | 744.50 | 514.80 | 555.30 |
| 06/2002 | 360.20 | 313.00 | 360.00 | 06/2005 | 314.00 | 275.50 | 283.90 | 06/2008 | 681.80 | 534.60 | 662.30 |
| 09/2002 | 434.40 | 361.50 | 419.00 | 09/2005 | 302.30 | 251.80 | 256.50 | 09/2008 | 693.90 | 427.60 | 430.10 |
| 12/2002 | 459.00 | 408.50 | 416.60 | 12/2005 | 263.40 | 228.00 | 230.10 | 12/2008 | 446.10 | 353.10 | 406.10 |

*Source: IntercontinentalExchange (ICE); formerly Winnipeg Commodity Exchange*

# SOYBEANS

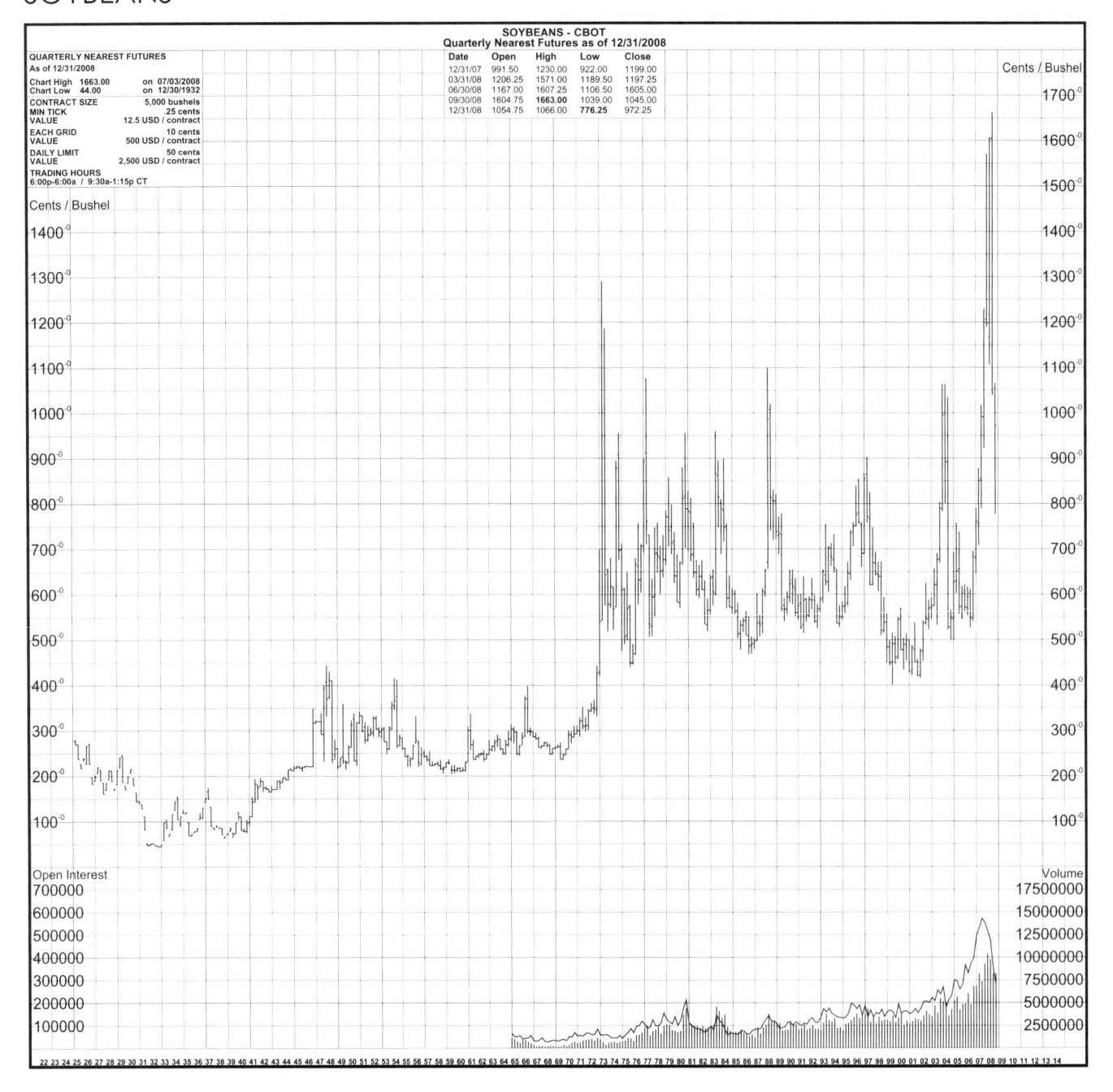

**SOYBEANS - CBOT**
Quarterly Nearest Futures as of 12/31/2008

| Date | Open | High | Low | Close |
|---|---|---|---|---|
| 12/31/07 | 991.50 | 1230.00 | 922.00 | 1199.00 |
| 03/31/08 | 1206.25 | 1571.00 | 1189.50 | 1197.25 |
| 06/30/08 | 1167.00 | 1607.25 | 1106.50 | 1605.00 |
| 09/30/08 | 1604.75 | 1663.00 | 1039.00 | 1045.00 |
| 12/31/08 | 1054.75 | 1066.00 | 776.25 | 972.25 |

**QUARTERLY NEAREST FUTURES**
As of 12/31/2008
Chart High 1663.00 on 07/03/2008
Chart Low 44.00 on 12/30/1932
CONTRACT SIZE 5,000 bushels
MIN TICK .25 cents
VALUE 12.5 USD / contract
EACH GRID 10 cents
VALUE 500 USD / contract
DAILY LIMIT 50 cents
VALUE 2,500 USD / contract
TRADING HOURS 6:00p-6:00a / 9:30a-1:15p CT

## Annual High, Low and Settle of Soybean Futures    In Cents per Bushel

| Year | High | Low | Settle | Year | High | Low | Settle | Year | High | Low | Settle |
|---|---|---|---|---|---|---|---|---|---|---|---|
| 1925 | 281.00 | 217.00 | 217.00 | 1939 | 97.00 | 64.00 | 97.00 | 1953 | 309.75 | 247.75 | 306.50 |
| 1926 | 271.00 | 183.00 | 183.00 | 1940 | 120.50 | 74.25 | 96.50 | 1954 | 415.75 | 261.00 | 285.00 |
| 1927 | 220.00 | 161.00 | 161.00 | 1941 | 194.00 | 91.25 | 174.50 | 1955 | 284.00 | 220.00 | 239.50 |
| 1928 | 213.00 | 169.00 | 170.00 | 1942 | 196.50 | 165.25 | 165.25 | 1956 | 331.50 | 220.00 | 246.50 |
| 1929 | 246.00 | 170.00 | 172.00 | 1943 | 192.00 | 165.25 | 186.00 | 1957 | 257.50 | 222.50 | 223.50 |
| 1930 | 216.00 | 144.00 | 144.00 | 1944 | 216.00 | 186.00 | 212.00 | 1958 | 235.50 | 205.25 | 217.50 |
| 1931 | 146.00 | 47.00 | 47.00 | 1945 | 222.00 | 210.00 | 219.00 | 1959 | 237.00 | 204.13 | 212.38 |
| 1932 | 52.00 | 44.00 | 44.00 | 1946 | 349.00 | 219.00 | 317.00 | 1960 | 232.00 | 208.75 | 230.13 |
| 1933 | 104.00 | 45.00 | 73.00 | 1947 | 401.25 | 231.50 | 394.00 | 1961 | 337.00 | 231.50 | 243.63 |
| 1934 | 154.00 | 81.00 | 111.00 | 1948 | 443.75 | 228.75 | 259.88 | 1962 | 257.00 | 232.00 | 246.88 |
| 1935 | 127.00 | 68.00 | 72.00 | 1949 | 360.00 | 214.25 | 229.63 | 1963 | 291.50 | 246.38 | 281.25 |
| 1936 | 130.00 | 76.00 | 130.00 | 1950 | 338.25 | 222.63 | 316.75 | 1964 | 298.50 | 245.50 | 281.63 |
| 1937 | 174.00 | 83.00 | 83.00 | 1951 | 342.13 | 271.63 | 291.00 | 1965 | 313.50 | 244.50 | 264.75 |
| 1938 | 93.00 | 63.00 | 67.00 | 1952 | 333.00 | 285.38 | 296.13 | 1966 | 398.00 | 268.00 | 296.50 |

Futures data begins 07/01/1959.    Data continued on page 212.    *Source: CME Group; Chicago Board of Trade*

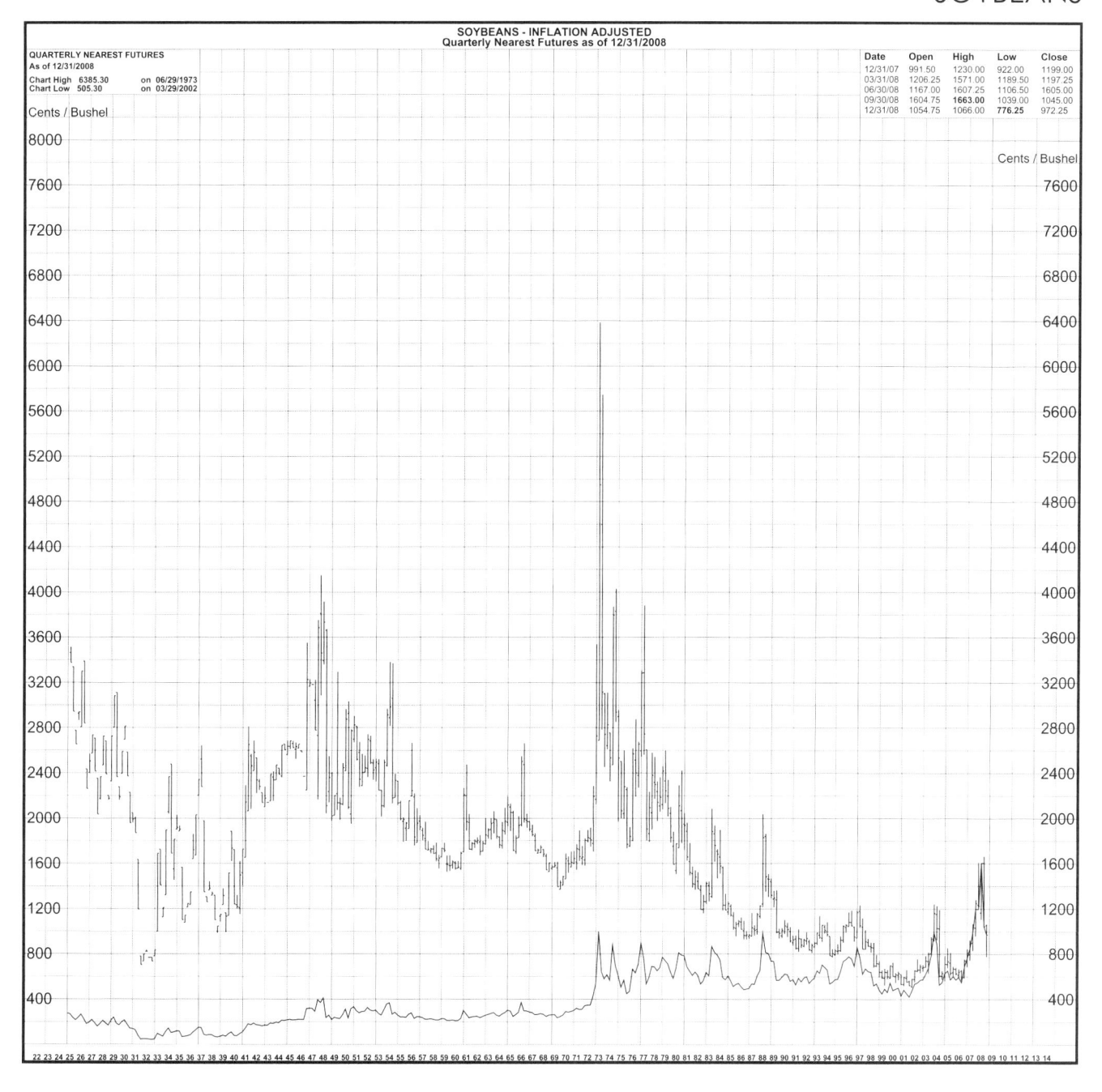

# SOYBEANS

**SOYBEANS - INFLATION ADJUSTED**
Quarterly Nearest Futures as of 12/31/2008

QUARTERLY NEAREST FUTURES
As of 12/31/2008
Chart High 6385.30 on 06/29/1973
Chart Low 505.30 on 03/29/2002

Cents / Bushel

| Date | Open | High | Low | Close |
|---|---|---|---|---|
| 12/31/07 | 991.50 | 1230.00 | 922.00 | 1199.00 |
| 03/31/08 | 1206.25 | 1571.00 | 1189.50 | 1197.25 |
| 06/30/08 | 1167.00 | 1607.25 | 1106.50 | 1605.00 |
| 09/30/08 | 1604.75 | 1663.00 | 1039.00 | 1045.00 |
| 12/31/08 | 1054.75 | 1066.00 | 776.25 | 972.25 |

## Annual High, Low and Settle of Soybeans    In Cents per Bushel

| Year | High | Low | Settle | Year | High | Low | Settle | Year | High | Low | Settle |
|---|---|---|---|---|---|---|---|---|---|---|---|
| 1925 | 281.00 | 217.00 | 217.00 | 1939 | 97.00 | 64.00 | 97.00 | 1953 | 309.75 | 247.75 | 306.50 |
| 1926 | 271.00 | 183.00 | 183.00 | 1940 | 120.50 | 74.25 | 96.50 | 1954 | 415.75 | 261.00 | 285.00 |
| 1927 | 220.00 | 161.00 | 161.00 | 1941 | 194.00 | 91.25 | 174.50 | 1955 | 284.00 | 220.00 | 239.50 |
| 1928 | 213.00 | 169.00 | 170.00 | 1942 | 196.50 | 165.25 | 165.25 | 1956 | 331.50 | 220.00 | 246.50 |
| 1929 | 246.00 | 170.00 | 172.00 | 1943 | 192.00 | 165.25 | 186.00 | 1957 | 257.50 | 222.50 | 223.50 |
| 1930 | 216.00 | 144.00 | 144.00 | 1944 | 216.00 | 186.00 | 212.00 | 1958 | 235.50 | 205.25 | 217.50 |
| 1931 | 146.00 | 47.00 | 47.00 | 1945 | 222.00 | 210.00 | 219.00 | 1959 | 237.00 | 207.00 | 215.00 |
| 1932 | 52.00 | 44.00 | 44.00 | 1946 | 349.00 | 219.00 | 317.00 | 1960 | 233.00 | 206.00 | 233.00 |
| 1933 | 104.00 | 45.00 | 73.00 | 1947 | 401.25 | 231.50 | 394.00 | 1961 | 334.00 | 232.00 | 246.00 |
| 1934 | 154.00 | 81.00 | 111.00 | 1948 | 443.75 | 228.75 | 259.88 | 1962 | 257.00 | 236.00 | 253.00 |
| 1935 | 127.00 | 68.00 | 72.00 | 1949 | 360.00 | 214.25 | 229.63 | 1963 | 293.00 | 254.00 | 284.00 |
| 1936 | 130.00 | 76.00 | 130.00 | 1950 | 338.25 | 222.63 | 316.75 | 1964 | 296.00 | 250.00 | 283.00 |
| 1937 | 174.00 | 83.00 | 83.00 | 1951 | 342.13 | 271.63 | 291.00 | 1965 | 311.25 | 246.00 | 267.00 |
| 1938 | 93.00 | 63.00 | 67.00 | 1952 | 333.00 | 285.38 | 296.13 | 1966 | 397.88 | 271.88 | 298.00 |

Chicago #2 Yellow through 12/1956, Chicago #1 Yellow 01/1957 to 03/26/1982    Data continued on page 213.
*Source: CME Group; Chicago Board of Trade*

# SOYBEANS

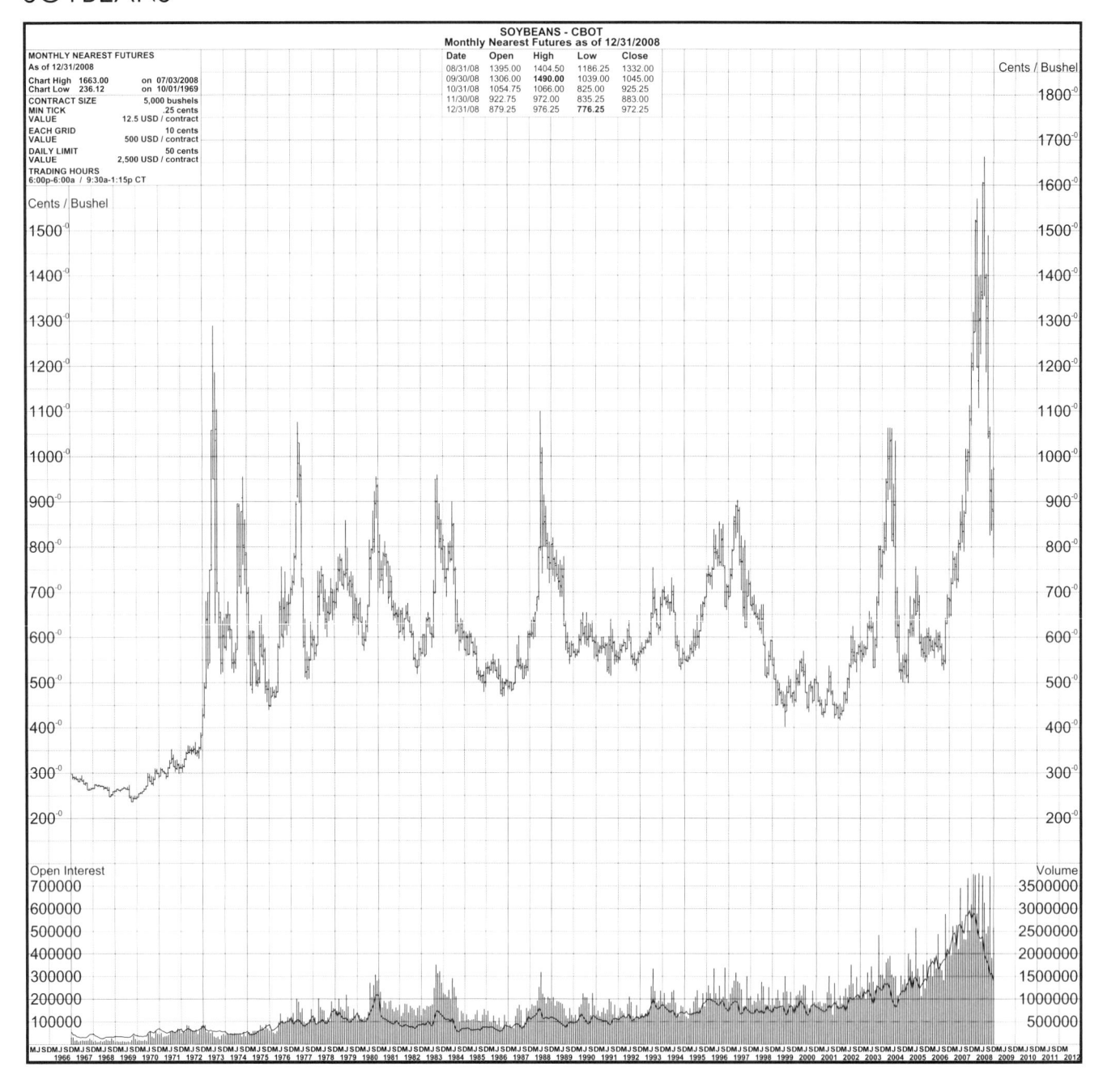

**SOYBEANS - CBOT**
Monthly Nearest Futures as of 12/31/2008

| Date | Open | High | Low | Close |
|---|---|---|---|---|
| 08/31/08 | 1395.00 | 1404.50 | 1186.25 | 1332.00 |
| 09/30/08 | 1306.00 | 1490.00 | 1039.00 | 1045.00 |
| 10/31/08 | 1054.75 | 1066.00 | 825.00 | 925.25 |
| 11/30/08 | 922.75 | 972.00 | 835.25 | 883.00 |
| 12/31/08 | 879.25 | 976.25 | 776.25 | 972.25 |

**MONTHLY NEAREST FUTURES**
As of 12/31/2008
Chart High 1663.00 on 07/03/2008
Chart Low 236.12 on 10/01/1969
CONTRACT SIZE 5,000 bushels
MIN TICK .25 cents
VALUE 12.5 USD / contract
EACH GRID 10 cents
VALUE 500 USD / contract
DAILY LIMIT 50 cents
VALUE 2,500 USD / contract
TRADING HOURS 6:00p-6:00a / 9:30a-1:15p CT

## Annual High, Low and Settle of Soybean Futures    In Cents per Bushel

| Year | High | Low | Settle | Year | High | Low | Settle | Year | High | Low | Settle |
|---|---|---|---|---|---|---|---|---|---|---|---|
| 1967 | 298.00 | 261.25 | 266.12 | 1981 | 827.50 | 596.00 | 610.50 | 1995 | 741.75 | 544.50 | 735.25 |
| 1968 | 275.75 | 247.25 | 260.50 | 1982 | 675.50 | 518.00 | 564.50 | 1996 | 856.00 | 659.75 | 690.50 |
| 1969 | 274.00 | 236.12 | 246.37 | 1983 | 960.00 | 555.50 | 814.50 | 1997 | 903.50 | 620.00 | 670.50 |
| 1970 | 310.25 | 246.00 | 292.75 | 1984 | 899.00 | 568.50 | 572.25 | 1998 | 694.00 | 509.25 | 537.75 |
| 1971 | 352.75 | 286.50 | 311.25 | 1985 | 614.00 | 478.00 | 531.25 | 1999 | 556.50 | 401.50 | 461.75 |
| 1972 | 444.00 | 301.25 | 426.25 | 1986 | 563.00 | 467.50 | 490.75 | 2000 | 570.50 | 433.50 | 499.50 |
| 1973 | 1,290.00 | 420.00 | 579.00 | 1987 | 614.50 | 479.50 | 607.00 | 2001 | 538.00 | 419.50 | 421.00 |
| 1974 | 956.00 | 521.00 | 697.00 | 1988 | 1,099.50 | 594.50 | 804.75 | 2002 | 625.00 | 415.50 | 569.50 |
| 1975 | 712.00 | 439.50 | 448.75 | 1989 | 820.50 | 540.00 | 568.00 | 2003 | 803.50 | 532.00 | 789.00 |
| 1976 | 757.00 | 446.00 | 706.50 | 1990 | 655.00 | 552.00 | 559.75 | 2004 | 1,064.00 | 501.00 | 547.75 |
| 1977 | 1,076.50 | 506.00 | 594.75 | 1991 | 640.00 | 514.00 | 554.75 | 2005 | 757.50 | 498.50 | 602.00 |
| 1978 | 758.00 | 550.25 | 676.50 | 1992 | 637.00 | 524.50 | 568.75 | 2006 | 695.75 | 526.50 | 683.50 |
| 1979 | 859.00 | 625.00 | 641.25 | 1993 | 755.00 | 561.75 | 704.25 | 2007 | 1,230.00 | 645.50 | 1,199.00 |
| 1980 | 956.00 | 569.50 | 788.75 | 1994 | 732.50 | 526.75 | 550.75 | 2008 | 1,663.00 | 776.25 | 972.25 |

Data continued from page 210.    Source: *CME Group; Chicago Board of Trade*

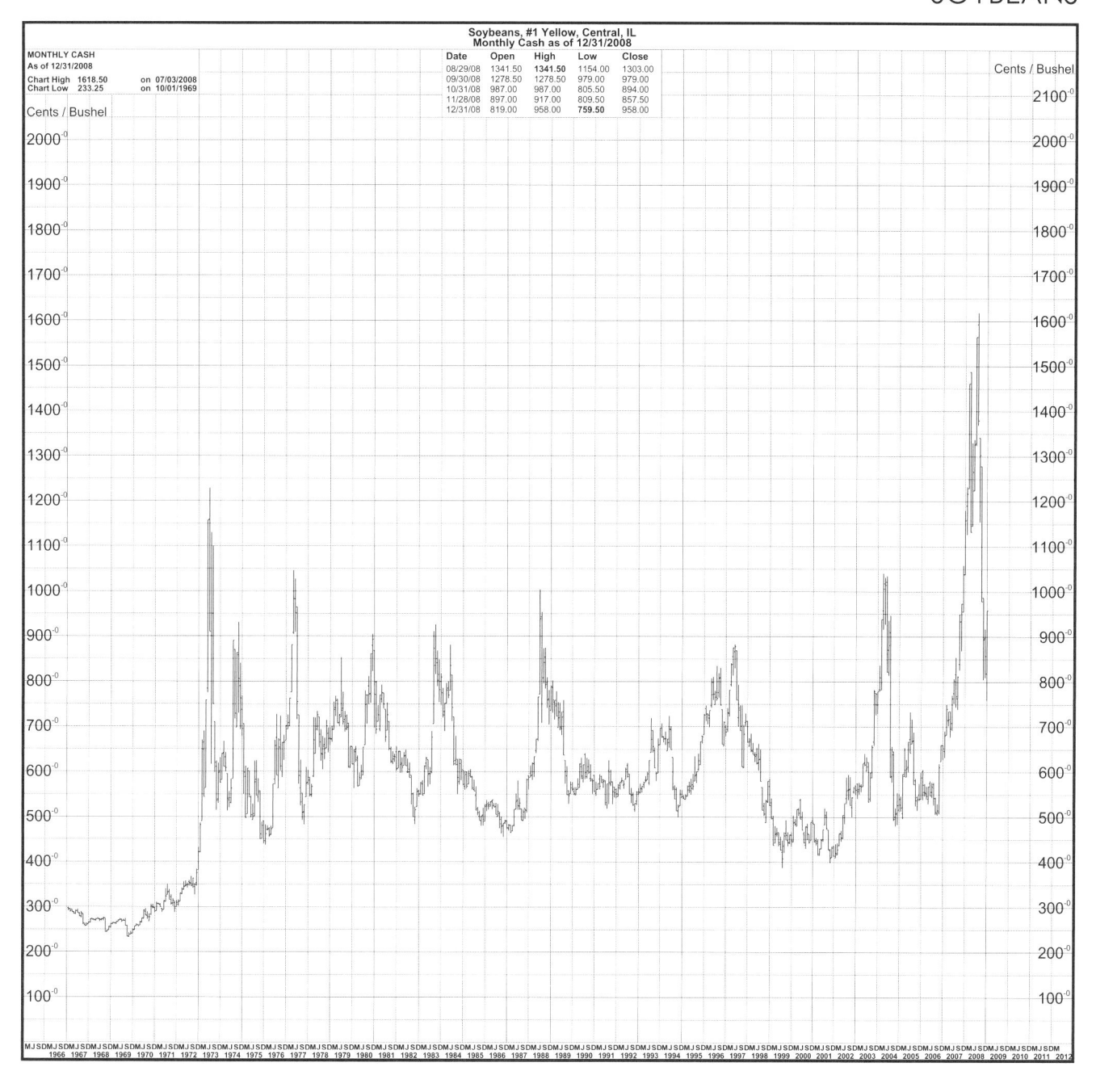

# SOYBEANS

Soybeans, #1 Yellow, Central, IL
Monthly Cash as of 12/31/2008

| Date | Open | High | Low | Close |
|---|---|---|---|---|
| 08/29/08 | 1341.50 | 1341.50 | 1154.00 | 1303.00 |
| 09/30/08 | 1278.50 | 1278.50 | 979.00 | 979.00 |
| 10/31/08 | 987.00 | 987.00 | 805.50 | 894.00 |
| 11/28/08 | 897.00 | 917.00 | 809.50 | 857.50 |
| 12/31/08 | 819.00 | 958.00 | 759.50 | 958.00 |

MONTHLY CASH
As of 12/31/2008
Chart High 1618.50 on 07/03/2008
Chart Low 233.25 on 10/01/1969
Cents / Bushel

## Annual High, Low and Settle of Soybeans   In Cents per Bushel

| Year | High | Low | Settle | Year | High | Low | Settle | Year | High | Low | Settle |
|---|---|---|---|---|---|---|---|---|---|---|---|
| 1967 | 298.38 | 257.00 | 265.63 | 1981 | 800.88 | 601.88 | 605.50 | 1995 | 728.50 | 539.00 | 725.50 |
| 1968 | 276.63 | 243.88 | 262.00 | 1982 | 648.50 | 483.50 | 551.00 | 1996 | 835.00 | 657.50 | 688.00 |
| 1969 | 274.25 | 233.25 | 248.63 | 1983 | 925.50 | 547.50 | 809.50 | 1997 | 882.50 | 609.00 | 666.00 |
| 1970 | 306.00 | 248.25 | 290.00 | 1984 | 881.00 | 550.00 | 571.50 | 1998 | 685.00 | 488.00 | 526.00 |
| 1971 | 350.00 | 287.25 | 309.25 | 1985 | 605.50 | 479.50 | 523.00 | 1999 | 542.00 | 387.50 | 447.50 |
| 1972 | 431.88 | 301.63 | 421.25 | 1986 | 537.50 | 454.00 | 475.50 | 2000 | 541.50 | 429.50 | 487.50 |
| 1973 | 1,228.75 | 419.88 | 575.63 | 1987 | 590.50 | 463.50 | 587.50 | 2001 | 520.00 | 398.50 | 413.63 |
| 1974 | 931.00 | 513.00 | 694.63 | 1988 | 1,004.00 | 581.50 | 789.00 | 2002 | 594.00 | 410.00 | 560.63 |
| 1975 | 705.63 | 440.25 | 445.88 | 1989 | 802.50 | 528.50 | 561.50 | 2003 | 782.63 | 533.63 | 779.00 |
| 1976 | 727.63 | 436.88 | 701.63 | 1990 | 641.00 | 548.00 | 557.00 | 2004 | 1,040.63 | 480.00 | 540.63 |
| 1977 | 1,046.25 | 482.63 | 587.00 | 1991 | 625.50 | 518.00 | 551.50 | 2005 | 733.63 | 497.00 | 588.00 |
| 1978 | 734.63 | 543.63 | 672.63 | 1992 | 619.50 | 511.50 | 555.50 | 2006 | 660.00 | 504.50 | 652.50 |
| 1979 | 853.00 | 607.88 | 616.25 | 1993 | 719.00 | 553.00 | 696.50 | 2007 | 1,180.50 | 632.00 | 1,158.00 |
| 1980 | 905.00 | 563.00 | 770.88 | 1994 | 723.50 | 500.00 | 545.50 | 2008 | 1,618.50 | 759.50 | 958.00 |

Chicago #1 Yellow to 03/26/1982, Central Illinois #1 Yellow 03/29/1982 to date.   Data continued from page 211.
*Source: CME Group; Chicago Board of Trade*

# SOYBEANS

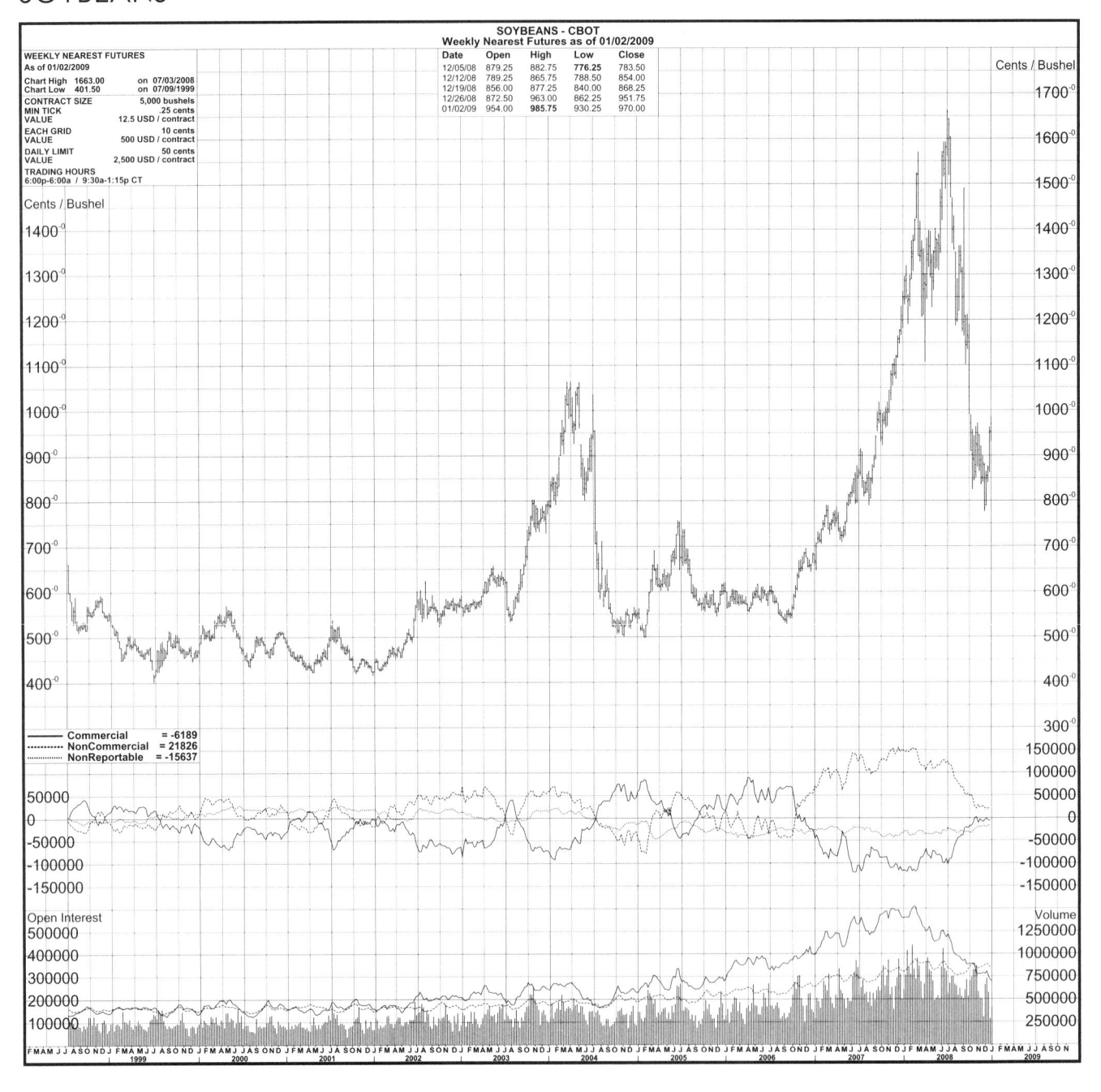

**SOYBEANS - CBOT**
Weekly Nearest Futures as of 01/02/2009

| Date | Open | High | Low | Close |
|---|---|---|---|---|
| 12/05/08 | 879.25 | 882.75 | 776.25 | 783.50 |
| 12/12/08 | 789.25 | 865.75 | 788.50 | 854.00 |
| 12/19/08 | 856.00 | 877.25 | 840.00 | 868.25 |
| 12/26/08 | 872.50 | 963.00 | 862.25 | 951.75 |
| 01/02/09 | 954.00 | **985.75** | 930.25 | 970.00 |

**WEEKLY NEAREST FUTURES** As of 01/02/2009
- Chart High 1663.00 on 07/03/2008
- Chart Low 401.50 on 07/09/1999
- CONTRACT SIZE: 5,000 bushels
- MIN TICK: .25 cents
- VALUE: 12.5 USD / contract
- EACH GRID: 10 cents
- VALUE: 500 USD / contract
- DAILY LIMIT: 50 cents
- VALUE: 2,500 USD / contract
- TRADING HOURS: 6:00p-6:00a / 9:30a-1:15p CT

Commercial = -6189
NonCommercial = 21826
NonReportable = -15637

## Quarterly High, Low and Settle of Soybean Futures   In Cents per Bushel

| Quarter | High | Low | Settle | Quarter | High | Low | Settle | Quarter | High | Low | Settle |
|---|---|---|---|---|---|---|---|---|---|---|---|
| 03/2000 | 548.50 | 455.75 | 545.50 | 03/2003 | 592.50 | 544.75 | 574.50 | 03/2006 | 622.00 | 561.00 | 571.50 |
| 06/2000 | 570.50 | 477.00 | 477.50 | 06/2003 | 658.00 | 573.00 | 621.25 | 06/2006 | 617.00 | 553.25 | 594.75 |
| 09/2000 | 504.00 | 433.50 | 490.50 | 09/2003 | 691.00 | 532.00 | 677.25 | 09/2006 | 613.00 | 526.50 | 547.50 |
| 12/2000 | 514.00 | 453.50 | 499.50 | 12/2003 | 803.50 | 669.00 | 789.00 | 12/2006 | 695.75 | 540.50 | 683.50 |
| 03/2001 | 500.00 | 428.00 | 428.50 | 03/2004 | 1,063.75 | 782.50 | 995.00 | 03/2007 | 791.00 | 645.50 | 761.25 |
| 06/2001 | 488.00 | 421.50 | 482.50 | 06/2004 | 1,064.00 | 800.75 | 893.00 | 06/2007 | 878.50 | 708.50 | 850.00 |
| 09/2001 | 538.00 | 450.50 | 451.25 | 09/2004 | 1,035.00 | 521.50 | 527.00 | 09/2007 | 1,017.75 | 789.00 | 991.25 |
| 12/2001 | 458.00 | 419.50 | 421.00 | 12/2004 | 566.00 | 501.00 | 547.75 | 12/2007 | 1,230.00 | 922.00 | 1,199.00 |
| 03/2002 | 480.50 | 415.50 | 476.25 | 03/2005 | 691.75 | 498.50 | 627.50 | 03/2008 | 1,571.00 | 1,189.50 | 1,197.25 |
| 06/2002 | 543.00 | 453.00 | 536.50 | 06/2005 | 757.50 | 602.00 | 651.75 | 06/2008 | 1,607.25 | 1,106.50 | 1,605.00 |
| 09/2002 | 625.00 | 532.00 | 545.75 | 09/2005 | 738.00 | 556.50 | 573.25 | 09/2008 | 1,663.00 | 1,039.00 | 1,045.00 |
| 12/2002 | 587.50 | 522.00 | 569.50 | 12/2005 | 619.50 | 544.25 | 602.00 | 12/2008 | 1,066.00 | 776.25 | 972.25 |

*Source: CME Group; Chicago Board of Trade*

# SOYBEANS

**Soybeans, #1 Yellow, Central, IL**
Weekly Cash as of 01/02/2009

| Date | Open | High | Low | Close |
|---|---|---|---|---|
| 12/05/08 | 819.00 | 819.00 | 759.50 | 759.50 |
| 12/12/08 | 796.50 | 836.00 | 790.50 | 833.50 |
| 12/19/08 | 824.50 | 851.50 | 824.50 | 849.50 |
| 12/26/08 | 865.00 | 894.50 | 865.00 | 894.50 |
| 01/02/09 | 918.50 | 958.00 | 918.50 | 955.00 |

WEEKLY CASH
As of 01/02/2009
Chart High 1618.50 on 07/03/2008
Chart Low 387.50 on 07/08/1999
Cents / Bushel

## Quarterly High, Low and Settle of Soybeans — In Cents per Bushel

| Quarter | High | Low | Settle | Quarter | High | Low | Settle | Quarter | High | Low | Settle |
|---|---|---|---|---|---|---|---|---|---|---|---|
| 03/2000 | 517.00 | 444.50 | 517.00 | 03/2003 | 576.63 | 541.00 | 568.00 | 03/2006 | 605.63 | 539.00 | 547.00 |
| 06/2000 | 541.50 | 471.00 | 471.00 | 06/2003 | 640.63 | 568.00 | 612.00 | 06/2006 | 580.50 | 529.50 | 567.50 |
| 09/2000 | 486.00 | 429.50 | 462.50 | 09/2003 | 660.00 | 533.63 | 654.63 | 09/2006 | 577.00 | 504.50 | 515.50 |
| 12/2000 | 497.50 | 441.50 | 487.50 | 12/2003 | 782.63 | 658.00 | 779.00 | 12/2006 | 660.00 | 507.50 | 652.50 |
| 03/2001 | 485.50 | 416.00 | 416.00 | 03/2004 | 1,040.63 | 779.00 | 1,006.63 | 03/2007 | 750.50 | 632.00 | 717.00 |
| 06/2001 | 472.00 | 414.50 | 472.00 | 06/2004 | 1,034.63 | 814.00 | 881.00 | 06/2007 | 807.50 | 677.50 | 802.00 |
| 09/2001 | 520.00 | 427.50 | 427.50 | 09/2004 | 947.00 | 492.63 | 496.00 | 09/2007 | 950.00 | 739.00 | 933.50 |
| 12/2001 | 435.63 | 398.50 | 413.63 | 12/2004 | 554.63 | 480.00 | 540.63 | 12/2007 | 1,180.50 | 868.50 | 1,158.00 |
| 03/2002 | 463.63 | 410.00 | 463.63 | 03/2005 | 654.00 | 497.00 | 605.00 | 03/2008 | 1,487.50 | 1,126.50 | 1,132.50 |
| 06/2002 | 530.63 | 445.63 | 530.63 | 06/2005 | 733.63 | 589.63 | 642.63 | 06/2008 | 1,565.00 | 1,146.00 | 1,565.00 |
| 09/2002 | 594.00 | 526.63 | 526.63 | 09/2005 | 717.00 | 525.00 | 537.63 | 09/2008 | 1,618.50 | 979.00 | 979.00 |
| 12/2002 | 569.63 | 501.00 | 560.63 | 12/2005 | 598.63 | 515.00 | 588.00 | 12/2008 | 987.00 | 759.50 | 958.00 |

Central Illinois #1 Yellow. *Source: CME Group; Chicago Board of Trade*

# SOYBEAN MEAL

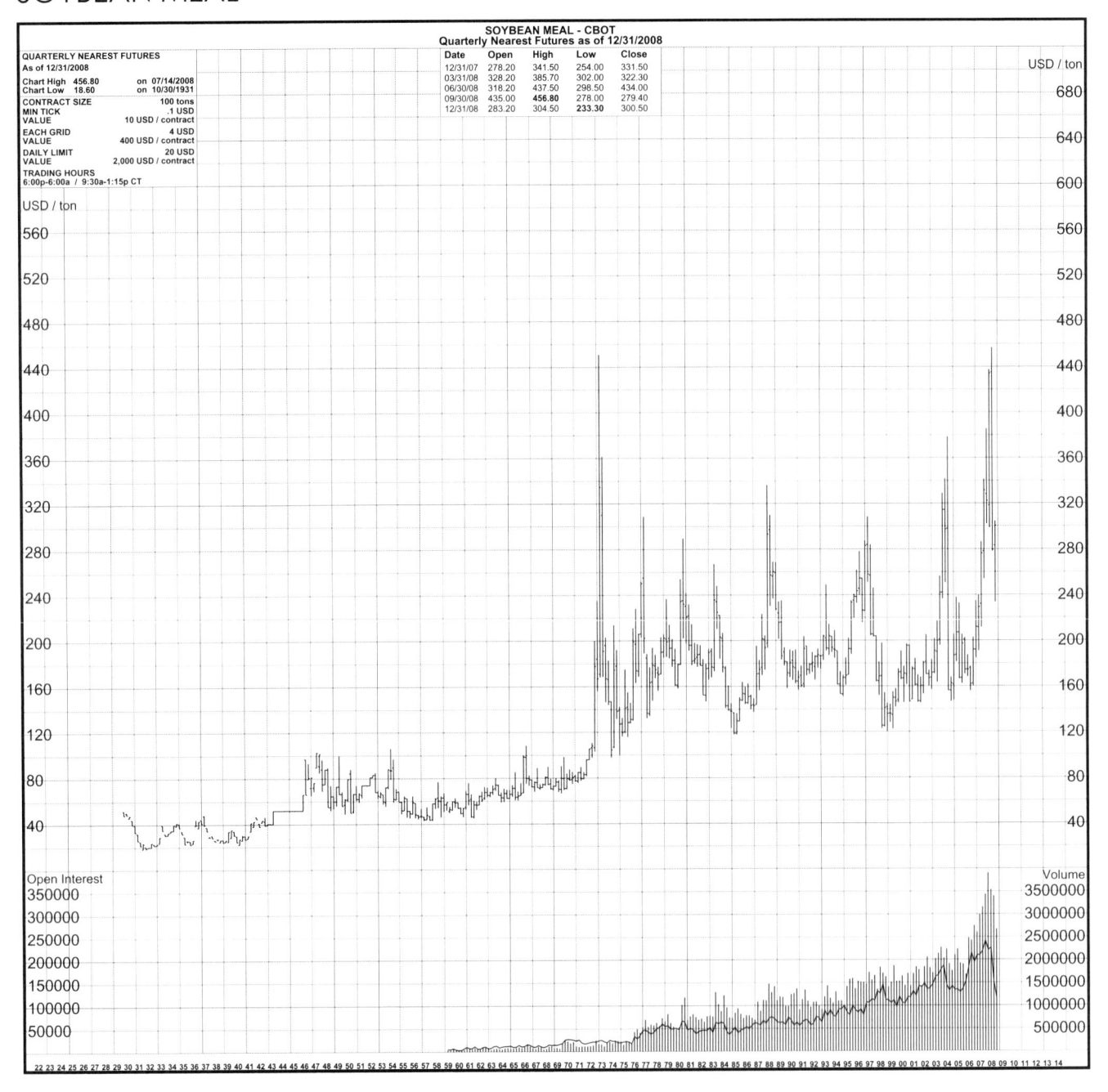

## Annual High, Low and Settle of Soybean Meal Futures  In Dollars per Ton

| Year | High | Low | Settle | Year | High | Low | Settle | Year | High | Low | Settle |
|---|---|---|---|---|---|---|---|---|---|---|---|
| 1925 | | | | 1939 | 34.95 | 24.45 | 34.95 | 1953 | 72.50 | 55.50 | 72.00 |
| 1926 | | | | 1940 | 33.90 | 22.25 | 29.60 | 1954 | 106.00 | 59.00 | 68.00 |
| 1927 | | | | 1941 | 42.50 | 26.60 | 42.50 | 1955 | 68.50 | 46.00 | 51.50 |
| 1928 | | | | 1942 | 46.60 | 37.90 | 39.00 | 1956 | 64.50 | 44.50 | 46.50 |
| 1929 | 58.30 | 53.05 | 53.05 | 1943 | 51.90 | 39.35 | 51.90 | 1957 | 55.00 | 43.00 | 43.50 |
| 1930 | 51.80 | 40.00 | 40.00 | 1944 | 52.00 | 51.90 | 52.00 | 1958 | 77.00 | 43.00 | 63.00 |
| 1931 | 39.30 | 18.60 | 23.00 | 1945 | 52.00 | 52.00 | 52.00 | 1959 | 67.00 | 49.00 | 59.90 |
| 1932 | 23.70 | 18.75 | 21.70 | 1946 | 97.00 | 52.00 | 80.70 | 1960 | 62.75 | 46.15 | 53.75 |
| 1933 | 39.20 | 21.70 | 30.50 | 1947 | 102.70 | 65.40 | 101.50 | 1961 | 76.00 | 45.05 | 56.90 |
| 1934 | 41.20 | 30.60 | 41.20 | 1948 | 96.50 | 52.00 | 64.50 | 1962 | 72.50 | 52.30 | 67.80 |
| 1935 | 40.70 | 22.85 | 25.50 | 1949 | 100.00 | 53.50 | 56.00 | 1963 | 80.00 | 63.50 | 74.20 |
| 1936 | 44.30 | 22.30 | 43.00 | 1950 | 88.00 | 49.00 | 66.50 | 1964 | 74.60 | 58.85 | 62.40 |
| 1937 | 48.35 | 28.80 | 28.80 | 1951 | 74.00 | 59.00 | 74.00 | 1965 | 85.50 | 60.70 | 64.55 |
| 1938 | 30.00 | 24.40 | 26.20 | 1952 | 85.00 | 68.00 | 68.00 | 1966 | 108.50 | 64.75 | 78.65 |

Futures data begins 07/01/1959.   44% protein.   Data continued on page 218.   *Source: CME Group; Chicago Board of Trade*

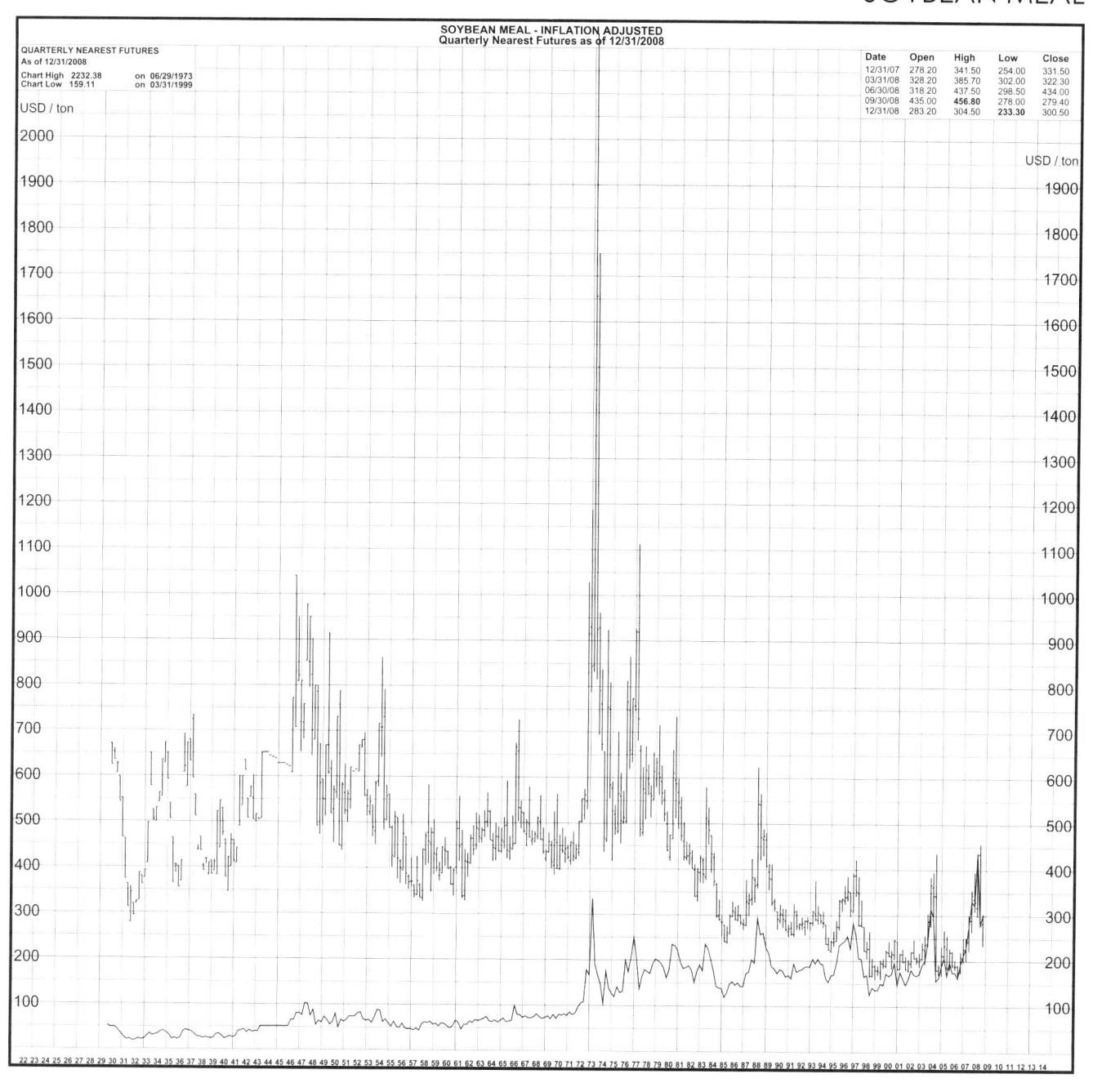

# SOYBEAN MEAL

**QUARTERLY NEAREST FUTURES**
As of 12/31/2008
Chart High 2232.38 on 06/29/1973
Chart Low 159.11 on 03/31/1999
USD / ton

SOYBEAN MEAL - INFLATION ADJUSTED
Quarterly Nearest Futures as of 12/31/2008

| Date | Open | High | Low | Close |
|---|---|---|---|---|
| 12/31/07 | 278.20 | 341.50 | 254.00 | 331.50 |
| 03/31/08 | 328.20 | 385.70 | 302.00 | 322.30 |
| 06/30/08 | 318.20 | 437.50 | 298.50 | 434.00 |
| 09/30/08 | 435.00 | **456.80** | 278.00 | 279.40 |
| 12/31/08 | 283.20 | 304.50 | **233.30** | 300.50 |

## Annual High, Low and Settle of Soybean Meal    In Dollars per Ton

| Year | High | Low | Settle | Year | High | Low | Settle | Year | High | Low | Settle |
|---|---|---|---|---|---|---|---|---|---|---|---|
| 1925 | | | | 1939 | 34.95 | 24.45 | 34.95 | 1953 | 72.50 | 55.50 | 72.00 |
| 1926 | | | | 1940 | 33.90 | 22.25 | 29.60 | 1954 | 106.00 | 59.00 | 68.00 |
| 1927 | | | | 1941 | 42.50 | 26.60 | 42.50 | 1955 | 68.50 | 46.00 | 51.50 |
| 1928 | | | | 1942 | 46.60 | 37.90 | 39.00 | 1956 | 64.50 | 44.50 | 46.50 |
| 1929 | 58.30 | 53.05 | 53.05 | 1943 | 51.90 | 39.35 | 51.90 | 1957 | 55.00 | 43.00 | 43.50 |
| 1930 | 51.80 | 40.00 | 40.00 | 1944 | 52.00 | 51.90 | 52.00 | 1958 | 77.00 | 43.00 | 63.00 |
| 1931 | 39.30 | 18.60 | 23.00 | 1945 | 52.00 | 52.00 | 52.00 | 1959 | 67.00 | 49.00 | 60.50 |
| 1932 | 23.70 | 18.75 | 21.70 | 1946 | 97.00 | 52.00 | 80.70 | 1960 | 63.50 | 43.00 | 54.00 |
| 1933 | 39.20 | 21.70 | 30.50 | 1947 | 102.70 | 65.40 | 101.50 | 1961 | 80.00 | 50.50 | 59.50 |
| 1934 | 41.20 | 30.60 | 41.20 | 1948 | 96.50 | 52.00 | 64.50 | 1962 | 80.50 | 57.00 | 72.00 |
| 1935 | 40.70 | 22.85 | 25.50 | 1949 | 100.00 | 53.50 | 56.00 | 1963 | 81.50 | 66.00 | 79.00 |
| 1936 | 44.30 | 22.30 | 43.00 | 1950 | 88.00 | 49.00 | 66.50 | 1964 | 78.00 | 61.50 | 66.00 |
| 1937 | 48.35 | 28.80 | 28.80 | 1951 | 74.00 | 59.00 | 74.00 | 1965 | 102.50 | 65.50 | 72.50 |
| 1938 | 30.00 | 24.40 | 26.20 | 1952 | 85.00 | 68.00 | 68.00 | 1966 | 107.00 | 69.50 | 86.00 |

Central Illinois 44% Protein.    Data continued on page 219.    *Source: CME Group; Chicago Board of Trade*

# SOYBEAN MEAL

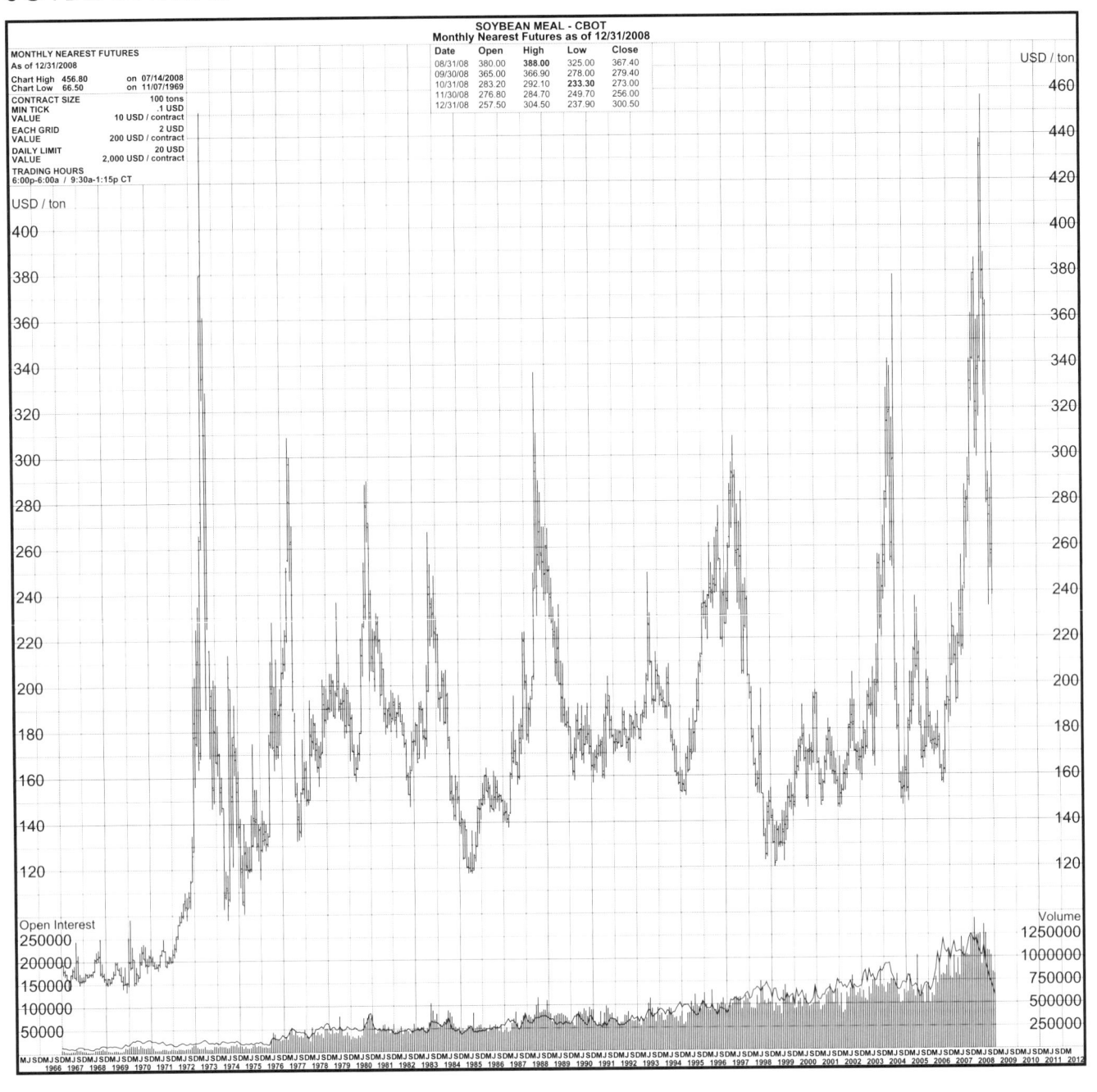

### Annual High, Low and Settle of Soybean Meal Futures — In Dollars per Ton

| Year | High | Low | Settle | Year | High | Low | Settle | Year | High | Low | Settle |
|---|---|---|---|---|---|---|---|---|---|---|---|
| 1967 | 89.00 | 68.10 | 71.90 | 1981 | 242.00 | 178.50 | 184.20 | 1995 | 235.00 | 151.10 | 233.20 |
| 1968 | 90.00 | 70.05 | 70.90 | 1982 | 197.00 | 146.80 | 175.60 | 1996 | 278.00 | 215.70 | 226.30 |
| 1969 | 90.50 | 66.50 | 79.70 | 1983 | 267.00 | 166.00 | 224.70 | 1997 | 308.50 | 203.00 | 203.80 |
| 1970 | 98.50 | 69.50 | 80.60 | 1984 | 222.50 | 138.50 | 139.60 | 1998 | 204.00 | 122.80 | 141.10 |
| 1971 | 89.70 | 75.70 | 83.00 | 1985 | 150.50 | 117.50 | 148.20 | 1999 | 158.00 | 120.00 | 146.70 |
| 1972 | 200.00 | 81.45 | 177.75 | 1986 | 163.90 | 140.10 | 143.30 | 2000 | 197.20 | 145.50 | 195.40 |
| 1973 | 451.00 | 146.50 | 167.00 | 1987 | 223.20 | 137.50 | 201.50 | 2001 | 196.00 | 145.80 | 147.10 |
| 1974 | 213.70 | 97.76 | 138.50 | 1988 | 336.50 | 174.30 | 260.50 | 2002 | 205.00 | 145.40 | 167.30 |
| 1975 | 175.00 | 100.50 | 128.40 | 1989 | 268.40 | 177.80 | 181.60 | 2003 | 256.50 | 157.10 | 241.90 |
| 1976 | 228.00 | 127.50 | 205.70 | 1990 | 192.00 | 158.00 | 164.50 | 2004 | 378.50 | 146.60 | 162.60 |
| 1977 | 308.70 | 132.00 | 163.40 | 1991 | 203.70 | 157.00 | 174.70 | 2005 | 238.00 | 148.10 | 197.30 |
| 1978 | 203.00 | 147.60 | 189.90 | 1992 | 192.80 | 165.50 | 187.40 | 2006 | 202.80 | 155.80 | 191.90 |
| 1979 | 236.50 | 177.00 | 182.80 | 1993 | 249.00 | 175.20 | 203.80 | 2007 | 341.50 | 184.70 | 331.50 |
| 1980 | 289.50 | 158.10 | 231.80 | 1994 | 209.00 | 153.00 | 153.20 | 2008 | 456.80 | 233.30 | 300.50 |

44% protein through September 1992 contract, 48% protein October 1992 contract to date.   Data continued from page 216.
Source: CME Group; Chicago Board of Trade

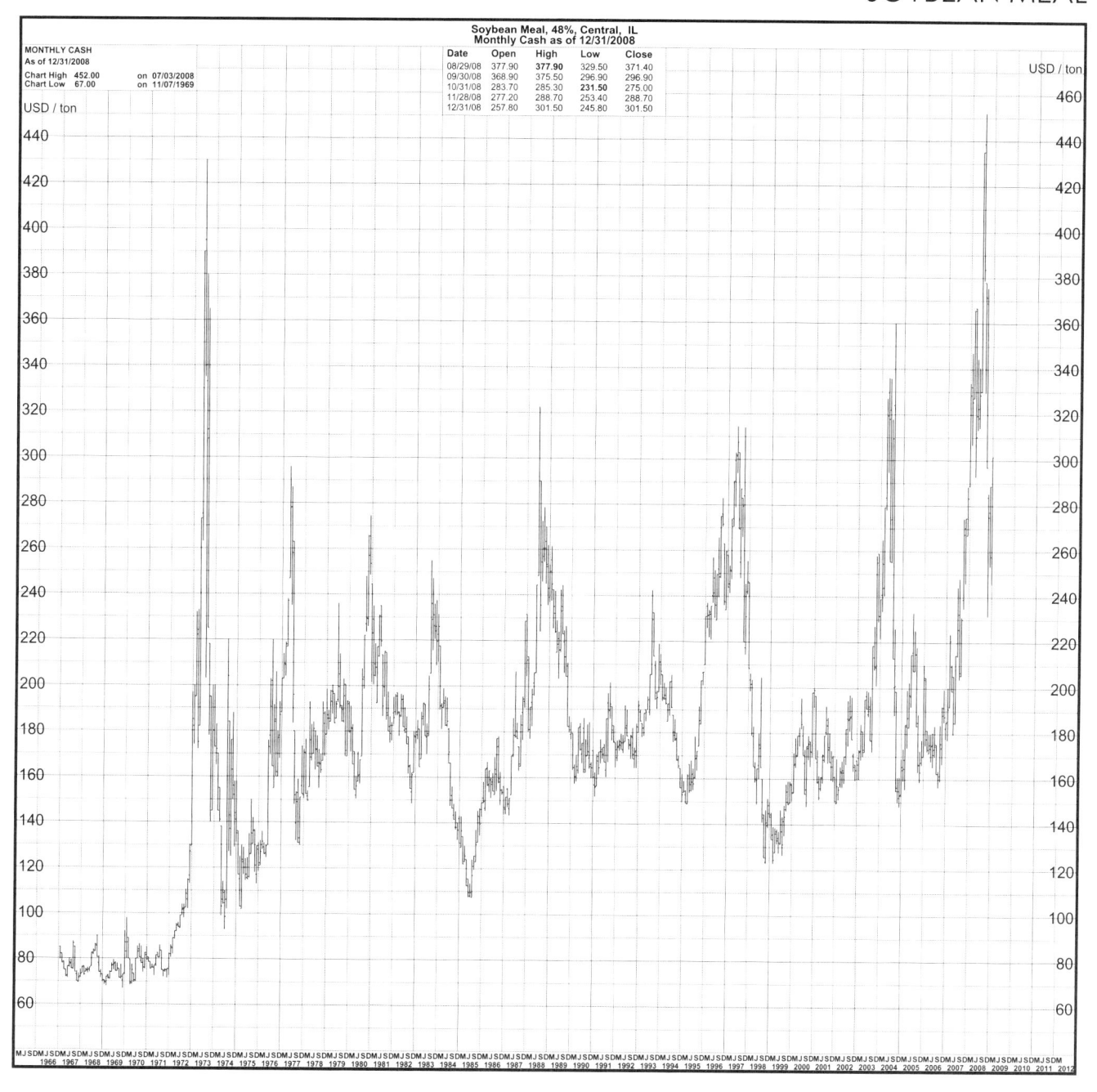

# SOYBEAN MEAL

| Soybean Meal, 48%, Central, IL Monthly Cash as of 12/31/2008 |||||
|---|---|---|---|---|
| Date | Open | High | Low | Close |
| 08/29/08 | 377.90 | 377.90 | 329.50 | 371.40 |
| 09/30/08 | 368.90 | 375.50 | 296.90 | 296.90 |
| 10/31/08 | 283.70 | 285.30 | 231.50 | 275.00 |
| 11/28/08 | 277.20 | 288.70 | 253.40 | 288.70 |
| 12/31/08 | 257.80 | 301.50 | 245.80 | 301.50 |

MONTHLY CASH
As of 12/31/2008
Chart High 452.00 on 07/03/2008
Chart Low 67.00 on 11/07/1969

## Annual High, Low and Settle of Soybean Meal — In Dollars per Ton

| Year | High | Low | Settle | Year | High | Low | Settle | Year | High | Low | Settle |
|---|---|---|---|---|---|---|---|---|---|---|---|
| 1967 | 87.50 | 69.50 | 73.00 | 1981 | 235.00 | 175.00 | 186.00 | 1995 | 231.00 | 149.00 | 231.00 |
| 1968 | 90.00 | 70.00 | 70.50 | 1982 | 197.00 | 148.50 | 179.75 | 1996 | 283.00 | 221.00 | 244.00 |
| 1969 | 92.00 | 67.00 | 87.00 | 1983 | 255.00 | 164.50 | 226.00 | 1997 | 314.50 | 208.50 | 208.50 |
| 1970 | 98.00 | 68.50 | 79.50 | 1984 | 217.50 | 131.00 | 131.00 | 1998 | 206.25 | 123.00 | 143.50 |
| 1971 | 86.00 | 71.50 | 82.00 | 1985 | 149.00 | 107.50 | 149.00 | 1999 | 159.00 | 123.00 | 154.25 |
| 1972 | 197.00 | 80.50 | 185.00 | 1986 | 178.00 | 144.00 | 147.00 | 2000 | 200.00 | 148.00 | 199.00 |
| 1973 | 430.00 | 140.00 | 173.00 | 1987 | 231.50 | 143.50 | 211.50 | 2001 | 196.50 | 150.50 | 150.50 |
| 1974 | 220.00 | 93.00 | 135.00 | 1988 | 322.50 | 177.00 | 250.50 | 2002 | 197.00 | 149.50 | 166.50 |
| 1975 | 150.00 | 102.00 | 121.00 | 1989 | 261.50 | 177.00 | 180.00 | 2003 | 259.00 | 160.00 | 239.00 |
| 1976 | 220.00 | 121.00 | 203.00 | 1990 | 186.25 | 157.50 | 160.50 | 2004 | 360.00 | 148.00 | 165.60 |
| 1977 | 296.00 | 130.00 | 170.50 | 1991 | 202.00 | 152.00 | 172.50 | 2005 | 232.90 | 155.70 | 203.80 |
| 1978 | 198.50 | 149.50 | 187.00 | 1992 | 194.00 | 164.50 | 192.00 | 2006 | 204.70 | 156.60 | 184.90 |
| 1979 | 236.00 | 169.00 | 179.50 | 1993 | 242.50 | 178.00 | 207.00 | 2007 | 333.70 | 177.20 | 328.50 |
| 1980 | 274.50 | 150.50 | 223.00 | 1994 | 205.50 | 150.00 | 153.00 | 2008 | 452.00 | 231.50 | 301.50 |

Central
*Source: CME Group; Chicago Board of Trade*

# SOYBEAN MEAL

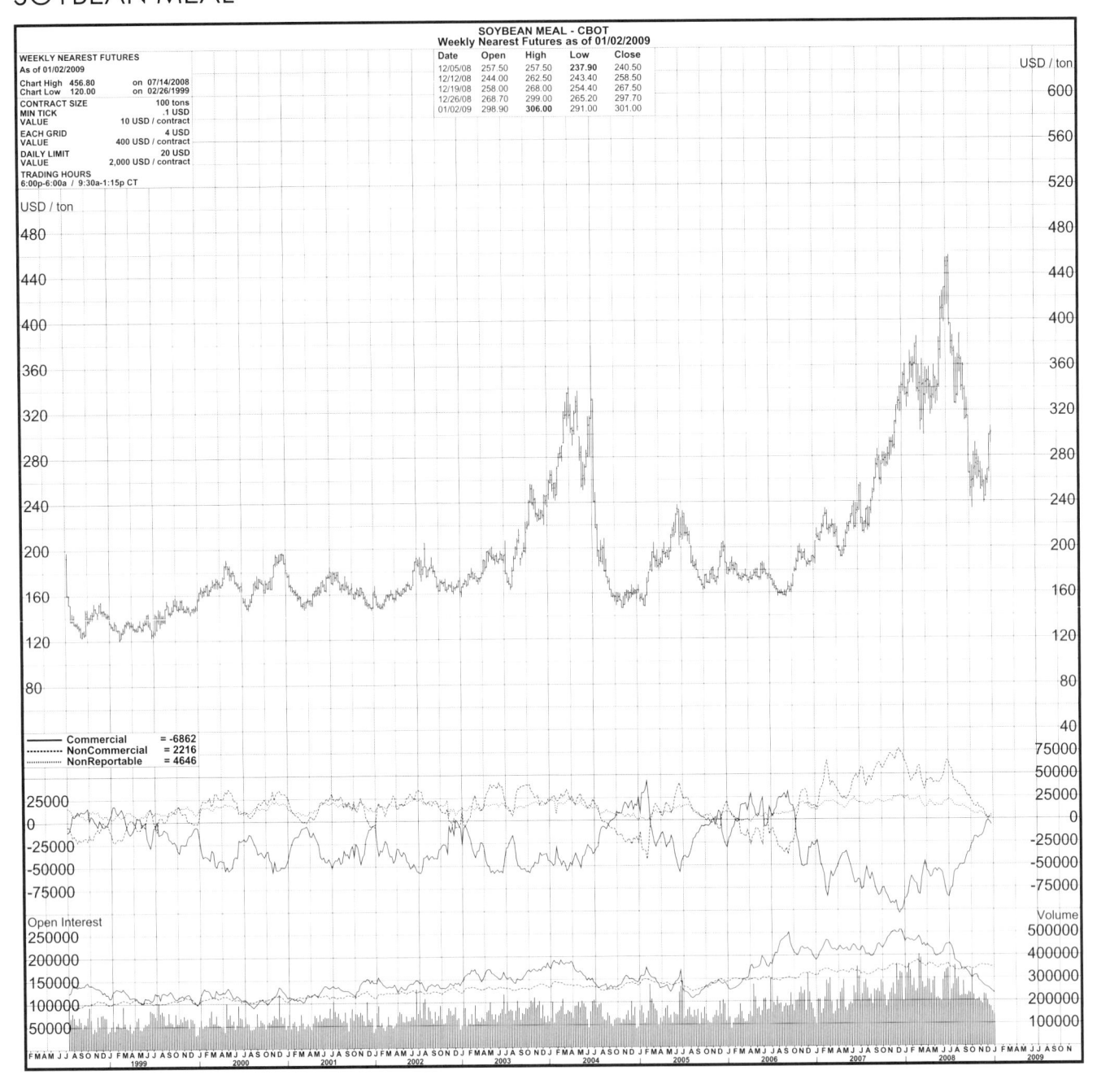

**WEEKLY NEAREST FUTURES**
As of 01/02/2009
Chart High 456.80 on 07/14/2008
Chart Low 120.00 on 02/26/1999
CONTRACT SIZE 100 tons
MIN TICK .1 USD
VALUE 10 USD / contract
EACH GRID 4 USD
VALUE 400 USD / contract
DAILY LIMIT 20 USD
VALUE 2,000 USD / contract
TRADING HOURS
6:00p-6:00a / 9:30a-1:15p CT

**SOYBEAN MEAL - CBOT**
Weekly Nearest Futures as of 01/02/2009

| Date | Open | High | Low | Close |
|---|---|---|---|---|
| 12/05/08 | 257.50 | 257.50 | 237.90 | 240.50 |
| 12/12/08 | 244.00 | 262.50 | 243.40 | 258.50 |
| 12/19/08 | 258.00 | 268.00 | 254.40 | 267.50 |
| 12/26/08 | 268.70 | 299.00 | 265.20 | 297.70 |
| 01/02/09 | 298.90 | 306.00 | 291.00 | 301.00 |

Commercial = -6862
NonCommercial = 2216
NonReportable = 4646

## Quarterly High, Low and Settle of Soybean Meal Futures    In Dollars per Ton

| Quarter | High | Low | Settle | Quarter | High | Low | Settle | Quarter | High | Low | Settle |
|---|---|---|---|---|---|---|---|---|---|---|---|
| 03/2000 | 175.50 | 145.50 | 172.20 | 03/2003 | 183.20 | 157.10 | 171.90 | 03/2006 | 202.50 | 170.50 | 174.60 |
| 06/2000 | 191.00 | 165.50 | 166.90 | 06/2003 | 201.80 | 170.80 | 190.80 | 06/2006 | 187.50 | 168.10 | 174.60 |
| 09/2000 | 177.50 | 145.70 | 171.30 | 09/2003 | 217.00 | 163.30 | 199.80 | 09/2006 | 177.50 | 155.80 | 161.90 |
| 12/2000 | 197.20 | 161.50 | 195.40 | 12/2003 | 256.50 | 195.60 | 241.90 | 12/2006 | 202.80 | 160.20 | 191.90 |
| 03/2001 | 196.00 | 146.50 | 146.70 | 03/2004 | 329.00 | 236.20 | 314.30 | 03/2007 | 234.60 | 184.70 | 211.80 |
| 06/2001 | 177.00 | 148.20 | 175.20 | 06/2004 | 342.00 | 250.70 | 297.50 | 06/2007 | 240.00 | 190.80 | 229.20 |
| 09/2001 | 184.50 | 160.10 | 161.40 | 09/2004 | 378.50 | 156.00 | 156.20 | 09/2007 | 286.50 | 211.40 | 276.30 |
| 12/2001 | 170.00 | 145.80 | 147.10 | 12/2004 | 168.00 | 146.60 | 162.60 | 12/2007 | 341.50 | 254.00 | 331.50 |
| 03/2002 | 168.00 | 145.40 | 160.30 | 03/2005 | 205.00 | 148.10 | 187.00 | 03/2008 | 385.70 | 302.00 | 322.30 |
| 06/2002 | 181.80 | 153.00 | 180.40 | 06/2005 | 238.00 | 181.30 | 207.00 | 06/2008 | 437.50 | 298.50 | 434.00 |
| 09/2002 | 205.00 | 170.10 | 170.30 | 09/2005 | 232.80 | 166.20 | 167.20 | 09/2008 | 456.80 | 278.00 | 279.40 |
| 12/2002 | 174.00 | 160.20 | 167.30 | 12/2005 | 205.40 | 162.30 | 197.30 | 12/2008 | 304.50 | 233.30 | 300.50 |

48% protein.    *Source: CME Group; Chicago Board of Trade*

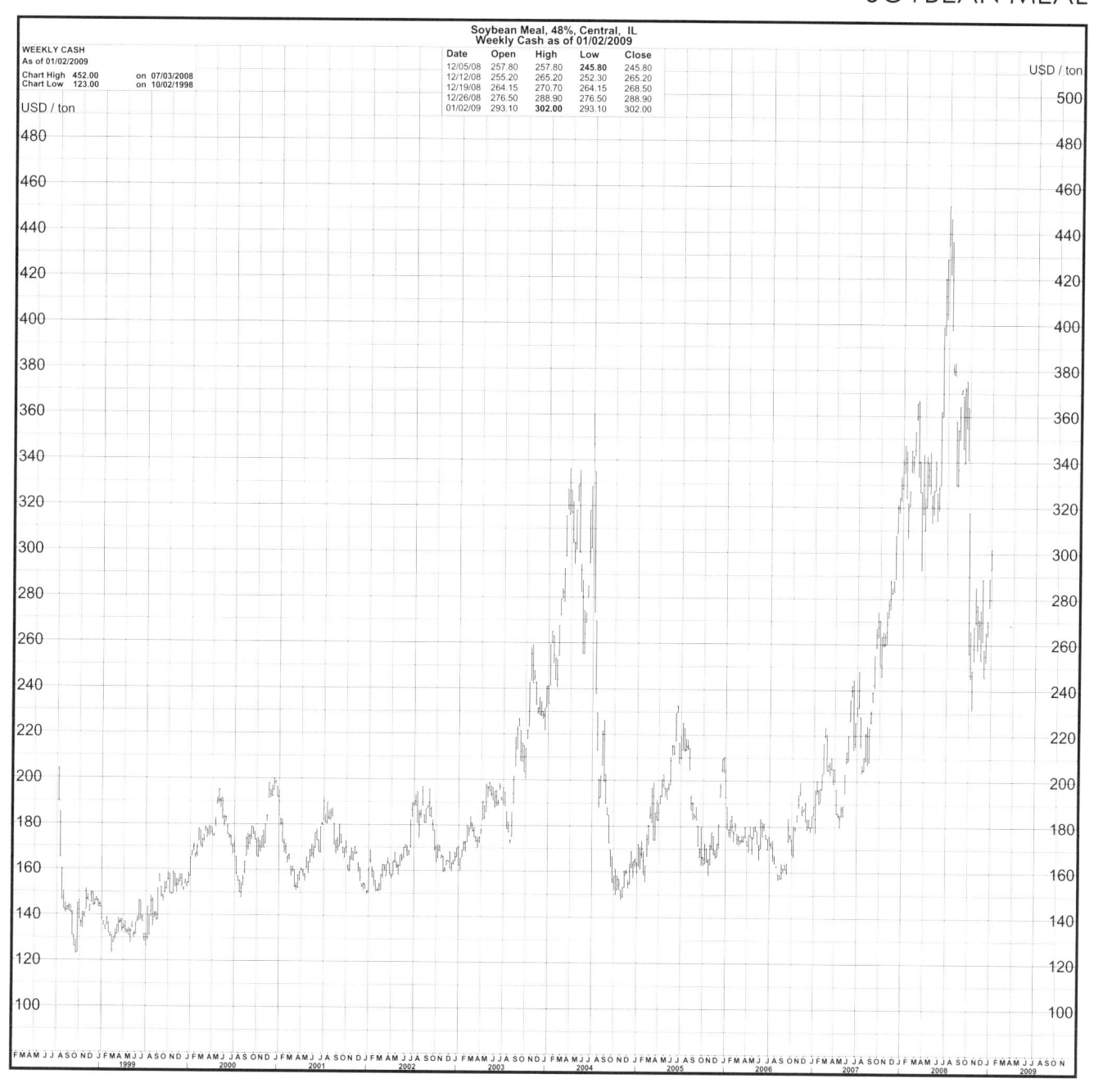

# SOYBEAN MEAL

**Soybean Meal, 48%, Central, IL**
Weekly Cash as of 01/02/2009

| Date | Open | High | Low | Close |
|---|---|---|---|---|
| 12/05/08 | 257.80 | 257.80 | 245.80 | 245.80 |
| 12/12/08 | 255.20 | 265.20 | 252.30 | 265.20 |
| 12/19/08 | 264.15 | 270.70 | 264.15 | 268.50 |
| 12/26/08 | 276.50 | 288.90 | 276.50 | 288.90 |
| 01/02/09 | 293.10 | 302.00 | 293.10 | 302.00 |

WEEKLY CASH
As of 01/02/2009
Chart High 452.00 on 07/03/2008
Chart Low 123.00 on 10/02/1998
USD / ton

## Quarterly High, Low and Settle of Soybean Meal    In Dollars per Ton

| Quarter | High | Low | Settle | Quarter | High | Low | Settle | Quarter | High | Low | Settle |
|---|---|---|---|---|---|---|---|---|---|---|---|
| 03/2000 | 179.00 | 154.00 | 179.00 | 03/2003 | 184.00 | 160.00 | 173.00 | 03/2006 | 204.70 | 171.60 | 175.10 |
| 06/2000 | 195.50 | 170.50 | 170.50 | 06/2003 | 199.00 | 172.00 | 192.00 | 06/2006 | 183.40 | 165.30 | 174.60 |
| 09/2000 | 179.00 | 148.00 | 175.50 | 09/2003 | 227.00 | 172.00 | 209.50 | 09/2006 | 183.80 | 156.60 | 175.65 |
| 12/2000 | 200.00 | 165.50 | 199.00 | 12/2003 | 259.00 | 201.00 | 239.00 | 12/2006 | 199.50 | 166.70 | 184.90 |
| 03/2001 | 196.50 | 151.00 | 152.00 | 03/2004 | 327.00 | 233.50 | 319.50 | 03/2007 | 223.60 | 177.20 | 198.80 |
| 06/2001 | 179.00 | 155.00 | 179.00 | 06/2004 | 336.00 | 255.00 | 309.50 | 06/2007 | 244.30 | 179.70 | 225.70 |
| 09/2001 | 192.00 | 167.00 | 167.50 | 09/2004 | 360.00 | 155.00 | 155.00 | 09/2007 | 274.30 | 203.90 | 267.50 |
| 12/2001 | 172.50 | 150.50 | 150.50 | 12/2004 | 168.90 | 148.00 | 165.60 | 12/2007 | 333.70 | 246.00 | 328.50 |
| 03/2002 | 169.00 | 149.50 | 163.50 | 03/2005 | 199.20 | 155.70 | 187.00 | 03/2008 | 366.70 | 292.80 | 310.30 |
| 06/2002 | 182.00 | 156.50 | 182.00 | 06/2005 | 232.90 | 182.70 | 207.50 | 06/2008 | 435.00 | 313.20 | 435.00 |
| 09/2002 | 197.00 | 174.50 | 177.50 | 09/2005 | 225.20 | 163.20 | 166.40 | 09/2008 | 452.00 | 296.90 | 296.90 |
| 12/2002 | 171.50 | 159.50 | 166.50 | 12/2005 | 210.30 | 158.80 | 203.80 | 12/2008 | 301.50 | 231.50 | 301.50 |

48% protein.    *Source: CME Group; Chicago Board of Trade*

# SOYBEAN OIL

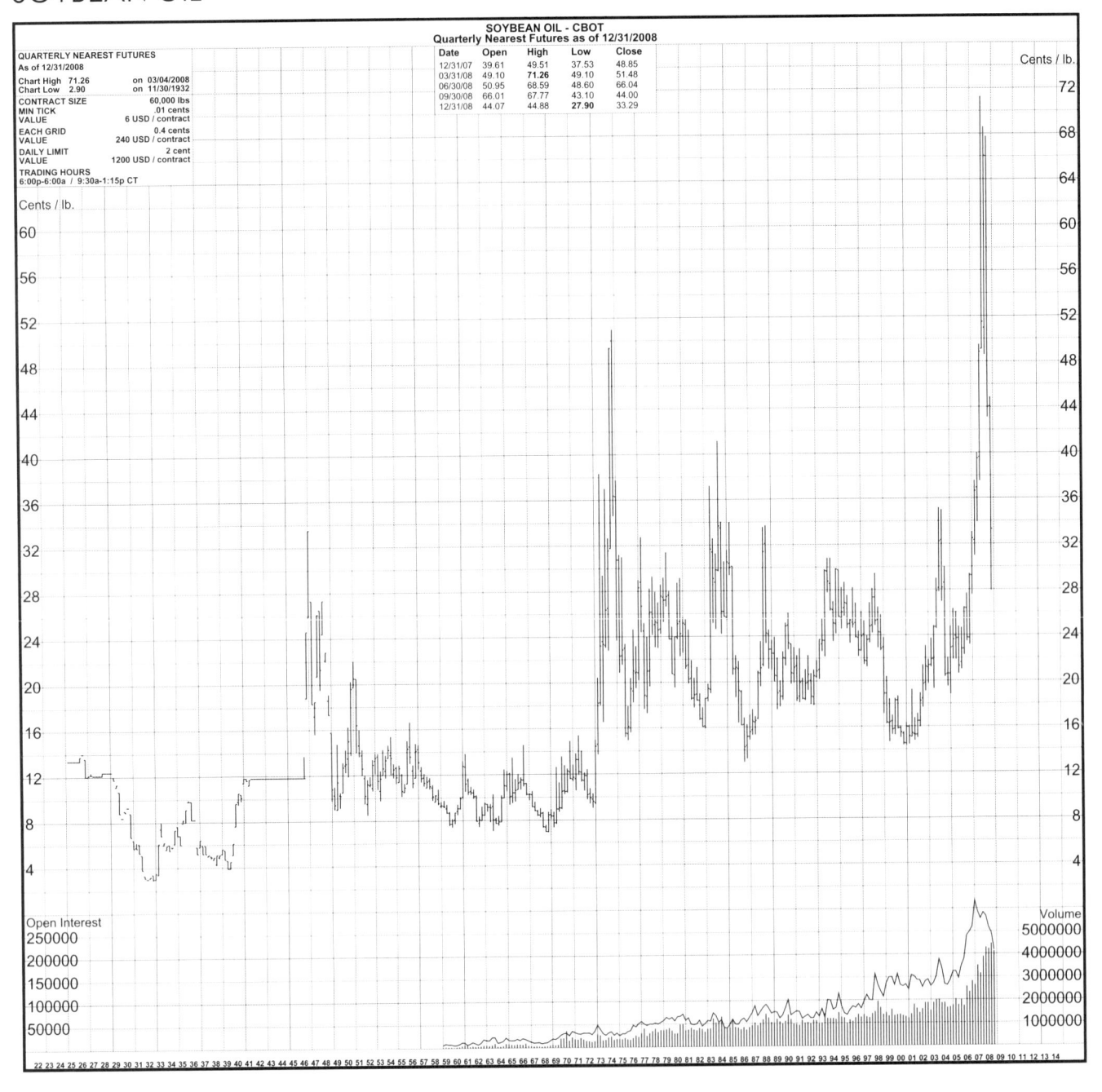

**SOYBEAN OIL - CBOT**
Quarterly Nearest Futures as of 12/31/2008

| Date | Open | High | Low | Close |
|---|---|---|---|---|
| 12/31/07 | 39.61 | 49.51 | 37.53 | 48.85 |
| 03/31/08 | 49.10 | 71.26 | 49.10 | 51.48 |
| 06/30/08 | 50.95 | 68.59 | 48.60 | 66.04 |
| 09/30/08 | 66.01 | 67.77 | 43.10 | 44.00 |
| 12/31/08 | 44.07 | 44.88 | 27.90 | 33.29 |

**QUARTERLY NEAREST FUTURES**
As of 12/31/2008
- Chart High: 71.26 on 03/04/2008
- Chart Low: 2.90 on 11/30/1932
- CONTRACT SIZE: 60,000 lbs
- MIN TICK: .01 cents
- VALUE: 6 USD / contract
- EACH GRID: 0.4 cents
- VALUE: 240 USD / contract
- DAILY LIMIT: 2 cent
- VALUE: 1200 USD / contract
- TRADING HOURS: 6:00p-6:00a / 9:30a-1:15p CT

## Annual High, Low and Settle of Soybean Oil Futures    In Cents per Pound

| Year | High | Low | Settle | Year | High | Low | Settle | Year | High | Low | Settle |
|---|---|---|---|---|---|---|---|---|---|---|---|
| 1925 | 13.38 | 13.25 | 13.38 | 1939 | 5.60 | 3.90 | 4.50 | 1953 | 14.25 | 9.75 | 12.60 |
| 1926 | 14.00 | 12.03 | 12.03 | 1940 | 10.50 | 5.10 | 10.10 | 1954 | 15.38 | 11.75 | 12.50 |
| 1927 | 12.38 | 12.02 | 12.12 | 1941 | 11.80 | 11.20 | 11.80 | 1955 | 12.88 | 10.13 | 10.90 |
| 1928 | 12.38 | 12.12 | 12.38 | 1942 | 11.80 | 11.80 | 11.80 | 1956 | 16.63 | 10.88 | 14.10 |
| 1929 | 12.38 | 8.80 | 8.80 | 1943 | 11.80 | 11.80 | 11.80 | 1957 | 14.63 | 10.88 | 11.40 |
| 1930 | 9.30 | 6.70 | 6.70 | 1944 | 11.80 | 11.80 | 11.80 | 1958 | 11.75 | 9.38 | 9.50 |
| 1931 | 6.40 | 3.80 | 3.80 | 1945 | 11.80 | 11.80 | 11.80 | 1959 | 9.40 | 7.51 | 7.66 |
| 1932 | 3.40 | 2.90 | 3.00 | 1946 | 24.60 | 11.80 | 24.60 | 1960 | 10.07 | 7.37 | 9.92 |
| 1933 | 8.00 | 3.00 | 6.20 | 1947 | 33.50 | 15.60 | 26.10 | 1961 | 13.85 | 9.93 | 10.43 |
| 1934 | 7.30 | 5.50 | 7.30 | 1948 | 27.30 | 17.30 | 17.30 | 1962 | 10.73 | 7.40 | 8.48 |
| 1935 | 9.10 | 6.00 | 9.10 | 1949 | 15.75 | 9.00 | 10.20 | 1963 | 10.30 | 7.05 | 8.06 |
| 1936 | 9.90 | 5.20 | 5.20 | 1950 | 20.25 | 10.50 | 19.60 | 1964 | 12.46 | 7.51 | 11.03 |
| 1937 | 6.40 | 5.00 | 5.10 | 1951 | 22.00 | 12.00 | 12.60 | 1965 | 13.50 | 9.36 | 10.61 |
| 1938 | 5.10 | 4.20 | 5.10 | 1952 | 13.38 | 8.50 | 12.90 | 1966 | 14.58 | 10.17 | 10.26 |

Futures data begins 07/01/1959.    Data continued on page 224.    *Source: CME Group; Chicago Board of Trade*

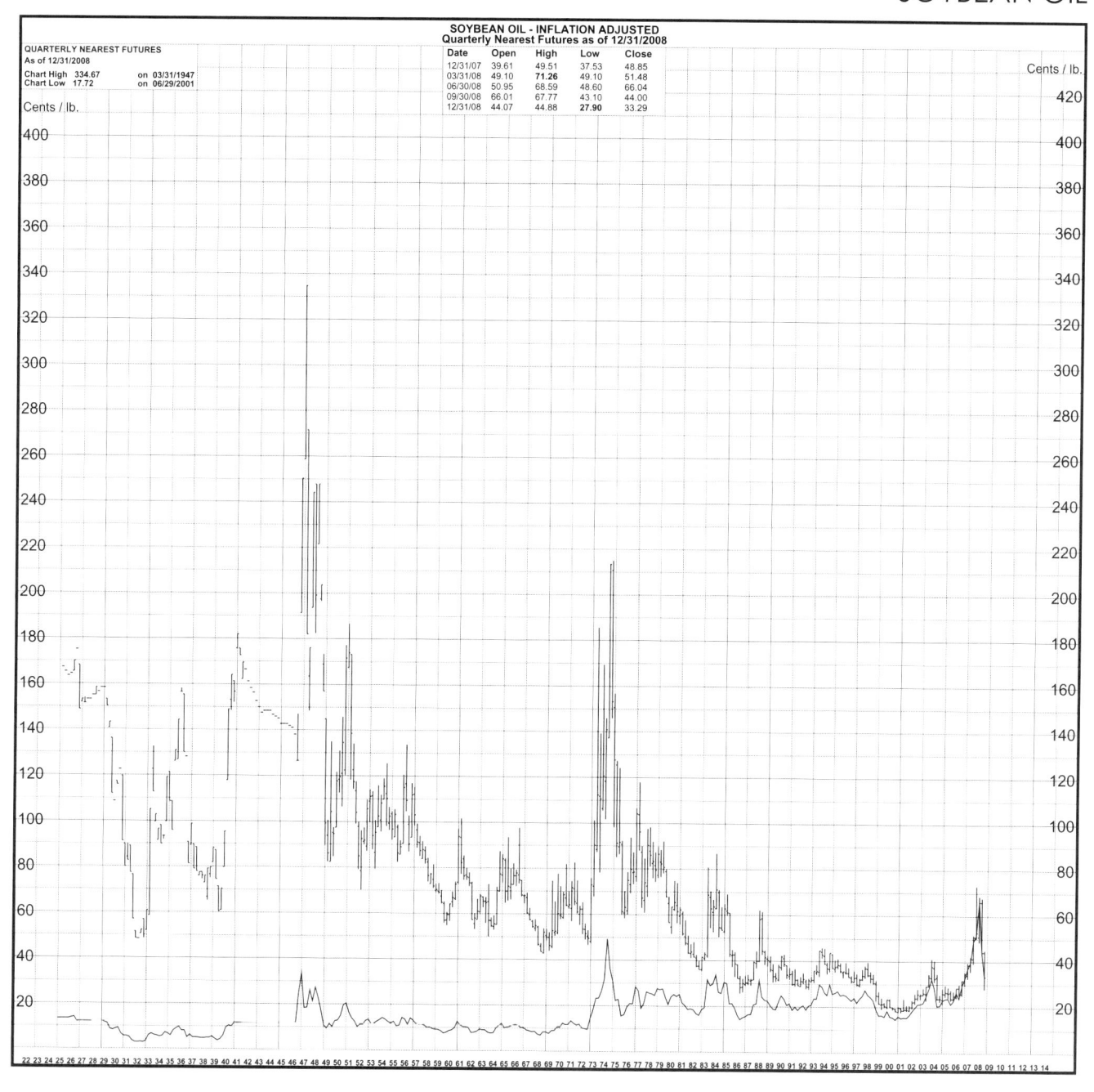

# SOYBEAN OIL

**QUARTERLY NEAREST FUTURES**
As of 12/31/2008
Chart High 334.67 on 03/31/1947
Chart Low 17.72 on 06/29/2001
Cents / lb.

**SOYBEAN OIL - INFLATION ADJUSTED**
Quarterly Nearest Futures as of 12/31/2008

| Date | Open | High | Low | Close |
|---|---|---|---|---|
| 12/31/07 | 39.61 | 49.51 | 37.53 | 48.85 |
| 03/31/08 | 49.10 | 71.26 | 49.10 | 51.48 |
| 06/30/08 | 50.95 | 68.59 | 48.60 | 66.04 |
| 09/30/08 | 66.01 | 67.77 | 43.10 | 44.00 |
| 12/31/08 | 44.07 | 44.88 | 27.90 | 33.29 |

## Annual High, Low and Settle of Soybean Oil — In Cents per Pound

| Year | High | Low | Settle | Year | High | Low | Settle | Year | High | Low | Settle |
|---|---|---|---|---|---|---|---|---|---|---|---|
| 1925 | 13.38 | 13.25 | 13.38 | 1939 | 5.60 | 3.90 | 4.50 | 1953 | 14.25 | 9.75 | 12.60 |
| 1926 | 14.00 | 12.03 | 12.03 | 1940 | 10.50 | 5.10 | 10.10 | 1954 | 15.38 | 11.75 | 12.50 |
| 1927 | 12.38 | 12.02 | 12.12 | 1941 | 11.80 | 11.20 | 11.80 | 1955 | 12.88 | 10.13 | 10.90 |
| 1928 | 12.38 | 12.12 | 12.38 | 1942 | 11.80 | 11.80 | 11.80 | 1956 | 16.63 | 10.88 | 14.10 |
| 1929 | 12.38 | 8.80 | 8.80 | 1943 | 11.80 | 11.80 | 11.80 | 1957 | 14.63 | 10.88 | 11.40 |
| 1930 | 9.30 | 6.70 | 6.70 | 1944 | 11.80 | 11.80 | 11.80 | 1958 | 11.75 | 9.38 | 9.50 |
| 1931 | 6.40 | 3.80 | 3.80 | 1945 | 11.80 | 11.80 | 11.80 | 1959 | 9.75 | 7.63 | 7.80 |
| 1932 | 3.40 | 2.90 | 3.00 | 1946 | 24.60 | 11.80 | 24.60 | 1960 | 10.90 | 7.50 | 10.90 |
| 1933 | 8.00 | 3.00 | 6.20 | 1947 | 33.50 | 15.60 | 26.10 | 1961 | 13.75 | 10.00 | 10.37 |
| 1934 | 7.30 | 5.50 | 7.30 | 1948 | 27.30 | 17.30 | 17.30 | 1962 | 10.63 | 7.50 | 8.60 |
| 1935 | 9.10 | 6.00 | 9.10 | 1949 | 15.75 | 9.00 | 10.20 | 1963 | 10.25 | 7.75 | 8.30 |
| 1936 | 9.90 | 5.20 | 5.20 | 1950 | 20.25 | 10.50 | 19.60 | 1964 | 12.82 | 7.75 | 12.00 |
| 1937 | 6.40 | 5.00 | 5.10 | 1951 | 22.00 | 12.00 | 12.60 | 1965 | 12.67 | 9.68 | 10.91 |
| 1938 | 5.10 | 4.20 | 5.10 | 1952 | 13.38 | 8.50 | 12.90 | 1966 | 14.64 | 10.34 | 10.38 |

Decatur, Illinois. Data continued on page 225. *Source: CME Group; Chicago Board of Trade*

# SOYBEAN OIL

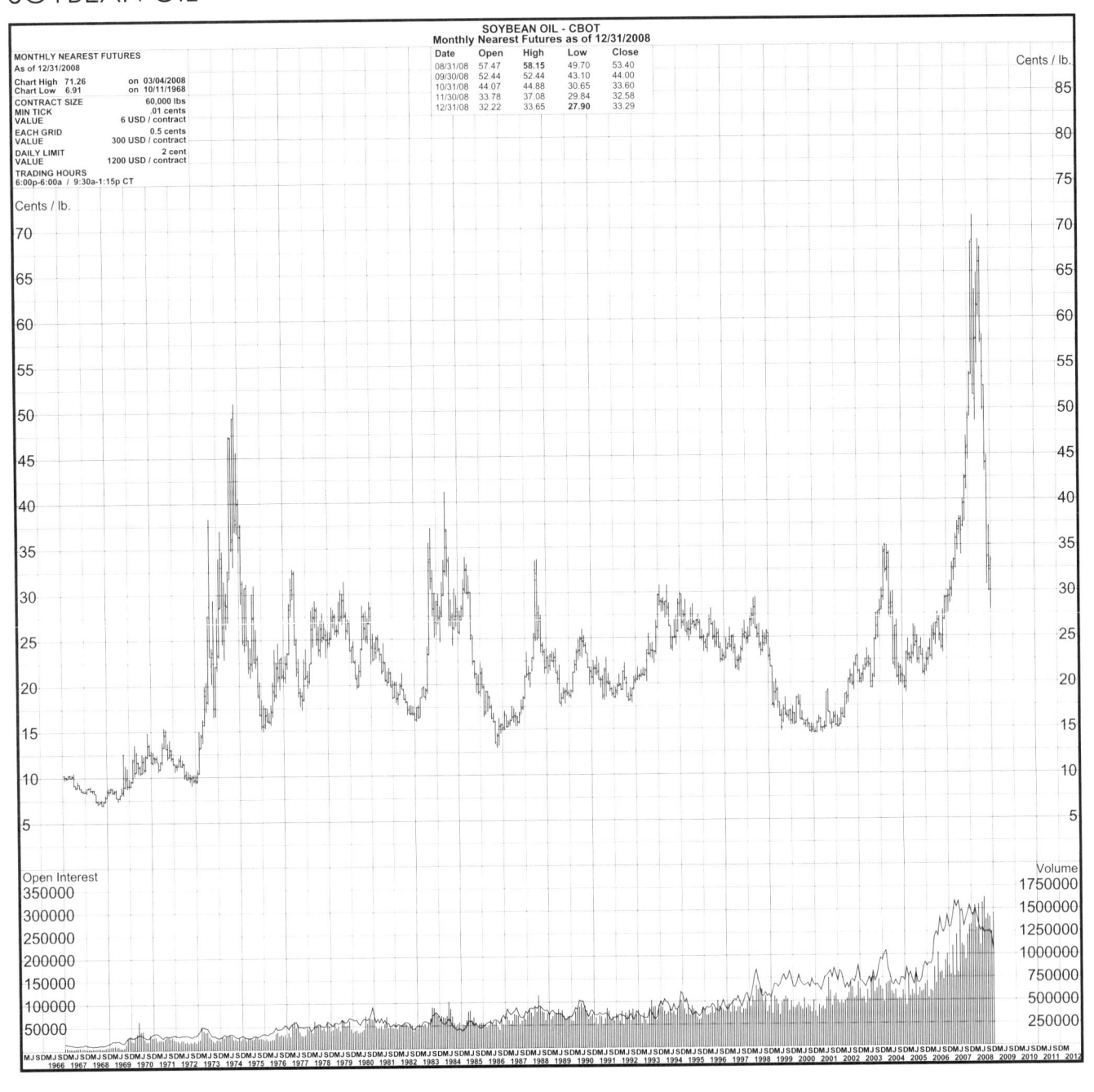

**MONTHLY NEAREST FUTURES**
As of 12/31/2008
Chart High 71.26 on 03/04/2008
Chart Low 6.91 on 10/11/1968
CONTRACT SIZE 60,000 lbs
MIN TICK .01 cents
VALUE 6 USD / contract
EACH GRID 0.5 cents
VALUE 300 USD / contract
DAILY LIMIT 2 cent
VALUE 1200 USD / contract
TRADING HOURS
6:00p-6:00a / 9:30a-1:15p CT

**SOYBEAN OIL - CBOT**
Monthly Nearest Futures as of 12/31/2008

| Date | Open | High | Low | Close |
|---|---|---|---|---|
| 08/31/08 | 57.47 | 58.15 | 49.70 | 53.40 |
| 09/30/08 | 52.44 | 52.44 | 43.10 | 44.00 |
| 10/31/08 | 44.07 | 44.88 | 30.65 | 33.60 |
| 11/30/08 | 33.78 | 37.08 | 29.84 | 32.58 |
| 12/31/08 | 32.22 | 33.65 | 27.90 | 33.29 |

## Annual High, Low and Settle of Soybean Oil Futures    In Cents per Pound

| Year | High | Low | Settle | Year | High | Low | Settle | Year | High | Low | Settle |
|---|---|---|---|---|---|---|---|---|---|---|---|
| 1967 | 10.55 | 8.37 | 8.44 | 1981 | 25.68 | 18.45 | 18.59 | 1995 | 29.75 | 24.57 | 24.97 |
| 1968 | 9.04 | 6.91 | 8.45 | 1982 | 21.32 | 16.08 | 16.08 | 1996 | 28.23 | 22.16 | 22.71 |
| 1969 | 12.65 | 7.32 | 9.05 | 1983 | 37.20 | 15.91 | 29.07 | 1997 | 26.87 | 21.25 | 24.79 |
| 1970 | 14.90 | 8.95 | 11.62 | 1984 | 41.15 | 24.21 | 25.72 | 1998 | 29.46 | 22.65 | 22.83 |
| 1971 | 15.40 | 10.57 | 11.47 | 1985 | 34.00 | 18.63 | 21.26 | 1999 | 23.80 | 14.65 | 15.75 |
| 1972 | 12.43 | 9.03 | 9.60 | 1986 | 21.82 | 12.95 | 15.18 | 2000 | 18.70 | 14.36 | 14.53 |
| 1973 | 38.33 | 9.36 | 23.35 | 1987 | 20.95 | 14.90 | 20.77 | 2001 | 19.26 | 14.35 | 15.27 |
| 1974 | 51.00 | 22.80 | 36.35 | 1988 | 33.70 | 19.57 | 22.82 | 2002 | 23.08 | 14.99 | 21.24 |
| 1975 | 37.75 | 15.20 | 15.55 | 1989 | 23.90 | 17.54 | 18.70 | 2003 | 29.00 | 19.30 | 27.87 |
| 1976 | 24.65 | 14.92 | 20.90 | 1990 | 26.00 | 18.37 | 20.74 | 2004 | 35.18 | 19.50 | 20.61 |
| 1977 | 32.75 | 17.27 | 20.99 | 1991 | 23.00 | 18.15 | 18.50 | 2005 | 26.31 | 18.82 | 21.30 |
| 1978 | 29.30 | 19.63 | 24.60 | 1992 | 22.29 | 17.89 | 20.47 | 2006 | 29.40 | 21.00 | 29.26 |
| 1979 | 31.40 | 23.75 | 23.78 | 1993 | 29.80 | 20.17 | 29.71 | 2007 | 49.51 | 27.58 | 48.85 |
| 1980 | 29.15 | 19.53 | 24.25 | 1994 | 30.82 | 23.48 | 29.83 | 2008 | 71.26 | 27.90 | 33.29 |

Data continued from page 222.    Source: *CME Group; Chicago Board of Trade*

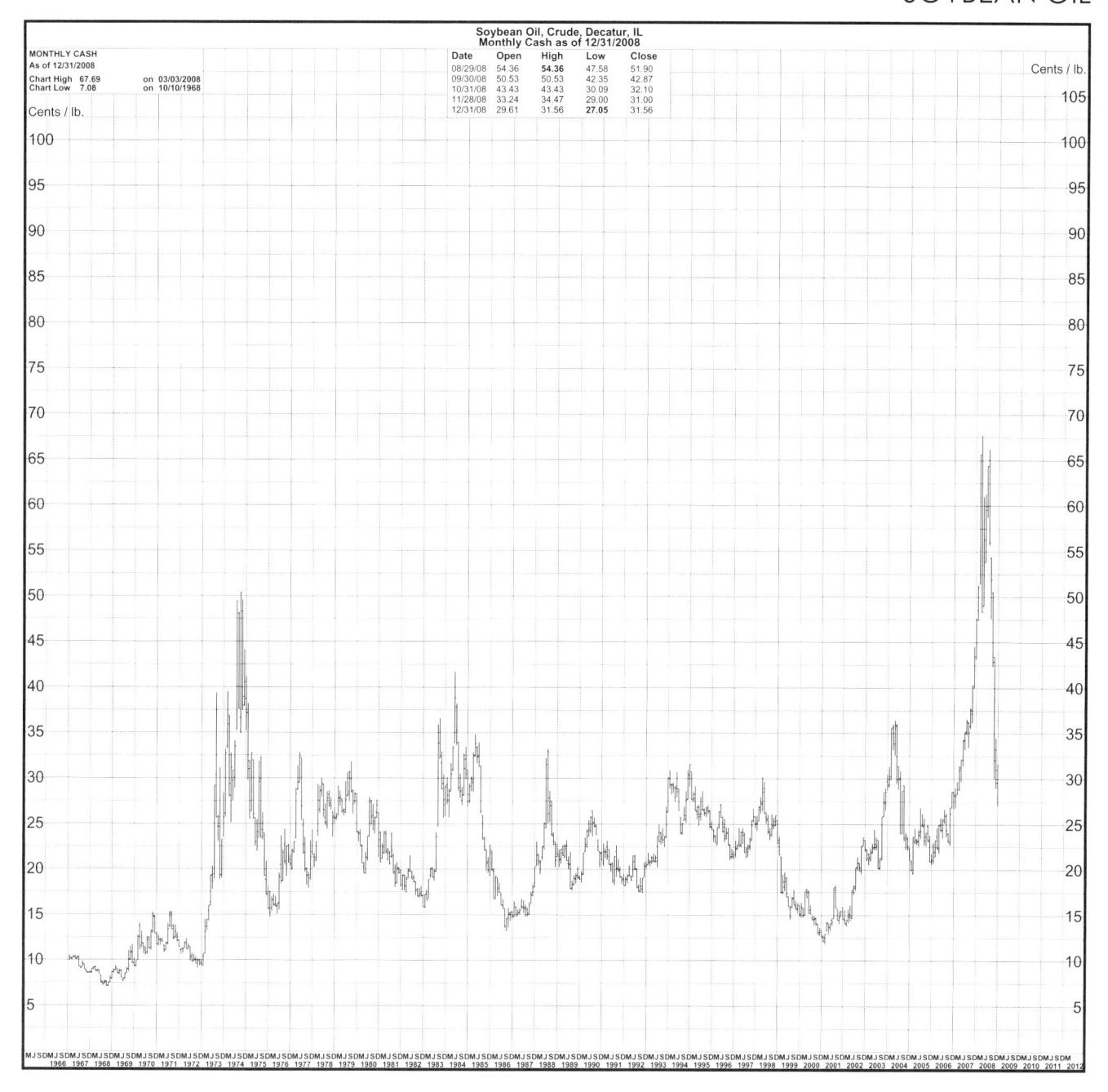

# SOYBEAN OIL

**MONTHLY CASH**
As of 12/31/2008
Chart High 67.69 on 03/03/2008
Chart Low 7.08 on 10/10/1968
Cents / lb.

Soybean Oil, Crude, Decatur, IL
Monthly Cash as of 12/31/2008

| Date | Open | High | Low | Close |
|---|---|---|---|---|
| 08/29/08 | 54.36 | 54.36 | 47.58 | 51.90 |
| 09/30/08 | 50.53 | 50.53 | 42.35 | 42.87 |
| 10/31/08 | 43.43 | 43.43 | 30.09 | 32.10 |
| 11/28/08 | 33.24 | 34.47 | 29.00 | 31.00 |
| 12/31/08 | 29.61 | 31.56 | 27.05 | 31.56 |

## Annual High, Low and Settle of Soybean Oil    In Cents per Pound

| Year | High | Low | Settle | Year | High | Low | Settle | Year | High | Low | Settle |
|---|---|---|---|---|---|---|---|---|---|---|---|
| 1967 | 10.49 | 8.51 | 8.64 | 1981 | 24.26 | 18.00 | 18.27 | 1995 | 30.75 | 24.38 | 24.56 |
| 1968 | 9.31 | 7.08 | 8.65 | 1982 | 21.48 | 15.88 | 15.88 | 1996 | 27.25 | 21.06 | 21.25 |
| 1969 | 11.73 | 7.61 | 9.36 | 1983 | 36.60 | 15.73 | 29.01 | 1997 | 26.72 | 21.32 | 25.04 |
| 1970 | 15.25 | 9.26 | 11.76 | 1984 | 41.68 | 25.67 | 28.22 | 1998 | 30.18 | 22.84 | 22.93 |
| 1971 | 15.38 | 10.79 | 11.47 | 1985 | 34.83 | 19.34 | 21.79 | 1999 | 23.67 | 14.53 | 15.15 |
| 1972 | 12.39 | 9.09 | 9.54 | 1986 | 22.02 | 13.27 | 14.88 | 2000 | 17.94 | 12.65 | 12.66 |
| 1973 | 39.35 | 9.35 | 25.68 | 1987 | 20.20 | 14.76 | 20.17 | 2001 | 18.35 | 11.83 | 14.62 |
| 1974 | 50.37 | 25.10 | 37.13 | 1988 | 33.25 | 19.45 | 21.69 | 2002 | 23.52 | 13.85 | 22.12 |
| 1975 | 38.25 | 15.65 | 15.65 | 1989 | 23.18 | 17.65 | 18.93 | 2003 | 30.52 | 20.05 | 29.25 |
| 1976 | 24.45 | 14.73 | 20.55 | 1990 | 26.46 | 18.60 | 21.01 | 2004 | 36.45 | 21.05 | 21.59 |
| 1977 | 32.87 | 17.90 | 21.59 | 1991 | 23.13 | 18.25 | 18.30 | 2005 | 26.83 | 19.49 | 21.05 |
| 1978 | 29.97 | 20.19 | 25.57 | 1992 | 21.60 | 17.42 | 20.47 | 2006 | 28.61 | 20.71 | 28.26 |
| 1979 | 31.85 | 24.10 | 24.10 | 1993 | 30.07 | 20.20 | 30.07 | 2007 | 47.68 | 26.82 | 47.47 |
| 1980 | 27.93 | 19.52 | 23.20 | 1994 | 31.57 | 23.85 | 31.57 | 2008 | 67.69 | 27.05 | 31.56 |

Decatur, Illinois Crude.    Data continued from page 223.    *Source: CME Group; Chicago Board of Trade*

225

# SOYBEAN OIL

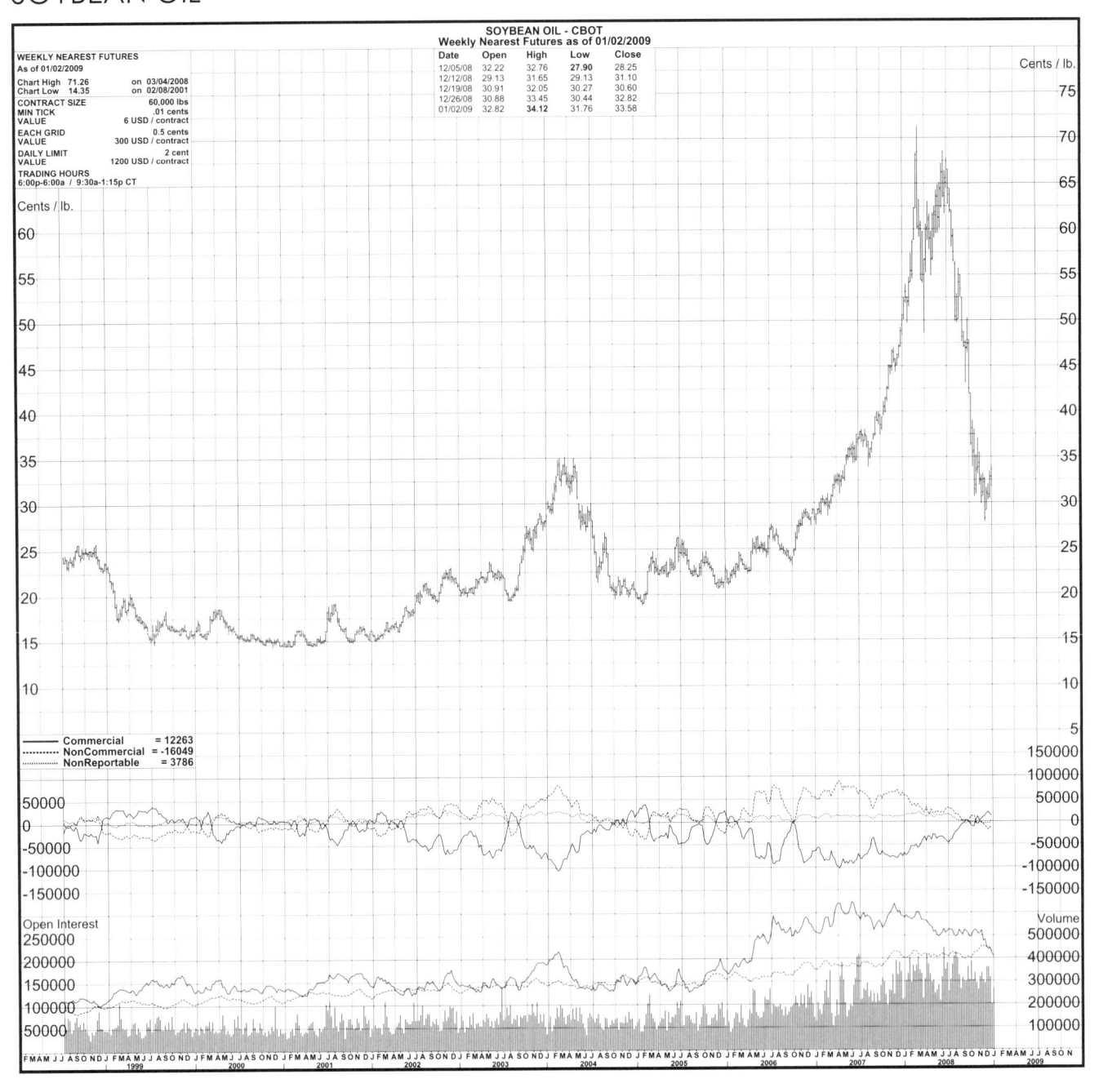

### Quarterly High, Low and Settle of Soybean Oil Futures — In Cents per Pound

| Quarter | High | Low | Settle | Quarter | High | Low | Settle | Quarter | High | Low | Settle |
|---|---|---|---|---|---|---|---|---|---|---|---|
| 03/2000 | 18.48 | 15.25 | 18.31 | 03/2003 | 21.86 | 19.75 | 21.37 | 03/2006 | 24.65 | 21.00 | 22.79 |
| 06/2000 | 18.70 | 15.75 | 15.86 | 06/2003 | 23.73 | 21.20 | 21.89 | 06/2006 | 26.45 | 22.25 | 26.36 |
| 09/2000 | 16.05 | 15.01 | 15.49 | 09/2003 | 24.82 | 19.30 | 24.71 | 09/2006 | 27.68 | 23.45 | 23.77 |
| 12/2000 | 15.52 | 14.36 | 14.53 | 12/2003 | 29.00 | 24.54 | 27.87 | 12/2006 | 29.40 | 23.15 | 29.26 |
| 03/2001 | 16.33 | 14.35 | 15.95 | 03/2004 | 35.18 | 27.80 | 32.23 | 03/2007 | 33.07 | 27.58 | 32.48 |
| 06/2001 | 16.09 | 14.42 | 15.14 | 06/2004 | 35.00 | 26.92 | 28.18 | 06/2007 | 37.57 | 30.98 | 36.63 |
| 09/2001 | 19.26 | 15.05 | 15.40 | 09/2004 | 30.00 | 20.34 | 20.52 | 09/2007 | 40.00 | 33.91 | 39.49 |
| 12/2001 | 16.75 | 14.75 | 15.27 | 12/2004 | 22.05 | 19.50 | 20.61 | 12/2007 | 49.51 | 37.53 | 48.85 |
| 03/2002 | 17.13 | 14.99 | 16.46 | 03/2005 | 24.75 | 18.82 | 22.90 | 03/2008 | 71.26 | 49.10 | 51.48 |
| 06/2002 | 18.95 | 15.94 | 18.25 | 06/2005 | 26.31 | 21.86 | 23.61 | 06/2008 | 68.59 | 48.60 | 66.04 |
| 09/2002 | 21.40 | 17.67 | 19.74 | 09/2005 | 26.05 | 21.85 | 23.72 | 09/2008 | 67.77 | 43.10 | 44.00 |
| 12/2002 | 23.08 | 19.09 | 21.24 | 12/2005 | 24.77 | 20.62 | 21.30 | 12/2008 | 44.88 | 27.90 | 33.29 |

*Source: CME Group; Chicago Board of Trade*

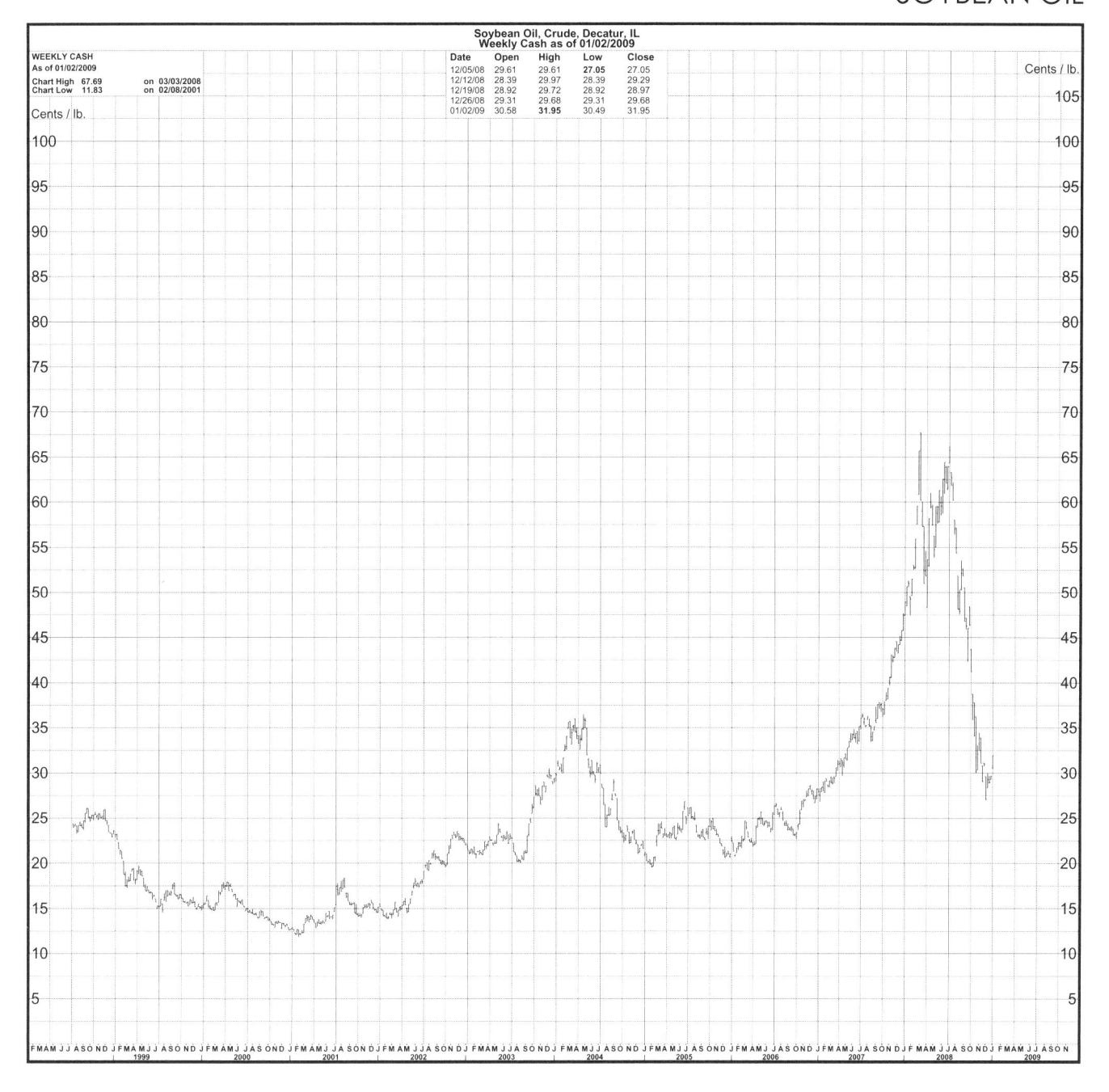

# SOYBEAN OIL

Soybean Oil, Crude, Decatur, IL
Weekly Cash as of 01/02/2009

| Date | Open | High | Low | Close |
|---|---|---|---|---|
| 12/05/08 | 29.61 | 29.61 | 27.05 | 27.05 |
| 12/12/08 | 28.39 | 29.97 | 28.39 | 29.29 |
| 12/19/08 | 28.92 | 29.72 | 28.92 | 28.97 |
| 12/26/08 | 29.31 | 29.68 | 29.31 | 29.68 |
| 01/02/09 | 30.58 | 31.95 | 30.49 | 31.95 |

WEEKLY CASH
As of 01/02/2009
Chart High 67.69 on 03/03/2008
Chart Low 11.83 on 02/08/2001

## Quarterly High, Low and Settle of Soybean Oil    In Cents per Pound

| Quarter | High | Low | Settle | Quarter | High | Low | Settle | Quarter | High | Low | Settle |
|---|---|---|---|---|---|---|---|---|---|---|---|
| 03/2000 | 17.63 | 14.75 | 17.63 | 03/2003 | 22.37 | 20.51 | 22.00 | 03/2006 | 24.66 | 20.71 | 22.42 |
| 06/2000 | 17.94 | 15.16 | 15.16 | 06/2003 | 24.45 | 21.85 | 22.64 | 06/2006 | 25.77 | 21.82 | 25.61 |
| 09/2000 | 15.04 | 13.89 | 14.11 | 09/2003 | 25.84 | 20.05 | 25.84 | 09/2006 | 26.69 | 23.01 | 23.15 |
| 12/2000 | 14.05 | 12.65 | 12.66 | 12/2003 | 30.52 | 25.90 | 29.25 | 12/2006 | 28.61 | 22.66 | 28.26 |
| 03/2001 | 14.33 | 11.83 | 14.20 | 03/2004 | 35.98 | 29.09 | 35.03 | 03/2007 | 31.47 | 26.82 | 30.98 |
| 06/2001 | 14.70 | 12.89 | 14.26 | 06/2004 | 36.45 | 28.87 | 29.98 | 06/2007 | 35.13 | 29.69 | 35.13 |
| 09/2001 | 18.35 | 14.52 | 14.52 | 09/2004 | 30.90 | 23.27 | 23.27 | 09/2007 | 37.84 | 33.42 | 37.61 |
| 12/2001 | 15.89 | 14.03 | 14.62 | 12/2004 | 24.11 | 21.05 | 21.59 | 12/2007 | 47.68 | 36.15 | 47.47 |
| 03/2002 | 15.71 | 13.85 | 14.84 | 03/2005 | 24.62 | 19.49 | 23.28 | 03/2008 | 67.69 | 47.43 | 48.35 |
| 06/2002 | 18.36 | 14.46 | 18.00 | 06/2005 | 26.83 | 22.55 | 24.29 | 06/2008 | 64.45 | 49.02 | 64.41 |
| 09/2002 | 21.39 | 17.71 | 20.22 | 09/2005 | 26.19 | 22.59 | 24.10 | 09/2008 | 66.24 | 42.35 | 42.87 |
| 12/2002 | 23.52 | 19.53 | 22.12 | 12/2005 | 24.99 | 20.59 | 21.05 | 12/2008 | 43.43 | 27.05 | 31.56 |

Decatur, Illinois Crude.    *Source: CME Group; Chicago Board of Trade*

# INDICES - COMMODITIES

## Current Outlook

Commodity prices collapsed in the second half of 2008, bringing an abrupt end to the largest commodity bull market in post-war history. That sell-off was caused by the global financial crisis and by the heavy liquidation of long positions by all manner of investors, speculators and hedge funds. Commodity prices are likely to remain weak until the global economy can recover from the financial shock.

Once the global recession is over, however, the commodity markets should be able to regain their balance and return to strength. Commodities are likely to see renewed demand in coming years once the theme of strong economic growth in the developing world gets back on track. The main drivers of economic growth and commodity demand in coming years will again be rising living standards in the developing world and the United Nations' projection for a 2.5 billion person increase in the world's population through 2050. When that demand emerges, commodity prices are likely to see a renewed rally as a signal to producers that they need to boost production to meet new demand.

## 1970s Commodity Bull Market

The second-largest commodity bull market in post-war history was the 146.7% rally in the Continuous Commodity Index (CCI) seen in 1971-74. That rally was driven by a sharp increase in inflation and related weakness in the dollar. As the nearby table shows, the average US inflation rate during that bull market was a lofty +4.9% and the dollar fell by an average of -7.5% per year. Inflation at the time stemmed from the Federal Reserve's overly easy monetary policy. The weak dollar stemmed from inflation and the fact that the dollar was adjusting downward after the Bretton Woods agreement broke down and currencies started floating.

In addition to inflation and a weak dollar, there were supply/demand factors in particular markets that helped drive the 1971-74 commodity bull market. Grain and soybean prices soared during that time largely because of huge Soviet grain and soybean purchases in 1972 and 1973. The 1971-74 bull market was also driven in its latter stages by the October 1973 Arab Oil Embargo, which caused oil prices to triple, thus pushing the CCI higher.

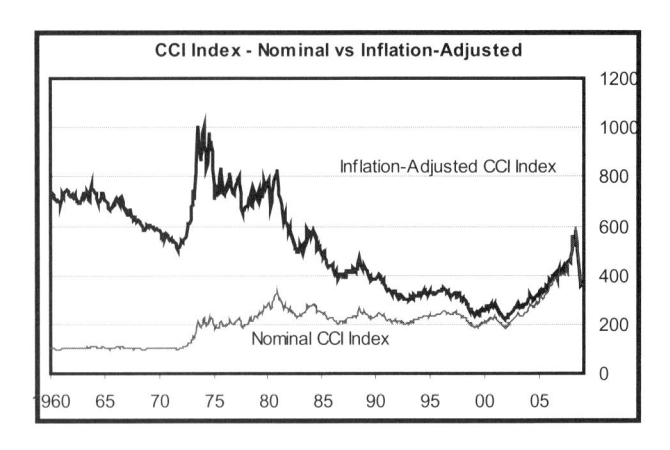

## 1977-80 Bull Market

After the CCI peaked in 1974, commodity prices moved sideways later in the 1970s as inflation and demand were undercut by the severe US recession seen in 1973-75. After the recession, however, commodity prices staged the third largest bull market in postwar history of +82.8% during 1977-80. Inflation was the key driver behind that rally. The US average annual CPI during that commodity bull market averaged an extraordinarily high +10.2%. The dollar was also weak during that time with an average annual -5.2% decline in the dollar index.

## 1980-2001 Bear Market

Fed Chairman Paul Volcker started to crack down on inflation in 1979, causing the double-dip recession in 1980 and 1981-82. Commodity prices were forced lower in the early-1980s by the double-dip recessions and the downward trend in inflation. Commodity prices were also pushed lower by the sharp rally in the dollar seen from 1980 until the 1985 Plaza Accord. Crude oil prices trended downward from 1981-85 and then plunged to $10 per barrel in March 1986, also undercutting the commodity indexes in the early to mid-1980s.

### Commodity Bull Markets Ranked by Percentage Gain in Continuous Commodity Index (1960-2009)

| Bull Market Period | Low | | High | | Percent Rally | Rally Duration (months) | Avg CPI (yr-yr%) | Avg Dollar Index (yr/yr%) | Correlation CRB-CPI | Correlation CRB-DXY |
|---|---|---|---|---|---|---|---|---|---|---|
| 2001-08 | Oct-01 | 182.83 | Jul-08 | 615.04 | 236.4% | 81 | 2.8% | -5.8% | 0.98 | -0.84 |
| 1971-74 | Oct-71 | 96.40 | Feb-74 | 237.80 | 146.7% | 28 | 4.9% | -7.5% | 0.97 | -0.79 |
| 1977-80 | Aug-77 | 184.70 | Nov-80 | 337.60 | 82.8% | 39 | 10.2% | -5.2% | 0.97 | -0.93 |
| 1986-88 | Jul-86 | 196.16 | Jun-88 | 272.19 | 38.8% | 23 | 3.2% | -13.3% | 0.89 | -0.68 |
| 1992-96 | Aug-92 | 198.17 | Apy-86 | 263.79 | 33.1% | 44 | 2.8% | -0.6% | 0.96 | -0.32 |

Note: Data is current through January 30, 2009. Source: Commodity Research Bureau

# INDICES - COMMODITIES

Although the CCI was volatile in the 1980s and 1990s, the general trend was downward. On an inflation-adjusted basis (see chart on previous page), it is easy to see that in reality commodity prices were in a serious bear market from 1980 until 2001. The main reasons for that commodity bear market included (1) the success of global central banks in taming inflation, and (2) greatly expanded supply in nearly all commodity markets due to improved technology and new producers coming into the markets (e.g., Brazil in the agricultural markets).

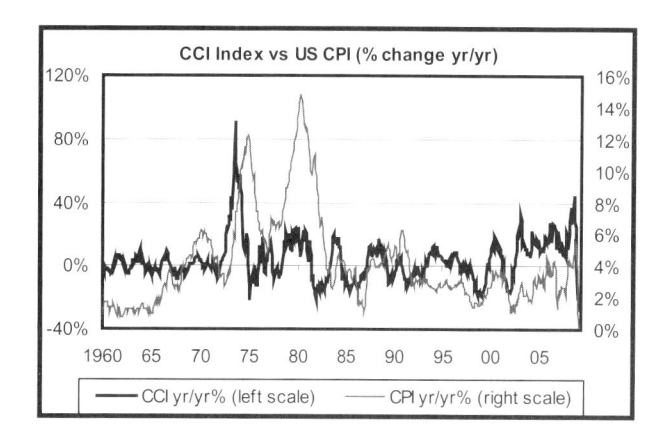

## 2001-08 Bull Market

Commodity prices hit a post-war low in inflation-adjusted terms in October 2001. Commodity prices were depressed in 2001 due to the post-bubble plunge in the US stock market, the US recession in 2001, and a US inflation rate that fell sharply through 2001 (i.e., from 3.7% in Jan-2001 to +1.1% by mid-2002).

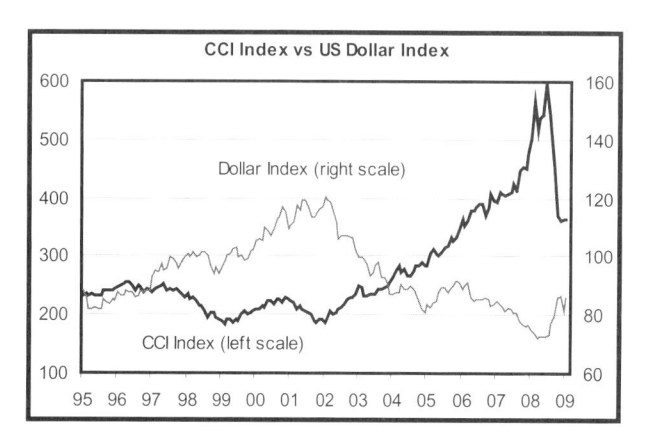

However, commodity prices bottomed out in October 2001 as the Federal Reserve was in the process of slashing interest rates to revive the economy and prevent an extremely damaging deflationary episode such as the one Japan experienced from 1990-2005. The Fed during 2001 slashed the funds rate target by 4.75 percentage points from 6.50% to 1.75%, and then cut the funds rate by another 0.75 percentage points to 1.00% by mid-2003. The Fed left the funds rate target at an extraordinarily low 1.00% for a year until June 2004 to ensure that a US recovery would take hold.

The Fed's sharp easing of monetary policy was the key reason why the dollar started plunging in early 2002 and fell by a total of 33% through late 2004. The dollar also plunged during 2002-04 because of the soaring US current account deficit, which is the broadest measure of US trade. The US current account deficit as a percentage of GDP was also already at 4% of GDP in 2002, but then proceeded to balloon to 6.3% of GDP by the end of 2004 and then hit its peak of 6.4% of GDP in Q3-2006.

The plunge in the dollar was the key reason behind the rally in the CCI during the first three years of the bull market from 2002 to 2004. The nearby chart illustrates the very strong negative correlation of -0.94 seen between the dollar index and the CCI over the 2002-04 period. Simply put, as the dollar went straight down, commodity prices went straight up. Yet inflation remained low over this period because the market had confidence in the Fed's inflation-fighting resolve and because globalization increased the supply of goods available throughout the world. This new competition meant that US companies could not raise prices without losing market share.

The commodity rally continued in 2005 but for different reasons. In 2005, the dollar started to recover because of the Fed's tighter monetary policy. Yet the CCI rallied even in the face of the stronger dollar because of strong demand in key commodity markets, driven in large part by China. China, with its truly massive scale of development, drove the prices of many commodities higher, particularly energy prices, metals prices, and construction materials prices.

The commodity rally stalled in 2006 as the US housing crisis started to emerge and concerns developed about weaker US and global demand for commodities. However, the commodity rally then kicked into high gear again in the latter half of 2007 when the Fed was forced into easing due to the fact that Wall Street firms started experiencing big losses on their mortgage portfolios. From August 2007 through the record high in July 2008, the CCI soared by 48.7%. That rally was driven by the Fed's interest rate cuts, the decline in the dollar over that period, and speculative fever.

As part of the 2007-08 commodity rally, crude oil prices nearly doubled from $78 in August 2007 to the record high of $147.27 in July 2008. Gold prices rallied from $675 in August 2007 to a record $1,033 in March 2008. Copper posted a record high of $4.27 per pound in May 2008 and silver peaked at $21.19 per ounce in March 2008.

# CONTINUOUS COMMODITY INDEX (CCI)

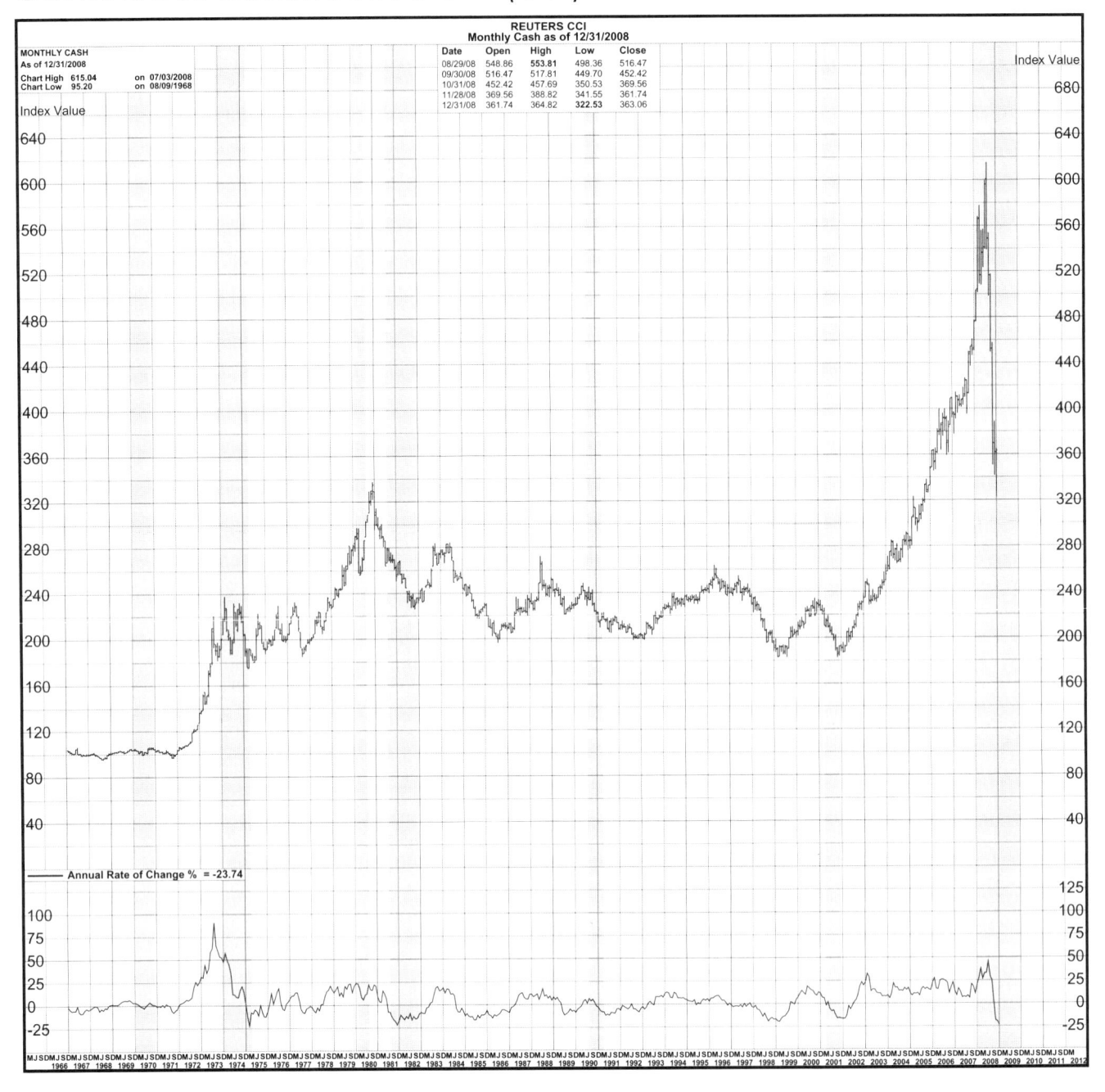

**REUTERS CCI Monthly Cash as of 12/31/2008**

| Date | Open | High | Low | Close |
|---|---|---|---|---|
| 08/29/08 | 548.86 | 553.81 | 498.36 | 516.47 |
| 09/30/08 | 516.47 | 517.81 | 449.70 | 452.42 |
| 10/31/08 | 452.42 | 457.69 | 350.53 | 369.56 |
| 11/28/08 | 369.56 | 388.82 | 341.55 | 361.74 |
| 12/31/08 | 361.74 | 364.82 | 322.53 | 363.06 |

MONTHLY CASH As of 12/31/2008
Chart High 615.04 on 07/03/2008
Chart Low 95.20 on 08/09/1968

Annual Rate of Change % = -23.74

## Annual High, Low and Settle of Continuous Commodity Index (CCI) — Index Value

| Year | High | Low | Settle | Year | High | Low | Settle | Year | High | Low | Settle |
|---|---|---|---|---|---|---|---|---|---|---|---|
| 1967 | 106.60 | 98.80 | 99.60 | 1981 | 314.50 | 250.50 | 254.90 | 1995 | 246.47 | 229.31 | 243.18 |
| 1968 | 102.00 | 95.20 | 100.80 | 1982 | 268.60 | 225.80 | 234.00 | 1996 | 263.79 | 235.99 | 239.61 |
| 1969 | 105.40 | 100.90 | 103.90 | 1983 | 283.80 | 232.10 | 277.60 | 1997 | 254.79 | 228.84 | 229.14 |
| 1970 | 106.40 | 99.10 | 102.50 | 1984 | 284.20 | 244.00 | 244.20 | 1998 | 236.08 | 187.89 | 191.22 |
| 1971 | 104.10 | 96.40 | 103.40 | 1985 | 248.10 | 217.30 | 229.37 | 1999 | 209.91 | 182.67 | 205.14 |
| 1972 | 136.30 | 103.40 | 135.90 | 1986 | 230.88 | 196.16 | 209.07 | 2000 | 234.38 | 201.43 | 227.83 |
| 1973 | 220.70 | 135.10 | 200.60 | 1987 | 238.21 | 204.24 | 232.53 | 2001 | 232.58 | 182.83 | 190.61 |
| 1974 | 237.80 | 187.30 | 203.90 | 1988 | 272.19 | 224.00 | 251.83 | 2002 | 238.39 | 186.38 | 234.52 |
| 1975 | 222.90 | 175.10 | 191.00 | 1989 | 252.37 | 220.82 | 229.93 | 2003 | 263.60 | 228.10 | 255.29 |
| 1976 | 229.70 | 191.20 | 204.70 | 1990 | 248.76 | 219.69 | 222.64 | 2004 | 292.49 | 257.49 | 283.90 |
| 1977 | 232.70 | 184.70 | 200.30 | 1991 | 222.96 | 204.43 | 208.08 | 2005 | 349.20 | 277.07 | 347.89 |
| 1978 | 237.40 | 198.90 | 227.60 | 1992 | 215.30 | 198.17 | 202.76 | 2006 | 409.65 | 345.49 | 394.89 |
| 1979 | 282.80 | 228.40 | 281.50 | 1993 | 226.76 | 198.38 | 226.31 | 2007 | 477.48 | 377.59 | 476.08 |
| 1980 | 337.60 | 256.30 | 308.50 | 1994 | 239.72 | 219.89 | 236.64 | 2008 | 615.04 | 322.53 | 363.06 |

1967=100.  Index data begins 09/04/1956.  *Source: Thomson Reuters*

# CONTINUOUS COMMODITY INDEX (CCI)

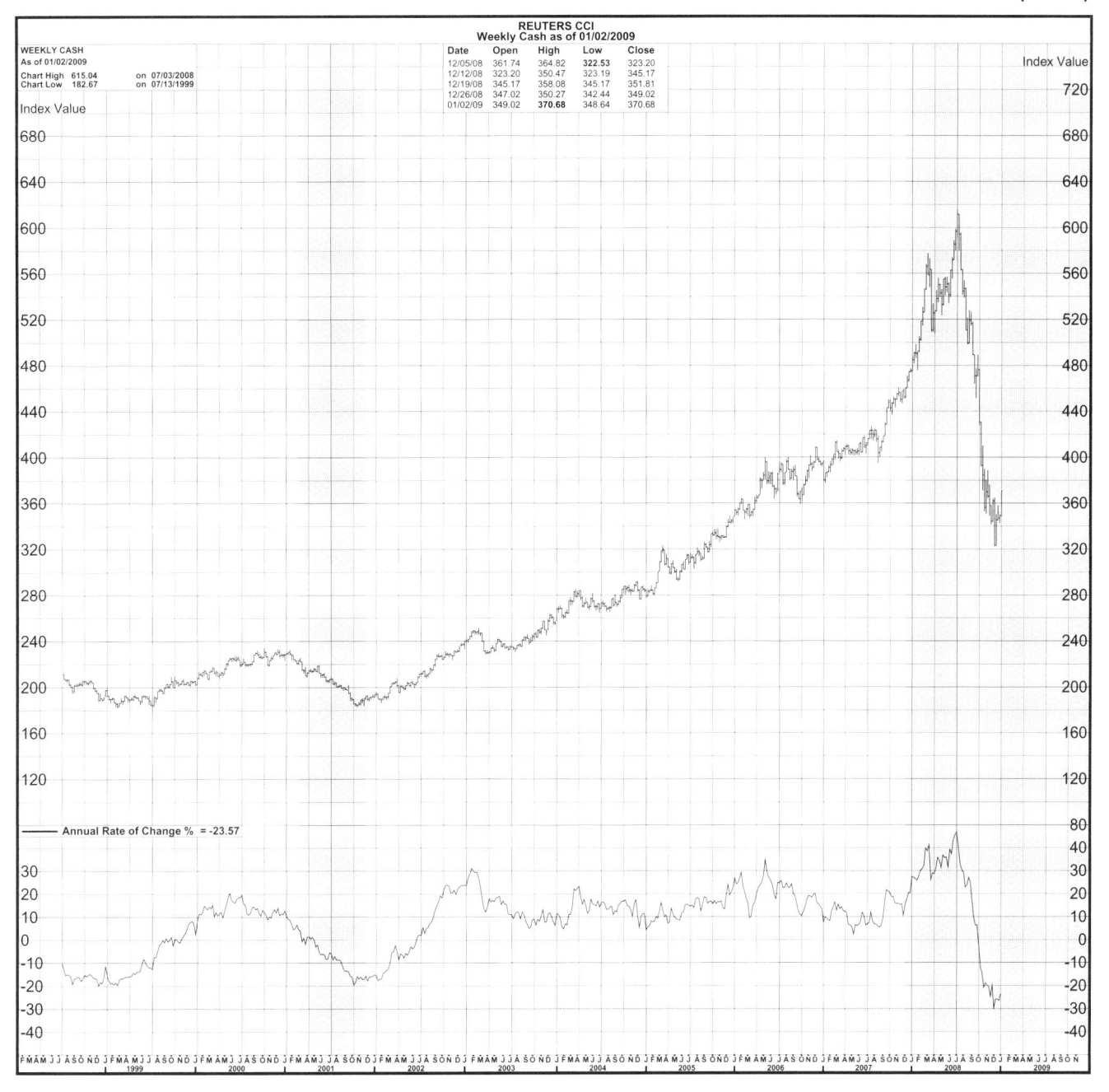

**WEEKLY CASH**
As of 01/02/2009
Chart High 615.04 on 07/03/2008
Chart Low 182.67 on 07/13/1999
Index Value

REUTERS CCI
Weekly Cash as of 01/02/2009

| Date | Open | High | Low | Close |
|---|---|---|---|---|
| 12/05/08 | 361.74 | 364.82 | 322.53 | 323.20 |
| 12/12/08 | 323.20 | 350.47 | 323.19 | 345.17 |
| 12/19/08 | 345.17 | 358.08 | 345.17 | 351.81 |
| 12/26/08 | 347.02 | 350.27 | 342.44 | 349.02 |
| 01/02/09 | 349.02 | 370.68 | 348.64 | 370.68 |

Annual Rate of Change % = -23.57

## Quarterly High, Low and Settle of Continuous Commodity Index (CCI)   Index Value

| Quarter | High | Low | Settle | Quarter | High | Low | Settle | Quarter | High | Low | Settle |
|---|---|---|---|---|---|---|---|---|---|---|---|
| 03/2000 | 217.88 | 201.43 | 214.37 | 03/2003 | 251.59 | 228.10 | 232.15 | 03/2006 | 365.66 | 345.49 | 361.91 |
| 06/2000 | 227.29 | 207.61 | 223.93 | 06/2003 | 242.16 | 228.77 | 233.78 | 06/2006 | 399.66 | 360.85 | 385.63 |
| 09/2000 | 232.20 | 217.42 | 226.57 | 09/2003 | 246.07 | 230.36 | 243.66 | 09/2006 | 399.90 | 359.07 | 370.10 |
| 12/2000 | 234.38 | 218.38 | 227.83 | 12/2003 | 263.60 | 241.68 | 255.29 | 12/2006 | 409.65 | 361.19 | 394.89 |
| 03/2001 | 232.58 | 210.24 | 210.26 | 03/2004 | 285.28 | 257.49 | 283.77 | 03/2007 | 414.62 | 377.59 | 407.45 |
| 06/2001 | 219.29 | 203.86 | 205.56 | 06/2004 | 284.42 | 264.34 | 265.94 | 06/2007 | 418.59 | 401.16 | 410.36 |
| 09/2001 | 209.27 | 188.24 | 190.49 | 09/2004 | 285.37 | 265.20 | 284.98 | 09/2007 | 450.36 | 395.03 | 447.56 |
| 12/2001 | 193.94 | 182.83 | 190.61 | 12/2004 | 292.49 | 276.15 | 283.90 | 12/2007 | 477.48 | 436.88 | 476.08 |
| 03/2002 | 205.45 | 186.38 | 204.92 | 03/2005 | 323.33 | 277.07 | 313.57 | 03/2008 | 577.64 | 475.91 | 516.38 |
| 06/2002 | 209.33 | 195.21 | 209.29 | 06/2005 | 315.79 | 292.06 | 306.91 | 06/2008 | 599.36 | 507.82 | 595.98 |
| 09/2002 | 229.62 | 207.24 | 226.53 | 09/2005 | 333.58 | 302.71 | 333.33 | 09/2008 | 615.04 | 449.70 | 452.42 |
| 12/2002 | 238.39 | 223.29 | 234.52 | 12/2005 | 349.20 | 326.09 | 347.89 | 12/2008 | 457.69 | 322.53 | 363.06 |

1967=100.   Index data begins 09/04/1956.   *Source: Thomson Reuters*

# REUTERS/JEFFERIES-CRB INDEX

**RJ/CRB Index Weekly Cash as of 01/02/2009**

| Date | Open | High | Low | Close |
|---|---|---|---|---|
| 12/05/08 | 242.20 | 244.04 | 208.58 | 208.60 |
| 12/12/08 | 208.60 | 236.10 | 208.60 | 226.96 |
| 12/19/08 | 226.96 | 231.40 | 218.59 | 220.08 |
| 12/26/08 | 218.87 | 219.57 | 210.33 | 215.28 |
| 01/02/09 | 215.28 | 233.93 | 214.93 | 233.92 |

WEEKLY CASH As of 01/02/2009
Chart High 473.97 on 07/03/2008
Chart Low 182.67 on 07/13/1999

Annual Rate of Change % = -36.13

## Quarterly High, Low and Settle of Reuters/Jefferies-CRB Index    Index Value

| Quarter | High | Low | Settle | Quarter | High | Low | Settle | Quarter | High | Low | Settle |
|---|---|---|---|---|---|---|---|---|---|---|---|
| 03/2000 | 217.88 | 201.43 | 214.37 | 03/2003 | 251.59 | 228.10 | 232.15 | 03/2006 | 350.96 | 316.06 | 333.18 |
| 06/2000 | 227.29 | 207.61 | 223.93 | 06/2003 | 242.16 | 228.77 | 233.78 | 06/2006 | 365.45 | 329.61 | 346.39 |
| 09/2000 | 232.20 | 217.42 | 226.57 | 09/2003 | 246.07 | 230.36 | 243.66 | 09/2006 | 358.43 | 296.81 | 305.58 |
| 12/2000 | 234.38 | 218.38 | 227.83 | 12/2003 | 263.60 | 241.68 | 255.29 | 12/2006 | 322.56 | 292.72 | 307.26 |
| 03/2001 | 232.58 | 210.24 | 210.26 | 03/2004 | 285.28 | 257.49 | 283.77 | 03/2007 | 318.85 | 284.61 | 316.88 |
| 06/2001 | 219.29 | 203.86 | 205.56 | 06/2004 | 284.42 | 264.34 | 265.94 | 06/2007 | 321.35 | 306.80 | 315.74 |
| 09/2001 | 209.27 | 188.24 | 190.49 | 09/2004 | 285.37 | 265.20 | 284.98 | 09/2007 | 338.22 | 299.01 | 333.67 |
| 12/2001 | 193.94 | 182.83 | 190.61 | 12/2004 | 292.49 | 276.15 | 283.90 | 12/2007 | 361.95 | 323.19 | 358.71 |
| 03/2002 | 205.45 | 186.38 | 204.92 | 03/2005 | 323.33 | 277.07 | 313.57 | 03/2008 | 422.12 | 349.05 | 386.89 |
| 06/2002 | 209.33 | 195.21 | 209.29 | 06/2005 | 313.91 | 292.06 | 300.00 | 06/2008 | 467.60 | 380.42 | 462.74 |
| 09/2002 | 229.62 | 207.24 | 226.53 | 09/2005 | 337.18 | 299.51 | 332.97 | 09/2008 | 473.97 | 337.44 | 345.50 |
| 12/2002 | 238.39 | 223.29 | 234.52 | 12/2005 | 336.42 | 310.81 | 331.83 | 12/2008 | 346.06 | 208.58 | 229.54 |

1967=100.    Data through 06/17/2005 is CCI.    *Source: Thomson Reuters*

# REUTERS/JEFFERIES-CRB TOTAL RETURN INDEX

**Quarterly High, Low and Settle of Reuters/Jefferies-CRB Total Return Index**  Index Value

| Quarter | High | Low | Settle | Quarter | High | Low | Settle | Quarter | High | Low | Settle |
|---|---|---|---|---|---|---|---|---|---|---|---|
| 03/2000 | 189.08 | 174.04 | 186.68 | 03/2003 | 214.03 | 197.50 | 200.92 | 03/2006 | 315.23 | 285.17 | 301.44 |
| 06/2000 | 207.52 | 182.09 | 195.06 | 06/2003 | 209.88 | 197.14 | 202.54 | 06/2006 | 332.34 | 300.26 | 317.15 |
| 09/2000 | 202.74 | 189.98 | 200.19 | 09/2003 | 212.32 | 200.34 | 210.87 | 09/2006 | 328.77 | 275.34 | 283.32 |
| 12/2000 | 211.22 | 194.82 | 203.47 | 12/2003 | 228.14 | 209.48 | 222.14 | 12/2006 | 301.62 | 271.67 | 288.44 |
| 03/2001 | 207.07 | 187.62 | 189.30 | 03/2004 | 250.33 | 224.03 | 249.10 | 03/2007 | 303.12 | 268.16 | 301.27 |
| 06/2001 | 197.31 | 182.57 | 183.78 | 06/2004 | 250.23 | 231.16 | 234.32 | 06/2007 | 308.76 | 293.57 | 303.84 |
| 09/2001 | 187.56 | 169.25 | 170.11 | 09/2004 | 249.35 | 229.06 | 249.04 | 09/2007 | 329.14 | 289.77 | 324.72 |
| 12/2001 | 171.37 | 163.56 | 168.51 | 12/2004 | 255.20 | 242.46 | 249.80 | 12/2007 | 358.95 | 314.89 | 352.33 |
| 03/2002 | 179.41 | 164.07 | 178.98 | 03/2005 | 284.41 | 243.43 | 276.15 | 03/2008 | 416.68 | 343.53 | 382.13 |
| 06/2002 | 182.33 | 170.68 | 179.55 | 06/2005 | 276.48 | 257.06 | 268.09 | 06/2008 | 463.78 | 375.76 | 458.96 |
| 09/2002 | 195.57 | 179.38 | 192.98 | 09/2005 | 297.97 | 263.63 | 295.06 | 09/2008 | 470.17 | 332.29 | 344.17 |
| 12/2002 | 202.15 | 189.16 | 199.55 | 12/2005 | 305.04 | 277.24 | 296.91 | 12/2008 | 344.70 | 207.97 | 228.88 |

Data through 06/16/2005 theoretical.  *Source: Thomson Reuters*

# CCI INDUSTRIALS SUB-INDEX

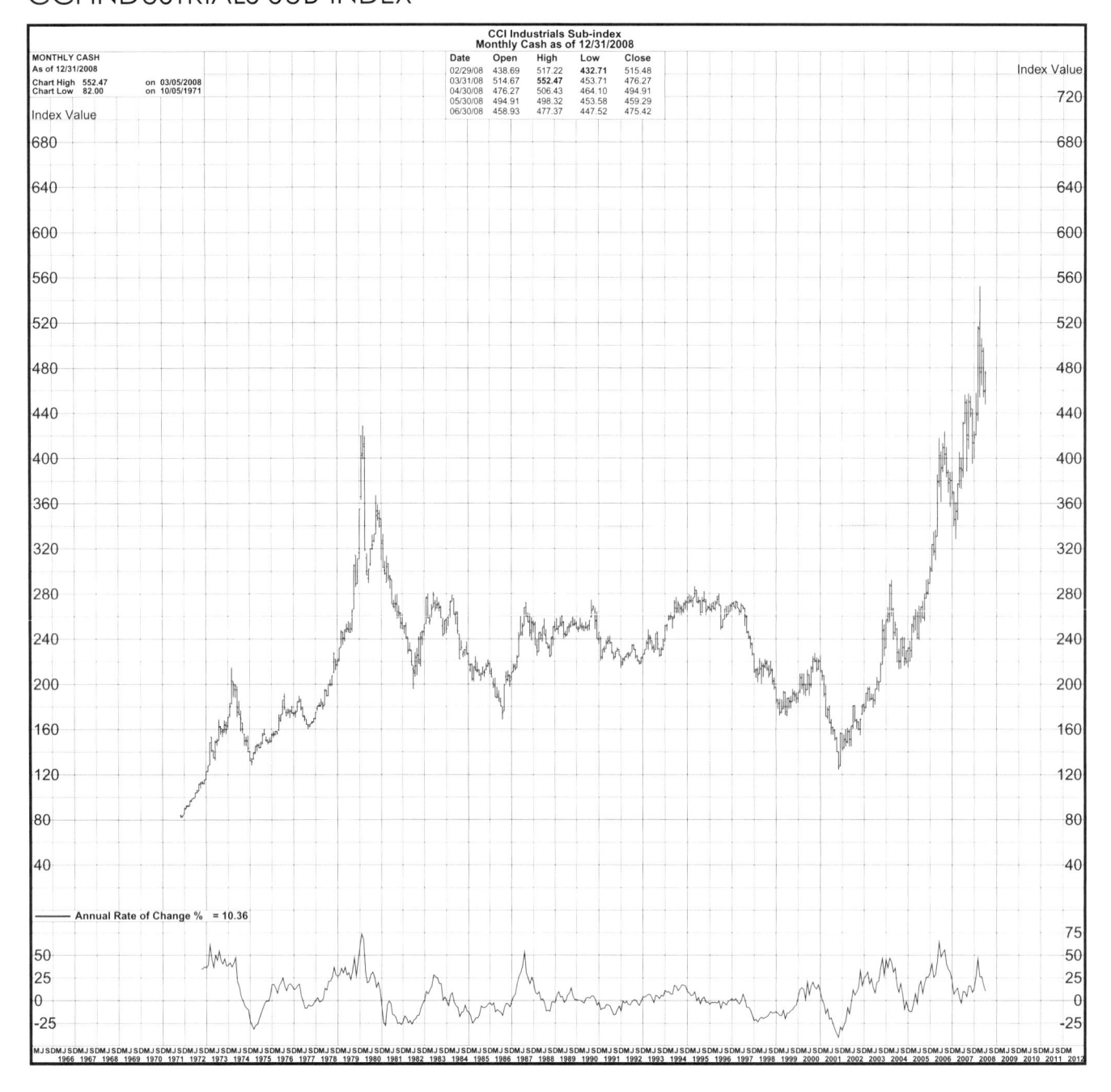

**Annual High, Low and Settle of CCI Industrials Sub-Index**   Index Value

| Year | High | Low | Settle | Year | High | Low | Settle | Year | High | Low | Settle |
|---|---|---|---|---|---|---|---|---|---|---|---|
| 1967 | | | | 1981 | 333.00 | 248.70 | 249.20 | 1995 | 286.88 | 261.03 | 265.50 |
| 1968 | | | | 1982 | 254.60 | 195.50 | 249.90 | 1996 | 280.33 | 247.96 | 271.12 |
| 1969 | | | | 1983 | 281.90 | 242.70 | 249.00 | 1997 | 273.97 | 210.14 | 210.91 |
| 1970 | | | | 1984 | 278.70 | 216.80 | 217.00 | 1998 | 223.07 | 182.56 | 185.30 |
| 1971 | 90.30 | 82.00 | 90.30 | 1985 | 224.70 | 202.10 | 211.70 | 1999 | 196.14 | 171.38 | 192.88 |
| 1972 | 122.90 | 89.70 | 122.80 | 1986 | 214.30 | 168.50 | 210.39 | 2000 | 227.84 | 189.34 | 210.99 |
| 1973 | 171.30 | 122.60 | 170.70 | 1987 | 272.33 | 210.71 | 252.47 | 2001 | 212.45 | 124.26 | 141.84 |
| 1974 | 214.80 | 132.10 | 132.10 | 1988 | 258.12 | 224.08 | 246.96 | 2002 | 183.06 | 142.65 | 176.61 |
| 1975 | 160.60 | 128.00 | 154.80 | 1989 | 261.00 | 240.59 | 249.64 | 2003 | 257.50 | 178.46 | 256.64 |
| 1976 | 192.20 | 152.50 | 173.60 | 1990 | 274.74 | 235.48 | 245.46 | 2004 | 292.64 | 213.10 | 232.09 |
| 1977 | 190.00 | 160.30 | 175.00 | 1991 | 242.99 | 214.28 | 217.18 | 2005 | 304.46 | 220.18 | 302.48 |
| 1978 | 228.30 | 176.10 | 222.10 | 1992 | 235.58 | 216.27 | 226.35 | 2006 | 423.86 | 299.60 | 368.79 |
| 1979 | 354.80 | 220.50 | 354.80 | 1993 | 251.97 | 223.94 | 251.73 | 2007 | 457.56 | 328.24 | 418.30 |
| 1980 | 429.00 | 289.40 | 324.60 | 1994 | 277.11 | 246.90 | 276.81 | 2008 | 552.47 | 419.86 | 475.42 |

1967=100.   Index data begins 09/23/1971.   *Source: Thomson Reuters*

# CCI INDUSTRIALS SUB-INDEX

**CCI Industrials Sub-index**
Weekly Cash as of 06/13/2008

| Date | Open | High | Low | Close |
|---|---|---|---|---|
| 05/16/08 | 484.94 | 495.67 | 476.93 | 493.54 |
| 05/23/08 | 493.54 | 493.65 | 471.96 | 479.00 |
| 05/30/08 | 479.00 | 489.79 | 453.58 | 459.29 |
| 06/06/08 | 458.93 | 463.73 | 447.52 | 462.21 |
| 06/13/08 | 462.21 | 477.37 | 456.01 | 475.42 |

WEEKLY CASH
As of 06/13/2008
Chart High 552.47 on 03/05/2008
Chart Low 124.26 on 10/25/2001

Annual Rate of Change % = 17.86

## Quarterly High, Low and Settle of CCI Industrials Sub-Index    Index Value

| Quarter | High | Low | Settle | Quarter | High | Low | Settle | Quarter | High | Low | Settle |
|---|---|---|---|---|---|---|---|---|---|---|---|
| 03/2000 | 209.80 | 190.50 | 200.09 | 03/2003 | 198.15 | 178.46 | 187.09 | 03/2006 | 336.66 | 299.60 | 330.91 |
| 06/2000 | 212.95 | 189.34 | 199.39 | 06/2003 | 196.23 | 178.98 | 195.93 | 06/2006 | 418.08 | 330.91 | 391.62 |
| 09/2000 | 227.84 | 196.70 | 220.74 | 09/2003 | 219.18 | 193.71 | 217.52 | 09/2006 | 423.86 | 383.31 | 387.46 |
| 12/2000 | 225.65 | 210.82 | 210.99 | 12/2003 | 257.50 | 217.16 | 256.64 | 12/2006 | 389.90 | 356.74 | 368.79 |
| 03/2001 | 212.45 | 171.20 | 171.28 | 03/2004 | 292.64 | 253.95 | 266.31 | 03/2007 | 377.59 | 328.24 | 376.99 |
| 06/2001 | 181.27 | 155.17 | 161.63 | 06/2004 | 267.65 | 219.24 | 228.16 | 06/2007 | 432.49 | 372.73 | 430.78 |
| 09/2001 | 162.31 | 139.84 | 140.21 | 09/2004 | 242.14 | 213.10 | 232.62 | 09/2007 | 457.56 | 388.31 | 449.85 |
| 12/2001 | 157.33 | 124.26 | 141.84 | 12/2004 | 241.64 | 214.81 | 232.09 | 12/2007 | 455.40 | 395.12 | 418.30 |
| 03/2002 | 161.29 | 142.65 | 158.09 | 03/2005 | 260.65 | 220.18 | 258.08 | 03/2008 | 552.47 | 419.86 | 476.27 |
| 06/2002 | 181.24 | 144.45 | 180.95 | 06/2005 | 269.67 | 239.04 | 264.67 | 06/2008 | 506.43 | 447.52 | 475.42 |
| 09/2002 | 181.36 | 159.05 | 160.11 | 09/2005 | 279.95 | 253.93 | 276.01 | 09/2008 | | | |
| 12/2002 | 183.06 | 154.54 | 176.61 | 12/2005 | 304.46 | 275.91 | 302.48 | 12/2008 | | | |

1967=100.    *Source: Thomson Reuters*

# CCI GRAINS & OILSEEDS SUB-INDEX

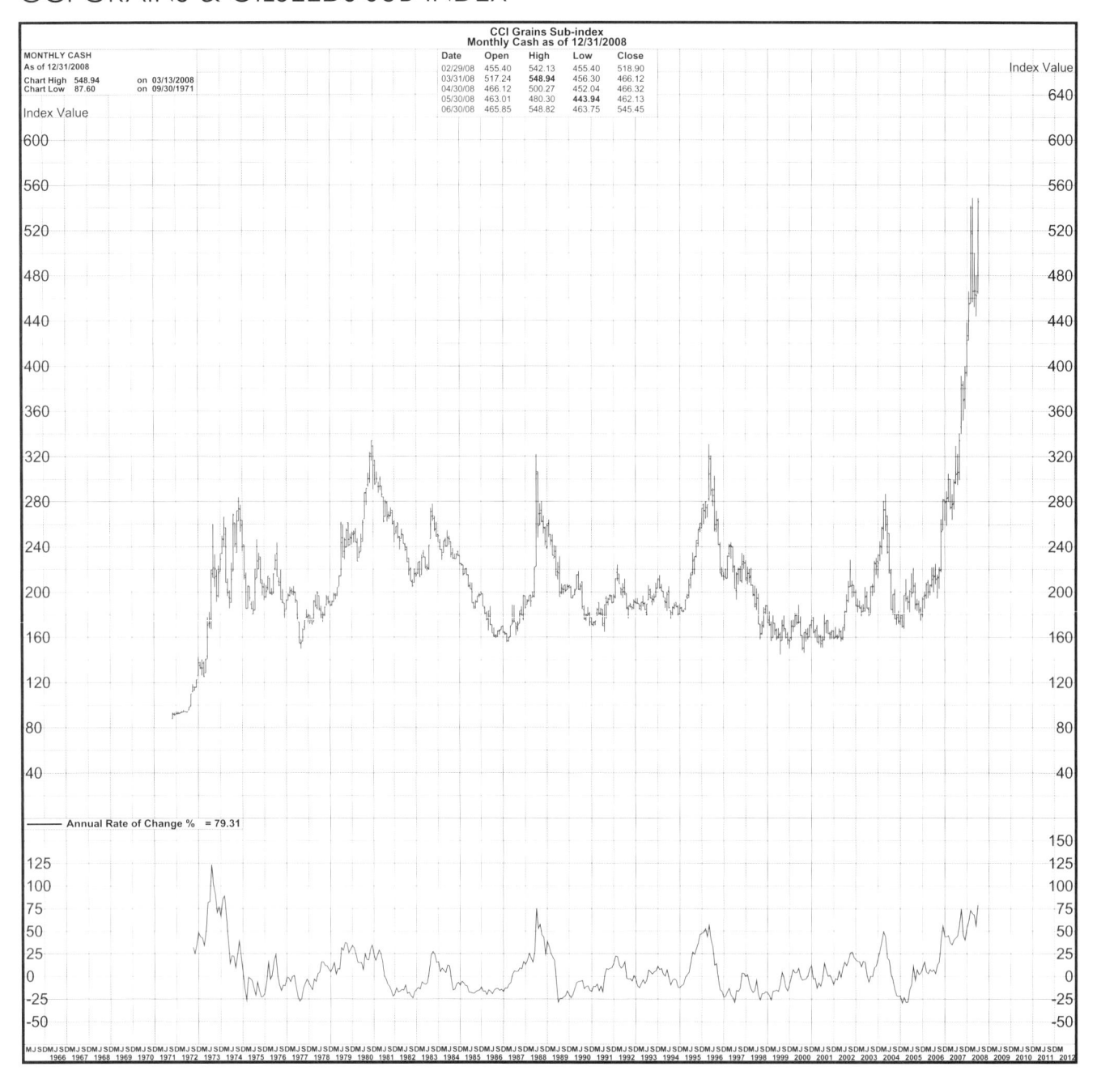

**CCI Grains Sub-index**
Monthly Cash as of 12/31/2008

| Date | Open | High | Low | Close |
|---|---|---|---|---|
| 02/29/08 | 455.40 | 542.13 | 455.40 | 518.90 |
| 03/31/08 | 517.24 | 548.94 | 456.30 | 466.12 |
| 04/30/08 | 466.12 | 500.27 | 452.04 | 466.32 |
| 05/30/08 | 463.01 | 480.30 | 443.94 | 462.13 |
| 06/30/08 | 465.85 | 548.82 | 463.75 | 545.45 |

MONTHLY CASH As of 12/31/2008
Chart High 548.94 on 03/13/2008
Chart Low 87.60 on 09/30/1971

Annual Rate of Change % = 79.31

## Annual High, Low and Settle of CCI Grains Sub-Index    Index Value

| Year | High | Low | Settle | Year | High | Low | Settle | Year | High | Low | Settle |
|---|---|---|---|---|---|---|---|---|---|---|---|
| 1967 | | | | 1981 | 317.10 | 243.60 | 251.30 | 1995 | 274.01 | 182.24 | 274.01 |
| 1968 | | | | 1982 | 261.10 | 204.20 | 215.10 | 1996 | 330.94 | 210.96 | 211.24 |
| 1969 | | | | 1983 | 278.00 | 213.20 | 249.60 | 1997 | 244.02 | 193.03 | 210.67 |
| 1970 | | | | 1984 | 254.50 | 224.50 | 224.90 | 1998 | 222.65 | 157.83 | 172.84 |
| 1971 | 94.20 | 87.60 | 92.50 | 1985 | 225.20 | 184.80 | 198.50 | 1999 | 182.96 | 144.63 | 156.64 |
| 1972 | 142.60 | 91.60 | 137.50 | 1986 | 198.50 | 159.10 | 164.63 | 2000 | 188.94 | 146.04 | 174.94 |
| 1973 | 259.80 | 124.70 | 228.90 | 1987 | 197.43 | 155.36 | 186.14 | 2001 | 181.12 | 150.62 | 159.04 |
| 1974 | 283.80 | 185.00 | 240.20 | 1988 | 322.00 | 186.45 | 258.47 | 2002 | 228.67 | 156.03 | 188.23 |
| 1975 | 246.70 | 180.60 | 195.60 | 1989 | 263.87 | 195.58 | 205.74 | 2003 | 233.61 | 178.33 | 225.75 |
| 1976 | 243.90 | 176.70 | 192.50 | 1990 | 218.72 | 169.68 | 171.18 | 2004 | 286.90 | 170.71 | 176.99 |
| 1977 | 205.50 | 149.50 | 179.00 | 1991 | 198.10 | 164.51 | 196.11 | 2005 | 221.67 | 167.32 | 193.79 |
| 1978 | 200.90 | 171.30 | 187.80 | 1992 | 224.36 | 176.25 | 190.43 | 2006 | 282.36 | 185.12 | 279.13 |
| 1979 | 262.00 | 187.40 | 251.90 | 1993 | 211.77 | 178.63 | 211.77 | 2007 | 438.54 | 258.39 | 426.98 |
| 1980 | 333.80 | 227.20 | 312.10 | 1994 | 215.14 | 176.01 | 185.50 | 2008 | 548.94 | 422.89 | 545.45 |

1967=100.   Index data begins 09/23/1971.   *Source: Thomson Reuters*

# CCI GRAINS & OILSEEDS SUB-INDEX

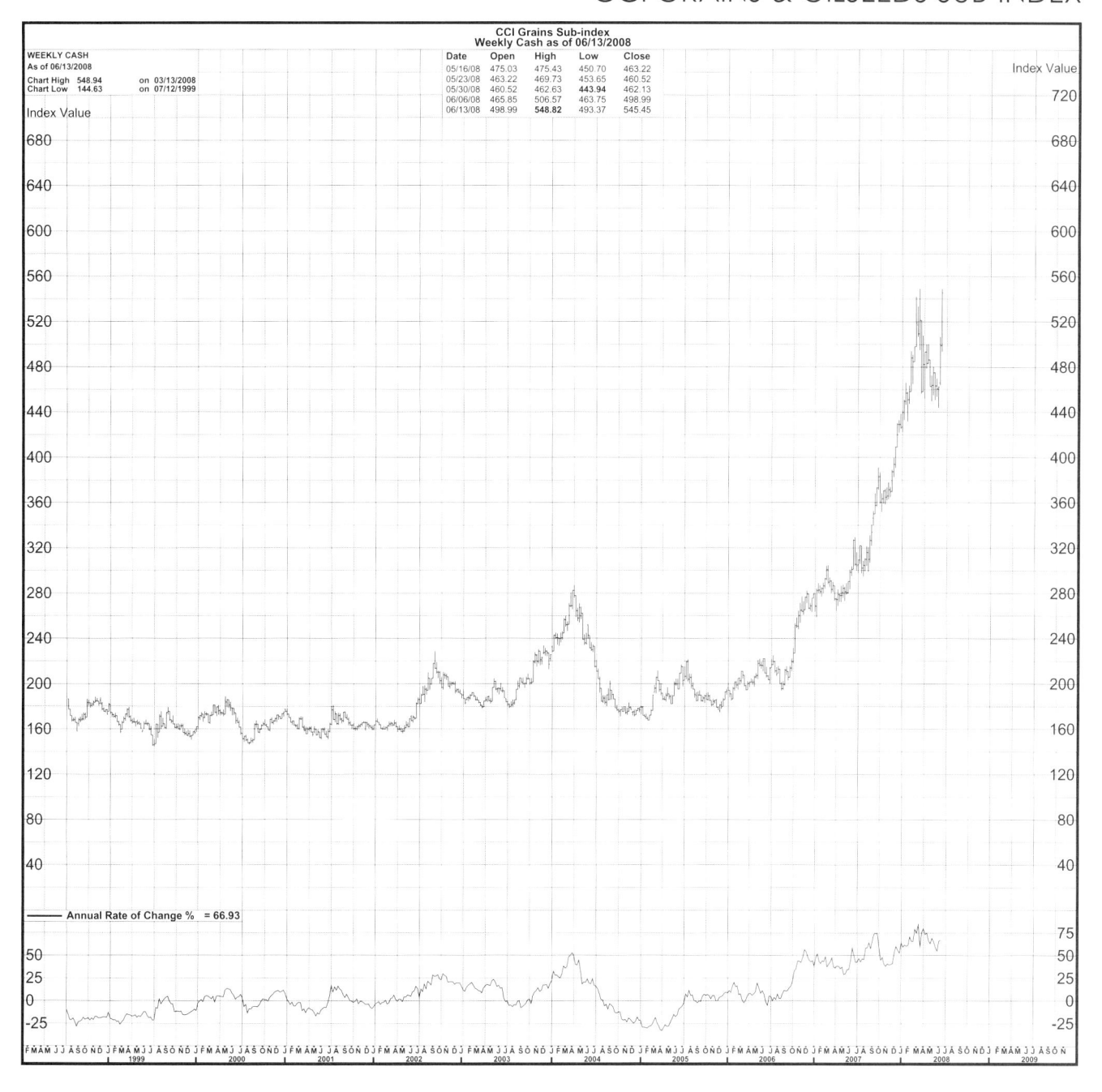

**CCI Grains Sub-index**
Weekly Cash as of 06/13/2008

| Date | Open | High | Low | Close |
|---|---|---|---|---|
| 05/16/08 | 475.03 | 475.43 | 450.70 | 463.22 |
| 05/23/08 | 463.22 | 469.73 | 453.65 | 460.52 |
| 05/30/08 | 460.52 | 462.63 | 443.94 | 462.13 |
| 06/06/08 | 465.85 | 506.57 | 463.75 | 498.99 |
| 06/13/08 | 498.99 | 548.82 | 493.37 | 545.45 |

WEEKLY CASH
As of 06/13/2008
Chart High 548.94 on 03/13/2008
Chart Low 144.63 on 07/12/1999

Annual Rate of Change % = 66.93

## Quarterly High, Low and Settle of CCI Grains Sub-Index — Index Value

| Quarter | High | Low | Settle | Quarter | High | Low | Settle | Quarter | High | Low | Settle |
|---|---|---|---|---|---|---|---|---|---|---|---|
| 03/2000 | 181.42 | 157.06 | 179.25 | 03/2003 | 194.35 | 178.33 | 182.69 | 03/2006 | 211.09 | 185.12 | 200.27 |
| 06/2000 | 188.94 | 161.19 | 161.43 | 06/2003 | 204.78 | 182.10 | 185.66 | 06/2006 | 222.29 | 196.82 | 213.62 |
| 09/2000 | 167.43 | 146.04 | 163.01 | 09/2003 | 207.67 | 178.41 | 205.04 | 09/2006 | 225.15 | 193.94 | 219.38 |
| 12/2000 | 174.96 | 157.60 | 174.94 | 12/2003 | 233.61 | 199.09 | 225.75 | 12/2006 | 282.36 | 217.64 | 279.13 |
| 03/2001 | 177.85 | 155.33 | 155.63 | 03/2004 | 280.73 | 227.31 | 272.63 | 03/2007 | 304.88 | 258.39 | 274.82 |
| 06/2001 | 162.56 | 150.62 | 157.73 | 06/2004 | 286.90 | 216.33 | 218.92 | 06/2007 | 329.59 | 263.74 | 304.20 |
| 09/2001 | 181.12 | 156.78 | 163.24 | 09/2004 | 220.61 | 175.85 | 176.21 | 09/2007 | 391.40 | 294.53 | 383.01 |
| 12/2001 | 166.66 | 158.06 | 159.04 | 12/2004 | 183.42 | 170.71 | 176.99 | 12/2007 | 438.54 | 351.60 | 426.98 |
| 03/2002 | 169.35 | 158.04 | 165.11 | 03/2005 | 211.78 | 167.32 | 194.31 | 03/2008 | 548.94 | 422.89 | 466.12 |
| 06/2002 | 183.37 | 156.03 | 182.72 | 06/2005 | 216.95 | 181.94 | 198.97 | 06/2008 | 548.82 | 443.94 | 545.45 |
| 09/2002 | 228.67 | 181.81 | 205.57 | 09/2005 | 221.67 | 183.06 | 189.25 | 09/2008 | | | |
| 12/2002 | 210.47 | 187.47 | 188.23 | 12/2005 | 195.55 | 174.46 | 193.79 | 12/2008 | | | |

1967=100. *Source: Thomson Reuters*

# CCI LIVESTOCK & MEATS SUB-INDEX

**CCI Livestock & Meats Sub-index**
Monthly Cash as of 12/31/2008

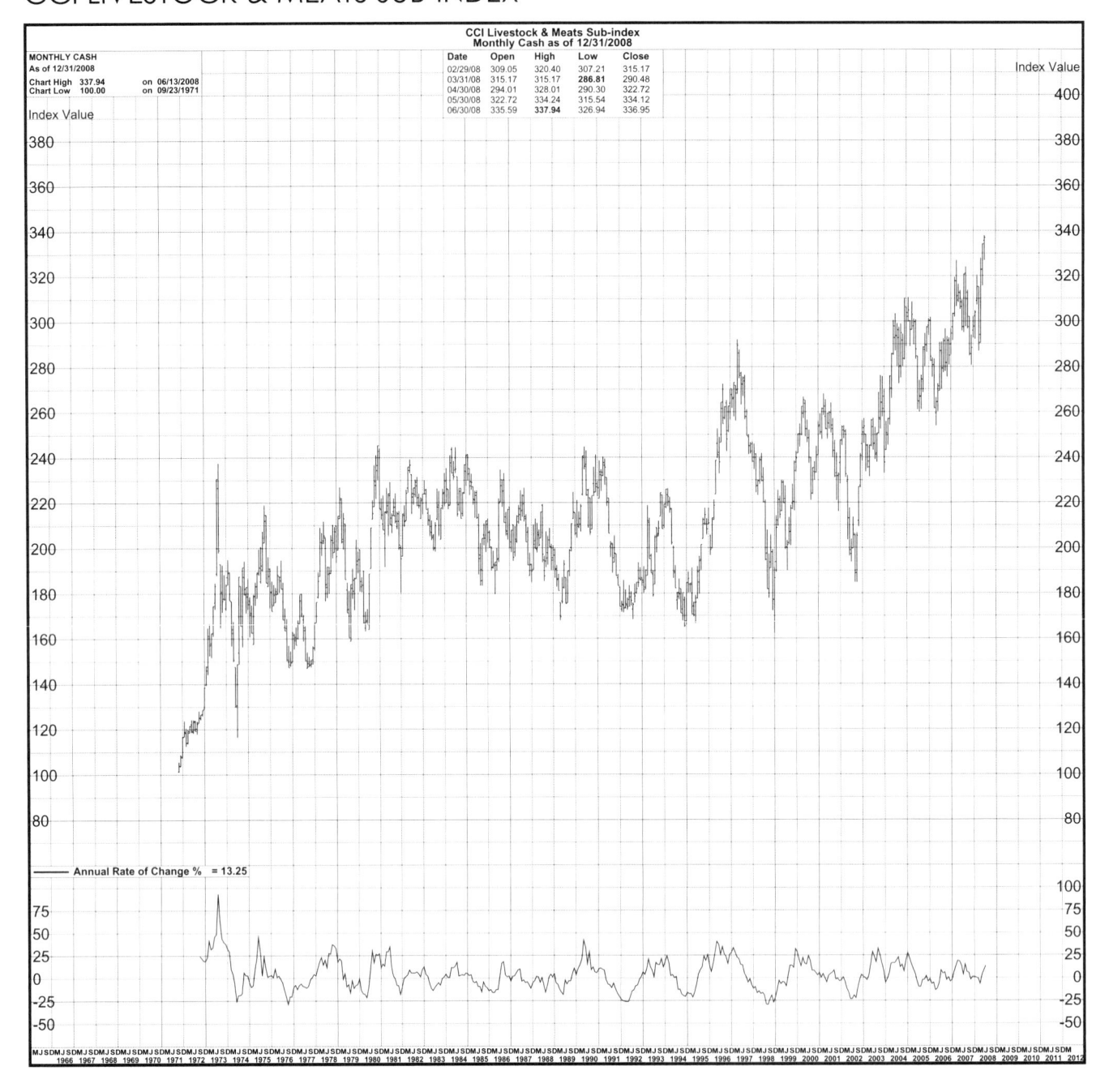

| Date | Open | High | Low | Close |
|---|---|---|---|---|
| 02/29/08 | 309.05 | 320.40 | 307.21 | 315.17 |
| 03/31/08 | 315.17 | 315.17 | 286.81 | 290.48 |
| 04/30/08 | 294.01 | 328.01 | 290.30 | 322.72 |
| 05/30/08 | 322.72 | 334.24 | 315.54 | 334.12 |
| 06/30/08 | 335.59 | 337.94 | 326.94 | 336.95 |

MONTHLY CASH As of 12/31/2008
Chart High 337.94 on 06/13/2008
Chart Low 100.00 on 09/23/1971

Annual Rate of Change % = 13.25

## Annual High, Low and Settle of CCI Livestock & Meats Sub-Index    Index Value

| Year | High | Low | Settle | Year | High | Low | Settle | Year | High | Low | Settle |
|---|---|---|---|---|---|---|---|---|---|---|---|
| 1967 | | | | 1981 | 229.30 | 180.60 | 195.30 | 1995 | 217.60 | 166.60 | 210.90 |
| 1968 | | | | 1982 | 239.20 | 196.40 | 219.90 | 1996 | 272.44 | 196.70 | 270.14 |
| 1969 | | | | 1983 | 233.20 | 198.40 | 229.70 | 1997 | 292.07 | 237.99 | 238.12 |
| 1970 | | | | 1984 | 244.60 | 213.00 | 240.80 | 1998 | 246.01 | 162.42 | 186.70 |
| 1971 | 116.80 | 100.00 | 116.60 | 1985 | 241.40 | 183.40 | 206.90 | 1999 | 242.59 | 189.21 | 239.61 |
| 1972 | 138.50 | 112.50 | 138.50 | 1986 | 234.70 | 179.60 | 200.16 | 2000 | 266.65 | 220.93 | 253.56 |
| 1973 | 237.60 | 139.40 | 183.70 | 1987 | 226.70 | 184.87 | 189.85 | 2001 | 268.06 | 215.98 | 247.41 |
| 1974 | 195.00 | 116.40 | 175.20 | 1988 | 219.34 | 185.30 | 199.10 | 2002 | 256.16 | 184.73 | 250.97 |
| 1975 | 219.00 | 157.60 | 180.80 | 1989 | 224.70 | 167.91 | 206.45 | 2003 | 276.19 | 231.38 | 237.77 |
| 1976 | 194.70 | 147.30 | 162.50 | 1990 | 244.73 | 204.43 | 226.61 | 2004 | 310.11 | 242.99 | 303.64 |
| 1977 | 180.20 | 147.00 | 166.90 | 1991 | 240.38 | 174.01 | 174.01 | 2005 | 310.55 | 260.03 | 300.28 |
| 1978 | 211.80 | 167.00 | 196.40 | 1992 | 193.63 | 168.32 | 185.67 | 2006 | 301.88 | 253.76 | 294.62 |
| 1979 | 227.00 | 158.90 | 195.00 | 1993 | 224.28 | 178.38 | 219.25 | 2007 | 327.00 | 280.64 | 297.68 |
| 1980 | 245.30 | 163.20 | 217.40 | 1994 | 226.34 | 164.91 | 184.64 | 2008 | 337.94 | 286.81 | 336.95 |

1967=100.    Index data begins 09/23/1971.    *Source: Thomson Reuters*

# CCI LIVESTOCK & MEATS SUB-INDEX

## Quarterly High, Low and Settle of CCI Livestock & Meats Sub-Index    Index Value

| Quarter | High | Low | Settle | Quarter | High | Low | Settle | Quarter | High | Low | Settle |
|---|---|---|---|---|---|---|---|---|---|---|---|
| 03/2000 | 262.49 | 241.78 | 262.37 | 03/2003 | 257.22 | 233.62 | 238.21 | 03/2006 | 301.88 | 261.38 | 261.65 |
| 06/2000 | 266.65 | 246.44 | 248.49 | 06/2003 | 257.32 | 231.38 | 246.04 | 06/2006 | 290.84 | 253.76 | 286.98 |
| 09/2000 | 252.17 | 220.93 | 235.41 | 09/2003 | 268.64 | 237.84 | 257.27 | 09/2006 | 296.79 | 269.98 | 281.64 |
| 12/2000 | 255.82 | 229.94 | 253.56 | 12/2003 | 276.19 | 233.12 | 237.77 | 12/2006 | 296.69 | 275.32 | 294.62 |
| 03/2001 | 268.06 | 247.84 | 262.42 | 03/2004 | 275.92 | 242.99 | 275.70 | 03/2007 | 327.00 | 291.51 | 311.09 |
| 06/2001 | 265.47 | 247.97 | 259.64 | 06/2004 | 303.47 | 265.88 | 293.58 | 06/2007 | 316.45 | 295.71 | 297.54 |
| 09/2001 | 264.03 | 231.06 | 231.65 | 09/2004 | 299.16 | 272.41 | 294.79 | 09/2007 | 324.03 | 295.03 | 297.49 |
| 12/2001 | 247.48 | 215.98 | 247.41 | 12/2004 | 310.11 | 280.26 | 303.64 | 12/2007 | 302.16 | 280.64 | 297.68 |
| 03/2002 | 254.05 | 231.21 | 232.60 | 03/2005 | 310.55 | 288.87 | 302.92 | 03/2008 | 320.40 | 286.81 | 290.48 |
| 06/2002 | 232.08 | 193.67 | 199.71 | 06/2005 | 301.13 | 260.92 | 264.65 | 06/2008 | 337.94 | 290.30 | 336.95 |
| 09/2002 | 213.57 | 184.73 | 205.31 | 09/2005 | 288.81 | 260.03 | 288.49 | 09/2008 | | | |
| 12/2002 | 256.16 | 209.38 | 250.97 | 12/2005 | 301.23 | 280.27 | 300.28 | 12/2008 | | | |

1967=100.   *Source: Thomson Reuters*

# CCI ENERGY SUB-INDEX

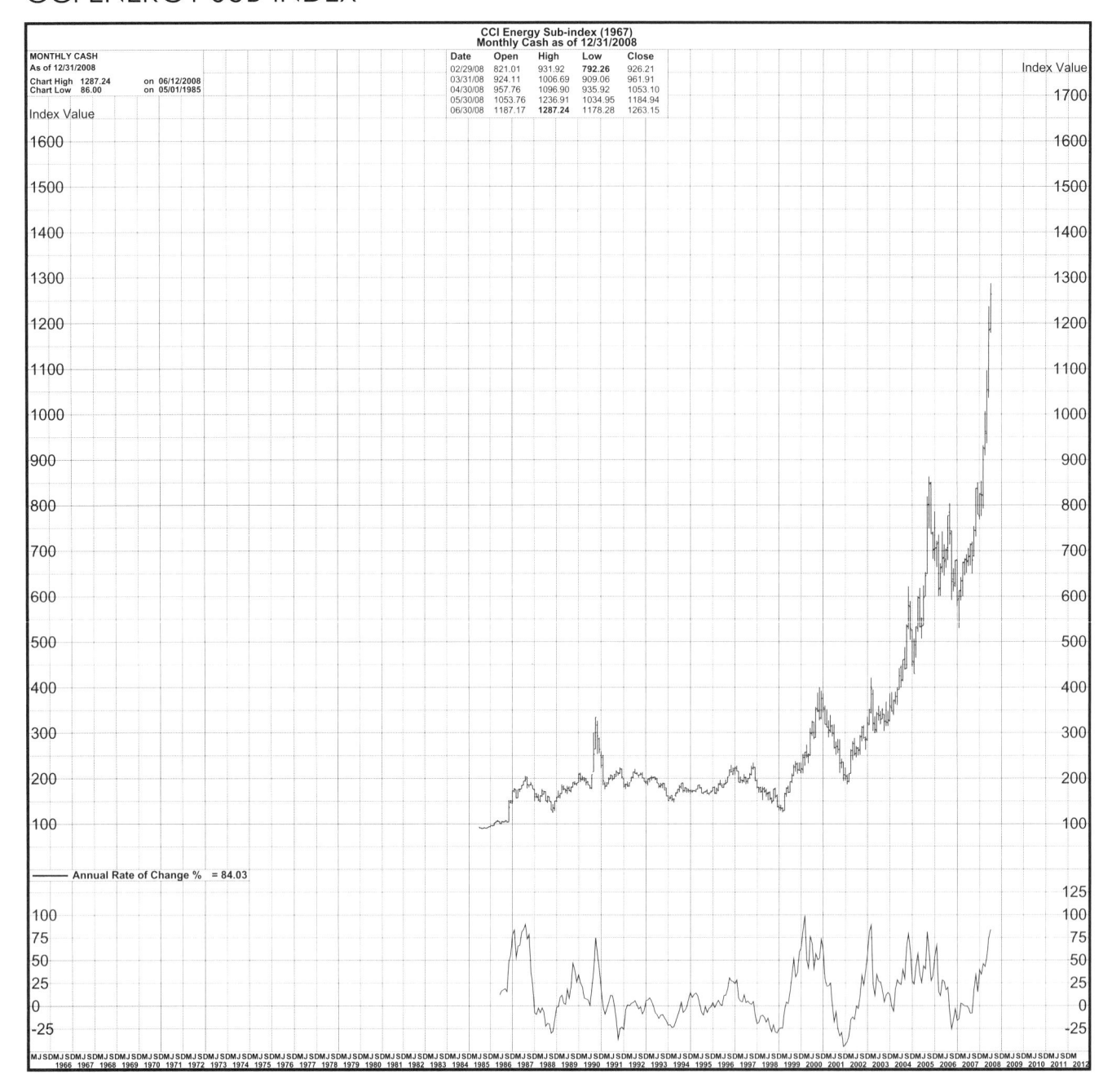

**CCI Energy Sub-index (1967)**
Monthly Cash as of 12/31/2008

MONTHLY CASH
As of 12/31/2008
Chart High 1287.24 on 06/12/2008
Chart Low 86.00 on 05/01/1985

| Date | Open | High | Low | Close |
|---|---|---|---|---|
| 02/29/08 | 821.01 | 931.92 | 792.26 | 926.21 |
| 03/31/08 | 924.11 | 1006.69 | 909.06 | 961.91 |
| 04/30/08 | 957.76 | 1096.90 | 935.92 | 1053.10 |
| 05/30/08 | 1053.76 | 1236.91 | 1034.95 | 1184.94 |
| 06/30/08 | 1187.17 | 1287.24 | 1178.28 | 1263.15 |

Annual Rate of Change % = 84.03

## Annual High, Low and Settle of CCI Energy Sub-Index — Index Value

| Year | High | Low | Settle | Year | High | Low | Settle | Year | High | Low | Settle |
|---|---|---|---|---|---|---|---|---|---|---|---|
| 1967 | | | | 1981 | | | | 1995 | 186.34 | 162.55 | 180.01 |
| 1968 | | | | 1982 | | | | 1996 | 229.31 | 165.60 | 224.04 |
| 1969 | | | | 1983 | | | | 1997 | 234.45 | 178.55 | 180.36 |
| 1970 | | | | 1984 | | | | 1998 | 181.80 | 129.20 | 134.96 |
| 1971 | | | | 1985 | 96.70 | 86.00 | 96.50 | 1999 | 237.59 | 124.97 | 220.99 |
| 1972 | | | | 1986 | 172.18 | 93.70 | 172.18 | 2000 | 399.38 | 210.45 | 355.78 |
| 1973 | | | | 1987 | 205.27 | 148.99 | 159.13 | 2001 | 360.20 | 193.76 | 204.87 |
| 1974 | | | | 1988 | 176.77 | 124.17 | 156.52 | 2002 | 335.31 | 186.36 | 320.67 |
| 1975 | | | | 1989 | 210.03 | 155.57 | 210.03 | 2003 | 421.31 | 298.76 | 358.74 |
| 1976 | | | | 1990 | 333.86 | 176.38 | 245.95 | 2004 | 621.83 | 338.00 | 457.27 |
| 1977 | | | | 1991 | 251.19 | 175.46 | 182.16 | 2005 | 863.37 | 429.79 | 705.34 |
| 1978 | | | | 1992 | 220.80 | 176.21 | 192.58 | 2006 | 804.10 | 578.05 | 591.55 |
| 1979 | | | | 1993 | 205.70 | 151.12 | 151.83 | 2007 | 850.46 | 529.28 | 825.13 |
| 1980 | | | | 1994 | 190.20 | 146.59 | 173.79 | 2008 | 1,287.24 | 775.59 | 1,263.15 |

1967=100.  Index data begins 05/01/1985.  Source: *Thomson Reuters*

# CCI ENERGY SUB-INDEX

**CCI Energy Sub-index (1967)**
Weekly Cash as of 06/13/2008

| Date | Open | High | Low | Close |
|---|---|---|---|---|
| 05/16/08 | 1170.45 | 1176.85 | 1149.10 | 1164.53 |
| 05/23/08 | 1164.53 | 1236.91 | 1159.74 | 1227.14 |
| 05/30/08 | 1227.14 | 1230.69 | 1179.37 | 1184.94 |
| 06/06/08 | 1187.17 | 1285.31 | 1178.28 | 1285.31 |
| 06/13/08 | 1285.31 | 1287.24 | 1241.09 | 1263.15 |

WEEKLY CASH
As of 06/13/2008
Chart High 1287.24 on 06/12/2008
Chart Low 124.97 on 02/16/1999

Annual Rate of Change % = 79.38

### Quarterly High, Low and Settle of CCI Energy Sub-Index    Index Value

| Quarter | High | Low | Settle | Quarter | High | Low | Settle | Quarter | High | Low | Settle |
|---|---|---|---|---|---|---|---|---|---|---|---|
| 03/2000 | 273.82 | 210.45 | 251.03 | 03/2003 | 421.31 | 303.30 | 320.87 | 03/2006 | 735.62 | 600.97 | 662.56 |
| 06/2000 | 326.23 | 232.37 | 323.44 | 06/2003 | 360.05 | 298.76 | 337.34 | 06/2006 | 742.61 | 644.90 | 701.14 |
| 09/2000 | 388.56 | 285.37 | 348.94 | 09/2003 | 354.37 | 303.08 | 324.77 | 09/2006 | 804.10 | 591.28 | 632.68 |
| 12/2000 | 399.38 | 326.59 | 355.78 | 12/2003 | 386.12 | 314.09 | 358.74 | 12/2006 | 679.66 | 578.05 | 591.55 |
| 03/2001 | 360.20 | 289.17 | 305.88 | 03/2004 | 390.65 | 338.00 | 379.91 | 03/2007 | 675.55 | 529.28 | 673.41 |
| 06/2001 | 339.07 | 264.54 | 266.86 | 06/2004 | 447.82 | 360.76 | 415.19 | 06/2007 | 705.88 | 645.60 | 686.39 |
| 09/2001 | 286.15 | 211.27 | 233.41 | 09/2004 | 537.91 | 412.67 | 534.50 | 09/2007 | 754.12 | 649.60 | 744.74 |
| 12/2001 | 243.03 | 193.76 | 204.87 | 12/2004 | 621.83 | 446.45 | 457.27 | 12/2007 | 850.46 | 730.61 | 825.13 |
| 03/2002 | 263.73 | 186.36 | 260.35 | 03/2005 | 600.24 | 429.79 | 597.25 | 03/2008 | 1,006.69 | 775.59 | 961.91 |
| 06/2002 | 288.53 | 239.15 | 265.89 | 06/2005 | 624.02 | 506.55 | 597.29 | 06/2008 | 1,287.24 | 935.92 | 1,263.15 |
| 09/2002 | 314.43 | 249.49 | 311.86 | 09/2005 | 863.37 | 599.93 | 847.12 | 09/2008 | | | |
| 12/2002 | 335.31 | 262.29 | 320.67 | 12/2005 | 851.76 | 676.76 | 705.34 | 12/2008 | | | |

1967=100.   *Source: Thomson Reuters*

# CCI PRECIOUS METALS SUB-INDEX

**MONTHLY CASH**
As of 12/31/2008
Chart High 1043.19 on 03/06/2008
Chart Low 133.50 on 01/26/1976

CCI Precious Metals Sub-index
Monthly Cash as of 12/31/2008

| Date | Open | High | Low | Close |
|---|---|---|---|---|
| 02/29/08 | 871.05 | 1007.89 | 856.02 | 1007.89 |
| 03/31/08 | 1008.56 | 1043.19 | 888.79 | 921.68 |
| 04/30/08 | 923.31 | 953.53 | 874.89 | 874.89 |
| 05/30/08 | 874.89 | 964.01 | 854.10 | 901.13 |
| 06/30/08 | 902.18 | 926.42 | 888.47 | 894.61 |

Annual Rate of Change % = 41.30

## Annual High, Low and Settle of CCI Precious Metals Sub-Index    Index Value

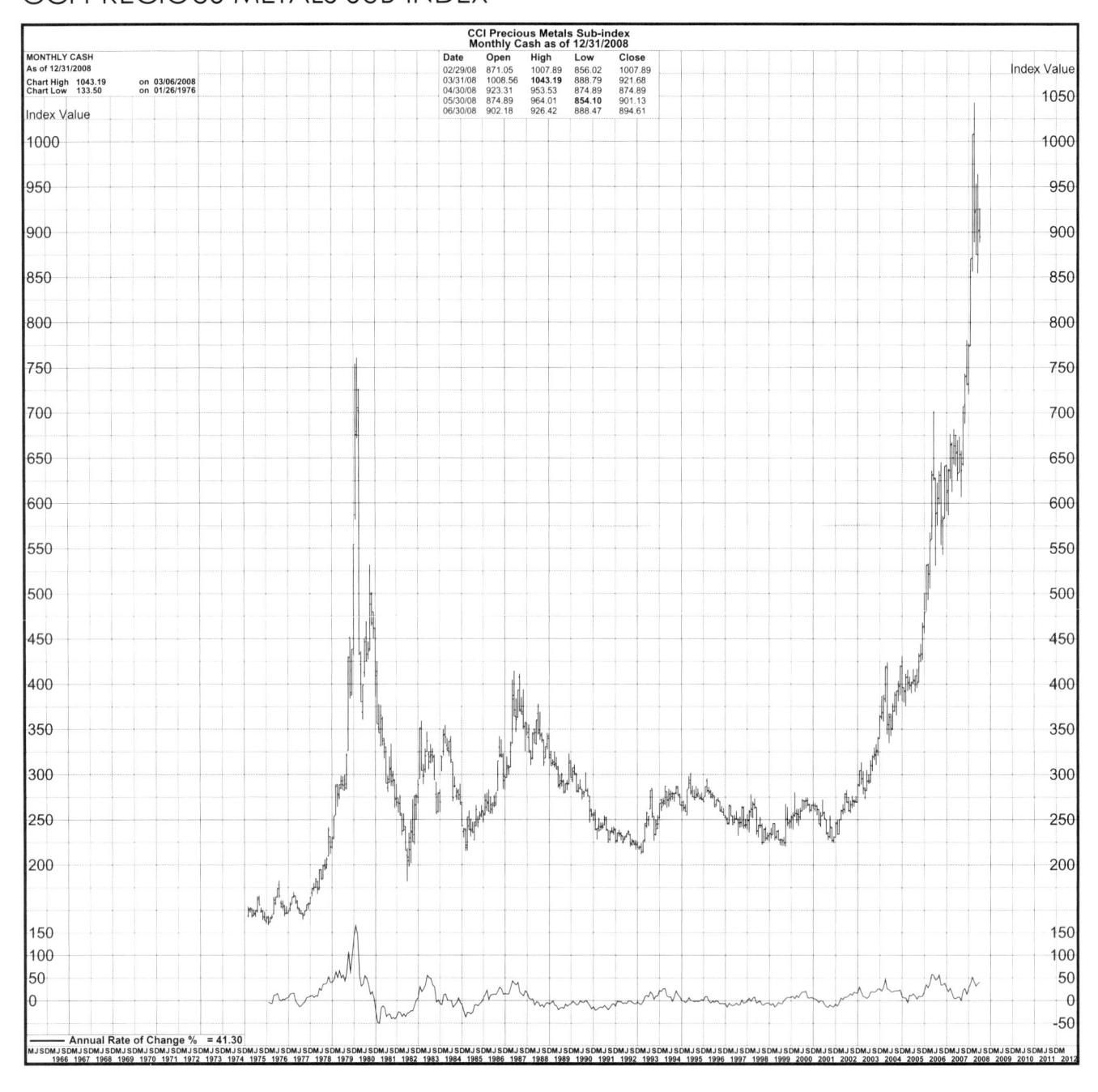

| Year | High | Low | Settle | Year | High | Low | Settle | Year | High | Low | Settle |
|---|---|---|---|---|---|---|---|---|---|---|---|
| 1967 | | | | 1981 | 425.00 | 262.80 | 269.30 | 1995 | 301.93 | 255.39 | 270.20 |
| 1968 | | | | 1982 | 294.20 | 181.60 | 288.60 | 1996 | 295.79 | 252.09 | 252.57 |
| 1969 | | | | 1983 | 359.20 | 256.80 | 269.50 | 1997 | 266.43 | 232.02 | 249.34 |
| 1970 | | | | 1984 | 354.50 | 242.50 | 243.30 | 1998 | 278.48 | 222.21 | 234.27 |
| 1971 | | | | 1985 | 266.40 | 215.10 | 256.60 | 1999 | 267.99 | 220.18 | 253.39 |
| 1972 | | | | 1986 | 342.40 | 255.10 | 296.63 | 2000 | 280.60 | 238.96 | 265.73 |
| 1973 | | | | 1987 | 414.66 | 296.44 | 346.37 | 2001 | 272.51 | 224.24 | 246.82 |
| 1974 | | | | 1988 | 378.36 | 309.34 | 318.67 | 2002 | 289.36 | 233.27 | 289.09 |
| 1975 | 166.30 | 135.20 | 141.00 | 1989 | 325.99 | 279.60 | 296.89 | 2003 | 365.80 | 272.71 | 364.08 |
| 1976 | 182.80 | 133.50 | 149.50 | 1990 | 311.28 | 246.50 | 257.76 | 2004 | 431.01 | 334.51 | 396.59 |
| 1977 | 170.20 | 139.60 | 163.80 | 1991 | 261.61 | 223.99 | 226.00 | 2005 | 499.79 | 375.66 | 478.08 |
| 1978 | 241.60 | 165.10 | 230.40 | 1992 | 238.94 | 216.49 | 219.06 | 2006 | 702.17 | 479.68 | 611.90 |
| 1979 | 554.10 | 228.50 | 554.10 | 1993 | 284.54 | 211.69 | 268.34 | 2007 | 780.62 | 586.36 | 773.57 |
| 1980 | 760.90 | 360.50 | 409.20 | 1994 | 287.73 | 259.12 | 269.62 | 2008 | 1,043.19 | 774.28 | 894.61 |

1967=100.   Index data begins 01/15/1975.   *Source: Thomson Reuters*

# CCI PRECIOUS METALS SUB-INDEX

**WEEKLY CASH**
As of 06/13/2008
Chart High 1043.19 on 03/06/2008
Chart Low 220.18 on 09/09/1999

Index Value

**CCI Precious Metals Sub-index**
Weekly Cash as of 06/13/2008

| Date | Open | High | Low | Close |
|---|---|---|---|---|
| 05/16/08 | 911.79 | 921.82 | 889.13 | 921.73 |
| 05/23/08 | 921.73 | 964.01 | 921.73 | 960.98 |
| 05/30/08 | 960.98 | 960.98 | 885.24 | 901.13 |
| 06/06/08 | 902.18 | 925.00 | 892.17 | 924.99 |
| 06/13/08 | 924.99 | 926.42 | 888.47 | 894.61 |

Annual Rate of Change % = 37.46

## Quarterly High, Low and Settle of CCI Precious Metals Sub-Index    Index Value

| Quarter | High | Low | Settle | Quarter | High | Low | Settle | Quarter | High | Low | Settle |
|---|---|---|---|---|---|---|---|---|---|---|---|
| 03/2000 | 280.60 | 238.96 | 256.92 | 03/2003 | 313.70 | 278.23 | 285.14 | 03/2006 | 567.76 | 479.68 | 558.69 |
| 06/2000 | 273.12 | 243.09 | 271.44 | 06/2003 | 305.10 | 272.71 | 293.27 | 06/2006 | 702.17 | 530.73 | 588.35 |
| 09/2000 | 274.19 | 261.05 | 266.93 | 09/2003 | 330.03 | 291.34 | 322.43 | 09/2006 | 645.63 | 553.52 | 578.52 |
| 12/2000 | 270.70 | 257.94 | 265.73 | 12/2003 | 365.80 | 310.58 | 364.08 | 12/2006 | 642.07 | 542.90 | 611.90 |
| 03/2001 | 268.56 | 244.94 | 245.45 | 03/2004 | 419.74 | 358.33 | 419.74 | 03/2007 | 676.91 | 586.36 | 650.27 |
| 06/2001 | 272.51 | 241.78 | 251.04 | 06/2004 | 424.05 | 334.51 | 350.90 | 06/2007 | 682.14 | 624.66 | 633.13 |
| 09/2001 | 254.58 | 227.16 | 242.01 | 09/2004 | 393.17 | 349.00 | 392.55 | 09/2007 | 707.38 | 606.72 | 706.89 |
| 12/2001 | 246.96 | 224.24 | 246.82 | 12/2004 | 431.01 | 380.99 | 396.59 | 12/2007 | 780.62 | 687.89 | 773.57 |
| 03/2002 | 261.42 | 233.27 | 260.55 | 03/2005 | 416.18 | 375.66 | 401.77 | 03/2008 | 1,043.19 | 774.28 | 921.68 |
| 06/2002 | 283.09 | 256.01 | 269.78 | 06/2005 | 416.77 | 389.86 | 404.47 | 06/2008 | 964.01 | 854.10 | 894.61 |
| 09/2002 | 276.69 | 257.40 | 271.22 | 09/2005 | 434.13 | 391.35 | 431.11 | 09/2008 | | | |
| 12/2002 | 289.36 | 264.58 | 289.09 | 12/2005 | 499.79 | 424.70 | 478.08 | 12/2008 | | | |

1967=100.   *Source: Thomson Reuters*

# CCI SOFTS SUB-INDEX

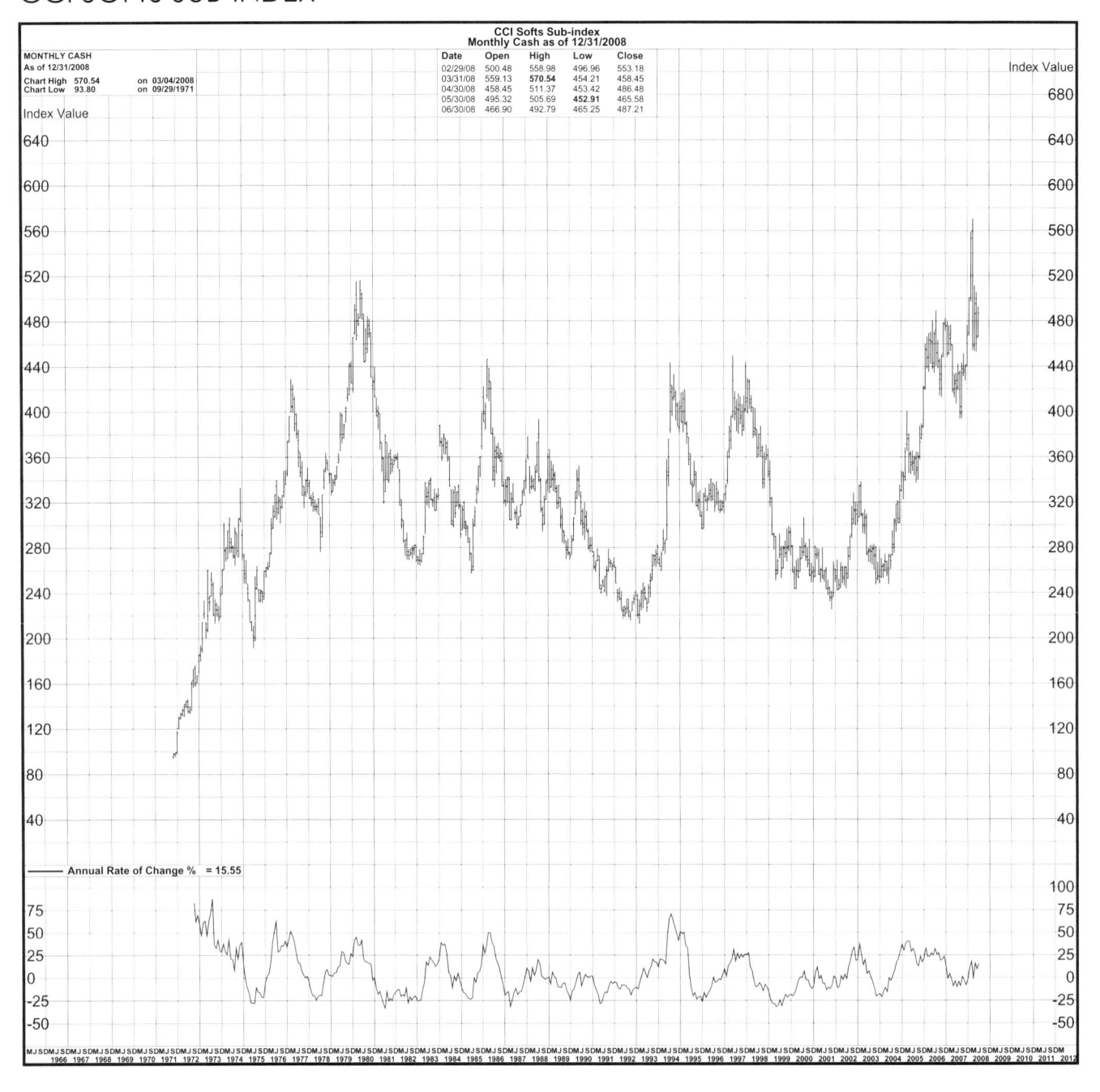

**MONTHLY CASH**
As of 12/31/2008
Chart High 570.54 on 03/04/2008
Chart Low 93.80 on 09/29/1971

**CCI Softs Sub-index**
Monthly Cash as of 12/31/2008

| Date | Open | High | Low | Close |
|---|---|---|---|---|
| 02/29/08 | 500.48 | 558.98 | 496.96 | 553.18 |
| 03/31/08 | 559.13 | 570.54 | 454.21 | 458.45 |
| 04/30/08 | 458.45 | 511.37 | 453.42 | 486.48 |
| 05/30/08 | 495.32 | 505.69 | 452.91 | 465.58 |
| 06/30/08 | 466.90 | 492.79 | 465.25 | 487.21 |

Annual Rate of Change % = 15.55

## Annual High, Low and Settle of CCI Softs Sub-Index — Index Value

| Year | High | Low | Settle | Year | High | Low | Settle | Year | High | Low | Settle |
|---|---|---|---|---|---|---|---|---|---|---|---|
| 1967 | | | | 1981 | 439.80 | 318.50 | 357.00 | 1995 | 418.91 | 295.38 | 297.01 |
| 1968 | | | | 1982 | 363.90 | 267.00 | 269.00 | 1996 | 341.05 | 295.69 | 326.54 |
| 1969 | | | | 1983 | 342.10 | 264.40 | 326.00 | 1997 | 449.99 | 320.88 | 408.73 |
| 1970 | | | | 1984 | 388.20 | 288.90 | 291.70 | 1998 | 429.33 | 331.65 | 344.82 |
| 1971 | 118.00 | 93.80 | 116.50 | 1985 | 398.20 | 256.90 | 398.20 | 1999 | 357.33 | 250.81 | 280.94 |
| 1972 | 186.20 | 120.40 | 185.40 | 1986 | 446.40 | 317.81 | 321.24 | 2000 | 306.50 | 243.34 | 254.43 |
| 1973 | 261.10 | 180.10 | 238.40 | 1987 | 358.45 | 296.37 | 356.09 | 2001 | 282.20 | 225.16 | 252.80 |
| 1974 | 333.20 | 238.90 | 274.10 | 1988 | 393.52 | 293.37 | 359.82 | 2002 | 328.36 | 241.94 | 303.69 |
| 1975 | 274.60 | 191.10 | 259.40 | 1989 | 366.43 | 268.79 | 271.69 | 2003 | 338.30 | 247.22 | 250.46 |
| 1976 | 348.50 | 253.90 | 348.10 | 1990 | 352.28 | 273.29 | 276.03 | 2004 | 347.84 | 247.78 | 343.51 |
| 1977 | 428.90 | 314.70 | 334.80 | 1991 | 279.09 | 236.89 | 264.37 | 2005 | 422.64 | 322.21 | 420.49 |
| 1978 | 363.90 | 276.00 | 345.00 | 1992 | 262.90 | 215.15 | 237.65 | 2006 | 489.41 | 412.48 | 475.85 |
| 1979 | 444.90 | 325.70 | 425.30 | 1993 | 282.37 | 212.47 | 265.92 | 2007 | 479.66 | 393.64 | 467.46 |
| 1980 | 516.10 | 400.20 | 426.00 | 1994 | 443.57 | 259.55 | 402.42 | 2008 | 570.54 | 452.91 | 487.21 |

1967=100.  Index data begins 09/23/1971.  *Source: Thomson Reuters*

# CCI SOFTS SUB-INDEX

**CCI Softs Sub-index**
Weekly Cash as of 06/13/2008

| Date | Open | High | Low | Close |
|---|---|---|---|---|
| 05/16/08 | 495.71 | 505.12 | 468.07 | 476.48 |
| 05/23/08 | 476.48 | 480.81 | 452.91 | 458.46 |
| 05/30/08 | 458.46 | 466.38 | 455.00 | 465.58 |
| 06/06/08 | 466.90 | 482.19 | 465.25 | 478.99 |
| 06/13/08 | 478.99 | 492.79 | 471.39 | 487.21 |

WEEKLY CASH As of 06/13/2008
Chart High 570.54 on 03/04/2008
Chart Low 225.16 on 10/10/2001

Annual Rate of Change % = 17.24

## Quarterly High, Low and Settle of CCI Softs Sub-Index    Index Value

| Quarter | High | Low | Settle | Quarter | High | Low | Settle | Quarter | High | Low | Settle |
|---|---|---|---|---|---|---|---|---|---|---|---|
| 03/2000 | 282.08 | 243.34 | 259.39 | 03/2003 | 338.30 | 292.39 | 299.56 | 03/2006 | 469.42 | 419.03 | 463.30 |
| 06/2000 | 288.36 | 253.00 | 275.89 | 06/2003 | 313.76 | 267.26 | 276.49 | 06/2006 | 480.81 | 434.08 | 468.69 |
| 09/2000 | 306.50 | 262.22 | 268.86 | 09/2003 | 283.26 | 260.67 | 272.18 | 09/2006 | 489.41 | 413.89 | 428.23 |
| 12/2000 | 287.81 | 249.03 | 254.43 | 12/2003 | 281.36 | 247.22 | 250.46 | 12/2006 | 482.99 | 412.48 | 475.85 |
| 03/2001 | 282.20 | 253.46 | 256.15 | 03/2004 | 274.56 | 252.81 | 267.49 | 03/2007 | 479.66 | 448.20 | 458.90 |
| 06/2001 | 280.19 | 248.98 | 259.63 | 06/2004 | 274.26 | 247.78 | 268.14 | 06/2007 | 458.90 | 406.71 | 421.63 |
| 09/2001 | 262.10 | 232.02 | 236.13 | 09/2004 | 318.60 | 272.34 | 318.29 | 09/2007 | 443.55 | 393.64 | 434.29 |
| 12/2001 | 267.61 | 225.16 | 252.80 | 12/2004 | 347.84 | 301.17 | 343.51 | 12/2007 | 476.46 | 427.17 | 467.46 |
| 03/2002 | 269.36 | 241.94 | 262.05 | 03/2005 | 400.82 | 322.21 | 376.04 | 03/2008 | 570.54 | 454.21 | 458.45 |
| 06/2002 | 264.17 | 243.81 | 256.95 | 06/2005 | 380.40 | 344.74 | 354.44 | 06/2008 | 511.37 | 452.91 | 487.21 |
| 09/2002 | 316.65 | 252.44 | 305.15 | 09/2005 | 364.91 | 336.91 | 359.61 | 09/2008 | | | |
| 12/2002 | 328.36 | 299.56 | 303.69 | 12/2005 | 422.64 | 357.56 | 420.49 | 12/2008 | | | |

1967=100.   *Source: Thomson Reuters*

# CRB SPOT INDEX

**CRB Spot Index**
Monthly Cash as of 12/31/2008

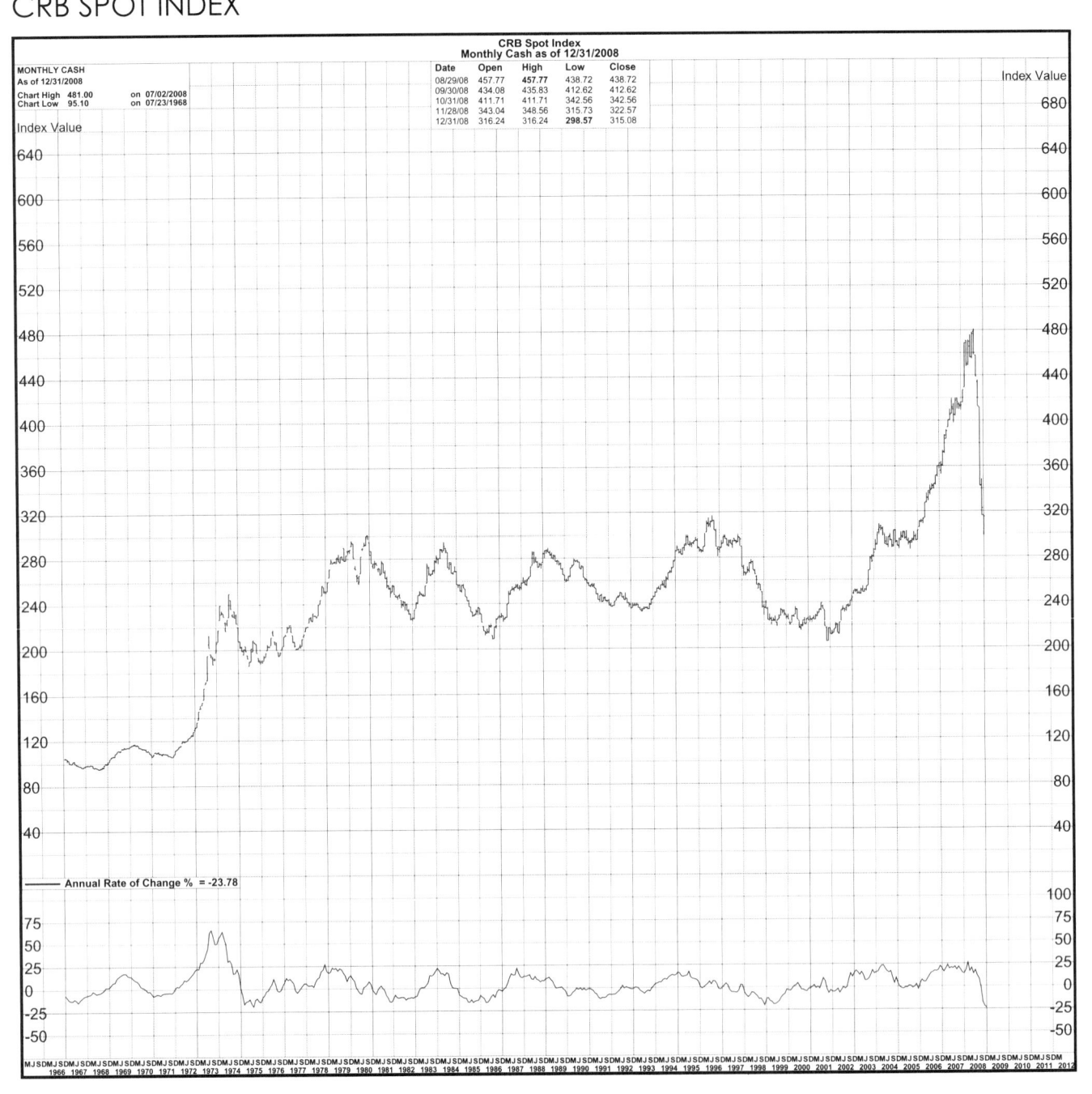

| Date | Open | High | Low | Close |
|---|---|---|---|---|
| 08/29/08 | 457.77 | 457.77 | 438.72 | 438.72 |
| 09/30/08 | 434.08 | 435.83 | 412.62 | 412.62 |
| 10/31/08 | 411.71 | 411.71 | 342.56 | 342.56 |
| 11/28/08 | 343.04 | 348.56 | 315.73 | 322.57 |
| 12/31/08 | 316.24 | 316.24 | 298.57 | 315.08 |

MONTHLY CASH As of 12/31/2008
Chart High 481.00 on 07/02/2008
Chart Low 95.10 on 07/23/1968

Annual Rate of Change % = -23.78

## Annual High, Low and Settle of CRB Spot Index — Index Value

| Year | High | Low | Settle | Year | High | Low | Settle | Year | High | Low | Settle |
|---|---|---|---|---|---|---|---|---|---|---|---|
| 1967 | 105.40 | 96.40 | 98.30 | 1981 | 286.80 | 246.20 | 250.00 | 1995 | 300.48 | 282.34 | 289.10 |
| 1968 | 101.50 | 95.10 | 100.80 | 1982 | 256.80 | 225.20 | 227.40 | 1996 | 317.00 | 280.81 | 288.22 |
| 1969 | 114.90 | 101.80 | 114.90 | 1983 | 278.40 | 226.60 | 277.80 | 1997 | 300.77 | 271.81 | 271.81 |
| 1970 | 117.40 | 106.20 | 106.20 | 1984 | 294.80 | 257.20 | 257.20 | 1998 | 278.23 | 228.66 | 235.22 |
| 1971 | 110.40 | 105.50 | 107.30 | 1985 | 257.70 | 228.30 | 236.70 | 1999 | 241.97 | 218.71 | 227.25 |
| 1972 | 131.60 | 108.20 | 131.60 | 1986 | 236.00 | 208.40 | 228.33 | 2000 | 236.22 | 215.29 | 223.99 |
| 1973 | 213.10 | 131.90 | 206.00 | 1987 | 258.68 | 223.77 | 258.21 | 2001 | 239.10 | 205.62 | 212.10 |
| 1974 | 249.90 | 207.30 | 207.90 | 1988 | 286.12 | 255.73 | 284.35 | 2002 | 246.42 | 211.20 | 244.31 |
| 1975 | 208.40 | 186.10 | 188.30 | 1989 | 289.18 | 260.60 | 260.60 | 2003 | 287.25 | 246.84 | 283.58 |
| 1976 | 217.30 | 188.70 | 201.90 | 1990 | 279.24 | 257.93 | 258.13 | 2004 | 309.10 | 285.36 | 292.97 |
| 1977 | 221.90 | 200.20 | 213.20 | 1991 | 258.78 | 238.24 | 238.24 | 2005 | 303.27 | 286.50 | 303.27 |
| 1978 | 256.50 | 216.20 | 250.30 | 1992 | 250.00 | 234.98 | 235.27 | 2006 | 362.51 | 305.89 | 362.35 |
| 1979 | 289.80 | 251.50 | 286.90 | 1993 | 246.55 | 232.09 | 245.44 | 2007 | 419.46 | 352.81 | 413.40 |
| 1980 | 300.90 | 257.40 | 283.50 | 1994 | 286.32 | 245.33 | 285.98 | 2008 | 481.00 | 298.57 | 315.08 |

1967=100.   Index data begins 01/07/1947.   *Source: Commodity Research Bureau*

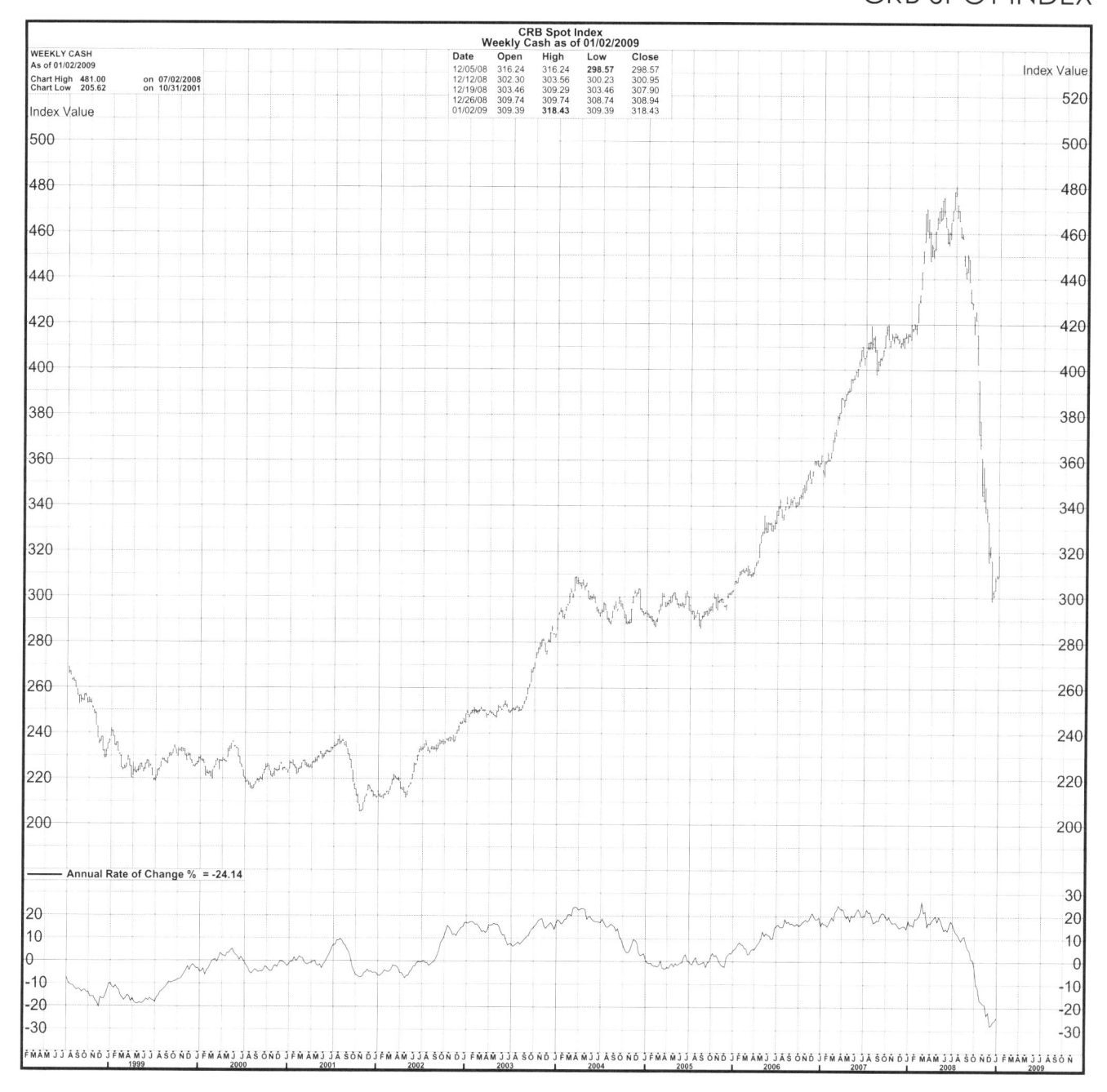

# CRB SPOT INDEX

## Quarterly High, Low and Settle of CRB Spot Index    Index Value

| Quarter | High | Low | Settle | Quarter | High | Low | Settle | Quarter | High | Low | Settle |
|---|---|---|---|---|---|---|---|---|---|---|---|
| 03/2000 | 229.71 | 219.78 | 228.01 | 03/2003 | 251.55 | 246.84 | 248.06 | 03/2006 | 313.87 | 305.89 | 313.17 |
| 06/2000 | 236.22 | 224.93 | 224.93 | 06/2003 | 254.53 | 246.98 | 249.06 | 06/2006 | 337.92 | 313.85 | 337.92 |
| 09/2000 | 223.95 | 215.29 | 223.95 | 09/2003 | 268.24 | 249.11 | 268.11 | 09/2006 | 344.51 | 334.16 | 344.05 |
| 12/2000 | 227.13 | 220.68 | 223.99 | 12/2003 | 287.25 | 268.23 | 283.58 | 12/2006 | 362.51 | 343.26 | 362.35 |
| 03/2001 | 228.10 | 222.01 | 224.72 | 03/2004 | 309.10 | 285.36 | 305.43 | 03/2007 | 387.64 | 352.81 | 386.91 |
| 06/2001 | 233.78 | 224.50 | 233.78 | 06/2004 | 307.47 | 291.16 | 291.16 | 06/2007 | 410.20 | 383.96 | 405.20 |
| 09/2001 | 239.10 | 218.65 | 218.65 | 09/2004 | 299.97 | 287.80 | 294.98 | 09/2007 | 419.46 | 397.97 | 417.74 |
| 12/2001 | 218.13 | 205.62 | 212.10 | 12/2004 | 303.75 | 288.11 | 292.97 | 12/2007 | 419.37 | 409.44 | 413.40 |
| 03/2002 | 221.82 | 211.20 | 219.64 | 03/2005 | 301.81 | 286.82 | 298.11 | 03/2008 | 470.66 | 415.74 | 450.32 |
| 06/2002 | 232.95 | 211.59 | 232.95 | 06/2005 | 302.83 | 294.15 | 294.15 | 06/2008 | 478.21 | 449.02 | 476.69 |
| 09/2002 | 237.21 | 231.05 | 237.21 | 09/2005 | 296.40 | 286.50 | 294.61 | 09/2008 | 481.00 | 412.62 | 412.62 |
| 12/2002 | 246.42 | 234.97 | 244.31 | 12/2005 | 303.27 | 293.64 | 303.27 | 12/2008 | 411.71 | 298.57 | 315.08 |

1967=100.    *Source: Commodity Research Bureau*

# CRB SPOT METALS SUB-INDEX

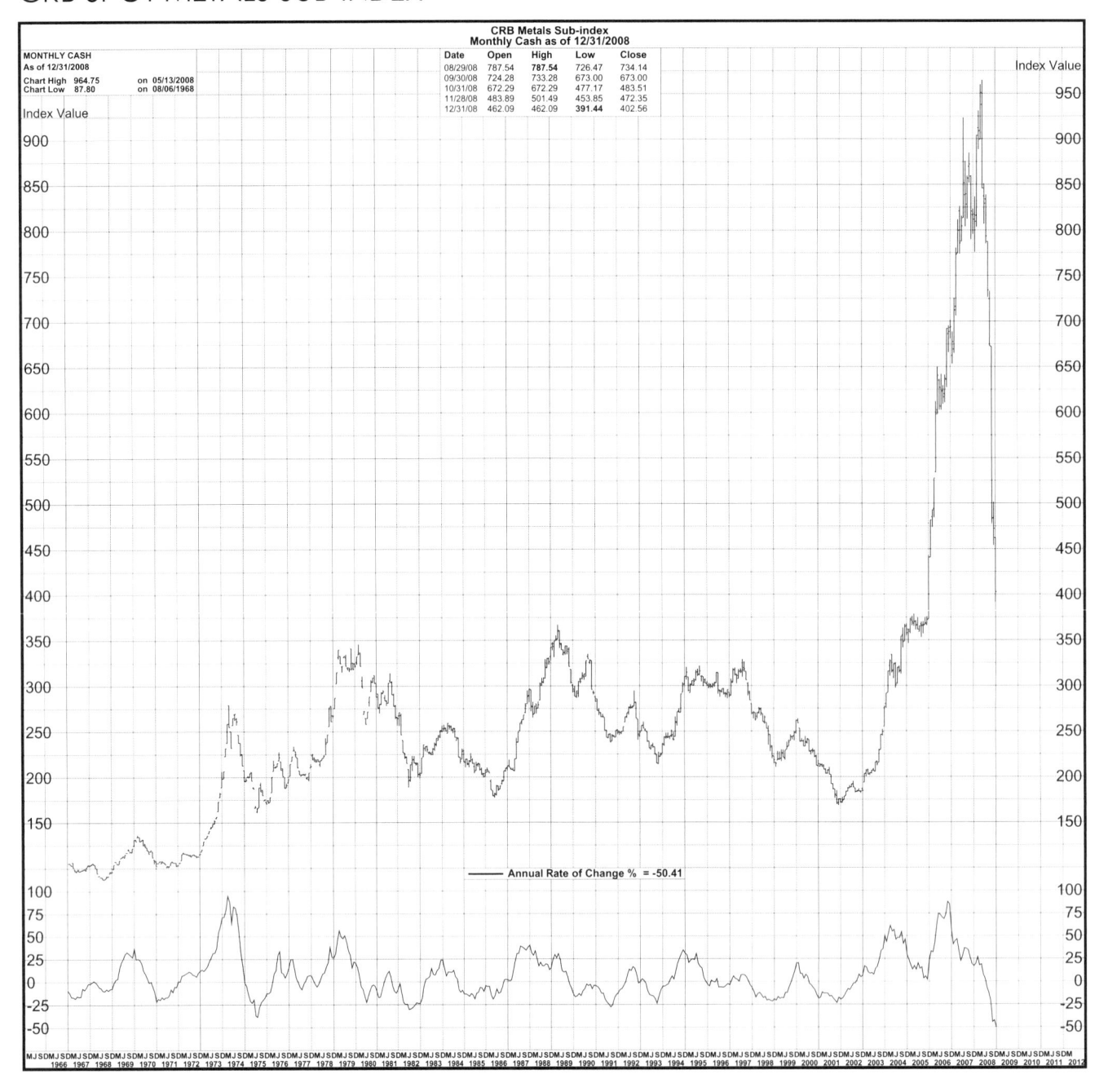

**CRB Metals Sub-index**
Monthly Cash as of 12/31/2008

| Date | Open | High | Low | Close |
|---|---|---|---|---|
| 08/29/08 | 787.54 | **787.54** | 726.47 | 734.14 |
| 09/30/08 | 724.28 | 733.28 | 673.00 | 673.00 |
| 10/31/08 | 672.29 | 672.29 | 477.17 | 483.51 |
| 11/28/08 | 483.89 | 501.49 | 453.85 | 472.35 |
| 12/31/08 | 462.09 | 462.09 | **391.44** | 402.56 |

MONTHLY CASH
As of 12/31/2008
Chart High 964.75 on 05/13/2008
Chart Low 87.80 on 08/06/1968

Annual Rate of Change % = -50.41

## Annual High, Low and Settle of CRB Metals Sub-Index   Index Value

| Year | High | Low | Settle | Year | High | Low | Settle | Year | High | Low | Settle |
|---|---|---|---|---|---|---|---|---|---|---|---|
| 1967 | 106.60 | 96.10 | 103.40 | 1981 | 314.20 | 256.20 | 264.20 | 1995 | 322.03 | 292.37 | 300.57 |
| 1968 | 105.60 | 87.80 | 96.00 | 1982 | 270.80 | 188.80 | 202.30 | 1996 | 314.72 | 285.88 | 289.90 |
| 1969 | 131.00 | 99.10 | 131.00 | 1983 | 256.00 | 204.10 | 250.40 | 1997 | 329.13 | 268.60 | 269.78 |
| 1970 | 136.40 | 102.60 | 102.60 | 1984 | 259.00 | 214.70 | 216.90 | 1998 | 276.33 | 214.38 | 218.51 |
| 1971 | 108.10 | 101.40 | 103.40 | 1985 | 226.50 | 199.40 | 207.70 | 1999 | 261.60 | 210.36 | 261.60 |
| 1972 | 117.90 | 105.70 | 116.00 | 1986 | 211.98 | 177.30 | 211.98 | 2000 | 264.00 | 211.82 | 214.03 |
| 1973 | 206.20 | 118.30 | 198.50 | 1987 | 296.72 | 206.71 | 296.72 | 2001 | 214.63 | 168.65 | 172.45 |
| 1974 | 279.00 | 196.10 | 196.10 | 1988 | 342.43 | 264.83 | 342.43 | 2002 | 195.23 | 171.46 | 184.50 |
| 1975 | 205.70 | 161.20 | 171.10 | 1989 | 367.15 | 292.78 | 296.49 | 2003 | 276.69 | 193.76 | 276.69 |
| 1976 | 227.70 | 172.00 | 197.80 | 1990 | 335.30 | 282.81 | 283.16 | 2004 | 367.73 | 275.47 | 357.69 |
| 1977 | 233.90 | 195.70 | 211.70 | 1991 | 285.85 | 238.11 | 248.51 | 2005 | 442.86 | 346.21 | 440.85 |
| 1978 | 278.00 | 211.50 | 267.30 | 1992 | 295.04 | 240.36 | 248.79 | 2006 | 701.71 | 440.78 | 693.88 |
| 1979 | 341.20 | 275.60 | 322.00 | 1993 | 260.68 | 214.08 | 236.27 | 2007 | 923.58 | 652.98 | 811.85 |
| 1980 | 346.00 | 257.60 | 288.30 | 1994 | 310.10 | 233.68 | 310.10 | 2008 | 964.75 | 391.44 | 402.56 |

1967=100.   Index data begins 01/07/1947.   *Source: Commodity Research Bureau*

# CRB SPOT METALS SUB-INDEX

**WEEKLY CASH**
As of 01/02/2009
Chart High 964.75 on 05/13/2008
Chart Low 168.65 on 11/07/2001

**CRB Metals Sub-index**
Weekly Cash as of 01/02/2009

| Date | Open | High | Low | Close |
|---|---|---|---|---|
| 12/05/08 | 462.09 | **462.09** | 426.43 | 426.43 |
| 12/12/08 | 432.82 | 437.56 | 425.31 | 425.31 |
| 12/19/08 | 424.94 | 424.94 | 414.56 | 414.56 |
| 12/26/08 | 400.14 | 400.14 | **391.44** | 391.44 |
| 01/02/09 | 393.01 | 421.42 | 392.92 | 421.42 |

Annual Rate of Change % = -49.65

## Quarterly High, Low and Settle of CRB Metals Sub-Index    Index Value

| Quarter | High | Low | Settle | Quarter | High | Low | Settle | Quarter | High | Low | Settle |
|---|---|---|---|---|---|---|---|---|---|---|---|
| 03/2000 | 264.00 | 238.39 | 239.01 | 03/2003 | 208.56 | 193.76 | 202.43 | 03/2006 | 527.52 | 440.78 | 527.52 |
| 06/2000 | 244.59 | 233.36 | 241.67 | 06/2003 | 209.23 | 201.50 | 206.36 | 06/2006 | 649.98 | 533.91 | 627.15 |
| 09/2000 | 240.65 | 224.05 | 227.89 | 09/2003 | 230.27 | 205.55 | 229.08 | 09/2006 | 642.24 | 602.43 | 636.97 |
| 12/2000 | 228.97 | 211.82 | 214.03 | 12/2003 | 276.69 | 229.71 | 276.69 | 12/2006 | 701.71 | 627.20 | 693.88 |
| 03/2001 | 214.63 | 207.97 | 207.97 | 03/2004 | 328.64 | 275.47 | 327.01 | 03/2007 | 780.95 | 652.98 | 773.13 |
| 06/2001 | 210.60 | 202.55 | 202.59 | 06/2004 | 334.58 | 297.34 | 300.89 | 06/2007 | 826.50 | 773.63 | 804.51 |
| 09/2001 | 202.11 | 176.59 | 180.41 | 09/2004 | 354.08 | 301.72 | 354.08 | 09/2007 | 923.58 | 803.98 | 856.92 |
| 12/2001 | 184.89 | 168.65 | 172.45 | 12/2004 | 367.73 | 341.51 | 357.69 | 12/2007 | 884.98 | 789.82 | 811.85 |
| 03/2002 | 184.12 | 171.46 | 183.85 | 03/2005 | 376.26 | 346.21 | 369.95 | 03/2008 | 931.12 | 775.75 | 909.03 |
| 06/2002 | 191.77 | 183.56 | 191.77 | 06/2005 | 378.72 | 361.01 | 361.42 | 06/2008 | 964.75 | 806.75 | 829.25 |
| 09/2002 | 195.23 | 182.37 | 184.25 | 09/2005 | 370.53 | 352.78 | 366.01 | 09/2008 | 839.01 | 673.00 | 673.00 |
| 12/2002 | 187.80 | 181.94 | 184.50 | 12/2005 | 442.86 | 365.67 | 440.85 | 12/2008 | 672.29 | 391.44 | 402.56 |

1967=100.   *Source: Commodity Research Bureau*

# CRB SPOT TEXTILES SUB-INDEX

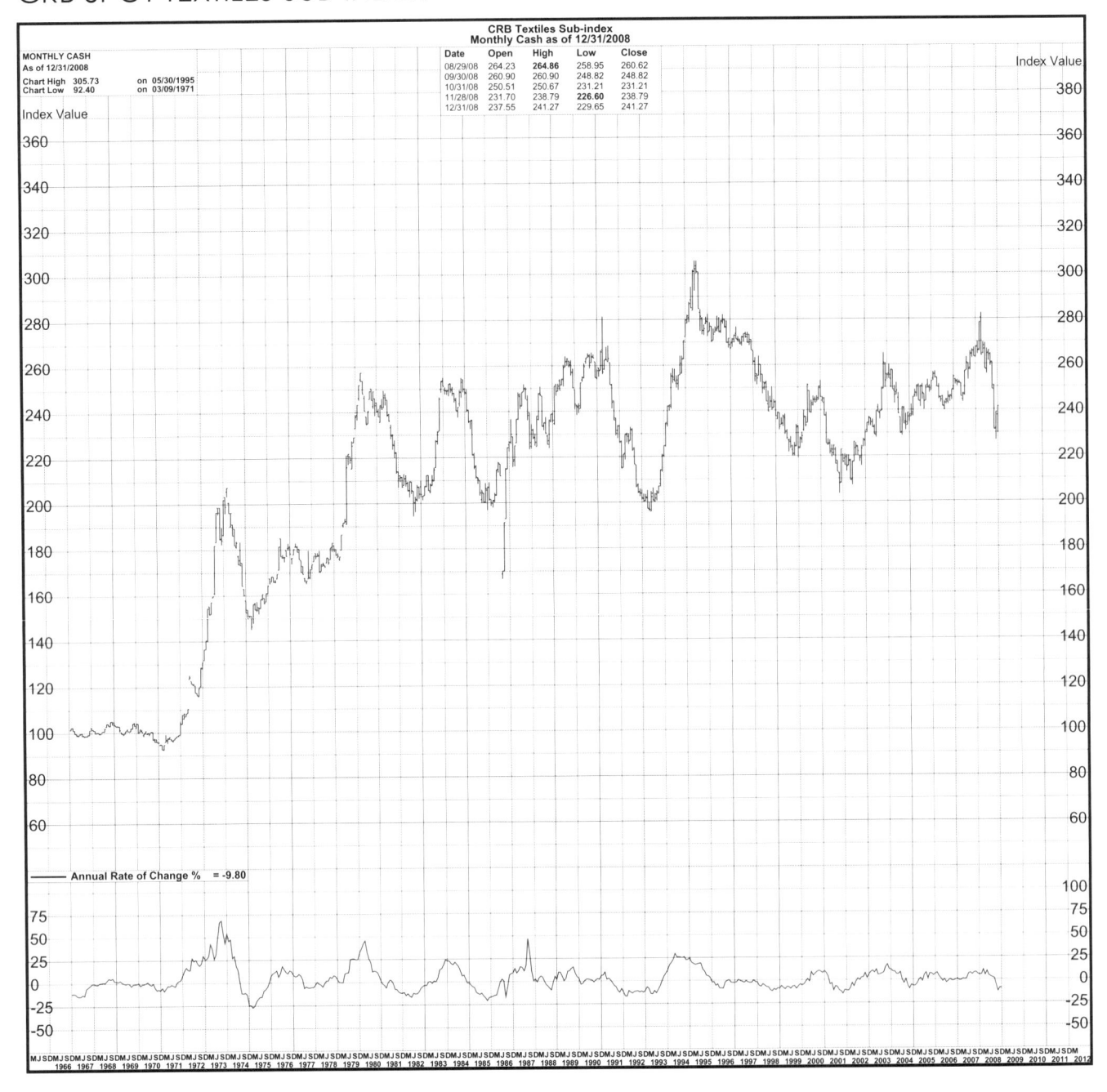

**CRB Textiles Sub-index Monthly Cash as of 12/31/2008**

| Date | Open | High | Low | Close |
|---|---|---|---|---|
| 08/29/08 | 264.23 | 264.86 | 258.95 | 260.62 |
| 09/30/08 | 260.90 | 260.90 | 248.82 | 248.82 |
| 10/31/08 | 250.51 | 250.67 | 231.21 | 231.21 |
| 11/28/08 | 231.70 | 238.79 | 226.60 | 238.79 |
| 12/31/08 | 237.55 | 241.27 | 229.65 | 241.27 |

MONTHLY CASH As of 12/31/2008
Chart High 305.73 on 05/30/1995
Chart Low 92.40 on 03/09/1971

Annual Rate of Change % = -9.80

## Annual High, Low and Settle of CRB Textiles Sub-Index   Index Value

| Year | High | Low | Settle | Year | High | Low | Settle | Year | High | Low | Settle |
|---|---|---|---|---|---|---|---|---|---|---|---|
| 1967 | 102.40 | 98.50 | 101.50 | 1981 | 249.50 | 207.00 | 211.00 | 1995 | 305.73 | 272.62 | 274.31 |
| 1968 | 105.10 | 99.50 | 103.70 | 1982 | 213.00 | 194.30 | 203.90 | 1996 | 282.16 | 266.83 | 267.43 |
| 1969 | 104.60 | 99.00 | 104.00 | 1983 | 254.90 | 201.30 | 251.20 | 1997 | 276.78 | 260.32 | 261.54 |
| 1970 | 104.10 | 95.40 | 95.80 | 1984 | 254.90 | 237.50 | 248.50 | 1998 | 264.02 | 237.33 | 237.47 |
| 1971 | 104.80 | 92.40 | 103.90 | 1985 | 249.80 | 196.70 | 206.70 | 1999 | 239.23 | 219.16 | 223.75 |
| 1972 | 130.90 | 103.80 | 130.90 | 1986 | 227.00 | 166.70 | 226.56 | 2000 | 253.02 | 223.32 | 245.74 |
| 1973 | 201.90 | 131.70 | 201.90 | 1987 | 251.88 | 215.72 | 231.79 | 2001 | 245.85 | 203.36 | 217.41 |
| 1974 | 207.30 | 152.50 | 152.50 | 1988 | 250.80 | 223.80 | 235.99 | 2002 | 230.93 | 207.01 | 230.15 |
| 1975 | 164.30 | 145.00 | 164.30 | 1989 | 264.16 | 234.03 | 243.02 | 2003 | 265.16 | 227.81 | 255.19 |
| 1976 | 185.00 | 165.20 | 178.20 | 1990 | 265.70 | 238.25 | 257.64 | 2004 | 260.19 | 228.68 | 237.87 |
| 1977 | 182.90 | 165.00 | 173.50 | 1991 | 281.41 | 226.23 | 226.23 | 2005 | 253.23 | 237.00 | 252.48 |
| 1978 | 182.90 | 170.20 | 179.40 | 1992 | 233.04 | 200.93 | 201.77 | 2006 | 256.89 | 239.76 | 254.40 |
| 1979 | 238.90 | 175.00 | 238.00 | 1993 | 224.69 | 195.96 | 224.69 | 2007 | 267.49 | 243.34 | 267.49 |
| 1980 | 257.30 | 234.70 | 240.40 | 1994 | 279.67 | 224.16 | 279.67 | 2008 | 282.52 | 226.60 | 241.27 |

1967=100.   Index data begins 01/07/1947.   *Source: Commodity Research Bureau*

# CRB SPOT TEXTILES SUB-INDEX

## Quarterly High, Low and Settle of CRB Textiles Sub-Index    Index Value

| Quarter | High | Low | Settle | Quarter | High | Low | Settle | Quarter | High | Low | Settle |
|---|---|---|---|---|---|---|---|---|---|---|---|
| 03/2000 | 239.99 | 223.32 | 236.96 | 03/2003 | 237.09 | 229.95 | 234.64 | 03/2006 | 256.89 | 249.93 | 249.93 |
| 06/2000 | 251.45 | 232.66 | 239.05 | 06/2003 | 239.47 | 227.81 | 239.47 | 06/2006 | 251.30 | 241.44 | 241.62 |
| 09/2000 | 246.29 | 238.63 | 243.30 | 09/2003 | 249.53 | 235.87 | 249.53 | 09/2006 | 247.98 | 239.76 | 245.89 |
| 12/2000 | 253.02 | 243.46 | 245.74 | 12/2003 | 265.16 | 249.13 | 255.19 | 12/2006 | 255.03 | 243.37 | 254.40 |
| 03/2001 | 245.85 | 225.38 | 225.38 | 03/2004 | 260.19 | 248.79 | 248.79 | 03/2007 | 253.39 | 250.27 | 251.77 |
| 06/2001 | 227.49 | 219.40 | 222.71 | 06/2004 | 251.97 | 238.12 | 238.38 | 06/2007 | 256.84 | 243.34 | 256.84 |
| 09/2001 | 224.75 | 212.96 | 212.96 | 09/2004 | 241.35 | 228.68 | 233.84 | 09/2007 | 265.74 | 253.00 | 264.41 |
| 12/2001 | 222.79 | 203.36 | 217.41 | 12/2004 | 238.66 | 231.05 | 237.87 | 12/2007 | 267.49 | 262.70 | 267.49 |
| 03/2002 | 220.84 | 213.13 | 217.62 | 03/2005 | 248.89 | 237.00 | 247.37 | 03/2008 | 282.52 | 263.80 | 263.80 |
| 06/2002 | 226.08 | 207.01 | 226.08 | 06/2005 | 251.27 | 241.21 | 250.35 | 06/2008 | 269.60 | 255.64 | 264.64 |
| 09/2002 | 225.75 | 217.32 | 219.07 | 09/2005 | 251.38 | 240.04 | 249.45 | 09/2008 | 265.97 | 248.82 | 248.82 |
| 12/2002 | 230.93 | 215.61 | 230.15 | 12/2005 | 253.23 | 247.39 | 252.48 | 12/2008 | 250.67 | 226.60 | 241.27 |

1967=100.    Source: Commodity Research Bureau

# CRB SPOT RAW INDUSTRIALS SUB-INDEX

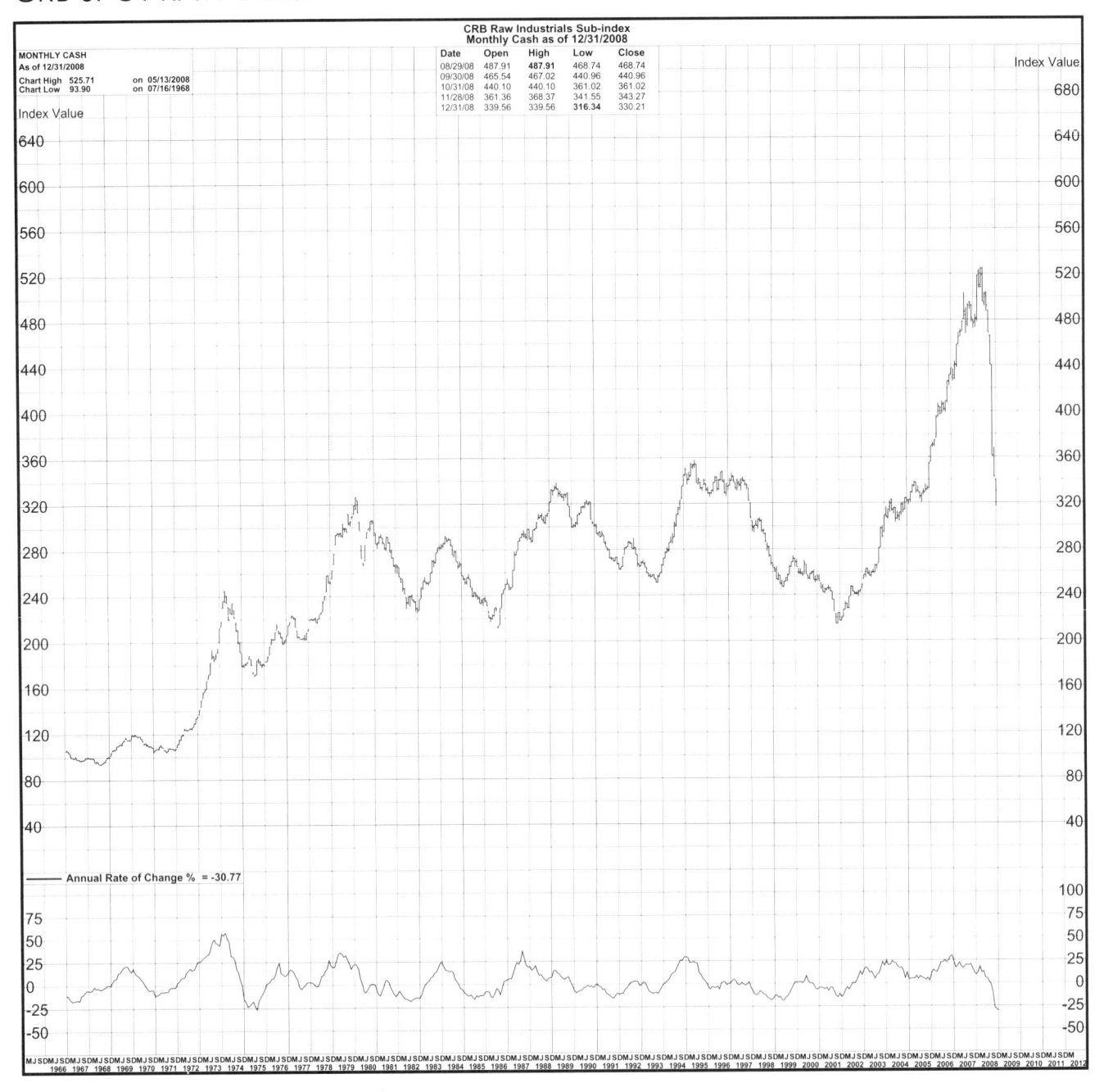

**CRB Raw Industrials Sub-index**
Monthly Cash as of 12/31/2008

| Date | Open | High | Low | Close |
|---|---|---|---|---|
| 08/29/08 | 487.91 | 487.91 | 468.74 | 468.74 |
| 09/30/08 | 465.54 | 467.02 | 440.96 | 440.96 |
| 10/31/08 | 440.10 | 440.10 | 361.02 | 361.02 |
| 11/28/08 | 361.36 | 368.37 | 341.55 | 343.27 |
| 12/31/08 | 339.56 | 339.56 | 316.34 | 330.21 |

MONTHLY CASH
As of 12/31/2008
Chart High 525.71 on 05/13/2008
Chart Low 93.90 on 07/16/1968

Annual Rate of Change % = -30.77

## Annual High, Low and Settle of CRB Raw Industrials Sub-Index — Index Value

| Year | High | Low | Settle | Year | High | Low | Settle | Year | High | Low | Settle |
|---|---|---|---|---|---|---|---|---|---|---|---|
| 1967 | 107.00 | 96.70 | 99.50 | 1981 | 295.20 | 260.90 | 265.80 | 1995 | 357.98 | 330.29 | 332.15 |
| 1968 | 100.70 | 93.90 | 100.20 | 1982 | 267.50 | 224.90 | 226.90 | 1996 | 348.08 | 325.50 | 334.92 |
| 1969 | 118.80 | 101.60 | 118.80 | 1983 | 284.50 | 227.60 | 281.60 | 1997 | 346.84 | 306.88 | 307.52 |
| 1970 | 120.20 | 104.70 | 104.70 | 1984 | 292.00 | 258.00 | 258.00 | 1998 | 307.26 | 263.49 | 265.32 |
| 1971 | 111.20 | 104.10 | 107.30 | 1985 | 259.10 | 231.00 | 237.60 | 1999 | 274.15 | 246.90 | 268.88 |
| 1972 | 135.60 | 109.00 | 135.60 | 1986 | 249.98 | 211.00 | 249.76 | 2000 | 270.87 | 250.46 | 255.81 |
| 1973 | 212.30 | 137.10 | 212.30 | 1987 | 297.81 | 245.21 | 297.81 | 2001 | 257.51 | 214.16 | 217.33 |
| 1974 | 245.60 | 179.20 | 179.20 | 1988 | 321.14 | 286.05 | 321.14 | 2002 | 249.48 | 216.70 | 248.56 |
| 1975 | 188.30 | 170.70 | 180.30 | 1989 | 338.54 | 298.99 | 300.40 | 2003 | 309.07 | 253.85 | 309.07 |
| 1976 | 216.30 | 183.10 | 205.40 | 1990 | 322.85 | 299.31 | 301.21 | 2004 | 324.30 | 302.90 | 321.50 |
| 1977 | 224.20 | 202.10 | 211.10 | 1991 | 302.16 | 267.25 | 267.25 | 2005 | 355.19 | 318.08 | 354.65 |
| 1978 | 258.60 | 216.30 | 251.90 | 1992 | 290.01 | 261.96 | 265.22 | 2006 | 437.28 | 355.77 | 437.28 |
| 1979 | 311.70 | 255.60 | 309.80 | 1993 | 271.13 | 250.72 | 266.50 | 2007 | 503.45 | 426.12 | 476.99 |
| 1980 | 326.90 | 266.40 | 293.50 | 1994 | 345.12 | 265.81 | 345.12 | 2008 | 525.71 | 316.34 | 330.21 |

1967=100. Index data begins 01/07/1947. *Source: Commodity Research Bureau*

# CRB SPOT RAW INDUSTRIALS SUB-INDEX

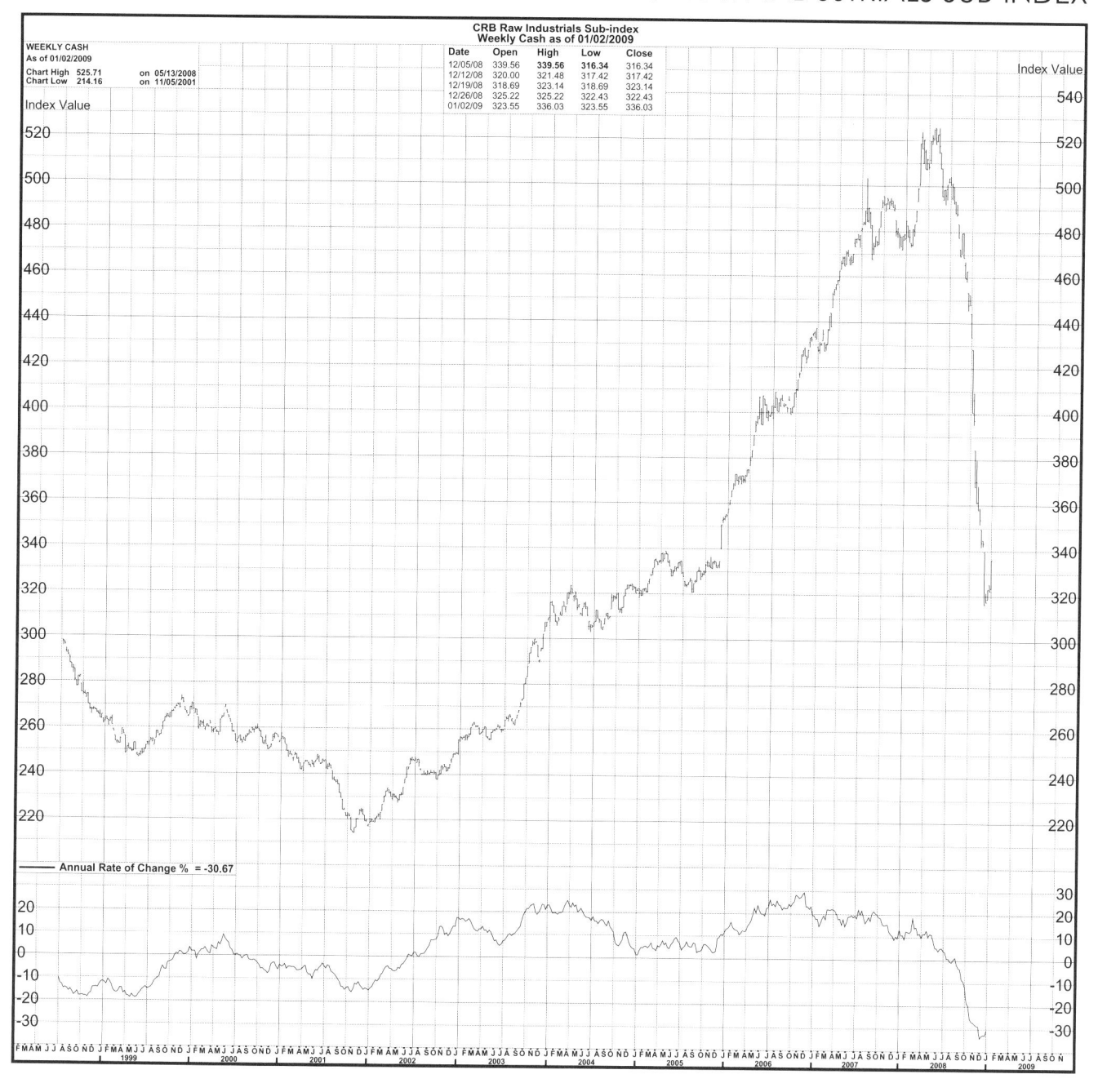

**CRB Raw Industrials Sub-index**
**Weekly Cash as of 01/02/2009**

| Date | Open | High | Low | Close |
|---|---|---|---|---|
| 12/05/08 | 339.56 | 339.56 | 316.34 | 316.34 |
| 12/12/08 | 320.00 | 321.48 | 317.42 | 317.42 |
| 12/19/08 | 318.69 | 323.14 | 318.69 | 323.14 |
| 12/26/08 | 325.22 | 325.22 | 322.43 | 322.43 |
| 01/02/09 | 323.55 | 336.03 | 323.55 | 336.03 |

WEEKLY CASH
As of 01/02/2009
Chart High 525.71 on 05/13/2008
Chart Low 214.16 on 11/05/2001

Annual Rate of Change % = -30.67

## Quarterly High, Low and Settle of CRB Raw Industrials Sub-Index    Index Value

| Quarter | High | Low | Settle | Quarter | High | Low | Settle | Quarter | High | Low | Settle |
|---|---|---|---|---|---|---|---|---|---|---|---|
| 03/2000 | 270.87 | 257.41 | 258.51 | 03/2003 | 263.11 | 253.85 | 258.01 | 03/2006 | 375.00 | 355.77 | 374.92 |
| 06/2000 | 270.02 | 256.54 | 257.98 | 06/2003 | 262.12 | 255.20 | 259.47 | 06/2006 | 407.33 | 376.77 | 402.91 |
| 09/2000 | 260.56 | 252.85 | 259.58 | 09/2003 | 280.62 | 259.26 | 280.62 | 09/2006 | 408.99 | 397.68 | 408.80 |
| 12/2000 | 261.55 | 250.46 | 255.81 | 12/2003 | 309.07 | 280.95 | 309.07 | 12/2006 | 437.28 | 406.89 | 437.28 |
| 03/2001 | 257.51 | 241.96 | 241.96 | 03/2004 | 322.14 | 305.60 | 319.17 | 03/2007 | 458.44 | 426.12 | 458.39 |
| 06/2001 | 248.25 | 240.99 | 246.21 | 06/2004 | 323.51 | 302.90 | 306.03 | 06/2007 | 478.68 | 458.32 | 478.26 |
| 09/2001 | 246.04 | 224.29 | 224.49 | 09/2004 | 319.69 | 303.99 | 318.33 | 09/2007 | 503.45 | 467.65 | 492.58 |
| 12/2001 | 225.07 | 214.16 | 217.33 | 12/2004 | 324.30 | 311.29 | 321.50 | 12/2007 | 495.46 | 472.14 | 476.99 |
| 03/2002 | 233.83 | 216.70 | 231.76 | 03/2005 | 335.63 | 318.08 | 335.00 | 03/2008 | 523.88 | 473.27 | 510.00 |
| 06/2002 | 247.34 | 227.43 | 247.34 | 06/2005 | 338.83 | 327.95 | 329.32 | 06/2008 | 525.71 | 491.89 | 502.04 |
| 09/2002 | 247.59 | 239.53 | 240.69 | 09/2005 | 332.03 | 320.49 | 328.75 | 09/2008 | 504.18 | 440.96 | 440.96 |
| 12/2002 | 249.48 | 237.87 | 248.56 | 12/2005 | 355.19 | 329.50 | 354.65 | 12/2008 | 440.10 | 316.34 | 330.21 |

1967=100.    *Source: Commodity Research Bureau*

# CRB SPOT FOODSTUFFS SUB-INDEX

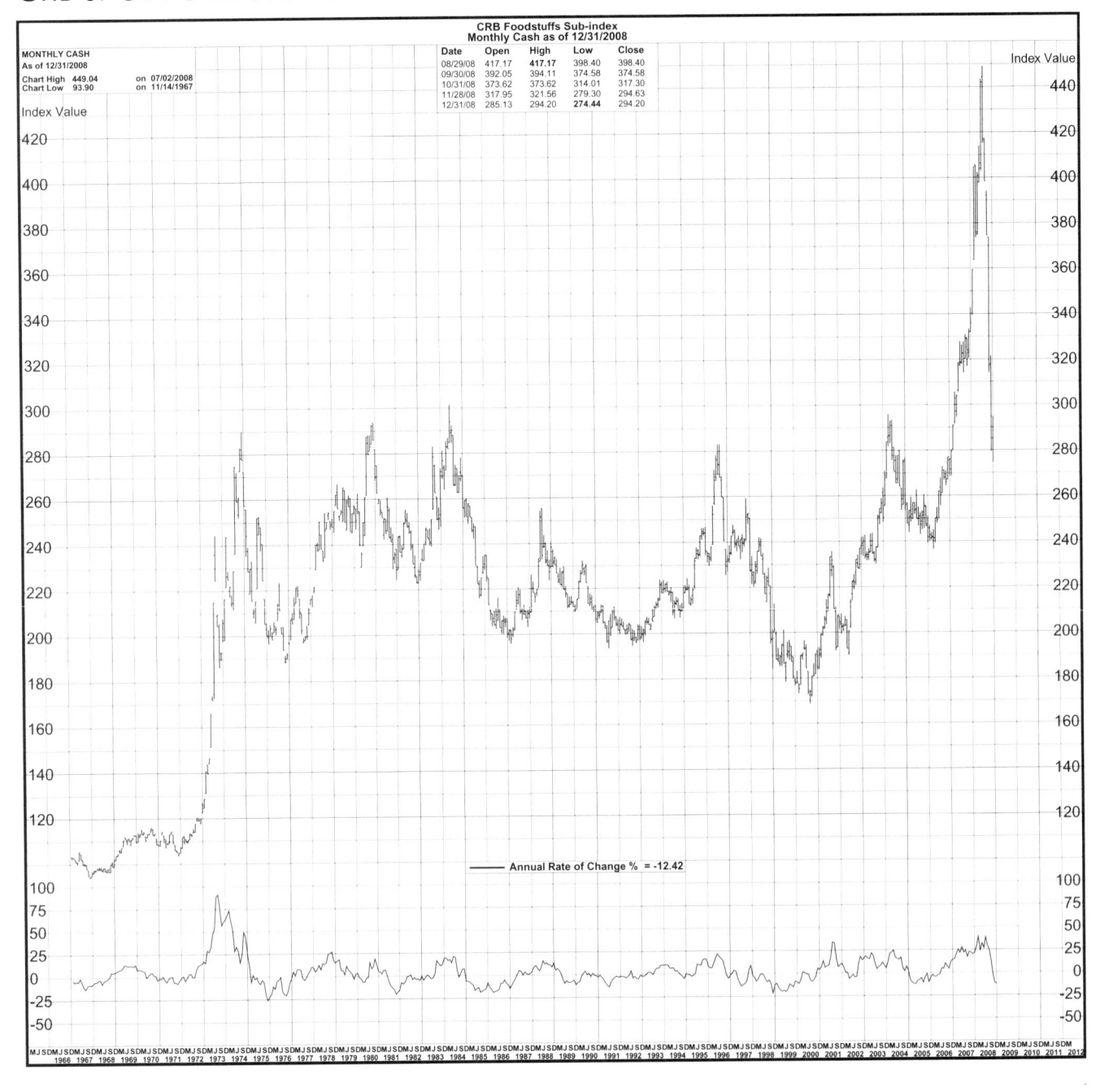

**CRB Foodstuffs Sub-index**
Monthly Cash as of 12/31/2008

| Date | Open | High | Low | Close |
|---|---|---|---|---|
| 08/29/08 | 417.17 | 417.17 | 398.40 | 398.40 |
| 09/30/08 | 392.05 | 394.11 | 374.58 | 374.58 |
| 10/31/08 | 373.62 | 373.62 | 314.01 | 317.30 |
| 11/28/08 | 317.95 | 321.56 | 279.30 | 294.63 |
| 12/31/08 | 285.13 | 294.20 | 274.44 | 294.20 |

MONTHLY CASH As of 12/31/2008
Chart High 449.04 on 07/02/2008
Chart Low 93.90 on 11/14/1967

Annual Rate of Change % = -12.42

## Annual High, Low and Settle of CRB Foodstuffs Sub-Index    Index Value

| Year | High | Low | Settle | Year | High | Low | Settle | Year | High | Low | Settle |
|---|---|---|---|---|---|---|---|---|---|---|---|
| 1967 | 105.60 | 93.90 | 96.50 | 1981 | 274.90 | 224.60 | 228.80 | 1995 | 246.80 | 212.23 | 236.39 |
| 1968 | 102.60 | 95.90 | 101.70 | 1982 | 255.30 | 222.80 | 228.00 | 1996 | 283.18 | 225.39 | 231.83 |
| 1969 | 113.00 | 101.90 | 109.50 | 1983 | 283.10 | 224.00 | 272.00 | 1997 | 259.21 | 227.26 | 227.26 |
| 1970 | 115.90 | 108.20 | 108.20 | 1984 | 301.40 | 255.90 | 255.90 | 1998 | 242.06 | 184.37 | 197.52 |
| 1971 | 114.20 | 103.50 | 107.30 | 1985 | 260.00 | 215.90 | 235.20 | 1999 | 212.74 | 176.76 | 178.10 |
| 1972 | 127.10 | 107.00 | 126.00 | 1986 | 235.00 | 198.48 | 200.41 | 2000 | 196.59 | 168.61 | 184.74 |
| 1973 | 244.40 | 124.70 | 206.00 | 1987 | 220.83 | 195.92 | 209.95 | 2001 | 235.78 | 183.96 | 204.61 |
| 1974 | 290.00 | 198.30 | 257.50 | 1988 | 255.28 | 209.71 | 238.33 | 2002 | 241.87 | 190.17 | 238.10 |
| 1975 | 255.80 | 200.30 | 200.30 | 1989 | 237.54 | 210.98 | 212.06 | 2003 | 263.46 | 230.27 | 250.24 |
| 1976 | 223.60 | 188.10 | 196.70 | 1990 | 232.42 | 205.33 | 206.39 | 2004 | 295.90 | 253.41 | 255.97 |
| 1977 | 222.00 | 196.90 | 216.10 | 1991 | 212.87 | 193.61 | 201.64 | 2005 | 262.61 | 239.08 | 241.73 |
| 1978 | 254.50 | 212.50 | 247.90 | 1992 | 207.45 | 194.55 | 197.72 | 2006 | 276.91 | 236.45 | 275.99 |
| 1979 | 266.70 | 245.20 | 256.70 | 1993 | 223.90 | 196.11 | 217.76 | 2007 | 342.76 | 268.39 | 335.94 |
| 1980 | 293.50 | 230.30 | 269.50 | 1994 | 223.58 | 206.53 | 217.82 | 2008 | 449.04 | 274.44 | 294.20 |

1967=100.   Index data begins 01/07/1947.   *Source: Commodity Research Bureau*

# CRB SPOT FOODSTUFFS SUB-INDEX

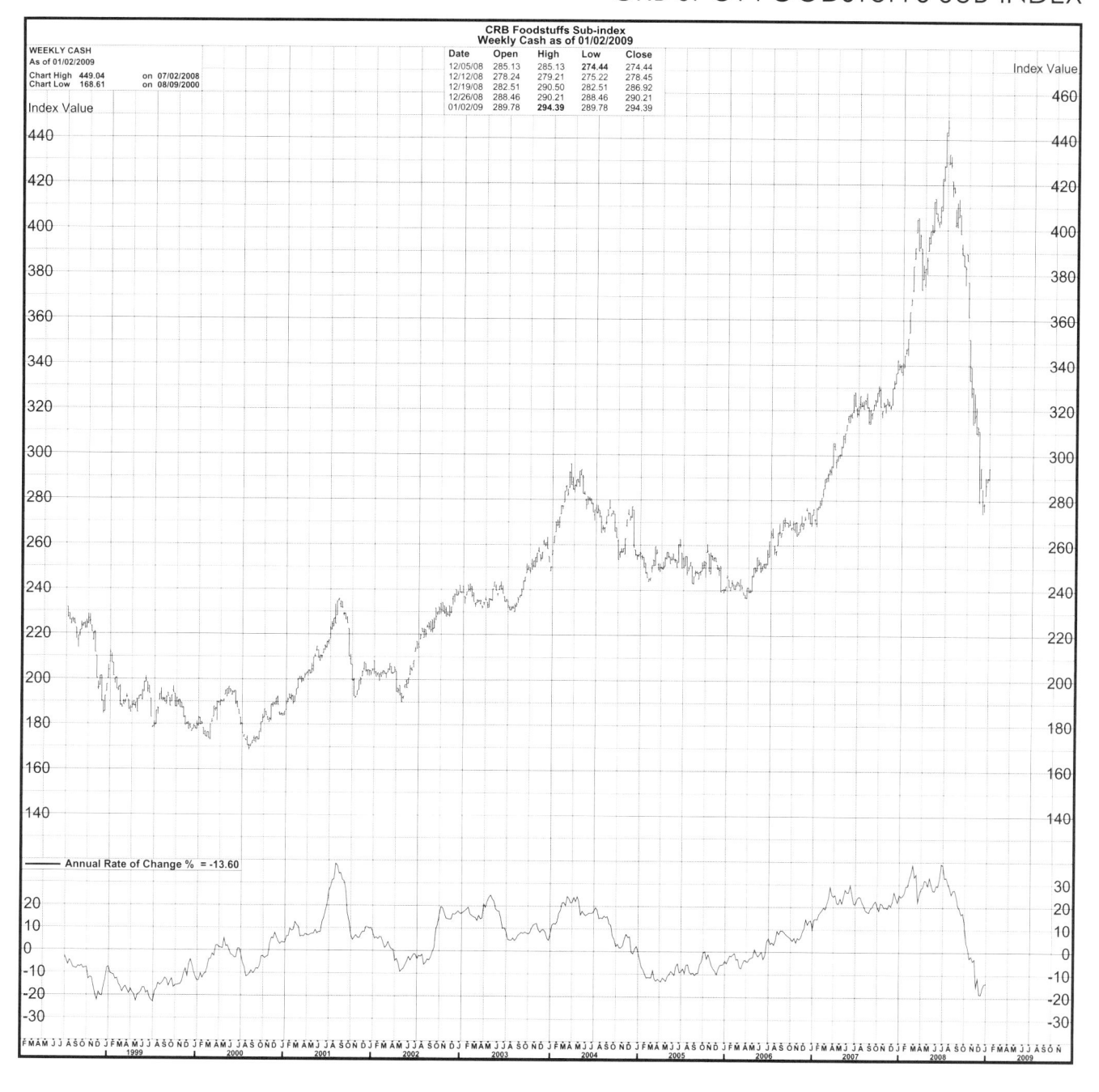

**WEEKLY CASH**
As of 01/02/2009
Chart High 449.04 on 07/02/2008
Chart Low 168.61 on 08/09/2000
Index Value

**CRB Foodstuffs Sub-index**
Weekly Cash as of 01/02/2009

| Date | Open | High | Low | Close |
|---|---|---|---|---|
| 12/05/08 | 285.13 | 285.13 | 274.44 | 274.44 |
| 12/12/08 | 278.24 | 279.21 | 275.22 | 278.45 |
| 12/19/08 | 282.51 | 290.50 | 282.51 | 286.92 |
| 12/26/08 | 288.46 | 290.21 | 288.46 | 290.21 |
| 01/02/09 | 289.78 | 294.39 | 289.78 | 294.39 |

Annual Rate of Change % = -13.60

## Quarterly High, Low and Settle of CRB Foodstuffs Sub-Index    Index Value

| Quarter | High | Low | Settle | Quarter | High | Low | Settle | Quarter | High | Low | Settle |
|---|---|---|---|---|---|---|---|---|---|---|---|
| 03/2000 | 190.05 | 173.16 | 190.05 | 03/2003 | 242.51 | 231.51 | 234.18 | 03/2006 | 247.00 | 236.45 | 241.30 |
| 06/2000 | 196.59 | 184.38 | 184.38 | 06/2003 | 243.76 | 231.70 | 234.58 | 06/2006 | 261.89 | 239.29 | 261.89 |
| 09/2000 | 182.89 | 168.61 | 180.79 | 09/2003 | 251.66 | 230.27 | 250.82 | 09/2006 | 272.61 | 255.65 | 267.98 |
| 12/2000 | 192.66 | 180.81 | 184.74 | 12/2003 | 263.46 | 247.33 | 250.24 | 12/2006 | 276.91 | 264.24 | 275.99 |
| 03/2001 | 202.82 | 183.96 | 201.79 | 03/2004 | 295.90 | 255.58 | 286.39 | 03/2007 | 305.67 | 268.39 | 302.65 |
| 06/2001 | 216.75 | 201.48 | 216.75 | 06/2004 | 293.37 | 270.73 | 270.73 | 06/2007 | 327.94 | 294.49 | 318.66 |
| 09/2001 | 235.78 | 210.32 | 210.32 | 09/2004 | 279.80 | 264.04 | 264.04 | 09/2007 | 330.98 | 313.99 | 328.99 |
| 12/2001 | 211.21 | 191.99 | 204.61 | 12/2004 | 277.01 | 253.41 | 255.97 | 12/2007 | 342.76 | 316.85 | 335.94 |
| 03/2002 | 208.28 | 199.18 | 203.09 | 03/2005 | 259.37 | 243.81 | 251.68 | 03/2008 | 405.44 | 339.26 | 375.92 |
| 06/2002 | 214.39 | 190.17 | 213.46 | 06/2005 | 262.61 | 249.40 | 249.67 | 06/2008 | 443.40 | 374.98 | 441.97 |
| 09/2002 | 232.08 | 213.80 | 232.08 | 09/2005 | 255.10 | 242.91 | 251.27 | 09/2008 | 449.04 | 374.58 | 374.58 |
| 12/2002 | 241.87 | 227.84 | 238.10 | 12/2005 | 260.53 | 239.08 | 241.73 | 12/2008 | 373.62 | 274.44 | 294.20 |

1967=100.   *Source: Commodity Research Bureau*

# CRB SPOT FATS & OILS SUB-INDEX

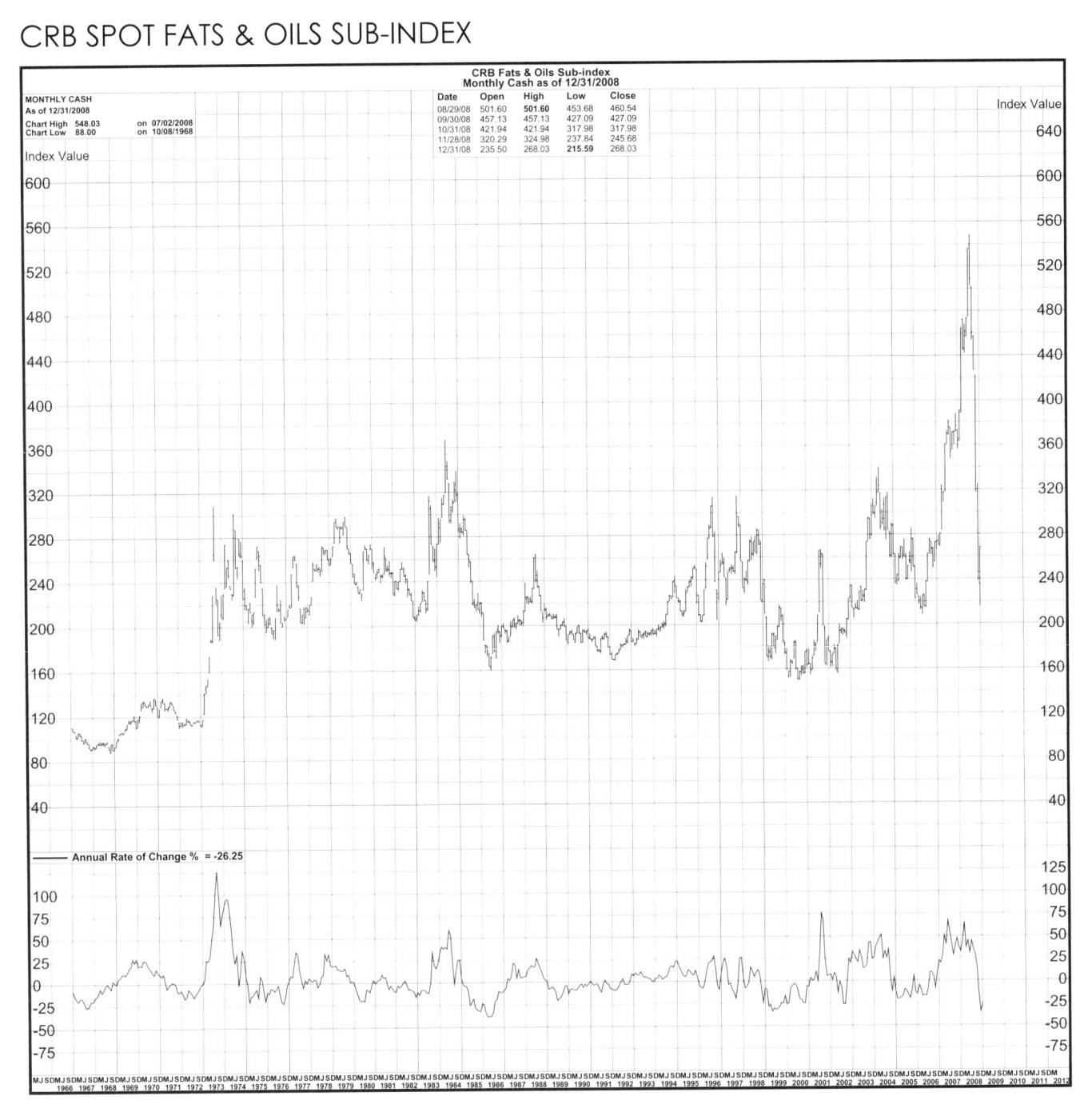

**MONTHLY CASH**
As of 12/31/2008
Chart High 548.03 on 07/02/2008
Chart Low 88.00 on 10/08/1968

**CRB Fats & Oils Sub-index Monthly Cash as of 12/31/2008**

| Date | Open | High | Low | Close |
|---|---|---|---|---|
| 08/29/08 | 501.60 | 501.60 | 453.68 | 460.54 |
| 09/30/08 | 457.13 | 457.13 | 427.09 | 427.09 |
| 10/31/08 | 421.94 | 421.94 | 317.98 | 317.98 |
| 11/28/08 | 320.29 | 324.98 | 237.84 | 245.68 |
| 12/31/08 | 235.50 | 268.03 | 215.59 | 268.03 |

Annual Rate of Change % = -26.25

## Annual High, Low and Settle of CRB Fats & Oils Sub-Index    Index Value

| Year | High | Low | Settle | Year | High | Low | Settle | Year | High | Low | Settle |
|---|---|---|---|---|---|---|---|---|---|---|---|
| 1967 | 110.70 | 90.50 | 93.10 | 1981 | 271.30 | 228.70 | 229.90 | 1995 | 253.28 | 206.82 | 226.68 |
| 1968 | 98.50 | 88.00 | 92.40 | 1982 | 257.70 | 205.70 | 205.70 | 1996 | 314.46 | 202.26 | 246.42 |
| 1969 | 121.40 | 93.40 | 110.20 | 1983 | 317.00 | 204.10 | 273.40 | 1997 | 315.23 | 216.70 | 257.08 |
| 1970 | 136.70 | 111.20 | 121.30 | 1984 | 366.90 | 273.20 | 287.10 | 1998 | 285.99 | 220.04 | 236.01 |
| 1971 | 137.20 | 109.70 | 111.70 | 1985 | 299.50 | 210.70 | 220.20 | 1999 | 240.47 | 166.42 | 174.78 |
| 1972 | 118.90 | 111.40 | 111.40 | 1986 | 220.80 | 159.60 | 199.79 | 2000 | 185.48 | 149.78 | 163.62 |
| 1973 | 308.50 | 112.00 | 209.10 | 1987 | 213.46 | 184.32 | 212.54 | 2001 | 266.74 | 154.27 | 175.82 |
| 1974 | 301.70 | 207.40 | 225.30 | 1988 | 263.51 | 202.43 | 214.70 | 2002 | 235.00 | 155.22 | 234.00 |
| 1975 | 272.20 | 200.40 | 202.10 | 1989 | 215.92 | 186.81 | 186.81 | 2003 | 308.13 | 205.23 | 297.20 |
| 1976 | 237.80 | 188.90 | 207.40 | 1990 | 200.23 | 182.74 | 188.67 | 2004 | 340.45 | 258.58 | 262.55 |
| 1977 | 263.70 | 202.90 | 214.80 | 1991 | 193.72 | 173.80 | 173.80 | 2005 | 285.99 | 221.76 | 223.41 |
| 1978 | 271.70 | 211.00 | 255.20 | 1992 | 196.60 | 168.16 | 184.97 | 2006 | 276.40 | 208.14 | 273.93 |
| 1979 | 298.40 | 256.00 | 257.40 | 1993 | 196.81 | 180.94 | 191.71 | 2007 | 387.96 | 269.31 | 363.44 |
| 1980 | 273.20 | 222.50 | 255.90 | 1994 | 244.05 | 189.45 | 236.17 | 2008 | 548.03 | 215.59 | 268.03 |

1967=100.    Index data begins 01/07/1947.    *Source: Commodity Research Bureau*

# CRB SPOT FATS & OILS SUB-INDEX

**CRB Fats & Oils Sub-index**
Weekly Cash as of 01/02/2009

| Date | Open | High | Low | Close |
|---|---|---|---|---|
| 12/05/08 | 235.50 | 235.50 | 226.61 | 226.61 |
| 12/12/08 | 229.36 | 229.36 | 215.59 | 215.59 |
| 12/19/08 | 220.14 | 242.98 | 220.14 | 241.24 |
| 12/26/08 | 256.69 | 256.69 | 255.41 | 255.41 |
| 01/02/09 | 259.07 | 268.85 | 259.07 | 268.85 |

WEEKLY CASH
As of 01/02/2009
Chart High 548.03 on 07/02/2008
Chart Low 149.78 on 08/11/2000

Annual Rate of Change % = -27.92

## Quarterly High, Low and Settle of CRB Fats & Oils Sub-Index  Index Value

| Quarter | High | Low | Settle | Quarter | High | Low | Settle | Quarter | High | Low | Settle |
|---|---|---|---|---|---|---|---|---|---|---|---|
| 03/2000 | 178.25 | 151.39 | 166.32 | 03/2003 | 234.37 | 205.23 | 214.32 | 03/2006 | 236.20 | 212.44 | 214.38 |
| 06/2000 | 185.48 | 158.67 | 160.42 | 06/2003 | 233.99 | 212.09 | 220.48 | 06/2006 | 238.42 | 208.14 | 238.00 |
| 09/2000 | 162.75 | 149.78 | 161.64 | 09/2003 | 273.36 | 219.11 | 273.36 | 09/2006 | 276.40 | 237.56 | 266.85 |
| 12/2000 | 178.21 | 155.38 | 163.62 | 12/2003 | 308.13 | 273.66 | 297.20 | 12/2006 | 273.93 | 249.59 | 273.93 |
| 03/2001 | 177.66 | 154.27 | 169.03 | 03/2004 | 331.13 | 294.23 | 317.85 | 03/2007 | 323.87 | 269.31 | 323.87 |
| 06/2001 | 207.77 | 171.14 | 207.77 | 06/2004 | 340.45 | 284.08 | 294.11 | 06/2007 | 372.96 | 308.46 | 369.51 |
| 09/2001 | 266.74 | 198.52 | 198.52 | 09/2004 | 317.40 | 274.90 | 283.74 | 09/2007 | 382.52 | 347.36 | 371.21 |
| 12/2001 | 198.14 | 162.58 | 175.82 | 12/2004 | 290.23 | 258.58 | 262.55 | 12/2007 | 387.96 | 356.30 | 363.44 |
| 03/2002 | 181.66 | 161.01 | 177.49 | 03/2005 | 262.77 | 235.02 | 259.41 | 03/2008 | 472.43 | 362.89 | 444.98 |
| 06/2002 | 199.87 | 155.22 | 193.62 | 06/2005 | 275.71 | 257.33 | 259.68 | 06/2008 | 535.78 | 441.80 | 535.78 |
| 09/2002 | 195.81 | 189.70 | 192.23 | 09/2005 | 263.95 | 238.50 | 254.11 | 09/2008 | 548.03 | 427.09 | 427.09 |
| 12/2002 | 235.00 | 187.14 | 234.00 | 12/2005 | 285.99 | 221.76 | 223.41 | 12/2008 | 421.94 | 215.59 | 268.03 |

1967=100.  *Source: Commodity Research Bureau*

# CRB SPOT LIVESTOCK SUB-INDEX

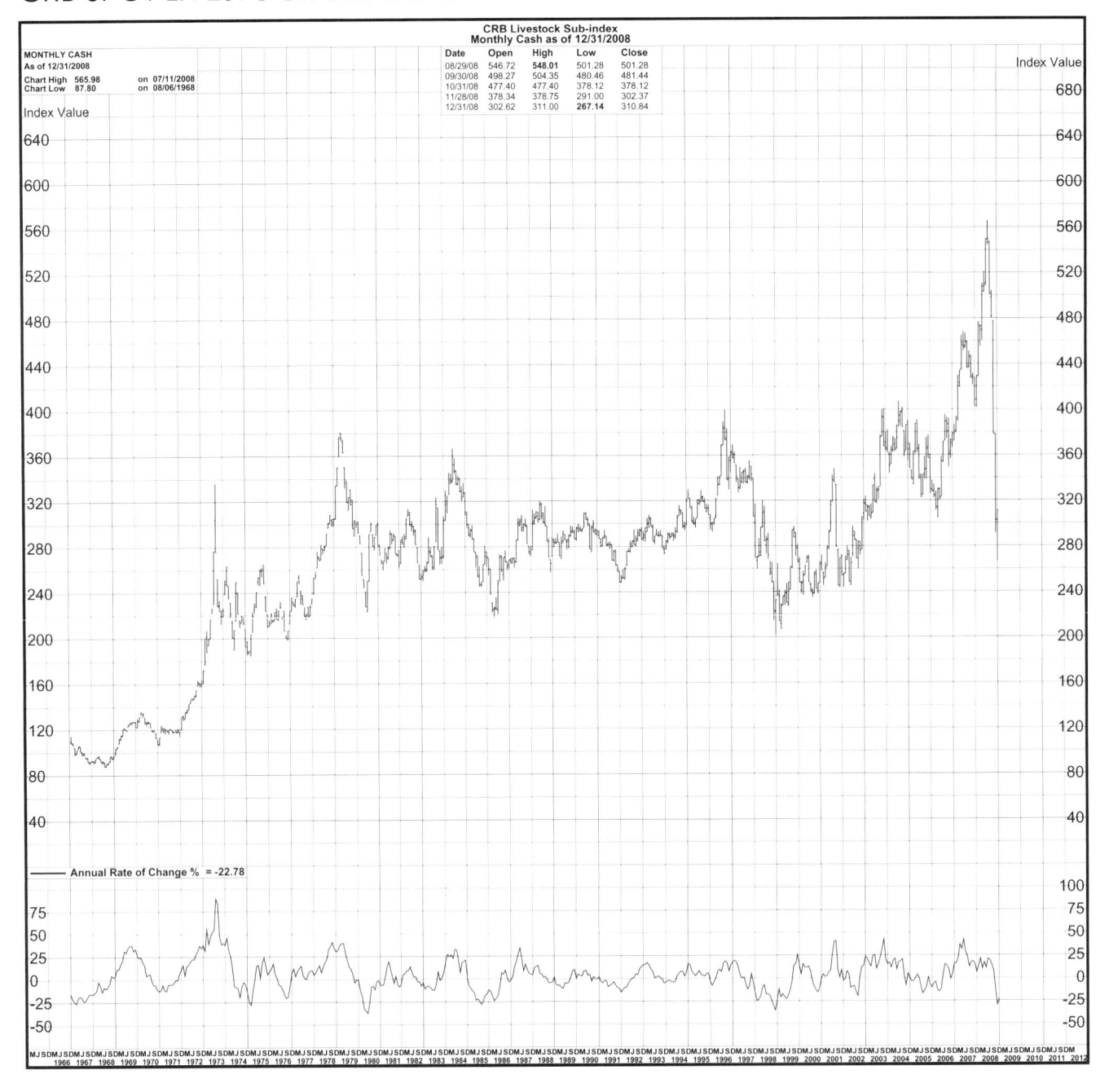

**CRB Livestock Sub-index Monthly Cash as of 12/31/2008**

| Date | Open | High | Low | Close |
|------|------|------|-----|-------|
| 08/29/08 | 546.72 | 548.01 | 501.28 | 501.28 |
| 09/30/08 | 498.27 | 504.35 | 480.46 | 481.44 |
| 10/31/08 | 477.40 | 477.40 | 378.12 | 378.12 |
| 11/28/08 | 378.34 | 378.75 | 291.00 | 302.37 |
| 12/31/08 | 302.62 | 311.00 | 267.14 | 310.84 |

MONTHLY CASH As of 12/31/2008
Chart High 565.98 on 07/11/2008
Chart Low 87.80 on 08/06/1968

Annual Rate of Change % = -22.78

## Annual High, Low and Settle of CRB Livestock Sub-Index — Index Value

| Year | High | Low | Settle | Year | High | Low | Settle | Year | High | Low | Settle |
|------|------|-----|--------|------|------|-----|--------|------|------|-----|--------|
| 1967 | 114.60 | 89.80 | 92.90 | 1981 | 295.00 | 259.80 | 264.20 | 1995 | 329.83 | 296.14 | 307.44 |
| 1968 | 97.80 | 87.80 | 96.50 | 1982 | 313.60 | 250.90 | 254.40 | 1996 | 399.67 | 292.73 | 363.01 |
| 1969 | 127.50 | 98.40 | 122.20 | 1983 | 323.90 | 250.20 | 303.10 | 1997 | 369.22 | 306.09 | 306.09 |
| 1970 | 136.20 | 106.80 | 106.80 | 1984 | 366.40 | 302.90 | 308.20 | 1998 | 320.31 | 201.75 | 232.28 |
| 1971 | 123.30 | 106.40 | 118.20 | 1985 | 310.60 | 245.10 | 271.10 | 1999 | 297.13 | 206.26 | 265.72 |
| 1972 | 163.40 | 120.10 | 163.10 | 1986 | 276.80 | 217.30 | 268.07 | 2000 | 272.11 | 234.91 | 265.51 |
| 1973 | 336.50 | 161.10 | 224.60 | 1987 | 307.91 | 261.46 | 280.14 | 2001 | 348.32 | 244.00 | 257.21 |
| 1974 | 263.50 | 190.10 | 192.80 | 1988 | 319.70 | 257.00 | 285.74 | 2002 | 320.63 | 243.62 | 317.79 |
| 1975 | 264.80 | 185.10 | 210.00 | 1989 | 298.22 | 269.53 | 286.98 | 2003 | 400.83 | 301.67 | 365.87 |
| 1976 | 232.40 | 198.70 | 223.90 | 1990 | 310.15 | 275.28 | 292.73 | 2004 | 407.25 | 343.74 | 365.02 |
| 1977 | 256.20 | 216.50 | 234.40 | 1991 | 294.48 | 248.50 | 248.62 | 2005 | 390.12 | 322.62 | 326.62 |
| 1978 | 308.20 | 239.10 | 305.10 | 1992 | 296.91 | 247.91 | 286.64 | 2006 | 395.37 | 304.32 | 378.58 |
| 1979 | 380.50 | 290.00 | 300.30 | 1993 | 307.55 | 272.74 | 274.28 | 2007 | 468.30 | 372.22 | 402.56 |
| 1980 | 302.50 | 223.10 | 281.00 | 1994 | 321.75 | 276.72 | 319.33 | 2008 | 565.98 | 267.14 | 310.84 |

1967=100. Index data begins 01/07/1947. *Source: Commodity Research Bureau*

# CRB SPOT LIVESTOCK SUB-INDEX

**Quarterly High, Low and Settle of CRB Livestock Sub-Index**   Index Value

| Quarter | High | Low | Settle | Quarter | High | Low | Settle | Quarter | High | Low | Settle |
|---|---|---|---|---|---|---|---|---|---|---|---|
| 03/2000 | 270.08 | 236.60 | 254.21 | 03/2003 | 323.77 | 301.67 | 306.09 | 03/2006 | 337.79 | 311.11 | 313.84 |
| 06/2000 | 272.11 | 248.24 | 248.24 | 06/2003 | 343.82 | 303.76 | 318.45 | 06/2006 | 358.88 | 304.32 | 354.16 |
| 09/2000 | 256.89 | 234.91 | 256.89 | 09/2003 | 377.45 | 317.28 | 375.53 | 09/2006 | 395.37 | 353.32 | 380.75 |
| 12/2000 | 265.83 | 237.75 | 265.51 | 12/2003 | 400.83 | 363.52 | 365.87 | 12/2006 | 392.44 | 349.29 | 378.58 |
| 03/2001 | 272.45 | 245.34 | 260.60 | 03/2004 | 382.21 | 343.74 | 364.12 | 03/2007 | 429.22 | 372.22 | 429.22 |
| 06/2001 | 320.21 | 262.04 | 315.84 | 06/2004 | 386.31 | 362.13 | 375.00 | 06/2007 | 468.30 | 418.96 | 454.81 |
| 09/2001 | 348.32 | 279.03 | 279.03 | 09/2004 | 407.25 | 384.23 | 384.23 | 09/2007 | 466.94 | 435.38 | 445.91 |
| 12/2001 | 277.54 | 244.00 | 257.21 | 12/2004 | 390.62 | 354.91 | 365.02 | 12/2007 | 447.17 | 402.56 | 402.56 |
| 03/2002 | 280.13 | 243.62 | 272.14 | 03/2005 | 369.79 | 333.63 | 363.04 | 03/2008 | 476.50 | 401.49 | 472.74 |
| 06/2002 | 297.43 | 245.49 | 288.93 | 06/2005 | 390.12 | 339.00 | 339.00 | 06/2008 | 549.60 | 460.62 | 549.56 |
| 09/2002 | 292.45 | 260.01 | 283.63 | 09/2005 | 358.65 | 322.62 | 347.21 | 09/2008 | 565.98 | 480.46 | 481.44 |
| 12/2002 | 320.63 | 272.09 | 317.79 | 12/2005 | 377.54 | 326.62 | 326.62 | 12/2008 | 477.40 | 267.14 | 310.84 |

1967=100.   *Source: Commodity Research Bureau*

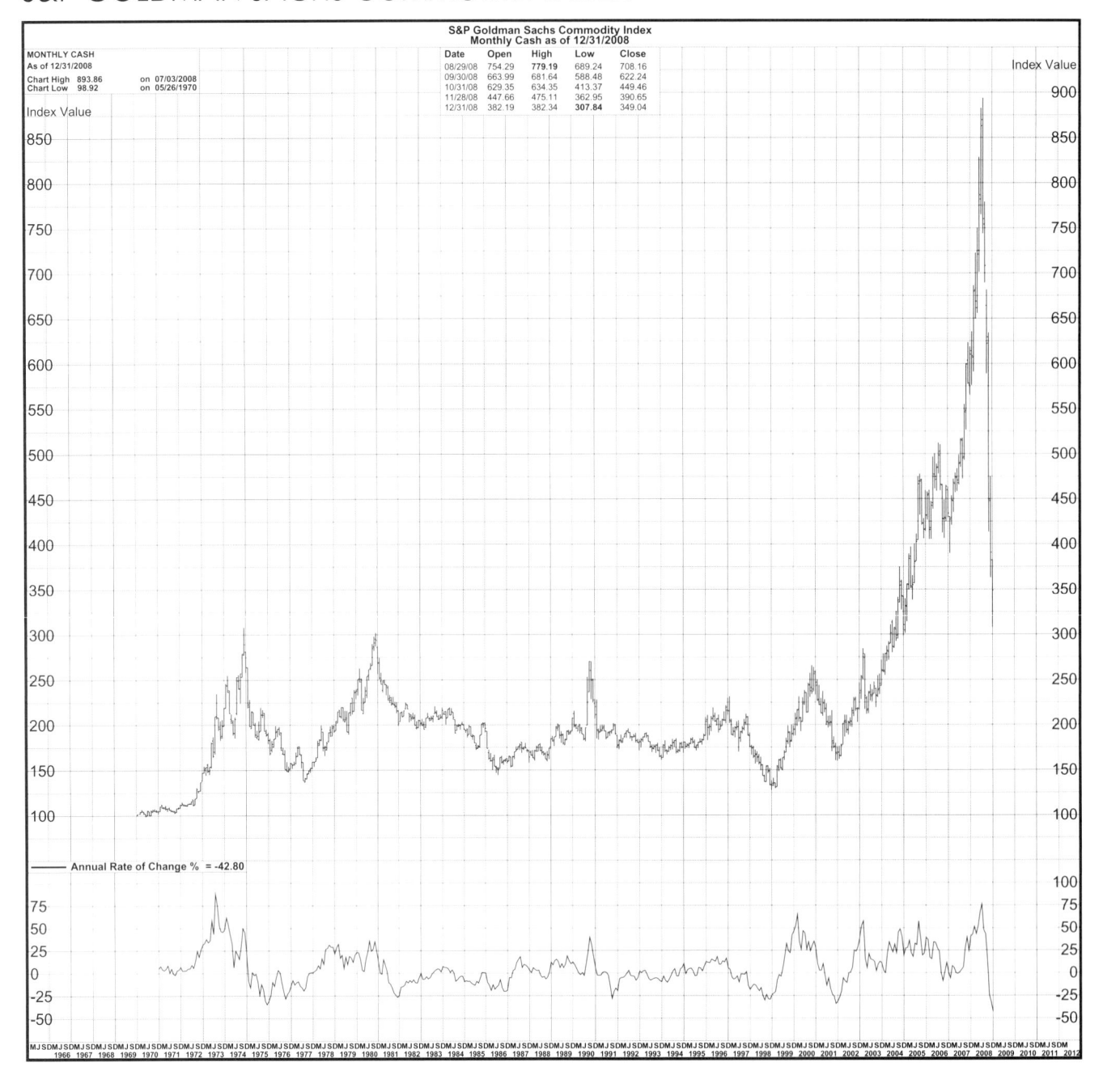

# S&P GOLDMAN SACHS COMMODITY INDEX

**MONTHLY CASH**
As of 12/31/2008
Chart High 893.86 on 07/03/2008
Chart Low 98.92 on 05/26/1970

S&P Goldman Sachs Commodity Index
Monthly Cash as of 12/31/2008

| Date | Open | High | Low | Close |
|---|---|---|---|---|
| 08/29/08 | 754.29 | 779.19 | 689.24 | 708.16 |
| 09/30/08 | 663.99 | 681.64 | 588.48 | 622.24 |
| 10/31/08 | 629.35 | 634.35 | 413.37 | 449.46 |
| 11/28/08 | 447.66 | 475.11 | 362.95 | 390.65 |
| 12/31/08 | 382.19 | 382.34 | 307.84 | 349.04 |

Annual Rate of Change % = -42.80

## Annual High, Low and Settle of S&P Goldman Sachs Commodity Index    Index Value

| Year | High | Low | Settle | Year | High | Low | Settle | Year | High | Low | Settle |
|---|---|---|---|---|---|---|---|---|---|---|---|
| 1967 | | | | 1981 | 274.33 | 199.09 | 201.65 | 1995 | 208.02 | 171.19 | 203.44 |
| 1968 | | | | 1982 | 225.07 | 194.93 | 201.46 | 1996 | 229.87 | 182.66 | 215.26 |
| 1969 | 100.00 | 100.00 | 100.00 | 1983 | 221.08 | 195.05 | 216.14 | 1997 | 231.82 | 169.69 | 175.62 |
| 1970 | 107.73 | 98.92 | 104.91 | 1984 | 219.40 | 190.55 | 195.53 | 1998 | 177.62 | 127.94 | 133.02 |
| 1971 | 112.35 | 102.31 | 111.93 | 1985 | 202.14 | 172.26 | 196.04 | 1999 | 199.61 | 129.38 | 194.54 |
| 1972 | 147.16 | 110.50 | 147.14 | 1986 | 193.08 | 144.33 | 159.27 | 2000 | 265.93 | 187.73 | 246.92 |
| 1973 | 234.93 | 144.31 | 218.73 | 1987 | 180.86 | 152.89 | 164.33 | 2001 | 250.40 | 160.12 | 169.15 |
| 1974 | 308.10 | 185.44 | 264.03 | 1988 | 184.41 | 159.39 | 184.41 | 2002 | 246.53 | 161.72 | 235.15 |
| 1975 | 264.03 | 179.07 | 183.46 | 1989 | 207.25 | 176.33 | 207.25 | 2003 | 284.61 | 211.63 | 260.54 |
| 1976 | 199.06 | 147.92 | 158.10 | 1990 | 270.41 | 181.56 | 219.97 | 2004 | 374.89 | 254.74 | 310.47 |
| 1977 | 176.66 | 137.03 | 159.33 | 1991 | 228.35 | 174.43 | 176.92 | 2005 | 478.08 | 301.32 | 431.72 |
| 1978 | 199.85 | 153.97 | 193.07 | 1992 | 196.04 | 171.70 | 181.01 | 2006 | 512.36 | 405.22 | 433.94 |
| 1979 | 239.61 | 189.20 | 237.81 | 1993 | 191.62 | 161.38 | 163.55 | 2007 | 623.63 | 389.81 | 610.17 |
| 1980 | 302.21 | 212.05 | 268.69 | 1994 | 185.01 | 163.41 | 180.84 | 2008 | 893.86 | 307.84 | 349.04 |

12/31/1969=100.    Index data begins 12/31/1969.    Source: CME Group; Chicago Mercantile Exchange

# S&P GOLDMAN SACHS COMMODITY INDEX

**S&P Goldman Sachs Commodity Index**
Weekly Cash as of 01/02/2009

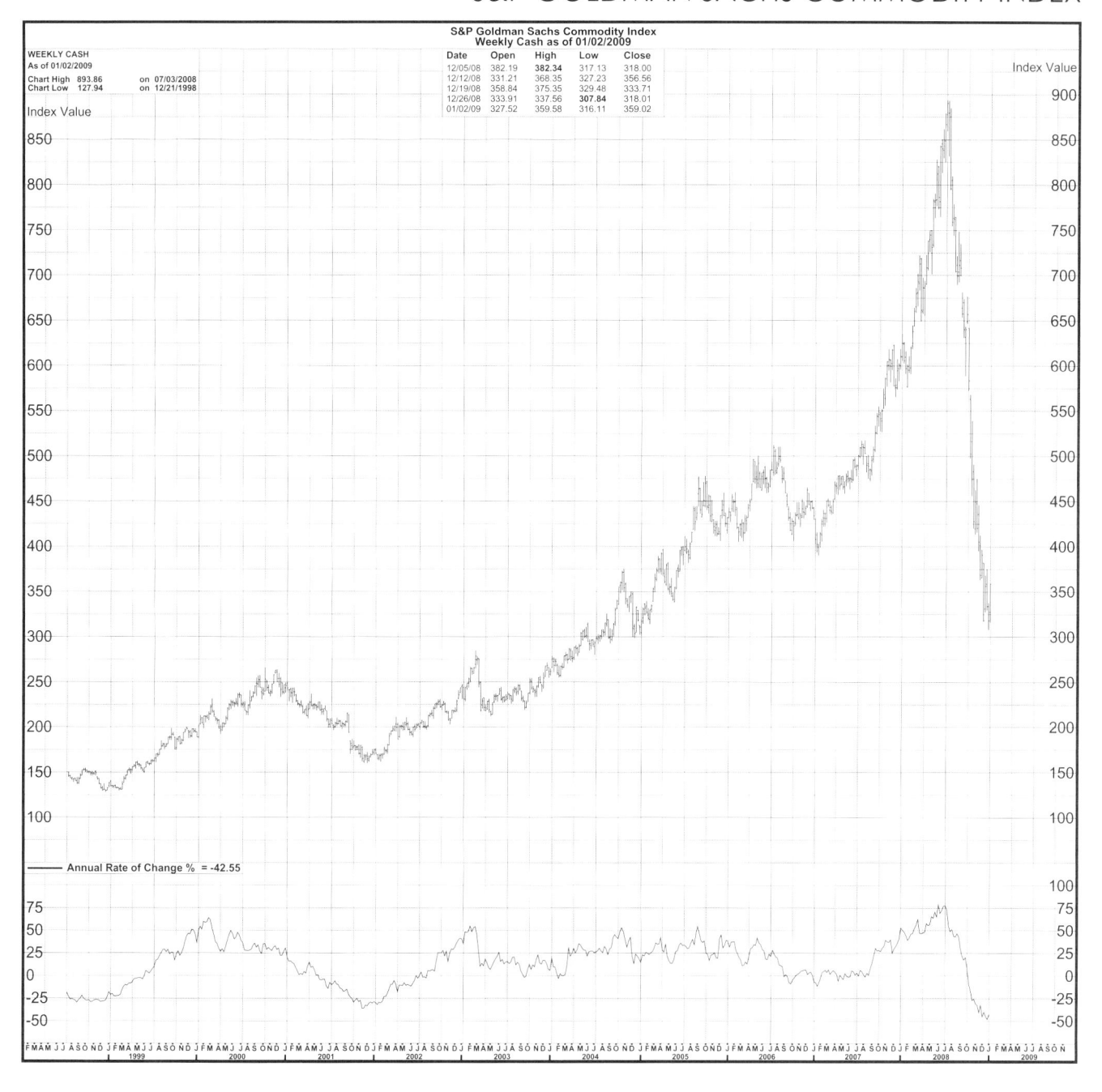

| Date | Open | High | Low | Close |
|---|---|---|---|---|
| 12/05/08 | 382.19 | 382.34 | 317.13 | 318.00 |
| 12/12/08 | 331.21 | 368.35 | 327.23 | 356.56 |
| 12/19/08 | 358.84 | 375.35 | 329.48 | 333.71 |
| 12/26/08 | 333.91 | 337.56 | 307.84 | 318.01 |
| 01/02/09 | 327.52 | 359.58 | 316.11 | 359.02 |

WEEKLY CASH
As of 01/02/2009
Chart High 893.86 on 07/03/2008
Chart Low 127.94 on 12/21/1998

Annual Rate of Change % = -42.55

## Quarterly High, Low and Settle of S&P Goldman Sachs Commodity Index    Index Value

| Quarter | High | Low | Settle | Quarter | High | Low | Settle | Quarter | High | Low | Settle |
|---|---|---|---|---|---|---|---|---|---|---|---|
| 03/2000 | 231.75 | 187.73 | 207.05 | 03/2003 | 284.61 | 216.90 | 232.28 | 03/2006 | 459.94 | 405.22 | 442.52 |
| 06/2000 | 238.44 | 192.36 | 235.71 | 06/2003 | 244.68 | 211.63 | 233.20 | 06/2006 | 500.53 | 438.71 | 484.68 |
| 09/2000 | 257.56 | 212.94 | 237.48 | 09/2003 | 247.72 | 218.81 | 232.63 | 09/2006 | 512.36 | 412.53 | 428.05 |
| 12/2000 | 265.93 | 233.33 | 246.92 | 12/2003 | 271.86 | 230.33 | 260.54 | 12/2006 | 465.28 | 406.37 | 433.94 |
| 03/2001 | 250.40 | 212.10 | 212.74 | 03/2004 | 287.54 | 254.74 | 282.12 | 03/2007 | 472.42 | 389.81 | 468.11 |
| 06/2001 | 237.45 | 199.19 | 202.66 | 06/2004 | 315.77 | 271.52 | 286.35 | 06/2007 | 499.11 | 456.86 | 489.15 |
| 09/2001 | 215.98 | 170.20 | 181.76 | 09/2004 | 341.24 | 284.61 | 337.73 | 09/2007 | 555.07 | 472.40 | 546.13 |
| 12/2001 | 186.92 | 160.12 | 169.15 | 12/2004 | 374.89 | 298.57 | 310.47 | 12/2007 | 623.63 | 526.36 | 610.17 |
| 03/2002 | 201.56 | 161.72 | 201.23 | 03/2005 | 389.43 | 301.32 | 383.87 | 03/2008 | 722.65 | 575.83 | 668.91 |
| 06/2002 | 211.08 | 186.38 | 202.78 | 06/2005 | 400.58 | 337.98 | 380.05 | 06/2008 | 882.81 | 655.70 | 862.81 |
| 09/2002 | 230.79 | 196.84 | 227.52 | 09/2005 | 478.08 | 381.05 | 469.56 | 09/2008 | 893.86 | 588.48 | 622.24 |
| 12/2002 | 246.53 | 202.51 | 235.15 | 12/2005 | 472.38 | 405.91 | 431.72 | 12/2008 | 634.35 | 307.84 | 349.04 |

12/31/1969=100.    *Source: CME Group; Chicago Mercantile Exchange*

# INDICES - EQUITIES

### US Stock Market History

The nearby chart of the Dow Jones Industrial Average (DJIA) going back to 1900 clearly shows the major phases for the US stock market. US stocks moved sideways in a volatile range during the 1900-1920 period. US stocks rallied sharply during the Roaring Twenties, but then plunged in 1929-1932 during the Great Depression. US stocks recovered later in the 1930s but then moved sideways during World War II. After World War II, the US stock market entered a long-term uptrend, with sharp corrections in the 1970s and more recently in 2000-02 and again in 2008-09. The nearby chart of the S&P 500 of the post-World War II period shows how poorly investors did in US stocks during the 1970s and early 1980s on an inflation-adjusted basis when stagflation prevailed in the US.

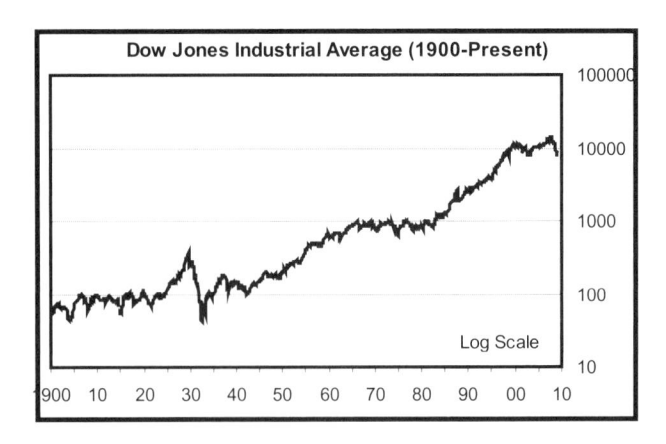

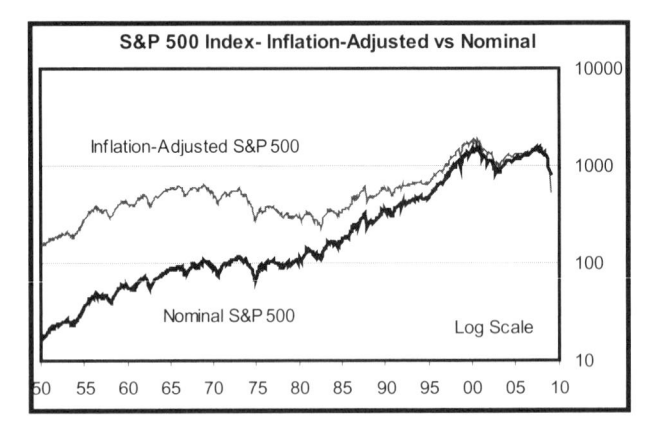

The lessons from these long-term charts are that stock investors tend to fare very well during periods of stable US economic growth and low inflation, and that they fare very poorly during periods of stagflation such as in the 1970s or during financial crises such as the Great Depression or the 2008-09 banking crisis. The charts also show that the stock market occasionally goes through bubble periods, such as during the Roaring Twenties and in the late-1990s, which later prompt painful corrections.

### 1929 Stock Market Crash

During the period from 1900 to 1920, the Dow Jones Industrial Average (DJIA) traded in a wide and volatile range. Several times during this period the DJIA fell by about 40% (e.g., in 1902-04, 1906-08, and 1910-15), but always rallied back within about 2 years.

After World War I ended in 1918, the US stock market traded in a volatile range for several years, but finally started to gather a head of steam after bottoming out in 1921. In fact, the DJIA from its low of 67.11 in 1921 more than quintupled over the following eight years to a record high of 381.17 in September 1929. The Roaring Twenties was a time of great optimism, with World War I in the past and with American industrial activity and productivity expanding greatly.

However, the 1929 Stock Market Crash brought the Roaring Twenties to an abrupt halt. The DJIA in just two days (October 28-29) plunged by an overall -23.6%. In the following two months, the DJIA continued lower for an overall sell-off of -47.9% from the peak. After a modest recovery in early 1930, the plunge resumed later in the year and the DJIA continued its plunge for another two years until finally bottoming in 1932 with a total loss of 90% from the 1929 peak. The 1929 Stock Market Crash helped set off the Great Depression, which of course resulted in mass unemployment and poverty across America.

There have been a variety of reasons given for the 1929 Stock Market Crash, including (1) rampant speculation during the 1920s and the use of excessive margin (up to 90%) to buy stocks, (2) overvaluation of stocks, particularly highly-levered public utility stocks and investment trusts, and (3) the Smoot-Hawley trade tariff bill which was passed in the midst of the crash and which would go on to cause a plunge in world trade.

After the 1929-32 crash, the US stock market rallied through most of the rest of the 1930s as America slowly came out of the Depression and as the economy began to expand again. However, the DJIA would not exceed its 1929 peak until 2-1/2 decades later in November 1954.

### Post-World War II Bull Market—1948 to 1973

The post-war period was a golden age for the US stock market. Stocks rallied sharply from 1949 to about 1966 as American business expanded its industrial base and profits. Moreover, macroeconomic conditions were very favorable with low inflation and low interest rates. The S&P 500 index rallied by a total of +675% from 15.51 at the end of World War II in August 1946 to the stock market peak of 102.24 seen in January 1973. That amounted to an average annual gain of +7.7%.

However, the stock market ran into trouble and turned sideways in the late-1960s on an inflation-adjusted basis as the US began to run a budget deficit in order to fund the

Vietnam War and President Johnson's Great Society social programs. The Federal Reserve monetized that deficit spending to keep interest rates low, thus allowing inflation to move higher. The US CPI, which averaged only 1.2% in the first-half of the 1960s, started rising in 1966 and by the end of 1969 it was over 6.0%.

**1973-75 Bear Market**

US macroeconomic conditions in the early 1970s deteriorated due to increased inflation, rising interest rates, and a decline in the dollar after the breakdown of the Bretton Woods agreement (which fixed the world's major currencies after World War II). The US economy and stock market were then hit with a major shock from the Arab Oil Embargo in October 1973, which was retaliation against the US for supporting Israel during the Yom Kippur War.

Crude oil prices (West Texas Intermediate oil) nearly tripled from $3.56 per barrel in July 1973 to $10.11 by early 1974. Crude oil prices then continued to rise steadily through the remainder of the 1970s, rising by another 50% to $15 per barrel by the end of 1978. The oil price shock caused inflation to soar from under 4.0% in 1972 to a peak of 12.3% two years later in 1974. The US experienced a long and grinding recession from November 1973 to March 1975.

The US stock market saw a serious bear market in 1973-74 due to the oil price shock and the US economic recession. The S&P 500 fell by a total of 48% during the 1973-74 bear market, from a high of 120.24 in January 1973 to the low of 62.28 in October 1974.

While the S&P 500 rose in the latter half of the 1970s on a nominal basis and recovered most of the losses seen in 1974-75, the earlier chart of the inflation-adjusted S&P500 shows that the US stock market on an inflation-adjusted basis actually continued to grind lower through the latter half of the 1970s. Stock investors did poorly over that time frame due to high inflation and continued damage from high oil prices to the US economy and corporate profits.

The US stock market then received another oil shock in 1980. Oil prices in 1979-80 more than doubled from $15 a barrel at the beginning of 1979 to a peak of $39.59 in June 1980 (which equates to $101 a barrel in 2008 dollars). That spike was caused by a near shut-down of Iranian oil production due to the Iranian revolution against the Shah of Iran.

Also during that time, Paul Volcker took over as Federal Reserve Chairman in August 1979 and started cracking down on the money supply to tame inflation. The Fed drove the federal funds rate as high as 20% in March 1980 and then again to 20% in May 1981. The combination of the oil and interest rate shocks caused double dip recessions in 1980 (Jan-July) and again in 1981-82 (July-81 to Nov-82).

The S&P 500 dropped by a total of -17% in Feb-March 1980, but then rallied through the remainder of 1980 as the US recession turned out to be short. However, the S&P 500 then again saw a bear market in 1981-82 totaling -27% (from 140.52 in Nov 1980 to 102.42 in Aug 1982) because of continued high oil prices and interest rates and the second phase of the double-dip recession.

**1982 Bull Market Begins**

Another golden age for the US stock market began in 1982 after the Federal Reserve got inflation under control and US interest rates started to fall. The devastating 1970s were finally over. The 10-year T-note yield, which peaked at about 16% in late 1981, moved lower through most of the 1980s and fell to 8% by 1990. The S&P 500 rallied sharply by a total of 229% from 1982 through 1987 (i.e., from a 102.42 low in August 1982 to a high of 336.77 in August 1987).

The infamous 1987 stock market crash then occurred on October 19, 1987, when the S&P 500 fell by -20.5% in a single day. The 1987 stock market crash of -20.5% was just slightly less than the 1929 Stock Market Crash of -23.6%, which was spread over two days (October 28-29, 1929).

The 1987 stock market crash was caused by a number of factors including (1) overvaluation in the stock market since the S&P 500 had rallied by 39% from the beginning of the year through the peak in August 1987, (2) the Fed's 150 basis point hike in the funds rate target to 7.50% in September 1987 from 6.00% in March 1987, and (3) suspicion that program trading and portfolio insurance worsened the slide due to sell stops and automated selling. The 1987 stock market crash was a global event as stock markets around the world plunged as well (UK -26.4%, Germany -9.3%, Japan -14.9%, Canada -22.5%, Australia -41.8%, Hong Kong -45.8%).

While the situation looked dire at the time, Fed Chairman Alan Greenspan, who had only been on the job for two months, quickly stepped in to calm the markets. The Fed flooded the financial system with liquidity to prevent any banking system defaults. Moreover, US corporations also helped to stem the panic by announcing large stock buyback programs to show that they thought the sell-off was overdone and that their stocks were trading at unreasonably cheap levels.

The US stock market after the 1987 stock market crash stabilized at its lower level very quickly. Within just two months the correction was over and the stock market was headed higher again. There was surprisingly little damage to the US economy, despite the huge loss in shareholder and household wealth that had just occurred. In less than two years, the S&P 500 had regained all of the losses seen during the 1987 stock market crash. While a momentous event at the time, the 1987 stock market crash is now just a blip in the overall 1982-2000 bull market.

# INDICES - EQUITIES

The S&P 500 in July-October 1990 saw a brief 3-month downdraft of -20.3% due to America's first war against Iraq, which caused another oil price spike and a US recession from July 1990 to March 1991. However, the S&P 500 was able to regain those losses within just four months.

The US stock market in the first half of the 1990s benefited as the Federal Reserve continued to cut interest rates in response to an improved inflation situation. The S&P 500 rallied by a total of 64% from the low of 294.51 seen in October 1990 to the high of 482.85 seen in January 1994. Inflation fell from an average of 5% in 1989-90 to an average of 3% in 1992-96. That allowed the Fed to cut the federal funds rate target from 9.75% in early 1989 to 3.00% by the end of 1992 and the funds rate remained at 3.00% into early 1994. The 10-year T-note yield fell sharply over that period from 9% in 1990 to the 6-8% range during the 1994-97 period. US GDP averaged strong growth of +3.6% in 1992-94. S&P 500 annual profit growth during the 1992-94 period was very strong at an average +14.3%.

**Bubble Market develops in the late-1990s.**

In the second-half of the 1990s, the US stock market entered an accelerated bull market that took the market to new record highs. The S&P 500 rallied by a total of +238% from the beginning of 1995 to the record high of 1552.87 posted in March 2000. The S&P 500 in the second half of the 1990s (1995-99) showed an average annual gain of an eye-popping +26.3% (+34.1% in 1995, +20.3% in 1996, +31.0% in 1997, +26.7% in 1998, +19.5% in 1999).

The late-1990s was a time of great optimism stemming from the technology and Internet boom, a structural increase in productivity, low interest rates, and low inflation-adjusted crude oil prices. The US economy performed very well in the latter half of the 1990s, averaging +4.0% annual GDP growth. Furthermore, average annual earnings growth for the S&P 500 companies during 1995-2000 was very strong at +12.6%, far exceeding the long-term average of +7.5%, as seen on the nearby chart.

In addition, foreign investors piled into the US stock market in the latter half of the 1990s, helping to drive stock prices even higher. Specifically, foreign ownership of US equities more than tripled from about $500 billion in 1995 to $1.6 trillion in 1999. Foreign investors accounted for 10% of the ownership of all US equities in 1999, up 4 percentage points from 6% in 1995.

However, it was speculative fever that eventually drove technology stock prices too high during the 1995-2000 stock boom. The bubble in technology stocks is best demonstrated by the Nasdaq Composite index during the 1995-2000 period, which rose nearly seven-fold from 751.96 at the beginning of 1995 to the peak of 5,132.52 in March 2000.

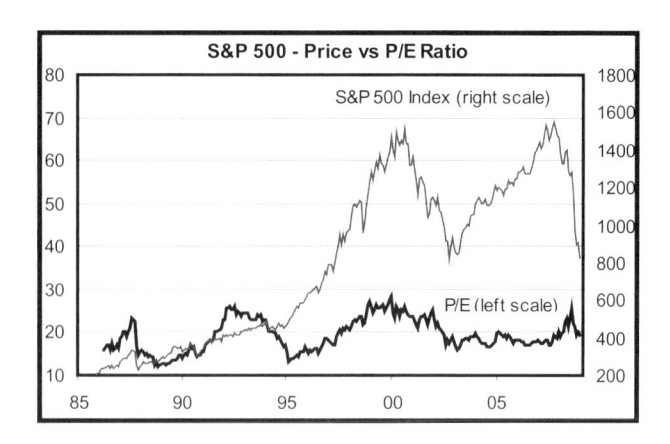

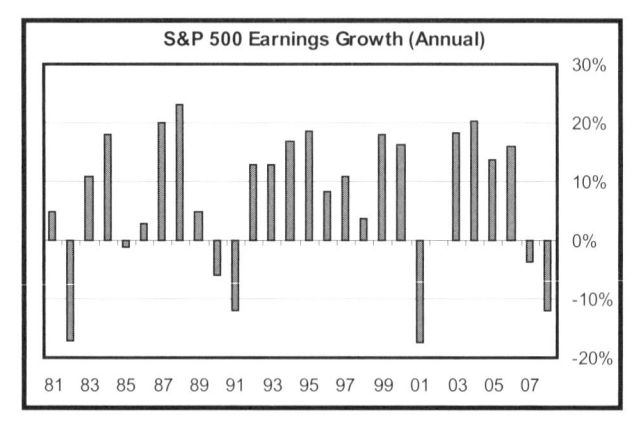

As early as 1996, Fed Chairman Greenspan realized that an equity bubble might be developing. Mr. Greenspan, in a now-famous speech delivered on December 15, 1996, asked the question about how the Fed can know when "irrational exuberance" has "unduly escalated asset values."

By early 2000, stock market valuations had become extreme. The Nasdaq Composite was trading at a price/earnings ratio of about 150, meaning that investors were willing to pay $150 for each dollar of current earnings in technology stocks. The price/earnings ratio for the S&P 500 based on forward-looking earnings was trading at 26 in March 2000, which was far above the average P/E ratio of 18 seen in the pre-bubble 1985-95 period.

**Equity bubble bursts, causing 2000-02 bear market**

The US stock market reached its peak in March 2000 and subsequently started its descent into the 2000-02 bear market. A variety of factors finally caught up with the stock market. Technology spending started slowing in early 2000 since corporations had already made their technology investments ahead of Y2K on fears of massive disruptions when the year 2000 began (which fortunately never occurred). In addition, the Fed raised its funds rate target by 175 basis points from 4.75% in mid-1999 to 6.50% in mid-2000. The US economy also started to stumble in the latter half of 2000, with GDP falling -0.5% in Q3-2000. After the equity bubble burst, household wealth plunged and consumer and business confidence was severely damaged. A full-blown, though short, recession then emerged from March to November 2001.

To make things worse, on September 11, 2001, al-Qaeda launched a terrorist attack on the World Trade Center and the Pentagon that shocked the nation. The attack occurred on a Tuesday morning. The New York Stock Exchange remained closed for the remainder of the week (Sep 11-14) but then reopened the following Monday. The S&P 500 fell by -13.5% in the subsequent 2 weeks, but then more than regained its losses within a month as confidence returned.

When 9/11 occurred, the Federal Reserve was already in the process of cutting interest rates because of the bursting of the equity bubble. However, 9/11 caused the Fed to continue to cut interest rates. In total, the Fed cut the federal funds rate by 475 basis points from 6.5% in late 2000 to 1.75% by the end of 2001. The Fed then cut by another 75 basis points to 1.00% by mid-2003.

The Fed was alarmed about the inability of the US economy to show sustained GDP growth of more than 2% annual growth in the 2001-02 time frame. The Fed was very worried that a deflationary period could emerge, such as the one seen in Japan from 1990-2005, in which the Fed would have trouble fighting a weak economy with monetary policy because the Fed would simply be "pushing on a string."

The US stock market finally bottomed out in October 2002. At the bottom of the bear market, the S&P 500 was down by a total of -50.5%, and the Nasdaq Composite was down by a total of -78.4%, from their record highs posted in March 2000.

**2002-07 bull market**

In October 2002, the US stock market finally turned higher as the Fed's extraordinarily easy monetary policy started to stimulate asset prices, including home prices and the equity market. Moreover, US consumer spending held up well and pulled the rest of the US economy through the soft period seen in 2001-03. By the end of 2003, GDP growth had recovered and then averaged a strong +3.5% in 2004-05.

Since the US had escaped deflation and the US economy was on the mend, the Fed in June 2004 started raising its funds rate target in 25 basis point increments at successive FOMC meetings. Over the 2-year period from June 2004 to June 2006, the Fed raised the funds rate target from 1%

to a peak of 5.25%. The US economy was resilient enough to absorb the Fed's slow tightening process and the US economy performed well from 2003-05. The US economy was also able to absorb the shock of crude oil prices more than doubling in price from $30 per barrel in late 2003 to a high of $70.85 in August 2005. The 2002-06 stock market rally was driven largely by a surge in corporate earnings. US corporations were able to produce double-digit annual earnings growth averaging +17.3% per year in 2003-05.

**2008-09 financial crisis and bear market**

The US stock market started to run into trouble in mid-2007 when the sub-prime mortgage crisis emerged and two Bear Stearns hedge funds became insolvent in June 2007. In addition, BNP Paribas froze redemptions from three of its mortgage security hedge funds in August 2007. US GDP was weak at –0.2% in Q4-2007 and +0.9% in Q2-2008. The Fed responded by starting to cut interest rates in September 2007. The S&P 500 was able to make a last run to a record high of 1576.09 in October 2007, but the stock market then sank for the rest of 2007.

The year 2008 was tumultuous for the stock market. The stock market moved lower in early 2008 as the housing market crisis became worse with increased foreclosures, falling home prices, and huge losses for banks and hedge funds holding mortgage securities. The crisis finally reached epic proportions in mid-September 2008 when Lehman Brothers was forced to declare bankruptcy. The S&P 500 then went into a terrifying decline during September-November 2008, falling by a total of 42% from the August close to the 11-1/2 year low of 741.02 posted in November 2008. The 2008 plunge completely erased the 2002/06 bull market and left the S&P 500 back to where it was in 1997.

As of early 2009, the situation for the US stock market remained grim. The US was in the midst of one of its worst recessions in post-war history and corporations were aggressively laying off employees to slash expenses. US consumers were shell-shocked by the crisis and responded by sharply cutting their spending. Earnings growth for the S&P 500 companies fell for six consecutive quarters through Q4-2008. Many US investors in 2008 completely lost their faith in stocks as they saw the value of their savings and retirement accounts evaporate. In addition, many investors yanked their money from overseas stock markets as they sought a safer home for their remaining capital.

Yet the situation in early 2009 was not completely hopeless. The stock market in early 2009 was trading at reasonably low levels. In mid-February 2009, the price/earnings ratio for the S&P 500 was trading at 19.8 against trailing earnings and at 12.7 against forward earnings.

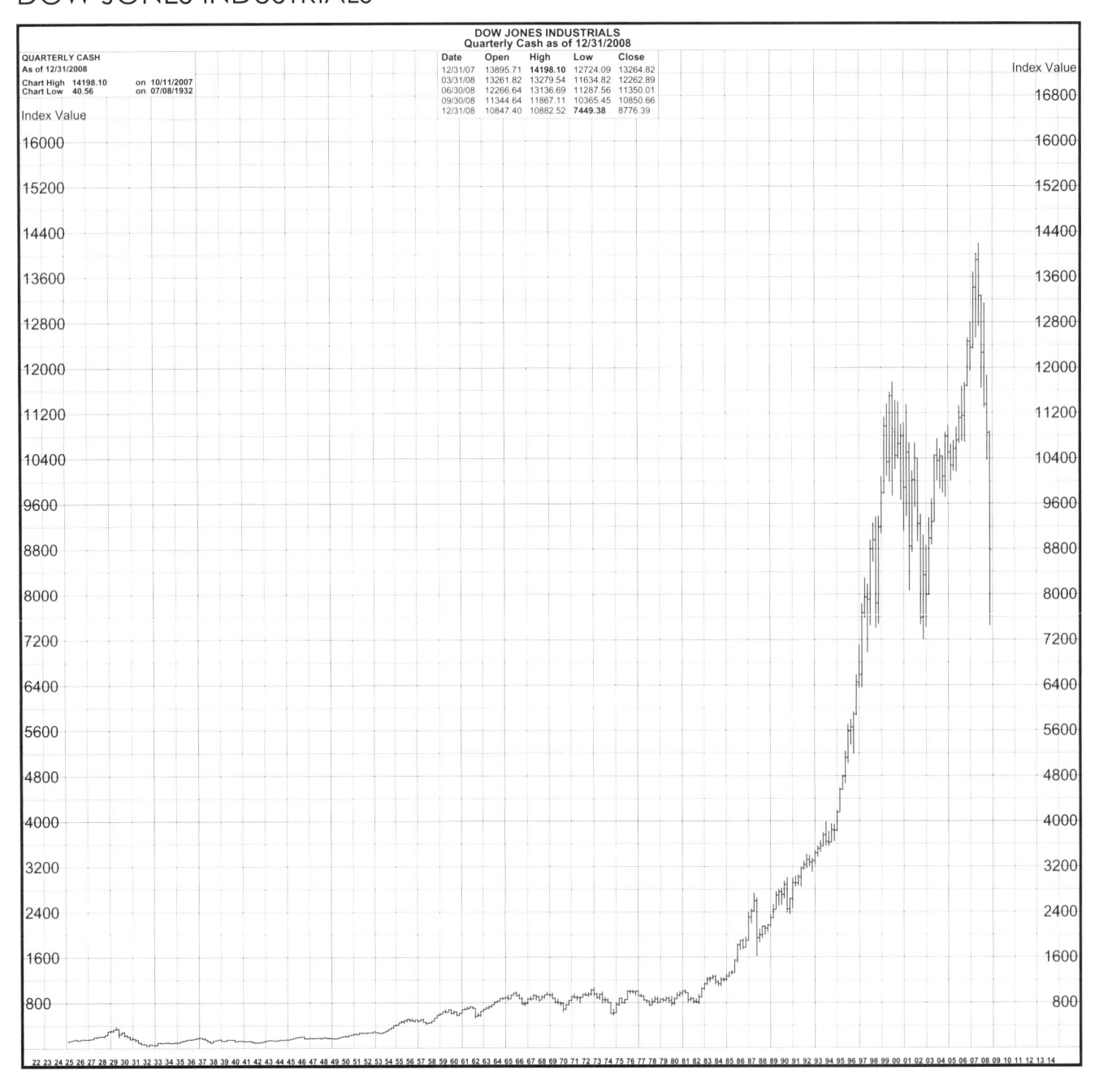

# DOW JONES INDUSTRIALS

**QUARTERLY CASH**
As of 12/31/2008
Chart High 14198.10 on 10/11/2007
Chart Low 40.56 on 07/08/1932

**DOW JONES INDUSTRIALS**
Quarterly Cash as of 12/31/2008

| Date | Open | High | Low | Close |
|---|---|---|---|---|
| 12/31/07 | 13895.71 | 14198.10 | 12724.09 | 13264.82 |
| 03/31/08 | 13261.82 | 13279.54 | 11634.82 | 12262.89 |
| 06/30/08 | 12266.64 | 13136.69 | 11287.56 | 11350.01 |
| 09/30/08 | 11344.64 | 11867.11 | 10365.45 | 10850.66 |
| 12/31/08 | 10847.40 | 10882.52 | 7449.38 | 8776.39 |

## Annual High, Low and Settle of Dow Jones Industrials Index    In Index Value

| Year | High | Low | Settle | Year | High | Low | Settle | Year | High | Low | Settle |
|---|---|---|---|---|---|---|---|---|---|---|---|
| 1925 | 159.39 | 115.00 | 156.66 | 1939 | 157.77 | 120.04 | 149.99 | 1953 | 295.03 | 254.36 | 280.90 |
| 1926 | 166.14 | 135.20 | 157.20 | 1940 | 153.29 | 110.41 | 131.13 | 1954 | 407.17 | 278.91 | 404.39 |
| 1927 | 200.93 | 152.73 | 200.70 | 1941 | 134.27 | 105.52 | 110.96 | 1955 | 490.75 | 385.65 | 488.40 |
| 1928 | 301.61 | 191.80 | 300.00 | 1942 | 120.19 | 92.69 | 119.40 | 1956 | 524.37 | 458.21 | 499.47 |
| 1929 | 386.10 | 195.35 | 248.48 | 1943 | 146.41 | 118.84 | 135.89 | 1957 | 523.11 | 416.15 | 435.69 |
| 1930 | 297.25 | 154.45 | 164.58 | 1944 | 152.75 | 134.10 | 151.93 | 1958 | 587.44 | 434.04 | 583.65 |
| 1931 | 196.96 | 71.79 | 77.90 | 1945 | 196.59 | 150.53 | 192.91 | 1959 | 683.90 | 571.73 | 679.36 |
| 1932 | 89.87 | 40.56 | 60.26 | 1946 | 213.36 | 160.49 | 177.20 | 1960 | 688.21 | 564.23 | 615.89 |
| 1933 | 110.53 | 49.68 | 98.67 | 1947 | 187.66 | 161.38 | 181.16 | 1961 | 741.30 | 606.09 | 731.14 |
| 1934 | 111.93 | 84.58 | 104.04 | 1948 | 194.49 | 164.07 | 177.30 | 1962 | 734.38 | 524.55 | 652.10 |
| 1935 | 149.42 | 95.95 | 144.13 | 1949 | 200.91 | 160.62 | 200.52 | 1963 | 773.07 | 643.57 | 762.95 |
| 1936 | 186.39 | 141.53 | 179.90 | 1950 | 236.63 | 193.94 | 235.42 | 1964 | 897.00 | 760.34 | 874.13 |
| 1937 | 195.59 | 112.54 | 120.85 | 1951 | 277.51 | 234.93 | 269.23 | 1965 | 976.61 | 832.74 | 969.26 |
| 1938 | 158.90 | 97.46 | 154.36 | 1952 | 293.50 | 254.70 | 291.90 | 1966 | 1,001.11 | 735.74 | 785.69 |

Data continued on page 268.    Source: New York Stock Exchange

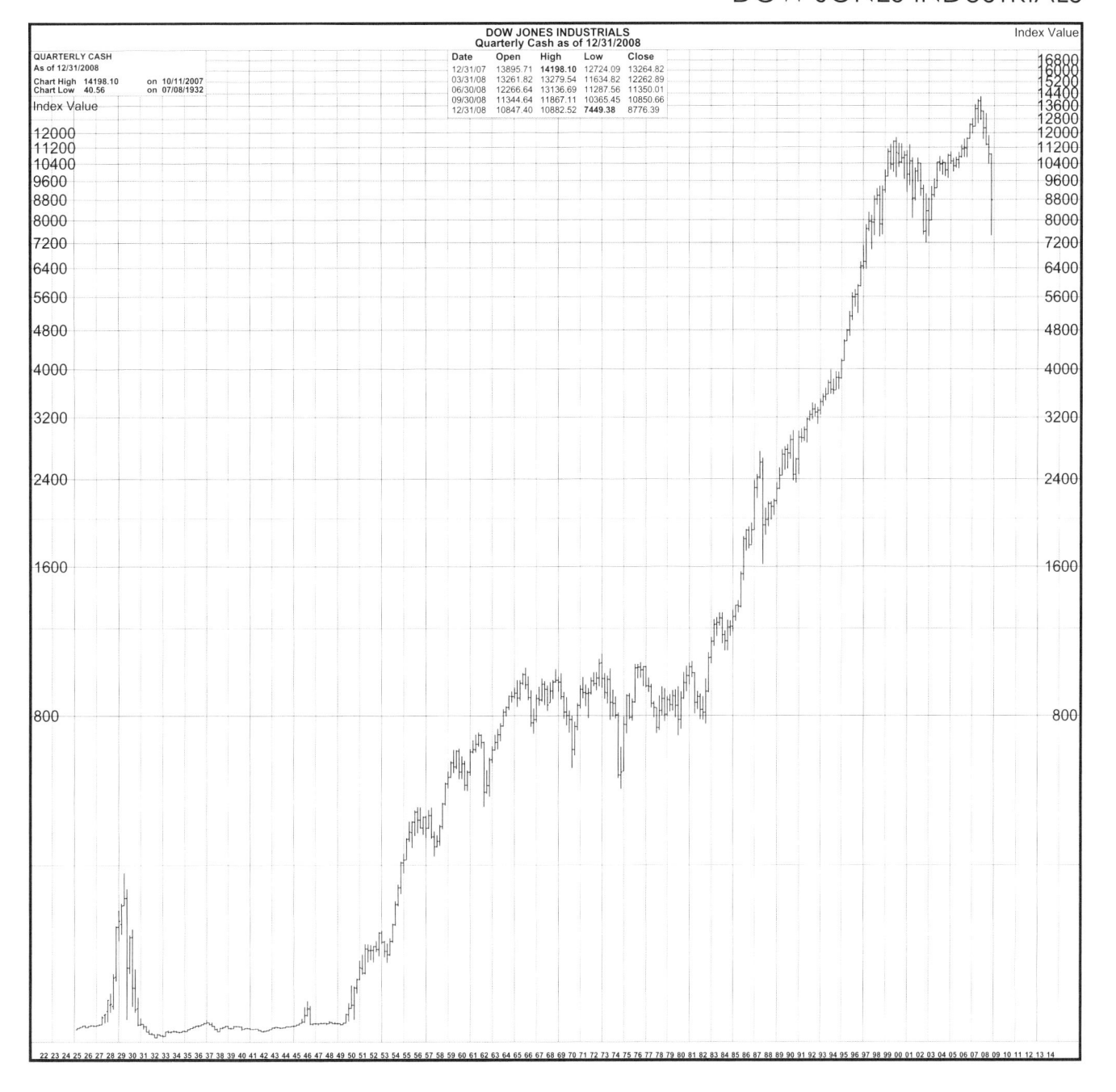

# DOW JONES INDUSTRIALS

**QUARTERLY CASH**
As of 12/31/2008
Chart High 14198.10 on 10/11/2007
Chart Low 40.56 on 07/08/1932

**DOW JONES INDUSTRIALS**
Quarterly Cash as of 12/31/2008

| Date | Open | High | Low | Close |
|---|---|---|---|---|
| 12/31/07 | 13895.71 | 14198.10 | 12724.09 | 13264.82 |
| 03/31/08 | 13261.82 | 13279.54 | 11634.82 | 12262.89 |
| 06/30/08 | 12266.64 | 13136.69 | 11287.56 | 11350.01 |
| 09/30/08 | 11344.64 | 11867.11 | 10365.45 | 10850.66 |
| 12/31/08 | 10847.40 | 10882.52 | 7449.38 | 8776.39 |

267

# DOW JONES INDUSTRIALS

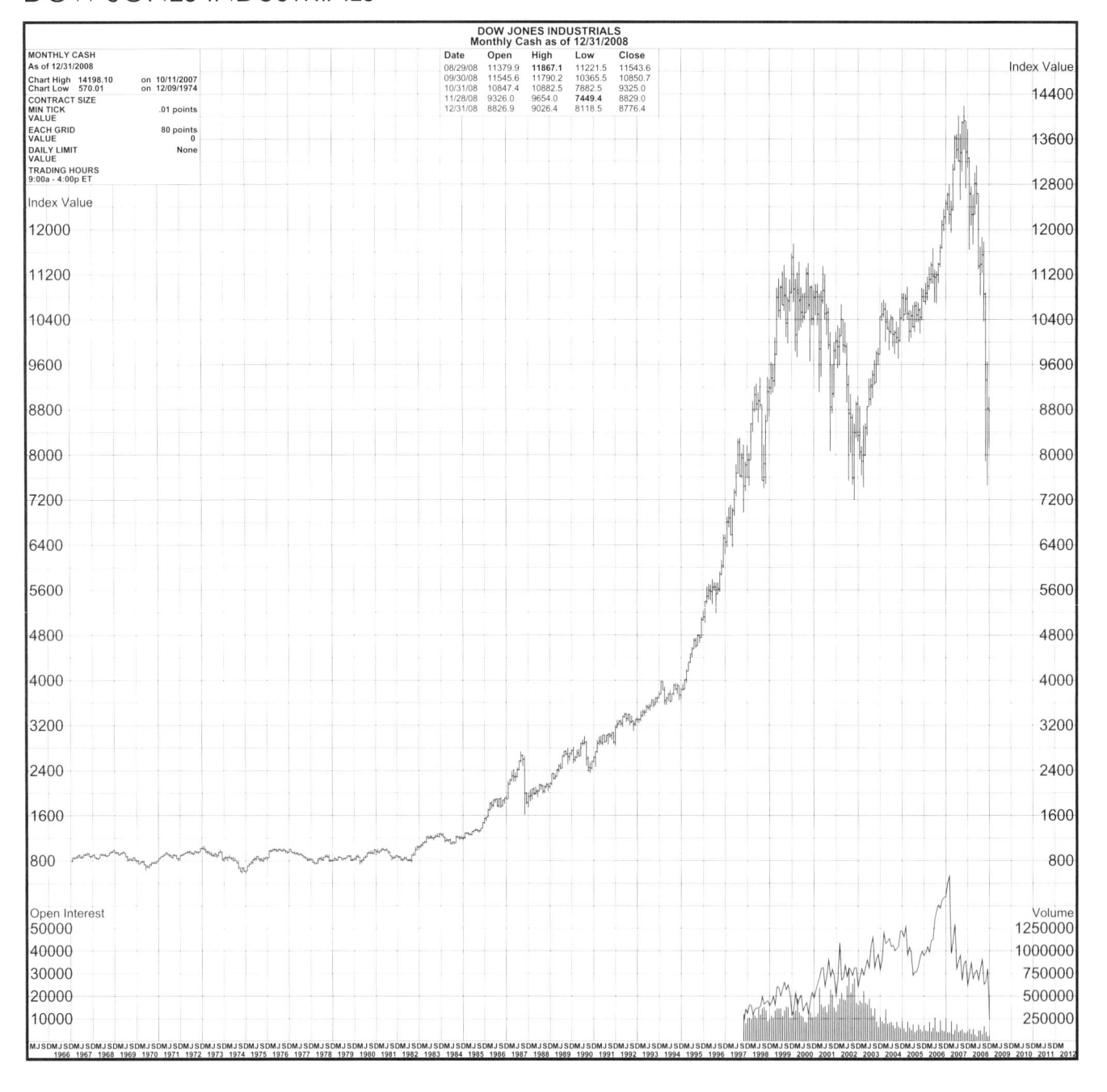

**DOW JONES INDUSTRIALS**
Monthly Cash as of 12/31/2008

| Date | Open | High | Low | Close |
|---|---|---|---|---|
| 08/29/08 | 11379.9 | 11867.1 | 11221.5 | 11543.6 |
| 09/30/08 | 11545.6 | 11790.2 | 10365.5 | 10850.7 |
| 10/31/08 | 10847.4 | 10882.5 | 7882.5 | 9325.0 |
| 11/28/08 | 9326.0 | 9654.0 | 7449.4 | 8829.0 |
| 12/31/08 | 8826.9 | 9026.4 | 8118.5 | 8776.4 |

MONTHLY CASH
As of 12/31/2008
Chart High 14198.10 on 10/11/2007
Chart Low 570.01 on 12/09/1974
CONTRACT SIZE
MIN TICK VALUE .01 points
EACH GRID VALUE 80 points
DAILY LIMIT VALUE None
TRADING HOURS 9:00a - 4:00p ET

## Annual High, Low and Settle of Dow Jones Industrials Index   In Index Value

| Year | High | Low | Settle | Year | High | Low | Settle | Year | High | Low | Settle |
|---|---|---|---|---|---|---|---|---|---|---|---|
| 1967 | 951.57 | 776.16 | 905.11 | 1981 | 1,030.98 | 807.45 | 875.00 | 1995 | 5,235.62 | 3,817.28 | 5,117.12 |
| 1968 | 994.65 | 817.61 | 943.75 | 1982 | 1,074.32 | 769.98 | 1,046.54 | 1996 | 6,589.53 | 5,014.52 | 6,448.27 |
| 1969 | 974.92 | 764.45 | 800.36 | 1983 | 1,291.67 | 1,020.24 | 1,258.63 | 1997 | 8,299.49 | 6,352.82 | 7,908.25 |
| 1970 | 848.23 | 627.46 | 838.92 | 1984 | 1,291.87 | 1,082.05 | 1,211.57 | 1998 | 9,380.20 | 7,400.30 | 9,181.43 |
| 1971 | 958.12 | 790.67 | 890.20 | 1985 | 1,563.76 | 1,180.99 | 1,546.67 | 1999 | 11,568.77 | 9,063.26 | 11,497.12 |
| 1972 | 1,042.44 | 882.75 | 1,020.02 | 1986 | 1,961.47 | 1,497.71 | 1,895.11 | 2000 | 11,750.28 | 9,654.64 | 10,786.85 |
| 1973 | 1,067.20 | 783.56 | 850.86 | 1987 | 2,736.61 | 1,616.21 | 1,938.82 | 2001 | 11,350.05 | 8,062.34 | 10,021.50 |
| 1974 | 904.02 | 570.01 | 616.24 | 1988 | 2,188.04 | 1,850.96 | 2,168.57 | 2002 | 10,673.10 | 7,197.49 | 8,341.63 |
| 1975 | 888.85 | 619.13 | 852.41 | 1989 | 2,795.97 | 2,131.79 | 2,753.20 | 2003 | 10,462.44 | 7,416.64 | 10,453.92 |
| 1976 | 1,026.26 | 848.63 | 1,004.65 | 1990 | 3,010.64 | 2,354.21 | 2,633.66 | 2004 | 10,868.07 | 9,708.40 | 10,783.01 |
| 1977 | 1,007.81 | 792.79 | 831.17 | 1991 | 3,188.05 | 2,457.67 | 3,168.83 | 2005 | 10,984.46 | 10,000.46 | 10,717.50 |
| 1978 | 917.27 | 736.75 | 805.01 | 1992 | 3,422.01 | 3,095.80 | 3,301.11 | 2006 | 12,529.88 | 10,661.15 | 12,463.15 |
| 1979 | 904.86 | 792.24 | 838.74 | 1993 | 3,799.92 | 3,231.96 | 3,754.09 | 2007 | 14,198.10 | 11,939.61 | 13,264.82 |
| 1980 | 1,009.39 | 729.95 | 963.98 | 1994 | 3,985.69 | 3,552.48 | 3,834.44 | 2008 | 13,279.54 | 7,449.38 | 8,776.39 |

Data continued from page 266.   *Source: New York Stock Exchange*

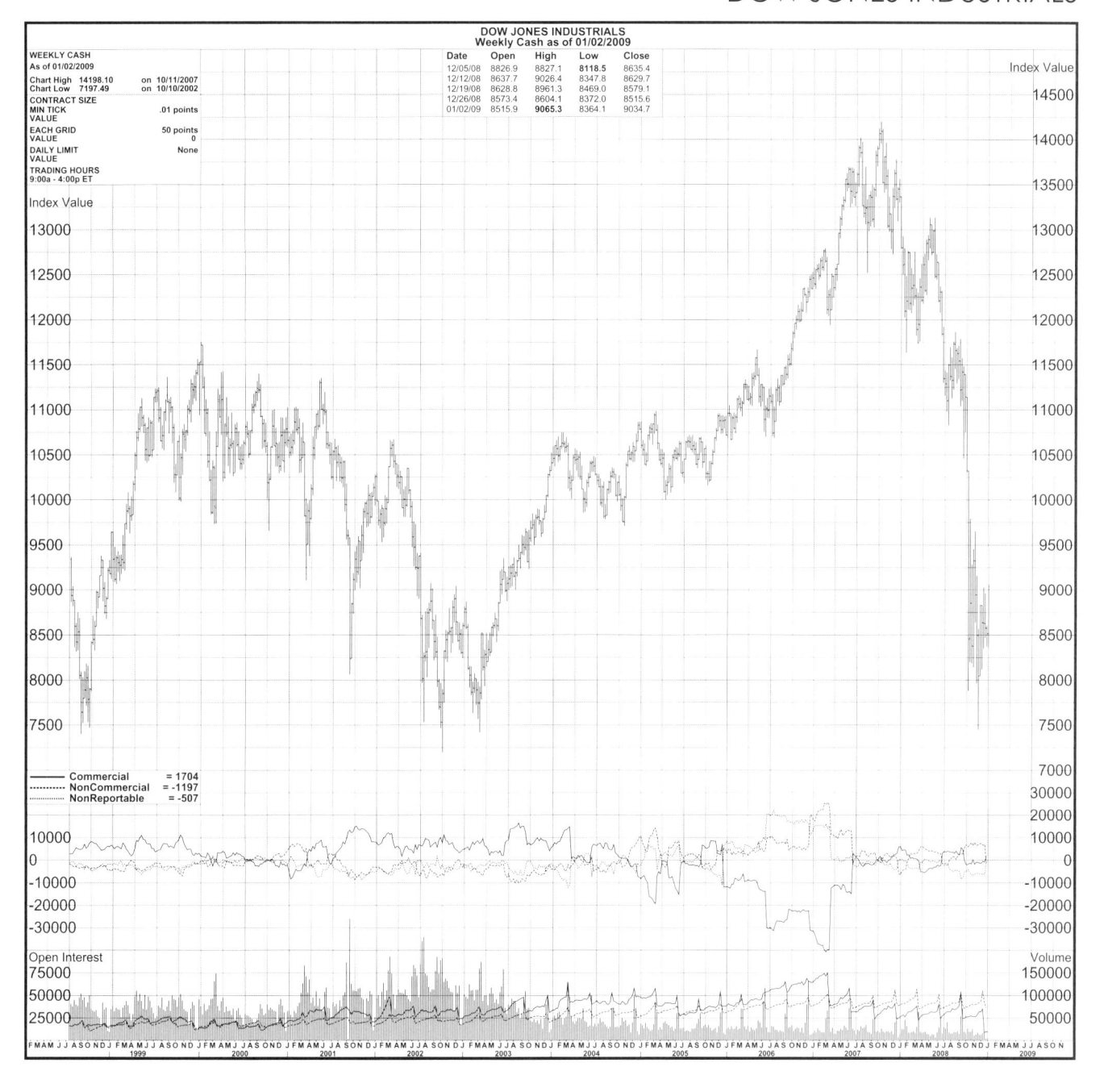

# DOW JONES INDUSTRIALS

**WEEKLY CASH**
As of 01/02/2009
Chart High 14198.10 on 10/11/2007
Chart Low 7197.49 on 10/10/2002
CONTRACT SIZE
MIN TICK VALUE .01 points
EACH GRID VALUE 50 points
DAILY LIMIT VALUE None
TRADING HOURS 9:00a - 4:00p ET

**DOW JONES INDUSTRIALS**
Weekly Cash as of 01/02/2009

| Date | Open | High | Low | Close |
|---|---|---|---|---|
| 12/05/08 | 8826.9 | 8827.1 | 8118.5 | 8635.4 |
| 12/12/08 | 8637.7 | 9026.4 | 8347.8 | 8629.7 |
| 12/19/08 | 8628.8 | 8961.3 | 8469.0 | 8579.1 |
| 12/26/08 | 8573.4 | 8604.1 | 8372.0 | 8515.6 |
| 01/02/09 | 8515.9 | 9065.3 | 8364.1 | 9034.7 |

Commercial = 1704
NonCommercial = -1197
NonReportable = -507

## Quarterly High, Low and Settle of Dow Jones Industrials Index   In Index Value

| Quarter | High | Low | Settle | Quarter | High | Low | Settle | Quarter | High | Low | Settle |
|---|---|---|---|---|---|---|---|---|---|---|---|
| 03/2000 | 11,750.28 | 9,731.81 | 10,921.92 | 03/2003 | 8,869.29 | 7,416.64 | 7,992.13 | 03/2006 | 11,334.96 | 10,661.15 | 11,109.32 |
| 06/2000 | 11,425.45 | 10,201.53 | 10,447.89 | 06/2003 | 9,352.77 | 7,979.69 | 8,985.44 | 06/2006 | 11,670.19 | 10,698.85 | 11,150.22 |
| 09/2000 | 11,401.19 | 10,393.09 | 10,650.92 | 09/2003 | 9,686.08 | 8,871.20 | 9,275.06 | 09/2006 | 11,741.99 | 10,683.32 | 11,679.07 |
| 12/2000 | 11,006.50 | 9,654.64 | 10,786.85 | 12/2003 | 10,462.44 | 9,276.80 | 10,453.92 | 12/2006 | 12,529.88 | 11,653.06 | 12,463.15 |
| 03/2001 | 11,035.14 | 9,106.54 | 9,878.78 | 03/2004 | 10,753.63 | 10,007.49 | 10,357.70 | 03/2007 | 12,795.93 | 11,939.61 | 12,354.35 |
| 06/2001 | 11,350.05 | 9,375.72 | 10,502.40 | 06/2004 | 10,570.81 | 9,852.19 | 10,435.48 | 06/2007 | 13,692.00 | 12,324.28 | 13,408.62 |
| 09/2001 | 10,679.12 | 8,062.34 | 8,847.56 | 09/2004 | 10,448.09 | 9,783.91 | 10,080.27 | 09/2007 | 14,021.95 | 12,517.94 | 13,895.63 |
| 12/2001 | 10,184.45 | 8,732.14 | 10,021.50 | 12/2004 | 10,868.07 | 9,708.40 | 10,783.01 | 12/2007 | 14,198.10 | 12,724.09 | 13,264.82 |
| 03/2002 | 10,673.10 | 9,529.46 | 10,403.94 | 03/2005 | 10,984.46 | 10,368.61 | 10,503.76 | 03/2008 | 13,279.54 | 11,634.82 | 12,262.89 |
| 06/2002 | 10,402.07 | 8,926.57 | 9,243.26 | 06/2005 | 10,656.29 | 10,000.46 | 10,274.97 | 06/2008 | 13,136.69 | 11,287.56 | 11,350.01 |
| 09/2002 | 9,410.38 | 7,460.78 | 7,579.58 | 09/2005 | 10,719.41 | 10,175.40 | 10,568.70 | 09/2008 | 11,867.11 | 10,365.45 | 10,850.66 |
| 12/2002 | 9,043.37 | 7,197.49 | 8,341.63 | 12/2005 | 10,959.79 | 10,156.46 | 10,717.50 | 12/2008 | 10,882.52 | 7,449.38 | 8,776.39 |

*Source: New York Stock Exchange*

## DOW JONES TRANSPORTS

**DOW JONES TRANSPORTS**
Monthly Cash as of 12/31/2008

| Date | Open | High | Low | Close |
|---|---|---|---|---|
| 08/29/08 | 5071.60 | 5293.41 | 4859.63 | 5103.40 |
| 09/30/08 | 5109.95 | 5259.34 | 4440.80 | 4616.01 |
| 10/31/08 | 4608.48 | 4623.59 | 3283.12 | 3885.83 |
| 11/28/08 | 3885.16 | 4094.39 | 2909.29 | 3512.20 |
| 12/31/08 | 3512.20 | 3638.96 | 3146.98 | 3537.15 |

MONTHLY CASH
As of 12/31/2008
Chart High 5536.57 on 05/19/2008
Chart Low 115.76 on 07/07/1970

### Annual High, Low and Settle of Dow Jones Transports Index   In Index Value

| Year | High | Low | Settle | Year | High | Low | Settle | Year | High | Low | Settle |
|---|---|---|---|---|---|---|---|---|---|---|---|
| 1967 | | | | 1981 | 451.93 | 326.18 | 380.30 | 1995 | 2,105.19 | 1,443.62 | 1,981.00 |
| 1968 | | | | 1982 | 468.90 | 288.97 | 448.38 | 1996 | 2,336.43 | 1,858.88 | 2,255.67 |
| 1969 | | | | 1983 | 613.14 | 434.24 | 596.69 | 1997 | 3,372.42 | 2,203.27 | 3,256.50 |
| 1970 | 184.04 | 115.76 | 171.52 | 1984 | 615.19 | 439.61 | 557.68 | 1998 | 3,701.42 | 2,282.18 | 3,149.31 |
| 1971 | 250.67 | 168.53 | 243.72 | 1985 | 729.17 | 550.04 | 708.33 | 1999 | 3,797.05 | 2,778.56 | 2,977.20 |
| 1972 | 278.27 | 210.19 | 227.17 | 1986 | 876.32 | 677.20 | 807.17 | 2000 | 3,017.18 | 2,260.78 | 2,946.60 |
| 1973 | 231.66 | 150.38 | 196.19 | 1987 | 1,104.19 | 653.86 | 747.86 | 2001 | 3,157.44 | 1,942.01 | 2,639.99 |
| 1974 | 204.89 | 124.30 | 143.44 | 1988 | 966.63 | 732.43 | 960.92 | 2002 | 3,050.98 | 2,008.31 | 2,309.96 |
| 1975 | 177.07 | 143.23 | 172.65 | 1989 | 1,540.54 | 946.14 | 1,177.81 | 2003 | 3,038.15 | 1,918.12 | 3,007.05 |
| 1976 | 238.06 | 172.07 | 237.03 | 1990 | 1,216.06 | 812.68 | 910.23 | 2004 | 3,823.96 | 2,743.46 | 3,798.05 |
| 1977 | 247.91 | 197.46 | 217.18 | 1991 | 1,358.55 | 887.37 | 1,358.00 | 2005 | 4,306.09 | 3,348.36 | 4,196.03 |
| 1978 | 264.95 | 198.19 | 206.56 | 1992 | 1,472.53 | 1,202.67 | 1,449.23 | 2006 | 5,013.67 | 4,059.87 | 4,560.20 |
| 1979 | 273.42 | 201.56 | 252.39 | 1993 | 1,789.47 | 1,441.18 | 1,762.32 | 2007 | 5,487.05 | 4,346.39 | 4,570.55 |
| 1980 | 430.18 | 229.79 | 398.10 | 1994 | 1,874.87 | 1,353.96 | 1,455.03 | 2008 | 5,536.57 | 2,909.29 | 3,537.15 |

*Source: New York Stock Exchange*

# DOW JONES TRANSPORTS

**DOW JONES TRANSPORTS**
Weekly Cash as of 01/02/2009

| Date | Open | High | Low | Close |
|---|---|---|---|---|
| 12/05/08 | 3512.20 | 3512.20 | 3179.25 | 3433.33 |
| 12/12/08 | 3431.63 | 3638.96 | 3146.98 | 3245.44 |
| 12/19/08 | 3245.49 | 3515.14 | 3167.24 | 3389.47 |
| 12/26/08 | 3390.96 | 3402.15 | 3282.35 | 3370.19 |
| 01/02/09 | 3368.74 | 3664.32 | 3283.48 | 3651.02 |

WEEKLY CASH As of 01/02/2009
Chart High 5536.57 on 05/19/2008
Chart Low 1918.12 on 03/12/2003

## Quarterly High, Low and Settle of Dow Jones Transports Index    In Index Value

| Quarter | High | Low | Settle | Quarter | High | Low | Settle | Quarter | High | Low | Settle |
|---|---|---|---|---|---|---|---|---|---|---|---|
| 03/2000 | 3,017.18 | 2,260.78 | 2,763.24 | 03/2003 | 2,425.83 | 1,918.12 | 2,131.21 | 03/2006 | 4,615.83 | 4,059.87 | 4,568.00 |
| 06/2000 | 2,979.25 | 2,605.43 | 2,645.37 | 06/2003 | 2,557.47 | 2,116.65 | 2,412.86 | 06/2006 | 5,013.67 | 4,410.16 | 4,928.89 |
| 09/2000 | 2,928.69 | 2,498.90 | 2,521.64 | 09/2003 | 2,825.07 | 2,370.58 | 2,673.86 | 09/2006 | 4,975.56 | 4,134.72 | 4,453.46 |
| 12/2000 | 2,964.07 | 2,348.70 | 2,946.60 | 12/2003 | 3,038.15 | 2,672.64 | 3,007.05 | 12/2006 | 4,891.05 | 4,416.02 | 4,560.20 |
| 03/2001 | 3,157.44 | 2,578.87 | 2,771.36 | 03/2004 | 3,090.07 | 2,743.46 | 2,895.43 | 03/2007 | 5,211.42 | 4,564.56 | 4,810.70 |
| 06/2001 | 3,010.24 | 2,606.26 | 2,833.56 | 06/2004 | 3,205.56 | 2,785.50 | 3,204.31 | 06/2007 | 5,348.47 | 4,785.80 | 5,098.88 |
| 09/2001 | 3,007.81 | 1,942.01 | 2,194.68 | 09/2004 | 3,271.62 | 2,959.58 | 3,243.51 | 09/2007 | 5,487.05 | 4,486.60 | 4,836.32 |
| 12/2001 | 2,662.08 | 2,119.77 | 2,639.99 | 12/2004 | 3,823.96 | 3,245.20 | 3,798.05 | 12/2007 | 5,023.46 | 4,346.39 | 4,570.55 |
| 03/2002 | 3,050.98 | 2,604.60 | 2,917.96 | 03/2005 | 3,889.97 | 3,454.74 | 3,715.97 | 03/2008 | 4,932.57 | 4,032.88 | 4,783.88 |
| 06/2002 | 2,919.96 | 2,578.71 | 2,730.32 | 06/2005 | 3,758.59 | 3,348.36 | 3,487.76 | 06/2008 | 5,536.57 | 4,779.33 | 4,948.03 |
| 09/2002 | 2,734.12 | 2,090.32 | 2,148.34 | 09/2005 | 3,821.96 | 3,473.33 | 3,740.55 | 09/2008 | 5,293.41 | 4,440.80 | 4,616.01 |
| 12/2002 | 2,416.91 | 2,008.31 | 2,309.96 | 12/2005 | 4,306.09 | 3,550.55 | 4,196.03 | 12/2008 | 4,623.59 | 2,909.29 | 3,537.15 |

*Source: New York Stock Exchange*

# DOW JONES UTILITIES

**MONTHLY CASH**
As of 12/31/2008
Chart High 555.71 on 01/08/2008
Chart Low 57.10 on 09/16/1974

**DOW JONES UTILITIES**
Monthly Cash as of 12/31/2008

| Date | Open | High | Low | Close |
|---|---|---|---|---|
| 08/29/08 | 484.81 | 487.61 | 458.37 | 477.52 |
| 09/30/08 | 477.70 | 480.60 | 420.25 | 428.45 |
| 10/31/08 | 428.45 | 431.65 | 294.30 | 378.42 |
| 11/28/08 | 378.29 | 395.11 | 331.77 | 382.24 |
| 12/31/08 | 381.83 | 381.87 | 339.45 | 370.76 |

## Annual High, Low and Settle of Dow Jones Utilities Index    In Index Value

| Year | High | Low | Settle | Year | High | Low | Settle | Year | High | Low | Settle |
|---|---|---|---|---|---|---|---|---|---|---|---|
| 1967 | | | | 1981 | 119.42 | 99.75 | 109.02 | 1995 | 226.66 | 180.79 | 225.40 |
| 1968 | | | | 1982 | 124.17 | 102.21 | 119.46 | 1996 | 239.59 | 202.84 | 232.53 |
| 1969 | | | | 1983 | 141.14 | 119.37 | 131.89 | 1997 | 273.44 | 207.80 | 273.07 |
| 1970 | 122.48 | 95.09 | 121.84 | 1984 | 150.13 | 119.56 | 149.36 | 1998 | 322.21 | 260.51 | 312.30 |
| 1971 | 129.12 | 107.55 | 117.75 | 1985 | 174.96 | 146.03 | 174.70 | 1999 | 336.03 | 268.59 | 283.36 |
| 1972 | 125.32 | 104.58 | 119.50 | 1986 | 219.75 | 168.09 | 205.84 | 2000 | 418.25 | 272.37 | 412.16 |
| 1973 | 121.45 | 83.81 | 89.37 | 1987 | 231.06 | 160.38 | 175.08 | 2001 | 412.48 | 270.26 | 293.94 |
| 1974 | 95.83 | 57.10 | 68.76 | 1988 | 190.02 | 166.25 | 186.28 | 2002 | 313.25 | 162.52 | 215.18 |
| 1975 | 88.19 | 69.53 | 83.65 | 1989 | 236.29 | 181.37 | 235.04 | 2003 | 267.90 | 186.54 | 266.90 |
| 1976 | 108.64 | 83.53 | 108.38 | 1990 | 236.23 | 188.76 | 209.70 | 2004 | 337.79 | 259.08 | 334.95 |
| 1977 | 119.09 | 104.23 | 111.28 | 1991 | 226.15 | 195.05 | 226.15 | 2005 | 438.74 | 323.79 | 405.11 |
| 1978 | 111.84 | 96.04 | 98.24 | 1992 | 226.02 | 200.23 | 221.02 | 2006 | 462.88 | 380.97 | 456.77 |
| 1979 | 110.86 | 97.70 | 106.60 | 1993 | 257.59 | 215.82 | 229.30 | 2007 | 555.07 | 443.78 | 532.53 |
| 1980 | 118.69 | 95.23 | 114.42 | 1994 | 229.77 | 172.03 | 181.52 | 2008 | 555.71 | 294.30 | 370.76 |

*Source: New York Stock Exchange*

# DOW JONES UTILITIES

**WEEKLY CASH**
As of 01/02/2009
Chart High 555.71 on 01/08/2008
Chart Low 162.52 on 10/10/2002

DOW JONES UTILITIES
Weekly Cash as of 01/02/2009

| Date | Open | High | Low | Close |
|---|---|---|---|---|
| 12/05/08 | 381.83 | 381.87 | 339.45 | 361.44 |
| 12/12/08 | 361.58 | 372.92 | 354.28 | 365.65 |
| 12/19/08 | 365.80 | 372.74 | 355.39 | 364.23 |
| 12/26/08 | 364.28 | 367.09 | 354.17 | 359.43 |
| 01/02/09 | 358.82 | 380.80 | 353.33 | 378.82 |

## Quarterly High, Low and Settle of Dow Jones Utilities Index — In Index Value

| Quarter | High | Low | Settle | Quarter | High | Low | Settle | Quarter | High | Low | Settle |
|---|---|---|---|---|---|---|---|---|---|---|---|
| 03/2000 | 317.82 | 272.37 | 291.77 | 03/2003 | 231.27 | 186.54 | 208.00 | 03/2006 | 427.50 | 388.79 | 389.01 |
| 06/2000 | 334.14 | 286.64 | 306.91 | 06/2003 | 256.99 | 207.85 | 250.99 | 06/2006 | 416.65 | 380.97 | 413.95 |
| 09/2000 | 402.28 | 306.88 | 398.22 | 09/2003 | 252.02 | 229.46 | 250.59 | 09/2006 | 443.49 | 411.81 | 428.40 |
| 12/2000 | 418.25 | 369.31 | 412.16 | 12/2003 | 267.90 | 243.26 | 266.90 | 12/2006 | 462.88 | 426.84 | 456.77 |
| 03/2001 | 412.48 | 330.95 | 381.42 | 03/2004 | 281.87 | 263.90 | 281.09 | 03/2007 | 505.15 | 443.78 | 500.18 |
| 06/2001 | 400.69 | 348.92 | 359.34 | 06/2004 | 283.52 | 259.08 | 277.89 | 06/2007 | 537.12 | 484.38 | 498.17 |
| 09/2001 | 374.26 | 286.95 | 301.67 | 09/2004 | 296.45 | 274.52 | 295.33 | 09/2007 | 521.32 | 460.68 | 501.54 |
| 12/2001 | 322.75 | 270.26 | 293.94 | 12/2004 | 337.79 | 295.30 | 334.95 | 12/2007 | 555.07 | 493.41 | 532.53 |
| 03/2002 | 308.59 | 270.89 | 305.73 | 03/2005 | 363.82 | 323.79 | 358.33 | 03/2008 | 555.71 | 466.74 | 479.00 |
| 06/2002 | 313.25 | 265.45 | 273.88 | 06/2005 | 389.28 | 349.25 | 386.59 | 06/2008 | 530.57 | 479.61 | 520.85 |
| 09/2002 | 274.06 | 186.49 | 214.87 | 09/2005 | 434.91 | 379.53 | 432.38 | 09/2008 | 527.28 | 420.25 | 428.45 |
| 12/2002 | 220.08 | 162.52 | 215.18 | 12/2005 | 438.74 | 378.95 | 405.11 | 12/2008 | 431.65 | 294.30 | 370.76 |

*Source: New York Stock Exchange*

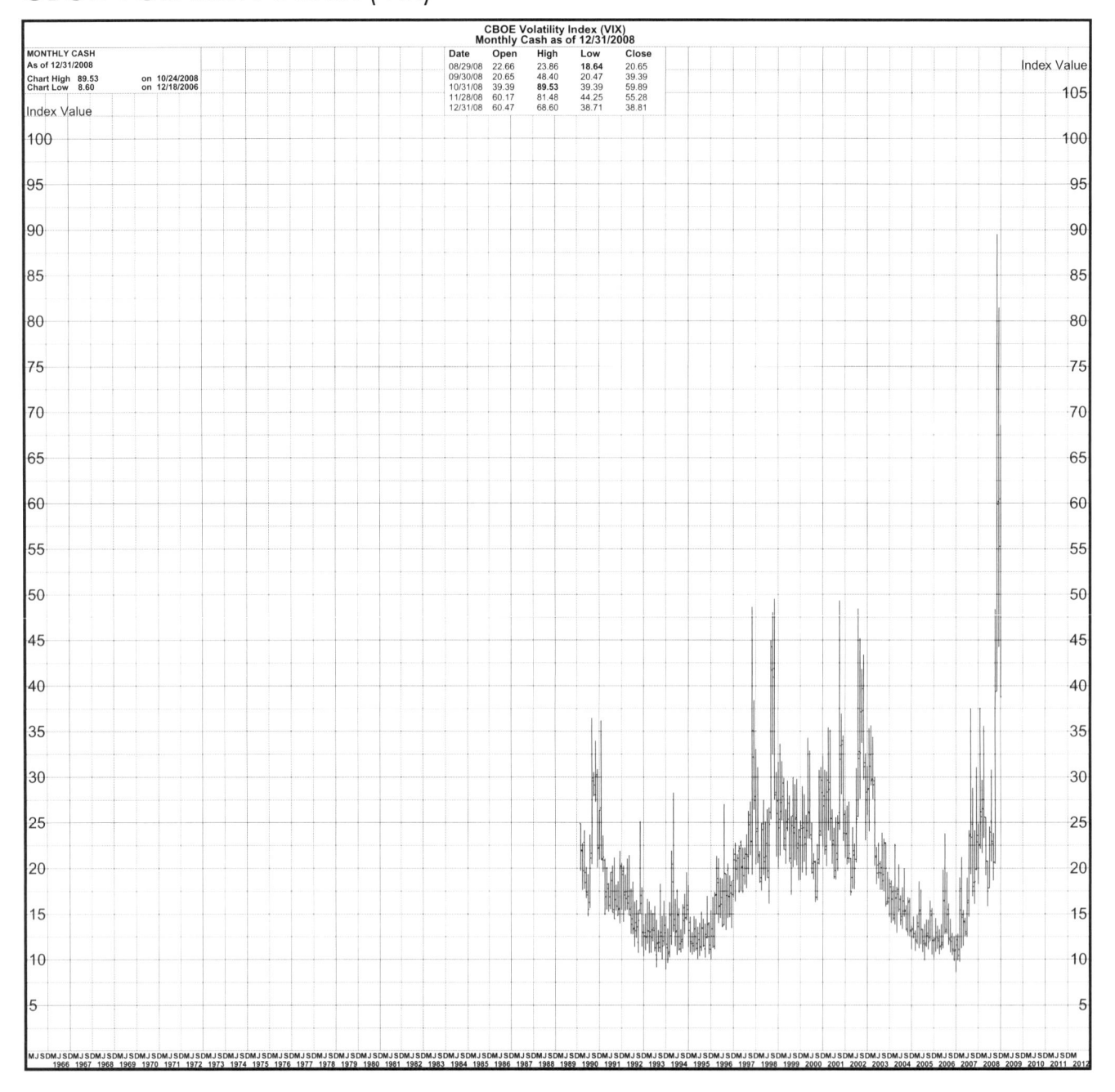

# CBOE VOLATILITY INDEX (VIX)

**MONTHLY CASH**
As of 12/31/2008
Chart High 89.53 on 10/24/2008
Chart Low 8.60 on 12/18/2006

CBOE Volatility Index (VIX)
Monthly Cash as of 12/31/2008

| Date | Open | High | Low | Close |
|---|---|---|---|---|
| 08/29/08 | 22.66 | 23.86 | 18.64 | 20.65 |
| 09/30/08 | 20.65 | 48.40 | 20.47 | 39.39 |
| 10/31/08 | 39.39 | 89.53 | 39.39 | 59.89 |
| 11/28/08 | 60.17 | 81.48 | 44.25 | 55.28 |
| 12/31/08 | 60.47 | 68.60 | 38.71 | 38.81 |

## Annual High, Low and Settle of CBOE Volatility Index (VIX)   In Index Value

| Year | High | Low | Settle | Year | High | Low | Settle | Year | High | Low | Settle |
|---|---|---|---|---|---|---|---|---|---|---|---|
| 1967 | | | | 1981 | | | | 1995 | 18.27 | 10.41 | 13.89 |
| 1968 | | | | 1982 | | | | 1996 | 28.45 | 12.66 | 21.67 |
| 1969 | | | | 1983 | | | | 1997 | 55.48 | 13.24 | 24.89 |
| 1970 | | | | 1984 | | | | 1998 | 60.63 | 16.73 | 25.41 |
| 1971 | | | | 1985 | | | | 1999 | 36.79 | 17.70 | 26.71 |
| 1972 | | | | 1986 | 28.41 | 15.75 | 18.71 | 2000 | 41.53 | 18.06 | 30.23 |
| 1973 | | | | 1987 | 172.79 | 10.43 | 39.45 | 2001 | 57.31 | 20.26 | 23.22 |
| 1974 | | | | 1988 | 52.60 | 15.22 | 18.53 | 2002 | 56.74 | 18.87 | 32.03 |
| 1975 | | | | 1989 | 51.71 | 11.60 | 17.39 | 2003 | 41.16 | 14.83 | 18.31 |
| 1976 | | | | 1990 | 40.01 | 15.51 | 23.55 | 2004 | 22.67 | 11.14 | 13.29 |
| 1977 | | | | 1991 | 38.21 | 12.16 | 20.17 | 2005 | 18.59 | 9.88 | 12.07 |
| 1978 | | | | 1992 | 27.28 | 11.89 | 13.55 | 2006 | 23.81 | 8.60 | 11.56 |
| 1979 | | | | 1993 | 18.00 | 8.86 | 11.46 | 2007 | 37.50 | 9.70 | 22.50 |
| 1980 | | | | 1994 | 25.31 | 9.25 | 13.44 | 2008 | 89.53 | 15.82 | 38.81 |

Index data begins 01/02/1990.   *Source: Chicago Board of Options Exchange*

# CBOE VOLATILITY INDEX (VIX)

**WEEKLY CASH**
As of 01/02/2009
Chart High 89.53 on 10/24/2008
Chart Low 8.60 on 12/18/2006

Index Value

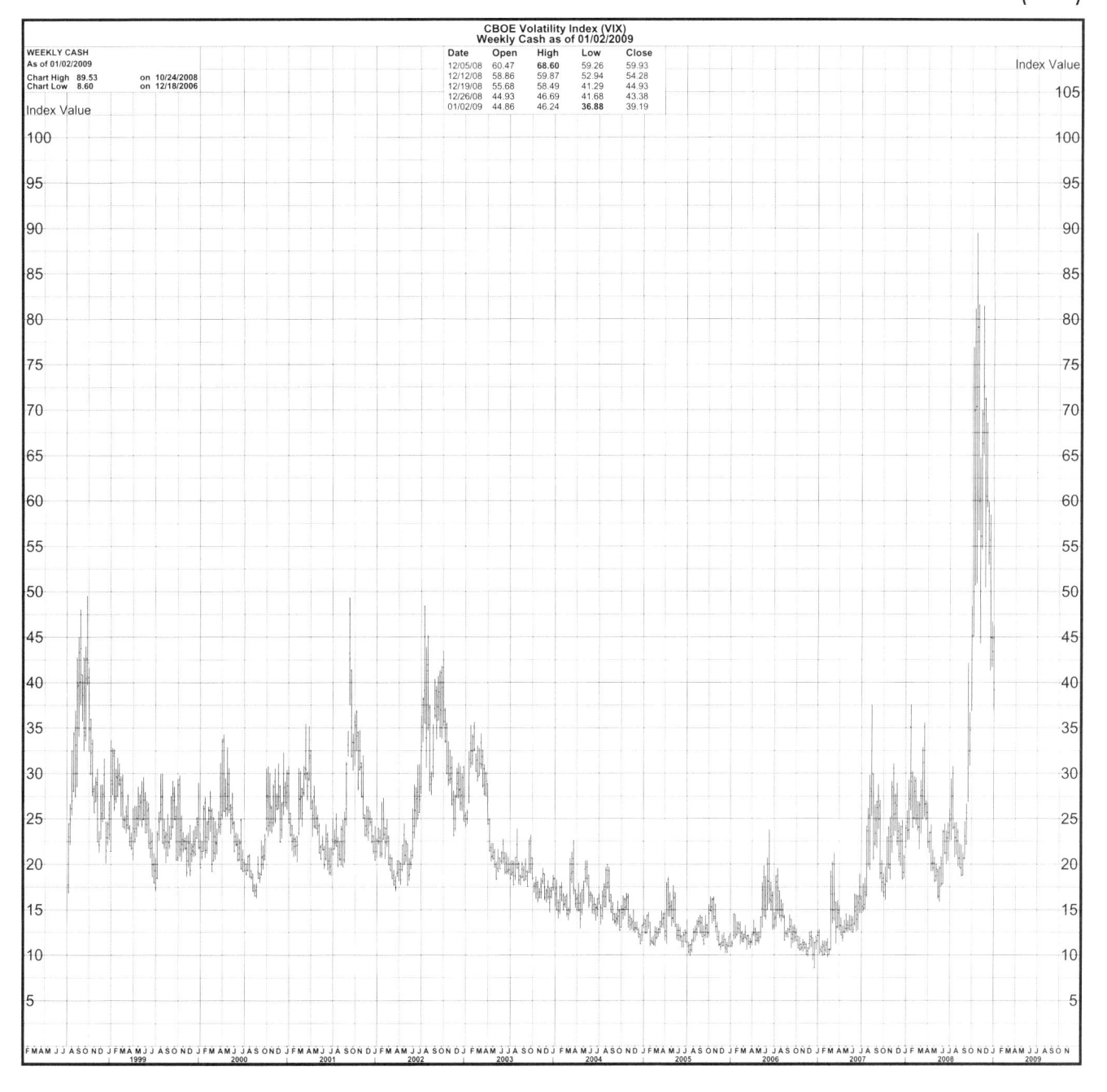

| Date | Open | High | Low | Close |
|---|---|---|---|---|
| 12/05/08 | 60.47 | 68.60 | 59.26 | 59.93 |
| 12/12/08 | 58.86 | 59.87 | 52.94 | 54.28 |
| 12/19/08 | 55.68 | 58.49 | 41.29 | 44.93 |
| 12/26/08 | 44.93 | 46.69 | 41.68 | 43.38 |
| 01/02/09 | 44.86 | 46.24 | 36.88 | 39.19 |

## Quarterly High, Low and Settle of CBOE Volatility Index (VIX)   In Index Value

| Quarter | High | Low | Settle | Quarter | High | Low | Settle | Quarter | High | Low | Settle |
|---|---|---|---|---|---|---|---|---|---|---|---|
| 03/2000 | 31.37 | 20.41 | 27.21 | 03/2003 | 41.16 | 26.19 | 33.37 | 03/2006 | 14.56 | 10.53 | 11.39 |
| 06/2000 | 41.53 | 22.02 | 22.26 | 06/2003 | 34.39 | 20.57 | 21.62 | 06/2006 | 23.81 | 11.02 | 13.08 |
| 09/2000 | 27.04 | 18.06 | 23.85 | 09/2003 | 25.88 | 18.79 | 22.72 | 09/2006 | 19.58 | 10.74 | 11.98 |
| 12/2000 | 37.72 | 22.34 | 30.23 | 12/2003 | 22.82 | 14.83 | 18.31 | 12/2006 | 12.91 | 8.60 | 11.56 |
| 03/2001 | 41.99 | 22.05 | 33.82 | 03/2004 | 22.67 | 13.83 | 16.74 | 03/2007 | 21.25 | 9.70 | 14.64 |
| 06/2001 | 40.70 | 20.89 | 21.63 | 06/2004 | 20.45 | 12.89 | 14.34 | 06/2007 | 18.98 | 11.46 | 16.23 |
| 09/2001 | 57.31 | 20.26 | 35.19 | 09/2004 | 19.97 | 13.16 | 13.34 | 09/2007 | 37.50 | 14.67 | 18.00 |
| 12/2001 | 38.56 | 22.04 | 23.22 | 12/2004 | 16.87 | 11.14 | 13.29 | 12/2007 | 31.09 | 16.08 | 22.50 |
| 03/2002 | 29.92 | 18.87 | 19.32 | 03/2005 | 14.89 | 10.90 | 14.02 | 03/2008 | 37.57 | 21.64 | 25.61 |
| 06/2002 | 36.01 | 19.88 | 29.13 | 06/2005 | 18.59 | 10.78 | 12.04 | 06/2008 | 25.61 | 15.82 | 23.95 |
| 09/2002 | 56.74 | 28.63 | 44.57 | 09/2005 | 14.41 | 9.88 | 11.92 | 09/2008 | 48.40 | 18.64 | 39.39 |
| 12/2002 | 50.48 | 26.41 | 32.03 | 12/2005 | 16.47 | 10.15 | 12.07 | 12/2008 | 89.53 | 38.71 | 38.81 |

*Source: Chicago Board of Options Exchange*

# NASDAQ 100 INDEX

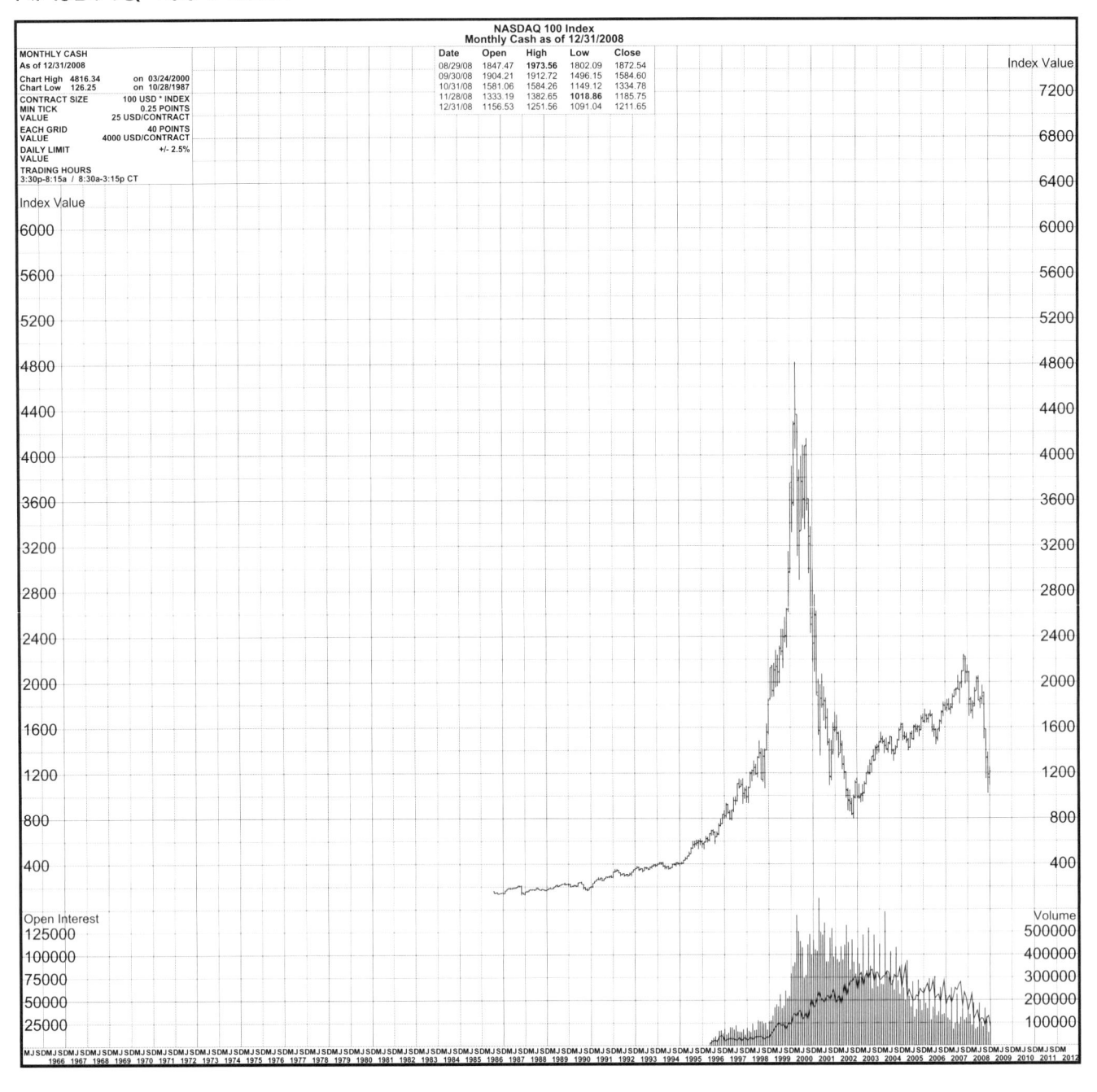

**MONTHLY CASH**
As of 12/31/2008

| | | |
|---|---|---|
| Chart High | 4816.34 | on 03/24/2000 |
| Chart Low | 126.25 | on 10/28/1987 |
| CONTRACT SIZE | | 100 USD * INDEX |
| MIN TICK | | 0.25 POINTS |
| VALUE | | 25 USD/CONTRACT |
| EACH GRID | | 40 POINTS |
| VALUE | | 4000 USD/CONTRACT |
| DAILY LIMIT VALUE | | +/- 2.5% |
| TRADING HOURS | | 3:30p-8:15a / 8:30a-3:15p CT |

**NASDAQ 100 Index — Monthly Cash as of 12/31/2008**

| Date | Open | High | Low | Close |
|---|---|---|---|---|
| 08/29/08 | 1847.47 | 1973.56 | 1802.09 | 1872.54 |
| 09/30/08 | 1904.21 | 1912.72 | 1496.15 | 1584.60 |
| 10/31/08 | 1581.06 | 1584.26 | 1149.12 | 1334.78 |
| 11/28/08 | 1333.19 | 1382.65 | 1018.86 | 1185.75 |
| 12/31/08 | 1156.53 | 1251.56 | 1091.04 | 1211.65 |

## Annual High, Low and Settle of NASDAQ 100 Index — In Index Value

| Year | High | Low | Settle | Year | High | Low | Settle | Year | High | Low | Settle |
|---|---|---|---|---|---|---|---|---|---|---|---|
| 1967 | | | | 1981 | | | | 1995 | 623.53 | 394.59 | 576.23 |
| 1968 | | | | 1982 | | | | 1996 | 873.00 | 526.80 | 821.36 |
| 1969 | | | | 1983 | | | | 1997 | 1,153.89 | 779.17 | 990.80 |
| 1970 | | | | 1984 | | | | 1998 | 1,848.36 | 933.01 | 1,836.03 |
| 1971 | | | | 1985 | | | | 1999 | 3,750.41 | 1,838.65 | 3,707.83 |
| 1972 | | | | 1986 | 164.55 | 133.28 | 141.41 | 2000 | 4,816.34 | 2,174.76 | 2,341.70 |
| 1973 | | | | 1987 | 214.03 | 126.25 | 156.25 | 2001 | 2,771.63 | 1,088.96 | 1,577.05 |
| 1974 | | | | 1988 | 192.77 | 151.57 | 177.41 | 2002 | 1,710.23 | 795.25 | 984.36 |
| 1975 | | | | 1989 | 238.85 | 172.95 | 223.84 | 2003 | 1,474.24 | 938.52 | 1,467.92 |
| 1976 | | | | 1990 | 246.82 | 162.55 | 200.53 | 2004 | 1,635.70 | 1,302.03 | 1,621.12 |
| 1977 | | | | 1991 | 332.67 | 190.90 | 330.70 | 2005 | 1,716.65 | 1,394.49 | 1,645.20 |
| 1978 | | | | 1992 | 363.20 | 287.67 | 360.19 | 2006 | 1,824.21 | 1,446.77 | 1,756.90 |
| 1979 | | | | 1993 | 401.81 | 326.56 | 398.28 | 2007 | 2,239.23 | 1,710.97 | 2,084.93 |
| 1980 | | | | 1994 | 418.99 | 350.03 | 404.27 | 2008 | 2,094.22 | 1,018.86 | 1,211.65 |

Index data begins 06/19/1986.  *Source: NASDAQ*

# NASDAQ 100 INDEX

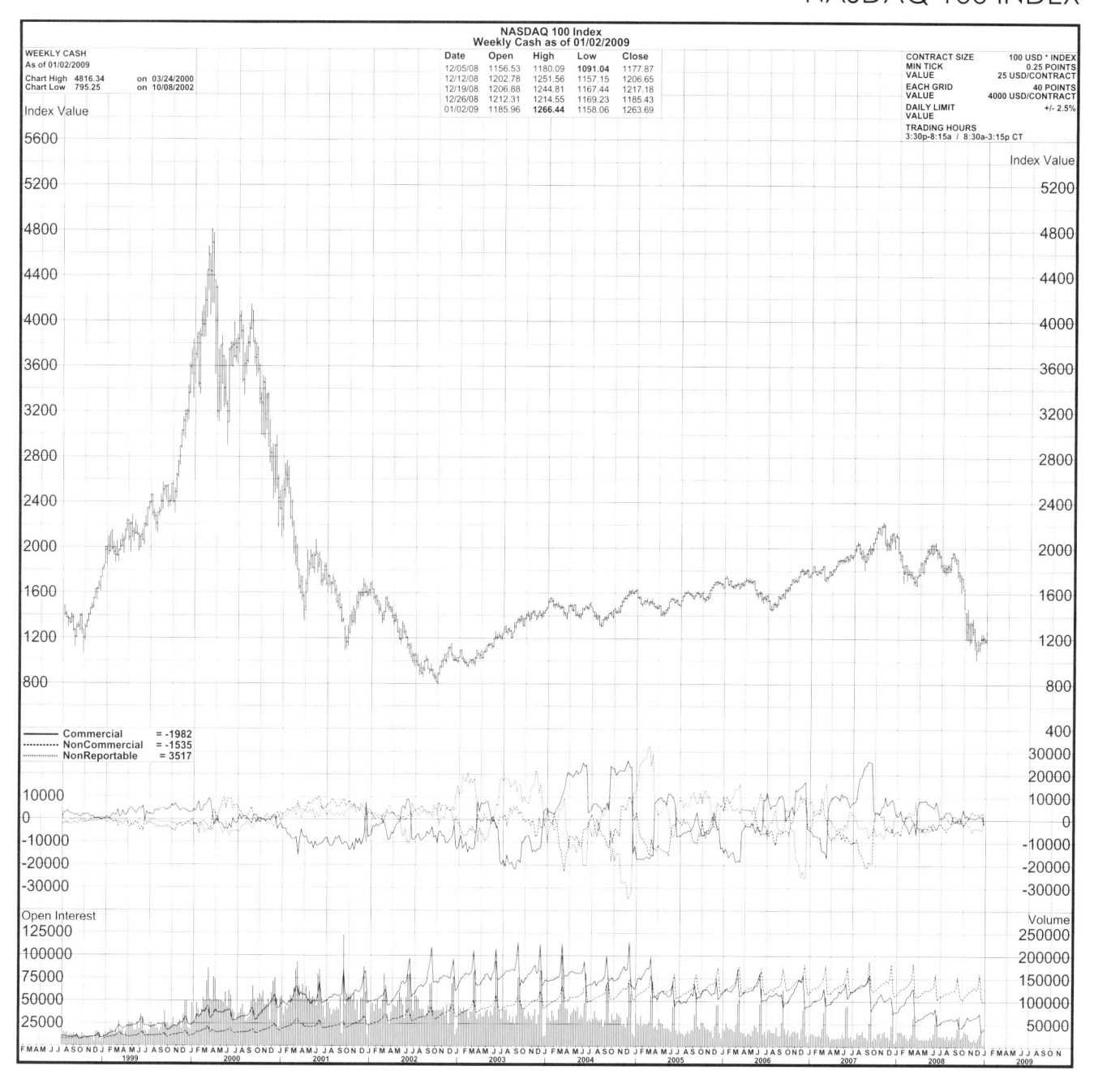

**WEEKLY CASH**
As of 01/02/2009
Chart High 4816.34 on 03/24/2000
Chart Low 795.25 on 10/08/2002

NASDAQ 100 Index
Weekly Cash as of 01/02/2009

| Date | Open | High | Low | Close |
|---|---|---|---|---|
| 12/05/08 | 1156.53 | 1180.09 | 1091.04 | 1177.87 |
| 12/12/08 | 1202.78 | 1251.56 | 1157.15 | 1206.65 |
| 12/19/08 | 1206.88 | 1244.81 | 1167.44 | 1217.18 |
| 12/26/08 | 1212.31 | 1214.55 | 1169.23 | 1185.43 |
| 01/02/09 | 1185.96 | 1266.44 | 1158.06 | 1263.69 |

CONTRACT SIZE: 100 USD * INDEX
MIN TICK: 0.25 POINTS
VALUE: 25 USD/CONTRACT
EACH GRID: 40 POINTS
VALUE: 4000 USD/CONTRACT
DAILY LIMIT VALUE: +/- 2.5%
TRADING HOURS: 3:30p-8:15a / 8:30a-3:15p CT

Commercial = -1982
NonCommercial = -1535
NonReportable = 3517

## Quarterly High, Low and Settle of NASDAQ 100 Index   In Index Value

| Quarter | High | Low | Settle | Quarter | High | Low | Settle | Quarter | High | Low | Settle |
|---|---|---|---|---|---|---|---|---|---|---|---|
| 03/2000 | 4,816.34 | 3,314.75 | 4,397.84 | 03/2003 | 1,104.32 | 938.52 | 1,018.66 | 03/2006 | 1,761.46 | 1,633.71 | 1,703.66 |
| 06/2000 | 4,355.70 | 2,897.27 | 3,763.79 | 06/2003 | 1,265.69 | 1,015.46 | 1,201.69 | 06/2006 | 1,750.23 | 1,511.53 | 1,575.23 |
| 09/2000 | 4,147.19 | 3,341.83 | 3,570.42 | 09/2003 | 1,406.61 | 1,180.11 | 1,303.70 | 09/2006 | 1,666.03 | 1,446.77 | 1,654.13 |
| 12/2000 | 3,613.86 | 2,174.76 | 2,341.70 | 12/2003 | 1,474.24 | 1,306.33 | 1,467.92 | 12/2006 | 1,824.21 | 1,623.07 | 1,756.90 |
| 03/2001 | 2,771.63 | 1,530.14 | 1,573.25 | 03/2004 | 1,559.47 | 1,368.08 | 1,438.41 | 03/2007 | 1,851.47 | 1,710.97 | 1,772.36 |
| 06/2001 | 2,073.98 | 1,348.52 | 1,834.37 | 06/2004 | 1,523.48 | 1,372.46 | 1,516.64 | 06/2007 | 1,948.58 | 1,761.65 | 1,934.10 |
| 09/2001 | 1,864.20 | 1,088.96 | 1,168.37 | 09/2004 | 1,514.82 | 1,302.03 | 1,412.74 | 09/2007 | 2,101.96 | 1,805.66 | 2,091.11 |
| 12/2001 | 1,734.58 | 1,131.32 | 1,577.05 | 12/2004 | 1,635.70 | 1,416.29 | 1,621.12 | 12/2007 | 2,239.23 | 1,980.18 | 2,084.93 |
| 03/2002 | 1,710.23 | 1,329.93 | 1,452.81 | 03/2005 | 1,635.45 | 1,458.26 | 1,482.53 | 03/2008 | 2,094.22 | 1,668.57 | 1,781.93 |
| 06/2002 | 1,481.74 | 979.87 | 1,051.41 | 06/2005 | 1,568.96 | 1,394.49 | 1,493.52 | 06/2008 | 2,055.82 | 1,776.60 | 1,837.09 |
| 09/2002 | 1,066.28 | 825.80 | 832.52 | 09/2005 | 1,628.57 | 1,484.46 | 1,601.66 | 09/2008 | 1,973.56 | 1,496.15 | 1,584.60 |
| 12/2002 | 1,155.68 | 795.25 | 984.36 | 12/2005 | 1,716.65 | 1,515.75 | 1,645.20 | 12/2008 | 1,584.26 | 1,018.86 | 1,211.65 |

*Source: NASDAQ*

# NASDAQ COMPOSITE INDEX

**NASDAQ Composite Index — Monthly Cash as of 12/31/2008**

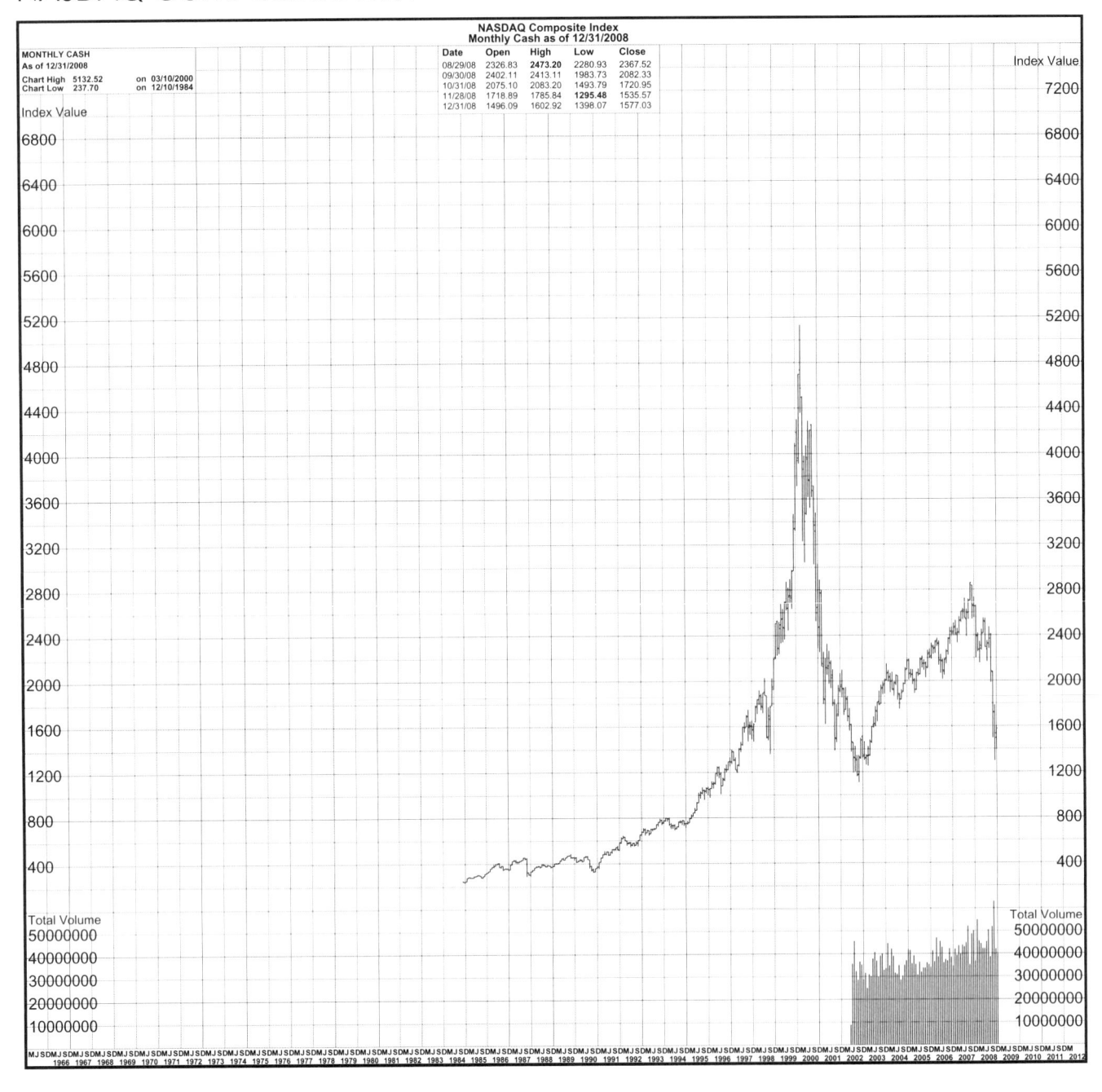

| Date | Open | High | Low | Close |
|---|---|---|---|---|
| 08/29/08 | 2326.83 | 2473.20 | 2280.93 | 2367.52 |
| 09/30/08 | 2402.11 | 2413.11 | 1983.73 | 2082.33 |
| 10/31/08 | 2075.10 | 2083.20 | 1493.79 | 1720.95 |
| 11/28/08 | 1718.89 | 1785.84 | 1295.48 | 1535.57 |
| 12/31/08 | 1496.09 | 1602.92 | 1398.07 | 1577.03 |

MONTHLY CASH As of 12/31/2008
Chart High 5132.52 on 03/10/2000
Chart Low 237.70 on 12/10/1984

## Annual High, Low and Settle of NASDAQ Composite Index — In Index Value

| Year | High | Low | Settle | Year | High | Low | Settle | Year | High | Low | Settle |
|---|---|---|---|---|---|---|---|---|---|---|---|
| 1967 | | | | 1981 | | | | 1995 | 1,074.85 | 740.47 | 1,052.13 |
| 1968 | | | | 1982 | | | | 1996 | 1,328.45 | 977.79 | 1,291.03 |
| 1969 | | | | 1983 | | | | 1997 | 1,748.62 | 1,194.39 | 1,570.35 |
| 1970 | | | | 1984 | 252.30 | 237.70 | 247.10 | 1998 | 2,200.63 | 1,357.09 | 2,192.69 |
| 1971 | | | | 1985 | 325.60 | 245.80 | 324.90 | 1999 | 4,090.61 | 2,193.13 | 4,069.31 |
| 1972 | | | | 1986 | 411.30 | 322.10 | 348.80 | 2000 | 5,132.52 | 2,288.16 | 2,470.52 |
| 1973 | | | | 1987 | 456.30 | 288.50 | 330.50 | 2001 | 2,892.36 | 1,387.06 | 1,950.40 |
| 1974 | | | | 1988 | 397.50 | 329.00 | 381.40 | 2002 | 2,098.88 | 1,108.49 | 1,335.51 |
| 1975 | | | | 1989 | 487.50 | 376.90 | 454.80 | 2003 | 2,015.23 | 1,253.22 | 2,003.37 |
| 1976 | | | | 1990 | 470.30 | 323.00 | 373.80 | 2004 | 2,185.56 | 1,750.82 | 2,175.44 |
| 1977 | | | | 1991 | 586.35 | 353.00 | 586.34 | 2005 | 2,278.16 | 1,889.91 | 2,205.32 |
| 1978 | | | | 1992 | 676.95 | 545.95 | 676.95 | 2006 | 2,470.95 | 2,012.78 | 2,415.29 |
| 1979 | | | | 1993 | 791.20 | 644.71 | 776.80 | 2007 | 2,861.51 | 2,331.57 | 2,652.28 |
| 1980 | | | | 1994 | 804.43 | 690.95 | 751.96 | 2008 | 2,661.50 | 1,295.48 | 1,577.03 |

Index data begins 10/11/1984.  *Source: NASDAQ*

# NASDAQ COMPOSITE INDEX

**Quarterly High, Low and Settle of NASDAQ Composite Index**   In Index Value

| Quarter | High | Low | Settle | Quarter | High | Low | Settle | Quarter | High | Low | Settle |
|---|---|---|---|---|---|---|---|---|---|---|---|
| 03/2000 | 5,132.52 | 3,711.09 | 4,572.83 | 03/2003 | 1,467.35 | 1,253.22 | 1,341.17 | 03/2006 | 2,353.13 | 2,189.91 | 2,339.79 |
| 06/2000 | 4,504.36 | 3,042.66 | 3,966.11 | 06/2003 | 1,686.10 | 1,338.23 | 1,622.80 | 06/2006 | 2,375.54 | 2,065.11 | 2,172.09 |
| 09/2000 | 4,289.06 | 3,521.14 | 3,672.82 | 09/2003 | 1,913.74 | 1,598.92 | 1,786.94 | 09/2006 | 2,273.30 | 2,012.78 | 2,258.43 |
| 12/2000 | 3,714.48 | 2,288.16 | 2,470.52 | 12/2003 | 2,015.23 | 1,796.09 | 2,003.37 | 12/2006 | 2,470.95 | 2,224.21 | 2,415.29 |
| 03/2001 | 2,892.36 | 1,794.21 | 1,840.26 | 03/2004 | 2,153.83 | 1,897.48 | 1,994.22 | 03/2007 | 2,531.42 | 2,331.57 | 2,421.63 |
| 06/2001 | 2,328.05 | 1,619.58 | 2,160.54 | 06/2004 | 2,079.12 | 1,865.40 | 2,047.79 | 06/2007 | 2,634.60 | 2,409.04 | 2,603.23 |
| 09/2001 | 2,181.05 | 1,387.06 | 1,498.80 | 09/2004 | 2,045.53 | 1,750.82 | 1,896.84 | 09/2007 | 2,724.74 | 2,386.69 | 2,701.50 |
| 12/2001 | 2,065.69 | 1,458.41 | 1,950.40 | 12/2004 | 2,185.56 | 1,899.33 | 2,175.44 | 12/2007 | 2,861.51 | 2,539.81 | 2,652.28 |
| 03/2002 | 2,098.88 | 1,696.55 | 1,845.35 | 03/2005 | 2,191.60 | 1,968.58 | 1,999.23 | 03/2008 | 2,661.50 | 2,155.42 | 2,279.10 |
| 06/2002 | 1,865.37 | 1,375.53 | 1,463.20 | 06/2005 | 2,106.57 | 1,889.91 | 2,056.96 | 06/2008 | 2,551.47 | 2,266.29 | 2,292.98 |
| 09/2002 | 1,459.84 | 1,160.07 | 1,172.06 | 09/2005 | 2,219.91 | 2,050.30 | 2,151.69 | 09/2008 | 2,473.20 | 1,983.73 | 2,082.33 |
| 12/2002 | 1,521.44 | 1,108.49 | 1,335.51 | 12/2005 | 2,278.16 | 2,025.95 | 2,205.32 | 12/2008 | 2,083.20 | 1,295.48 | 1,577.03 |

*Source: NASDAQ*

# S&P 500 INDEX

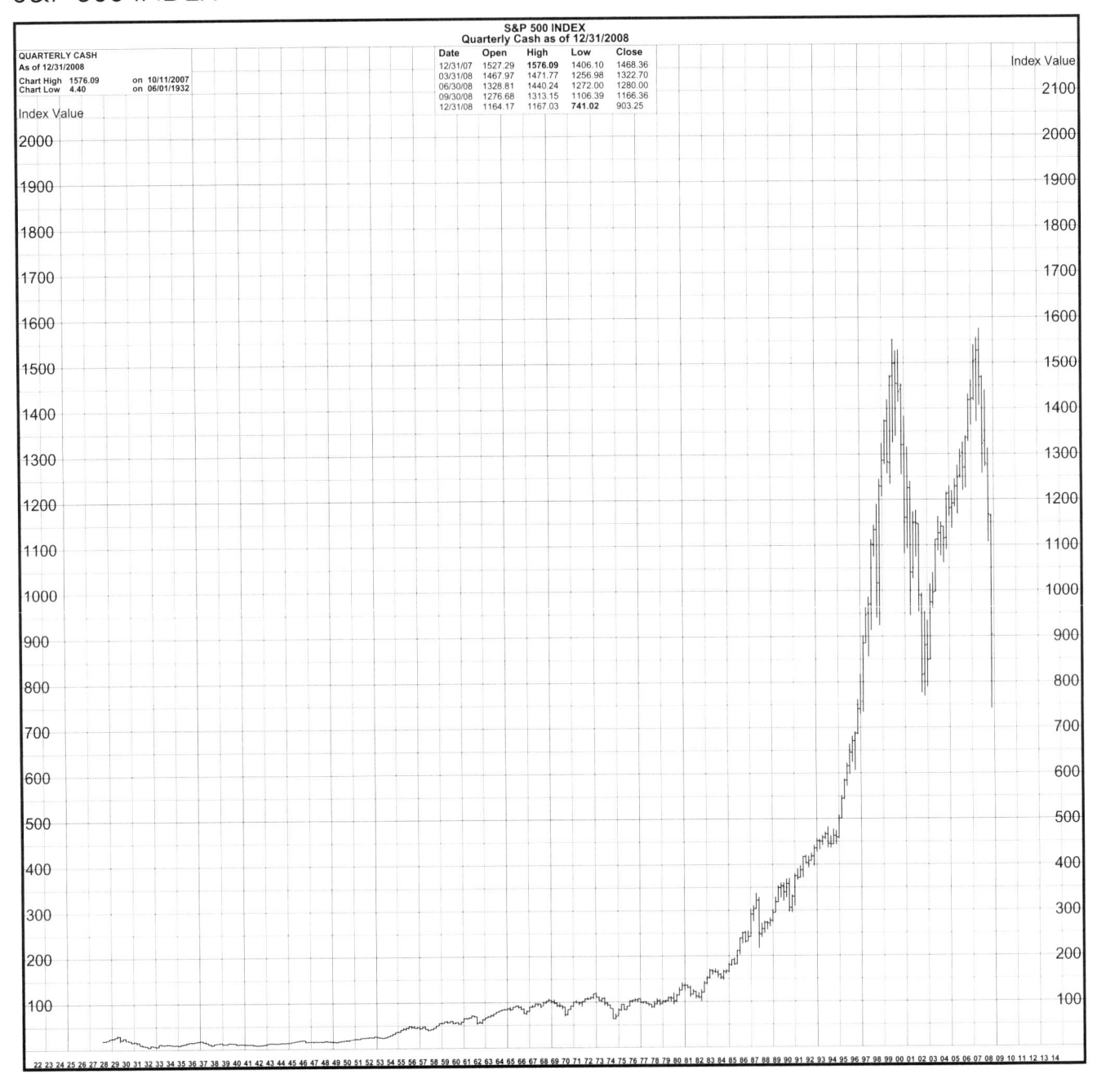

**S&P 500 INDEX**
Quarterly Cash as of 12/31/2008

| Date | Open | High | Low | Close |
|---|---|---|---|---|
| 12/31/07 | 1527.29 | 1576.09 | 1406.10 | 1468.36 |
| 03/31/08 | 1467.97 | 1471.77 | 1256.98 | 1322.70 |
| 06/30/08 | 1328.81 | 1440.24 | 1272.00 | 1280.00 |
| 09/30/08 | 1276.68 | 1313.15 | 1106.39 | 1166.36 |
| 12/31/08 | 1164.17 | 1167.03 | 741.02 | 903.25 |

QUARTERLY CASH
As of 12/31/2008
Chart High 1576.09 on 10/11/2007
Chart Low 4.40 on 06/01/1932

## Annual High, Low and Settle of S&P 500 Index     In Index Value

| Year | High | Low | Settle | Year | High | Low | Settle | Year | High | Low | Settle |
|---|---|---|---|---|---|---|---|---|---|---|---|
| 1925 | | | | 1939 | 13.23 | 10.31 | 12.46 | 1953 | 26.66 | 22.71 | 24.81 |
| 1926 | | | | 1940 | 12.77 | 9.09 | 10.58 | 1954 | 35.98 | 24.80 | 35.98 |
| 1927 | | | | 1941 | 10.86 | 8.38 | 8.69 | 1955 | 46.41 | 34.58 | 45.48 |
| 1928 | 24.28 | 16.97 | 24.20 | 1942 | 9.77 | 7.47 | 9.77 | 1956 | 49.74 | 43.11 | 46.67 |
| 1929 | 31.83 | 17.66 | 21.45 | 1943 | 12.64 | 9.88 | 11.67 | 1957 | 49.13 | 38.98 | 39.99 |
| 1930 | 25.92 | 14.44 | 15.34 | 1944 | 13.28 | 11.60 | 13.28 | 1958 | 55.21 | 40.33 | 55.21 |
| 1931 | 18.17 | 7.72 | 8.12 | 1945 | 17.67 | 13.21 | 17.36 | 1959 | 60.71 | 53.58 | 59.89 |
| 1932 | 9.31 | 4.40 | 6.92 | 1946 | 19.25 | 14.12 | 15.30 | 1960 | 60.39 | 52.30 | 58.11 |
| 1933 | 12.20 | 5.56 | 9.97 | 1947 | 16.14 | 13.74 | 15.30 | 1961 | 72.64 | 57.57 | 71.55 |
| 1934 | 11.82 | 8.36 | 9.47 | 1948 | 17.06 | 13.84 | 15.20 | 1962 | 71.13 | 52.32 | 63.10 |
| 1935 | 13.46 | 8.06 | 13.43 | 1949 | 16.79 | 13.55 | 16.79 | 1963 | 75.02 | 62.69 | 75.02 |
| 1936 | 17.69 | 13.40 | 17.18 | 1950 | 20.43 | 16.66 | 20.43 | 1964 | 86.28 | 75.43 | 84.75 |
| 1937 | 18.67 | 10.17 | 10.55 | 1951 | 23.83 | 20.69 | 23.73 | 1965 | 92.63 | 81.60 | 92.43 |
| 1938 | 13.79 | 8.50 | 13.14 | 1952 | 26.59 | 23.09 | 26.57 | 1966 | 94.06 | 73.20 | 80.33 |

Index data begins 01/03/1928.     Data continued on page 282.     *Source: CME Group; Chicago Mercantile Exchange*

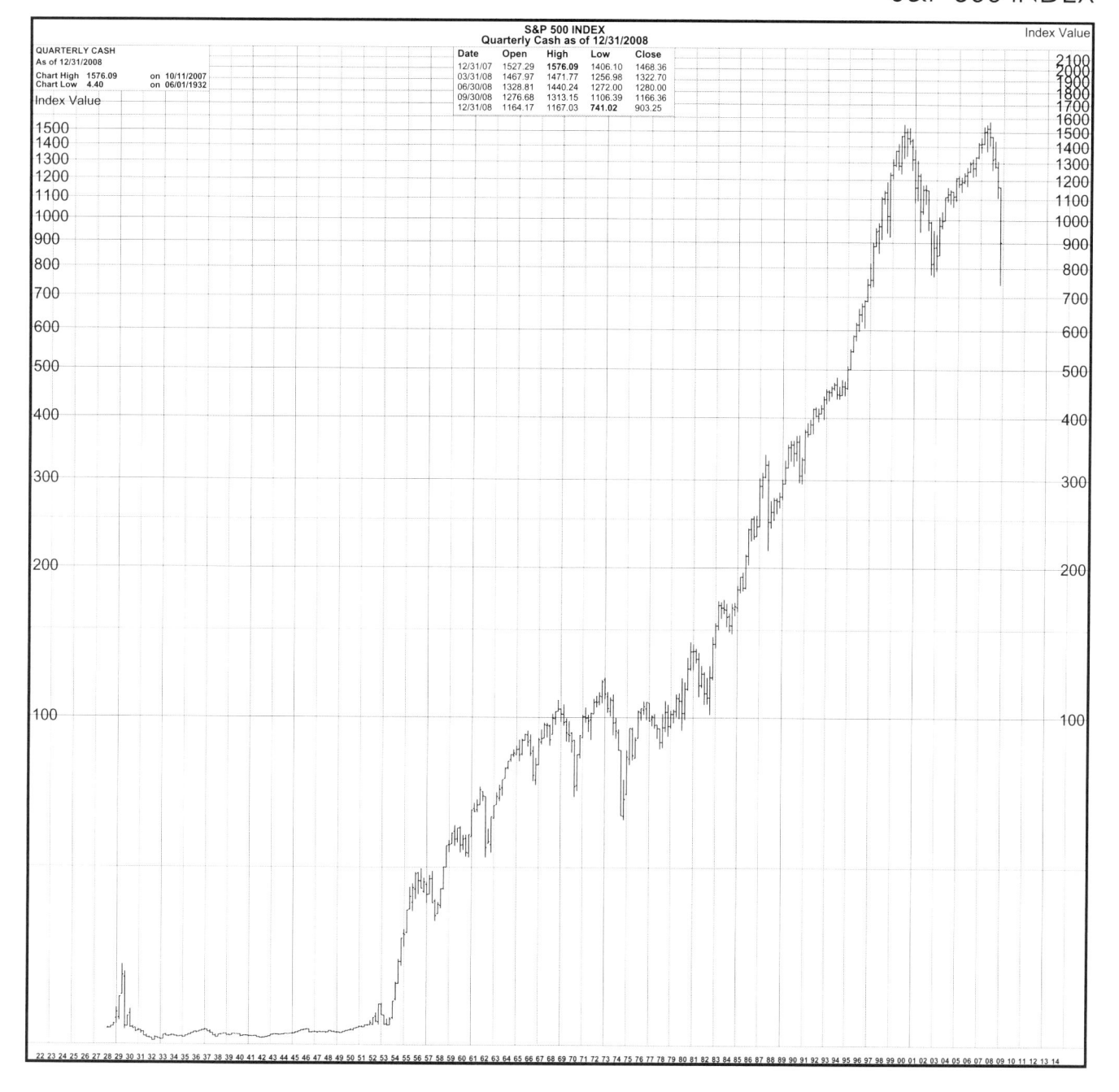

# S&P 500 INDEX

**S&P 500 INDEX**
Quarterly Cash as of 12/31/2008

| Date | Open | High | Low | Close |
|---|---|---|---|---|
| 12/31/07 | 1527.29 | 1576.09 | 1406.10 | 1468.36 |
| 03/31/08 | 1467.97 | 1471.77 | 1256.98 | 1322.70 |
| 06/30/08 | 1328.81 | 1440.24 | 1272.00 | 1280.00 |
| 09/30/08 | 1276.68 | 1313.15 | 1106.39 | 1166.36 |
| 12/31/08 | 1164.17 | 1167.03 | 741.02 | 903.25 |

QUARTERLY CASH
As of 12/31/2008
Chart High 1576.09 on 10/11/2007
Chart Low 4.40 on 06/01/1932
Index Value

# S&P 500 INDEX

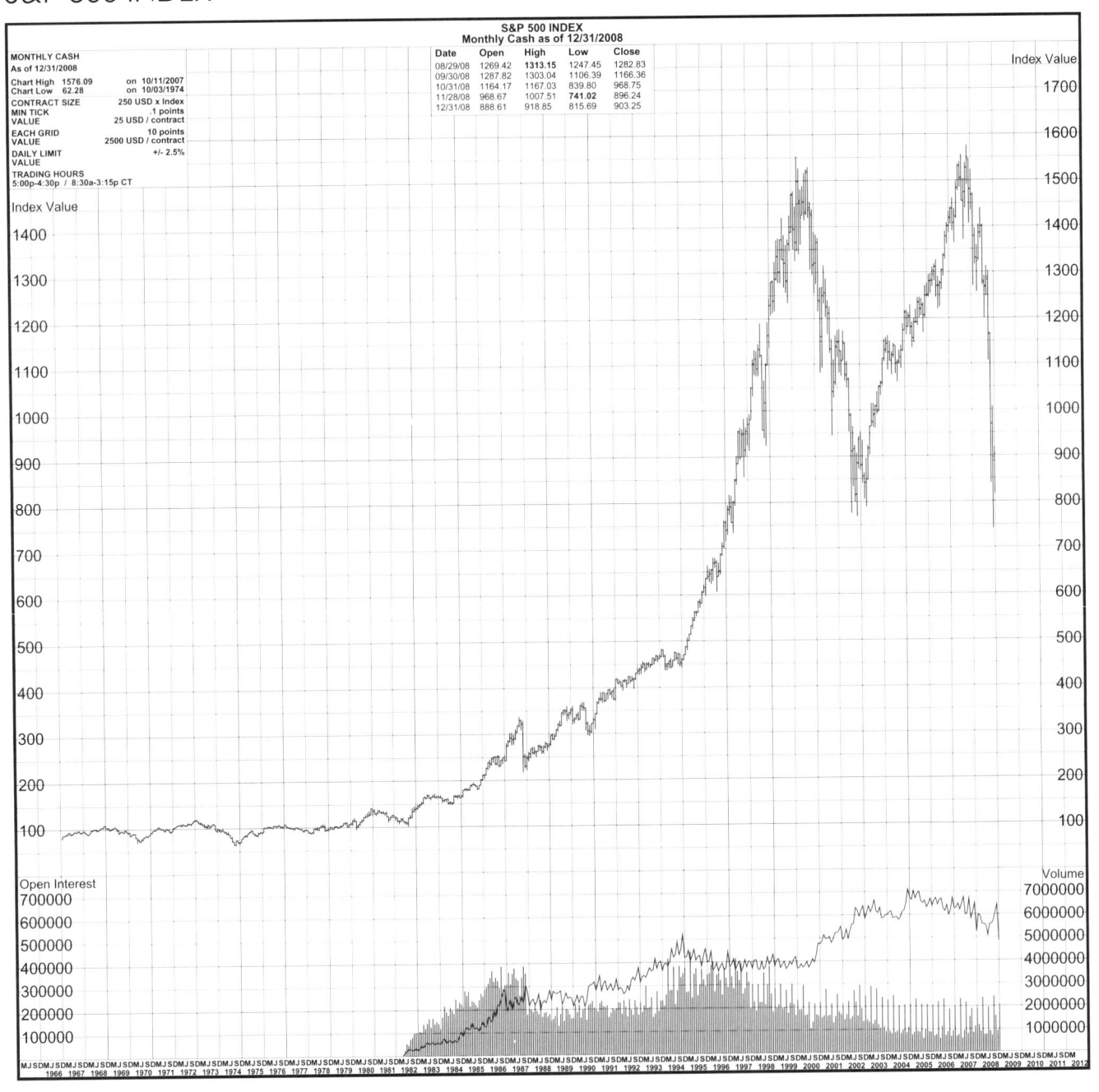

**S&P 500 INDEX — Monthly Cash as of 12/31/2008**

| Date | Open | High | Low | Close |
|---|---|---|---|---|
| 08/29/08 | 1269.42 | 1313.15 | 1247.45 | 1282.83 |
| 09/30/08 | 1287.82 | 1303.04 | 1106.39 | 1166.36 |
| 10/31/08 | 1164.17 | 1167.03 | 839.80 | 968.75 |
| 11/28/08 | 968.67 | 1007.51 | 741.02 | 896.24 |
| 12/31/08 | 888.61 | 918.85 | 815.69 | 903.25 |

**MONTHLY CASH** As of 12/31/2008
Chart High 1576.09 on 10/11/2007
Chart Low 62.28 on 10/03/1974
CONTRACT SIZE 250 USD x Index
MIN TICK .1 points
VALUE 25 USD / contract
EACH GRID 10 points
VALUE 2500 USD / contract
DAILY LIMIT VALUE +/- 2.5%
TRADING HOURS 5:00p-4:30p / 8:30a-3:15p CT

## Annual High, Low and Settle of S&P 500 Index — In Index Value

| Year | High | Low | Settle | Year | High | Low | Settle | Year | High | Low | Settle |
|---|---|---|---|---|---|---|---|---|---|---|---|
| 1967 | 97.59 | 80.38 | 96.47 | 1981 | 140.32 | 110.19 | 122.55 | 1995 | 622.88 | 457.20 | 615.93 |
| 1968 | 108.37 | 87.72 | 103.86 | 1982 | 145.33 | 101.44 | 140.64 | 1996 | 762.12 | 597.29 | 740.74 |
| 1969 | 106.16 | 89.20 | 92.06 | 1983 | 172.65 | 138.08 | 164.93 | 1997 | 986.25 | 729.55 | 970.43 |
| 1970 | 93.46 | 69.29 | 92.00 | 1984 | 170.41 | 147.26 | 167.24 | 1998 | 1,244.93 | 912.83 | 1,229.23 |
| 1971 | 104.77 | 90.16 | 101.95 | 1985 | 213.08 | 163.36 | 211.28 | 1999 | 1,473.10 | 1,206.59 | 1,469.25 |
| 1972 | 119.12 | 101.67 | 118.05 | 1986 | 254.86 | 202.60 | 242.16 | 2000 | 1,552.87 | 1,254.07 | 1,320.28 |
| 1973 | 120.24 | 92.16 | 97.55 | 1987 | 337.89 | 216.47 | 247.09 | 2001 | 1,383.37 | 944.75 | 1,148.08 |
| 1974 | 99.80 | 62.28 | 68.56 | 1988 | 283.77 | 240.17 | 277.72 | 2002 | 1,176.97 | 768.63 | 879.82 |
| 1975 | 95.61 | 70.04 | 90.19 | 1989 | 360.44 | 273.81 | 353.40 | 2003 | 1,112.56 | 788.90 | 1,111.92 |
| 1976 | 107.83 | 90.90 | 107.46 | 1990 | 369.78 | 294.51 | 330.23 | 2004 | 1,217.33 | 1,060.72 | 1,211.92 |
| 1977 | 107.00 | 90.71 | 95.10 | 1991 | 418.32 | 309.35 | 417.09 | 2005 | 1,275.80 | 1,136.22 | 1,248.29 |
| 1978 | 108.05 | 86.45 | 96.11 | 1992 | 442.65 | 392.41 | 435.71 | 2006 | 1,431.81 | 1,219.29 | 1,418.30 |
| 1979 | 112.16 | 95.22 | 107.94 | 1993 | 471.29 | 426.88 | 466.45 | 2007 | 1,576.09 | 1,363.98 | 1,468.36 |
| 1980 | 141.96 | 94.24 | 135.76 | 1994 | 482.85 | 435.86 | 459.27 | 2008 | 1,471.77 | 741.02 | 903.25 |

Data continued from page 280. *Source: CME Group; Chicago Mercantile Exchange*

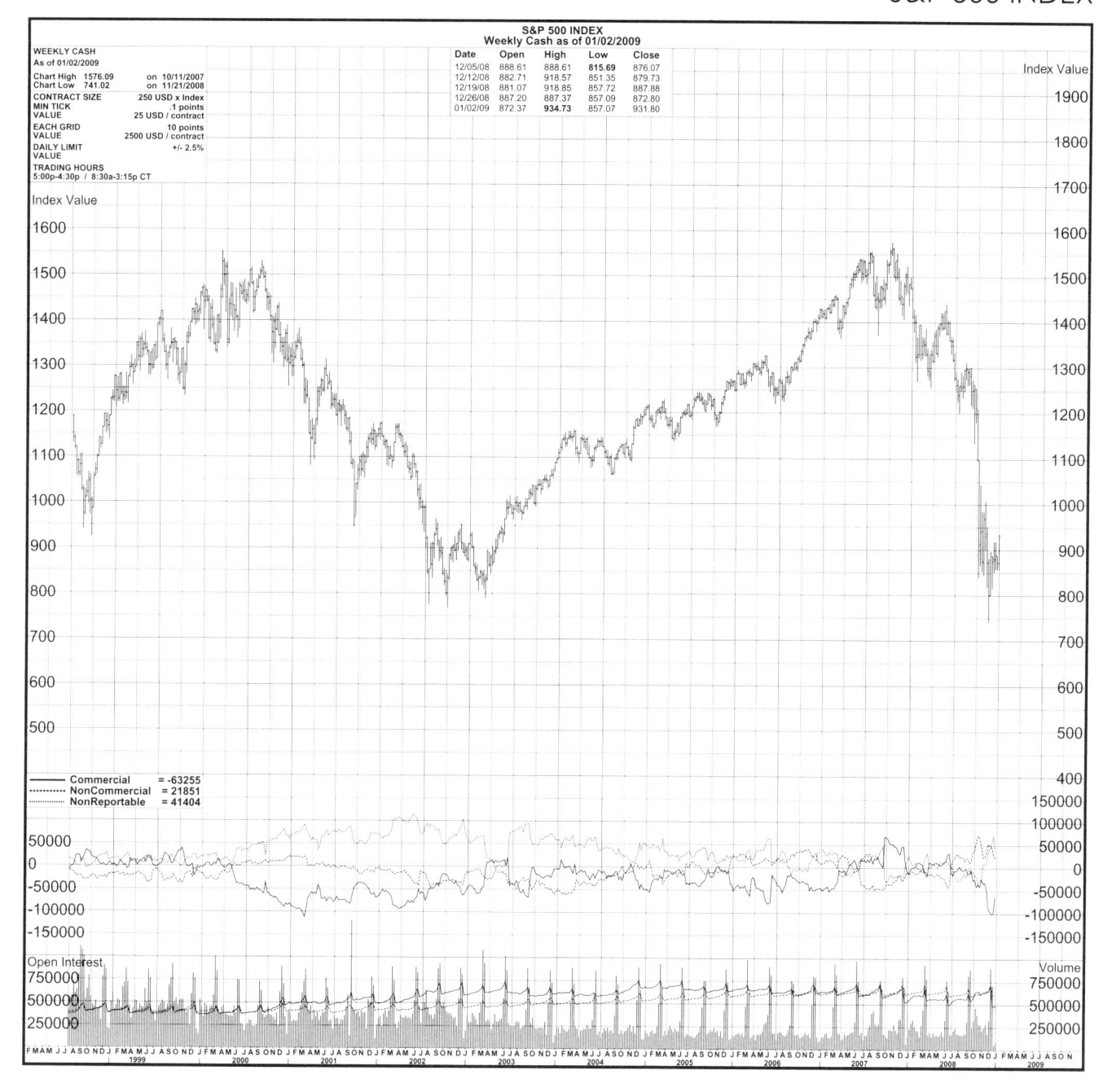

# S&P 500 INDEX

**WEEKLY CASH**
As of 01/02/2009
Chart High 1576.09 on 10/11/2007
Chart Low 741.02 on 11/21/2008
CONTRACT SIZE 250 USD x Index
MIN TICK .1 points
VALUE 25 USD / contract
EACH GRID 10 points
VALUE 2500 USD / contract
DAILY LIMIT +/- 2.5%
VALUE
TRADING HOURS
5:00p-4:30p / 8:30a-3:15p CT

**S&P 500 INDEX**
Weekly Cash as of 01/02/2009

| Date | Open | High | Low | Close |
|---|---|---|---|---|
| 12/05/08 | 888.61 | 888.61 | 815.69 | 876.07 |
| 12/12/08 | 882.71 | 918.57 | 851.35 | 879.73 |
| 12/19/08 | 881.07 | 918.85 | 857.72 | 887.88 |
| 12/26/08 | 887.20 | 887.37 | 857.09 | 872.80 |
| 01/02/09 | 872.37 | 934.73 | 857.07 | 931.80 |

Commercial = -63255
NonCommercial = 21851
NonReportable = 41404

## Quarterly High, Low and Settle of S&P 500 Index   In Index Value

| Quarter | High | Low | Settle | Quarter | High | Low | Settle | Quarter | High | Low | Settle |
|---|---|---|---|---|---|---|---|---|---|---|---|
| 03/2000 | 1,552.87 | 1,325.02 | 1,498.58 | 03/2003 | 935.05 | 788.90 | 848.18 | 03/2006 | 1,310.88 | 1,245.74 | 1,294.82 |
| 06/2000 | 1,527.19 | 1,339.40 | 1,454.60 | 06/2003 | 1,015.33 | 847.85 | 974.50 | 06/2006 | 1,326.70 | 1,219.29 | 1,270.20 |
| 09/2000 | 1,530.09 | 1,413.89 | 1,436.51 | 09/2003 | 1,040.29 | 960.84 | 995.97 | 09/2006 | 1,340.28 | 1,224.54 | 1,335.85 |
| 12/2000 | 1,454.82 | 1,254.07 | 1,320.28 | 12/2003 | 1,112.56 | 997.12 | 1,111.92 | 12/2006 | 1,431.81 | 1,327.10 | 1,418.30 |
| 03/2001 | 1,383.37 | 1,081.19 | 1,160.33 | 03/2004 | 1,163.23 | 1,087.06 | 1,126.21 | 03/2007 | 1,461.57 | 1,363.98 | 1,420.86 |
| 06/2001 | 1,315.93 | 1,091.99 | 1,225.71 | 06/2004 | 1,150.57 | 1,076.32 | 1,140.84 | 06/2007 | 1,540.56 | 1,416.37 | 1,503.35 |
| 09/2001 | 1,239.78 | 944.75 | 1,040.94 | 09/2004 | 1,140.80 | 1,060.72 | 1,114.58 | 09/2007 | 1,555.90 | 1,370.60 | 1,526.75 |
| 12/2001 | 1,173.62 | 1,026.76 | 1,148.08 | 12/2004 | 1,217.33 | 1,090.19 | 1,211.92 | 12/2007 | 1,576.09 | 1,406.10 | 1,468.36 |
| 03/2002 | 1,176.97 | 1,074.36 | 1,147.39 | 03/2005 | 1,229.11 | 1,163.69 | 1,180.59 | 03/2008 | 1,471.77 | 1,256.98 | 1,322.70 |
| 06/2002 | 1,147.84 | 952.92 | 989.82 | 06/2005 | 1,219.59 | 1,136.22 | 1,191.33 | 06/2008 | 1,440.24 | 1,272.00 | 1,280.00 |
| 09/2002 | 994.46 | 775.68 | 815.28 | 09/2005 | 1,245.86 | 1,183.55 | 1,228.81 | 09/2008 | 1,313.15 | 1,106.39 | 1,166.36 |
| 12/2002 | 954.28 | 768.63 | 879.82 | 12/2005 | 1,275.80 | 1,168.20 | 1,248.29 | 12/2008 | 1,167.03 | 741.02 | 903.25 |

*Source: CME Group; Chicago Mercantile Exchange*

# S&P MIDCAP 400 INDEX

**S&P MidCap 400 Index**
Monthly Cash as of 12/31/2008

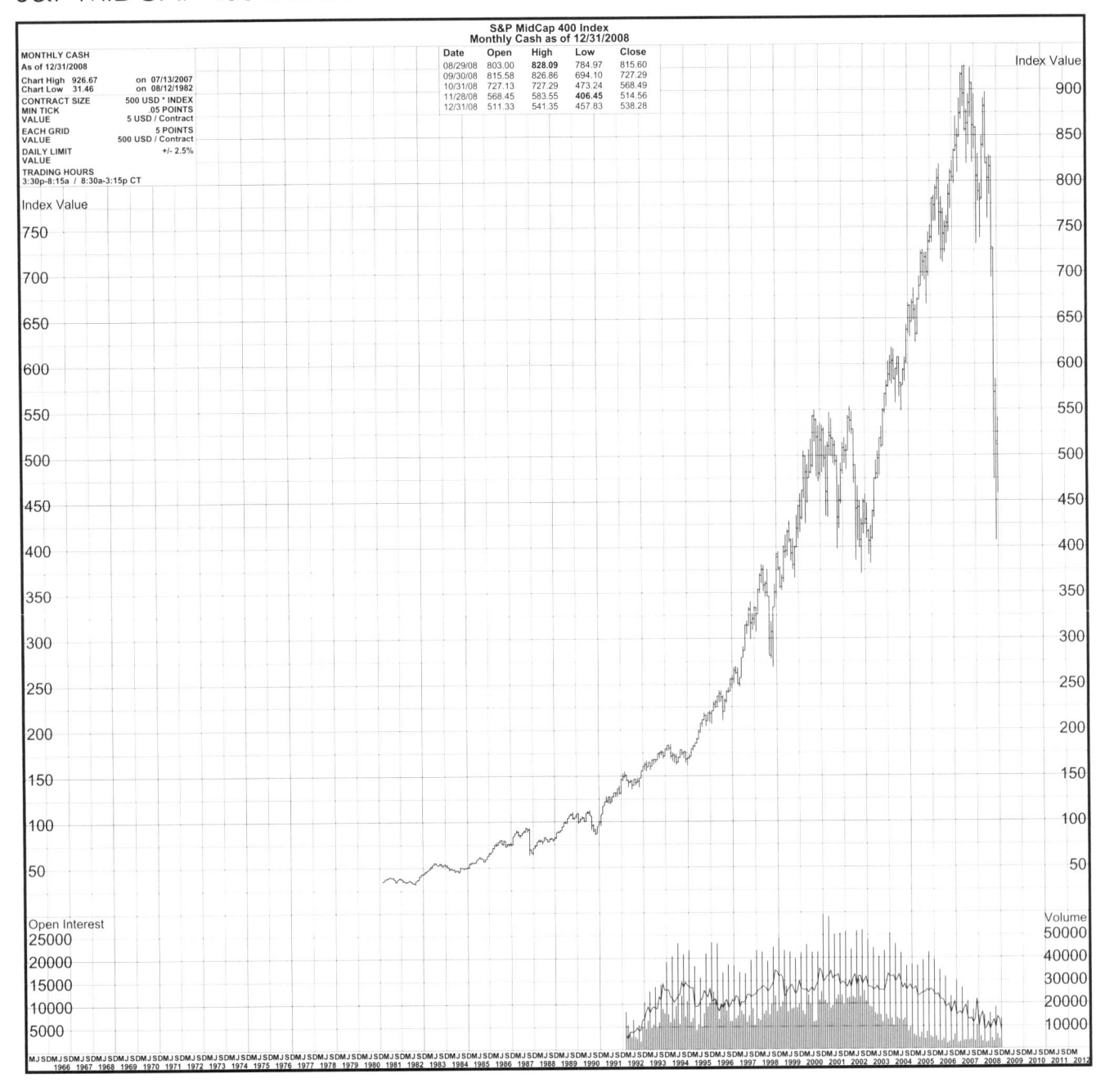

| Date | Open | High | Low | Close |
|---|---|---|---|---|
| 08/29/08 | 803.00 | 828.09 | 784.97 | 815.60 |
| 09/30/08 | 815.58 | 826.86 | 694.10 | 727.29 |
| 10/31/08 | 727.13 | 727.29 | 473.24 | 568.49 |
| 11/28/08 | 568.45 | 583.55 | 406.45 | 514.56 |
| 12/31/08 | 511.33 | 541.35 | 457.83 | 538.28 |

MONTHLY CASH As of 12/31/2008
Chart High 926.67 on 07/13/2007
Chart Low 31.46 on 08/12/1982
CONTRACT SIZE 500 USD * INDEX
MIN TICK .05 POINTS
VALUE 5 USD / Contract
EACH GRID 5 POINTS
VALUE 500 USD / Contract
DAILY LIMIT VALUE +/- 2.5%
TRADING HOURS 3:30p-8:15a / 8:30a-3:15p CT

## Annual High, Low and Settle of S&P 400 MidCap Index — In Index Value

| Year | High | Low | Settle | Year | High | Low | Settle | Year | High | Low | Settle |
|---|---|---|---|---|---|---|---|---|---|---|---|
| 1967 | | | | 1981 | 40.32 | 33.64 | 37.67 | 1995 | 220.73 | 167.93 | 217.84 |
| 1968 | | | | 1982 | 43.56 | 31.46 | 43.56 | 1996 | 259.29 | 206.34 | 255.58 |
| 1969 | | | | 1983 | 55.96 | 43.30 | 52.50 | 1997 | 340.40 | 247.27 | 333.37 |
| 1970 | | | | 1984 | 53.56 | 44.37 | 50.63 | 1998 | 392.31 | 268.66 | 392.31 |
| 1971 | | | | 1985 | 66.02 | 49.67 | 65.98 | 1999 | 445.10 | 352.35 | 444.67 |
| 1972 | | | | 1986 | 80.76 | 64.52 | 74.34 | 2000 | 549.63 | 415.98 | 516.76 |
| 1973 | | | | 1987 | 93.91 | 63.13 | 70.74 | 2001 | 547.51 | 397.54 | 508.31 |
| 1974 | | | | 1988 | 83.11 | 70.75 | 82.78 | 2002 | 554.01 | 370.83 | 429.79 |
| 1975 | | | | 1989 | 110.82 | 81.95 | 108.78 | 2003 | 581.92 | 381.82 | 576.01 |
| 1976 | | | | 1990 | 112.88 | 85.39 | 100.00 | 2004 | 666.99 | 548.29 | 663.31 |
| 1977 | | | | 1991 | 146.59 | 95.16 | 146.59 | 2005 | 752.00 | 623.57 | 738.05 |
| 1978 | | | | 1992 | 160.58 | 135.12 | 160.56 | 2006 | 822.03 | 710.53 | 804.37 |
| 1979 | | | | 1993 | 179.44 | 155.02 | 179.38 | 2007 | 926.67 | 796.64 | 858.20 |
| 1980 | | | | 1994 | 184.95 | 161.55 | 169.44 | 2008 | 897.37 | 406.45 | 538.28 |

Index data begins 01/02/1981.    *Source: CME Group; Chicago Mercantile Exchange*

# S&P MIDCAP 400 INDEX

**WEEKLY CASH**
As of 01/02/2009
Chart High 926.67 on 07/13/2007
Chart Low 268.66 on 10/08/1998
CONTRACT SIZE 500 USD * INDEX
MIN TICK .05 POINTS
VALUE 5 USD / Contract
EACH GRID 5 POINTS
VALUE 500 USD / Contract
DAILY LIMIT +/- 2.5%
VALUE
TRADING HOURS
3:30p-8:15a / 8:30a-3:15p CT

S&P MidCap 400 Index
Weekly Cash as of 01/02/2009

| Date | Open | High | Low | Close |
|---|---|---|---|---|
| 12/05/08 | 511.33 | 514.56 | 457.83 | 498.12 |
| 12/12/08 | 499.30 | 526.51 | 481.30 | 507.52 |
| 12/19/08 | 507.48 | 537.54 | 486.80 | 523.39 |
| 12/26/08 | 523.37 | 523.70 | 499.14 | 514.90 |
| 01/02/09 | 514.78 | 553.40 | 501.58 | 551.34 |

## Quarterly High, Low and Settle of S&P 400 MidCap Index    In Index Value

| Quarter | High | Low | Settle | Quarter | High | Low | Settle | Quarter | High | Low | Settle |
|---|---|---|---|---|---|---|---|---|---|---|---|
| 03/2000 | 505.63 | 415.98 | 499.69 | 03/2003 | 448.02 | 381.82 | 409.47 | 03/2006 | 795.50 | 732.57 | 792.11 |
| 06/2000 | 506.90 | 425.65 | 481.77 | 06/2003 | 495.12 | 407.81 | 480.21 | 06/2006 | 818.87 | 713.09 | 764.87 |
| 09/2000 | 549.63 | 480.18 | 538.81 | 09/2003 | 532.04 | 473.90 | 510.42 | 09/2006 | 770.44 | 710.53 | 754.25 |
| 12/2000 | 540.65 | 471.17 | 516.76 | 12/2003 | 581.92 | 510.42 | 576.01 | 12/2006 | 822.03 | 744.09 | 804.37 |
| 03/2001 | 533.82 | 433.44 | 459.92 | 03/2004 | 618.46 | 574.60 | 603.56 | 03/2007 | 870.89 | 796.64 | 848.47 |
| 06/2001 | 547.51 | 432.38 | 518.56 | 06/2004 | 616.94 | 557.37 | 607.69 | 06/2007 | 925.90 | 847.63 | 895.51 |
| 09/2001 | 519.18 | 397.54 | 432.02 | 09/2004 | 607.69 | 548.29 | 593.20 | 09/2007 | 926.67 | 818.78 | 885.06 |
| 12/2001 | 514.51 | 420.03 | 508.31 | 12/2004 | 666.99 | 580.67 | 663.31 | 12/2007 | 924.07 | 820.06 | 858.20 |
| 03/2002 | 543.87 | 484.75 | 541.10 | 03/2005 | 683.36 | 629.29 | 658.87 | 03/2008 | 859.43 | 731.29 | 779.51 |
| 06/2002 | 554.01 | 469.31 | 489.52 | 06/2005 | 695.91 | 623.57 | 684.94 | 06/2008 | 897.37 | 779.47 | 818.99 |
| 09/2002 | 489.88 | 384.93 | 407.38 | 09/2005 | 725.02 | 685.08 | 716.33 | 09/2008 | 828.09 | 694.10 | 727.29 |
| 12/2002 | 457.22 | 370.83 | 429.79 | 12/2005 | 752.00 | 665.23 | 738.05 | 12/2008 | 727.29 | 406.45 | 538.28 |

*Source: CME Group; Chicago Mercantile Exchange*

# S&P 100 INDEX

**MONTHLY CASH**
As of 12/31/2008
Chart High 846.19 on 03/24/2000
Chart Low 46.35 on 03/06/1978

**S&P 100 Index (OEX) Monthly Cash as of 12/31/2008**

| Date | Open | High | Low | Close |
|---|---|---|---|---|
| 08/29/08 | 585.69 | 608.81 | 576.86 | 590.83 |
| 09/30/08 | 593.46 | 601.50 | 515.52 | 543.49 |
| 10/31/08 | 543.71 | 548.43 | 397.34 | 464.19 |
| 11/28/08 | 464.25 | 482.76 | 361.32 | 432.89 |
| 12/31/08 | 428.95 | 445.85 | 395.55 | 431.54 |

## Annual High, Low and Settle of S&P 100 Index — In Index Value

| Year | High | Low | Settle | Year | High | Low | Settle | Year | High | Low | Settle |
|---|---|---|---|---|---|---|---|---|---|---|---|
| 1967 | | | | 1981 | 70.58 | 56.13 | 59.77 | 1995 | 299.18 | 212.94 | 292.96 |
| 1968 | | | | 1982 | 72.79 | 51.66 | 71.09 | 1996 | 369.87 | 285.16 | 359.99 |
| 1969 | | | | 1983 | 87.33 | 69.78 | 83.06 | 1997 | 474.99 | 355.11 | 459.94 |
| 1970 | | | | 1984 | 85.00 | 72.92 | 82.54 | 1998 | 615.90 | 431.76 | 604.03 |
| 1971 | | | | 1985 | 104.09 | 80.30 | 103.00 | 1999 | 798.38 | 598.01 | 792.83 |
| 1972 | | | | 1986 | 121.49 | 97.91 | 115.54 | 2000 | 846.19 | 656.67 | 686.45 |
| 1973 | | | | 1987 | 167.02 | 105.85 | 119.13 | 2001 | 725.07 | 480.02 | 584.28 |
| 1974 | | | | 1988 | 134.12 | 115.06 | 131.93 | 2002 | 600.80 | 384.96 | 444.75 |
| 1975 | | | | 1989 | 167.62 | 129.83 | 164.68 | 2003 | 550.90 | 400.24 | 550.78 |
| 1976 | 59.41 | 50.00 | 58.23 | 1990 | 175.95 | 139.67 | 155.24 | 2004 | 578.13 | 518.67 | 575.29 |
| 1977 | 57.92 | 48.76 | 51.03 | 1991 | 193.87 | 145.42 | 192.78 | 2005 | 586.81 | 542.77 | 570.00 |
| 1978 | 58.04 | 46.35 | 52.99 | 1992 | 202.18 | 181.69 | 198.32 | 2006 | 665.95 | 559.02 | 660.41 |
| 1979 | 58.19 | 52.39 | 55.53 | 1993 | 217.44 | 193.65 | 214.73 | 2007 | 734.51 | 624.81 | 685.65 |
| 1980 | 71.01 | 51.03 | 68.83 | 1994 | 223.60 | 201.17 | 214.32 | 2008 | 687.47 | 361.32 | 431.54 |

Index data begins 01/02/1976.   Source: Chicago Board of Options Exchange

# S&P 100 INDEX

**WEEKLY CASH**
As of 01/02/2009
Chart High 846.19 on 03/24/2000
Chart Low 361.32 on 11/21/2008
Index Value

**S&P 100 Index (OEX)**
Weekly Cash as of 01/02/2009

| Date | Open | High | Low | Close |
|---|---|---|---|---|
| 12/05/08 | 428.95 | 428.95 | 395.55 | 424.48 |
| 12/12/08 | 428.26 | 445.85 | 411.95 | 425.22 |
| 12/19/08 | 425.39 | 441.17 | 415.46 | 424.18 |
| 12/26/08 | 423.81 | 424.15 | 411.75 | 417.93 |
| 01/02/09 | 418.65 | 445.78 | 411.62 | 444.52 |

## Quarterly High, Low and Settle of S&P 100 Index    In Index Value

| Quarter | High | Low | Settle | Quarter | High | Low | Settle | Quarter | High | Low | Settle |
|---|---|---|---|---|---|---|---|---|---|---|---|
| 03/2000 | 846.19 | 716.55 | 815.06 | 03/2003 | 475.09 | 400.24 | 429.13 | 03/2006 | 596.28 | 568.37 | 587.75 |
| 06/2000 | 830.09 | 721.58 | 790.25 | 06/2003 | 512.67 | 429.54 | 490.39 | 06/2006 | 604.06 | 559.02 | 579.56 |
| 09/2000 | 834.87 | 754.85 | 759.83 | 09/2003 | 522.91 | 484.41 | 498.56 | 09/2006 | 622.12 | 562.88 | 620.03 |
| 12/2000 | 773.97 | 656.67 | 686.45 | 12/2003 | 550.90 | 499.25 | 550.78 | 12/2006 | 665.95 | 617.71 | 660.41 |
| 03/2001 | 725.07 | 548.19 | 591.63 | 03/2004 | 573.44 | 532.00 | 551.13 | 03/2007 | 671.47 | 624.81 | 649.89 |
| 06/2001 | 680.02 | 554.43 | 632.00 | 06/2004 | 562.86 | 526.53 | 553.87 | 06/2007 | 707.76 | 647.12 | 692.77 |
| 09/2001 | 642.10 | 480.02 | 533.10 | 09/2004 | 554.43 | 518.67 | 534.86 | 09/2007 | 720.26 | 640.50 | 714.49 |
| 12/2001 | 599.97 | 526.93 | 584.28 | 12/2004 | 578.13 | 521.90 | 575.29 | 12/2007 | 734.51 | 657.14 | 685.65 |
| 03/2002 | 600.80 | 544.82 | 577.87 | 03/2005 | 586.81 | 555.05 | 561.86 | 03/2008 | 687.47 | 583.64 | 613.71 |
| 06/2002 | 577.19 | 471.24 | 490.12 | 06/2005 | 574.37 | 542.88 | 558.07 | 06/2008 | 658.72 | 577.27 | 581.09 |
| 09/2002 | 495.03 | 384.96 | 407.25 | 09/2005 | 578.22 | 553.50 | 566.80 | 09/2008 | 608.81 | 515.52 | 543.49 |
| 12/2002 | 487.94 | 387.80 | 444.75 | 12/2005 | 584.33 | 542.77 | 570.00 | 12/2008 | 548.43 | 361.32 | 431.54 |

*Source: Chicago Board of Options Exchange*

# RUSSELL 2000 INDEX

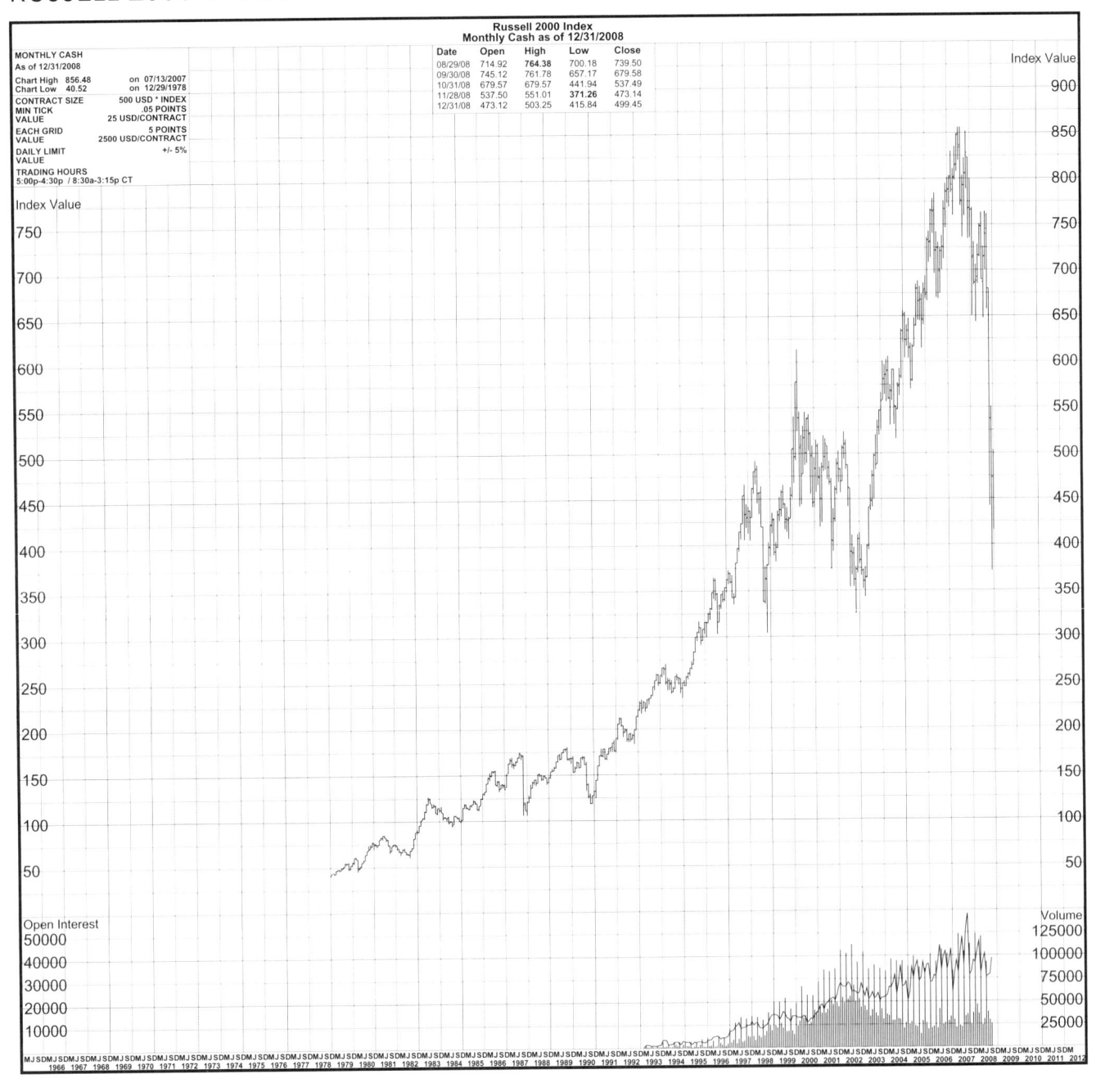

**Russell 2000 Index**
Monthly Cash as of 12/31/2008

| Date | Open | High | Low | Close |
|---|---|---|---|---|
| 08/29/08 | 714.92 | **764.38** | 700.18 | 739.50 |
| 09/30/08 | 745.12 | 761.78 | 657.17 | 679.58 |
| 10/31/08 | 679.57 | 679.57 | 441.94 | 537.49 |
| 11/28/08 | 537.50 | 551.01 | **371.26** | 473.14 |
| 12/31/08 | 473.12 | 503.25 | 415.84 | 499.45 |

**MONTHLY CASH** As of 12/31/2008
Chart High 856.48 on 07/13/2007
Chart Low 40.52 on 12/29/1978
CONTRACT SIZE 500 USD * INDEX
MIN TICK .05 POINTS
VALUE 25 USD/CONTRACT
EACH GRID 5 POINTS
VALUE 2500 USD/CONTRACT
DAILY LIMIT +/- 5%
TRADING HOURS 5:00p-4:30p / 8:30a-3:15p CT

## Annual High, Low and Settle of Russell 2000 Index — In Index Value

| Year | High | Low | Settle | Year | High | Low | Settle | Year | High | Low | Settle |
|---|---|---|---|---|---|---|---|---|---|---|---|
| 1967 | | | | 1981 | 85.16 | 65.37 | 73.67 | 1995 | 316.98 | 246.38 | 315.97 |
| 1968 | | | | 1982 | 91.01 | 60.33 | 88.90 | 1996 | 364.96 | 299.45 | 362.61 |
| 1969 | | | | 1983 | 126.99 | 88.29 | 112.27 | 1997 | 466.21 | 335.18 | 437.02 |
| 1970 | | | | 1984 | 116.69 | 93.95 | 101.49 | 1998 | 492.28 | 303.87 | 421.97 |
| 1971 | | | | 1985 | 129.87 | 101.21 | 129.87 | 1999 | 504.75 | 381.96 | 504.75 |
| 1972 | | | | 1986 | 155.30 | 128.23 | 135.00 | 2000 | 614.16 | 440.76 | 483.53 |
| 1973 | | | | 1987 | 174.44 | 106.07 | 120.42 | 2001 | 519.89 | 373.62 | 488.50 |
| 1974 | | | | 1988 | 152.08 | 120.43 | 147.37 | 2002 | 523.79 | 324.90 | 383.09 |
| 1975 | | | | 1989 | 180.95 | 146.33 | 168.30 | 2003 | 566.74 | 343.06 | 556.91 |
| 1976 | | | | 1990 | 171.08 | 118.45 | 132.20 | 2004 | 656.11 | 515.90 | 651.57 |
| 1977 | | | | 1991 | 189.93 | 124.52 | 189.91 | 2005 | 693.63 | 570.03 | 673.22 |
| 1978 | 40.52 | 40.52 | 40.52 | 1992 | 221.01 | 183.40 | 221.01 | 2006 | 801.01 | 666.58 | 787.66 |
| 1979 | 55.91 | 40.81 | 55.91 | 1993 | 260.41 | 216.43 | 258.59 | 2007 | 856.48 | 734.38 | 766.03 |
| 1980 | 77.70 | 45.36 | 74.80 | 1994 | 271.08 | 233.89 | 250.36 | 2008 | 768.47 | 371.26 | 499.45 |

Index data begins 12/29/1978.   Source: IntercontinentalExchange (ICE); formerly New York Board of Trade (NYBOT)

# RUSSELL 2000 INDEX

**Russell 2000 Index**
Weekly Cash as of 01/02/2009

| Date | Open | High | Low | Close |
|---|---|---|---|---|
| 12/05/08 | 473.12 | 473.12 | 415.84 | 461.09 |
| 12/12/08 | 461.09 | 491.78 | 440.71 | 468.43 |
| 12/19/08 | 468.43 | 497.54 | 445.80 | 486.26 |
| 12/26/08 | 486.26 | 486.93 | 460.85 | 476.77 |
| 01/02/09 | 476.77 | 508.45 | 461.02 | 505.84 |

WEEKLY CASH
As of 01/02/2009
Chart High 856.48 on 07/13/2007
Chart Low 303.87 on 10/08/1998
CONTRACT SIZE 500 USD * INDEX
MIN TICK .05 POINTS
VALUE 25 USD/CONTRACT
EACH GRID 5 POINTS
VALUE 2500 USD/CONTRACT
DAILY LIMIT NONE
VALUE
TRADING HOURS
9:30a - 4:15p ET

Commercial = -1400
NonCommercial = 901
NonReportable = 499

## Quarterly High, Low and Settle of Russell 2000 Index    In Index Value

| Quarter | High | Low | Settle | Quarter | High | Low | Settle | Quarter | High | Low | Settle |
|---|---|---|---|---|---|---|---|---|---|---|---|
| 03/2000 | 614.16 | 467.56 | 539.08 | 03/2003 | 399.55 | 343.06 | 364.54 | 03/2006 | 767.17 | 666.58 | 765.14 |
| 06/2000 | 545.90 | 441.56 | 517.23 | 06/2003 | 465.73 | 363.73 | 448.37 | 06/2006 | 784.62 | 669.88 | 724.58 |
| 09/2000 | 545.71 | 487.39 | 521.37 | 09/2003 | 520.61 | 441.22 | 487.68 | 09/2006 | 738.17 | 668.58 | 725.59 |
| 12/2000 | 523.41 | 440.76 | 483.53 | 12/2003 | 566.74 | 488.29 | 556.91 | 12/2006 | 801.01 | 712.16 | 787.66 |
| 03/2001 | 515.22 | 419.70 | 450.53 | 03/2004 | 603.16 | 556.13 | 590.31 | 03/2007 | 830.02 | 760.06 | 800.71 |
| 06/2001 | 519.89 | 424.64 | 510.69 | 06/2004 | 606.42 | 530.68 | 591.52 | 06/2007 | 856.42 | 798.17 | 833.70 |
| 09/2001 | 508.59 | 373.62 | 404.86 | 09/2004 | 591.38 | 515.90 | 572.94 | 09/2007 | 856.48 | 735.95 | 805.45 |
| 12/2001 | 494.71 | 393.00 | 488.50 | 12/2004 | 656.11 | 562.82 | 651.57 | 12/2007 | 852.07 | 734.38 | 766.03 |
| 03/2002 | 509.19 | 457.05 | 506.46 | 03/2005 | 654.30 | 603.75 | 615.07 | 03/2008 | 768.47 | 643.29 | 687.97 |
| 06/2002 | 523.79 | 441.76 | 462.65 | 06/2005 | 648.16 | 570.03 | 639.66 | 06/2008 | 763.27 | 684.89 | 689.66 |
| 09/2002 | 461.79 | 354.11 | 362.27 | 09/2005 | 688.51 | 638.93 | 667.80 | 09/2008 | 764.38 | 647.37 | 679.58 |
| 12/2002 | 413.64 | 324.90 | 383.09 | 12/2005 | 693.63 | 614.76 | 673.22 | 12/2008 | 676.21 | 371.26 | 499.45 |

*Source: IntercontinentalExchange (ICE); formerly New York Board of Trade (NYBOT)*

# VALUE LINE INDEX

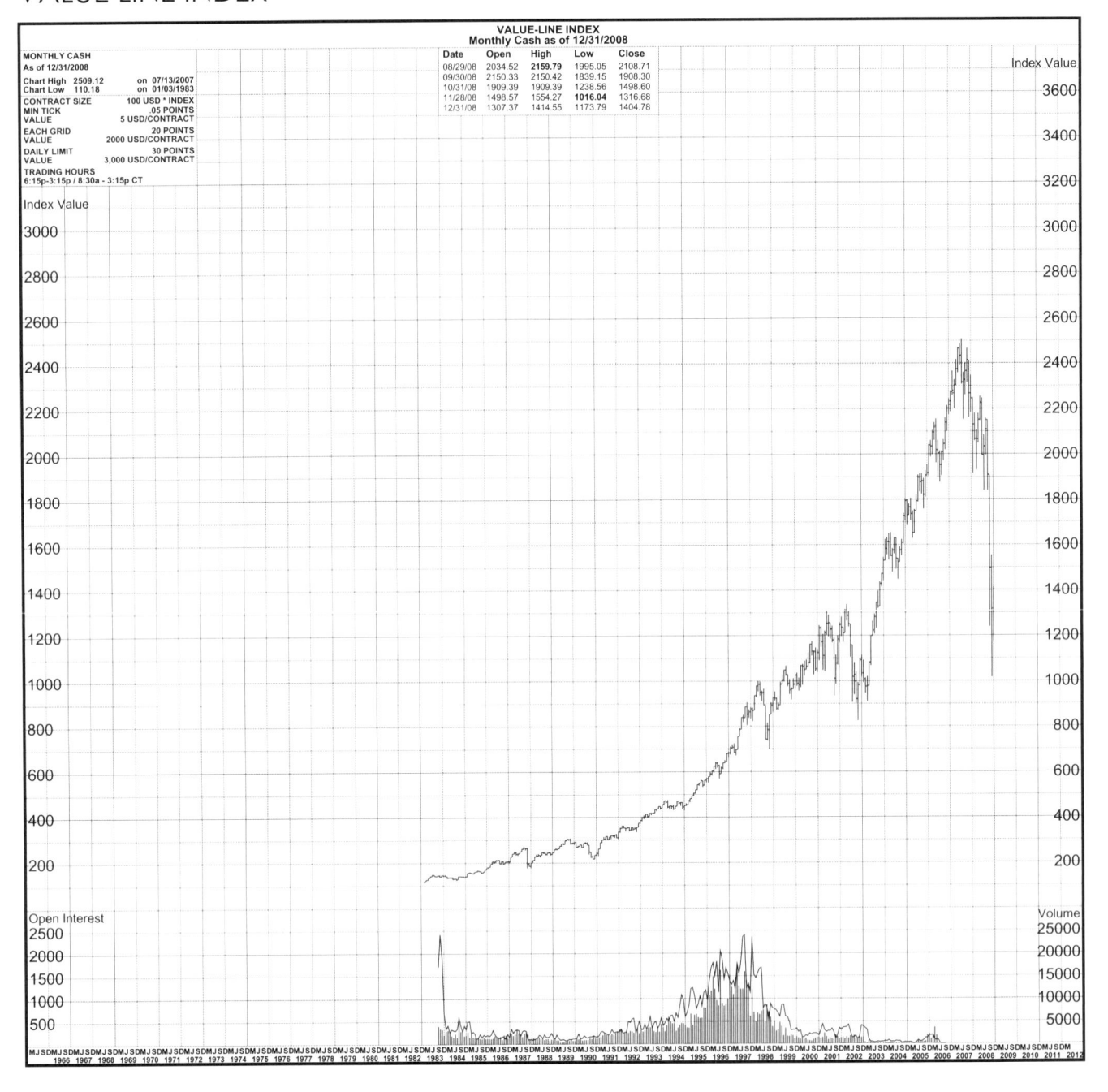

**VALUE-LINE INDEX**
Monthly Cash as of 12/31/2008

| Date | Open | High | Low | Close |
|---|---|---|---|---|
| 08/29/08 | 2034.52 | 2159.79 | 1995.05 | 2108.71 |
| 09/30/08 | 2150.33 | 2150.42 | 1839.15 | 1908.30 |
| 10/31/08 | 1909.39 | 1909.39 | 1238.56 | 1498.60 |
| 11/28/08 | 1498.57 | 1554.27 | 1016.04 | 1316.68 |
| 12/31/08 | 1307.37 | 1414.55 | 1173.79 | 1404.78 |

MONTHLY CASH As of 12/31/2008
Chart High 2509.12 on 07/13/2007
Chart Low 110.18 on 01/03/1983
CONTRACT SIZE 100 USD * INDEX
MIN TICK 05 POINTS
VALUE 5 USD/CONTRACT
EACH GRID 20 POINTS
VALUE 2000 USD/CONTRACT
DAILY LIMIT 30 POINTS
VALUE 3,000 USD/CONTRACT
TRADING HOURS 6:15p-3:15p / 8:30a - 3:15p CT

## Annual High, Low and Settle of Value-Line Index   In Index Value

| Year | High | Low | Settle | Year | High | Low | Settle | Year | High | Low | Settle |
|---|---|---|---|---|---|---|---|---|---|---|---|
| 1967 | | | | 1981 | | | | 1995 | 571.20 | 450.32 | 569.91 |
| 1968 | | | | 1982 | | | | 1996 | 686.65 | 552.31 | 682.62 |
| 1969 | | | | 1983 | 150.23 | 110.18 | 144.10 | 1997 | 906.20 | 670.94 | 876.84 |
| 1970 | | | | 1984 | 148.69 | 124.60 | 140.18 | 1998 | 999.91 | 699.44 | 927.84 |
| 1971 | | | | 1985 | 179.66 | 139.19 | 179.66 | 1999 | 1,067.98 | 871.42 | 1,025.80 |
| 1972 | | | | 1986 | 213.82 | 176.68 | 203.14 | 2000 | 1,176.20 | 956.69 | 1,124.76 |
| 1973 | | | | 1987 | 271.17 | 176.93 | 200.08 | 2001 | 1,311.09 | 934.49 | 1,247.13 |
| 1974 | | | | 1988 | 248.56 | 201.85 | 245.51 | 2002 | 1,337.54 | 824.77 | 1,033.75 |
| 1975 | | | | 1989 | 307.55 | 243.68 | 290.15 | 2003 | 1,545.05 | 910.60 | 1,530.52 |
| 1976 | | | | 1990 | 294.88 | 215.35 | 241.52 | 2004 | 1,803.83 | 1,448.33 | 1,794.19 |
| 1977 | | | | 1991 | 335.32 | 229.57 | 335.30 | 2005 | 1,955.17 | 1,627.84 | 1,916.74 |
| 1978 | | | | 1992 | 386.10 | 331.76 | 386.09 | 2006 | 2,243.69 | 1,874.87 | 2,216.74 |
| 1979 | | | | 1993 | 456.15 | 382.19 | 455.88 | 2007 | 2,509.12 | 2,152.63 | 2,245.58 |
| 1980 | | | | 1994 | 476.76 | 431.10 | 452.53 | 2008 | 2,255.21 | 1,016.04 | 1,404.78 |

Index data begins 01/03/1983.   *Source: Kansas City Board of Trade*

# VALUE LINE INDEX

**VALUE-LINE INDEX**
Weekly Cash as of 01/02/2009

**WEEKLY CASH**
As of 01/02/2009
Chart High 2509.12 on 07/13/2007
Chart Low 699.44 on 10/08/1998
CONTRACT SIZE 100 USD * INDEX
MIN TICK .05 POINTS
VALUE 5 USD/CONTRACT
EACH GRID 10 POINTS
VALUE 1000 USD/CONTRACT
DAILY LIMIT 30 POINTS
VALUE 3,000 USD/CONTRACT
TRADING HOURS
6:15p-3:15p / 8:30a - 3:15p CT

| Date | Open | High | Low | Close |
|---|---|---|---|---|
| 12/05/08 | 1307.37 | 1307.37 | 1173.79 | 1286.86 |
| 12/12/08 | 1297.44 | 1381.22 | 1262.50 | 1327.44 |
| 12/19/08 | 1329.71 | 1399.89 | 1272.50 | 1372.35 |
| 12/26/08 | 1372.30 | 1372.66 | 1305.66 | 1342.67 |
| 01/02/09 | 1342.27 | 1459.49 | 1304.62 | 1454.77 |

## Quarterly High, Low and Settle of Value-Line Index — In Index Value

| Quarter | High | Low | Settle | Quarter | High | Low | Settle | Quarter | High | Low | Settle |
|---|---|---|---|---|---|---|---|---|---|---|---|
| 03/2000 | 1,070.16 | 956.69 | 1,067.12 | 03/2003 | 1,093.05 | 910.60 | 979.13 | 03/2006 | 2,105.37 | 1,903.40 | 2,095.25 |
| 06/2000 | 1,093.79 | 982.56 | 1,062.57 | 06/2003 | 1,263.64 | 976.80 | 1,222.44 | 06/2006 | 2,156.12 | 1,894.76 | 2,003.89 |
| 09/2000 | 1,176.20 | 1,062.62 | 1,130.82 | 09/2003 | 1,396.38 | 1,206.33 | 1,326.97 | 09/2006 | 2,064.40 | 1,874.87 | 2,044.67 |
| 12/2000 | 1,147.64 | 1,027.11 | 1,124.76 | 12/2003 | 1,545.05 | 1,326.97 | 1,530.52 | 12/2006 | 2,243.69 | 2,019.11 | 2,216.74 |
| 03/2001 | 1,245.47 | 1,047.51 | 1,110.97 | 03/2004 | 1,650.47 | 1,530.24 | 1,611.47 | 03/2007 | 2,366.25 | 2,185.89 | 2,303.00 |
| 06/2001 | 1,311.09 | 1,041.98 | 1,254.79 | 06/2004 | 1,655.20 | 1,479.53 | 1,631.15 | 06/2007 | 2,487.03 | 2,301.00 | 2,431.47 |
| 09/2001 | 1,255.50 | 934.49 | 1,010.70 | 09/2004 | 1,630.65 | 1,448.33 | 1,576.11 | 09/2007 | 2,509.12 | 2,152.63 | 2,365.37 |
| 12/2001 | 1,258.03 | 985.79 | 1,247.13 | 12/2004 | 1,803.83 | 1,551.30 | 1,794.19 | 12/2007 | 2,467.61 | 2,161.83 | 2,245.58 |
| 03/2002 | 1,315.60 | 1,170.12 | 1,310.00 | 03/2005 | 1,805.50 | 1,684.89 | 1,735.57 | 03/2008 | 2,249.29 | 1,916.18 | 2,050.82 |
| 06/2002 | 1,337.54 | 1,104.72 | 1,158.78 | 06/2005 | 1,822.31 | 1,627.84 | 1,791.95 | 06/2008 | 2,255.21 | 1,994.58 | 1,994.64 |
| 09/2002 | 1,159.21 | 901.29 | 920.52 | 09/2005 | 1,915.54 | 1,788.90 | 1,879.39 | 09/2008 | 2,159.79 | 1,839.15 | 1,908.30 |
| 12/2002 | 1,114.29 | 824.77 | 1,033.75 | 12/2005 | 1,955.17 | 1,757.86 | 1,916.74 | 12/2008 | 1,909.39 | 1,016.04 | 1,404.78 |

*Source: Kansas City Board of Trade*

# DAX INDEX

DEUTSCHER AKTIENINDEX (DAX)
Monthly Cash as of 12/30/2008

| Date | Open | High | Low | Close |
|---|---|---|---|---|
| 08/29/08 | 6461.0 | 6626.7 | 6219.1 | 6422.3 |
| 09/30/08 | 6400.9 | 6553.9 | 5658.2 | 5831.0 |
| 10/31/08 | 5865.1 | 5876.9 | 4014.6 | 4988.0 |
| 11/28/08 | 5053.9 | 5302.6 | 4035.0 | 4669.4 |
| 12/31/08 | 4653.1 | 4850.4 | 4304.0 | 4810.2 |

MONTHLY CASH
As of 12/30/2008
Chart High 8151.6 on 07/13/2007
Chart Low 319.9 on 01/18/1967

## Annual High, Low and Settle of DAX Index   In Index Value

| Year | High | Low | Settle | Year | High | Low | Settle | Year | High | Low | Settle |
|---|---|---|---|---|---|---|---|---|---|---|---|
| 1967 | 503.20 | 319.90 | 503.20 | 1981 | 548.20 | 468.30 | 490.40 | 1995 | 2,320.22 | 1,893.63 | 2,253.88 |
| 1968 | 603.20 | 509.50 | 555.60 | 1982 | 554.60 | 476.60 | 552.80 | 1996 | 2,914.61 | 2,271.40 | 2,888.69 |
| 1969 | 659.20 | 548.40 | 622.40 | 1983 | 777.00 | 530.00 | 774.00 | 1997 | 4,459.89 | 2,833.78 | 4,249.69 |
| 1970 | 629.10 | 443.90 | 443.90 | 1984 | 820.90 | 692.70 | 820.90 | 1998 | 6,217.83 | 3,833.71 | 5,002.39 |
| 1971 | 542.20 | 423.80 | 473.50 | 1985 | 1,366.20 | 820.30 | 1,366.20 | 1999 | 6,992.92 | 4,605.27 | 6,958.14 |
| 1972 | 596.90 | 471.20 | 536.40 | 1986 | 1,586.00 | 1,248.60 | 1,432.30 | 2000 | 8,136.16 | 6,110.26 | 6,433.61 |
| 1973 | 581.00 | 386.30 | 396.30 | 1987 | 1,570.30 | 945.90 | 1,000.00 | 2001 | 6,795.14 | 3,539.18 | 5,160.10 |
| 1974 | 436.40 | 372.30 | 401.80 | 1988 | 1,343.84 | 931.18 | 1,327.87 | 2002 | 5,467.31 | 2,519.30 | 2,892.63 |
| 1975 | 566.20 | 411.20 | 563.20 | 1989 | 1,805.01 | 1,268.69 | 1,790.37 | 2003 | 3,996.28 | 2,188.75 | 3,965.16 |
| 1976 | 593.80 | 486.70 | 509.00 | 1990 | 1,976.43 | 1,320.43 | 1,398.23 | 2004 | 4,272.18 | 3,618.58 | 4,256.08 |
| 1977 | 567.60 | 491.40 | 549.30 | 1991 | 1,728.30 | 1,311.82 | 1,577.90 | 2005 | 5,469.96 | 4,157.51 | 5,408.26 |
| 1978 | 611.70 | 525.00 | 575.10 | 1992 | 1,814.64 | 1,413.68 | 1,545.05 | 2006 | 5,993.90 | 5,290.49 | 5,970.08 |
| 1979 | 593.30 | 492.20 | 497.80 | 1993 | 2,284.56 | 1,514.31 | 2,266.68 | 2007 | 8,151.57 | 6,444.70 | 8,067.32 |
| 1980 | 535.20 | 473.90 | 480.90 | 1994 | 2,282.60 | 1,953.23 | 2,106.58 | 2008 | 8,100.64 | 4,014.60 | 4,810.20 |

Index data begins 10/01/1959.   Source: Eurex

# DAX INDEX

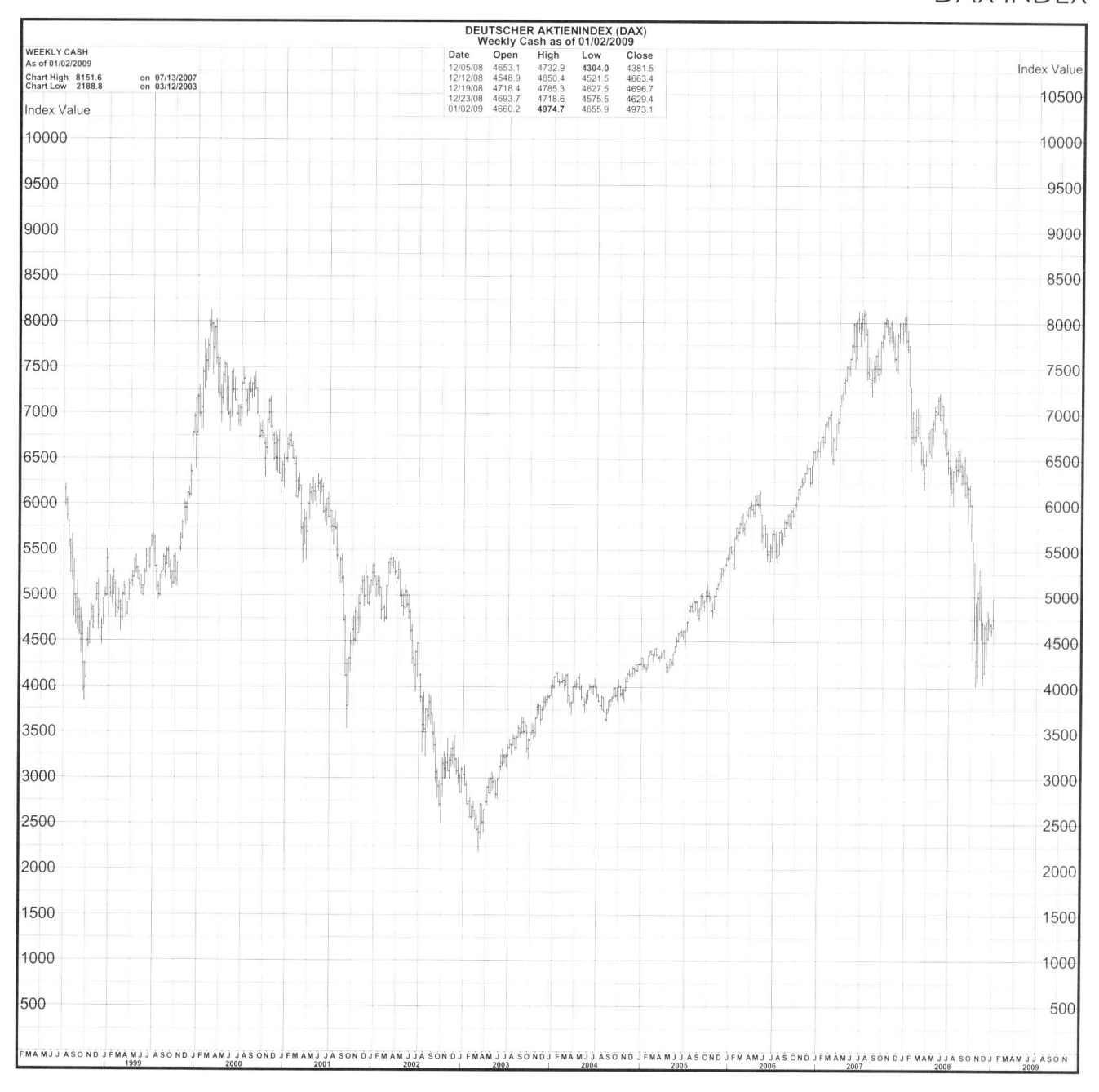

**WEEKLY CASH**
As of 01/02/2009
Chart High 8151.6 on 07/13/2007
Chart Low 2188.8 on 03/12/2003

**DEUTSCHER AKTIENINDEX (DAX)**
Weekly Cash as of 01/02/2009

| Date | Open | High | Low | Close |
|---|---|---|---|---|
| 12/05/08 | 4653.1 | 4732.9 | 4304.0 | 4381.5 |
| 12/12/08 | 4548.9 | 4850.4 | 4521.5 | 4663.4 |
| 12/19/08 | 4718.4 | 4785.3 | 4627.5 | 4696.7 |
| 12/23/08 | 4693.7 | 4718.6 | 4575.5 | 4629.4 |
| 01/02/09 | 4660.2 | 4974.7 | 4655.9 | 4973.1 |

## Quarterly High, Low and Settle of DAX Index    In Index Value

| Quarter | High | Low | Settle | Quarter | High | Low | Settle | Quarter | High | Low | Settle |
|---|---|---|---|---|---|---|---|---|---|---|---|
| 03/2000 | 8,136.16 | 6,388.91 | 7,599.39 | 03/2003 | 3,157.25 | 2,188.75 | 2,423.87 | 03/2006 | 5,993.90 | 5,290.49 | 5,970.08 |
| 06/2000 | 7,641.53 | 6,794.08 | 6,898.21 | 06/2003 | 3,324.44 | 2,395.72 | 3,220.58 | 06/2006 | 6,162.37 | 5,243.71 | 5,683.31 |
| 09/2000 | 7,503.32 | 6,468.46 | 6,798.12 | 09/2003 | 3,676.88 | 3,119.35 | 3,256.78 | 09/2006 | 6,031.55 | 5,365.06 | 6,004.33 |
| 12/2000 | 7,185.66 | 6,110.26 | 6,433.61 | 12/2003 | 3,996.28 | 3,217.40 | 3,965.16 | 12/2006 | 6,629.33 | 5,944.57 | 6,596.92 |
| 03/2001 | 6,795.14 | 5,351.48 | 5,829.95 | 03/2004 | 4,175.48 | 3,692.40 | 3,856.70 | 03/2007 | 7,040.20 | 6,444.70 | 6,917.03 |
| 06/2001 | 6,337.47 | 5,383.99 | 6,058.38 | 06/2004 | 4,156.89 | 3,710.02 | 4,052.73 | 06/2007 | 8,131.73 | 6,891.80 | 8,007.32 |
| 09/2001 | 6,131.97 | 3,539.18 | 4,308.15 | 09/2004 | 4,101.52 | 3,618.58 | 3,892.90 | 09/2007 | 8,151.57 | 7,190.36 | 7,861.51 |
| 12/2001 | 5,341.86 | 4,157.60 | 5,160.10 | 12/2004 | 4,272.18 | 3,838.98 | 4,256.08 | 12/2007 | 8,117.79 | 7,444.62 | 8,067.32 |
| 03/2002 | 5,467.31 | 4,706.01 | 5,397.29 | 03/2005 | 4,435.31 | 4,160.83 | 4,348.77 | 03/2008 | 8,100.64 | 6,167.82 | 6,534.97 |
| 06/2002 | 5,379.64 | 3,946.70 | 4,382.56 | 06/2005 | 4,637.34 | 4,157.51 | 4,586.28 | 06/2008 | 7,231.86 | 6,308.24 | 6,418.32 |
| 09/2002 | 4,483.03 | 2,719.49 | 2,769.03 | 09/2005 | 5,061.84 | 4,444.94 | 5,044.12 | 09/2008 | 6,626.70 | 5,658.20 | 5,831.02 |
| 12/2002 | 3,476.83 | 2,519.30 | 2,892.63 | 12/2005 | 5,469.96 | 4,762.75 | 5,408.26 | 12/2008 | 5,876.93 | 4,014.60 | 4,810.20 |

*Source: Eurex*

# CAC-40 INDEX

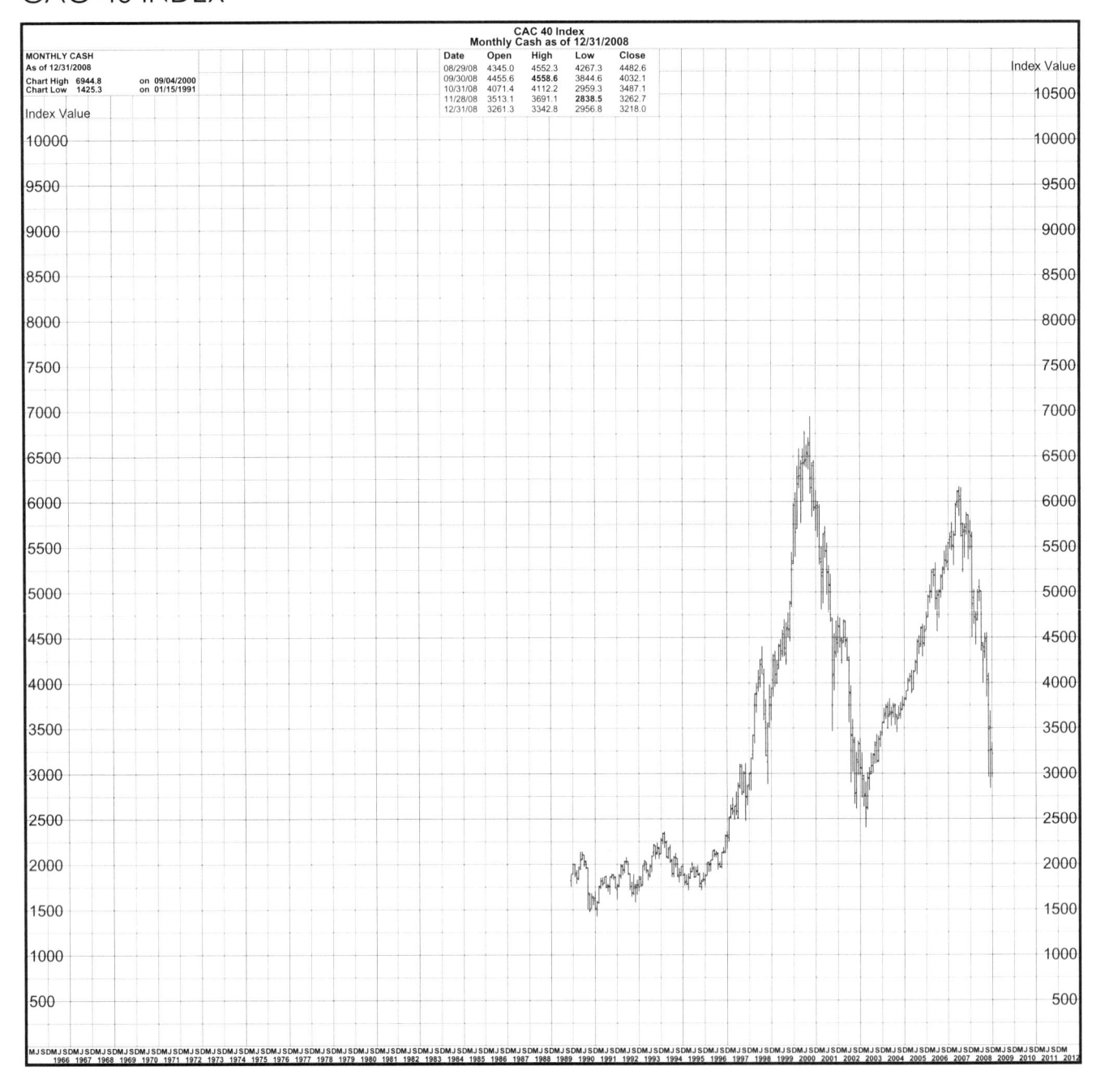

**CAC 40 Index — Monthly Cash as of 12/31/2008**

| Date | Open | High | Low | Close |
|---|---|---|---|---|
| 08/29/08 | 4345.0 | 4552.3 | 4267.3 | 4482.6 |
| 09/30/08 | 4455.6 | 4558.6 | 3844.6 | 4032.1 |
| 10/31/08 | 4071.4 | 4112.2 | 2959.3 | 3487.1 |
| 11/28/08 | 3513.1 | 3691.1 | 2838.5 | 3262.7 |
| 12/31/08 | 3261.3 | 3342.8 | 2956.8 | 3218.0 |

Monthly Cash As of 12/31/2008
Chart High 6944.8 on 09/04/2000
Chart Low 1425.3 on 01/15/1991

## Annual High, Low and Settle of CAC-40 Index    In Index Value

| Year | High | Low | Settle | Year | High | Low | Settle | Year | High | Low | Settle |
|---|---|---|---|---|---|---|---|---|---|---|---|
| 1967 | | | | 1981 | | | | 1995 | 2,025.15 | 1,711.80 | 1,871.97 |
| 1968 | | | | 1982 | | | | 1996 | 2,358.65 | 1,873.14 | 2,315.73 |
| 1969 | | | | 1983 | | | | 1997 | 3,114.00 | 2,251.53 | 2,998.91 |
| 1970 | | | | 1984 | | | | 1998 | 4,404.94 | 2,809.73 | 3,942.66 |
| 1971 | | | | 1985 | | | | 1999 | 5,979.54 | 3,845.77 | 5,958.32 |
| 1972 | | | | 1986 | | | | 2000 | 6,944.77 | 5,388.85 | 5,926.42 |
| 1973 | | | | 1987 | | | | 2001 | 5,999.18 | 3,463.07 | 4,624.58 |
| 1974 | | | | 1988 | | | | 2002 | 4,720.04 | 2,612.03 | 3,063.91 |
| 1975 | | | | 1989 | 2,005.92 | 1,751.33 | 2,001.08 | 2003 | 3,566.76 | 2,401.15 | 3,557.90 |
| 1976 | | | | 1990 | 2,141.13 | 1,472.59 | 1,517.93 | 2004 | 3,856.01 | 3,452.41 | 3,821.16 |
| 1977 | | | | 1991 | 1,897.26 | 1,425.26 | 1,765.66 | 2005 | 4,780.05 | 3,804.92 | 4,715.23 |
| 1978 | | | | 1992 | 2,080.80 | 1,577.74 | 1,857.78 | 2006 | 5,553.86 | 4,564.69 | 5,541.76 |
| 1979 | | | | 1993 | 2,289.48 | 1,755.90 | 2,268.22 | 2007 | 6,168.15 | 5,217.70 | 5,627.25 |
| 1980 | | | | 1994 | 2,360.98 | 1,796.82 | 1,881.15 | 2008 | 5,665.94 | 2,838.50 | 3,217.97 |

Index data begins 10/27/1989.    *Source: Euronext Paris*

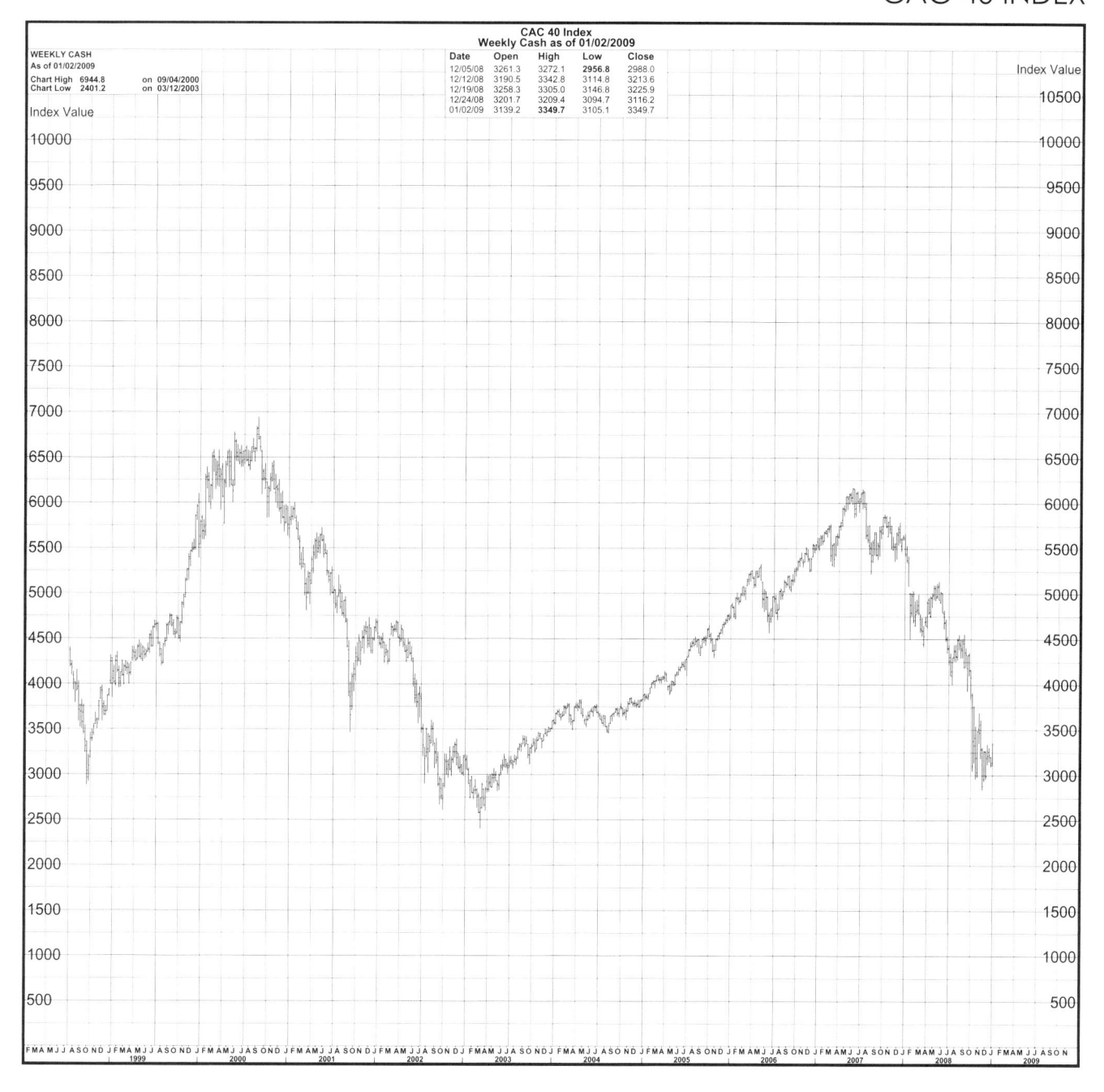

# CAC-40 INDEX

**CAC 40 Index**
Weekly Cash as of 01/02/2009

| Date | Open | High | Low | Close |
|---|---|---|---|---|
| 12/05/08 | 3261.3 | 3272.1 | 2956.8 | 2988.0 |
| 12/12/08 | 3190.5 | 3342.8 | 3114.8 | 3213.6 |
| 12/19/08 | 3258.3 | 3305.0 | 3146.8 | 3225.9 |
| 12/24/08 | 3201.7 | 3209.4 | 3094.7 | 3116.2 |
| 01/02/09 | 3139.2 | 3349.7 | 3105.1 | 3349.7 |

WEEKLY CASH
As of 01/02/2009
Chart High 6944.8 on 09/04/2000
Chart Low 2401.2 on 03/12/2003

## Quarterly High, Low and Settle of CAC-40 Index    In Index Value

| Quarter | High | Low | Settle | Quarter | High | Low | Settle | Quarter | High | Low | Settle |
|---|---|---|---|---|---|---|---|---|---|---|---|
| 03/2000 | 6,590.35 | 5,388.85 | 6,286.05 | 03/2003 | 3,232.34 | 2,401.15 | 2,618.46 | 03/2006 | 5,247.31 | 4,719.33 | 5,220.85 |
| 06/2000 | 6,780.66 | 5,761.47 | 6,446.54 | 06/2003 | 3,228.60 | 2,599.28 | 3,084.10 | 06/2006 | 5,329.16 | 4,564.69 | 4,965.96 |
| 09/2000 | 6,944.77 | 6,085.40 | 6,266.63 | 09/2003 | 3,435.79 | 3,008.72 | 3,134.99 | 09/2006 | 5,285.34 | 4,710.61 | 5,250.01 |
| 12/2000 | 6,459.50 | 5,673.87 | 5,926.42 | 12/2003 | 3,566.76 | 3,122.36 | 3,557.90 | 12/2006 | 5,553.86 | 5,196.07 | 5,541.76 |
| 03/2001 | 5,999.18 | 4,804.40 | 5,180.45 | 03/2004 | 3,789.33 | 3,489.53 | 3,625.23 | 03/2007 | 5,771.69 | 5,295.58 | 5,634.16 |
| 06/2001 | 5,728.52 | 4,872.92 | 5,225.33 | 06/2004 | 3,831.54 | 3,520.61 | 3,732.99 | 06/2007 | 6,168.15 | 5,620.70 | 6,054.93 |
| 09/2001 | 5,299.90 | 3,463.07 | 4,079.02 | 09/2004 | 3,773.64 | 3,452.41 | 3,640.61 | 09/2007 | 6,156.16 | 5,217.70 | 5,715.69 |
| 12/2001 | 4,735.21 | 3,914.39 | 4,624.58 | 12/2004 | 3,856.01 | 3,599.37 | 3,821.16 | 12/2007 | 5,882.07 | 5,358.76 | 5,627.25 |
| 03/2002 | 4,720.04 | 4,210.30 | 4,688.02 | 03/2005 | 4,108.00 | 3,804.92 | 4,067.78 | 03/2008 | 5,665.94 | 4,416.71 | 4,707.07 |
| 06/2002 | 4,688.16 | 3,561.24 | 3,897.99 | 06/2005 | 4,254.80 | 3,882.42 | 4,229.35 | 06/2008 | 5,142.10 | 4,348.31 | 4,434.85 |
| 09/2002 | 3,973.93 | 2,666.04 | 2,777.45 | 09/2005 | 4,620.85 | 4,089.27 | 4,600.02 | 09/2008 | 4,558.56 | 3,844.63 | 4,032.10 |
| 12/2002 | 3,393.04 | 2,612.03 | 3,063.91 | 12/2005 | 4,780.05 | 4,288.15 | 4,715.23 | 12/2008 | 4,112.24 | 2,838.50 | 3,217.97 |

*Source: Euronext Paris*

# FTSE 100 INDEX

**MONTHLY CASH**
As of 12/31/2008
Chart High 6950.6 on 12/30/1999
Chart Low 978.7 on 07/12/1984

**FTSE 100 INDEX**
Monthly Cash as of 12/31/2008

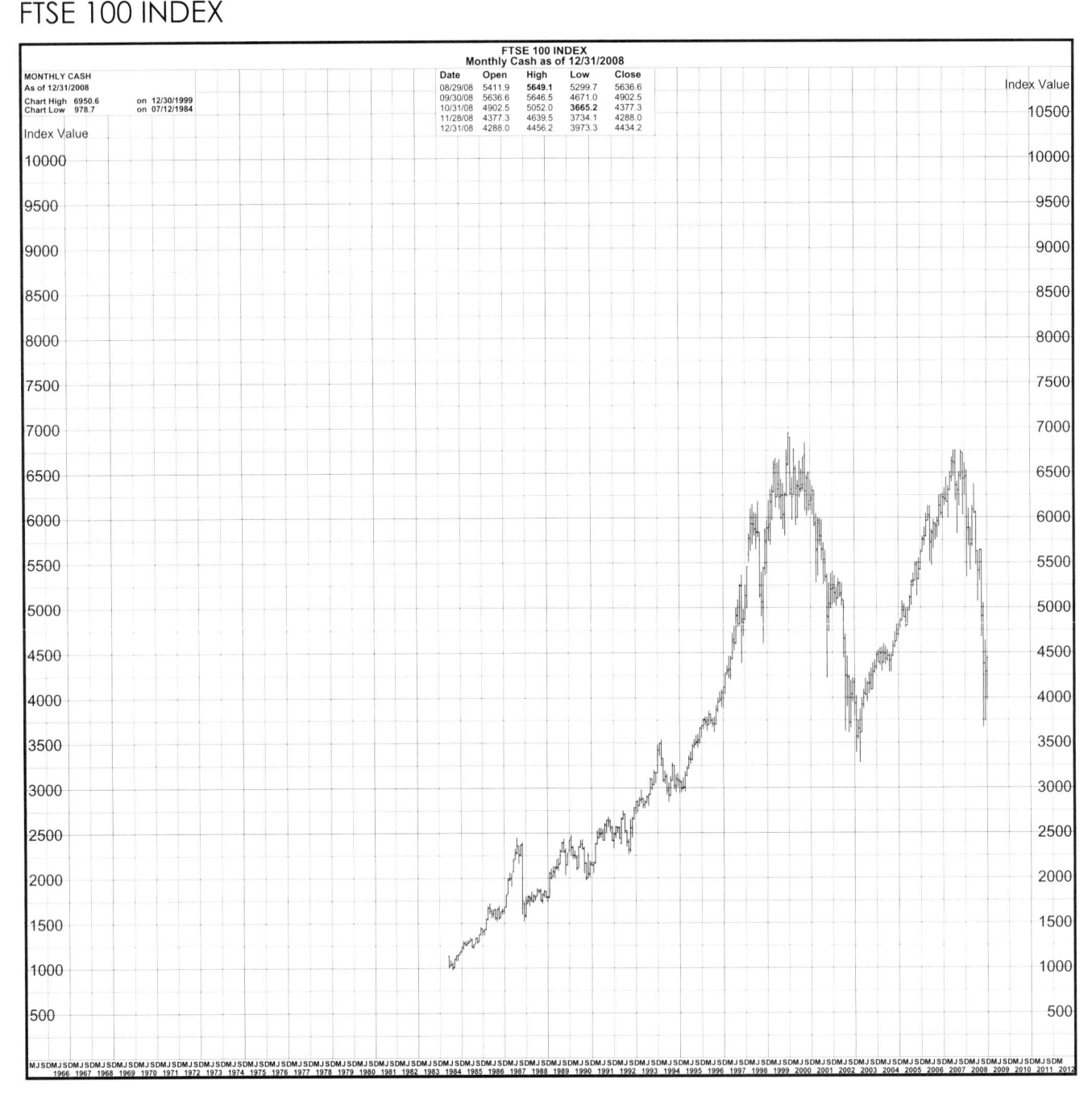

| Date | Open | High | Low | Close |
|---|---|---|---|---|
| 08/29/08 | 5411.9 | 5649.1 | 5299.7 | 5636.6 |
| 09/30/08 | 5636.6 | 5646.5 | 4671.0 | 4902.5 |
| 10/31/08 | 4902.5 | 5052.0 | 3665.2 | 4377.3 |
| 11/28/08 | 4377.3 | 4639.5 | 3734.1 | 4288.0 |
| 12/31/08 | 4288.0 | 4456.2 | 3973.3 | 4434.2 |

## Annual High, Low and Settle of FTSE 100 Index   In Index Value

| Year | High | Low | Settle | Year | High | Low | Settle | Year | High | Low | Settle |
|---|---|---|---|---|---|---|---|---|---|---|---|
| 1967 | | | | 1981 | | | | 1995 | 3,690.6 | 2,949.4 | 3,689.3 |
| 1968 | | | | 1982 | | | | 1996 | 4,123.2 | 3,612.6 | 4,118.5 |
| 1969 | | | | 1983 | | | | 1997 | 5,367.3 | 4,036.9 | 5,135.5 |
| 1970 | | | | 1984 | 1,231.3 | 978.7 | 1,231.2 | 1998 | 6,183.7 | 4,599.2 | 5,882.6 |
| 1971 | | | | 1985 | 1,460.7 | 1,199.6 | 1,412.6 | 1999 | 6,950.6 | 5,697.7 | 6,930.2 |
| 1972 | | | | 1986 | 1,721.7 | 1,365.7 | 1,679.0 | 2000 | 6,900.2 | 5,915.2 | 6,222.5 |
| 1973 | | | | 1987 | 2,449.1 | 1,515.0 | 1,712.7 | 2001 | 6,360.3 | 4,219.8 | 5,217.4 |
| 1974 | | | | 1988 | 1,892.2 | 1,687.5 | 1,793.1 | 2002 | 5,362.3 | 3,609.9 | 3,940.4 |
| 1975 | | | | 1989 | 2,435.7 | 1,782.4 | 2,422.7 | 2003 | 4,491.8 | 3,277.5 | 4,476.9 |
| 1976 | | | | 1990 | 2,479.4 | 1,974.1 | 2,143.5 | 2004 | 4,826.2 | 4,283.0 | 4,814.3 |
| 1977 | | | | 1991 | 2,683.7 | 2,052.3 | 2,493.1 | 2005 | 5,647.2 | 4,765.4 | 5,618.8 |
| 1978 | | | | 1992 | 2,848.9 | 2,260.9 | 2,846.5 | 2006 | 6,271.4 | 5,467.4 | 6,220.8 |
| 1979 | | | | 1993 | 3,480.8 | 2,727.6 | 3,418.4 | 2007 | 6,754.1 | 5,821.7 | 6,456.9 |
| 1980 | | | | 1994 | 3,539.2 | 2,844.7 | 3,065.5 | 2008 | 6,534.7 | 3,665.2 | 4,434.2 |

Index data begins 04/02/1984.   *Source: Euronext Liffe*

# FTSE 100 INDEX

## Quarterly High, Low and Settle of FTSE 100 Index    In Index Value

| Quarter | High | Low | Settle | Quarter | High | Low | Settle | Quarter | High | Low | Settle |
|---|---|---|---|---|---|---|---|---|---|---|---|
| 03/2000 | 6,900.2 | 5,972.7 | 6,540.2 | 03/2003 | 4,025.5 | 3,277.5 | 3,613.3 | 03/2006 | 6,047.0 | 5,618.8 | 5,964.6 |
| 06/2000 | 6,635.7 | 5,915.2 | 6,312.7 | 06/2003 | 4,218.8 | 3,612.3 | 4,031.2 | 06/2006 | 6,137.1 | 5,467.4 | 5,833.4 |
| 09/2000 | 6,838.6 | 6,075.1 | 6,294.2 | 09/2003 | 4,329.6 | 3,951.5 | 4,091.3 | 09/2006 | 6,002.9 | 5,654.6 | 5,960.8 |
| 12/2000 | 6,514.7 | 6,017.2 | 6,222.5 | 12/2003 | 4,491.8 | 4,091.3 | 4,476.9 | 12/2006 | 6,271.4 | 5,897.3 | 6,220.8 |
| 03/2001 | 6,360.3 | 5,279.6 | 5,633.7 | 03/2004 | 4,566.2 | 4,291.3 | 4,385.7 | 03/2007 | 6,451.4 | 5,999.8 | 6,308.0 |
| 06/2001 | 5,995.4 | 5,354.3 | 5,642.5 | 06/2004 | 4,601.6 | 4,363.0 | 4,464.1 | 06/2007 | 6,751.3 | 6,293.9 | 6,607.9 |
| 09/2001 | 5,726.1 | 4,219.8 | 4,903.4 | 09/2004 | 4,630.7 | 4,283.0 | 4,570.8 | 09/2007 | 6,754.1 | 5,821.7 | 6,466.8 |
| 12/2001 | 5,411.2 | 4,730.7 | 5,217.4 | 12/2004 | 4,826.2 | 4,551.6 | 4,814.3 | 12/2007 | 6,751.7 | 6,026.9 | 6,456.9 |
| 03/2002 | 5,362.3 | 5,015.5 | 5,271.8 | 03/2005 | 5,077.8 | 4,765.4 | 4,894.4 | 03/2008 | 6,534.7 | 5,338.7 | 5,702.1 |
| 06/2002 | 5,292.3 | 4,442.9 | 4,656.4 | 06/2005 | 5,138.2 | 4,773.7 | 5,113.2 | 06/2008 | 6,377.0 | 5,470.9 | 5,625.9 |
| 09/2002 | 4,708.7 | 3,609.9 | 3,721.8 | 09/2005 | 5,508.4 | 5,022.1 | 5,477.7 | 09/2008 | 5,649.1 | 4,671.0 | 4,902.5 |
| 12/2002 | 4,224.8 | 3,663.4 | 3,940.4 | 12/2005 | 5,647.2 | 5,130.9 | 5,618.8 | 12/2008 | 5,052.0 | 3,665.2 | 4,434.2 |

*Source: Euronext Liffe*

# HANG SENG INDEX

**HANG SENG INDEX**
Monthly Cash as of 12/31/2008

| Date | Open | High | Low | Close |
|---|---|---|---|---|
| 08/29/08 | 22497.9 | 22881.3 | 20350.5 | 21261.9 |
| 09/30/08 | 20999.3 | 21066.6 | 16283.7 | 18016.2 |
| 10/31/08 | 17870.4 | 18285.7 | 10676.3 | 13968.7 |
| 11/28/08 | 14436.0 | 15317.8 | 11814.8 | 13888.2 |
| 12/31/08 | 13775.3 | 15781.1 | 13344.6 | 14387.5 |

MONTHLY CASH As of 12/31/2008
Chart High 31958.4 on 10/30/2007
Chart Low 1645.0 on 04/11/1986

## Annual High, Low and Settle of Hang Seng Index — In Index Value

| Year | High | Low | Settle | Year | High | Low | Settle | Year | High | Low | Settle |
|---|---|---|---|---|---|---|---|---|---|---|---|
| 1967 | | | | 1981 | | | | 1995 | 10,073.00 | 6,890.00 | 10,073.00 |
| 1968 | | | | 1982 | | | | 1996 | 13,744.00 | 10,070.00 | 13,451.00 |
| 1969 | | | | 1983 | | | | 1997 | 16,820.00 | 8,775.00 | 10,722.00 |
| 1970 | | | | 1984 | | | | 1998 | 11,926.00 | 6,544.00 | 10,048.58 |
| 1971 | | | | 1985 | | | | 1999 | 17,138.11 | 9,000.24 | 16,962.10 |
| 1972 | | | | 1986 | 2,543.00 | 1,645.00 | 2,524.00 | 2000 | 18,397.57 | 13,596.63 | 15,095.53 |
| 1973 | | | | 1987 | 3,968.00 | 1,876.00 | 2,302.00 | 2001 | 16,274.67 | 8,894.36 | 11,397.21 |
| 1974 | | | | 1988 | 2,774.00 | 2,199.00 | 2,687.00 | 2002 | 12,021.72 | 8,772.48 | 9,321.29 |
| 1975 | | | | 1989 | 3,329.00 | 2,022.00 | 2,836.00 | 2003 | 12,740.50 | 8,331.87 | 12,575.94 |
| 1976 | | | | 1990 | 3,559.00 | 2,697.00 | 3,024.00 | 2004 | 14,339.06 | 10,917.65 | 14,230.14 |
| 1977 | | | | 1991 | 4,309.00 | 2,970.00 | 4,297.00 | 2005 | 15,508.57 | 13,320.53 | 14,876.43 |
| 1978 | | | | 1992 | 6,470.00 | 4,284.00 | 5,512.00 | 2006 | 20,049.03 | 14,843.97 | 19,964.72 |
| 1979 | | | | 1993 | 11,959.00 | 5,431.00 | 11,888.00 | 2007 | 31,958.41 | 18,659.23 | 27,812.65 |
| 1980 | | | | 1994 | 12,599.00 | 7,670.00 | 8,191.00 | 2008 | 27,853.60 | 10,676.29 | 14,387.48 |

Index data begins 04/11/1986.   *Source: Hong Kong Futures Exchange*

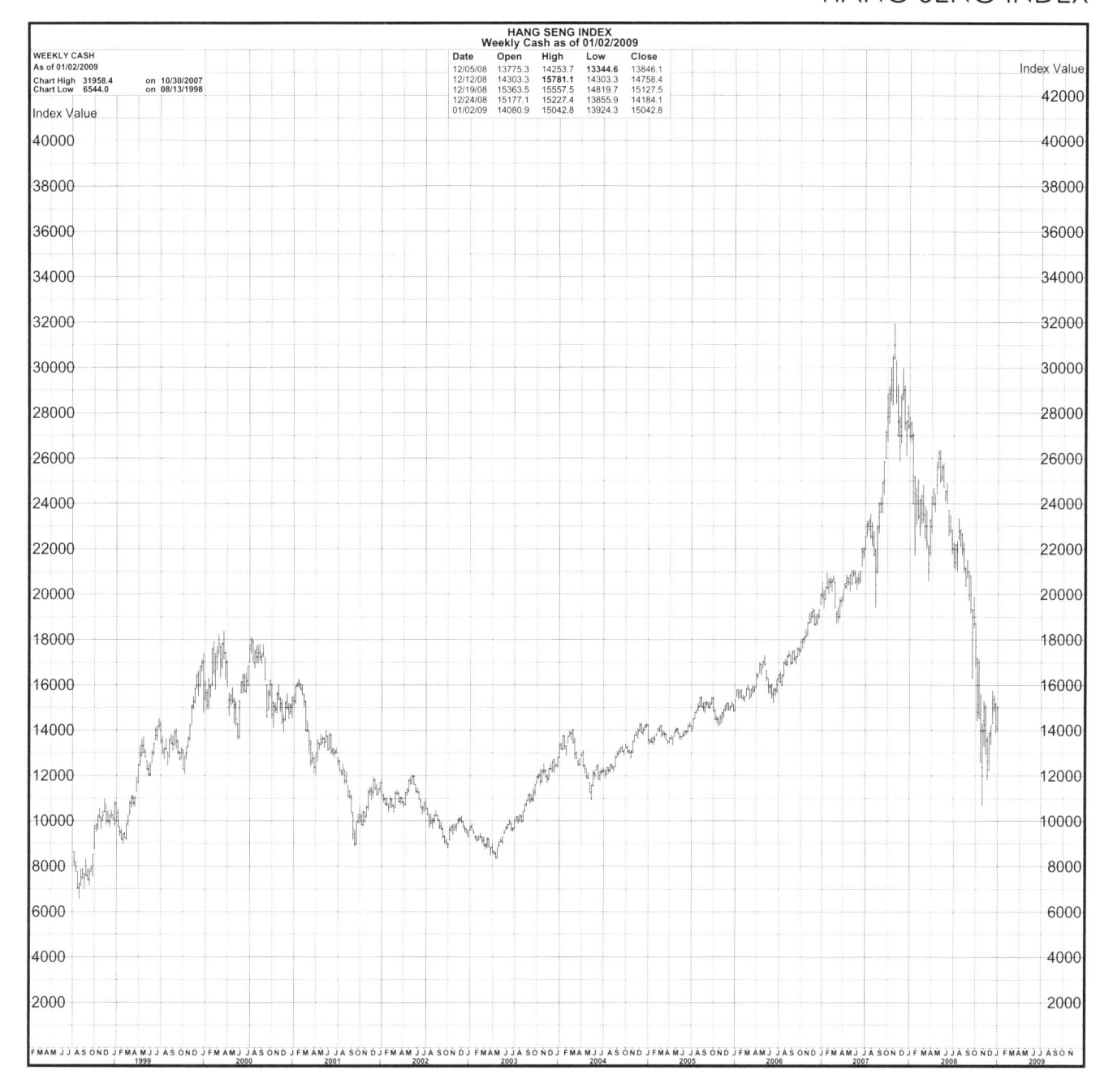

# HANG SENG INDEX

**HANG SENG INDEX**
Weekly Cash as of 01/02/2009

| Date | Open | High | Low | Close |
|---|---|---|---|---|
| 12/05/08 | 13775.3 | 14253.7 | 13344.6 | 13846.1 |
| 12/12/08 | 14303.3 | 15781.1 | 14303.3 | 14758.4 |
| 12/19/08 | 15363.5 | 15557.5 | 14819.7 | 15127.5 |
| 12/24/08 | 15177.1 | 15227.4 | 13855.9 | 14184.1 |
| 01/02/09 | 14080.9 | 15042.8 | 13924.3 | 15042.8 |

WEEKLY CASH
As of 01/02/2009
Chart High 31958.4 on 10/30/2007
Chart Low 6544.0 on 08/13/1998

## Quarterly High, Low and Settle of Hang Seng Index     In Index Value

| Quarter | High | Low | Settle | Quarter | High | Low | Settle | Quarter | High | Low | Settle |
|---|---|---|---|---|---|---|---|---|---|---|---|
| 03/2000 | 18,397.57 | 14,763.97 | 17,406.54 | 03/2003 | 9,892.70 | 8,586.70 | 8,634.45 | 03/2006 | 15,999.31 | 14,843.97 | 15,805.04 |
| 06/2000 | 17,458.06 | 13,596.63 | 16,155.78 | 06/2003 | 10,067.86 | 8,331.87 | 9,577.12 | 06/2006 | 17,328.43 | 15,204.86 | 16,267.62 |
| 09/2000 | 18,125.57 | 14,538.88 | 15,648.98 | 09/2003 | 11,444.72 | 9,512.20 | 11,229.80 | 09/2006 | 17,683.45 | 15,948.76 | 17,543.05 |
| 12/2000 | 16,245.61 | 13,894.19 | 15,095.53 | 12/2003 | 12,740.50 | 11,372.50 | 12,575.94 | 12/2006 | 20,049.03 | 17,428.10 | 19,964.72 |
| 03/2001 | 16,274.67 | 12,396.97 | 12,760.64 | 03/2004 | 14,058.21 | 12,400.35 | 12,681.67 | 03/2007 | 20,971.46 | 18,659.23 | 19,800.93 |
| 06/2001 | 13,989.16 | 12,061.55 | 13,042.53 | 06/2004 | 13,126.15 | 10,917.65 | 12,285.75 | 06/2007 | 22,085.59 | 19,672.94 | 21,772.73 |
| 09/2001 | 13,236.98 | 8,894.36 | 9,950.70 | 09/2004 | 13,356.88 | 11,862.68 | 13,120.03 | 09/2007 | 27,254.97 | 19,386.72 | 27,142.47 |
| 12/2001 | 11,957.83 | 9,758.98 | 11,397.21 | 12/2004 | 14,339.06 | 12,743.42 | 14,230.14 | 12/2007 | 31,958.41 | 25,861.73 | 27,812.65 |
| 03/2002 | 11,905.55 | 10,387.49 | 11,032.92 | 03/2005 | 14,272.54 | 13,320.53 | 13,516.88 | 03/2008 | 27,853.60 | 20,572.92 | 22,849.20 |
| 06/2002 | 12,021.72 | 10,291.16 | 10,598.55 | 06/2005 | 14,365.05 | 13,337.44 | 14,201.06 | 06/2008 | 26,387.37 | 21,773.67 | 22,102.01 |
| 09/2002 | 10,939.56 | 9,014.58 | 9,072.21 | 09/2005 | 15,508.57 | 13,920.87 | 15,428.52 | 09/2008 | 23,369.05 | 16,283.72 | 18,016.21 |
| 12/2002 | 10,246.86 | 8,772.48 | 9,321.29 | 12/2005 | 15,493.00 | 14,189.47 | 14,876.43 | 12/2008 | 18,285.68 | 10,676.29 | 14,387.48 |

*Source: Hong Kong Futures Exchange*

# NIKKEI 225 INDEX

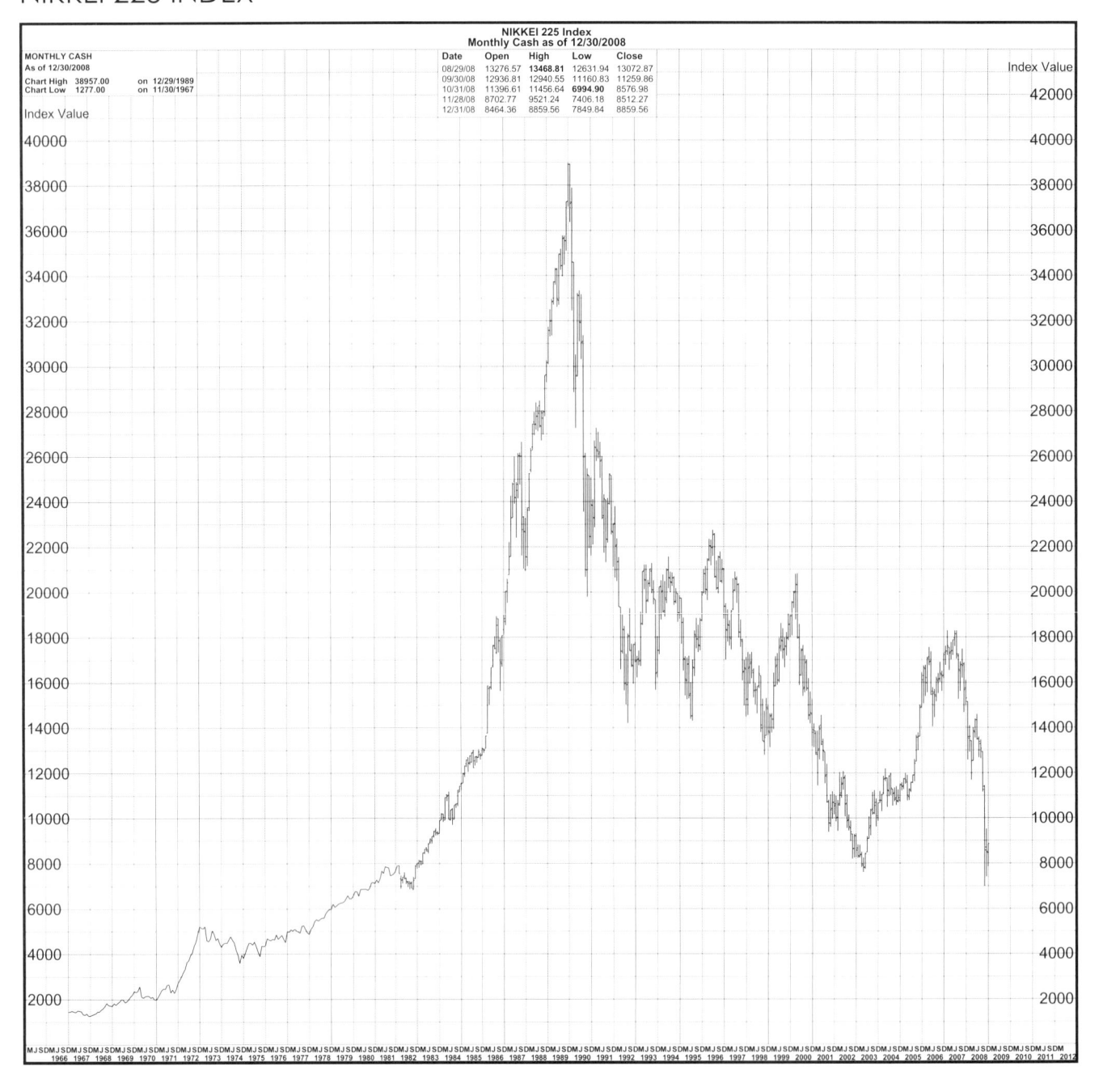

**NIKKEI 225 Index Monthly Cash as of 12/30/2008**

| Date | Open | High | Low | Close |
|---|---|---|---|---|
| 08/29/08 | 13276.57 | 13468.81 | 12631.94 | 13072.87 |
| 09/30/08 | 12936.81 | 12940.55 | 11160.83 | 11259.86 |
| 10/31/08 | 11396.61 | 11456.64 | 6994.90 | 8576.98 |
| 11/28/08 | 8702.77 | 9521.24 | 7406.18 | 8512.27 |
| 12/31/08 | 8464.36 | 8859.56 | 7849.84 | 8859.56 |

MONTHLY CASH As of 12/30/2008
Chart High 38957.00 on 12/29/1989
Chart Low 1277.00 on 11/30/1967

## Annual High, Low and Settle of Nikkei 225 Index   In Index Value

| Year | High | Low | Settle | Year | High | Low | Settle | Year | High | Low | Settle |
|---|---|---|---|---|---|---|---|---|---|---|---|
| 1967 | 1,506.00 | 1,277.00 | 1,283.00 | 1981 | 7,867.00 | 7,150.00 | 7,682.00 | 1995 | 20,023.00 | 14,295.00 | 19,868.00 |
| 1968 | 1,840.00 | 1,312.00 | 1,715.00 | 1982 | 8,026.00 | 6,849.00 | 8,016.00 | 1996 | 22,750.70 | 18,819.92 | 19,361.00 |
| 1969 | 2,360.00 | 1,759.00 | 2,360.00 | 1983 | 9,893.00 | 7,803.00 | 9,893.00 | 1997 | 20,910.79 | 14,488.21 | 15,258.74 |
| 1970 | 2,574.00 | 1,987.00 | 1,987.00 | 1984 | 11,577.00 | 9,703.00 | 11,542.00 | 1998 | 17,352.95 | 12,787.90 | 13,842.17 |
| 1971 | 2,714.00 | 2,099.00 | 2,714.00 | 1985 | 13,128.00 | 11,558.00 | 13,083.00 | 1999 | 19,036.08 | 13,122.61 | 18,934.34 |
| 1972 | 5,208.00 | 2,857.00 | 5,208.00 | 1986 | 18,988.00 | 12,881.00 | 18,820.00 | 2000 | 20,833.21 | 13,182.51 | 13,785.69 |
| 1973 | 5,226.00 | 4,307.00 | 4,307.00 | 1987 | 26,646.00 | 18,525.00 | 21,564.00 | 2001 | 14,556.11 | 9,382.95 | 10,542.62 |
| 1974 | 4,773.00 | 3,595.00 | 3,817.00 | 1988 | 30,264.00 | 21,148.00 | 30,159.00 | 2002 | 12,081.43 | 8,197.22 | 8,578.95 |
| 1975 | 4,533.00 | 3,886.00 | 4,359.00 | 1989 | 38,957.00 | 30,082.00 | 38,915.00 | 2003 | 11,238.63 | 7,603.76 | 10,676.64 |
| 1976 | 4,991.00 | 4,507.00 | 4,991.00 | 1990 | 38,950.00 | 19,781.00 | 23,848.00 | 2004 | 12,195.66 | 10,299.43 | 11,488.76 |
| 1977 | 5,264.00 | 4,866.00 | 4,866.00 | 1991 | 27,270.00 | 21,123.00 | 22,983.00 | 2005 | 16,445.56 | 10,770.58 | 16,111.43 |
| 1978 | 6,002.00 | 5,112.00 | 6,002.00 | 1992 | 23,801.00 | 14,194.00 | 16,924.00 | 2006 | 17,563.37 | 14,045.53 | 17,225.83 |
| 1979 | 6,591.00 | 6,073.00 | 6,569.00 | 1993 | 21,281.00 | 15,671.00 | 17,417.00 | 2007 | 18,300.39 | 14,669.85 | 15,307.78 |
| 1980 | 7,165.00 | 6,556.00 | 7,116.00 | 1994 | 21,573.00 | 17,242.00 | 19,723.00 | 2008 | 15,156.66 | 6,994.90 | 8,859.56 |

Index data begins 05/1949.   *Source: Singapore Exchange*

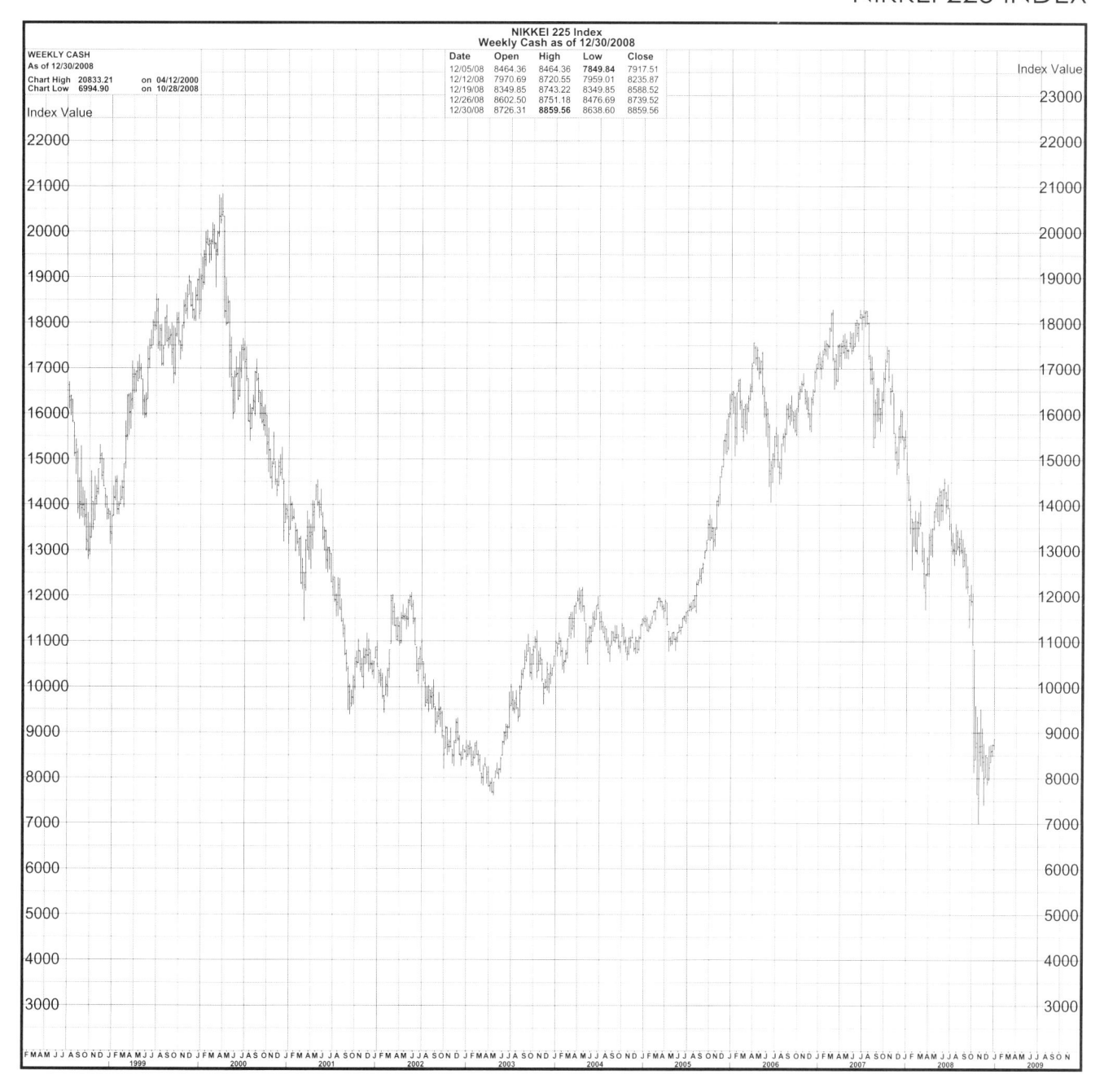

# NIKKEI 225 INDEX

```
NIKKEI 225 Index
Weekly Cash as of 12/30/2008
Date      Open      High      Low       Close
12/05/08  8464.36   8464.36   7849.84   7917.51
12/12/08  7970.69   8720.55   7959.01   8235.87
12/19/08  8349.85   8743.22   8349.85   8588.52
12/26/08  8602.50   8751.18   8476.69   8739.52
12/30/08  8726.31   8859.56   8638.60   8859.56
```

WEEKLY CASH
As of 12/30/2008
Chart High  20833.21  on 04/12/2000
Chart Low    6994.90  on 10/28/2008

## Quarterly High, Low and Settle of Nikkei 225 Index    In Index Value

| Quarter | High | Low | Settle | Quarter | High | Low | Settle | Quarter | High | Low | Settle |
|---|---|---|---|---|---|---|---|---|---|---|---|
| 03/2000 | 20,809.79 | 18,068.10 | 20,337.32 | 03/2003 | 8,829.06 | 7,824.82 | 7,972.71 | 03/2006 | 17,125.64 | 15,059.52 | 17,059.66 |
| 06/2000 | 20,833.21 | 15,870.25 | 17,411.05 | 06/2003 | 9,188.95 | 7,603.76 | 9,083.11 | 06/2006 | 17,563.37 | 14,045.53 | 15,505.18 |
| 09/2000 | 17,661.11 | 15,394.71 | 15,747.26 | 09/2003 | 11,160.19 | 9,078.74 | 10,219.05 | 09/2006 | 16,414.94 | 14,437.24 | 16,127.58 |
| 12/2000 | 16,192.78 | 13,182.51 | 13,785.69 | 12/2003 | 11,238.63 | 9,614.60 | 10,676.64 | 12/2006 | 17,301.69 | 15,615.56 | 17,225.83 |
| 03/2001 | 14,186.62 | 11,433.88 | 12,999.70 | 03/2004 | 11,869.00 | 10,299.43 | 11,715.39 | 03/2007 | 18,300.39 | 16,532.91 | 17,287.65 |
| 06/2001 | 14,556.11 | 12,511.66 | 12,969.05 | 06/2004 | 12,195.66 | 10,489.84 | 11,858.87 | 06/2007 | 18,297.00 | 16,999.05 | 18,138.36 |
| 09/2001 | 12,929.66 | 9,382.95 | 9,774.68 | 09/2004 | 11,988.12 | 10,545.89 | 10,823.57 | 09/2007 | 18,295.27 | 15,262.10 | 16,785.69 |
| 12/2001 | 11,186.75 | 9,604.09 | 10,542.62 | 12/2004 | 11,500.95 | 10,575.23 | 11,488.76 | 12/2007 | 17,488.97 | 14,669.85 | 15,307.78 |
| 03/2002 | 12,034.04 | 9,420.85 | 11,024.94 | 03/2005 | 11,975.46 | 11,212.63 | 11,668.95 | 03/2008 | 15,156.66 | 11,691.00 | 12,525.54 |
| 06/2002 | 12,081.43 | 10,060.72 | 10,621.84 | 06/2005 | 11,911.90 | 10,770.58 | 11,584.01 | 06/2008 | 14,601.27 | 12,521.84 | 13,481.38 |
| 09/2002 | 11,050.69 | 8,969.26 | 9,383.29 | 09/2005 | 13,678.44 | 11,540.93 | 13,574.30 | 09/2008 | 13,603.31 | 11,160.83 | 11,259.86 |
| 12/2002 | 9,320.11 | 8,197.22 | 8,578.95 | 12/2005 | 16,445.56 | 12,996.29 | 16,111.43 | 12/2008 | 11,456.64 | 6,994.90 | 8,859.56 |

*Source: Singapore Exchange*

# SPI 200 INDEX

**SPI 200 INDEX**
Monthly Cash as of 12/31/2008

| Date | Open | High | Low | Close |
|---|---|---|---|---|
| 08/29/08 | 4977.4 | 5146.3 | 4758.5 | 5135.6 |
| 09/30/08 | 5128.7 | 5177.2 | 4527.4 | 4600.5 |
| 10/31/08 | 4636.7 | 4832.5 | 3724.8 | 4018.0 |
| 11/28/08 | 4018.0 | 4340.5 | 3217.5 | 3742.5 |
| 12/31/08 | 3742.5 | 3742.5 | 3474.1 | 3722.3 |

MONTHLY CASH
As of 12/31/2008
Chart High 6851.5 on 11/01/2007
Chart Low 173.5 on 09/30/1974

## Annual High, Low and Settle of SPI 200 Index  In Index Value

| Year | High | Low | Settle | Year | High | Low | Settle | Year | High | Low | Settle |
|---|---|---|---|---|---|---|---|---|---|---|---|
| 1967 | 320.0 | 216.6 | 301.6 | 1981 | 737.4 | 545.8 | 595.5 | 1995 | 2,237.4 | 1,817.2 | 2,203.0 |
| 1968 | 419.7 | 300.1 | 405.5 | 1982 | 595.5 | 443.1 | 485.4 | 1996 | 2,426.5 | 2,092.4 | 2,424.6 |
| 1969 | 441.8 | 368.3 | 441.8 | 1983 | 775.3 | 487.9 | 775.3 | 1997 | 2,797.3 | 2,210.0 | 2,616.5 |
| 1970 | 448.2 | 320.2 | 348.7 | 1984 | 787.9 | 646.3 | 726.1 | 1998 | 2,893.7 | 2,386.7 | 2,813.4 |
| 1971 | 350.3 | 273.6 | 340.8 | 1985 | 1,052.1 | 715.2 | 1,003.8 | 1999 | 3,156.9 | 2,771.1 | 3,152.5 |
| 1972 | 431.9 | 331.1 | 408.6 | 1986 | 1,473.2 | 1,010.8 | 1,473.2 | 2000 | 3,343.7 | 2,883.0 | 3,154.7 |
| 1973 | 429.9 | 287.2 | 297.5 | 1987 | 2,312.4 | 1,149.3 | 1,318.8 | 2001 | 3,425.2 | 2,828.0 | 3,359.9 |
| 1974 | 362.1 | 173.5 | 201.6 | 1988 | 1,657.6 | 1,169.6 | 1,487.2 | 2002 | 3,443.9 | 2,842.6 | 2,975.5 |
| 1975 | 299.3 | 195.8 | 299.3 | 1989 | 1,786.6 | 1,411.9 | 1,649.8 | 2003 | 3,317.5 | 2,666.3 | 3,299.8 |
| 1976 | 353.0 | 273.5 | 291.4 | 1990 | 1,713.7 | 1,266.5 | 1,280.7 | 2004 | 4,055.0 | 3,252.9 | 4,050.6 |
| 1977 | 322.4 | 283.5 | 322.3 | 1991 | 1,697.7 | 1,199.8 | 1,651.4 | 2005 | 4,775.8 | 3,926.6 | 4,763.4 |
| 1978 | 382.9 | 298.0 | 366.1 | 1992 | 1,688.9 | 1,355.6 | 1,549.9 | 2006 | 5,684.4 | 4,751.1 | 5,669.9 |
| 1979 | 472.8 | 369.1 | 458.9 | 1993 | 2,173.6 | 1,487.4 | 2,173.6 | 2007 | 6,851.5 | 5,483.3 | 6,339.8 |
| 1980 | 746.2 | 509.1 | 713.5 | 1994 | 2,350.1 | 1,814.5 | 1,912.7 | 2008 | 6,385.7 | 3,217.5 | 3,722.3 |

Index data begins 07/1936.  *Source: Sydney Futures Exchange*

# SPI 200 INDEX

**WEEKLY CASH**
As of 01/02/2009
Chart High 6851.5 on 11/01/2007
Chart Low 2386.7 on 09/01/1998

**SPI 200 INDEX**
Weekly Cash as of 01/02/2009

| Date | Open | High | Low | Close |
|---|---|---|---|---|
| 12/05/08 | 3742.5 | 3742.5 | 3485.2 | 3489.9 |
| 12/12/08 | 3489.9 | 3670.8 | 3474.1 | 3510.4 |
| 12/19/08 | 3510.4 | 3664.4 | 3507.7 | 3615.7 |
| 12/24/08 | 3615.7 | 3627.7 | 3494.3 | 3582.2 |
| 01/02/09 | 3582.2 | 3767.5 | 3572.7 | 3713.8 |

## Quarterly High, Low and Settle of SPI 200 Index — In Index Value

| Quarter | High | Low | Settle | Quarter | High | Low | Settle | Quarter | High | Low | Settle |
|---|---|---|---|---|---|---|---|---|---|---|---|
| 03/2000 | 3,276.7 | 3,016.2 | 3,133.3 | 03/2003 | 3,062.0 | 2,666.3 | 2,848.6 | 03/2006 | 5,139.5 | 4,751.1 | 5,129.7 |
| 06/2000 | 3,260.0 | 2,883.0 | 3,257.6 | 06/2003 | 3,089.0 | 2,829.8 | 2,998.9 | 06/2006 | 5,406.7 | 4,758.3 | 5,073.9 |
| 09/2000 | 3,343.7 | 3,131.9 | 3,246.1 | 09/2003 | 3,249.8 | 2,977.5 | 3,176.2 | 09/2006 | 5,164.2 | 4,899.9 | 5,154.1 |
| 12/2000 | 3,321.8 | 3,120.5 | 3,154.7 | 12/2003 | 3,317.5 | 3,158.8 | 3,299.8 | 12/2006 | 5,684.4 | 5,113.9 | 5,669.9 |
| 03/2001 | 3,313.7 | 3,088.6 | 3,096.9 | 03/2004 | 3,456.1 | 3,252.9 | 3,415.3 | 03/2007 | 6,052.1 | 5,499.0 | 5,995.0 |
| 06/2001 | 3,425.2 | 3,100.5 | 3,425.2 | 06/2004 | 3,556.4 | 3,341.0 | 3,532.9 | 06/2007 | 6,409.2 | 5,915.8 | 6,274.9 |
| 09/2001 | 3,419.5 | 2,828.0 | 2,988.0 | 09/2004 | 3,673.1 | 3,467.1 | 3,665.0 | 09/2007 | 6,594.4 | 5,483.3 | 6,567.8 |
| 12/2001 | 3,376.0 | 2,994.8 | 3,359.9 | 12/2004 | 4,055.0 | 3,654.6 | 4,050.6 | 12/2007 | 6,851.5 | 6,105.1 | 6,339.8 |
| 03/2002 | 3,443.9 | 3,322.3 | 3,363.3 | 03/2005 | 4,266.9 | 4,026.1 | 4,109.9 | 03/2008 | 6,385.7 | 5,039.6 | 5,355.7 |
| 06/2002 | 3,372.1 | 3,124.5 | 3,163.2 | 06/2005 | 4,321.7 | 3,926.6 | 4,277.5 | 06/2008 | 5,980.8 | 5,144.7 | 5,215.3 |
| 09/2002 | 3,205.9 | 2,909.5 | 2,928.3 | 09/2005 | 4,679.1 | 4,213.6 | 4,641.2 | 09/2008 | 5,231.9 | 4,527.4 | 4,600.5 |
| 12/2002 | 3,047.6 | 2,842.6 | 2,975.5 | 12/2005 | 4,775.8 | 4,311.1 | 4,763.4 | 12/2008 | 4,832.5 | 3,217.5 | 3,722.3 |

*Source: Sydney Futures Exchange*

# LIVESTOCK & MEATS

## Cattle

Cattle prices were strong during the 2002-05 period. Cattle prices in 2002-03 rallied sharply due to strong US domestic demand, strong export demand for high-quality grain-fed US beef, and the declining trend seen in the size of the US cattle herd since 1996 (and more generally since 1975). Prices surged on these factors in late 2003 to a then-record high. However, cattle prices then plunged in December 2003 and early 2004 after the dairy cow in Washington state was found to have Mad Cow disease. That led to more than 50 countries suspending US beef imports, including Japan which is the most important export destination for US beef. US beef exports plunged to near zero in a matter of days, causing cattle prices to plunge. However, cattle prices quickly recovered in 2004-05 due to continued strong US domestic demand and the relatively quick action by producers to reduce supplies.

Cattle prices in early 2006 plunged on a combination of factors including (1) high slaughter numbers and cattle weights, (2) price competition tied to huge poultry inventories which resulted from bird flu overseas, and (3) virtually non-existent US beef exports due to the continued overseas bans on US beef. Cattle prices then rallied in the second half of 2006 and remained strong through mid-2008 when cattle prices were boosted by the big commodity bull market.

Cattle prices were also boosted in early 2007 as US beef exports to Asia improved. Beef sales to Japan rose more than four-fold after Japanese restrictions on US beef were lifted. Sales to South Korea also rose after that country finally lifted its U.S. beef import ban. US cattle exports, after hitting a record low of 21.2 million head in 2005, tripled to 66.3 million head by 2007 and then rose to about 110 million head by 2008. Still, US cattle exports in 2008 were one-sixth of the record high of 678 million head in 2001 before mad-cow emerged. The USDA projects that it will take more than a decade for the US to rebuild its overseas beef export markets.

The surge in corn and feed prices that started in late 2006 was bearish for cattle in the short-term because it encouraged producers to send more cattle to slaughter. However, the surge in feed costs was bullish longer-term since it reduced herd sizes and raised costs for cattle producers.

Cattle prices in the latter half of 2008 fell sharply due to (1) the general plunge in commodity prices, (2) the financial crisis, which made it more difficult and expensive for cattle feeder lots to finance herds, and (3) the global recession which reduced demand for beef and encouraged switching to less expensive proteins. High slaughter rates pushed down prices, but the smaller herd sizes will eventually pave the way for a recovery in cattle prices.

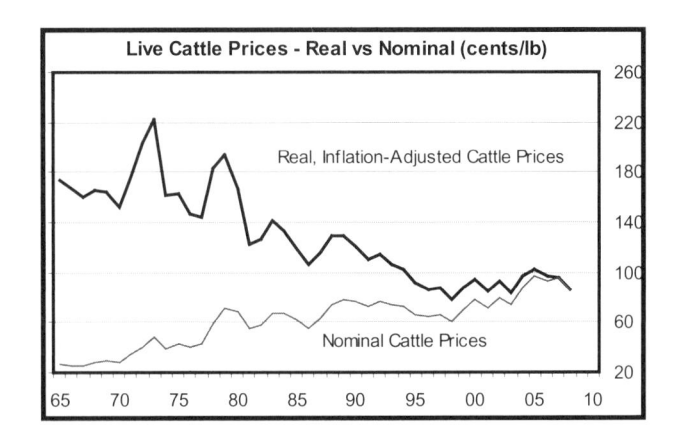

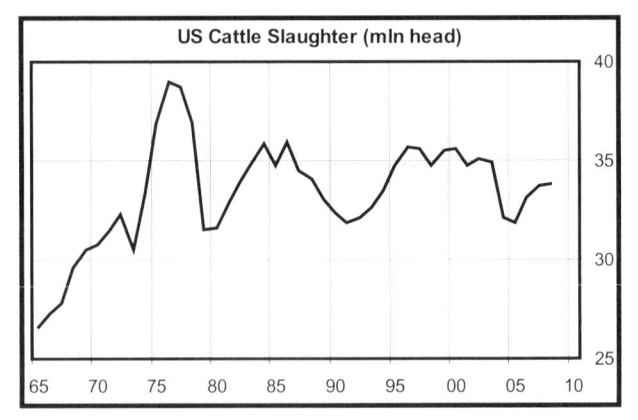

### Cattle Market Events

**1975—US cattle numbers peak**—Cattle herd numbers in the US peak at 132 million head, having nearly doubled from 1940, but then enter a steady downtrend to current levels near 95 million.

**1985—US per-capita beef consumption peaks**—US per-capita beef consumption peaks in 1985 at 79.3 pounds per year but then falls sharply in the 1990s (due to health concerns about eating beef) and finally stabilizes near 66 pounds.

**1989—World cattle numbers peak**—World cattle numbers grow steadily in the 1980s but then peak in 1989 at 1.10 billion head, and then trend lower to 1.02 billion in 2005.

**2001—Brazil cattle herd soars**—Brazil cattle herd numbers, which were stable near 150 million head in the 1990s, surge starting in 2001 to 170 million by 2005, as Brazil puts more emphasis on meat production and the export of higher-value agriculture products.

**May 2003**—First case of Mad Cow disease (BSE) is found in Canada, prompting the US to suspend the import of Canadian cattle.

**December 2003**—First case of BSE is found in the US in a Canadian-born dairy cow in Washington state. More than 50 countries suspend US beef exports.

# LIVESTOCK & MEATS

## Hogs

Lean hog prices showed more than the usual volatility starting in the mid-1990s. There were major declines to 3-decade lows in 1998 and again in 2002. The plunge in hog prices in 1998 was caused by an overexpansion of pork production in 1996-97 when prices were high. That expansion caused an industry disaster in 1998 when hog prices plunged and many smaller hog farmers were forced out of business. In addition, Asian demand for pork was reduced in late-1997 and 1998 by the Asian financial crisis. Hog prices recovered in 2000-01 but then plunged again in 2002 as US hog farmers again overproduced and caused another pork glut. Oversupply was exacerbated by an increase in the flow of Canadian live hogs into the US by 1.9 million head annually from 1999 through 2001.

Hog prices in 2003 and 2004 recovered as the US economy improved after the 2001 recession and as US hog exports were strong starting in 2002. In addition, herd sizes and slaughter rates were relatively low during that period. Hog prices faded in 2005 and early 2006 on adequate hog supplies supply and competition from poultry, which was cheap due to a glut of domestic poultry inventories tied to bird flu in Asia. Yet bird flu and mad cow diseased sparked stronger demand in Asia for US pork as consumers avoided poultry and beef.

Lean hog prices surged to a record high of 90 cents/lb in August 2008 as hog prices were caught up in the commodity bull market frenzy. Hog prices then fell sharply in late 2008 on the general commodity market meltdown and the financial crisis, which emerged in September 2008. The global recession hurt pork demand and the financial crisis caused hog farmers to sharply reduce their herds due to financing problems. Indeed, due to high feed costs in 2007 and the financial crisis in 2008, the US hog slaughter surged to 109 million head in 2007 and a record 116 million in 2008 as farmers liquidated their herds. However, the smaller herd sizes and restricted supplies should eventually lead to higher hog prices when demand reemerges.

The long-term outlook for the pork market is generally favorable, according to the USDA's "Agricultural Baseline Projections to 2017." Domestic demand for pork should grow at roughly the same rate as the US population since the USDA is projecting that US per-capita pork consumption will remain stable at 51-52 pounds per year. The USDA is projecting steady growth in US pork exports, driven by increasing global demand for meat and the efficiency of US pork production facilities. However, the USDA expects strong pork competition from Canada and Mexico for exports to the Pacific Rim. The USDA believes that continued high feed costs(driven by strong ethanol producer demand for corn) will cause lower pork production in the 2009-12 period, but that pork production will eventually rebound as the market adjusts to higher feed costs.

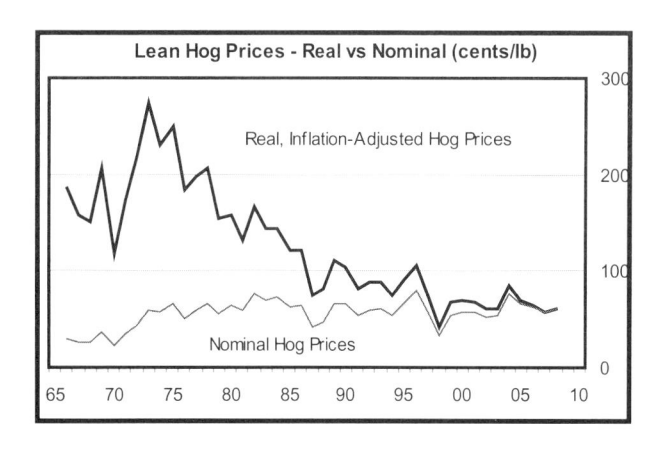

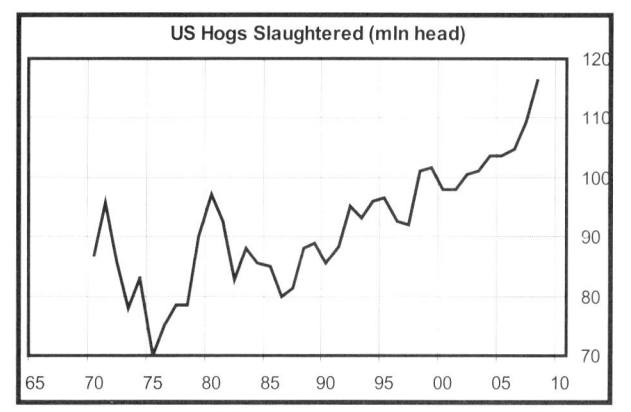

## Hog Market Events

**1970s—Hog prices rally**—Hog prices rallied sharply in the early-1970s due to high inflation and a general rise in commodity prices. Hog prices in 1975 reached an inflation-adjusted record high close of 257 cents per pound (2006 dollars) due to tight supplies caused by a sharp drop in pork production in the first half of the 1970s. On an inflation-adjusted basis, hog prices are currently only about one-fourth of the record high of 257 cents per pound posted in 1975.

**1980s—Lower pork production supports prices**—In 1980, the number of US hogs slaughtered reached a then-record high of 97.2 million head, causing hog prices to plunge to 37 cents per pound. However, the number of hogs slaughtered then fell sharply by -4.8% in 1981 then and by -10.4% in 1982, leading to a sharp rally in pork prices to the all-time record high of 91.80 cents per pound in August 1982.

**1990s—Pork exports surge in the 1990s**—Between 1994 and 1998, the volume of US pork exports tripled due to efficient new plants, genetics, and the penetration of the Japanese market. In 1995, US pork exports exceeded imports for the first time in post-war history. US pork exports now account for more than 12% of production, versus 1% of production in the late 1980s.

**1998—Hog prices drop to 30-year lows**—Due to a severe production glut, hog prices in 1998 fell to levels not seen since the early-1970s and inflation-adjusted prices fall to levels not seen since the Depression.

305

# CATTLE, FEEDER

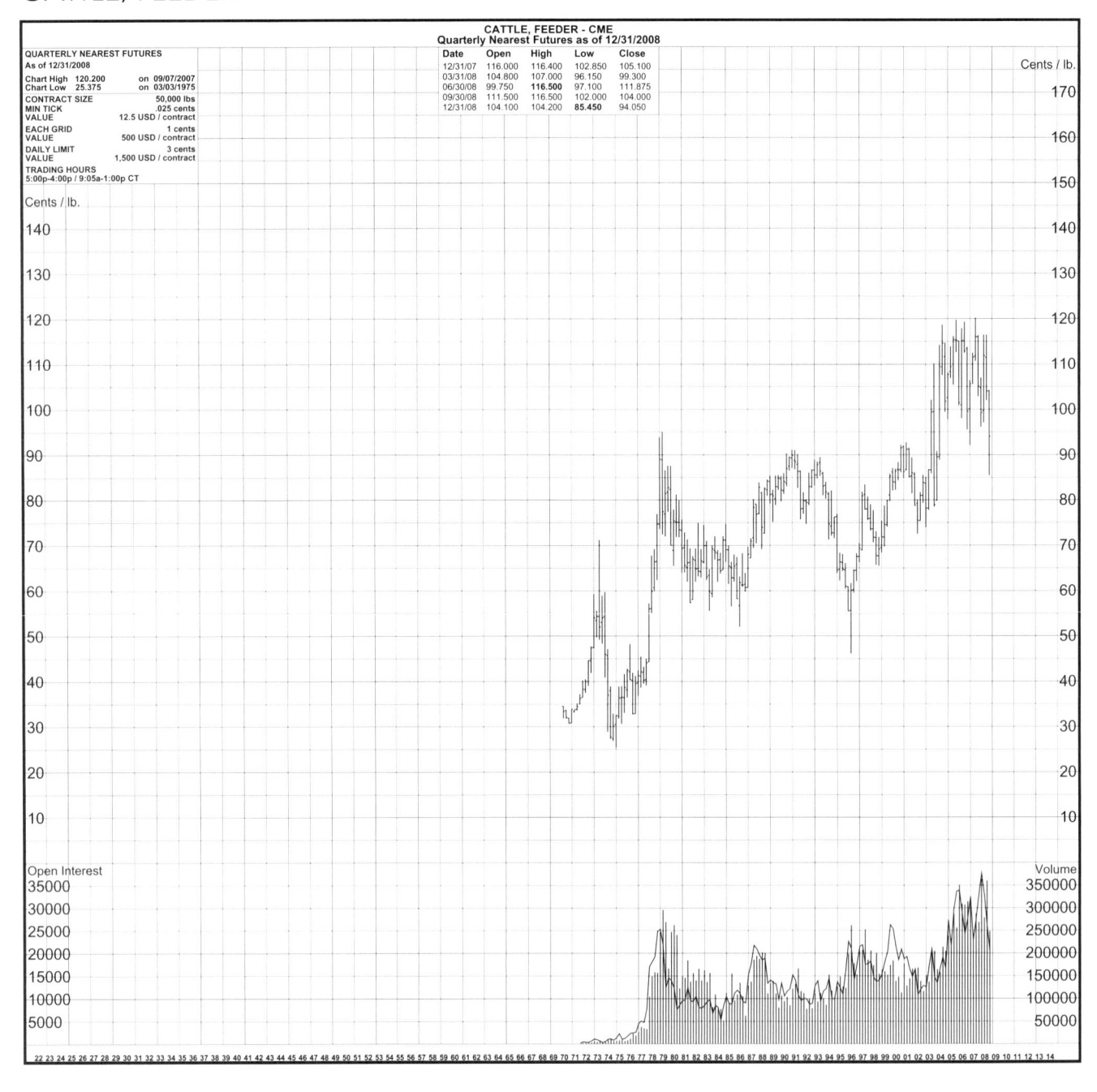

**CATTLE, FEEDER - CME**
Quarterly Nearest Futures as of 12/31/2008

| Date | Open | High | Low | Close |
|---|---|---|---|---|
| 12/31/07 | 116.000 | 116.400 | 102.850 | 105.100 |
| 03/31/08 | 104.800 | 107.000 | 96.150 | 99.300 |
| 06/30/08 | 99.750 | 116.500 | 97.100 | 111.875 |
| 09/30/08 | 111.500 | 116.500 | 102.000 | 104.000 |
| 12/31/08 | 104.100 | 104.200 | 85.450 | 94.050 |

**QUARTERLY NEAREST FUTURES**
As of 12/31/2008
Chart High 120.200 on 09/07/2007
Chart Low 25.375 on 03/03/1975
CONTRACT SIZE 50,000 lbs
MIN TICK .025 cents
VALUE 12.5 USD / contract
EACH GRID 1 cents
VALUE 500 USD / contract
DAILY LIMIT 3 cents
VALUE 1,500 USD / contract
TRADING HOURS 5:00p-4:00p / 9:05a-1:00p CT

## Annual High, Low and Settle of Feeder Cattle Futures   In Cents per Pound

| Year | High | Low | Settle | Year | High | Low | Settle | Year | High | Low | Settle |
|---|---|---|---|---|---|---|---|---|---|---|---|
| 1967 | | | | 1981 | 75.700 | 57.250 | 57.350 | 1995 | 76.900 | 60.450 | 61.025 |
| 1968 | | | | 1982 | 74.900 | 58.000 | 66.525 | 1996 | 68.250 | 46.150 | 67.525 |
| 1969 | | | | 1983 | 74.450 | 55.500 | 69.225 | 1997 | 83.400 | 66.250 | 75.875 |
| 1970 | 35.45 | 30.69 | 30.75 | 1984 | 72.000 | 61.950 | 71.200 | 1998 | 79.050 | 65.450 | 69.175 |
| 1971 | 37.25 | 30.85 | 36.300 | 1985 | 74.750 | 56.500 | 65.450 | 1999 | 85.850 | 68.450 | 85.350 |
| 1972 | 47.750 | 36.475 | 47.400 | 1986 | 68.300 | 52.000 | 60.725 | 2000 | 92.200 | 82.050 | 91.500 |
| 1973 | 71.200 | 47.250 | 54.000 | 1987 | 80.200 | 60.725 | 76.875 | 2001 | 92.750 | 81.400 | 86.025 |
| 1974 | 59.750 | 26.800 | 30.100 | 1988 | 84.550 | 69.150 | 84.150 | 2002 | 86.200 | 72.525 | 83.800 |
| 1975 | 41.650 | 25.375 | 38.650 | 1989 | 85.600 | 75.150 | 84.850 | 2003 | 110.170 | 73.950 | 78.925 |
| 1976 | 48.250 | 32.675 | 39.525 | 1990 | 90.350 | 79.650 | 89.400 | 2004 | 118.700 | 79.800 | 101.800 |
| 1977 | 45.500 | 36.800 | 44.100 | 1991 | 91.100 | 75.700 | 78.050 | 2005 | 119.750 | 97.800 | 115.250 |
| 1978 | 76.900 | 44.300 | 74.675 | 1992 | 86.750 | 74.700 | 86.625 | 2006 | 119.350 | 95.500 | 99.600 |
| 1979 | 95.150 | 71.950 | 82.700 | 1993 | 89.500 | 81.000 | 83.050 | 2007 | 120.200 | 92.100 | 105.100 |
| 1980 | 87.600 | 65.475 | 73.450 | 1994 | 84.000 | 71.250 | 76.225 | 2008 | 116.500 | 85.450 | 94.050 |

Futures begin trading 11/30/1971.   *Source: CME Group; Chicago Mercantile Exchange*

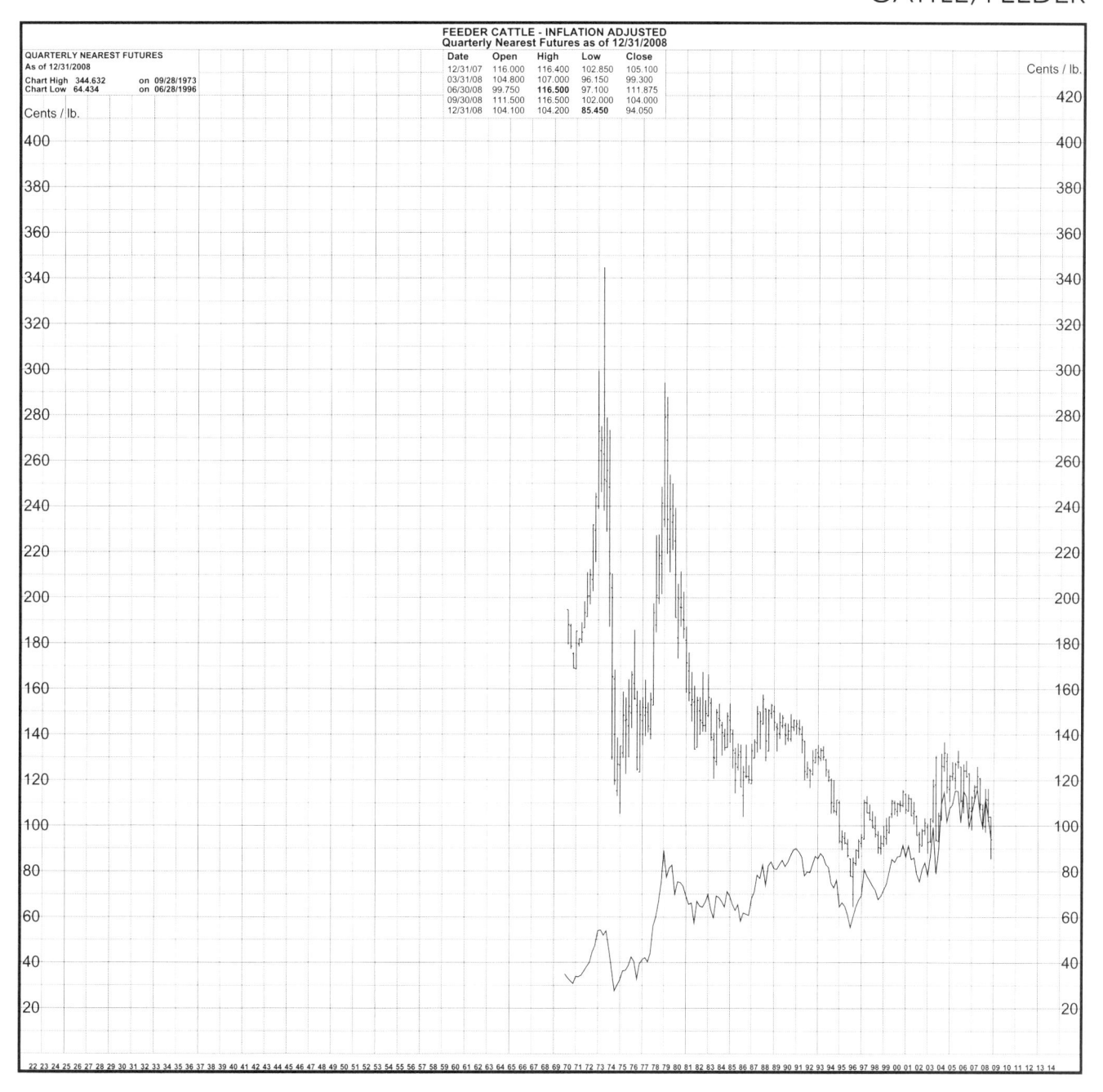

# CATTLE, FEEDER

**QUARTERLY NEAREST FUTURES**
As of 12/31/2008
Chart High 344.632 on 09/28/1973
Chart Low 64.434 on 06/28/1996
Cents / lb.

**FEEDER CATTLE - INFLATION ADJUSTED**
Quarterly Nearest Futures as of 12/31/2008

| Date | Open | High | Low | Close |
|---|---|---|---|---|
| 12/31/07 | 116.000 | 116.400 | 102.850 | 105.100 |
| 03/31/08 | 104.800 | 107.000 | 96.150 | 99.300 |
| 06/30/08 | 99.750 | 116.500 | 97.100 | 111.875 |
| 09/30/08 | 111.500 | 116.500 | 102.000 | 104.000 |
| 12/31/08 | 104.100 | 104.200 | 85.450 | 94.050 |

## Annual High, Low and Settle of Feeder Cattle — In Cents per Pound

| Year | High | Low | Settle | Year | High | Low | Settle | Year | High | Low | Settle |
|---|---|---|---|---|---|---|---|---|---|---|---|
| 1967 | | | | 1981 | 75.13 | 59.00 | 59.50 | 1995 | 85.75 | 62.63 | 64.13 |
| 1968 | | | | 1982 | 70.50 | 59.50 | 65.00 | 1996 | 69.63 | 54.25 | 68.75 |
| 1969 | | | | 1983 | 74.50 | 59.75 | 65.00 | 1997 | 93.75 | 68.75 | 85.37 |
| 1970 | 35.45 | 30.69 | 30.75 | 1984 | 71.75 | 62.00 | 70.00 | 1998 | 90.88 | 68.88 | 74.75 |
| 1971 | 37.40 | 30.85 | 37.38 | 1985 | 74.50 | 60.38 | 65.00 | 1999 | 97.00 | 75.63 | 95.75 |
| 1972 | 44.81 | 37.35 | 44.81 | 1986 | 69.15 | 58.00 | 65.50 | 2000 | 106.88 | 89.50 | 98.88 |
| 1973 | 65.40 | 45.31 | 47.50 | 1987 | 88.75 | 65.50 | 82.00 | 2001 | 109.88 | 83.63 | 95.31 |
| 1974 | 52.25 | 26.50 | 26.50 | 1988 | 95.75 | 78.90 | 91.25 | 2002 | 96.06 | 81.00 | 89.25 |
| 1975 | 41.20 | 24.75 | 39.50 | 1989 | 96.40 | 84.50 | 90.25 | 2003 | 112.25 | 75.00 | 75.70 |
| 1976 | 46.20 | 34.25 | 35.75 | 1990 | 102.13 | 88.00 | 100.50 | 2004 | 128.50 | 73.63 | 113.19 |
| 1977 | 43.50 | 35.45 | 42.75 | 1991 | 105.25 | 86.00 | 86.00 | 2005 | 131.80 | 108.00 | 122.63 |
| 1978 | 76.25 | 42.75 | 76.25 | 1992 | 94.75 | 83.75 | 90.63 | 2006 | 131.75 | 97.68 | 97.96 |
| 1979 | 97.75 | 75.50 | 85.75 | 1993 | 102.50 | 89.00 | 91.25 | 2007 | 119.29 | 94.10 | 104.13 |
| 1980 | 90.00 | 68.00 | 75.00 | 1994 | 95.00 | 76.13 | 82.63 | 2008 | 113.61 | 88.58 | 92.93 |

Oklahoma City.  *Source: CME Group; Chicago Mercantile Exchange*

# CATTLE, FEEDER

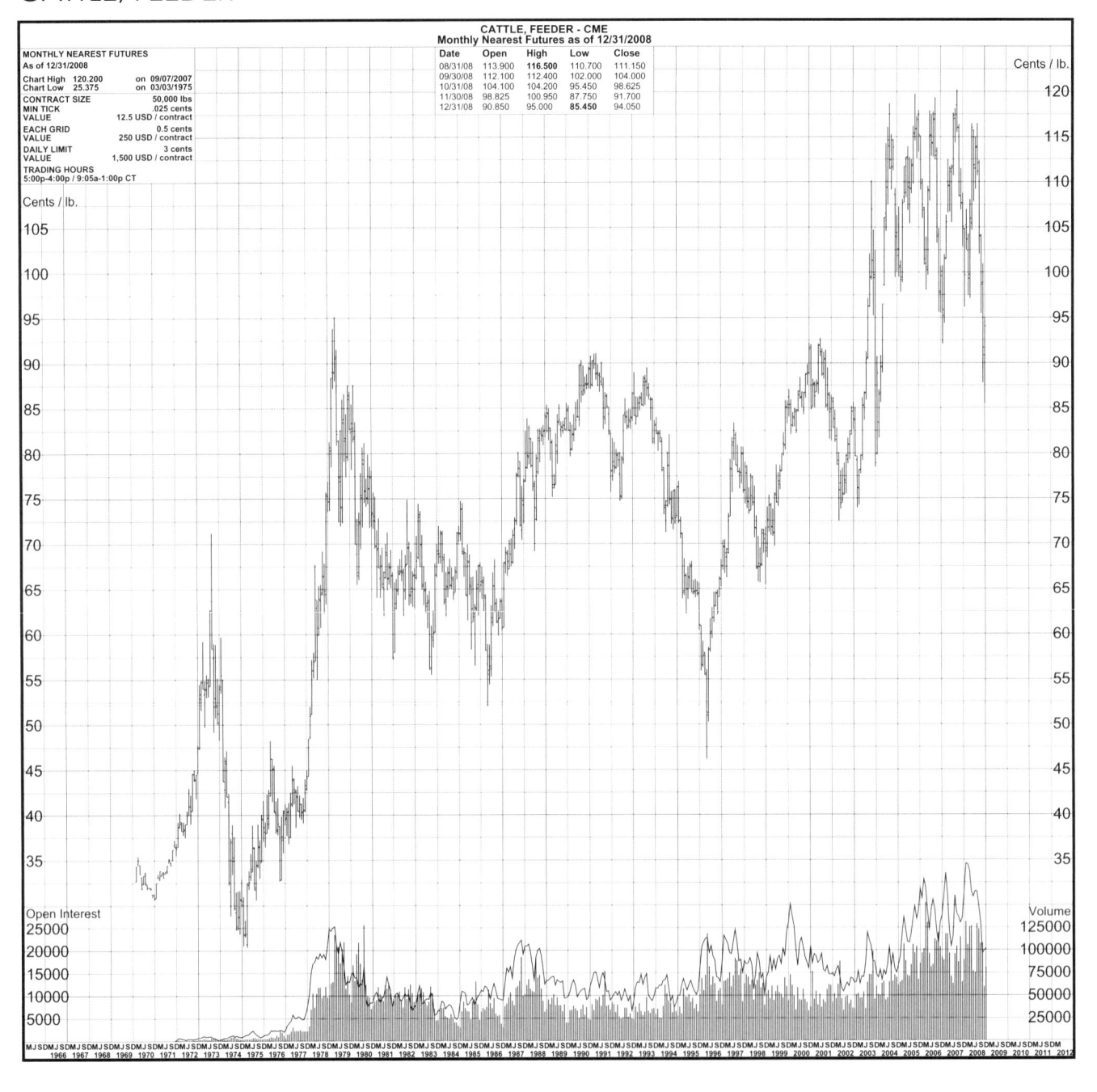

## CATTLE, FEEDER - CME
Monthly Nearest Futures as of 12/31/2008

| Date | Open | High | Low | Close |
|---|---|---|---|---|
| 08/31/08 | 113.900 | 116.500 | 110.700 | 111.150 |
| 09/30/08 | 112.100 | 112.400 | 102.000 | 104.000 |
| 10/31/08 | 104.100 | 104.200 | 95.450 | 98.625 |
| 11/30/08 | 98.825 | 100.950 | 87.750 | 91.700 |
| 12/31/08 | 90.850 | 95.000 | 85.450 | 94.050 |

**MONTHLY NEAREST FUTURES**
As of 12/31/2008
Chart High 120.200 on 09/07/2007
Chart Low 25.375 on 03/03/1975
CONTRACT SIZE 50,000 lbs
MIN TICK .025 cents
VALUE 12.5 USD / contract
EACH GRID 0.5 cents
VALUE 250 USD / contract
DAILY LIMIT 3 cents
VALUE 1,500 USD / contract
TRADING HOURS 5:00p-4:00p / 9:05a-1:00p CT

## Annual High, Low and Settle of Feeder Cattle Futures    In Cents per Pound

| Year | High | Low | Settle | Year | High | Low | Settle | Year | High | Low | Settle |
|---|---|---|---|---|---|---|---|---|---|---|---|
| 1967 |  |  |  | 1981 | 75.700 | 57.250 | 57.350 | 1995 | 76.900 | 60.450 | 61.025 |
| 1968 |  |  |  | 1982 | 74.900 | 58.000 | 66.525 | 1996 | 68.250 | 46.150 | 67.525 |
| 1969 |  |  |  | 1983 | 74.450 | 55.500 | 69.225 | 1997 | 83.400 | 66.250 | 75.875 |
| 1970 | 35.45 | 30.69 | 30.75 | 1984 | 72.000 | 61.950 | 71.200 | 1998 | 79.050 | 65.450 | 69.175 |
| 1971 | 37.25 | 30.85 | 36.300 | 1985 | 74.750 | 56.500 | 65.450 | 1999 | 85.850 | 68.450 | 85.350 |
| 1972 | 47.750 | 36.475 | 47.400 | 1986 | 68.300 | 52.000 | 60.725 | 2000 | 92.200 | 82.050 | 91.500 |
| 1973 | 71.200 | 47.250 | 54.000 | 1987 | 80.200 | 60.725 | 76.875 | 2001 | 92.750 | 81.400 | 86.025 |
| 1974 | 59.750 | 26.800 | 30.100 | 1988 | 84.550 | 69.150 | 84.150 | 2002 | 86.200 | 72.525 | 83.800 |
| 1975 | 41.650 | 25.375 | 38.650 | 1989 | 85.600 | 75.150 | 84.850 | 2003 | 110.170 | 73.950 | 78.925 |
| 1976 | 48.250 | 32.675 | 39.525 | 1990 | 90.350 | 79.650 | 89.400 | 2004 | 118.700 | 79.800 | 101.800 |
| 1977 | 45.500 | 36.800 | 44.100 | 1991 | 91.100 | 75.700 | 78.050 | 2005 | 119.750 | 97.800 | 115.250 |
| 1978 | 76.900 | 44.300 | 74.675 | 1992 | 86.750 | 74.700 | 86.625 | 2006 | 119.350 | 95.500 | 99.600 |
| 1979 | 95.150 | 71.950 | 82.700 | 1993 | 89.500 | 81.000 | 83.050 | 2007 | 120.200 | 92.100 | 105.100 |
| 1980 | 87.600 | 65.475 | 73.450 | 1994 | 84.000 | 71.250 | 76.225 | 2008 | 116.500 | 85.450 | 94.050 |

Futures begin trading 11/30/1971.    Source: *CME Group; Chicago Mercantile Exchange*

# CATTLE, FEEDER

**Cattle, Oklahoma City Avg**
Monthly Cash as of 12/31/2008

| Date | Open | High | Low | Close |
|---|---|---|---|---|
| 08/29/08 | 110.790 | 113.610 | 110.790 | 111.320 |
| 09/30/08 | 111.480 | 112.360 | 106.170 | 106.170 |
| 10/31/08 | 105.620 | 105.620 | 95.740 | 95.740 |
| 11/28/08 | 96.190 | 97.740 | 91.860 | 93.580 |
| 12/31/08 | 94.350 | 94.350 | 88.580 | 92.930 |

MONTHLY CASH
As of 12/31/2008
Chart High 131.800 on 05/09/2005
Chart Low 24.750 on 01/31/1975

## Annual High, Low and Settle of Feeder Cattle    In Cents per Pound

| Year | High | Low | Settle | Year | High | Low | Settle | Year | High | Low | Settle |
|---|---|---|---|---|---|---|---|---|---|---|---|
| 1967 | | | | 1981 | 75.13 | 59.00 | 59.50 | 1995 | 85.75 | 62.63 | 64.13 |
| 1968 | | | | 1982 | 70.50 | 59.50 | 65.00 | 1996 | 69.63 | 54.25 | 68.75 |
| 1969 | | | | 1983 | 74.50 | 59.75 | 65.00 | 1997 | 93.75 | 68.75 | 85.37 |
| 1970 | 35.45 | 30.69 | 30.75 | 1984 | 71.75 | 62.00 | 70.00 | 1998 | 90.88 | 68.88 | 74.75 |
| 1971 | 37.40 | 30.85 | 37.38 | 1985 | 74.50 | 60.38 | 65.00 | 1999 | 97.00 | 75.63 | 95.75 |
| 1972 | 44.81 | 37.35 | 44.81 | 1986 | 69.15 | 58.00 | 65.50 | 2000 | 106.88 | 89.50 | 98.88 |
| 1973 | 65.40 | 45.31 | 47.50 | 1987 | 88.75 | 65.50 | 82.00 | 2001 | 109.88 | 83.63 | 95.31 |
| 1974 | 52.25 | 26.50 | 26.50 | 1988 | 95.75 | 78.90 | 91.25 | 2002 | 96.06 | 81.00 | 89.25 |
| 1975 | 41.20 | 24.75 | 39.50 | 1989 | 96.40 | 84.50 | 90.25 | 2003 | 112.25 | 75.00 | 75.70 |
| 1976 | 46.20 | 34.25 | 35.75 | 1990 | 102.13 | 88.00 | 100.50 | 2004 | 128.50 | 73.63 | 113.19 |
| 1977 | 43.50 | 35.45 | 42.75 | 1991 | 105.25 | 86.00 | 86.00 | 2005 | 131.80 | 108.00 | 122.63 |
| 1978 | 76.25 | 42.75 | 76.25 | 1992 | 94.75 | 83.75 | 90.63 | 2006 | 131.75 | 97.68 | 97.96 |
| 1979 | 97.75 | 75.50 | 85.75 | 1993 | 102.50 | 89.00 | 91.25 | 2007 | 119.29 | 94.10 | 104.13 |
| 1980 | 90.00 | 68.00 | 75.00 | 1994 | 95.00 | 76.13 | 82.63 | 2008 | 113.61 | 88.58 | 92.93 |

Oklahoma City.   *Source: CME Group; Chicago Mercantile Exchange*

309

# CATTLE, FEEDER

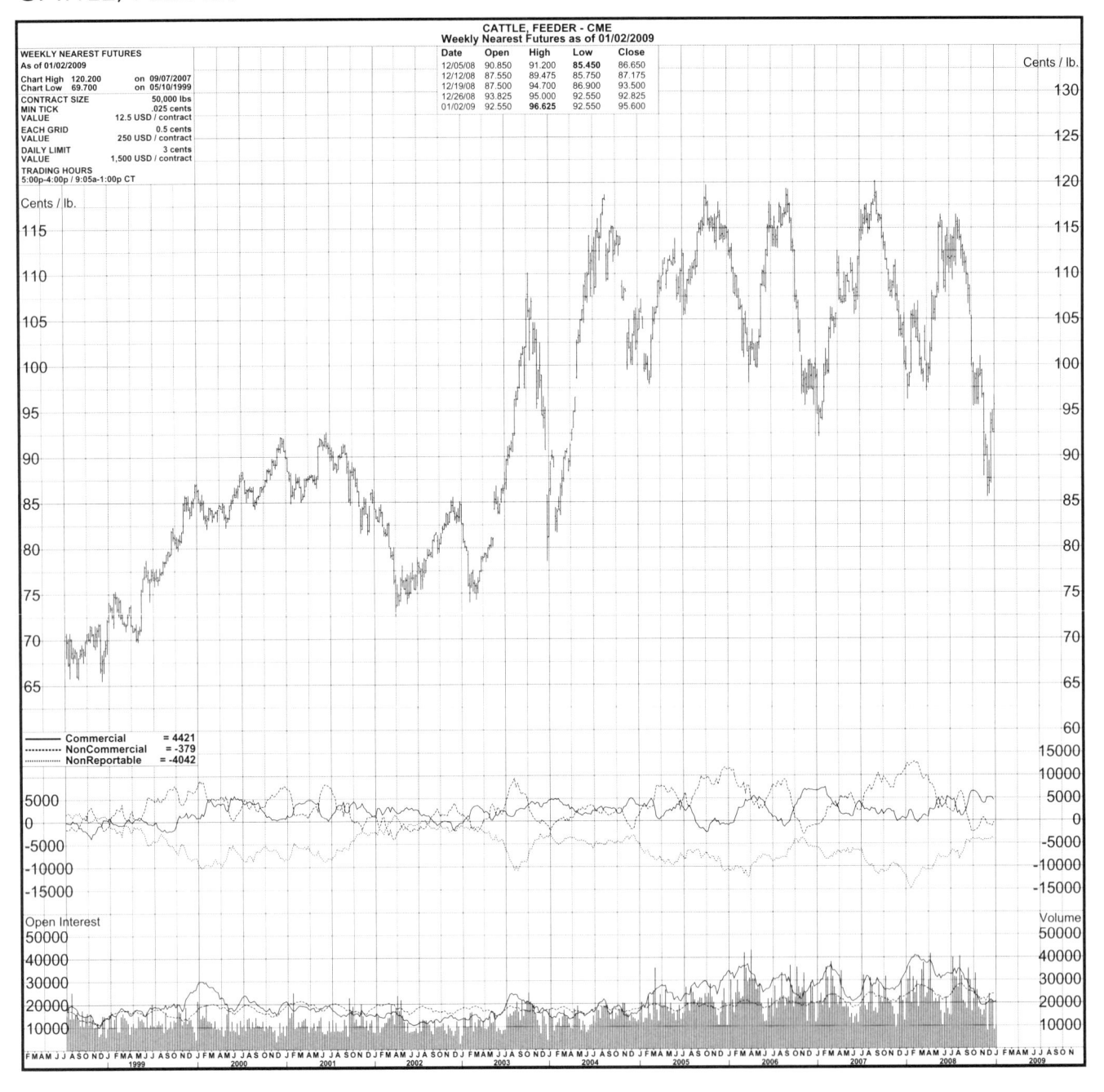

## Quarterly High, Low and Settle of Feeder Cattle Futures   In Cents per Pound

| Quarter | High | Low | Settle | Quarter | High | Low | Settle | Quarter | High | Low | Settle |
|---|---|---|---|---|---|---|---|---|---|---|---|
| 03/2000 | 87.100 | 82.050 | 84.025 | 03/2003 | 85.100 | 73.950 | 78.150 | 03/2006 | 115.100 | 100.800 | 101.475 |
| 06/2000 | 86.950 | 82.175 | 86.450 | 06/2003 | 86.800 | 77.750 | 86.700 | 06/2006 | 117.920 | 98.000 | 115.200 |
| 09/2000 | 88.400 | 84.250 | 86.650 | 09/2003 | 102.100 | 85.850 | 99.375 | 09/2006 | 119.350 | 112.450 | 112.900 |
| 12/2000 | 92.200 | 86.100 | 91.500 | 12/2003 | 110.170 | 78.500 | 78.925 | 12/2006 | 113.800 | 95.500 | 99.600 |
| 03/2001 | 92.050 | 84.800 | 86.300 | 03/2004 | 90.840 | 79.800 | 89.500 | 03/2007 | 106.370 | 92.100 | 105.590 |
| 06/2001 | 92.750 | 86.500 | 91.225 | 06/2004 | 114.250 | 88.850 | 109.400 | 06/2007 | 112.500 | 105.500 | 111.550 |
| 09/2001 | 91.600 | 85.025 | 85.200 | 09/2004 | 118.700 | 107.500 | 114.625 | 09/2007 | 120.200 | 110.700 | 116.040 |
| 12/2001 | 89.450 | 81.400 | 86.025 | 12/2004 | 114.750 | 99.400 | 101.800 | 12/2007 | 116.400 | 102.850 | 105.100 |
| 03/2002 | 86.200 | 78.750 | 78.750 | 03/2005 | 108.100 | 97.800 | 107.675 | 03/2008 | 107.000 | 96.150 | 99.300 |
| 06/2002 | 80.100 | 72.525 | 75.500 | 06/2005 | 113.920 | 106.850 | 109.425 | 06/2008 | 116.500 | 97.100 | 111.875 |
| 09/2002 | 81.700 | 75.400 | 80.950 | 09/2005 | 116.200 | 105.400 | 115.425 | 09/2008 | 116.500 | 102.000 | 104.000 |
| 12/2002 | 85.600 | 79.300 | 83.800 | 12/2005 | 119.750 | 112.600 | 115.250 | 12/2008 | 104.200 | 85.450 | 94.050 |

*Source: CME Group; Chicago Mercantile Exchange*

# CATTLE, FEEDER

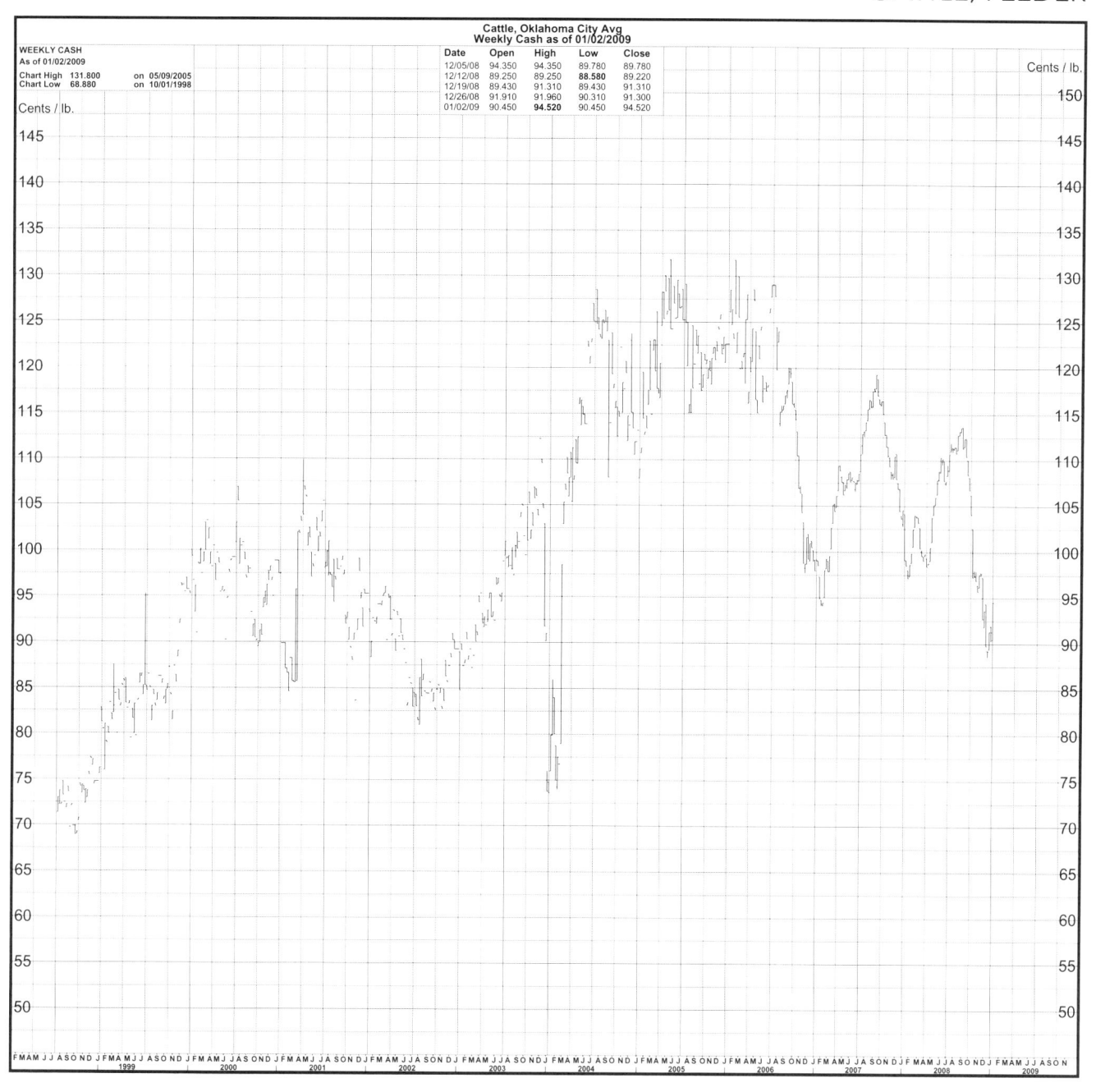

**Cattle, Oklahoma City Avg**
**Weekly Cash as of 01/02/2009**

| Date | Open | High | Low | Close |
|---|---|---|---|---|
| 12/05/08 | 94.350 | 94.350 | 89.780 | 89.780 |
| 12/12/08 | 89.250 | 89.250 | 88.580 | 89.220 |
| 12/19/08 | 89.430 | 91.310 | 89.430 | 91.310 |
| 12/26/08 | 91.910 | 91.960 | 90.310 | 91.300 |
| 01/02/09 | 90.450 | 94.520 | 90.450 | 94.520 |

WEEKLY CASH
As of 01/02/2009
Chart High 131.800 on 05/09/2005
Chart Low 68.880 on 10/01/1998

## Quarterly High, Low and Settle of Feeder Cattle   In Cents per Pound

| Quarter | High | Low | Settle | Quarter | High | Low | Settle | Quarter | High | Low | Settle |
|---|---|---|---|---|---|---|---|---|---|---|---|
| 03/2000 | 103.25 | 91.00 | 99.75 | 03/2003 | 95.38 | 84.81 | 95.38 | 03/2006 | 131.75 | 116.19 | 117.38 |
| 06/2000 | 100.50 | 90.25 | 99.25 | 06/2003 | 98.88 | 91.69 | 98.88 | 06/2006 | 129.06 | 115.13 | 129.06 |
| 09/2000 | 106.88 | 90.50 | 90.50 | 09/2003 | 105.06 | 97.38 | 99.56 | 09/2006 | 129.06 | 113.67 | 115.77 |
| 12/2000 | 98.88 | 89.50 | 98.88 | 12/2003 | 112.25 | 75.00 | 75.70 | 12/2006 | 115.44 | 97.68 | 97.96 |
| 03/2001 | 102.13 | 84.63 | 101.88 | 03/2004 | 110.75 | 73.63 | 108.00 | 03/2007 | 106.09 | 94.10 | 106.09 |
| 06/2001 | 109.88 | 97.13 | 104.25 | 06/2004 | 127.00 | 105.38 | 125.13 | 06/2007 | 109.43 | 106.23 | 108.52 |
| 09/2001 | 105.38 | 94.38 | 97.81 | 09/2004 | 128.50 | 108.06 | 116.31 | 09/2007 | 119.29 | 108.81 | 116.40 |
| 12/2001 | 99.13 | 83.63 | 95.31 | 12/2004 | 123.75 | 110.56 | 113.19 | 12/2007 | 116.42 | 102.79 | 104.13 |
| 03/2002 | 96.06 | 88.38 | 94.81 | 03/2005 | 126.13 | 108.00 | 118.75 | 03/2008 | 103.99 | 97.16 | 99.31 |
| 06/2002 | 94.94 | 83.13 | 85.50 | 06/2005 | 131.80 | 120.50 | 125.25 | 06/2008 | 110.32 | 98.43 | 108.92 |
| 09/2002 | 88.13 | 81.00 | 82.81 | 09/2005 | 129.13 | 115.13 | 120.88 | 09/2008 | 113.61 | 106.17 | 106.17 |
| 12/2002 | 90.94 | 82.63 | 89.25 | 12/2005 | 125.81 | 118.25 | 122.63 | 12/2008 | 105.62 | 88.58 | 92.93 |

Oklahoma City.   *Source: CME Group; Chicago Mercantile Exchange*

311

# CATTLE, LIVE

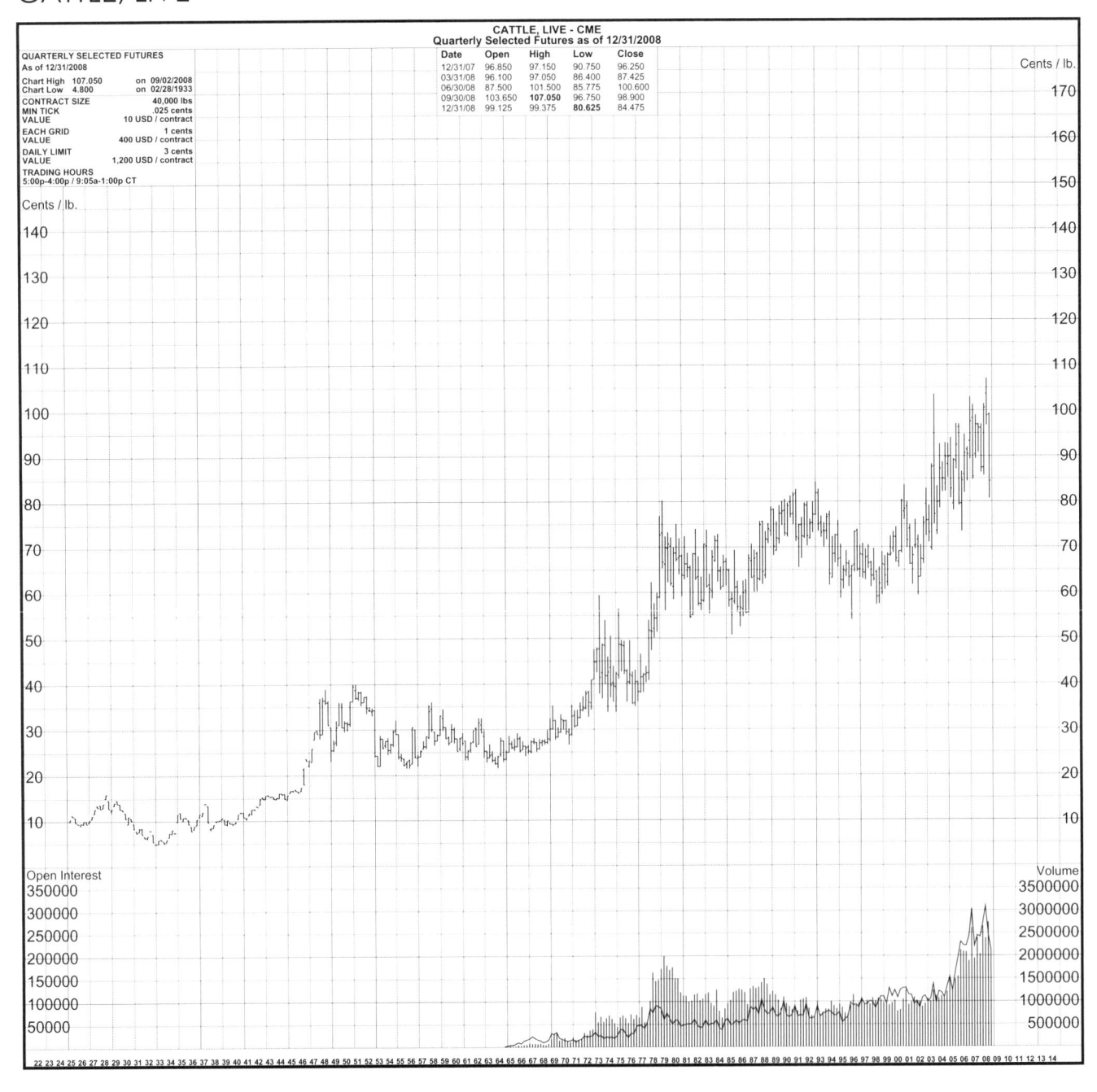

**QUARTERLY SELECTED FUTURES**
As of 12/31/2008
Chart High 107.050 on 09/02/2008
Chart Low 4.800 on 02/28/1933
CONTRACT SIZE 40,000 lbs
MIN TICK .025 cents
VALUE 10 USD / contract
EACH GRID 1 cents
VALUE 400 USD / contract
DAILY LIMIT 3 cents
VALUE 1,200 USD / contract
TRADING HOURS
5:00p-4:00p / 9:05a-1:00p CT

**CATTLE, LIVE - CME**
Quarterly Selected Futures as of 12/31/2008

| Date | Open | High | Low | Close |
|---|---|---|---|---|
| 12/31/07 | 96.850 | 97.150 | 90.750 | 96.250 |
| 03/31/08 | 96.100 | 97.050 | 86.400 | 87.425 |
| 06/30/08 | 87.500 | 101.500 | 85.775 | 100.600 |
| 09/30/08 | 103.650 | 107.050 | 96.750 | 98.900 |
| 12/31/08 | 99.125 | 99.375 | 80.625 | 84.475 |

## Annual High, Low and Settle of Live Cattle Futures — In Cents per Pound

| Year | High | Low | Settle | Year | High | Low | Settle | Year | High | Low | Settle |
|---|---|---|---|---|---|---|---|---|---|---|---|
| 1925 | 11.28 | 8.97 | 9.72 | 1939 | 10.64 | 9.03 | 9.44 | 1953 | 34.25 | 22.00 | 26.00 |
| 1926 | 10.00 | 9.07 | 9.43 | 1940 | 12.06 | 9.08 | 11.85 | 1954 | 30.00 | 24.50 | 29.50 |
| 1927 | 13.57 | 9.70 | 13.08 | 1941 | 12.57 | 10.23 | 12.57 | 1955 | 32.00 | 22.00 | 22.25 |
| 1928 | 15.91 | 12.83 | 12.86 | 1942 | 15.30 | 12.39 | 14.85 | 1956 | 30.50 | 21.50 | 24.00 |
| 1929 | 14.59 | 11.92 | 12.74 | 1943 | 15.71 | 14.84 | 14.87 | 1957 | 28.50 | 22.00 | 28.50 |
| 1930 | 12.62 | 9.42 | 10.17 | 1944 | 16.07 | 14.81 | 14.87 | 1958 | 36.00 | 26.50 | 28.75 |
| 1931 | 9.43 | 7.11 | 7.11 | 1945 | 16.91 | 14.71 | 16.59 | 1959 | 34.50 | 26.50 | 27.00 |
| 1932 | 7.91 | 5.44 | 5.44 | 1946 | 23.64 | 16.14 | 23.19 | 1960 | 31.25 | 25.25 | 28.00 |
| 1933 | 6.01 | 4.80 | 5.17 | 1947 | 29.82 | 21.94 | 29.08 | 1961 | 29.25 | 23.25 | 27.00 |
| 1934 | 8.06 | 5.35 | 7.41 | 1948 | 39.00 | 28.00 | 31.00 | 1962 | 32.50 | 26.25 | 29.25 |
| 1935 | 11.91 | 9.90 | 10.62 | 1949 | 36.00 | 23.00 | 35.50 | 1963 | 29.75 | 22.75 | 23.25 |
| 1936 | 10.38 | 7.80 | 10.38 | 1950 | 36.25 | 29.50 | 36.25 | 1964 | 28.25 | 21.50 | 23.450 |
| 1937 | 13.97 | 9.69 | 9.69 | 1951 | 40.00 | 35.25 | 36.00 | 1965 | 28.600 | 23.200 | 26.225 |
| 1938 | 10.16 | 7.91 | 10.16 | 1952 | 37.50 | 33.00 | 34.25 | 1966 | 29.200 | 24.100 | 25.950 |

Futures begin trading 11/30/1964. *Source: CME Group; Chicago Mercantile Exchange*

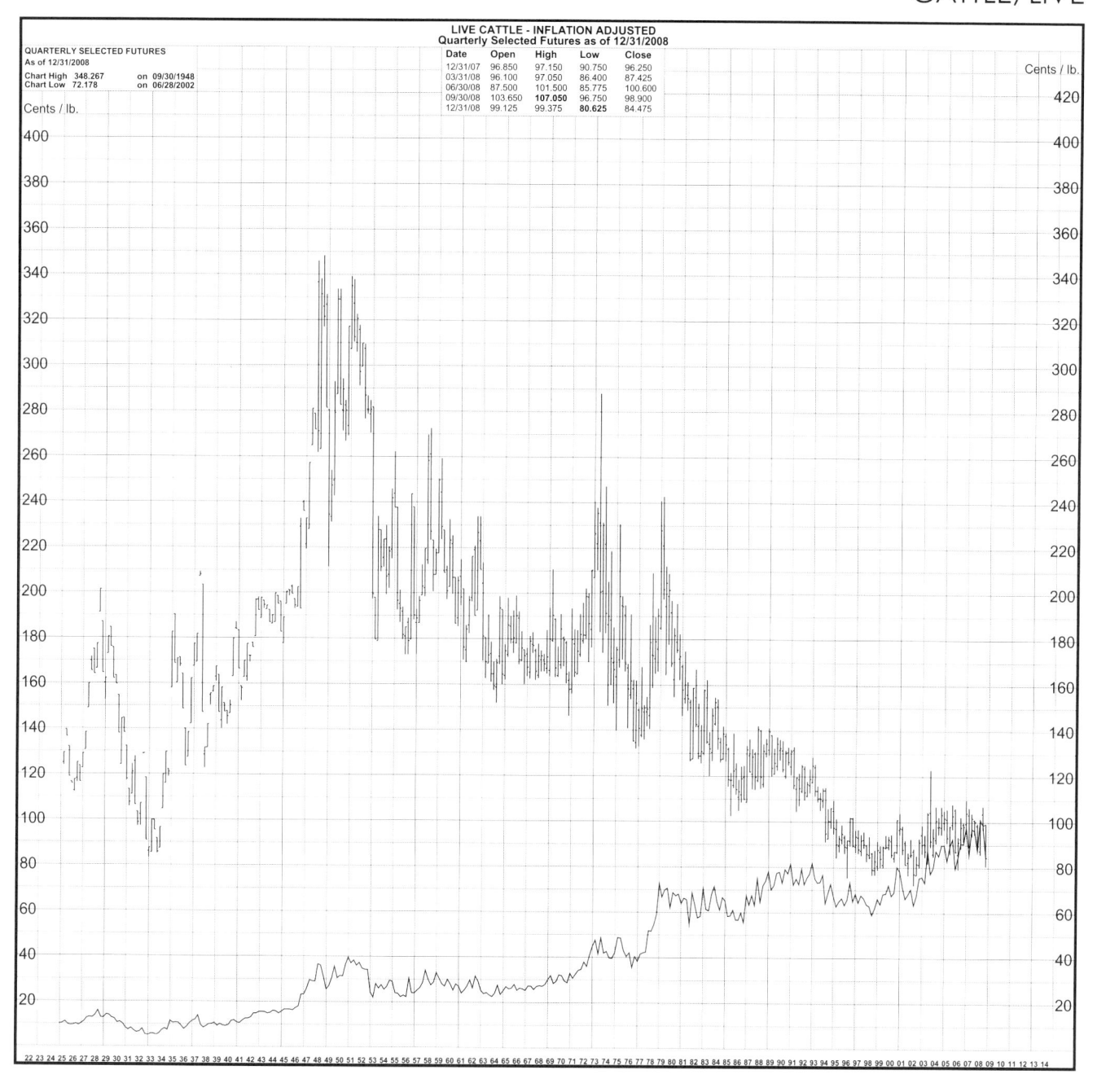

# CATTLE, LIVE

**LIVE CATTLE - INFLATION ADJUSTED**
Quarterly Selected Futures as of 12/31/2008

| Date | Open | High | Low | Close |
|------|------|------|------|-------|
| 12/31/07 | 96.850 | 97.150 | 90.750 | 96.250 |
| 03/31/08 | 96.100 | 97.050 | 86.400 | 87.425 |
| 06/30/08 | 87.500 | 101.500 | 85.775 | 100.600 |
| 09/30/08 | 103.650 | **107.050** | 96.750 | 98.900 |
| 12/31/08 | 99.125 | 99.375 | 80.625 | 84.475 |

QUARTERLY SELECTED FUTURES
As of 12/31/2008
Chart High 348.267 on 09/30/1948
Chart Low 72.178 on 06/28/2002

## Annual High, Low and Settle of Live Cattle — In Cents per Pound

| Year | High | Low | Settle | Year | High | Low | Settle | Year | High | Low | Settle |
|------|------|------|--------|------|------|------|--------|------|------|------|--------|
| 1925 | 11.28 | 8.97 | 9.72 | 1939 | 10.64 | 9.03 | 9.44 | 1953 | 34.25 | 22.00 | 26.00 |
| 1926 | 10.00 | 9.07 | 9.43 | 1940 | 12.06 | 9.08 | 11.85 | 1954 | 30.00 | 24.50 | 29.50 |
| 1927 | 13.57 | 9.70 | 13.08 | 1941 | 12.57 | 10.23 | 12.57 | 1955 | 32.00 | 22.00 | 22.25 |
| 1928 | 15.91 | 12.83 | 12.86 | 1942 | 15.30 | 12.39 | 14.85 | 1956 | 30.50 | 21.50 | 24.00 |
| 1929 | 14.59 | 11.92 | 12.74 | 1943 | 15.71 | 14.84 | 14.87 | 1957 | 28.50 | 22.00 | 28.50 |
| 1930 | 12.62 | 9.42 | 10.17 | 1944 | 16.07 | 14.81 | 14.87 | 1958 | 36.00 | 26.50 | 28.75 |
| 1931 | 9.43 | 7.11 | 7.11 | 1945 | 16.91 | 14.71 | 16.59 | 1959 | 34.50 | 26.50 | 27.00 |
| 1932 | 7.91 | 5.44 | 5.44 | 1946 | 23.64 | 16.14 | 23.19 | 1960 | 31.25 | 25.25 | 28.00 |
| 1933 | 6.01 | 4.80 | 5.17 | 1947 | 29.82 | 21.94 | 29.08 | 1961 | 29.25 | 23.25 | 27.00 |
| 1934 | 8.06 | 5.35 | 7.41 | 1948 | 39.00 | 28.00 | 31.00 | 1962 | 32.50 | 26.25 | 29.25 |
| 1935 | 11.91 | 9.90 | 10.62 | 1949 | 36.00 | 23.00 | 35.50 | 1963 | 29.75 | 22.75 | 23.25 |
| 1936 | 10.38 | 7.80 | 10.38 | 1950 | 36.25 | 29.50 | 36.25 | 1964 | 28.25 | 21.50 | 25.50 |
| 1937 | 13.97 | 9.69 | 9.69 | 1951 | 40.00 | 35.25 | 36.00 | 1965 | 30.00 | 25.00 | 27.00 |
| 1938 | 10.16 | 7.91 | 10.16 | 1952 | 37.50 | 33.00 | 34.25 | 1966 | 32.00 | 24.50 | 25.25 |

Chicago: All Grades to 12/1947; Good 01/1948 to 12/1964; Choice 01/1965 to 07/1971.   Data continued on page 315.
*Source: CME Group; Chicago Mercantile Exchange*

# CATTLE, LIVE

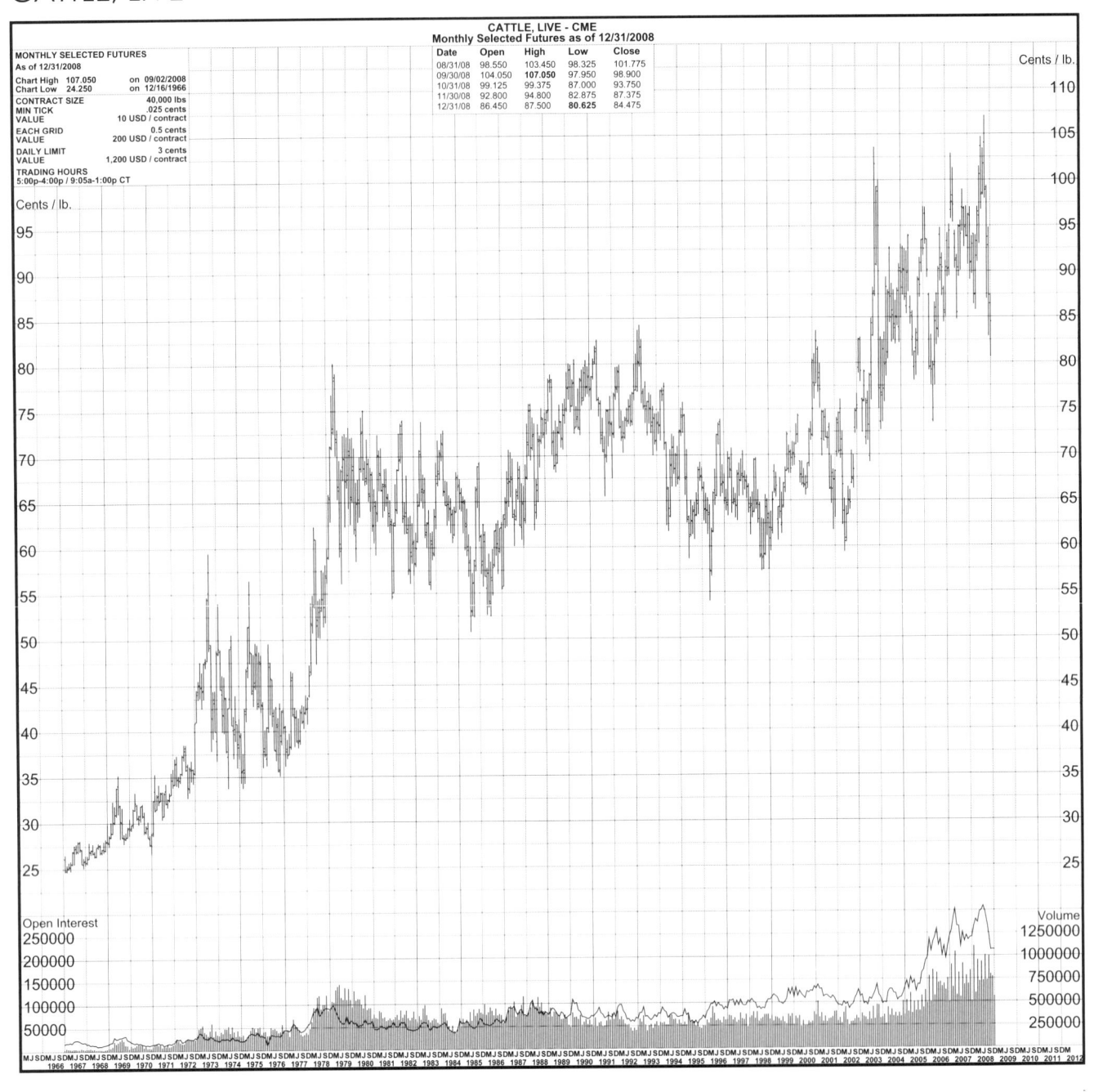

**CATTLE, LIVE - CME**
Monthly Selected Futures as of 12/31/2008

| Date | Open | High | Low | Close |
|---|---|---|---|---|
| 08/31/08 | 98.550 | 103.450 | 98.325 | 101.775 |
| 09/30/08 | 104.050 | 107.050 | 97.950 | 98.900 |
| 10/31/08 | 99.125 | 99.375 | 87.000 | 93.750 |
| 11/30/08 | 92.800 | 94.800 | 82.875 | 87.375 |
| 12/31/08 | 86.450 | 87.500 | 80.625 | 84.475 |

**MONTHLY SELECTED FUTURES** As of 12/31/2008
- Chart High 107.050 on 09/02/2008
- Chart Low 24.250 on 12/16/1966
- CONTRACT SIZE: 40,000 lbs
- MIN TICK: .025 cents
- VALUE: 10 USD / contract
- EACH GRID: 0.5 cents
- VALUE: 200 USD / contract
- DAILY LIMIT: 3 cents
- VALUE: 1,200 USD / contract
- TRADING HOURS: 5:00p-4:00p / 9:05a-1:00p CT

## Annual High, Low and Settle of Live Cattle Futures     In Cents per Pound

| Year | High | Low | Settle | Year | High | Low | Settle | Year | High | Low | Settle |
|---|---|---|---|---|---|---|---|---|---|---|---|
| 1967 | 28.100 | 24.675 | 25.700 | 1981 | 72.400 | 54.375 | 54.650 | 1995 | 75.825 | 58.650 | 66.425 |
| 1968 | 29.850 | 25.525 | 27.925 | 1982 | 74.000 | 55.100 | 58.325 | 1996 | 73.950 | 54.000 | 64.975 |
| 1969 | 35.250 | 27.400 | 29.300 | 1983 | 73.825 | 55.350 | 67.850 | 1997 | 70.800 | 62.800 | 66.450 |
| 1970 | 33.350 | 26.600 | 28.725 | 1984 | 72.875 | 60.500 | 66.675 | 1998 | 69.725 | 57.300 | 62.000 |
| 1971 | 35.900 | 28.550 | 34.200 | 1985 | 69.350 | 50.725 | 61.150 | 1999 | 72.450 | 59.450 | 68.475 |
| 1972 | 40.900 | 32.700 | 40.875 | 1986 | 62.975 | 52.425 | 55.525 | 2000 | 80.400 | 65.525 | 80.225 |
| 1973 | 59.500 | 36.750 | 48.600 | 1987 | 70.725 | 55.700 | 63.125 | 2001 | 83.600 | 61.750 | 68.175 |
| 1974 | 54.000 | 33.750 | 39.550 | 1988 | 75.750 | 61.825 | 73.950 | 2002 | 76.650 | 59.350 | 75.350 |
| 1975 | 56.500 | 33.750 | 42.925 | 1989 | 79.150 | 68.150 | 77.375 | 2003 | 103.600 | 69.175 | 77.200 |
| 1976 | 49.600 | 35.100 | 40.400 | 1990 | 81.250 | 72.225 | 77.200 | 2004 | 92.950 | 72.650 | 89.850 |
| 1977 | 46.600 | 36.150 | 42.375 | 1991 | 82.700 | 65.500 | 72.400 | 2005 | 97.125 | 78.050 | 92.450 |
| 1978 | 62.350 | 40.725 | 58.925 | 1992 | 80.000 | 70.250 | 77.125 | 2006 | 97.050 | 73.450 | 90.425 |
| 1979 | 80.250 | 56.050 | 70.675 | 1993 | 84.300 | 70.000 | 73.450 | 2007 | 102.920 | 84.750 | 96.250 |
| 1980 | 75.125 | 58.500 | 68.075 | 1994 | 77.925 | 61.650 | 72.675 | 2008 | 107.050 | 80.625 | 84.475 |

*Source: CME Group; Chicago Mercantile Exchange*

# CATTLE, LIVE

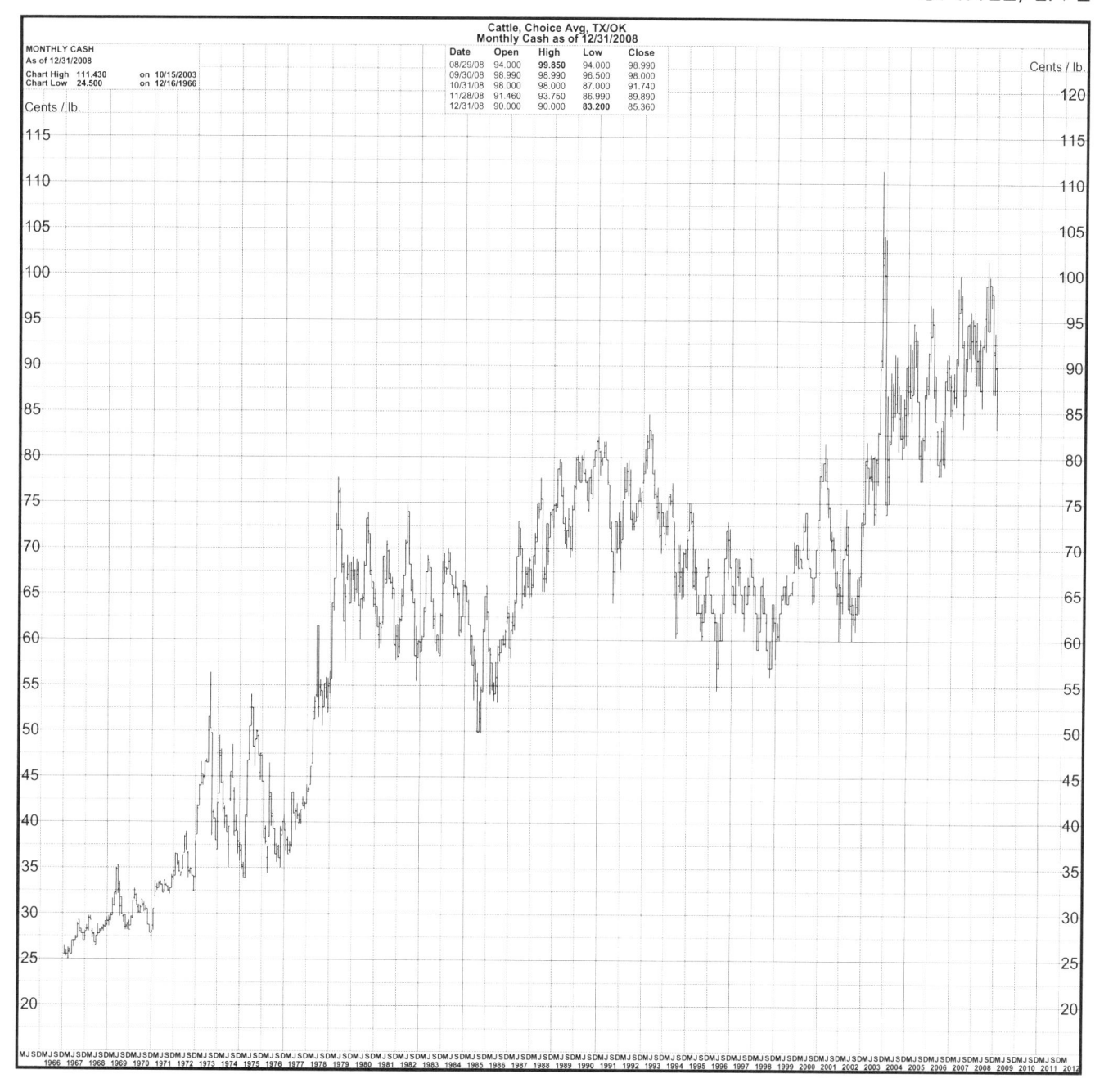

**Cattle, Choice Avg, TX/OK**
Monthly Cash as of 12/31/2008

| Date | Open | High | Low | Close |
|---|---|---|---|---|
| 08/29/08 | 94.000 | 99.850 | 94.000 | 98.990 |
| 09/30/08 | 98.990 | 98.990 | 96.500 | 98.000 |
| 10/31/08 | 98.000 | 98.000 | 87.000 | 91.740 |
| 11/28/08 | 91.460 | 93.750 | 86.990 | 89.890 |
| 12/31/08 | 90.000 | 90.000 | 83.200 | 85.360 |

MONTHLY CASH
As of 12/31/2008
Chart High 111.430 on 10/15/2003
Chart Low 24.500 on 12/16/1966
Cents / lb.

## Annual High, Low and Settle of Live Cattle   In Cents per Pound

| Year | High | Low | Settle | Year | High | Low | Settle | Year | High | Low | Settle |
|---|---|---|---|---|---|---|---|---|---|---|---|
| 1967 | 29.25 | 25.00 | 28.00 | 1981 | 70.81 | 57.75 | 58.19 | 1995 | 75.00 | 60.00 | 65.00 |
| 1968 | 29.75 | 26.50 | 29.15 | 1982 | 74.75 | 55.50 | 59.75 | 1996 | 73.00 | 54.50 | 66.00 |
| 1969 | 35.25 | 28.15 | 28.15 | 1983 | 69.25 | 58.25 | 66.12 | 1997 | 70.00 | 61.00 | 66.00 |
| 1970 | 32.75 | 27.00 | 28.00 | 1984 | 70.00 | 60.40 | 65.88 | 1998 | 67.00 | 56.00 | 60.25 |
| 1971 | 34.65 | 28.10 | 34.60 | 1985 | 65.90 | 49.75 | 63.00 | 1999 | 70.87 | 60.00 | 68.00 |
| 1972 | 39.00 | 32.40 | 37.50 | 1986 | 63.75 | 53.10 | 59.12 | 2000 | 78.00 | 64.00 | 78.00 |
| 1973 | 56.40 | 37.00 | 42.10 | 1987 | 73.00 | 58.00 | 65.75 | 2001 | 81.55 | 60.03 | 64.21 |
| 1974 | 49.50 | 35.00 | 36.90 | 1988 | 77.75 | 65.25 | 74.75 | 2002 | 74.46 | 60.00 | 74.00 |
| 1975 | 54.00 | 33.90 | 44.45 | 1989 | 80.00 | 69.00 | 79.75 | 2003 | 111.43 | 72.76 | 75.22 |
| 1976 | 46.50 | 34.40 | 39.10 | 1990 | 82.25 | 74.00 | 81.00 | 2004 | 91.38 | 73.86 | 87.35 |
| 1977 | 44.10 | 36.50 | 43.40 | 1991 | 81.75 | 64.00 | 70.75 | 2005 | 96.76 | 77.50 | 93.34 |
| 1978 | 61.50 | 43.30 | 55.55 | 1992 | 79.75 | 71.00 | 78.25 | 2006 | 96.56 | 78.00 | 87.43 |
| 1979 | 77.75 | 55.70 | 67.00 | 1993 | 84.75 | 69.50 | 70.50 | 2007 | 100.00 | 83.27 | 92.92 |
| 1980 | 73.95 | 60.00 | 63.62 | 1994 | 77.25 | 60.25 | 71.00 | 2008 | 101.59 | 83.20 | 85.36 |

Chicago: Choice 01/1965 to 07/1971; Omaha: Choice 08/1971 to 08/1987; Texas/Oklahoma Average 09/1987 to date.   Data continued from page 313
*Source: CME Group; Chicago Mercantile Exchange*

# CATTLE, LIVE

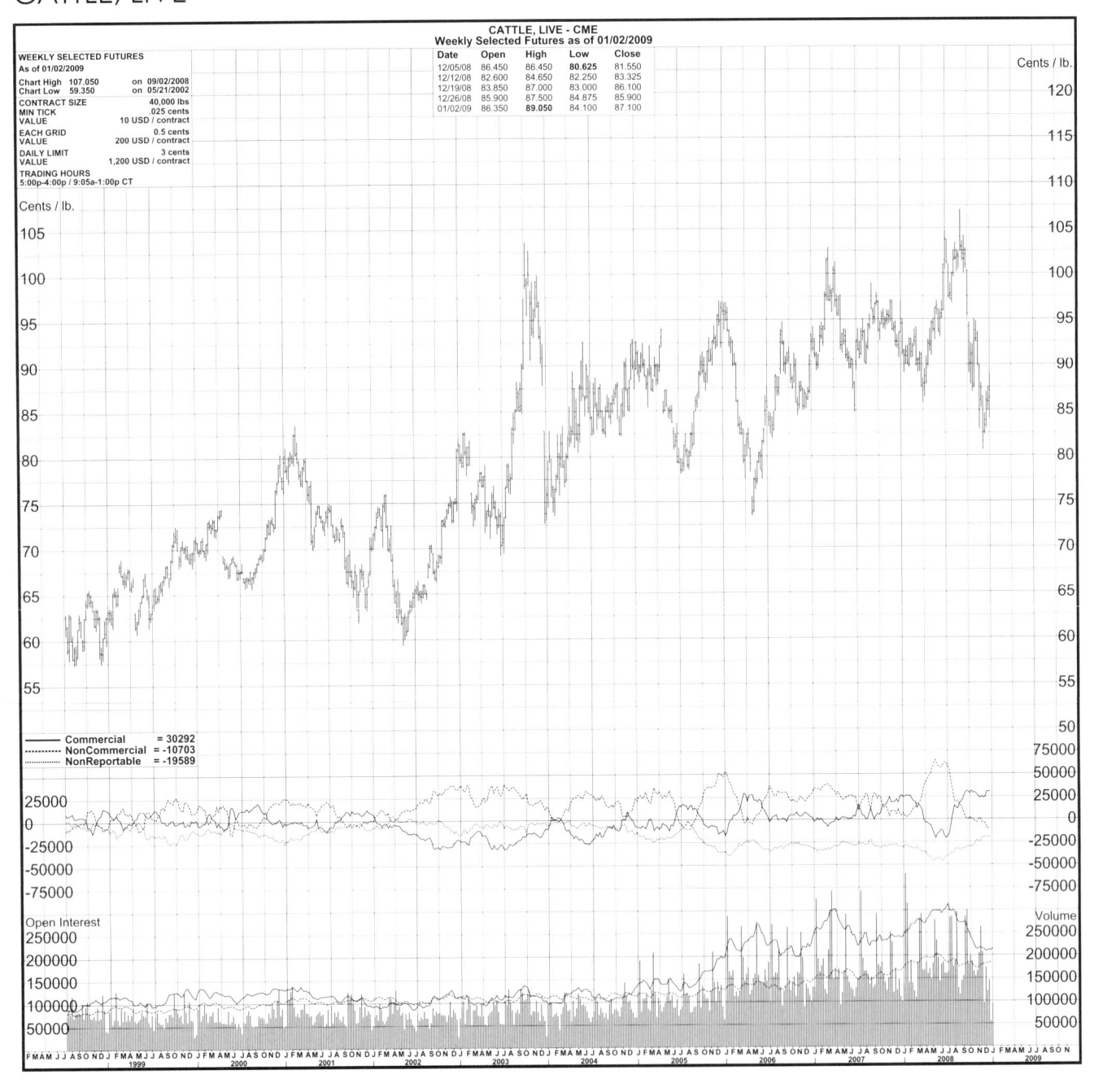

**CATTLE, LIVE - CME**
Weekly Selected Futures as of 01/02/2009

| Date | Open | High | Low | Close |
|---|---|---|---|---|
| 12/05/08 | 86.450 | 86.450 | 80.625 | 81.550 |
| 12/12/08 | 82.600 | 84.650 | 82.250 | 83.325 |
| 12/19/08 | 83.850 | 87.000 | 83.000 | 86.100 |
| 12/26/08 | 85.900 | 87.500 | 84.875 | 85.900 |
| 01/02/09 | 86.350 | 89.050 | 84.100 | 87.100 |

**WEEKLY SELECTED FUTURES** As of 01/02/2009
- Chart High 107.050 on 09/02/2008
- Chart Low 59.350 on 05/21/2002
- CONTRACT SIZE 40,000 lbs
- MIN TICK .025 cents
- VALUE 10 USD / contract
- EACH GRID 0.5 cents
- VALUE 200 USD / contract
- DAILY LIMIT 3 cents
- VALUE 1,200 USD / contract
- TRADING HOURS 5:00p-4:00p / 9:05a-1:00p CT

Commercial = 30292
NonCommercial = -10703
NonReportable = -19589

## Quarterly High, Low and Settle of Live Cattle Futures    In Cents per Pound

| Quarter | High | Low | Settle | Quarter | High | Low | Settle | Quarter | High | Low | Settle |
|---|---|---|---|---|---|---|---|---|---|---|---|
| 03/2000 | 73.400 | 68.725 | 72.175 | 03/2003 | 82.850 | 72.400 | 75.800 | 03/2006 | 97.050 | 79.150 | 79.500 |
| 06/2000 | 74.450 | 66.575 | 67.475 | 06/2003 | 79.200 | 71.000 | 73.225 | 06/2006 | 86.650 | 73.450 | 84.550 |
| 09/2000 | 69.100 | 65.525 | 69.075 | 09/2003 | 88.300 | 69.175 | 87.600 | 09/2006 | 94.800 | 81.950 | 90.650 |
| 12/2000 | 80.400 | 68.650 | 80.225 | 12/2003 | 103.600 | 74.975 | 77.200 | 12/2006 | 92.000 | 84.425 | 90.425 |
| 03/2001 | 83.600 | 76.050 | 78.350 | 03/2004 | 83.400 | 72.650 | 79.825 | 03/2007 | 102.920 | 89.350 | 97.600 |
| 06/2001 | 79.950 | 69.825 | 71.525 | 06/2004 | 92.700 | 78.500 | 87.250 | 06/2007 | 101.350 | 84.750 | 85.500 |
| 09/2001 | 74.925 | 66.150 | 66.225 | 09/2004 | 88.700 | 82.050 | 85.075 | 09/2007 | 99.000 | 89.400 | 96.950 |
| 12/2001 | 69.900 | 61.750 | 68.175 | 12/2004 | 92.950 | 82.200 | 89.850 | 12/2007 | 97.150 | 90.750 | 96.250 |
| 03/2002 | 76.075 | 69.550 | 70.425 | 03/2005 | 92.750 | 85.350 | 89.825 | 03/2008 | 97.050 | 86.400 | 87.425 |
| 06/2002 | 72.600 | 59.350 | 63.400 | 06/2005 | 94.050 | 80.700 | 82.775 | 06/2008 | 101.500 | 85.775 | 100.600 |
| 09/2002 | 70.475 | 63.400 | 67.400 | 09/2005 | 89.400 | 78.050 | 89.125 | 09/2008 | 107.050 | 96.750 | 98.900 |
| 12/2002 | 76.650 | 66.250 | 75.350 | 12/2005 | 97.125 | 87.150 | 92.450 | 12/2008 | 99.375 | 80.625 | 84.475 |

*Source: CME Group; Chicago Mercantile Exchange*

# CATTLE, LIVE

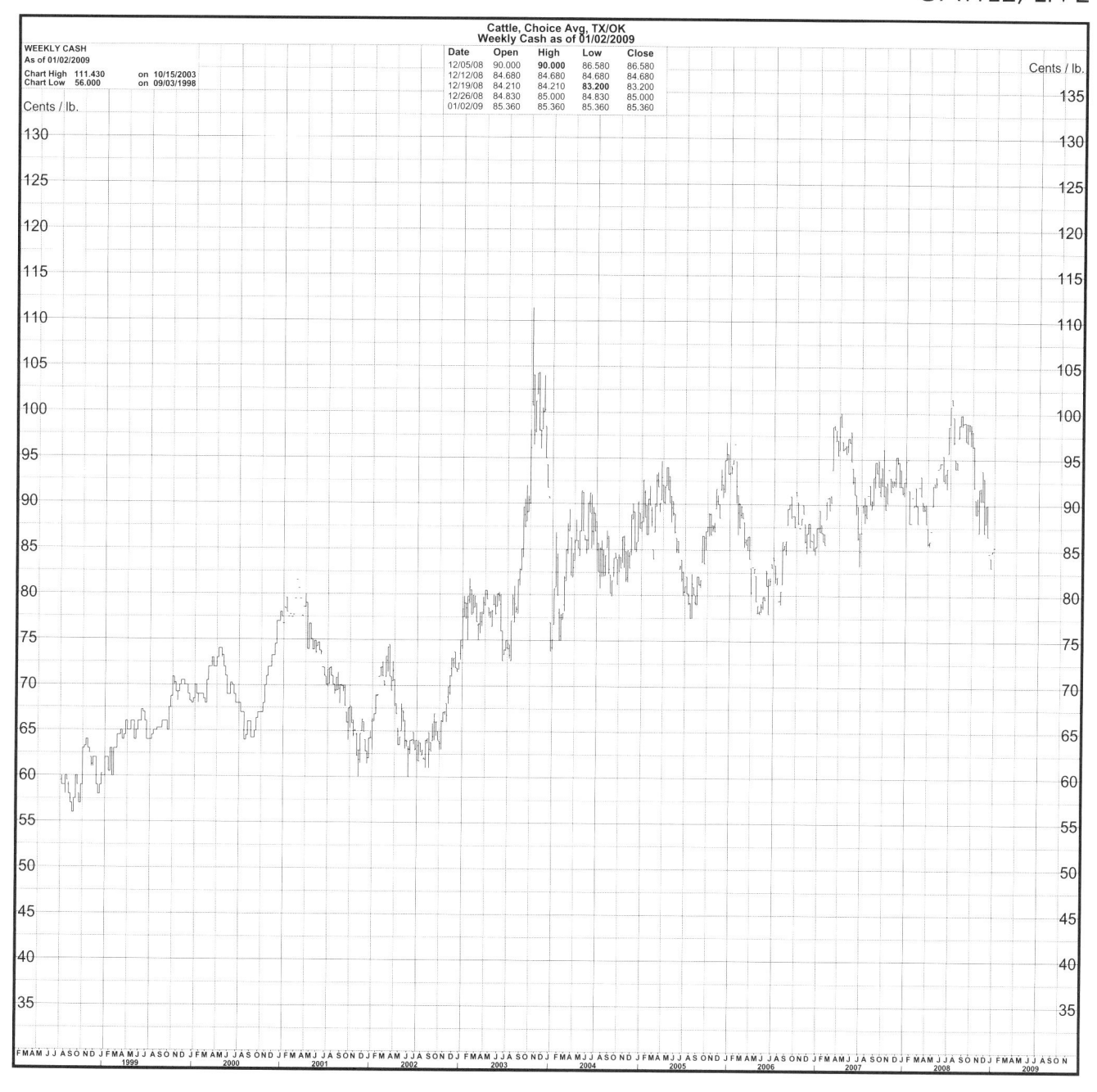

**WEEKLY CASH**
As of 01/02/2009
Chart High 111.430 on 10/15/2003
Chart Low 56.000 on 09/03/1998
Cents / lb.

Cattle, Choice Avg, TX/OK
Weekly Cash as of 01/02/2009

| Date | Open | High | Low | Close |
|---|---|---|---|---|
| 12/05/08 | 90.000 | 90.000 | 86.580 | 86.580 |
| 12/12/08 | 84.680 | 84.680 | 84.680 | 84.680 |
| 12/19/08 | 84.210 | 84.210 | 83.200 | 83.200 |
| 12/26/08 | 84.830 | 85.000 | 84.830 | 85.000 |
| 01/02/09 | 85.360 | 85.360 | 85.360 | 85.360 |

## Quarterly High, Low and Settle of Live Cattle    In Cents per Pound

| Quarter | High | Low | Settle | Quarter | High | Low | Settle | Quarter | High | Low | Settle |
|---|---|---|---|---|---|---|---|---|---|---|---|
| 03/2000 | 73.00 | 68.00 | 72.00 | 03/2003 | 81.78 | 72.85 | 77.88 | 03/2006 | 96.56 | 84.03 | 84.03 |
| 06/2000 | 74.00 | 68.00 | 68.00 | 06/2003 | 80.42 | 72.76 | 73.91 | 06/2006 | 83.48 | 78.00 | 83.08 |
| 09/2000 | 68.00 | 64.00 | 67.00 | 09/2003 | 92.00 | 72.78 | 89.75 | 09/2006 | 90.89 | 79.00 | 87.54 |
| 12/2000 | 78.00 | 67.00 | 78.00 | 12/2003 | 111.43 | 75.00 | 75.22 | 12/2006 | 91.37 | 84.50 | 87.43 |
| 03/2001 | 81.55 | 76.75 | 77.58 | 03/2004 | 89.38 | 73.86 | 84.60 | 03/2007 | 98.64 | 85.59 | 95.41 |
| 06/2001 | 80.00 | 71.05 | 71.05 | 06/2004 | 91.38 | 83.00 | 88.96 | 06/2007 | 100.00 | 83.27 | 84.90 |
| 09/2001 | 72.04 | 65.93 | 65.93 | 09/2004 | 88.00 | 79.92 | 82.34 | 09/2007 | 94.86 | 86.92 | 92.10 |
| 12/2001 | 67.72 | 60.03 | 64.21 | 12/2004 | 90.22 | 81.22 | 87.35 | 12/2007 | 96.04 | 89.50 | 92.92 |
| 03/2002 | 74.46 | 63.00 | 69.48 | 03/2005 | 94.75 | 84.00 | 94.69 | 03/2008 | 94.99 | 87.44 | 87.44 |
| 06/2002 | 72.66 | 60.00 | 64.00 | 06/2005 | 94.01 | 80.00 | 80.00 | 06/2008 | 98.91 | 85.50 | 98.91 |
| 09/2002 | 66.90 | 61.00 | 64.99 | 09/2005 | 87.02 | 77.50 | 87.01 | 09/2008 | 101.59 | 94.00 | 98.00 |
| 12/2002 | 74.00 | 63.00 | 74.00 | 12/2005 | 96.76 | 86.50 | 93.34 | 12/2008 | 98.00 | 83.20 | 85.36 |

Omaha: Texas/Oklahoma Average.    *Source: CME Group; Chicago Mercantile Exchange*

# HOGS, LEAN

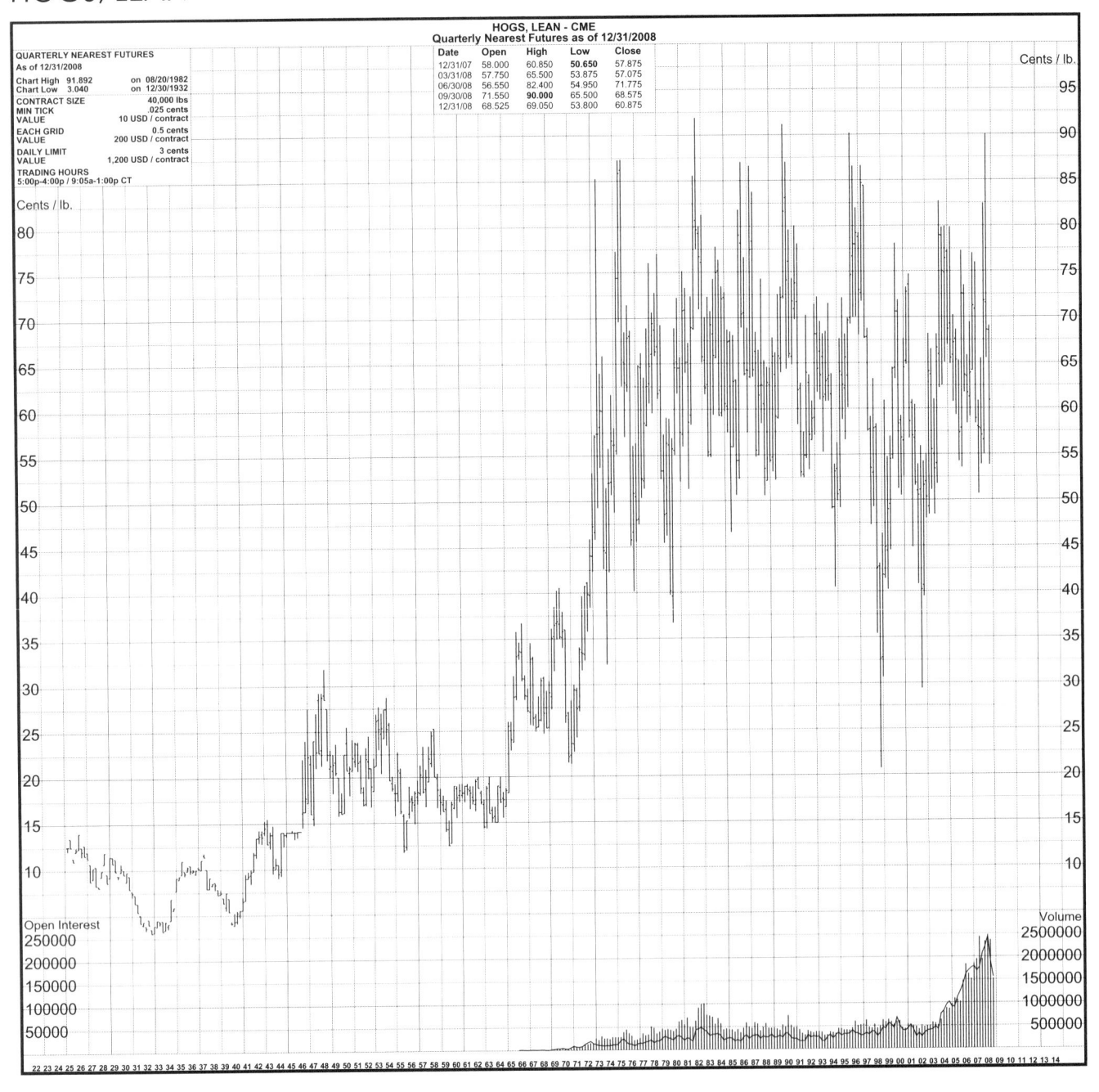

**HOGS, LEAN - CME**
Quarterly Nearest Futures as of 12/31/2008

| Date | Open | High | Low | Close |
|---|---|---|---|---|
| 12/31/07 | 58.000 | 60.850 | 50.650 | 57.875 |
| 03/31/08 | 57.750 | 65.500 | 53.875 | 57.075 |
| 06/30/08 | 56.550 | 82.400 | 54.950 | 71.775 |
| 09/30/08 | 71.550 | 90.000 | 65.500 | 68.575 |
| 12/31/08 | 68.525 | 69.050 | 53.800 | 60.875 |

**QUARTERLY NEAREST FUTURES**
As of 12/31/2008
Chart High 91.892 on 08/20/1982
Chart Low 3.040 on 12/30/1932
CONTRACT SIZE 40,000 lbs
MIN TICK .025 cents
VALUE 10 USD / contract
EACH GRID 0.5 cents
VALUE 200 USD / contract
DAILY LIMIT 3 cents
VALUE 1,200 USD / contract
TRADING HOURS
5:00p-4:00p / 9:05a-1:00p CT

## Annual High, Low and Settle of Lean Hogs Futures   In Cents per Pound

| Year | High | Low | Settle | Year | High | Low | Settle | Year | High | Low | Settle |
|---|---|---|---|---|---|---|---|---|---|---|---|
| 1925 | 13.55 | 10.38 | 10.97 | 1939 | 7.77 | 5.38 | 5.38 | 1953 | 27.70 | 18.50 | 25.35 |
| 1926 | 14.01 | 11.48 | 11.57 | 1940 | 5.60 | 3.85 | 5.50 | 1954 | 28.75 | 18.50 | 18.75 |
| 1927 | 11.96 | 8.32 | 8.32 | 1941 | 10.00 | 5.55 | 9.70 | 1955 | 22.75 | 11.75 | 12.00 |
| 1928 | 11.89 | 8.08 | 8.61 | 1942 | 14.25 | 9.75 | 13.50 | 1956 | 19.00 | 12.00 | 18.25 |
| 1929 | 11.44 | 9.06 | 9.34 | 1943 | 15.50 | 9.50 | 10.25 | 1957 | 23.35 | 16.75 | 20.00 |
| 1930 | 10.67 | 7.92 | 7.92 | 1944 | 14.00 | 9.00 | 13.75 | 1958 | 25.25 | 16.63 | 18.60 |
| 1931 | 7.65 | 4.20 | 4.20 | 1945 | 14.25 | 13.25 | 14.00 | 1959 | 18.75 | 12.50 | 12.50 |
| 1932 | 4.58 | 3.04 | 3.04 | 1946 | 24.00 | 13.40 | 17.75 | 1960 | 19.25 | 12.75 | 18.50 |
| 1933 | 4.51 | 3.12 | 3.25 | 1947 | 27.50 | 14.75 | 22.75 | 1961 | 19.25 | 16.50 | 18.25 |
| 1934 | 6.82 | 3.41 | 5.89 | 1948 | 31.85 | 21.25 | 22.50 | 1962 | 20.00 | 16.25 | 17.25 |
| 1935 | 10.95 | 7.70 | 9.57 | 1949 | 23.65 | 15.75 | 16.25 | 1963 | 20.00 | 14.35 | 15.50 |
| 1936 | 10.47 | 9.48 | 9.96 | 1950 | 25.50 | 16.00 | 21.00 | 1964 | 20.00 | 15.00 | 17.50 |
| 1937 | 11.77 | 7.90 | 7.90 | 1951 | 24.10 | 18.25 | 18.85 | 1965 | 31.00 | 16.75 | 28.70 |
| 1938 | 9.12 | 7.24 | 7.24 | 1952 | 24.50 | 16.75 | 19.00 | 1966 | 36.757 | 15.50 | 28.851 |

Futures begin trading 02/28/1966.   Data through December 1996 contract; "Live Hogs" / .74; adjusted to correspond to "Lean Hogs".   Data continued on page 320.   *Source: CME Group; Chicago Mercantile Exchange*

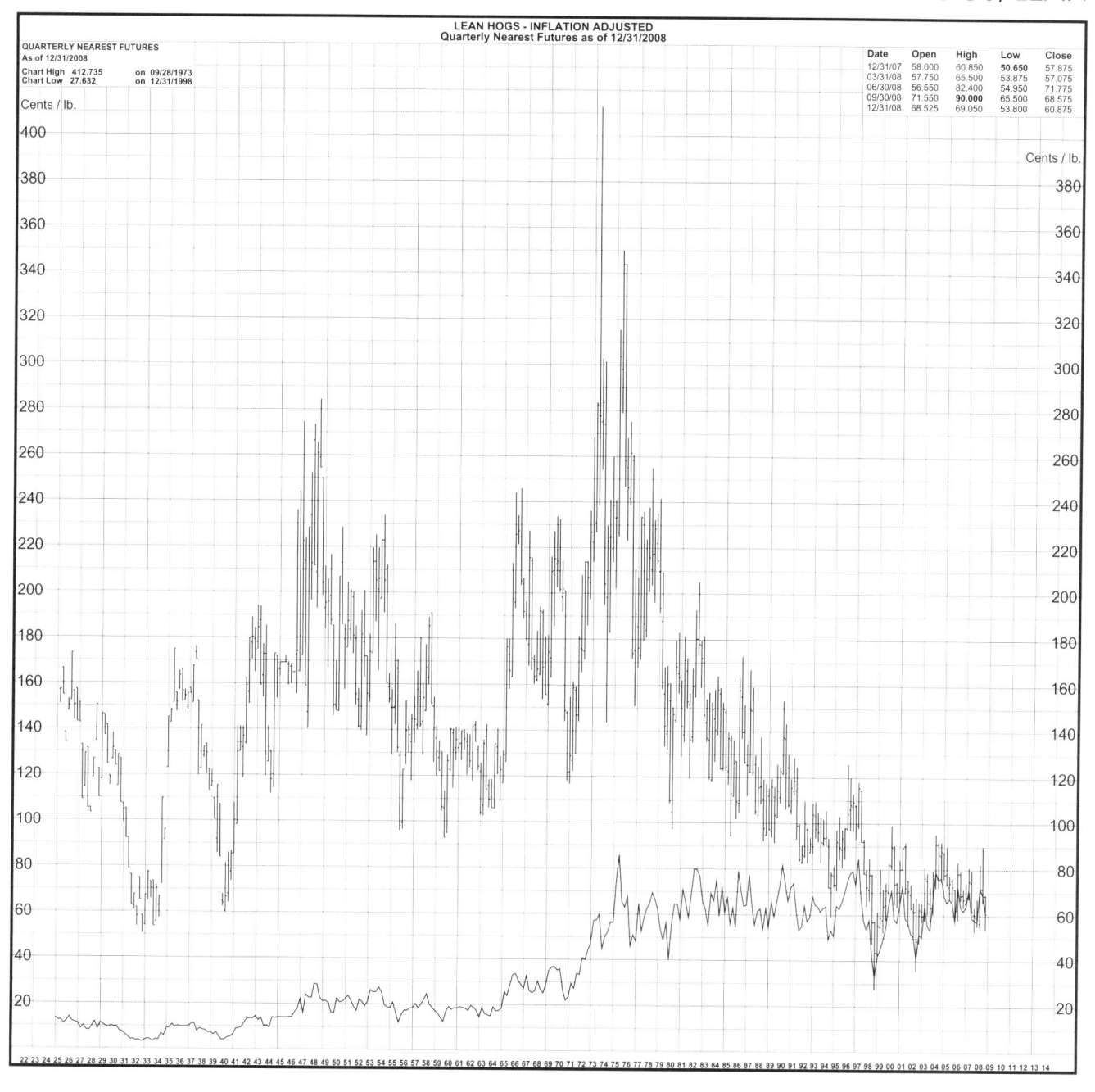

# HOGS, LEAN

**LEAN HOGS - INFLATION ADJUSTED**
Quarterly Nearest Futures as of 12/31/2008

QUARTERLY NEAREST FUTURES
As of 12/31/2008
Chart High 412.735 on 09/28/1973
Chart Low 27.632 on 12/31/1998
Cents / lb.

| Date | Open | High | Low | Close |
|---|---|---|---|---|
| 12/31/07 | 58.000 | 60.850 | 50.650 | 57.875 |
| 03/31/08 | 57.750 | 65.500 | 53.875 | 57.075 |
| 06/30/08 | 56.550 | 82.400 | 54.950 | 71.775 |
| 09/30/08 | 71.550 | 90.000 | 65.500 | 68.575 |
| 12/31/08 | 68.525 | 69.050 | 53.800 | 60.875 |

## Annual High, Low and Settle of Lean Hogs    In Cents per Pound

| Year | High | Low | Settle | Year | High | Low | Settle | Year | High | Low | Settle |
|---|---|---|---|---|---|---|---|---|---|---|---|
| 1925 | 13.55 | 10.38 | 10.97 | 1939 | 7.77 | 5.38 | 5.38 | 1953 | 27.70 | 18.50 | 25.35 |
| 1926 | 14.01 | 11.48 | 11.57 | 1940 | 5.60 | 3.85 | 5.50 | 1954 | 28.75 | 18.50 | 18.75 |
| 1927 | 11.96 | 8.32 | 8.32 | 1941 | 10.00 | 5.55 | 9.70 | 1955 | 22.75 | 11.75 | 12.00 |
| 1928 | 11.89 | 8.08 | 8.61 | 1942 | 14.25 | 9.75 | 13.50 | 1956 | 19.00 | 12.00 | 18.25 |
| 1929 | 11.44 | 9.06 | 9.34 | 1943 | 15.50 | 9.50 | 10.25 | 1957 | 23.35 | 16.75 | 20.00 |
| 1930 | 10.67 | 7.92 | 7.92 | 1944 | 14.00 | 9.00 | 13.75 | 1958 | 25.25 | 16.63 | 18.60 |
| 1931 | 7.65 | 4.20 | 4.20 | 1945 | 14.25 | 13.25 | 14.00 | 1959 | 18.75 | 12.50 | 12.50 |
| 1932 | 4.58 | 3.04 | 3.04 | 1946 | 24.00 | 13.40 | 17.75 | 1960 | 19.25 | 12.75 | 18.50 |
| 1933 | 4.51 | 3.12 | 3.25 | 1947 | 27.50 | 14.75 | 22.75 | 1961 | 19.25 | 16.50 | 18.25 |
| 1934 | 6.82 | 3.41 | 5.89 | 1948 | 31.85 | 21.25 | 22.50 | 1962 | 20.00 | 16.25 | 17.25 |
| 1935 | 10.95 | 7.70 | 9.57 | 1949 | 23.65 | 15.75 | 16.25 | 1963 | 20.00 | 14.35 | 15.50 |
| 1936 | 10.47 | 9.48 | 9.96 | 1950 | 25.50 | 16.00 | 21.00 | 1964 | 20.00 | 15.00 | 17.50 |
| 1937 | 11.77 | 7.90 | 7.90 | 1951 | 24.10 | 18.25 | 18.85 | 1965 | 31.00 | 16.75 | 28.70 |
| 1938 | 9.12 | 7.24 | 7.24 | 1952 | 24.50 | 16.75 | 19.00 | 1966 | 30.50 | 21.00 | 22.00 |

Chicago: Top.    Data continued on page 321.    *Source: CME Group; Chicago Mercantile Exchange*

# HOGS, LEAN

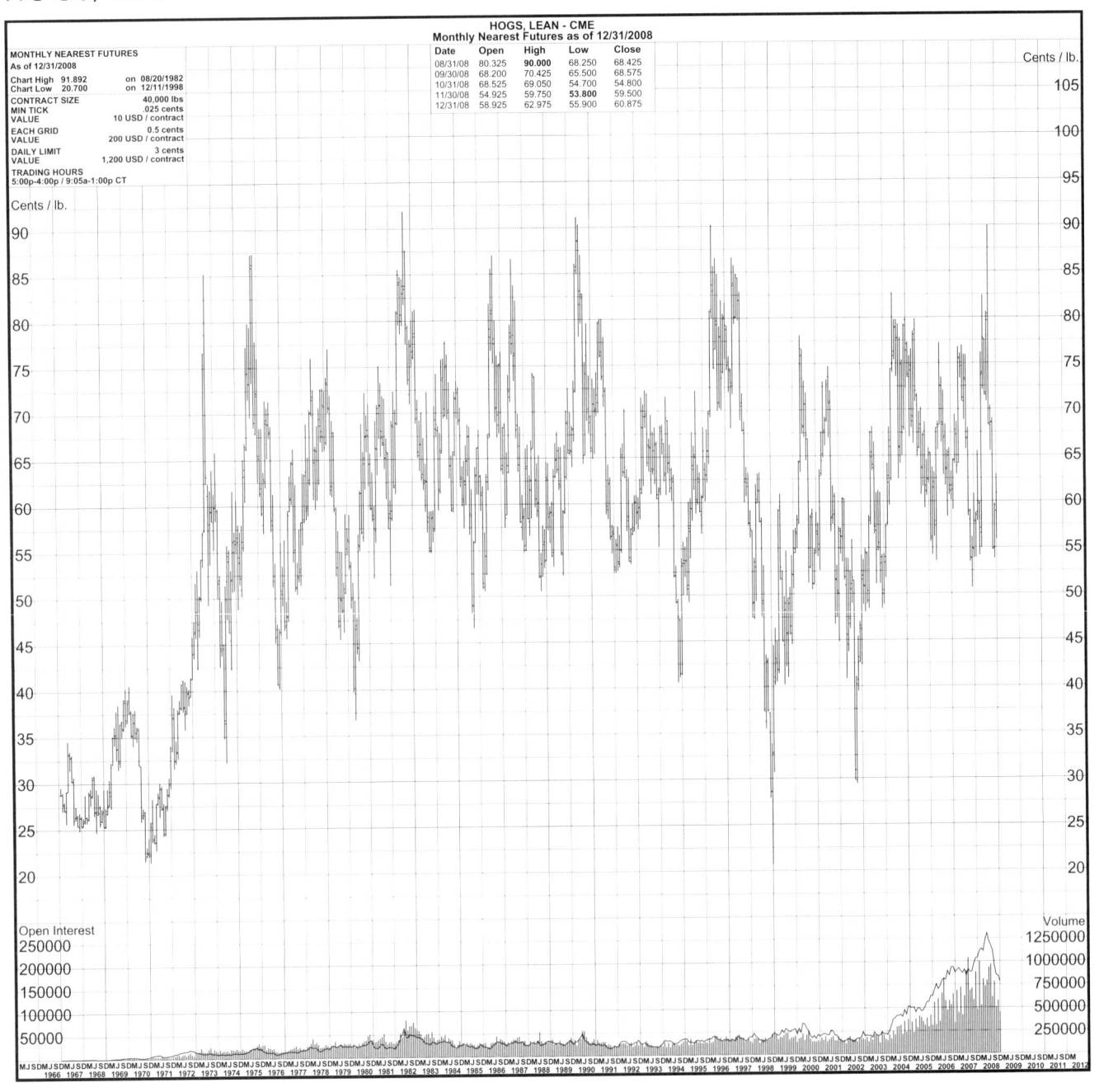

**MONTHLY NEAREST FUTURES**
As of 12/31/2008
Chart High 91.892 on 08/20/1982
Chart Low 20.700 on 12/11/1998
CONTRACT SIZE 40,000 lbs
MIN TICK .025 cents
VALUE 10 USD / contract
EACH GRID 0.5 cents
VALUE 200 USD / contract
DAILY LIMIT 3 cents
VALUE 1,200 USD / contract
TRADING HOURS
5:00p-4:00p / 9:05a-1:00p CT

**HOGS, LEAN - CME**
Monthly Nearest Futures as of 12/31/2008

| Date | Open | High | Low | Close |
|---|---|---|---|---|
| 08/31/08 | 80.325 | 90.000 | 68.250 | 68.425 |
| 09/30/08 | 68.200 | 70.425 | 65.500 | 68.575 |
| 10/31/08 | 68.525 | 69.050 | 54.700 | 54.800 |
| 11/30/08 | 54.925 | 59.750 | 53.800 | 59.500 |
| 12/31/08 | 58.925 | 62.975 | 55.900 | 60.875 |

## Annual High, Low and Settle of Lean Hogs Futures    In Cents per Pound

| Year | High | Low | Settle | Year | High | Low | Settle | Year | High | Low | Settle |
|---|---|---|---|---|---|---|---|---|---|---|---|
| 1967 | 34.595 | 24.865 | 25.338 | 1981 | 75.135 | 51.284 | 58.581 | 1995 | 72.162 | 49.189 | 65.642 |
| 1968 | 30.912 | 24.662 | 25.270 | 1982 | 91.892 | 58.311 | 76.689 | 1996 | 90.169 | 60.135 | 79.225 |
| 1969 | 40.270 | 25.203 | 36.892 | 1983 | 81.284 | 54.764 | 69.257 | 1997 | 86.600 | 57.550 | 57.700 |
| 1970 | 40.608 | 21.486 | 22.128 | 1984 | 77.804 | 59.189 | 72.061 | 1998 | 63.275 | 20.700 | 32.650 |
| 1971 | 34.088 | 21.351 | 33.851 | 1985 | 72.770 | 46.554 | 63.007 | 1999 | 60.925 | 30.650 | 54.500 |
| 1972 | 45.878 | 31.554 | 44.054 | 1986 | 87.027 | 50.608 | 63.851 | 2000 | 78.100 | 50.500 | 56.825 |
| 1973 | 85.270 | 42.331 | 59.865 | 1987 | 86.622 | 54.797 | 55.507 | 2001 | 74.700 | 44.850 | 57.050 |
| 1974 | 65.912 | 32.162 | 56.622 | 1988 | 74.257 | 50.541 | 62.872 | 2002 | 60.425 | 29.400 | 51.600 |
| 1975 | 87.365 | 48.784 | 65.507 | 1989 | 72.534 | 52.230 | 65.811 | 2003 | 68.200 | 48.000 | 53.425 |
| 1976 | 71.453 | 40.135 | 50.845 | 1990 | 91.149 | 63.986 | 66.047 | 2004 | 82.700 | 51.750 | 76.400 |
| 1977 | 66.216 | 45.574 | 58.547 | 1991 | 80.068 | 52.568 | 53.108 | 2005 | 79.850 | 59.275 | 65.275 |
| 1978 | 76.047 | 58.176 | 66.351 | 1992 | 70.270 | 52.466 | 58.953 | 2006 | 77.250 | 53.550 | 61.700 |
| 1979 | 77.061 | 45.439 | 56.318 | 1993 | 72.264 | 55.270 | 61.284 | 2007 | 76.975 | 50.650 | 57.875 |
| 1980 | 72.230 | 36.689 | 64.527 | 1994 | 71.554 | 40.507 | 53.176 | 2008 | 90.000 | 53.800 | 60.875 |

Data through December 1996 contract; "Live Hogs" / .74; adjusted to correspond to "Lean Hogs".    Data continued from page 318.
*Source: CME Group; Chicago Mercantile Exchange*

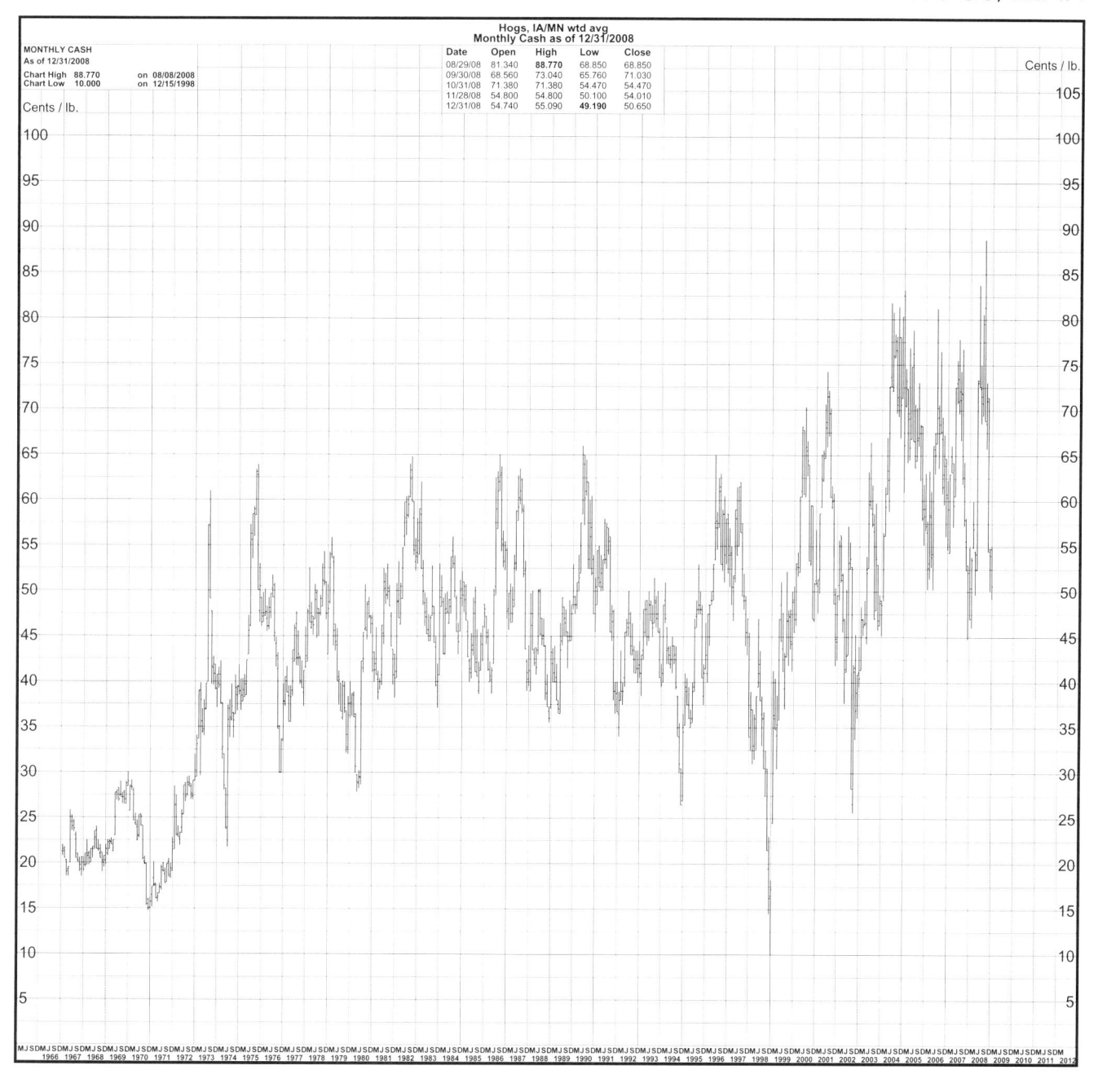

# HOGS, LEAN

**MONTHLY CASH**
As of 12/31/2008
Chart High 88.770 on 08/08/2008
Chart Low 10.000 on 12/15/1998
Cents / lb.

Hogs, IA/MN wtd avg
Monthly Cash as of 12/31/2008

| Date | Open | High | Low | Close |
|---|---|---|---|---|
| 08/29/08 | 81.340 | 88.770 | 68.850 | 68.850 |
| 09/30/08 | 68.560 | 73.040 | 65.760 | 71.030 |
| 10/31/08 | 71.380 | 71.380 | 54.470 | 54.470 |
| 11/28/08 | 54.800 | 54.800 | 50.100 | 54.010 |
| 12/31/08 | 54.740 | 55.090 | 49.190 | 50.650 |

## Annual High, Low and Settle of Lean Hogs    In Cents per Pound

| Year | High | Low | Settle | Year | High | Low | Settle | Year | High | Low | Settle |
|---|---|---|---|---|---|---|---|---|---|---|---|
| 1967 | 25.85 | 18.50 | 19.25 | 1981 | 53.00 | 38.00 | 40.40 | 1995 | 53.00 | 35.00 | 43.00 |
| 1968 | 24.00 | 19.00 | 21.50 | 1982 | 64.80 | 40.40 | 55.50 | 1996 | 65.00 | 40.00 | 55.00 |
| 1969 | 30.00 | 20.75 | 29.00 | 1983 | 62.00 | 37.10 | 49.25 | 1997 | 62.00 | 34.00 | 34.00 |
| 1970 | 29.15 | 14.75 | 15.75 | 1984 | 56.00 | 43.00 | 49.50 | 1998 | 47.00 | 10.00 | 17.25 |
| 1971 | 22.80 | 15.15 | 22.25 | 1985 | 51.00 | 38.65 | 48.00 | 1999 | 52.22 | 24.48 | 45.53 |
| 1972 | 32.00 | 21.50 | 30.20 | 1986 | 65.00 | 38.70 | 47.75 | 2000 | 70.31 | 46.24 | 50.94 |
| 1973 | 61.00 | 29.50 | 40.75 | 1987 | 63.50 | 39.00 | 41.25 | 2001 | 74.24 | 41.83 | 49.57 |
| 1974 | 42.30 | 21.75 | 38.95 | 1988 | 50.30 | 35.50 | 43.25 | 2002 | 57.24 | 25.66 | 40.46 |
| 1975 | 63.90 | 36.80 | 46.50 | 1989 | 53.00 | 36.50 | 49.35 | 2003 | 66.46 | 41.39 | 48.53 |
| 1976 | 51.75 | 29.95 | 37.85 | 1990 | 66.00 | 45.50 | 50.50 | 2004 | 83.21 | 49.00 | 66.14 |
| 1977 | 47.70 | 35.55 | 42.80 | 1991 | 58.00 | 36.50 | 36.70 | 2005 | 78.82 | 55.14 | 57.26 |
| 1978 | 54.35 | 42.20 | 48.00 | 1992 | 50.00 | 34.00 | 41.00 | 2006 | 81.21 | 50.23 | 59.10 |
| 1979 | 55.90 | 32.00 | 37.50 | 1993 | 51.50 | 38.50 | 39.75 | 2007 | 77.84 | 44.79 | 47.03 |
| 1980 | 50.70 | 27.85 | 41.25 | 1994 | 51.00 | 26.50 | 34.50 | 2008 | 88.77 | 46.06 | 50.65 |

Chicago: Top to 03/1968; Farrowing 04/1968 to 05/1970; Omaha: Average 06/1970 to 11/1998; Iowa/S. Minn. 12/1998 to date.    Data continued from page 319.    *Source: CME Group; Chicago Mercantile Exchange*

# HOGS, LEAN

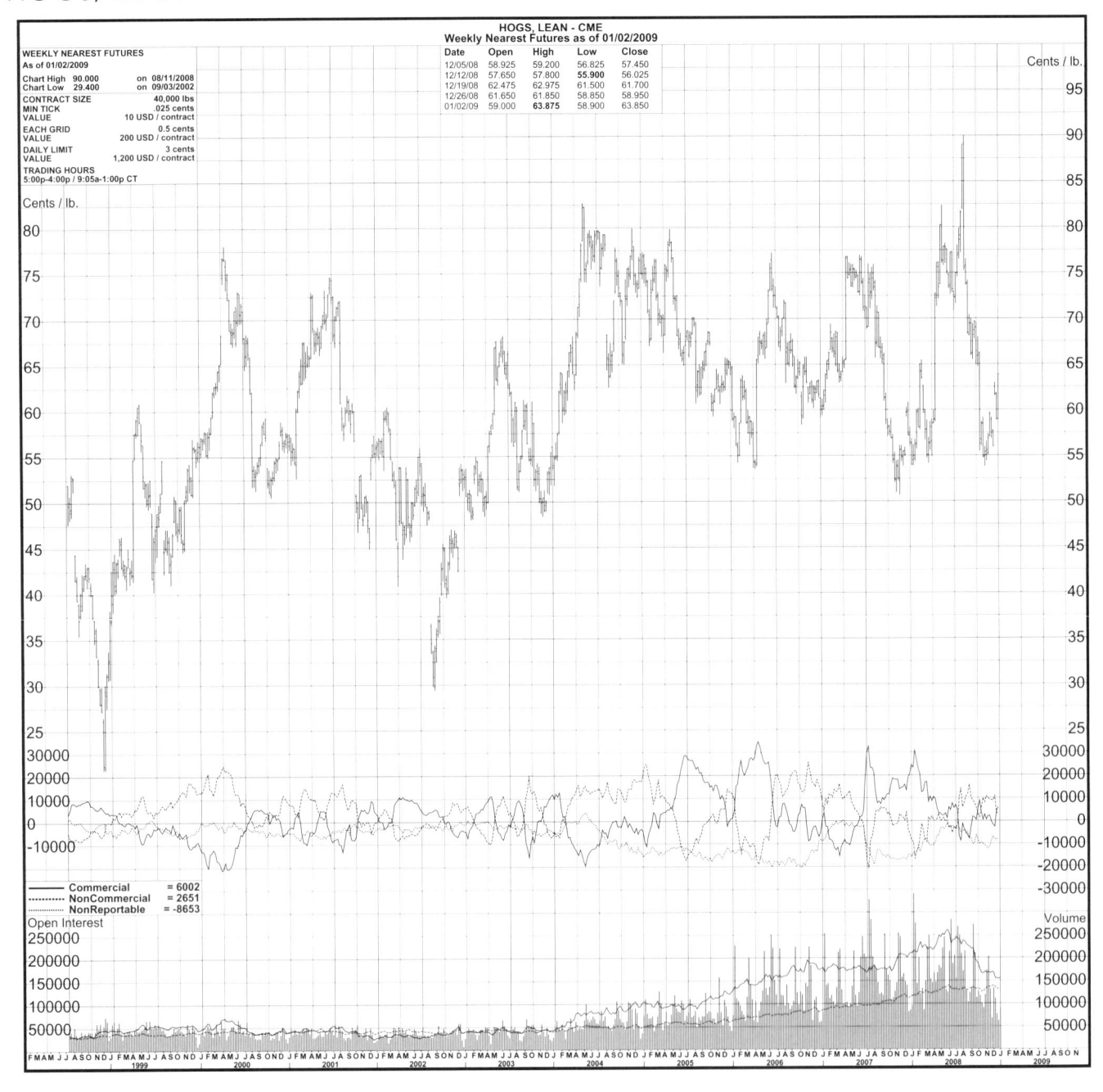

## Quarterly High, Low and Settle of Lean Hogs Futures   In Cents per Pound

| Quarter | High | Low | Settle | Quarter | High | Low | Settle | Quarter | High | Low | Settle |
|---|---|---|---|---|---|---|---|---|---|---|---|
| 03/2000 | 64.500 | 54.450 | 64.350 | 03/2003 | 54.950 | 48.000 | 50.325 | 03/2006 | 65.325 | 54.225 | 57.350 |
| 06/2000 | 78.100 | 63.250 | 70.600 | 06/2003 | 68.200 | 48.400 | 64.050 | 06/2006 | 77.250 | 53.550 | 72.550 |
| 09/2000 | 71.900 | 51.225 | 58.350 | 09/2003 | 66.525 | 51.100 | 55.525 | 09/2006 | 73.475 | 61.725 | 63.625 |
| 12/2000 | 59.250 | 50.500 | 56.825 | 12/2003 | 61.025 | 48.400 | 53.425 | 12/2006 | 65.850 | 58.350 | 61.700 |
| 03/2001 | 67.675 | 52.600 | 64.475 | 03/2004 | 68.150 | 51.750 | 66.650 | 03/2007 | 69.450 | 59.100 | 63.850 |
| 06/2001 | 73.275 | 64.800 | 72.750 | 06/2004 | 82.700 | 62.225 | 78.950 | 06/2007 | 76.975 | 64.100 | 71.225 |
| 09/2001 | 74.700 | 56.750 | 58.600 | 09/2004 | 79.800 | 62.500 | 75.000 | 09/2007 | 75.975 | 58.350 | 58.900 |
| 12/2001 | 60.950 | 44.850 | 57.050 | 12/2004 | 79.925 | 65.050 | 76.400 | 12/2007 | 60.850 | 50.650 | 57.875 |
| 03/2002 | 60.425 | 51.550 | 51.875 | 03/2005 | 77.350 | 67.000 | 68.700 | 03/2008 | 65.500 | 53.875 | 57.075 |
| 06/2002 | 53.950 | 40.825 | 50.525 | 06/2005 | 79.850 | 64.850 | 65.525 | 06/2008 | 82.400 | 54.950 | 71.775 |
| 09/2002 | 55.925 | 29.400 | 40.200 | 09/2005 | 70.225 | 60.725 | 67.200 | 09/2008 | 90.000 | 65.500 | 68.575 |
| 12/2002 | 54.250 | 39.450 | 51.600 | 12/2005 | 68.650 | 59.275 | 65.275 | 12/2008 | 69.050 | 53.800 | 60.875 |

*Source: CME Group; Chicago Mercantile Exchange*

# HOGS, LEAN

**WEEKLY CASH**
As of 01/02/2009
Chart High 88.770 on 08/08/2008
Chart Low 10.000 on 12/15/1998
Cents / lb.

Hogs, IA/MN wtd avg
Weekly Cash as of 01/02/2009

| Date | Open | High | Low | Close |
|---|---|---|---|---|
| 12/05/08 | 54.740 | 54.740 | 53.820 | 54.020 |
| 12/12/08 | 54.090 | 55.090 | 53.420 | 53.420 |
| 12/19/08 | 53.010 | 53.010 | 50.290 | 50.290 |
| 12/26/08 | 51.190 | 51.190 | **49.190** | 49.390 |
| 01/02/09 | 49.570 | 51.500 | 49.570 | 51.500 |

## Quarterly High, Low and Settle of Lean Hogs    In Cents per Pound

| Quarter | High | Low | Settle | Quarter | High | Low | Settle | Quarter | High | Low | Settle |
|---|---|---|---|---|---|---|---|---|---|---|---|
| 03/2000 | 60.44 | 46.24 | 60.44 | 03/2003 | 49.02 | 41.39 | 46.52 | 03/2006 | 63.33 | 50.27 | 53.79 |
| 06/2000 | 70.31 | 60.34 | 65.94 | 06/2003 | 66.46 | 44.25 | 59.13 | 06/2006 | 81.21 | 50.23 | 70.25 |
| 09/2000 | 66.61 | 52.85 | 59.50 | 09/2003 | 61.75 | 47.01 | 53.60 | 09/2006 | 76.49 | 60.79 | 61.52 |
| 12/2000 | 59.42 | 46.66 | 50.94 | 12/2003 | 52.98 | 45.16 | 48.53 | 12/2006 | 67.30 | 54.62 | 59.10 |
| 03/2001 | 65.16 | 47.60 | 62.33 | 03/2004 | 66.99 | 49.00 | 63.35 | 03/2007 | 66.12 | 54.30 | 59.50 |
| 06/2001 | 74.24 | 62.18 | 71.46 | 06/2004 | 81.82 | 58.83 | 76.00 | 06/2007 | 77.84 | 60.54 | 72.10 |
| 09/2001 | 72.15 | 59.12 | 59.93 | 09/2004 | 81.39 | 69.28 | 78.03 | 09/2007 | 76.77 | 57.25 | 57.93 |
| 12/2001 | 60.85 | 41.83 | 49.57 | 12/2004 | 83.21 | 60.93 | 66.14 | 12/2007 | 58.15 | 44.79 | 47.03 |
| 03/2002 | 56.20 | 45.54 | 46.83 | 03/2005 | 76.89 | 64.23 | 65.89 | 03/2008 | 59.96 | 46.06 | 54.16 |
| 06/2002 | 57.24 | 37.69 | 53.20 | 06/2005 | 78.82 | 63.69 | 63.72 | 06/2008 | 83.78 | 52.43 | 71.53 |
| 09/2002 | 55.49 | 25.66 | 41.21 | 09/2005 | 73.05 | 62.22 | 68.24 | 09/2008 | 88.77 | 65.76 | 71.03 |
| 12/2002 | 45.29 | 33.72 | 40.46 | 12/2005 | 68.28 | 55.14 | 57.26 | 12/2008 | 71.38 | 49.19 | 50.65 |

Iowa/S. Minn.    *Source: CME Group; Chicago Mercantile Exchange*

# PORK BELLIES

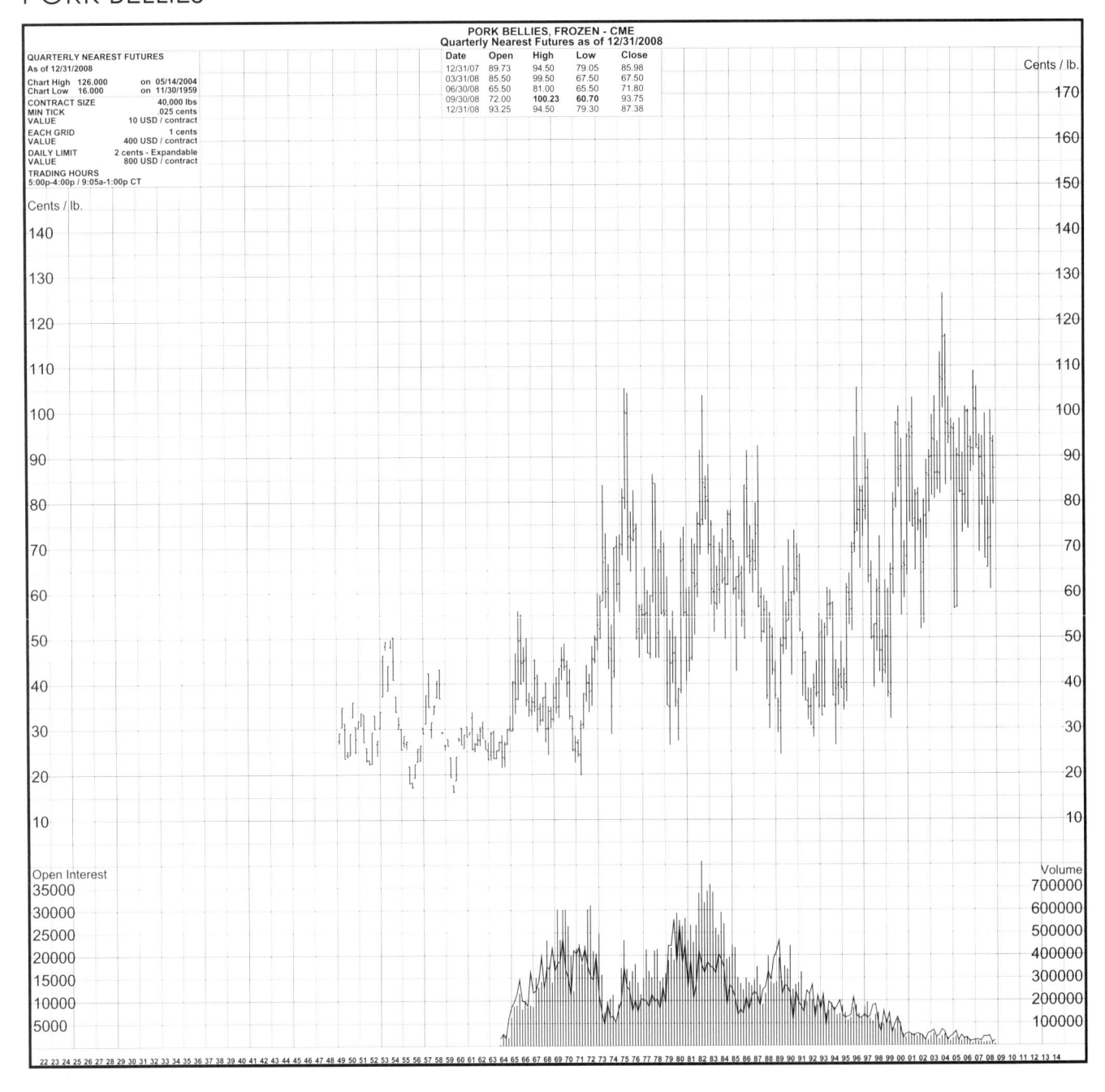

**QUARTERLY NEAREST FUTURES**
As of 12/31/2008
Chart High 126.000 on 05/14/2004
Chart Low 16.000 on 11/30/1959
CONTRACT SIZE 40,000 lbs
MIN TICK .025 cents
VALUE 10 USD / contract
EACH GRID 1 cents
VALUE 400 USD / contract
DAILY LIMIT 2 cents - Expandable
VALUE 800 USD / contract
TRADING HOURS
5:00p-4:00p / 9:05a-1:00p CT

**PORK BELLIES, FROZEN - CME**
Quarterly Nearest Futures as of 12/31/2008

| Date | Open | High | Low | Close |
|---|---|---|---|---|
| 12/31/07 | 89.73 | 94.50 | 79.05 | 85.98 |
| 03/31/08 | 85.50 | 99.50 | 67.50 | 67.50 |
| 06/30/08 | 65.50 | 81.00 | 65.50 | 71.80 |
| 09/30/08 | 72.00 | 100.23 | 60.70 | 93.75 |
| 12/31/08 | 93.25 | 94.50 | 79.30 | 87.38 |

## Annual High, Low and Settle of Pork Belly Futures — In Cents per Pound

| Year | High | Low | Settle | Year | High | Low | Settle | Year | High | Low | Settle |
|---|---|---|---|---|---|---|---|---|---|---|---|
| 1925 | | | | 1939 | | | | 1953 | 49.25 | 30.25 | 44.00 |
| 1926 | | | | 1940 | | | | 1954 | 50.25 | 30.00 | 31.00 |
| 1927 | | | | 1941 | | | | 1955 | 30.00 | 18.00 | 18.00 |
| 1928 | | | | 1942 | | | | 1956 | 26.38 | 17.00 | 26.38 |
| 1929 | | | | 1943 | | | | 1957 | 42.38 | 28.00 | 31.50 |
| 1930 | | | | 1944 | | | | 1958 | 43.13 | 28.88 | 29.25 |
| 1931 | | | | 1945 | | | | 1959 | 27.75 | 16.00 | 16.13 |
| 1932 | | | | 1946 | | | | 1960 | 30.25 | 18.63 | 28.75 |
| 1933 | | | | 1947 | | | | 1961 | 23.75 | 24.975 | 26.750 |
| 1934 | | | | 1948 | | | | 1962 | 31.750 | 25.500 | 25.500 |
| 1935 | | | | 1949 | 34.75 | 23.50 | 23.50 | 1963 | 29.700 | 23.000 | 25.250 |
| 1936 | | | | 1950 | 36.00 | 23.88 | 27.75 | 1964 | 30.000 | 21.425 | 29.750 |
| 1937 | | | | 1951 | 33.50 | 22.75 | 23.13 | 1965 | 56.000 | 29.425 | 49.400 |
| 1938 | | | | 1952 | 33.00 | 22.25 | 27.50 | 1966 | 55.250 | 32.650 | 34.250 |

Futures begin trading 09/18/1961.   Data continued on page 326.   *Source: CME Group; Chicago Mercantile Exchange*

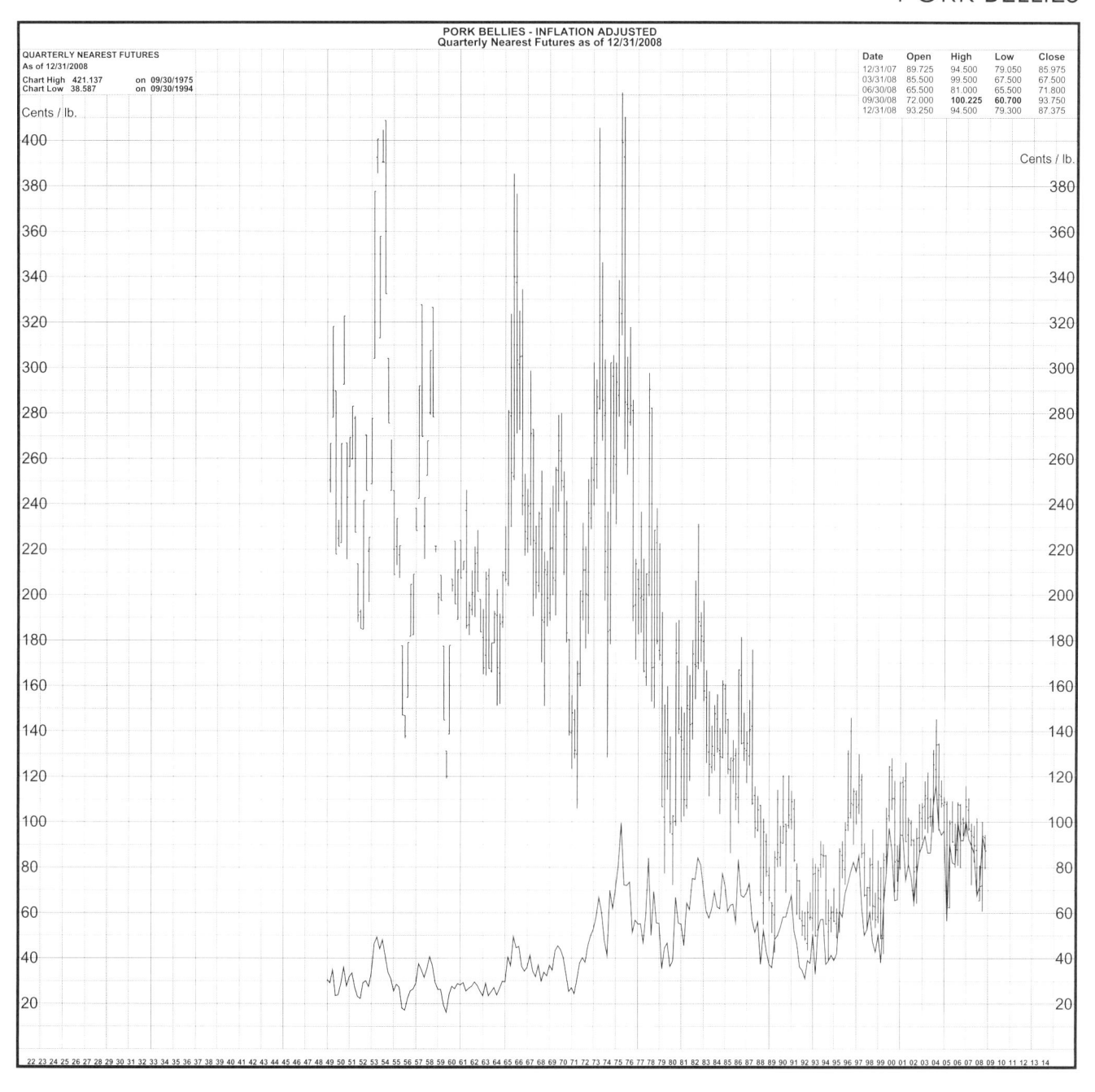

# PORK BELLIES

**PORK BELLIES - INFLATION ADJUSTED**
Quarterly Nearest Futures as of 12/31/2008

QUARTERLY NEAREST FUTURES
As of 12/31/2008
Chart High 421.137 on 09/30/1975
Chart Low 38.587 on 09/30/1994

| Date | Open | High | Low | Close |
|---|---|---|---|---|
| 12/31/07 | 89.725 | 94.500 | 79.050 | 85.975 |
| 03/31/08 | 85.500 | 99.500 | 67.500 | 67.500 |
| 06/30/08 | 65.500 | 81.000 | 65.500 | 71.800 |
| 09/30/08 | 72.000 | 100.225 | 60.700 | 93.750 |
| 12/31/08 | 93.250 | 94.500 | 79.300 | 87.375 |

## Annual High, Low and Settle of Pork Bellies    In Cents per Pound

| Year | High | Low | Settle | Year | High | Low | Settle | Year | High | Low | Settle |
|---|---|---|---|---|---|---|---|---|---|---|---|
| 1925 | | | | 1939 | | | | 1953 | 49.25 | 30.25 | 44.00 |
| 1926 | | | | 1940 | | | | 1954 | 50.25 | 30.00 | 31.00 |
| 1927 | | | | 1941 | | | | 1955 | 30.00 | 18.00 | 18.00 |
| 1928 | | | | 1942 | | | | 1956 | 26.38 | 17.00 | 26.38 |
| 1929 | | | | 1943 | | | | 1957 | 42.38 | 28.00 | 31.50 |
| 1930 | | | | 1944 | | | | 1958 | 43.13 | 28.88 | 29.25 |
| 1931 | | | | 1945 | | | | 1959 | 27.75 | 16.00 | 16.13 |
| 1932 | | | | 1946 | | | | 1960 | 30.25 | 18.63 | 28.75 |
| 1933 | | | | 1947 | | | | 1961 | 35.88 | 24.25 | 24.25 |
| 1934 | | | | 1948 | | | | 1962 | 31.25 | 23.75 | 23.75 |
| 1935 | | | | 1949 | 34.75 | 23.50 | 23.50 | 1963 | 30.50 | 20.50 | 24.50 |
| 1936 | | | | 1950 | 36.00 | 23.88 | 27.75 | 1964 | 28.00 | 20.50 | 27.00 |
| 1937 | | | | 1951 | 33.50 | 22.75 | 23.13 | 1965 | 55.00 | 27.25 | 49.50 |
| 1938 | | | | 1952 | 33.00 | 22.25 | 27.50 | 1966 | 53.00 | 32.00 | 33.50 |

Chicago: 12-14 lb.    Data continued on page 327.    *Source: CME Group; Chicago Mercantile Exchange*

# PORK BELLIES

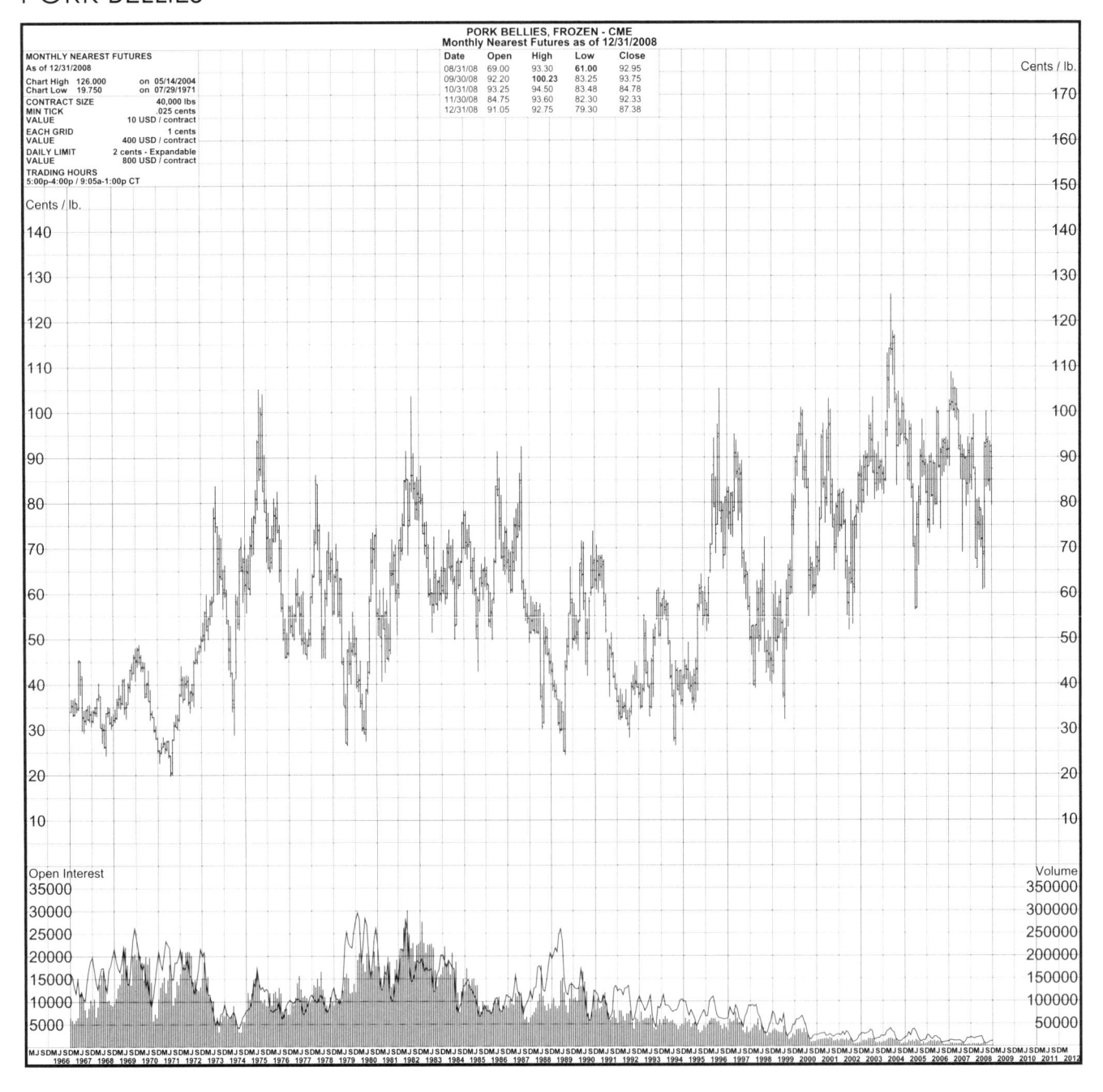

**PORK BELLIES, FROZEN - CME**
Monthly Nearest Futures as of 12/31/2008

| Date | Open | High | Low | Close |
|---|---|---|---|---|
| 08/31/08 | 69.00 | 93.30 | 61.00 | 92.95 |
| 09/30/08 | 92.20 | 100.23 | 83.25 | 93.75 |
| 10/31/08 | 93.25 | 94.50 | 83.48 | 84.78 |
| 11/30/08 | 84.75 | 93.60 | 82.30 | 92.33 |
| 12/31/08 | 91.05 | 92.75 | 79.30 | 87.38 |

**MONTHLY NEAREST FUTURES**
As of 12/31/2008
Chart High 126.000 on 05/14/2004
Chart Low 19.750 on 07/29/1971
CONTRACT SIZE 40,000 lbs
MIN TICK .025 cents
VALUE 10 USD / contract
EACH GRID 1 cents
VALUE 400 USD / contract
DAILY LIMIT 2 cents - Expandable
VALUE 800 USD / contract
TRADING HOURS 5:00p-4:00p / 9:05a-1:00p CT

## Annual High, Low and Settle of Pork Belly Futures    In Cents per Pound

| Year | High | Low | Settle | Year | High | Low | Settle | Year | High | Low | Settle |
|---|---|---|---|---|---|---|---|---|---|---|---|
| 1967 | 45.450 | 29.250 | 31.850 | 1981 | 71.950 | 40.450 | 61.375 | 1995 | 64.300 | 34.000 | 58.275 |
| 1968 | 40.400 | 24.225 | 32.200 | 1982 | 103.500 | 58.850 | 81.100 | 1996 | 105.250 | 51.500 | 82.350 |
| 1969 | 48.100 | 31.550 | 45.400 | 1983 | 88.300 | 51.250 | 61.725 | 1997 | 95.200 | 49.500 | 50.025 |
| 1970 | 48.875 | 25.100 | 25.375 | 1984 | 78.200 | 49.700 | 77.300 | 1998 | 72.475 | 39.000 | 42.750 |
| 1971 | 37.950 | 19.750 | 37.900 | 1985 | 78.200 | 42.650 | 63.825 | 1999 | 81.950 | 32.100 | 78.150 |
| 1972 | 50.650 | 33.600 | 49.700 | 1986 | 91.400 | 49.650 | 66.850 | 2000 | 101.100 | 54.875 | 65.875 |
| 1973 | 83.800 | 47.350 | 60.300 | 1987 | 92.500 | 49.000 | 51.325 | 2001 | 103.000 | 63.775 | 81.425 |
| 1974 | 72.500 | 28.750 | 61.900 | 1988 | 59.450 | 30.050 | 43.050 | 2002 | 89.350 | 51.825 | 86.200 |
| 1975 | 105.100 | 55.650 | 72.250 | 1989 | 65.900 | 24.275 | 49.900 | 2003 | 103.300 | 77.600 | 86.475 |
| 1976 | 82.550 | 45.600 | 56.850 | 1990 | 73.800 | 41.725 | 63.100 | 2004 | 126.000 | 81.700 | 94.250 |
| 1977 | 65.650 | 45.400 | 59.400 | 1991 | 70.750 | 36.075 | 36.225 | 2005 | 98.400 | 56.300 | 82.150 |
| 1978 | 86.250 | 45.600 | 55.550 | 1992 | 44.875 | 28.050 | 37.750 | 2006 | 101.050 | 73.125 | 91.775 |
| 1979 | 71.050 | 26.350 | 46.650 | 1993 | 61.150 | 32.700 | 57.150 | 2007 | 108.800 | 68.900 | 85.975 |
| 1980 | 74.500 | 27.300 | 55.575 | 1994 | 60.700 | 26.350 | 41.375 | 2008 | 100.225 | 60.700 | 87.375 |

Data continued from page 324.    *Source: CME Group; Chicago Mercantile Exchange*

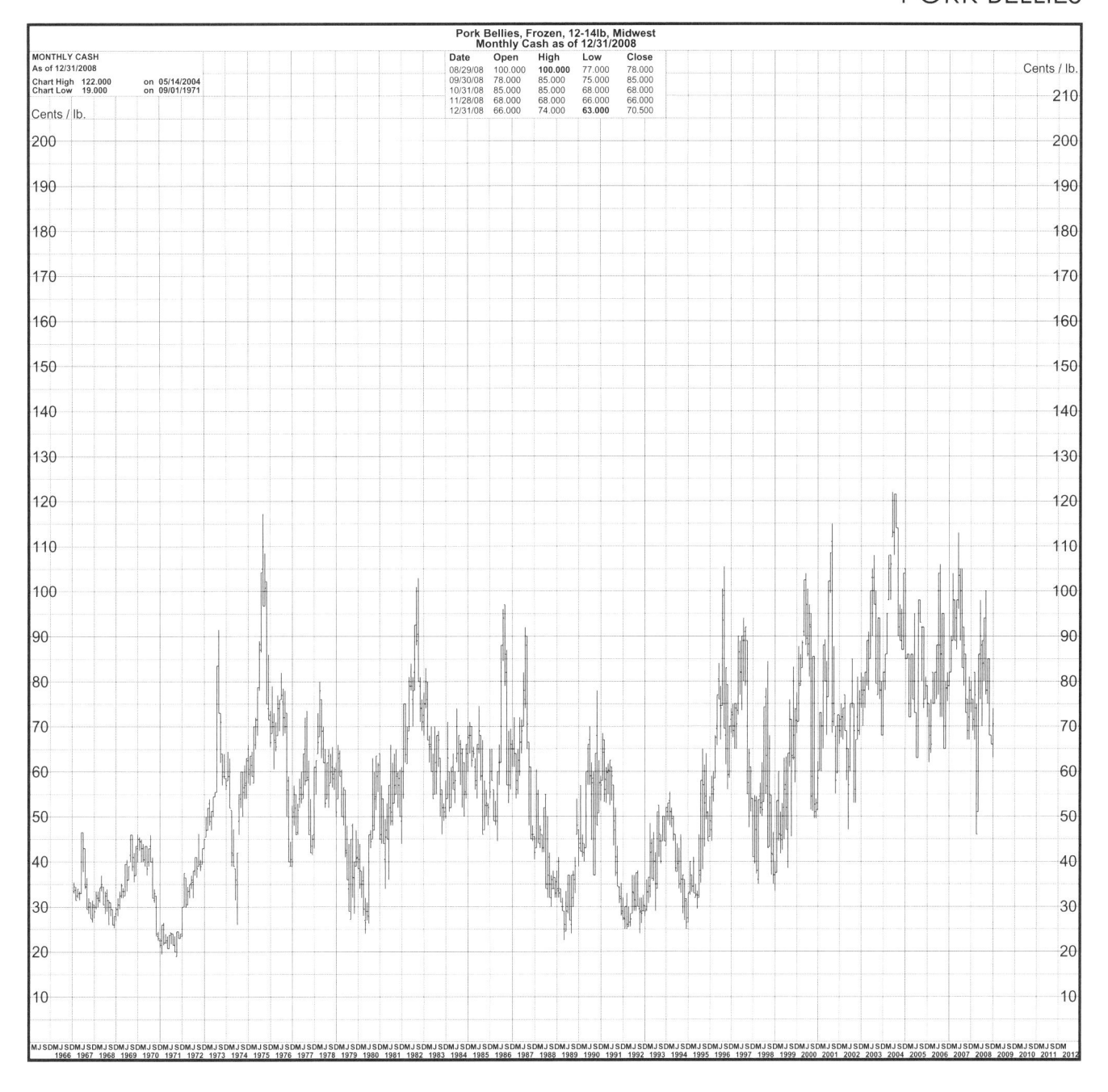

# PORK BELLIES

**Pork Bellies, Frozen, 12-14lb, Midwest**
Monthly Cash as of 12/31/2008

| Date | Open | High | Low | Close |
|---|---|---|---|---|
| 08/29/08 | 100.000 | 100.000 | 77.000 | 78.000 |
| 09/30/08 | 78.000 | 85.000 | 75.000 | 85.000 |
| 10/31/08 | 85.000 | 85.000 | 68.000 | 68.000 |
| 11/28/08 | 68.000 | 68.000 | 66.000 | 66.000 |
| 12/31/08 | 66.000 | 74.000 | 63.000 | 70.500 |

MONTHLY CASH As of 12/31/2008
Chart High 122.000 on 05/14/2004
Chart Low 19.000 on 09/01/1971

## Annual High, Low and Settle of Pork Bellies   In Cents per Pound

| Year | High | Low | Settle | Year | High | Low | Settle | Year | High | Low | Settle |
|---|---|---|---|---|---|---|---|---|---|---|---|
| 1967 | 46.50 | 26.50 | 29.00 | 1981 | 66.00 | 34.00 | 60.00 | 1995 | 65.00 | 29.50 | 49.00 |
| 1968 | 37.00 | 25.25 | 29.50 | 1982 | 103.00 | 54.00 | 75.00 | 1996 | 105.50 | 44.50 | 73.00 |
| 1969 | 46.00 | 28.00 | 45.00 | 1983 | 83.00 | 46.00 | 54.00 | 1997 | 94.00 | 41.00 | 41.00 |
| 1970 | 46.00 | 21.00 | 21.50 | 1984 | 74.00 | 50.00 | 67.50 | 1998 | 84.50 | 33.50 | 37.50 |
| 1971 | 30.00 | 19.00 | 30.00 | 1985 | 74.50 | 46.00 | 55.50 | 1999 | 83.25 | 37.50 | 71.00 |
| 1972 | 46.25 | 30.00 | 45.00 | 1986 | 97.00 | 44.50 | 65.00 | 2000 | 104.00 | 49.50 | 58.50 |
| 1973 | 91.50 | 45.50 | 57.00 | 1987 | 92.00 | 40.50 | 42.00 | 2001 | 115.00 | 55.13 | 69.00 |
| 1974 | 66.00 | 26.00 | 59.50 | 1988 | 60.50 | 30.00 | 34.00 | 2002 | 85.00 | 47.00 | 78.00 |
| 1975 | 117.25 | 57.00 | 66.50 | 1989 | 54.00 | 22.50 | 43.00 | 2003 | 108.00 | 68.00 | 82.00 |
| 1976 | 82.00 | 39.00 | 50.00 | 1990 | 78.00 | 37.00 | 57.00 | 2004 | 122.00 | 78.00 | 85.00 |
| 1977 | 73.50 | 41.50 | 61.00 | 1991 | 68.50 | 27.00 | 27.50 | 2005 | 98.00 | 63.00 | 75.00 |
| 1978 | 80.00 | 50.00 | 51.00 | 1992 | 38.00 | 24.00 | 29.00 | 2006 | 106.00 | 62.00 | 82.00 |
| 1979 | 66.00 | 27.25 | 38.50 | 1993 | 52.50 | 29.00 | 52.00 | 2007 | 113.00 | 67.00 | 76.00 |
| 1980 | 64.00 | 24.00 | 45.00 | 1994 | 55.50 | 25.00 | 33.00 | 2008 | 100.00 | 46.00 | 70.50 |

Chicago: 12-14 lb. to 09/1975; Midwest: 12-14 lb. 10/1975 to date   Data continued from page 325.   *Source: CME Group; Chicago Mercantile Exchange*

327

# PORK BELLIES

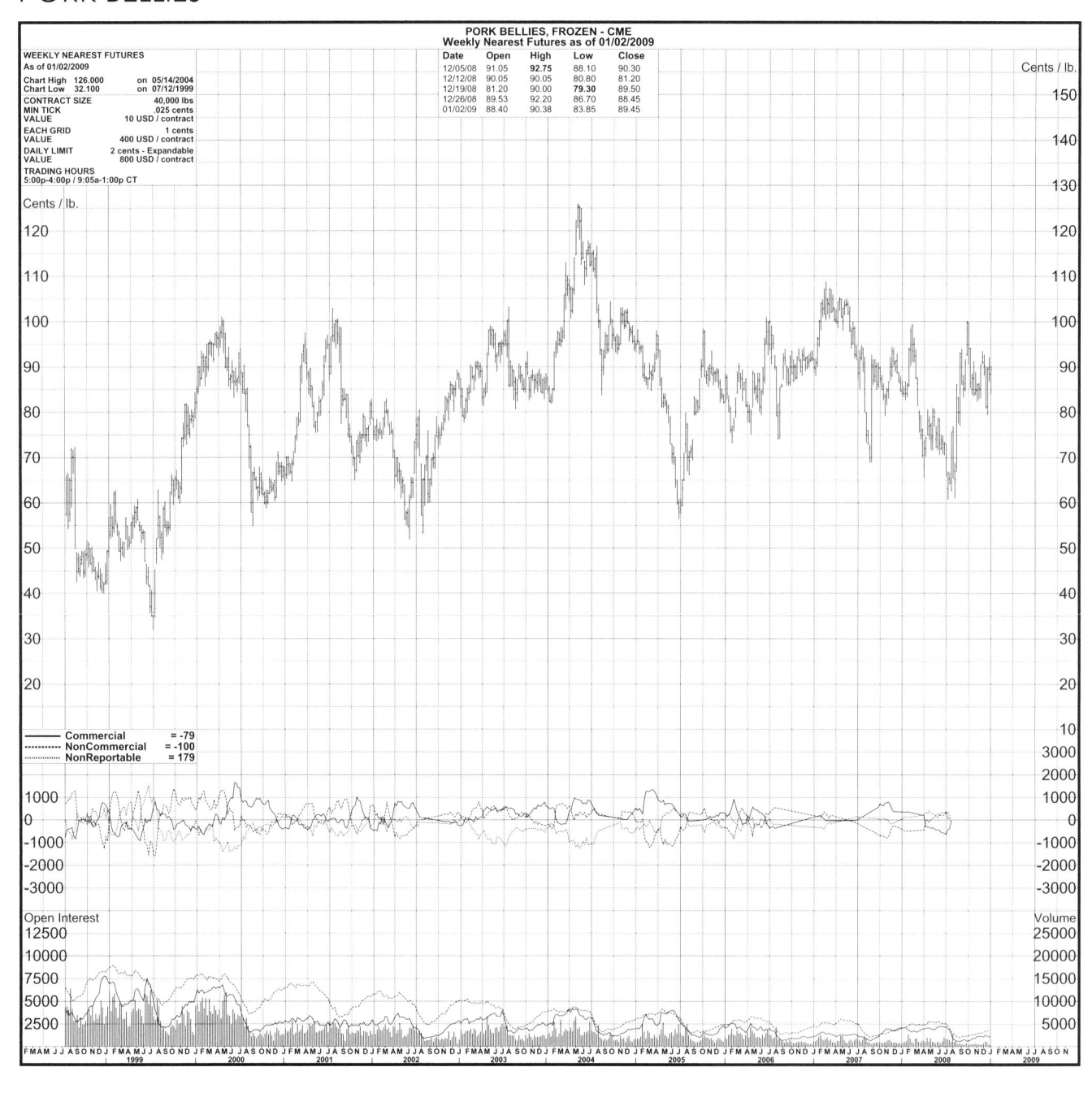

**Quarterly High, Low and Settle of Pork Belly Futures** In Cents per Pound

| Quarter | High | Low | Settle | Quarter | High | Low | Settle | Quarter | High | Low | Settle |
|---|---|---|---|---|---|---|---|---|---|---|---|
| 03/2000 | 97.700 | 78.500 | 97.300 | 03/2003 | 91.400 | 77.600 | 89.725 | 03/2006 | 90.900 | 73.125 | 81.350 |
| 06/2000 | 101.100 | 83.050 | 87.075 | 06/2003 | 99.200 | 81.300 | 93.850 | 06/2006 | 101.050 | 74.950 | 99.975 |
| 09/2000 | 93.950 | 54.875 | 65.550 | 09/2003 | 103.300 | 80.550 | 86.350 | 09/2006 | 100.350 | 74.000 | 92.025 |
| 12/2000 | 71.400 | 58.700 | 65.875 | 12/2003 | 93.400 | 82.525 | 86.475 | 12/2006 | 94.400 | 86.575 | 91.775 |
| 03/2001 | 95.000 | 63.775 | 94.350 | 03/2004 | 113.000 | 81.700 | 107.375 | 03/2007 | 108.800 | 87.900 | 100.400 |
| 06/2001 | 97.550 | 75.400 | 94.150 | 06/2004 | 126.000 | 100.600 | 116.275 | 06/2007 | 105.450 | 91.600 | 92.400 |
| 09/2001 | 103.000 | 74.375 | 74.475 | 09/2004 | 117.000 | 83.600 | 97.375 | 09/2007 | 94.800 | 68.900 | 89.675 |
| 12/2001 | 82.600 | 64.925 | 81.425 | 12/2004 | 103.150 | 92.650 | 94.250 | 12/2007 | 94.500 | 79.050 | 85.975 |
| 03/2002 | 83.000 | 73.450 | 75.825 | 03/2005 | 98.250 | 84.600 | 96.250 | 03/2008 | 99.500 | 67.500 | 67.500 |
| 06/2002 | 76.275 | 51.825 | 64.350 | 06/2005 | 97.300 | 56.300 | 56.500 | 06/2008 | 81.000 | 65.500 | 71.800 |
| 09/2002 | 80.600 | 53.050 | 76.775 | 09/2005 | 91.750 | 56.500 | 90.275 | 09/2008 | 100.225 | 60.700 | 93.750 |
| 12/2002 | 89.350 | 71.800 | 86.200 | 12/2005 | 98.400 | 81.800 | 82.150 | 12/2008 | 94.500 | 79.300 | 87.375 |

*Source: CME Group; Chicago Mercantile Exchange*

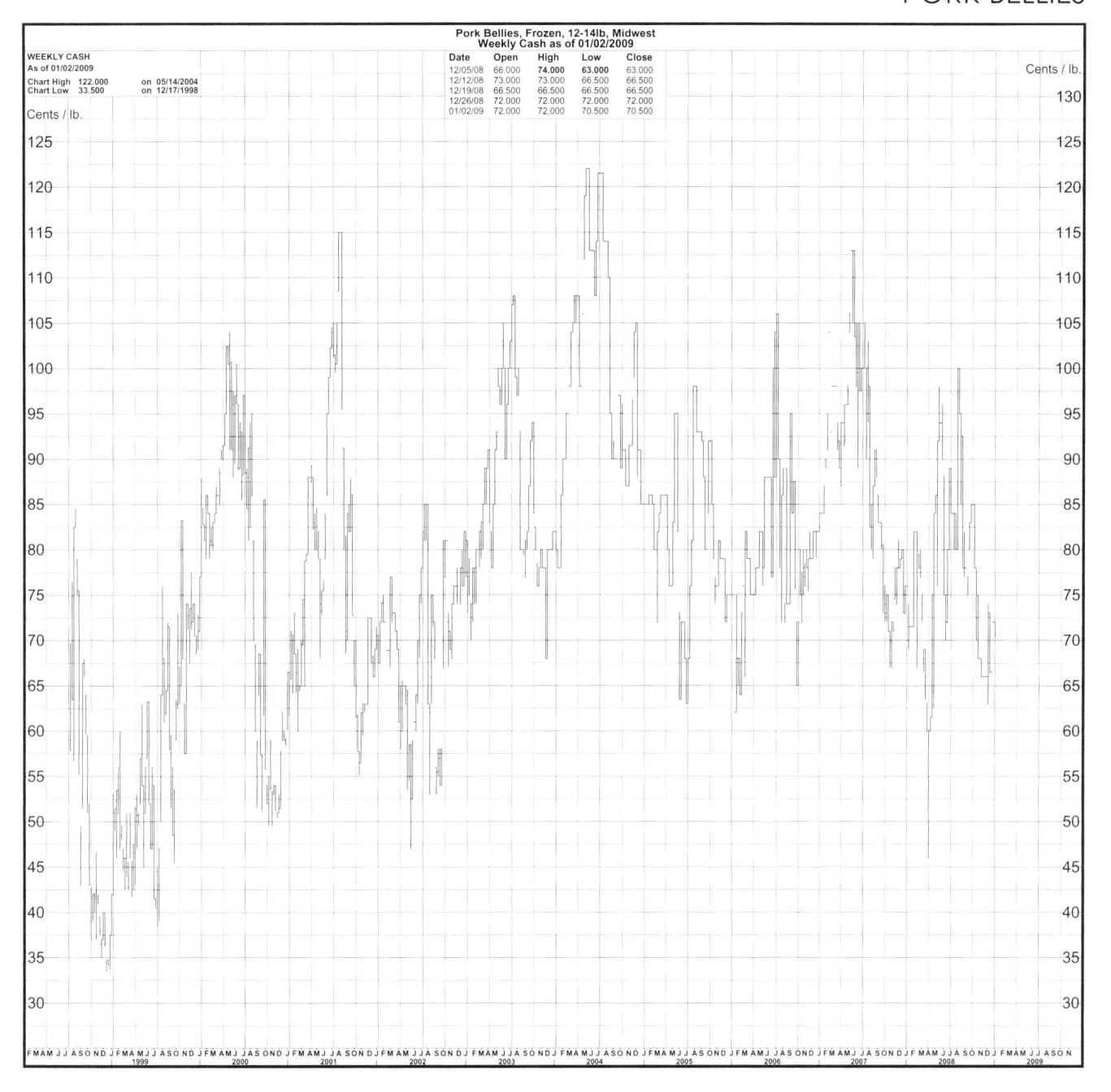

# PORK BELLIES

**Pork Bellies, Frozen, 12-14lb, Midwest**
Weekly Cash as of 01/02/2009

| Date | Open | High | Low | Close |
|---|---|---|---|---|
| 12/05/08 | 66.000 | 74.000 | 63.000 | 63.000 |
| 12/12/08 | 73.000 | 73.000 | 66.500 | 66.500 |
| 12/19/08 | 66.500 | 66.500 | 66.500 | 66.500 |
| 12/26/08 | 72.000 | 72.000 | 72.000 | 72.000 |
| 01/02/09 | 72.000 | 72.000 | 70.500 | 70.500 |

WEEKLY CASH As of 01/02/2009
Chart High 122.000 on 05/14/2004
Chart Low 33.500 on 12/17/1998

## Quarterly High, Low and Settle of Pork Bellies   In Cents per Pound

| Quarter | High | Low | Settle | Quarter | High | Low | Settle | Quarter | High | Low | Settle |
|---|---|---|---|---|---|---|---|---|---|---|---|
| 03/2000 | 89.00 | 71.00 | 88.50 | 03/2003 | 89.00 | 70.00 | 89.00 | 03/2006 | 82.00 | 62.00 | 75.00 |
| 06/2000 | 104.00 | 85.50 | 86.00 | 06/2003 | 105.00 | 78.00 | 100.00 | 06/2006 | 104.00 | 75.00 | 104.00 |
| 09/2000 | 97.00 | 51.25 | 85.50 | 09/2003 | 108.00 | 77.00 | 94.00 | 09/2006 | 106.00 | 65.00 | 65.00 |
| 12/2000 | 85.50 | 49.50 | 58.50 | 12/2003 | 94.00 | 68.00 | 82.00 | 12/2006 | 82.00 | 65.00 | 82.00 |
| 03/2001 | 88.00 | 60.00 | 88.00 | 03/2004 | 108.00 | 78.00 | 105.00 | 03/2007 | 104.00 | 82.00 | 89.00 |
| 06/2001 | 102.25 | 68.00 | 102.25 | 06/2004 | 122.00 | 98.00 | 121.50 | 06/2007 | 113.00 | 87.00 | 100.00 |
| 09/2001 | 115.00 | 68.50 | 72.75 | 09/2004 | 121.50 | 89.00 | 89.00 | 09/2007 | 105.00 | 73.00 | 73.00 |
| 12/2001 | 72.50 | 55.13 | 69.00 | 12/2004 | 105.00 | 85.00 | 85.00 | 12/2007 | 81.00 | 67.00 | 76.00 |
| 03/2002 | 77.00 | 67.00 | 69.00 | 03/2005 | 86.00 | 72.00 | 86.00 | 03/2008 | 82.00 | 46.00 | 46.00 |
| 06/2002 | 75.00 | 47.00 | 75.00 | 06/2005 | 95.00 | 63.00 | 63.00 | 06/2008 | 98.00 | 51.00 | 89.00 |
| 09/2002 | 85.00 | 53.00 | 67.00 | 09/2005 | 98.00 | 63.00 | 92.00 | 09/2008 | 100.00 | 75.00 | 85.00 |
| 12/2002 | 82.00 | 67.00 | 78.00 | 12/2005 | 92.00 | 72.00 | 75.00 | 12/2008 | 85.00 | 63.00 | 70.50 |

Midwest: 12-14 lb.   *Source: CME Group; Chicago Mercantile Exchange*

# HIDES

## Hides / Heavy Native Steers
### Monthly Cash as of 12/31/2008

| Date | Open | High | Low | Close |
|---|---|---|---|---|
| 08/29/08 | 86.88 | 88.25 | 86.88 | 86.88 |
| 09/30/08 | 86.88 | 86.88 | 84.25 | 84.75 |
| 10/31/08 | 86.13 | 86.88 | 81.75 | 81.75 |
| 11/28/08 | 81.75 | 82.50 | 64.50 | 64.50 |
| 12/31/08 | 64.50 | 64.50 | 40.75 | 42.00 |

Monthly Cash as of 12/31/2008
Chart High 112.50 on 04/23/2001
Chart Low 8.25 on 02/08/1968

## Annual High, Low and Settle of Hides    In Cents per Pound

| Year | High | Low | Settle | Year | High | Low | Settle | Year | High | Low | Settle |
|---|---|---|---|---|---|---|---|---|---|---|---|
| 1967 | 13.25 | 9.25 | 10.00 | 1981 | 50.25 | 40.00 | 41.00 | 1995 | 103.00 | 72.00 | 72.00 |
| 1968 | 13.25 | 8.25 | 11.25 | 1982 | 47.00 | 37.00 | 37.00 | 1996 | 104.00 | 72.00 | 91.00 |
| 1969 | 18.75 | 10.75 | 12.50 | 1983 | 62.00 | 36.50 | 54.50 | 1997 | 103.50 | 77.00 | 78.50 |
| 1970 | 14.50 | 10.00 | 10.00 | 1984 | 71.00 | 46.00 | 46.00 | 1998 | 87.75 | 65.50 | 69.25 |
| 1971 | 18.00 | 10.00 | 17.00 | 1985 | 65.00 | 41.00 | 59.50 | 1999 | 81.50 | 63.00 | 77.00 |
| 1972 | 45.50 | 17.00 | 33.00 | 1986 | 71.00 | 56.00 | 61.00 | 2000 | 88.50 | 73.37 | 86.25 |
| 1973 | 40.00 | 26.00 | 26.00 | 1987 | 91.50 | 61.00 | 82.00 | 2001 | 112.50 | 66.00 | 68.00 |
| 1974 | 29.00 | 11.50 | 11.50 | 1988 | 100.00 | 75.00 | 78.00 | 2002 | 89.00 | 64.50 | 84.50 |
| 1975 | 31.50 | 10.50 | 26.50 | 1989 | 102.00 | 78.00 | 90.00 | 2003 | 90.00 | 75.13 | 86.25 |
| 1976 | 41.00 | 26.50 | 33.00 | 1990 | 102.00 | 82.00 | 85.00 | 2004 | 87.63 | 73.50 | 78.00 |
| 1977 | 42.00 | 32.00 | 38.00 | 1991 | 90.00 | 70.00 | 70.00 | 2005 | 84.13 | 75.25 | 78.63 |
| 1978 | 60.00 | 34.00 | 53.50 | 1992 | 83.00 | 67.00 | 79.00 | 2006 | 91.63 | 78.13 | 91.63 |
| 1979 | 97.00 | 53.00 | 57.00 | 1993 | 83.00 | 74.00 | 78.50 | 2007 | 99.88 | 80.38 | 82.25 |
| 1980 | 63.00 | 32.00 | 44.00 | 1994 | 96.00 | 72.00 | 90.25 | 2008 | 90.75 | 40.75 | 42.00 |

Heavy Native Steers.    Source: U.S. Department of Agriculture

# HIDES

```
Hides / Heavy Native Steers
Weekly Cash as of 01/02/2009
WEEKLY CASH
As of 01/02/2009
Chart High  112.50   on 04/23/2001
Chart Low    40.75   on 12/04/2008
Cents / lb.

Date       Open    High    Low    Close
12/05/08   64.50   64.50   40.75  40.75
12/12/08   40.75   40.75   40.75  40.75
12/19/08   40.75   43.25   40.75  43.25
12/26/08   43.75   43.75   43.25  43.25
01/02/09   43.25   43.25   42.00  42.00
```

## Quarterly High, Low and Settle of Hides   In Cents per Pound

| Quarter | High | Low | Settle | Quarter | High | Low | Settle | Quarter | High | Low | Settle |
|---|---|---|---|---|---|---|---|---|---|---|---|
| 03/2000 | 79.25 | 74.25 | 79.25 | 03/2003 | 88.38 | 81.00 | 84.50 | 03/2006 | 86.50 | 78.13 | 83.00 |
| 06/2000 | 81.75 | 73.50 | 76.00 | 06/2003 | 88.50 | 75.13 | 80.75 | 06/2006 | 89.75 | 82.75 | 88.25 |
| 09/2000 | 88.50 | 73.37 | 88.50 | 09/2003 | 90.00 | 80.00 | 85.25 | 09/2006 | 89.50 | 84.50 | 89.25 |
| 12/2000 | 88.50 | 82.00 | 86.25 | 12/2003 | 87.75 | 84.25 | 86.25 | 12/2006 | 91.63 | 86.75 | 91.63 |
| 03/2001 | 97.50 | 79.75 | 97.50 | 03/2004 | 87.63 | 78.88 | 82.38 | 03/2007 | 98.13 | 91.00 | 97.75 |
| 06/2001 | 112.50 | 90.25 | 95.87 | 06/2004 | 84.50 | 78.25 | 83.75 | 06/2007 | 99.88 | 88.25 | 89.75 |
| 09/2001 | 97.50 | 71.25 | 71.25 | 09/2004 | 86.63 | 82.50 | 85.75 | 09/2007 | 89.75 | 84.50 | 86.50 |
| 12/2001 | 74.50 | 66.00 | 68.00 | 12/2004 | 83.88 | 73.50 | 78.00 | 12/2007 | 86.50 | 80.38 | 82.25 |
| 03/2002 | 84.25 | 64.50 | 84.25 | 03/2005 | 81.75 | 75.25 | 80.88 | 03/2008 | 84.50 | 77.38 | 83.75 |
| 06/2002 | 88.50 | 80.50 | 84.25 | 06/2005 | 84.13 | 77.75 | 81.00 | 06/2008 | 90.75 | 82.25 | 86.25 |
| 09/2002 | 87.13 | 83.25 | 87.13 | 09/2005 | 83.75 | 79.25 | 80.75 | 09/2008 | 89.13 | 84.25 | 84.75 |
| 12/2002 | 89.00 | 76.00 | 84.50 | 12/2005 | 82.00 | 78.63 | 78.63 | 12/2008 | 86.88 | 40.75 | 42.00 |

Heavy Native Steers.   *Source: U.S. Department of Agriculture*

# TALLOW

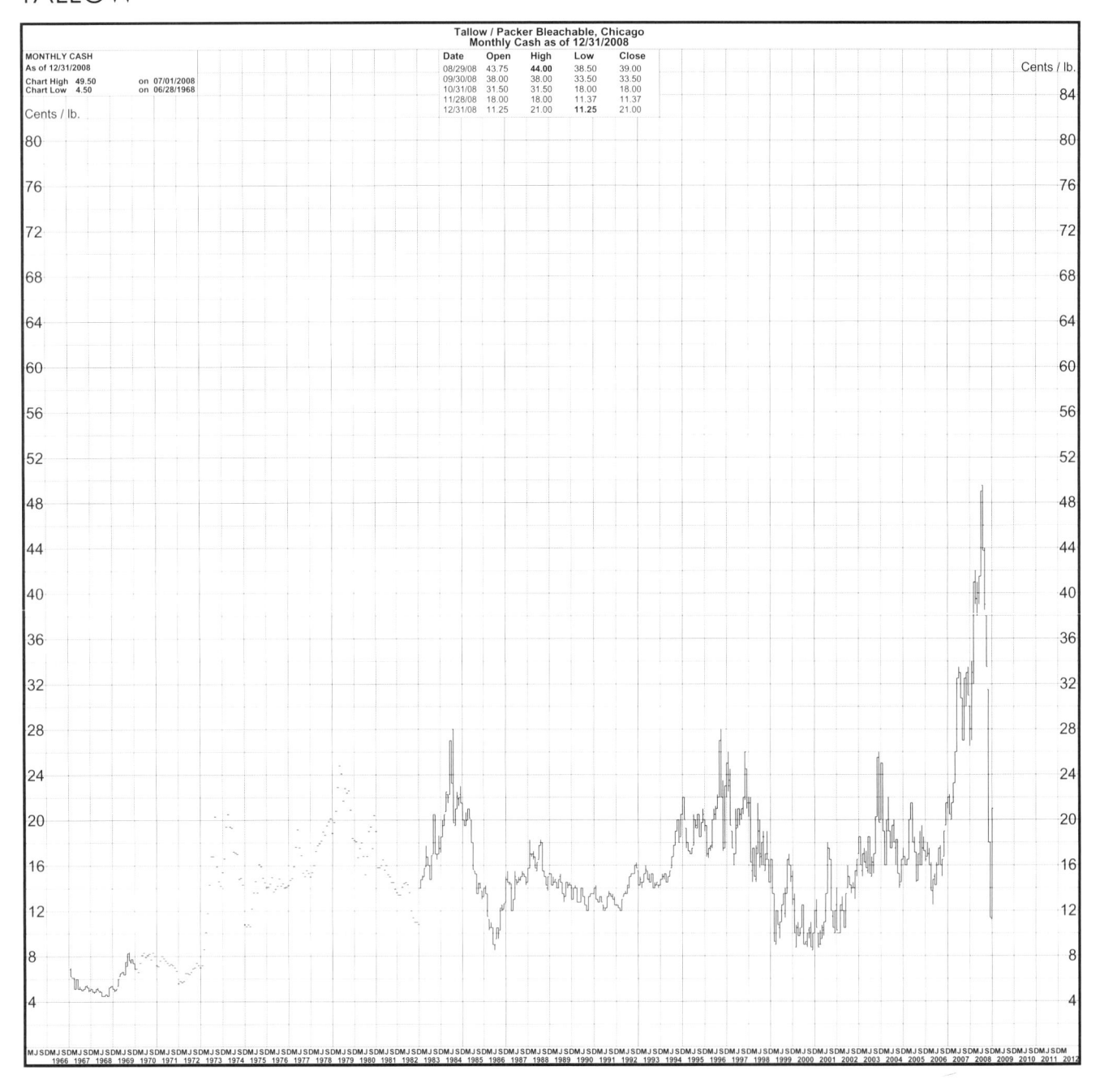

**Tallow / Packer Bleachable, Chicago**
Monthly Cash as of 12/31/2008

| Date | Open | High | Low | Close |
|---|---|---|---|---|
| 08/29/08 | 43.75 | 44.00 | 38.50 | 39.00 |
| 09/30/08 | 38.00 | 38.00 | 33.50 | 33.50 |
| 10/31/08 | 31.50 | 31.50 | 18.00 | 18.00 |
| 11/28/08 | 18.00 | 18.00 | 11.37 | 11.37 |
| 12/31/08 | 11.25 | 21.00 | 11.25 | 21.00 |

MONTHLY CASH As of 12/31/2008
Chart High 49.50 on 07/01/2008
Chart Low 4.50 on 06/28/1968

## Annual High, Low and Settle of Tallow   In Cents per Pound

| Year | High | Low | Settle | Year | High | Low | Settle | Year | High | Low | Settle |
|---|---|---|---|---|---|---|---|---|---|---|---|
| 1967 | 7.00 | 4.88 | 5.13 | 1981 | 16.50 | 13.60 | 13.60 | 1995 | 22.00 | 17.00 | 19.50 |
| 1968 | 5.38 | 4.50 | 5.13 | 1982 | 14.50 | 10.80 | 10.80 | 1996 | 28.00 | 16.63 | 25.00 |
| 1969 | 8.38 | 4.88 | 6.88 | 1983 | 20.50 | 14.00 | 18.50 | 1997 | 26.00 | 16.00 | 21.50 |
| 1970 | 8.30 | 6.60 | 7.20 | 1984 | 28.00 | 18.50 | 20.00 | 1998 | 22.00 | 14.50 | 16.50 |
| 1971 | 8.00 | 5.60 | 5.60 | 1985 | 21.00 | 13.00 | 14.00 | 1999 | 17.00 | 9.00 | 13.00 |
| 1972 | 7.40 | 5.70 | 7.00 | 1986 | 15.00 | 8.50 | 14.75 | 2000 | 13.50 | 8.50 | 12.00 |
| 1973 | 20.30 | 7.20 | 15.40 | 1987 | 15.75 | 12.00 | 15.75 | 2001 | 18.00 | 8.75 | 10.25 |
| 1974 | 20.50 | 10.80 | 10.80 | 1988 | 18.25 | 13.75 | 15.25 | 2002 | 18.50 | 10.00 | 18.50 |
| 1975 | 16.10 | 10.60 | 14.10 | 1989 | 15.25 | 12.75 | 13.00 | 2003 | 26.00 | 15.00 | 25.00 |
| 1976 | 14.95 | 13.69 | 14.25 | 1990 | 14.25 | 12.00 | 14.00 | 2004 | 25.00 | 14.00 | 16.75 |
| 1977 | 19.15 | 14.70 | 15.00 | 1991 | 14.25 | 12.00 | 12.50 | 2005 | 21.50 | 14.50 | 16.50 |
| 1978 | 20.12 | 15.38 | 18.83 | 1992 | 16.25 | 12.00 | 14.25 | 2006 | 22.00 | 12.50 | 22.00 |
| 1979 | 24.80 | 18.20 | 18.20 | 1993 | 16.00 | 14.00 | 14.75 | 2007 | 33.50 | 20.00 | 28.00 |
| 1980 | 20.40 | 15.20 | 19.00 | 1994 | 22.00 | 14.50 | 22.00 | 2008 | 49.50 | 11.25 | 21.00 |

Bleachable.   *Source: U.S. Department of Agriculture*

# TALLOW

## Tallow / Packer Bleachable, Chicago
Weekly Cash as of 01/02/2009

| Date | Open | High | Low | Close |
|---|---|---|---|---|
| 12/05/08 | 11.25 | 11.25 | 11.25 | 11.25 |
| 12/12/08 | 11.25 | 11.25 | 11.25 | 11.25 |
| 12/19/08 | 11.75 | 14.50 | 11.75 | 14.50 |
| 12/26/08 | 18.37 | 18.37 | 18.25 | 18.25 |
| 01/02/09 | 18.75 | 21.00 | 18.75 | 21.00 |

WEEKLY CASH As of 01/02/2009
Chart High 49.50 on 07/01/2008
Chart Low 8.50 on 11/01/2000

## Quarterly High, Low and Settle of Tallow     In Cents per Pound

| Quarter | High | Low | Settle | Quarter | High | Low | Settle | Quarter | High | Low | Settle |
|---|---|---|---|---|---|---|---|---|---|---|---|
| 03/2000 | 13.50 | 8.75 | 9.75 | 03/2003 | 18.50 | 15.00 | 16.25 | 03/2006 | 18.00 | 13.75 | 13.75 |
| 06/2000 | 12.50 | 9.00 | 9.00 | 06/2003 | 18.50 | 15.25 | 15.25 | 06/2006 | 16.25 | 12.50 | 16.00 |
| 09/2000 | 10.50 | 8.75 | 10.50 | 09/2003 | 20.25 | 15.00 | 20.25 | 09/2006 | 17.75 | 15.00 | 16.50 |
| 12/2000 | 12.00 | 8.50 | 12.00 | 12/2003 | 26.00 | 19.75 | 25.00 | 12/2006 | 22.00 | 16.75 | 22.00 |
| 03/2001 | 13.00 | 8.75 | 9.00 | 03/2004 | 25.00 | 16.00 | 19.00 | 03/2007 | 23.25 | 20.00 | 23.25 |
| 06/2001 | 13.50 | 9.50 | 13.50 | 06/2004 | 22.00 | 17.50 | 19.50 | 06/2007 | 33.50 | 23.25 | 33.00 |
| 09/2001 | 18.00 | 12.00 | 12.00 | 09/2004 | 20.00 | 15.25 | 15.25 | 09/2007 | 33.00 | 27.00 | 32.50 |
| 12/2001 | 14.00 | 10.00 | 10.25 | 12/2004 | 17.50 | 14.00 | 16.75 | 12/2007 | 33.50 | 26.50 | 28.00 |
| 03/2002 | 13.25 | 10.00 | 12.00 | 03/2005 | 20.00 | 16.00 | 20.00 | 03/2008 | 42.00 | 27.00 | 39.50 |
| 06/2002 | 16.00 | 10.50 | 15.00 | 06/2005 | 21.50 | 17.13 | 17.13 | 06/2008 | 49.00 | 38.00 | 49.00 |
| 09/2002 | 15.00 | 13.50 | 14.00 | 09/2005 | 19.00 | 14.50 | 16.00 | 09/2008 | 49.50 | 33.50 | 33.50 |
| 12/2002 | 18.50 | 13.00 | 18.50 | 12/2005 | 19.50 | 16.00 | 16.50 | 12/2008 | 31.50 | 11.25 | 21.00 |

Bleachable.    *Source: U.S. Department of Agriculture*

# METALS

## Gold

### Gold and Silver—Current Outlook

During the global financial crisis that emerged in force in late 2008, gold regained some of its luster as a safe haven during times of crisis. Market participants during late 2008 and early 2009 were not enamored of any paper currencies. Currencies in the emerging world plunged as investors withdrew investments from vulnerable emerging markets.

The dollar only showed strength in late 2008 because of demand for emergency dollar liquidity, not because of any fundamental belief in the US economy or monetary policy. The safest alternative in that environment was gold and gold was able to regain some strength in early 2009 and overcome about two-thirds of the sharp downward correction seen during March-October 2008.

**Gold prices during Bretton Woods (1945-71)**

During the Bretton Woods period of 1945-1971, gold was fixed at about $35 per ounce. Bretton Woods was the global currency management system that fixed global currencies in terms of the dollar and also fixed gold in terms of the dollar at $35 per ounce. However, President Nixon on August 15, 1971 announced that the US government would no longer convert dollars into gold.

That was the end of the Bretton Woods system and currency rates and gold prices have since floated freely.

**Gold soars in the 1970s**

After Bretton Woods broke down and gold started to trade freely, gold prices started to rally sharply. Gold prices were driven higher mainly by the sharp inflation pressures that emerged from (1) deficit spending for President Johnson's Great Society and the Vietnam war in the 1960s and early 1970s, (2) the oil spike in 1973 tied to the Arab oil embargo, and (3) monetary mismanagement by the Federal Reserve. The Fed at that time used interest rate targeting and refused to raise interest rates fast enough to curb inflation, trying to avoid a recession. But in the end, the Fed did more harm than good by waiting to curb inflation.

US inflation finally peaked at +14.8% yr/yr in March 1980, shortly after Paul Volcker took over from G. William Miller as Fed Chairman and started clamping down on the money supply. By no coincidence, gold peaked at roughly the same time in January 1980 at $850 (London PM gold fix) and then started a steep descent.

**Gold moves lower during the 1980s and 1990s**

Fed Chairman Volcker's stiff monetarist medicine took a toll on both the US economy and gold prices. The US economy experienced a double-dip recession in 1980 and 1981-82. Gold sold off sharply during that time as the double-dip recessions caused inflation to fall and undercut demand for gold. Gold was also undercut in the first half of the 1980s by the sharp rally in the dollar.

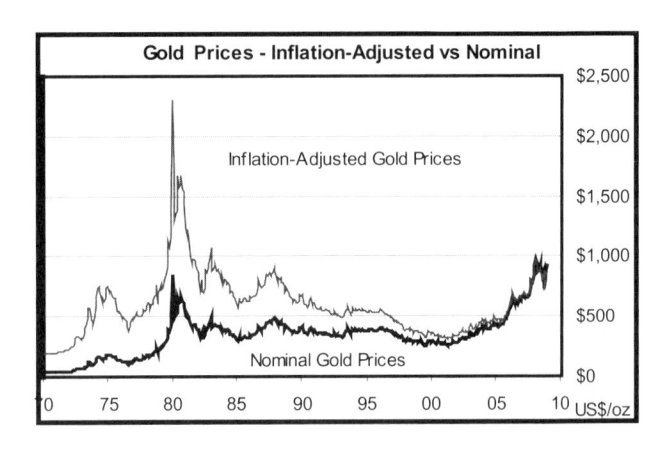

During the latter-half of the 1980s and the first half of the 1990s, gold was relatively stable and traded in the range of $300-500 per ounce. However, gold on an inflation-adjusted basis moved steadily lower from the early 1980s all the way until 2001. On an inflation-adjusted basis (in 2008 dollars), gold fell from the peak of $2,304 in January 1980, to $573 in 1990, and then to a 35-year low of $309 in 2001.

Gold was also pressured over this time frame by heavy selling by central banks. Central banks started selling gold due to increased trust in paper currencies and the high cost of holding gold reserves. In fact, according to the World Gold Council, the world's central banks as a whole have slashed their ownership of gold by 22% from a peak of 38,300 metric tons in 1965 to the current level of 29,697 metric tons, which is the lowest level since about 1950. During the disinflationary 1980s and 1990s, the heavy selling by central banks forced gold prices lower. However, more recently, the strong demand seen in the marketplace has been able to absorb continued central bank selling.

The plunge in inflation-adjusted gold prices from 1980 through 2001 demoralized gold investors, and more importantly, mining companies. Gold mining almost doubled during the 1980s, but was then largely stagnant after 1990. Mining companies refused to invest the large amount of capital needed to open new mines because of low prices and rising mining expenses. Thus, by the time demand started to reemerge in 2001, mining companies were caught flat-footed without the ability to boost supply to take advantage of higher prices.

**2001-08 bull market**

Gold prices more tripled in value from 2001 through

2008. Gold futures prices traded as low as $255.00 per ounce in early 2001, but then entered a steady rally up to $1,033.90 per ounce by March 2008. That rally was driven mainly by the 42% plunge in the US dollar index over that time frame. The plunge in the dollar increased the value of real assets such as gold in terms of the depreciated currency. The rally in gold was also driven by stagnant annual gold mine production from 2000 through 2008 near 2,500 metric tons.

Gold prices were driven higher from 2005 through 2008 by the continued decline in the dollar and by strong investment demand and speculative buying. Gold demand in 2007 hit a record $78.55 billion, according to the World Gold Council. In 2007, investment demand rose +15%, jewelry demand rose +20%, and net inflows into ETF funds totaled 253 metric tons ($5.8 billion). Strong investment demand stemmed from both speculative fever and from inflation fears in light of sharply higher crude oil prices.

Gold futures prices hit a record high of $1,033.90 in March 2008, exceeding the previous record high of $850.00 seen on January 21, 1980 (London gold PM fix). However, on an inflation-adjusted basis, the nominal peak seen in 2008 of $1033.90 was less than half the peak of $2,304 seen in January 1980 (in 2008 dollars).

After peaking in March 2008, gold prices then plunged by 34% through the remainder of 2008, posting a 1-1/3 year low of $681 in October 2008. That sell-off was driven by the emerging global recession, the banking crisis, and heavy long liquidation pressure by speculators. Gold prices were also pushed lower by the sharp rally in the dollar that emerged in the wake of the banking crisis in mid-September as investors scrambled for dollar liquidity. However, gold prices were then able to recover to the $900 area by January 2009 due to general mistrust of paper currencies and concerns that the cost of the massive bailout plans implemented by the US and European governments would eventually prove to be inflationary.

### Silver

Silver, like gold, has also been a store of value and a medium of exchange for thousands of years. However, silver has more importance as a metal for use in photography and industrial applications. Data from the Silver Institute for 2004 shows that the bulk of silver supply goes to industrial applications (367 million ounces), photography (181 million ounces), and jewelry and silverware (248 million ounces). Only 41 million ounces goes for silver coins and medals, and another 41 million ounces for implied net investment. Silver therefore trades not only as a precious metal, but also as an industrial metal. The strength of the world economy and industrial demand is therefore an important demand driver for silver prices.

Silver prices in January 1980 posted their all-time record high of $48.00 per ounce (NY daily close), which was equivalent to $130 per ounce in current 2008 dollars (using the Dec-2008 CPI as the base to deflate the silver series). Silver was driven to that record high in 1980 by the same inflation-driven fundamentals that caused the surge in gold prices.

However, silver was also pushed sharply higher by Nelson Bunker Hunt's infamous attempt to corner the silver market. The Hunt family and a group of wealthy Arabs in 1973 started amassing more than 200 million ounces of silver, amounting to about one-half of the world's deliverable supply. However, the silver market then crashed when the New York Metals Exchange changed its trading rules and the Federal Reserve intervened. Nelson Bunker Hunt eventually filed for bankruptcy and was convicted of manipulating the markets.

Silver prices traded on a generally depressed note in the 1980s and 1990s due to the Federal Reserve's generally successful anti-inflation policy and a steady increase in silver mining output. Starting in 2004, silver became caught up in the general commodity bull market and started to rally. Silver futures prices more than tripled from the 2003 close of $5.965 per ounce to the 28-year high of $21.185 in March 2008. That rally was driven by investor demand for silver and also by industrial demand for silver from rapidly-developing countries such as China. Barclays came out with the first exchange-traded fund (ETF) holding silver in 2006. By early 2009, Barclay's iShares Silver Trust was one of many silver ETFs and the Barclay's ETF alone had $3.2 billion of assets under management.

Silver prices in late 2008 plunged by 60% as the commodity markets corrected downward on the global financial crisis. However, silver prices were able to recover by more than $4 per ounce in early 2009 to the $13 area due to crisis demand for precious metals. Looking forward, silver in coming years should see revived industrial demand when the global recession is over, thus providing firm underpinning for silver prices.

# ALUMINUM

**MONTHLY SELECTED FUTURES**
As of 12/31/2008
Chart High 1.5000 on 07/11/2008
Chart Low .2450 on 12/01/1966
CONTRACT SIZE 44,000 pounds
MIN TICK .05 cents
VALUE 20 USD / contract
EACH GRID 0.01 cents
VALUE 4 USD / contract
DAILY LIMIT 20 cents
VALUE 8,000 USD / contract
TRADING HOURS
6:00p-5:15p / 7:50a-1:15p ET

**ALUMINUM - COMEX**
Monthly Selected Futures as of 12/31/2008

| Date | Open | High | Low | Close |
|---|---|---|---|---|
| 08/31/08 | 1.3400 | 1.3400 | 1.2375 | 1.2375 |
| 09/30/08 | 1.2300 | 1.2300 | 1.1225 | 1.1225 |
| 10/31/08 | 1.1175 | 1.1175 | .9100 | .9425 |
| 11/30/08 | .9500 | .9750 | .8110 | .8135 |
| 12/31/08 | .7985 | .7985 | .6785 | .7280 |

### Annual High, Low and Settle of Aluminum    In USD per Pound

| Year | High | Low | Settle | Year | High | Low | Settle | Year | High | Low | Settle |
|---|---|---|---|---|---|---|---|---|---|---|---|
| 1925 | .2800 | .2700 | .2800 | 1939 | .2000 | .2000 | .2000 | 1953 | .2150 | .2000 | .2150 |
| 1926 | .2700 | .2685 | .2685 | 1940 | .2000 | .1700 | .1700 | 1954 | .2220 | .2150 | .2220 |
| 1927 | .2637 | .2426 | .2426 | 1941 | .1700 | .1500 | .1500 | 1955 | .2442 | .2220 | .2440 |
| 1928 | .2390 | .2390 | .2390 | 1942 | .1500 | .1500 | .1500 | 1956 | .2710 | .2440 | .2710 |
| 1929 | .2390 | .2390 | .2390 | 1943 | .1500 | .1500 | .1500 | 1957 | .2710 | .2600 | .2600 |
| 1930 | .2430 | .2330 | .2330 | 1944 | .1500 | .1500 | .1500 | 1958 | .2600 | .2400 | .2470 |
| 1931 | .2330 | .2330 | .2330 | 1945 | .1500 | .1500 | .1500 | 1959 | .2600 | .2470 | .2600 |
| 1932 | .2330 | .2330 | .2330 | 1946 | .1500 | .1500 | .1500 | 1960 | .2600 | .2600 | .2600 |
| 1933 | .2330 | .2330 | .2330 | 1947 | .1500 | .1500 | .1500 | 1961 | .2600 | .2400 | .2400 |
| 1934 | .2330 | .2050 | .2050 | 1948 | ---- | ---- | ---- | 1962 | .2400 | .2250 | .2250 |
| 1935 | .2050 | .2050 | .2050 | 1949 | ---- | ---- | ---- | 1963 | .2300 | .2250 | .2300 |
| 1936 | .2050 | .2050 | .2050 | 1950 | ---- | ---- | ---- | 1964 | .2450 | .2300 | .2450 |
| 1937 | .2050 | .2000 | .2000 | 1951 | .1900 | .1900 | .1900 | 1965 | .2450 | .2450 | .2450 |
| 1938 | .2000 | .2000 | .2000 | 1952 | .2000 | .1900 | .2000 | 1966 | .2450 | .2450 | .2450 |

Data continued on page 337.    Source: CME Group; New York Mercantile Exchange

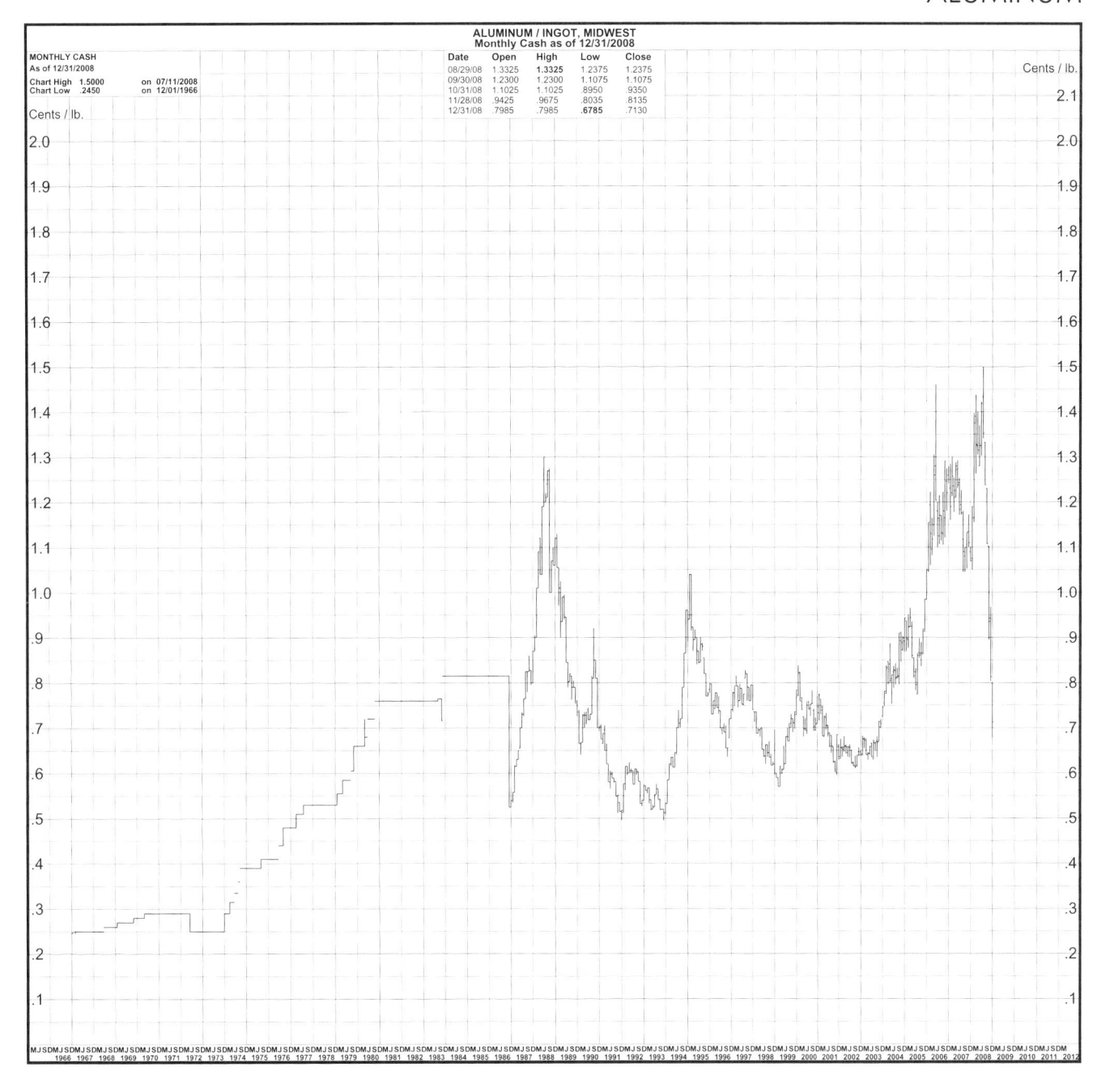

# ALUMINUM

**ALUMINUM / INGOT, MIDWEST**
Monthly Cash as of 12/31/2008

| Date | Open | High | Low | Close |
|---|---|---|---|---|
| 08/29/08 | 1.3325 | **1.3325** | 1.2375 | 1.2375 |
| 09/30/08 | 1.2300 | 1.2300 | 1.1075 | 1.1075 |
| 10/31/08 | 1.1025 | 1.1025 | .8950 | .9350 |
| 11/28/08 | .9425 | .9675 | .8035 | .8135 |
| 12/31/08 | .7985 | .7985 | **.6785** | .7130 |

MONTHLY CASH
As of 12/31/2008
Chart High 1.5000 on 07/11/2008
Chart Low .2450 on 12/01/1966

## Annual High, Low and Settle of Aluminum — In USD per Pound

| Year | High | Low | Settle | Year | High | Low | Settle | Year | High | Low | Settle |
|---|---|---|---|---|---|---|---|---|---|---|---|
| 1967 | .2500 | .2450 | .2500 | 1981 | .7600 | .7600 | .7600 | 1995 | 1.0400 | .7700 | .7975 |
| 1968 | .2600 | .2500 | .2600 | 1982 | .7600 | .7600 | .7600 | 1996 | .7975 | .6350 | .7400 |
| 1969 | .2800 | .2600 | .2800 | 1983 | .8150 | .7160 | .8150 | 1997 | .8275 | .7350 | .7400 |
| 1970 | .2900 | .2800 | .2900 | 1984 | .8150 | .8150 | .8150 | 1998 | .7350 | .5950 | .6000 |
| 1971 | .2900 | .2900 | .2900 | 1985 | .8150 | .8150 | .8150 | 1999 | .7835 | .5700 | .7835 |
| 1972 | .2900 | .2500 | .2500 | 1986 | .8150 | .5250 | .5400 | 2000 | .8385 | .6800 | .7465 |
| 1973 | .2900 | .2500 | .2900 | 1987 | .8700 | .5350 | .8700 | 2001 | .7760 | .5955 | .6365 |
| 1974 | .3900 | .2900 | .3900 | 1988 | 1.3000 | .8700 | 1.1200 | 2002 | .6815 | .6110 | .6390 |
| 1975 | .4100 | .3900 | .4100 | 1989 | 1.1300 | .7250 | .7350 | 2003 | .7470 | .6290 | .7460 |
| 1976 | .4800 | .4100 | .4800 | 1990 | .9200 | .6400 | .7025 | 2004 | .9425 | .7475 | .9425 |
| 1977 | .5300 | .4800 | .5300 | 1991 | .7075 | .4963 | .5175 | 2005 | 1.0510 | .7750 | 1.0510 |
| 1978 | .5300 | .5300 | .5300 | 1992 | .6225 | .5125 | .5713 | 2006 | 1.4600 | 1.0450 | 1.2500 |
| 1979 | .6600 | .5300 | .6600 | 1993 | .5763 | .4950 | .5325 | 2007 | 1.3000 | 1.0450 | 1.0700 |
| 1980 | .7600 | .6600 | .7600 | 1994 | .9600 | .5325 | .9400 | 2008 | 1.5000 | .6785 | .7130 |

Data continued from page 336.    *Source: CME Group; New York Mercantile Exchange*

337

# ALUMINUM

**ALUMINUM - COMEX**
Weekly Selected Futures as of 01/02/2009

| Date | Open | High | Low | Close |
|---|---|---|---|---|
| 12/05/08 | .7985 | **.7985** | .6910 | .6910 |
| 12/12/08 | .6960 | .7210 | .6910 | .6910 |
| 12/19/08 | .6785 | .6985 | **.6785** | .6985 |
| 12/26/08 | .7160 | .7160 | .7110 | .7110 |
| 01/02/09 | .6985 | .7455 | .6985 | .7455 |

**WEEKLY SELECTED FUTURES**
As of 01/02/2009
Chart High 1.5000 on 07/11/2008
Chart Low .5700 on 02/26/1999
CONTRACT SIZE 44,000 pounds
MIN TICK .05 cents
VALUE 20 USD / contract
EACH GRID 0.005 cents
VALUE 2 USD / contract
DAILY LIMIT 20 cents
VALUE 8,000 USD / contract
TRADING HOURS
6:00p-5:15p / 7:50a-1:15p ET

## Quarterly High, Low and Settle of Aluminum Futures    In USD per Pound

| Quarter | High | Low | Settle | Quarter | High | Low | Settle | Quarter | High | Low | Settle |
|---|---|---|---|---|---|---|---|---|---|---|---|
| 03/2000 | .8375 | .7350 | .7350 | 03/2003 | .6840 | .6385 | .6410 | 03/2006 | 1.2290 | 1.0500 | 1.1250 |
| 06/2000 | .7590 | .6825 | .7500 | 06/2003 | .6680 | .6280 | .6355 | 06/2006 | 1.4600 | 1.1100 | 1.1640 |
| 09/2000 | .7835 | .7285 | .7580 | 09/2003 | .6815 | .6310 | .6705 | 09/2006 | 1.2350 | 1.1055 | 1.1935 |
| 12/2000 | .7695 | .6950 | .7460 | 12/2003 | .7540 | .6730 | .7490 | 12/2006 | 1.3000 | 1.1370 | 1.2500 |
| 03/2001 | .7760 | .6860 | .6860 | 03/2004 | .8465 | .7510 | .8270 | 03/2007 | 1.3000 | 1.1600 | 1.2310 |
| 06/2001 | .7325 | .6805 | .6865 | 06/2004 | .8880 | .7530 | .8280 | 06/2007 | 1.2925 | 1.1735 | 1.1835 |
| 09/2001 | .6890 | .6220 | .6310 | 09/2004 | .8950 | .7960 | .8950 | 09/2007 | 1.2265 | 1.0450 | 1.1150 |
| 12/2001 | .6850 | .5960 | .6395 | 12/2004 | .9470 | .8350 | .9470 | 12/2007 | 1.1800 | 1.0675 | 1.0700 |
| 03/2002 | .6965 | .6330 | .6620 | 03/2005 | .9700 | .8725 | .9420 | 03/2008 | 1.4375 | 1.0500 | 1.3275 |
| 06/2002 | .6690 | .6345 | .6560 | 06/2005 | .9430 | .7900 | .7955 | 06/2008 | 1.4300 | 1.2800 | 1.4180 |
| 09/2002 | .6515 | .6110 | .6160 | 09/2005 | .9010 | .7750 | .8730 | 09/2008 | 1.5000 | 1.1225 | 1.1225 |
| 12/2002 | .6615 | .6150 | .6420 | 12/2005 | 1.0595 | .8700 | 1.0595 | 12/2008 | 1.1175 | .6785 | .7280 |

*CME Group; New York Mercantile Exchange*

# ALUMINUM

**ALUMINUM / INGOT, MIDWEST**
Weekly Cash as of 01/02/2009

| Date | Open | High | Low | Close |
|---|---|---|---|---|
| 12/05/08 | .7985 | .7985 | .6910 | .6910 |
| 12/12/08 | .6960 | .7210 | .6910 | .6910 |
| 12/19/08 | .6785 | .6985 | .6785 | .6985 |
| 12/26/08 | .7160 | .7160 | .7110 | .7110 |
| 01/02/09 | .6985 | .7305 | .6860 | .7305 |

WEEKLY CASH
As of 01/02/2009
Chart High 1.5000 on 07/11/2008
Chart Low .5700 on 02/26/1999
Cents / lb.

## Quarterly High, Low and Settle of Aluminum — In USD per Pound

| Quarter | High | Low | Settle | Quarter | High | Low | Settle | Quarter | High | Low | Settle |
|---|---|---|---|---|---|---|---|---|---|---|---|
| 03/2000 | .8385 | .7395 | .7395 | 03/2003 | .6825 | .6380 | .6405 | 03/2006 | 1.2225 | 1.0450 | 1.1180 |
| 06/2000 | .7580 | .6800 | .7500 | 06/2003 | .6660 | .6290 | .6355 | 06/2006 | 1.4600 | 1.1000 | 1.1640 |
| 09/2000 | .7835 | .7260 | .7540 | 09/2003 | .6810 | .6310 | .6675 | 09/2006 | 1.2225 | 1.1055 | 1.1800 |
| 12/2000 | .7695 | .6920 | .7465 | 12/2003 | .7470 | .6695 | .7460 | 12/2006 | 1.2910 | 1.1210 | 1.2500 |
| 03/2001 | .7760 | .6820 | .6820 | 03/2004 | .8465 | .7475 | .8000 | 03/2007 | 1.3000 | 1.1600 | 1.2250 |
| 06/2001 | .7325 | .6805 | .6865 | 06/2004 | .8865 | .7530 | .8280 | 06/2007 | 1.2925 | 1.1715 | 1.1835 |
| 09/2001 | .6890 | .6220 | .6250 | 09/2004 | .9095 | .7960 | .9095 | 09/2007 | 1.2265 | 1.0450 | 1.1000 |
| 12/2001 | .6850 | .5955 | .6365 | 12/2004 | .9425 | .8460 | .9425 | 12/2007 | 1.1725 | 1.0525 | 1.0700 |
| 03/2002 | .6815 | .6320 | .6600 | 03/2005 | .9655 | .8685 | .9440 | 03/2008 | 1.4375 | 1.0500 | 1.3275 |
| 06/2002 | .6630 | .6340 | .6560 | 06/2005 | .9350 | .7830 | .7955 | 06/2008 | 1.4225 | 1.2800 | 1.4180 |
| 09/2002 | .6515 | .6110 | .6130 | 09/2005 | .8980 | .7750 | .8660 | 09/2008 | 1.5000 | 1.1075 | 1.1075 |
| 12/2002 | .6570 | .6140 | .6390 | 12/2005 | 1.0510 | .8630 | 1.0510 | 12/2008 | 1.1025 | .6785 | .7130 |

*CME Group; New York Mercantile Exchange*

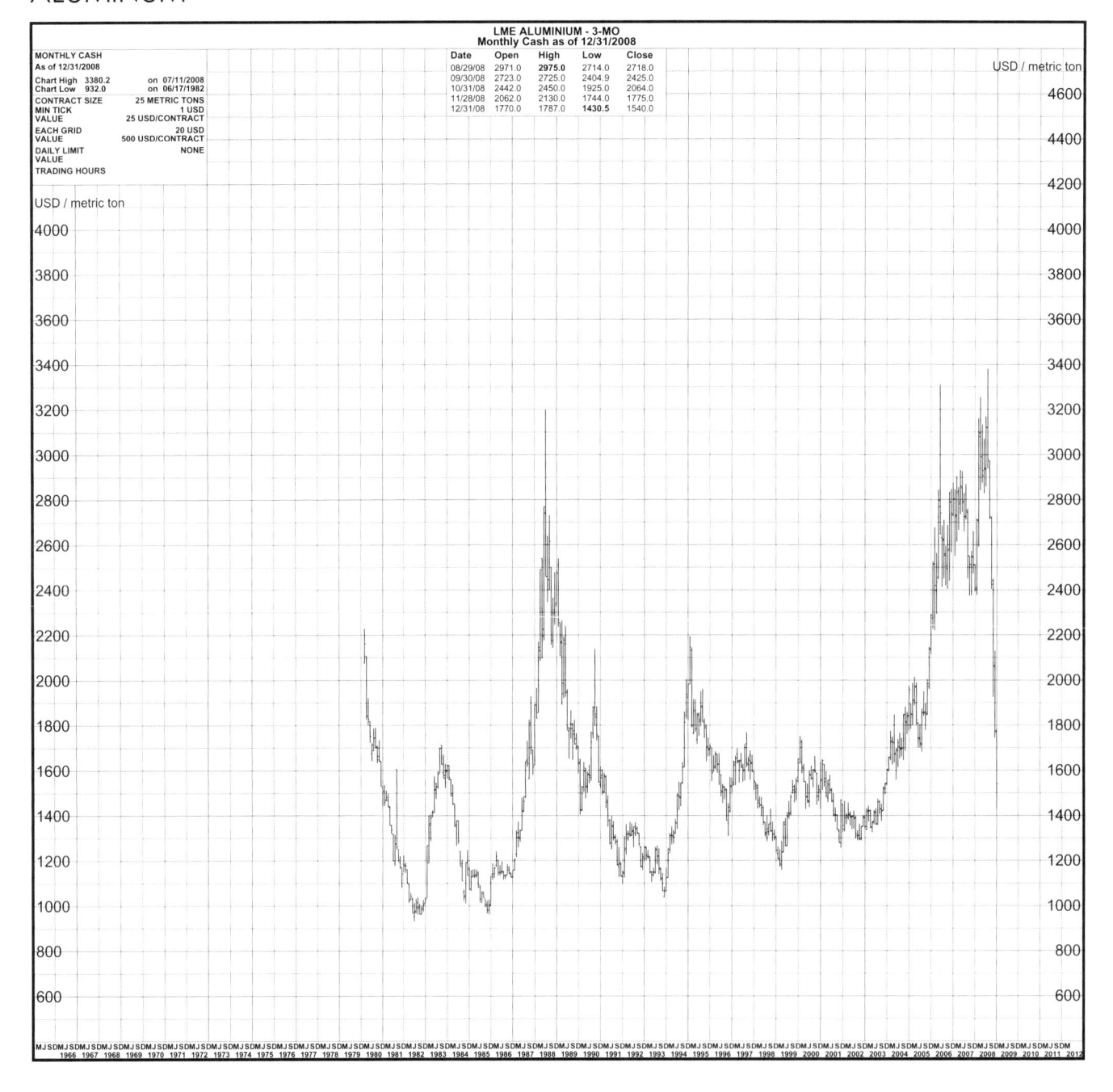

# ALUMINUM

## Annual High, Low and Settle of Aluminium   In USD per Metric Ton

| Year | High | Low | Settle | Year | High | Low | Settle | Year | High | Low | Settle |
|---|---|---|---|---|---|---|---|---|---|---|---|
| 1967 | | | | 1981 | 1,605.4 | 1,079.2 | 1,181.6 | 1995 | 2,194.0 | 1,640.0 | 1,706.0 |
| 1968 | | | | 1982 | 1,193.2 | 932.0 | 1,029.0 | 1996 | 1,699.0 | 1,309.0 | 1,546.0 |
| 1969 | | | | 1983 | 1,711.8 | 1,035.2 | 1,621.9 | 1997 | 1,770.0 | 1,514.0 | 1,552.0 |
| 1970 | | | | 1984 | 1,623.9 | 1,010.6 | 1,074.3 | 1998 | 1,546.0 | 1,237.0 | 1,245.0 |
| 1971 | | | | 1985 | 1,162.6 | 961.9 | 1,129.7 | 1999 | 1,651.0 | 1,158.0 | 1,650.0 |
| 1972 | | | | 1986 | 1,241.0 | 1,115.0 | 1,157.7 | 2000 | 1,752.0 | 1,428.0 | 1,554.0 |
| 1973 | | | | 1987 | 1,930.0 | 1,157.1 | 1,892.0 | 2001 | 1,649.0 | 1,255.0 | 1,355.0 |
| 1974 | | | | 1988 | 3,200.0 | 1,830.0 | 2,475.0 | 2002 | 1,465.0 | 1,289.0 | 1,350.0 |
| 1975 | | | | 1989 | 2,540.0 | 1,587.0 | 1,630.0 | 2003 | 1,607.0 | 1,324.0 | 1,600.0 |
| 1976 | | | | 1990 | 2,138.0 | 1,405.0 | 1,568.0 | 2004 | 1,972.0 | 1,558.0 | 1,958.0 |
| 1977 | | | | 1991 | 1,605.0 | 1,097.0 | 1,150.0 | 2005 | 2,289.5 | 1,681.0 | 2,288.4 |
| 1978 | | | | 1992 | 1,370.5 | 1,124.0 | 1,259.5 | 2006 | 3,310.0 | 2,220.0 | 2,803.2 |
| 1979 | | | | 1993 | 1,267.0 | 1,037.0 | 1,124.0 | 2007 | 2,932.0 | 2,375.0 | 2,402.8 |
| 1980 | 2,230.0 | 1,445.2 | 1,508.7 | 1994 | 2,005.0 | 1,124.0 | 1,981.0 | 2008 | 3,380.2 | 1,430.5 | 1,540.0 |

3-month Forward.   *Source: London Metal Exchange*

# ALUMINUM

## LME ALUMINIUM - 3-MO
### Weekly Cash as of 01/02/2009

| Date | Open | High | Low | Close |
|---|---|---|---|---|
| 12/05/08 | 1770.0 | 1787.0 | 1485.0 | 1491.0 |
| 12/12/08 | 1500.0 | 1573.3 | 1478.0 | 1495.0 |
| 12/19/08 | 1520.0 | 1540.0 | 1430.5 | 1515.0 |
| 12/24/08 | 1522.0 | 1585.0 | 1500.0 | 1537.0 |
| 01/02/09 | 1550.0 | 1585.0 | 1465.0 | 1575.0 |

**WEEKLY CASH** As of 01/02/2009
- Chart High 3380.2 on 07/11/2008
- Chart Low 1158.0 on 03/05/1999
- CONTRACT SIZE: 25 METRIC TONS
- MIN TICK: 1 USD
- VALUE: 25 USD/CONTRACT
- EACH GRID: 10 USD
- VALUE: 250 USD/CONTRACT
- DAILY LIMIT VALUE: NONE
- TRADING HOURS

## Quarterly High, Low and Settle of Aluminium    In USD per Metric Ton

| Quarter | High | Low | Settle | Quarter | High | Low | Settle | Quarter | High | Low | Settle |
|---|---|---|---|---|---|---|---|---|---|---|---|
| 03/2000 | 1,752.0 | 1,548.0 | 1,549.5 | 03/2003 | 1,444.0 | 1,335.0 | 1,346.0 | 03/2006 | 2,678.2 | 2,220.0 | 2,435.0 |
| 06/2000 | 1,601.0 | 1,428.0 | 1,582.0 | 06/2003 | 1,432.0 | 1,324.0 | 1,365.0 | 06/2006 | 3,310.0 | 2,413.0 | 2,620.0 |
| 09/2000 | 1,664.0 | 1,525.0 | 1,595.5 | 09/2003 | 1,475.0 | 1,359.0 | 1,420.5 | 09/2006 | 2,710.0 | 2,405.0 | 2,575.0 |
| 12/2000 | 1,635.0 | 1,429.5 | 1,554.0 | 12/2003 | 1,607.0 | 1,420.0 | 1,600.0 | 12/2006 | 2,875.0 | 2,440.8 | 2,803.2 |
| 03/2001 | 1,649.0 | 1,481.0 | 1,487.0 | 03/2004 | 1,775.0 | 1,594.0 | 1,724.0 | 03/2007 | 2,905.0 | 2,550.0 | 2,780.0 |
| 06/2001 | 1,581.0 | 1,458.0 | 1,462.0 | 06/2004 | 1,847.0 | 1,558.0 | 1,722.0 | 06/2007 | 2,932.0 | 2,657.8 | 2,725.0 |
| 09/2001 | 1,500.0 | 1,334.0 | 1,339.0 | 09/2004 | 1,850.0 | 1,645.0 | 1,845.5 | 09/2007 | 2,870.0 | 2,375.0 | 2,512.8 |
| 12/2001 | 1,471.0 | 1,255.0 | 1,355.0 | 12/2004 | 1,972.0 | 1,685.0 | 1,958.0 | 12/2007 | 2,661.0 | 2,376.0 | 2,402.8 |
| 03/2002 | 1,465.0 | 1,328.0 | 1,403.0 | 03/2005 | 2,015.0 | 1,782.0 | 1,970.0 | 03/2008 | 3,255.0 | 2,377.0 | 2,990.0 |
| 06/2002 | 1,422.0 | 1,338.0 | 1,388.0 | 06/2005 | 1,990.0 | 1,700.0 | 1,719.5 | 06/2008 | 3,169.0 | 2,828.0 | 3,120.3 |
| 09/2002 | 1,398.0 | 1,289.0 | 1,295.0 | 09/2005 | 1,951.0 | 1,681.0 | 1,851.0 | 09/2008 | 3,380.2 | 2,404.9 | 2,425.0 |
| 12/2002 | 1,402.0 | 1,289.0 | 1,350.0 | 12/2005 | 2,289.5 | 1,843.8 | 2,288.4 | 12/2008 | 2,450.0 | 1,430.5 | 1,540.0 |

3-month Forward.    *Source: London Metal Exchange*

# COPPER

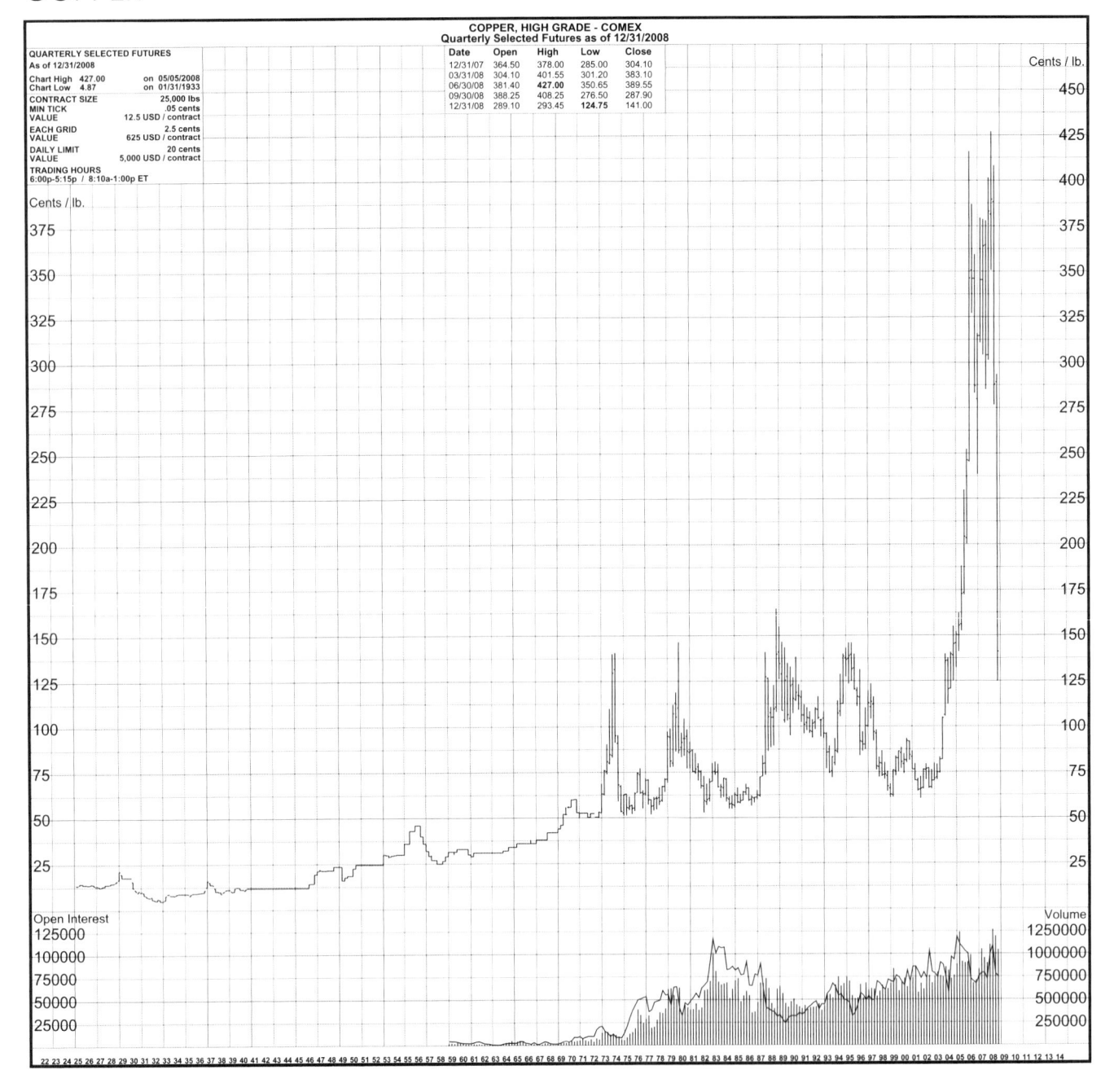

**COPPER, HIGH GRADE - COMEX**
Quarterly Selected Futures as of 12/31/2008

| Date | Open | High | Low | Close |
|---|---|---|---|---|
| 12/31/07 | 364.50 | 378.00 | 285.00 | 304.10 |
| 03/31/08 | 304.10 | 401.55 | 301.20 | 383.10 |
| 06/30/08 | 381.40 | 427.00 | 350.65 | 389.55 |
| 09/30/08 | 388.25 | 408.25 | 276.50 | 287.90 |
| 12/31/08 | 289.10 | 293.45 | 124.75 | 141.00 |

**QUARTERLY SELECTED FUTURES**
As of 12/31/2008
Chart High 427.00 on 05/05/2008
Chart Low 4.87 on 01/31/1933
CONTRACT SIZE 25,000 lbs
MIN TICK .05 cents
VALUE 12.5 USD / contract
EACH GRID 2.5 cents
VALUE 625 USD / contract
DAILY LIMIT 20 cents
VALUE 5,000 USD / contract
TRADING HOURS
6:00p-5:15p / 8:10a-1:00p ET

## Annual High, Low and Settle of High-Grade Copper Futures    In Cents per Pound

| Year | High | Low | Settle | Year | High | Low | Settle | Year | High | Low | Settle |
|---|---|---|---|---|---|---|---|---|---|---|---|
| 1925 | 14.79 | 13.45 | 13.96 | 1939 | 12.37 | 9.87 | 12.37 | 1953 | 30.00 | 24.50 | 29.50 |
| 1926 | 14.26 | 13.44 | 13.44 | 1940 | 12.09 | 10.69 | 11.87 | 1954 | 30.00 | 29.50 | 30.00 |
| 1927 | 13.95 | 12.46 | 13.95 | 1941 | 11.87 | 11.87 | 11.87 | 1955 | 43.00 | 30.00 | 43.00 |
| 1928 | 15.94 | 13.96 | 15.94 | 1942 | 11.87 | 11.87 | 11.87 | 1956 | 46.00 | 36.00 | 36.00 |
| 1929 | 21.26 | 16.72 | 17.87 | 1943 | 11.87 | 11.87 | 11.87 | 1957 | 36.00 | 27.00 | 27.00 |
| 1930 | 17.87 | 9.70 | 10.49 | 1944 | 11.87 | 11.87 | 11.87 | 1958 | 29.00 | 25.00 | 29.00 |
| 1931 | 10.02 | 6.67 | 6.72 | 1945 | 11.87 | 11.87 | 11.87 | 1959 | 35.35 | 27.44 | 31.68 |
| 1932 | 7.21 | 4.91 | 4.91 | 1946 | 19.37 | 11.87 | 19.37 | 1960 | 35.00 | 27.50 | 27.71 |
| 1933 | 8.87 | 4.87 | 8.00 | 1947 | 22.19 | 19.45 | 21.37 | 1961 | 32.60 | 26.67 | 30.21 |
| 1934 | 8.87 | 7.87 | 8.87 | 1948 | 23.50 | 21.50 | 23.50 | 1962 | 31.05 | 27.95 | 28.77 |
| 1935 | 9.12 | 7.87 | 9.12 | 1949 | 23.50 | 16.00 | 18.50 | 1963 | 30.59 | 28.67 | 30.50 |
| 1936 | 10.89 | 9.12 | 10.89 | 1950 | 24.50 | 18.50 | 24.50 | 1964 | 61.80 | 30.40 | 36.95 |
| 1937 | 15.87 | 10.11 | 10.11 | 1951 | 24.50 | 24.50 | 24.50 | 1965 | 60.85 | 36.25 | 57.25 |
| 1938 | 11.12 | 8.87 | 11.12 | 1952 | 24.50 | 24.50 | 24.50 | 1966 | 82.75 | 46.25 | 53.90 |

Futures data begins 07/01/1959.    Data continued on page 344.    *CME Group; New York Mercantile Exchange*

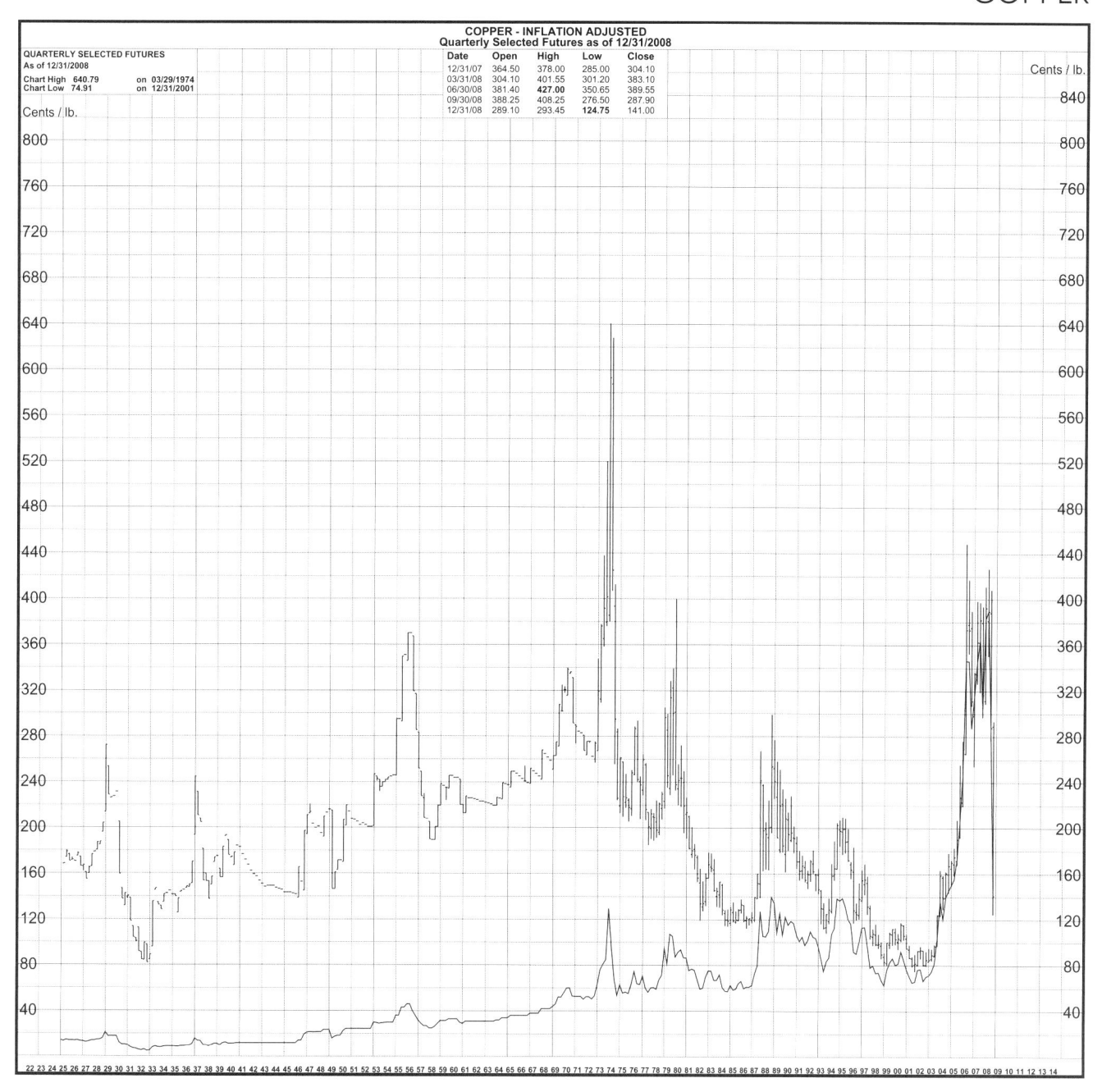

# COPPER

**QUARTERLY SELECTED FUTURES**
As of 12/31/2008
Chart High 640.79 on 03/29/1974
Chart Low 74.91 on 12/31/2001
Cents / lb.

**COPPER - INFLATION ADJUSTED**
Quarterly Selected Futures as of 12/31/2008

| Date | Open | High | Low | Close |
|---|---|---|---|---|
| 12/31/07 | 364.50 | 378.00 | 285.00 | 304.10 |
| 03/31/08 | 304.10 | 401.55 | 301.20 | 383.10 |
| 06/30/08 | 381.40 | 427.00 | 350.65 | 389.55 |
| 09/30/08 | 388.25 | 408.25 | 276.50 | 287.90 |
| 12/31/08 | 289.10 | 293.45 | 124.75 | 141.00 |

## Annual High, Low and Settle of Copper    In Cents per Pound

| Year | High | Low | Settle | Year | High | Low | Settle | Year | High | Low | Settle |
|---|---|---|---|---|---|---|---|---|---|---|---|
| 1925 | 14.79 | 13.45 | 13.96 | 1939 | 12.37 | 9.87 | 12.37 | 1953 | 30.00 | 24.50 | 29.50 |
| 1926 | 14.26 | 13.44 | 13.44 | 1940 | 12.09 | 10.69 | 11.87 | 1954 | 30.00 | 29.50 | 30.00 |
| 1927 | 13.95 | 12.46 | 13.95 | 1941 | 11.87 | 11.87 | 11.87 | 1955 | 43.00 | 30.00 | 43.00 |
| 1928 | 15.94 | 13.96 | 15.94 | 1942 | 11.87 | 11.87 | 11.87 | 1956 | 46.00 | 36.00 | 36.00 |
| 1929 | 21.26 | 16.72 | 17.87 | 1943 | 11.87 | 11.87 | 11.87 | 1957 | 36.00 | 27.00 | 27.00 |
| 1930 | 17.87 | 9.70 | 10.49 | 1944 | 11.87 | 11.87 | 11.87 | 1958 | 29.00 | 25.00 | 29.00 |
| 1931 | 10.02 | 6.67 | 6.72 | 1945 | 11.87 | 11.87 | 11.87 | 1959 | 33.00 | 29.00 | 33.00 |
| 1932 | 7.21 | 4.91 | 4.91 | 1946 | 19.37 | 11.87 | 19.37 | 1960 | 33.00 | 30.00 | 30.00 |
| 1933 | 8.87 | 4.87 | 8.00 | 1947 | 22.19 | 19.45 | 21.37 | 1961 | 31.00 | 29.00 | 31.00 |
| 1934 | 8.87 | 7.87 | 8.87 | 1948 | 23.50 | 21.50 | 23.50 | 1962 | 31.00 | 31.00 | 31.00 |
| 1935 | 9.12 | 7.87 | 9.12 | 1949 | 23.50 | 16.00 | 18.50 | 1963 | 31.00 | 31.00 | 31.00 |
| 1936 | 10.89 | 9.12 | 10.89 | 1950 | 24.50 | 18.50 | 24.50 | 1964 | 34.00 | 31.00 | 34.00 |
| 1937 | 15.87 | 10.11 | 10.11 | 1951 | 24.50 | 24.50 | 24.50 | 1965 | 36.00 | 34.00 | 36.00 |
| 1938 | 11.12 | 8.87 | 11.12 | 1952 | 24.50 | 24.50 | 24.50 | 1966 | 38.00 | 36.00 | 36.00 |

New York: Pig Ingots 01/1910 to 10/1986.    Data continued on page 345.    *CME Group; New York Mercantile Exchange*

# COPPER

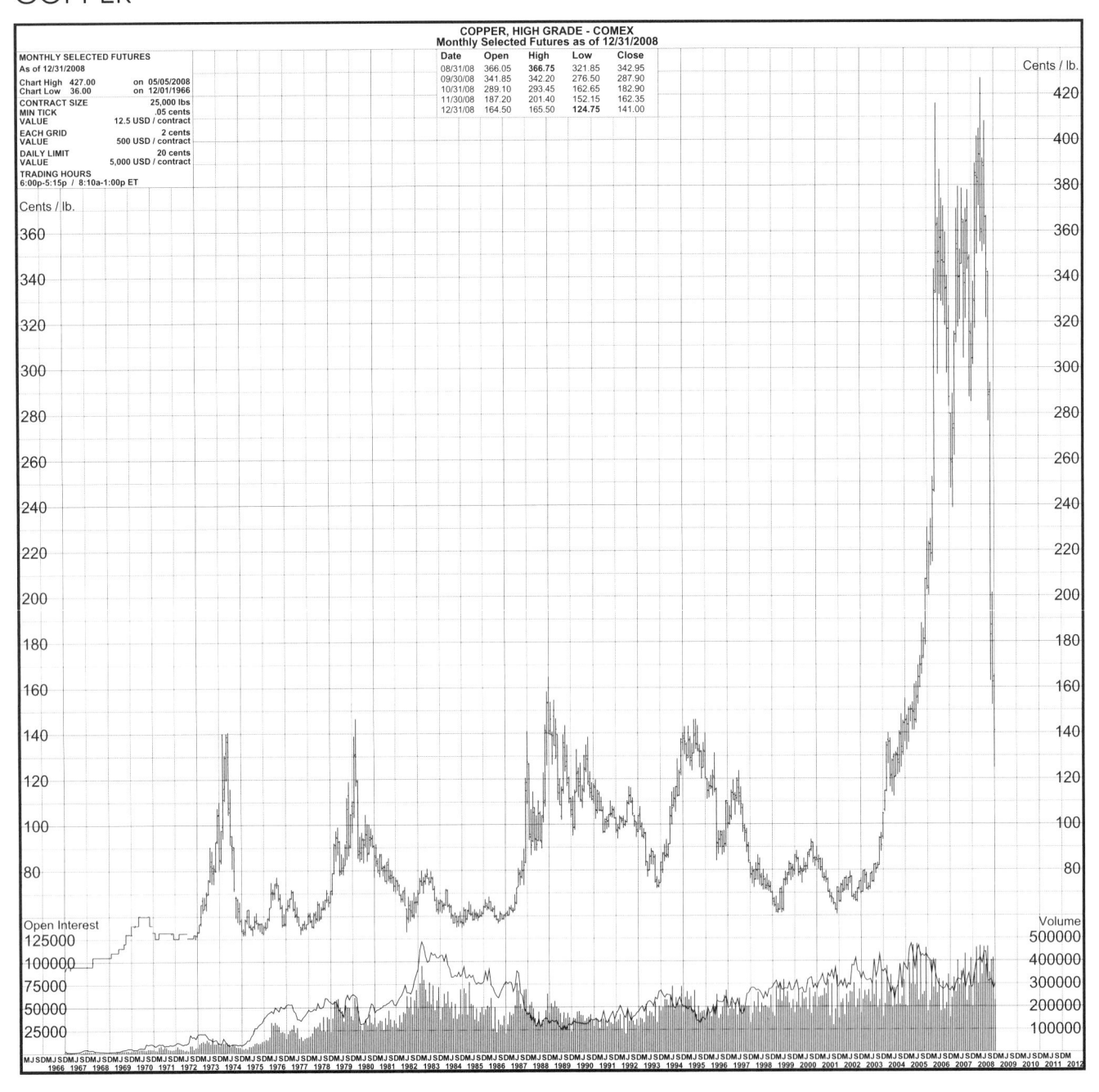

**COPPER, HIGH GRADE - COMEX**
Monthly Selected Futures as of 12/31/2008

| Date | Open | High | Low | Close |
|---|---|---|---|---|
| 08/31/08 | 366.05 | 366.75 | 321.85 | 342.95 |
| 09/30/08 | 341.85 | 342.20 | 276.50 | 287.90 |
| 10/31/08 | 289.10 | 293.45 | 162.65 | 182.90 |
| 11/30/08 | 187.20 | 201.40 | 152.15 | 162.35 |
| 12/31/08 | 164.50 | 165.50 | 124.75 | 141.00 |

**MONTHLY SELECTED FUTURES** As of 12/31/2008
Chart High 427.00 on 05/05/2008
Chart Low 36.00 on 12/01/1966
CONTRACT SIZE 25,000 lbs
MIN TICK .05 cents
VALUE 12.5 USD / contract
EACH GRID 2 cents
VALUE 500 USD / contract
DAILY LIMIT 20 cents
VALUE 5,000 USD / contract
TRADING HOURS 6:00p-5:15p / 8:10a-1:00p ET

## Annual High, Low and Settle of High-Grade Copper Futures    In Cents per Pound

| Year | High | Low | Settle | Year | High | Low | Settle | Year | High | Low | Settle |
|---|---|---|---|---|---|---|---|---|---|---|---|
| 1967 | 64.90 | 41.40 | 56.50 | 1981 | 91.70 | 70.40 | 75.70 | 1995 | 146.10 | 120.00 | 120.55 |
| 1968 | 76.30 | 43.30 | 50.80 | 1982 | 76.10 | 52.80 | 69.65 | 1996 | 131.40 | 83.90 | 100.25 |
| 1969 | 76.40 | 50.50 | 72.75 | 1983 | 80.90 | 60.75 | 67.00 | 1997 | 123.60 | 76.10 | 78.10 |
| 1970 | 78.00 | 45.05 | 48.90 | 1984 | 71.80 | 54.90 | 57.20 | 1998 | 86.70 | 64.40 | 67.20 |
| 1971 | 58.70 | 44.05 | 48.75 | 1985 | 66.55 | 55.70 | 64.15 | 1999 | 86.40 | 60.90 | 86.30 |
| 1972 | 53.40 | 45.85 | 50.25 | 1986 | 68.55 | 56.60 | 61.15 | 2000 | 93.40 | 74.10 | 84.30 |
| 1973 | 109.90 | 49.85 | 84.80 | 1987 | 141.00 | 60.05 | 127.40 | 2001 | 86.40 | 60.50 | 65.90 |
| 1974 | 140.70 | 53.20 | 53.60 | 1988 | 164.75 | 86.50 | 139.75 | 2002 | 79.45 | 65.65 | 70.25 |
| 1975 | 63.20 | 51.30 | 55.30 | 1989 | 154.75 | 101.95 | 106.40 | 2003 | 105.10 | 70.00 | 104.55 |
| 1976 | 77.30 | 53.80 | 63.20 | 1990 | 138.40 | 95.00 | 116.85 | 2004 | 155.00 | 105.40 | 145.25 |
| 1977 | 71.80 | 51.90 | 60.30 | 1991 | 119.70 | 96.05 | 97.55 | 2005 | 229.90 | 132.35 | 204.20 |
| 1978 | 71.75 | 54.70 | 71.05 | 1992 | 116.70 | 93.70 | 103.60 | 2006 | 416.00 | 200.25 | 287.10 |
| 1979 | 119.00 | 69.25 | 105.20 | 1993 | 108.00 | 72.00 | 83.30 | 2007 | 379.50 | 238.50 | 304.10 |
| 1980 | 146.50 | 77.05 | 86.55 | 1994 | 140.00 | 78.50 | 138.60 | 2008 | 427.00 | 124.75 | 141.00 |

Data th
*CME Group; New York Mercantile Exchange*

# COPPER

**Copper, Scrap #2 Wire, NY**
Monthly Cash as of 12/31/2008

| Date | Open | High | Low | Close |
|---|---|---|---|---|
| 08/29/08 | 362.85 | 362.85 | 323.50 | 342.95 |
| 09/30/08 | 332.25 | 335.40 | 288.80 | 288.80 |
| 10/31/08 | 279.70 | 279.70 | 167.50 | 184.40 |
| 11/28/08 | 183.75 | 195.10 | 156.85 | 162.35 |
| 12/31/08 | 160.35 | 160.35 | 124.75 | 139.50 |

MONTHLY CASH
As of 12/31/2008
Chart High 407.75 on 07/02/2008
Chart Low 36.00 on 12/01/1966
Cents / lb.

## Annual High, Low and Settle of Copper    In Cents per Pound

| Year | High | Low | Settle | Year | High | Low | Settle | Year | High | Low | Settle |
|---|---|---|---|---|---|---|---|---|---|---|---|
| 1967 | 38.00 | 36.00 | 38.00 | 1981 | 89.00 | 78.00 | 78.00 | 1995 | 149.00 | 121.00 | 126.00 |
| 1968 | 42.00 | 38.00 | 42.00 | 1982 | 79.00 | 63.00 | 72.00 | 1996 | 130.00 | 87.00 | 103.00 |
| 1969 | 56.00 | 42.00 | 52.00 | 1983 | 84.00 | 65.00 | 68.00 | 1997 | 122.00 | 77.00 | 77.00 |
| 1970 | 60.25 | 53.00 | 53.00 | 1984 | 76.00 | 60.00 | 63.00 | 1998 | 86.00 | 65.00 | 66.00 |
| 1971 | 53.00 | 50.00 | 50.25 | 1985 | 71.00 | 61.00 | 66.50 | 1999 | 88.00 | 61.00 | 85.25 |
| 1972 | 52.52 | 50.25 | 50.50 | 1986 | 70.50 | 60.00 | 63.25 | 2000 | 92.85 | 74.20 | 84.65 |
| 1973 | 68.10 | 50.50 | 68.10 | 1987 | 150.00 | 62.50 | 150.00 | 2001 | 86.70 | 60.40 | 65.30 |
| 1974 | 85.60 | 68.00 | 68.60 | 1988 | 168.00 | 93.50 | 156.75 | 2002 | 78.35 | 65.30 | 69.70 |
| 1975 | 68.60 | 60.60 | 63.60 | 1989 | 163.00 | 102.75 | 109.00 | 2003 | 104.30 | 70.90 | 104.30 |
| 1976 | 74.00 | 63.60 | 65.00 | 1990 | 138.65 | 99.12 | 120.00 | 2004 | 154.25 | 106.25 | 148.70 |
| 1977 | 74.00 | 60.00 | 63.00 | 1991 | 122.00 | 100.25 | 101.25 | 2005 | 228.00 | 139.50 | 216.15 |
| 1978 | 72.00 | 60.00 | 71.25 | 1992 | 120.00 | 97.44 | 105.50 | 2006 | 407.55 | 213.00 | 285.40 |
| 1979 | 107.00 | 71.25 | 103.00 | 1993 | 110.50 | 79.00 | 86.00 | 2007 | 377.20 | 240.45 | 303.05 |
| 1980 | 138.00 | 79.25 | 86.25 | 1994 | 143.00 | 84.50 | 143.00 | 2008 | 407.75 | 124.75 | 139.50 |

New York: Pig Ingots to 10/1986; Midwest: Pig Ingots 11/1986 to date.    Data continued from page 343.    *CME Group; New York Mercantile Exchange*

# COPPER

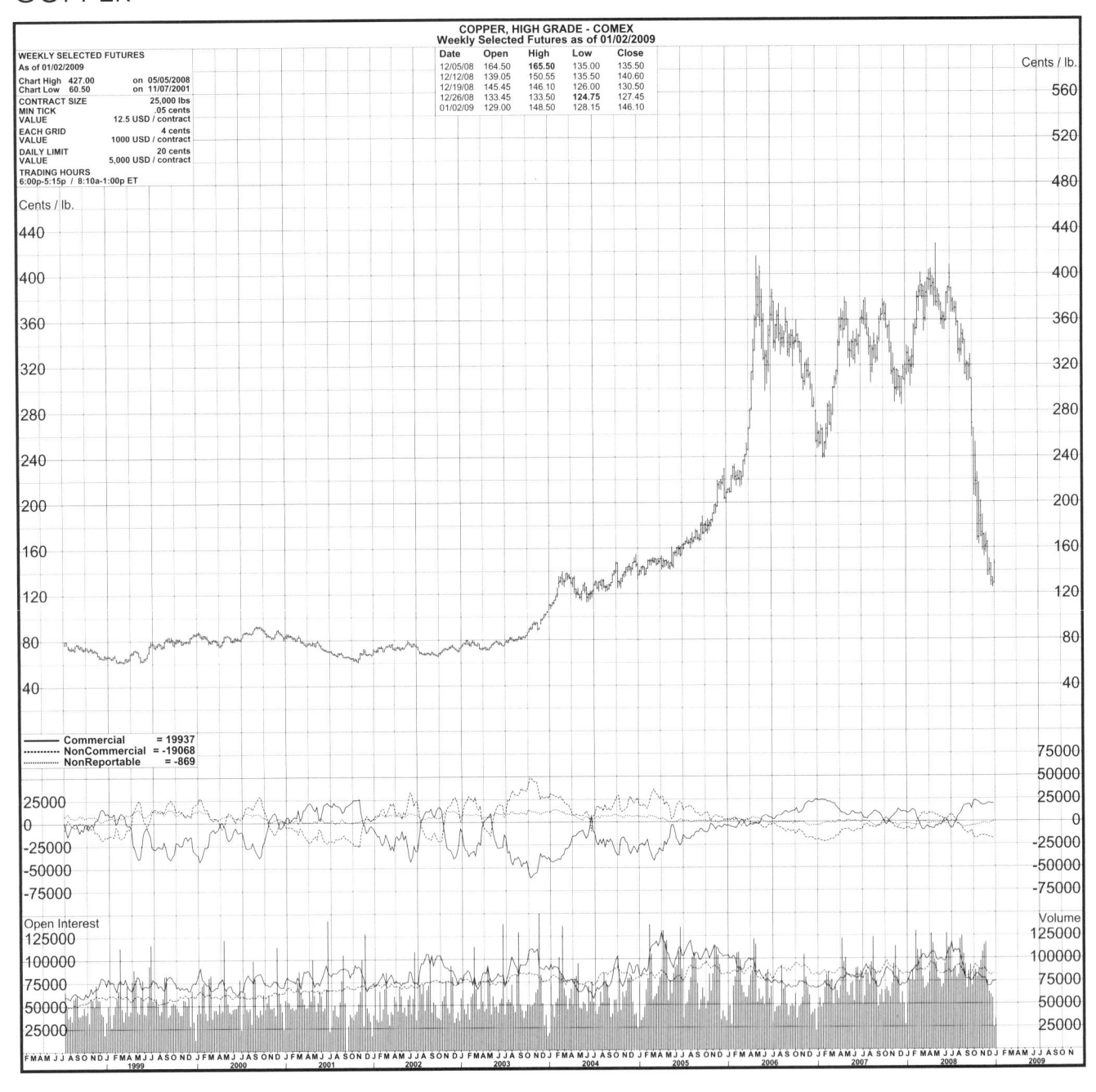

## COPPER, HIGH GRADE - COMEX
### Weekly Selected Futures as of 01/02/2009

| Date | Open | High | Low | Close |
|---|---|---|---|---|
| 12/05/08 | 164.50 | **165.50** | 135.00 | 135.50 |
| 12/12/08 | 139.05 | 150.55 | 135.50 | 140.60 |
| 12/19/08 | 145.45 | 146.10 | 126.00 | 130.50 |
| 12/26/08 | 133.45 | 133.50 | **124.75** | 127.45 |
| 01/02/09 | 129.00 | 148.50 | 128.15 | 146.10 |

**WEEKLY SELECTED FUTURES** As of 01/02/2009
- Chart High 427.00 on 05/05/2008
- Chart Low 60.50 on 11/07/2001
- CONTRACT SIZE: 25,000 lbs
- MIN TICK: .05 cents
- VALUE: 12.5 USD / contract
- EACH GRID: 4 cents
- VALUE: 1000 USD / contract
- DAILY LIMIT VALUE: 20 cents / 5,000 USD / contract
- TRADING HOURS: 6:00p-5:15p / 8:10a-1:00p ET

Commercial = 19937
NonCommercial = -19068
NonReportable = -869

## Quarterly High, Low and Settle of High-Grade Copper Futures    In Cents per Pound

| Quarter | High | Low | Settle | Quarter | High | Low | Settle | Quarter | High | Low | Settle |
|---|---|---|---|---|---|---|---|---|---|---|---|
| 03/2000 | 88.50 | 76.90 | 80.50 | 03/2003 | 79.85 | 70.00 | 71.45 | 03/2006 | 252.35 | 200.25 | 246.30 |
| 06/2000 | 85.10 | 74.10 | 81.55 | 06/2003 | 79.30 | 70.70 | 74.80 | 06/2006 | 416.00 | 245.30 | 346.25 |
| 09/2000 | 93.40 | 80.05 | 92.05 | 09/2003 | 83.20 | 74.25 | 81.85 | 09/2006 | 387.00 | 327.00 | 346.05 |
| 12/2000 | 92.00 | 81.30 | 84.30 | 12/2003 | 105.10 | 81.75 | 104.55 | 12/2006 | 359.50 | 283.00 | 287.10 |
| 03/2001 | 86.40 | 76.30 | 76.40 | 03/2004 | 139.85 | 105.40 | 136.00 | 03/2007 | 316.00 | 238.50 | 314.60 |
| 06/2001 | 79.60 | 70.20 | 70.45 | 06/2004 | 137.70 | 112.15 | 120.50 | 06/2007 | 379.50 | 310.75 | 345.35 |
| 09/2001 | 71.50 | 64.40 | 65.20 | 09/2004 | 140.80 | 120.50 | 139.60 | 09/2007 | 378.70 | 304.10 | 364.00 |
| 12/2001 | 72.55 | 60.50 | 65.90 | 12/2004 | 155.00 | 124.80 | 145.25 | 12/2007 | 378.00 | 285.00 | 304.10 |
| 03/2002 | 76.60 | 65.65 | 76.35 | 03/2005 | 152.00 | 132.35 | 150.25 | 03/2008 | 401.55 | 301.20 | 383.10 |
| 06/2002 | 79.45 | 70.75 | 76.75 | 06/2005 | 162.50 | 141.00 | 155.35 | 06/2008 | 427.00 | 350.65 | 389.55 |
| 09/2002 | 77.20 | 65.95 | 66.60 | 09/2005 | 188.20 | 152.35 | 172.75 | 09/2008 | 408.25 | 276.50 | 287.90 |
| 12/2002 | 76.30 | 65.70 | 70.25 | 12/2005 | 229.90 | 172.25 | 204.20 | 12/2008 | 293.45 | 124.75 | 141.00 |

*CME Group; New York Mercantile Exchange*

# COPPER

**Copper, Scrap #2 Wire, NY**
Weekly Cash as of 01/02/2009

| Date | Open | High | Low | Close |
|---|---|---|---|---|
| 12/05/08 | 160.35 | 160.35 | 135.50 | 135.50 |
| 12/12/08 | 147.80 | 148.65 | 140.60 | 140.60 |
| 12/19/08 | 138.50 | 138.50 | 126.95 | 130.50 |
| 12/26/08 | 131.70 | 131.70 | 124.75 | 127.45 |
| 01/02/09 | 129.70 | 144.40 | 129.70 | 144.40 |

WEEKLY CASH
As of 01/02/2009
Chart High 407.75 on 07/02/2008
Chart Low 60.40 on 11/07/2001

## Quarterly High, Low and Settle of Copper   In Cents per Pound

| Quarter | High | Low | Settle | Quarter | High | Low | Settle | Quarter | High | Low | Settle |
|---|---|---|---|---|---|---|---|---|---|---|---|
| 03/2000 | 87.50 | 75.75 | 80.00 | 03/2003 | 79.50 | 71.25 | 71.25 | 03/2006 | 250.35 | 213.00 | 248.80 |
| 06/2000 | 84.60 | 74.20 | 81.55 | 06/2003 | 78.75 | 70.90 | 74.80 | 06/2006 | 407.55 | 257.35 | 346.25 |
| 09/2000 | 92.85 | 80.35 | 91.55 | 09/2003 | 82.75 | 74.60 | 81.30 | 09/2006 | 382.95 | 331.65 | 345.90 |
| 12/2000 | 90.95 | 81.85 | 84.65 | 12/2003 | 104.30 | 81.85 | 104.30 | 12/2006 | 356.00 | 283.00 | 285.40 |
| 03/2001 | 86.70 | 75.85 | 75.85 | 03/2004 | 139.45 | 106.25 | 135.55 | 03/2007 | 314.35 | 240.45 | 314.35 |
| 06/2001 | 79.50 | 70.45 | 70.45 | 06/2004 | 137.10 | 114.45 | 120.50 | 06/2007 | 377.20 | 317.40 | 345.35 |
| 09/2001 | 75.00 | 64.60 | 64.60 | 09/2004 | 140.00 | 122.00 | 140.00 | 09/2007 | 375.40 | 312.95 | 363.05 |
| 12/2001 | 72.20 | 60.40 | 65.30 | 12/2004 | 154.25 | 125.75 | 148.70 | 12/2007 | 374.95 | 287.00 | 303.05 |
| 03/2002 | 76.60 | 65.30 | 76.05 | 03/2005 | 152.35 | 139.50 | 151.05 | 03/2008 | 398.95 | 305.05 | 386.35 |
| 06/2002 | 78.35 | 71.00 | 76.75 | 06/2005 | 168.95 | 143.35 | 155.35 | 06/2008 | 402.80 | 353.25 | 387.50 |
| 09/2002 | 76.80 | 66.00 | 66.00 | 09/2005 | 187.65 | 153.65 | 180.15 | 09/2008 | 407.75 | 288.80 | 288.80 |
| 12/2002 | 75.65 | 65.60 | 69.70 | 12/2005 | 228.00 | 183.40 | 216.15 | 12/2008 | 279.70 | 124.75 | 139.50 |

Midwest: Pig Ingots.   *CME Group; New York Mercantile Exchange*

347

# COPPER

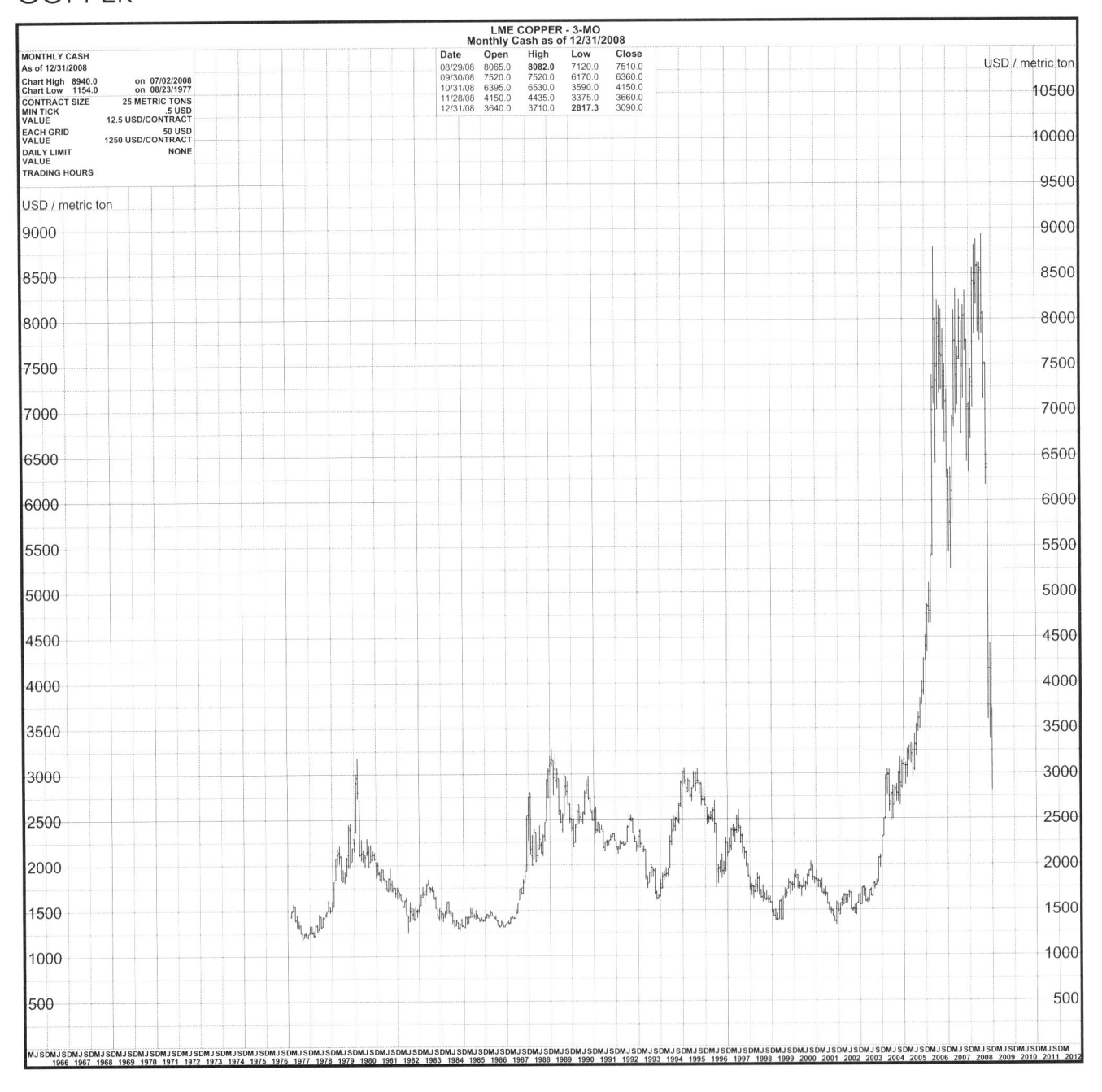

**LME COPPER - 3-MO**
Monthly Cash as of 12/31/2008

| Date | Open | High | Low | Close |
|---|---|---|---|---|
| 08/29/08 | 8065.0 | 8082.0 | 7120.0 | 7510.0 |
| 09/30/08 | 7520.0 | 7520.0 | 6170.0 | 6360.0 |
| 10/31/08 | 6395.0 | 6530.0 | 3590.0 | 4150.0 |
| 11/28/08 | 4150.0 | 4435.0 | 3375.0 | 3660.0 |
| 12/31/08 | 3640.0 | 3710.0 | 2817.3 | 3090.0 |

MONTHLY CASH
As of 12/31/2008
Chart High 8940.0 on 07/02/2008
Chart Low 1154.0 on 08/23/1977
CONTRACT SIZE 25 METRIC TONS
MIN TICK .5 USD
VALUE 12.5 USD/CONTRACT
EACH GRID 50 USD
VALUE 1250 USD/CONTRACT
DAILY LIMIT NONE
VALUE
TRADING HOURS

## Annual High, Low and Settle of Copper — In USD per Metric Ton

| Year | High | Low | Settle | Year | High | Low | Settle | Year | High | Low | Settle |
|---|---|---|---|---|---|---|---|---|---|---|---|
| 1967 | | | | 1981 | 2,041.0 | 1,630.0 | 1,727.0 | 1995 | 3,072.0 | 2,650.0 | 2,657.0 |
| 1968 | | | | 1982 | 1,713.0 | 1,250.0 | 1,538.0 | 1996 | 2,710.0 | 1,745.0 | 2,127.0 |
| 1969 | | | | 1983 | 1,847.0 | 1,387.0 | 1,464.0 | 1997 | 2,608.0 | 1,720.0 | 1,747.0 |
| 1970 | | | | 1984 | 1,603.0 | 1,274.0 | 1,318.0 | 1998 | 1,905.0 | 1,466.0 | 1,485.0 |
| 1971 | | | | 1985 | 1,535.0 | 1,305.0 | 1,426.0 | 1999 | 1,890.0 | 1,376.0 | 1,880.5 |
| 1972 | | | | 1986 | 1,500.0 | 1,313.0 | 1,369.0 | 2000 | 2,036.0 | 1,639.0 | 1,833.0 |
| 1973 | | | | 1987 | 2,750.0 | 1,356.0 | 2,750.0 | 2001 | 1,845.0 | 1,336.0 | 1,483.0 |
| 1974 | | | | 1988 | 3,200.0 | 1,995.0 | 3,125.0 | 2002 | 1,719.0 | 1,440.0 | 1,560.0 |
| 1975 | | | | 1989 | 3,280.0 | 2,353.0 | 2,400.0 | 2003 | 2,303.0 | 1,557.0 | 2,301.0 |
| 1976 | | | | 1990 | 2,980.0 | 2,197.0 | 2,610.0 | 2004 | 3,179.5 | 2,307.0 | 3,150.0 |
| 1977 | 1,579.0 | 1,154.0 | 1,309.0 | 1991 | 2,640.0 | 2,160.0 | 2,193.0 | 2005 | 4,518.0 | 2,875.0 | 4,395.0 |
| 1978 | 1,620.0 | 1,210.0 | 1,604.0 | 1992 | 2,570.0 | 2,119.0 | 2,310.3 | 2006 | 8,800.0 | 4,330.0 | 6,324.9 |
| 1979 | 2,466.0 | 1,546.0 | 2,242.0 | 1993 | 2,392.0 | 1,613.0 | 1,785.0 | 2007 | 8,335.0 | 5,250.0 | 6,695.0 |
| 1980 | 3,181.0 | 1,856.0 | 1,949.0 | 1994 | 3,030.0 | 1,736.0 | 3,023.0 | 2008 | 8,940.0 | 2,817.3 | 3,090.0 |

3-month Forward. *Source: London Metal Exchange*

# COPPER

**WEEKLY CASH** As of 01/02/2009
Chart High 8940.0 on 07/02/2008
Chart Low 1336.0 on 11/07/2001
CONTRACT SIZE 25 METRIC TONS
MIN TICK .5 USD
VALUE 12.5 USD/CONTRACT
EACH GRID 50 USD
VALUE 1250 USD/CONTRACT
DAILY LIMIT NONE
VALUE
TRADING HOURS

**LME COPPER - 3-MO**
Weekly Cash as of 01/02/2009

| Date | Open | High | Low | Close |
|---|---|---|---|---|
| 12/05/08 | 3640.0 | 3710.0 | 2991.0 | 3075.0 |
| 12/12/08 | 3075.3 | 3380.0 | 3020.3 | 3165.0 |
| 12/19/08 | 3240.0 | 3280.0 | 2850.2 | 2926.0 |
| 12/24/08 | 2980.0 | 3065.0 | 2817.3 | 2845.0 |
| 01/02/09 | 2850.0 | 3265.0 | 2844.0 | 3210.5 |

## Quarterly High, Low and Settle of Copper   In USD per Metric Ton

| Quarter | High | Low | Settle | Quarter | High | Low | Settle | Quarter | High | Low | Settle |
|---|---|---|---|---|---|---|---|---|---|---|---|
| 03/2000 | 1,940.0 | 1,726.0 | 1,761.0 | 03/2003 | 1,755.0 | 1,557.0 | 1,590.5 | 03/2006 | 5,510.3 | 4,330.0 | 5,385.0 |
| 06/2000 | 1,851.0 | 1,639.0 | 1,790.0 | 06/2003 | 1,738.0 | 1,571.0 | 1,655.0 | 06/2006 | 8,800.0 | 5,390.0 | 7,320.0 |
| 09/2000 | 2,036.0 | 1,761.0 | 1,997.0 | 09/2003 | 1,834.0 | 1,640.0 | 1,798.0 | 09/2006 | 8,210.0 | 7,000.0 | 7,590.0 |
| 12/2000 | 1,987.0 | 1,783.0 | 1,833.0 | 12/2003 | 2,303.0 | 1,798.0 | 2,301.0 | 12/2006 | 7,890.0 | 6,250.0 | 6,324.9 |
| 03/2001 | 1,845.0 | 1,683.0 | 1,688.5 | 03/2004 | 3,051.0 | 2,307.0 | 2,990.0 | 03/2007 | 6,935.0 | 5,250.0 | 6,875.0 |
| 06/2001 | 1,753.0 | 1,556.0 | 1,568.0 | 06/2004 | 3,044.0 | 2,475.0 | 2,649.0 | 06/2007 | 8,335.0 | 6,807.0 | 7,560.2 |
| 09/2001 | 1,584.0 | 1,425.0 | 1,446.5 | 09/2004 | 3,020.0 | 2,653.0 | 2,997.5 | 09/2007 | 8,212.0 | 6,730.0 | 8,030.0 |
| 12/2001 | 1,595.0 | 1,336.0 | 1,483.0 | 12/2004 | 3,179.5 | 2,650.0 | 3,150.0 | 12/2007 | 8,315.0 | 6,317.0 | 6,695.0 |
| 03/2002 | 1,678.0 | 1,440.0 | 1,652.0 | 03/2005 | 3,308.0 | 2,875.0 | 3,288.0 | 03/2008 | 8,820.0 | 6,675.0 | 8,390.0 |
| 06/2002 | 1,719.0 | 1,563.0 | 1,687.0 | 06/2005 | 3,435.0 | 2,960.0 | 3,319.0 | 06/2008 | 8,880.0 | 7,760.0 | 8,560.0 |
| 09/2002 | 1,692.0 | 1,450.0 | 1,459.0 | 09/2005 | 3,835.0 | 3,188.0 | 3,769.5 | 09/2008 | 8,940.0 | 6,170.0 | 6,360.0 |
| 12/2002 | 1,677.0 | 1,441.0 | 1,560.0 | 12/2005 | 4,518.0 | 3,750.0 | 4,395.0 | 12/2008 | 6,530.0 | 2,817.3 | 3,090.0 |

3-month Forward.   *Source: London Metal Exchange*

# GOLD

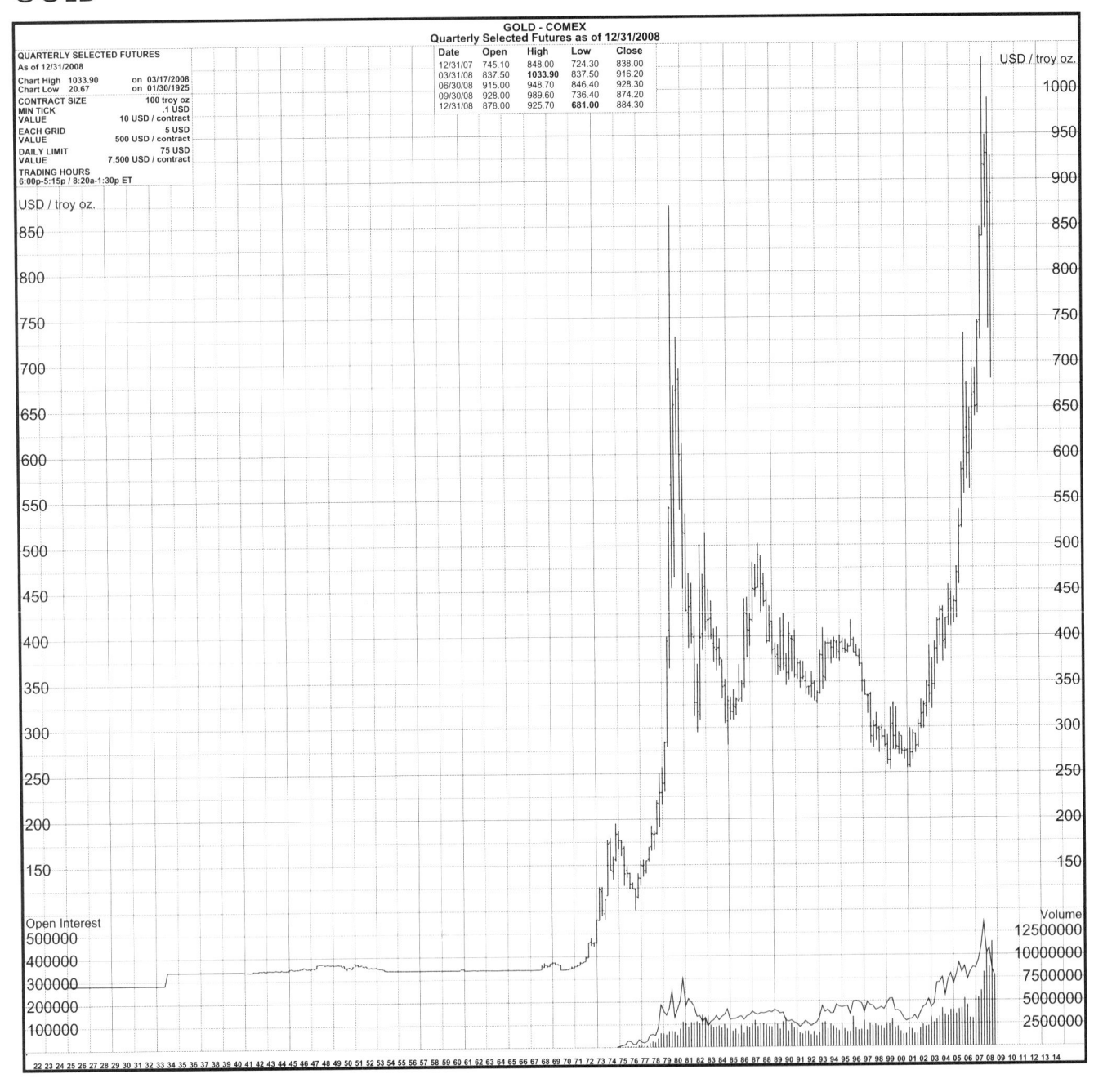

**QUARTERLY SELECTED FUTURES**
As of 12/31/2008
Chart High 1033.90 on 03/17/2008
Chart Low 20.67 on 01/30/1925
CONTRACT SIZE 100 troy oz
MIN TICK .1 USD
VALUE 10 USD / contract
EACH GRID 5 USD
VALUE 500 USD / contract
DAILY LIMIT 75 USD
VALUE 7,500 USD / contract
TRADING HOURS
6:00p-5:15p / 8:20a-1:30p ET

**GOLD - COMEX**
Quarterly Selected Futures as of 12/31/2008

| Date | Open | High | Low | Close |
|---|---|---|---|---|
| 12/31/07 | 745.10 | 848.00 | 724.30 | 838.00 |
| 03/31/08 | 837.50 | 1033.90 | 837.50 | 916.20 |
| 06/30/08 | 915.00 | 948.70 | 846.40 | 928.30 |
| 09/30/08 | 928.00 | 989.60 | 736.40 | 874.20 |
| 12/31/08 | 878.00 | 925.70 | 681.00 | 884.30 |

## Annual High, Low and Settle of Gold    In USD per Troy Ounce

| Year | High | Low | Settle | Year | High | Low | Settle | Year | High | Low | Settle |
|---|---|---|---|---|---|---|---|---|---|---|---|
| 1925 | 20.67 | 20.67 | 20.67 | 1939 | 35.00 | 35.00 | 35.00 | 1953 | 39.25 | 35.25 | 35.50 |
| 1926 | 20.67 | 20.67 | 20.67 | 1940 | 35.00 | 35.00 | 35.00 | 1954 | 35.50 | 35.25 | 35.25 |
| 1927 | 20.67 | 20.67 | 20.67 | 1941 | 35.50 | 34.25 | 35.50 | 1955 | 35.25 | 35.15 | 35.15 |
| 1928 | 20.67 | 20.67 | 20.67 | 1942 | 36.25 | 35.00 | 35.50 | 1956 | 35.20 | 35.15 | 35.20 |
| 1929 | 20.67 | 20.67 | 20.67 | 1943 | 36.50 | 35.50 | 36.50 | 1957 | 35.25 | 35.15 | 35.25 |
| 1930 | 20.67 | 20.67 | 20.67 | 1944 | 36.75 | 36.00 | 36.25 | 1958 | 35.25 | 35.25 | 35.25 |
| 1931 | 20.67 | 20.67 | 20.67 | 1945 | 38.25 | 36.25 | 37.25 | 1959 | 35.25 | 35.25 | 35.25 |
| 1932 | 20.67 | 20.67 | 20.67 | 1946 | 39.50 | 37.75 | 38.25 | 1960 | 36.50 | 35.20 | 36.50 |
| 1933 | 20.67 | 20.67 | 20.67 | 1947 | 43.25 | 37.50 | 43.00 | 1961 | 36.50 | 35.15 | 35.50 |
| 1934 | 35.00 | 35.00 | 35.00 | 1948 | 43.25 | 41.50 | 42.00 | 1962 | 35.50 | 35.20 | 35.45 |
| 1935 | 35.00 | 35.00 | 35.00 | 1949 | 42.50 | 40.50 | 40.50 | 1963 | 35.42 | 35.25 | 35.25 |
| 1936 | 35.00 | 35.00 | 35.00 | 1950 | 41.50 | 36.50 | 40.25 | 1964 | 35.35 | 35.25 | 35.35 |
| 1937 | 35.00 | 35.00 | 35.00 | 1951 | 44.00 | 40.00 | 40.00 | 1965 | 35.50 | 35.28 | 35.50 |
| 1938 | 35.00 | 35.00 | 35.00 | 1952 | 40.75 | 38.15 | 38.70 | 1966 | 35.50 | 35.30 | 35.40 |

U.S. Government
*CME Group; New York Mercantile Exchange*

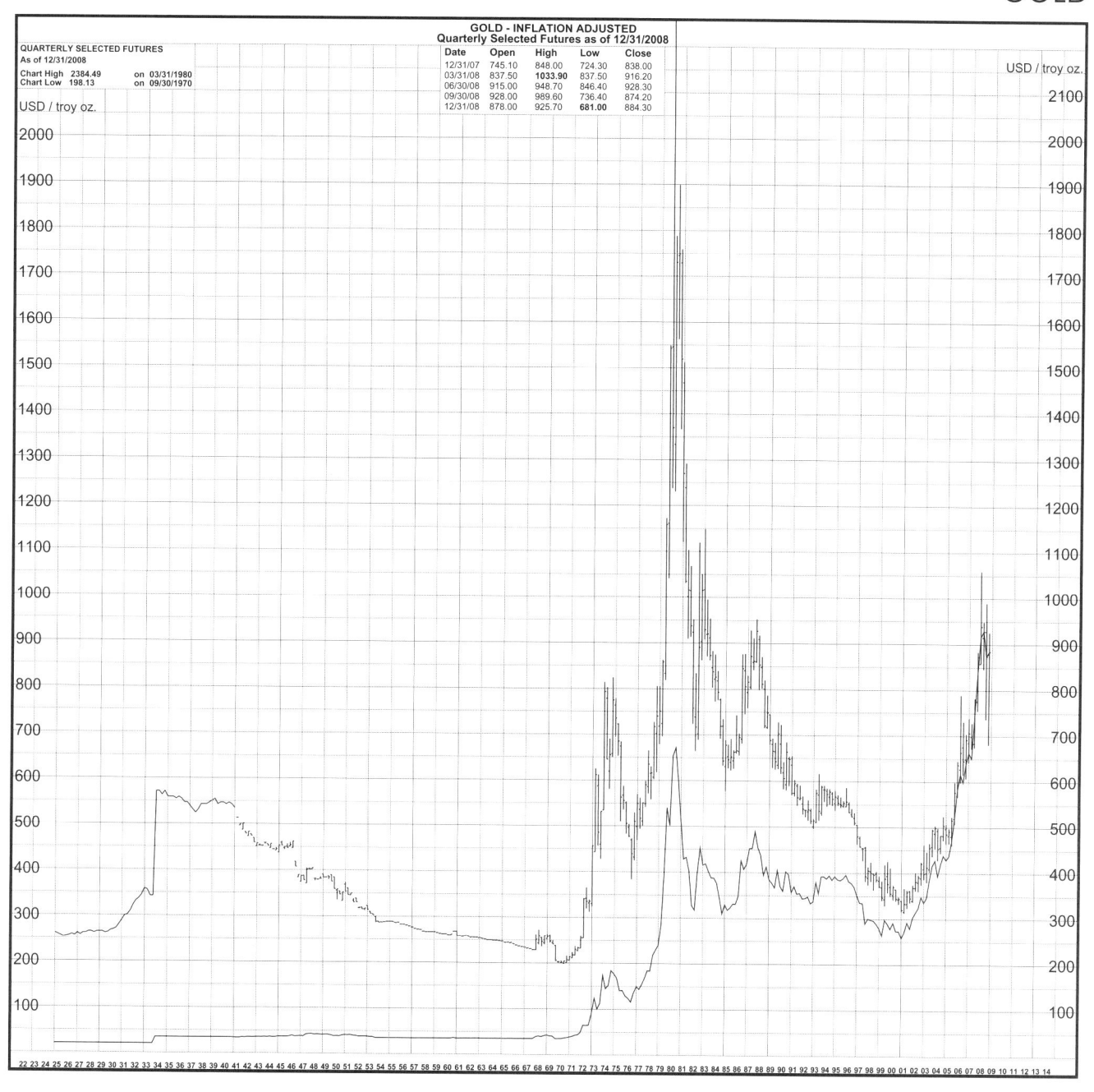

# GOLD

**QUARTERLY SELECTED FUTURES**
As of 12/31/2008
Chart High 2384.49 on 03/31/1980
Chart Low 198.13 on 09/30/1970
USD / troy oz.

**GOLD - INFLATION ADJUSTED**
Quarterly Selected Futures as of 12/31/2008

| Date | Open | High | Low | Close |
|---|---|---|---|---|
| 12/31/07 | 745.10 | 848.00 | 724.30 | 838.00 |
| 03/31/08 | 837.50 | 1033.90 | 837.50 | 916.20 |
| 06/30/08 | 915.00 | 948.70 | 846.40 | 928.30 |
| 09/30/08 | 928.00 | 989.60 | 736.40 | 874.20 |
| 12/31/08 | 878.00 | 925.70 | 681.00 | 884.30 |

## Annual High, Low and Settle of Gold   In USD per Troy Ounce

| Year | High | Low | Settle | Year | High | Low | Settle | Year | High | Low | Settle |
|---|---|---|---|---|---|---|---|---|---|---|---|
| 1925 | 20.67 | 20.67 | 20.67 | 1939 | 35.00 | 35.00 | 35.00 | 1953 | 39.25 | 35.25 | 35.50 |
| 1926 | 20.67 | 20.67 | 20.67 | 1940 | 35.00 | 35.00 | 35.00 | 1954 | 35.50 | 35.25 | 35.25 |
| 1927 | 20.67 | 20.67 | 20.67 | 1941 | 35.50 | 34.25 | 35.50 | 1955 | 35.25 | 35.15 | 35.15 |
| 1928 | 20.67 | 20.67 | 20.67 | 1942 | 36.25 | 35.00 | 35.50 | 1956 | 35.20 | 35.15 | 35.20 |
| 1929 | 20.67 | 20.67 | 20.67 | 1943 | 36.50 | 35.50 | 36.50 | 1957 | 35.25 | 35.15 | 35.25 |
| 1930 | 20.67 | 20.67 | 20.67 | 1944 | 36.75 | 36.00 | 36.25 | 1958 | 35.25 | 35.25 | 35.25 |
| 1931 | 20.67 | 20.67 | 20.67 | 1945 | 38.25 | 36.25 | 37.25 | 1959 | 35.25 | 35.25 | 35.25 |
| 1932 | 20.67 | 20.67 | 20.67 | 1946 | 39.50 | 37.75 | 38.25 | 1960 | 36.50 | 35.20 | 36.50 |
| 1933 | 20.67 | 20.67 | 20.67 | 1947 | 43.25 | 37.50 | 43.00 | 1961 | 36.50 | 35.15 | 35.50 |
| 1934 | 35.00 | 35.00 | 35.00 | 1948 | 43.25 | 41.50 | 42.00 | 1962 | 35.50 | 35.20 | 35.45 |
| 1935 | 35.00 | 35.00 | 35.00 | 1949 | 42.50 | 40.50 | 40.50 | 1963 | 35.42 | 35.25 | 35.25 |
| 1936 | 35.00 | 35.00 | 35.00 | 1950 | 41.50 | 36.50 | 40.25 | 1964 | 35.35 | 35.25 | 35.35 |
| 1937 | 35.00 | 35.00 | 35.00 | 1951 | 44.00 | 40.00 | 40.00 | 1965 | 35.50 | 35.28 | 35.50 |
| 1938 | 35.00 | 35.00 | 35.00 | 1952 | 40.75 | 38.15 | 38.70 | 1966 | 35.50 | 35.30 | 35.40 |

U.S. Government
*CME Group; New York Mercantile Exchange*

# GOLD

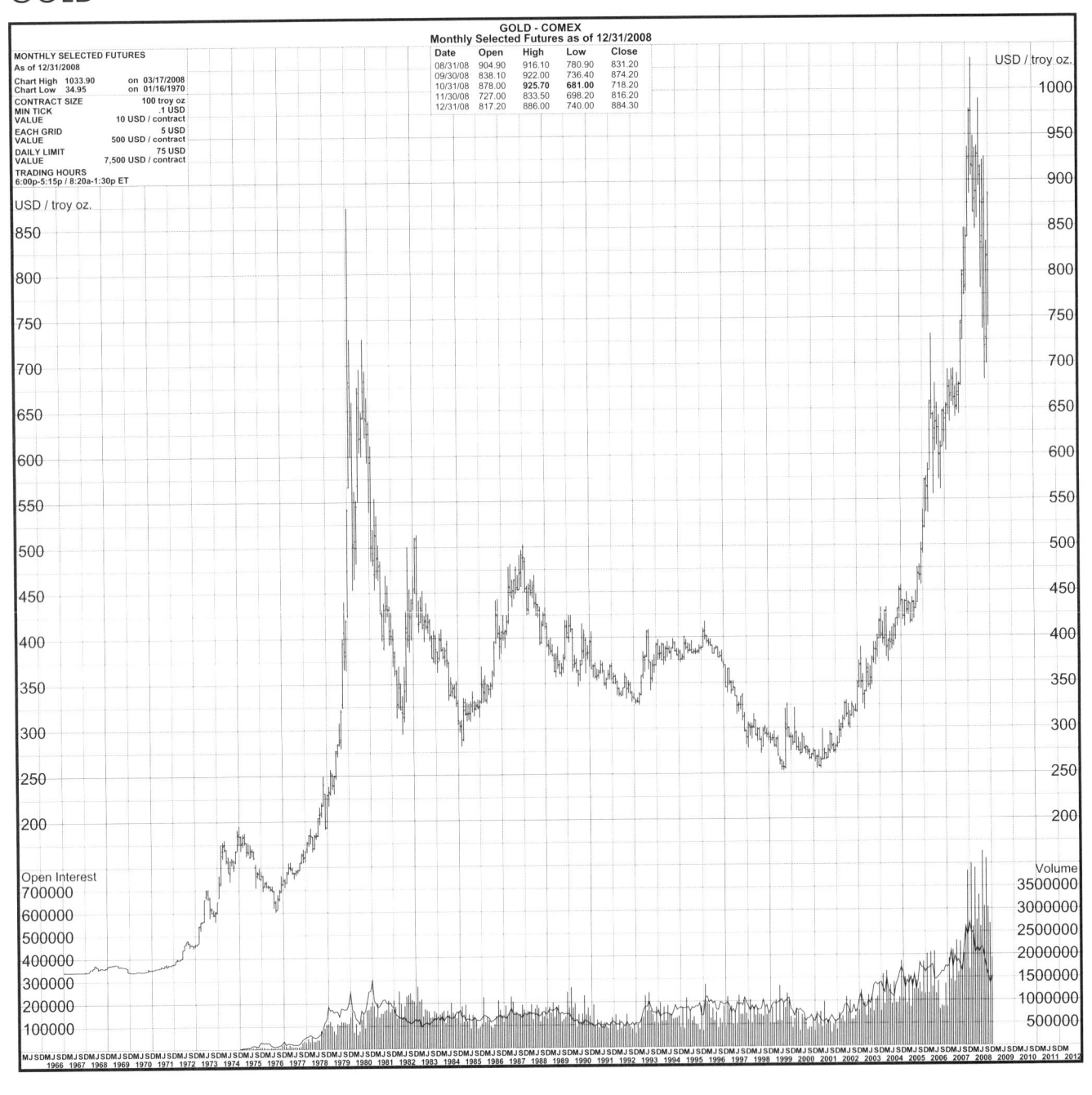

**GOLD - COMEX Monthly Selected Futures as of 12/31/2008**

| Date | Open | High | Low | Close |
|---|---|---|---|---|
| 08/31/08 | 904.90 | 916.10 | 780.90 | 831.20 |
| 09/30/08 | 838.10 | 922.00 | 736.40 | 874.20 |
| 10/31/08 | 878.00 | 925.70 | 681.00 | 718.20 |
| 11/30/08 | 727.00 | 833.50 | 698.20 | 816.20 |
| 12/31/08 | 817.20 | 886.00 | 740.00 | 884.30 |

**MONTHLY SELECTED FUTURES** As of 12/31/2008
- Chart High 1033.90 on 03/17/2008
- Chart Low 34.95 on 01/16/1970
- CONTRACT SIZE: 100 troy oz
- MIN TICK: .1 USD
- VALUE: 10 USD / contract
- EACH GRID: 5 USD
- VALUE: 500 USD / contract
- DAILY LIMIT: 75 USD
- VALUE: 7,500 USD / contract
- TRADING HOURS: 6:00p-5:15p / 8:20a-1:30p ET

### Annual High, Low and Settle of Gold Futures — In USD per Troy Ounce

| Year | High | Low | Settle | Year | High | Low | Settle | Year | High | Low | Settle |
|---|---|---|---|---|---|---|---|---|---|---|---|
| 1967 | 35.50 | 35.27 | 35.50 | 1981 | 612.00 | 387.50 | 402.80 | 1995 | 401.00 | 372.00 | 388.10 |
| 1968 | 43.25 | 35.85 | 42.05 | 1982 | 501.00 | 294.70 | 453.00 | 1996 | 417.50 | 366.00 | 369.20 |
| 1969 | 44.05 | 35.20 | 35.45 | 1983 | 514.00 | 372.00 | 388.00 | 1997 | 369.40 | 281.50 | 289.90 |
| 1970 | 39.30 | 34.95 | 37.65 | 1984 | 410.50 | 304.70 | 309.70 | 1998 | 315.60 | 271.60 | 289.20 |
| 1971 | 44.25 | 37.70 | 43.85 | 1985 | 342.20 | 281.20 | 331.10 | 1999 | 327.50 | 252.50 | 289.60 |
| 1972 | 70.30 | 44.30 | 65.20 | 1986 | 443.00 | 328.00 | 406.90 | 2000 | 322.00 | 264.40 | 273.60 |
| 1973 | 126.45 | 64.20 | 112.30 | 1987 | 502.30 | 389.00 | 488.90 | 2001 | 298.60 | 255.00 | 279.00 |
| 1974 | 195.50 | 116.80 | 183.90 | 1988 | 488.50 | 391.80 | 412.30 | 2002 | 350.80 | 277.20 | 348.20 |
| 1975 | 187.50 | 127.40 | 141.00 | 1989 | 419.70 | 356.50 | 405.20 | 2003 | 418.40 | 319.30 | 416.10 |
| 1976 | 141.50 | 101.00 | 135.70 | 1990 | 425.00 | 346.00 | 396.20 | 2004 | 456.50 | 371.30 | 438.40 |
| 1977 | 169.90 | 127.50 | 167.50 | 1991 | 406.90 | 343.00 | 355.20 | 2005 | 538.50 | 410.10 | 518.90 |
| 1978 | 249.40 | 165.50 | 229.00 | 1992 | 361.50 | 328.90 | 333.10 | 2006 | 732.00 | 517.60 | 638.00 |
| 1979 | 543.00 | 216.60 | 541.00 | 1993 | 409.00 | 325.80 | 391.90 | 2007 | 848.00 | 603.00 | 838.00 |
| 1980 | 873.00 | 453.00 | 599.50 | 1994 | 398.60 | 369.10 | 384.40 | 2008 | 1,033.90 | 681.00 | 884.30 |

Futures begin trading 12/31/1974. Data continued from page 350. *CME Group; New York Mercantile Exchange*

# GOLD

**Gold Composite — Monthly Cash as of 12/31/2008**

| Date | Open | High | Low | Close |
|---|---|---|---|---|
| 08/29/08 | 914.23 | 917.02 | 772.73 | 831.18 |
| 09/30/08 | 835.86 | 925.52 | 736.55 | 870.85 |
| 10/31/08 | 870.72 | 932.11 | 682.75 | 722.30 |
| 11/28/08 | 726.50 | 830.82 | 700.02 | 817.94 |
| 12/31/08 | 818.58 | 890.49 | 741.59 | 881.70 |

MONTHLY CASH As of 12/31/2008
Chart High 1032.80 on 03/17/2008
Chart Low 34.95 on 01/16/1970
USD / troy oz.

## Annual High, Low and Settle of Gold — In USD per Troy Ounce

| Year | High | Low | Settle | Year | High | Low | Settle | Year | High | Low | Settle |
|---|---|---|---|---|---|---|---|---|---|---|---|
| 1967 | 35.50 | 35.27 | 35.50 | 1981 | 599.25 | 391.25 | 401.00 | 1995 | 397.75 | 371.20 | 386.85 |
| 1968 | 43.25 | 35.85 | 42.05 | 1982 | 481.00 | 296.75 | 456.90 | 1996 | 417.90 | 366.30 | 367.45 |
| 1969 | 44.05 | 35.20 | 35.45 | 1983 | 509.25 | 374.25 | 381.50 | 1997 | 368.15 | 282.00 | 288.80 |
| 1970 | 39.30 | 34.95 | 37.65 | 1984 | 405.85 | 307.50 | 308.30 | 1998 | 314.70 | 271.50 | 288.00 |
| 1971 | 44.25 | 37.70 | 43.85 | 1985 | 341.15 | 284.25 | 329.70 | 1999 | 337.50 | 252.00 | 287.50 |
| 1972 | 70.30 | 44.30 | 65.20 | 1986 | 438.35 | 326.55 | 397.00 | 2000 | 319.00 | 262.62 | 271.90 |
| 1973 | 126.45 | 64.20 | 112.30 | 1987 | 499.75 | 390.00 | 484.05 | 2001 | 296.00 | 254.35 | 278.95 |
| 1974 | 195.50 | 116.80 | 186.75 | 1988 | 483.90 | 395.30 | 410.90 | 2002 | 354.25 | 277.05 | 348.05 |
| 1975 | 185.50 | 128.90 | 140.35 | 1989 | 415.50 | 355.75 | 402.90 | 2003 | 417.75 | 319.15 | 415.65 |
| 1976 | 139.20 | 102.20 | 134.75 | 1990 | 423.75 | 345.85 | 394.00 | 2004 | 456.87 | 371.70 | 438.44 |
| 1977 | 168.10 | 130.10 | 164.96 | 1991 | 410.00 | 342.80 | 354.00 | 2005 | 541.00 | 410.40 | 517.03 |
| 1978 | 242.75 | 165.95 | 226.00 | 1992 | 361.00 | 328.80 | 333.10 | 2006 | 730.40 | 511.96 | 636.60 |
| 1979 | 515.50 | 217.10 | 512.00 | 1993 | 408.90 | 325.50 | 390.20 | 2007 | 845.90 | 602.34 | 833.60 |
| 1980 | 850.00 | 481.50 | 586.00 | 1994 | 398.00 | 369.50 | 382.70 | 2008 | 1,032.80 | 682.75 | 881.70 |

Black Market to 02/1968; Handy and Harman 03/1968 to 05/1990; Composite 06/1990 to date.   Data continued from page 351.
*CME Group; New York Mercantile Exchange*

# GOLD

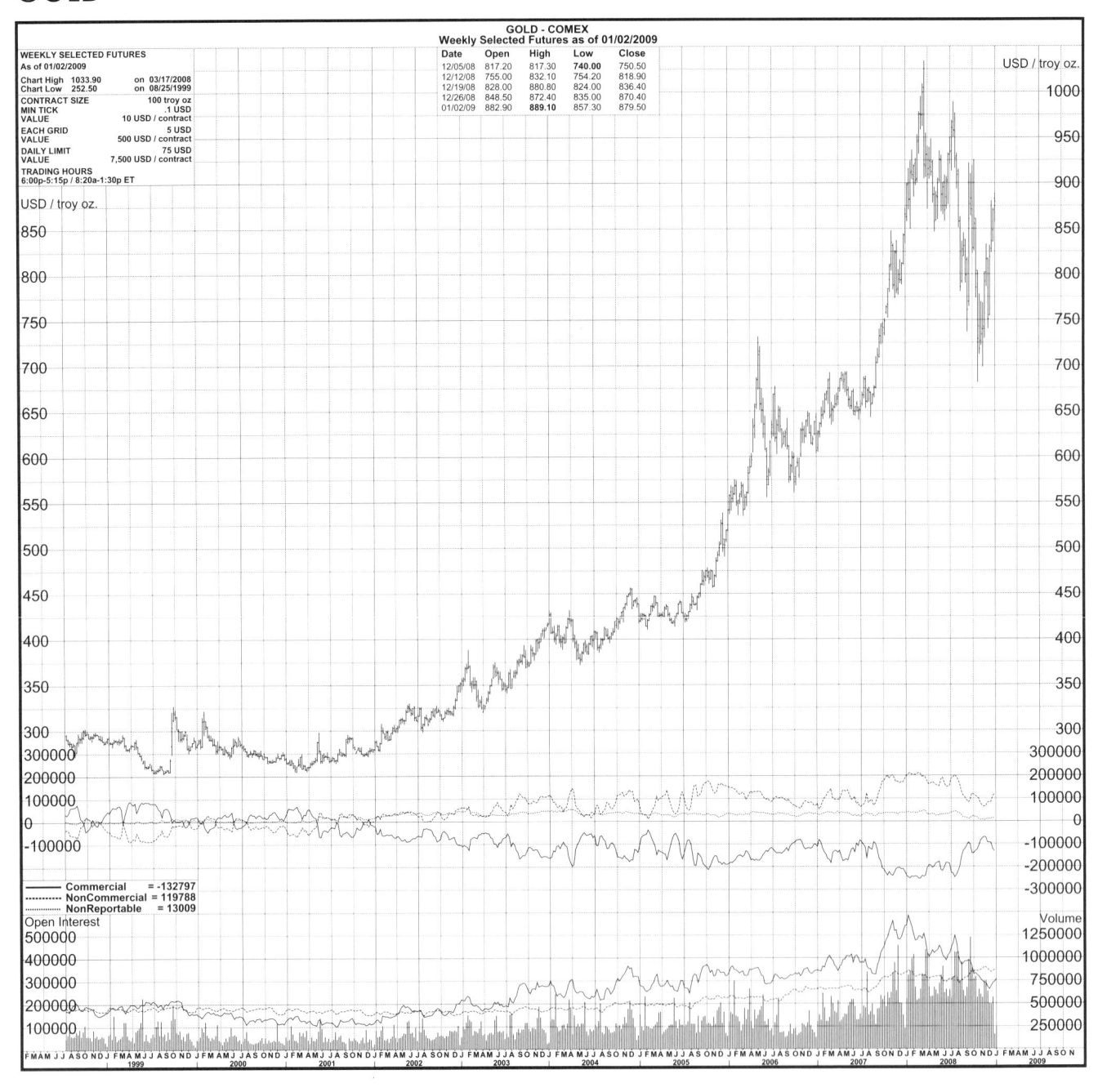

**GOLD - COMEX**
Weekly Selected Futures as of 01/02/2009

| Date | Open | High | Low | Close |
|---|---|---|---|---|
| 12/05/08 | 817.20 | 817.30 | 740.00 | 750.50 |
| 12/12/08 | 755.00 | 832.10 | 754.20 | 818.90 |
| 12/19/08 | 828.00 | 880.80 | 824.00 | 836.40 |
| 12/26/08 | 848.50 | 872.40 | 835.00 | 870.40 |
| 01/02/09 | 882.90 | 889.10 | 857.30 | 879.50 |

**WEEKLY SELECTED FUTURES**
As of 01/02/2009
Chart High 1033.90 on 03/17/2008
Chart Low 252.50 on 08/25/1999
CONTRACT SIZE 100 troy oz
MIN TICK .1 USD / contract
VALUE 10 USD / contract
EACH GRID 5 USD
VALUE 500 USD / contract
DAILY LIMIT 75 USD
VALUE 7,500 USD / contract
TRADING HOURS
6:00p-5:15p / 8:20a-1:30p ET

Commercial = -132797
NonCommercial = 119788
NonReportable = 13009

## Quarterly High, Low and Settle of Gold Futures    In USD per Troy Ounce

| Quarter | High | Low | Settle | Quarter | High | Low | Settle | Quarter | High | Low | Settle |
|---|---|---|---|---|---|---|---|---|---|---|---|
| 03/2000 | 322.00 | 274.50 | 278.40 | 03/2003 | 388.90 | 325.80 | 335.90 | 03/2006 | 589.60 | 517.60 | 581.80 |
| 06/2000 | 294.30 | 269.50 | 291.50 | 06/2003 | 374.90 | 319.30 | 346.30 | 06/2006 | 732.00 | 555.00 | 616.00 |
| 09/2000 | 289.70 | 269.50 | 273.60 | 09/2003 | 393.80 | 340.60 | 385.40 | 09/2006 | 677.50 | 571.00 | 598.60 |
| 12/2000 | 277.20 | 264.40 | 273.60 | 12/2003 | 418.40 | 368.00 | 416.10 | 12/2006 | 649.50 | 560.50 | 638.00 |
| 03/2001 | 275.00 | 255.00 | 257.90 | 03/2004 | 431.50 | 388.20 | 427.30 | 03/2007 | 692.50 | 603.00 | 663.00 |
| 06/2001 | 298.60 | 255.00 | 271.30 | 06/2004 | 432.00 | 371.30 | 393.00 | 06/2007 | 693.30 | 640.00 | 650.90 |
| 09/2001 | 296.00 | 264.10 | 292.40 | 09/2004 | 418.80 | 385.00 | 418.70 | 09/2007 | 745.70 | 642.90 | 742.80 |
| 12/2001 | 292.90 | 271.20 | 279.00 | 12/2004 | 456.50 | 410.30 | 438.40 | 12/2007 | 848.00 | 724.30 | 838.00 |
| 03/2002 | 308.00 | 277.20 | 302.60 | 03/2005 | 448.00 | 410.10 | 428.70 | 03/2008 | 1,033.90 | 837.50 | 916.20 |
| 06/2002 | 330.30 | 297.50 | 313.90 | 06/2005 | 442.50 | 413.20 | 437.10 | 06/2008 | 948.70 | 846.40 | 928.30 |
| 09/2002 | 328.00 | 298.00 | 323.90 | 09/2005 | 475.70 | 418.20 | 469.00 | 09/2008 | 989.60 | 736.40 | 874.20 |
| 12/2002 | 350.80 | 309.80 | 348.20 | 12/2005 | 538.50 | 456.10 | 518.90 | 12/2008 | 925.70 | 681.00 | 884.30 |

*CME Group; New York Mercantile Exchange*

# GOLD

**Gold Composite Weekly Cash as of 01/02/2009**

| Date | Open | High | Low | Close |
|---|---|---|---|---|
| 12/05/08 | 818.58 | 818.58 | 741.59 | 755.92 |
| 12/12/08 | 755.22 | 834.94 | 754.62 | 822.06 |
| 12/19/08 | 824.13 | 882.25 | 821.80 | 838.29 |
| 12/26/08 | 838.55 | 872.95 | 829.80 | 869.15 |
| 01/02/09 | 871.35 | 890.49 | 856.60 | 875.95 |

WEEKLY CASH
As of 01/02/2009
Chart High 1032.80 on 03/17/2008
Chart Low 252.00 on 08/26/1999
USD / troy oz.

## Quarterly High, Low and Settle of Gold    In USD per Troy Ounce

| Quarter | High | Low | Settle | Quarter | High | Low | Settle | Quarter | High | Low | Settle |
|---|---|---|---|---|---|---|---|---|---|---|---|
| 03/2000 | 319.00 | 275.50 | 278.40 | 03/2003 | 389.05 | 325.70 | 337.35 | 03/2006 | 589.51 | 511.96 | 582.95 |
| 06/2000 | 293.75 | 269.70 | 289.60 | 06/2003 | 374.65 | 319.15 | 346.40 | 06/2006 | 730.40 | 542.27 | 616.00 |
| 09/2000 | 289.50 | 268.85 | 273.65 | 09/2003 | 393.75 | 340.55 | 385.35 | 09/2006 | 676.41 | 570.94 | 598.93 |
| 12/2000 | 277.35 | 262.62 | 271.90 | 12/2003 | 417.75 | 366.50 | 415.65 | 12/2006 | 649.96 | 559.30 | 636.60 |
| 03/2001 | 274.40 | 254.35 | 257.45 | 03/2004 | 430.40 | 387.95 | 426.40 | 03/2007 | 688.73 | 602.34 | 663.74 |
| 06/2001 | 296.00 | 255.05 | 270.35 | 06/2004 | 431.08 | 371.70 | 394.17 | 06/2007 | 694.19 | 639.48 | 649.50 |
| 09/2001 | 294.50 | 264.75 | 292.45 | 09/2004 | 419.09 | 385.55 | 418.51 | 09/2007 | 745.92 | 642.25 | 743.00 |
| 12/2001 | 293.75 | 271.45 | 278.95 | 12/2004 | 456.87 | 409.50 | 438.44 | 12/2007 | 845.90 | 721.22 | 833.60 |
| 03/2002 | 308.55 | 277.05 | 302.45 | 03/2005 | 447.05 | 410.40 | 428.55 | 03/2008 | 1,032.80 | 834.95 | 916.95 |
| 06/2002 | 330.55 | 297.70 | 314.45 | 06/2005 | 443.70 | 413.85 | 435.30 | 06/2008 | 952.76 | 846.27 | 925.59 |
| 09/2002 | 327.95 | 298.95 | 323.55 | 09/2005 | 475.50 | 418.25 | 469.35 | 09/2008 | 988.02 | 736.55 | 870.85 |
| 12/2002 | 354.25 | 308.75 | 348.05 | 12/2005 | 541.00 | 455.50 | 517.03 | 12/2008 | 932.11 | 682.75 | 881.70 |

Composite.    *CME Group; New York Mercantile Exchange*

355

# LEAD

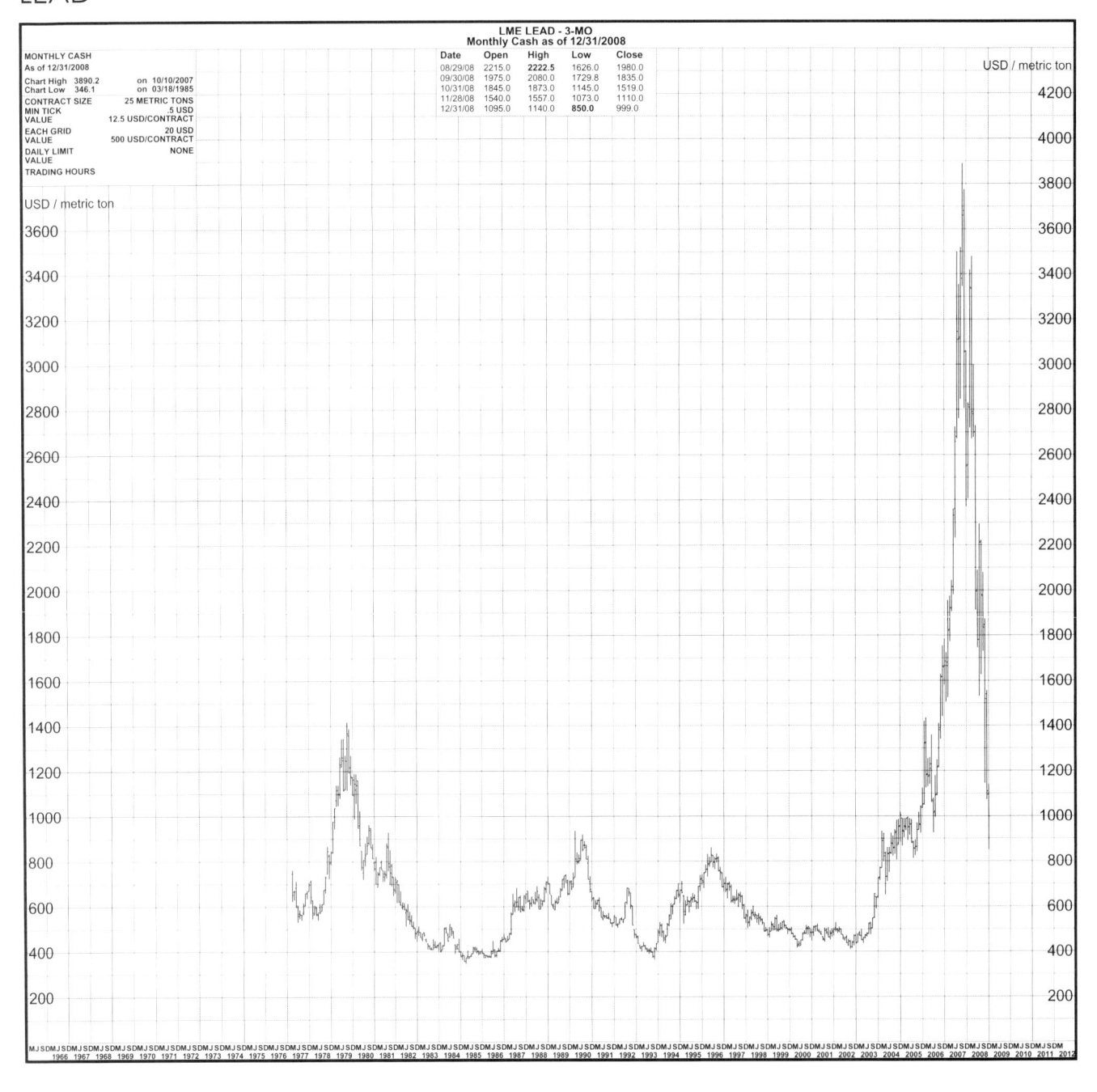

## Annual High, Low and Settle of Lead   In USD per Metric Ton

| Year | High | Low | Settle | Year | High | Low | Settle | Year | High | Low | Settle |
|---|---|---|---|---|---|---|---|---|---|---|---|
| 1967 | | | | 1981 | 929.1 | 647.6 | 721.1 | 1995 | 742.0 | 523.0 | 714.0 |
| 1968 | | | | 1982 | 719.1 | 445.1 | 487.4 | 1996 | 861.0 | 666.5 | 700.0 |
| 1969 | | | | 1983 | 514.7 | 403.6 | 436.2 | 1997 | 731.0 | 525.0 | 564.0 |
| 1970 | | | | 1984 | 522.8 | 378.6 | 378.6 | 1998 | 603.0 | 466.0 | 474.0 |
| 1971 | | | | 1985 | 423.4 | 346.1 | 391.6 | 1999 | 562.0 | 460.0 | 495.5 |
| 1972 | | | | 1986 | 480.6 | 371.1 | 462.4 | 2000 | 517.0 | 415.0 | 484.0 |
| 1973 | | | | 1987 | 684.1 | 438.8 | 656.9 | 2001 | 523.0 | 441.0 | 497.0 |
| 1974 | | | | 1988 | 731.9 | 588.0 | 700.8 | 2002 | 530.0 | 409.0 | 436.0 |
| 1975 | | | | 1989 | 743.0 | 584.5 | 707.0 | 2003 | 727.0 | 435.0 | 724.0 |
| 1976 | | | | 1990 | 935.0 | 624.0 | 633.0 | 2004 | 1,019.0 | 651.0 | 1,004.0 |
| 1977 | 762.9 | 530.9 | 697.8 | 1991 | 643.0 | 509.0 | 560.0 | 2005 | 1,125.0 | 812.0 | 1,051.0 |
| 1978 | 867.4 | 540.7 | 843.4 | 1992 | 684.0 | 459.0 | 463.0 | 2006 | 1,785.0 | 924.8 | 1,665.2 |
| 1979 | 1,417.5 | 838.0 | 1,094.5 | 1993 | 499.0 | 365.0 | 488.0 | 2007 | 3,890.2 | 1,505.0 | 2,550.0 |
| 1980 | 1,190.6 | 719.2 | 768.3 | 1994 | 703.0 | 435.0 | 673.0 | 2008 | 3,480.0 | 850.0 | 999.0 |

3-month Forward.   Source: London Metal Exchange

# LEAD

```
                    LME LEAD - 3-MO
                 Weekly Cash as of 01/02/2009
WEEKLY CASH       Date      Open    High    Low     Close
As of 01/02/2009  12/05/08  1095.0  1140.0  921.3   940.0
Chart High  3890.2  on 10/10/2007   12/12/08  975.0   1045.0  956.0   1020.0
Chart Low   409.0   on 09/24/2002   12/19/08  1020.0  1050.0  851.0   875.0
CONTRACT SIZE    25 METRIC TONS    12/24/08  900.0   924.8   850.0   850.0
MIN TICK         .5 USD            01/02/09  890.0   1120.0  860.0   1120.0
VALUE            12.5 USD/CONTRACT
EACH GRID        20 USD
VALUE            500 USD/CONTRACT
DAILY LIMIT      NONE
VALUE
TRADING HOURS
```

## Quarterly High, Low and Settle of Lead    In USD per Metric Ton

| Quarter | High | Low | Settle | Quarter | High | Low | Settle | Quarter | High | Low | Settle |
|---|---|---|---|---|---|---|---|---|---|---|---|
| 03/2000 | 509.0 | 449.5 | 453.0 | 03/2003 | 500.0 | 438.0 | 449.5 | 03/2006 | 1,435.0 | 1,049.0 | 1,175.0 |
| 06/2000 | 454.0 | 415.0 | 450.0 | 06/2003 | 483.0 | 435.0 | 479.0 | 06/2006 | 1,360.0 | 924.8 | 1,015.0 |
| 09/2000 | 517.0 | 445.0 | 504.0 | 09/2003 | 550.0 | 474.0 | 547.0 | 09/2006 | 1,410.5 | 995.0 | 1,380.0 |
| 12/2000 | 513.0 | 446.0 | 484.0 | 12/2003 | 727.0 | 547.0 | 724.0 | 12/2006 | 1,785.0 | 1,340.0 | 1,665.2 |
| 03/2001 | 523.0 | 466.0 | 492.5 | 03/2004 | 933.0 | 714.0 | 822.0 | 03/2007 | 1,975.2 | 1,505.0 | 1,920.0 |
| 06/2001 | 498.0 | 447.0 | 455.0 | 06/2004 | 862.0 | 651.0 | 837.0 | 06/2007 | 2,725.0 | 1,905.0 | 2,657.9 |
| 09/2001 | 508.0 | 441.0 | 462.0 | 09/2004 | 940.0 | 822.0 | 925.0 | 09/2007 | 3,520.0 | 2,670.0 | 3,400.0 |
| 12/2001 | 503.0 | 451.0 | 497.0 | 12/2004 | 1,019.0 | 805.0 | 1,004.0 | 12/2007 | 3,890.2 | 2,371.0 | 2,550.0 |
| 03/2002 | 530.0 | 479.0 | 498.0 | 03/2005 | 991.0 | 867.0 | 989.0 | 03/2008 | 3,480.0 | 2,405.0 | 2,790.0 |
| 06/2002 | 500.0 | 445.0 | 461.0 | 06/2005 | 996.0 | 880.0 | 880.0 | 06/2008 | 3,000.0 | 1,745.0 | 1,780.0 |
| 09/2002 | 471.0 | 409.0 | 419.0 | 09/2005 | 970.0 | 812.0 | 938.0 | 09/2008 | 2,293.8 | 1,531.0 | 1,835.0 |
| 12/2002 | 477.0 | 413.0 | 436.0 | 12/2005 | 1,125.0 | 923.9 | 1,051.0 | 12/2008 | 1,873.0 | 850.0 | 999.0 |

3-month Forward.    Source: *London Metal Exchange*

# NICKEL

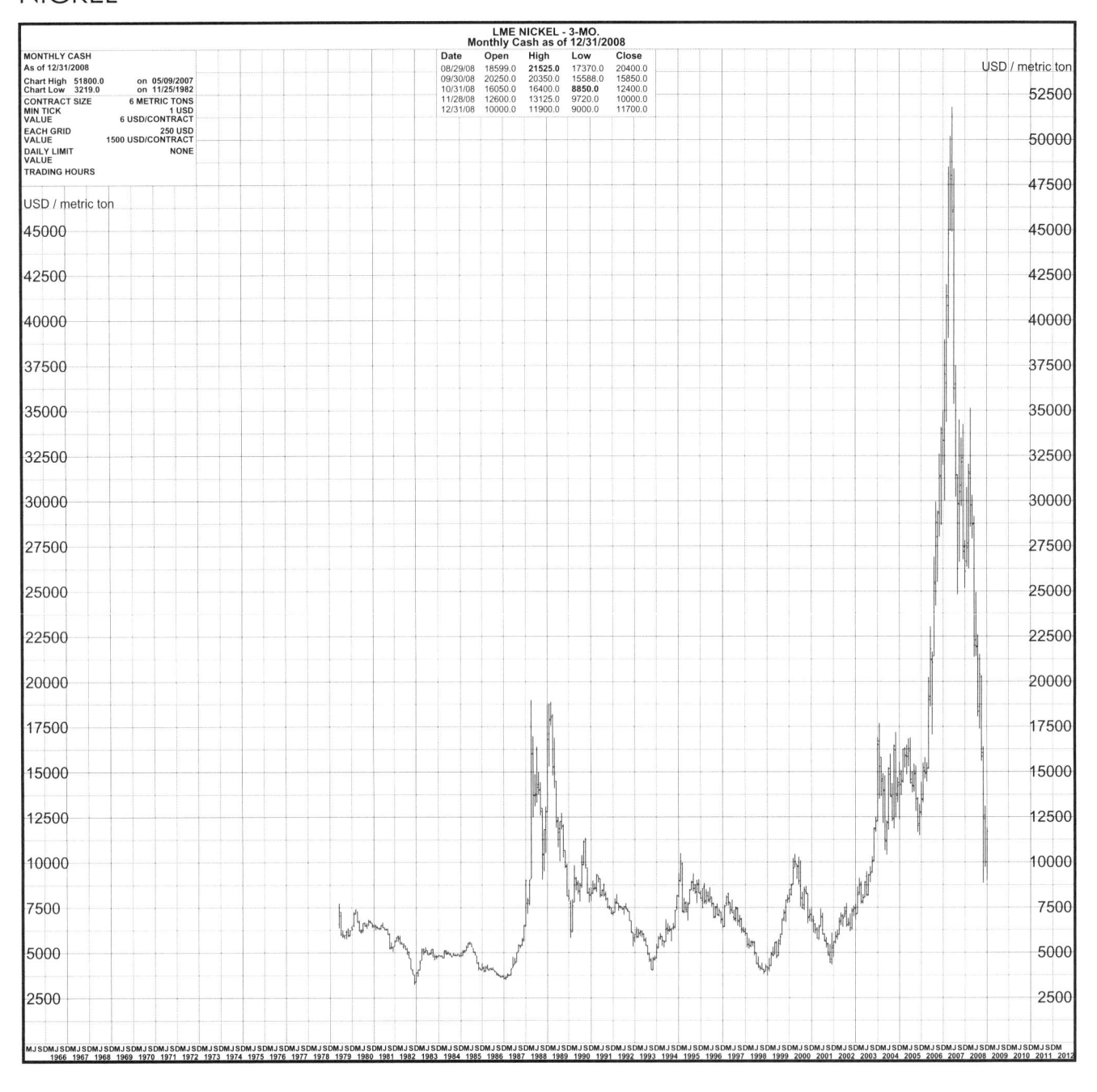

```
                    LME NICKEL - 3-MO.
                  Monthly Cash as of 12/31/2008
MONTHLY CASH       Date     Open    High    Low     Close
As of 12/31/2008   08/29/08 18599.0 21525.0 17370.0 20400.0
Chart High 51800.0 on 05/09/2007  09/30/08 20250.0 20350.0 15588.0 15850.0
Chart Low   3219.0 on 11/25/1982  10/31/08 16050.0 16400.0  8850.0 12400.0
CONTRACT SIZE  6 METRIC TONS      11/28/08 12600.0 13125.0  9720.0 10000.0
MIN TICK              1 USD       12/31/08 10000.0 11900.0  9000.0 11700.0
VALUE        6 USD/CONTRACT
EACH GRID         250 USD
VALUE        1500 USD/CONTRACT
DAILY LIMIT         NONE
VALUE
TRADING HOURS
```

## Annual High, Low and Settle of Nickel   In USD per Metric Ton

| Year | High | Low | Settle | Year | High | Low | Settle | Year | High | Low | Settle |
|---|---|---|---|---|---|---|---|---|---|---|---|
| 1967 | | | | 1981 | 6,701 | 5,051 | 5,647 | 1995 | 10,500 | 6,770 | 8,010 |
| 1968 | | | | 1982 | 5,962 | 3,219 | 3,906 | 1996 | 8,850 | 6,360 | 6,465 |
| 1969 | | | | 1983 | 5,313 | 3,665 | 4,842 | 1997 | 8,320 | 5,920 | 6,070 |
| 1970 | | | | 1984 | 5,168 | 4,701 | 4,825 | 1998 | 6,080 | 3,775 | 4,170 |
| 1971 | | | | 1985 | 5,602 | 4,000 | 4,131 | 1999 | 8,515 | 3,940 | 8,500 |
| 1972 | | | | 1986 | 4,356 | 3,541 | 3,568 | 2000 | 10,450 | 6,610 | 6,830 |
| 1973 | | | | 1987 | 9,039 | 3,484 | 8,995 | 2001 | 7,450 | 4,320 | 5,575 |
| 1974 | | | | 1988 | 19,000 | 7,154 | 16,800 | 2002 | 7,760 | 5,470 | 7,130 |
| 1975 | | | | 1989 | 18,900 | 7,850 | 8,000 | 2003 | 16,900 | 7,140 | 16,500 |
| 1976 | | | | 1990 | 11,350 | 5,800 | 8,300 | 2004 | 17,700 | 10,400 | 14,875 |
| 1977 | | | | 1991 | 9,350 | 7,050 | 7,215 | 2005 | 16,901 | 11,480 | 13,500 |
| 1978 | | | | 1992 | 8,245 | 5,320 | 6,020 | 2006 | 34,950 | 13,300 | 33,326 |
| 1979 | 7,748 | 5,748 | 6,302 | 1993 | 6,440 | 4,030 | 5,305 | 2007 | 51,800 | 24,800 | 26,100 |
| 1980 | 7,404 | 6,057 | 6,477 | 1994 | 9,400 | 5,240 | 8,975 | 2008 | 35,150 | 8,850 | 11,700 |

3-month Forward.   *Source: London Metal Exchange*

# NICKEL

**WEEKLY CASH** As of 01/02/2009
Chart High 51800.0 on 05/09/2007
Chart Low 3775.0 on 12/08/1998
CONTRACT SIZE 6 METRIC TONS
MIN TICK 1 USD
VALUE 6 USD/CONTRACT
EACH GRID 250 USD
VALUE 1500 USD/CONTRACT
DAILY LIMIT NONE
VALUE
TRADING HOURS

**LME NICKEL - 3-MO.**
Weekly Cash as of 01/02/2009

| Date | Open | High | Low | Close |
|---|---|---|---|---|
| 12/05/08 | 10000.0 | 10500.0 | 9011.0 | 9085.0 |
| 12/12/08 | 9200.0 | 11500.0 | 9000.0 | 10550.0 |
| 12/19/08 | 10700.0 | 10715.0 | 9375.0 | 10300.0 |
| 12/24/08 | 10300.0 | 10500.0 | 9580.0 | 9625.0 |
| 01/02/09 | 9800.0 | 13550.0 | 9700.0 | 12900.0 |

## Quarterly High, Low and Settle of Nickel    In USD per Metric Ton

| Quarter | High | Low | Settle | Quarter | High | Low | Settle | Quarter | High | Low | Settle |
|---|---|---|---|---|---|---|---|---|---|---|---|
| 03/2000 | 10,450 | 8,135 | 10,020 | 03/2003 | 9,140 | 7,140 | 7,780 | 03/2006 | 15,802 | 13,300 | 15,200 |
| 06/2000 | 10,300 | 7,550 | 8,010 | 06/2003 | 9,500 | 7,700 | 8,210 | 06/2006 | 23,050 | 15,150 | 21,050 |
| 09/2000 | 8,690 | 7,340 | 8,300 | 09/2003 | 10,330 | 8,160 | 10,065 | 09/2006 | 29,950 | 21,400 | 29,300 |
| 12/2000 | 8,260 | 6,610 | 6,830 | 12/2003 | 16,900 | 10,025 | 16,500 | 12/2006 | 34,950 | 28,000 | 33,326 |
| 03/2001 | 7,050 | 5,750 | 5,810 | 03/2004 | 17,700 | 12,150 | 14,000 | 03/2007 | 48,500 | 30,000 | 44,800 |
| 06/2001 | 7,450 | 5,710 | 6,020 | 06/2004 | 15,250 | 10,400 | 15,175 | 06/2007 | 51,800 | 35,350 | 36,200 |
| 09/2001 | 6,070 | 4,805 | 4,910 | 09/2004 | 16,500 | 11,850 | 16,425 | 09/2007 | 37,500 | 24,800 | 30,501 |
| 12/2001 | 6,090 | 4,320 | 5,575 | 12/2004 | 17,200 | 12,350 | 14,875 | 12/2007 | 34,250 | 25,177 | 26,100 |
| 03/2002 | 6,950 | 5,470 | 6,690 | 03/2005 | 16,350 | 13,700 | 15,900 | 03/2008 | 35,150 | 26,250 | 29,755 |
| 06/2002 | 7,540 | 6,410 | 7,160 | 06/2005 | 16,901 | 14,325 | 14,590 | 06/2008 | 30,325 | 21,355 | 21,905 |
| 09/2002 | 7,760 | 6,160 | 6,360 | 09/2005 | 15,450 | 12,825 | 13,500 | 09/2008 | 22,599 | 15,588 | 15,850 |
| 12/2002 | 7,680 | 6,260 | 7,130 | 12/2005 | 14,451 | 11,480 | 13,500 | 12/2008 | 16,400 | 8,850 | 11,700 |

3-month Forward.    *Source: London Metal Exchange*

# PALLADIUM

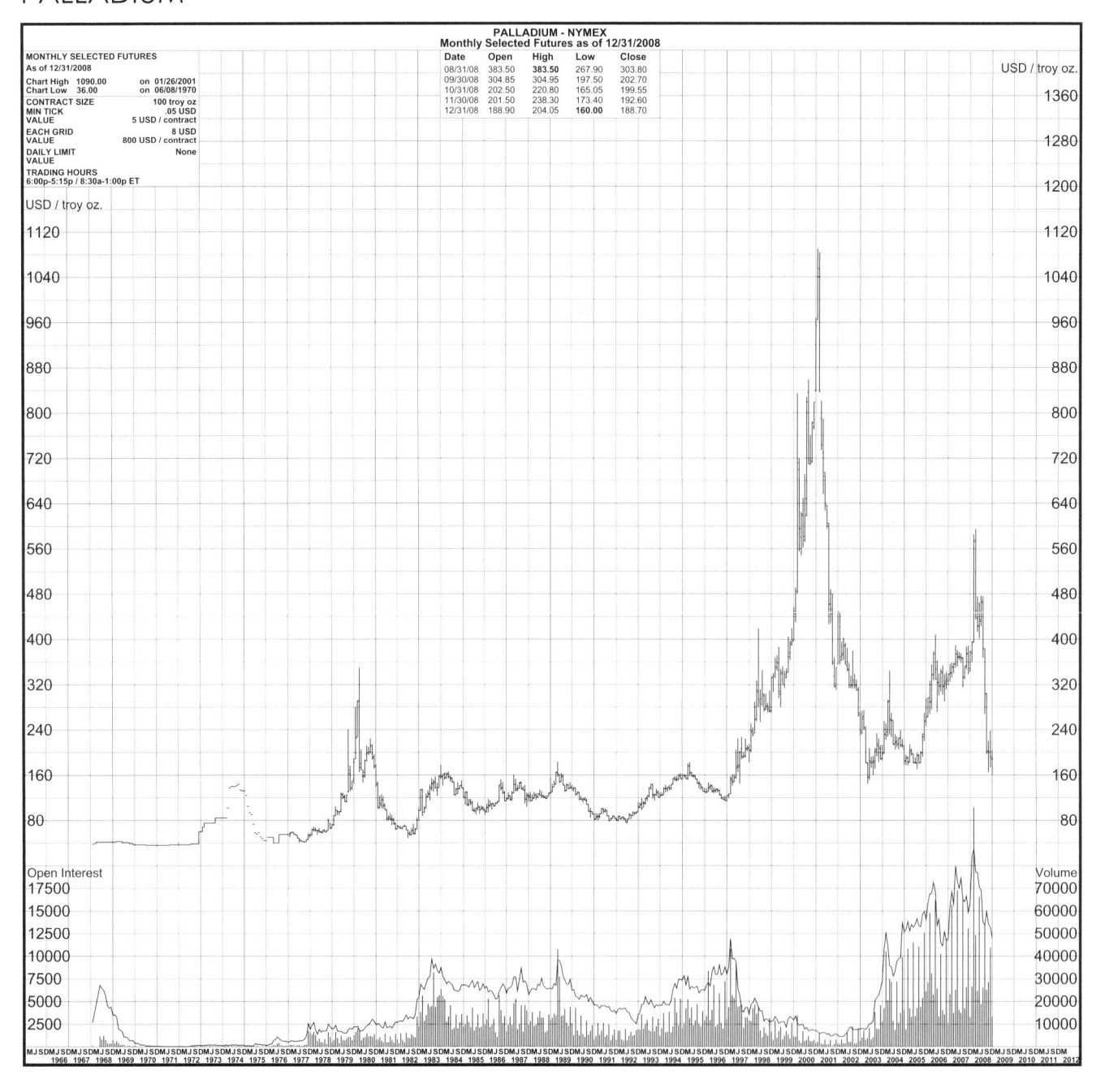

**PALLADIUM - NYMEX**
Monthly Selected Futures as of 12/31/2008

| Date | Open | High | Low | Close |
|---|---|---|---|---|
| 08/31/08 | 383.50 | 383.50 | 267.90 | 303.80 |
| 09/30/08 | 304.85 | 304.95 | 197.50 | 202.70 |
| 10/31/08 | 202.50 | 220.80 | 165.05 | 199.55 |
| 11/30/08 | 201.50 | 238.30 | 173.40 | 192.60 |
| 12/31/08 | 188.90 | 204.05 | 160.00 | 188.70 |

**MONTHLY SELECTED FUTURES**
As of 12/31/2008
Chart High 1090.00 on 01/26/2001
Chart Low 36.00 on 06/08/1970
CONTRACT SIZE 100 troy oz
MIN TICK .05 USD
VALUE 5 USD / contract
EACH GRID 8 USD
VALUE 800 USD / contract
DAILY LIMIT None
VALUE
TRADING HOURS
6:00p-5:15p / 8:30a-1:00p ET

## Annual High, Low and Settle of Palladium Futures   In USD per Troy Ounce

| Year | High | Low | Settle | Year | High | Low | Settle | Year | High | Low | Settle |
|---|---|---|---|---|---|---|---|---|---|---|---|
| 1967 |  |  |  | 1981 | 149.00 | 63.00 | 69.30 | 1995 | 182.90 | 128.80 | 129.65 |
| 1968 | 42.00 | 37.00 | 42.00 | 1982 | 102.00 | 48.00 | 97.50 | 1996 | 147.00 | 114.50 | 124.05 |
| 1969 | 43.00 | 37.00 | 37.00 | 1983 | 178.00 | 88.00 | 157.45 | 1997 | 227.60 | 120.25 | 203.15 |
| 1970 | 37.00 | 36.00 | 36.00 | 1984 | 166.75 | 120.00 | 121.50 | 1998 | 419.00 | 200.00 | 332.15 |
| 1971 | 37.00 | 36.00 | 37.00 | 1985 | 132.00 | 89.75 | 95.40 | 1999 | 456.95 | 280.00 | 449.20 |
| 1972 | 60.00 | 37.00 | 60.00 | 1986 | 153.00 | 94.00 | 118.30 | 2000 | 975.00 | 430.20 | 954.45 |
| 1973 | 84.00 | 60.00 | 84.00 | 1987 | 160.00 | 103.65 | 123.60 | 2001 | 1,090.00 | 310.00 | 448.00 |
| 1974 | 143.80 | 84.00 | 132.50 | 1988 | 155.95 | 113.00 | 129.00 | 2002 | 447.00 | 229.70 | 238.00 |
| 1975 | 124.32 | 44.00 | 44.00 | 1989 | 184.00 | 129.25 | 135.50 | 2003 | 275.00 | 145.00 | 197.50 |
| 1976 | 55.00 | 40.00 | 55.00 | 1990 | 139.90 | 80.55 | 81.25 | 2004 | 344.70 | 177.75 | 185.25 |
| 1977 | 59.80 | 40.10 | 53.50 | 1991 | 102.50 | 77.50 | 80.65 | 2005 | 297.10 | 170.20 | 261.50 |
| 1978 | 83.35 | 52.40 | 72.50 | 1992 | 112.00 | 74.50 | 104.45 | 2006 | 409.00 | 262.00 | 338.50 |
| 1979 | 240.50 | 70.10 | 182.50 | 1993 | 145.00 | 98.00 | 124.35 | 2007 | 389.50 | 315.20 | 378.20 |
| 1980 | 350.00 | 139.00 | 142.25 | 1994 | 164.00 | 122.50 | 160.25 | 2008 | 595.10 | 160.00 | 188.70 |

Futures data begins 01/03/1977.   *CME Group; New York Mercantile Exchange*

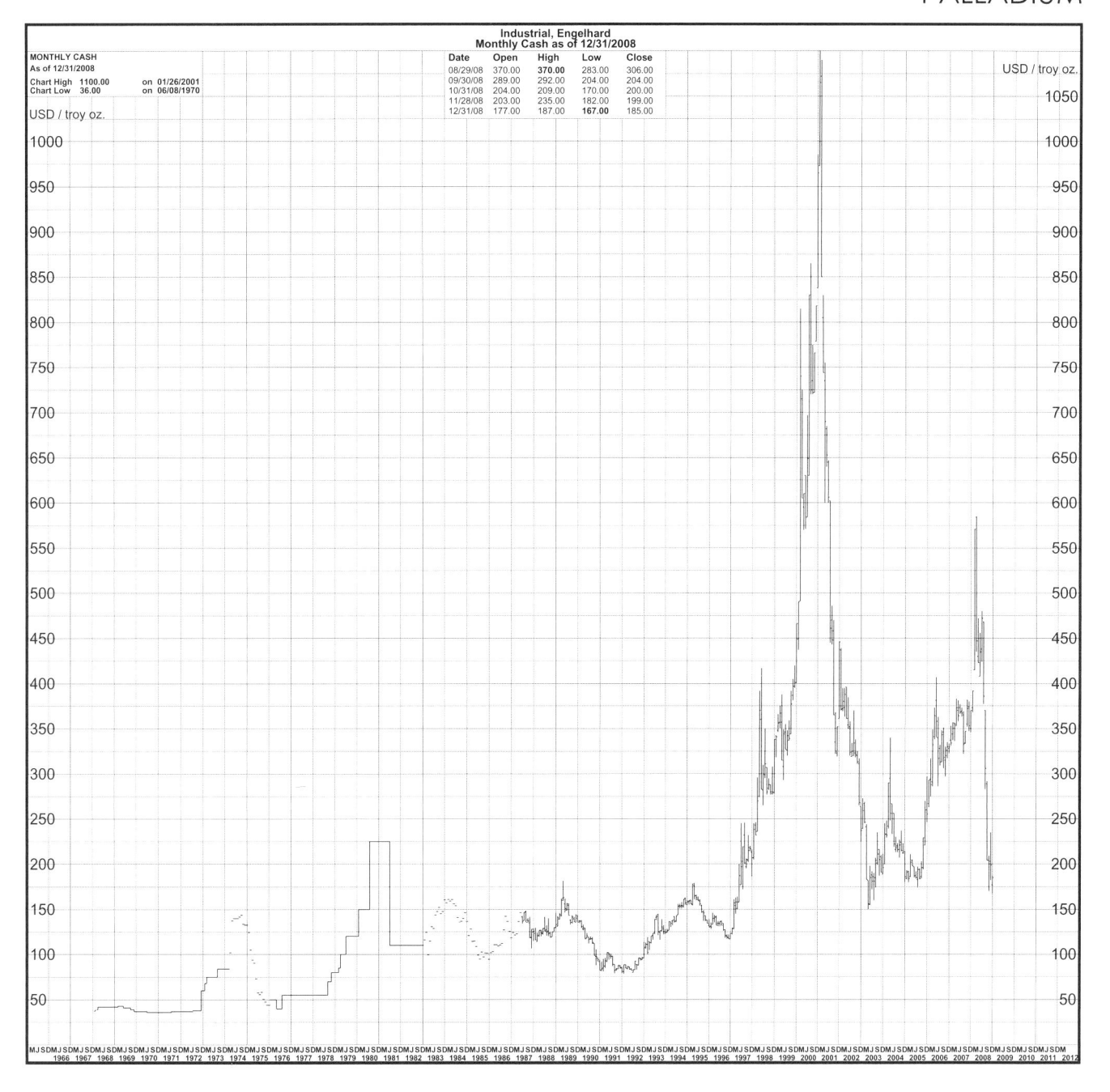

# PALLADIUM

**Monthly Cash as of 12/31/2008** — Industrial, Engelhard

| Date | Open | High | Low | Close |
|---|---|---|---|---|
| 08/29/08 | 370.00 | 370.00 | 283.00 | 306.00 |
| 09/30/08 | 289.00 | 292.00 | 204.00 | 204.00 |
| 10/31/08 | 204.00 | 209.00 | 170.00 | 200.00 |
| 11/28/08 | 203.00 | 235.00 | 182.00 | 199.00 |
| 12/31/08 | 177.00 | 187.00 | 167.00 | 185.00 |

Chart High 1100.00 on 01/26/2001
Chart Low 36.00 on 06/08/1970

**Annual High, Low and Settle of Palladium**   In USD per Troy Ounce

| Year | High | Low | Settle | Year | High | Low | Settle | Year | High | Low | Settle |
|---|---|---|---|---|---|---|---|---|---|---|---|
| 1967 | | | | 1981 | 225.00 | 110.00 | 110.00 | 1995 | 179.00 | 130.00 | 130.00 |
| 1968 | 42.00 | 37.00 | 42.00 | 1982 | 110.00 | 110.00 | 110.00 | 1996 | 146.00 | 117.00 | 123.00 |
| 1969 | 43.00 | 37.00 | 37.00 | 1983 | 160.69 | 99.55 | 160.69 | 1997 | 246.00 | 122.00 | 207.00 |
| 1970 | 37.00 | 36.00 | 36.00 | 1984 | 161.10 | 135.83 | 136.72 | 1998 | 417.00 | 205.00 | 338.00 |
| 1971 | 37.00 | 36.00 | 37.00 | 1985 | 127.88 | 94.50 | 94.50 | 1999 | 466.00 | 293.00 | 466.00 |
| 1972 | 60.00 | 37.00 | 60.00 | 1986 | 142.30 | 101.83 | 118.15 | 2000 | 985.00 | 437.00 | 965.00 |
| 1973 | 84.00 | 60.00 | 84.00 | 1987 | 148.50 | 106.50 | 125.50 | 2001 | 1,100.00 | 319.00 | 446.00 |
| 1974 | 143.80 | 84.00 | 132.50 | 1988 | 146.00 | 114.25 | 133.00 | 2002 | 439.00 | 225.00 | 237.00 |
| 1975 | 124.32 | 44.00 | 44.00 | 1989 | 181.50 | 131.00 | 135.50 | 2003 | 273.00 | 150.00 | 196.00 |
| 1976 | 55.00 | 40.00 | 55.00 | 1990 | 138.00 | 82.75 | 82.75 | 2004 | 340.00 | 180.00 | 186.00 |
| 1977 | 55.00 | 55.00 | 55.00 | 1991 | 102.50 | 79.00 | 81.00 | 2005 | 297.00 | 174.00 | 255.00 |
| 1978 | 80.00 | 55.00 | 80.00 | 1992 | 114.00 | 78.50 | 107.00 | 2006 | 407.00 | 263.00 | 330.00 |
| 1979 | 120.00 | 80.00 | 120.00 | 1993 | 145.00 | 100.00 | 124.00 | 2007 | 383.00 | 322.00 | 370.00 |
| 1980 | 225.00 | 120.00 | 225.00 | 1994 | 163.00 | 124.00 | 158.00 | 2008 | 585.00 | 167.00 | 185.00 |

*CME Group; New York Mercantile Exchange*

# PALLADIUM

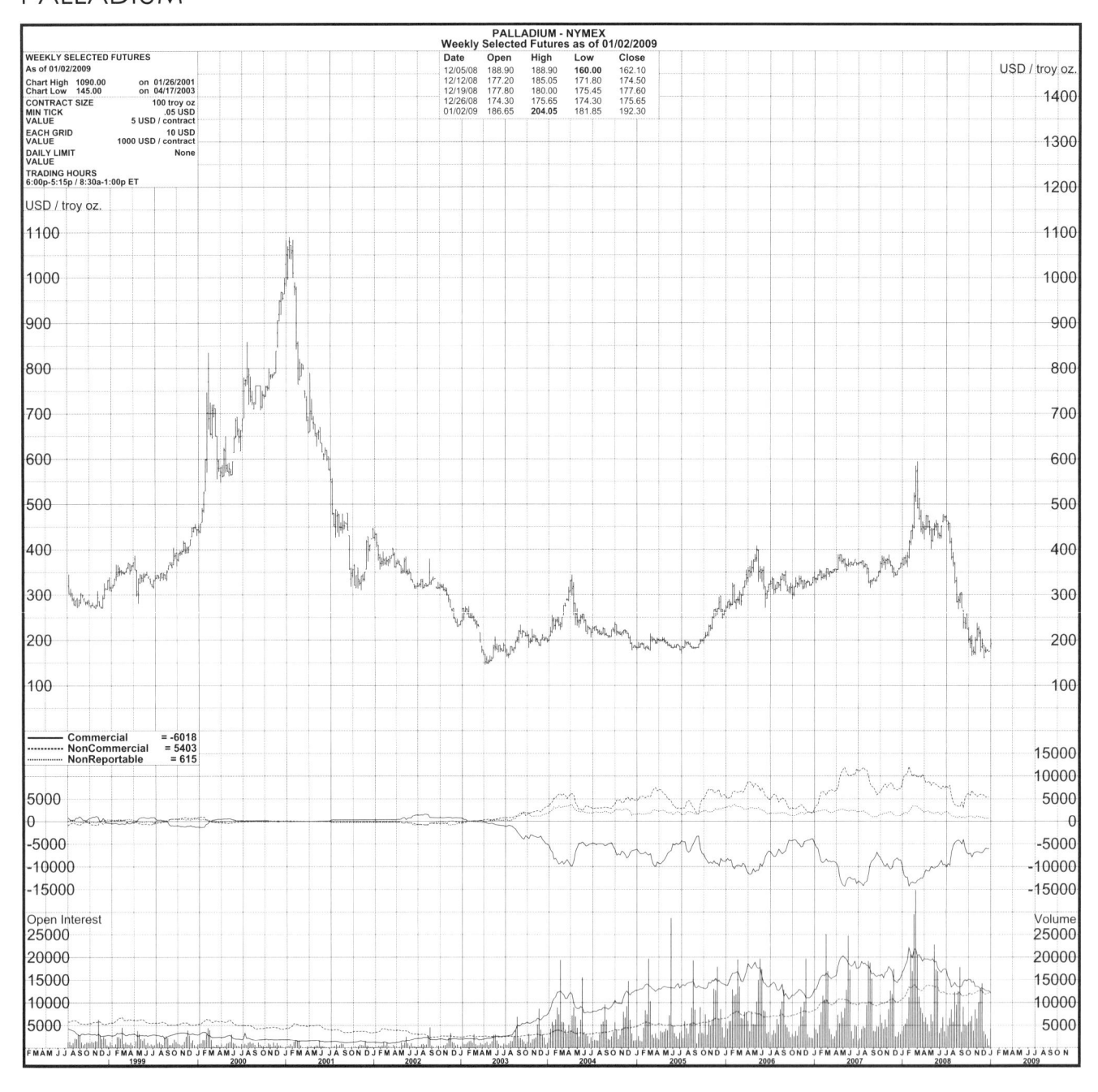

## Quarterly High, Low and Settle of Palladium Futures   In USD per Troy Ounce

| Quarter | High | Low | Settle | Quarter | High | Low | Settle | Quarter | High | Low | Settle |
|---|---|---|---|---|---|---|---|---|---|---|---|
| 03/2000 | 835.00 | 430.20 | 595.50 | 03/2003 | 275.00 | 178.00 | 182.45 | 03/2006 | 355.80 | 262.00 | 336.80 |
| 06/2000 | 692.15 | 547.50 | 647.95 | 06/2003 | 208.00 | 145.00 | 181.35 | 06/2006 | 409.00 | 271.00 | 323.50 |
| 09/2000 | 859.00 | 618.00 | 714.85 | 09/2003 | 234.00 | 160.00 | 215.15 | 09/2006 | 354.05 | 301.00 | 316.40 |
| 12/2000 | 975.00 | 712.25 | 954.45 | 12/2003 | 225.00 | 182.50 | 197.50 | 12/2006 | 343.10 | 290.10 | 338.50 |
| 03/2001 | 1,090.00 | 734.00 | 744.00 | 03/2004 | 293.50 | 198.00 | 289.95 | 03/2007 | 358.90 | 325.20 | 357.25 |
| 06/2001 | 789.90 | 595.00 | 599.95 | 06/2004 | 344.70 | 213.00 | 214.95 | 06/2007 | 389.50 | 350.20 | 368.50 |
| 09/2001 | 605.00 | 355.00 | 357.00 | 09/2004 | 232.40 | 205.00 | 224.75 | 09/2007 | 375.80 | 315.20 | 351.95 |
| 12/2001 | 449.50 | 310.00 | 448.00 | 12/2004 | 239.20 | 177.75 | 185.25 | 12/2007 | 389.00 | 338.00 | 378.20 |
| 03/2002 | 447.00 | 355.50 | 388.90 | 03/2005 | 215.00 | 177.00 | 203.55 | 03/2008 | 595.10 | 360.10 | 450.20 |
| 06/2002 | 394.00 | 314.00 | 318.80 | 06/2005 | 207.00 | 180.50 | 181.95 | 06/2008 | 476.85 | 401.50 | 464.75 |
| 09/2002 | 380.00 | 313.00 | 319.00 | 09/2005 | 202.70 | 170.20 | 199.80 | 09/2008 | 475.90 | 197.50 | 202.70 |
| 12/2002 | 329.00 | 229.70 | 238.00 | 12/2005 | 297.10 | 192.10 | 261.50 | 12/2008 | 238.30 | 160.00 | 188.70 |

*CME Group; New York Mercantile Exchange*

# PALLADIUM

**WEEKLY CASH**
As of 01/02/2009
Chart High 1100.00 on 01/26/2001
Chart Low 150.00 on 04/25/2003
CONTRACT SIZE 100 troy oz
MIN TICK .05 USD
VALUE 5 USD / contract
EACH GRID 5 USD
VALUE 500 USD / contract
DAILY LIMIT None
VALUE
TRADING HOURS
6:00p-5:15p / 8:30a-1:00p ET

**Industrial, Engelhard**
**Weekly Cash as of 01/02/2009**

| Date | Open | High | Low | Close |
|---|---|---|---|---|
| 12/05/08 | 177.00 | 177.00 | **167.00** | 167.00 |
| 12/12/08 | 177.00 | 183.00 | 173.00 | 173.00 |
| 12/19/08 | 177.00 | 180.00 | 175.00 | 179.00 |
| 12/26/08 | 179.00 | 179.00 | 175.00 | 175.00 |
| 01/02/09 | 187.00 | **187.00** | 185.00 | 186.00 |

## Quarterly High, Low and Settle of Palladium     In USD per Troy Ounce

| Quarter | High | Low | Settle | Quarter | High | Low | Settle | Quarter | High | Low | Settle |
|---|---|---|---|---|---|---|---|---|---|---|---|
| 03/2000 | 815.00 | 437.00 | 605.00 | 03/2003 | 273.00 | 183.00 | 183.00 | 03/2006 | 349.00 | 263.00 | 332.00 |
| 06/2000 | 697.00 | 570.00 | 649.00 | 06/2003 | 198.00 | 150.00 | 181.00 | 06/2006 | 407.00 | 286.00 | 317.00 |
| 09/2000 | 865.00 | 630.00 | 722.00 | 09/2003 | 235.00 | 160.00 | 211.00 | 09/2006 | 351.00 | 306.00 | 318.00 |
| 12/2000 | 985.00 | 722.00 | 965.00 | 12/2003 | 216.00 | 187.00 | 196.00 | 12/2006 | 335.00 | 297.00 | 330.00 |
| 03/2001 | 1,100.00 | 744.00 | 744.00 | 03/2004 | 290.00 | 200.00 | 290.00 | 03/2007 | 357.00 | 331.00 | 355.00 |
| 06/2001 | 755.00 | 600.00 | 606.00 | 06/2004 | 340.00 | 219.00 | 222.00 | 06/2007 | 383.00 | 353.00 | 368.00 |
| 09/2001 | 602.00 | 365.00 | 365.00 | 09/2004 | 230.00 | 207.00 | 221.00 | 09/2007 | 373.00 | 322.00 | 347.00 |
| 12/2001 | 446.00 | 319.00 | 446.00 | 12/2004 | 237.00 | 180.00 | 186.00 | 12/2007 | 382.00 | 346.00 | 370.00 |
| 03/2002 | 439.00 | 363.00 | 388.00 | 03/2005 | 211.00 | 180.00 | 202.00 | 03/2008 | 585.00 | 368.00 | 447.00 |
| 06/2002 | 396.00 | 320.00 | 324.00 | 06/2005 | 205.00 | 184.00 | 185.00 | 06/2008 | 480.00 | 408.00 | 472.00 |
| 09/2002 | 370.00 | 318.00 | 321.00 | 09/2005 | 203.00 | 174.00 | 196.00 | 09/2008 | 468.00 | 204.00 | 204.00 |
| 12/2002 | 325.00 | 225.00 | 237.00 | 12/2005 | 297.00 | 194.00 | 255.00 | 12/2008 | 235.00 | 167.00 | 185.00 |

*CME Group; New York Mercantile Exchange*

# PLATINUM

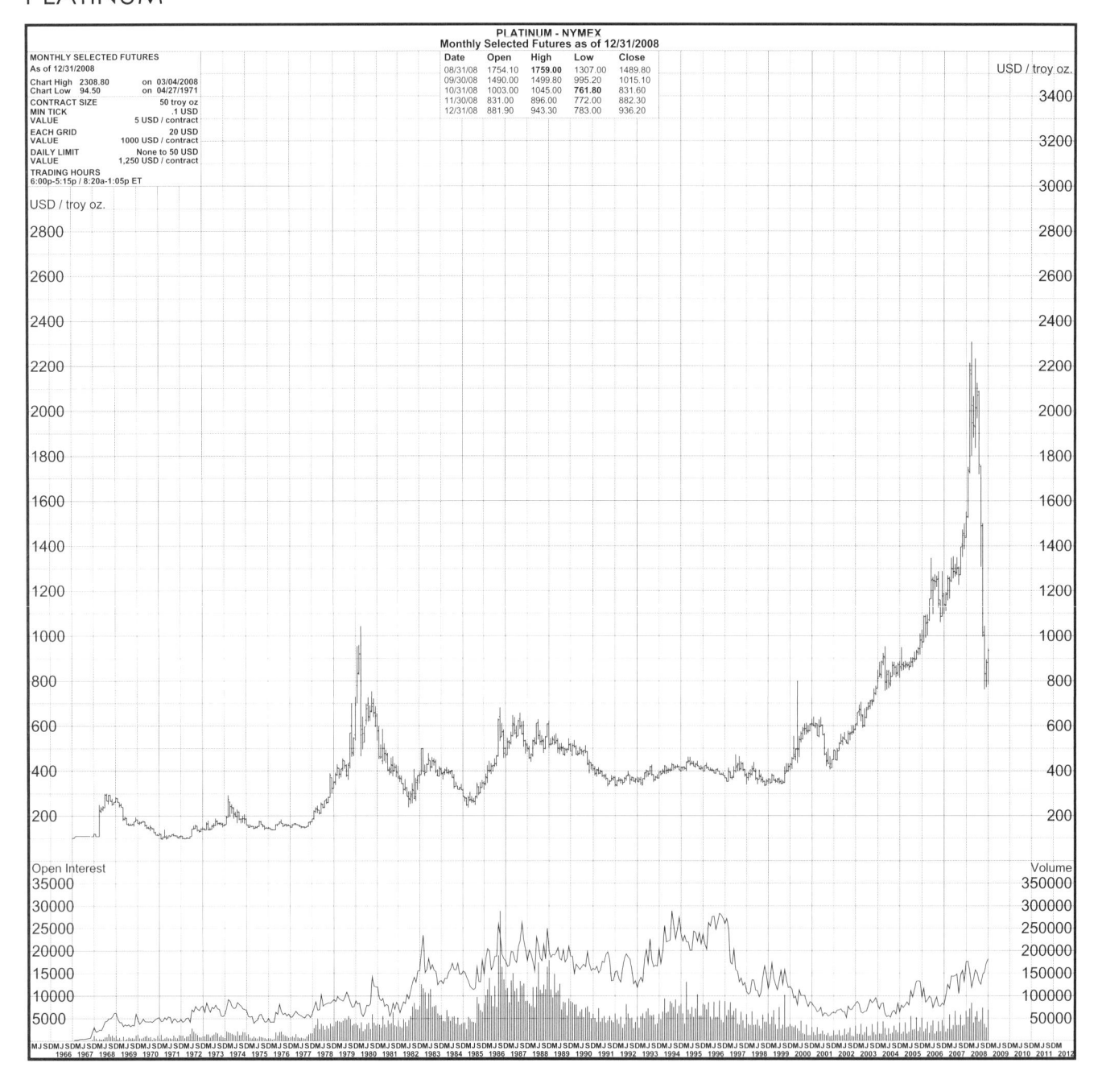

## PLATINUM - NYMEX
Monthly Selected Futures as of 12/31/2008

| Date | Open | High | Low | Close |
|---|---|---|---|---|
| 08/31/08 | 1754.10 | 1759.00 | 1307.00 | 1489.80 |
| 09/30/08 | 1490.00 | 1499.80 | 995.20 | 1015.10 |
| 10/31/08 | 1003.00 | 1045.00 | 761.80 | 831.60 |
| 11/30/08 | 831.00 | 896.00 | 772.00 | 882.30 |
| 12/31/08 | 881.90 | 943.30 | 783.00 | 936.20 |

**MONTHLY SELECTED FUTURES** As of 12/31/2008
Chart High 2308.80 on 03/04/2008
Chart Low 94.50 on 04/27/1971
CONTRACT SIZE 50 troy oz
MIN TICK .1 USD
VALUE 5 USD / contract
EACH GRID 20 USD
VALUE 1000 USD / contract
DAILY LIMIT None to 50 USD
VALUE 1,250 USD / contract
TRADING HOURS 6:00p-5:15p / 8:20a-1:05p ET

## Annual High, Low and Settle of Platinum Futures — In USD per Troy Ounce

| Year | High | Low | Settle | Year | High | Low | Settle | Year | High | Low | Settle |
|---|---|---|---|---|---|---|---|---|---|---|---|
| 1967 | 120.00 | 102.93 | 120.00 | 1981 | 599.00 | 365.50 | 373.20 | 1995 | 463.00 | 397.00 | 398.20 |
| 1968 | 300.50 | 214.00 | 280.00 | 1982 | 409.00 | 238.00 | 383.10 | 1996 | 436.90 | 369.00 | 369.30 |
| 1969 | 281.50 | 153.10 | 168.00 | 1983 | 502.00 | 375.00 | 390.50 | 1997 | 473.80 | 339.50 | 370.80 |
| 1970 | 180.10 | 112.50 | 120.50 | 1984 | 417.50 | 285.50 | 287.70 | 1998 | 440.00 | 332.00 | 364.50 |
| 1971 | 140.00 | 94.50 | 110.00 | 1985 | 359.80 | 236.00 | 340.30 | 1999 | 435.00 | 341.00 | 430.20 |
| 1972 | 161.60 | 96.00 | 141.70 | 1986 | 682.00 | 334.00 | 470.70 | 2000 | 800.00 | 408.00 | 609.60 |
| 1973 | 188.80 | 134.60 | 160.10 | 1987 | 658.50 | 469.00 | 500.60 | 2001 | 641.10 | 406.00 | 493.00 |
| 1974 | 293.50 | 159.50 | 159.50 | 1988 | 630.00 | 439.50 | 516.60 | 2002 | 610.50 | 445.20 | 604.40 |
| 1975 | 179.50 | 137.00 | 146.90 | 1989 | 566.20 | 466.20 | 487.30 | 2003 | 847.70 | 590.00 | 811.30 |
| 1976 | 184.50 | 135.00 | 149.50 | 1990 | 536.90 | 387.50 | 408.70 | 2004 | 954.00 | 756.00 | 863.70 |
| 1977 | 186.90 | 144.20 | 186.40 | 1991 | 421.50 | 330.00 | 338.70 | 2005 | 1,026.00 | 843.20 | 973.00 |
| 1978 | 390.00 | 183.00 | 349.00 | 1992 | 400.00 | 330.00 | 354.10 | 2006 | 1,347.00 | 972.00 | 1,139.30 |
| 1979 | 730.00 | 337.00 | 692.60 | 1993 | 427.50 | 335.50 | 394.90 | 2007 | 1,551.50 | 1,109.00 | 1,528.40 |
| 1980 | 1,045.00 | 465.00 | 578.00 | 1994 | 435.40 | 379.00 | 414.70 | 2008 | 2,308.80 | 761.80 | 936.20 |

Futures begin trading 03/04/1968.   *CME Group; New York Mercantile Exchange*

# PLATINUM

**MONTHLY CASH**
As of 12/31/2008
Chart High 2275.00 on 03/04/2008
Chart Low 100.00 on 12/30/1966
USD / troy oz.

**Free Market**
Monthly Cash as of 12/31/2008

| Date | Open | High | Low | Close |
|---|---|---|---|---|
| 08/29/08 | 1680.00 | 1680.00 | 1328.00 | 1485.00 |
| 09/30/08 | 1390.00 | 1420.00 | 1010.00 | 1010.00 |
| 10/31/08 | 1015.00 | 1036.00 | 760.00 | 823.00 |
| 11/28/08 | 820.00 | 880.00 | 780.00 | 872.00 |
| 12/31/08 | 815.00 | 912.00 | 798.00 | 912.00 |

## Annual High, Low and Settle of Platinum    In USD per Troy Ounce

| Year | High | Low | Settle | Year | High | Low | Settle | Year | High | Low | Settle |
|---|---|---|---|---|---|---|---|---|---|---|---|
| 1967 | 120.00 | 102.93 | 120.00 | 1981 | 475.00 | 420.00 | 475.00 | 1995 | 461.50 | 398.25 | 398.25 |
| 1968 | 120.00 | 109.00 | 120.00 | 1982 | 475.00 | 475.00 | 475.00 | 1996 | 431.50 | 367.00 | 369.50 |
| 1969 | 130.00 | 120.00 | 130.00 | 1983 | 475.00 | 475.00 | 475.00 | 1997 | 497.00 | 342.50 | 363.00 |
| 1970 | 130.00 | 130.00 | 130.00 | 1984 | 475.00 | 475.00 | 475.00 | 1998 | 429.00 | 334.25 | 360.25 |
| 1971 | 130.00 | 120.00 | 120.00 | 1985 | 475.00 | 276.75 | 340.30 | 1999 | 457.00 | 342.00 | 443.00 |
| 1972 | 130.00 | 120.00 | 130.00 | 1986 | 675.50 | 341.30 | 477.50 | 2000 | 622.00 | 405.00 | 619.00 |
| 1973 | 158.00 | 130.00 | 158.00 | 1987 | 632.00 | 461.00 | 500.00 | 2001 | 637.00 | 415.00 | 480.00 |
| 1974 | 190.00 | 158.00 | 190.00 | 1988 | 623.50 | 446.00 | 520.50 | 2002 | 602.00 | 453.00 | 598.00 |
| 1975 | 190.00 | 155.00 | 155.00 | 1989 | 563.75 | 470.00 | 488.50 | 2003 | 840.00 | 603.00 | 813.00 |
| 1976 | 175.00 | 155.00 | 162.00 | 1990 | 532.00 | 391.50 | 411.75 | 2004 | 936.00 | 767.00 | 861.00 |
| 1977 | 180.00 | 162.00 | 180.00 | 1991 | 423.00 | 333.00 | 338.25 | 2005 | 1,004.00 | 844.00 | 965.00 |
| 1978 | 300.00 | 180.00 | 280.00 | 1992 | 391.00 | 332.75 | 353.50 | 2006 | 1,360.00 | 982.00 | 1,120.00 |
| 1979 | 350.00 | 280.00 | 350.00 | 1993 | 422.00 | 338.25 | 394.00 | 2007 | 1,547.00 | 1,122.00 | 1,528.00 |
| 1980 | 420.00 | 350.00 | 420.00 | 1994 | 425.50 | 378.00 | 417.00 | 2008 | 2,275.00 | 760.00 | 912.00 |

*CME Group; New York Mercantile Exchange*

# PLATINUM

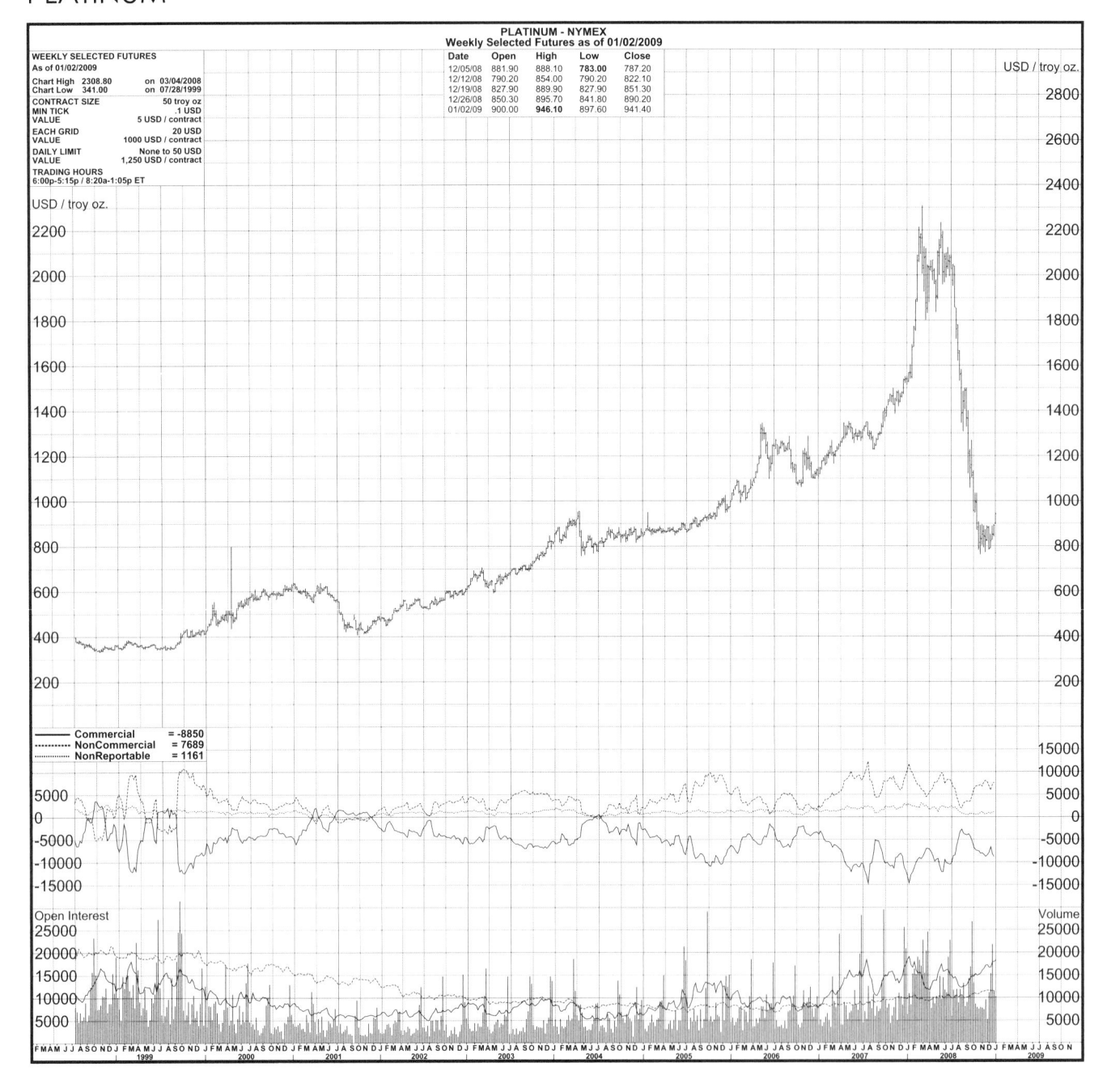

## PLATINUM - NYMEX
Weekly Selected Futures as of 01/02/2009

| Date | Open | High | Low | Close |
|---|---|---|---|---|
| 12/05/08 | 881.90 | 888.10 | 783.00 | 787.20 |
| 12/12/08 | 790.20 | 854.00 | 790.20 | 822.10 |
| 12/19/08 | 827.90 | 889.90 | 827.90 | 851.30 |
| 12/26/08 | 850.30 | 895.70 | 841.80 | 890.20 |
| 01/02/09 | 900.00 | 946.10 | 897.60 | 941.40 |

**WEEKLY SELECTED FUTURES** As of 01/02/2009
Chart High 2308.80 on 03/04/2008
Chart Low 341.00 on 07/28/1999
CONTRACT SIZE 50 troy oz
MIN TICK .1 USD
VALUE 5 USD / contract
EACH GRID 20 USD
VALUE 1000 USD / contract
DAILY LIMIT None to 50 USD
VALUE 1,250 USD / contract
TRADING HOURS 6:00p-5:15p / 8:20a-1:05p ET

Commercial = -8850
NonCommercial = 7689
NonReportable = 1161

## Quarterly High, Low and Settle of Platinum Futures    In USD per Troy Ounce

| Quarter | High | Low | Settle | Quarter | High | Low | Settle | Quarter | High | Low | Settle |
|---|---|---|---|---|---|---|---|---|---|---|---|
| 03/2000 | 555.00 | 408.00 | 496.40 | 03/2003 | 707.00 | 599.50 | 648.40 | 03/2006 | 1,095.00 | 972.00 | 1,059.40 |
| 06/2000 | 800.00 | 433.10 | 565.50 | 06/2003 | 684.00 | 590.00 | 670.60 | 06/2006 | 1,347.00 | 1,065.00 | 1,246.70 |
| 09/2000 | 614.00 | 539.00 | 578.80 | 09/2003 | 718.80 | 669.00 | 706.90 | 09/2006 | 1,287.90 | 1,124.00 | 1,141.20 |
| 12/2000 | 630.50 | 564.00 | 609.60 | 12/2003 | 847.70 | 705.00 | 811.30 | 12/2006 | 1,289.00 | 1,059.60 | 1,139.30 |
| 03/2001 | 641.10 | 554.50 | 555.00 | 03/2004 | 924.00 | 810.00 | 908.70 | 03/2007 | 1,269.90 | 1,109.00 | 1,248.30 |
| 06/2001 | 639.00 | 548.00 | 560.10 | 06/2004 | 954.00 | 756.00 | 791.50 | 06/2007 | 1,353.80 | 1,240.00 | 1,279.00 |
| 09/2001 | 567.20 | 420.10 | 433.30 | 09/2004 | 885.80 | 775.00 | 861.00 | 09/2007 | 1,395.50 | 1,226.50 | 1,395.20 |
| 12/2001 | 493.00 | 406.00 | 493.00 | 12/2004 | 887.00 | 813.00 | 863.70 | 12/2007 | 1,551.50 | 1,350.00 | 1,528.40 |
| 03/2002 | 527.00 | 445.20 | 521.70 | 03/2005 | 950.00 | 843.20 | 870.60 | 03/2008 | 2,308.80 | 1,523.60 | 2,024.40 |
| 06/2002 | 572.00 | 513.00 | 537.30 | 06/2005 | 905.00 | 846.50 | 883.50 | 06/2008 | 2,234.90 | 1,835.00 | 2,069.50 |
| 09/2002 | 578.00 | 516.00 | 564.50 | 09/2005 | 938.50 | 860.30 | 930.30 | 09/2008 | 2,089.60 | 995.20 | 1,015.10 |
| 12/2002 | 610.50 | 559.00 | 604.40 | 12/2005 | 1,026.00 | 914.50 | 973.00 | 12/2008 | 1,045.00 | 761.80 | 936.20 |

*CME Group; New York Mercantile Exchange*

# PLATINUM

**Free Market**
Weekly Cash as of 01/02/2009

| Date | Open | High | Low | Close |
|---|---|---|---|---|
| 12/05/08 | 815.00 | 815.00 | 798.00 | 798.00 |
| 12/12/08 | 846.00 | 848.00 | 800.00 | 800.00 |
| 12/19/08 | 836.00 | 860.00 | 836.00 | 853.00 |
| 12/26/08 | 863.00 | 885.00 | 855.00 | 885.00 |
| 01/02/09 | 909.00 | 931.00 | 900.00 | 931.00 |

WEEKLY CASH As of 01/02/2009
Chart High 2275.00 on 03/04/2008
Chart Low 334.25 on 10/30/1998
CONTRACT SIZE 50 troy oz
MIN TICK .1 USD
VALUE 5 USD / contract
EACH GRID 10 USD
VALUE 500 USD / contract
DAILY LIMIT None to 50 USD
VALUE 1,250 USD / contract
TRADING HOURS 6:00p-5:15p / 8:20a-1:05p ET

## Quarterly High, Low and Settle of Platinum    In USD per Troy Ounce

| Quarter | High | Low | Settle | Quarter | High | Low | Settle | Quarter | High | Low | Settle |
|---|---|---|---|---|---|---|---|---|---|---|---|
| 03/2000 | 573.00 | 414.00 | 482.00 | 03/2003 | 704.00 | 603.00 | 642.00 | 03/2006 | 1,084.00 | 982.00 | 1,076.00 |
| 06/2000 | 598.00 | 405.00 | 558.00 | 06/2003 | 685.00 | 603.00 | 667.00 | 06/2006 | 1,335.00 | 1,070.00 | 1,232.00 |
| 09/2000 | 610.00 | 532.00 | 569.00 | 09/2003 | 718.00 | 665.00 | 710.00 | 09/2006 | 1,282.00 | 1,130.00 | 1,145.00 |
| 12/2000 | 622.00 | 570.00 | 619.00 | 12/2003 | 840.00 | 710.00 | 813.00 | 12/2006 | 1,360.00 | 1,055.00 | 1,120.00 |
| 03/2001 | 637.00 | 563.00 | 563.00 | 03/2004 | 917.00 | 815.50 | 917.00 | 03/2007 | 1,251.00 | 1,122.00 | 1,248.00 |
| 06/2001 | 628.00 | 555.00 | 558.00 | 06/2004 | 936.00 | 767.00 | 793.00 | 06/2007 | 1,338.00 | 1,238.00 | 1,276.00 |
| 09/2001 | 560.00 | 429.00 | 429.00 | 09/2004 | 885.00 | 776.00 | 854.00 | 09/2007 | 1,384.00 | 1,244.00 | 1,384.00 |
| 12/2001 | 480.00 | 415.00 | 480.00 | 12/2004 | 884.00 | 821.50 | 861.00 | 12/2007 | 1,547.00 | 1,356.00 | 1,528.00 |
| 03/2002 | 524.00 | 453.00 | 516.00 | 03/2005 | 877.00 | 844.00 | 864.00 | 03/2008 | 2,275.00 | 1,534.00 | 2,044.00 |
| 06/2002 | 565.00 | 516.00 | 545.00 | 06/2005 | 900.00 | 856.00 | 884.00 | 06/2008 | 2,185.00 | 1,880.00 | 2,069.00 |
| 09/2002 | 574.00 | 520.00 | 563.00 | 09/2005 | 930.00 | 860.00 | 929.00 | 09/2008 | 2,080.00 | 1,010.00 | 1,010.00 |
| 12/2002 | 602.00 | 557.00 | 598.00 | 12/2005 | 1,004.00 | 914.00 | 965.00 | 12/2008 | 1,036.00 | 760.00 | 912.00 |

*CME Group; New York Mercantile Exchange*

# SILVER

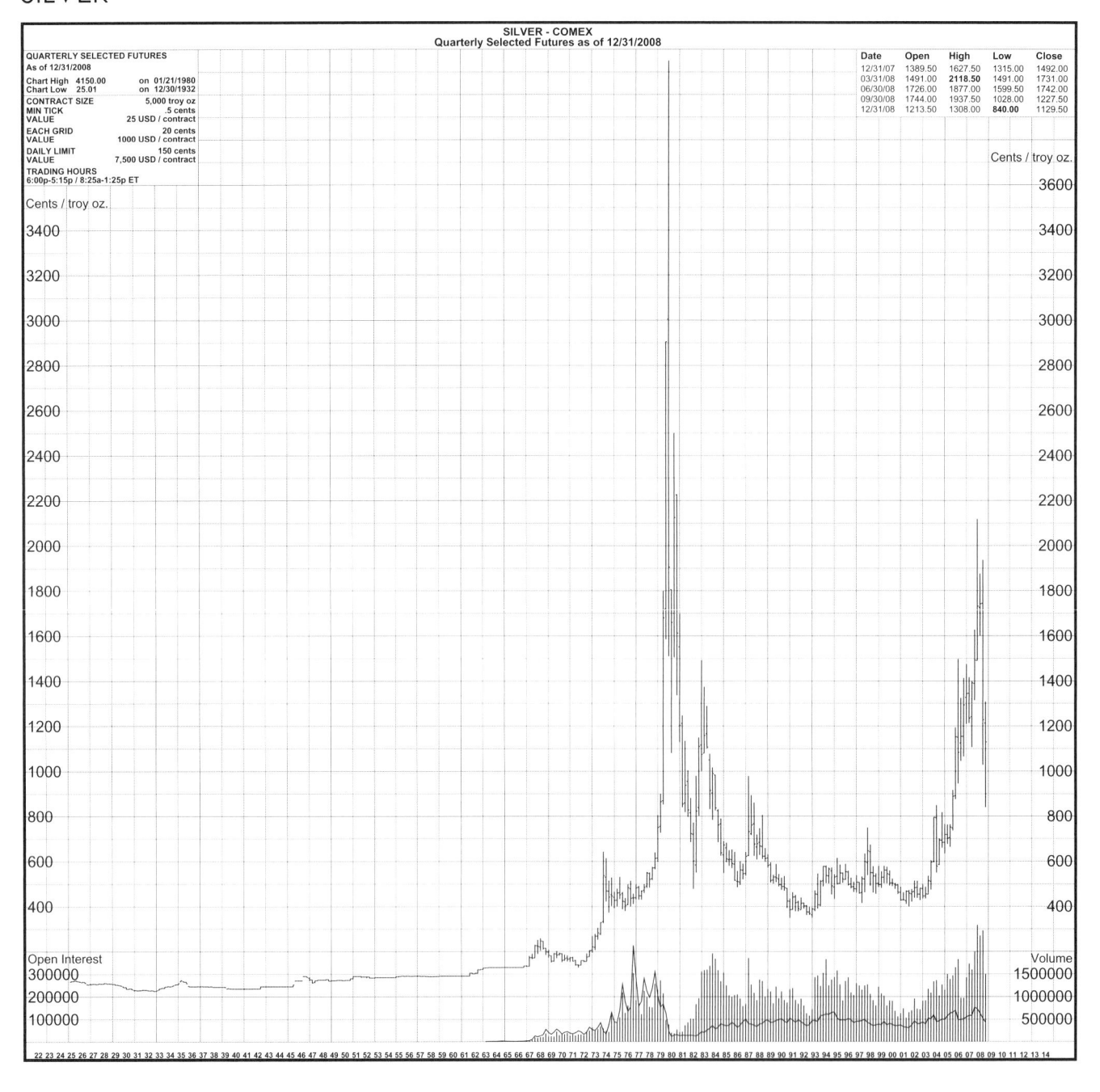

## SILVER - COMEX
### Quarterly Selected Futures as of 12/31/2008

**QUARTERLY SELECTED FUTURES**
As of 12/31/2008
Chart High 4150.00 on 01/21/1980
Chart Low 25.01 on 12/30/1932
CONTRACT SIZE 5,000 troy oz
MIN TICK .5 cents
VALUE 25 USD / contract
EACH GRID 20 cents
VALUE 1000 USD / contract
DAILY LIMIT 150 cents
VALUE 7,500 USD / contract
TRADING HOURS
6:00p-5:15p / 8:25a-1:25p ET

| Date | Open | High | Low | Close |
|---|---|---|---|---|
| 12/31/07 | 1389.50 | 1627.50 | 1315.00 | 1492.00 |
| 03/31/08 | 1491.00 | 2118.50 | 1491.00 | 1731.00 |
| 06/30/08 | 1726.00 | 1877.00 | 1599.50 | 1742.00 |
| 09/30/08 | 1744.00 | 1937.50 | 1028.00 | 1227.50 |
| 12/31/08 | 1213.50 | 1308.00 | **840.00** | 1129.50 |

## Annual High, Low and Settle of Silver Futures    In Cents per Troy Ounce

| Year | High | Low | Settle | Year | High | Low | Settle | Year | High | Low | Settle |
|---|---|---|---|---|---|---|---|---|---|---|---|
| 1925 | 71.57 | 66.90 | 68.89 | 1939 | 42.75 | 34.75 | 34.96 | 1953 | 85.25 | 83.25 | 85.25 |
| 1926 | 67.79 | 53.47 | 53.47 | 1940 | 34.95 | 34.75 | 34.75 | 1954 | 85.25 | 85.25 | 85.25 |
| 1927 | 57.96 | 54.72 | 57.96 | 1941 | 35.12 | 34.75 | 35.12 | 1955 | 92.00 | 85.25 | 90.50 |
| 1928 | 60.30 | 57.02 | 57.33 | 1942 | 44.75 | 35.12 | 44.75 | 1956 | 91.63 | 90.00 | 91.38 |
| 1929 | 57.00 | 48.47 | 48.47 | 1943 | 44.75 | 44.75 | 44.75 | 1957 | 91.38 | 89.63 | 89.63 |
| 1930 | 45.00 | 32.63 | 32.63 | 1944 | 44.75 | 44.75 | 44.75 | 1958 | 90.38 | 88.63 | 89.88 |
| 1931 | 32.22 | 26.77 | 30.12 | 1945 | 70.75 | 44.75 | 70.75 | 1959 | 91.63 | 89.88 | 91.38 |
| 1932 | 30.14 | 25.01 | 25.01 | 1946 | 90.12 | 70.75 | 86.73 | 1960 | 91.50 | 91.38 | 91.38 |
| 1933 | 43.55 | 25.40 | 43.55 | 1947 | 86.25 | 59.75 | 74.63 | 1961 | 104.75 | 91.38 | 104.75 |
| 1934 | 54.39 | 44.19 | 54.39 | 1948 | 77.50 | 70.00 | 70.00 | 1962 | 122.00 | 101.00 | 120.50 |
| 1935 | 74.36 | 54.42 | 58.42 | 1949 | 73.25 | 70.00 | 73.25 | 1963 | 129.50 | 121.00 | 129.50 |
| 1936 | 47.25 | 44.75 | 45.35 | 1950 | 80.00 | 71.75 | 80.00 | 1964 | 131.70 | 128.50 | 131.70 |
| 1937 | 45.46 | 43.81 | 43.81 | 1951 | 90.16 | 80.00 | 88.00 | 1965 | 131.80 | 128.00 | 129.70 |
| 1938 | 44.75 | 42.75 | 42.75 | 1952 | 88.00 | 82.75 | 83.25 | 1966 | 131.20 | 128.70 | 130.90 |

Futures begin trading 06/12/1963.    Data continued on page 370.    *CME Group; New York Mercantile Exchange*

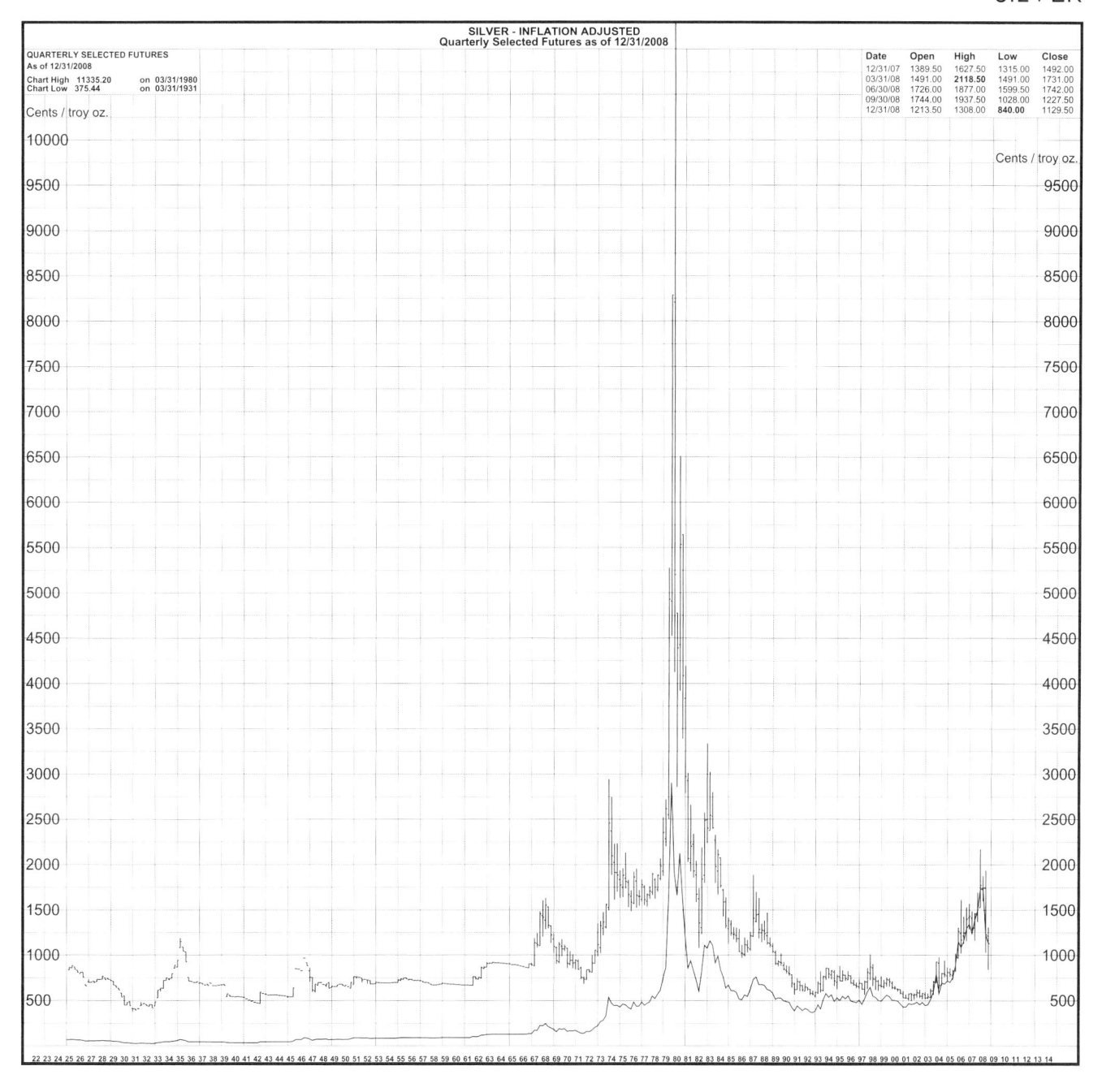

# SILVER

## SILVER - INFLATION ADJUSTED
Quarterly Selected Futures as of 12/31/2008

| Date | Open | High | Low | Close |
|---|---|---|---|---|
| 12/31/07 | 1389.50 | 1627.50 | 1315.00 | 1492.00 |
| 03/31/08 | 1491.00 | 2118.50 | 1491.00 | 1731.00 |
| 06/30/08 | 1726.00 | 1877.00 | 1599.50 | 1742.00 |
| 09/30/08 | 1744.00 | 1937.50 | 1028.00 | 1227.50 |
| 12/31/08 | 1213.50 | 1308.00 | 840.00 | 1129.50 |

QUARTERLY SELECTED FUTURES
As of 12/31/2008
Chart High 11335.20 on 03/31/1980
Chart Low 375.44 on 03/31/1931
Cents / troy oz.

## Annual High, Low and Settle of Silver   In Cents per Troy Ounce

| Year | High | Low | Settle | Year | High | Low | Settle | Year | High | Low | Settle |
|---|---|---|---|---|---|---|---|---|---|---|---|
| 1925 | 71.57 | 66.90 | 68.89 | 1939 | 42.75 | 34.75 | 34.96 | 1953 | 85.25 | 83.25 | 85.25 |
| 1926 | 67.79 | 53.47 | 53.47 | 1940 | 34.95 | 34.75 | 34.75 | 1954 | 85.25 | 85.25 | 85.25 |
| 1927 | 57.96 | 54.72 | 57.96 | 1941 | 35.12 | 34.75 | 35.12 | 1955 | 92.00 | 85.25 | 90.50 |
| 1928 | 60.30 | 57.02 | 57.33 | 1942 | 44.75 | 35.12 | 44.75 | 1956 | 91.63 | 90.00 | 91.38 |
| 1929 | 57.00 | 48.47 | 48.47 | 1943 | 44.75 | 44.75 | 44.75 | 1957 | 91.38 | 89.63 | 89.63 |
| 1930 | 45.00 | 32.63 | 32.63 | 1944 | 44.75 | 44.75 | 44.75 | 1958 | 90.38 | 88.63 | 89.88 |
| 1931 | 32.22 | 26.77 | 30.12 | 1945 | 70.75 | 44.75 | 70.75 | 1959 | 91.63 | 89.88 | 91.38 |
| 1932 | 30.14 | 25.01 | 25.01 | 1946 | 90.12 | 70.75 | 86.73 | 1960 | 91.50 | 91.38 | 91.38 |
| 1933 | 43.55 | 25.40 | 43.55 | 1947 | 86.25 | 59.75 | 74.63 | 1961 | 104.75 | 91.38 | 104.75 |
| 1934 | 54.39 | 44.19 | 54.39 | 1948 | 77.50 | 70.00 | 70.00 | 1962 | 122.00 | 101.00 | 120.50 |
| 1935 | 74.36 | 54.42 | 58.42 | 1949 | 73.25 | 70.00 | 73.25 | 1963 | 129.30 | 121.00 | 129.30 |
| 1936 | 47.25 | 44.75 | 45.35 | 1950 | 80.00 | 71.75 | 80.00 | 1964 | 129.30 | 129.30 | 129.30 |
| 1937 | 45.46 | 43.81 | 43.81 | 1951 | 90.16 | 80.00 | 88.00 | 1965 | 129.30 | 129.30 | 129.30 |
| 1938 | 44.75 | 42.75 | 42.75 | 1952 | 88.00 | 82.75 | 83.25 | 1966 | 129.30 | 129.30 | 129.30 |

Data continued on page 371.   *CME Group; New York Mercantile Exchange*

# SILVER

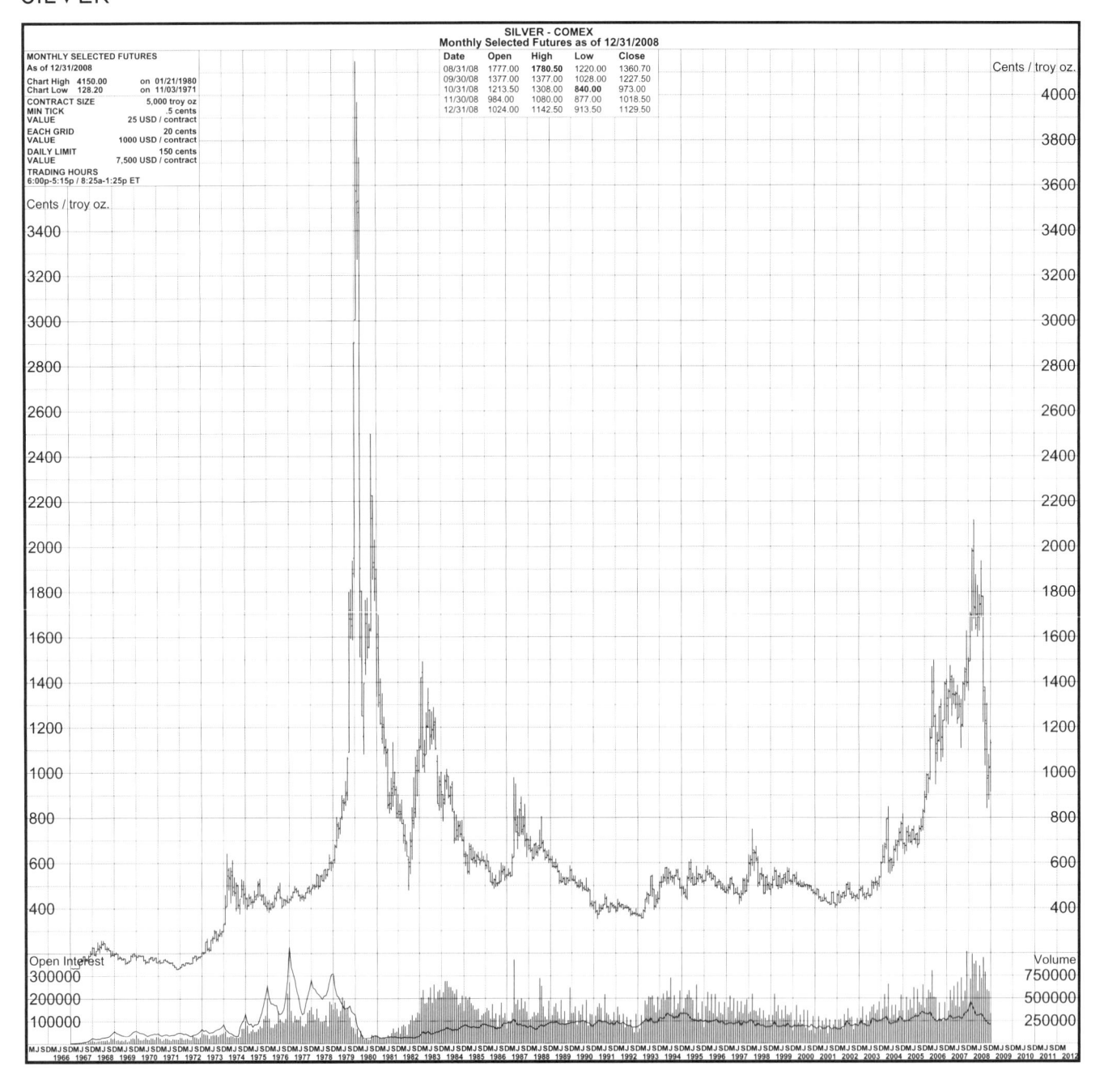

## SILVER - COMEX
### Monthly Selected Futures as of 12/31/2008

| Date | Open | High | Low | Close |
|---|---|---|---|---|
| 08/31/08 | 1777.00 | 1780.50 | 1220.00 | 1360.70 |
| 09/30/08 | 1377.00 | 1377.00 | 1028.00 | 1227.50 |
| 10/31/08 | 1213.50 | 1308.00 | 840.00 | 973.00 |
| 11/30/08 | 984.00 | 1080.00 | 877.00 | 1018.50 |
| 12/31/08 | 1024.00 | 1142.50 | 913.50 | 1129.50 |

**MONTHLY SELECTED FUTURES**
As of 12/31/2008
- Chart High 4150.00 on 01/21/1980
- Chart Low 128.20 on 11/03/1971
- CONTRACT SIZE: 5,000 troy oz
- MIN TICK: .5 cents
- VALUE: 25 USD / contract
- EACH GRID VALUE: 20 cents / 1000 USD / contract
- DAILY LIMIT VALUE: 150 cents / 7,500 USD / contract
- TRADING HOURS: 6:00p-5:15p / 8:25a-1:25p ET

## Annual High, Low and Settle of Silver Futures    In Cents per Troy Ounce

| Year | High | Low | Settle | Year | High | Low | Settle | Year | High | Low | Settle |
|---|---|---|---|---|---|---|---|---|---|---|---|
| 1967 | 230.25 | 128.80 | 226.00 | 1981 | 1,697.00 | 797.00 | 829.00 | 1995 | 616.00 | 434.00 | 520.70 |
| 1968 | 259.00 | 184.00 | 198.20 | 1982 | 1,150.00 | 478.00 | 1,110.00 | 1996 | 589.00 | 464.00 | 479.00 |
| 1969 | 206.90 | 151.00 | 184.10 | 1983 | 1,493.00 | 832.00 | 915.50 | 1997 | 635.00 | 415.50 | 598.80 |
| 1970 | 195.00 | 152.10 | 166.00 | 1984 | 1,017.00 | 624.50 | 638.00 | 1998 | 750.00 | 456.00 | 502.00 |
| 1971 | 177.20 | 128.20 | 138.40 | 1985 | 689.00 | 548.00 | 590.50 | 1999 | 581.00 | 482.00 | 545.30 |
| 1972 | 205.50 | 138.70 | 204.70 | 1986 | 642.00 | 485.00 | 546.00 | 2000 | 560.00 | 455.00 | 463.50 |
| 1973 | 331.30 | 195.40 | 329.70 | 1987 | 979.50 | 536.50 | 677.00 | 2001 | 488.00 | 401.50 | 458.80 |
| 1974 | 643.00 | 326.10 | 447.00 | 1988 | 806.00 | 598.00 | 613.00 | 2002 | 515.00 | 421.00 | 481.20 |
| 1975 | 532.00 | 388.00 | 423.60 | 1989 | 631.00 | 502.00 | 527.30 | 2003 | 605.00 | 434.60 | 596.50 |
| 1976 | 515.00 | 380.00 | 439.00 | 1990 | 544.50 | 393.00 | 424.70 | 2004 | 850.00 | 549.50 | 683.70 |
| 1977 | 500.00 | 430.50 | 484.90 | 1991 | 464.00 | 350.50 | 391.20 | 2005 | 917.00 | 635.00 | 889.00 |
| 1978 | 640.00 | 482.20 | 613.70 | 1992 | 441.00 | 362.00 | 369.00 | 2006 | 1,497.00 | 876.00 | 1,293.50 |
| 1979 | 2,905.00 | 598.00 | 2,905.00 | 1993 | 547.00 | 351.00 | 511.70 | 2007 | 1,627.50 | 1,106.00 | 1,492.00 |
| 1980 | 4,150.00 | 1,080.00 | 1,612.00 | 1994 | 582.00 | 453.00 | 491.70 | 2008 | 2,118.50 | 840.00 | 1,129.50 |

Data continued from page 368.    *CME Group; New York Mercantile Exchange*

# SILVER

**Silver Composite Monthly Cash as of 12/31/2008**

| Date | Open | High | Low | Close |
|---|---|---|---|---|
| 08/29/08 | 1774.00 | 1778.60 | 1241.45 | 1360.70 |
| 09/30/08 | 1372.80 | 1376.11 | 1026.50 | 1201.70 |
| 10/31/08 | 1203.90 | 1298.77 | 845.76 | 980.40 |
| 11/28/08 | 984.69 | 1079.30 | 880.40 | 1030.60 |
| 12/31/08 | 1029.90 | 1159.46 | 916.70 | 1137.45 |

MONTHLY CASH As of 12/31/2008
Chart High 4800.00 on 01/21/1980
Chart Low 128.80 on 11/03/1971

### Annual High, Low and Settle of Silver    In Cents per Troy Ounce

| Year | High | Low | Settle | Year | High | Low | Settle | Year | High | Low | Settle |
|---|---|---|---|---|---|---|---|---|---|---|---|
| 1967 | 217.00 | 129.30 | 210.00 | 1981 | 1,645.00 | 795.00 | 825.00 | 1995 | 613.00 | 436.00 | 518.00 |
| 1968 | 256.50 | 181.00 | 190.00 | 1982 | 1,121.00 | 488.50 | 1,090.00 | 1996 | 587.00 | 468.00 | 477.00 |
| 1969 | 202.50 | 154.00 | 180.00 | 1983 | 1,474.50 | 834.00 | 895.00 | 1997 | 638.00 | 418.00 | 593.00 |
| 1970 | 193.00 | 157.00 | 163.50 | 1984 | 1,003.50 | 626.00 | 636.00 | 1998 | 787.00 | 462.00 | 502.00 |
| 1971 | 175.20 | 128.80 | 138.00 | 1985 | 673.50 | 557.00 | 583.00 | 1999 | 582.00 | 482.00 | 540.00 |
| 1972 | 204.80 | 138.70 | 204.20 | 1986 | 619.50 | 487.00 | 536.50 | 2000 | 551.00 | 455.00 | 457.00 |
| 1973 | 328.40 | 196.20 | 328.40 | 1987 | 1,020.00 | 536.00 | 669.50 | 2001 | 484.00 | 404.00 | 462.00 |
| 1974 | 670.00 | 327.00 | 437.00 | 1988 | 799.00 | 601.00 | 602.00 | 2002 | 515.00 | 423.00 | 478.00 |
| 1975 | 522.50 | 391.00 | 416.50 | 1989 | 617.00 | 501.50 | 518.00 | 2003 | 601.00 | 434.00 | 594.00 |
| 1976 | 510.00 | 381.50 | 437.50 | 1990 | 539.00 | 392.00 | 422.00 | 2004 | 845.00 | 545.50 | 682.28 |
| 1977 | 496.00 | 430.00 | 478.00 | 1991 | 463.00 | 352.00 | 390.00 | 2005 | 926.94 | 632.60 | 881.60 |
| 1978 | 629.60 | 482.90 | 607.40 | 1992 | 439.00 | 363.00 | 368.00 | 2006 | 1,521.30 | 869.40 | 1,289.50 |
| 1979 | 2,800.00 | 596.10 | 2,800.00 | 1993 | 551.00 | 353.00 | 510.00 | 2007 | 1,621.20 | 1,106.19 | 1,479.42 |
| 1980 | 4,800.00 | 1,080.00 | 1,565.00 | 1994 | 585.00 | 454.00 | 488.00 | 2008 | 2,134.90 | 845.76 | 1,137.45 |

Handy and Harman: to 05/1990; Composite: 06/1990 to date.    Data continued from page 369.    *CME Group; New York Mercantile Exchange*

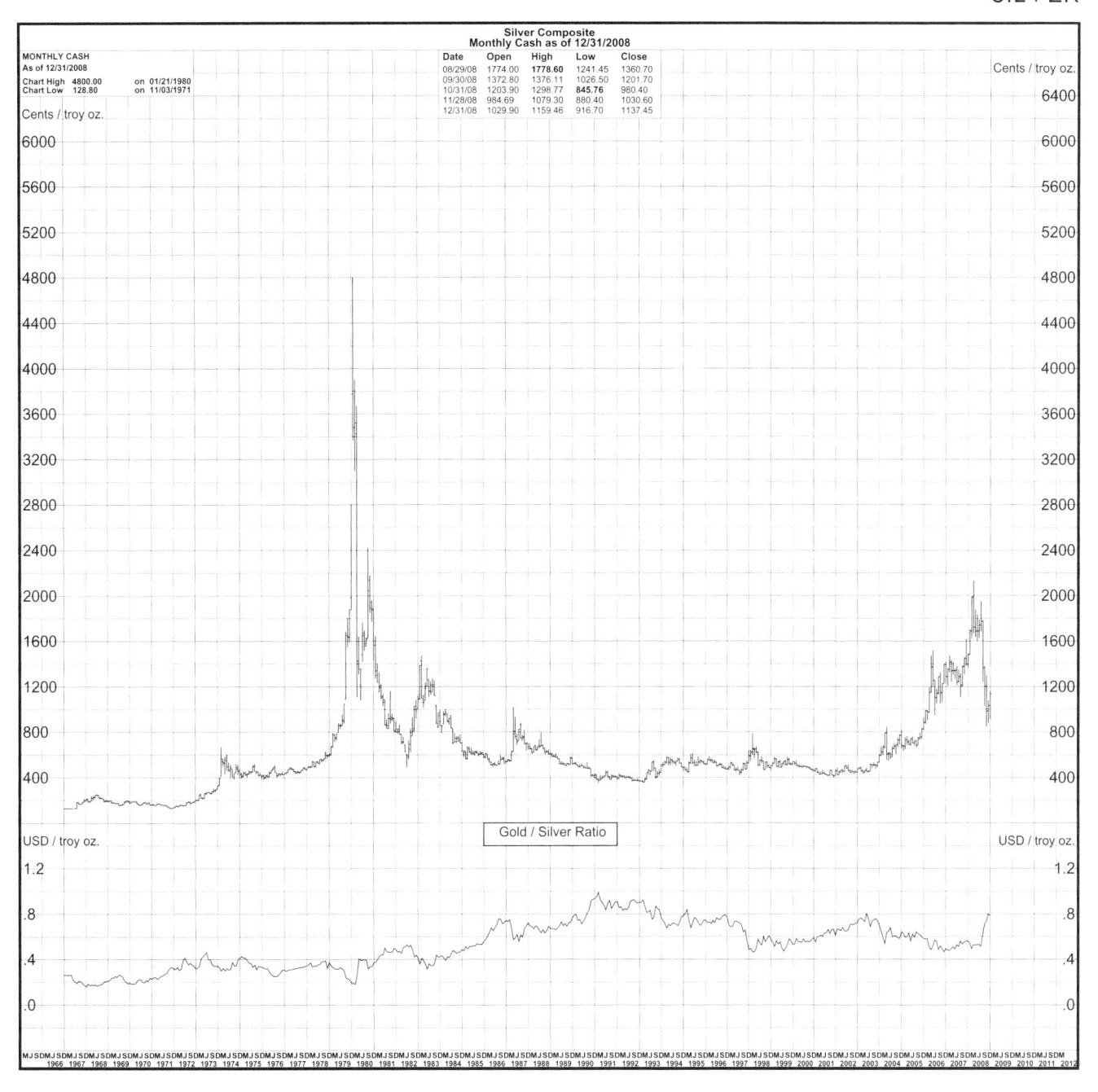

# SILVER

**SILVER - COMEX Weekly Selected Futures as of 01/02/2009**

| Date | Open | High | Low | Close |
|---|---|---|---|---|
| 12/05/08 | 1024.00 | 1025.00 | 913.50 | 940.10 |
| 12/12/08 | 1023.50 | 1044.50 | 965.00 | 1019.90 |
| 12/19/08 | 1039.00 | 1141.00 | 1030.00 | 1081.90 |
| 12/26/08 | 1082.90 | 1082.90 | 1023.30 | 1050.30 |
| 01/02/09 | 1096.50 | 1160.00 | 1065.00 | 1149.00 |

**WEEKLY SELECTED FUTURES** As of 01/02/2009
- Chart High 2118.50 on 03/17/2008
- Chart Low 401.50 on 11/21/2001
- CONTRACT SIZE 5,000 troy oz
- MIN TICK .5 cents
- VALUE 25 USD / contract
- EACH GRID 20 cents
- VALUE 1000 USD / contract
- DAILY LIMIT 150 cents
- VALUE 7,500 USD / contract
- TRADING HOURS 6:00p-5:15p / 8:25a-1:25p ET

Commercial = -30680
NonCommercial = 20240
NonReportable = 10440

## Quarterly High, Low and Settle of Silver Futures    In Cents per Troy Ounce

| Quarter | High | Low | Settle | Quarter | High | Low | Settle | Quarter | High | Low | Settle |
|---|---|---|---|---|---|---|---|---|---|---|---|
| 03/2000 | 560.00 | 492.00 | 504.50 | 03/2003 | 498.00 | 434.60 | 446.50 | 03/2006 | 1,194.00 | 876.00 | 1,152.00 |
| 06/2000 | 524.00 | 490.00 | 503.30 | 06/2003 | 488.00 | 435.00 | 455.70 | 06/2006 | 1,497.00 | 945.00 | 1,083.30 |
| 09/2000 | 504.50 | 477.50 | 494.80 | 09/2003 | 536.50 | 454.50 | 514.20 | 09/2006 | 1,326.00 | 1,045.00 | 1,154.00 |
| 12/2000 | 498.50 | 455.00 | 463.50 | 12/2003 | 605.00 | 474.50 | 596.50 | 12/2006 | 1,414.00 | 1,065.00 | 1,293.50 |
| 03/2001 | 488.00 | 427.00 | 429.50 | 03/2004 | 795.00 | 595.00 | 794.50 | 03/2007 | 1,474.50 | 1,209.50 | 1,345.00 |
| 06/2001 | 463.50 | 427.00 | 429.20 | 06/2004 | 850.00 | 549.50 | 577.60 | 06/2007 | 1,417.00 | 1,212.50 | 1,235.30 |
| 09/2001 | 471.80 | 411.00 | 467.50 | 09/2004 | 701.00 | 583.00 | 693.80 | 09/2007 | 1,400.00 | 1,106.00 | 1,392.00 |
| 12/2001 | 473.00 | 401.50 | 458.80 | 12/2004 | 819.00 | 660.00 | 683.70 | 12/2007 | 1,627.50 | 1,315.00 | 1,492.00 |
| 03/2002 | 477.50 | 421.00 | 465.00 | 03/2005 | 764.00 | 635.00 | 718.00 | 03/2008 | 2,118.50 | 1,491.00 | 1,731.00 |
| 06/2002 | 515.00 | 439.00 | 483.30 | 06/2005 | 763.00 | 677.00 | 702.80 | 06/2008 | 1,877.00 | 1,599.50 | 1,742.00 |
| 09/2002 | 514.00 | 438.00 | 454.80 | 09/2005 | 764.50 | 663.00 | 751.20 | 09/2008 | 1,937.50 | 1,028.00 | 1,227.50 |
| 12/2002 | 482.00 | 428.00 | 481.20 | 12/2005 | 917.00 | 736.00 | 889.00 | 12/2008 | 1,308.00 | 840.00 | 1,129.50 |

*CME Group; New York Mercantile Exchange*

# SILVER

**Silver Composite — Weekly Cash as of 01/02/2009**

| Date | Open | High | Low | Close |
|---|---|---|---|---|
| 12/05/08 | 1029.90 | 1029.90 | 916.70 | 951.70 |
| 12/12/08 | 951.30 | 1053.70 | 948.30 | 1029.50 |
| 12/19/08 | 1029.60 | 1159.46 | 1026.60 | 1088.50 |
| 12/26/08 | 1085.20 | 1107.80 | 1012.82 | 1069.60 |
| 01/02/09 | 1071.73 | 1159.06 | 1068.50 | 1158.04 |

WEEKLY CASH — As of 01/02/2009
Chart High 2134.90 on 03/17/2008
Chart Low 404.00 on 11/21/2001
Cents / troy oz.

## Quarterly High, Low and Settle of Silver    In Cents per Troy Ounce

| Quarter | High | Low | Settle | Quarter | High | Low | Settle | Quarter | High | Low | Settle |
|---|---|---|---|---|---|---|---|---|---|---|---|
| 03/2000 | 551.00 | 492.00 | 500.00 | 03/2003 | 496.00 | 434.00 | 446.00 | 03/2006 | 1,192.50 | 869.40 | 1,150.70 |
| 06/2000 | 519.00 | 489.00 | 501.00 | 06/2003 | 489.00 | 435.00 | 456.00 | 06/2006 | 1,521.30 | 947.60 | 1,106.60 |
| 09/2000 | 503.00 | 475.00 | 484.00 | 09/2003 | 535.00 | 454.00 | 512.00 | 09/2006 | 1,327.60 | 1,044.60 | 1,145.70 |
| 12/2000 | 493.00 | 455.00 | 457.00 | 12/2003 | 601.00 | 473.00 | 594.00 | 12/2006 | 1,417.82 | 1,058.60 | 1,289.50 |
| 03/2001 | 484.00 | 428.00 | 428.00 | 03/2004 | 792.80 | 593.00 | 791.50 | 03/2007 | 1,474.40 | 1,205.56 | 1,337.40 |
| 06/2001 | 468.00 | 428.00 | 429.00 | 06/2004 | 845.00 | 545.50 | 576.80 | 06/2007 | 1,414.50 | 1,212.80 | 1,237.60 |
| 09/2001 | 467.00 | 413.00 | 463.00 | 09/2004 | 699.80 | 581.80 | 689.00 | 09/2007 | 1,385.40 | 1,106.19 | 1,374.60 |
| 12/2001 | 469.00 | 404.00 | 462.00 | 12/2004 | 817.00 | 655.50 | 682.28 | 12/2007 | 1,621.20 | 1,309.00 | 1,479.42 |
| 03/2002 | 488.00 | 423.00 | 466.00 | 03/2005 | 764.08 | 632.60 | 715.53 | 03/2008 | 2,134.90 | 1,480.10 | 1,722.60 |
| 06/2002 | 514.00 | 440.00 | 484.00 | 06/2005 | 761.00 | 676.60 | 704.40 | 06/2008 | 1,876.86 | 1,599.10 | 1,741.50 |
| 09/2002 | 515.00 | 438.00 | 454.00 | 09/2005 | 759.60 | 664.40 | 745.40 | 09/2008 | 1,947.50 | 1,026.50 | 1,201.70 |
| 12/2002 | 481.00 | 428.00 | 478.00 | 12/2005 | 926.94 | 731.50 | 881.60 | 12/2008 | 1,298.77 | 845.76 | 1,137.45 |

Composite.    *CME Group; New York Mercantile Exchange*

# TIN

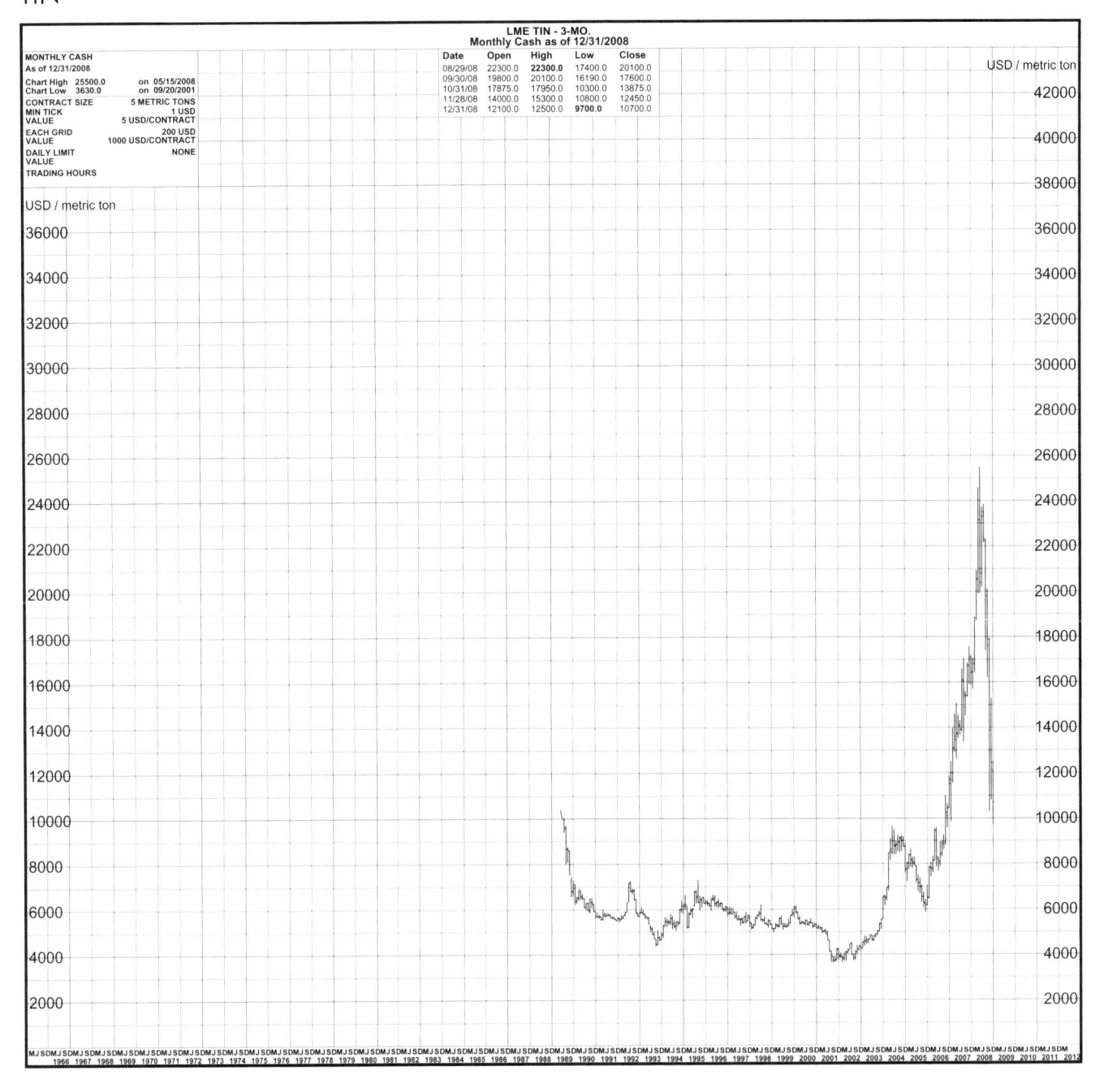

## LME TIN - 3-MO. Monthly Cash as of 12/31/2008

| Date | Open | High | Low | Close |
|---|---|---|---|---|
| 08/29/08 | 22300.0 | 22300.0 | 17400.0 | 20100.0 |
| 09/30/08 | 19800.0 | 20100.0 | 16190.0 | 17600.0 |
| 10/31/08 | 17875.0 | 17950.0 | 10300.0 | 13875.0 |
| 11/28/08 | 14000.0 | 15300.0 | 10800.0 | 12450.0 |
| 12/31/08 | 12100.0 | 12500.0 | 9700.0 | 10700.0 |

**MONTHLY CASH** As of 12/31/2008
Chart High 25500.0 on 05/15/2008
Chart Low 3630.0 on 09/20/2001
CONTRACT SIZE 5 METRIC TONS
MIN TICK 1 USD
VALUE 5 USD/CONTRACT
EACH GRID 200 USD
VALUE 1000 USD/CONTRACT
DAILY LIMIT NONE
TRADING HOURS

## Annual High, Low and Settle of Tin    In USD per Metric Ton

| Year | High | Low | Settle | Year | High | Low | Settle | Year | High | Low | Settle |
|---|---|---|---|---|---|---|---|---|---|---|---|
| 1967 | | | | 1981 | | | | 1995 | 7,310.0 | 5,170.0 | 6,325.0 |
| 1968 | | | | 1982 | | | | 1996 | 6,650.0 | 5,680.0 | 5,840.0 |
| 1969 | | | | 1983 | | | | 1997 | 6,130.0 | 5,235.0 | 5,420.0 |
| 1970 | | | | 1984 | | | | 1998 | 6,210.0 | 5,100.0 | 5,170.0 |
| 1971 | | | | 1985 | | | | 1999 | 6,150.0 | 4,960.0 | 6,100.0 |
| 1972 | | | | 1986 | | | | 2000 | 6,175.0 | 5,160.0 | 5,180.0 |
| 1973 | | | | 1987 | | | | 2001 | 5,320.0 | 3,630.0 | 3,940.0 |
| 1974 | | | | 1988 | | | | 2002 | 4,550.0 | 3,630.0 | 4,280.0 |
| 1975 | | | | 1989 | 10,440.0 | 6,570.0 | 7,100.0 | 2003 | 6,570.0 | 4,260.0 | 6,525.0 |
| 1976 | | | | 1990 | 7,150.0 | 5,650.0 | 5,705.0 | 2004 | 9,650.0 | 6,150.0 | 7,765.0 |
| 1977 | | | | 1991 | 5,990.0 | 5,500.0 | 5,605.0 | 2005 | 8,650.0 | 5,850.0 | 6,500.0 |
| 1978 | | | | 1992 | 7,250.0 | 5,447.0 | 5,850.0 | 2006 | 11,850.0 | 6,450.0 | 11,510.0 |
| 1979 | | | | 1993 | 6,130.0 | 4,360.0 | 4,900.0 | 2007 | 17,575.0 | 9,849.0 | 16,400.0 |
| 1980 | | | | 1994 | 6,400.0 | 4,730.0 | 6,210.0 | 2008 | 25,500.0 | 9,700.0 | 10,700.0 |

3-month Forward.    Source: London Metal Exchange

# TIN

## LME TIN - 3-MO. Weekly Cash as of 01/02/2009

**WEEKLY CASH**
As of 01/02/2009
Chart High 25500.0 on 05/15/2008
Chart Low 3630.0 on 09/20/2001
CONTRACT SIZE 5 METRIC TONS
MIN TICK 1 USD
VALUE 5 USD/CONTRACT
EACH GRID 100 USD
VALUE 500 USD/CONTRACT
DAILY LIMIT NONE
VALUE
TRADING HOURS

| Date | Open | High | Low | Close |
|---|---|---|---|---|
| 12/05/08 | 12100.0 | 12500.0 | 11390.0 | 11520.0 |
| 12/12/08 | 11600.0 | 12270.0 | 11400.0 | 11500.0 |
| 12/19/08 | 11600.0 | 11600.0 | 10305.0 | 10500.0 |
| 12/24/08 | 10600.0 | 10600.0 | 9800.0 | 9855.0 |
| 01/02/09 | 9750.0 | 11650.0 | 9700.0 | 11600.0 |

## Quarterly High, Low and Settle of Tin   In USD per Metric Ton

| Quarter | High | Low | Settle | Quarter | High | Low | Settle | Quarter | High | Low | Settle |
|---|---|---|---|---|---|---|---|---|---|---|---|
| 03/2000 | 6,175.0 | 5,320.0 | 5,345.0 | 03/2003 | 4,820.0 | 4,260.0 | 4,540.0 | 03/2006 | 8,325.0 | 6,450.0 | 8,150.0 |
| 06/2000 | 5,550.0 | 5,270.0 | 5,510.0 | 06/2003 | 4,850.0 | 4,480.0 | 4,650.0 | 06/2006 | 9,602.0 | 7,675.0 | 8,100.0 |
| 09/2000 | 5,605.0 | 5,275.0 | 5,390.0 | 09/2003 | 5,070.0 | 4,585.0 | 5,035.0 | 09/2006 | 9,275.0 | 7,860.0 | 8,850.0 |
| 12/2000 | 5,410.0 | 5,160.0 | 5,180.0 | 12/2003 | 6,570.0 | 5,030.0 | 6,525.0 | 12/2006 | 11,850.0 | 8,825.0 | 11,510.0 |
| 03/2001 | 5,320.0 | 4,950.0 | 4,975.0 | 03/2004 | 8,480.0 | 6,150.0 | 8,475.0 | 03/2007 | 14,600.0 | 9,849.0 | 13,450.0 |
| 06/2001 | 5,115.0 | 4,610.0 | 4,660.0 | 06/2004 | 9,650.0 | 8,150.0 | 8,760.0 | 06/2007 | 15,100.0 | 12,600.0 | 13,900.0 |
| 09/2001 | 4,625.0 | 3,630.0 | 3,740.0 | 09/2004 | 9,235.0 | 8,410.0 | 9,140.0 | 09/2007 | 17,050.0 | 13,348.0 | 15,400.0 |
| 12/2001 | 4,295.0 | 3,650.0 | 3,940.0 | 12/2004 | 9,250.0 | 7,600.0 | 7,765.0 | 12/2007 | 17,575.0 | 15,350.0 | 16,400.0 |
| 03/2002 | 4,070.0 | 3,630.0 | 4,040.0 | 03/2005 | 8,650.0 | 7,200.0 | 8,125.0 | 03/2008 | 20,950.0 | 15,700.0 | 20,550.0 |
| 06/2002 | 4,480.0 | 3,700.0 | 4,460.0 | 06/2005 | 8,300.0 | 7,150.0 | 7,300.0 | 06/2008 | 25,500.0 | 19,900.0 | 23,305.0 |
| 09/2002 | 4,550.0 | 3,720.0 | 4,120.0 | 09/2005 | 7,500.0 | 6,300.0 | 6,555.0 | 09/2008 | 23,850.0 | 16,190.0 | 17,600.0 |
| 12/2002 | 4,415.0 | 4,010.0 | 4,280.0 | 12/2005 | 7,050.0 | 5,850.0 | 6,500.0 | 12/2008 | 17,950.0 | 9,700.0 | 10,700.0 |

3-month Forward.   *Source: London Metal Exchange*

# ZINC

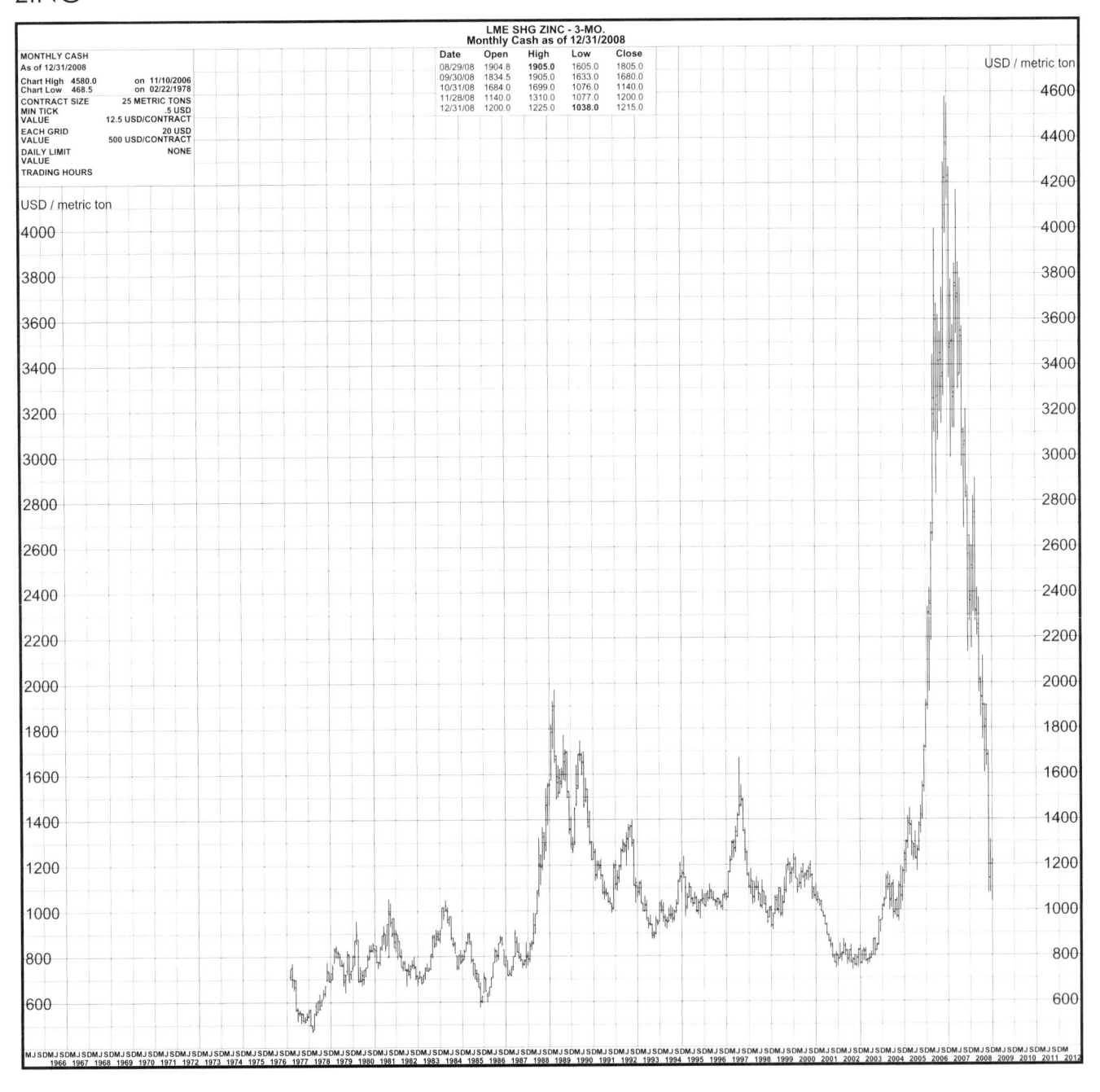

## LME SHG ZINC - 3-MO.
Monthly Cash as of 12/31/2008

| Date | Open | High | Low | Close |
|---|---|---|---|---|
| 08/29/08 | 1904.8 | 1905.0 | 1605.0 | 1805.0 |
| 09/30/08 | 1834.5 | 1905.0 | 1633.0 | 1680.0 |
| 10/31/08 | 1684.0 | 1699.0 | 1076.0 | 1140.0 |
| 11/28/08 | 1140.0 | 1310.0 | 1077.0 | 1200.0 |
| 12/31/08 | 1200.0 | 1225.0 | 1038.0 | 1215.0 |

MONTHLY CASH As of 12/31/2008
Chart High 4580.0 on 11/10/2006
Chart Low 468.5 on 02/22/1978
CONTRACT SIZE 25 METRIC TONS
MIN TICK .5 USD
VALUE 12.5 USD/CONTRACT
EACH GRID 20 USD
VALUE 500 USD/CONTRACT
DAILY LIMIT NONE
VALUE
TRADING HOURS

### Annual High, Low and Settle of Zinc — In USD per Metric Ton

| Year | High | Low | Settle | Year | High | Low | Settle | Year | High | Low | Settle |
|---|---|---|---|---|---|---|---|---|---|---|---|
| 1967 | | | | 1981 | 1,054.5 | 746.1 | 903.3 | 1995 | 1,239.0 | 963.0 | 1,024.0 |
| 1968 | | | | 1982 | 895.0 | 667.9 | 690.0 | 1996 | 1,118.0 | 1,000.5 | 1,060.0 |
| 1969 | | | | 1983 | 918.5 | 680.3 | 914.6 | 1997 | 1,674.0 | 1,054.5 | 1,107.0 |
| 1970 | | | | 1984 | 1,049.3 | 740.2 | 782.7 | 1998 | 1,185.0 | 923.0 | 934.0 |
| 1971 | | | | 1985 | 905.2 | 574.8 | 708.7 | 1999 | 1,245.0 | 914.0 | 1,245.0 |
| 1972 | | | | 1986 | 890.4 | 601.4 | 794.3 | 2000 | 1,235.0 | 1,042.0 | 1,042.0 |
| 1973 | | | | 1987 | 916.2 | 711.3 | 787.8 | 2001 | 1,081.0 | 745.0 | 787.0 |
| 1974 | | | | 1988 | 1,575.0 | 771.0 | 1,555.0 | 2002 | 874.5 | 738.0 | 767.0 |
| 1975 | | | | 1989 | 1,975.0 | 1,275.0 | 1,292.0 | 2003 | 1,023.0 | 757.0 | 1,017.0 |
| 1976 | | | | 1990 | 1,750.0 | 1,220.0 | 1,257.0 | 2004 | 1,262.0 | 950.0 | 1,246.0 |
| 1977 | 771.6 | 507.2 | 559.6 | 1991 | 1,273.0 | 989.0 | 1,115.0 | 2005 | 1,925.0 | 1,160.0 | 1,909.0 |
| 1978 | 775.2 | 468.5 | 726.3 | 1992 | 1,397.0 | 1,032.0 | 1,081.0 | 2006 | 4,580.0 | 1,877.0 | 4,205.7 |
| 1979 | 848.3 | 641.0 | 759.1 | 1993 | 1,134.0 | 873.5 | 1,030.0 | 2007 | 4,270.0 | 2,135.0 | 2,360.0 |
| 1980 | 956.4 | 670.5 | 828.6 | 1994 | 1,214.0 | 918.0 | 1,162.0 | 2008 | 2,900.0 | 1,038.0 | 1,215.0 |

3-month Forward.   Source: London Metal Exchange

# ZINC

**WEEKLY CASH**
As of 01/02/2009
Chart High 4580.0 on 11/10/2006
Chart Low 738.0 on 08/13/2002
CONTRACT SIZE 25 METRIC TONS
MIN TICK .5 USD
VALUE 12.5 USD/CONTRACT
EACH GRID 20 USD
VALUE 500 USD/CONTRACT
DAILY LIMIT NONE
VALUE
TRADING HOURS

LME SHG ZINC - 3-MO.
Weekly Cash as of 01/02/2009

| Date | Open | High | Low | Close |
|---|---|---|---|---|
| 12/05/08 | 1200.0 | 1225.0 | 1051.0 | 1070.0 |
| 12/12/08 | 1095.0 | 1137.0 | 1038.0 | 1070.0 |
| 12/19/08 | 1085.0 | 1160.0 | 1063.8 | 1140.0 |
| 12/24/08 | 1155.0 | 1196.0 | 1130.5 | 1150.0 |
| 01/02/09 | 1165.0 | 1298.0 | 1118.0 | 1280.0 |

## Quarterly High, Low and Settle of Zinc    In USD per Metric Ton

| Quarter | High | Low | Settle | Quarter | High | Low | Settle | Quarter | High | Low | Settle |
|---|---|---|---|---|---|---|---|---|---|---|---|
| 03/2000 | 1,235.0 | 1,073.0 | 1,116.0 | 03/2003 | 834.0 | 763.0 | 777.0 | 03/2006 | 2,705.0 | 1,877.0 | 2,655.0 |
| 06/2000 | 1,204.0 | 1,090.0 | 1,161.0 | 06/2003 | 819.0 | 757.0 | 800.0 | 06/2006 | 4,000.0 | 2,620.0 | 3,220.0 |
| 09/2000 | 1,216.0 | 1,128.0 | 1,152.0 | 09/2003 | 877.0 | 795.0 | 844.0 | 09/2006 | 3,740.0 | 3,065.0 | 3,344.9 |
| 12/2000 | 1,160.0 | 1,042.0 | 1,042.0 | 12/2003 | 1,023.0 | 843.0 | 1,017.0 | 12/2006 | 4,580.0 | 3,260.0 | 4,205.7 |
| 03/2001 | 1,081.0 | 992.0 | 993.5 | 03/2004 | 1,169.0 | 1,010.0 | 1,110.0 | 03/2007 | 4,270.0 | 2,990.0 | 3,255.2 |
| 06/2001 | 994.0 | 889.0 | 890.0 | 06/2004 | 1,153.5 | 958.0 | 992.0 | 06/2007 | 4,170.5 | 3,119.9 | 3,350.2 |
| 09/2001 | 895.0 | 788.0 | 799.5 | 09/2004 | 1,124.0 | 950.0 | 1,108.0 | 09/2007 | 3,780.0 | 2,680.0 | 3,045.0 |
| 12/2001 | 818.0 | 745.0 | 787.0 | 12/2004 | 1,262.0 | 1,000.0 | 1,246.0 | 12/2007 | 3,205.0 | 2,135.0 | 2,360.0 |
| 03/2002 | 874.5 | 771.0 | 842.0 | 03/2005 | 1,450.0 | 1,160.0 | 1,375.0 | 03/2008 | 2,900.0 | 2,150.0 | 2,320.0 |
| 06/2002 | 854.0 | 758.0 | 822.0 | 06/2005 | 1,392.0 | 1,215.0 | 1,230.0 | 06/2008 | 2,420.0 | 1,850.0 | 1,940.0 |
| 09/2002 | 849.0 | 738.0 | 759.0 | 09/2005 | 1,460.2 | 1,170.0 | 1,420.0 | 09/2008 | 2,120.0 | 1,605.0 | 1,680.0 |
| 12/2002 | 844.0 | 748.0 | 767.0 | 12/2005 | 1,925.0 | 1,399.0 | 1,909.0 | 12/2008 | 1,699.0 | 1,038.0 | 1,215.0 |

3-month Forward.    *Source: London Metal Exchange*

# CRB ENCYCLOPEDIA CD

## Table of Contents

*Chapter 1: Installation*
    QuickSearch ................................................. 317
*Chapter 2: Searching and Browsing*
    Selecting Text to Search .............................. 317
    Types of Searches......................................... 317
    Search Operators .......................................... 318
    Conducting a Search ..................................... 318
    Search Results ............................................... 319
    Reader Preferences ....................................... 319
    Table of Contents Browsing ........................ 319
*Chapter 3: Viewing Images*
    Finding Images ............................................. 320
    Finding Embedded Images.......................... 320
    Zooming Hyper-linked Images .................... 320

*Chapter 4: Printing*
    Print Hints ..................................................... 321
    Printing Text or Images .............................. 321
    Print Setup .................................................... 322
    Page Layout .................................................. 322
*Chapter 5: User Annotations*
    Using Bookmarks......................................... 322
    Using Notes .................................................. 322

CRB Encyclopedia CD Copyright © Commodity Research Bureau, a Barchart.com, Inc. company. All rights reserved.

QuickSearch is a trademark of dataDisc, Inc.
Segments of this manual reprinted with permission by dataDisc, Inc.

Factual information contained in the CRB Yearbooks CD has been obtained from sources believed to be reliable but are not necessarily inclusive and are not guaranteed in any way and should not be construed as a representation by us.

---

## Chapter 1: Installation

### Installing QuickSearch

To run QuickSearch, you will need:
- A computer with a 120 Mhz or faster processor, running any current Windows 2000®, XP®, Vista® or Macintosh operating system
- At least 32 MB of total RAM installed on your computer; for best performance, we recommend at least 64 MB
- A CD-ROM drive

To Install:
1) Place the disc in the CD-ROM drive. If installation does not start automatically proceed to step 2.
2) Click Start; Select Run
3) Type D:\Autoplay, where D is the letter representing your CD-ROM drive. Press the enter key and follow the instructions.

## Chapter 2: Searching and Browsing

### Selecting Text to Search

Searches can be conducted across all the text in a *QuickSearch* document (full-text), restricted to a specific field (fielded search), or restricted to a selected table of contents section.

**Everywhere in text** - searches the full text of the *QuickSearch* document (except for user-defined notes and bookmarks). Choose **Everywhere in text** in the Search dialog box to specify a full-text search.

**Fielded Search** - searches a specific field and ignores all text outside of that field. To specify a fielded search:

1) Click **Selected field** under **Select where to search**.
2) Select a field from the list of available fields.

**Current Table of Contents section** - restricts a research only to a Table of Contents (TOC) section.

1) Click the TOC section in the TOC window.
2) Click the Search button on the toolbar OR select Search/Search from the main menu.
3) Click *Current Table of Contents section* under *Select where to search*.

Note: Search results will represent the selected TOC Section and its sublevels.

### Types of Searches

**Search for Phrase**
Type an exact phrase you wish to find, e.g. "Business is the key." Use quotation marks around the search text to distinguish a *phrase search* from a *word search* or choose *Search for phrase* in the **Search/More>>** dialog box. The QuickSearch default setting is a phrase search.

**Search for Words**
Two types of word searches may be conducted - single words or words in proximity as determined by **Search Operators**. To conduct a word search, choose *Search for word(s)* in the **Search/More>>** dialog box.

1) **Single Word** - Enter any single word, e.g. BUSINESS, to find all occurrences in the document.
2) **Words in Proximity** - Enter any series of words that you wish to find near each other (e.g. BUSINESS INCREASE). Before conducting a *proximity search*, define a search range/proximity in the **Search/ More>>** dialog box. The default setting is 4 words. A typical sentence has 10 words, a typical paragraph has 25 words, and a typical page has 500 words.

**Refine Last Search**

The **Refine last search** feature can be used to modify your most recent search. (See the Advanced Searching section of this chapter.)

*Search Operators*

Boolean, wildcard and phrase search operators are available by selecting **MORE>>** in the **Search** dialog box. Double-click on any operator to add it to the Search command line *or* type the operator in the **Type the text to find** box.

**To see example of each operator:**
- Click the **Search** button and then the **More>>** button.
  OR
- Select **Search/Search** from the main menu and **More>>**.
- Click once on the operator you wish to view.

**The following operators are available for a word search:**

**AND (&)** - BUSINESS AND INCREASE - Returns all occurrences of BUSINESS and INCREASE in the specified search range that are near each other. "Near" is defined using the Word Proximity setting in the **Search/ More>>** dialog box.

**OR (|)** - BUSINESS OR INCREASE - Returns all occurrences of the words in the specified search range without regard to proximity.

NOT (~) - BUSINESS NOT INCREASE - Returns all occurrences of the word BUSINESS that are not near the word INCREASE in the specified search range. "Near" is defined using the Word Proximity setting in the **Search/ More>>** dialog box.

**Wildcard (*)** - Use the asterisk (*) at the end of any part of a word to represent any character or combination of characters. For example, BUSI* may return hits such as *business*, *businesses*, *busing*, and *Businowski*. The wildcard operator cannot be used in a phrase search.

*Conducting a Search*

**Basic Searching**

1) Click the Search button on the Reader toolbar OR select Search/Search from the main menu.
2) In the **Search** dialog box, select where to search choosing one of the following:
   - Everywhere in text
   - Selected field*
   - Current Table of Contents

*Note: Click a field or a TOC entry before choosing Selected field or Current Table of Contents section.

3) Type the search text (word, words within proximity or phrase) in the *Type the text to find* box or double click on any entry in the **Word Wheel** to select it as search text.
4) Click **Search** in the dialog box. "Hits" will be highlighted in the text and displayed in context in a separate **Hit List** window. The number of hits also will be displayed on the status bar at the bottom of the screen.

**Advanced Searching**

**Search for Words**
1) Begin a search by completing steps 1-3 of a Basic Search.
2) Select **More>>** to expand the Search dialog box and change to a *Search for Word(s)* and/or select other **Search Operators** which alter the nature of the search to be conducted. A *Search for Phrase* is conducted unless you select another type of search.
3) Specify the **Word Proximity** in the **Search/ More>>** dialog box, if you are conducting an AND or NOT search. The default proximity is 4 words.
4) Click **Search** in the dialog box. "Hits" will be highlighted in the text and displayed in context in a separate **Hit List** window. The number of hits also will be displayed on the status bar at the bottom of the screen.

**Refine Last Search**

To refine the last research:
1) Begin a search by completing steps 1-3 of a Basic Search. Click the **More>>** button on the **Search** dialog box to access all search parameters.
2) Click the **Refine last search** box in the lower left corner of the **Search** dialog box.
3) Select the **Boolean** operator to be applied to the refined search (just to the right of the *Refine last search* check box).
4) Preview the format for the refined search in the *Refined Search box* at the bottom of the **Search** dialog box.
5) Type the **[New text to Find]** word(s) in the *Type the text to find box* at the top of the **Search** dialog box.
6) Click **Search**.

**Example:**

Your first search in the Constitution was for the word "House." If you want to narrow the search results to include only hits of "House" which are not near "senate," you can return to the **Search** dialog box, select **Refine last search**, select the *NOT* operator, specify the word proximity, type "Senate" in the *Type the text* to find box at the top of the **Search** dialog box and click the **Search** button. The **Hit List** will display only hits of "House" which were not located near "Senate" ("near" depends on the proximity that you specified). The final search command would look as follows:

(House) ~ (Senate)

This search could be further refined by selecting **Refine last search** and repeating the steps above.

**Example:**

If you want to find only occurrences of "House *NOT* Senate" which are near "Representative," return to the Search dialog box, select **Refine last search**, select the *AND* operator, specify the word proximity, type "Representatives" in the Type the text to find box at the top of the **Search** dialog box and click on the **Search** button. The **Hit List** would display only hits of "House" which were near "Representatives" but not located near "Senate" ("near" depends on the proximity that you specified). The final search command would look as follows:

[(House) ~ (Senate)] & (Representatives)

*Search Results*

**Browsing Search Results**

**Hit List**

After conducting a search, each occurrence of the e search text in the document will be displayed in context in a separate **Hit List** window. Double click on any entry in the **Hit List** to move to the corresponding section of text.

**Highlighted Hits in the Text**

After conducting a search, each occurrence of the search text is highlighted in the text of the document.

1) Click the **First/Previous/Next/Last (Hit)** buttons to move between highlighted hits in the text.
2) The number of the current hit being viewed and the total number of hits are displayed in the Status bar at the bottom of the screen.

**Removing the Hit List**

1) Click the **Clear** button on the toolbar *OR* select **Search/Clear Search** from the main menu to remove the current **Hit List** window and the highlighting from the hits in the text.
2) Turn off the **Hit List** for future searches by selecting **Edit/Preferences** to open the **Document Preferences** dialog box. Click the **Reader** tab to open **Reader Preferences**. Deselect *Show Hit List?*.

*Reader Preferences*

Select **Edit/Preferences** from the main menu to open the **Document Preference** dialog box. The box includes three tabs: **Reader**, **Author**, and **Stopper Word List**.

**Reader Preferences include:**

**CD-ROM Drive Letter**

Every CD-ROM player is assigned a drive letter. (It is usually the last drive letter after your other drives.)

**Default Word Search Proximity**

Set the default proximity (the number of words between selected words) to be applied in multiple word (non-phrase) searches.

**Show Hit List?**

Click **Show Hit List?** to open a **Hit List** automatically after conducting a Search. The Hit List shows "hits" - items found - when you do a search. Browse hits by clicking the **Next/Previous Hit** buttons on the toolbar or selecting **Search/Search** from the main menu. All hits will be highlighted in the text even if a **Hit List** is not activated.

**TOC Window Color**

Click the **TOC Window Color** button to open a dialog box containing table of Contest background color options. Select from a present color chart, or create a custom color and select it. Click **OK**.
  **SAVE YOUR DOCUMENT** after you select preferences!

*Table of Contents Browsing*

**Hyperlinks**

The Table of Contents (TOC) provides a convenient method for accessing any section of the ***QuickSearch*** document. Each TOC entry is hyper-linked to the corresponding section of text; just click on an entry and ***QuickSearch*** automatically will move the corresponding section to the text window.

**Multiple Levels**

***QuickSearch*** TOC's may include up to 32 levels. If there are sublevels in a TOC section, a "+" will appear in front of the TOC entry. To open the next level, click on the "+".

**Automatic Tracing**

As you move through a ***QuickSearch*** document (scroll, Next Hit, Previous Hit, etc.) the Table of Contents will "track" your location in the document automatically. A box outline indicates the current TOC section.

# Chapter 3: Viewing Images

A ***QuickSearch*** document may contain ***hyperlinked*** or ***embedded*** images. Different methods are used for finding and viewing each type of image

*Finding Images*

**Finding Hyperlinked Images**

You can find hyperlinked images in a QuickSearch document by using any of the following options:
- **List** of images
- **Next/Previous Image** buttons or menu selections
- **Search** feature
- **Special formatting**/camera icon

*Image List* - Open a comprehensive list of hyperlinked images in the document.
1) Click the **Image List** button on the Toolbar **OR** select **Search/Image List** from the main menu.
2) Double click on an image title in the **Image List** to open the image.

*Browsing Images* - You can browse through images using the **Next/Previous Image** buttons or menu selections.
1) Select **Nest/Previous Image** buttons **OR** Search/First (Nest, Previous, Last) Image from the main menu.
2) The **Next and Previous Image** buttons or menu selections move the reader sequentially through images in the document.
3) The **First** and **Last Image** menu selections move only to the first or last image in the document.

**Searching for Words in Hyperlinked Image Titles** - As each hyper-linked image file is added to a ***QuickSearch*** document, it is given an *Image Title*. The Image Title appears with an optional camera icon at the point you have chosen in the text window. The Image Title is indexed with other text and may be found using a word or phrase search (see Chapter 1 - *Searching & Browsing*).

*Look for Special Formatting/Camera Icon* – Hyper-linked images can be found by looking for words that have special formatting (the default is double-underlined text). Double click on the specially formatted text to open the image. A camera icon may precede the specially formatted image title. The image can also be opened by clicking on the camera icon.

*Finding Embedded Images*

Embedded images appear in the text at the point you have chosen. They may be found by:
- Scrolling through text
- Conducting a search for words/phrases that appear near the image.

**Scrolling for an Embedded Image**
Use the vertical scroll bar to scan text and locate embedded images.

**Searching for an Embedded Image\***
Search for text that has been placed near an image and marked as hidden.

*Note: **Titles of embedded images will *NOT* appear on an Image List**. The Image List feature is only for hyper-linked images.

*Zooming Hyper-linked Images*

**Marquee Image Zooming\***

*Marquee Image Zooming* allows you to select a portion of a **hyper-linked image** and enlarge it to the size of the image window. ***QuickSearch*** allows you to zoom to a single pixel.

*Note: Marquee Image Zooming **is available *ONLY* for hyper-linked images**.

1) Click a hyperlinked image title or camera icon to open the image window.
2) Click on and hold the left mouse button and drag a box around the image area you want to enlarge.
3) When the area is defined, release the mouse button. The area selected will fill the Image Window.
4) Steps 2 and 3 may be repeated to continuing zooming.
5) To return the image to its original size, click once on the image with the left mouse button.

**Image Panning**

**Image Panning** allows you to use the horizontal/vertical scroll bars* to move around a **hyperlinked** image that has been enlarged by Marquee zooming.

Click an arrow on the scroll bar **OR** click and drag the horizontal or vertical scroll bar button to move the image across the screen.

*Note: **Scroll bars do not appear on-screen until an image has been zoomed**.

**Scale to Gray**

Some 1 bit (black & white) hyperlinked images can be sharpened by using the **Scale to Gray** feature. **Scale to Gray** will fill in missing pixels to improve the quality of an image. This feature is particularly useful for viewing scanned document images.

**To use Scale to Gray:**
1) Open a hyperlinked image
2) Select **View/Scale to Gray** from the main menu
3) **Scale to Gray** will remain active until it is deselected.

381

# Chapter 4: Printing

The **Print** feature will print text and images in the following forms:
- Highlighted lines or blocks of text
- Selected Tables of Contents section(s)
- Search results ("hit" lists)
- Embedded images
- Hyper-linked images
- Zoomed portions of Hyper-linked images

### *Print Hints*

Highlighted text, images and TOC sections will print in order as they are found in the document.

The printed size of Zoomed and Hyper-linked images may vary between portrait and landscape page orientation settings (found via **File/Print Setup**).

You can print *multiple* TOC sections by:
- Using the **Shift** key to select a series of adjacent TOCs.
- Using the **CTRL** key to individually select specific TOCs.
- Using the **Shift** and **CTRL** keys alternately to select specific TOC groupings.

Printing specifications can be set from the Windows Print Manager utility.
Make **Print Setup** modifications *before* you **Print**.

### *Printing Text or Images*

To Print portions of a document:
1) Highlight lines and/or block(s) of text.
2) Click the **Print** button on the toolbar.
OR
Select the **File/Print** from the main menu.
OR
Press **CTRL+P**.

To Print a *Single* TOC section:
1) Click the TOC heading in the **Table of Contents** window.
2) Click the **Print** button on the toolbar.
OR
Select the **File/Print TOC selection(s)** from the main menu.
OR
Click the **right mouse** button and select **Print TOC selection(s)**.
OR
Press **CTRL+P**.
*Note: All the sublevels in the TOC section will be printed.

To Print Multiple TOC sections:
1) Click the first TOC section you want to print from the **Table of Contents** window.
2) Press and hold the **CTRL** key while you click the order TOC sections you want to print. They do not have to be adjacent.
3) When you have finished selecting TOCs, click the **Print** button on the toolbar.
OR
Select **File/Print TOC selection(s)** from the main menu.
OR
Click the **right mouse** button and select **Print TOC selection(s)**.
OR
Press **CTRL+P**.

To Print adjacent TOC sections:
1) Click the *first* TOC section you want to print from the **Table of Contents** window.
2) Press and hold the **Shift** key, and click the last TOC section in the series (all TOC sections between the first and last will be selected automatically).
3) Click the **Print** button on the toolbar.
*OR*
Select **File/Print TOC selection** from the main menu.
*OR*
Click the **right mouse** button and select **Print TOC selection(s)**.
OR
Press **CTRL+P**.

*Note: **Multiple TOC Selection functions (highlighting using the** Shift **and/or** CTRL **keys) can be used in combination to select specific TOC groupings.**

To Print Embedded Images:
1) Highlight (double click) the embedded image(s) you want ant to print.
2) Click the **Print** button on the Toolbar.
OR
Select **File/Print** from the main menu.
OR
Press **CTRL+P**.

To Print a Hyperlinked Image:
You can print a **Hyperlinked Image** or a zoomed portion of a Hyperlinked Image.
1) Open the image by double clicking the **Image title** and/or the **camera icon**.
*OR*
Click the Image List button on the toolbar and double click the Image title from the list.
2) Click the Print button on the Toolbar.
*OR*
Select File/Print from the main menu.
*OR*
Press **CTRL+P**.

*Print Setup*

The Print Setup option allows you to select printer type, page orientation, paper size, paper source, and printer properties (paper, graphics, fonts, device options). Make these selections **before** you print.

To change the Print Setup:
1) Select **File/Print Setup** from the main menu.
2) In the **Print Setup** dialog box, click the down arrow in the **Name** pull down menu, select a printer type and enter it in the **Name** window (or click **Network** to access Network printer options).
3) To select new printer properties select **Properties** and make modifications.
4) Select **Landscape** or **Portrait**.
5) Select **OK** to exit.

**Page Layout**

You can adjust the top, bottom, left, and right margins of a printed page as follows:
1) Select **File/Page Layout** from the main menu.
2) In the **Page Parameters** dialog box, set margins (in inches) and click **OK**.

## Chapter 5: User Annotations

The reader may customize a ***QuickSearch*** document by adding "margin" Bookmarks and Notes.

Annotate functions enable the reader to make customized **Bookmarks** in the text and make private, unsearchable comments about a document with **Notes**. The **Bookmark** feature enables the reader to "save his place," while the **Notes** feature allows the reader to "write in the margins" of the text.

*Using Bookmarks*

To add a Bookmark to a document:
1) Highlight a portion of text or place the cursor where you would like to add the Bookmark.
2) Click on the **Bookmark** icon on the Reader toolbar *OR* select **Annotate/Bookmark** from the main menu or select **Insert Bookmark** from the **right mouse** button menu. If text has been highlighted, it is shown in the **Edit Bookmark/Name** text box. If not, enter a name for the bookmark in the text box.
3) Click **Add** to place the selected text in the **Current Bookmarks** list.
4) Click **Go to** to scroll text to the point where the bookmark appears.
5) Click **Close** to close the Bookmark dialog box.

To go to a Bookmark:
1) Click on the **Bookmark** button on the toolbar *OR* select **Insert Bookmark** from the **right mouse** button menu to open the list of Current Bookmarks.
2) Highlight the bookmark you want to move to in the text.
3) Click **Go to**. The selected text will move to the top of the text window.

To edit a Bookmark:
1) Click on the **Bookmark** icon on the toolbar *OR* select **Annotate/Bookmark** from the main menu *OR* select **Insert Bookmark** from the **right mouse** button menu to open the dialog box containing current bookmarks.
2) In the **Current Bookmarks** list, click on the bookmark you wish to edit. It will appear in the **Edit Bookmark/Name** window.
3) Make changes and click **Add**.

To remove a Bookmark:
1) Click the **Bookmark** icon on the Reader toolbar or select **Insert Bookmark** from the **right mouse** button menu to open the dialog box containing current bookmarks.
2) In the **Current Bookmarks** list, click on the bookmark you wish to remove. It will appear in the **Edit Bookmark/Name** text box.
3) Click **Remove**.

*Using Notes*

To add a Note to a document:
1) Place the cursor in the text window where you want the note to appear.
2) Click on the **Notepad** button *OR* select **Annotate/Notes/Insert** from the main menu *OR* select **Insert Note** from the **right mouse** button menu to open the **Notepad** dialog box.
3) Type in the note and click **Save**; a Notepad icon appears in the left margin next to the specified line of text.

To View a Note:
1) Double click the **Notepad** icon in the left margin.
2) The **Notepad** dialog box displays the note.

To Edit a Note:
1) Double click the icon of the note you want to edit.
2) Make changes to text.
3) Click **Save**.

To Remove a Note:
1) Place the cursor on the **Notepad** icon and select **Annotate/Note/Delete** from the main menu *OR* select **Delete Note** from the **right mouse** button menu.
2) A dialog box will ask you to confirm the note deletion.
3) Click **Yes**. The icon will disappear after scrolling in the document.

# CRB Wall Charts and Desk Sets

Designed to help you easily spot market reversals and critical turning points, CRB Historical Wall Charts and Desk Sets will show you in one quick look how seasonal patterns and long-term trends create profitable trading opportunities. Our charts let you plot trendlines according to actual market performance, rather than charting on market averages. Each chart offers plenty of room for updating and adding trendlines.

## Historical Wall Charts

Printed each fall, Wall Charts are available for the top 35 markets. More than just a poster measuring 22½"h x 34"w, these ten-year charts use the nearest futures contract and show open/high/low/settle prices with total volume and total open interest and Commitment of Traders data for each week through the last week of September.

**Agricultural Markets:** Corn, Oats, Soybeans, Soybean Meal, Soybean Oil, Wheat, Kansas City Wheat, Cotton #2, Cocoa, Coffee, Sugar #11, Feeder Cattle, Live Cattle, Lean Hogs and Pork Bellies.

**Financial Markets:** U.S. Dollar Index, British Pound, Canadian Dollar, Euro FX, Japanese Yen, Swiss Franc, Eurodollars, 5-Year T-Notes, 10-Year T-Notes 30-Year T-Bonds, Copper, Gold Silver, Crude Oil, Heating Oil #2, Unleaded Gasoline Natural Gas, S&P 500 Index, NASDAQ 100 Index and Dow Jones Industrials

## Historical Desk Sets

Printed each winter, the Desk Set includes 48 markets*. By allowing you to take the longest possible view of these markets, our Desk Set helps you identify potential trends and plan your strategy accordingly. Measuring 12½"h x 17"w, this spiral-bound set includes 10 years of weekly trading ranges with total volume and open interest and Commitment of Traders data and 35 years of monthly price activity with total volume and open interest through the end of December on adjacent pages.

*__Additional Markets:__ Lumber, Orange Juice, Australian Dollar, Mexican Peso, 2-Year T-Notes, Palladium, Platinum, SPI 200 Index, DAX Index, Hang Seng Index, Nikkei 225 Index, FTSE 100 Index, Continuous Commodity Index (CCI), CRB Spot Index, CRB Foodstuffs Sub-Index and CRB Raw Industrials Sub-Index.

*For more information, visit www.crbtrader.com, or call 800-621-5271*

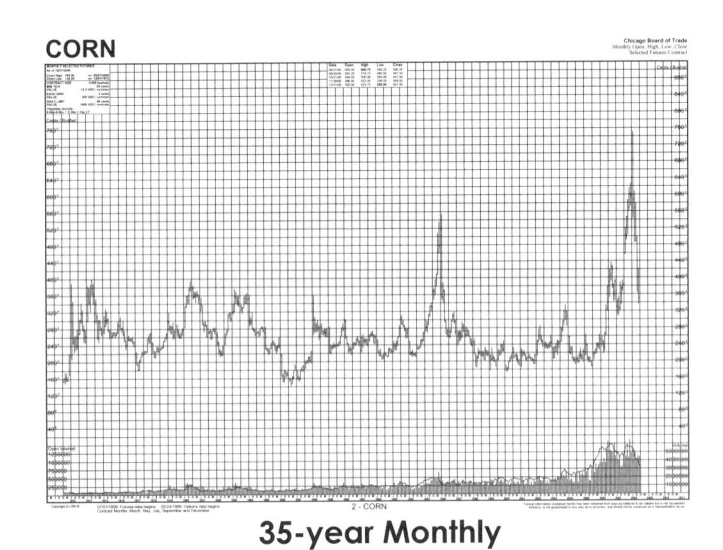

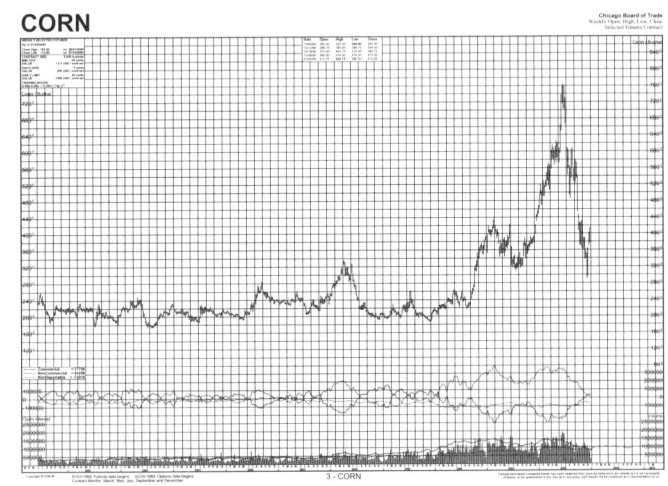

**35-year Monthly**

**10-year Weekly**

Commodity Research Bureau • 330 South Wells Street • Suite 612 • Chicago IL, 60606 • USA
Phone: 312.554.8456 or 800.621.5271 • Fax: 312.939.4135 • info@crbtrader.com • www.crbtrader.com